The Impeachment and Trial of
Andrew Johnson, President
of the United States

The Impeachment and Trial of Andrew Johnson, President of the United States

The complete record of the impeachment in the House of Representatives, the preliminary proceedings in the Senate, the articles of impeachment, and the full proceedings in the court of impeachment of the Senate of the United States.

BY THE UNITED STATES CONGRESS

DOVER PUBLICATIONS, INC., NEW YORK

Published in Canada by General Publishing Company, Ltd., 30 Lesmill Road, Don Mills, Toronto, Ontario.

Published in the United Kingdom by Constable and Company, Ltd., 10 Orange Street, London WC 2.

This Dover edition, first published in 1974, is an unabridged republication of the work originally published in 1868 by T. B. Peterson & Brothers, Philadelphia, in 1868 under the title *The Great Impeachment and Trial of Andrew Johnson.*

International Standard Book Number: 0-486-23093-7

Manufactured in the United States of America
Dover Publications, Inc.
180 Varick Street
New York, N. Y. 10014

CONTENTS.

THE
GREAT IMPEACHMENT
AND
TRIAL OF ANDREW JOHNSON,
President of the United States.

The impeachment of Andrew Johnson forms an important epoch in the history of the United States; he was the first President brought to the bar of the Senate to answer the charge of high crimes and misdemeanors. Before Mr. Johnson's accession to the Presidency, and for a few months after his assumption of that high office, his politics were of the extreme Republican or Radical school. During the summer and autumn of 1865, Mr. Johnson undertook to restore the State Governments of the Commonwealths which had receded from and waged war against the national authority. This important task Mr. Johnson sought to accomplish on principles directly opposed to his previous political professions. The Thirty-Ninth Congress at its first session dissented from the reconstruction views of the President; the President, however, paid little heed to the wishes of Congress, and insisted on carrying out what he termed his policy. Congressmen of extreme views, former political associates of Mr. Johnson, boldly denounced his reconstruction measures on the floor of the House of Representatives, and even in the more dignified Senate, the Executive's Southern policy was severely criticised.

Mr. Johnson saw fit to notice these strictures of Senators and Representatives, and in numerous public speeches he spoke of Congress in the bitterest terms. Nor did he confine himself to words alone. In all his official acts he evinced a determination to weaken the influence of the majority of Congress. The Representatives were quite as determined as the Executive, and his unfriendly acts were repaid by legislation specially framed to defeat his plans of Southern restoration. The breach between Congress and the Executive grew wider and wider, and when the second session of the Thirty-ninth Congress opened, the Radical Representatives were determined to examine the official conduct of the President, with a view to impeachment. At the head of the first impeachment movement was James M. Ashley, of Ohio. On the 17th of December, 1866, he introduced a resolution for the appointment of a select committee to inquire whether any acts had been done by any officer of the Government of the United States, which, in contemplation of the Constitution, are high crimes and misdemeanors. This resolution, requiring a two-thirds majority for its adoption, was not agreed to. On the 7th day of January, 1867, Representatives Benjamin F. Loan, of Missouri, and John R. Kelso, of the same State, offered resolutions aiming at the impeachment of the Executive, and on the same day Mr. Ashley formally charged President Johnson with the commission of high crimes and misdemeanors. The resolutions of Messrs. Loan and Kelso, and the charges of Mr. Ashley, were referred to the Judiciary Committee.

On the 28th of February following, a majority of the Judiciary Committee reported that they had taken testimony of a character sufficient to justify a further investigation, and regretted their inability to dispose definitely of the important subject committed to their charge, and bequeathed their unfinished labors to the succeeding Congress.

The Fortieth Congress.

On the 4th day of March, 1867, the Fortieth Congress convened; it was composed largely of members who had served in the previous body. On the fourth day of the session, Mr. Ashley proposed that the Judiciary Committee continue the investigations with reference to the impeachment of the President. This proposition was agreed to, and was immediately followed by a resolution from Sidney Clarke, of Kansas, requesting the committee to report on the first day of the meeting of the House after the recess. This latter provision was not complied with by the committee; there was a mid-summer session, short and busy; but the impeachment investigation was not heard of until the 25th day of November, 1867, when three reports were presented to Congress— one majority and two minority; the majority report recommended the impeachment of the President for high crimes and misdemeanors. The two minority reports, each signed by two members of the committee, advocated the suppression of any further proceedings. The reports were received and laid over until the 6th of December, a spirited discussion took place, and was prolonged until the close of the day's session. On the 7th the final vote was taken, and it stood—for impeachment, 56; against impeachment, 109; and thus ended the first attempt to bring Andrew Johnson to trial.

The Second Effort.

The next movement toward impeachment grew out of a series of letters which had passed between President Johnson and General Grant in the surrender of the War Office by the latter to Secretary Stanton, in conformity with the action of the Senate. This correspondence was read in the House on the 4th of February, 1868, and referred to the Reconstruction Committee. The object of this reference was to enable the committee to decide whether Mr. Johnson had or was disposed to place such obstruction in the way of the acts of Congress as to render his impeachment necessary. The committee examined witnesses, and deliberated upon the project until the 13th inst., when they decided against presenting articles of impeachment.

An Impeachment Effected.

With the failure of the second attempt, those in favor of impeachment abandoned all hopes of their project ever succeeding. And this feeling was shared by the nation at large.

The President determined otherwise, and on the 21st of February, Congress and the country were startled by the following communication, which was on that day submitted to the House of Representatves, by the Secretary of War, Hon. Edwin M. Stanton:—

War Department. Washington City, Feb. 21, 1868.—Sir:—General Thomas has just delivered to me a copy of the inclosed order, which you will please communicate to the House of Representatives.

Your obedient servant,
Edwin M. Stanton, Secretary of War.
Hon. Schuyler Colfax, Speaker of the House of Representatives.

Executive Mansion, Washington, Feb. 21, 1868.—Sir:—By virtue of power and authority vested in me, as President, by the Constitution and laws of the United States, you are hereby removed from office, as Secretary of the Department of War, and your functions as such will terminate upon receipt of this communication. You will transfer to Brevet Major-General Lorenzo Thomas, Adjutant-General of the Army, who has this day been authorized and empowered to act as Secretary of War ad interim, all records, papers, and other public property now in your custody and charge. Respectfully, yours,

(Signed)   Andrew Johnson,
President of the United States.
To the Hon. Edwin M. Stanton, Washington, D. C.

The House at once referred this action of the President's to the Reconstruction Committee, with authority to report upon it at any time. The Representatives friendly to the President next endeavored to obtain an adjournment until Monday, the 24th, Saturday being Washington's birthday. The Republican members voted solidly against this proposition. Just before the close of

the day's session, Hon. John Covode offered the following resolution as a question of privilege:—

Resolved, That Andrew Johnson, President of the United States, be impeached for high crimes and misdemeanors.

This resolution was also referred to the Committee on Reconstruction.

The unexpected action of the President in the case of Mr. Stanton took the Senate quite aback, and that body considered the matter in Executive Session, and after a secret deliberation of seven hours' duration, the following resolution was adopted:—

Whereas, The Senate has received and considered the communication of the President, stating that he had removed Edwin M. Stanton, Secretary of War, and had designated the Adjutant-General of the Army to act as Secretary of War ad interim; therefore,
Resolved, By the Senate of the United States, that under the Constitution and laws of the United States, the President has no power to remove the Secretary of War and to designate any other officer to perform the duty of that office ad interim.

Excitement Throughout the Country.

The country was thrown into the wildest state of excitement by the action of the President ; it was generally admitted that he had defied Congress. The Republicans urged immediate impeachment, the Democrats argued that the President's course was justified by the Constitution of the United States. Civil war was presaged; the ultra Democrats avowed their readiness to support the President against impeachment by force of arms, and the Executive Mansion was exposed to a fire of telegraphic despatches advising Mr. Johnson to stand firm, and proffers of men and arms. The Radical Republicans favored the President of the Senate and Speaker of the House with missives of sympathy and encouragement; they, too, were ready to resort to arms. But this was merely the smoke of the conflict, the majority of the people were opposed to the employment of force. All were anxious, but none but a few desperate adventurers thought of initiating civil strife.

The 22d of February, 1868, in Congress.

Meanwhile Congress went coolly and determinedly to its work. It convened on the anniversary of Washington's birth, and at ten minutes past two o'clock, Hon. Thaddeus Stevens arose to make a report from the Committee on Reconstruction.

The Speaker gave an admonition to the spectators in the gallery and to members on the floor to preserve order during the proceedings about to take place, and to manifest neither approbation nor disapprobation.

Mr. Stevens then said:—From the Committee on Reconstruction I beg leave to make the following report:—That, in addition to the papers referred to the committee, the committee find that the President, on the 21st day of February, 1868, signed and ordered a commission or letter of authority to one Lorenzo Thomas, directing and authorizing said Thomas to act as Secretary of War ad interim, and to take possession of the books, records, papers and other public property in the War Department, of which the following is a copy :—

EXECUTIVE MANSION, WASHINGTON, D. C., February 21, 1868.—Sir:—The Hon. Edwin M. Stanton having been removed from office as Secretary of War, you are hereby authorized and empowered to act as Secretary of War *ad interim*, and will immediately enter upon the discharge of the duties pertaining to that office. Mr. Stanton has been instructed to transfer to you all records, books, papers and other public property intrusted to his charge. Respectfully yours,
(Signed) ANDREW JOHNSON.
To Brevet Major-General Lorenzo Thomas, Adjutant-General United States Army, Washington, D. C.
(Official copy.)
Respectfully furnished to Hon. Edwin M. Stanton.
(Signed) L. THOMAS,
Secretary of War *ad interim*.

Upon the evidence collected by the committee, which is hereafter presented, and in virtue of the powers with which they have been invested by the House, they are of the opinion that Andrew Johnson, President of the United States, be impeached of high crimes and misdemeanors. They therefore recommend to the House the adoption of the accompanying resolution.

THADDEUS STEVENS, C. T. HURLBURD,
GEORGE S. BOUTWELL, J. F. FARNSWORTH,
JOHN A. BINGHAM, F. C. BEAMAN,
H. E. PAINE.

Resolved, That Andrew Johnson, President of the United States, be impeached of high crimes and misdemeanors.

The report having been read, Mr. Stevens said : "Mr. Speaker, it is not my intention, in the first instance, to discuss the question, and if there be no desire on the other side to discuss it, we are willing that the question shall be taken on the knowledge which the House already has. Indeed, the fact of removing a man from office while the Senate is in session, without the consent of the Senate, is of itself, if there was nothing else, always considered a high crime and misdemeanor, and was never practiced. But I will not discuss this question unless gentlemen on the other side desire to discuss it."

Gentlemen on the other side did anxiously desire to discuss the question ; and a very lively debate ensued, terminating at quarter after eleven o'clock at night. The debate was reopened at ten o'clock on Monday morning and continued until five in the afternoon, when the House proceeded, amid great but suppressed excitement, to vote on the resolution, as follows :—

Resolved, That Andrew Johnson, President of the United States, be impeached of high crimes and misdemeanors.

During the vote excuses were made for the absence of Messrs. Robinson, Benjamin, Washburn (Ind.), Williams (Ind.), Van Horn (Mo.), Trimble (Tenn.), Pomeroy, Donnelly, Koontz, Maynard, and Shellabarger.

The Speaker stated that he could not consent that his constituents should be silent on so grave an occasion , and therefore, as a member of the House, he voted yea.

The vote resulted—yeas, 126 ; nays, 47, as follows :—

YEAS.

Allison, Ames, Anderson, Arnell, Ashley (Nev.), Ashley (Ohio), Bailey, Baker, Baldwin, Banks, Beaman, Beatty, Benton, Bingham, Blaine, Blair, Boutwell, Bromwell, Broomall, Buckland, Butler, Cake, Churchill, Clarke (Ohio), Clarke, (Kan.), Cobb, Coburn, Cook, Cornell, Covode, Cullom, Dawes, Dodge, Driggs, Eckley, Eggleston, Eliot, Farnsworth, Ferris, Ferry, Fields, Gravely, Griswold, Halsey, Harding, Higby, Hill, Hooper, Hopkins, Hubbard (Ia.), Hubbard (W.Va.) Hulburd, Hunter, Ingersoll, Jenckes, Judd, Julian, Kelley, Kelsey, Ketcham, Kitchen, Laflin, Lawrence (Pa.), Lawrence (Ohio), Lincoln, Loan, Logan, Loughridge, Lynch, Mallory, Marvin, McCarthy, McClurg, Mercur, Miller, Moore, Moorhead, Morrell, Mullins, Myers, Newcomb, Nunn, O'Neill, Orth, Paine, Perham, Peters, Pike, Pile, Plants, Poland, Polsley, Price, Raum, Robertson, Sawyer, Schenck, Scofield, Seyle, Shanks, Smith, Spalding, Starkweather, Stevens (N. H.) Stevens (Pa.), Stokes, Taffee, Taylor, Trowbridge, Twitchell, Upson, Van Aernam, Van Horn (N.Y.), Van Wyck, Ward, Washburn (Wis.), Washburne (Ill.), Washburn (Mass) Welker, Williams (Pa.), Wilson (Iowa), Wilson (Ohio), Williams (Pa.), Windom, Woodbridge, And Speaker—126.

NAYS.

Adams, Archer, Axtell, Barnes, Barnum, Beck, Boyer, Brooks, Burr, Cary, Chanler, Eldridge, Fox, Getz, Glossbrenner, Golladay, Grover, Haight, Holman, Hotchkiss, Hubbard (Conn.), Humphrey, Johnson, Jones, Kerr, Knott, Marshall, McCormick, McCullough, Morgan, Morrissey, Mungen, Niblack, Nicholson, Phelps, Pruyn, Randall, Ross, Sitgreaves, Stewart, Stone, Taber, Trimble (Ky.), Van Auken, Van Trump, Wood, Woodward—47.

The announcement of the result elicited no manifestation, but the immense audience which had filled the galleries and corridors all the day, gradually dispersed till it was reduced to less than one-fourth its original number.

Mr. Stevens moved to reconsider the vote by which the resolution was agreed to, and also moved to lay the motion to reconsider on the table.

The latter motion was agreed to, this being the parliamentary mode of making a decision final.

Mr. Stevens then moved the following resolution :—

Resolved, That a committee of two be appointed to go to the Senate, and at the bar thereof, in the name of the House of Representatives and of all the people of the United States, to impeach Andrew Johnson, President of the United States, of high crimes and misdemeanors, and acquaint the Senate that the House of Representatives will, in due time, exhibit particular articles of impeachment against him, and make good the same, and that the committee do demand that the Senate take the order for the appearance of said Andrew Johnson to answer to said impeachment.

Second, *Resolved*, that a committee of seven be appointed to prepare and report articles of impeachment against Andrew Johnson, President of the United States, with power to send for persons, papers and records, and to take testimony under oath.

The Democratic members attempted to resort to fillibustering, but were cut off, after an ineffectual effort, by a motion to suspend the rules, so as to bring the House immediately to a vote on the resolutions. The rules were suspended, and the resolutions were adopted. Yeas, 124; nays, 42.

The Speaker then announced the two comitees as follows:—

Committee of two to announce to the Senate the action of the House—Messrs. Stevens (Pa.), and Bingham (Ohio.)

The committee of seven to prepare articles of impeachment, consists of Messrs. Boutwell (Mass.), Stevens (Pa.), Bingham, (Ohio), Wilson, (Ia.), Logan, (Ill.), Julian, (Ind.), and Ward (N. Y.)

The House at twenty minutes past six adjourned.

Impeachment Under the Constitution.

The views and opinions of the fathers of the Republic on the subject of impeaching and removing from office the Executive of the government, may be readily gathered from the following debate in the Federal Convention:—

In the Convention which formed the Constitution of the United States, on June 2, 1787, Mr. Williamson, seconded by Mr. Davie, moved that the President be removed on impeachment and conviction of malpractice or neglect of duty, which was agreed to.

On July 20, Mr. Pinckney and Mr. Gouverneur Morris moved to strike out this provision. Mr. Pinckney observed that the President ought not to be impeachable while in office.

Mr. Davie said:—If he be not impeachable while in office, he will spare no efforts or means whatever to get himself re-elected. He considered this as an essential security for the good behavior of the Executive. Mr. Williamson concurred in making the Executive impeachable while in office.

Mr. Gouverneur Morris said:—He can do no criminal act without coadjutors, who may be punished. In case he should be re-elected that will be a sufficient proof of his innocence. Besides, who is to impeach? *Is the impeachment to suspend his functions?* If it is not, the mischief will go on. If it is, the impeachment will be nearly equivalent to a displacement, and will render the Executive dependent on those who are to impeach.

Colonel Mason remarked:—No point is of more importance than that the right of impeachment should be continued. Shall any man be above justice? Above all, shall that man be above it who can commit the most extensive injustice? When great crimes were committed, he was for punishing the principal as well as the coadjutors. There had been much debate and difficulty as to the mode of choosing the Executive. He approved of that which had been adopted at first, namely, of referring the appointment to the National Legislature. One objection against electors was the danger of their being corrupted by their candidates, and this furnished a peculiar reason in favor of impeachments while in office. Shall the man who has practiced corruption, and by that means procured his appointment in the first instance, be suffered to escape punishment by repeating his guilt?

Dr. Franklin was for retaining the clause as favorable to the Executive. History furnishes one example of a first magistrate being brought formally to justice. Everybody cried out against this as unconstitutional. What was the practice before this in cases where the Chief Magistrate rendered himself obnoxious? Why, recourse was had to assassination, in which he was not only deprived of his life, but of the opportunity of vindicating his character. It would be the best way, therefore, to provide in the Constitution for the regular punishment of the Executive where his misconduct should deserve it, and for his honorable acquittal where he should be unjustly accused.

Mr. Gouverneur Morris would admit corruption and some other few offenses to be such as ought to be impeachable; but he thought the cases ought to be enumerated and defined.

Mr. Madison thought it indispensable that some provision should be made for defending the community against the incapacity, negligence or perfidy of the Chief Magistrate. The limitation of the period of his service was not a sufficient security. He might lose his capacity after his appointment. He might pervert his administration into a scheme of peculation or oppression. He might betray his trust to foreign powers. The case of the executive magistracy was very distinguishable from that of the Legislature or any other public body holding offices of limited duration. It could not be presumed that all or even the majority of the members of an assembly would either lose their capacity for discharging or be bribed to betray their trust. Besides the restraints of their personal integrity and honor, the difficulty of acting in concert for purposes of corruption was a security to the public. And if one or a few members only should be seduced, the soundness of the remaining members would maintain the integrity and fidelity of the body. In the case of the executive magistracy, which was to be administered by a single man, loss of capacity or corruption was more within the compass of probable events, and either of them might be fatal to the republic.

Mr. Pinckney did not see the necessity of impeachments. He was sure they ought not to issue from the Legislature, who would, in that case, hold them as a rod over the Executive, and by that means effectually destroy his independence. His revisionary power, in particular, would be rendered altogether insignificant.

Mr. Gerry urged the necessity of impeachment. A good magistrate will not fear them. A bad one ought to be kept in fear of them. He hoped the maxim would not be adopted here that the Chief Magistrate could do no wrong.

Mr. Rufus King thought that unless the Executive was to hold his place during good behavior, he ought not to be liable to impeachment.

Mr. Randolph said the propriety of impeachments was a favorite principle with him. Guilt wherever found, ought to be punished. The Executive will have great opportunities for abusing his power, particularly in time of war, when the military force, and in some respects, the public money, will be in his hands. Should no punishment be provided, it will be irregularly inflicted by tumults and insurrections.

Dr. Franklin mentioned the case of the Prince of Orange during the late war. An arrangement was made between France and Holland, by which their two fleets were to unite at a certain time and place. The Dutch fleet did not appear. Everybody began to wonder at it. At length it was suspected that the Stadtholder was at the bottom of the matter. This suspicion prevailed more and more. Yet as he could not be impeached, and no regular examination took place, he remained in his office; and strengthening his own party, as the party opposed him became formidable, he gave birth to the most violent animosities and contentions. Had he been impeachable, a regular and peaceable inquiry would have taken place, and he would, if guilty, have been duly punished; if innocent, restored to the confidence of the public.

After further remarks by Mr. King, Mr Wilson and Mr. Pinckney, Mr. Gouverneur Morris said his opinion had been changed by the arguments used in the discussion. He was now sensible of the necessity of impeachment, if the Executive was to continue for any length of time in office. Our Executive was like a magistrate having a hereditary interest in his office. He may be bribed by a greater interest to betray his trust; and no one would say that we ought to expose ourselves to the danger of seeing our first magistrate in foreign pay, without being able to guard against it by displacing him. One would think the King of England well secured against bribery. He has, as it were, a fee simple in the whole kingdom. Yet Charles II was bribed by Louis XIV. The Executive ought, therefore, to be impeached for treachery. Corrupting his electors and incapacity were other causes of impeachment. For the latter he should be punished, not as a man, but as an officer, and punished only by degradation from his office. This magistrate is not the king, but the prime minister. The people are the king. When we make him amenable to justice, however, we should take care to provide some mode that will not make him dependent on the Legislature.

On the 6th day of September the clause referring to the Senate the trial of impeachment against the President, for treason and bribery, was taken up.

Colonel Mason said:—Why is the provision restrained to treason and bribery only? Treason, as defined in the Constitution, will not reach many great and dangerous offenses. Hastings is not guilty of treason. Attempts to subvert the Constitution may not be treason, as above defined. As bills of attainder, which have saved the British Constitution, are forbidden, it is the more necessary to extend the power of impeachments. He moved to add, after "bribery," "or maladministration."

Mr. Gerry seconded him.

Mr. Madison objected. So vague a term will be equivalent to a tenure during the pleasure of the Senate.

Mr. Gouverneur Morris remarked:—It will not be put in force, and can do no harm. An election every four years will prevent maladministration.

Colonel Mason withdrew "maladministration" and substituted "other high crimes and misdemeanors against the State." And the proposition as amended was adopted.

Mr. Madison objected to a trial of the President by the Senate, especially as he was to be impeached by the other branch of the Legislature, and for any act which might be called a misdemeanor. He would prefer the Supreme Court for the trial of impeachments; or, rather, a tribunal of which that should form a part.

Mr. Gouverneur Morris thought no other tribunal than the Senate could be trusted. The Supreme Court were too few in number, and might be warped or corrupted. He was against a dependence of the Executive on the Legislature, considering legislative tyranny the great danger to be apprehended; but there could be no danger that the Senate would say untruly, on their oaths that the President was guilty of crimes or faults, especially as in four years he can be turned out.

After some further debate, the clause was amended by adding the words "and every member shall be on oath," and as adopted reads as follows:—

"The Senate of the United States shall have power to try all impeachments, but no person shall be convicted without the concurrence of two-thirds of the members present, and every member shall be on oath."

The Senate Notified.

On the day following the passage of the Impeachment Resolution (Tuesday, February 25), the House of Representatives officially notified the Senate of its action.

While Senator Garrett Davis (Ky.) was addressing the Chair, the Doorkeeper announced a committee of the House of Representatives, and Messrs. Stevens and Bingham entered and stood facing the President pro tem., while a large number of members of the House ranged themselves in a semi-circle behind.

When order was restored, Mr. STEVENS read, in a firm voice, as follows:—

Mr. President:—In obedience to the order of the House of Representatives, we have appeared before you; and in the name of the House of Representatives and of all the people of the United States, we do impeach Andrew Johnson, President of the United States, of high crimes and misdemeanors in office. And we further inform the Senate that the House of Representatives will, in due time, exhibit particular articles of impeachment against him, and make good the same. And in their name we demand that the Senate take due order for the appearace of the said Andrew Johnson to answer to the said impeachment.

The President *pro tem.*—The Senate will take order in the premises.

Mr. Stevens was then furnished with a chair, and sat in the spot whence he had addressed the Chair.

Mr. HOWARD (Mich.) addressed the Chair, but

Mr. DAVIS insisted that he had the floor, having given way only for the reception of a message from the House.

The Chair said the Senator certainly had the floor.

Mr. DAVIS said:—" Mr. President, I was about to renew my remarks, when Mr. Howard asked whether this was not a question of privilege?"

The Chair did not know that there was any rule about it.

Mr. DAVIS.—Mr. President, no question of privilege.

Mr. HOWARD.—I call the Senator to order, and claim that this is a privileged question.

The President *pro tem.*—There is a question of order raised, which the Chair will submit to the Senate for its decision.

Mr. DAVIS—I will just ask—

The President *pro tem.*—The question of order must be settled before the Senator can proceed.

Mr. JOHNSON—Mr. President, I should like to know what the question of order is.

The President *pro tem.*—The question is whether the Senator must give way to a privileged question.

Mr. HOWARD said the House of Representatives having sent a committee announcing that in due time they will present articles of impeachment against Andrew Johnson, President of the United States, and asking that the Senate take order in reference thereto, the message of the House had been received, and the subject-matter was now before the Senate, and his contemplated motion was the appointment of a select committee to whom it should be referred, and he thought that was a question of privilege.

Mr. DAVIS replied that he had given way in deference to the universal usage established by courtesy between the two Houses for the reception of a message from the House. When that message was delivered, he had a right to resume the floor, and the Senator could not take it from him to make a privileged motion, or any motion.

Mr. EDMUNDS thought the Senator from Kentucky was entitled to the floor, while he did not admit the propriety as a matter of taste, or the delicacy of his insisting upon it. (Laughter.)

Mr. DAVIS preferred to settle such questions for himself, without regard to the Senator's opinion or judgment. Had he been asked to yield the floor, he would not have hesitated for an instant, but when it was attempted to take the floor from him, he denied the right to it; and the Chair having decided in his favor, he would now complete his remarks. They were not long. (Laughter.)

Mr. CONNESS hoped the Senator from Kentucky, always contentious, would yield his undoubted right on this occasion.

Mr. DAVIS said it must first be decided by the Senate whether he had the right or not, and then he would waive or not as seemed proper.

The Chair put the question, and the Senate voted to allow Mr. Davis to continue.

Mr. DAVIS, with much cheerfulness—I now yield the floor for the purpose indicated by the Senator from Michigan. (Laughter.)

Mr. HOWARD (Mich.) offered the following:—

Resolved, That the message of the House of Representatives relative to the impeachment of Andrew Johnson, President of the United States, be referred to a select committee of seven, to consider the same and report thereon.

Mr. BAYARD (Del.) had no objection to the resolution, but would call attention to the fact that this was a mere notice that the House of Representatives intended to impeach the President. Impeachment could not be acted upon until articles of impeachment were presented, and the Senate had no authority as a legislative body to act in relation to a question of impeachment, the Constitution requiring them to be organized into a court, with the Chief Justice President when the question of impeachment came before them. Until that time they could entertain no motion in regard to the fact; that the court would be called upon to make its own orders, under the Constitution and laws.

Mr. HOWARD said the course pointed out by the Senator was not according to the precedent furnished by the case of Judge Peck, in the year 1830. In that case, according to the journals of the Senate, a message was brought from the House of Representatives by Mr. Buchanan and Mr. Henry Storrs, two of their members, and was in the following words:—

"Mr. President:—We have been directed, in the name of the House of Representatives and of all the people of the United States, to impeach James H. Peck, Judge of the District Court of the United States for the District of Missouri, of high misdemeanors in office, and to acquaint the Senate that the House will in due time exhibit particular articles of impeachment against him, and make good the same. We have also been directed to demand that the Senate take order for the appearance of the said James H. Peck to answer to said impeachment," and they withdrew.

"The Senate proceeded to consider the last mentioned message, and, on motion of Mr. Tazewell, it was resolved that it be referred to a select committee, to consist of three members, to consider and report thereon. Ordered, that Mr, Tazewell, Mr. Webster and Mr. Bell be the committee."

That was a preliminary proceeding, and this case was precisely similar to it.

Mr. POMEROY (Kan.) said the mode of preliminary proceeding had always been precisely the same as in the case just read. When the managers appeared on the part of the House of Representatives, they presented their articles to the Court of Impeachment. This, however, was only the presentation—the notice always given to the Senate.

Mr. JOHNSON (Md.) had no doubt the mode proposed by the Senator from Michigan (Mr. Howard) was proper. He believed that in all preceding cases, a committee had been appointed to take into consideration the message received from the House, and to recommend such measures as were deemed advisable; and he knew no reason why that should not be done here. Perhaps, however, it would be more advisable to delay the resolution for a day, and let the matter be disposed of by the Senate.

Mr. CONKLING (N. Y.), referring to the case of the impeachment by the Senate of Judge Humphreys, of Tennessee, suggested that the words "to be appointed by the Chair," be included in the resolution.

Mr. HOWARD accepted the amendment.

The resolution was unanimously adopted.

Articles of Impeachment.

Meanwhile the House Committee appointed to draw up the articles of impeacment examined numerous witnesses and proceeded carefully to prepare the charges and specifications against the Executive, and on the last day of February they reported the results of their labors as follows:—

Articles exhibited by the House of Representatives of the United States, in the name of themselves and all the people of the United States, against Andrew Johnson, President of the United States, as maintenance and support of their impeachment against him for high crimes and misdemeanor in office:—

Article 1. That said Andrew Johnson, President of the United States, on the 21st day of February, in the year of our Lord, 1868, at Washington, in the District of Columbia, unmindful of the high duties of his oath of office and of the requirements of the Constitution, that he should take care that the laws be faithfully executed, did unlawfully, in violation of the Constitution and laws of the United States, issue an order in writing for the removal of Edwin M. Stanton from the office of Secretary of the Department of War, said Edwin M. Stanton having been, therefor, duly appointed and commissioned by and with the advice and consent of the Senate of the United States as such Secretary; and said Andrew Johnson, President of the United States, on the 12th day of August, in the year of our Lord 1867, and during the recess of said Senate, having suspended by his order Edwin M. Stanton from said office, and within twenty days after the first day of the next meeting of said Senate, on the 12th day of December, in the year last aforesaid, having reported to said Senate such suspension, with the evidence and reasons for his action in the case, and the name of the person designated to perform the duties of such office temporarily, until the next meeting of the Senate, and said Senate thereafterwards, on the 13th day of January, in the year of our Lord 1868, having duly considered the evidence and reasons reported by said Andrew Johnson for said suspension, did refuse to concur in said suspension; whereby and by force of the provisions of an act entitled "an act regulating the tenure of civil offices," passed March 2, 1867, said Edwin M. Stanton did forthwith resume the functions of his office, whereof the said Andrew Johnson had then and there due notice, and the said Edwin M. Stanton, by reason of the premises, on said 21st day of February, was lawfully entitled to hold said office of Secretary for the Department of War, which said order for the removal of said Edwin

M. Stanton is, in substance, as follows, that is to say:—

EXECUTIVE MANSION, WASHINGTON, D. C., Feb. 21, 1868. —Sir:—By virtue of the power and authority vested in me, as President, by the Constitution and laws of the United States, you are hereby removed from the office of Secretary for the Department of War, and your functions as such will terminate upon receipt of this communication. You will transfer to Brevet Major-General L. Thomas, Adjutant-General of the Army, who has this day been authorized and empowered to act as Secretary of War *ad interim*, all books, papers and other public property now in your custody and charge. Respectfully, yours,
ANDREW JOHNSON.
To the Hon. E. M. Stanton, Secretary of War.

Which order was unlawfully issued, and with intent then are there to violate the act entitled "An act regulating the tenure of certain civil offices," passed March 2, 1867, and contrary to the provisions of said act, and in violation thereof, and contrary to the provisions of the Constitution of the United States, and without the advice and consent of the Senate of the United States, the said Senate then and there being in session, to remove said E. M. Stanton from the office of Secretary for the Department of War, whereby said Andrew Johnson, President of the United States, did then and there commit, and was guilty of a high misdemeanor in office.

Article 2. That on the 21st day of February, in the year of our Lord 1868, at Washington, in the District of Columbia, said Andrew Johnson, President of the United States, unmindful of the high duties of his oath of office, and in violation of the Constitution of the United States, and contrary to the provisions of an act entitled "An act regulating the tenure of certain civil offices," passed March 2, 1867, without the advice and consent of the Senate, then and there being in session, and without authority of law, did appoint one L. Thomas to be Secretary of War *ad interim*, by issuing to said Lorenzo Thomas a letter of authority, in substance as follows, that is to say:—

EXECUTIVE MANSION, WASHINGTON, D. C., Feb. 21, 1868. —Sir:—The Hon. Edwin M. Stanton having been this day removed from office as Secretary of the Department of War, you are hereby authorized and empowered to act as Secretary of War *ad interim*, and will immediately enter upon the discharge of the duties pertaining to that office. Mr. Stanton has been instructed to transfer to you all the records, books, papers and other public property now in his custody and charge. Respectfully yours,
ANDREW JOHNSON.
To Brevet Major-General Lorenzo Thomas, Adjutant-General United States Army, Washington, D. C.

Whereby said Andrew Johnson, President of the United States, did then and there commit, and was guilty of a high misdemanor in office.

Article 3. That said Andrew Johnson, President of the United States, on the 21st day of February, in the year of our Lord one thousand eight hundred and sixty-eight, at Washington in the District of Columbia, did commit, and was guilty of a high misdemeanor in office, in this:—That without authority of law, while the Senate of the United States was then and there in session, he did appoint one Lorenzo Thomas to be Secretary for the Department of War, *ad interim*, without the advice and consent of the Senate, and in violation of the Constitution of the United States, no vacancy having happened in said office of Secretary for the Department of War during the recess of the Senate, and no vacancy existing in said office at the time, and which said appointment so made by Andrew Johnson of said Lorenzo Thomas is in substance as follows, that is to say:—

EXECUTIVE MANSION, WASHINGTON, D. C., Feb. 21, 1868. —Sir:—The Hon. E. M. Stanton having been this day removed from office as Secretary for the Department of War, you are hereby authorized and empowered to act as Secretary of War *ad interim*, and will immediately enter upon the discharge of the duties pertaining to that office. Mr. Stanton has been instructed to transfer to you all the records, books, papers, and other public property now in his custody and charge. Respectfully yours,
ANDREW JOHNSON.
To Brevet Major-General L. Thomas, Adjutant-General United States Army, Washington, D. C.

Article 4. That said Andrew Johnson, President of the United States, unmindful of the high duties of his office, and of his oath of office, in violation of the Constitution and laws of the United States, on the 21st day of February, in the year of our Lord 1868, at Washington, in the District of Columbia, did unlawfully conspire with one Lorenzo Thomas, and with other persons to the House of Representatives unknown, with intent, by intimidation and threats, to hinder and prevent Edwin M. Stanton, then and there, the Secretary for the Department of War, duly appointed under the laws of the United States, from holding said office of Secretary for the Department of War, contrary to and in violation of the Constitution of the United States, and of the provisions of an act entitled "An act to define and punish certain conspiracies," approved July 31, 1861, whereby said Andrew Johnson, President of the United States, did then and there commit and was guilty of high crime in office.

Article 5. That said Andrew Johnson, President of the United States, unmindful of the high duties of his office and of his oath of office, on the 21st of February, in the year of our Lord one thousand eight hundred and sixty-eight, and on divers others days and times in said year before the 28th day of said February, at Washington, in the District of Columbia, did unlawfully conspire with one Lorenzo Thomas, and with other persons in the House of Representatives unknown, by force to prevent and hinder the execution of an act entitled "An act regulating the tenure of certain civil offices," passed March 2, 1867, and in pursuance of said conspiracy, did attempt to prevent E. M. Stanton, then and there being Secretary for the Department of War, duly appointed and commissioned under the laws of the United States, from holding said office, whereby the said Andrew Johnson, President of the United States, did then and there commit and was guilty of high misdemeanor in office.

Article 6. That Andrew Johnson, President of the United States, unmindful of the duties of his high office and of his oath of office, on the 21st day of February, in the year of our Lord 1868, at Washington, in the District of Columbia, did unlawfully conspire with one Lorenzo Thomas, by force to seize, take and possess the property of the United States at the War Department, contrary to the provisions of an act entitled "An act to define and punish certain conspiracies," approved July 31, 1861, and with intent to violate and disregard an act entitled "An act regulating the tenure of certain civil offices," passed March 2, 1867, whereby said Andrew Johnson, President of the United States, did then and there commit a high crime in office.

Article 7. That said Andrew Johnson, President of the United States, unmindful of the high duties of his office, and of his oath of office, on the 21st day of February, in the year of our Lord 1868, and on divers other days in said year, before the 28th day of said February, at Washington, in the District of Columbia, did unlawfully conspire with one Lorenzo Thomas to prevent and hinder the execution of an act of the United States, entitled "An act regulating the tenure of certain civil office," passed March 2, 1867, and in pursuance of said conspiracy, did unlawfully attempt to prevent Edwin M. Stanton, then and there being Secretary for the Department of War, under the laws of the United States, from holding said office to which he had been duly appointed and commissioned, whereby said Andrew Johnson, President of the United States, did there and then commit and was guilty of a high misdemeanor in office.

Article 8. That said Andrew Johnson, President of the United States, unmindful of the high duties of his office, and of his oath of office, on the 21st day of February, in the year of our Lord, 1868, at Washington, in the District of Columbia, did unlawfully conspire with one Lorenzo Thomas, to seize, take and possess the property of the United States in the War Department, with intent to violate and disregard the act entitled "An act regulating the tenure of certain civil offices," passed March 2, 1867, whereby said Andrew Johnson, President of the United States, did then and there commit a high misdemeanor in office.

Article 9. That said Andrew Johnson, President of the United States, on the 22d day of February, in the year of our Lord 1868, at Washington, in the District of Columbia, in disregard of the Constitution and the law of Congress duly enacted, as Commander-in-Chief, did bring before himself, then and there, William H. Emory, a Major-General by brevet in the Army of the United States, actually in command of the Department of Washington, and the military forces therefor, and did then and there, as Commander-in-Chief, declare to, and instruct said Emory, that part of a law of the United States, passed March 2, 1867, entitled "an act for making appropriations for the support of the army for the year ending June 30, 1868, and for other purposes," especially the second section thereof, which provides, among other things,

that all orders and instructions relating to military operations issued by the President and Secretary of War, shall be issued through the General of the Army, and in case of his inability, through the next in rank was unconstitutional, and in contravention of the commission of Emory, and therefore not binding on him, as an officer in the Army of the United States, which said provisions of law had been therefore duly and legally promulgated by General Order for the government and direction of the Army of the United States, as the said Andrew Johnson then and there well knew, with intent thereby to induce said Emory, in his official capacity as Commander of the Department of Washington, to violate the provisions of said act, and to take and receive, act upon and obey such orders as he, the said Andrew Johnson, might make and give, and which should not be issued through the General of the Army of the United States, according to the provisions of said act, whereby said Andrew Johnson, President of the United States, did then and there commit, and was guilty of a high misdemeanor in office; and the House of Representatives, by protestation, saving to themselves the liberty of exhibition, at any time hereafter, any further articles of their accusation or impeachment against the said Andrew Johnson, President of the United States, and also of replying to his answers, which will make up the articles herein preferred against him, and of offering proof to the same and every part thereof, and to all and every other article, accusation or impeachment which shall be exhibited by them as the case shall require, do demand that the said Andrew Johnson may be put to answer the high crimes and misdemeanors in office herein charged against him, and that such proceedings, examinations, trials and judgments may be thereupon had and given as may be agreeable to law and justice.

An animated debate sprang up on the question of the adoption of the above articles, which was continued until March 2, when they were adopted, and Speaker Colfax announced as managers of the impeachment trial on the part of the House, Messrs. Thaddeus Stevens, B. F. Butler, John H. Bingham, George S. Boutwell, J. F. Wilson, T. Williams and John A. Logan.

It was then ordered that the articles agreed to by the House to be exhibited in its name and in the name of all the people of the United States, against Andrew Johnson, President of the United States, in maintenance of the impeachment against him for high crimes and misdemeanors in office, be carried to the Senate by the managers appointed to conduct such impeachment.

General Butler's Supplementary Article.

On the 2d of March, General Butler proposed an additional article, but as the vote on the previous articles was taken on that day, final action was postponed until the 3d, when General Butler again reported it, remarking that, with but a single exception, the managers favored the adoption of the article. He strongly urged the reception of the charges he had prepared, saying:—

"The articles already adopted presented only the bone and sinew of the offenses of Andrew Johnson. He wanted to clothe that bone and sinew with flesh and blood, and to show him before the country as the quivering sinner that he is, so that hereafter, when posterity came to examine these proceedings, it might not have cause to wonder that the only offense charged against Andrew Johnson was a merely technical one. He would have him go down to posterity as the representative man of this age, with a label upon him that would stick to him through all time."

The article was adopted. Yeas, 87; nays, 41—the only Republicans voting in the negative being Messrs. Ashley (Nev.), Coburn, Griswold, Laflin, Mallory, Marvin, Pomeroy, Smith, Wilson, (Ia.), Wilson (Ohio), Windom and Woodbridge.

This article was made the tenth on the list, and is as follows:—

Article 10. That said Andrew Johnson, President of the United States, unmindful of the high duties of his high office and the dignity and proprieties thereof, and of the harmony and courtesies which ought to exist and be maintained between the executive and legislative branches of the Government of the United States, designing and intending to set aside the rightful authorities and powers of Congress, did attempt to bring into disgrace, ridicule, hatred, contempt and reproach, the Congress of the United States, and the several branches thereof, to impair and destroy the regard and respect of all the good people of the United States for the Congress and the legislative power thereof, which all officers of the government ought inviolably to preserve and maintain, and to excite the odium and resentment of all good people of the United States against Congress and the laws by it duly and constitutionally enacted; and in pursuance of his said design and intent, openly and publicly, and before divers assemblages of citizens of the United States, convened in divers parts thereof, to meet and receive said Andrew Johnson as the Chief Magistrate of the United States, did, on the eighteenth day of August, in the year of our Lord one thousand eight hundred and sixty-six, and on divers other days and times, as well before as afterwards, make and declare, with a loud voice, certain intemperate, inflammatory and scandalous harangues, and therein utter loud threats and bitter menaces, as well against Congress as the laws of the United States duly enacted thereby, amid the cries, jeers and laughter of the multitudes then assembled in hearing, which are set forth in the several specifications hereinafter written, in substance and effect, that is to say:—

THE SPECIFICATIONS.

"Specification First. In this, that at Washington, in the District of Columbia, in the Executive Mansion, to a committee of citizens who called upon the President of the United States, speaking of and concerning the Congress of the United States, heretofore, to wit:— On the 18th day of August, in the year of our Lord, 1866, in a loud voice, declare in substance and effect, among other things, that is to say:—

" 'So far as the Executive Department of the government is concerned, the effort has been made to restore the Union, to heal the breach, to pour oil into the wounds which were consequent upon the struggle, and, to speak in a common phrase, to prepare, as the learned and wise physician would, a plaster healing in character and co-extensive with the wound. We thought and we think that we had partially succeeded, but as the work progresses, as reconstruction seemed to be taking place, and the country was becoming reunited, we found a disturbing and moving element opposing it. In alluding to that element it shall go no further than your Convention, and the distinguished gentleman who has delivered the report of the proceedings, I shall make no reference that I do not believe, and the time and the occasion justify. We have witnessed in one department of the government every endeavor to prevent the restoration of peace, harmony and union. We have seen hanging upon the verge of the government, as it were, a body called or which assumes to be the Congress of the United States, while in fact it is a Congress of only part of the States. We have seen this Congress pretend to be for the Union, when its every step and act tended to perpetuate disunion and make a disruption of States inevitable. We have seen Congress gradually encroach, step by step, upon constitutional rights, and violate day after day, and month after month, fundamental principles of the government. •We have seen a Congress that seemed to forget that there was a limit to the sphere and scope of legislation. We have seen a Congress in a minority assume to exercise power which, if allowed to be consummated, would result in despotism or monarchy itself.'

"Specification Second. In this, that at Cleveland, in the State of Ohio, heretofore to wit:—On the third day of September, in the year of our Lord, 1866, before a public assemblage of citizens and others, said Andrew Johnson, President of the United States, speaking of and concerning the Congress of the United States, did, in a loud voice, declare in substance and effect, among other things, that is to say:—

" 'I will tell you what I did do—I called upon your Congress that is trying to break up the government. In conclusion, beside that Congress had taken much pains to poison the constituents against him, what has Congress done? Have they done anything to restore the union of the States? No. On the contrary, they had done everything to prevent it; and because he stood now where he did when the Rebellion commenced, he had been denounced as a traitor. Who had run greater risks or made greater sacrifices than himself? But Congress, factious and domineering, had undertaken to poison the minds of the American people.'

"Specification Third. In this case, that at St. Louis, in the State of Missouri, heretofore to wit:—On the 8th day of September, in the year of our Lord 1866, before a public assemblage of citizens and others, said Andrew Johnson, President of the United States, speaking of acts concerning the Congress of the United States, did, in a loud voice, declare in substance and effect, among other things, that is to say:—

" 'Go on; perhaps if you had a word or two on the subject of New Orleans you might understand more about it than you do, and if you will go back and ascertain the cause of the riot at New Orleans, perhaps you will not be so prompt in calling out "New Orleans." If you will take up the riot of New Orleans and trace it back to its source and its immediate cause, you will find out who was responsible for the blood that was shed there. If you will take up the riot at New Orleans and trace it back to the Radical Congress, you will find out that the riot at New Orleans was substantially planned. If you will take up the proceedings in their caucuses you will understand that they knew that a convention was to be called which was extinct by its powers having expired; that it was said that the intention was that a new government was to be organized, and on the organization of that government the intention was to enfranchise one portion of the population, called the colored population, and who had been emancipated, and at the same time disfranchise white men. When you design to talk about New Orleans you ought to understand what you are talking about. When you read the speeches that were made, and take up the facts on the Friday and Saturday before that convention sat, you will find that speeches were made incendiary in their character, exciting that portion of the population—the black population —to arm themselves and prepare for the shedding of blood. You will also find that convention did assemble in violation of law, and the intention of that convention was to supersede the organized authorities in the State of Louisiana, which had been organized by the government of the United States, and every man engaged in that rebellion, in that convention, with the intention of superseding and upturning the civil government which had been recognized by the Government of the United States. I say that he was a traitor to the Constitution of the United States, and hence you find that another rebellion was commenced, having its origin in the Radical Congress. So much for the New Orleans riot. And there was the cause and the origin of the blood that was shed, and every drop of blood that was shed is upon their skirts and they are responsible. I could test this thing a little closer, but will not do it here to-night. But when you talk about the causes and consequences that resulted from proceedings of that kind, perhaps, as I have been introduced here and you have provoked questions of this kind, though it does not provoke me, I will tell you a few wholesome things that have been done by this Radical Congress in connection with New Orleans and the extension of the elective franchise. I know that I have been traduced and abused. I know it has come in advance of me here, as elsewhere, that I have attempted to exercise an arbitrary power in resisting laws that were intended to be forced upon the government; that I had exercised that power; that I had abandoned the party that elected me, and that I was a traitor, because I exercised the veto power in attempting, and did arrest for a time, that which was called a "Freedmen's Bureau" bill. Yes, that I was a traitor. And I have been traduced; I have been slandered; I have been maligned; I have been called Judas Iscariot, and all that. Now, my countrymen, here to-night, it is very easy to indulge in epithets; it is easy to call a man a Judas, and cry out traitor, but when he is called upon to give arguments and facts he is very often found wanting. Judas Iscariot—Judas! There was a Judas, and he was one of the twelve Apostles. O, yes, the twelve Apostles had a Christ, and he never could have had a Judas unless he had twelve Apostles. If I have played the Judas who has been my Christ that I have played the Judas with? Was it Thad. Stevens? Was it Wendell Phillips? Was it Charles Sumner? They are the men that stop and compare themselves with the Savior, and everybody that differs with them in opinion, and tries to stay and arrest their diabolical and nefarious policy is to be denounced as a Judas. Well, let me say to you, if you will stand by me in this action, if you will stand by me in trying to give the people a fair chance—soldiers and citizens—to participate in these offices, God be willing, I will kick them out. I will kick them out just as fast as I can. Let me say to you, in concluding, that what I have said is what I intended to say; I was not provoked into this, and care not for their menaces, the taunts and the jeers. I care not for threats, I do not intend to be bullied by enemies, nor overawed by my friends. But, God willing, with your help, I will veto their measures whenever any of them come to me.'

" Which said utterances, declarations, threats and harangues, highly censurable in any, are peculiarly indecent and unbecoming in the Chief Magistrate of the United States, by means whereof the said Andrew Johnson has brought the high office of the President of the United States into contempt, ridicule and disgrace, to the great scandal of all good citizens, whereby said Andrew Johnson, President of the United States, did commit, and was then and there guilty of a high misdemeanor in office.

The Eleventh Article.

On the same day Mr. Bingham offered still another article, stating that it had received the unanimous vote of the managers, and he moved the previous question on its adoption. After slight objections from Messrs. Brooks and Eldridge it was adopted by the same vote as the previous articles.

Article 11. That the said Andrew Johnson, President of the United States, unmindful of the high duties of his office and his oath of office, and in disregard of the Constitution and laws of the United States, did, heretofore, to wit:—On the 18th day of August, 1866, at the city of Washington, and in the District of Columbia, by public speech, declare and affirm in substance, that the Thirty-ninth Congress of the United States was not a Congress of the United States authorized by the Constitution to exercise legislative power under the same, but on the contrary, was a Congress of only part of the States, thereby denying and intending to deny, that the legislation of said Congress was valid or obligatory upon him, the said Andrew Johnson, except in so far as he saw fit to approve the same, and also thereby denying the power of the said Thirty-ninth Congress to propose amendments to the Constitution of the United States. And in pursuance of said declaration, the said Andrew Johnson, President of the United States, afterwards, to wit:—On the 21st day of February, 1868, at the city of Washington, D. C., did, unlawfully and in disregard of the requirements of the Constitution that he should take care that the laws be faithfully executed, attempt to prevent the execution of an act entitled "An act regulating the tenure of certain civil offices," passed March 2, 1867, by unlawfully devising and contriving and attempting to devise and contrive means by which he should prevent Edwin M. Stanton from forthwith resuming the functions of the office of Secretary for the Department of War, notwithstanding the refusal of the Senate to concur in the suspension theretofore made by the said Andrew Johnson of said Edwin M. Stanton from said office of Secretary for the Department of War; and also by further unlawfully devising and contriving, and attempting to devise and contrive means then and there to prevent the execution of an act entitled "An act making appropriations for the support of the army for the fiscal year ending June 30, 1868, and for other purposes," approved March 20, 1867. And also to prevent the execution of an act entitled "An act to provide for the more efficient government of the Rebel States," passed March 2, 1867. Whereby the said Andrew Johnson, President of the United States, did then, to wit, on the 21st day of February, 1868, at the

city of Washington, commit and was guilty of a high misdemeanor in office.

Impeachment Articles Read to the Senate.

On the 4th of March, 1868, at five minutes past one o'clock, members of the House entered the Senate, preceded by the Sergeant-at-Arms of the Senate. As they stepped inside the bar of the Senate, the Sergeant-at-Arms announced, in a loud voice, "The Managers of the House of Representatives, to present articles of impeachment." The managers walked to the front part of the Senate Chamber, close to the President's desk, and took seats, while the members of the House ranged themselves around the seats of the Senators.

After silence was restored, Mr. Bingham arose and said, holding the articles in his hand:—"The Managers of the House of Representatives, by order of the House of Representatives, are ready at the bar of the Senate, if it will please the Senate to hear them, to present the articles of impeachment, in maintenance of the impeachment preferred against Andrew Johnson, President of the United States, by the House of Representatives."

Hon. B. F. Wade, President of the Senate, then said:—"The Sergeant-at-Arms will make proclamation."

The Sergeant-at-arms then said:—"Hear ye! hear ye! hear ye! All persons are commanded to keep silence, on pain of imprisonment, while the House of Representatives is exhibiting to the Senate of the United States, articles of impeachment against Andrew Johnson, President of the United States."

Mr. Bingham then rose and commenced reading the articles.

Every person kept perfectly still while Mr. Bingham was reading the articles. The galleries were closely packed, and hundreds of people stood in the halls and corridors, unable to get even a glimpse of the inside proceedings.

At the conclusion of the reading of the articles, which occupied thirty minutes, President Wade said:—"The Senate will take due order and cognizance of the articles of impeachment, of which due notice will be given by the Senate to the House of Representatives."

The House then withdrew, with Mr. Dawes as Chairman of the House Committee of the Whole on the State of the Union, to the hall of the House.

Opening of the Trial.

On the day following the presentation of the articles of impeachment to the Senate, the trial was formally opened. At the conclusion of the morning hour, Vice President Wade announced that all legislative and executive business of the Senate is ordered to cease, for the purpose of proceeding to business connected with the impeachment of the President of the United States. The chair is vacated for that purpose.

The Chief Justice then advanced up the aisle, clad in his official robe, assisted by Mr. Pomeroy, chairman of the committee appointed for that purpose, with Judge Nelson, of the Supreme Court, on his right; Messrs. Buckalew and Wilson, the other members of the committee, bringing up the rear, with members of the House, who stood behind the bar of the Senate.

The Chief Justice, having ascended to the President's chair, said, in a measured and impressive voice:—

"Senators—In obedience to notice, I have appeared to join with you in forming a Court of Impeachment for the trial of the President of the United States, and I am now ready to take oath."

Oath of the Chief Justice.

The following oath was then administered to the Chief Justice by Judge Nelson:—

"I do solemnly swear that in all things appertaining to the trial of the impeachment of Andrew Johnson, President of the United States, I will do impartial justice, according to the Constitution and laws. So help me God."

The Chief Justice then said:—Senators, the oath will now be administered to the Senators as they will be called by the Secretary in succession,

The Senators Sworn.

The Secretary called the roll, each Senator advancing in turn and taking the oath prescribed in the rules as given above. The only Senators absent were Doolittle (Vt.), Patterson (N. H.), Saulsbury (Del.) and Edmunds (Vt.)

Hon. B. F. Wade Challenged.

When the name of Senator Wade was called,

Mr. HENDRICKS rose and put the question to the presiding officer, whether Senator from Ohio, being the person who would succeed to the Presidential office, was entitled to sit as a judge in the case.

Remarks of Mr. Sherman.

Mr. SHERMAN argued that the Constitution itself settled that question. It provided that the presiding officer should not preside on the trial of the President, but being silent as to his right to be a member of the court, it followed by implication that he had the right to be a member of the court, each State was entitled to be represented by two Senators.

The Senate had already seen a Senator who was related to the President by marriage take the oath, and he could see no difference between interest on the ground of affinity and the interest which the Senator from Ohio might be supposed to have. Besides, the Senator from Ohio was only the presiding officer of the Senate *pro tempore*, and might or might not continue as such to the close of these proceedings. He, therefore, hoped that the oath would be administered to the Senator from Ohio.

Reverdy Johnson's Views.

Mr. JOHNSON (Md.) assimilated this case to an ordinary judicial proceeding, and reminded the Senate that no judge would be allowed to sit in a case where he holds a direct interest. Was it right, he said, to subject a Senator to such great temptation—the whole Executive power of the nation, with twenty-five thousand dollars a year? He submitted, therefore, that it was due to the cause of impartial justice that such precedent should not be established as would bring the Senate in disrepute. Why was it that the Chief Justice now presided? It was because the fathers of the republic thought that he who was to be entitled to benefits should not be permitted ever to preside where he could only vote in case of a tie vote. He did not know that the question could be decided at once. It was a grave and important question, and would be so considered by the country, and he submitted whether it was not proper to postpone its decision till to-morrow, in order, particularly, that the precedents of the English House of Lords might be examined. He moved, therefore, that the question be postponed till to-morrow.

Mr. DAVIS (Ky.) argued that the question was to be decided on principle, and that principle was to be found in the Constitution. It was thought the man who was to succeed the President in case of removal from office should not take part in the trial of the President. If the case of Mr. Wade did not come within the letter of the Constitution, it did come clearly within its principle and meaning.

Mr. MORRILL (Me.) argued that there was no party before the court to make the objection, and that it did not lie in the province of one Senator to raise an objection against a fellow Senator. When the party appeared here, then objection could be made and argued; but not here and now. It seemed to him that there was no option and no discretion but to administer the oath to all the Senators.

Mr. HENDRICKS (Ind.) argued that it was inherent in a court to judge of its own qualification, and it was not for a Senator to present the question. It was for the court itself to determine whether a member claiming a seat in the court was entitled to it; therefore, the question was not immaturely made. The suggestion of Senator Sherman that Senator Wade might not continue to be President of the Senate, was no answer to the objection. When he should cease to be the presiding officer of the Senate he could be sworn in, but now, at this time, he was incompetent.

In the case of Senator Stockton, of New Jersey, the question had been decided. There it was held that the Senator, being interested in the result of the vote, had no right to vote. One of the standing rules of the Senate itself was, that no Senator should vote where he had an interest in the result of the vote, but in his judgment the constitutional ground was even higher than the question of interest. The Vice President was not allowed, by the Constitution, to keep order in the Senate during an impeachment trial. He hoped he need not disclaim any personal feeling in the matter. He made the point now because he thought the Constitution itself had settled it that no man should help to deprive the President of his office when that man himself was to fill the office. He hoped that, in view of the importance of the question, the motion made by the Senator from Maryland would prevail.

Mr. WILLIAMS (Ore.) held that the objection was entirely immature. If this body was the Senate, then the presiding officer of the Senate should preside, and if it was not, was there any court organized to decide the question? He never heard that one juror could challenge another juror, or that one judge could challenge another judge. Had a court ever been known to adopt a rule that a certain member of it should or should not participate in its proceedings. It was a matter entirely for the judge himself.

Mr. DAVIS asked the question whether, if a Vice President came here to present himself as a member of the court, the court itself could not exclude him?

Mr. WILLIAMS did not think that a parallel case, for by the very words of the Constitution the Vice President was excluded. It did not follow that because this court was organized as the Constitution required, a Senator having any interest would participate in the trial. He might, when the time came on for trial, decline to participate. If any Senator should insist, notwithstanding the rule of the Senate referred to, on his right to vote, even on a question where he had an interest, he had a constitutional right to do so.

Mr. FESSENDEN (Me.) suggested that the administration of the oath to the Senator from Ohio be passed over for the present until all the other Senators are sworn.

Mr. CONNESS (Cal.) objected, that there was no right on the part of the Senate to raise a question as to the right of another Senator, and he preferred that a vote be now taken and the question decided. The question as to whether a Senator had such an interest in the result as to keep him from participating in the trial, was a matter for the Senator alone.

Mr. FESSENDEN explained that his intention was simply that all the other Senators should be sworn, so as to be able to act upon the question as a duly organized court.

He cared nothing about it, however, one way or another, and he had no opinion to express on the subject.

Can a Senator be Excluded from the Senate?

Mr. HOWARD (Mich.) sustained the right of the Senator from Ohio to be sworn and to participate in the trial. He did not understand on what ground this objection could be sustained. They were not acting in their ordinary capacity as a Senate, but were acting as a court. What right had the members of the Senate, not yet sworn, to vote on this objection? How was the subject to be got at? Could the members already sworn exclude a Senator? That would be a strange deposition. As the Senate was now fixed it had no right to pass a resolution or an order. It was an act simply *coram non judice*. He suggested, therefore, that the objection be withdrawn for the present.

The President Might Ask a Question.

Mr. MORTON (Ind.) argued that there was no person here authorized to make the objection, because it was the right of a party to waive the objection of interest on the part of a judge or juror, and the President when he came here for trial might say, "Why was not the Senator from Ohio sworn?" The theory of his colleague (Mr. Hendricks) was false. This impeachment was to be tried by the Senate. The Senator from Ohio was a member of this body, and his rights as such could not be taken from him. His election as Presiding officer took from him none of his rights as Senator; but aside from that, he repeated, that there was no person here entitled to raise the question.

A Precedent Cited.

Mr. JOHNSON (Md.) urged the propriety of his motion, that the question should be postponed till to-morrow. It was a question in which the people of the United States were concerned, and by no conduct of his, by no waiver of his rights could the court be organized in any other way than the Constitution provides. He repelled the intimation that the body was not a court but was a Senate. As the Senate, he argued, its powers were only legislative, and it had no judicial powers except as a court. So had all their predecessors ruled. In the celebrated impeachment case of Justice Chase, the Senate acted on the idea that they were acting as a court, not as a Senate.

The Senators were to declare on their oaths, to decide the question of guilty or not guilty, and declare the judgment; and who had ever heard of a Senate declaring a judgment. The very fact that the Chief Justice had to preside showed that this was a court of the highest character. As to the argument that a Senator had a right to vote on a question wherein he had an interest, he asked who had ever heard before of such a proposition. The courts had even gone so far as to declare that a judgment pronounced by a judge in a case where he had personal interest was absolutely void, on the general principle that no man had a right to be a judge in his own case. In conclusion, he suspended the motion, and moved that the other members be now sworn.

Mr. Wade's Rights.

Mr. SHERMAN (Ohio) declared that the right of his colleague to take the oath, and his duty to do it was clear in his own mind. If hereafter the question of interest was raised against him it could be discussed and decided. The case of Senator Stockton, to which reference had been made, was a case in point. Notwithstanding the question of the legality of his election, no one questioned his right to be sworn in the first instance. It was only when his case came up for decision that his right to vote on that case was disputed and refused, and he (Mr. Sherman) had ever doubted the correctness of that decision. The same question came up in his own case when he was a candidate for the Speakership of the House of Representatives.

He had taken his oath as a member of the House, and he had a right, if he had chosen to exercise it, to cast his vote for himself. He claimed that the State of Ohio had a right to be represented on this trial by its two Senators. His colleague should decide for himself whether he would participate in the trial and vote on questions arising in it. Questions had been introduced in this debate which he thought should not have been introduced. The only question at issue was, should or should not the Senator from Ohio be sworn in.

Why the Challenge was Made.

Mr. BAYARD (Del.) argued against the right of Senator Wade to take the oath, the object of the Constitution being to exclude the person who was to be benefited by the deposition of the President from taking part in the proceeding leading to such deposition. He proceeded to argue that the character of the body in trying impeachment was that of a court, not that of a Senate. He could not conceive on what ground the questions as to the character of the body was introduced, except it was that Senators, in cutting themselves loose from the restraints of their judicial character, might give a full swing to their partisan passions. If he stood in the same position as the Senator from Ohio, the wealth of the world would not tempt him to sit in such a case.

Mr. Sumner Looks up Law and Equity.

Mr. SUMNER (Mass.) declined to follow Senators in the discussion of the question as to whether this body was a Senate or was a court. Its powers were plainly laid down in the Constitution. The Constitution had not given the body a name, but it had given it powers, and those powers it was now exercising. Distinguished Senators on the other side had stated that the Constitution intended to prevent Senators who were to benefit by the result of impeachment from participating in the trial of the accused. Where did they find that interest? Where did they find the reason alleged for the provision as to the Chief Justice presiding? It was not to be found in the Constitution itself, nor in the papers of Mr. Madison, nor in the *Federalist*, nor in any cotemporaneous publications.

The first that was to be found of that idea was in Rawle's Commentaries on the Constitution, published in 1825, and the next that was to be found of it was ten years later, in Story's Commentaries, where, in a note, Rawle is cited. If they were to trust to the lights of history, the reason for the introduction of this clause was because the framers of the Constitution had contemplated the suspension of the President during impeachment, and because, therefore, the Vice President could not be in the Senate he would be discharging the Executive functions.

Mr. SUMNER referred to the constitutional debates in support of his theory, particularly citing the words of James Madison in the debate in the Virginia Convention, to the effect that the House might impeach the President, that the Senate might convict him, and that they (meaning either the Senate or the Senate and House of Representatives jointly) could suspend him from office, when his duties would devolve upon the Vice President. Here, he argued, was an authentic reason for that provision of the Constitution providing that when the President was on trial the Chief Justice should preside.

He submitted that the Senate could not proceed upon the theory of the Senators on the other side. The text could not be extended from its plain and simple meaning. As to the question of interest, he asked who could put into the one scale the great interests of the public justice, and into the other paltry personal temptation. He believed that if the Senator from Ohio was allowed to hold those scales, the one containing personal interest would "kick the beam."

Speech of Mr. Howe.

Mr. HOWE (Wis.) thought the question would not be a very difficult one if they were willing to read what was written, and to abide by it. It was written that the Senate should be composed of two Senators from each State, and it was elsewhere written that Ohio was a State. It was also written that the Senate should have the power to try impeachments—the Senate, and no one else. He conceived, therefore, that that was the end of the law. Whatever after question of delicacy there might be, the question of law was clear, that the Senator from Ohio was entitled to participate in this trial. If the Constitution were silent on the subject, no one would have challenged the right of the presiding officer of the Senate to preside on this trial. The Constitution, however, had provided for that question, and had gone no further. If any objection did exist to the Senator from Ohio, the only party who had a right to raise the objection was not here and was not represented here.

Mr. DRAKE (Mo.) argued that if the objection had any legal validity whatever, it was one which had to be passed upon affirmatively or negatively by some body, and he wanted to know what that body was? Was it so passed upon by the presiding officer of the Senate? He hardly thought so. Was it to be passed upon by this body itself? Then come in the difficulty that there were still four Senators unsworn. It might have been among the first or the very first one, and then would have had to be decided by Senators, not one of whom had been sworn.

Mr. THAYER (Neb.) discussed the question as to whether this was a court or not. They had to come down to the plain words of the Constitution, "The Senate shall have power to try impeachments." If this body was a court now, where did the transformation take place? It was the Senate when it met at twelve o'clock, and had not since adjourned; nor could it be said at what particular point of time the transformation took place, if at all. If the question of interest was to be raised in the case of the Senator from Ohio, it ought with greater reason be raised against the Senator from Tennessee (Mr. Patterson), who was so closely allied with the President. Besides every Senator who might succeed to the office of presiding officer was also interested but one degree less than the Senator from Ohio. The Senator from Ohio could not be deprived of his vote except by a gross usurpation of power. Suppose ten or fifteen Senators were closely allied to the accused, the objection might be made, and the whole movement defeated by reducing the body below a quorum.

Mr. HOWARD rose to call the attention of the chair to the real matter before the body, and to inquire whether the pending motion, that other Senators be sworn in, was in order.

Chief Justice CHASE replied affirmatively.

Mr. HOWARD rose to call the attention of the chair to the real question before the Senate, and asked whether the pending motion, that other Senators be sworn, was not in order?

The Chief Justice said that the Senator from Indiana having objected to the Senator from Ohio taking the oath, there was now a motion that the remaining names be called, omitting the name of the Senator from Ohio.

Mr. Howard said there was no rule requiring the names to be called in alphabetical order. The remaining names could be called now. He saw no necessity for further discussion of this motion, and thought it was merely a question of order. It seemed to him that it must be held that the trial had commenced, and that as the Senate had the sole power to try impeachments, and as the Constitution also prescribed the administration of an oath, it was out of order to interfere with the taking of that oath.

Mr. Buckalew asked if the rules did not provide that, the presiding officer shall submit all questions to the Senate; but assuming it to be a question of order, he contended that the clause was intended to apply to the old form of taking votes by States. The Senate had already adopted a rule for excluding votes in a particular case—a rule founded in justice. The argument was that the Senator had a right under the Constitution to represent Ohio.

On several occasions recently, Senators had presented themselves and had been denied admission. Here they were organized into a court to decide the gravest possible questions. The objection was made at the proper time, and if not now made, a number of members not qualified to act might take part in the proceedings and be judges in the case. It was not only their right but their duty to raise the question now. They are acting under the Constitution, most of them having been sworn already, and the Chief Justice being there to add dignity and disinterestedness to the deliberations; and if they properly raised the question to be decided at the earliest possible moment, it was a question arising under the Senate, and they must meet it before they could organize. He was content to take the decision of the Chief Justice of the United States and the opinion of a distinguished commentator, in preference to that of the Senator from Massachusetts. Objections were always made to jurors before they were sworn; if not, it would be too late.

Mr. Frelinghuysen (N. J.) asked whether the Senator supposed the accused waived his right of challenge by the Senators being all sworn? He would challenge, if at all, after they were organized, and, therefore, this was not the time to make objection.

Mr. Buckalew said he was not talking of challenges. It had not been put upon that ground by the Senator from Indiana (Mr. Hendricks). Challenge was a right given by statute.

Mr. Morton replied to Mr. Buckalew, and said the Constitution had made the tribunal itself, and they had no right to constitute one. It was not important what they called the Senate now, but it was material that they should sit as the Constitution authorized them, in the trial of an impeachment—as a Senate.

The Senator from Ohio being a member of the Senate, and the Senate performing duties imposed upon it by the Constitution, it was idle for them to talk about organizing a court, when the Constitution placed certain duties upon them.

At 4·30 P. M., Mr. Grimes (Ia.), after premising that the Chief Justice having sat since 11 A. M., must be fatigued, moved to adjourn.

Mr. Howard suggested that as a court they could not adjourn the Senate, and Mr. Grimes moved to adjourn the court until to-morrow morning.

The Chief Justice put the motion and declared it carried, and vacated the chair.

PROCEEDINGS OF THURSDAY, MARCH 5.

The Chief Justice was again escorted to the chair by Mr. Pomeroy, the chairman of the committee appointed for that purpose.

The Secretary of the Senate read the minutes of the court yesterday, including the adjournment of the Senate.

The Chief Justice then stated the question to be—an objection having been made to the swearing-in of the Senator from Ohio (Mr. Wade)—a motion to postpone the swearing-in of that Senator until the remaining members have been sworn.

He also announced that Mr. Dixon (Conn.) had the floor.

Mr. Dixon—Mr. President—

A Point of Order.

Mr. Howard (Mich.)—Mr. President, I rise to a point of order

The Chief Justice—The Senator will state his point of order.

Mr. Howard—By the Constitution, the Senate, sitting on the trial of impeachment, is to be on oath or affirmation. Each member of the Senate, by the Constitution, is a component member of the body for that purpose. There can, therefore, be no trial unless that oath or affirmation be taken by the respective Senators who are present. The Constitution of the United States is imperative, and when a member presents himself to take the oath, I hold that, as a rule of order, it is the duty of the presiding officer to administer the oath, and that the proposition to take the oath cannot be postponed. Other members have no control over the question. That is the simple duty devolved upon the presiding officer of the body who administers the oath.

Further, sir:—The Senate, on the second day of the present month, adopted rules for their government in proceedings of this kind. Rule third declares that, before proceeding to the consideration of the articles of impeachment, the presiding officer shall administer the oath hereinafter provided to the members of the Senate then present. Mr. Wade is present and ready, and the other members if they appear, whose duty it is to take the oath. The form of the oath is also prescribed by our present rules as follows :—

"I solemnly swear (or affirm as the case may be), that in all the things appertaining to the trial of the impeachment of Andrew Johnson, now pending, I will do impartial justice according to the Constitution and laws. So help me God."

That is the form of oath prescribed by our rules. It is the form in which the presiding officer of this body himself is sworn. It is the form in which we all (thus far) have been sworn; and so far as the rules are concerned, I insist that they have already been adopted and recognized by us, so far as it is possible, during the condition in which we now are, of organizing ourselves for the discharge of our present duties. I, therefore, make the point of order, that the objection made to the swearing in of Mr. Wade, is out of order, under the rules and under the Constitution of the United States, and I ask the court respectfully, but earnestly, that the President of the Senate, the Chief Justice of the Supreme Court of the United States, now presiding in the body, do decide the question without debate. I object to any further debate.

Mr. Dixon—The question before the Senate is whether under this rule the Senator from Ohio—

Mr Drake (Mo.)—I call the Senator from Connecticut to order.

The Chief Justice—The Senator from Conecticut is called to order. The Senator from Michigan (Mr. Howard) has made a point of order to be submitted to the consideration of the body. During the proceedings for the organization of the Senate for the trial of an impeachment of the President, the Chair regards the general rules of the Senate obligatory, and the Senate must determine itself every question which arises, unless the Chair is permitted to determine. In a case of this sort, affecting so nearly the organization of this body, the Chair feels himself constrained to submit the question of order to the Senate. Will the Senator from Michigan state his point of order in writing?

Mr. DIXON—Mr. President, I rise to a point of order.

The Chief Justice—A point of order is already pending, and this point cannot be made until the other is decided.

Mr. DIXON—I desire to know whether a point of order cannot be made with regard to that question.

The Chief Justice—The Chair is of opinion that no point of order can be made pending another point of order.

Mr. HOWARD prepared his point of order and sent it to the Chair.

The Chief Justice—Senators, the point of order submitted by the Senator from Michigan is as follows:—"That the objection raised to administering the oath to Mr. Wade is out of order, and the motion of the Senator from Maryland to postpone the administering of the oath to Mr. Wade until other Senators are sworn, is also out of order under the rules adopted by the Senate of 2d of March inst., and under the Constitution of the United States." The question is open to debate.

Mr. DIXON—Mr. President.

The Chief Justice—The Senator from Connecticut.

Mr. DRAKE—I call the Senator to order. Under the rules of the Senate questions of order are not debatable.

Mr. DIXON was understood to say that questions of order referred to the Senate were debatable.

Mr. DRAKE—I do not so understand the rules of the Senate. There can be debate upon an appeal from the decision of the Chair, but there can be no debate in the first instance upon a question of order, as I understand the rules of the Senate.

The Chief Justice—The Chair rules that a question of order is debatable when submitted to the Senate.

Mr. DRAKE—If I am mistaken in the rules of the Senate on that subject I would like to be corrected, but I take it I am not.

The Chief Justice—The Senator from Missouri is out of order, unless he appeals from the decision of the Chair.

Mr. DRAKE asked leave to read the sixth rule, providing that when a member shall be called to order by the President or a Senator, he shall sit down, and not proceed without leave of the Senate, and that every question of order shall be decided by the President, without debate, and subject to an appeal to the Senate.

Mr. POMEROY said the rule applied to submission to the Senate, without a question was not debatable.

Mr. DIXON said the question was now presented in a different shape from that presented yesterday by the Senator from Michigan, when he reminded them that after all this was a question of order, and ought to be so decided. The question now was, whether it was a question of the orderly proceedings of this body. The Senator from Ohio could take the oath. On that question he proposed to address the Senate. At the adjournment

yesterday, he was about remarking that the President of the United States was about to be tried before this body, in its judicial capacity, whether called a court or not, upon articles of impeachment presented by the House of Representatives.

If upon that trial (continued Mr. Dixon), he should be convicted, the judgment of the body may extend to his removal from office and to his disqualification after to hold any office of profit or trust under the United States. How far the judgment will extend, in case of conviction, of course it is impossible for any one now to say. In all human probability it would extend at least as far as to his removal from office. In that event, the very moment the judgment was rendered, the office of President of the United States, with all its power and all its attributes, would be vested in the Senator from Ohio, now holding the office of President of this body. The office would vest in the President of the Senate for the time being. The question before this body now is for this tribunal to decide whether, upon the trial of a person holding the office of President of the Senate, and in whom the office of President of the United States, upon conviction, rests, can be a judge upon that trial, sir, is the question before this tribunal.

Mr. SHERMAN called the Senator to order. He claimed that the Senator was not in order in speaking upon the general question of the impeachment when a point of order was submitted to the Senate by the Chair. He thought they should adhere to the rules of the Senate.

The Chief Justice intimated that the Senator from Connecticut should speak within the rules.

Mr. DIXON said that if permitted to go on without interruption, he had proposed to go into the general merits of the question, but as it appeared to be the opinion of the Senate that he could not do so, he would not trespass on its attention in that regard. He proposed to discuss the question under the Constitution of the United States and rules of order.

Mr. HOWARD—I call the Senator from Connecticut to order, and ask whether it is now in order to take an appeal from the decision of the Chair?

Mr. DIXON submitted that there was not such a question of order as the Senator had a right to raise. The only question he had a right to raise was, whether he (Mr. Dixon) was out of order.

Mr. HOWARD—Very well; I raise that question distinctly, and call the Senator to order. I make the point that the twenty-third rule, adopted by the Senate, declares that all orders and decisions shall be taken by yeas and nays, without debate.

The Chief Justice, in deciding the point of order, said the twenty-third rule is a rule for the proceedings of the Senate when organized for the trial of an impeachment. It is not yet organized, and in the opinion of the chair the twenty-third rule does not apply at present.

Mr. DRAKE appealed from the decision.

The Chief Justice Sustained.

The Chief Justice re-stated the decision, and stated that the question was, shall the opinion of the chair stand as the judgment of the Senate?

The question was taken by yeas and nays, and resulted—Yeas, 24; nays, 20, as follows:—

YEAS.—Messrs. Anthony, Buckalew, Corbett, Davis, Dixon, Fessenden, Fowler, Frelinghuysen, Grimes, Henderson, Hendricks, Johnson, McCreery, Morrill (Me.), Norton, Patterson (Tenn.), Pomeroy, Ross, Saulsbury, Sherman, Sprague, Van Winkle, Willey and Williams—24.

NAYS.—Messrs. Cameron, Cattell, Chandler, Cole, Conkling, Conness, Drake, Ferry, Harlan, Howard, Morgan, Morrill (Vt.), Morton, Nye, Stewart, Sumner, Thayer, Tipton, Wilson and Yates—20.

So the decision of the Chair was sustained.

The announcement of the result was followed by manifestations of applause, which were promptly checked.

Speech of Mr. Dixon.

Mr. DIXON then proceeded with his argument, and said he was not unmindful of the high character of the Senator from Ohio, and did not forget what he had learned from his observations in the Senate for nearly twelve years of his just and generous nature. He acknowledged most cheerfully that that Senator was as much raised above the imperfections and frailties of this weak, depraved, corrupt human nature, as it was possible for any member to be.

Mr. CONNESS raised the question of order, that the Senator was not confining himself within the limits of the debate.

The Chief Justice said he was greatly embarrassed in attempting to ascertain the precise scope of debate to be indulged in, and therefore he was not prepared to say that the Senator from Connecticut was out of order.

Mr. DIXON continued his remarks, and said he did not suppose that, in disavowing any personal objection to the Senator from Ohio, he was infringing the rules of debate. If any advantage or profit was to accrue to that honorable Senator from the trial, what was it? What was the nature of his interest? The Senator from Massachusetts (Mr. Sumner) had spoken of it as a matter of trifling consequence, but it was nothing less than the high office of President of the United States. It was the highest object of human ambition in this country, and perhaps in the world.

Mr. STEWART (Nev.) called the Senator from Connecticut to order. He was discussing the main question, not the question of order.

The Chief Justice remarked that he had already said it was very difficult to determine the precise limits of debate on the point of order taken by the Senator from Michigan. The nature of the objection taken by the Senator from Indiana (Mr. Hendricks), and the validity of that objection must necessarily become the subject of debate, and he was unable to pronounce the Senator from Connecticut out of order.

Mr. DIXON resumed his speech. He ventured to say that with the great temptation of the Presidency operating on the human mind, it would be nothing short of miraculous if the Senator from Ohio could be impartial. Nothing short of the power of Omnipotence operating directly on the human heart, could, under such circumstance, make any human being impartial. It might be said that the objection made was not within the letter of the Constitution. The Constitution did not, he admitted, expressly prohibit a member of the Senate acting as presiding officer *pro tempore*, from acting as a judge in a case of impeachment. He was not prepared to say that the Senator from Ohio came within the letter of the express prohibition of the Constitution, but he certainly came within its spirit; and he assumed that the Senate was here to act, not on the letter, but on the spirit of the Constitution.

There was no prohibition in the Constitution that the presiding officer *pro tempore* on a trial of this kind shall vote. The provision only was, that the Vice President of the United States shall not preside or give the casting vote in a trial of this kind. The reason of that provision has already been explained. That reason was so manifest that it was not necessary to give it. It was that there was such a direct interest in the Vice President in the result of the trial, that it was deemed improper that he should preside in a proceeding through which a vacancy might be created. The framers of the Constitution knew that the provisions of the common law prevented

a man being a judge in his own case. They knew that, as had been said by a learned commentator, the omnipotence of Parliament was limited in that respect, and even that omnipotent body could not make a man judge in his own case. If it would shock humanity, if it would violate every feeling of justice throughout the world, for the Vice President to act, would it have less effect in relation to the presiding officer *pro tempore?* No language could depict the impropriety of a Senator acting as a judge in a case which, in a certain event, was to place him in the Presidential chair.

The President of the United States could not waive his objection in this case. It was a question in which the people of the United States were doubly interested, and it must be decided by the laws and Constitution, and by the great rules of right. The objection was not as had been argued. It was premature, for there were many preliminary questions on which, if the Senator from Ohio were now sworn, he might proceed to vote. If there was anything desirable in a trial it was that, in the first place, it should be impartially just, and that, in the second place, it must appear to the public mind that it was impartially just.

If the Senate were to decide that the Senator from Ohio, who is to be benefitted by the deposition of the President, could take part in the trial, there would certainly be some doubt entertained in the public mind of the fairness of the trial. If history should have to record that fact, the sympathies of the civilized world would be with the deposed President.

Mr. Hendricks Withdraws His Challenge.

Mr. HENDRICKS said that in making the objection, he did not question the general proposition of the right of the Senator from Ohio to vote on all proper questions, but he claimed that by his own acts he had accepted a position which disqualified him from sitting as a judge in this case.

It was, therefore, his own act, and not the act of the Senate, that disqualified him. This question necessarily arose often in the organization of bodies composed of many members. It often occurred in the House of Representatives, when members were called to be sworn, and it had necessarily to be decided before the organization was complete. The question must, therefore, be decided here. Substantially this body was a court. It had not to consider legislative questions at all. The judgment of each Senator was controlled altogether by questions of law and fact, and the body was, therefore, in its very essence and nature, a judicial body. The Senate ceased to be a body for the consideration of legislative questions, and became a body for the consideration of judicial questions.

The first step in passing from one character to the other character was the appearance of the Chief Justice of the United States in the chair. The next step was that Senators should take the oath that as judges they would be fair and just, and the question arose in this stage as to the competency of a certain Senator. The question was whether the Senator from Ohio could participate in the trial. He (Mr. Hendricks) had held in the Stockton case that a Senator might vote on a question where he had an interest, but the Senate had decided differently, and he held to the decision of the Senate. He was somewhat surprised to hear the Senator from Massachusetts (Mr. Sumner) argue now in the contrary view. He believed that the objection was made at the proper time, but as some of the Senators who had sustained the general objection, particularly the Senator from Delaware (Mr. Bayard), seemed to intimate that the objection might be reserved and made at another time, he would withdraw it.

Mr. HENDRICKS having thus withdrawn his objection, the motion offered by Senator Johnson and the question of order submitted by Senator Howard fell to the ground.

Senator Wade Sworn.

Senator Wade thereupon came forward and took the oath administered by the Chief Justice. The other Senators who had not already been sworn were called on one by one, and took the oath, and then, the Chief Justice, rising, said, "All the Senators having taken the oath required by the Constitution, the court is now organized for the purpose of proceeding with the trial of the impeachment of Andrew Johnson. The Sergeant-at-Arms will make proclamation."

A Proclamation.

The Sergeant-at-Arms then made the formal proclamation in these words:—"Hear ye! Hear ye! Hear ye! All persons are commanded to keep silence on pain of imprisonment, while the Senate of the United States is sitting for the trial of articles of impeachment against Andrew Johnson, President of the United States."

Mr. HOWARD—I submit the following order:—

Ordered, That the Secretary of the Senate inform the managers of the House of Representatives that the Senate is now organized.

Mr. Howard's Motion Adopted.

The Chief Justice—Before submitting that question to the Senate the Chief Justice thinks it his duty to submit to the Senate the rules of procedure. In the judgment of the Chief Justice the Senate is now organized as a distinct body from the Senate sitting in its legislative capacity. It performs a distinct function; the members are under a different oath, and the presiding officer is not the President *pro tempore*, but the Chief Justice of the United States. Under these circumstances the Chair conceives that rules adopted by the Senate in its legislative capacity are not rules for the government of the Senate sitting for the trial of an impeachment, unless they be also adopted by that body.

In this judgment of the Chair, if it be erroneous, he desires to be corrected by the judgment of the court or the Senate, sitting for the trial of the impeachment of the President—which in his judgment are synonymous terms—and therefore, if he be permitted to do so, he will take the sense of the Senate upon this question, whether the rules adopted on the 2d of March shall be considered as the rules of proceedings in this body.

Cries of "question," "question."

The Chief Justice put the question.

There was but one faint "no," apparently on the Democratic side.

The Chief Justice—The yeas have it, by the sound. The rules will be considered as the rules of this body.

To Mr. Howard—Will the Senator have the goodness to repeat his motion?

Mr. HOWARD repeated his motion, given above, which was put, and declared adopted.

Entrance of the Managers.

After a few minutes' delay, at a quarter before three o'clock, the doors were thrown open. The Sergeant-at-Arms announced "The Managers of the impeachment on the part of the House of Representatives," and the managers entered and proceeded up the aisle, arm in arm, Messrs. Bingham and Butler in the advance. Mr. Stevens did not appear.

The Chief Justice—The managers on the part of the House of Representatives will take the seats assigned to them.

They took their seats accordingly, inside the bar.

Order having been restored,

Mr. BINGHAM rose and said (in an almost inaudible tone, until admonished by Senators near him to speak louder)—We are instructed by the House of Representatives and its managers to demand that the Senate take process against Andrew Johnson, President of the United States, that he answer at the bar of the Senate the articles of impeachment heretofore presented by the House of Representatives, through its managers, by the Senate.

Summons Against the President.

Mr. Bingham having taken his seat,

Mr. HOWARD offered the following:—

Ordered, That a summons be issued, as required by the rules of procedure and practice in the Senate when sitting in the trial of impeachments, to Andrew Johnson, returnable on Friday, the 13th day of March inst., at one o'clock P. M.

The question was put on agreeing to the order. It was declared carried and directed to be executed.

Mr. HOWARD—I move that the Senate, sitting upon the trial of impeachment, do now adjourn.

Several Senators addressed the Chair simultaneously, but Mr. ANTHONY was recognized. He offered an amendment to rule seven, to strike out the last clause, providing that "the presiding officer may, in the first instance, submit to the Senate, without a division, all questions of evidence and incidental questions; but the same shall, on the demand of one-fifth of the members present, be decided by the yeas and nays," and insert in lieu thereof the following:—

"The presiding officer of the court may rule all questions of evidence and incidental questions, which ruling shall stand as the judgment of the court, unless some member of the court shall ask that a formal vote be taken thereon, in which case it shall be submitted to the court for decision; or he may, at his option, in the first instance, submit any such question to a vote of the members of the court."

The amendment would restore the rule to its original form before the amendment.

Mr. ANTHONY did not desire to press his amendment immediately, and at his suggestion it was laid on the table.

Mr. HOWARD then moved that the court adjourn to the time at which the summons was made returnable, Friday, the 13th inst.

Mr. SUMNER—Before that motion is put I should like to ask my friend, the Senator from Rhode Island (Mr. Anthony), whether, under the rule now adopted, he regards that as debatable?

Mr. ANTHONY—No.

Mr. SUMNER—By these rules it is provided as follows:—All the orders and decisions shall be made and had by yeas and nays, which shall be entered on the record without debate, except when the doors shall be closed for discussion.

Mr. ANTHONY—I have not read the rules in reference to the question, and I do not desire to press the motion at present.

Adjournment of the Court.

The Chief Justice—There is nothing before the Senate but the motion to adjourn.

The motion to adjourn was carried, and the Chief Justice declared the court adjourned until Friday, the 13th inst., at 1 o'clock, and vacated the chair. The managers then retired.

The Summons Served.

The summons was served on the President by the Sergeant-at-Arms of the Senate, on the afternoon of Saturday, March 7. On receiving the document, Mr. Johnson replied, that he would attend to the matter.

PROCEEDINGS OF FRIDAY, MARCH 13.

The Reply to the Summons.

On Friday, March 13, the day fixed for the reply of the President to the summons of the Court of Impeachment, the favored ticket-holders to seats in the galleries commenced pouring into the Capitol by ten o'clock, and by eleven o'clock the ladies' gallery was packed by as brilliant an audience as upon a full dress opera night. None were permitted to pass the Supreme Court door without a ticket, and guards were placed at half a dozen points from thence on to the entrance of the galleries. A heavy police force was on hand, and the rules were rigidly enforced, and hundreds of strangers, ignorant of the necessity of obtaining tickets, were turned back disappointed. The Senators' seats were arranged as before. In the open space in front of the President's chair were two long tables, each furnished with seven chairs—one intended for the managers, and the other for the counsel. Back of the Senators' seats, and filling the entire lobby, were about two hundred chairs for the accommodation of the members of the House, the Judiciary and others entitled to the floor.

Senators Howard and Anthony were in their seats early, and by one o'clock half the Senators had appeared and ranged themselves in little knots discussing the momentous business of the day.

It was noticeable that not a single negro was in the galleries. The section usually occupied by them was filled with ladies. There was no rush and no crowding of door aisles. Everything was conducted with perfect order and decorum.

The Prayer.

The Chaplain invoked a blessing upon those now entering upon this high and important duty, and upon whom rest the eyes of the country and of the world, that they may be guided by Divine wisdom, that all their acts may be characterized by justice, and that the High Court may be led to such a verdict as God will approve, and to which all the people shall respond heartily, "Amen."

The morning hour of the Senate was occupied with the usual legislative routine.

Report of the Sergeant-at-Arms.

The Sergeant-at-Arms then subscribed to the following affidavit, read by the Clerk:—

"The foregoing writ of summons, addressed to Andrew Johnson, President of the United States, and the foregoing precept, addressed to me, were this day served upon the said Andrew Johnson, by delivering to and leaving with him copies of the same at the Executive Mansion, the usual place of abode of the said Andrew Johnson, on Saturday, the 7th day of March, instant, at seven o'clock.
(Signed)   GEORGE G. BROWN,
Sergeant-at-Arms of the United States Senate.

The President Called.

The Chief Justice—The Sergeant-at-Arms will call the accused.

The Sergeant-at-Arms, in a loud voice:—"Andrew Johnson, President of the United States! Andrew Johnson, President of the United States! Appear and answer the articles of impeachment exhibited against you by the House of Representatives of the United States."

The doors were thrown open at this point, and every eye was turned that way for a moment, but Mr. Butler entered and took his seat with the other managers.

Mr. JOHNSON (Md.) rose and said something in a voice inaudible in the gallery, whereupon the Chief Justice said:—The Sergeant-at-Arms will inform the counsel of the President.

The President's counsel, Messrs. Stanbery, Curtis and Nelson, were ushered in at the side door, and took seats at the table to the right of the chair, Mr. Stanbery on the right, the others in the order named.

Mr. CONKLING offered the following, by direction of the committee, in order, he said, to correct a clerical error:—

Ordered, That the twenty-third rule of the Senate for proceedings on the trial of impeachment be amended by inserting after the word "debate," in the second line, the following words:—"Subject, however, to the operation of rule seven," so that if amended it will read as follows:—"23d. All the orders and decisions shall be made and had by yeas and nays, which shall be entered on the record, and without debate, subject, however, to the operation of rule seven," &c.

Rule seven provides that the presiding officer may, in the first instance, submit to the Senate, without a division, all questions of evidence and incidental questions.

Mr. CONKLING explained that such was the original intention, but that the qualifying words were accidentally omitted. The order was adopted.

At twenty minutes past one o'clock the Sergeant-at-Arms announced the members of the House of Representatives, and the members entered and distributed themselves as far as possible among the chairs and sofas not already occupied by those having the *entree* to the Chamber under the rules. Many, however, did not find seats at once.

The Plea of the President.

Mr. STANBERY then rose and said:—Mr. Chief Justice, my brothers Curtis, Nelson and myself, are here this morning as counsel for the President. I have his authority to enter his plea, which, by your leave, I will proceed to read.

Mr. Stanbery read the plea of President Johnson.

A Professional Statement.

Mr. STANBERY—I have also a professional statement in support of the application; whether it is in order to offer it now the Chair will decide.

The Chief Justice—The appearance will be considered as entered. You can proceed.

Mr. Stanbery then read his statement as follows:—

In the matter of the impeachment of Andrew Johnson, President of the United States, Henry Stanbery, Benjamin R. Curtis, Jeremiah S. Black, William M. Evarts and Thomas A. R. Nelson, of counsel for the respondent, move the court for the allowance of forty days for the preparation of the answer to the articles of impeachment, and, in support of the motion, make the following professional statement:—

The articles are eleven in number, involving many questions of law and fact. We have, during the limited time and opportunity offered us, considered, as far as possible, the field of investigation which must be explored in the preparation of the answer, and the conclusion at which we have arrived is that, with the utmost diligence, the time we have asked is reasonable and necessary. The precedents as to time for answer upon impeachment before the Senate, to which we have had opportunity to refer, are those of Judge Chase and Judge Peck.

In the case of Judge Chase, time was allowed from the 3d of January until the 11th of February next succeeding, to put his answer, a period of thirty-two days; but in this case there was but a single article.

Judge Peck asked for time from the 10th to the 25th of May to put in his answer, and it was granted. It appears that Judge Peck had been long cognizant of the ground laid for his impeachment, and had been present before the committee of the House upon the examination of the witnesses, and had been permitted by the House of Representatives to present to that body an elaborate answer to the charges.

It is apparent that the President is fairly entitled to more time than was allowed in either of the foregoing cases. It is proper to add that the respondents in those cases were lawyers fully capable of preparing their own answers, and that no pressing official duties interfered with their attention to that business.

Whereas, the President, not being a lawyer, must rely on his counsel; the charges involve his acts, relations and intentions, as to all which his counsel must be fully advised upon consultation with him, step by step, in the preparation of his defense. It is seldom that a case requires such constant communication between client and counsel as this, and yet such communication can only be had at such intervals as are allowed to the President from the usual hours that must be devoted to his high official duties.

We further beg leave to suggest for the consideration of this honorable court, that counsel, careful as well for their own reputation as of the interests of their client, in a case of such magnitude as this, so out of the ordinary range of professional experience, where so much responsibility is felt, they submit to the candid consideration of the court that they have a right to ask for themselves such opportunity to discharge that duty as seems to them to be absolutely necessary.
(Signed)
     HENRY STANBERY,
     BENJAMIN R. CURTIS,
     JEREMIAH S. BLACK,
     WILLIAM M. EVARTS,
     THOMAS A. R. NELSON,
March 13, 1868.   Counsel for respondent.

Mr. Bingham's Replication.

Mr. BINGHAM, Chairman of the Managers on the part of the House, said—

Mr. President—I am instructed by the managers, on the part of the House, to suggest that under the eighth rule adopted by the Senate for the government of these proceedings, after the appearance of the accused, a motion for a continuance is not allowed, the language of the rule being that if the accused appear and file an answer, the case shall proceed as on the general issue. If he do not appear, the case shall proceed as on the general issue. The managers appeared at the bar of the Senate, impressed with the belief that the rule meant precisely what it says, and that in default of appearance the trial would proceed as on a plea of not guilty; if, on appearance, no answer was filed, the trial shall still, according to the language of the rule, proceed as on a plea of not guilty.

Address of Judge Curtis.

Mr. CURTIS, of the counsel for the President, said:—

Mr. Chief Justice:—If the construction which the managers have put upon the rule be correct, the counsel for the President have been entirely misled by the phraseology of the rule. They (the counsel for the President) have construed the rule in the light of similar rules existing in courts of justice—for instance, in a court of equity. The order in the subpœna is to appear on a certain day and answer the plea; but certainly it was never understood that they were to answer the plea on the day of their appearance. So it is in a variety of other legal proceedings. Parties are summoned to appear on a certain day, but the day when they are to answer is either fixed by some general rule of the tribunal, or there will be a special order in the particular case.

Now, here we find a rule by which the President is commanded to appear on this day, and answer and abide. Certainly that part of the rule which relates to abiding has reference to future proceedings and to the final result of the case. And so, as we have construed the rule, the part of it which relates to answering has reference to a future proceeding. We submit, therefore, as counsel for the President, that the interpretation which is put upon the rule by the honorable managers is not the correct one.

Reply of Judge Wilson for the Managers.

Mr. WILSON, one of the Managers, said:—Mr. President—I desire to say, in behalf of the Managers, that we do not see how it would be possible for the eighth rule adopted by the Senate to mislead the respondent or his counsel. That rule provides that upon the presentation of articles of impeachment and the organization of the Senate as hereinbefore provided, a writ of summons shall issue to the accused, reciting said articles, and notifying him to appear before the Senate upon a day and at a place to be fixed by the Senate and named in such writ, and file his answer to said articles of impeachment, and to stand and abide such orders and judgments of the Senate thereon. The rule further provides that if the accused after service shall fail to appear, either in person or by attorney, on the day so fixed therefor, as aforesaid, or appearing shall fail to file an answer to such articles of impeachment, the trial shall proceed nevertheless as upon a plea of not guilty.

The learned counsel in the professional statement submitted to the Senate, refer to the cases of Judge Chase and Judge Peck, and I presume that in the examination of the records of those cases, the attention of the counsel was directed to the rules adopted by the Senate for the government of its action on the argument of those case.

By reference to the rules adopted by the Senate for the trial of Judge Peck, we find that a very material change has been made by the Senate in the adoption of the present rule. The rule in the case of Judge Peck, being the third rule, prescribed the form of summons, and required that on a day to be fixed the respondent should then and there appear and answer.

The same rule was adopted in the Chase case, but the present rule is in those cases the words to which I have called the attention of the Senate:—"That he shall appear and file his answer to said articles of impeachment; and that, appearing in person, shall he fail to file his answer to such articles, the trial shall proceed, nevertheless, as on a plea of not guilty." I submit, therefore, Mr. President, that the change which has been made in the rule for the goverment of this case must have been made for some good reason. What that reason may have been may be made a subject of discussion in this case hereafter, but the change meets us on the presentation of this motion, and we, therefore, on the part of the House of Representatives, which we are here representing, ask that the rule adopted by the Senate for the government of this case may be enforced. It is for the Senate to say whether this rule shall be sustained as a rule to govern the case, or whether it shall be changed; but standing as a rule at this time, we ask for its enforcement.

Mr. Stanbery Criticises the Action of the Managers.

Mr. STANBERY said the action taken by the honorable managers is so singular that in the whole course of my practice I have not met with an example of it. The President of the United States, Mr. Chief Justice, is arraigned on impeachment by the House of Representatives, a case of the greatest magnitude that we have ever had, and it, as to time, is to be treated as if it were a case before a police court, to be put through with railroad speed, on the first day of the trial. Where do my learned friends find a precedent for calling on the trial on this day?

They say:—"We have notified you to appear here to answer on a given day." We are here. We enter our appearance. As my learned friend, Mr. Curtis, has said, you have used precisely the language that is used in a subpœna in chancery. But who ever heard that, when a defendant in chancery made his appearance, he must appear with his answer ready to go on with the case, and must enter on the trial? Of course we come here to enter our appearance. We state that we are ready to answer. We do not wish the case to go by default. We want time, reasonable time; nothing more. Consider that it is but a few days since the President was served with the summons; that as yet all his counsel are not present. Your Honor will observe that of five counsel who signed this professional statement, two are not present, and could not be present, and one of them I am sure is not in the city. Not one of them, on looking at these articles, suspected that it was the intention to bring on the trial at this day. Yet, we understand the gentlemen on the other side to say, read these rules according to their letter, and you must go on.

If the gentlemen are right, if we are here to answer to-day, and to go on with the trial to-day, then this is the day for trial. But article nine says:—"At 12·30 P. M. of the day appointed for the return of the summons against the person impeached"—showing that this is the return day and not the trial day. The managers say that, according to the letter of the eighth rule, this is the trial day, and that we must go on and file our answer, or that without answer the court shall enter the plea of "not guilty" on the general issue, and proceed at once. But we say that this is the return day and not the day of trial.

The tenth rule says:—"The person impeached shall be then called to appear and answer." The defendant appears to answer, states his willingness to answer, and only asks time.

The eleventh rule says:— "At 12·30 P. M. of the day appointed for the trial." That is not this day. This day, which the managers would make the first day of the trial, is in the Senate's own rules put down for the return day, and there must be some day fixed for the trial to suit the convenience of the parties, so that the letter of one rule answers the letter of another rule.

But pray, Mr. Chief Justice, is it possible that, under these circumstances, we are to be caught in this trap of the letter? As yet there has not been time to prepare an answer to a single one of these articles. As yet the President has been engaged in procuring his counsel, and all the time occupied with so much consultation as was necessary to fix the shortest time when, in our judgment, we will be ready to proceed with the trial. Look back through the whole line of impeachment cases, even in the worst times. Go back to the Star Chamber, and everywhere, and you will find that even there English fair play prevailed.

This is the first instance to be found on record anywhere where, on appearance day, the defendant was required to answer immediately, and proceed with the trial. We have not a witness summoned; we hardly know what witnesses to summon. We are entirely at sea. Mr. Chief Justice, I submit to this court whether we are to be caught in this way. "Strike, but hear." Give us the opportunity that men have in common civil cases, where they are allowed hardly less than thirty days to answer, and most frequently sixty days. Give us time; give us reasonable time, and then we shall be prepared for the trial and for the sentence of the court, whatever it may be.

Remarks of the Chief Justice.

The Chief Justice, rising, said:—

The Chief Justice would state, at the start, that he is embarrassed in the construction of the rules. The twenty-second rule provides that the case on each side may be opened by one person. He understood that as referring to the case when the evidence and the case are ready for argument. The twentieth rule provides that all preliminary or interlocutory questions and all motions shall be argued for not exceeding one hour on each side, unless the Senate shall, by order, extend the time; whether that is intended to apply to the whole argument on each side, or to the arguments of each counsel who may address the court, is a question which the Chief Justice is at a loss to solve. In the present case he has allowed the argument to proceed without attempting to restrict it, and unless the Senate order otherwise he will proceed in that course.

Mr. BINGHAM said:—It was not my purpose when I raised the question under the rule prescribed by the Senate, to touch in any way on the merits of any application which might be made for the extension of the time for the preparation of the trial. The only object I had in view, Mr. President, was to see whether the Senate were disposed to abide by its own rules, and by raising the question to remind the Senators of what they know—that in this proceeding they are a rule and a law unto themselves. Neither the common law nor the civil law furnishes any rule whatever for the conduct of this trial, save it may be the rules which govern the matter of evidence. There is nothing more clearly settled in this country, and in that country whence we derive our laws generally, than the proposition which we have just stated, and hence it follows that the Senate shall prescribe rules for the conduct of the trial; and having prescribed rules, my associate managers and myself deem it important to inquire whether those rules, on the very threshold of these proceedings, were to be disregarded and set aside. I may be pardoned for saying that I am greatly surprised at the hasty words which dropped from the lips of my learned and accomplished friend, Mr. Stanbery, who has just taken his seat—that he failed to discriminate between the objection made here and the objection which might hereafter be made, for the motion for the continuance of the trial.

But, Mr. President, there is nothing clearer—nothing better known to my learned and accomplished friend, than that the making up of the issue before any tribunal of justice and the trial are very distinct transactions. This is perfectly well understood. A very remarkable case in the State trials lies before me, where Lord Holt presided over the trial of Sir Richard Brown, Preston and others, for high treason; and when counsel appeared, as the gentlemen appear this morning in this court, to ask for a continuance, the answer which fell from the lips of the Lord Chief Justice perpetually was:—We are not to consider the question of the trial, until a plea be pleaded. Because, as his lordship very well remarked, it may happen that no trial will be required. Perchance you may plead guilty to the indictment, and so the rule lying before us contemplated. The last clause of it provides that if the defendant appears and shall plead guilty, there may be no further proceedings in the case; no trial about it. Nothing would remain to be done but to pronounce judgment under the Constitution.

It is time enough for us to talk about trial when we have an issue. The rule is a plain one—a simple one, and I may be pardoned for saying that I fail to perceive anything in rules ten and eleven, to which the learned counsel have referred, which in any kind of construction can be applied to limit the effect of the words in rule eight, to wit:—"That if the party fail to appear, either in person or by counsel, on the day named in the summons, the trial shall proceed on the plea of not guilty;" and further:—"That if failing on the day named in the summons, either in person or by attorney, he failed to answer the articles, the trial shall, nevertheless, proceed as on a plea of not guilty."

When words are plain in written law there is an end of construction. They must be followed. The managers so thought when they appeared at this bar. All that they ask is that the rule be enforced—not a postponement for forty days, to be met at the end of that time, perhaps, with a dilatory plea and a motion, if you please, to quash the articles, or with a question raising the inquiry whether this is the Senate of the United States.

It seems to me, if I may be pardoned in making one other remark, that in prescribing both these rules, that the summons shall issue to be returned on a certain day—given, as in this case, six days in advance—it was intended thereby to enable the party, on the day fixed for his appearance, to come to this bar and make his answer to those articles. I may be pardoned for saying, further, what is doubtless known to every one within the hearing of my voice, that technical rules do in no way control, or limit or temper the action of this body; that under the plea of not guilty every conceivable defense which this party can make to these articles—if they be articles at all—if they be prepared by a competent tribunal at all—can be attempted.

Why, then, this delay of forty days to draw up an answer? What we desire to know on behalf of the House of Representatives—by whose authority we appear here—is whether an answer is to be filed, in accordance with the rule, and if it be not filed, whether the rule itself is to be enforced by the Senate, and a plea of not guilty entered upon the accused? That is our inquiry. It is not my purpose to enter on the discussion at all as to the postponing of the day for the progress of the trial. My desire is for the present to see whether, under this rule and by force of this rule, we can obtain an issue.

The Chief Justice—Senators, the counsel for the President submit a motion that forty days be allowed for the preparation of his answer. The rule requires that as every question shall be taken without debate, you who are in favor of agreeing to that motion say yea.

Senator EDMUNDS (Vt.) rising, said:—Mr. President, on that subject, I submit the following order:—

"*Ordered*, That the respondent file his answer to the articles of impeachment on or before the first day of April next, and that the managers of the impeachment file their replication thereto within three days thereafter, and that the matter stand for trial on Monday, April 6, 1868."

Senator MORTON (Ind.)—I move that the Senate retire for the purpose of consultation.

Mr. BINGHAM—I am instructed by the managers to request that the Senate shall pass on the motion under the eighth rule, and reject the application to defer the day of answer.

The Chief Justice—The Chief Justice will regard the motion of the Senator from Vermont (Mr. Edmunds) as an amendment to the motion submitted by the counsel for the President.

Senator CONKLING (N. Y.)—What is to become of the motion of the Senator from Indiana (Mr. Morton).

Senator SUMNER—What was the motion of the Senator from Indiana?

Senator CONKLING—That the Senate retire for the purpose of consultation.

Senator SUMNER—That is the true motion.

The Chief Justice put the question and declared it carried, and the Senate then retired from the Chamber at 2 o'clock P. M.

The galleries thinned considerably while the court held a long consultation, and the floor presented very much the appearance of a county court room, when the jury had retired, and the court was in recess, not half the House and other occupants of the floor remaining, and they scattered in knots among the Senators' seats and elsewhere. The managers, meanwhile, occasionally consulted or pored over books bound in law calf. Mr. Stevens discussed with apparent relish some raw oysters brought him from the refectory. The President *pro tem.*, Mr. Wade, was on the floor during most of the time occupied by the consultation.

At seven minutes past 4 o'clock the Senators reentered and took their seats, when order was restored.

Order of the Court.

The Chief Justice said:—The motion made by counsel is overruled, and the Senate adopts the order which will be read by the Secretary.

The Secretary read the order as follows:—

Ordered, That the respondent answer to the articles of impeachment on or before Monday, the 23d day of March instant.

The Replication.

Mr. BINGHAM—Mr. President, I am instructed by the managers to submit to the consideration of the Senate the following motion, and ask that it may be reported by the Secretary.

The Secretary read as follows:—

Ordered, That before the filing of replication by the managers on the part of the House of Representatives, the trial of Andrew Johnson, President of the United States, upon the articles of impeachment exhibited by the House of Representatives, shall proceed forthwith.

The Chair put the question, and said the yeas appeared to have it; but the yeas and nays were demanded, with the following result:—

YEAS.—Messrs. Cameron, Cattell, Chandler. Cole. Conklin, Conness, Corbett, Drake, Ferry, Harlan, Howard, Morgan, Morton, Nye. Patterson (N. H.), Pomeroy, Ramsey, Ross, Stewart, Sumner, Thayer, Tipton, Williams, Wilson and Yates—25.

NAYS.—Messrs. Anthony, Bayard, Buckalew, Davis' Dixon, Edmunds, Fessenden, Fowler, Frelinghuysen' Grimes, Henderson, Hendricks, Howe, Johnson, McCreery, Morrill (Me.), Morrill (Vt.), Norton, Patterson (Tenn.), Saulsbury, Sherman, Sprague, Trumbull, Van Winkle, Vickers and Willey—26.

So the order was not agreed to.

Mr. Wade did not vote.

Mr. SHERMAN offered the following order, which was read:—

Ordered, That the trial of the articles of impeachment shall proceed on the 6th of April next.

Mr. HOWARD—I hope not, Mr. President.

Mr. WILSON moved to amend by making it the 1st instead of the 6th of April next.

Mr. BUTLER—I would like to inquire of the President of the Senate if the managers on the part of the House of Representatives have a right to be heard upon this matter?

The Chief Justice—The Chair is of opinion that the managers have a right to be heard.

Speech of Gen. Butler.

Mr. BUTLER—Mr. President and gentlemen of the Senate:—However ungracious it may seem on the part of the managers representing the House of Representatives, and thereby representing the people of the United States, in pressing an early trial of the accused, yet our duty to those who send us here—representing their wishes, speaking in their behalf and by their command—the peace of the country, the interests of the people, all seem to require that we should urge the speediest possible trial.

Among the reasons why the trial is sought to be delayed, the learned counsel who appear for the accused have brought to the attention of the Senate precedents in early days. We are told that railroad speed was not to be used on this trial. Sir, why not; railroads have effected everything else in this world; telegraphs have brought places together that were thousands of miles apart.

It takes infinitely less time, if I may use so strong an expression, to bring a witness from California now than it took to send to Philadelphia for one in the case of the trial of Judge Chase; and, therefore, we must not shut our eyes to the fact that there are railroads and there are telegraphs to give the accused the privilege of calling his counsel together, and of getting answers from any witnesses that he may have summoned and to bring them here. It should have an important bearing on the course we are to take that I respectfully submit is not to be overlooked.

Railroads and telegraphs have changed the order of things. In every other business of life we recognize that fact, why should we not in this? Passing from that which is but an incident—a detail, perhaps—will you allow me to suggest that the ordinary course of justice, the ordinary delays of courts, the ordinary term given in ordinary cases, for men to answer when called before courts of justice, have no application to this case. Not even, sir, when cases are heard and determined before the Supreme Court of the United States, are the rules applicable to this particular case, for this reason, if for no other, that when ordinary trials are had, when ordinary questions are examined at the bar of any court of justice, there is no danger to the Commonwealth in delay; the Republic may take no detriment if the trial is delayed.

To give the accused time interferes with nobody; to give him indulgence hurts no one—may help him. But here the House of Representatives have presented at the bar of the Senate, in the most solemn form, the chief ruler of the nation, and they say—and they desire your judgment upon the accusation—that he has usurped power which does not belong to him; that he is, at the same time, breaking the laws solemnly enacted by you, and those that have sent you here—by the Congress of the United States—and that he still proposes so to do.

Sir, who is the criminal? I beg pardon of the counsel for the respondent, he is the Chief Executive of the nation! When I have said that, I have taken out from all rule this trial, because, I submit with deference, sir, that for the first time in the history of the world has a nation brought its ruler to the bar of its highest court, under the rules and forms provided by the Constitution; above all rule and all analogy—all likeness to an ordinary trial ceases there.

I say that the Chief Executive, who is the commander of your armies; who claims that command; who controls, through his subordinates, your Treasury; who controls your navy; who controls all elements of power; who controls your foreign relations; who may complicate, in an hour of passion or prejudice, the whole nation by whom he is arraigned as the respondent at your bar; and mark me, sir, I respectfully submit that the very question here at issue this day, this hour, is whether he shall control, beyond the reach of your laws and outside of your laws, the army of the United States? That is the one great question here at issue—whether he shall set aside your laws; set aside the decrees of the Senate and the laws enacted by Congress; setting aside every law; claiming the Executive power only that he shall control the great military arm of this government, and control it, if he pleases, to your ruin and the ruin of the country.

Again, sir, do we not know, may we not upon this motion assume, the fact that the whole business of the War Department of this country pauses until this trial goes on. He will not recognize, as we all know, the Secretary of War whom this body has declared the legal Secretary of War, and whom Congress, under a power legitimately exercised, has recognized as the legal Secretary of War; and do we not know, also, that while he has appointed a Secretary of War *ad interim,* he dare not recognize him, and this day, and this hour, the whole business of the War Department stops.

Mr. Butler reminded the Senate that a gallant officer of the army, if confirmed by them to-day, who, by right, ought to have his commission and his pay commence immediately his appointment reached him, would have to wait if this motion prevailed for forty days, as long as it took God to destroy this world by a flood (laughter), and for what? I wonder that the intelligent and able counsel might delay the trial still longer when one department of the government was already thrown into confusion while they were blamed.

But, he continued, that is not all. The great pulse of the nation beats in perturbation while this strictly constitutional but wholly anomalous proceeding goes on, and it passes fitfully when we pause, and goes forward when we go forward, and the very question to-day in this country is arising out of the desire of men to have business interests settled, to have prosperity return, to have the spring open as auspiciously under our laws as it will under the laws of nature. I say the very pulse of the nation beats here, and beating fitfully requires us to still it by bringing this respondent to justice, from which God give him deliverance, if he so deserves, at the earliest possible hour consistent with his right.

Mr. Butler then urged that while all the time shown to be necessary when the case comes to trial should be granted, no time should be fixed in advance. They should not presume in advance that the respondent could not get ready. Let him put in his answer, and then, if he showed the absence of necessary witnesses, the managers would either acquiesce in a proper delay or admit all that he sought to prove by the testimony. He would not deny the respondent a single indulgence consistent with public safety. They asked no more privileges than they were willing to grant to him.

The great act for which he was to be brought to the bar was committed on the 21st of February. He knew its consequences just as well as they did. The House of Representatives had dealt with it on the 22d. On the 4th of March they had brought it before the Senate, with what they called its legal consequences; and now they were here ready for trial—instant trial. Some Judges had sat twenty-two hours in the day on the trial of great crimes; and they, God giving them strength, would sit here every day and every hour, to bring this trial to a conclusion.

He knew exactly what he had done; they had granted him more time, and now they ask that he should be prepared then to meet them. He hoped hereafter no man anywhere would say that the charges upon which Andrew Johnson was arraigned were frivolous, unsubstantial, or of no effect, when counsel of the highest respectability, who would not, for their lives, say what they did not believe, told the Senate that with all their legal ability they could not put in an answer to the charges, so grave were they, in less than forty days, yea fifty days.

Mr. Butler concluded after recapitulating the considerations which he thought ought to influence them in deciding this question by reminding them that a speedy termination of the trial either way would bring quiet to the country, and praying them not to decide this question, upon which the life of the nation depends—the greatest question that ever came before any body—on any the ordinary analogies of law.

Mr. NELSON, of counsel for the President, said:—
I have endeavored, in coming here, to divest my mind of the idea that we are engaged in a political discussion, and have tried to be impressed only with the thought that we appear before a tribunal sworn to try the great question which has been submitted for its consideration, and to dispense justice and equity between two of the greatest powers, if I may so express myself, of the land. I have come here under the impression that there is much force in the observation which the honorable manager (Butler) made, that this tribunal is not to be governed by the rigid rules of law, but is disposed to allow the largest liberty, both to the honorable managers on the part of the House of Representatives and the counsel on behalf of the President.

I have supposed, therefore, that there was nothing improper in our making an appeal to this tribunal for time to answer the charges preferred, and that, instead of that appeal being denied, much more liberality would be extended by the Senate of the nation, sitting as a court of impeachment, than we could ever expect on a trial in a court of common law.

It is not my purpose, Mr. Chief Justice, to enter at this stage into a discussion of the charges, although it would seem to be invited by one or two of the observations made by the honorable manager (Butler). He has told you that it is right in a case of this kind to proceed with railroad speed, and that in consequence of the great improvements of the age, the investigation of this case can be proceeded with much more speedily than it could have been a few years ago. The charges made here are charges of the greatest importance. The questions which will have to be considered by this honorable body are questions in which not only the representatives of the people are concerned, but in which the people themselves have the deepest and most lasting interest.

Questions are raised here in reference to differences of opinion between the Executive of the nation and the honorable Congress, as to their constitutional powers, and as to the rights which they respectively claim. These are questions of the utmost gravity, and are questions which, in the view that we entertain of them, should receive a most deliberate consideration on the part of the Senate. I trust that I may be pardoned by the Chief Justice and Senators for making an allusion to a statute which has long been in force in the State from which I come. I only do it for the purpose of making a brief argument by analogy.

We have a statute in Tennessee which has been long in force, and which provides that where a bill of indictment is found against an individual, and he knows that, owing to excitement or other cause, he may not have a fair trial at the first term of the court, his case shall be continued to the next term of the court. The mode of proceeding at law is not a mode of railroad speed. If there is anything under heaven, Mr. Chief Justice, which gives to judicial proceedings a claim to the consideration and approbation of mankind, it is the fact that justice and courts hasten slowly in the investigation of cases presented to them.

Nothing is done or presumed to be done in a state of excitement. Every moment is allowed for calm and mutual deliberation. Courts are in the habit of investigating cases slowly, carefully, cautiously, and when they form their judgment and pronounce their opinions, and when these opinions are published to the world they meet the sanction of judicial and legal minds everywhere, and meet the approbation and confidence of the people before whom they are promulgated. If this is so, and this is one of the proudest characteristics in the form of judicial proceedings in courts, so much more ought it be so in an exalted and honorable body like this, composed of the greatest men of the United States—of Senators revered and honored by their countrymen, and who from their position are preserved free from reproach and to be calm in their deliberations.

I need not tell you, sir, nor need I tell these honorable Senators whom I address on this occasion—many of whom are lawyers, and many of whom have been clothed, in times past, with the judicial ermine—that in the courts of law the vilest criminal who ever was arraigned in the United States has been given time to prepare for trial; and right not only to be heard by counsel, no matter how great his crime may be, the malignity of the offense with which he has been charged, still he is tried according to the forms of law, and is allowed to have counsel. Continuances are granted to him, and if he is unable to obtain justice, time is given him and all manner of preparation is allowed him. If this is so in courts of common law where they are fettered and bound by the iron rule to which I have alluded, how much more so ought it to be in a great tribunal like this, which does not follow the forms of law, and which is seeking alone to obtain justice. It is necessary for me to remind you and the honorable Senators, that upon a page of foolscap there may be a bill of indictment prepared against an individual which might require weeks in the investigation.

It is unnecessary to remind this honorable body that it is an easy thing to make charges, but that it is often a laborious and difficult thing to make a defense against those accusations.

Reasoning from the analogy found by such proceedings at law, I earnestly maintain before this honorable body that suitable time should be given us to answer the charges preferred here.

A large number of the charges involve an inquiry running back to the very foundation of the government; they involve an examination of the precedents that have been sanctioned by different administrations; they involve, in short, the most extensive range of inquiry; and the last two charges presented by the House of Representatives, if I may be pardoned for using an expression of the view I entertain of them, open up Pandora's box, and will cause the investigation as to the great differences of opinion which existed between the President and Congress—an inquiry which, so far as I can perceive, will be at most interminable in its character.

Now, what do we ask here for the President of the United States, the highest officer in this land? We ask simply that he may be allowed time for his defense. On whose judgment is he to rely in relation to that? He must, in a great part, rely on the judgment of his counsel, to whom he has entrusted his defense. We, who are professionally responsible, have asserted, in the presence of this Senate, in the face of the nation and of the whole world, that we believe we will require the number of days to prepare the President's answer, which was stated in the proposition submitted to the Senate. Such is still our opinion. Are these grave charges to be rushed through the Senate, sitting as a judicial tribunal, in hot haste, and with railroad speed, and without giving the President an opportunity to answer them—that same opportunity which you would give to the meanest criminal?

I do not believe, Mr. Chief Justice and honorable Senators, that you will hesitate one moment in giving us all the time that we deem necessary for preparing our defense, and what may be necessary to enable this body judiciously, carefully, deliberately and cautiously, and with a view of its accountability not only to its constituents, but to posterity, to decide this case.

I have no doubt that the honorable Senators, in justice to themselves and in justice to the great land which they represent, will endeavor to conduct this investigation in a manner that will stamp the impress of honor and justice upon them and upon their proceedings, not only now, but in all time to come, after all of us shall have passed away from the stage of human action.

Mr. Chief Justice, this is an exalted tribunal. I say it in no spirit of compliment, but because I feel it. I feel that there is no more exalted tribunal that could be convened under the sun, and I may say, in answer to an observation of one of the honorable managers, that I, for one, as an American citizen, feel proud that we have assembled here to-day, and assembled under the circumstances which have brought us together.

It is one of the first instances in the history of the world in which the ruler of a people has been presented by a portion of the representatives of the people for trial before a Senate sitting as a judicial tribunal. While that is so, it is equally true on the other hand that the President, through his counsel, comes here and submits himself to the jurisdiction of this court—submits himself calmly, peaceable and with a confident reliance on the justice of the honorable Senate which is to hear his case.

Mr. Chief Justice—I sincerely hope that the resolution offered by the Senator from Ohio will meet the approval of this honorable body. I hope that time will be given, and that these proceedings which in all time to come, will be quoted as a precedent, will be conducted with that gravity, that dignity, and that decorum which are fit and becoming in the representatives of a free and great people.

Senator CONKLING submitted, as an amendment, the following:—

Ordered, That unless otherwise ordered by the Senate for cause shown, the trial of the pending impeachment shall be proceeded with immediately after the replication shall be filed.

The Chief Justice decided the amendment out of order as an amendment to an amendment offered by Senator Wilson.

Senator WILSON withdrew his amendment so that Senator Conkling's amendment to the motion of Senator Sherman might be in order.

Mr. BINGHAM said, I am instructed by the managers to say, that the proposition just suggested by the honorable Senator from New York, is entirely satisfactory to the managers on the part of the House, and to say further, that we believe it is in perfect accord with the precedents in this country. The Senate will, doubtless, remember, that in the trial of the Chase case, when a day was fixed for the trial, the Senate adopted an order which was substantially the same as now suggested. It was as follows:—

"*Ordered,* That the 4th day of February next shall be the day for receiving the answer and proceeding on the trial of impeachment against Samuel Chase."

If nothing further had been said touching the original proposition, we would have been content and satisfied to leave the question, without further remark, to the decision of the Senate; but in view of what has been said, we beg leave to respond that we are chargeable with no indecent haste when we ask that no unnecessary delay shall interpose between the people and the trial of a man who has been charged with having violated the greatest trust ever committed to a single person; trusts which involve the highest interests of the whole people; trusts which involve the peace of the whole country; trusts which involve in some sense the success of this last great experiment of republican government on earth. We may be pardoned, further, for saying that it strikes us with somewhat of surprise, without intending the slightest possible disrespect to any member of this honorable body, that any proposition should be entertained for a continuance in a trial like this when no formal application has been made by the accused himself.

To be sure, a motion was interposed here to-day, in the face of the rules and of the law of this body, for leave to file an answer at the end of forty days. The Senate has disposed of that motion, and in a manner, we venture to say, satisfactory to the whole country, as it is certainly satisfactory to the Representatives of the people at this bar.

And now, sir, that being disposed of, and the Senate having determined the day on which answer shall be filed, we submit, with all due respect to the Senate that it is but just to the people of the country that we shall await the incoming of that answer and the replication thereto by the Representatives of the people, and then see and know what colorable excuse will be offered either by the President accused in his own person, or through his representatives, why this trial would be delayed a single hour.

If he be innocent of those grave accusations, the truth will soon be ascertained by this enlightened body, and he has the right, in the event of the facts so appearing, to a speedy deliverance, while the country has a right to a speedy determination of this most important question. If, on the other hand, he be guilty of those grave and serious charges, what man is there, within this body or outside of it, ready to say that he should, for a day or an hour longer, disgrace the high position which has been held hitherto only by the noblest and most enlightened and most trustworthy of the land?

We think that the executive power of this nation should only be represented in the hands of the men who are faithful to these great trusts of the people. This issue has been made with the President of the United States, and while we admit that there should be no indecent haste, we do demand in the name of the people, most respectfully, that there shall be no unnecessary delay, and no delay at all, unless good cause be shown for delay in the mode and manner hitherto observed in proceedings of this kind.

Senator JOHNSON inquired whether there was any period fixed within which replication was to be filed?

Mr. BINGHAM replied that replication could only be filed with the consent, and after consultation with the House; but he had no doubt that it would be done within one or two days after answer was filed.

Senator CONKLING called for the enforcement of the eighteenth and twenty-third rules, requiring motions to be voted on without debate.

The Chief Justice ruled that debate was not in order.

Senator JOHNSON said he had simply been making an inquiry,

The question being on Senator Conkling's amendment to Senator Sherman's motion, the yeas and nays were taken, and resulted:—Yeas, 40; nays, 10, as follows:—

YEAS.—Messrs. Anthony, Cameron, Cattell, Chandler, Cole, Conkling, Conness, Corbett, Drake, Edmunds, Ferry, Fessenden, Fowler, Frelinghuysen, Grimes, Harlan, Henderson, Howard, Howe, Morgan, Morrill (Me.), Morrill (Vt.), Morton, Nye, Patterson (N. H.), Pomeroy, Ramsey, Ross, Sherman, Sprague, Stewart, Sumner, Thayer, Tipton, Trumbull, Van Winkle, Willey, Williams, Wilson and Yates.

NAYS.—Messrs. Bayard, Buckalew, Davis, Dixon, Hendricks, McCreery, Patterson (Tenn.), Saulsbury and Vickers.

Senator SHERMAN'S motion, as amended, was then agreed to; so it was ordered that unless otherwise ordered by the Senate, for cause shown, the trial of the pending impeachment shall proceed immediately after replication shall be filed.

On motion of Senator HOWARD, it was ordered that the Senate, sitting as a Court of Impeachment, adjourn until the 23d of the present month, at one o'clock in the afternoon.

PROCEEDINGS OF MONDAY, MARCH 23.

The choice seats in the gallery were secured at an early hour by the ladies, who occupied, at the opening of the Senate, about three-fourths of the space allotted to the public, as on the occasion of the organization of the Senate into a court.

The floor was arranged as before. The Chaplain again invoked a blessing upon those now coming to the consideration of grave and momentous matters relating to both individual and to the national welfare, praying that God would preside over this high council, and that justice be done in the name of God, and of all the people of this great nation.

The Trial.

At half-past twelve o'clock the Chair announced that according to rule all legislative and executive business would cease, and directed the Secretary of the Senate to notify the House.

Mr. TRUMBULL (Ill.) called for the reading of the rule, saying that he understood that one o'clock was the hour appointed,

The rule was read providing that on the day set apart for the trial the Senate shall cease Executive business and legislation, and proceed to the trial of the impeachment.

Mr. EDMUNDS (Vt.) called attention to a subsequent order introduced by Mr. Howard, of the Committee of Seven, adjourning the court until one o'clock to-day. This, he said, was the day set apart for receiving the answer, not for proceeding to the trial.

Several Senators suggested to leave it to the decision of the Chair.

The Chair decided that the rule was imperative, and business must now cease.

Mr. EDMUNDS respectfully appealed from the decision of the Chair.

The Chair announced the question to be, Shall the decision of the Chair stand as the judgment of the Senate, but at the suggestion of Mr. TRUMBULL, Mr. Edmunds withdrew the appeal, and the Secretary of the Senate was again directed to notify the House that the Senate was ready to proceed with the trial of the impeachment.

During the interregnum Mr. Stevens entered quietly at a side door, and took his seat at the manager's table.

Chief Justice Chase Enters.

At 1 P. M. the President *pro tem.* vacated the chair, the Chief Justice entered by the side door to the left of the chair, and called the Senate to order.

The Sergeant-at-Arms made the usual proclamation commanding silence, whereupon the managers appeared at the door.

The Sergeant-at-Arms announced "the managers of the impeachment on the part of the House of Representatives," and the Chief Justice said, "The managers will take the seats assigned by the Senate." Messrs. Bingham and Boutwell led the way up the aisle, and they took their seats.

In the meantime Messrs. Stanbery, Curtis, Nelson, Evarts and Groesbeck seated themselves at their table in the order named, Mr. Stanbery occupying the extreme right.

The Sergeant-at-Arms then announced "the House of Representatives," and the members of the House appeared, preceded by Mr. Washburne, on the arm of Mr. McPherson, Clerk of the House, and took their seats outside the bar.

By direction of the Chief Justice, the Secretary of the Senate then read the minutes of the proceedings of Friday, the 13th inst.

Mr. DOOLITTLE (Wis.) was called by the Clerk, and came forward and took the oath.

Senator DAVIS (Ky.) said—Mr. Chief Justice, I rise to make the same proposition to this court that I made to the Senate. I think now is the appropriate time, before the Senate proceeds to make up the case. I, therefore, submit to the court a motion in writing.

The Secretary read as follows:—

Mr. Davis, a member of the Senate in the Court of Impeachment, moved the court to make this order:—

That the Constitution having invested the Senate with the sole power to try the articles of impeachment of the President of the United States, preferred by the House of Representatives, and having provided that the Senate shall be composed of two Senators from each State, to be chosen by the Legislature thereof; and the States of Virginia, North Carolina, South Carolina, Georgia, Alabama, Mississippi, Arkansas, Texas, Louisiana and Florida, having each chosen two Senators who have been excluded from their seats respectively:—

Ordered, That the Court of Impeachment for the trial of the President cannot be legally and constitutionally formed while the Senators from the States aforesaid are thus excluded from the Senate, and which objection continues until Senators from those States are permitted to take their seats in the Senate, subject to all constitutional exceptions and objections to their return and qualification severally.

Senator HOWARD—Mr. President—

The Chief Justice—The question must be decided without debate.

Senator HOWARD—I object to the receiving of the paper.

Senator CONNESS (Cal.)—I desire to submit a motion which will meet the case. I move that the motion be not received, upon which I call for the yeas and nays.

Senator HOWE (Wis.)—I rise to submit a question of order.

The Chief Justice—The Senator will state his point of order.

Senator HOWE—I would ask if the motion offered by the Senator from Kentucky be in order?

The Chief Justice—The motion comes before the Senate in the form of a motion, submitted by a member of the Senate, sitting as a court of impeachment. The twenty-third rule requires that all the orders and decisions shall be made and had by yeas and nays, which shall be entered on the record, and without debate, subject, however, to the operation of rule seven. The seventh rule requires the presiding officer to, in the first instance, submit to the Senate, without a divison, all questions of evidence and incidential questions, but the same shall, on demand of one-fifth of the members present, be decided by yeas and nays. The question then, being on a proposition submitted by a Senator under the twenty-third rule, it is in order.

Mr. CONNESS—Mr. President, is the motion submitted by me in order?

The Chief Justice—No sir.

The call for the yeas and nays were ordered, and they were called. Messrs. Davis and McCreery only voting yea. Messrs. Saulsbury, Bayard and Wade did not vote. So the motion was not agreed to.

Mr. STANBERY then rose and said—Mr. Chief Justice, in obedience to the order of this honorable court, made at the last session, that the answer of the President should be filed to-day, we have it ready. The counsel for the President, abandoning all other business—some of us leaving our courts, our cases and our clients—have devoted every hour to the consideration of this case. The labor has been incessant. We have devoted, as I say, not only every hour ordinarily devoted to business, but many required for necessary rest and recreation have been consumed in it. It is a matter of regret that the court did not allow us more time for preparation; nevertheless, we hope that the answer will be found in all respects sufficient. Such as it is, we are now ready to read and file it.

Mr. CURTIS proceeded to read the answer.

The President's Answer.

To the Senate of the United States sitting as a court of impeachment for the trial of Andrew Johnson, President of the United States.

The answer of the said Andrew Johnson, President of the United States, to the articles of impeachment exhibited against him by the House of Representatives of the United States.

Answer to article 1. For answer to the first article he says that Edwin M. Stanton was appointed Secretary for the Department of War on the 15th day of January, 1862, by Abraham Lincoln, then President of the United States, during the first term of his Presidency, and was commissioned according to the Constitution and the laws of the United States to hold said office during the pleasure of the President; that the office of Secretary for the Department of War was created by an act of the First Congress in its first session, passed on the 7th day of August, A. D. 1789, and in and by that act it was provided and enacted that the said Secretary for the Department of War shall perform and execute such duties as shall from time to time be enjoined on and intrusted to him by the President of the United States, agreeably to the Constitution, relative to the subjects within the scope of the said department; and furthermore, that the said Secretary shall conduct the business of the said department in such a manner as the President of the United States shall from time to time order and instruct; and this respondent, further answering, says that, by force of the act aforesaid and by reason of his appointment, the said Stanton became the principal officer in one of the Executive

Departments of the government, within tne true intent and meaning of the second section of the second article of the Constitution of the United States; and according to the true intent and meaning of that provision of the Constitution of the United States, and in accordance with the settled and uniform practice of each and every President of the United States, the said Stanton then became, and so long as he should continue to hold the said office of Secretary for the Department of War, must continue to be one of the advisers of the President of the United States, as well as the person intrusted to act for and represent the President in matters enjoined upon him or intrusted to him by the President touching the department aforesaid, and for whose conduct in such capacity subordinate to the President, the President is, by the Constitution and laws of the United States, made responsible; and this respondent further answering, says;—He succeeded to the office of President of the United States upon and by reason of the death of Abraham Lincoln, then President of the United States, on the 15th day of April, 1865, and the said Stanton was then holding the said office of Secretary for the Department of War, under and by reason of the appointment and commission aforesaid, and not having been removed from the said office by this respondent, the said Stanton continued to hold the same under the appointment and commission aforesaid, at the pleasure of the President, until the time hereinafter particularly mentioned, and at no time received any appointment or commission, save as above detailed.

And this respondent further answering, says that on and prior to the fifth day of August, A. D. 1867, this respondent, the President of the United States, responsible for the conduct of the Secretary for the Department of War, and having the constitutional right to resort to and rely upon the person holding that office for advice concerning the great and difficult public duties enjoined on the President by the Constitution and laws of the United States, became satisfied that he could not allow the said Stanton to continue to hold the office of Secretary for the Department of War without hazzard of the public interest; that the relations between the said Stanton and the President no longer permitted the President to resort to him for advice, or to be, in the judgment of the President, safely responsible for his conduct of the affairs of the Department of War, as by law required, in accordance with the orders and instructions of the President.

And thereupon, by force of the Constitution and laws of the United States, which devolve on the President the power and the duty to control the conduct of the business of that Executive Department of the government, and by reason of the constitutional duty of the President to take care that the laws be faithfully executed, this respondent did necessarily consider and did determine that the said Stanton ought no longer to hold the said office of Secretary for the Department of War, and this respondent, by virtue of the power and authority vested in him as President of the United States by the Constitution and laws of the United States to give effect to such, his decision and determination, did, on the 5th day of August, A. D. 1867, address to the said Stanton a note, of which the following is a true copy:—

"Sir:—Public considerations of a high character constrain me to say that your resignation as Secretary of War will be accepted.

To which note the said Stanton made the following reply:—

WAR DEPARTMENT, WASHINGTON, August 5, 1867.—Sir:—Your note of this day has been received, stating that public considerations of a high character constrain you to say that my resignation as Secretary of War will be accepted. In reply, I have the honor to say that public considerations of a high character, which alone have induced me to continue at the head of this department, constrain me not to resign the office of Secretary of War before the next meeting of Congress.

Very respectfully, yours,
(Signed) EDWIN M. STANTON.

This respondent, as President of the United States, was thereon of opinion that, having regard to the necessary official relations and duties of the Secretary for the Department of War to the President of the United States, according to the Constitution and laws of the United States, and having regard to the responsibility of the President for the conduct of the said Secretary; and having regard to the paramount executive authority of the office which the respondent holds under the Constitution and laws of the United States, it was impossible, consistently with the public interests, to allow the said Stanton to continue to hold the said office of Secretary for the Department of War; and it then became the official duty of the respondent, as President of the United States, to consider and decide what act or acts should and might lawfully be done by him, as President of the United States, to cause the said Stanton to surrender the said office.

This respondent was informed, and verily believes, that it was practically settled by the first Congress of the United States, and had been so considered and uniformly and in great numbers of instances, acted on by each Congress and President of the United States in succession, from President Washington to and including President Lincoln, and from the first Congress to the Thirty-ninth Congress; that the Constitution of the United States conferred on the President, as part of the Executive power, and as one of the necessary means and instruments of performing the Executive duty expressly imposed on him by the Constitution of taking care that the laws be faithfully executed, the power at any and all times of removing from office all executive officers for cause to be judged of by the President alone.

This respondent had, in pursuance of the Constitution, required the opinion of each principal officer of the Executive departments upon this question of constitutional executive power and duty, and had been advised by each of them, including the said Stanton, Secretary for the Department of War, that under the Constitution of the United States this power was lodged by the Constitution in the President of the United States, and that consequently it could be lawfully exercised by him, and the Congress could not deprive him thereof: and this respondent, in his capacity of President of the United States, and because in that capacity, he was both enabled and bound to use his best judgment upon this question did, in good faith, and with an honest desire to arrive at the truth, come to the conclusion and opinon, and did make the same known to the honorable the Senate of the United States, by a message dated on the second day of March, 1867, a true copy whereof is hereunto annexed and marked A, that the power last mentioned was conferred, and the duty of exercising it in fit cases was imposed on the President by the Constitution of the United States, and that the President could not be deprived of this power or relieved of this duty; nor could the same be vested by law in the President and the Senate jointly, either in part or whole, and this has ever since remained, and was the opinion of this respondent at the time when he was forced, as aforesaid, to consider and decide what act or acts should and might lawfully be done by this respondent, as President of the United States, to cause the said Stanton to surrender the said office. This respondent was also then aware that by the first section of an act regulating the tenure of certain civil offices, passed March 2, 1867, by a constitutional majority of both Houses of Congress, it was enacted as follows:—

That every person holding any civil office to which he has been appointed by and with the advice and consent of the Senate, and every person who shall hereafter be appointed to any such office, and shall become duly qualified to act therein, is and shall be entitled to hold such office until a successor shall have been in like manner appointed and duly qualified, except as herein otherwise provided. * * * *Provided*, That the Secretaries of State, of the Treasury, of War, of the Navy, and of the Interior, the Postmaster-General and the Attorney-General, shall hold their offices respectively for and during the term of the President by whom they may have been appointed, and for one month thereafter, subject to removal by and with the advice and consent of the Senate.

This respondent was also aware that this act was understood and intended to be an expression of the opinion of the Congress by which that act was passed; that the power to remove executive officers for cause might, by law, be taken from the President, and vested in him and the Senate jointly; and although this respondent had arrived at and still retained the opinion above expressed, and veritably believed, as he still believes, that the said first section of the last mentioned act was and is wholly inoperative and void, by reason of its conflict with the Constitution of the United States; yet, inasmuch as the same had been enacted by the constitutional majority in each of the two Houses of that Congress, this respondent considered it to be proper to be examined and decided whether the particular case of the said Stanton, on which it was this respondent's duty to act, was within or without the terms of that first section of the act, or if within it, whether the President had not the power, according to the terms of the act, to remove the said Stanton from the office of Secretery for the Department of War, and having, in his capacity of

President of the United States, so examined and considered, did form the opinion that the case of the said Stanton and his tenure of office were not affected by the first section of the last-named act. And this respondent further answering, says, that although a case thus existed which, in his judgment, as President of the United States, called for the exercise of the Executive power to remove the said Stanton from the office of Secretary for the Department of War; and although this respondent was of opinion, as is above shown, that under the Constitution of the United States the power to remove the said Stanton from the said office was vested in the President of the United States; and although this respondent was also of the opinion, as is above shown, that the case of the said Stanton was not affected by the first section of the last-named act; and although each of the said opinions had been formed by this respondent upon an actual case, requiring him, in his capacity of President of the United States, to come to some judgment and determination thereon, yet the respondent, as President of the United States, desired and determined to avoid if possible any question of the construction and effect of the said first section of the last-named act, and also the broader question of the executive power conferred on the President of the United States by the Constitution of the United States to remove one of the principal officers of one of the Executive Departments for cause seeming to him sufficient; and this respondent also desired and determined that, if from causes over which he could exert no control, it should become absolutely necessary to raise and have in some way determined either or both of the said last-named questions, it was in accordance with the Constitution of the United States, and was required of the President thereby, that questions of so much gravity and importance, upon which the Legislature and Executive Departments of the government had disagreed, which involved powers considered by all branches of the government during its entire history down to the year 1867, to have been confided by the Constitution of the United States to the President, and to be necessary for the complete and proper execution of his constitutional duties, should be in some proper way submitted to that judicial department of the government intrusted by the Constitution with the power, and subjected by it to the duty, not only of determining finally the Constitution and effect of all acts of Congress, by comparing them with the Constitution of the United States, and pronouncing them inoperative when found in conflict with that fundamental law which the people have enacted for the government of all their servants, and to these ends:—

First. That through the action of the Senate of the United States, the absolute duty of the President to substitute some fit person in the place of Mr. Stanton as one of his advisers, who is as a principal of a subordinate office, whose official conduct he was responsible for, and had a lawful right to control, might, if possible, be accomplished without the necessity of raising any one of the questions aforesaid; and second, if these duties could not so be performed, then that these questions, or such of them as might necessarily arise, should be judicially determined in manner aforesaid, and for no other end or purpose. This respondent, as President of the United States, on the 12th day of August, 1867, seven days after the reception of the letter of the said Stanton of the 5th of August, herein before stated, did issue to the said Stanton the order following, viz.:—

EXECUTIVE MANSION, WASHINGTON, Aug. 12, 1867.—Sir: —By virtue of the power and authority vested in me as President, by the Constitution and laws of the United States, you are hereby suspended from office as Secretary of War, and will cease to exercise any and all functions pertaining to the same. You will at once transfer to Gen. Ulysses S. Grant, who has this day been authorized and empowered to act as Secretary of War ad interim, all records, books, papers and other public property now in your custody and charge.

Hon. E. M. Stanton, Secretary of War.

To which said order the said Stanton made the following reply:—

"WAR DEPARTMENT, WASHINGTON CITY, Aug. 12, 1867.— Sir:—Your note of this date has been received, informing me that, by virtue of the powers vested in you as President by the Constitution and laws of the United States, I am suspended from office as Secretary of War, and will cease to exercise any and all functions pertaining to the same, and also directing me at once to transfer to General Ulysses S. Grant, who has this day been authorized and empowered to act as Secretary of War ad interim, all records, books, papers and other public property now in my custody and charge. Under a sense of public duty I am compelled to deny your right, under the Constitution and laws of the United States, without the advice and consent of the Senate, and without legal cause, to suspend me from office as Secretary of War for the exercise of any or all functions pertaining to the same, and without such advice and consent to compel me to transfer to any person the records, books, papers and public property in my custody as Secretary; but inasmuch as the General commanding the armies of the United States has been appointed ad interim, and has notified me that he has accepted the appointment, I have no alternative but to submit, under protest, to superior force.
"To the President."

And this respondent, further answering, says that it is provided in and by the second section of an act to regulate the tenure of certain civil offices, that the President may suspend an officer from the performance of the duties of the office held by him, for certain causes therein designated, until the next meeting of the Senate, and until the case shall be acted on by the Senate; that this respondent, as President of the United States, was advised, and he verily believed and still believes, that the executive power of removal from office confided to him by the Constitution as aforesaid, includes the power of suspension from office at the pleasure of the President; and this respondent, by the order aforesaid, did suspend the said Stanton from office, not until the next meeting of the Senate or until the Senate should have acted upon the case, but by force of the power and authority vested in him by the Constitution and laws of the United States, indefinitely, and at the pleasure of the President; and the order, in form aforesaid, was made known to the Senate of the United States on the 12th day of December, A. D. 1867, as will be more fully hereinafter stated.

And this respondent further answering, says in and by the act of February 12, 1795, it was among other things provided and enacted that in case of vacancy in the office of Secretary for the Department of War, it shall be lawful for the President, in case that he shall think it necessary to authorize any person to perform the duties of that office, until a successor be appointed, or such vacancy filled, but not exceeding the term of six months; and this respondent being advised and believing that such law was in full force, and not repealed, by an order dated August 12, 1867, did authorize and empower Ulysses S. Grant, General of the armies of the United States, to act as Secretary of War ad interim, in the form of which similar authority had theretofore been given, not until the next meeting of the Senate, and until the Senate should act on the case, but at the pleasure of the President, subject only to the limitation of six months in the said last mentioned act contained, and a copy of the last named order was made known to the Senate of the United States on the 12th day of December, A. D. 1867, as will be hereinafter more fully stated, and in pursuance of the design and intention aforesaid, if it should become necessary, to submit the said question to a judicial determination, this respondent, at or near the date of the last mentioned order, did make known such his purpose to obtain a judicial decision of the said questions, or such of them as might be necessary; and this respondent further answering, says that in further pursuance of his intention and design, if possible, to perform what he judged to be his imperative duty to prevent the said Stanton from longer holding the office of Secretary for the Department of War, and at the same time avoiding, if possible, any question respecting the extent of the power of removal from executive office confided to the President by the Constitution of the United States, and any question respecting the construction and effect of the first section of the said "act regulating the tenure of certain civil officers," while he should not by any act of his abandon and relinquish either a power which he believed the Constitution had conferred on the President of the United States to enable him to perform the duties of his office, or a power designedly left to him by the first section of the act of Congress last aforesaid, this respondent did on the 12th day of December, 1867, transmit to the Senate of the United States a message, a copy whereof is hereunto annexed and marked B, wherein he made known the orders aforesaid, and the reasons which had induced the same, so far as this respondent then considered it material and necessary that the same should be set forth, and reiterated his views concerning the constitutional power of removal vested in the President, and also expressed his views concerning the construction of the said first section of the last-mentioned act as respected the power of the President to remove the said Stanton from the said office of Secretary for the Department of War; well, hoping that this respondent could thus perform what he then believed and still believes to be his imperative duty in reference to the said Stanton, without derogating from the powers which this respondent believed were confided to the President by the Constitution and laws, and without the necessity of raising judicially any questions respecting the same. And this respondent, further answering, says that this hope not having been realized, the President was compelled either to allow the said Stanton to resume the said office and remain therein, contrary to the settled convictions of the President formed as aforesaid, respecting the power confided to him and the duties required of him by the Constitution of the United States, and contrary to the opinion formed as aforesaid, that the first section of the last-mentioned act did not affect the case of the said Stanton, and contrary to the fixed belief of the President, that he could no longer advise with or trust, or be responsible for the said Stanton in the said office of Secretary for the Department of War, or else he was compelled to take such steps as might, in the judgment of the President, be lawful and necessary to raise for a judicial decision the questions affecting the lawful right of the said Stanton to resume the said office, or the power of the said Stanton to persist in refusing to quit the said office, if he should persist in actually refusing to quit the same; to this end and to this end only, this respondent did, on the 21st day of February, 1868, issue the order for the removal of the said Stanton, in the said first article mentioned and set forth, and the order authorizing the said Lorenzo F. Thomas to act as Secretary of War *ad interim*, in the said second article set forth; and this respondent proceeding to answer specifically each substantial allegation in said first article, says:—

He denies that the said Stanton on the 21st day of February, 1868, was lawfully in possession of the said office of Secretary for the Department of War. He denies that the said Stanton on the day last-mentioned was lawfully entitled to hold the said office against the will of the President of the United States. He denies that the said order for the removal of the said Stanton was unlawfully issued. He denies that the said order was issued with intent to violate the act entitled "An act to regulate the tenure of certain civil offices." He denies that the said order was a violation of the last-mentioned act. He denies that the said order was a violation of the Constitution of the United States, or of any law thereof, or of his oath of office. He denies that the said order was issued with an intent to violate the Constitution of the United States, or any law thereof, or this respondent's oath of office; and he respectfully but earnestly insists that not only was it issued by him in the performance of what he believed to be an imperative official duty, but in the performance of what this honorable court will consider was in point of fact an imperative official duty; and he denies that any and all substantive matters in the said first article contained, in manner and form as the same are therein stated and set forth, do by law constitute a high misdemeanor in office within the true intent and meaning of the Constitution of the United States.

Answer to Article 2.

For answer to the second article this respondent says that he admits he did issue and deliver to said Lorenzo Thomas the said writing set forth in said second article, bearing date at Washington, D. C., February 21, 1868, addressed to Brevet Major-General Lorenzo Thomas, Adjutant-General United States Army, Washington; and he further admits that the same was so issued without the advice and consent of the Senate of the United States, then in session, but he denies that he thereby violated the Constitution of the United States, or any law thereof, or that he did thereby intend to violate the Constitution of the United States, or the provisions of any act of Congress; and this respondent refers to his answer to said first article for a full statement of the purposes and intentions with which said order was issued, and adopts the same as a part of his answer to this article; and further denies that there was then and there no vacancy in the said office of Secretary for the Department of War, that he did then and there commit or was guilty of a high misdemeanor in office, and this respondent maintains and will insist:—

First, that at the date and delivery of said writing, there was a vacancy existing in the office of Secretary for the Department of War. Second, that notwithstanding the Senate of the United States was then in session, it was lawful and according to long and well-established usage, to empower and authorize the said Thomas to act as Secretary of War *ad interim*. Third, that if the said act regulating the tenure of civil officers be held to be a valid law, no provisions of the same were violated by the issuing of said order, or by the designation of said Thomas to act as Secretary of War *ad interim*.

Answer to Article 3.

And for answer to said third article, this respondent says that he abides by his answer to said first and second articles in so far as the same are responsive to the allegations contained in the said third article; and, without here again repeating the same answer, prays the same be taken as an answer to this third article, as fully as if here again set out at length; and as to the new allegation contained in said third article, that this respondent did appoint the said Thomas to be Secretary for the Department of War *ad interim*, this respondent denies that he gave any other authority to said Thomas than such as appears in said written authority set out in said article, by which he authorized and empowered said Thomas to act as Secretary for the Department of War *ad interim*; and he denies that the same amounts to an appointment, and insists that it is only a designation of an officer of that department to act temporarily as Secretary for the Department of War *ad interim* until an

appointment should be made; but whether the said written authority amounts to an appointment or to a temporary authority or designation, this respondent denies that in any sense he did thereby intend to violate the Constitution of the United States, or that he thereby intended to give the said order, the character or effect of an appointment in the constitutional or legal sense of that term; he further denies that there was no vacancy in said office of Secretary for the Department of War existing at the date of said written authority.

Answer to Article 4.

For answer to said fourth article, this respondent denies that on the said 21st day of February, 1868, at Washington aforesaid, or at any other time or place, he did unlawfully conspire with the said Lorenzo Thomas, or with the said Thomas or any other person or persons, with intent, by intimidations and threats, unlawfully to hinder and prevent the said Stanton from holding said office of Secretary for the Department of War, in violation of the Constitution of the United States, or of the provisions of the said act of Congress, in said article mentioned, or that he did then and there commit, or was guilty of a high crime in office; on the contrary thereof, protesting that the said Stanton was not then and there lawfully the Secretary for the Department of War, this respondent stated that his sole purpose in authorizing the said Thomas to act as Secretary for the Department of War, *ad interim*, was, as is fully stated in his answer to the said first article, to bring the question of the right of the said Stanton to hold said office, notwithstanding his said suspension, and notwithstanding the said order of removal, and notwithstanding the said authority of the said Thomas to act as Secretary of War, *ad interim*, to the test of a final decision by the Supreme Court of the United States, in the earliest practicable mode by which the question could be brought before that tribunal. This respondent did not conspire or agree with the said Thomas, or any other person or persons, to use intimidation or threats to hinder or prevent the said Stanton from holding the said office of Secretary for the Department of War; nor did this respondent at any time command or advise the said Thomas, or any other person or persons, to resort to or use either threats or intimidation for that purpose. The only means in the contemplation or purpose of respondent to be used are set forth fully in the said orders of February 21, the first addressed to Mr. Stanton and the second to the said Thomas.

By the first order the respondent notified Mr. Stanton that he was removed from the said office, and that his functions as Secretary for the Department of War were to terminate upon the receipt of that order, and he also thereby notified the said Stanton that the said Thomas had been authorized to act as Secretary for the Department of War *ad interim*, and ordered the said Stanton to transfer to him all the records, books, papers, and other public property in his custody and charge, and by the second order notified the said Thomas of the removal from office of the said Stanton, and authorized him to act as Secretary for the Department of War *ad interim*, and directed him to immediately enter upon the discharge of the duties pertaining to that office, and to receive the transfer of all the records, books, papers, and other public property from Mr. Stanton then in his custody and charge. Respondent gave no instructions to the said Thomas to use intimidation or threats to enforce obedience to these orders.

He gave him no authority to call in the aid of the military or any other force to enable him to obtain possession of the office, or of the books, papers, records or property thereof; the only agency resorted to, or intended to be resorted to, was by means of the said Executive orders requiring obedience. But the Secretary for the Department of War refused to obey these orders, and still holds undisturbed possession and custody of that department, and of the records, books, papers and other public property therein. Respondent further states that, in execution of the orders so given by this respondent to the said Thomas, he, the said Thomas, proceeded in a peaceful manner to demand of the said Stanton a surrender to him of the public property in the said department, and to vacate the possession of the same, and to allow him, the said Thomas, peaceably to exercise the duties devolved upon him by authority of the President. That, as this respondent has been informed and believes, the said Stanton peremptorily refused obedience to the orders issued.

Upon such refusal no force or threat of force was used by the said Thomas, by authority of the President or otherwise, to enforce obedience, either then or at any subsequent time; and his respondent doth here except to the sufficiency of the allegations contained in said fourth article, and states for ground of exception that it is not stated that there was any agreement between this respondent and the said Thomas, or any other person or persons, to use intimidation and threats; nor is there any allegation as to the nature of said intimidation and threats, or that there was any agreement to carry them into execution, or that any step was taken, or agreed to be taken, to carry them into execution; and that the allegation in said article that the intent of said conspiracy to use intimidation and threats, is wholly insufficient, inasmuch as it is not alleged that the said intent formed the basis or became a part of any agreement between the said alleged conspirators; and furthermore, that there is no allegation of any conspiracy or agreement to use intimidation or threats.

Answer to Article 5.

And for answer to the said fifth article, this respondent denies that on the said 21st day of February, 1868, or at any other time or times in the same year, before the said 2d day of March, 1868, or at any prior or subsequent time, at Washington aforesaid, or at any other place, this respondent did unlawfully conspire with the said Thomas, or any other persons, to prevent or hinder the execution of the said act entitled "An act regulating the tenure of certain civil offices," or that, in pursuance of said alleged conspiracy, he did unlawfully attempt to prevent the said Edwin M. Stanton from holding said office of Secretary for the Department of War, or that he did thereby commit, or that he was thereby guilty of a high misdemeanor in office. Respondent protesting that said Stanton was not then and there Secretary for the Department of War, begs leave to refer to his answer given to the fourth article, and to his answer given to the first article, as to his intent and purpose in issuing the order for the removal of Mr. Stanton; and the said respondent prays equal benefit therefrom, as if the same were here again repeated and fully set forth. And this respondent excepts to the sufficiency of the said fifth article, and states his ground for such exception, that it is not alleged by what means, or by what agreement the said alleged conspiracy was formed or agreed to be carried out, or in what way the same was intended to be carried out, or what were acts done in pursuance thereof.

Answer to Article 6.

And for answer to the said sixth article this respondent denies that on the said 21st day of February, 1868, at Washington aforesaid, or at any other time or place, he did unlawfully conspire with the said Thomas by force to seize, take or possess the property of the United States in the Department of War, contrary to the provisions of the said acts referred to in the said article, or either of them, or with intent to violate either of them; respondent, protesting that the said Stanton was not then and there Secretary for the Department of War, not only denies the said conspiracy as charged, but also denies any unlawful intent in reference to the custody and charge of the property of the United States in the said Department of War, and again refers to his former answer for a full statement of his intent and purpose in the premises.

Answer to Article 7.

And for answer to said seventh article, respondent denies that on the said 21st day of February, 1868, at Washington aforesaid, or at any other time and place, he did unlawfully conspire with said Thomas, with intent unlawfully to seize, take or possess the property of the United States in the Department of War, with intent to violate or disregard the said act in said seventh article referred to, or that he did then and there commit a high misdemeanor in office; respondent, protesting that the said Stanton was not then and there Secretary for the Department of War, again refers to his former answers in so far as they are applicable to show the intent with which he proceeded in the premises, and prays equal benefit therefrom as if the same were here again fully repeated. Respondent further takes exception to the sufficiency of the allegations of this article as to the conspiracy alleged, upon the same ground as stated in the exception set forth in his answer to said article fourth.

Answer to Article 8.

And for answer to the said eighth article, this respondent denies that on the 21st day of February, 1868, at Washington aforesaid, or at any other time and place, he did issue and deliver to the said Thomas the said letter of authority set forth in the said eighth article, with the intent unlawfully to control the disbursement of the money appropriated for the military service and for the Department of War; this respondent, protesting that there was a vacancy in the office of Secretary for the Department of War, admits that he did issue the said letter of authority, and he denies that the same was with any unlawful intent whatever, either to violate the Constitution of the United States, or any act of Congress. On the contrary, this respondent again affirms that his sole intent to vindicate his authority as President of the United States, and by peaceful means to bring the question of the right of the said Stanton to continue to hold the said office of Secretary of War to to a final decision before the Supreme Court of the United States, as has been hereinbefore set forth, and he prays the same benefit from his answer in the premises as if the same were here again repeated at length.

Answer to Article 9.

And for answer to the said ninth article, the respondent states, that on the said 22d day of February, 1868, the following note was addressed to the said Emory, by the private Secretary of respondent:—

EXECUTIVE MANSION, WASHINGTON, D. C., Feb. 22, 1868.—General:—The President desires me to say that he will be pleased to have you call upon him as early as possible. Respectfully and truly yours,

WILLIAM G. MOORE, United States Army.

General Emory called at the Executive Mansion according to this request. The object of respondent was to be advised by General Emory, Commandant of the Department of Washington, what changes had been made in the military affairs of the Department. Respondent had been informed that various changes had been made, which in no wise had been brought to his notice, or reported to him from the Department of War, or from any other quarter had he obtained the facts. General Emory had explained in detail the changes which had taken place. Said Emory called the attention of respondent to a general order which he referred to, and which this respondent then sent for. When it was produced it was as follows:—

WAR DEPARTMENT, ADJUTANT-GENERAL'S OFFICE,

WASHINGTON, D. C., March 14, 1867.—General Orders, No. 17:—The following acts of Congress are published for the information and government of all concerned:—

Public. No. 85. To making appropriations for the support of the army for year ending June 30, 1868, and for other purposes.

Section 2. *And be it further enacted*, That the headquarters of the General of the United States Army shall be at the city of Washington, and all orders and instructions relating to military operations issued by the President or Secretary of War shall be issued through the General of the Army, and in case of his inability, through the next in rank. The General of the Army shall not be removed, suspended, or relieved from command, or assigned to duty elsewhere than at the said headquarters, except at his own request, without the previous approval of the Senate, and any orders or instructions relating to military operations issued contrary to the requirements of this section shall be null and void; and any officer who shall issue orders or instructions contrary to the provisions of this section shall be deemed guilty of a misdemeanor in office, and any officer of the army who shall transmit, convey, or obey any orders or instructions issued contrary to the provisions of this section, knowing that such orders were so issued, shall be liable to impeachment for not less than two or more than twenty years upon conviction thereof in any court of competent jurisdiction. Approved March 2. 1867.

By order of the Secretary of War.

E. D. TOWNSEND,
Assistant Adjutant-General.

Official—Assistant Adjutant-General, A. G. O., No. 172.

General Emory not only called the attention of respondent to this order but to the fact that it was in conformity with a section contained in an appropriation act passed by Congress. Respondent, after reading the order, observed, "this is not in accordance with the Constitution of the United States, which makes me Commander-in-Chief of the Army and Navy, or of the language of the commission which you hold." General Emory then stated that this law had met respondent's approval. Respondent then said in reply in substance, "Am I to understand that the President of the United States cannot give an order but through the General-in-Chief or General Grant?" General Emory again reiterated the statement that it had met respondent's approval, and that it was the opinion of some of the leading lawyers of the country that this order was constitutional, with some further conversation. Respondent then inquired the names of the lawyers who had given the opinion, and he mentioned the names of two. Respondent then said that the object of the law was very evident, referring to the clause in the Appropriation act upon which the order purported to be based. This, according to respondent's recollection, was the substance of the conversation had with General Emory.

Respondent denies that any allegations in the said article of any instructions or declarations given to the said Emory, then or at any other time, contrary to or in addition to what is hereinbefore set forth, are true. Respondent denies that in the said conversation with the said Emory he had any other intent than to express the opinion then given to the said Emory; nor did he then or at any time request or order the said Emory to disobey any law or any order issued in conformity with any law, nor intend to offer any inducements to the said Emory to violate any law. What this respondent then said to General Emory was simply the expression of an opinion which he then fully believed to be sound, and which he yet believes to be so—that by the express provisions of the Constitution this respondent, as President, is made the Commander-in-Chief of the armies of the United States, and as such he is to be respected; and that his orders, whether issued through the General-in-Chief or by any other channel of communication, are entitled to respect and obedience; and that such constitutional power cannot be taken from him by virtue of any act of Congress. Respondent doth therefore deny that by the expression of such opinion he did commit or was guilty of a high misdemeanor in office; and this respondent doth further say that the said article nine lays no foundation whatever for the conclusion stated in the said article, that the respondent, by reason of the allegations therein contained, was guilty of a high misdemeanor in office.

In reference to the statement made by General Emory that this respondent had approved of said act of Congress containing the section referred to, the respondent admits that his formal approval was given to said act, but accompanied the same by the following message addressed and sent with the act to the House of Representatives, in which the said act originated, and from which it came to respondent:—

"To the House of Representatives:—The act entitled "An act making appropriations for the support of the army for the year ending June 30, 1868, and for other purposes," contains provisions to which I must call attention. These provisions are contained in the second section, which, in certain cases, virtually deprives the President of his constitutional functions as Commander-in-Chief of the Army, and in the sixth section, which denies to ten States of the Union their constitutional right to protect themselves, in any emergency, by means of their own militia. These provisions are out of place in an appropriation act, but I am compelled to defeat these necessary appropriations if I withhold my signature to the act. Pressed by these considerations, I feel constrained to return the bill with my signature, but to accompany it with my earnest protest against the sections which I have indicated.

"Washington, D. C., March 22, 1867."

Respondent, therefore, did no more than to express to said Emory the same opinion which he had so expressed to the House of Representatives.

Answer to Article 10.

And in answer to the tenth article and specifications thereof, the respondent says that on the 14th and 15th days of August, in the year 1866, a political convention of delegates, from all or most of the States and territories of the Union, was held in the city of Philadelphia, under the name and style of the "National Union Convention," for the purpose of maintaining and advancing certain political views and opinions before the people of the United States, and for their support and adoption in the exercise of the constitutional suffrage in the elections of representatives and delegates in Congress, which were soon to occur in many of the States and territories of the Union, which said Convention in the course of its proceedings, and in furtherance of the objects of the same, adopted a declaration of principles, and an address to the people of the United States, and appointed a committee of two of its members from each State, and of one from each Territory, and one from the District of Columbia, to wait upon the President of the United States and present to him a copy of the proceedings of the Convention. That on the 15th day of said month of August this committee waited upon the President of the United States at the Executive mansion, and was received by him in one of the rooms thereof; and by their chairman, the Hon. Reverdy Johnson, then and now a Senator of the United States, acting and speaking in their behalf, presented a copy of the proceedings of the Convention, and addressed the President of the United States in a speech, of which a copy, according to a published report of the same, and as the respondent believes, substantially a correct report, is hereto annexed, as a part of this answer, and marked, exhibit C.

That thereupon and in reply to the address of said committee by their chairman, this respondent addressed the said committee so waiting upon him in one of the rooms of the Executive mansion, and this respondent believes that this, his address to said committee, is the occasion referred to in the first specification of the tenth article; but this respondent does not admit that the passages therein set forth, as if extracts from a speech or address of this respondent upon said occasion, correctly or justly present his speech or address upon said occasion; but on the contrary this respondent demands and insists that if this honorable court shall deem the said article and the said first specification thereof to contain allegation of matter cognizable by this honorable court, as a high misdemeanor in office, within the intent and meaning of the Constitution of the United States, and shall receive or allow proof in support of the same, that proof shall be required to be made of the actual speech and address of this respondent on said occasion, which this respondent denies that said article and specification contains, or correctly or justly represents. And this respondent, further answering the tenth article and the specifications thereof, says that at Cleveland, in the State of Ohio, and on the 3d day of September, in the year 1866, he was attended by a large assemblage of his fellow citizens, and in deference and obedience to their call and demand, he addressed them upon matters of public and political consideration, and this respondent believes that said occasion and address are referred to in the second specification of the tenth article; but this respondent does not admit that the passages therein set forth, as if extracts from a speech of this respondent on said occasion, correctly or justly present his speech or address upon said occasion, but, on the contrary, this respondent demands and insists that, if this honorable court shall deem the said article, and the said second specification thereof to contain allegation of matter cognizable by this honorable court as a high misdemeanor in office, within the intent and meaning of the Constitution of the United States, and shall receive or allow proof in support of the same, that proof shall be required to be made of the actual speech and address of this respondent on said occasion, which this respondent denies that said article and specification contains, or correctly or justly represents.

And this respondent, further answering the tenth article and the specifications thereof, says that at St. Louis, in the State of Missouri, and on the 8th day of September, in the year 1866, he was attended by a numerous assemblage of his fellow-citizens, and in deference and obedience to their call and demand, he addressed them upon matters of public and political consideration, and this respondent believes that said occasion and address are referred to in the third specification of the tenth article; but this respondent does not admit that the passages therein set forth as if extracts from a speech of this respondent on said occasion, correctly or justly present his speech or address upon said occasion; but on the contrary, this respondent demands and insists that if this honorable court shall deem the said article and the said third specification thereof to contain allegation of matter cognizable by this honorable court as a high misdemeanor in office, within the intent and meaning of the Constitution of the United States, and shall receive or allow proof in support of the same, that proof shall be required to be made of the actual speech and address of this respondent on said occasion, which this respondent denies that the said article and specification contains, or correctly or justly represents.

And this respondent further answering the tenth article, protesting that he has not been unmindful of the high duties of his office, or of the harmony or courtesies which ought to exist and be maintained between the executive and legislative branches of the government of the United States; denies that he has ever intended or designed to set aside the rightful authority or powers of Congress, or attempted to bring into disgrace, ridicule, hatred, contempt or reproach, the Congress of the United States, or either branch, or to impair or destroy the regard or respect of all or any of the good people of the United States for the Congress or the rightful power thereof, or to excite the odium or resentment of all or any of the good people of the United States against Congress and the laws by it duly and constitutionally enacted.

This respondent further says, that at all times he has, in his official acts as President, recognized the authority of the several Congresses of the United States as constituted and organized during his administration of the office of President of the United States; and this respondent, further answering, says that he has from time to time, under his Constitutional right and duty as President of the United States, communicated to Congress his views and opinions in regard to such acts or resolutions thereof as, being submitted to him as President of the United States, in pursuance of the Constitution, seemed to this respondent to require such communication; and he has from time to time, in the exercise of that freedom of speech which belongs to him as a citizen of the United States, and in his political relations as President of the United States to the people of the United States as upon fit occasions a duty of the highest obligation expressed to his fellow citizens his views and opinions, respecting them as such, and proceedings of Congress, and that in such addresses to his fellow citizens, and in such his communications to Congress he has expressed his views, opinions and judgment of and concerning the actual constitution of the two houses of Congress, without representation therein of certain states of the Union, and of the effect that in wisdom and justice, in the opinion and judgment of this respondent, Congress in its legislation and proceedings should given to this political circumstance, and whatsoever he has thus communicated to Congress, or addressed to his fellow-citizens or any assemblage thereof, this respondent says was and is within and according to his right and privilege as an American citizen, and his right and duty as President of the United States; and this respondent, not waiving or at all disparaging his right of freedom of opinion and of freedom of speech, as hereinbefore or hereinafter more particularly set forth, but claiming and insisting upon the same.

Further answering the said tenth article, says that the views and opinions expressed by this respondent in his said addresses to the assemblages of his fellow citizens, as in said article or in this answer thereto mentioned, are not, and were not intended to be other or different from those expressed by him in his communications to Congress; that the eleven States lately in insurrection never had ceased to be States of the Union, and that they were then entitled to representation in Congress by loyal Representatives and Senators, as fully as the other States of the Union, and that, consequently, the Congress as then constituted was not, in fact, a Congress of all the States, but a Congress of only a part of the States. This respondent, always protesting against the unauthorized exclusion therefrom of the said eleven States, nevertheless gave his assent to all laws passed by said Congress, which did not, in his opinion and judgment, violate the Constitution, exercising his constitutional authority of returning bills to said Congress with his objections, when they appeared to him to be unconstitutional or inexpedient.

But further, this respondent has also expressed the opinion, both in his communications to Congress and in his addresses to the people, that the policy adopted by Congress in reference to the States lately in insurrection did not tend to peace and harmony and union, but, on the contrary, did tend to disunion and the permanent disruption of the States, and that in following its said policy laws had been passed by Congress in violation of the fundamental principles of the government, and which tended to consolidation and despotism, and such being his deliberate opinions, he would have felt himself unmindful of the high duties of his office if he had failed to express them in his communications to Congress or in his addresses to the people, when called upon by them to express his opinions on matters of public and political consideration.

And this respondent, further answering the tenth article, says that he has always claimed and insisted, and now claims and insists, that both in his personal and private capacity of a citizen of the United States, and in the political relations of the President of the United States to the people of the United States—whose servant, under the duties and responsibilities of the Constitution of the United States, the President of the United States is, and should always remain—this respondent had and has the full right, and, in his office of President of the United States, is held to the high duty of, forming, and and on fit occasions expressing opinions of and concerning the legislation of Congress, proposed or completed, in respect of its wisdom, expediency, justice, worthiness, objects, purposes and public and political motives and tendencies, and within and as a part of such right and duty, to form and on fit occasions to express opinions of and concerning the public character and conduct, views, purposes, objects, motives and tendencies of all men engaged in the public service, as well in Congress as otherwise, and under no other rules or limits upon this right of freedom of opinion and of freedom of speech, or of responsibility and amenability for the actual exercise of such freedom of opinion and freedom of speech, than attend upon such rights and their exercise on the part of all other citizens of the United States, and on the part of all their public servants. And this respondent, further answering said tenth article, says that the several occasions on which, as is alleged in the several specifications of said article, this respondent addressed his fellow citizens on subjects of public and political consideration, were not nor was any one of them sought or planned by this respondent, but on the contrary each of said occasions arose upon the exercise of a lawful and accustomed right of the people of the United States to call upon their public servants and express to them their opinions, wishes and feelings upon matters of public and political consideration, and to invite from such public servants an expression of their opinions, views and feelings on matters of public and political consideration. And this respondent claims and insists, before this honorable court, and before all the people of the United States, that of or concerning this, his right of freedom of opinion and of freedom of speech, and this his exercise of such rights on all matters of public and political consideration, and in respect of all public servants or persons whatsoever engaged in or connected therewith, this respondent, as a citizen or as President of the United States, is not subject to question, inquisition, impeachment or inculpation, in any form or manner whatsoever.

And this respondent says that neither the said tenth article nor any specification thereof nor any allegation therein contained touches or relates to any official act or doing of this respondent in the office of President of the United States, or in the discharge of any of its constitutional or legal duties or responsibilities, but that the said article and the specifications and allegations thereof wholly and in every part thereof, question only the discretion or propriety of freedom of opinion or freedom of speech, as exercised by this respondent as a citizen of the United States in his personal right and capacity, and without allegation or imputation against this respondent of the violation of any law of the United States, touching or relating to the freedom of speech or its exercise by the citizens of the United States, or by this respondent as one of the said citizens or otherwise; and he denies that by reason of any matters in the said article or its specifications alleged, he has said or done anything indecent or unbecoming in the Chief Magistrate of the United States, or that he has brought the high office of the President of the United States into contempt, ridicule or disgrace, or that he has committed or has been guilty of a high misdemeanor in office.

Answer to Article 11.

And in answer to the eleventh article, this respondent denies that on the 18th day of August, in the year 1866, at the city of Washington, in the District of Columbia, he did, by public speech or otherwise, declare or affirm in substance or at all, that the Thirty-ninth Congress of the United States was not a Congress of the United States, authorized by the Constitution to exercise legislative power under the same, or that he did then and there declare or affirm that the said Thirty-ninth Congress was a Congress of only part of the States, in any sense or meaning, other than that eleven States of the Union were denied representation therein; or that he made any or either of the declarations or affirmations on this behalf in the said article, alleged as denying, or intending to deny that the legislation of said Thirty-ninth Congress was not valid or obligatory upon this respondent, except so far as this respondent saw fit to approve the same; and as to the allegation in said article that he did thereby intend, or made to be understood that the said Congress had not power to propose amendments to the Constitution, this respondent says that in said address he said nothing in reference to the subject of amendments of the Constitution, nor was the question of the competency of the said Congress to propose such amendments without the participation of said States in any way mentioned or considered or referred to by this respondent, nor in what he did say had he any intent regarding the same, and he denies the allegation so made to the contrary thereof; but this respondent in further answer to, and in respect of the said allegations of the said eleventh article herein before traversed and denied, claims and insists upon his personal and official right of freedom of opinion and freedom of speech, and his duty in his political relations as President of the United States to the people of the United States, in the exercise of such freedom of opinion and freedom of speech in the same manner, form and effect as he has in this behalf stated the same in his answer to the said tenth article, and with the same effect as if he here repeated the same. And he further claims and insists, as in said answer to said tenth article he has claimed and insisted, that he is not subject to question of impeachment or inculpation in any form or manner, of or concerning such rights of freedom of opinion or freedom of speech, or his said alleged exercise thereof. And this respondent further denies that on the 21st day of February, in the year 1868, or at any other time, at the city of Washington, in the District of Columbia, in pursuance of any such declaration as is in that behalf in the said eleventh article alleged, or otherwise, he did, unlawfully and in disregard of the requirement of the Constitution, that he should take care that the laws should be faithfully executed, attempt to prevent the execution of an act entitled "an act regulating the tenure of certain civil offices," passed March 2, 1867, by unlawfully devising or contriving, or attempting to devise or contrive measures by which he should prevent Edwin M. Stanton from forthwith resuming the functions of Secretary for the Department of War; or by unlawfully devising or contriving, or attempting to devise or contrive means to prevent the execution of an act entitled "an act making appropriations for the support of the army for the fiscal year ending June 30, 1868, and for other purposes," approved March 2, 1867; or to prevent the execution of an

act entitled "an act to provide for the more efficient government of the Rebel States," passed March 21, 1867.

And this respondent, further answering the said eleventh article, says that he has in his answer to the first article set forth in detail the acts, steps, and proceedings done and taken by this respondent to and towards or in the matter of the suspension or removal of the said Edwin M. Stanton in or from the office of Secretary for the Department of War, with the times, modes, circumstances, intents, views, purposes, and opinions of official obligation and duty under and with which such acts, steps, and proceedings were done and taken; and he makes answer to this eleventh article of the matter in his answer to the first article, pertaining to the suspension or removal of said Edwin M. Stanton, to the same intent and effect as if they were here repeated and set forth.

And this respondent further answering the said eleventh article denies that by means or reason of anything in said article alleged, this respondent as President of the United States, did, on the 21st day of February, 1868, or any other day or time commit, or that he was guilty of a high misdemeanor in office, and this respondent further answering the said eleventh article, says that the same and the matters therein contained do not charge or allege the commission of any act whatever by this respondent in his office of President of the United States; not the omission by this respondent of any act of official obligation or duty in his office of President of the United States, nor does the said article nor matters there contained name, designate, describe or define any act or mode or form of device, contrivance or means, or of attempt at device, contrivance or means, whereby this respondent can know or understand what act or mode or form of attempt, device, contrivance or means, or of attempt at device, contrivance or means are imputed to or charged against this respondent, in his office of President of the United States, or intended so to be, or whereby this respondent can more fully or definitely make answer unto said article than he hereby does.

And this respondent, in submitting to this honorable court this, his answer to the articles of impeachment exhibited against him, respectfully reserves the right to amend and add to the same from time to time, as may become necessary or proper, and when and as such necessity and propriety shall appear.
(Signed)

ANDREW JOHNSON,
HENRY STANBERY,
B. R. CURTIS,
THOMAS A. R. NELSON,
WILLIAM EVARTS,
W. S. GROESBECK,
Of Counsel.

Messrs. Stanbery and Evarts successively relieved Mr. Curtis in the reading, which occupied until about three o'clock.

At the conclusion the Chief Justice put the question on receiving the answer and ordering it to be filed, which was agreed to.

Mr. BOUTWELL—Mr. President, by direction of the managers on the part of the House of Representatives, I have the honor to present a copy of the answer filed by Andrew Johnson, President of the United States, to the articles of impeachment presented by the House of Representatives; and to say that it is the expectation of the managers that they will be able, at one o'clock to-morrow, after consultation with the House, to present a fit replication to the answer. (Sensation in the galleries).

Mr. EVARTS, of counsel—Chief Justice:—The counsel for the President think it proper, unless some objection show now be made, to bring to the attention of the honorable court the matter of provision for the allowance of time given for the preparation for the trial which shall be accorded to the President and his counsel, after the replication of the House of Representatives to the President shall be submitted to this court. In the application which was made on the 13th inst., for time for preparation and submission of answer which had been presented to the court, were included in our consideration of that time that we so asked, with the expectation and intention or carrying on with all due diligence, at the same time, the preparation of the answer and the preparation for the trial.

The action of the court, and its determination of the time within which the answers should properly be presented, has obliged us, as may be well understood by this court, to devote our whole time to the preparation of the answer, and we have had no time to consider the various questions of law and offset, and the forms for the production of the same, which rest upon the responsibility and lie within the duty of counsel in all matters requiring judicial consideration. We, therefore, if the honorable court please, submit now the request that the President and his counsel may be allowed the period of thirty days after the filing of the replication on the part of the House of Representatives to the answer of the President for the preparation for trial, and before it shall actually proceed; and I beg leave to send to the Chief Justice a written minute of that proposition, signed by counsel.

The Chief Justice stated the question to be on the motion of Mr. Boutwell, of the managers.

Senator SUMNER misapprehending the question, said:—Before the vote, I wish to inquire if the honorable managers on the part of the House desire to be heard?

The Chief Justice explained the question to be on the motion on the part of the managers, which was then put and agreed to.

The Secretary read the application of the counsel for the President, which was addressed " To the Senate of the United States, sitting as a Court of Impeachment," representing that after the replication to this answer shall have been filed, it will, in the opinion and judgment of the counsel, require not less than thirty days for preparation for the trial. Signed by counsel for the President.

Mr. HOWARD—If it be in order, I move that that application lie on the table until the replication of the House of Representatives has been filed.

Mr. BINGHAM—Mr. President, before that motion takes effect, if it be the pleasure of the Senate, the managers are ready to consider this application.

The Chief Justice was stating the question to be on the motion of Mr. Howard, when

Mr. HOWARD withdrew the motion.

Mr. LOGAN, of the managers, objected to the application, as not containing any reason to justify the Senate in postponing the trial, not that they desired to force it on with unnecessary rapidity, but because such reasons should be given in an application for time as would be adhered to in a court of law. Counsel had merely asked an opportunity to prepare themselves. They had had and would have had during the trial an equal opportunity with the managers for preparation. The application did not state that any material witnesses could not be procured, or that time for their procurement was required, before the commencement of the trial. The answer admitted the facts of the appointments, &c., charged in the first article. They were within the knowledge of the President, who, being charged by these articles with high crimes and misdemeanors, his counsel, if there was any reason for this application, should have stated it.

On the trial of Judges Chase and Peck, and other trials here and in other countries, such applications were accompanied with reasons for asking delay, such as necessary witnesses, records, &c., at a distance, the examination of decisions, &c., and were sworn to by the respondent to the articles of impeachment. The learned counsel on the other side had, doubtless, examined the authorities on such trials, and knew that these things were requisite on an application for a continuance of a case in a court of law, because of the absence of a witness. It was usual to state on affidavit what it was expected to prove by the witness, his residence, that he could be procured at a certain time, and that the facts could not be proven by any other witness.

In this application none of these requirements were complied with; it simply asked time to prepare for the trial of this cause; that is, time to examine authorities, to prepare arguments, and for naught else. Time should not be given in this more than in any other case, unless for good cause shown, as provided by order of the Senate. Showing cause meant that necessity should be shown for the continuance of the trial. He reminded them, that in the trial of Judge Chase an application had been made for a period of time for four days more than proved to be necessary to try the whole cause.

In the trial of Queen Caroline of England, in answer to an application for time to procure witnesses, &c., which was granted merely out of courtesy to the Queen, the Attorney-General protested against its becoming a precedent in the trial of future causes. He (Mr. Logan) insisted that no more time should be given in this case than is absolutely necessary to try the cause, since no necessity for an extension had been shown whereby the court could judge of its materiality. If it were granted, there would probably be, at the end of that period, an application for twenty or thirty days more, for the purpose of procuring witnesses living in Sitka, or some other remote part of the country.

He would say, whether it was considered proper or not, that no more time should be granted in the trial of the President than in the trial of the poorest man that lives. They were amenable to the same laws, and subject to the same laws. The managers had accused the President of intentionally obstructing the laws, and other serious offenses, which, if true, showed that it was dangerous for him to remain the chief magistrate of this nation, and, therefore, time should not be given unless sufficient reasons were shown.

To the allegation that time would be given to an ordinary criminal he would say, that the managers considered the President a criminal, and had so charged, but the counsel had not, as required in the case of ordinary criminals, shown reasons for the delay. Mr. Logan reiterated and enlarged upon the view that the nature of the crime charged was such that delay was dangerous.

The managers were here to enter their protest against any extension of time whatever, after the filing of their replication to-morrow, at one o'clock, at which time they would ask leave to state their case to the Senate, and follow it up with their evidence, the other side following with theirs. He asked that the Senate, sitting as a Court of Impeachment, examine carefully whether or not any facts are shown to justify this application, and whether due diligence had been employed in procuring witnesses and getting ready for trial. They protested against such an application being made without even an affidavit to support it.

Mr. EVARTS denied that because courts other than those called for a special purpose and with limited authority, have established regulations bearing upon the right of defendant in civil or criminal prosecutions, having established terms of court, and well recognized and understood habits in conduct of judicial action, that should influence the proceedings of this body. The time had not arrived for the counsel for the accused to consider what issues are to be prepared on their side, and they felt no occasion to present an affidavit on matters so completely within the cognizance of the court, obedient, said he, to the orders of the court.

Observant, as we propose at all times to be, of that public necessity and duty which requires on the part of the President of the United States and his counsel, not less than on the part of the House of Representatives and its manager, that diligence should be used, and that we as counsel should be withdrawn from all other professional or personal avocations, yet we cannot recognize in presence of this court, that it is an answer to an application for reasonable time to consider and prepare to subpœna and produce, in all things to arrange, and in all things to be ready for the actual procedure of the trial. Nor, with great respect to the honorable managers in this great procedure, do we deem a sufficient answer to our desire to be relieved from undue pressure of haste upon our part, that equal pressure of haste may have been entailed upon them.

Mr. EVARTS proceeded to say that the ability of the counsel to proceed with the trial was not to be measured by that of the managers, the latter having the power, and having exercised it for a considerable period, of summoning witnesses and calling for papers. He thought if the court would give due attention and respect to the statement of counsel, they would see that very considerable range of subjects and practical considerations presented themselves to their attention and judgment. They were placed in the condition of a defendant who, upon issue joined, desired time to prepare for trial, in which the ordinary course was as a matter of absolute universal custom to allow a continuance.

They asked no more time than in the interests of justice and of duty should be given to the poorest man in the country. Measures of justice and duty had no respect to poverty or station whatever. If on the part of the managers, or of the accused, from any cause, a proper delay for the production of a witness was required, it would be the duty of the court to take it into consideration and provide for it. It would be a departure from the general habit of all courts if, after issue joined, they were not allowed reasonable time before they were called upon to proceed with the case.

Mr. WILSON, of the managers, said the managers had determined, so far as was in their power, this case should not be taken out of the line of the precedent, and would therefore resist all application for unreasonable delay, and they have prepared to meet the question now. The first step taken by the respondent's counsel, on the 13th inst., are the precedents on the trial of Judge Chase. On the return day of the summons, he appeared and applied for time to answer, coupling with it a request for time to prepare for trial, which he supported with a solemn affidavit that he could not be prepared sooner than the 5th of the succeeding March, and therefore asked for time until the commencement of the next session of Congress.

The application was denied, and he was required to answer on the 4th of February succeeding, and five days before the expiration of the time declared by him to be necessary, the case was concluded by an acquittal, so complete had been the preparation.

In the case of Judge Peck, he appeared on the return day, three days after the service of summons, and applied for and was granted time to answer. In this case, however, notwithstanding the rule of the Senate requiring the filing of the answer then, they were met with an application for forty days.

The Senate allowed ten days for the answer. In that answer he found the strongest argument against any delay of this case, the respondent therein, had a right under the Constitution, as among his just powers to do the very acts charged against him at the bar of the Senate. This in ordinary cases might not be a weighty consideration, but here the respondent was not only to obey the law like all citizens, but to execute it, being clothed with the whole executive power of the nation.

In the opinion of the House of Representatives he had not discharged that duty as required by his oath of office, and for that failure and for a positive breach of the law, they arraigned him at this bar. With the admission in the answer he asked time to make good his declarations, holding in his hands this immense Executive power, no provision having been made for its surrender—holding that power over the nation with which he has disturbed and is disturbing the repose of the Republic. They felt it their duty to urge a speedy progress towards the trial of this case, which should guarantee the rights of the people, at the same time observing the rights that belong to the accused.

But for the order adopted by the Senate on the 13th inst., this application could not have been made, but the case must have been discussed on the threshold. That order had now the effect of this rule:—

"*Ordered,* That unless otherwise ordered by the Senate, for cause shown, the trial of the pending impeachment shall proceed immedialy after the replication be filed."

He submitted that there was not sufficient cause shown in this application to justify the Senate, in the exercise of a sound discretion, in granting the time asked for. That discretion was not without the rule itself. It must act upon some rule, and put itself within the bounds of reason, and he denied that this was such an application as to justify its exercise in giving one hour's delay.

It would be observed that the respondent was carefully kept out of this motion. In all the cases of which he (Mr. Wilson) had any knowledge in this country, the respondent, even when judges taken from the bench, had asked in their own names for delay, supporting the application by affidavits, covering the features of the case and unfolding the line of their defense, asking a reasonable time in which to prepare for trial. We therefore ask, he continued, that when this case is thus kept out of the ordinary channel, the Senate will regard in the same degree the voice of the House of Representatives as prescribed by the managers, and put this respondent upon his speedy trial, to the end that peace may be restored to the country by the healing of the breach between the two departments of the government, and that all things may again move in this land as they did in times past, and before this unfortunate conflict occurred. Therefore, sir, in the name of the Representatives, we ask that this application, as it is now presented, may be denied.

Mr. HENDERSON moved to postpone the decision of the question.

Mr. STANBERY on behalf of the President, said:—On the 13th of this month we entered our appearance, and this honorable court made an order that we should have till the 23d (this day), to file an answer. It gave the managers leave to file their replication without limit as to time, but provided that on the filing of their replication the case should proceed to trial, unless reasonable cause were shown for further delay. The honorable court, therefore, meant us to have time to prepare for trial if we should show reasonable ground for the application. Now what has happened, Mr. Chief Justice.

What has been stated to this honorable court, composed in a great measure of members of the bar, by members of the bar on their professional honor, we have stated that since we had this leave to file the answer every hour and every moment of our time has

been occupied in preparing it. Not an instant has been lost. We refused all other applications and devoted ourselves exclusively to this duty day and night; and I am sorry to be obliged to say that even the day sacred to other uses has been employed in this duty.

Allow me further to say to this honorable court, that not until within a few minutes before we came into court this morning, was the answer concluded. Certainly it was intended on the 13th to give us time, not merely to prepare our answer, but to prepare for that still more important thing, the trial. I hope I shall obtain credit with this honorable court, when I say that we have been so pressed with the duty of making up the issues and preparing the answer, that we have not had an opportunity of asking the President what witnesses he should produce.

We have been so pressed that the communications which we have received from the honorable managers in reference to the admission of testimony and facilities of proof, we have had to reply to by saying:—"We have not yet, gentlemen, a moment's time to consider it; all that we know of the case is, that it charges transactions not only here, but in Cleveland, St. Louis and other distant points, and the managers have sent us a list of witnesses who are to testify in matters of which they intend to make proof against us. But we have not had an opportunity of knowing what witnesses we are to produce. We have not subpoenaed any.

Now mark the advantages which all this time the honorable managers have had over us. As I understand, and it will not be denied, almost every day they have been engaged in the preparation of this case. Their articles were framed long ago. While we were engaged in preparing our answer they have been, as I understand, most industriously engaged in preparing their witnesses. Day after day witnesses have been called before them and examined. We had no such power and no such opportunity. We are here without any preparation—without having had a moment's time to consult with our client or among ourselves.

The managers say that our anxiety is to prepare ourselves, whereas they are all prepared—completely prepared. So far as counsel is concerned, I am very happy to hear that they are. I should be very far from saying that I am equally prepared. I have had no time to look at anything else except this necessary and all-absorbing duty of preparing the answer. Now, if the Senate says we shall go on when this replication comes in to-morrow, it places me in a position in which I never have been before in all my practice, with a formidable array of counsel against me, and yet not a witness summoned, not a document prepared, all unarmed and defenseless.

I beg this honorable court to give us time. If it cannot give us all the time we ask, let it give us some time at least, within which, by the utmost diligence, we can make what preparations we deem necessary, and without which we cannot safely go to trial. Gentlemen of the other side complained that we should have been ready on the 13th, and read against us a rule that that was the day fixed for not only the appearance, but filing the answer. They read out of the rule that old formula which has come down from five hundred years back, in reference to appearing and answering. It is the same language adopted in those early times when the defendant was called upon and answered by parole; but then our ancestors would not answer on the day of appearance, but always asked and had time for answer.

Mr. BINGHAM, one of the managers, rose to reply.

The Chief Justice intimated that when counsel make any motion to the court, the counsel who make the motion have invariably the right to close the argument.

Mr. BINGHAM said, with all due respect to the ruling of the presiding officer of the Senate, I beg leave to remind the Senate, that from time immemorial in proceedings of this kind, the right of the Commons in England, and of the representatives of the people in the United States to close all debates, has never been called in question. On the contrary, in Melbourne's case, Lord Erskine, who presided, said when the question was presented, that he owed it to the Commons to protest against the immemorial usage being denied to the Commons of England of being heard in response finally to whatever might be said in behalf of the accused at the bar of the Peers.

Lord Erskine's decision has never been questioned, and I believe it has been the continued rule in England for about five hundred years. In the first case ever tried in the Senate of the Under States under the Constitution, the case of Blount, although the accused had interposed a plea to the jurisdictions, the argument was closed by the manager on the part of the House. I had risen for the purpose of making some response to the remarks last made; but as the presiding officer has interposed the objection to the Senate, I do not deem it proper for me to proceed further until the Senate shall have passed on the question.

Senator HOWARD said he rose to move to lay the motion of the counsel on the table.

Mr. BOUTWELL, one of the managers, remarked that it seemed to the managers, and to himself, especially, a matter of so much importance as to whether the managers should have the closing argument, that he wished, and they wished, that to be decided now.

Senator HOWARD said that it was not his intention to shut off debate or discussion, either on the part of the managers or on the part of counsel for the accused, and if there was any desire on the part of either to proceed with the discussion he would withdraw his motion to lay on the table.

Mr. BINGHAM then said—I deeply regret, Mr. President, that the counsel for the accused have made any question here, or any intimation, if you please, that a question is made or intended to be made by the managers touching the entire sincerity with which they ask this time. I am sure that nothing was further from our purpose than that. The gentleman who last took his seat (Mr. Stanbery) spoke of having presented this application on their honor. No man questions their honor—no man who knows them will question their honor—but we must be pardoned for saying that it is altogether unusual, on questions of this kind, to allow continuance to be obtained on a mere point of honor.

The rule of the Senate which was adopted on the 13th inst., is the ordinary rule in courts of law, namely, that the trial shall proceed unless for cause shown further time shall be allowed. I submit that a question of this magnitude has never been decided on the mere presentation of counsel in this country or any other country. The point of continuance arising on a question of this sort, I venture to say, has never been decided affirmatively, at least in favor of such a proposition, on the mere statement of counsel. If Andrew Johnson will say that there are witnesses not within the process of this court, but whose attendance he can hope to procure if time be allowed him; and if he will make affidavit before this tribune that they are material, and will set forth in his affidavit what he expects to prove by them. I concede that on such a showing there would be something on which the Senate might probably act, but instead of that he throws himself back on his counsel, and has them to make their statement here that it will require thirty days of time in which to prepare for trial. He sent those gentlemen at the bar of this tribunal on the 13th inst., to notify the Senate, on their honor, that it would require forty days to prepare an answer, and now he sends them back, upon their honors, to notify the Senate that it will require thirty days to prepare for trial.

I take it, sir, that the counsel for the accused have quite as much time for preparation, if this trial shall proceed to-morrow, as had the managers on the part of the House, who are charged with duties by the people which they are not permitted to lay aside from day to day, in the other end of the Capitol. I think, on the showing made here this day by the President of the United States, unless very good cause is shown, and that, too, under the obligation of his own oath at the bar of the Senate, that not another hour's continuance should be allowed him after the case shall have been put at issue. We asked leave to suggest to the Senate that we hoped on to-morrow, by leave of the people's representatives, to put this case at issue by filing a replication. That is all the delay we desire.

They have had the opportunity for process ever since the 13th inst., and they are guilty of gross neglect—I do not speak of the counsel, but of the accused—in not having the witnesses subpœnaed; and yet not a single summons has been required by him, under the rule and order of this tribunal, to bring to the bar a single witness on his behalf. He has shown a total neglect; and yet he comes here with a confession and avoidance of the matters presented by the House of Representatives, and tells the Senate, and tells the country that he defies their power, thus trifling with the great power which the people, for various purposes, have reposed in the hands of their Representatives and Senators in Congress assembled.

What is this power of impeachment if the President of the United States, holding the whole executive power of the nation, is permitted, when arraigned at the bar of the Senate, in the name of all the people, and charged with high crimes and misdemeanors, in that he has violated his oath, in that he has violated the Constitution of the country, in that he has violated the peoples' laws, and attempted by his violation to lay hands upon the peoples' treasury? What, I say, is this great defensive power worth if the President, on a mere statement of counsel, be permitted to postpone for further inquiry for thirty days, until he prepare to do what?

Until he prepare to make good his elaborate statement set forth in his answer that the Constitution is but a ca-

binet in his hands, and that he defies our power to restrain him When I heard this discussion going on, I thought of the weighty words of that great man whose luminous intellect shed lustre on the jurisprudence of his country and the great State of New York for more than one-third of a century, when he wrote it down in his commentaries on the laws—commentaries that will live as long as our language lives—that if the President of the United States will not be restrained from abusing the trust committed to him by the people, either by the obligations of his oath or by the written requirement of the Constitution that he shall take care that the laws be faithfully executed, or by the other provision that his term of office is limited to the short tenure of four years; nor yet by the decent respect to the public opinion of the country, there remains the tremendous power lodged by the people under the Constitution in the hands of their representatives to arrest him by impeachment in the abuse of the great trust committed to his hands.

Faithful to the duties imposed upon us by our oaths as the representatives of the people, we have interposed that remedy by arresting the man. He comes to-day to answer us, and he says to us, "I defy your impeachment; by the Executive power reposed in me by the Constitution, I claim, in the presence of the Senate and in the presence of the country, the right. without challenge, let or hindrance, to suspend every Executive officer of this government, at my pleasure." I venture to say, before the enlightened bar of public opinion in America, that by those motives incorporated, in his answer the President is as guilty of malfeasance and misdemeanor in office, as ever man was guilty of malfeasance and misdemeanor in office since the nations began to be on earth. What, that he will suspend all the executive officers of the government at his pleasure, not by force of the Tenure of Office act, to which he makes reference, and which he says is void and of no effect, but by force of the Constitution of the United States; that, too, while the Senate is in session. What does he mean by it?

Let the Senate answer when it comes to vote on this proposition for the extension of time. Does he mean by it that he will vacate the offices and not fill them? Does he mean by that, your money appropriated for carrying on and administering the government shall remain locked up in the vaults of the Treasury, and shall not be applied, or does he mean by it that he will repeal what he has already done in the presence of the Senate and in violation of the Constitution and the laws, and will remove without the consent of the Senate, and will appoint while the Senate is in session, without its consent and advice, just such persons as will answer his own purpose? Is that what he means by it? If it is, it is a very easy method of repealing the Constitution of the United States. I admit that it is a time honored rule of law, the gathered wisdom of a thousand years, that the accused has the right to a speedy and impartial trial.

I claim that the people also have a right to a speedy and impartial trial, and that the question pending here touches in some sort the rights of the people. In their name we demand here a speedy and impartial trial. If the President is not guilty, we ask in behalf of the country that he shall be declared innocent of the offenses of which he stands charged. If it be the judgment of the Senate that he has laid violent hands on the Constitution of the country, and rent it to tatters in the presence of its custodians, the sooner that judgment is pronounced the better. In this view of the case the public interests demand that the trial shall proceed until, by the solemn oath of the accused, made at the bar, it shall be made to appear that he cannot proceed on account of the absence of witnesses material to him, and until he states what he expects to prove by them.

I venture to say that he can make no showing of that sort which we are not ready to meet, by saying that we will admit that his witnesses will swear to his statements, and let him have the benefit of that. Nearly all the testimony involved in the issue is documentary. Much of it is official. It will occur to the Senate that as this trial progresses, they will have as much time for preparation by the time that the case closes on the part of the government as we have had. We make no boast of any superior preparation of this matter. We desire simply to discharge our duty as best we can. We assume no superiority over counsel, as was intimated by the gentleman (Mr. Stanbery). We desire simply to discharge our duty here; to discharge it promptly, to discharge it faithfully.

We appeal to the Senate to grant us the opportunity of doing so, that justice may be done between the people of the United States and the President of the United States; that the Constitution which he had violated may be vindicated, and that the wrong he has committed against an outraged and betrayed people may be speedily redressed.

Mr. BUTLER, another of the managers, said he would like to call the attention of the Senate to the position in which the managers would be placed if the question of time were not settled now. If a replication were made at all, he thought he could say for his associates that it would be simply a gaining of issue to the answer, and therefore, and for that purpose, it might be considered already filed. The managers would have to be ready at all hazards by to-morrow to go on with the case, with the uncertainty of having the court, or rather, "he begged pardon," the Senate postponing the trial for thirty days.

He therefore agreed with the counsel for the defense, that it was better for all that the question should be settled now. He knew he spoke for the managers and for the House of Representatives when he urged that the question should be settled now. Our subpœnas, said he, are out. Our witnesses have been called. We want to know when to bring them here. We have got to come here sure, and we will be here. (Laughter, which was promptly suppressed by the Chair.) That is all we ask. Therefore I trust that the Senate will fix, at this time, the hour and the day that this trial shall certainly proceed.

Senator HENDERSON offered the following:—

Ordered, That the application of counsel for the President to be allowed thirty days to prepare for the trial of impeachment, be postponed until after the replication is filed.

The question was taken by yeas and nays, and resulted as follows:—

YEAS—Messrs. Anthony, Buckalew, Cattell, Cole, Dixon, Doolittle. Edmunds, Fessenden, Fowler, Frelinghuysen, Grimes, Henderson, Hendricks, Johnson, McCreery, Morrill (Me.), Norton, Patterson (Tenn.), Ross, Saulsbury, Sherman, Sprague, Trumbull, Van Winkle and Vickers—25.

NAYS—Messrs. Bayard, Cameron, Chandler, Conkling, Conness, Corbett, Cragin, Davis, Drake, Ferry, Harlan, Howard, Howe, Morgan, Morrill (Vt.), Morton, Nye, Patterson (N. H.), Pomeroy, Ramsey, Stewart, Sumner. Thayer, Tipton, Willey, Williams, Wilson and Yates—21.

Senator HOWARD moved that the motion of the counsel for the accused be laid on the table.

Senator DRAKE made the question of order that it was not in order to move to lay on the table a proposition of the counsel for the accused, or of the managers.

The Chief Justice sustained the point of order, and the motion was received.

The question recurring on the application of counsel for the President that they be allowed thirty days to prepare for the trial.

The question was taken by yeas and nays, and resulted—yeas, 11; nays, 41, as follows:—

YEAS—Messrs. Bayard, Buckalew, Davis, Dixon, Doolittle, Hendricks, Johnson, McCreery, Patterson, of Tennessee, Saulsbury and Vickers.

NAYS.—Messrs. Anthony, Cameron, Cattell, Chandler, Conkling, Conness, Corbett, Cragin, Drake, Edmunds, Ferry, Fessenden, Fowler, Frelinghuysen, Grimes, Harlan, Henderson, Howard, Howe, Morgan, Morrill (Me.), Morrill (Vt.), Morton, Nye, Patterson (N. H.), Pomeroy, Ramsey, Ross, Sherman, Sprague, Stewart, Thayer, Trumbull, Upson, Van Winkle, Willey, Williams, Wilson and Yates.

The application was rejected.

Mr. EVARTS then submitted the following:—

Counsel for the President now move that there be allowed for preparation to the President of the United States for the trial, after the replication shall be filed and before the trial shall be required to proceed, such reasonable time as shall be now fixed by the Senate.

Senator JOHNSON inquired whether it was in order to amend that motion.

The Chief Justice informed him that it was in order to submit an independent proposition.

Mr. JOHNSON—I move, then, that ten days be allowed after the filing of the replication.

Mr. SHERMAN then moved that the Senate, sitting as a court of impeachment, adjourn till to-morrow at one o'clock.

The motion was agreed to.

The Chief Justice thereupon vacated the Chair, which was resumed by the presiding officer of the Senate, and the Senate, at 4·45 P. M. adjourned.

PROCEEDINGS OF TUESDAY, MARCH 24.

The Replication of the Managers.

During the morning session of the Senate, the Clerk of the House appeared and announced that the House had adopted a replication to the answer of the President of the United States to the articles of impeachment.

One o'clock having arrived, the President *pro tem.* vacated the chair for the Chief Justice, who entered and took his seat, ordering proclamation, which was made accordingly by the Sergeant-at-Arms.

In the meantime the counsel for the President, Messrs. Stanbery, Curtis, Evarts, Nelson and Groesbeck, entered and took their seats.

At five minutes past one o'clock the managers were announced and took their seats, with the exception of Mr. Stevens.

The House was announced immediately, and the members disposed themselves outside the bar.

The minutes of the session of yesterday were read by the Secretary.

The Secretary read the announcement of the adoption of the replication by the House.

Mr. BOUTWELL, one of the managers, then rose and said:—

Mr. President:—I am charged by the managers with the duty of presenting the replication offered by the House. He read the replication, as follows:—

Replication.

Replication of the House of Representatives of the United States to the answer of Andrew Johnson, President of the United States, to the articles of impeachment exhibited against him by the House of Representatives.

The House of Representatives of the United States have considered the several answers of Andrew Johnson, President of the United States, to the several articles of impeachment against him by them exhibited in the name of themselves and of all the people of the United States, and reserving to themselves all the advantage of exception to the insufficiency of the answer to each and all of the several articles of impeachment exhibited against the said Andrew Johnson, President of the United States, do deny each and every averment in said several answers, or either of them, which denies or traverses the acts, intents, crimes or misdemeanors charged against the said Andrew Johnson in said articles of impeachment, or either of them, and for replication to the said answer do say that the said Andrew Johnson, President of the United States, is guilty of the high crimes and misdemeanors mentioned in said articles, and that the House of Representatives are ready to prove the same.

At the conclusion of the reading, Senator JOHNSON said:—Mr. Chief Justice, I move that an authenticated copy be presented to the counsel for the President.

The motion was agreed to.

Time for Preparation

The Chief Justice—Last evening a motion was pending on the part of the counsel for the President, that such time should be allowed for their preparation as the Senate should please to determine; thereupon the Senator from Maryland (Mr. Johnson) presented an order which will be read by the Secretary.

The Secretary read the order providing that ten days time be allowed.

Mr. SUMNER—Mr. President, I send to the Chair an amendment, to come immediately after the word "ordered," being in the nature of a substitute.

The Secretary read the amendment, as follows:—

That now that replication has been filed, the Senate, adhering to its rule already adopted, shall proceed with the trial from day to day, Sundays excepted, unless otherwise ordered or reasons shown.

Mr. EDMUNDS—I move that the Senate retire to consider that order.

Senator SUMNER, and others—No, no.

The yeas and nays were demanded and ordered, resulting as follows:—

YEAS—Messrs. Anthony, Bayard, Buckalew, Corbett, Davis, Dixon, Doolittle, Edmunds, Fessenden, Fowler, Frelinghuysen, Grimes, Henderson, Hendricks, Howe, Johnson, McCreery, Morrill, (Me.); Morrill, (Vt.); Norton, Patterson, (N. H.); Patterson, (Tenn.); Saulsbury, Sprague, Van Winkle, Vickers, Willey and Williams—29.

NAYS—Messrs. Cameron, Cattell, Chandler, Cole, Conkling, Conness, Cragin, Drake, Ferry, Harlan, Howard, Morgan, Nye, Pomeroy, Ramsey, Ross, Sherman, Stewart, Sumner, Thayer, Tipton, Trumbull and Wilson—23.

So the Senate retired for consideration at 1·25.

Consultation.

After the Senators had retired, Mr. Stevens was discovered sitting to the left and rear of the President's desk, having entered unnoticed during the proceedings. In the meantime the galleries, hitherto very quiet, rippled with fans and chit-chat, in the assurance that the curtain was down, while on the floor the seats sacred to Senators were invaded by knots of members and others in conversation.

The Private Consultation.

When the Senate had retired for consultation, Mr. JOHNSON modified the resolution he had previously submitted in the Chamber, by providing that the trial of the President shall commence on Thursday, April 2.

Mr. WILLIAMS moved that the further consideration of the respondent's application for time be postponed until the managers have opened their case and submitted their evidence.

This was disagreed to by a vote of 42 nays to 9 yeas, as follows:—

YEAS.—Messrs. Anthony, Chandler, Dixon, Grimes, Harlan, Howard, Morgan, Patterson (Tenn.) and Williams.

NAYS.—Messrs. Bayard, Buckalew, Cameron, Cattell, Cole, Conkling, Conness, Cragin, Davis, Doolittle, Drake, Edmunds, Ferry, Fessenden, Fowler, Frelinghuysen, Henderson, Hendricks, Howe, Johnson, McCreery, Morrill (Me.), Morrill (Vt.), Morton, Norton, Nye, Patterson, (N. H.) Pomeroy, Ramsey, Ross, Saulsbury, Sherman, Sprague, Stewart, Sumner, Thayer, Tipton, Trumbull, Van Winkle, Vickers, Willey and Wilson.

Absent or not voting.—Messrs. Corbett, Wade and Yates.

Mr. SUMNER had offered the following amendment, which he subsequently withdrew:—

Now that replication has been filed, the Senate, adhering to its rule, already adopted, will proceed with the trial from day to day, Sundays excepted, unless otherwise ordered, or reason shown.

Mr. CONKLING moved an amendment to Mr. Johnson's resolution, by striking out Thursday, April 2, and inserting Monday, March 30, as the time when the trial shall commence.

This was agreed to. Yeas, 28; nays, 24, as follows:—

YEAS.—Messrs. Cameron, Cattell, Chandler, Cole, Conkling, Conness, Cragin, Drake, Ferry, Harlan, Howard, Howe, Morgan, Morrill (Me.), Morrill (Vt.), Morton, Nye, Patterson (N. H.), Pomeroy, Ramsey, Ross, Stewart, Sumner, Thayer, Tipton, Willey, Williams, Wilson—28.

NAYS.—Messrs. Anthony, Bayard, Buckalew, Corbett, Davis, Dixon, Doolittle, Edmunds, Fessenden, Fowler, Frelinghuysen, Grimes, Henderson, Hendricks, Johnson, McCreery, Norton, Patterson (Tenn.), Saulsbury, Sherman, Sprague, Trumbull, Van Winkle and Vickers—24.

Absent or not voting. –Messrs. Wade and Yates.

Other modifications were made to the original resolution, when it was adopted as read in open Senate.

Return of the Senate.

At 3·25 P. M. the Senate reappeared, having been out exactly two hours.

Order having been restored, the Chief Justice said:—

I am directed to inform the counsel that the Senate has agreed to an order, in response to their application, which will now be read:—

"Ordered—That the Senate will commence the trial of the President, upon the articles of impeachment exhibited against him, on Monday, the 30th day of March inst., and proceed therein with all despatch under the rules of the Senate sitting upon the trial of an impeachment."

After a momentary pause the Chief Justice asked:—

Have the counsel for the President anything to propose?

The counsel bowed in acquiescence to the decision.

Mr. BUTLER, of the managers—If the Chair will allow me, I will give notice to the witnesses to appear here on Monday, the 30th inst., at 12½ o'clock.

The Court Adjourns.

On motion of Senator WILSON, the Court was then adjourned till the date named, at half-past twelve o'clock, and the Chief Justice vacated the Chair, which was immediately resumed by the President *pro tem.*, Mr. Wade, who called the Senate to order.

PROCEEDINGS OF MONDAY, MARCH 30.

WASHINGTON, March 30.—At 12·30 the President *pro tem* of the Senate vacated the Chair, which was immediately taken by the Chief Justice.

The Sergeant-at-Arms made a proclamation commanding silence.

The President's counsel entered and took their seats as before, at 12·45, and the Sergeant-at-Arms announced the managers on the part of the House of Representatives, who took their places, with the exception of Mr. Stevens, who entered soon afterward, and took a seat slightly apart from the managers' table.

The House of Representatives was then announced, and the members appeared headed by Mr. Washburne, of Illinois, on the arm of the Clerk of the House, and were seated.

The minutes of the last day of the trial were read, and Mr. Butler commenced his opening at a quarter before one o'clock.

Opening Argument of Mr. Butler.

Mr. President and Gentlemen of the Senate:—The onerous duty has fallen to my fortune to present to you, imperfectly as I must, the several propositions of fact and of law upon which the House of Representatives will endeavor to sustain the cause of the people against the President of the United States, now pending at your bar.

The high station of the accused, the novelty of the proceeding, the gravity of the business, the importance of the questions to be presented to your adjudication, the possible momentous result of the issues, each and all must plead for me to claim your attention for as long a time as your patience may endure.

Now, for the first time in the history of the world, has a nation brought before its highest tribunal its Chief Executive Magistrate for trial and possible deposition from office, upon charges of maladministration of the powers and duties of that office. In other times, and in other lands, it has been found that despotisms could only be tempered by assassination, and nations living under constitutional governments even, have found no mode by which to rid themselves of a tyrannical, imbecile, or faithless ruler, save by overturning the very foundation and frame work of the government itself. And, but recently, in one of the most civilized and powerful governments of the world, from which our own institutions have been largely modeled, we have seen a nation submit for years to the rule of an insane king, because its constitution contained no method for his removal.

Our fathers, more wisely, founding our government, have provided for such and all similar exigencies a conservative, effectual, and practical remedy by the constitutional provision that the "President, Vice President, and all civil officers of the United States *shall* be removed from office on impeachment for and conviction of treason, bribery, or other high crimes and misdemeanors." The Constitution leaves nothing to implication, either as to the persons upon whom, or the body by whom, or the tribunal before which, or the offenses for which, or the manner in which this high power should be exercised; each and all are provided for by express words of imperative command.

The House of Representatives shall solely impeach; the Senate only shall try; and in case of conviction the judgment shall alone be removal from office and disqualification for office, one or both. These mandatory provisions became necessary to adapt a well-known procedure of the mother country to the institutions of the then infant republic. But a single incident only of the business was left to construction, and that concerns the offenses or incapacities which are the groundwork of impeachment. This was wisely done, because human foresight is inadequate, and human intelligence fails in the task of anticipating and providing for, by positive enactment, all the infinite gradations of a human wrong and sin, by which the liberties of a people and the safety of a nation may be endangered from the imbecility, corruption and unhallowed ambition of its rulers.

It may not be uninstructive to observe that the framers of the Constitution, while engaged in their glorious and, I trust, ever-enduring work, had their attention aroused and their minds quickened most signally upon this very topic. In the previous year only Mr. Burke, from his place in the House of Commons, in England, had preferred charges for impeachment against Warren Hastings, and three days before our convention sat he was impeached at the bar of the House of Lords for misbehavior in office as the ruler of a people whose numbers were counted by millions. The mails were then bringing across the Atlantic, week by week, the eloquent accusations of Burke, the gorgeous and burning denunciations of Sheridan, in behalf of the oppressed people of India, against one who had wielded over them more than regal power. May it not have been that the trial then in progress was the determining cause why the framers of the Constitution left the description of offenses, because of which the conduct of an officer might be inquired of, to be defined by the laws and usages of Parliament as found in the precedents of the mother country, with which our fathers were as familiar as we are with our own?

In the light, therefore, of these precedents, the question arises, *What are impeachable offenses* under the provisions of our Constitution?

To analize, to compare, to reconcile these precedents, is a work rather for the closet than the forum. In order, therefore, to spare your attention, I have preferred to state the result to which I have arrived, and that you may see the authorities and discussions, both in this country and in England, from which we deduce our propositions, so far as applicable to this case, I pray leave to lay before you, at the close of my argument, a brief of all the precedents and authorities upon this subject, in both countries, for which I am indebted to the exhaustive and learned labors of my friend, the honorable William Lawrence, of Ohio, member of the Judiciary Committee of the House of Representatives, in which I fully concur and which I adopt.

We define, therefore, an impeachable high crime or misdemeanor to be *one in its nature or consequences subversive of some fundamental or essential principle of government, or highly prejudicial to the public interest, and this may consist of a violation of the Constitution, of law, of an official oath, or of duty, by an act committed or omitted, or, without violating a positive law, by the abuse of discretionary powers from improper motives, or for any improper purpose.*

The first criticism which will strike the mind on a cursory examination of this definition is, that some of the enumerated acts are not within the common-law definition of crimes. It is but common learning that in the English precedents the words "high crimes and misdemeanors" are universally used; but any malversation in office, highly prejudicial to the public interest, or subversive of some fundamental principle of government by which the safety of a people may be in danger, is a high crime against the nation, as the term is used in parliamentary law.

Hallam, in his Constitutional History of England, certainly deduces this doctrine from the precedents, and especially Lord Danby, case 11, State Trials, 600, of which he says:—

The Commons, in impeaching Lord Danby, went a great way towards establishing the principle that no minister can shelter himself behind the throne by pleading obedience to the orders of his sovereign. He is answerable for the *justice, the honesty, the utility of all measures emanating* from the Crown, as well as for their *legality;* and thus the executive administration is, or ought to be, subordinate in all great matters of policy to the superintendence and virtual control of the two houses of Parliament.

Mr. Christian, in his notes to the Commentaries of Blackstone, explains the collocation and use of the words "high crimes and misdemeanors" by saying:—

When the words "high crimes and misdemeanors" are used in prosecutions by impeachment, the words "high crimes" have no definite signification, but are used merely to give greater solemnity to the charge.

A like interpretation must have been given by the framers of the Constitution, because a like definition to ours was in the mind of Mr. Madison, to whom more than to any other we are indebted for the phraseology of our Constitution, for, in the first Congress, when *discussing* the power to remove an officer by the President, which is one of the very material questions before the Senate at this moment, he uses the following words:—

The danger consists mainly in this:—That the President can displace from office a man whose merits require he should be continued in it. In the first place, he will be impeachable by the House for such an act of maladministration, for I contend that the wanton removal of meritorious officers would subject him to impeachment and removal from his own high trust.

Strengthening this view, we find that within ten years afterwards impeachment was applied by the very men who framed the Constitution to the acts of public officers, which under no common law definition could be justly called crimes or misdemeanors, either high or low. Leaving, however, the correctness of our proposition to be sustained by the authorities we furnish, we are naturally brought to the consideration of the method of the procedure, and the nature of the proceedings in cases of impeachment, and the character and powers of the tribunal by which high crimes and misdemeanors are to be adjudged or determined.

One of the important questions which meets us at the outset is, Is this proceeding a trial, as that term is understood so far as relates to the rights and duties of a court and jury upon an indictment for crime? Is it not rather more in the nature of an inquest of office?

The Constitution seems to have determined it to be the latter, because, under its provisions the right to retain and hold office is the only subject that can be finally adjudicated; all preliminary inquiry being carried on solely to determine that question and that alone.

All investigations of fact are in some sense trials, but not in the sense in which the word is used by courts.

Again, as a correlative question:—

Is this body, now sitting to determine the accusation of the House of Representatives against the President of the United States, the Senate of the United States, or a court?

I trust, Mr. President and Senators, I may be pardoned for making some suggestions upon these topics, because to us it seems these are questions not of forms, but of substance. If this body here is a court in any manner as contra-distinguished from the Senate, then we agree that many, if not all the analogies of the procedures of courts must obtain; that the common-law incidents of a trial in court must have place: that you may be bound in your proceedings and adjudication by the rules and precedents of the common or statute law; that the interest, bias or preconceived opinions or affinities to the party, of the judges, may be open to inquiry, and even the rules of order and precedents in courts should have effect; that the managers of the House of Representatives must conform to those rules as they would be applicable to public or private prosecutors of crime in courts, and that the accused may claim the benefit of the rule in criminal cases, that he may only be convicted when the evidence makes the fact clear beyond reasonable doubt, instead of by a preponderance of the evidence.

We claim and respectfully insist that this tribunal has none of the attributes of a judicial court, as they are commonly received and understood. Of course, this question must be largely determined by the express provisions of the Constitution, and in it there is no word, as is well known to you, Senators, which gives the slightest coloring to the idea that this is a court, save that in the trial of this particular respondent, the Chief Justice of the Supreme Court must preside. But even this provision can have no determining effect upon the question, because, is not this the same tribunal in all its powers, incidents and duties, when other civil officers are brought to its bar for trial, when the Vice President (not a judicial officer) must preside? Can it be contended for a moment that this is the Senate of the United States when sitting on the trial of all other officers, and a court only when the President is at the bar? solely because in this case, the Constitution has designated the Chief Justice as the presiding officer?

The fact that Senators are sitting for this purpose on oath or affirmation does not influence the argument, because it is well understood that this was but a substitute for the obligation of honor under which, by the theory of the British Constitution, the peers of England were supposed to sit in like cases.

A peer of England makes answer in a court of chancery upon honor, when a common person must answer upon oath. But our fathers, sweeping away all distinctions of caste, require every man alike, acting in a solemn proceeding like this, to take an oath. Our Constitution holds all good men alike honorable, and entitled to honor.

The idea that this tribunal was a court seems to have crept in because of the analogy to similar proceedings in trials before the House of Lords.

Analogies have ever been found deceptive and illusory. Before such analogy is invoked we must not forget that the Houses of Parliament at first, and latterly the House of Lords, claimed and exercised jurisdiction over all crimes, even where the punishment extended to life and limb. By express provision of our Constitution all such jurisdiction is taken from the Senate, and "the judicial power of the United States is vested in one Supreme Court, and such inferior courts as from time to time Congress may ordain and establish." We suggest, therefore, that we are in the presence of the Senate of the United States, convened as a constitutional tribunal, to inquire into and determine whether Andrew Johnson, because of malversation in office, is longer fit to retain the office of President of the United States, or hereafter to hold any office of honor or profit.

I respectfully submit that thus far your mode of proceeding has no analogy to that of a court. You issue a summons to give the respondent notice of the case pending against him. You do not sequester his person—you do not require his personal appearance even; you proceed against him, and will *go on* to determine his cause in his absence, and make the final order therein. How different is each step from those of ordinary criminal procedure.

A constitutional tribunal solely, you are bound by no law, either statute or common, which may limit your constitutional prerogative. You consult no precedents, save those of the law and custom of parliamentary bodies. You are a law unto yourselves, bound only by the natural principles of equity and justice, and that *salus populi suprema est lex.*

Upon these principles and parliamentary law no judges can aid you, and, indeed, in late years, the judges of England in the trial of impeachment, declined to speak to a question of parliamentary law, even at the request of the House of Peers, although they attended on them in their robes of office.

Nearly five hundred years ago, in 1338, the House of Lords resolved, in the case of Belknap and the other judges, "that these matters, when brought before them, shall be discussed and adjudged by the course of Parliament, and not by the civil law, nor by the common law of the land used in other inferior courts." And that regulation, which was in contravention of the opinion of all the judges of England, and against the remonstrance of Richard II, remains the unquestioned law of England to this day.

Another determining quality of the tribunal, distinguishing it from a court and the analogies of ordinary legal proceedings, and showing that it is a Senate only, is that there can be no right of challenge by either party to any of its members for favor or malice, affinity or interest.

This has been held from the earliest times in Parliament, even when that was the high court of judicature of the realm, sitting to punish all crimes against the peace.

In the case of the Duke of Somerset (1 Howell's State Trials, p. 521), as early as 1551, it was held that the Duke of Northumberland and the Marquis of Northampton and the Earl of Pembroke, for an attempt upon whose lives Somerset was on trial, should sit in judgment upon him against the objection of the accused because "a peer of the realm might not be challenged."

Again, the Duke of Northumberland, (ibid, 1st State Trials, p. 765,) Marquis of Northampton and Earl of Warwick, on trial for their crimes, A. D. 1553, before the Court of the Lord High Steward of England, being one of the prisoners, inquired whether any such persons as were equally culpable in that crime, and those by whose letters and commandments he was directed in all his doings, might be his judges or pass upon his trial at his death. It was answered that:—

"If any were as deeply to be touched as himself in that case, yet as long as no attainder of record were against them, they were nevertheless persons able in the law to pass upon any trial, and not to be challenged therefor, but at the Prince's pleasure.

Again, on the trial of the Earls of Essex and Southampton (ibid., 1 State Trials, p. 1335) for high treason, before all the justices of England, A. D. 1600, the Earl of Essex desired to know of my Lord Chief Justice whether he might challenge any of the peers or no. Whereunto the Lord Chief Justice answered 'No.' "

Again, in Lord Audley's case (ibid 3 State Trials, page 402. A. D. 1631), it was questioned whether a peer might challenge his peers, as in the case of common jurats. It was answered by all the judges, after consultation, "he might not." [This case was of more value, because it was an indictment for being accessory to rape upon his own wife, and had no political influence in it whatever.] The same point was ruled in the Countess of Essex's case, on trial for treason. (Moore's Reports, 621.)

In the Earl of Portland's case, A. D. 1701 (ibid, State Trials, page 288), the Commons objected that Lord Sommers, the Earl of Oxford and Lord Halifax, who had been impeached by the Commons before the House of Lords for being concerned in the same acts for which Portland was being brought to trial, voted and acted with the House of Lords in the preliminary proceedings of said trial, and were upon a committee of conference in relation thereto. But the lords, after discussion, solemnly resolved "That no lord of Parliament, impeached of high crimes and misdemeanors, can be precluded from voting on any occasion except on his own trial."

In the trial of Lord Viscount Melville, A. D. 1806, (ibid. 29 State Trials, p. 1398), some observations having been made as to the possible bias of some portion of the peers (by the counsel for defendant), Mr. Whitebread, one of the managers on the part of the Commons, answered as follows:—

"My lords, as to your own court, something has been thrown out about the possibility of a challenge. Upon such a subject it will not be necessary to say more than this, which has been admitted—that an order was given by the House of Commons to prosecute Lord Melville in a court of law where he would have the *right* to challenge his jurors. * * * What did the noble Viscount then do by the means of one of his friends? * * * From the mouth of that learned gentleman came at last the successful motion—"That Henry, Viscount of Melville, be impeached of high crimes and misdemeanors." I am justified, then, in saying that he is here by his own option * * * But, my lords, a challenge to your lord-hips! Is not every individual peer the guardian of his own honor?

In the trial of Warren Hastings the same point was ruled, or, more properly speaking, taken for granted, for of the more than one hundred and seventy peers who commenced the trial, but twenty-nine sat and pronounced the verdict at the close. and some of these were peers created since the trial began, and had not heard either the opening or much of the evidence; and during the trial there had been by death, succession and creation, more than one hundred and eighty changes in the House of Peers, who were his judges.

We have abundant authority, also, on this point in our own country. In the case of Judge Pickering, who was tried March, 1804, for drunkenness in office, although undefended in form, yet he had all his rights preserved. This trial being postponed a session, three Senators—Samuel Smith, o. Maryland; Israel Smith, of Vermont, and John Smith, of New York—who had all been members of the House of Representatives, and there voted in favor of impeaching Judge Pickering, were Senators when his trial came off.

Mr. Smith, of New York, raised the question asking to be excused from voting. Mr. Smith, of Maryland, declared "he would not be influenced from his duty by any false delicacy; that he, for his part, felt no delicacy upon the subject; the vote he had given in the other House to impeach Judge Pickering, would have no influence upon him in the court; his constituents had a right to his vote, and he would not by any act of his deprive, or consent to deprive them of their right, but would claim and exercise it upon this as upon every other question that might be submitted to the Senate while he had the honor of a seat."

A vote being had upon the question, it was determined that these gentlemen should sit and vote on the trial. This passed in the affirmative, by a vote of 19 to 7, and all the gentlemen sat and voted on every question during the trial.

On the trial of Samuel Chase before the Senate of the United States, no challenge was attempted, although the case was decided by an almost strict party vote in high party times, and doubtless many of the Senators had formed and expressed opinions upon his conduct. That arbitrary judge, but learned lawyer, knew too much to attempt any such futile movement as a challenge to a Senator. Certain it is that the proprieties of the occasion were not marred by the worse than anomalous proceeding of the challenge of one Senator to another, especially before the defendant had appeared.

Nor did the managers exercise the right of challenge, although Senators Smith and Mitchell of New York were members of the Senate on the trial, and voted *not guilty* on every article, who had been members of the House when the articles were found, and had there voted steadily against the whole proceeding.

Judge Peck's case, which was tried in 1831, affords another instance in point.

The conduct of Judge Peck had been the subject of much animadversion and comment by the public, and had been for four years pending before the Congress of the United States before it finally came to trial. It was not possible but that many of the Senate had both formed and expressed opinions upon Peck's proceedings, and yet it never occurred to that good lawyer to make objections to his triers. Nor did the managers challenge, although Webster, of Massachusetts, was a member of the committee of the House of Representatives, to whom the petition for impeachment was referred, and which, after examination, reported thereon "leave to withdraw," and Sprague, of Maine, voted against the proceedings in the House, while Livingston, of Louisiana, voted for them.

All of these gentlemen sat upon the trial, and voted as they did in the House. A very remarkable and instructive case was that of Judge Addison, of Pennsylvania, in 1804. There, after the articles of impeachment were framed, the trial was postponed to another session of the Legislature. Meanwhile, three members of the House of Representatives who had voted for the articles of impeachment were elected to the Senate, and became the triers of the articles of impeachment of which they had solemnly voted the respondent to be guilty.

To their sitting on the trial Judge Addison objected, but after an exhaustive argument his objection was overruled, 17 to 6. Two of the minority were the gentlemen who had voted him guilty, and who themselves objected to sitting on the trial.

Thus stands the case upon authority. How does it stand upon principle?

In a conference held in 1691, between the lords and commons, on a proposition to limit the number of judges, the lords made answer:—

"That in the case of impeachment, which are the groans of the people, and for the highest crimes, and carry with them a greater supposition of guilt than any other accusation, there all the lords must judge."

There have been many instances in England where this necessity, that no peer be excused from sitting on such trials, has produced curious results. Brothers have sat upon the trials of brothers; fathers upon the trials of sons and daughters; uncles upon the trials of nephews and nieces; no excuse being admitted.

One, and a most peculiar and painful instance, will suffice upon this point to illustrate the strength of the rule. In the trial of Anne Boleyn, the wife of one sovereign of England, and the mother of another, her father, Lord Rochefort, and her uncle, the Duke of Norfolk, sat as judges and voted guilty, although one of the charges against daughter and niece was a criminal intimacy with her brother, the son and nephew of the judges.

It would seem impossible that in a proceeding before such a tribunal so constituted, there could be a challenge, because as the number of triers is limited by law, and as there are not now, and never have been, any provisions either in England or in this country for substituting another for the challenged party, as a talesman is substituted in a jury, the accused might escape punishment altogether by challenging a sufficient number to prevent a quorum; or the accusers might oppress the respondent by challenging all persons favorable to him until the necessary unanimity for conviction was secured.

This proceeding being but an inquest of office, and, except in a few rare instances, always partaking, more or less, of political considerations, and required to be discussed, before presentation to the triers, by the co-ordinate branch of the legislature, it is impossible that Senators should not have opinions and convictions upon the subject matter more or less decidedly formed before the case reaches them. If, therefore, challenges could be allowed because of such opinions, as in the case of jurors, no trial could go forward, because every intelligent Senator could be objected to upon one side or the other.

I should have hardly dared to trouble the Senate with such minuteness of citation and argument upon this point, were it not that certain persons and papers outside of this body, by sophistries drawn from the analogies of the proceedings in courts before juries, have endeavored, in advance, to prejudice the public mind, but little instructed in this topic, because of the infrequency of impeachments, against the legal validity and propriety of the proceedings upon this trial.

I may be permitted, without offense, further to state, that these and similar reasons have prevented the managers from objecting, by challenge or otherwise, to the competency of one of the triers, of near affinity to the accused.

We believe it is his right, nay, his duty, to the State he represents, to sit upon the trial as he would upon any other matter which should come before the Senate. His seat and vote belongs to his constituents, and not to himself, to be used, according to his best judgment, upon every grave matter that comes before the Senate.

Again, as political considerations are in this trial, raising questions of interest to the constituents of every Senator, it is his right and duty to express himself as fully and freely upon such questions as upon any other, even to express a belief in the guilt or innocence of the accused, or to say he will sustain him in the course he is taking, although he so says after accusation brought.

Let me illustrate. Suppose that after this impeachment had been voted by the House of Representatives, the constituents of any Senator had called a public meeting to sustain the President against what they were pleased to term the "tyrannical acts of Congress towards him in impeaching him," and should call upon their Senator to attend and take part in such meeting, I do not conceive that it would or ought to be legally objected against him as a disqualification to sit upon this trial, upon the principles I have stated, if he should attend the meeting or favor the object, or if his engagements in the Senate prevented his leaving.

I have not been able to find any legal objection in the books to his writing a letter to such meeting, containing, among other things, statements like the following:—

SENATE CHAMBER, Feb. 24, 1868.—Gentlemen:—My public and professional engagements will be such on the 4th of March that I am reluctantly compelled to decline your invitation to be present and address the meeting to be held in your city on that day. * * * * * * *

That the President of the United States has sincerely endeavored to preserve those (our free institutions) from violation I have no doubt, and I have, therefore, throughout the unfortunate difference of opinion between him and Congress sustained him. And this I shall continue to do so long as he shall prove faithful to duty. With my best thanks for the honor you have done me by your invitation, and regretting that it is not in my power to accept it,

I remain, with regard, your obedient servant,
REVERDY JOHNSON.

We should have as much right to expect his vote on a clearly proven case of guilty, as had King Henry the Eighth to hope for the vote of her father against his wife. He got it.

King Henry knew the strength of his case, and we know the strength of ours against this respondent.

If it is said that this is an infelicity, it is a sufficient and decisive answer that it is the infelicity of a precise constitutional provision, which provides that the Senate shall have the sole power to try impeachment, and the only security against bias or prejudice on the part of any Senator is that two-thirds of the Senators present are necessary for conviction.

To this rule there is but one possible exception, founded on both reason and authority, that a Senator may not be a judge in his own case. I have thought it necessary, before to determine the nature and attributes of the tribunal, before we attend to the scope and meaning of the accusation before it.

The first eight articles set out in several distinct forms the acts of the respondent in removing Mr. Stanton from office, and appointing Mr. Thomas, *ad interim*, differing in legal effect in the purposes for which and the intent with which either or both of the acts were done, and the legal duties and rights infringed, and the acts of Congress violated in so doing

All the articles allege these acts to be in contravention of his oath of office, and in disregard of the duties thereof.

If they are so, however, the President might have the *power* to do them under the law; still, being so done, they are acts of official misconduct, and, as we have seen, impeachable.

The President has the legal power to do many acts which, if done, in disregard of his duty, or for improper purposes, then the exercise of that power is an official misdemeanor.

Ex. gr: he has the power of pardon; if exercised in a given case for a corrupt motive, as for the payment of money, or wantonly pardoning all criminals, it would be a misdemeanor. Examples might be multiplied indefinitely.

Article first, stripped of legal verbiage, alleges that, having suspended Mr. Stanton and reported the same to the Senate, which refused to concur in the suspension, and Stanton having rightfully resumed the duties of his office, the respondent, with knowledge of the facts, issued an order, which is recited, for Stanton's removal, with intent to violate the act of March 2, 1867, to regulate the tenure of certain civil offices, and with the further intent to remove Stanton from the office of Secretary of War, then in the lawful discharge of its duties, in contravention of said act without the advice and consent of the Senate, and against the Constitution of the United States.

Article 2 charges that the President, without authority of law, on the 21st of February, 1868, issued letter of authority to Lorenzo Thomas to act as Secretary of War *ad interim*, the Senate being in session, in violation of the Tenure of Office act, and with intent to violate it and the Constitution, there being no vacancy in the office of Secretary of War.

Article 3 alleges the same act as done without authority of law, and alleges an intent to violate the Constitution.

Article 4 charges that the President conspired with Lorenzo Thomas and divers other persons, with intent, by *intimidation and threats*, to prevent Mr. Stanton from holding the office of Secretary of War, in violation of the Constitution and of the act of July 31, 1861.

Article 5 charges the same conspiracy with Thomas to prevent Mr. Stanton's holding his office, and thereby to prevent the execution of the civil tenure act.

Article 6 charges that the President conspired with Thomas to seize and possess the property under the control of the War Department by *force*, in contravention of the act of July 31, 1861, and with intent to disregard the civil tenure of office act.

Article 7 charges the same conspiracy, with intent only to violate the civil tenure of office act.

Articles 3d, 4th, 5th, 6th, and 7th may be considered together, as to the proof to support them.

It will be shown that having removed Stanton and appointed Thomas, the President sent Thomas to the War Office to obtain possession; that having been met by Stanton with a denial of his rights, Thomas retired, and after consultation with the President, Thomas asserted his purpose to take possession of the War Office by force, making his boast in several public places of his intentions so to do, but was prevented by being promptly arrested by process from the court.

This will be shown by the evidence of Hon. Mr. Van Horn, a member of the House, who was present when the demand for possession of the War Office was made by General Thomas, already made public.

By the testimony of the Hon. Mr. Burleigh, who, after that, in the evening of the twenty-first of February, was told by Thomas that he intended to take possession of the War Office by force the following morning, and invited him up to see the performance. Mr. Burleigh attended, but the act did not come off, for Thomas had been arrested and held to bail.

By Thomas boasting at Willards' Hotel on the same evening that he should call on General Grant for military force to put him in possession of the office, and he did not see how Grant could refuse it.

Article 8 charges that the appointment of Thomas was made for the purpose of getting control of the disbursement of the moneys appropriated for the military service and Department of War.

In addition to the proof already adduced, it will be shown that after the appointment of Thomas, which must have been known to the members of his Cabinet, the President caused a formal notice to be served on the Secretary of the Treasury, to the end that the Secretary might answer the requisitions for money of Thomas, and this was only prevented by the firmness with which Stanton retained possession of the books and papers of the War Office.

It will be seen that every fact charged in Article 1 is admitted by the answer of the respondent; the intent is also admitted as charged; that is to say, to set aside the civil tenure of office act, and to remove Mr. Stanton from the office for the Secretary of the Department of War without the advice and consent of the Senate, and, if not justified, contrary to the provisions of the Constitution itself.

The only question remaining is, does the respondent justify himself by the Constitution and laws?

On this he avers, that by the Constitution, there is "conferred on the President, as a part of the executive power, the power at any and all times of removing from office all executive officers for cause, to be judged of by the President alone, and that he verily believes that the executive power of removal from office, confided to him by the Constitution, as aforesaid, includes the power of suspension from office indefinitely."

Now, these offices, so vacated, must be filled, temporarily at least, by his appointment, because government must go on; there can be no interregnum in the execution of the laws in an organized government; he claims, therefore, of necessity, the right to fill their places with appointments of his choice, and that this power cannot be restrained or limited in any degree by any law of Congress, because, he avers, "that the power was conferred, and the duty of exercising it in fit cases was imposed on the President by the Constitution of the United States, and that the President could not be deprived of this power, or relieved of this duty, nor could the same be vested by law in the President and the Senate jointly, either in part or whole."

This, then, is the plain and inevitable issue before the Senate and the American people:—

Has the President, under the Constitution, the more than kingly prerogative at will to remove from office and suspend from office indefinitely, all executive officers of the United States, either civil, military or naval, at any and all times, and fill the vacancies with creatures of his own appointment, for his own purposes, without any restraint whatever, or possibility of restraint by the Senate or by Congress through laws duly enacted?

The House of Representatives, in behalf of the people, join this issue by affirming that the exercise of such powers is a high misdemeanor in office.

If the affirmation is maintained by the respondent, then, so far as the first eight articles are concerned—unless such corrupt purposes are shown as will of themselves make the exercise of a legal power a crime—the respondent must go and ought to go quit and free.

Therefore, by these articles and the answers thereto, the momentous question, here and now, is raised whether the *Presidential office itself* (*if it has the prerogatives and power claimed for it*) *ought, in fact, to exist as a part of the constitutional government of a free people,* while by the last three articles the simpler and less important inquiry is to be determined, whether Andrew Johnson has so conducted himself that he ought longer to hold any constitutional office whatever. The latter sinks to merited insignificance compared with the grandeur of the former.

If that is sustained, then a right and power hitherto unclaimed and unknown to the people of the country is engrafted on the Constitution, most alarming in its extent, most corrupting in its influence, most dangerous in its tendencies, and most tyrannical in its exercise.

Whoever, therefore, votes "not guilty" on these articles, votes to enchain our free institutions, and to prostrate them at the feet of any man who, being President, may choose to control them.

For this most stupendous and unlimited prerogative the respondent cites no line and adduces no word of constitutional enactment—indeed he could not, for the only mention of removal from office in the Constitution is as a part of the judgment in case of impeachment, and the only power of appointment is by nomination to the Senate of officers to be appointed by their advice and consent, save a qualified and limited power of appointment by the President when the Senate is not in session. Whence then does the respondent by his answer claim to have derived this power? I give him the benefit of his own words, "that it was practically settled by the first Congress of the United States." Again, I give him the benefit of his own phrases as set forth in his message to the Senate of 2d of March, 1867, made a part of his answer:—"The question was decided by the House of Representatives by a vote of 34 to 20, (in this, however, he is mistaken,) and in the Senate by the casting vote of the Vice President." In the same answer he admits that before he undertook the exercise of this most dangerous and stupendous power, after seventy-five years of study and examination of the Constitution by the people living under it, another Congress has decided that there was no such unlimited power. So that he admits that this tremendous power which he claims from the legislative construction of one Congress by a vote of 34 to 20 in the House, and a tie vote in the Senate, has been denied by another House of more than three times the number of members by a vote of 133 to 37; and by a Senate of more than double the number of Senators by a vote of 38 to 10, and this, too, after he had presented to them all the arguments in its favor that he could find to sustain his claim of power.

If he derives this power from the practical settlement of one Congress of a legislative construction of the constitutional provisions, why may not such construction be as practically settled more authoritatively by the greater unanimity of another Congress—yea, as we shall see, of many other Congresses?

The great question, however, still returns upon us—whence comes this power?—how derived or conferred? Is it unlimited and unrestrained? illimitable and unrestrainable, as the President claims it to be?

In presenting this topic it will be my duty, and I shall attempt to do nothing more, than to state the propositions of law and the authorities to support them so far as they may come to my knowledge, leaving the argument and illustrations of the question to be extended in the close by abler and better hands.

If a power of removal in the Executive is found at all in the Constitution, it is admitted to be an implied one, either from the power of appointment, or because "the executive power is vested in the President."

Has the executive power granted by the Constitution by these words any limitations? Does the Constitution invest the President with all executive power, prerogatives, privileges and immunities enjoyed by executive officers of other countries—kings and emperors—without limitation? If so, then the Constitution has been much more liberal in granting powers to the Executive than to the legislative branch of the government, as that has only "all legislative powers herein granted (which) shall be vested in the Congress of the United States;" not all uncontrollable legislative powers, as there are many limitations upon that power as exercised by the Parliament of England for example. So there are many executive powers expressly limited in the Constitution, such as declaring war, making rules and regulations for the government of the army and navy, and coining money.

As some executive powers are limited by the Constitution itself, is it not clear that the words "the executive power is vested in the President," do not confer on him all executive powers, but must be construed with reference to other constitutional provisions granting or regulating specific powers? The executive power of appointment is clearly limited by the words "he shall nominate and by and with the advice and consent of the Senate, shall appoint ambassadors, * * * and all other officers of the United States whose appointments are not herein otherwise provided for, and which shall be established by law."

Is it not, therefore, more in accordance with the theory of the Constitution to imply the power of removal from the power of appointment, restrained by like limitations, than to imply it solely as a prerogative of executive power and therefore illimitable and uncontrollable? Have the people anywhere else in the Constitution granted illimitable and uncontrollable powers either to the executive or any other branch of the government? Is not the whole power of government one of checks, balances, and limitations? Is it to be believed that our fathers, just escaping from the oppressions of monarchical power, and so dreading it that they feared the very name of king, gave this more than kingly power to the Executive, illimitable and uncontrollable, and that too by implication merely?

Upon this point our proposition is, that the Senate being in session, and an office, not an inferior one, within the terms of the Constitution being filled, the President has the implied power of inaugurating the removal *only* by nomination of a successor to the Senate, which, when consented to, works the full removal and supersedes of the incumbent. Such has been, it is believed, the practice of the government from the beginning, down to the act about which we are inquiring. Certain it is that Mr. Webster, in the Senate, in 1835, so asserted without contradiction, using the following language:—

"If one man be Secretary of State, and another be appointed, the first goes out by the mere force of the appointment of the other, without any previous act of removal whatever. And this is the practice of the government, and has been from the first. In all the removals which have been made they have generally been effected simply by making other appointments. I cannot find a case to the contrary. There is no such thing as any distinct official act of removal. I have looked into the practice, and caused inquiries to be made in the departments, and I do not learn that any such proceeding is known as an entry or record of the removal of an officer from office, and the President would only act in such cases by causing some proper record or entry to be made as proof of the fact of removal. I am aware that there have been some cases in which notice has been sent to persons in office that their services are or will be, after a given day, dispensed with. These are usually cases in which the object is, not to inform the incumbent that he is removed, but to tell him that a successor either is, or by a day named will be, appointed. If there be any instances in which such notice is given, without express reference to the appointment of a successor, they are few; and even in these such reference must be implied, because in no case is there any distinct official act of removal, as I can find, unconnected with the act of appointment."

This would seem to reconcile all the provisions of the Constitution, the right of removal being in the President, to be executed *sub modo*, as is the power of appointment, the appointment, when consummated, making the removal.

This power was elaborately debated in the first Congress upon the bills establishing a Department of Foreign Affairs and the War Department. The debate arose on the motion, in Committee of the Whole, to strike out, after the title of the officer, the words, "to be removable from office by the President of the United States." It was four days discussed in Committee of the Whole in the House, and the clause retained by a vote of 20 yeas to 34 nays, which seemed to establish the power of removal as either by a legislative grant or construction of the Constitution. But the triumph of its friends was short-lived, for when the bill came up in the House, Mr. Benson moved to amend it by altering the second section of the bill, so as to *imply* only the power of removal to be in the President, by inserting, that "whenever the principal officer shall be removed from office by the President of the United States, or in any other case of vacancy, the chief clerk shall, during such vacancy, have charge and custody of all records, books, and papers appertaining to the department."

Mr. Benson "declared he would move to strike out the words in the first clause, to be removable by the President, which appeared somewhat like a grant. Now the mode he took would evade that point and establish a legis-

lative construction of the Constitution. He also hoped his amendment would succeed in reconciling both sides of the House to the decision and quieting the minds of the gentlemen."

After debate the amendment was carried, 30 to 18. Mr. Benson then moved to strike out the words "to be removable by the President of the United States," which was carried, 31 to 19; and so the bill was engrossed and sent to the Senate.

The debates of that body being in secret session, we have no record of the discussion which arose on the motion of Mr. Benson establishing the implied power of removal; but after very elaborate consideration, on several successive days, the words implying this power in the President were retained by the casting vote of the elder Adams, the Vice President. So, if this claimed "legislative settlement" was only established by the vote of the second executive officer of the government. Alas! most of our woes in this government have come from Vice Presidents. When the bill establishing the War Department came up, the same words, "to be removable by the President" were struck out, on the motion of one of the opponents of the recognition of the power, by a vote of 24 to 22, a like amendment to that of the second section of the act establishing the Department of State being inserted. When, six years afterwards, the Department of the Navy was established, no such recognition of the power of the President to remove was inserted; and as the measure passed by a strict party vote, 47 yeas to 41 nays, it may well be conceived that its advocates did not care to load it with this constitutional question, when the executive power was about passing into other hands, for one cannot read the debates upon this question without being impressed with the belief that reverence for the character of Washington largely determined the argument in the first Congress. Neither party did or could have looked forward to such an executive administration as we have this day.

It has generally been conceded in subsequent discussions that here was a legislative determination of this question; but I humbly submit that, taking the whole action of Congress together, it is very far from being determined. I should hardly have dared, in view of the eminent names of Holmes, Clay, Webster and Calhoun, that have heretofore made the admission, to have ventured the assertion, were it not that in every case they, as does the President and his counsel, rely on the first vote in the Committee of the Whole, sustaining the words "to be removable by the President," and in no instance take any notice of the subsequent proceedings in the House by which these words were taken out of the bill. This may have happened because "Eliot's Debates," which is the authority most frequently cited in these discussions, stops with the vote in Committee, and takes no notice of the further discussion. But whatever may be the effect of this legislative construction, the cotemporaneous and subsequent practice of the government shows that the President made no removals except by nominations to the Senate when in session, and superseding officers by a new commission to the confirmed nominee. Mr. Adams, in that remarkable letter to Mr. Pickering, in which he desires his resignation, requests him to send it early, in order that he may nominate to the Senate, then about to sit; and he, in fact, removes Mr. Pickering by a nomination. Certainly no such unlimited power has ever been claimed by any of the earlier Presidents, as has now been set up for the President by his most remarkable, aye, criminal answer.

It will not have escaped attention that no determination was made by that legislative construction as to *how* the removal, if in the President's power, should be made, which is now the question in dispute. *That* has been determined by the universal practice of the government, with exceptions, if any, so rare as not to be worthy of consideration; so that we now claim the law to be what the practice has ever been. If, however, we concede the power of removal to be in the President as an implied power, yet we believe it cannot be successfully contended upon any authorities or constant practice of the government that the execution of that power may not be regulated by the Congress of the United States, under the clause in the Constitution which "vests in Congress the power to make all laws which shall be necessary and proper for carrying into execution * * * all powers vested by this Constitution in the Government of the United States, or in any department or office thereof."

The power of regulation of the tenure of office, and the manner of removal, has always been exercised by Congress, unquestioned, until now.

On the 15th of May, 1820 (Vol. 3 Stat. at Large, p. 582), Congress provided for the term of office of certain officers therein named to be four years, but made them removable at pleasure. By the second section of the same act Congress removed from office all the officers therein commissioned, in providing a date when each commission should expire, thus asserting a legislative power of removal from office; sometimes by passing acts which appear to concede the power to the President to remove at pleasure, sometimes restricting that power in their acts by the most stringent provisions. Sometimes conferring the power of removal, and sometimes that of appointment—the acts establishing the territorial officers being most conspicuous in this regard.

Upon the whole, no claim of exclusive right over removals or appointments seems to have been made either by the Executive or by Congress. No bill was ever vetoed on this account until now.

In 1818, Mr. Wirt, then Attorney-General, giving the earliest official opinion on this question coming from that office, said that only where Congress had not undertaken to restrict the tenure of office, by the act creating it, would a commission issue to run during the pleasure of the President; but if the tenure was fixed by law, then commission must conform to the law. No constitutional scruples as to the power of Congress to limit the tenure of office seem to have disturbed the mind of that great lawyer. But this was before any attempt had been made by any President to arrogate to himself the official patronage for the purpose of party or personal aggrandisement, which gives the only value to this opinion as an authority. Since the Attorney-General's office has become a political one I shall not trouble the Senate with citing or examining the opinions of its occupants.

In 1826, a committee of the Senate, consisting of Mr. Benton, of Missouri, chairman; Mr. Macon, of North Carolina; Mr. Van Buren, of New York; Mr. Dickerson, of New Jersey; Mr. Johnson, of Kentucky; Mr. White, of Tennessee; Mr. Holmes, of Maine; Mr. Hayne, of South Carolina, and Mr. Findlay, of Pennsylvania, was appointed to take into consideration the question of restraining the power of the President over removals from office, who made a report through their chairman, Mr. Benton, setting forth the extent of the evils arising from the power of appointment to and removal from office by the President, declaring that the Constitution had been changed in this regard, and that "construction and legislation have accomplished this change," and submitted two amendments to the Constitution, one providing a direct election of the President by the people, and another "that no Senator or Representative should be appointed to any place until the expiration of the Presidential term in which such person shall have served as Senator or Representative," as remedies for some of the evils complained of; but the committee say, that "not being able to reform the Constitution, in the election of President they must go to work upon his powers, and trim down these by *statutory enactments*, whenever it can be done by law, and with a just regard to the proper efficiency of government, and for this purpose reported six bills—one, to regulate the publication of the laws and public advertisements; another, *to secure in office* faithful collectors and disbursers of the revenues, and to displace defaulters—the first section of which vacated the commissions of "all officers, after a given date, charged with the collection and disbursement of the public moneys who had failed to account for such moneys on or before the 30th day of September preceding;" and the second section enacted that "at the same time a nomination is made to fill a vacancy occasioned by the exercise of the President's power to remove from office, the fact of the removal shall be stated to the Senate with a report of the reasons for which such officers may have been removed; also a bill to regulate the appointment of postmasters, and a bill to prevent military and naval officers from being dismissed the service at the pleasure of the President, by inserting a clause in the commission of such officers that "it is to continue in force during good behavior," and "that no officer shall ever hereafter be dismissed the service except in pursuance of the sentence of a court-martial, or upon address to the President from the two houses of Congress."

Is it not remarkable that exactly correlative measures to these have been passed by the Thirty-ninth Congress, and are now the subject of controversy at this bar?

It does not seem to have occurred to this able committee that Congress had not the power to curb the Executive in this regard, because they asserted the practice of dismissing from office "to be a dangerous violation of the Constitution."

In 1830 Mr. Holmes introduced and discussed in the Senate a series of resolutions which contained, among other things, "the right of the Senate to inquire, and the duty of the President to inform them, when and for what causes any officer has been removed in the recess." In 1835 Mr. Calhoun, Mr. Southard, Mr. Bibb, Mr. Webster, Mr. Benton, and Mr. King, of Georgia, of the Senate, were elected a committee to consider the subject of Executive patronage, and the means of limiting it. That committee, with but one dissenting voice (Mr. Benton), reported a bill which provided in its third section, "that in all nominations made by the President to the Senate, to fill vacancies occasioned by removal from office, the fact of the removal shall be stated to the Senate at the same time that the nomination is made, with a statement of the reasons for such removal."

It will be observed that this is the precise section reported by Mr. Benton in 1826, and passed to a second reading in the Senate. After much discussion the bill passed the Senate, 31 yeas, 16 nays—an almost two-thirds vote. Thus it would seem that the ablest men of that day, of both political parties, subscribed to the power of Congress to limit and control the President in his removal from office.

One of the most marked instances of this power in Congress will be found in the act of February 25, 1863, providing for a national currency and the office of comptroller. (Statute at Large, vol. 12, p. 665). This controls both the appointment and the removal of that officer, enacting that he shall be appointed on the nomination of the Secretary of the Treasury, by and with the advice and consent of the Senate, and shall hold his office for the term of five years, unless sooner removed by the President, by and with the advice and consent of the Senate. This was substantially re-enacted June 3, 1864, with the addition that "he shall be removed upon reasons to be communicated to the Senate."

Where were the vigilant gentlemen then, in both Houses, who now so denounce the power of Congress to regulate the appointment and removal of officers by the President as unconstitutional?

It will be observed that the Constitution makes no difference between the officers of the army and navy and officers in the civil service, so far as their appointments

and commissions, removals and dismissals, are concerned. Their commissions have ever run, "to hold office during the pleasure of the President;" yet Congress, by the act of 17th July, 1862, (Statutes at Large, volume 12, page 596) enacted "that the President of the United States be and hereby is authorized and requested to dismiss and discharge from the military service, either in the army, navy, marine corps or volunteer force, in the United States service, any officer for any cause which, in his judgment, either renders such officer unsuitable for, or whose dismission would promote the public service."

Why was it necessary to authorize the President so to do if he had the constitutional power to dismiss a military officer at pleasure?—and his powers, whatever they are, as is not doubted, are the same as in a civil office. The answer to this suggestion may be that this act was simply one of supererogation, only authorizing him to do what he was empowered already to do, and, therefore, not specially pertinent to this discussion.

But on 13th of July, 1866, Congress enacted "that no officer in the military or naval service *shall*, in time of peace, *be dismissed* from service except upon, and in pursuance of, the sentence of a court-martial to that effect." What becomes, then, of the respondent's objection that Congress cannot regulate his power of removal from office? In the snow-storm of his vetoes, why did no flake light down on this provision? It concludes the whole question here at issue. It is approved; approval signed Andrew Johnson.

It will not be claimed, however, if the Tenure of Office act is constitutional (and that question I shall not argue, except as has been done incidentally, for reasons hereafter to be stated), that he could remove Mr. Stanton, provided the office of Secretary of War comes within its provisions and one claim made here before you, by the answer, is that that office is excepted by the terms of the law. Of course, I shall not argue to the Senate, composed mostly of those who passed the bill, what their wishes and intentions were. Upon that point I cannot aid them, but the construction of the act furnishes a few suggestions. First let us determine the exact status of Mr. Stanton at the moment of its passage. The answer admits Mr. Stanton was appointed and commissioned and duly qualified as Secretary of War, under Mr. Lincoln, in pursuance of the act of 1789. In the absence of any other legislation or action of the President, he legally held his office during the term of his natural life. This consideration is an answer to every suggestion as to the Secretary holding over from one Presidential term to another.

On the 2d of March, 1867, the Tenure of Office act provided in substance that all civil officers duly qualified to act by appointment, with the advice and consent of the Senate, shall be entitled to hold such office until a successor shall have been in like manner appointed and duly qualified, except as herein otherwise provided, to wit.—*Provided,* That the Secretaries shall hold their office during the term of the President by whom they may have been appointed, and for one month thereafter, subject to removal by and with the advice and consent of the Senate."

By whom was Mr. Stanton appointed? By Mr. Lincoln, whose Presidential term was he holding under when the bullet of Booth became a proximate cause of this trial? Was not his appointment in full force at that hour? Has any act of the respondent up to the 12th day of August last vitiated or interfered with that appointment? Whose Presidential term is the respondent now serving out? His own, or Mr. Lincoln's? If his own, he is entitled to four years up to the anniversary of the murder, because each Presidential term is four years by the Constitution, and the regular recurrence of those terms is fixed by the act of May 8, 1792. If he is serving out the remainder of Mr. Lincoln's term, then his term of office expires on the 4th of March, 1869, if it does not before.

Is not the statement of these propositions their sufficient argument? If Mr. Stanton's commission was vacated in any way by the "Tenure of Office act," then it must have ceased one month after the 4th of March, 1865, to wit, April 4, 1865. Or, if the Tenure of Office act had no retroactive effect, then his commission must have ceased if it had the effect to vacate his commission at all on the passage of the act, to wit, 2d March, 1867; and, in that case, from that day to the present he must have been exercising his office in contravention of the second section of the act, because he was not commissioned in accordance with its provisions. And the President, by "employing" him in so doing from 2d March to 12th August, became guilty of a high misdemeanor under the provision of the sixth section of said act; so that if the President shall succeed in convincing the Senate that Mr. Stanton has been acting as Secretary of War against the Tenure of Office act, which he will do if he convince them that that act vacated in any way Mr. Stanton's commission, or that he himself was not serving out the remainder of Mr. Lincoln's Presidential term, then the House of Representatives have but to report another article for this misdemeanor to remove the President upon his own confession.

It has been said, however, that in the discussion at the time of the passage of this law, observations were made by Senators tending to show that it did not apply to Mr. Stanton, because it was asserted that no member of the Cabinet of the President would wish to hold his place against the wishes of his chief, by whom he had been called into council; and these arguments have been made the ground work of attack upon a meritorious officer, which may have so influenced the minds of Senators that it is my duty to observe upon them, to meet arguments to the prejudice of my cause.

Without stopping to deny the correctness of the general

proposition, there seems to be at least two patent answers to it.

The respondent did not call Mr. Stanton into his council. The blow of the assassin did call the respondent to preside over a Cabinet of which Mr. Stanton was then an honored member, beloved of its chief; and if the respondent deserted the principles under which he was elected, betrayed his trust, and sought to return Rebels whom the valor of our armies had subdued, again into power, are not these reasons, not only why Mr. Stanton should not desert his post, but, as a true patriot, maintain it all the more firmly against this unlooked-for treachery?

Is it not known to you, Senators, and to the country, that Mr. Stanton retains this unpleasant and distasteful position not of his own will alone, but at the behest of a majority of those who represent the people of this country in both houses of its Legislature, and after the solemn decision of the Senate that any attempt to remove him without their concurrence is unconstitutional and unlawful.

To desert it now, therefore, would be to imitate the treachery of his accidental chief. But whatever may be the construction of the Tenure of Civil Office act by others, or as regards others, Andrew Johnson, the respondent, is concluded upon it.

He permitted Mr. Stanton to exercise the duties of his office in spite of it, if that office were affected by it. He suspended him under its provisions; he reported that suspension to the Senate, with his reasons therefor, in accordance with its provisions, and the Senate, acting under it, declined to concur with him, whereby Mr. Stanton was reinstated. In the well-known language of the law, is not the responsdent estopped by his solemn official acts from denying the legality and constitutional propriety of Mr. Stanton's position?

Before proceeding further, I desire most earnestly to bring to the attention of the Senate the averments of the President in his answer, by which he justifies his action in attempting to remove Mr. Stanton, and the reasons which controlled him in so doing. He claims that on the 12th day of August last he had become fully of the opinion that he had the power to remove Mr. Stanton or any other executive officer, or suspend him from office and to appoint any other person to act instead "indefinitely and at his pleasure;" that he was fully advised and believed, as he still believes, that the Tenure of Civil Office act was unconstitutional, inoperative and void in all its provisions, and that he had then determined at all hazards, if Stanton could not be otherwise got rid of, to remove him from office in spite of the provisions of that act and the action of the Senate under it, if for no other purpose, in order to raise for a judicial decision the question affecting the lawful right of said Stanton to persist in refusing to quit the office.

Thus it appears that with full intent to resist the power of the Senate, to hold the Tenure of Office act void, and to exercise this illimitable power claimed by him, he did suspend Mr. Stanton, apparently in accordance with the provisions of the act; he did send the message to the Senate within the time prescribed by the act; he did give his reasons for the suspension to the Senate, and argued them at length, accompanied by what he claimed to be the evidence of the official misconduct of Mr. Stanton, and thus invoked the action of the Senate to assist him in displacing a high officer of the government under the provisions of an act which he at that very moment believed to be unconstitutional, inoperative and void, thereby showing that he was willing to make use of a void act and the Senate of the United States as his tools to do that which he believed neither had any constitutional power to do.

Did not every member of the Senate, when that message came in announcing the suspension of Mr. Stanton, understand and believe that the President was acting in this case as he had done in every other case, under the provisions of this act? Did not both sides discuss the question under its provisions? Would any Senator upon this floor, on either side, demean himself as to consider the question one moment if he had known it was then within the intent and purpose of the President of the United States to treat the deliberations and action of the Senate as void and of no effect if its decision did not comport with his views and purposes; and yet, while acknowledging the intent was in his mind to hold as naught the judgment of the Senate if it did not concur with his own, and remove Mr. Stanton at all hazards, and as I charge it upon him here, as a fact no man can doubt, with the full knowledge also that the Senate understood that he was acting under the provisions of the Tenure of Office act, still thus deceiving them, when called to answer for a violation of that act in his solemn answer he makes the shameless avowal that he did not transmit to the Senate of the United States a "message wherein he made known the orders aforesaid and the reasons which induced the same, so far as the respondent then considered it material and necessary that the same should be set forth."

True it is, there is not one word, one letter, one implication in that message that the President was not acting in good faith under the Tenure of Office act, and desiring the Senate to do the same. So the President of the United States, with a determination to assert at all hazards the tremendous power of removal of every officer, without the consent of the Senate, did not deem it "material or necessary" that the Senate should know that he had suspended Mr. Stanton indefinitely against the provisions of the Tenure of Office act, with full intent at all hazards to remove him, and that the solemn deliberations of the Senate, which the President of the United States was then calling upon them to make in a matter of the highest governmental concern, were only to be of use in case they suited his purpose; that it was not "material or necessary" for the Senate to know that its high decision was futile and useless; that the President was playing fast and loose with this branch of the government—a sort of "heads I win, tails you loose" game—which was never before exercised save by thimble-riggers and sharpers.

If Andrew Johnson never committed any other offense; if we know nothing of him save from this avowal, we should have a full picture of his mind and heart, painted in colors of living light, so that no man will ever mistake his mental and moral lineaments hereafter.

Instead of open and frank dealing, as becomes the head of a great government in every relation of life, and especially needful from the highest executive officer of the government to the highest legislative branch thereof; instead of a manly, straightforward bearing, claiming openly and distinctly the rights which he believed pertained to his high office, and yielding to the other branches, fairly and justly, those which belong to them, we find him, upon his own written confession, keeping back his claims of power, concealing his motives, covering his purposes, attempting by indirection and subterfuge to do that as the ruler of a great nation which, if it be done at all, should have been done boldly, in the face of day; and upon this position he must stand before the Senate and the country if they believe his answer, which I do not, that he had at that time these intents and purposes in his mind, and they are not the subterfuge and evasion and after-thought which a criminal brought to bay makes to escape the consequences of his acts.

Senators! he asked you for time in which to make his answer. You gave him ten days, and this is the answer he makes! If he could do this in ten days, what should we have had if you had given him forty? You show him a mercy in not extending the time for answer.

In the appointment of General Grant *ad interim*, he acted under the act of February 13, 1795, and was subject to its limitations. By the act of August 7, 1789, creating the Department of War, (1st Statutes at Large, page 49), "in case of any vacancy" no provision is made for any appointment of an acting or an *ad interim* Secretary. In that case the records and papers are to be turned over for safe keeping to the custody of the chief clerk. This apparent omission to provide for an executive emergency was attempted to be remedied by Congress by the act of May 8, 1792, (1st Statutes, 281), which provides "that in case of death, absence from the seat of government, or sickness of the Secretary of State, Secretary of the Treasury, or of the Secretary of the War Department, or of any officer of either of the said departments whose appointment is not in the head thereof, whereby they cannot perform the duties of their respective offices, it shall be lawful for the President of the United States, in case he shall think it necessary, to authorize any person or persons, at his discretion, to perform the duties of the said respective offices until a successor be appointed, or until such absence or inability by sickness shall cease."

It will be observed that this act provides for vacancies by death, absence, or sickness only, whereby the head of a department or any officer in it cannot perform his duty, but makes no provision for vacancy by removal.

Two difficulties were found in that provision of law; first, that it provided only for certain enumerated vacancies; and also, it authorizes the President to make an acting appointment of any person for any length of time. To meet these difficulties the act of 13th of February 1795, was passed, (1st Stat. at Large, 415), which provides "in case of vacancy, whereby the Secretaries or any officer in any of the departments cannot perform the duties of his office, the President may appoint any person to perform the duties for a period not exceeding six months."

Thus the law stood as to acting appointments in all of the departments (except the Navy and Interior, which had no provision for any person to act in place of the Secretary), until the 19th of February, 1863, when, by the second section of an act approved at that date (12th Stat., 646), it was "provided that no person acting or assuming to act as a civil, military or naval officer shall have any money paid to him as salary in any office which is not authorized by some previously existing law. The state of the law upon this subject at that point of time is thus:—In case of death, absence or sickness, or of any vacancy whereby a Secretary or other officer of the State, War or Treasury Department could not perform the duties of the office, any person could be authorized by the President to perform those duties for the space of six months.

For the Departments of the Interior and the Navy provision had been made for the appointment of an assistant secretary, but no provision in case of vacancy in his office, and a restriction put upon any officers acting when not authorized by law, from receiving any salary whatever.

To meet those omissions, and to meet the case of resignation of any officer of an executive department, and also to meet what was found to be a defect in allowing the President to appoint any person to those high offices for the space of six months, whether such person had any acquaintance with the duties of the department or not, an act was passed February 20, 1863, (12 Stat., p. 656,) which provides that in case of the death, resignation, absence from the seat of government, or sickness of the head of an executive department of the government, or of any officer of either of the said departments whose appointment is not in the head thereof, whereby they cannot perform the duties of their respective offices, it shall be lawful for the President of the United States, in case he shall think it necessary, to authorize the head of any other executive department or other officer in either of said departments whose appointment is vested in the President, at his discretion, to perform the duties of the said respective offices until a successor be appointed, or until such absence or inability shall cease. Therefore, in case of the death, resignation, sickness, or absence of a head of an executive department, whereby the incumbent could not perform the duties of his office, the President might authorize the head of another executive department to perform the duties of the vacant office, and in case of like disability of any officer of an executive department other than the head, the President might authorize an officer of the same department to perform his duties for the space of six months.

It is remarkable that in all these statutes, from 1789 down, no provision is made for the case of a removal, or that anybody is empowered to act for the removed officer, the chief clerk being empowered to take charge of the books and papers only.

Does not this series of acts conclusively demonstrate a legislative construction of the Constitution that there could be no removal of the chief of an executive department by the act of the President save by the nomination and appointment of his successor, if the Senate were in session, or a qualified appointment till the end of the next session, if the vacancy happened or was made in a recess?

Let us now apply this state of the law to the appointment of Major-General Thomas Secretary of War *ad interim*, by Executive order. Mr. Stanton had neither died nor resigned, was not sick nor absent. If he had been, under the act of March 3, 1863, which repeals all inconsistent acts, the President was authorized only to appoint the head of another executive department to fill his place *ad interim*. Such was not General Thomas. He was simply an officer of the army, the head of a bureau or department of the War Department, and not eligible under the law to be appointed; so that his appointment was an illegal and void act.

There have been two cases of *ad interim* appointments which illustrate and confirm this position; the one was the appointment of Lieutenant-General Scott Secretary of War *ad interim*, and the other the appointment of General Grant *ad interim* upon the suspension of Mr. Stanton, in August last.

The appointment of General Scott was legal, because that was done before the restraining act of March 2, 1863, which requires the detail of the head of another department to act *ad interim*.

The appointment of General Grant to take the place of Mr. Stanton during his suspension would have been illegal under the acts I have cited he being an officer of the army and not the head of a department, if it had not been authorized by the second section of the Tenure of Office act, which provides that in case of suspension, and no other, the President may designate "some suitable person to perform temporarily the duties of such office until the next meeting of the Senate." Now, General Grant was such "suitable person," and was properly enough appointed under that provision.

This answers one ground of the defense which is taken by the President that he did not suspend Mr. Stanton under the Tenure of Office act, but by his general power of suspension and removal of an officer. If the President did not suspend Stanton under the Tenure of Office act, because he deemed it unconstitutional and void, then there was no law authorizing him to appoint General Grant, and that appointment was unauthorized by law and a violation of his oath of office.

But the Tenure of Civil Office bill by its express terms forbids any employment, authorization or appointment of any person in civil office, where the appointment is by and with the advice and consent of the Senate, while the Senate is in session. If this act is constitutional, i. e., if it is not so far in conflict with the paramount law of the land as to be inoperative and void, then the removal of Mr. Stanton and the appointment of General Thomas are both in direct violation of it, and are declared by it to be high misdemeanors.

The intent with which the President has done this is not doubtful, nor are we obliged to rely upon the principle of law that a man must be held to intend the legal consequences of all his acts.

The President admits that he intended to set aside the Tenure of Office act, and thus contravene the Constitution, if that law was unconstitutional.

Having shown that the President wilfully violated an act of Congress, without justification, both in the removal of Stanton and the appointment of Thomas, for the purpose of obtaining wrongfully the possession of the War Office by force, if need be, and certainly by threats and intimidations, for the purpose of controlling its appropriations through its *ad interim* chief, who shall say that Andrew Johnson is not guilty of the high crimes and misdemeanors charged against him in the first eight articles?

The respondent makes answer to this view that the President, believing this Civil Tenure law to be unconstitutional, had a right to violate it, for the purpose of bringing the matter before the Supreme Court for its adjudication.

We are obliged, *in limine*, to ask the attention of the Senate to this consideration, that they may take it with them as our case goes forward.

We claim that the question of the constitutionality fo any law of Congress is, upon this trial, a totally irrelevant one; because all the power or right in the President to judge upon any supposed conflict of an act of Congress with the paramount law of the Constitution is exhausted when he has examined a bill sent him and returned it with his objections. If then passed over his veto it becomes as valid as if in fact signed by him.

The Constitution has provided three methods, all equally potent, by which a bill brought into either House may become a law:—

First. By passage by vote of both Houses, in due form, with the President's signature;

Second. By passage by vote of both Houses, in due form, and the President's neglect to return it within ten days, with his objections;

Third. By passage by vote of both Houses, in due form, a veto by the President, a reconsideration by both Houses, and a passage by a two-thirds vote.

The Constitution substitutes this reconsideration and passage as an equivalent to the President's signature. After that he and all other officers must execute the law, whether in fact constitutional or not.

For the President to refuse to execute a law duly passed because he thought it unconstitutional, after he had vetoed it for that reason, would, in effect, be for him to execute his veto. and leave the law unexecuted.

It may be said he may do this at his peril. True; but that peril is to be impeached for violating his oath of office, as is now being done.

If, indeed, laws duly passed by Congress affecting generally the welfare of any considerable portion of the people had been commonly, or as a usage declared by the Supreme Court unconstitutional, and therefore inoperative, there might seem to be some palliation, if not justification, to the Executive to refuse to execute a law in order to have its constitutionality tested by the Supreme Court.

It is possible to conceive of so flagrant a case of unconstitutionality as to be such shadow of justification to the Executive, provided at the same time one conceives an equally flagrant case of stupidity, ignorance and imbecility, or worse, in the Representatives of the people and in the Senate of the United States; but both conceptions are so rarely possible and absurd as not to furnish a ground of governmental action.

How stands the fact? Has the Supreme Court so frequently declared the laws of Congress in conflict with the Constitution as to afford the President just ground for belief, or hope even, that the court will do so in a given instance? I think I may safely assert, as a legal fact, that since the first decision of the Supreme Court till the day of this arraignment no law passed by Congress, affecting the general welfare, has ever, by the judgment of that court, been set aside or held for naught because of unconstitutionality as the ground-work of its decision.

In three cases only has the judgment of that court been influenced by the supposed conflict between the law and the Constitution, and they were cases affecting the court itself and its own duties, and where the law seemed to interfere with its own prerogatives.

Touching privileges and prerogatives have been the shipwreck of many a wholesome law. It is the sore spot, the sensitive nerve of all tribunals, parliamentary or judicial.

The first case questioning the validity of a law of Congress is Hayburn's (2 Dallas, 409), where the court decided upon the unconstitutionality of the act of March 23, 1792, Statutes at Large, vol. 1, p. 244, which conferred upon the court the power to decide upon and grant certificates of invalid pensions. The court held that such power could not be conferred upon the court as an original jurisdiction, the court receiving all its original jurisdiction from the provisions of the Constitution. This decision would be nearly unintelligible were it not explained in a note to the case in United States vs. Ferreira (13 Howard, p. 52), reporting United States vs. Todd, decided February 17, 1794.

We learn, however, from both cases, the cause of this unintelligibility of the decision in Hayburn's case. When the same question came up at the Circuit Court in New York, the judges being of opinion that the law could not be executed by them as judges, because it was unconstitutional, yet determined to obey it until the case could be adjudicated by the whole court. They therefore, not to violate the law, did execute it as commissioners until it was repealed, which was done the next year.

The judges on the circuit in Pennsylvania all united in a letter to the Executive, most humble apologizing, with great regret, that their convictions of duty did not permit them to execute the law according to its terms, and took special care that this letter should accompany their decision, so that they might not be misunderstood.

Both examples it would have been well for this respondent to have followed before he undertook to set himself to violate an act of Congress.

The next case where the court decided upon any conflict between the Constitution and the law is Gordon vs. United States, tried in April, 1865, seventy-one years afterward, two Justices dissenting, without any opinion being delivered by the court.

The court here dismissed an appeal from the Court of Claims, alleging that, under the Constitution, no appellate jurisdiction could be exercised over the Court of Claims under an act of Congress which gave revisory power to the Secretary of the Treasury over a decision of the Court of Claims. This decision is little satisfactory, as it is wholly without argument or authority cited.

The next case is ex parte Garland (4 Wallace, 333), known as the Attorney's Oath case, where the court decided that an attorney was not an officer of the United States, and, therefore, might practice before that court without taking the test oath.

The reasoning of the court in that case would throw doubt on the constitutionality of the law of Congress, but the decision of the invalidity of the law was not necessary to the decision of the case, which did not command a unanimity in the court, as it certainly did not the assent of the Bar.

Yet in this case it will be observed that the court made a rule requiring the oath to be administered to the attorneys in obedience of the law until it came before them in a cause duly brought up for decision. The Supreme Court obeyed the law up to the time it was set aside. They did not violate it to make a test case.

Here is another example to this respondent, as to his duty in the case, which he will wish he had followed, I may venture to say, when he hears the judgment of the Senate upon the impeachment now pending.

There are several other cases wherein the validity of acts of Congress have been discussed before the Supreme Court, but none where the decision has turned on that point.

In Marbury vs. Madison (1 Cranch, 137), Chief Justice Marshall dismissed the case for want of jurisdiction, took opportunity to deliver a chiding opinion against the administration of Jefferson before he did so.

In the Dred Scot case, so familiar to the public, the court decided it had no jurisdiction, but gave the government and the people a lecture on their political duties.

In the case of Fisher vs. Blight (2 Cranch, 358), the constitutionality of a law was very much discussed, but was held valid by the decision of the court.

In United States vs, Coombs (12 Peters, 72), although the power to declare a law of Congress in conflict with the Constitution was claimed in the opinion of the court *arguendo*, yet the law itself was sustained.

The case of Pollard vs. Hagan (3 Howard, 212), and the two cases, Goodtitle vs. Kibbe (9 Howard, 271), Hallett vs. Beebe (13 Howard. 25), growing out of the same controversy, have been thought to impugn the validity of two private acts of Congress, but a careful examination will show that it was the operation, and not the validity of the acts which came in question and made the basis of the decision.

Thus it may be seen that the Supreme Court, in three instances only, have apparently, by its decision, impugned the validity of an act of Congress because of a conflict with the Constitution, and in each case a question of the rights and prerogatives of the court or its officers has been in controversy.

The cases where the constitutionality of an act of Congress has been doubted in the *obiter dicta* of the court, but were not the basis of decision, are open to other criticisms.

In Marbury vs. Madison, Chief Justice Marshall had just been serving as Secretary of State, in an opposing administration to the one whose acts he was trying to overturn as Chief Justice.

In the Dred Scott case, Chief Justice Taney—selected by General Jackson to remove the deposits. because his bitter partisanship would carry him through where Duane halted and was removed—delivered the opinion of the court, whose *obiter dicta* fanned the flame of dissension which led to the civil war through which the people have just passed, and against that opinion the judgment of the country has long been recorded.

When *ex parte* Garland was decided, the country was just emerging from a conflict of arms, the passions and excitement of which had found their way upon the bench, and some of the judges, just coming from other service of the government and from the bar, brought with them opinions. But I forbear. I am treading on dangerous ground. Time has not yet laid its softening and correcting hand long enough upon this decision to allow me further to comment upon it in this presence.

Mr. President and Senators, can it be said that the possible doubts thrown on three or four acts of Congress, as to their constitutionality, during a judicial experience of seventy-five years—hardly one to a generation—is a sufficient warrant to the President of the United States to set aside and violate any act of Congress whatever, upon the plea that he believed the Supreme Court would hold it unconstitutional when a case involving the question should come before it, and especially one much discussed on its passage, to which the whole mind of the country was turned during the progess of the discussion, upon which he had argued with all his power his constitutional objections, and which, after careful reconsiderations had been passed over his veto.

Indeed, will you hear an argument as a Senate of the United States, a majority of whom voted for that very bill, upon its constitutionality in the trial of an executive officer for wilfully violating it before it had been doubted by any court?

Bearing upon this question, however, it may be said that the President removed Mr. Stanton for the very purpose of testing the constitutionality of this law before the courts, and the question is asked, will you condemn him as for a crime for so doing? If this plea were a true one, it ought not to avail; but it is a subterfuge. We shall show you that he has taken no step to submit the question to any court, although more than a year has elapsed since the passage of the act.

On the contrary, the President has recognized its validity and acted upon it in every department of the government, save in the War Department, and there except in regard to the head thereof solely. We shall show you he long ago caused all the forms of commissions and official bonds of all the civil officers of the government to be altered to conform to its requirement. Indeed, the fact will not be denied—nay, in the very case of Mr. Stanton, he suspended him under its provisions, and asked this very Senate, before whom he is now being tried for its violation, to pass upon the sufficiency of his reasons for acting under it in so doing according to its terms; yet, rendered reckless and mad by the patience of Congress under his usurpation of other powers, and his disregard of other laws, he boldly avows in his letter to the General of the Army that he intends to disregard its provisions, and summons the commander of the troops of this department to seduce him from his duty so as to be able to command, in violation of another act of Congress, sufficient military power to enforce his unwarranted decrees.

The President knew, or ought to have known; his official adviser, who now appears as his counsel, could, and did tell him, doubtless, that he alone, as Attorney-General, could file an information in the nature of a *quo warranto* to determine this question of the validity of the law.

Mr. Stanton, if ejected from office, was without remedy, because a series of decisions has settled the law to be that an ejected officer cannot reinstate himself, either by *quo warranto, mandamus*, or other appropriate remedy in the courts.

If the President had really desired solely to test the constitutionality of the law or his legal right to remove Mr. Stanton, instead of his defiant message to the Senate on the 21st of February, informing them of the removal, but not suggesting this purpose which is thus shown to be an afterthought, he would have said in substance:–"Gentlemen of the Senate, in order to test the constitutionality of the law entitled 'An act regulating the tenure of certain civil offices,' which I verily believe to be unconstitutional and void, I have issued an order of removal of E. M. Stanton from the office of Secretary of the Department of War. I felt myself constrained to make this removal lest Mr. Stanton should answer the information in the nature of a *quo warranto*, which I intend the Attorney-General shall file at an early day, by saying that he holds the office of Secretary of War by the appointment and authority of Mr. Lincoln, which has never been revoked. Anxious that there shall be no collision or disagreement between the several departments of the government and the Executive, I lay before the Senate this message, that the reasons for my action, as well as the action itself, for the purpose indicated, may meet your concurrence."

Had the Senate received such a message, the representatives of the people might never have deemed it necessary to impeach the President for such an act to insure the safety of the country, even if they had denied the accuracy of his legal position.

On the contrary, he issued a letter of removal, peremptory in form, intended to be so in effect, ordering an officer of the army, Lorenzo Thomas, to take possession of the office and eject the incumbent, which he claimed he would do by force, even at the risk of inaugurating insurrection, civil commotion and war.

Whatever may be the decision of the legal question involved when the case comes before the final judicial tribunal, who shall say that such conduct of the Executive, under the circumstances, and in the light of the history of current events and his concomitant action, is not in Andrew Johnson a high crime and misdemeanor? Imagine, if it were possible, the consequence of a decision by the Senate in the negative—a verdict of not guilty upon this proposition.

A law is deliberately passed with all the form of legislative procedure; is presented to the President for his signature; is returned by him to Congress with his objections; is thereupon reconsidered, and by a yea and nay vote of three-quarters of the representatives of the people in the popular branch, and three-fourths of the Senators representing the States in the higher branch, is passed again, notwithstanding the veto; is acquiesced in by the President—by all departments of the government conforming thereto for quite a year, no court having doubted its validity. Now its provisions are wilfully and designedly violated by the President, with intent to usurp to himself the very powers which the law was designed to limit, for the purpose of displacing a meritorious officer whom the Senate just before had determined ought not and should not be removed; for which high-handed act the President is impeached in the name of all the people of the United States, by three-fourths of the House of Representatives, and presented at the bar of the Senate, and by the same Senate that passed the law; nay, more, by the very Senators who, when the proceeding came to their knowledge, after a re-deliberation of many hours, solemnly declared the act unlawful and in violation of the Constitution; yet that act of usurpation is declared not to be a high misdemeanor in office by their solemn verdict of not guilty upon their oaths.

Would not such a judgment be a conscious self-abnegation of the intelligent capacity of the representatives of the people in Congress assembled to frame laws for their guidance in accordance with the principles and terms of their Constitution, and frame of their government?

Would it not be a notification—an invitation, rather—standing to all time, to any bold, bad, aspiring man to seize the liberties of the people, which they had shown themselves incapable of maintaining or defending, and playing the role of a Cæsar or Napoleon here, to establish a despotism, while this, the last and greatest experiment of freedom and equality of right in the people, following the long line of buried republics, sink to its tomb amid the blows of usurped power from which free representative government shall arise to the light of a morn of resurrection never more—never more, forever.

Article ninth charges that Major-General Emory, being in command of the Military Department of Washington, the President called him before him and instructed him that the act of March 2, 1867, which provides that all orders from the President shall be issued through the General of the Army, was unconstitutional and inconsistent with his commission, with intent to induce General Emory to take orders directly from himself and thus hinder the execution of the Civil Tenure act, and to prevent Mr. Stanton from holding his office of Secretary of War.

If the transaction set forth in this article stood alone, we might well admit that doubts might arise as to the sufficiency of the proof. But the surroundings are so pointed and significant as to leave no doubt in the mind of an impartial man as to the interests and purposes of the President. No one would say that the President might not properly send to the commander of this department to make inquiry as to the disposition of his forces, but the question is with what intent and purpose did the President send for General Emory at the time he did?

Time here is an important element of the act. Congress had passed an act in March, 1867, restraining the President from issuing military orders save through the General of the Army. The President had protested against that act. On the 12th of August he had attempted to get possession of the War Office by the removal of the incumbent, but could only do so by appointing the General of the Army thereto. Failing in his attempt to get full possession of the office, through the Senate, he had determined, as he admits, to remove Stanton at all hazards, and endeavored to prevail on the General to aid him in so doing. He declines. For that the respondent quarrels with him, denounces him in the newspapers, and accuses him of bad faith and untruthfulness. Thereupon, asserting his prerogatives as Commander-in-Chief, he creates a new military Department of the Atlantic. He attempts to bribe Lieutenant-General Sherman to take command of it, by promotion to the rank of General by brevet, trusting that his military services would compel the Senate to confirm him.

If the respondent can get a general by brevet appointed, he can then, by simple order, put him on duty according to his brevet rank, and thus have a general of the army in command at Washington, through whom he can transmit his orders and comply with the act which he did not dare transgress, as he had approved it, and get rid of the hated General Grant. Sherman spurned the bribe. The respondent, not discouraged, appointed Major-General George H. Thomas to the same brevet rank, but Thomas declined.

What stimulated the ardor of the President just at that time, almost three years after the war closed, but just after the Senate had reinstated Stanton, to reward military service by the appointment of generals by brevet? Why did his zeal of promotion take that form and no other? There were many other meritorious officers of lower rank desirous of promotion. The purpose is evident to every thinking mind. He had determined to set aside Grant, with whom he had quarreled, either by force or fraud, either in conformity with or in spite of the act of Congress, and control the military power of the country. On the 1st of February (for all these events cluster nearly about the same point of time), he appoints Lorenzo Thomas Secretary of War, and orders Stanton out of the office; Stanton refuses to go; Thomas is about the streets declaring that he will put him out by force—"kick him out"—he has caught his master's word.

On the evening of the 21st a resolution looking to impeachment is offered in the House.

The President, on the morning of the 22d, "as early as practicable," is seized with a sudden desire to know how many troops there were in Washington. What for, just then? Was that all he wanted to know? If so, his Adjutant-General could have given him the official morning report, which would have shown the condition and station of every man. But that was not all. He directs the commander of the department to come as early as practicable.

Why this haste to learn the number of troops? Observe, this order does not go through General Grant, as by law it ought to have done. General Emory, not knowing what is wanted, of course obeyed the order as soon as possible. The President asked him if he remembered the conversation which he had with him when he first took command of the department, as to the strength of the garrison of Washington and the general disposition of the troops in department? Emory replied that "he did distinctly;" that was last September.

Then, after explaining to him fully as to all the changes, the President asked for recent changes of troops. Emory denied they could have been made without the order going through him, and then, with soldierly frankness, (as he evidently suspected what the President was after), said by law no order could come to him save through the General of the Army, and that had been approved by the President and promulgated in general order, No. 17. The President wished to see it. It was produced. General Emory says, "Mr. President, I will take it as a great favor if you will permit me to call your attention to this order or act."

Why a favor to Emory? Because he feared that he was to be called upon by the President to do something in contravention of that law. The President read it and said:— "This is not in accordance with the Constitution of the United States, which makes me Commander-in-Chief of the Army and Navy, or with the language of your commission." Emory then said:—"That is not a matter for the officers to determine. There was the order sent to us approved by him, and we were all governed by that order." He said. "Am I to understand, then, that the President of the United States cannot give an order but through General Grant?" General Emory then made the President a short speech, telling him that the officers of the army had been consulting lawyers on the subject, Reverdy Johnson and Robert J. Walker, and were advised they were bound to obey that order. Said he, "I think it right to tell you the army are a unit on this subject." After a short pause, "seeing there was nothing more to say," General Emory left. What made all the officers consult lawyers about obeying a law of the United States? What influence had been at work with them? The course of the President.

In his message to Congress, in December, he had declared that the time might come when he would resist a law of Congress by force. How could General Emory tell that in the judgment of the President that time had not come, and hence was anxious to assure the President that he could not oppose the law.

In his answer to the first article he asserts that he had fully come to the conclusion to remove Mr. Stanton at all events. notwithstanding the law and the action of the Senate; in other words, he intended to make, and did make, executive resistance to the law duly enacted. The consequence of such resistance he has told us in his message:—

*   *   *   *   *   *   *   *

Where an act has been passed according to the forms of the Constitution by the supreme legislative authority, and is regularly enrolled among the public statutes of the country, Executive resistance to it, especially in times of high party excitement, would be likely to produce violent collision between the respective adherents of the two branches of the government. This would be simply civil war, and civil war must be resorted to only as the last remedy for the worst evils.

*   *   *   *   *   *   *   *

It is true that cases may occur in which the Executive would be compelled to stand on its rights, and maintain them, regardless of all consequences.

*   *   *   *   *   *   *   *

He admits, in substance, that he told Emory that the law was wholly unconstitutional, and, in effect, took away all his power as Commander-in-Chief. Was it not just such a law as he had declared he would resist? Do you not believe that if General Emory had yielded in the least to his suggestions the President would have offered him promotion to bind him to his purposes, as he did Sherman and Thomas?

Pray remember that this is not the case of one gentleman conversing with another on mooted questions of law, but it is the President, the Commander-in-Chief, "the fountain of all honor and source of all power" in the eye of a military officer, teaching that officer to disobey a law which he himself has determined is void, with the power to promote the officer if he finds him an apt pupil.

Is it not a high misdemeanor for the President to assume to instruct the officers of the army that the laws of Congress are not to be obeyed?

Article ten alleges that, intending to set aside the rightful authority and powers of Congress, and to bring into disgrace and contempt the Congress of the United States, and to destroy confidence in and to excite odium against Congress and its laws, he, Andrew Johnson, President of the United States, made divers speeches set out therein, whereby he brought the office of President into contempt, ridicule, and disgrace.

To sustain these charges there will be put in evidence the short-hand notes of the reporters in each instance who took these speeches, or examined the sworn copies thereof, and in one instance where the speech was examined and corrected by the private secretary of the President himself.

To the charges of this article the respondent answers that a convention of delegates (whom he does not say) sat in Philadelphia for certain political purposes mentioned, and appointed a committee to wait upon the respondent as President of the United States; that they were received, and their Chairman, the Hon. Reverdy Johnson, then and now a Senator of the United States, addressed the respondent in a speech, a copy of which the respondent believes is from a substantially correct report, is made a part of the answer; that the respondent made a reply to the address of the committee. While, however, he gives us in his answer a copy of the speech made to him by Mr. Reverdy Johnson, taken from a newspaper, he wholly omits to give us an authorized version of his own speech, about which he may be supposed to know quite as much, and thus saved us some testimony. He does not admit that the extracts from his speech in the articles are correct, nor does he deny that they are so?

In regard to the speech at Cleveland, he again does not admit that the extracts correctly or justly present his speech; but again he does not deny that it does so far as the same is set out.

As to the speech at St. Louis, he does not deny that he made it; says only that he does not admit it, and requires, in each case, that the whole speech shall be proved. In that, I beg leave to assure him and the Senate, his wishes shall be gratified in their fullest fraction. The Senate shall see the performance, so far as is in our power to photograph the scene by evidence, on all those occasions, and shall hear every material word that he said.

His defense, however, to the article is that "he felt himself in duty bound to express opinions of and concerning the public character, conduct, views, purposes, motives and tendencies of all men engaged in the public service, as well in Congress as otherwise," "and that for anything he may have said on either of those occasions he is justified under the constitutional right of freedom of opinion and freedom of speech, and is not subject to greater inquisition, impeachment or inculpation in any manner or form whatsoever." He denies, however, that by reason of any matter in said article or its specification alleged he has said or done anything indecent or unbecoming in the Chief Magistrate of the United States, or tending to bring his high office into contempt, ridicule or disgrace.

The issue, then, finally, is this:—That those utterances of his, in the manner and form in which they are alleged to have been made, and under the circumstances and at the time they were made, are decent and becoming the President of the United States, and do not tend to bring the office into ridicule and disgrace.

We accept the issues. They are two:—

First. That he has the right to say what he did of Congress in the exercise of freedom of speech; and, second, that what he did say in those speeches was a highly gentlemanlike and proper performance in a citizen, and still more becoming in a President of the United States.

Let us first consider the graver matter of the assertion of the right to cast contumely upon Congress; to denounce it as a "body hanging on the verge of the government;" "pretending to be a Congress when in fact it was not a Congress;" "a Congress pretending to be for the Union, when its every step and act tended to perpetuate disunion, and make a disruption of the States inevitable;" "a Congress in a minority assuming to exercise a power which, if allowed to be consummated, would result in despotism and monarchy itself;" "a Congress which had done everything to prevent the union of the States;" "a Congress factious and domineering;" "a Radical Congress which gave origin to another rebellion;" "a Congress upon whose skirts was every drop of blood that was shed in the New Orleans riots."

You will find these denunciations had a deeper meaning than mere expressions of opinion. It may be taken as an axiom in the affairs of nations that no usurper has ever seized upon the legislature of his country until he has familiarized the people with the possibility of so doing by vituperation and decrying it. Denunciatory attacks upon the legislature have always preceded; slanderous abuse of the individuals composing it have always accompanied a seizure by a despot of the legislative power of a country.

Two memorable examples in modern history will spring to the recollection of every man. Before Cromwell drove out by the bayonet the Parliament of England, he and his partisans had denounced it, derided it, decried it and defamed it, and thus brought it into ridicule and contempt. He vilified it with the same name which it is a significant fact the partisans of Johnson, by a concerted cry, applied to the Congress of the United States when he commenced his memorable pilgrimage and crusade against it. It is a still more significant fact that the justification made by Cromwell and by Johnson for setting aside the authority of Parliament and Congress, respectively, was precisely the same, to wit: that they were elected by part of the people only.

When Cromwell, by his soldiers, finally entered the hall of Parliament to disperse its members, he attempted to cover the enormity of his usurpation by denouncing this man personally as a libertine, that as a drunkard, another as the betrayer of the liberties of the people. Johnson started out on precisely the same course, but forgetting the parallel too early he proclaims this patriot an assassin that statesman a traitor; threatens to hang that man whom the people delight to honor, and breathes out "threatenings and slaughter" against this man whose services in the cause of human freedom has made his name a household word wherever the language is spoken. There is, however, an appreciable difference between Cromwell and Johnson, and there is a like difference in the results accomplished by each.

When Bonaparte extinguished the legislature of France, he waited until through his press and his partisans, and by his own denunciations, he brought its authority into disgrace and contempt; and when, finally, he drove the council of the nation from their chamber, like Cromwell, he justified himself by personal abuse of the individuals themselves as they passed by him.

That the attempt of Andrew Johnson to overthrow Congress has failed, is because of the want of ability and power, not of malignity and will.

We are too apt to overlook the danger which may come from words:—

"We are inclined to say that is only talk—wait till some act is done, and then it will be time to move. But words may be, and sometimes are, things—living, burning things that set a world on fire."

As a most notable instance of the power of words, look at the inception of the Rebellion through which we have just passed. For a quarter of a century the nation took no notice of the talk of disunion and Secession which was heard in Congress and on the "stump" until in the South a generation was taught them by word, and the word suddenly burst forth into terrible, awful war. Does any one doubt that if Jackson had hanged Calhoun in 1832 for talking nullification and Secession, which was embryo treason, the cannon of South Carolina against Fort Sumter would never been heard with all their fearful and deadly consequences? Nay, more; if the United States officers, Senators, and Representatives, had been impeached or disqualified from office in 1832 for advocating Secession on the "stump," as was done in 1862 by Congress, then our sons and brothers, now dead in battle, or starved in prison, had been alive and happy, and a peaceful solution of the question of slavery had been found.

Does any one doubt that if the intentions of the respondent could have been carried out, and his denunciations had weakened the Congress in the affections of the people, so that those who had in the North sympathized with the Rebellion could have elected such a minority even of the Representatives to Congress as, together with those sent up from the governments organized by Johnson in the rebellious States, they should have formed a majority of both or either House of Congress, that the President would have recognized such body as the legitimate Congress, and attempted to carry out its decrees by the aid of the army and navy and the Treasury of the United States, over which he now claims such unheard-of and illimitable powers, and thus lighted the torch of civil war?

In all earnestness, Senators, I call each one of you, upon his conscience, to say whether he does not believe, by such preponderance of evidence drawn from the acts of the respondent since he has been in office, that if the people had not been, as they ever have been, true and loyal to their Congress and themselves, such would not have been the result of these usurpations of power in the Executive.

Is it, indeed, to be seriously argued here that there is a constitutional right in the President of the United States, who, during his official life, can never lay aside his official character to denounce, malign, abuse, ridicule and contemn, openly and publicly, the Congress of the United States—a co-ordinate branch of the government.

It cannot fail to be observed that the President (shall I dare to say his counsel, or are they compelled by the exigencies of their defense,) have deceived themselves as to the gravamen of the charge in this article? It does not raise the question of freedom of speech, but of propriety and decency of speech and conduct in a high officer of the government.

Andrew Johnson, the private citizen, as I may reverently hope and trust he soon will be, has the full constitutional right to think and speak what he pleases; in the manner he pleases, and where he pleases, provided always he does not bring himself within the purview of the common law offenses of being a common railer and brawler, or a common scold, which he may do (if a male person is ever liable to commit that crime); but the dignity of station, the proprieties of position, the courtesies of office, all of which are a part of the common law of the land, require the President of the United States to observe that gravity of deportment, that fitness of conduct, that appropriateness of demeanor, and those amenities of behavior which are a part of his high official functions.

He stands before the youth of the country the exemplar of all that is of worth in ambition, and all that is to be sought in aspiration; he stands before the men of the country as the grave magistrate who occupies, if he does not fill, the place once occupied by Washington; nay, far higher and of greater consequence, he stands before the world as the representative of free institutions, as the type of a man whom the suffrages of a free people have chosen as their chief. He should be the living evidence of how much better, higher, nobler, and more in the image of God is the elected ruler of a free people than a hereditary monarch coming into power by the accident of birth; and when he disappoints all these hopes and all these expectations, and becomes the ribald, scurrilous blasphemer, bandying epithets and taunts with a jeering mob, shall he be heard to say that such conduct is not a high misdemeanor in office? Nay, that disappointing the hopes, causing the cheeks to burn with shame, exposing to the taunts and ridicule of every nation the good name and fame of the chosen institutions of thirty millions of people, is it not the highest possible crime and misdemeanor in office? and under the circumstances, the gravamen of these charges? The words are not alleged to be either false or defamatory, because it is not within the power of any man, however high his official position, in effect to slander the citizens of the United States, in the ordinary sense of that word, so as to call on Congress to answer as to truth of the accusation. We do not go in, therefore, to any question of truth or falsity. We rest upon the scandal of the scene. We would as soon think, in the trial of an indictment against a termagant as a common scold, of summoning witnesses to prove that what she said was not true. It is the noise and disturbance in the neighborhood that is the offense, and not a question of the provocation or irritation which causes the outbreak.

At the risk of being almost offensive, but protesting that if so it is not my fault, but that of the person whose acts I am describing, let me but faintly picture to you the scene at Cleveland and St. Louis.

It is evening; the President of the United States on a journey to do homage at the tomb of an illustrious statesman, accompanied by the head of the Army and Navy and Secretary of State, has arrived in the great central city of the continent. He has been welcomed by the civic authorities. He has been escorted by a procession of the benevolent charitable societies, and citizens and soldiers to his hotel. He has returned thanks in answer to an address of the Mayor to the citizens who have received him. The hospitality of the city has provided a banquet for him and his suite, when he is again expected to address the chosen guests of the city, where all things may be conducted in decency and in order.

While he was resting, as one would have supposed he would have to do, from the fatigues of the day, a noisy crowd of men and boys, washed and unwashed, drunk and sober, black and white, assemble in the street, who make night hideous by their bawling; quitting the drawing-room without the advice of his friends, the President of the United States rushes forth on to the balcony of the hotel to address what proves to have been a mob, and this he calls in his answer a "fit occasion on which he has held to the high duty of expressing opinions of and concerning the legislation of Congress, proposed or completed, in respect of its wisdom, expediency, justice, worthiness, objects, purposes, and public and political motives and tendencies.

Observe now, upon this fit occasion, like in all respects to that at Cleveland, when the President is called upon by the constitutional requirements of his office to explain "the evidence, expediency, justice, worthiness, objects, purposes and tendencies of the acts of Congress," what he says and the manner in which he says it. Does he speak with the gravity of a Marshall when expounding constitutional law? Does he use the polished sentences of a Wirt? Or, failing in these, which may be his misfortune, does he, in plain homely words of truth and soberness, endeavor to instruct the men and youth before him in their duty to obey the laws and to reverence their rulers, and to prize their institutions of government? Although he may have been mistaken in the aptness of the occasion for such didactic instructions, still good teaching is never thrown away. He shows, however, by his language, as he had shown at Cleveland, that he meant to adapt himself to the occasion. He had hardly opened his mouth, as we shall show you, when some one in the crowd cried, "How about our British subjects?"

The Chief Executive, supported by his Secretary of State, so that all the foreign relations and diplomatic service were fully represented, with a dignity that not even his counsel can appreciate, and with an amenity which must have delighted Downing street, answers:—"We will attend to John Bull after awhile, so far as that is concerned." The mob, ungrateful, receive this bit of expression of opinion upon the justice, worthiness, objects, purposes and public and political motives and tendencies of our relations with the Kingdom of Great Britain, as they fell from the honored lips of the President of the United States. with laughter, and the more unthinking, with cheers.

Having thus disposed of our diplomatic relations with the first naval and commercial nation on earth, the President next proceeds to instruct in the manner aforesaid and for the purpose aforesaid to this noisy mob, on the subject of the riots, upon which his answer says, "it is the constitutional duty of the President to express opinion for the purposes aforesaid." A voice calls out "New Orleans! —go on!" After a graceful exordium, the President expresses his high opinion that a massacre, wherein his pardoned and unpardoned Rebel associates and friends deliberately shot down and murdered unarmed Union men without provocation—even Horton, the minister of the living God, as his hands were raised to the Prince of Peace, praying, in the language of the great martyr:— "Father, forgive them, for they know not what they do!" —was the result of the laws passed by the legislative department of your government in the words following, that is to say—

"If you will take up the riot at New Orleans, and trace it back to its source, or to its immediate cause, you will find out who was responsible for the blood that was shed there.

"If you take up the riot at New Orleans, and take it back to the Radical Congress—."

This, as we might expect, was received by the mob, composed, doubtless, in large part of unrepentant Rebels, with great cheering, and cries of "Bully!" It was "bully" for them to learn, on the authority of the President of the United States, that they might shoot down Union men and patriots and lay the sin of the murder upon the Congress of the United States! And this was another bit of opinion, which the counsel say it was the high duty of the President to express upon the justice, the worthiness, objects, "purposes and public political motives and tendencies of the legislation of your Congress." After some further debate with the mob some one, it seems, had called "Traitor."

The President of the United States. on this fitting, constitutional occasion, immediately took this as personal, and replies to it:—"Now, my countrymen, it is very easy to indulge in epithets; it is very easy to call a man a Judas, and cry out traitor; but when he is called upon to give arguments and facts, he is very often found wanting."

What were the "facts that were found wanting," which, in the mind of the President, prevented him from being a Judas Iscariot? He shall state the wanting facts in his own language on this occasion, when he is exercising his high constitutional prerogative.

"Judas Iscariot! Judas! There was a Judas once; one of the twelve Apostles. Oh! yes; the twelve Apostles had a Christ. (A voice, 'and a Moses too;' great laughter.) The twelve Apostles had a Christ, and he never could have had a Judas unless he had had the twelve Apostles. If I have played the Judas, who has been my Christ that I have played the Judas with? Was it Thad. Stevens? Was it Wendell Phillips? Was it Charles Sumner?"

If it were not that the blasphemy shocks us, we should gather from all this that it dwelt in the mind of the President of the United States, that the only reason why he was not a Judas was that he had not been able to find a Christ towards whom to play the Judas.

It would appear that this "opinion," given in pursuance of his constitutional obligation, was received with cheers and hisses. Whether the cheers were that certain patriotic persons named by him might be hanged, or the hissing was because of the inability of the President to play the part of Judas, for the reasons before stated, I am sorry to say the evidence will not inform us.

His answer makes the President say that it is his "duty to express opinions concerning the public characters, and the conduct, views, purposes, objects, motives and tendencies of all men engaged in the public service."

Now, as "the character, motives, tendencies, purposes, objects and views of Judas alone had opinions expressed" about them on this fit occasion (although he seemed to desire to have some others, whose names he mentioned, hanged), I shall leave his counsel to inform you what were the public services of Judas Iscariot, to say nothing of Moses, which it was the constitutional duty and right of the President of the United States to discuss on this particularly "fit occasion."

But I will not pursue this revolting exhibition any further.

I will only show you at Cleveland the crowd and the President of the United States, in the darkness of night, bandying epithets with each other, crying:—"Mind your dignity, Andy;" "Don't get mad, Andy;" "Bully for you, Andy."

I hardly dare shock, as I must, every sense of propriety by calling your attention to the President's allusion to the death of the sainted martyr, Lincoln, as the means by which he attained his office; and if it can be justified in any man, public or private, I am entirely mistaken in the commonest properties of life. The President shall tell his own story:—

"There was two years ago a ticket before you for the Presidency. I was placed upon that ticket with a distinguished citizen now no more. (Voices—'It's a pity!') 'Too bad!' 'Unfortunate!') Yes; I know there are some who say 'unfortunate!' Yes; unfortunate for some that God rules on high and deals in justice. (Cheers.) Yes, unfortunate; the ways of Providence are mysterious and incomprehensible, controlling all who exclaim 'unfortunate.'"

Article 11 charges that the President having denied in a public speech on the 18th of August, 1866, at Washington. that the Thirty-ninth Congress was authorized to exercise legislative power, and denying that the legislation of said Congress was valid or obligatory upon him, or that it had power to propose certain amendments to the Constitution, did attempt to prevent the execution of the act entitled "An act Regulating the Tenure of Certain Civil Offices," by unlawfully attempting to devise means by which to prevent Mr. Stanton from resuming the functions of the office of Secretary of the Department of War, notwithstanding the refusal of the Senate to concur in his suspension, and that he also contrived means to prevent the execution of an act of March 2, 1867, which provides that all military orders shall be issued through the General of the Army of the United States; and also another act of the same 2d of March, commonly known as the Reconstruction act. To sustain this charge proof will be given of his denial of the authority of Congress, as charged; also his letter to the General of the Army, in which he admits that he endeavored to prevail on him, by promises of pardon and indemnity, to disobey the requirements of the Tenure of Office act, and to hold the office of Secretary of War against Mr. Stanton after he had been reinstated by the Senate; that he chided the General for not acceding to his request, and declared that had he known that he (Grant) would not have acceded to his wishes, he would have taken other means to prevent Mr. Stanton from resuming his office; his admissions in his answer, was that his purpose was, from the first suspension of Mr. Stanton, on August 12, 1867, to oust him from his office, notwithstanding the decision of the Senate under the act; his order to General Grant to refuse to recognize any order of Mr. Stanton purporting to come from himself after he was so reinstated, and his order to General Thomas, as an officer of the army of the United States, to take possession of the War Office, not transmitted, as it should have been, through the General of the Army; and the declarations of General Thomas that, as an officer of the Army of the United States, he felt bound to obey the orders of the Commander-in-Chief.

To prove further the purpose and intent with which his declarations were made, and his denial of the power of Congress to propose amendments to the Constitution as one of the means employed by him to prevent the execution of the acts of Congress, we shall show he has opposed and hindred the pacification of the country and the return of the insurrectionary States to the Union, and has advised the Legislature of the State of Alabama not to adopt the Constitutional Amendment, known as the fourteenth article. when appealed to to know if it was best for the Legislature so to do, and this, to, after that amendment had been adopted by a majority of the loyal State Legislatures, and after, in the election of 1866, it had been sustained by an overwhelming majority of the loyal people of the United States. I do not propose comment further on this article, because, if the Senate shall have decided that all the acts charged in the preceding articles are justified by law, then so large a part of the intent and purposes with which the respondent is charged in this article would fail of proof, that it would be difficult to say whether he might not, with equal impunity, violate the laws known as the Reconstruction acts, which in his message he declares "as plainly unconstitutional as any that can be inaugurated." If that be so, why should he not violate them? If, therefore, the judgment of the Senate shall sustain us upon the other articles, we shall take judgment upon this by confession, as the respondent declares in the same message that he does not intend to execute them.

Is it wonderful at all that such a speech, which seems to have been unprovoked and coolly uttered, should have elicited the single response from the crowd, "Bully for you?"

I go no further. I might follow this ad nauseam. I grant the President of the United States further upon this disgraceful scene the mercy of my silence. Tell me, now, who can read this account of this exhibition, and reflect that the result of our institutions of government has been to place such a man, so lost to decency and propriety of conduct, so unfit, in the high office of ruler of this nation, without blushing and hanging his head in shame as the finger of scorn and contempt for republican democracy is pointed at him by some advocate of monarchy in the old world?

What answer have you when an intelligent foreigner says, "Look! see! this is the culmination of the ballot unrestrained in the hands of a free people in a country where any man may aspire to the office of President. Is not our government of an hereditary king or emperor a better one, where at least our sovereign is born a gentleman, than to have such a thing as this for a ruler?"

Yes, we have an answer. We can say this man was not the choice of the people for the President of the United States. He was thrown to the surface by the whirlpool of a civil war, and carelessly, we grant, was elected to the second place in the government, without thought that he might ever fill the first. By murder most foul, he succeeded to the Presidency, and is the elect of an assassin to that high office, and not of the people. "It was a grievous fault, and grievously have we answered it;" but let me tell you, oh, advocate of monarchy, that our form of goverment gives us a remedy for such misfortune, which yours, with its divine right of kings, does not. We can remove, as we are about to do, from the office he has disgraced, by the sure, safe and constitutional method of impeachment; while your king, if he becomes a buffoon, or a jester, or a tyrant, can only be displaced through revolution, bloodshed and civil war. This—this, oh monarchist! is the crowning glory of our institutions; because of which, if for no other reason, our form of government claims precedence over all other governments of the earth.

To the bar of this high tribunal, invested with all its great powers and duties, the House of Representatives has brought the President of the United States by the most solemn form of accusation, charging him with high crimes and misdemeanors in office, as set forth in the several articles which I have thus feebly presented to your attention. Now, it seems necessary that I should briefly touch upon and bring freshly to your remembrance the history of some of the events of his administration of affairs in high office, in order that the intents with which and the purposes for which the respondent committed the acts alleged against him may be fully understood.

Upon the first reading of the articles of impeachment, the question might have arisen in the mind of some Senator, why are these acts of the President only presented by the House, when history informs us that others equally dangerous to the liberties of the people, if not more so, and others of equal usurpation of powers, if not greater, are passed by in silence?

To such possible inquiry we reply, that the acts set out in the first eight articles are but the culmination of a series of wrongs, malfeasances and usurpations committed by the respondent, and, therefore, need to be examined in the light of his precedent and concomitant acts, to grasp their scope and design. The last three articles presented show the perversity and malignity with which he acted, so that the man, as he is known to us, may be clearly spread upon record, to be seen and known of all men hereafter.

What has been the respondent's course of administration? For the evidence we rely upon common fame and current history, as sufficient proof. By the common law, common fame, *si oriatur apud bonos et graves*, was ground of indictment even; more than two hundred and forty years ago it was determined in Parliament that common fame is a good ground for the proceeding of this House, either to inquire of here or to transmit to the complaint, if the House find cause, to the King or Lords."

Now, is it not well known to all good and brave men, (*bonos et graves*,) that Andrew Johnson entered the office of President of the United States at the close of an armed Rebellion, making loud denunciations, frequently and everywhere, "that traitors ought to be punished, and treason should be made odious; that the loyal and true men of the South should be fostered and encouraged; and, if there were but few of them, to such only should be given in charge the reconstruction of the disorganized States."

Do not all men know that soon afterwards he changed his course, and only made treason odious, so far as he was concerned, by appointing traitors to office, and by indiscriminate pardon to all who "came in unto him?" Who does not know that Andrew Johnson initiated, of his own will, a course of reconstruction of the Rebel States, which, at at the time, he claimed was provisional only, and until the meeting of Congress an its action thereon?

Who does not know that when Congress met and undertook to legislate upon this very subject of reconstruction, of which he had advised them in his message, which they alone had the power to do, Andrew Johnson, last aforesaid, again changed his course, and declared that Congress had no power to legislate upon that subject, but that the two houses had only the power separately to judge of the qualifications of the members who might be sent to each by rebellious constituencies, acting under State organizations which Andrew Johnson had called into existence by his late fiat, the electors of which were voting by his permission and under his limitations?

Who does not know that when Congress, assuming its rightful power to propose amendments to the Constitution, had passed such an amendment, and had submitted it to the States as a measure of pacification, Andrew Johnson advised and counseled the Legislatures of the States lately in Rebellion, as well as others, to reject the amendment, so that it might not operate as law and thus establish equality of suffrage in all the States and equality of rights in the number of the Electoral College and in the number of the Representatives to the Congress of the United States.

Lest any one should doubt the correctness of this piece of history, or the truth of this common fame, we shall show you that, while the Legislature of Alabama was deliberating upon the reconsideration of the vote whereby it had rejected the constitutional amendment, the fact being brought to the knowledge of Andrew Johnson, and his advice asked, he, by a telegraphic message under his own hand, here to be produced, to show his intent and purposes, advised the Legislature against passing the amendment, and to remain firm in their opposition to Congress.

We shall show like advice of Andrew Johnson upon the same subject to the Legislature of South Carolina, and this, too, in the winter of 1867, after the action of Congress in proposing the constitutional amendments had been sustained in the previous election by an overwhelming majority. Thus we charge that Andrew Johnson, President of the United States, not only endeavors to thwart the constitutional action of Congress, and bring it to naught but, also to hinder and oppose the execution of the will of the loyal people of the United States, expressed in the only mode in which it can be done, through the ballot box, in the election of their representatives. Who does not know that from the hour he began these, his usurpations of power, he everywhere denounced Congress, the legality and constitutionality of its action, and defied its legitimate power; and for that purpose announced his intention and carried out his purpose, as far as he was able, of removing every true man from office who sustained the Congress of the United States? And it is to carry out this plan of action that he claims the unlimited power of removal, for the illegal exercise of which he stands before you to-day.

Who does not know that in pursuance of the same plan he used his veto power indiscriminately to prevent the passage of wholesome laws, enacted for the pacification of the country, and when laws were passed by the constitutional majorities over his vetoes he made the most determined opposition, both open and covert, to them; and for the purpose of making that opposition effectual he endeavored to array, and did array, all the people lately in rebellion to set themselves against Congress, and against the true and loyal men, their neighbors, so that murders, assassinations and massacres were rife all over the Southern States, which he encouraged by his refusal to consent that a single murderer should be punished, though thousands of good men have been slain; and, further, that he attempted, by military orders, to prevent the execution of acts of Congress by the military commanders who were charged therewith. These, and his concurrent acts show conclusively that his attempt to get control of the military force of the government, by the seizure of the Department of War, was done in pursuance of his general design, if it were possible, to overthrow the Congress of the United States, and he now claims, by his answer, the right to control at his own will, for the execution of this very design, every officer of the army, navy, civil and diplomatic service of the United States. He asks you here, Senators, by your solemn adjudication, to confirm him in that right—to invest him with that power, to be used with the intents and for the purposes which he has already shown.

The responsibility is with you; the safeguards of the Constitution against usurpation are in your hands; the interests and hopes of free institutions wait upon your action. The House of Representatives has done its duty. We have presented the facts in the constitutional manner; we have brought the criminal to your bar, and demand judgment at your hands for his great crimes.

Never again, if Andrew Johnson go quit and free this day, can the people of this or any other country, by constitutional checks or guards, stay the usurpation of Executive power. I speak, therefore, not the language of exaggeration, but the words of truth and soberness, in saying that the future political welfare and liberties of all men hang trembling on the decision of the hour.

Recess.

At five minutes before three o'clock, Senator WILSON interrupted Mr. Butler to move that the Senate take a recess of ten minutes.

Mr. BUTLER—I am very much obliged to the Senator.

The Chief Justice put the question on the motion and declared it adopted, and the Senate took a recess accordingly.

Business Resumed.

The Chief Justice promptly called the Senate to order at the expiration of the ten minutes, and Mr. Butler concluded his opening at seventeen minutes before four. His description of the scenes at St. Louis caused several audible titters in the gallery, particularly, when bowing low to the President's counsel, he reiterated with emphasis the words "high constitutional prerogative."

Mr. BINGHAM of the managers, then rose and said:—Mr. President, the managers on the part of the House are ready to proceed with the testimony to make good the articles of impeachment exhibited by the House of Representatives against the President of the United States, and my associate, Mr. Wilson, will present the testimony.

Mr. WILSON—I wish to state in behalf of the managers that, notwithstanding the meaning of the document which we deem important to be presented in evidence have been set out in the exhibits accompanying the answers, and also in some of the answers, we still are of the opinion that it is proper for us to produce the documents originally, by way of guarding against any mishap that might arise from imperfect copies set out in the answer.

I offer, first, on behalf of the managers, a certified

copy of the oath of office of the President of the United States, which I will read:—

I do solemnly swear that I will faithfully execute the office of President of the United States, and will, to the best of my ability, preserve, protect and defend the Constitution. (Signed.)   ANDREW JOHNSON.

To which is attached the following certificate:—

I, Salmon P. Chase. Chief Justice of the Supreme Court of the United States, hereby certify, that on the 15th day of April, 1865, at the City of Washington, in the District of Columbia, personally appeared Andrew Johnson, Vice President, upon whom, by the death of Abraham Lincoln. late President, the duties of the office of President have devolved, and took and subscribed the oath of office above, &c. (Signed.)   SALMON P. CHASE, Chief Justice.

Mr. WILSON read the attestation of the document by Frederick W. Seward, acting Secretary of State, and continued, I now offer the nomination of Mr. Stanton as Secretary of War, by President Lincoln. It is as follows:—

IN EXECUTIVE SESSION SENATE OF THE UNITED STATES, January 13, 1862.—The following message was received from the President of the United States, by Mr. Nicolay, his Secretary:—

To the Senate of the United States:—I nominate Edwin M. Stanton, of Pennsylvania, to be Secretary of War, in place of Simon Cameron, nominated to be Minister to Russia. (Signed.)   ABRAHAM LINCOLN.

Executive Mansion, January 13, 1862.

I next offer the ratification of the Senate in Executive session, upon the said nomination:—

IN EXECUTIVE SESSION, SENATE OF THE UNITED STATES, Jan. 15, 1862.

Resolved, That the Senate advise and consent to the appointment of Edwin M. Stanton, of Pennsylvania, to be Secretary of War, agreeably to the appointment.

Mr. WILSON read the certification of the Secretary of the Senate.

I next offer a copy of the communication made to the Senate December 12, 1867, by the President. As this document is somewhat lengthy, I will not read it unless desired.

It is the message of the President of the United States assigning his reasons for the suspension of the Secretary of War.

Several Senators—"Read it."

Mr. WILSON proceeded to read the somewhat lengthy document at twenty minutes past four o'clock.

Senator SHERMAN rose and said:—Mr. President, if the honorable managers would allow me, I would move to adjourn.

Mr. STANBERY said as far as the counsel were concerned they would dispense with the reading.

Senator SHERMAN—I move that the Senate, sitting as a court of impeachment, adjourn until to-morrow, at the usual hour.

Mr. SUMNER suggested an adjournment until 10 o'clock to-morrow, but the Chief Justice put the question on Mr. Sherman's motion, and declared it carried.

The Chief Justice then vacated the chair.

PROCEEDINGS OF TUESDAY, MARCH 31.

The Senate met at noon. After the presentation of a few unimportant petitions, the Chair was vacated, and immediately assumed by the Chief Justice.

The Sergeant-at-Arms made the usual proclamation, and the managers and members of the House were successively announced and took their seats. The counsel for the President also entered and were seated.

The galleries, at the opening, were not more than half full.

Additional Evidence.

Mr. WILSON, on the part of the managers, said in continuation of the documentary evidence, I now offer a resolution passed by the Senate in Executive Session, in response to the message of the President, notifying the Senate of the suspension of Hon. Edwin M. Stanton as Secretary of War. Also, the resolution adopted in Executive Session of the Senate, January 13, 1868, declaring that the Senate did not concur in the suspension of Edwin M. Stanton from

the office of Secretary of War, was read and put in evidence, together with the order of the same date directing the Secretary of the Senate to communicate an official and authenticated copy thereof [to the President, Mr. Stanton and General Grant.

Mr. WILSON then produced and offered in evidence an extract from the Journal of the Senate in Executive Session of February 21, 1868, showing the proceedings of the Senate on the message of the President, announcing that he had suspended Mr. Stanton from office.

Mr. WILSON also produced and' offered in evidence an authentic copy of the commission of Edwin M. Stanton as Secretary of War; stating at the same time that that was the only commission under which the managers claim that Mr. Stanton had acted as Secretary of War. The commission is in the usual form, and contains a provision that Edwin M. Stanton shall have and hold the office, with all the powers, privileges and emoluments pertaining to the same, during the pleasure of the President of the United States for the time being. It is dated June 15, 1862, and signed by Abraham Lincoln.

The First Witness.

The first witness called by the managers was William McDonald, one of the clerks of the Senate. Before proceeding to examine him, Mr. BUTLER asked, in behalf of the managers, that the witnesses who were in attendance should be allowed to remain on the floor of the Senate.

The Chief Justice intimated that they had better remain in the room assigned to them by the Sergeant-at-Arms until they were called.

The witness took his stand by the left of the Secretary's desk, and was sworn by the Secretary in the following form, and with uplifted hand:—

"You do swear, that the evidence you shall give in the case now pending, the United States vs. Andrew Johnson, shall be the truth, the whole truth, and nothing but the truth, so help you God."

The examination was conducted by Mr. Butler, as follows:—

Question. State your name and office. Answer. William J. McDonald, Chief Clerk of the Senate.

Look at this paper, and read the certificate which appears to be signed by your name.

Witness reads as follows:—

OFFICE OF THE SECRETARY OF THE SENATE OF THE UNITED STATES, WASHINGTON, February 27, 1868.—An attested copy of the foregoing resolutions was left by me at the office of the President of the United States, in the Executive Mansion, he not being present, about 9 o'clock P. M., on the 13th of January, 1868,
W. J. McDONALD,
Chief Clerk of the Senate of the United States.

Q. Is that certificate a correct one of the acts done? Is it a correct certificate of the acts done, and the paper was left as that certificate states? A. It was.

Read this other certificate.

Witness reads as follows:—

OFFICE OF THE SECRETARY OF THE SENATE OF THE UNITED STATES, WASHINGTON, Feb. 21, 1868.—An attested copy of the foregoing resolution was delivered by me into the hands of the President of the United States, at his office in the Executive mansion, at about 10 o'clock P. M., on the 21st of February, 1868.   W. J. McDONALD,
Chief Clerk of the Senate of the United States.

Q. Do you make the same statement as regards this service? A. Yes, sir, the same statement.

Mr. WILSON then read the resolutions of the Senate of January 13, 1868, and February 22, 1868, to the service of which the last witness had testified. The resolution of January 13, 1868, is that by which the Senate refuses to concur in the suspension of Mr. Stanton, and the resolution of February 22, 1868, is that by which the Senate resolves that under the Constitution and laws of the United State, the President has no power to remove the Secretary of War and to designate another officer to perform the duties of that office ad interim.

Mr. Jones' Testimony.

The next witness called was J. W. Jones, who was examined by Mr. Butler, as follows:—

Q. State your name and position? A. J.W. Jones, Keeper of the Stationery of the Senate.

Q. You are an officer of the Senate? Yes.

Q. State whether or not you know Major-General Lorenzo Thomas, Adjutant-General of the United States Army? A. I do.

Q. How long have you known him? A. I have known him six or seven years.

Q. Were you employed by the Secretary of the Senate to serve on him a notice of the proceedings of the Senate? A. I was.

Q. Looking at this memorandum, when did you attempt to make the service? A. On the 21st of February, 1868.

Where "Ad Interim" was Found.

Q. Where did you find him? A. I found him at the Marines' Hall Masked Ball.

Q. Was he masked? A. He was.

Q. How did you know it was he? A. I saw his shoulder-straps and asked him to unmask.

Q. Did he do so? A. He did.

Q. After ascertaining that it was he, what did you do? A. I handed him a copy of the resolution of the Senate.

Q. About what time of the day or night? A. About eleven o'clock at night.

Q. Did you make the service then? A. I did.

Q. Have you certified the facts? A. Yes.

Q. Is that certificate there? A. It is.

Q. Will you read it? A. Witness said as follows:—
Certified copy of the foregoing resolution has been delivered to Brevet Major-General Lorenzo Thomas, Adjutant-General of the United States Army, and the same was by me delivered to the hands of General Thomas, about the hour of eleven o'clock P. M. on the 21st of February, 1868.
J. W. JONES.

Q. Is that certificate true? A. It is.

Mr. WILSON then read the proceedings in Executive Session of the Senate on February 21, 1868, the copy of which was served on General Thomas.

Mr. Creecy on the Stand.

The next witness called was Charles C. Creecy, who was examined by Mr. BUTLER, as follows:—

Q. State your full name and official position. A. James C. Creecy, Appointing Clerk of the Treasury Department.

Q. Look at this bundle of papers and give me the form of commission used in the Treasury Department before the passage of the act of March 2, 1867. Witness produced and handed the paper to Mr. Butler.

Q. Was this the ordinary form, or one used without any exception? A. It was the ordinary form.

Complaints were made on the part of Senators and of the counsel for the President, that it was impossible to hear what was said by the witness, and Mr. BUTLER suggested that, if it were not considered improper, he would repeat the witness' answers.

Mr. EVARTS replied that the counsel preferred that the witness should speak out so as to be heard.

Senator TRUMBULL suggested that the witness should stand further from the counsel, and the witness accordingly took his position at the right-hand side of the Secretary's desk, when the examination was continued.

Q. For the class of appointments for which such commissions would be issued, was there any other form used before that time? A. I think that is the form for a permanent commission.

Q. Now give the form that has been used in the Treasury Department since the passage of the act of March 2, 1867.

Mr. STANBERY, counsel for the President, asked Mr. Butler to be kind enough to state the object of the testimony.

Mr. BUTLER replied, the object of this testimony is to show that, prior to the passage of the act of March 2, 1867, known as the Civil Tenure of Office bill, a certain form of commission was used and issued by the President of the United States, and that after the passage of the Civil Tenure of Office bill, a new form was made conforming to the Civil Tenure of Office act, thus showing that the President acted on the Tenure of Office act as an actual valid law.

Mr. BUTLER resumed the examination as follows:—

Q. I see there are certain interlineations in this form. Do you speak of the form before it was interlined, or subsequently? A. This commission shows the changes that have been made conformably to the Tenure of Office bill.

Q. There is a portion of that paper in print and a portion in writing; do I understand you that the printed portion was the form before the Tenure of Office bill was passed? A. Yes.

Q. And the written portion shows the changes? A. Yes.

Read with a loud voice the printed portion of the commission.

Senator CONNESS suggested that the reading had better be done by the Clerk, and the commission, in its original and in its altered form, was read by the Secretary of the Senate.

In the original form the office was to be held "during the pleasure of the President of the United States for the time being." In the altered form these words were struck out, and the following words substituted: "Until a successor shall have been appointed and duly qualified."

The examination was resumed.

Q. Since that act has any other form of commission been used than the one as altered for such appointments? A. No, sir.

Q. Have you now the form of the official bond of officers used prior to the Civil Tenure of Office act? A. I have.

Witness produces it.

Q. Has there been any change made in it? A. No sir.

Q. Please give me a copy of the commission issued for temporary appointments since the Tenure of Office act.

Witness hands the paper to Mr. Butler.

Q. State whether the printed part of this paper was the part in use prior to the Tenure of Office act? A. It was.

Q. Was any change made in the form of commission? A. Yes.

The commission was read by the Secretary of the Senate, showing that the words "during the pleasure of the President of the United States for the time being" were struck out, and the words "unless this commission is sooner revoked by the President of the United States for the time being," substituted.

Q. State whether before these changes were made the official opinion of the Solicitor of the Treasury was taken? A. It was.

Q. Have you it here? A. I have.

Witness hands the paper to Mr. Butler.

After a moment Mr. Butler said he withdrew the question.

Q. Do you know whether, since the alteration of this form, any commissions have been issued, signed by the President, as altered. A. Yes, sir.

Q. Has the President signed both the temporary and permanent forms of commissions, as altered? A. Yes, sir.

Mr. Edmund Cooper's Case.

Q. Look at this paper, last handed to you, and state what it is? A. It is a commission issued to Mr. Edmund Cooper, Assistant Secretary of the Treasury.

Q. Under what date? A. The third of November, 1867.

Q. Who was the Assistant Secretary of the Treasury at the time of issuing that commission? A. Mr. E. E. Chandler.

Q. Do you happen to remember, as a matter of memory, whether the Senate was then in session? A. I think it was not.

Q. State whether Mr. Cooper qualified and went into office under the first commission? A. He did not qualify under the first commission.

Q. What is the second paper I handed to you? A. It is a letter of authority to Mr. Cooper to act as Assistant Secretary of the Treasury.

Mr. EVARTS asked whether the other paper was considered as read, and Mr. BUTLER replied that it was.

Mr. EVARTS asked, when are we to know the contents of these papers, if they are not read?

Mr. BUTLER stated that they were the same as read.

Mr. EVARTS responded, well, let it be so stated; we know nothing whatever about them.

The Secretary of the Senate read the comission of Mr. Cooper, dated November 3, 1867, which provides that he shall hold his office to the end of the next session of the Senate, and no longer, subject to the conditions prescribed by law. He also read the letter of authority of December 22, 1867, which recites that a vacancy had occurred in the office of Assistant Secretary of the Treasury, and that in pursuance of the authority of the act of Congress of 1799, Edward Cooper is authorized to perform the duties of the Assistant Secretary of the Treasury until a successor be appointed, or such vacancy be filled.

The examination was continued by Mr. BUTLER.

Q. How did Mr. Chandler get out of office? A. He resigned.

Q. Have you a copy of his resignation? A. I have not.

Q. Can you state from memory at what time his resignation took effect? A. I cannot; it was only a day or two before the appointment of Mr. Cooper.

The witness was cross-examined by Mr. CURTIS, as follows:—

Q. Can you fix the day when this change in the form of the commission was first made? A. I think it was about the fourth day after the passage of the act.

Q. With what confidence do you speak; do you from recollection? A. I speak from the decision of the Secretary of the Treasury on the subject, which was given on the 6th of March.

Q. Then you would fix the date as the 6th of March? A. Yes, sir.

Senator HOWARD again complained that it was impossible for the Senators to hear the testimony, and Mr. CURTIS repeated it as follows:—

The question was for the witness to fix the date when this change in the form of the permanent commission first occurred?

Q. Will you now state what that date was, according to your best recollection? A. It was the 6th of March, 1867.

Burt Van Horn sworn on the part of the managers.

"Ad Interim" and the War Office.

Mr. BUTLER—Q. Will you state whether you were present at the War Department when Major-General Lorenzo Thomas, Adjutant-General of the United States Army, was there to make demand for the office, property, books and records? A. I was.

Q. When was it? A. It was on Saturday, the 22d of February.

Q. About what time of day? A. Perhaps a few minutes after eleven o'clock.

Q. February of what year? A. 1868.

Q. Who were present? A. (Reading.) Gen. Charles H. Van Wyck, of New York; General J. M. Dodge, of Iowa; Hon. Freeman Clark, of New York; Hon. J. K. Moorhead, of Pennsylvania; Hon. Columbus Delano, of Ohio; Hon. W. D. Kelley, of Pennsylvania, and Thomas W. Ferry, of Michigan, and myself; the Secretary of War, Mr. Stanton, and his son, were also present.

Q. Please state what took place. A. The gentlemen and myself were in the Secretary's office—the office he usually occupies as Secretary of War; General Thomas came in, apparently from the President's; came into the building and came up stairs; when he came into the Secretary's room first, he said, "Good morning, Mr. Secretary; good morning, gentlemen;" the Secretary replied, "Good morning;" and, I believe, we all said good morning; then he began the conversation as follows (reading):—"I am Secretary of War *ad interim*, and am ordered by the President of the United States to take charge of the office;" Mr. Stanton replied as follows:—"I order you to repair to your room and exercise your functions as Adjutant-General of the Army;" Mr. Thomas replied to this, "I am Secretary of War *ad interim*, and I shall not obey your orders; but I shall obey the orders of the President, who has ordered me take charge of the War Department;" Mr. Stanton replied to this as follows:—"As Secretary of War, I order you to repair to your place as Adjutant-General;" Mr. Thomas replied:—"I will not do so;" Mr. Stanton then said, in reply to General Thomas:— "Then you may stand there, if you please, but you cannot act as Secretary of War; if you do, you do so at your peril;" Mr. Thomas replied to this:—"I shall act as Secretary of War;" this was the conversation in the Secretary's room.

Q. What happened then? A. After that they went to the room of General Schriver, opposite to the Secretary's room.

Q. Who went first? A. General Thomas went first; he had some conversation with General Schriver that I did not hear; he was followed by Mr. Stanton, by General Moorhead and Mr. Ferry, and then by myself; some little conversation was had that I did not hear, but after I got into the room—it was but a moment after they went in, however—Mr. Stanton addressed Mr. Thomas as follows, which I understood was the summing up of the conversation.

Mr. EVARTS—Never mind about that.

Witness—Mr. Stanton said, "Then you claim to be here as Secretary of War, and refuse to obey my orders?" Mr. Thomas said, "I do, sir; I shall require the mails of the War Department to be delivered to me, and shall transact all the business of the War Department;" that was the substance of the conversation which I heard, and, in fact, the conversation as I heard it.

By Mr. BUTLER—Q. Did you make any memorandum afterwards? A. I made it at the time; I had paper in my hand at the time, and I took it down as the conversation occurred; it was copied off by a clerk in the presence of the gentlemen with me.

Q. What was done after that? Where did Mr. Thomas go? A. It was then after eleven o'clock; the rest of us came in from the House, and I left Mr. Thomas in the room with General Schriver.

Cross-examined by Mr. STANBERY.

The witness stated that he went to the War Department to see the Secretary of War on public business, the time being a rather exciting one; went there to talk with him on public affairs, namely, on the subject of the removal; did talk with on that subject; went there in company with Mr. Clark, of New York; arrived there a little before eleven o'clock; General Moorhead and Mr. Ferry were there when he arrived; thought Mr. Delano was there; also two or three others came in afterwards; could not say what there business was; they did not state it to him; General Thomas then came into the room; when the conversation between Gen. Thomas and the Secretary began, witness had a large envelope and pencil in his pocket, and when the conversation took place it occurred to him that it might be well to know what they said; witness did not know that he was in the habit of making memoranda of conversation; nobody requested him to do it; it was of his own motion; after the conversation was ended witness thought General Thomas went out first, and the Secretary of War followed but a moment after; witness did not state what his object was, and did not recollect that the Secretary requested any of the gentlemen to go with him; witness followed upon his own motion; did not know that all went in; General Moorhead and another went in before him; they followed the Secretary very soon, perhaps a minute after he went in; could not say what had taken place before he went in; witness heard some conversation, but did not know what it was then; the conversation he had detailed followed; witness had his pencil and envelope in his hand when he went in; did not know where that envelope is now; it was probably destroyed; copied it off immediately at the Secretary's table; could not say that it was destroyed; had no knowledge of it—the document; what he had been reading from was not manuscript, it was a copy of his testimony before the committee, taken from the notes he wrote; read them to a young man in the Secretary's office, who copied them; did not know that it was important to keep the original; did not know the name of the clerk who took the copy; preserved the notes until he testified before the committee; could not say how long he preserved them; could not say what has become of the envelope; had not searched for it; suggested of his own motion, after he returned to the Secretary's room, that the notes should be written out; a young man was there ready to do it; was not aware that anything else took place in General Schriver's room than what he had testified to; could not say who left the room first; left Secretary Stanton there and went into the Secretary's room; could not say whether Mr. Stanton came in while the notes were being copied or not; saw Mr. Stanton sitting then in his own office, after he left the room; did not know what took place between them afterwards; saw no friendly greeting between Mr. Stanton and General Thomas while in General Schriver's room; the notes he took on the envelope were questions and answers, of which the copy was an exact transcript, though it did not exhibit the whole conversation; and one expression occurred to him now that General Thomas used, and that he did not get down; the notes covered all the conversation of any importance; what he wrote was *verbatim*, question and answer; did not take it in short hand; the conversation was very slow and deliberate; General Thomas said very little in that conversation; Mr. Stanton did not ask General Thomas if he wished him to vacate immediately, or if he would give him time to arrange his private papers.

Re-Direct examination by Mr. BUTLER.—The remark referred to by him in his cross-examination that occurred to him now, and that he had not written out, was from General Thomas, to the effect that he did not wish anything unpleasant; that was what Thomas said.

Re-Cross-examination by Mr. STANBERY.—Q. This emphasis on the words, "I don't know its materiality," did he speak that word in the ordinary way? A. He spoke it in the way I have mentioned; he said he did not want any "unpleasantness;" witness said this occurred in the first part of the conversation, before General Thomas went to his room; had taken part of the conversation before that; did not think it material.

Mr. BINGHAM—I suppose it is not for the witness to swear what he thought about it.

Mr. EVARTS—Examining as to the completeness or the perfection of the witness' memory. It is certainly material to know why he omitted some parts and testified to others.

Mr. BINGHAM withdrew the objection.

James K. Moorhead sworn on behalf of the managers.

Direct examination by Mr. BUTLER.—Witness is a member of the House of Representatives, and was present at the War Department on the morning of Saturday, February 22, understanding that General Thomas was to be there that morning to take possession of the Department; went there from his boarding-house, in company with Mr. Burleigh, who, he understood, had some conversation with General Thomas the night before; Mr. Van Horn had correctly stated what took place, and witness could corroborate the statement.

Objection by Mr. Curtis.

Witness proceeded to say that General Thomas went over to General Schriver's room; he was followed by Mr. Stanton and himself; Stanton there put a question to General Thomas, and asked witness to remember it, which induced him to make a memorandum of it; that he thought he still had among his papers; it was made briefly and roughly, but so that he could understand it; Mr. Stanton said, "General Thomas, you profess to be here as Secretary of War, and refuse to obey my orders;" General Thomas replied, "I do, sir."

After that had passed, witness walked to the door leading into the hall, when he heard something that attracted his attention, and he returned; Mr. Stanton then said, "General Thomas requires the mails of the department to be delivered to him;" General Thomas said, "I require the mails of the department to be delivered to me, and I will transact the business of the office;" witness then asked General Thomas if he made use of those words, and he assented and added, "You may make as full a copy as you please;" that was all the memorandum witness made, and he made it at that time and place.

Cross-examined by Mr. STANBERY.—Witness had not made a memorandum of the number of persons he found at Mr. Stanton's office when he arrived there, and could not remember all of them; there were a number of members of Congress; he had seen Mr. Van Horn and Judge Kelley there; had been there just about half an hour when General Thomas came in; saw him through the windows, which were open towards the White House, coming, somebody having announced the fact; he came alone.

Q. Was he armed in any way? A. No, sir; not that I know of.

(Witness here made an observation inaudible in the reporter's gallery, but which caused considerable merriment on the floor.)

When General Thomas came in he said, "Good morning, Mr. Secretary." "Good morning, gents;" thought Mr. Stanton asked him if he had any business with him; Mr. Stanton was sometimes sitting and sometimes standing; did not notice which he was doing when he spoke; thought he did not ask him to take a seat, and that witness did not take one; General Thomas then said he was there as Secretary ad interim, appointed by the President, and came to take possession; nothing was said before that; Mr. Stanton said, "I am Secretary of War; you are Adjutant-General; I order you to your room;" General Thomas replied that he would not obey the order; that he was Secretary of War, and then retired to General Shriver's room; Mr. Stanton asked witness to accompany him; did not know what he wanted him for; supposed he was going to have further conversation; Mr. Van Horn also followed; thought there was some unimportant conversation before what he had detailed, but could not remember it; it was joking, or something of that kind, to no purpose; they did not seem to be in any passion; not hostile; witness did not recollect any of the jokes that passed; left the room shortly after the remark that Mr. Stanton asked him to remember; had got back into Mr. Stanton's room before that, and was induced to return from overhearing conversation that he thought was important, whereupon Mr. Stanton told him he wanted him to remember the remark in regard to the mails of the department and

that he (General Thomas) was there as Secretary of War; witness came out first from General Schriver's room; Mr. Stanton remained but a very short time; it was then near twelve o'clock, and he and the other members went to the Capitol, leaving the rest of the company there; do not remember who stayed, a number of gentlemen; could not remember whether military or civilians; thought he had seen General Grant there during the morning, but not while General Thomas was there, and do not recollect General Thomas using the expression that he "wished no unpleasantness."

Q. Did there appear to be any unpleasantness? A. General Thomas wanted to get in, I think, and Mr. Stanton wanted to keep him out.

Q. But there was nothing offensive on either side? A. Nothing very belligerent on either side.

Q. Was there any joking in Mr. Stanton's room, as well as in General Schriver's room? A. I do not know, sir.

Q. No occasion for a laugh? A. It was more stern in Mr. Stanton's room; Mr. Stanton ordered General Thomas to leave.

Q. That is the only thing that looked like sternness? A. Yes, sir.

Re-Direct examination by Mr. BUTLER.—Q. The President's counsel has asked you if on that occasion he was armed; will you allow me to ask if on that occasion he was masked. (Laughter). A. He was not, sir.

Walter A. Burleigh sworn on behalf of the managers.

Direct examination by Mr. BUTLER.—Q. What is your name and position? A. My name is Walter A. Burleigh, and I am a Delegate from Daeota Territory.

Q. Do you know L. Thomas, Adjutant-General of the Army. A. I do.

Q. How long have you known him? A. For several years; I don't know how long.

Q. Have you been on terms of intimacy with him? A. I have.

Q. Has he been at your house since you have been here? Yes, sir.

Q. Do you remember an occasion when you had a conversation with Mr. Moorhead about visiting Mr. Stanton's office? A. I recollect going to the Secretary of War with Mr. Moorhead on the morning of the 22d of February, I think, last.

Q. On the evening before had you seen General Thomas? A. I had.

Q. Where? A. At his house.

Q. What time in the evening? A. In the early part of the evening; I cannot say precisely the hour.

Q. Had you a conversation with him? A. Yes, sir.

Mr. STANBERY—What is the relevancy of that? What is the object?

Mr. BUTLER—The object is to show the intent and purpose with which General Thomas went to the War Department on the morning of the 22d; that he went with the intent and purpose of taking possession by force; that he alleged that intent and purpose; that in consequence of that allegation, Mr. Burleigh invited General Moorhead and went up to the War Office; from the conversation what I expect to prove in this—after the President of the United States had appointed General Thomas, and given him directions to take the War Office, and after he had made a quiet visit there on the 21st, on the evening of the 22d he told Mr. Burleigh that the next day he was going to take possession by force. Mr. Burleigh said to him—

Mr. STANBERY—No matter about that. We object to the testimony.

Mr. BUTLER—Then you don't know what you have to object to, if you don't know what it is. (Laughter).

The Chief Justice decided the testimony admissible, speaking in a very low tone.

Senator DRAKE—I suppose the matter of admitting the testimony is a matter for the Senate, and not for the presiding officer. The questions should be submitted, I think, to the Senate. I take exception to the presiding officer undertaking to decide that point.

The Chief Justice, rising—The Chief Justice is of opinion that he should decide upon objections to evidence. If he is incorrect in that opinion, it is for the Senate to correct him.

Senator DRAKE—I appeal from the decision of the Chair, and demand the decision of the Senate.

Senator FOWLER asked that the question be stated.

The Chief Justice—The Chief Justice would state

to the Senate that in his judgement it is his duty to decide on questions of evidence in the first instance, and that if any Senator desires that the question shall then be submitted to the Senate, it is his duty to do it. So far as he is aware, this is the uniform course of practice on trials of persons impeached in the Senate of the United States.

Senator DRAKE—My position, Mr. President, is that there is nothing in the rules of this Senate, sitting upon the trial of an impeachment, that gives that authority to the presiding officer over the body. That is my position of order.

Senator JOHNSON—I call the Senator to order. The question is not debateable.

Mr. BUTLER—If the President pleases, is not this question debateable?

The Chief Justice—It is debateable by the managers and the counsel for the President.

Mr. BUTLER—We have the honor, Mr. President, and gentlemen of the Senate, to object to the ruling just attempted to be made by the presiding officer of the Senate, and with the utmost submission, but with an equal degree of firmness, we must insist upon our objection, because otherwise it would always put the managers in the condition, when the ruling is against them, of appealing to the Senate as a body against the ruling of the chair. We have been too long in parliamentary and other bodies not to know how much disadvantage it is to be put in that position—the position of apparent appeal from the decision of the chair, either real or apparent, and we are glad that the case has come up upon a ruling of the presiding officer which is in our favor, so that we are not invidious in making the objection.

Although we learn from what has fallen from the presiding officer that he understands that the precedents are in the direction of his intimation, yet if we understand the position taken the precedents are not in support of that position. Lest I should have the misfortune to misstate the position of the presiding officer of the Senate, I will state it as I understand it. I understand his position to be that primarily, as a judge in a court has a right to do, the presiding officer claims the right to rule a question of law, and then if any member of the court chooses to object it may be taken in the nature of an appeal by one member of the court. If I am incorrect in my statement of the position of the presiding officer, I would be glad to be corrected.

The Chief Justice—The Chair will state that under the rules of this body he is the presiding officer. He is so in virtue of his office under the Constitution. He is Chief Justice of the United States, and therefore, when the President is tried by the Senate, it is his duty to preside in that body, and, as he understands, he is therefore the President of the Senate, sitting as a Court of Impeachment; the rule of the Senate is the 7th rule, reading:—

"The presiding officer may in the first instance, submit to the Senate, without a division, all questions of evidence and incidental questions."

He is not required by that rule to submit these questions in the first instance; but for the despatch of business, as is usual in the Supreme Court, he may express his opinion in the first instance, and if the Senate, who constitutes the court, or any member of the court desires to ask the opinion of the Senate as a court, it is his duty then to ask for the opinion of the court.

Mr. BUTLER—May I respectfully inquire whether that extends to the managers as to a question of law to be submitted to this court?

The Chief Justice—The Chief Justice thinks not. It is a matter for the court.

Mr. BUTLER—Then it immediately becomes a very important and momentous substance, because the presiding officer of the court, who is not a member of the court, and has no hand in the court, as we understand it, except on a question of equal division, gives a decision which prevents the House of Representatives from asking even that the Senate shall pass upon it, and, therefore, if this is the rule, our hands are tied, and it was in order to get the exact rule that we have asked the presiding officer of the Senate to state, as he has kindly and frankly stated the exact position. Now then, I say again—

The Chief Justice—The Chief Justice thinks it right and proper for the managers to propose any question they see fit to the Senate, but it is for the Senate themselves to determine.

Mr. BUTLER—As I understand it, we propose a question to the Senate, and the Chief Justice decides that we cannot get it decided without a decision of the Chief Justice, to which we object respectfully as we ought, firmly as we must. Now, upon the question of precedent, sorry I am to be obliged to deny the position taken by the presiding officer of the Senate.

I understand that this is a question the precedents for which have been established for many years. Not expecting the question would arise, I have not at this moment at my hands all the books, but I can give the leading case where the question arose. If I am not mistaken it arose on the trial of Lord Stafford, in the thirty-second year of King Charles the second, and that the House of Lords had a rule prior to the trial of Lord Stafford, by which the Commons were bound to address the Lord High Steward as "His Grace," or "My Lord," precisely as the counsel for the respondent think themselves obliged to address the presiding officer of this body as "Mr. Chief Justice."

When the preliminaries of the trial of Stafford were settled, the Commons objected that they, as a part of the Parliament of Great Britain, ought not to be called upon, through their managers, to address any individual whatever, but that the address should be made to the lords.

A committee of conference thereupon was had, and the rule previously adopted in the House of Commons was considered, and the rule adopted and reported that in the trial the Managers of the House of Commons should not address the Lord High Steward, and should not ask anything of him, but should address the House as "My Lords," showing the reason and giving as a reason that the Lord High Steward was but a Speaker *pro tem.*, presiding over the body during the trial.

When Lord Stafford came to trial the House of Lords instructed him that he must address the lords, and not the Lord High Steward at all. From that day to the latest trial in Parliament, which is Lord Cardigan's in 1841, the Earl of Cardigan being brought before the House of Lords, and Lord Chief Justice Denman sitting on that trial, the universal address has been, by counsel, prisoners, managers and everybody, "My Lord." There was to be no recognition of any superior right in the presiding officer over any other member of the court, nor did that matter stop here.

In more than one case this question has arisen. In Lord Macclesfield's case, if I remember rightly, the question arose in this way:—Whether the presiding officer should decide questions, and he left it wholly to the House of Lords, saying to the lords, "You may decide as you please." Again, when Lord Erskine presided at the trial of Lord —, which was a trial early in the century, coming up with as much form as any other trial, and with as much regard for form and for the preservation of decency and order, the question was put to him, whether he would call points of law, and he expressly disclaimed that power.

Again, in Lord Cardigan's case, to which I have just referred, before Lord Chief Justice Denman, upon a question of evidence in regard to the admissibility of a card, on which the name of "Harvey Garnett Tuckett" was placed, the question being whether the man's name was Harvey Garnett Phipps Tuckett, or Harvey Garnett Tuckett, Lord Denman decided that he would submit to the lords if the counsel desired to press the question, but the counsel did not desire him to settle it; and the other side went on to argue, and when the Attorney-General of England had finished his argument, Lord Denman arose and apologized for having allowed him to argue, and said he hoped it would not be taken as a precedent, but saying he did not think it quite right for him to interfere, and when finally the lords withdrew and Lord Denman was giving the opinion to the lords of the guilt or innocence of the party, he apologized to the lords for giving an opinion in advance, saying that he was only one of them, as he was independent of his office of Lord High Steward, and that his opinion was no more or less than any of theirs, and he had only spoken, first, because somebody must speak. He says, using this remarkable language:—"This is not a court and jury. You, my lords, exercise the functions of both judge and jury, and the whole matter is with you."

Now, then, in the light of authority, in the light of the precedent, in which the presiding officer appeals, in the light of reason, and in the light of principle, we are bound to object. And this is not a mere question of form. All forms are waived, but it is a question of substance. It is a question, whether the House of Representatives can get, on its own motion to the Senate, a question of law, if the Chief Justice, who is presiding, is to stand between the Senate and them.

It is a question of vital importance; but if it was of no

importance I could not yield one hair, because no jot or tittle of the rights of the House of Representatives shall fall to the ground by reason of any inattention or yielding of mine. Let me state it again, because to me it seems an invasion of the privilege of the House of Representatives. It is, that when the House of Representatives states a question of law to the Senate of the United States on the trial of the President of the United States, the Chief Justice presiding in the Senate, sitting as a court, can stand between the House of Representatives and the Senate and decide the question. Then, by the courtesy of some members of the Senate, the House of Representatives, through its managers, can get that question of law decided by the Senate.

I should be inclined to deem it my duty, and the duty of the other managers, if we were put in that position, to ask instructions of the House, before we allowed the rights of the House to be bound hand and foot, at the beck of any man. I do not care who he may be, for it is, I respectfully submit, a question of the most momentous consequence; not of so much consequence now, when we have a learned, able, honest, candid and patriotic Chief Justice of the United States; but let us look forward to the time, which may come, in the history of this nation, when we get a Jeffries as Lord High Steward.

We desire that the precedents of this good time, with good men, when everything is quiet, when the country will not be disturbed by the precedent. We desire that the precedent be so settled that it will hold a Jeffries as it did of old; for it brings to my mind an instance of Jeffries' conduct on an exactly similar question, when, on the trial of Lord Stanley, Jeffries being Lord High Steward, said to the Earl, as he came to plead (I give the substance of the words), "you had better confess, and throw yourself on the mercy of the king, your master; he is the fountain of your mercy, and it will be better for you to do it," and the Earl Stanley (if I remember the name aright), replied to him. "Are you, sir, one of my judges that gives me that advice; are you on my trial for my death?" and Jeffries quailed before the indignant eye of the man with whose right he tried to interfere, and said, "No, I am not one of your judges, and am only advising you as your friend."

I want the precedent fixed in as good times as there were before Jeffries, so that if we ever have the misfortune to have such a Chief Justice as we have Andrew Johnson in the chair of the President, the precedent will be so settled that they cannot in any way be disturbed, but will be securely fixed for all time.

The Chief Justice repeated his decision, to the effect that it was his right and duty, under the rules, to decide preliminary questions, in the first instance without submitting them to the Senate, and that if any Senator demanded the judgment of the Senate upon them, they might then be submitted to the Senate.

Senator DRAKE—I raise the question that the presiding officer of the Senate has no right to make a decision of that kind.

The Chief Justice (determinedly)—The Senator is not in order.

Senator DRAKE (not heeding the Chief Justice)—I demand that that question be put to the Senate.

The Chief Justice (with still more determination)—The Senator is not in order.

Senator CONKLING—I ask whether the question is to the competency of the proposed testimony, or as to whether the presiding officer be competent to decide that question.

The Chief Justice—It is the question whether the Chair in the first instance, is capable of deciding on that question or that the Clerk will proceed to call the yeas and nays.

Senator CONKLING—Before the yeas and nays are called, I beg that the latter clause of the seventh rule be read.

Senator HOWARD read the whole rule.

The rule was read as follows:—The presiding officer of the Senate shall direct all necessary preparations in the Senate Chamber, and the presiding officer upon the trial shall direct all the forms of proceeding while the Senate are sitting for the purpose of trying an impeachment, and all forms during the trial, not otherwise specially provided for. The presiding officer may in the first instance submit to the Senate without a division all questions of evidence and incidental questions, but the same shall on demand of one-fifth of the members present, be decided by yeas and nays.

Mr. BINGHAM, one of the managers, rose to call the attention of the Senate to the language of the rule just read, and submitted, with all due respect to the presiding officer, that that rule meant nothing more than this, "that if no question be raised by the Senate, and one-fifth of the Senators do not demand the yeas and nays, it authorized the presiding officer simply to take the sense of the Senate on all questions without a division," and there it ended. He begged leave further to say, in connection with what had fallen from his associate (Mr. Butler), that he looked on this question as settled by the very terms of the Constitution itself; the Constitution, he argued, providing that the Senate shall have the sole power to try impeachments.

The expression, "the sole power," necessarily means, as the Senate will doubtless agree, "the only power." It includes everything pertaining to the trial, and every judgment that may be made is a part of the trial, whether it be on a preliminary question or on the final question. It seems to me the word was incorporated in the Constitution, touching proceedings in impeachment, in the very light of the long-continued usages and practice of Parliament. It is settled in the very elaborate and exhaustive report of the Commons of England, on the Lord's Journal, that the peers alone decide all the questions of law and fact arising in such trials. In other words, it is settled that the peers alone are the judges in every case of the law and the fact; that the Lord Chancellor presiding is a ministerial officer, to keep order, to present to the consideration of the peers the various questions as they arise, and to take their judgment upon them. There his authority stops.

This question is considered so well settled that it is carried into the great text book of the law, and finds a place in the Institutes of Coke, wherein it is declared that "the peers are the judges of the law and the facts, and conduct the whole proceedings according to the law and usage of Parliament." It is as I understand this question as it is presented here. I agree with my associate that it is of very great importance, not only touching the admissibility of evidence, but touching every other question that can arise; for example, questions which may involve the validity or legality of any of the charges preferred in those articles.

We understand that the question is, whether the Senate shall decide that the presiding officer himself, not being a member of this body, which is invested with the sole power to try impeachments, and, therefore, to decide all questions in the trial, can himself make a decision, which decision is to stand as the judgment of this tribunal, unless reversed by subsequent action of the Senate. That we understand to be the question submitted, and on which the Senate is now to vote. It is suggested to me by my associate, Mr. Butler, that this also involves the further proposition that the managers, in the event of such decision being made by the presiding officer, cannot even call for a review of that decision by the Senate.

Senator WILSON moved that the Senate retire for consultation.

Mr. CONKLING and others—"No, no."

Mr. SHERMAN sent to the Secretary's desk a paper, which was read, as follows:—

"I ask the managers what are the precedents in the cases of impeachment in the United States on this point. Did the Vice President as presiding officer, decide preliminary questions or did he submit them in the first instance to the Senate?"

Mr. BOUTWELL, one of the managers, said—"I am not disposed to ask the attention of the Senate further to this matter, as a question concerning the rights of the House. In proceedings of this kind, it seems to me of the gravest character, and yet I can very well understand that the practical assertion on all questions arising here of the principle for which the managers—on behalf of the House—stand, would be calculated to delay the proceedings, and very likely involve us, at times, in difficulty.

In what I said I spoke with the highest personal respect for the Chief Justice who presides here, feeling that, in the rulings, he may make on questions of law, and of the admissibility of testimony, he would always be guided by that conscientious regard for the right for which he is distinguished; but, after all, I foresee if the managers here, acting for the House in the case now before the Senate and before the country, and acting, I may say, in behalf of other generations, and of other men, who, unfortunately, may be similarly situated in future times, were now to make the surrender of the right that the Chief Justice of the Supreme Court of the United States, sitting here as the presiding officer of this body for a specified purpose, and for no other, has a power to decide even in a preliminary and a conditional way, questions that may be vital to the final decision of this tribunal on the guilt or innocence of the person arraigned.

Here they should make a surrender, which would in substance abandon the constitutional rights of the House of Representatives and the constitutional rights of the Senate sitting as a tribunal to to try impeachment, presented by the House of Representatives; and, with all due deference, I say that the language of the Constitution, "when the President of the United States is tried the Chief Justice shall preside," is conclusive on this whole matter. He presides here, not as a member of this body, for if that were assumed then the claim would be not only in derogation, but in violation of another provision of the Constitution, which concedes to the Senate the sole power of trying all impeachments, and I know of no language that can be used more specific in its character, more conclusive in its terms.

It includes, as we here maintain, all those men chosen under the Constitution, and representing here the several States of the Union, whatever may be their faults; whatever may be their interests; whatever may be their capacity; whatever may be their affiliations with or to the person accused, sitting here as a tribunal to decide the questions under the Constitution, with all the felicities, and with all the infelicities which belong to the tribunal itself under the Constitution, with no power to change it in any particular, and is exclusive—I say it with all due deference—of every other man, whatever his station, rank or position elsewhere; whatever his relations to this body under the Constitution, the Senate has the sole power to try all impeachments, and no person elsewhere can in any way interfere to control or affect its decision or judgment in the slightest degree. Therefore, Mr. President, it must follow as a constitutional right that the Senate itself, without advice, as a matter of right, must decide every incidental question which, by any possibility, can control the ultimate judgment of the Senate on the great question of the guilt or innocence of the party accused. If, under any circumstances, the testimony of any witness may be denied or admitted on judgment of any person or of any authority except this tribunal before which we here stand, then the party accused and impeached by the House of Representatives, may be acquitted or may be convicted on authorities, or by influences separate and distinct from the judgment and opinion of the Senate itself..

On this point, I think there can finally be no difference of opinion; but, Mr. President, some of the managers, not having had an opportunity to consult with my associates on that point, and speaking, therefore, with deference to what may be their judgment, the judgment of the House, I should be very willing for myself. to proceed in the conduct of this case on the understanding that the right is here and is now solemnly asserted by the Senate for itself, and as a precedent for all its successors, that every question of law or evidence arising here is to be decided by the Senate, without consultation with or the influence of the presiding officer.

However worthy it is, as I know it to be worthy of consideration, the Constitution standing between the Senate here and the presiding officer there, I hold that the judgment must be exclusively here; still it should be willing that in all this proceeding the presiding officer of the Senate shall give his opinion or his ruling. If you please, on incidental questions of law and evidence, as they arise, the understanding being that any member of the Senate, or any one of the managers, or any one acting as counsel for the respondent, may have it settled by the judgment of the Senate, whether the ruling of the presiding officer is correct or otherwise.

In the trial of Lord Melville (vol. 29, State Trials), Lord Erskine evidently acted upon this idea. A question of the admissibility of evidence having been argued by the managers on one side, and by the counsel for the respondent on the other side, Lord Erskine said:—" If any noble lord is desirous that this subject should be a matter of further consideration in the Chamber of Parliament, it will be proper that he should now move an adjournment. If not, I have formed an opinion, and shall declare it;" and on that theory he administered the duties of the chair.

With respect to the rights of the House of Representatives and to the rights of the respondent, I should not, for myself, object; but I cannot conscientiously, even in his presence, consent to the doctrine as a matter of right, that the presiding officer of the Senate is to decide this question under such circumstances, that it is not in the power of the managers to take the judgment of the court as to whether the decision is right or wrong.

Mr. BINGHAM, one of the managers, rose to call the attention of the Senate to an abstract which he had made on the question. It was to the effect that Judges of the realm and the Barons of the Exchequer were no part of the House of Lords, except for mere ministerial purposes; that the Peers are not triers or jurors only, but are also judges both of law and of fact, and that the judges ought not to give an opinion in a matter of Parliament.

[NOTE.—This brief condensation is all that it was possible for the reporter to make, on account of the impossibility of hearing distinctly in the gallery, and of the total lack of facilities for properly reporting these most important proceedings.—REPORTER.]

Mr. BUTLER, referring to the question put by Mr. Sherman some time back, cited a precedent in case of the impeachment of Judge Chase, where the question whether a witness should be permitted to refer to his notes in order to refresh his memory on the stand, and where the President put the question to the Senate, which was decided in the negative. Yeas, 16; nays, 18.

Mr. EVARTS, on behalf of the President, said:—Mr. Chief Justice and Senators:—I rise to make but a single observation in reference to a position or an argument presented by one of the honorable managers to aid the judgment of the Senate on the question submitted to it.

That question we understand to be, whether, according to the rules of this body, the Chief Justice presiding shall determine, preliminarily, interlocutory questions of evidence and of law as they arise, subject to the decision of the Senate on presentation by any Senator of the question to it. Now the honorable manager, Mr. Boutwell, recognizing the great inconvenience that would arise in retarding of the trial from that appeal to so numerous a body on every interlocutory question, while he insists on the magnitude and importance of the right to determine, intimates that the managers will allow the Chief Justice to decide unless they see reason to object.

In behalf of the counsel for the President, I have only this to say, that we shall take from this court the rule as to whether the first preliminary decision is to be made by the Chief Justice, or to be made by the whole body, and that we shall not submit to the choice of the managers as to how far that rule shall be departed from. Whatever the rule is, we shall abide by, but if the court determine that the proper plan is for the whole body to decide on every interlocutory question, we shall claim as a matter of right, and as a matter of course, that that proceeding shall be adopted.

Senator WILSON renewed his motion, that the Senate retire for consultation.

The vote was taken by yeas and nays, and resulted: —Yeas, 25; nays, 25, as follows:—

YEAS.—Messrs. Anthony, Buckalew, Cole, Conness, Corbett, Davis, Dixon, Edmunds, Fowler, Grimes, Hendricks, Howe, Johnson. McCreery, Morrill (Me.), Morrill (Vt.), Morton, Norton, Patterson (N. H.), Patterson (Tenn.), Pomeroy, Ross, Vickers, Williams and Wilson—25.

NAYS.—Messrs. Cameron, Cattell, Chandler, Conkling, Cragin, Doolittle, Drake, Ferry, Fessenden, Frelinghuysen, Henderson, Howard, Morgan, Nye, Ramsey, Saulsbury, Sherman, Sprague, Stewart, Sumner, Thayer, Tipton, Trumbull, Van Winkle and Willey—25.

It being a tie vote, the Chief Justice voted yea, thus giving practical effect to the position assumed by him, as to his right to vote.

The circumstance created some flutter on the floor and much amusement in the galleries.

The Senate, headed by the Chief Justice, then, at three o'clock. retired for consultation, and soon after the galleries began to thin out. The members of the House gathered in knots and indulged in boisterous conversation, and the counsel for the President consulted quietly together. One, two, three hours passed, and still the Senators did not return to their Chamber.

The few spectators in the galleries dawdled listlessly. Most of the members of the House sought other scenes more charming, and the general appearance of things was listless and uninteresting. At last, at twenty minutes past six, the Senate returned, and the Chief Justice, having called the body to order, said:—

The Senate has had under consideration the question which was discussed before it retired, and has directed me to report the following rule:—

Rule 7. The presiding officer of the Senate shall direct all necessary preparations in the Senate Chamber, and the presiding officer of the Senate shall direct all the forms of proceedings when the Senate is sitting for the purpose of trying an impeachment, and all forms during the trial, not otherwise especially provided for; and the presiding officer, on the trial, may rule on all questions of evidence and on incidental questions, which decision will stand as the judgment of the Senate, for decision; or he may, at his option, in the first instance, submit any such question to a vote of the members of the Senate.

Mr. BUTLER intimated that the managers desired to retire for consultation.

Senator TRUMBULL said that unless the managers desired the Senate to continue in session, he would now move an adjournment.

The managers intimated that they did not.

Senator TRUMBULL then made the motion for adjournment to twelve o'clock to-morrow, which was carried.

The Chief Justice vacated the Chair, and the Senate having resumed its legislative session adjourned at twenty minutes past six.

The Senate Consultation.

When the Senate retired from their Chamber this afternoon, Mr. Henderson moved to postpone the pending question on appeals, with a view to take up the rules. This was agreed to by the following vote:—

YEAS—Messrs. Anthony, Bayard, Buckalew, Cameron, Cattell, Cole, Corbett, Cragin, Davis. Dixon, Doolittle, Edmunds, Fessenden, Fowler, Frelinghuysen Henderson, Hendricks, Johnson. McCreery, Morrill (Vt.), Norton, Patterson (N. H.), Patterson (Tenn.), Pomeroy, Ross, Saulsbury, Sprague, Trumbull, Van Winkle, Vickers, Willey and Williams—32.

NAYS.—Messrs. Chandler, Conkling, Conness, Drake. Ferry, Howard, Howe, Morgan, Morrill (Me.), Morton, Nye, Ramsey, Sherman, Stewart, Sumner, Thayer, Tipton and Wilson—18.

Mr. HENDERSON then moved amendments to the seventh rule, when a motion was made and disagreed to to strike out from the same the words which provide that the rulings on questions of evidence and incidental questions shall stand as the judgment of the Senate.

Mr. SUMNER offered an amendment to Mr. Henderson's proposition, as follows:—

That the Chief Justice, presiding in the Senate, in the trial of the President of the United States, is not a member of the Senate, and has no authority, under the Constitution, to vote on any question during the trial.

This was rejected by the following vote:—

Yeas.—Messrs. Cameron, Cattell, Chandler, Conkling, Conness, Corbett, Cragin, Drake, Howard, Morgan, Morrill (Me.), Morton, Nye, Pomeroy, Ramsey, Stewart, Sumner, Thayer, Tipton, Trumbull, Williams and Wilson—22.

Nays.—Messrs. Bayard, Buckalew, Cole, Davis, Dixon, Doolittle, Edmunds, Ferry, Fessenden, Fowler, Frelinghuysen, Henderson, Hendricks, Howe, Johnson, McCreery, Morrill (Vt.), Norton, Patterson (N.H.), Patterson (Tenn.), Ross, Sherman, Sprague, Van Winkle, Vickers and Willey—26.

Mr. Drake moved an amendment to Mr. Henderson's proposition, as follows:—"It is the judgment of the Senate, that, under the Constitution, the Chief Justice presiding over the Senate, in the pending trial, has no privilege of ruling questions of law arising therein, but that all such questions should be submitted to and decided by the Senate. This was disagreed to by the following vote:—

Yeas.—Messrs. Cameron, Cattell, Chandler, Cole, Conkling, Conness, Drake, Ferry, Howard, Howe, Morgan, Morrill (Me.), Morton, Nye, Ramsey, Stewart, Sumner, Thayer, Tipton and Wilson—20.

Nays.—Messrs. Anthony, Bayard, Buckalew, Corbett, Cragin, Davis, Dixon, Doolittle, Edmunds, Fessenden, Fowler, Frelinghuysen, Henderson, Hendricks, Johnson, McCreery, Morrill (Vt.), Morton, Patterson (N. H.), Patterson (Tenn.), Pomeroy, Ross, Saulsbury, Sherman, Van Winkle, Vickers, Willey—30.

Mr. SHERMAN submitted the following, which was rejected by a vote of 25 to 25:—

"That under the rules, and in accordance with the precedents in the United States in cases of impeachment, all questions, other than those of order, should be submitted to the Senate."

Finally, the Senators agreed to Mr. Henderson's amendment to the seventh rule, as reported at the close of the trial report.

The following was the final vote:—

YEAS—Messrs. Anthony, Bayard, Buckalew, Cameron, Corbett, Cragin, Davis, Dixon, Doolittle, Edmunds, Fessenden, Fowler, Frelinghuysen, Henderson, Hendricks, Johnson, McCreery, Morrill (Vt.), Norton, Patterson (N. H.), Patterson (Tenn.), Pomeroy, Ross, Saulsbury, Sherman, Sprague, Trumbull, Van Winkle, Vickers, Willey and Williams—31.

NAYS—Messrs. Cattell, Chandler, Cole, Conkling, Drake Ferry, Howard, Howe, Morgan, Morrill (Me.), Norton, Nye, Ramsey, Stewart, Sumner, Thayer, Tipton and Wilson—13.

PROCEEDINGS OF WEDNESDAY, APRIL I.

The Opening Prayer.

The Senate met at 12 o'clock. Prayer was offered by Rev. James J. Kane, of Brooklyn, N. Y. He asked a blessing upon this great court, assembled for the trial of the most momentous question which has arisen during the existence of the nation; the records of the past show that a like crisis in other nations has been followed by war and bloodshed. He prayed that God would avert the danger. Many in our borders sought a pretext to make the sword leap from the scabbard and make it drunk with the blood of their fellows. He asked that God would turn to naught the counsel of the ungodly and the craftiness of the enemies of our country; to remember the blood that has already been shed, as well of our martyred President as of those who died in the field or hospital for the country.

He especially prayed that the representatives of the people should be endowed with wisdom and discretion; that the Executive be guided by wisdom, whether he remain President or not, and that all his acts be marked by prudence and moderation; that his constitutional advisers be also guided by the spirit of wisdom, as well as all the rest of those in authority over us; that the nation may be prepared to receive the decision of the great event and abide by it; that our especial blessing may rest upon those who have the management of this trial, so that the result may redound to the honor and glory of God.

Arrival of the Managers.

At ten minutes past twelve o'clock the Sergeant-at-Arms of the Senate announced the managers of the impeachment on the part of the House of Representatives.

All the managers, except Mr. Stevens, entered and took seats at the tables on the left side of the area, in front of the Secretary's desk. Subsequently Mr. Stevens comes in and takes his seat. The counsel for the President are already seated at the right hand side. The Sergeant-at-arms then announced the House of Representatives of the United States. The members of the House enter in pairs, headed by Mr. Washburne (Ill.), Chairman of the Committee of the Whole, attended by Mr. McPherson, Clerk, and Mr. Buxton, Assistant Doorkeeper, and closely followed by the Speaker, Mr. Dawes, Mr. Covode and Mr. Windom. These take their seats on chairs in the front aisle. The members generally file off to the right and left, and take the chairs that are placed on the eastern and western angles.

The Journal.

The Secretary then proceeded to read the journal of the proceedings yesterday. The reading occupied a quarter of an hour.

Senator SUMNER (Mass.) then rose and said, Mr. President, I send to the Chair an order in the nature of a correction of the journal.

The Chief Justice ordered the paper to be read.

The Clerk read it, as follows:—

It appearing, on the reading of the journal of yesterday, that on a question where the Senate was equally divided, the Chief Justice presiding on the trial of the President gave the casting vote, it is hereby declared that, in the judgment of the Senate, such vote was without authority of the Constitution of the United States.

On that question Senator SUMNER asked for the yeas and nays.

The vote was taken, and it resulted—Yeas 21, nays 27, as follows:—

YEAS.—Messrs. Cameron, Chandler, Cole, Conkling, Conness, Cragin, Drake, Howard, Howe, Morgan, Morrill (Me.), Morton, Pomeroy, Ramsey, Stewart, Sumner, Thayer, Tipton, Trumbull, Williams, and Wilson—21.

NAYS—Messrs. Anthony. Bayard, Buckalew, Corbett, Davis, Dixon, Doolittle, Edmunds, Ferry, Fessenden, Fowler, Frelinghuysen, Grimes, Henderson, Hendricks, Johnson, McCreery, Morrill (Vt.), Norton, Patterson (N. H.), Patterson (Tenn.), Ross, Sherman, Sprague, Van Winkle, Vickers, and Willey—27.

So the order was rejected.

The Contested Interrogatory.

The Secretary then read the following form of question proposed by Mr. Butler, one of the managers, to the witness, W. A. Burleigh, who was on the stand yesterday:—"You said yesterday, in answer to my question, that you had a conversation with General Lorenzo Thomas on the evening of the 21st of February last. State if he said anything as to means by which he intended to obtain, or was directed by the President to obtain possession of the War Department. State all that he said as nearly as you can."

Mr. STANBERY, counsel for the President, objected to the question.

The Chief Justice was about to submit to the Senate, when

Senator FRELINGHUYSEN submitted the following question in writing to the managers:—"Do the managers intend to connect this conversation between the witness and General Thomas with the respondents?"

Mr. BUTLER, one of the manages, rose and said that if that question was to be argued before the Senate the managers would endeavor to answer it.

On the question being repeated by the Chief Justice,

Mr. BUTLER rose and said:—If the question is to be argued on the one side the other will endeavor to answer the question submitted by the Senator from New Jersey.

In the course of the argument Senator TRUMBULL called for the reading of the question to the witness.

After it was read the Chief Justice asked whether the managers proposed to answer the question of the Senator from New Jersey.

Mr. BUTLER again rose. If there is to be no argument I will answer the question proposed, but if there is to be an argument on the part of the counsel for the President, we propose as a more convenient method to answer the question in the course of our argument. I can say that we do propose to connect the respondent with the question.

Argument of Mr. Stanbery.

The Chief Justice was about to put the question, when Mr. STANBERY rose to argue it. He said:—Mr. Chief Justice and Senators. We have at length reached the domain of law, where we have to argue no longer questions of mere form and modes of procedure, but questions that are proper to be argued by lawyers and to be decided by a court.

The question now, Mr. Chief Justice and Senators, is whether any foundation has been laid, either in the articles themselves or in any testimony as yet given, for using any of the declarations of General Thomas in evidence against the President. General Thomas is not on trial. It is the President and the President alone that is on trial, and the testimony to be offered must be testimony which is binding on him. It is agreed that the President was not present on the evening of the 21st of February, when General Thomas made those declarations. They were made in the absence of the President. He had no opportunity of hearing them or of contradicting them. If they are to be used against him they must be made by some person speaking for him, by authority. First of all, what foundation is there for the declarations of Gen. Thomas to be given in evidence, as to what he intended to do, or what the President had authorized him to do?

It will be seen, that by the first article the offense charged against the President is, that he issued a written order to Mr. Stanton for his removal, adding that General Thomas was authorized to receive the transfer of the books, records, papers and property of the department. Now the offense laid in that article is not as to anything that was done under the order; not as to any animus by which it was issued; but the order in itself is simply the gravamen of the offense. So much for the first article. Now, what is the second? It is that on the same day, the 21st of February, 1868, the President issued a letter of authority to General Thomas, and the gravamen there is the issuing of that letter of authority, not anything done under it. What next?

The third article goes upon the same letter of authority, and charges the issuing of it to be an offense intended to violate a certain act. Then we come to the fourth article. Senators will observe that in the three first articles the offense charged is issuing certain orders in violation either of the Constitution or the act known as the Tenure of Office act, but in the fourth article the managers of the House proceed to charge us with an entirely new offense against a totally

different statute, and that is a conspiracy between General Thomas and the President, and other persons unknown; by force, in one article, and by intimidation in another, to endeavor to prevent Mr. Stanton from holding the office of Secretary of War, and that in pursuance of that conspiracy certain acts were done which are not named, with intent to violate the conspiracy act of July 31, 1861. These are the only charges which have any relevancy to the question now pending.

I need not refer to the other articles, in which the offenses charged against the President arise out of his relations to General Emory, his speeches made at the Executive mansion, in August, 1866; at Cleveland, on the 3d of September, 1866, and at St. Louis, on the 8th of September, 1866. Now what proof has yet been made under these first eight articles? The proof is simply, so far as this question is concerned, the production in evidence of the order removing Mr. Stanton, and of the order to General Thomas. There they are to speak for themselves. As yet we have not had one particle of what was said by the President, either before or after the issuing of the orders.

The only foundation yet laid for the introduction of the testimony used is the production of the President's orders. The attempt now is, by the declarations of General Thomas, to show with what intent the President issued these orders, not by producing General Thomas here to testify as to what the President told him, but without having General Thomas sworn at all, to bind the President by General Thomas' declarations, not made under oath, and made without any cross-examination or contradiction. Now, Senators, what foundation is laid to show the authority given by the President to General Thomas to speak for him as to his intent. You must find that foundation, if at all, in the orders themselves. What are those orders? I will read them. The first is the order to Mr. Stanton:—

EXECUTIVE MANSION, WASHINGTON, D. C., Feb. 21, 1868.—Sir:—By virtue of the power and authority vested in me as President by the Constitution and laws of the United States, you are hereby removed from office as Secretary for the Department of War, and your functions as such will terminate upon receipt of this communication.

You will transfer to Brevet Major-General Lorenzo Thomas, Adjutant-General of the army, who has this day been authorized and empowered to act as Secretary of War ad interim, all records, books, papers and other public property now in your custody and charge.

Respectfully yours,   ANDREW JOHNSON.
To Hon. Edwin M. Stanton, Washington, D. C.

So much for that. Then comes the order to General Thomas, which I will read to the Senate:—

Sir:—Hon. Edwin M. Stanton having been this day removed from office as Secretary for the Department of War, you are hereby authorized and empowered to act as Secretary of War ad interim, and will immediately enter upon the duties pertaining to that office.

Mr. Stanton has been instructed to transfer to you all the records, books, papers and other public property now in his custody and charge

Respectfully, yours,   ANDREW JOHNSON.
To Brevet Major-General Lorenzo Thomas, Adjutant-General United States Army, Washington, D. C.

There they are. They are orders made by the President to two of his subordinates—an order directing one of them to vacate his office and transfer the public property in his possession to another party, and an order to that other party to take possession of the office and to act as Secretary of War ad interim.

Gentlemen, does that make a conspiracy? Is that proof of a conspiracy, or tending to a conspiracy? Does that make General Thomas an agent of the President, in such a sense as that the President would be bound by everything he says or does even within the scope of his agency? If it makes him his agent, does this letter of authority authorize him to do anything but that which he is commanded to do—go there and demand possession, and receive a transfer of the records of the department? Does it authorize him to go beyond the letter and meaning of authority given him? Why certainly not.

In the first place, it must be either on the footing of a conspiracy between General Thomas and the President, or on the policy of an agency in which the President is principal, and General Thomas is the agent. That the declarations of General Thomas, either as co-conspirator or as agent, are to be given against the President. There is no other ground on which these hearsay declarations could be given as evidence.

I agree that when a conspiracy is established, or when it is partially established, when testimony is given tending to prove it, and a proper foundation laid of a conspiracy in which A, B and C are concerned, then the declarations of one of the conspirators, made while the conspiracy is in process and made in furtherance of the conspiracy, not outside of it, may be given in evidence as against the other co-conspirators and binds the others. So, too, I agree, that where an agency is established either by parole, proof or by writing, and when established by writing that is the measure of the agency, and you cannot extend it by parole. The acts done and the declarations made in pursuance of that agency, are binding on the principal.

Now, I ask this honorable court where there is anything like a conspiracy here? Where is there any proof establishing any agency between General Thomas and the President, in which the President is the principal and General Thomas the agent? I do not admit that this letter of authority constitutes such agency at all. I do not admit that the President is bound by any declarations made by General Thomas on the footing of his being an agent of the President; but if he were, if this were a case of principal and agent, then I say that the letter of authority to General Thomas is that which binds the President, and nothing beyond it. The object here is to show that General Thomas declared that it was his intention, and the intention of the President, in executing that authority, to use force, intimidation and threats. Suppose a principal gives authority to his agent to go and take possession of a house in the occupancy of another, does that authorize him when he goes there to commit an assault and battery on the tenant, or to drive him out *vi et armis?*

Is the principal to be made a criminal by the act of his agent, acting simply on the authority to take peaceable possession of a house, by the consent of the party in posession, or is the principal to be bound by the declaration of the agent when the authority is in writing and does not authorize such a declaration? Who of us here would be safe in giving any authority to another if that were the rule by which we were to be governed? What, Senators, has the President done that he is to be held, either as a conspirator or as a principal giving authority to an agent? Does the President appoint General Thomas as his agent in any individual matter of his, to take possession of an office which belongs to him, or to take possession of papers that are his property? Not at all. What is the nature of this order? It is in the customary form; it is the designation of an officer already known to the law, to do what? To exercise a positive duty; to perform the duties of a public officer.

The President is the only authority which gives this power. Is the person whom he appoints his agent? When he accepts the appointment, does he act under these circumstances as the agent of the principal to carry out a private enterprise or perform a private action? Certainly not. He at once becomes the officer of the law, liable as a public officer to removal and impeachment, to indictment and prosecution for anything that he does in violation of his duty. Are all the officers of the United States who have been appointed in this way the agents of the President when the President gives them a commission, either a permanent or temporary one, to fill a vacancy or to fill an office? Are the persons so designated and appointed his agents? Is he bound by everything they do? If they take a bribe, is it a bribe to him? If they commit an assault and battery, is the assault and battery committed by him? If they exceed their authority does he become liable? Why, not at all. If third parties are injured by them in the exercise of the power which he has given them, he can give third parties the power to come back upon the President as the responsible party, on the principle of *respondent superior.* Why there is no principle of law or justice in it. He clothes him not with his authority, but with the authority of his office. A public officer is appointed; he stands under obligations not to his principal, not to the President, but to the law itself; and if he does any act which injures a third person, or violates any law, it is he who is responsible and not the President.

Senators:—I should almost apologize to this honorable court, composed as it is so largely of lawyers, for arguing so clear a point. I understood the learned manager (Mr. Butler) to say that they expected hereafter to connect the President with these declarations of General Thomas.

Mr. BUTLER—I did not say hereafter.

Mr. STANBERY—Does the learned manager say that he has heretofore done it?

Mr. BUTLER made an answer not heard by the reporters.

Mr. STANBERY—You mean that you expect to do it, not that you have done it. I understood the gentleman to say, in answer to the question put by the Senator, that he did expect to show a connection between the President and those declarations of General Thomas. If he did not say that he meant nothing, or he meant one thing and said another. I agree that there are exceptions to the introduction of testimony in cases of conspiracy, and perhaps in cases of agency, and that in extreme cases where it is impossible to have preliminary proof given, the statement of the counsel, made on their professional honor, is taken that the testimony offered is intended to be introductory to the testimony to be afterwards offered.

But in this case we have heard no reason why the ordinary rule should be reversed, and why testimony which is *prima facie* inadmissible should be offered in the assurance that a foundation would be hereafter laid to it. What reason is there for this deviation from the ordinary rule? Is it a matter of taste for the counsel to begin at the wrong end, and introduce what is clearly inadmissible, and to say:—"We will give you the superstructure first and the foundation afterwards?" Was such a thing as that ever heard of? I repeat that there may be extreme cases, founded on the direct assurance of counsel before a court, where the court will allow testimony which is *prima facie* inadmissible to be heard on the statement that the counsel would afterwards connect it. I think it is hardly necessary for me to argue the question further.

Authorities Demanded.

Mr. Stanbery having sat down,

Mr. BUTLER rose and asked that the usual rule be enforced, that counsel, in making their arguments, shall cite the authorities on which the arguments rest.

The Chief Justice remarked that that was undoubtedly the rule.

Mr. STANBERY said:—Mr. Chief Justice, we will allow this question to stand without citing authorities.

Mr. Butler's Reply.

Mr. BUTLER then rose and said:—Mr. President and Senators:—The gravity of the question presented to the Senate for its decision has induced the President's counsel to argue at length, knowing that largely on that question, and on the testimony to be adduced under it on one of these articles of impeachment, the fate of their client must stand. It is the great question, and, therefore, I must ask the attention of the Senate and of the presiding officer, as well I may, to some considerations which, in my mind, determine it. But, before I do that, I beg leave to state the exact status of the case up to the point at which the question is propounded. And I may say, without offense to the learned counsel for the President, that in making the objection, they have entirely ignored the answer of the President. It appears, then, that on or about the 12th of August last, the President conceived the idea of removing Edwin M. Stanton from the office of Secretary of War, at all hazards, claiming the right and power to do so against the provisions of the act known as "the Civil Tenure of Office act."

Therefore the decision of the question in one of its aspects will decide the great question here at issue at this hour, which is, is that act to be treated as a law? Is it an act of Congress, valid and not to be infringed by the act of any executive officer? Because, if that is a law, then the President admits that he undertook to remove Mr. Stanton in violation of that law, and that he issued the order to General Thomas for that purpose only. His palliation is, that he did so to make a judicial case. But he intended to issue the order to General Thomas, and General Thomas was to act under it in violation of the provisions of that act. Am I not right on this proposition? That being so, then we have the President on his side intending to violate the law, and we have him then issuing the order in violation of the law. We have him then calling to his aid in the violation of that law, an officer of the army.

Now, then, in the light of that law, what is the next thing we find? We find that the President issued an order to General Thomas to take possession of the War Department. Counsel say that it is an order in the usual form. I take issue with them. There are certain ear-marks about that order which show that it is not in the usual form. It is in the words of an imperative command. It is not "You are authorized and empowered to take possession of the War Department, etc., but it is, "You will immediately enter upon the discharge of the duties pertaining to that office." Now, then, we must take another thing which appears in this case beyond all possibility of cavil, and that is, that the President knew at the time that Mr. Stanton had claimed the right, on the 12th of August, not to be put out of that office, and that when he went out of it, that he notified the President solemnly that he only went out in obedience to superior force.

The President had authorized the General of the armies of the United States to take possession of the office, and that for all legal purposes, and for all actual purposes, was equivalent to his using the whole of the army of the United States to take possession; because if the General of the Army thought that the order was legal, he had a right to use the whole of the army of the United States to carry it out. Therefore I say that the President was notified that Mr. Stanton had only yielded, on leaving that office at first, to superior force.

Mr. Stanton had yielded wisely and patriotically, because if he had not yielded a collision might have been brought on, which would have, in the language of the late Rebels—and General Thomas belongs to them—"raised a civil war." Now, then, the President knew that Mr. Stanton at first said, "I only yield this office to superior force." Mr. Stanton having yielded the office, the General of the Army had, in obedience to the high behests of the Senate, restored it to him, and Mr. Stanton had been reinstated in it, in obedience to the high behests of the Senate. Thus he felt that he was still more fortified than at first. It he would not yield at first on the 12th of August, 1867, except to superior force, do you believe, Senators—is any man so besotted as to believe—that the President did not know that Mr. Stanton meant to hold it against everything but force?

He had seen Mr. Stanton sustained by the vote of the Senate. He had seen that an attempt to remove him was illegal and unconstitutional, and then, for for the purpose of bringing this to the issue, the President of the United States issued his order to Gen. Thomas, another officer of the army, "You will immediately enter upon the discharge of the duties pertaining to that office." What then? He had come to the conclusion to violate a law, and to take possession of the War Office. He had sent the order to Gen. Thomas, and General Thomas had agreed with him to take possession of the office by some means.

Thus we have the agreement between two minds to do an unlawful act, and that, I believe, is the definition of conspiracy all over the world. Let me repeat it; you have the agreement between the President, on his part, to do what has been declared an unlawful act, and you have General Thomas consenting to do it, and therefore you have an agreement of two minds to do an unlawful act; and that, I say, makes a conspiracy, so far as I understand the law. So, that on that conspiracy we shall rest this evidence under article seventh, which alleges that Andrew Johnson did unlawfully conspire with one Lorenzo Thomas, with intent unlawfully to seize, take and possess the property of the United States in the Department of War.

Then there is another ground on which this testimony can stand, and that is on the ground of principal and agent. Let me examine that ground, if you please. He claims that every Secretary, every Attorney-General, every officer of this government lives by his will, upon his breath only, are his servants only, and are responsible to him alone, not to the Senate or to Congress, or to either branch of Congress. They are responsible to him. He appoints them to such offices as he choses, and he claims this right illimitably, and he says in his message to you of the 2d of March, 1868, that if any one of his secretaries had said to him that he could not agree with him on the constitutionality of the act of March 2, 1867, he would have turned him out at once. All that had passed General Thomas knew as well as anybody else.

Now, then, what is the Secretary's commission, whether *ad interim* or permanent? It is that "he shall perform and execute such duties as, from time to time, shall be enjoined upon him or intrusted to him by the President of the United States, agreeably to the Constitution, relative to the land and naval forces; or to such other matters respecting the military and naval forces as the President of the United States shall assign to the department;" and that "the said principal officer shall conduct the business of such department as the President, from time to time, shall order or direct." Therefore, his commission is to do precisely as the President desires him to do, anything which pertains to the office; and he stands there as the agent of his principal. To do what?

What was Mr. Thomas authorized to do by the President? It was to obtain the War Office. Was he authorized to do anything else that we hear of at that time? No. What do we propose to show? Having shown that he was authorized to take it; having shown that he agreed with the President to take it; having put in testimony that the two are connected together in the pursuit of one common object, the President wanting General Thomas to get in, and General Thomas wanting to get in, and both agreeing and concerting means together to get in, the question is, by every rule of law, after we have shown the acts, the declarations, however naked they may be, of either of these two parties, about the common object. The very question we propose is to ask the general declarations of General Thomas about the common object. Now, the case does not indeed stop here, because we shall show that he was then talking about the common object. We asked Mr. Burleigh if he was a friend of General Thomas. He said "Yes." If they were intimate. "Yes."

I have already told you that Burleigh was a friend of the President. That he needed somebody to aid in this enterprise. There was to be some moral support to the enterprise, and we propose to show that General Thomas was endeavoring to get one or two members of the House of Representatives to support him in this enterprise, and was laying out a plan; and that he asked him to go with him and support him in the enterprise, and be there aiding and abetting. This is the testimony we propose to show, and that is the way we propose to connect him with the enterprise. That is the exact condition of things.

Now the proposition is, having shown the common object, when lawful or unlawful, makes no difference, but, as we contend, an unlawful object; having shown that the act of the two parties was one thing; having shown the argument of one with the other to do the act, can we not put in the declaration of both parties in regard to that act? Does not the act of one become the act of the other? Why have not my learned friends objected to what was said to Mr. Stanton? The President was not there. General Thomas was not upon oath. Why did not we put in the act of General Thomas there yesterday? It was because of what he was doing in relation to the thing itself.

Mr. STANBERY—It was within the authority.

Mr. BUTLER—Ah! that was within the authority. How was it within the authority? It was within the authority because the President had commanded him to take possession.

Now, then, we wish to know the means by which he was to take possession. How was that to be done, and what was it to be done with? They say—and only for the gravity of the occasion I could not help thinking it a tremendous joke—they say you should call the other conspirator, on the threat of one conspirator to show the conspiracy. Was that ever done in any court, one conspirator to turn king's witness, or state's witness against the other? Was that ever done? Never, sir.

Mr. BUTLER here quoted from Roscoe's Criminal Evidence, 390, in order, he said, to show that they were not bound to put in all their evidence at once, and that from the acts and declarations of the criminals themselves they could prove the conspiracy. He also read from 12 Wheaton, 469 and 470, the case of a slaver fitted out at Baltimore for the West Indies, wherein the declaration of one of the principals was admitted in evidence, to show the object of the voyage. It was agreed that the object in this case was to get the War Department at all hazards. It was admitted in the answer. The conspirators had been notified that Stanton would not deliver it, except by force. They then set out to provide ways and means. It would be shown that at this very conversation Thomas declared that if he had not been arrested he would have used force. Were they, then, to be told that the President could do this and that, and yet that they could not put in what the agent said. While he was pursuing this matter, suppose Thomas had gone to General Emory and said he wanted him to take this department by force, as no doubt he intended to do, until he found the hand of the law laid upon him. They expected to show by these declarations and to leave no doubt in the mind of any Senator what this purpose was. He (Mr. Butler) thought there was no doubt in the mind of any man what that purpose was.

The learned counsel for the respondent had said they had now got to a question of law fit to be argued by lawyers to lawyers. Implying that all other questions argued in this high court have not been fit to be argued either by lawyers or to lawyers. It was for them to defend themselves against that sort of imputation. He had supposed the great questions they had been arguing were not only fit to be argued by lawyers to lawyers, but by statesmen to statesmen. He insisted that this was not a question to be narrowed down to the attorney's office, but one to be viewed in the light of law, in the light of jurisprudence by the Senate of the United States. This was not a case where the court might go one way and the jury another. They were both court and jury, and he held that they should receive testimony in regard to all the acts and declarations of this Secretary *ad interim.* In this view the managers were fortunate in being sustained by the precedents.

The Question.

Mr. CURTIS, of counsel, asked for the reading of the question.

The Secretary read as follows:—"You said yesterday, in answer to my question, that you had a conversation with General Lorenzo Thomas on the evening of the 21st of February last. State if he said anything by which he intended to obtain, or was directed by the President to obtain, possession of the War Department? If so, state all that he said as nearly as you can.

Remarks of Mr. Curtis.

Mr. CURTIS—Mr. Chief Justice:—It will be observed that this question contains two distinct branches. The first inquires of the witness for declarations of General Thomas respecting his own intent. The second inquires of the witness for declarations of General Thomas respecting instructions given to him by the President. Now, in reference to the first branch—that is, the independent intent of General Thomas himself—I am not aware that that subject matter is anywhere an issue. General Thomas is not on trial. It is the President who is on trial. It is his intent or purpose; his directions; the unlawful means which he is charged with having adopted and endeavored to carry into effect, which constitute the criminality of these charges which relate to this subject, and, therefore, it seems to be that it is a sufficient objection to the first part of this question that it relates to a subject matter wholly immaterial in this case, in regard to which the most legitimate evidence which could be adduced ought in no manner to effect the case of the President, because the President is not charged here with any ill intentions or illegal intentions of General Thomas.

But he is charged here with reference to his own illegal intentions and views solely, for with them alone can he be charged; and, therefore, I respectfully submit, Mr. Chief Justice, that that branch of the question which seeks to draw into this case independent of the evidence, the intentions of General Thomas, aside from instructions given to him, or views communicated to him by the President himself, is utterly immaterial, and ought not to be allowed to be proved by any evidence, whether competent or incompetent. In the next place, I submit the evidence which is offered to prove the intention of General Thomas, if that fact were in issue here, and had been proved for any effect upon the President's case, is not admissible in this trial. The intent of a party, as every lawyer knows, is a fact, and it is a fact to be proved by legal, admissible evidence, just as much as any other fact.

It is common for a person not a lawyer to say that the true way to ascertain a man's intent is to take what he says as his intent, because when it is expressed that is the best evidence. All that is true. But inasmuch as he is not sworn before us—inasmuch as it is not given by him on the stand in the presence of the accused, with an opportunity for cross-examination—unless you can bring the case within one of the exceptions which exist in the court (one of them, as has been said by my associate, being the case of principal and agent, the other being the case of co-conspirators), I do not propose to go over the grounds which were so clearly put, as it seems to me, by my associate.

I think it must have been understood perfectly well the grounds upon which it is our intention to rest these declarations of General Thomas that he was not the agent of the President; that he received from his superior officer an order to do a certain thing, and in no sense thereby became the agent of that superior officer, nor did that superior officer become accountable for the manner in which he was carrying out that order, and that this is most especially true when the nature of the order is the designation of one public officer to occupy another public office and discharge its

duties, in which case, whatever the designated person does he does on his own account, and by force of his own views, unless he has received some special instructions in regard to the mode of carrying it out.

We submit, then, in the first place, that the intentions of General Thomas are immaterial, and the President cannot be affected by them. Secondly, if they were material they must be proved by sworn evidence, and not by hearsay statements. The other part of the question appears to me to admit of a little question.

It is proposed to inquire of the witness what was said by General Thomas respecting directions or instructions given to him by the President, which presents the naked case of an attempt to prove the authority of an agent by the agent's own declarations.

The question is whether the President gave instructions to General Thomas in regard to the particular manner or means by which this order was to be carried out. Upon its facts the order is intelligible. We understand it to be in the usual form. There is no allusion made to the exercise of force, threats or intimidation of any kind. Now they propose to superadd to this written order by means of the declarations of the agent himself, that he had authority to use threats, intimidation or force, and no lawyer will say that that can be done, unless there is first laid the foundation for it by showing that the parties were connected together as conspirators.

I agree that if they could show a conspiracy between the President and General Thomas, to which these declarations relate, then the declaration of one of them in reference to the subject matter of that conspiracy would be evidence against them. Now, what is the case as it stands before you, and as was accepted by the honorable manager himself? He starts out with a proposition that the President, in his answer, has admitted his intention to remove Mr. Stanton from office. That, he says, was an illegal intention; that, he says, was an intention to carry out by means of the order given to General Thomas, and when the President, he says, gave that order to General Thomas, and General Thomas accepted it and undertook to execute it, there was an agreement between them to do an illegal act.

Well, what was the illegal act? We have got what he called conspiracy to remove Mr. Stanton, and if that be contrary to the Tenure of Office law, that is an illegal act, I agree; but is that the illegal act which they are now undertaking to prove? Is that the extent of the conspiracy which they are now undertaking to show? Not at all. They are going altogether beyond that.

They now undertake to say that the President conspired with General Thomas, by various threats or intimidations, to commit a totally distinct crime under the conspiracy act. Yet they have shown only an agreement to remove Mr. Stanton; and with the limit of the conspiracy, as they call it, circumscribed within the intention merely to remove Mr. Stanton, they now attempt to prove the assumption of a conspiracy to remove him by force; that is, without having proved a conspiracy to remove him without force, they ask leave to give in evidence the declarations of these co-conspirators to show a conspiracy to remove him with force.

I respectfully submit that they must first show the conspiracy which they, themselves, pretend they have given evidence of; as soon as they get to the limit of that conspiracy of which they allege they have given some proof, let them then show this totally different conspiracy, namely:—A conspiracy to turn out Mr. Stanton by force. They must produce some evidence of that other conspiracy, before they can use the declarations of other parties as evidence against them.

But, sir, I do not think that this should be permitted. It is an entire misconception of the relations between these two parties of the Commander-in-Chief and the subordinate officer, the one receiving an order from the other; there is no evidence here tending to prove any conspiracy. The learned manager (Mr. Butler) has said that an agreement between two persons to do an unlawful act is a conspiracy. Well, it may be, but when the Commander-in-Chief gives an order to a subordinate officer to do an act, and the subordinate officer assents or goes to do it, is that done by agreement?

Does it derive its force and character and operation from any agreement between them? any concurrence in their minds, by which the two parties agree together to accomplish something, which, without that agreement, could not be done? Is it not as plain as day that military obedience is not conspiracy, and cannot be conspiracy? Is it not as plain as day that it is the duty of a subordinate officer, when he receives an order from his commanding officer, to execute that order?

General Thomas obeyed the order of the President on the ground of military obedience; was that a conspiracy? There can be no such thing as a conspiracy between the commander-in-chief and the subordinate officer. He is not liable for the fact that the commander-in-chief issues the order, and the subordinate officer obeys it. I therefore respectfully submit that the honorable managers have not only not proven even a conspiracy to remove Mr. Stanton by force, but they have offered no evidence to prove any conspiracy at all. It rests exactly where the written orders place it—an order from a superior officer to an inferior officer, and an assertion by him to execute that order. It has been said by the manager in the course of his argument, that if we took his view of the case we ought to have objected to the testimony of the declarations of General Thomas made when he went into the War Department on Saturday, the 22d of February. We could not make an objection to the testimony of what he then said. That was competent evidence.

He was there in pursuance of the order given to him by the President. He was doing what the President authorized him to do, namely, delivering an order to Mr. Stanton, he being for that purpose merely the messenger of the President, and having executed that, he was to take possession under the other order. Of course the President authorized him to demand possession, and that demand was as much an act capable of proof and proper to be proved as any other act done in the matter. Therefore we could have made no such exception as would have fallen within the range of any of the exceptions which we now take.

The learned manager relies also upon certain authorities which he has produced in books. The first is a case in Roscoe's Criminal Law, page 690, showing that under some circumstances the conspiracy may be proved before the person on trial had joined the conspiracy. I see no difficulty in that. The first thing is to prove the conspiracy which is a separate and independent fact. Now, in that case the government undertook to show in the first place that there was a conspiracy, and had proved it by testimony as to the assembling together of a body of men for the purpose of militia training, &c.

Having proved the conspiracy, they then gave evidence to show that the defendant had subsequently formed the conspiracy. That was all relevant and proper. If the managers will take the first step here and, in support of their articles, will show, by evidence, a conspiracy existing between the President and General Thomas, then they may go on giving evidence of the declarations of one or both of them, and until they do, I submit that they cannot give such evidence. The case in 2 Carrington, cited by the managers, was the case of a joint act of three persons falsely imprisoning a fourth.

There was a conspiracy—there was a false imprisonment—the immediate act done in pursuance of the conspiracy, and the court decided in that case that a declaration, made subsequent to the imprisonment, as to what were the intentions of one of the conspirators might be given in evidence against the others. The case cited from 12th Wheaton was one where the owner of a ship, having authorized the master to fit out the vessel as a slaver, the declarations of the master were given in evidence, to show the object and purpose of the voyage.

Unquestionably if he had made him his agent to carry on a sailing voyage, he had made him his agent for the purpose of doing all acts necessary to carry it out, and what was the act that was given in evidence? It was an attempt to engage a person to go on the voyage in a subordinate position. In the course of that attempt the master stated to him what the character and purpose of the voyage were, so that the case falls within the lines of the authorities and principles on which we rest.

We submit, therefore, to the Senate that neither of these questions should be allowed to be put to the witness. I ought to say that the statement by the manager that the answer of the President admits his intention to remove Mr. Stanton from office illegally and at all hazards is not so. The manager is mistaken if he has so read the answer. The answer distinctly says that the President believed, after the gravest consideration, that Mr. Stanton's case was not within the Tenure of Office act; and the answer further says that

he never authorized General Thomas to employ threats, force or intimidation. If the manager is to refer to the answer as an evidence for one purpose he must take it as it stands.

Argument of Mr. Bingham.

Mr. BINGHAM, one of the managers, next rose to make an argument in support of the ruling of the Chief Justice. He said, I have listened to the learned counsel who have argued in support of the objection. Admitting their premises, it would be but just to them and just to myself to say that their conclusions follow, but I deny their premises. There is nothing in the record to justify their assuming here for the purpose of this question, that we are restricted to the article which alleges that this conspiracy was to be executed by force.

There is nothing in the case as it stands before the Senate which justifies the assumption that the Senate is to be restricted in the decision of this question to the other article, which alleges that this conspiracy was to be executed by threats or intimidation. There is nothing in the question propounded by my associate to the witness, which justifies the assumption made here that the witness is to testify that any force was to be employed at all. Though if he were so to testify, I contend on all the authorities that it is admissible.

The Senate will notice that in Article 5 there is no allegation of force; no allegation of threats, or intimidation. Article 5 simply alleges an unlawful conspiracy entered into between the accused and General Thomas to violate the Civil Tenure of Office act. My associate was right in all his authorities, that if two or more agree together to violate a law of the land it is a conspiracy. In Article 5 there is no averment of force or threat or intimidation, but simply an allegation that a conspiracy was entered into between the accused, Lorenzo Thomas and other persons unknown to prevent the execution of the Tenure of Office act.

That rule declares that any interference with its provisions is a misdemeanor; and, of course, if a combination be entered into between two or more to prevent its execution that combination itself amounts to a conspiracy. The counsel have succeeded most admirably in diverting the attention of the Senate from the question which underlies the admissibility of this evidence, and which controls it.

I refer now specifically to Article 5, in which we claim this question arises. That article alleges that said Andrew Johnson, President of the United States, unmindful of the high duties of his office, on the 21st day of February, in the year of our Lord 1868, and on divers other days and times in such year, before the 2d day of March, 1868, at Washington, in the District of Columbia, did unlawfully conspire with one Lorenzo Thomas, and with other persons to the House of Representatives unknown, to prevent and hinder the execution of an act entitled an act regulating the tenure of certain civil offices, passed March 2, 1867, and in pursuance of said conspiracy did unlawfully attempt to prevent Edwin M. Stanton, then and there being Secretary for the Department of War, duly appointed and commissioned under the law of the United States, from holding said office, whereby the said Andrew Johnson, President of the United States, did then and there commit and was guilty of high misdemeanors in office.

Now, the Tenure of Office act recited in that article expressly, that persons holding civil office at the time of its enactment, who have heretofore been appointed by and with the advice and consent of the Senate, and every person who shall thereafter be appointed to any such office, and shall be duly qualified to act therein, is and shall be entitled to hold said office until his successor shall have been in like manner appointed and duly qualified, that is to say, by and with the advice and consent of the Senate.

The act then provides that the President of the United States may, during the recess of the Senate, on evidence satisfactory to the President, showing that an officer is guilty of misdemeanor in office, suspend such officer and designate some other person to perform the duties until the case be acted on by the Senate; and that if the Senate shall concur in such suspension, and consent to the removal of that officer, it shall so certify to the President, who may thereupon remove such officer and appoint another. But if the Senate shall refuse to concur, such officer so appointed shall forthwith resume the functions of his office.

The sixth section of the same act provides that every removal, appointment or employment made contrary to the provisions of the act, shall be deemed to be a high misdemeanor. The conspiracy entered into here between the two parties, was to prevent the execution of that law. This is so plain that no man can mistake it. The President, in the presence of this tribunal, nor General Thomas either, can shelter himself by the intimation that it was a military order to a subordinate military officer.

I wish to show, in the presence of the Senate, that if that were so it would be competent for the President of the United States to shelter himself or any of his subordinates by issuing a military order to-morrow, directed to Adjutant-General Thomas, or any other officer of the Army of the United States, to depose the Congress of the nation. This is an afterthought. It is no military order. It is a letter of authority within the express words of the statutes, and in violation of it. The evidence is that General Thomas accepted and acted on it.

The evidence was given yesterday, and was received without objection. It is now too late to make the objection. It is perfectly justifiable in this tribunal for me to say further, and to say it on my own honor as one of the managers of the House, that we rely not simply on the declaration of General Thomas to show the purpose of the accused to disregard this statute—to violate its plain provisions—but we expect, by the written confession of the accused himself, to show to this Senate this day, or as soon thereafter as can be done, that his declared determination in any event was to deny the authority of the Senate.

There was no intimation given to the Senate of this intended interference; the President grasped the power in his own hands, as if repealing the law of the nation, and challenging the representatives of the nation to bring him to this bar to answer; and now, when we attempt to progress with the trial, according to the known and established rules of evidence in all courts of justice, we are met with the plausible and ingenious—more plausible and more ingenious than some remarks of the learned counsel for the accused —that the declaration of one co-conspirator cannot be given in evidence against another, as to the mode of executing the conspiracy.

I state it perhaps a little more strongly than the counsel did; but that was exactly the significance of his remarks. I would like to know whence he derives any such authority. A declaration made, the execution of a conspiracy by a co-conspirator is admisible even as to the mode in which he would execute and carry out the design. It is not admissible simply against himself, but admissible against his co-conspirators.

It is admissible against them, not to establish the original conspiracy, but to prove the intent and purpose of the conspirators. The conspiracy is complete whenever the agreement is entered into to violate the law, no matter whether an overt act be committed afterwards in pursuance of it or not. But the overt acts which are committed afterwards by any one of the conspirators in pursuance of the conspiracy is evidence against him and against his co-conspirators.

That is precisely the ground on which the ruling was made, yesterday by the presiding officer of the court. That is the ground on which we stand to-day. I quite agree with the learned counsel for the accused, that the declaration of a purpose to do some act independent of the original design of the conspiracy, and to commit some subsequent independent crime, is evidence against no person but himself. But how can the Senate judge of that when not one word has dropped from the lips of the witness as to how the conspirators were going to carry the conspiracy into effect. General Thomas was in perfect accord with the accused, as he entered on this duty. He did not act that day as Adjutant-General; he acted as Secretary of War *ad interim*. He so denominated himself in the presence of the Secretary.

He declared he was Secretary of War in accordance with the authority which he carried on his person, and now we are to be told that, because he is not on trial at this tribunal, his declaration cannot be admitted as testimony, while the counsel himself has read the text going to show that if they were jointly indicted, as they may be hereafter, in pursuance of the judgment of this tribunal, this declaration would be clearly admissible. Lorenzo Thomas is not a civil officer of the government, and cannot be impeached; the power of the House of Representatives cannot extend beyond the President, Vice President and other civil officers. To be sure, Mr. Thomas claims to be a civil officer, and he is one. The President of the United States has proven by this combination with

him, to repeal the statutes and the Constitution of this country.

I have thus spoken for the purpose of showing the significance and importance which the counsel for the accused attach to it. It is not simply that they desire that this testimony shall be ruled out, but they desire to get in in some shape a judgment on the part of the Senate on the main question, whether Andrew Johnson is guilty of a crime, even though it be proved hereafter that his purpose was to defy the final judgment of the Senate itself, and the authority of the law. I understand from the intimation of one of his counsel, that if this were a conspiracy, then the acceptance by General Grant of the appointment as Secretary of War *ad interim*, was also a conspiracy.

The Senate will see very clearly that that does not follow. It involves a very different question, for the reason that the Senate expressly authorizes the President, for reasons satisfactory to himself, during the recess of the Senate, to suspend the Secretary of War and to appoint a Secretary *ad interim*, on the condition, nevertheless, that he should, within twenty days after the next session of the Senate, report his action, with the evidence therefor, and ask the decision of the Senate. He did so act. There was no conspiracy in that action of his, and it is not alleged that he did not thus recognize the obligations of the law, and did suspend the Secretary of War, and did appoint a Secretary *ad interim*, and did, within twenty days, thereafter, report the facts to the Senate, together with his reason.

The Senate, in pursuance of the act, did pronounce judgment in the case of suspension, and did reverse the action of the President. The Senate notified him thereof, and in the meantime he entered into this combination to defeat the action of the Senate and to overthrow the majesty of the law. And now, when we bring his co-conspirator into court on the written letter of authority issued in direct violation of the law while the Senate was in session, we are met with the objection that the declaration of the co-conspirator cannot be put in evidence against the accused.

I beg leave to say that I believe it will turn out that there will be enough in this conversation between Burleigh and Thomas to show to the satisfaction of the Senators that General Thomas did not simply desire to acquaint Burleigh of how this conspiracy between himself and Johnson was to be executed, but that relying on his personal friendship he desired Mr. Burleigh to be present on that occasion. I think I have said all that I think is necessary. I leave the question to the decision of the Senate, perfectly assured that the Senate will hear first and decide afterwards.

It certainly is very competent for the Senate, as it is competent for any other court of justice in the trial of cases where a question of doubt arises, to hear the evidence, and afterwards, as the Senators are judges both for the law and of the facts, they may dismiss so much of it as is found incompetent. I insist that there is no particle of law in which this testimony can be now excluded.

Senator JOHNSON sent to the Secretary a slip of paper, which was read, as follows:—

The honorable managers are requested to say whether evidence hereafter will be produced to show-

1st. That the President before the time when the declarations as which they propose to prove were made, authorized him to obtain possession of the office by force, threats, or intimation if necessary. 2d. That the President had knowledge that such declarations had been made and had approved of them.

Mr. BINGHAM, on behalf of the managers, said, I am instructed by my associates, and I am in accord with them, that we do not deem it our duty to make answer to so personal a question as that, and it will certainly occur to the Senate why we should not do it.

Mr. EVARTS rose to close the discussion, but Mr. BINGHAM raised the question, that under the rule limiting discussion on interlocutory questions the hour of the counsel for the President had expired, and that, at all events, the right to close the discussion lay with the managers.

The Chief Justice remarked that the twentieth rule made a limit as to time, and the twenty-first rule made a limit as to the persons who might address the court. He was not certain whether the limit of one hour applied to each counsel who spoke, or to all the counsel on one side, and he proposed to have that point decided by the Senate.

The Chief Justice put the question as to whether the twentieth rule should be understood as limiting discussion on interlocutory questions to one hour on each side, and it was decided affirmatively without a division.

Senator CONKLING then moved that the counsel for the President having been under misapprehension as to the application of the rule, have permission in this instance to submit any additional remarks they desire to make.

Mr. EVARTS remarked that the counsel for the President did not understand that they had yet occupied three full hours in debate.

The Chief Justice remarked that they had.

Mr. EVARTS said that they did not desire to transcend the rule, but that they supposed that they had still some few moments unoccupied. He had reason, however, with the intention of claiming only, as part of the counsel for the President, the right of closing as well as opening, according to ordinary rules of interlocutory discussion.

Senator CONKLING thereupon withdrew his motion.

The Chief Justice directed the Secretary to read the question to which objection was made, and it was read, as follows:—

Question proposed by Mr. BUTLER—You said yesterday, in answer to my question, that you had a conversation with General Thomas on the evening of February 21. State if he said anything as to the means by which he intended to obtain or was directed by the President to obtain possession of the War Department? State all he said, and as nearly as you can.

Senator DRAKE claimed that the yeas and nays must be taken on all questions under the rule.

The Chief Justice decided that it would not be necessary to have the yeas and nays taken, unless demanded by one-fifth of the members present.

Senator JOHNSON remarked that the question which he had submitted had probably not been heard by all the members of the Senate, and he asked that it be read again before the vote be taken.

Mr. BOUTWELL remarked, on behalf of the managers, that they had declined to answer the question because it seemed to them in the nature of an argument.

The vote was taken on allowing the question put by Mr. Butler to the witness to be asked, and it resulted yeas, 39; nays, 11; as follows:—

YEAS.—Messrs. Anthony, Cameron, Cattell, Chandler, Cole, Conkling, Conness, Corbett, Cragin, Drake, Edmunds, Ferry, Fessenden, Fowler, Frelinghuysen, Grimes, Henderson, Howe, Morgan, Morrill (Me.), Morrill (Vt.), Morton, Nye, Patterson (N. H.), Pomeroy, Ross, Sherman, Sprague, Stewart, Sumner, Thayer, Tipton, Trumbull, Van Winkle, Willey, Williams and Wilson—39.

NAYS.—Messrs. Bayard, Buckalew, Davis, Dixon, Doolittle, Hendricks, Johnson, McCreery, Norton, Patterson (Tenn.) and Vickers—11.

The witness W. H. Burleigh was recalled and examined by Mr. Butler.

You said yes, to-day, in answer to my question that you had a conversation with General Thomas on the evening of the 21st of February. State if he said anything as to the means by which he intended to obtain, or was directed by the President to obtain, possession of the War Department.

Witness—On the evening of the 21st of February I went to General Thomas'; I invited Mr. Smith to go with me to his house (some portions of the testimony at this point were inaudible in the reporters' gallery); I told him I heard he had been appointed Secretary of War, and he said he had been appointed that day; I think he said that after receiving his appointment from the President he went to the War Office to show his appointment to Mr. Stanton, and also his order to take the office. He said that the Secretary remarked to him—(here again the witness became inaudible.) I asked him when he was going to take possession. He remarked that he would take possession next morning at 10 o'clock. I think he also said that he had issued some orders. He asked me to come and see him. I asked whether I would find him in the Secretary's room, and he said yes; that he would be there punctually at ten o'clock. Said I, suppose Mr. Stanton objects to it, what would you do? His reply was, that if Stanton objected, he would use force. Said I, suppose he bolts his doors against you. Said he, if he does, I will break them down. I think that was about all the conversation we had at the time.

Q. Were you at the office at any time before he assumed the duties of Secretary ad interim, and after he assumed the duties of Adjutant-General? A. Yes sir; I was there two or three times.

Q. Did you hear him say anything to the officers or to the clerks of the department as to what his intentions were when he came into control of the department?

In reply to a question by Mr. Evarts, Mr. Butler replied that he referred to the time after General Thomas was restored to the office of Adjutant-General, and before he was appointed Secretary of War ad interim.

Mr. EVARTS—Then your inquiry is as to declarations antecedent to the action of the President.

Mr. BUTLER—The object is to show attempts on the part of General Thomas to seduce the officers of the War Department by telling them what he would do for them when he got control, precisely as Absalom sat at the gates of Israel, and attempted to seduce the people from their allegiance to David, the King, by telling what he would do when he came to the throne.

Mr. EVARTS objected to the question.

The Senate took a recess of ten minutes, after which Mr. Butler withdrew the question and put another, as follows:—

Q. I observe that you did not answer the whole of my question. I asked you whether anything was said by him in that conversation as to the orders he had received from the President? A. During the conversation General Thomas said he would use force if necessary, and stated that he was required by the President to take possession of the department, and that he was bound to obey the President, as his superior officer. This was in connection with the conversation about force, and in connection with his making the demand.

Q. After General Thomas was restored to the office of Adjutant-General, did you hear him make any statement to officers or clerks as to the rules or orders of Mr. Stanton which he would revoke or rescind in favor of the officers or employees when he would have control of affairs there?

Mr. EVARTS objected to the question, as irregular and immaterial to any issue in the case.

Mr. BUTLER argued that it came within the question last discussed. He said, we charge that the whole procedure of taking up this disgraced officer and restoring him to the War Office, knowing that he was an old enemy of Mr. Stanton's, who had deposed him from his official station, was part of the conspiracy. Mr. Thomas then goes to seducing the clerks, to getting them ready to rely upon him when he should be brought into the War Office.

Now I propose to show the acts of one of these co-conspirators clustering about the point of time just before he was going to break down the doors of the War Office with crowbars and axes. I propose to show him endeavoring to seduce the clerks and employees of the War Department from their allegiance, and this entirely comes within the rule which is made.

Mr. EVARTS said:—Mr. Chief Justice and Senators:—The question which led to the introduction of the statement of General Thomas to this witness as to his intentions, and as to the President's instructions to him (General Thomas), was based upon the claim that the order of the President on the 21st of February for the removal of Mr. Stanton and for General Thomas to take possession of the office, created and is proved a conspiracy, and that thereafter, in that proof, declarations and intentions will be given in evidence. That step has been gained in the judgment of this honorable court in conformity with the rules of law and evidence.

That being gained, it is solemnly argued that if no conspiracy is proved, you can introduce declarations made thereafter. You can, by the same rule, introduce declarations made heretofore. That is the only argument presented to the court for the admission of this evidence. So far as the statement of the learned managers relates to the office, the position, the character and the conduct of General Thomas, it is sufficient for me to say, that not one particle of evidence has been given in this case bearing on any one of those topics.

If General Thomas had been a disgraced officer; if those aspersions and those revilings are just, they are not justified by any evidence before this court. If, as a matter of fact applicable to the situation on which this proof is sought to be introduced, the former employment of General Thomas and his recent restoration to the active duties of Adjutant-General are pertinent, let them be proved, and then we have, at least, the basis of fact of General Thomas previous relation to the War Department, and Mr. Stanton, and to the office of Adjutant-General.

And now, having pointed out to this honorable court that the declarations sought to be given in evidence of General Thomas to affect the President, are confessedly of a period antecedent to the date at which any evidence whatever is before this court, bringing the President and General Thomas in connection. I might leave it safely there; but what is there in the nature of the general proof sought to be introduced which should affect the President of the United States with any responsibility for those general and vague statements of an officer of what he might and could or would do, if thereafter he should come into possession of the War Department.

Mr. BINGHAM rose and said:—Mr. President, I desire to say a word or two in reply to the counsel. I am willing to concede that what may have been said by General Thomas before the transaction is not admissible. That is, however, subject to the exception that the Senate, being the triers of the facts as well as of the law, may allow declarations of this sort to be proved. If there is any doubt that we are permitted to show that some arrangement was entered into between those parties, or, if you please, that a voluntary act was committed by General Thomas, in order to commend himself to the chief of the conspirators, The general rule is laid down in Roscoe, page 76, that the acts and declarations of other persons in the conspiracy may be given in evidence, if referable to the case, and yet I admit that if it was so remote as not in probability to connect itself with the transaction, it ought not to be received. The testimony in this case indicates a purpose on the part of General Thomas to make his arrangements with the employees of the War Department.

The Chief Justice—The Chief Justice is of opinion that no sufficient foundation has been laid for the introduction of this testimony, there having been no evidence as to the existence of a conspiracy prior to the time to which the question relates. I will put the question to the Senate if any Senator demands it.

Senator HOWARD demanded the question to be put.

Mr. BUTLER rose and said that he was about to ask the Senate if it would not relax the rule, so as to allow the managers on the part of the House of Representatives, when they have a question which they deem of consequence to their case, to have the question put to the Senate on the motion of the House of Representatives.

The Secretary read, by direction of the Chief Justice, the question to which objection had been made, and the Chief Justice put the question to the Senate, whether that should be allowed to be proposed to the witness.

The vote was taken and resulted, yeas, 28; nays, 22, as follows:—

YEAS.—Messrs. Anthony, Cameron, Cattell, Chandler, Cole, Conkling, Conness, Corbett, Cragin, Drake, Henderson, Howard, Howe, Morgan, Morrill (Vt.), Morton, Nye, Patterson (N. H.), Pomeroy, Ramsey, Ross, Sprague, Stewart, Sumner, Thayer, Tipton, Trumbull and Wilson —28.

NAYS—Messrs! Bayard, Buckalew, Davis, Dixon, Doolittle, Edmunds, Ferry, Fessenden, Fowler, Frelinghuysen, Grimes, Hendricks, Johnson, McCreery, Morrill (Me.), Norton, Patterson (Tenn.), Sherman, Van Winkle, Vickers, Willey and Williams—22.

So the question was allowed, and the examination was continued.

Mr. BUTLER, however, modifying his question as follows:—Q. Were you present at the War Department on the occasion referred to. A. I was.

Q. Did you hear General Thomas make any statements to the officers and clerks, or either of them, belonging to the War Office, as to the rules and orders of Mr. Stanton or the office, which he (Thomas) would revoke, relax or rescind in favor of the government employees when he got control of the department. If so, state what that conversation was? A. Soon after General Thomas was restored I visited his office and wanted him to take a walk with me; this, I think, was not more than a week or ten days before his appointment as Secretary of War.

Mr. EVARTS interrupted the witness, and said the question allowed by the Senate, he understood to relate to statements made by General Thomas, at the War Office, to clerks of the department, but the witness was now going on to state what took place between himself and General Thomas.

The witness was allowed to proceed, and he stated that General Thomas said he had made arrangements for all the heads of divisions in the office to stop on that morning, as he wanted to address them; I offered to go out but he told me to remain, and four or five

officers brought their clerks in, and he made an address to each company as they came in, stating that he did not propose to hold them strictly to the letter of their instructions, but that they might come and go as they pleased, as he would regard them as gentlemen who would do their duty. Afterwards I told the General that he would make a fine politician, as I thought he understood human nature; he described the rules as harsh and arbitrary. General Thomas had been away from the Adjutant-General's Office for a considerable time; he was sent South, I believe.

Q. Since you heard this conversation about breaking down the doors of the War Office by force have you seen General Thomas? A. Yes, I have. I gave my testimony before the Board of Managers, and General Thomas told me that he had been summoned before the managers. I saw him the other day.

Various questions were put to witness to elicit a statement of a recent conversation in which General Thomas had acknowledged the correctness of the evidence given by witness before the managers, but Mr. Evarts objected, but finally the objections were overruled by the Chief Justice, and the witness proceeded as follows:—

In the forepart of last week, on meeting General Thomas he said the only thing that prevented him taking possession of the War Office was his arrest. Witness did not recollect what he said to General Thomas.

Cross-examination by Mr. STANBERY.

Witness had business with General Thomas; at his interview at the War Department, prior to the appointment as Secretary of War; had heard before that he was restored to his position as Adjutant-General; saw there a number of the heads of bureaus and their clerks; could not name them; would not say how came in first; General Williams was present; General Thomas addressed each of the heads of the bureaus and clerks separately, to four or five of them making nearly the same address to each; could not give the exact language, but it was to the effect that he had come back to assume the duties of the office; that he was glad to see them; that he proposed to relax somewhat the arbitrary rules of the office; that he did not wish to hold them to such a strict accountability; that he expected them to discharge their duties, and that was all he cared about.

Witness understood General Thomas to mean by the office he had returned to, the office of the Adjutant-General; did not understand that General Thomas gave any orders at that time; there were only heads of departments connected with the Adjutant-General's office.

Q. Did you hear or see anything improper at that time? A. I don't know that I am a judge of what is proper or improper in the Adjutant-General's office; there was nothing very offensive.

Samuel Wilkeson sworn direct. Examination by Mr. Butler.

Q. Do you know Lorenzo Thomas, Adjutant-General of the United States army? A. I do.

Q. How long have you known him? A. Between six and seven years.

Q. Have you had any conversation with him relative to the change in the War Department? If so, state as near as you can what it was. A. I had a conversation with him respecting that change on the 21st day of February.

Q. What time in the day? A. Between one and two o'clock in the afternoon.

Q. Where? A. At the War Department, at his office.

Q. State what took place at this interview? A. I asked him to tell me what had occurred that morning between him and the Secretary of War, in his endeavor to take possession of the War Department; he hesitated to do so, until I told him the town was filled with rumors of the change that had been made and the removal of Mr. Stanton and the appointment of himself. He then said that since the affair had become public he felt relieved to speak to me about it. He drew from his pocket a copy of the original order of the President of the United States directing him to take possession of the War Department immediately. He told me that he had taken, as a witness of his action, General Williams, and came up in the War Department and had shown to Edwin M. Stanton the order of the President, and had demanded by virtue of that order the possession of the War Department and its books and papers. He told me that E. M. Stanton, after reading the order, had asked him if he would allow him sufficient time to gather ogether his books, papers and other personal property and take them away with him; that he told him he would allow him all the necessary time to do so, and had then withdrawn from Mr. Stanton's room. He further told me that day being Friday that the next day would be a "dies non," being Saturday, the anniversary of Washington's Birthday, when he had directed that the War Department would be closed; the next day was Sunday, and that on Monday he should demand possession of the War Department and its property, and if that demand was refused, or resisted, that he should apply to the General-in-Chief of the Army for a force sufficient to enable him to take possession of the War Department, and he added that he didn't see how the General of the Army could refuse to obey his demand for that force. He then added that, under the order which the President had given him, he had no election to pursue any other course than the one he had indicated; that he was a subordinate officer, directed by an order from a superior officer, and that he must pursue that course.

Q. Did you see him afterwards, and have any conversation with him on the subject? A. I did, sir.

Q. When was that? A. That evening.

Q. Where? A. At Willard's Hotel.

Q. What did he say there? A. He then said that he should next day demand possession of the War Department, and that if the demand was resisted, he would apply to General Grant for a force to enable him to take possession; and he also repeated his declaration that he couldn't see how General Grant could refuse to obey that demand for force.

Q. Were these conversations earnest or otherwise on his part? A. Do you mean by earnestness that he meant what he said?

Q. Yes. A. Then they were in that sense, earnest. (Laughter.)

Cross-examination by Mr. STANBERY.

Witness stated that he had been a journalist by profession for a number of years; that he had been in Washington during the sessions of Congress for the last seven years; General Thomas said he had issued an order to close the War Department on Saturday; did not say when it had been issued; could not say whether it was issued by him as Adjutant-General or as Secretary of War.

By Mr. BUTLER—Q. State whether in either of these conversation he said that he was Secretary of War? A. Yes, sir, he claimed to be Secretary of War.

George W. Kassner, sworn.—Direct examination by Mr. BUTLER.—He said he was a citizen of Delaware, and had known General Thomas ever since he had left West Point, and had lived in the same county with him; saw him about the 7th of March, in the East room of the White House, at a levee about ten o'clock in the morning; he introduced himself to General Thomas, who did not recognize him; he told Thomas that the "eyes of Delaware were upon him," and would require him to stand firm; he replied that he would not disappoint his friends, and in a day or two he would "kick that fellow out;" he did not mention any names, but witness thought he referred to the Secretary of War.

Witness was cross-examined at great length by Mr. STANBERY, and his eccentric manner and responses created bursts of laughter. Among other things, he said:—Before I left him I renewed the expression of the wishes of Delaware. (Laughter.) I first communicated the conversation I had to Mr. Tanner, going along the street that night, and also to several others in Washington, and among the rest to a gentleman from Delaware named Smith, but his name was not John.

[The serio-comic manner of the witness kept the Senate in a roar during the examination, which was continued for some time, and led the Chief Justice to remark that the cross-examination was too protracted, and served no good purpose.]

Mr. BUTLER proposed to ask this witness as to General Thomas having been called before the board of managers after witness had been examined, and that the evidence was read to General Thomas and he had assented to its correctness.

Mr. CURTIS, one of counsel, objected, and after a short argument waived it for the present.

The court adjourned till twelve o'clock to-morrow, and the Senate went into Executive session, and soon afterwards adjourned.

PROCEEDINGS OF THURSDAY, APRIL 2.

The Senate met at 12 o'clock, and the Chair was immediately vacated for the Chief Justice, who said that the Sergeant-at-Arms will open the court by proclamation.

The Sergeant-at-Arms made the proclamation in due form, and at 12·10 the managers were announced and took their places, and in turn were immediately followed by about a dozen of the members of the House of Representatives.

The journal was read.

The Seventh Rule.

Mr. DRAKE (Mo.), immediately after the reading of the journal was concluded, rose and said:—Mr. President, I send to the Chair, and ask the adoption of an amendment to the rules.

The Secretary read the amendment, as follows:—

To amend Rule 7 by adding the following:—Upon all such questions the votes shall be without a decision, unless the yeas and nays be demanded by one-fifth of the members present, as required by the presiding officer, when the same shall be taken.

At the suggestion of Mr. DRAKE, Rule 7 was read. It provides that the Chief Justice shall rule upon all questions of evidence and incidental questions as in the first instance.

Mr. HENDRICKS (Ind.)—I suppose by the rules it stands over one day.

The Chief Justice—If any Senator objects.

Mr. CONKLING (N. Y.)—Under what rule?

A brief colloquy ensued between Messrs. Hendricks and Conkling, which was inaudible in the reporters' gallery. The motion was then laid over.

Karsner Recalled.

Mr. STANBERY, of counsel, then rose and said:—Mr. Chief Justice, before the managers proceed with another witness, we wish to recall, for a moment, Mr. Karsner.

Mr. BUTLER, of the managers—I submit that if Mr. Karsner is to be recalled—the examination and cross-examination having been finished on both sides—he must be called as a witness for the respondent, and the proper time will be when they begin their case.

Mr. STANBERY—We will call him but a moment.

Chief Justice to Mr. Butler—Have you any objections to his being called?

Mr. BUTLER—No, sir.

George W. Karsner took the stand again.

By Mr. STANBERY—Q. Mr. Karsner, where did you stay that night on the 9th of March, after you had the conversation with General Thomas? A. I stayed at the house of my friend, Mr. Tanner.

Q. What is the employment of Mr. Tanner? A. I believe he is engaged in one of the departments in Washington.

Q. In which. A. I think the War Department.

Q. Do you recollect whether or not the next morning you accompanied Mr. Tanner to the War Department? A. I don't recollect that; sometimes I did, sometimes I didn't; sometimes I was engaged; other times I did accompany him.

Q. At any time did you go to the War Department to see Mr. Stanton with regard to your testimony? A. I saw Mr. Stanton.

Q. What about? A. Nothing in particular; only I was introduced to him.

Q. Who by? A. Mr. Tanner.

Why he Wanted to See Mr. Stanton.

Q. What was your object in seeing him? A. Well, I had seen all the great men in Washington, and I wished to see Mr. Stanton.

Q. In that conversation with Mr. Stanton was any reference made to your conversation with General Thomas? A. I think there was.

Q. Didn't you receive a note from Mr. Stanton at that time—a memoranda? A. No sir.

Q. Did he give you any direction where to go? A. No sir.

Q. Did he speak about your being examined as a witness before the committee, or that you should be? A. There was something to that effect.

Mr. STANBERY—That's all.

Mr. BUTLER—That's all, Mr. Karsner.

Congressman Ferry's Testimony.

Thomas W. Ferry, member of Congress from Michigan, was next called, and being sworn, was examined by Mr. BUTLER, as follows:—

Q. Were you present at the War Office on the morning of the 22d of February, when General Thomas came there? A. I was.

Q. At the time when some demand was made. A. Yes.

Q. State whether you paid attention to what was going on there, and whether you made any memorandum of it? A. I did pay attention, and I made a memorandum of the occurrences so far as I observed them.

Q. Have you that memorandum with you? A. I have.

Q. Please state, assisting your memory by that memorandum, what took place, in the order as well as you can, and as distinctly as you can? A. The memorandum covers the occurrences as distinctly as I can positively state them; I wrote it immediately after the appearance of General Thomas, and is more accurate and perfect than I can state from memory.

Unless objected to, you may read it.

Mr. STANBERY—We shall make no objection.

The witness then read the memorandum, as follows:—

WAR DEPARTMENT, WASHINGTON CITY, February 22, 1868.—In the presence of Secretary Stanton, Judge Kelley, Mr. Moorhead, General Dodge, General Van Wyck, Mr. Van Horn, Mr. Delano and Mr. Freeman Clarke.—At twenty-five minutes to twelve o'clock Adjutant-General Thomas came to the office of the Secretary of War, saying "Good morning." The Secretary replied, "Good morning, sir." Then looking around, General Thomas said, "I do not wish to disturb these gentlemen, and I will wait." The Secretary replied, "Nothing private here, sir. What do you want?" General Thomas demanded of Secretary Stanton to surrender the Secretary of War's office. Mr. Stanton denied it to him, and ordered him back to his own office as Adjutant-General. General Thomas refused to go, and said:—"I claim the office of Secretary of War, and demand it, by order of the President." Mr. Stanton—"I deny your authority to act on that order, and I order you back to your own office." General Thomas said:—"I will stand here. I want no unpleasantness in the presence of these gentlemen." Mr. Stanton—"You can stand there if you please, but you cannot act as Secretary of War. I am Secretary of War, and I order you to go out of this office to your own." General Thomas—"I refuse to go, and I will stand here." Mr. Stanton—"How are you to get possession? Do you mean to use force? General Thomas, "I do not care to use force, but my mind is made up as to what I am to do. I want no unpleasantness. I shall stay here and act as Secretary of War." Mr. Stanton—"You shall not. I order you, as your superior, back to your own office." General Thomas—"I will not obey you, but will stand here." Mr. Stanton—"You can stand here or not, as you please; but I order you out of this office to your own office; I am Secretary of War." General Thomas then went into an opposite room, crossed the hall to General Schriver's office, and commenced ordering General Schriver and General E. D. Townsend. Mr. Stanton entered, followed by Mr. Moorhead and Mr. Ferry, and ordered these officers not to obey or pay any attention to General Thomas. He said, "I deny his authority as Secretary of War ad interim, and forbid obedience to his directions; I am Secretary of War, and I now order you out of this office to your own office." General Thomas—"I shall not go; I shall discharge the functions of Secretary of War." Mr. Stanton—"You will not." General Thomas—"I shall require the employees of the War Department to deliver to me the mails, and shall transact the business of the office." Mr. Stanton—"You shall not have them, and I order you to your own office."

Cross-examination by Mr. STANBERY:—

Q. Did the conversation stop there? A. So far as I heard it did.

Q. You then left the office? A. I did; I left General Thomas in General Schriver's room, and returned to the Secretary of War's room; the Secretary of War remained for a few moments in General Schriver's room and then returned to his own room.

Q. How early on the morning of the 22d of February did you go to the office of the Secretary of War? A. My impression is it was about a quarter past eleven o'clock in the morning.

Q. Had you been there at all the night before? A. I had not been.

The storm which passed over the city made the Hall so dark that the gas had to be lighted at this point.

The testimony was then resumed.

Q. Did you hear the order given by General Thomas in General Schriver's room? A. Yes, sir.

Q. Were you in General Schriver's room at the time? A. I believe I was the first who followed Mr. Stanton into Gen. Schriver's room, and Mr. Moorhead came second.

General Emory on the Stand.

General William H. Emory sworn, and examined by Mr. Butler,

Q. What is your rank and your command in the army? A. I am Colonel of the Fifth Cavalry, and brevet major-general in the army; my command is the Department of Washington.

Q. How long have you been in command of that department? A. Since the 1st of September, 1867.

Q. Soon after you went into command of the department did you have any conversations with the President of the United States as to the troops in the department, or their stations? A. Yes.

Q. Before proceeding to give that conversation state to the Senate the extent of the Department of Washington, its territorial limits. A. The Department of Washington consists of the District of Columbia, Maryland and Delaware, excluding Fort Delaware.

Q. State, as well as you can, and if you cannot give it all, the substance of the conversations which you had with the President when you first entered on the command? A. It is impossible for me to give anything like the conversation; I can only give the substance of it, it occurred so long ago; he asked me about the location of the troops, and I told him the strength of each post, and, as nearly as I could recollect, the commanding officer of each post.

Q. Go on. A. That was the substance and important part of the conversation; there was some conversation as to whether more troops should be sent here or not, I recommending that there should be more troops here, and referring the President to the report of General Canby, my predecessor, recommending that there should be always at the seat of government at least a brigade of infantry, a battery of artillery, and a squadron of cavalry; some conversation was had with reference to the formation of a military force in Maryland, which was then going on.

Q. What military force? A. The force organized by the State of Maryland.

Q. Please state, as nearly as you can, what you said to the President in substance relative to the formation of that military force? A. I merely stated that I could not see the object of it, and that I did not like the organization, and saw no necessity for it.

Q. Did you state what your objections were to the organization? A. I think it likely I did, but I cannot recollect exactly at this time what they were; I think it likely that I stated that they were clothed in a uniform which was offensive to our people—some portions of it—and that they were officered by gentlemen who had been in the Southern army.

Q. By "offensive uniform," do you mean gray? A. Yes.

Q. Do you recollect anything else at the time? A. Nothing else.

Q. Did you call at that time upon the President at your own suggestion and of your own mind, or were you sent for? A. I was sent for.

Q. When again did he send for you for any such purpose? A. I think it was the 22d of February.

Q. In what manner did you receive the message? A. I received a note from Colonel Moore.

Q. Who is Colonel Moore? A. He is private Secretary to the President, and an officer in the army.

Q. Have you that note? A. I have not; it may be in my desk at the office.

Q. Did you produce that note before the committee of the House of Representatives? A. I read from it.

Q. Have you since seen that note as copied in its proceedings? A. I have.

Q. State whether this (handing a paper to the witness) is a correct copy. A. It is a correct copy.

Please read it.

The witness read as follows:—

EXECUTIVE MANSION, WASHINGTON, D. C., Feb. 22, 1868. —General:—The President directs me to state that he will be pleased to have you call upon him as early as practicable.

Very respectfully and truly, yours,
WM. G. MOORE, U. S. A.

Q. How early did you call? A. I called immediately.

Q. How early in the day? A. I think it was about mid-day.

Q. Who did you find in the President's room? A. I found the President alone.

Q. State as nearly as you can what took place there? A. I will try and state the substance of it; the words I cannot undertake to state exactly; the President asked me if I recollected the conversation he had with me when I first took command of the department; I told him that I recollected the fact of the conversation distinctly, and he then asked me what changes had been made; I told him no material changes, but such as had been made I could state at once; I went on to state that in the fall six companies of the Twenty-ninth Infantry had been brought to this city to winter, but as an offset to them the Twelfth Infantry had been detached to South Carolina on the requisition of the Commander of that district; two companies of artillery had been detached by my predecessor; one of them, detached for the purpose of aiding in putting down the Fenian difficulties had been returned to the command, and that, although the number of companies had been increased, the numerical strength of the command was very much the same, growing out of the order reducing the artillery and infantry companies from the maximum of war establishment to the minimum of peace establishment; the President said, I do not refer to these changes; I replied that if he would state to me the changes he referred to, or who made a report of the changes, perhaps I might be more explicit; he said, I refer to the changes within a day or two, or something to that effect; I told him that no changes had been made; that under a recent order issued for the government of the army of the United States, founded on the law of Congress, all orders had to be transmitted through General Grant to the army, and, in like manner, all orders coming from General Grant to any of his subordinate officers must necessarily come, if in my department, through me; that if by chance an order had been given to any junior officer of mine, it was his duty at once to report the fact; the President asked me, "What order do you refer to?" I replied, "Order No. 15, in the series of 1867;" he stated he would like to see the order, and a messenger was despatched for it; at that time a gentleman came in who, I supposed, had business in no way connected with the business I had on hand, and I withdrew to the farther end of the room; while there the messenger came with the book of orders, and handed it to me; as soon as the visitor had withdrawn I returned to the President with the book in my hand, and stated that I would take it as a favor if he would permit me to call his attention to that order; that it had been passed in an appropriation bill, and that I thought it not unlikely it has escaped his attention; he took the order and read it, and observed:—"This is not in conformity with the Constitution of the United States, which makes me Commander-in-Chief, or with the terms of your commission."

Senator HOWARD called upon the witness to repeat his language.

Witness—He said "This is not in conformity with the Constitution of the United States, which makes me Commander-in-Chief, or with the terms of your commission." I replied that "is the order which you have approved and issued to the army for our government," or something to that effect; I cannot recollect the exact words, nor do I pretend to give the exact words of the President; he said, "I am to understand that the President of the United States cannot give an order except through the General of the Army, or through General Grant;" I said, in reply, that was my impression, and that was the opinion which the army entertained, and that I thought the army was, on that subject, a unit; I also said, "I think it only fair, Mr. President, to say to you that when this order came out there was considerable discussion on the subject as to what were the obligations of an officer under the order, and some eminent lawyers were consulted; I, myself, consulted one, and the opinion was given me decidedly, not equivocally, that we were bound by the order, constitutional or not constitutional."

Q. Did you state to him who the lawyers were who had been consulted? A. Yes.

Q. What did you state on that subject? A. Well, perhaps in reference to that a part of my statement was not altogether correct; in regard to myself I consulted Mr. Robert J. Walker.

Q. State what you said to the President, whether correct or otherwise? A. I stated that I had consulted Mr. Robert J. Walker, in reply to his question as to who it was that was consulted, and that I understood other officers had consulted Mr. Reverdy Johnson.

Q. Did you say to him what opinion had been given by those lawyers? A. I stated that the lawyers whom I consulted stated to me that we were bound by it undoubtedly, and that I understood from officers whom I supposed had consulted Mr. Johnson, that he was of the same opinion.

Q. What did the President reply to that? A. The President said the object of the law was evident; there the conversation ended by my thanking him for the courtesy with which he had allowed me to express my own opinion.

C. Did you then withdraw? A. I then withdrew.

Q. Did you see General Thomas that morning? A. I have no recollection of it.

Q. State whether this paper is an official copy of the order to which you refer? A. No, sir; it is only a part of the order; the order which I had in my hand has the appropriation bill in front of it; that is perhaps another from the Adjutant-General's office, but it is the substance of the order, or a part of it.

Q. Is it, so far as it concerns this matter? A. So far as it concerns this matter it is the same order, but not the same copy; or, more properly speaking, the same edition; there are two editions of the order; one containing the whole of the appropriation bill, and this is a section of the appropriation bill.

Q. Is this (handing the witness another paper) an official copy? A. Yes.

Q. This, I observe, is headed Order No. 15, and you said the order was No. 17. Do you refer to the same or a different order? A. I refer to the same order. I think Order 17 is the one containing the Appropriation bill; I think that is the one on file in my office that made the confusion in the first place; I said Order 15 or 17, but Order 17, I think, embraces the Appropriation bill.

Mr. BUTLER (handing the order to the President's counsel)—This is No. 15, and covers the section of the act.

Mr. EVARTS said—Then we will treat this as Order No. 17, unless there should be a difference.

Mr. BUTLER said:—There is no difference; and he read the order as follows:—

GENERAL ORDERS No. 15.—WAR DEPARTMENT, ADJUTANT-GENERAL'S OFFICE, WASHINGTON, March 12, 1867.—The following extract from an act of Congress is published for the information and government of all concerned:—"An act making an appropriation for the support of the army, for the year ending June 30, 1868, and for other purposes. Section 2. And be it further enacted, That the headquarters of the General of the Army of the United States shall be at the city of Washington, and all orders and instructions relating to military operations issued by the President or Secretary of War shall be issued through the General of the Army, and in case of his absence through the next in rank. The General of the Army shall not be retired, suspended, or removed from command, or assigned to duty elsewhere than at headquarters, except at his own request, with the previous approval of the Senate, and any orders or instructions relating to military operations issued contrary to the requirements of this section shall be null and void, and any officer issuing orders or instructions contrary to the provisions of this section shall be deemed guilty of a misdemeanor in office, and any officer of the army who shall transmit or obey any order or instruction so issued, contrary to the provisions of this section, knowing that such orders were so issued, shall be liable to imprisonment for not less than two years and not more than twenty years, on conviction thereof in any court of competent jurisdiction. Approved, March 2, 1867."

By order of the Secretary of War.

E. D. TOWNSEND, Assistant Adjutant-General.

Q. You are still in command of this department? A. I am.

Cross-examined by Mr. STANBERY—Q. The paper which you had, and which was read by the President on that day, was marked Order No. 17—15 or 17. In that paper marked 17, was the whole appropriation acted, printed and set out? A. Yes.

Q. In other respects it was like this? A. In other respects it was like that; the copy on file at my office contains the Appropriation bill, and I may have confounded them.

Q. Is it your impression that the paper which you had at the President's, or which was read by you at the President's, is the same as the one in your office? A. That is my impression.

Q. As I understood you, when this document, or No. 17, was sent to the officers of the army, there was a discussion among them. A. Yes.

Q. I see that this document contains no construction of the act, but simply gives the act for their information? That is so.

Q. On reading the act discussion arose among the officers of the army? A. Yes.

Q. As to its meaning, or what? A. A discussion with a view of ascertaining what an officer's obligations under the act were.

Q. You had received no instruction from the War Department or elsewhere, except what was contained in this document itself? A. None whatever.

Q. It left you, then, to construe the act? A. Yes.

Q. On that, you say, to settle your doubts, you applied to an eminent lawyer? A. I had no doubts myself, but to settle the doubts of others, I did.

Q. And the gentleman to whom you applied was Mr. Robert J. Walker? A. Yes.

Q. Was it he who advised you that you were bound to obey only orders given through General Grant, whether it was constitutional or unconstitutional to send orders in that way? A. It was only the question whether we were bound by the order.

Q. I understood you to say that the answer was constitutional or unconstitutional. A. Then I made a mistake. My question was, whether we were bound by it. I would like to correct that.

Q. You said in a former answer that the advice was that you were bound to obey the order whether it was constitutional or not, until it was decided? A. We had no right to judge of the constitutionality.

Q. That was the advice you got? A. Yes.

Q. Decided by whom and where? A. By the Supreme Court; and not only that, but a new order would have to be promulgated making this null and void and of no effect.

Q. When you said to the President that he approved something, did you speak in reference to that Order No. 17, which contains the whole of the act? Did you mean to say that he had approved the order or the act? A. So far as we were concerned, the order and the act were the same thing, and, if you will observe, it is marked "approved;" that means by the President.

Q. What is marked "approved," the order or the act? A. The act is marked "approved;" the order contains nothing but the act; not a word beside.

Q. Then the approval was to the act? A. I consider the order and the act the same.

Q. But the word "approved" that you speak of is to the act? A. So far as that is concerned, the order and act are the same thing.

Mr. WILSON, on behalf of the managers, produced and put in evidence an authenticated copy of General Emory's commission to rank of Major-General by brevet, to rank as such from the 12th day of March, 1865, for gallant and meritorious services at the battle of ——.

Mr. WILSON read the order assigning General Emory to the command of Washington, and continued:—We now offer the order under which General Thomas resumed his duties as Adjutant-General of the Army of the United States. (Reading it). We now offer the original letter of General Grant, requesting the President to put in writing the verbal order that he had given him prior to the date of this letter. Both the letter and the order of the President are the original documents. (Reads the request.) On that letter is the following indorsement (reading the indorsement):—"By the President, made in compliance with the request."

The next document which we produce is a letter written by the President of the United States to Gen. Grant, dated February 10, 1868. It is the original letter. ·I send it to the counsel that they may examine it.

Senator HOWARD—Is that an original?

Mr. WILSON—It is the original.

Mr. STANBERY, after examining it, said:—Mr. Chief Justice, it appears that this is a letter purporting to be a part of the correspondence between General Grant and the President. I ask the honorable managers whether it is their intention to produce the entire correspondence?

Mr. WILSON—It is not our intention to produce anything beyond this letter, which we now offer.

Mr. STANBERY (returning the letter)—No other part of the correspondence but this letter?

Mr. WILSON—That is all we propose now to offer.

Mr. STANBERY—I wish the honorable managers to state what is the purpose of introducing this letter—what is the object—for what charge?

Mr. WILSON—I may state, as the special object for the introduction of this letter, that it is to show the declaration of the President as to his intent to prevent the Secretary of War (Mr. Stanton) resuming the duties of the office of Secretary of War, in defiance of the Senate. Do you desire it read (to Mr. Stanbery)?

Mr. STANBERY—Oh, yes! of course.

Mr. WILSON read the letter, which is that in which the President inclosed the testimony of his Cabinet on the question of veracity between himself and General Grant, which letter Mr. Wilson did not read.

Mr. STANBERY—I ask the honorable manager if he has read all that he intends to? In that letter certain letters were referred to, of which it is explanatory. Do you propose to read them?

Mr. WILSON—All has been read that we propose to offer.

Mr. STANBERY—You do not propose to offer the papers and document that accompany that letter?

Mr. WILSON—I wish to state to the counsel that we offered a letter of the President of the United States. We proposed to offer it, we have offered it, it is in evidence; that is the entire evidence.

Mr. STANBERY—We ask that the documents referred to be read, that accompany it and explain it.

Mr. WILSON—We offer, sir, nothing but the letter. If the counsel have anything to offer when they come to make up their case, we will consider it then.

Mr. STANBERY—Suppose there were a postscript.

Mr. WILSON—There is no postscript, though. (Laughter.) It is there as written by the President.

Mr. STANBERY—We will ask a ruling upon that point. On the first page of the letter the matter is referred to which you read. He read portions of the letter, emphasizing the President's quotation from General Grant's letter, referring to a former letter of the President's as "containing many gross misrepresentations," also the portion referring to the letters inclosed, saying he left them to speak for themselves without comment. That, Mr. Stanbery continued, is the answer to the statement.

Mr. WILSON—I suppose the counsel will not claim that this is not the letter complete? That is all we propose to offer now. This letter is in evidence.

Mr. STANBERY—We submit that the gentlemen are bound to produce them.

Mr. WILSON—The objection is too late, if it had any force at the proper time. The letter is submitted and has been read, and is in evidence now.

The Chief Justice made a statement inaudible to the gallery, which was understood to favor Mr. Wilson's point.

Mr. EVARTS—Our point is, Mr. Chief Justice, that those inclosures form a part of the communication made by the President to General Grant, and we assumed that they would be read as a part of this letter, as a matter of course.

Mr. BINGHAM—We desire to state, Mr. President, that we are not aware of any obligation, by any rule of evidence whatever, in this written statement of the accused, to admit in evidence the statement referred to generally by him. in that written statement, of third persons. In the first place their evidence, we claim, would not be evidence against the President at all; they would be hearsay; they would not be the best evidence of what the parties had said. The matters contained in the letter of the President show that the papers, which we are asked to produce here, have relation to a question of fact between himself and General Grant.

This question of fact as far as the President is concerned, is assumed by the President in this letter by himself, and for himself, and includes him, and we insist that if forty members of his Cabinet were to write otherwise he could not ask this question. It includes him; it is his own declaration about a matter of dispute between himself and General Grant; and that which is referred to in this letter is no part of the matter upon which we rely in this accusation against the President.

Mr. STANBERY—We rely upon it.

Mr. BINGHAM—Of course the gentleman relies upon it, and they ask us to read a matter which is no part of the evidence at all. It is not the highest evidence if we are to have the testimony of the members of the Cabinet about a material matter; and, as I have said, this letter claims that this is a material fact. I claim that, so far as they are concerned, they are unsworn letters and unsworn testimony, and that, by no rule of evidence, is competent.

I admit that if the letter, according to the statement here, showed a statement adopted by the President in regard to the matter of the charges, it would be a different question; that it would take it then outside of the rules of evidence. But anybody can see that that is not the point at all. I assert that it is not competent to offer in evidence the statement of any Cabinet officer whatever; that it has not any bearing upon the letter now read, to show that his purpose was to prevent the execution of the Tenure of Office law, and prevent the Secretary of War, after being confirmed by the Senate, and the appointment of General Thomas being non-concurred in, from entering upon and forthwith performing, as the law requires, the duties of his office. That is the point of this letter. We introduce it for the purpose of showing the President's intention; we say, that in every point of view, the letter being offered for the reasons I have already stated, those statements are foreign to the case, and we are under no obligation to introduce them, and in my judgment have no right to introduce them.

Mr. EVARTS—Mr. Chief Justice:—The counsel for the President will reduce their objections to writing.

The objection was prepared accordingly by Mr. Curtis, and by direction of the Chief Justice, the Clerk read it as follows:—"The counsel for the President object that the letter is not in evidence in the case unless the honorable managers shall also read the inclosures therein referred to, and by the latter made part of the same."

Mr. STANBERY—Is the question now before your Honor or before the court?

The Chief Justice—It is before the court, sir.

Mr. STANBERY—The managers read a letter from the President to use against him certain statements made in it, and perhaps the whole. We do not know the object. They say the object is to prove a certain intent with regard to the exclusion of Mr. Stanton from office. In that letter the President has referred to certain documents which are inclosed in it, as throwing light upon the question and explaining his own views.

Now I put it to the honorable Senators, suppose he had copied these letters himself in the body of the letter, and had said just as he says here:—"I refer you to these; these are part of my communication," would any one doubt that although they came from other persons he can, if he chooses, use them as explanatory of his letter, or alone; and he sends along with it certain explanatory matters, and he took the trouble of putting them in the body of his letter. Now suppose he attaches it and make it a part, calls it an exhibit, attaches it to the letter by tack or seal, or otherwise, would it not be read as a part of the communication, as the very matter is introduced as explanatory, without which he is not willing to introduce that letter? Not at all. Is it not fair to read with it the letters that are a part of it? It seems to me that they must read the whole of what the President said in order to give his views, not merely the letter.

Mr. WILSON—The managers do not suppress anything. We have received from the files of the proper department a letter complete in itself, a letter written by the President, and signed by the President, in which, it is true, he refers to certain statements made by members of the Cabinet touching a question of veracity pending between the President and General Grant. Now, we insist that that question has nothing to do with this case—everything contained in the letter which can, by any possibility, be considered as the elements of the case, is tendered by offering the letter itself; and the statements of the President, referring to the said inclosures, show that those inclosures relate exclusively to that question of veracity pending between himself and General Grant, and are in no wise connected with the question between the President and the representatives of the people.

The Chief Justice stated the case, (not so as to be heard by the reporter, however).

Mr. WILSON—We expect to use the letter for any proper purpose connected with the issues of the case. We read the whole of it.

The Chief Justice—The Chair will put the question to the consideration of the Senate.

Senator CONKLING—I offer the following request: —It calls for the reading of the matter referred to by the counsel.

The Secretary read the request as follows:—The counsel for the respondent will please read the words in the letter relied upon touching the inclosure.

Mr. STANBERY read it as follows:—

"General:—The extraordinary character of your letter of the 3d inst. would seem to preclude any reply on my part, but the manner in which publicity has been given to the correspondence of which that letter forms a part, the grave questions which are involved, induce me to take this mode of giving, as a proper sequel to the communications which have passed between us, the statements of five members of the Cabinet, who were present on the occasion of our conversation on the 14th ult. Copies of the letters which they have addressed to me upon this subject, are accordingly herewith inclosed."

The Chief Justice stated the question.

Mr. FRELINGHUYSEN called for the yeas and nays, which were ordered.

Senator DRAKE—I desire to ask whether, if these objections are sustained, has it the effect of ruling out the letter altogether?

The Chief Justice—No, sir.

In reply to a query from Senator Anthony, the Chief Justice stated that the effect of an affirmative vote would be to sustain the objection of the President's counsel.

Senator HENDERSON—I presume the Senator desires to know whether the letter can afterwards be read as evidence if the objection should be sustained.

The Objection not Sustained.

The Chief Justice—It will exclude only the letters. The yeas and nays were called, with the following result:—

YEAS.—Messrs. Bayard, Conkling, Davis, Dixon, Doolittle, Fowler, Grimes, Henderson, Hendricks, Johnson, McCreery, Morrill (Vt.), Norton, Patterson (Tenn.), Ross, Sprague, Trumbull, Van Winkle, Vickers, Willey—20.

NAYS.—Messrs. Anthony, Buckalew, Cameron, Cattell, Chandler, Cole, Conness, Corbett, Cragin, Drake, Edmunds, Ferry, Fessenden, Frelinghuysen, Howard, Howe, Morgan, Morrill (Me.), Nye, Patterson (N. H.), Pomeroy, Ramsey, Sherman, Stewart, Sumner, Thayer, Tipton, Williams, Wilson—29.

So the objection was not sustained.

Thomas' Appointment.

Mr. WILSON—We now offer a copy of a letter of appointment by the President, appointing Lorenzo Thomas Secretary of War ad interim, that is certified to by Gen. Thomas. I submit it to the court for examination. I call attention to one thing connected with it. We offer it for the purpose of showing that General Thomas attempted to act as Secretary of War ad interim. His signature is attached to that document as such. If we are not called upon to prove his signature, we will not offer any evidence for the purpose.

He read the paper, as well as the following indorsement:—

Official copy, respectfully furnished to Edwin M. Stanton. L. THOMAS, Secretary of War ad interim.

Received 10 P. M., Feb. 21, 1868.

Mr. STANBERY—That is in the handwriting of Mr. Stanton?

Mr. BUTLER—That is in the handwriting of Mr. Stanton.

Mr. WILSON—We next offer copies of the order removing Mr. Stanton; the letter of authority appointing General Thomas, with certain indorsements thereon, forwarded by the President to the Secretary of the Treasury for his information. I submit that.

After inspection by Messrs. Stanbery and Curtis,

Mr. WILSON asked:—"Have the counsel for the respondent any objection to the introduction read negatively?"

The papers were read.

Examination of Colonel Wallace.

George W. Wallace, sworn and examined by Mr. Butler. Q. What is your rank in the army? A. Lieutenant-Colonel Twelfth Infantry, commanding the garrison of Washington since August last.

Q. What time in August? A. The latter part of the month; the exact day I do not recollect.

Q. State if at any time you were sent for to go to the Executive Mansion about the 23d of February? A. On the 22d of February I received a note from Colonel Moore that he desired to see me the following morning at the Executive Mansion.

Q. Who is Colonel Moore? A. He is on the Staff of the President, and is an officer of the army.

Q. Does he act as secretary to the President? A. I believe he does.

Q. About what time of the night did you receive the note? A. About seven o'clock.

Q. Was there any time designated when you were to call? A. Merely in the morning—Sunday morning.

Q. Did you go? A. I did.

Q. What time in the morning? A. About ten o'clock.

Q. Did you meet Colonel Moore there? A. I did.

Q. What was the business? A. He desired to see me in reference to a matter relating to myself personally.

Q. How? A. Sometime in December my name had been submitted to the Senate for a brevet; the papers had been returned to the Executive Mansion, and on looking over them Colonel Moore was of opinion that my name had been set aside; his object was to notify me of that fact, in order that I might make use of influence, and have the matter rectified.

Q. After that, did he say anything about your seeing the President? A. I asked him how the President was; he replied, very well; do you desire to see him? to which I replied, certainly, and in the course of a few minutes I was admitted to the presence of the Executive.

Q. Was a messenger sent in to know if the President would see you? A. That I am unable to answer.

Q. Did Colonel Moore leave the room where you were conversing with him before you went in to see the President. A. He left the room to bring out this package of papers, and for no other object that I am aware of.

Q. Did he go into the office where the President was only for that purpose? A. Yes sir.

Q. He brought the package and explained to you that your name appeared to have been rejected? A. Yes sir.

Q. And then you went in to see the President? A. I did; I went in at my own request.

Q. When you had passed the usual salutations, what was the first thing he said to you? A. The President asked me if any changes had been made in the garrison within a short time, in moving the troops. •

Q. You mean the garrison of Washington? A. Yes

Q. What did you tell him on that subject? A. I reported that four companies of the Twelfth Infantry had been sent to the Fifth District, and that beyond that no other changes had been made; I omitted to mention another company which I have since thought of.

Q. Did he ever send for you on such an errand before?

Mr. EVARTS suggested that the President had not sent for him on this occasion.

Mr. BUTLER modified his question. Did he ever get you into his room, directly or indirectly, in order to put such a question as that before?

Mr. EVARTS objected to the question because it assumed that the witness had stated that on his inquiry how the President was? the Secretary said:—"Would you like to see him?" and he said, "Certainly," and went into his room. That was certainly not getting him into the room directly or indirectly.

Mr. BUTLER—I assume one thing, Mr. President, and the counsel assumes another.

Mr. EVARTS—I follow the testimony. I assume nothing.

Mr. BUTLER—I again say that I assume the theory on the testimony, and I think the testimony was that the witness went there by the procurement of the President. I shall so argue when I come to it. But without parleying about that, I will put the question in this form:—

Q. Were you ever in that like position in reference to the President before? A. Never.

Q. Did he say to you anything on that subject as to his having asked the same question from your commander, General Emory, on the previous day, and of his having told him the same as you did? A. No, sir.

Q. Did he speak of it as a thing which he did know already?

Mr. EVARTS suggested that the witness should state what the President said.

Mr. STANBERY also objected to this mode of examination in chief, saying that it was a mode of examining witnesses which was altogether new to counsel.

Mr. BUTLER withdrew the question, and asked was there anything more said? A. Nothing more.

Q. On your part or on his? A. On neither.

Q. Did you find out the next day that you had been rejected by the Senate? A. I used the word "rejected" in my testimony before the committee, but I don't know that that was the right expression; when I come to reflect upon it the words used by Colonel Moore were, "set aside;" my own view of the matter was, that I had been rejected.

Q. Why do you change, now on the stand, the word "rejected" for the words "set aside?"

Mr. EVARTS—He does not change. He said "set aside" before. It is you that makes the change.

Mr. BUTLER—I understand what he said. (To the witness.)—Q. Why do you now change and say that you do not think Colonel Moore used that language. A. I have a perfect right to make use of such language as I think proper as a witness.

Mr. BUTLER—Entirely so, sir; but I only ask you why you use it? A. My reason is to correct any misapprehension in regard to the expression of Colonel Moore; my own view of it was that it amounted to a rejection; he said, "set aside;" he used that language I think.

Q. Did he make any difference between "set aside" and "rejected" at that time? A. That is a question I never thought of.

Q. Did he advise you to use influence with Senators to get yourself confirmed?

Mr. STANBERY asked what that had to do with the question?

Mr. BUTLER said he wanted to understand what the witness meant by rejected?

The witness was not cross-examined, but the court took a recess for ten minutes.

Mr. Stevens has a Fall.

During the recess Mr. Stevens, in attempting to reach a chair, fell on the floor of the Senate Chamber. Several Senators ran to his assistance, raised him and helped him to a chair. He appeared not to be much hurt.

After the recess Mr. Butler put in evidence the order restoring General Thomas to the Adjutant-General's office. The order is dated Headquarters of the army, February 14, 1868, and is as follows:—

General L. Thomas, Adjutant-General, Sir:—Gen. Grant directs me to say that the President of the United States desires you to assume your duties as Adjutant-General of the army.

Very respectfully,   C. B. COMSTOCK,
                    Brevet Brigadier-General.

Mr. Chandler's Testimony.

William E. Chandler was then sworn and examined by Mr. Butler.

Q. I believe you were once Assistant Secretary of the Treasury? A. I was.

Q. From what time to what time? A. From June, 1865, till November 30, 1867.

Q. While in the discharge of the duties of the office did you learn the office routine or practice by which money is taken from the Treasury for the use of the War Department? A. I did.

Q. State the steps by which it is drawn from the Treasury by the War Department. A. By requisition of the Secretary of War on the Secretary of the Treasury, which requisition is passed through the hands of the accounting officers of the department, and is then honored by the issue of a warrant signed by the Secretary of the Treasury, on which the money is paid by the Treasurer of the United States.

Q. Please state the accounting officers through which it passes. A. The Second Comptroller of the Treasury has the control of war and navy accounts; several of the auditing officers pass upon the war requisitions—the Second Auditor, the Third Auditor, and possibly others.

Q. Please trace a requisition through the War Department. A. My attention has not been called to the subject until now and I am not certain that I can state accurately the process in any given case; it is my impression, however, that a requisition from the Secretary of War would come to the Secretary of the Treasury and pass through the Secretary's office to the office of the Second Comptroller of the Treasury, for the purpose of ascertaining whether or not the appropriations on which the draft is to be made has been drawn; the requisition would pass from the office of the Comptroller through the office of the Auditor and then back to the Secretary of the Treasury; thereupon, in the warrant room of the Secretary of the Treasury, a warrant for the payment of the money would be issued, which would also pass through the office of the Comptroller, being countersigned by him; then it would pass into the office of the Register of the Treasury to be then registered, and thence to the Treasurer of the United States, who, on this requisition, would issue his draft for the payment of the money; that is substantially the process, though I am not sure I have stated the different steps of it accurately.

Q. Would it go to the Second Auditor first? A. Quite possibly the requisition would go first to the Second or Third Auditor, and then to the Comptroller.

Q. Is there any method known to you by which the President of the United States, or any other person, can get money from the Treasury of the United States, for the use of the War Department, except through a requisition on the Secretary of War? A. There is not.

Q. What is the course of issuing a commission to an officer of the Treasury Department who has been confirmed by the Senate? A. A commission is prepared in the department and signed by the Secretary; it is then forwarded to the President, and signed by him; it is then returned to the Treasury Department, where, in the case of a bonded officer, it is held until his oath and bond have been filed and approved; in the case of an officer not required by law to give bond, the commission is held until he qualifies by taking the oath; it is my impression that that is the usual form; there are some officers of the Treasury Department whose commissions are countersigned by the Secretary of State, instead of by the Secretary of the Treasury; for instance, an assistant secretary's commission has to be countersigned by the Secretary of State, and not by the Secretary of the Treasury; and suppose the commission of the Secretary of the Treasury himself; it issues from the office of the Secretary of State.

Q. On the 20th of November, 1867, was there any vacancy in the office of Assistant Secretary of the Treasury? A. There was not.

Q. Was there a vacancy up to the 30th of November? A. There was not.

Q. Do you know Edmund Cooper?

Sharp Sparring.

Mr. STANBERY asked the object of offering that testimony?

Mr. BUTLER replied—The object is to show one of the ways and means described in the eleventh article, by which the President proposed to get control of the moneys of the Treasury Department and of the War Department. If the counsel has any other question to ask, I shall be very glad to answer it?

Mr. STANBERY—That is not a sufficient answer to the question.

Mr. BUTLER—It is sufficient for the time.

Mr. EVARTS—What part of the eleventh article do you propose to connect this testimony with?

Mr. BUTLER—With both the eighth and eleventh articles. The eighth article says, that said Andrew Johnson, unmindful of the high duties of his office, and of his oath of office, with intent unlawfully to control the disbursements of the moneys appropriated for the military service and for the Department of War, did so and so. One of his means for doing it was to place his Private Secretary in the office of the Assistant Secretary of the Treasury. The Assistant Secretary of the Treasury, as I understand it, is allowed by law to sign warrants.

Mr. EVARTS said the managers propose to prove that there being no vacancy in the office of Assistant Secretary of the Treasury, the President proposed to appoint Edmund Cooper Assistant Secretary. That is the idea, is it? We object to its relevancy under the eighth article. As to the eleventh article, the honorable court will remember that in our answer we stated that there was no suggesting of ways and means, or of attempts of ways and means, whereby we could answer it; the only allegations there being that, in pursuance of a speech which he made on the 18th of August, 1867, and afterwards, on the 21st of February, 1868, at the city of Washington, in the District of Columbia, unlawfully and in disregard of the requirements of the Constitution, prevent the execution of the Tenure of Office act.

The only allegations in that article are, that on the 21st of February, 1868, the President did attempt to prevent the execution of the Tenure of Office act by unlawfully contriving means to prevent Edwin M. Stanton from resuming his place in the War Department, and now proof is offered here substantively of efforts in November, 1867, to appoint Edmund Cooper as Assistant Secretary of the Treasury. We object to such proof.

Mr. BUTLER—The objection is two-fold; one is that the evidence is not competent; the other is that the pleading is not sufficient. It is said that the pleading is too general.

If we were to find an indictment at common law for a conspiracy, and were to make the allegations too general, the only objection to that would be that it did not sufficiently inform the defendants what facts should be given in evidence; and the remedy for a defendant in that case is to move for specifications, or a bill of particulars; therefore, indictments for conspiracy are generally drawn as was the indictment in the Martha Washington case, giving one general count, and then several specific counts, setting out specific acts, in the nature of specifications, so that if the pleader fails in sustaining the specific acts, the plea may hold good under the general count.

We need not, I say, discuss the question of pleadings. The only question is, is this testimony competent. The difficulty that rests in the mind of my learned friends on the other side, is that they cluster everything about the 21st of February. They seem to forget that the 21st of February was only the culmination of a purpose formed long before, as in the President's answer is set forth, to wit, as early as the 12th

of August, 1867. He says that he determined then to get Mr. Stanton out at any rate.

I used the words yesterday "at all hazards," and, perhaps, that may be subject to criticism.

Now, then, there are many things for the President to do. He must get control of the War Office; but what good will that do if he could not get somebody in the Treasury Department who should be his servant, his slave, dependent upon his breath to answer the requisitions of his pseudo-officer whom he might appoint to the War Department, and, therefore, he begins early. The appointment of Mr. Cooper as Assistant Secretary of the Treasury was, therefore, a means on the part of the President to get his hands into the Treasury of the United States.

We show the Senate that, although Mr. McCulloch, the Secretary of the Treasury, must have known that Thomas was appointed Secretary of War *ad interim*, the President took pains to serve upon him an attested copy of his appointment, in order that he and Mr. Cooper might recognize it. I have yet to learn that it was ever objected anywhere that, when I am tracing a man's motives and when I am tracing his course, I have not a right to put in any act that he does, everything that comes out of his mouth, as part of my proof.

Let us see if that is not sustained by authority. The question arose in the trial of James Watts, for high treason, in 1817, before one of the best lawyers in England, Lord Ellenborough. The objection there was precisely the one that the learned counsel here raises. It was alleged that certain treasonable speeches had been made. They were not set out in form, but it was claimed that they could not be proved as overt acts.

The question then was whether certain other speeches could be put in as tending to show the animus with which the first set of speeches had been made.

Lord Ellenborough closed the description by saying, "If there had been no overt act under which this evidence was receivable, it is a universal rule of evidence, that what a party says may be given in evidence against himself to explain any part of his conduct to which it bears reference." The counsel for the defense said—"We do not object that it is not evidence, but that it is not proof of the overt act." Lord Ellenborough said there can be no doubt that whatever proceeds from the mouth of a man may be given in evidence against him, to show the intention with which he acts, *a fortiori*, when it is under his own hand. If his declarations may be given in evidence, why not his acts.

I would not trouble the presiding officer, and I would not have troubled the Senators upon this matter, had it not been that there may be other acts, all clustering around this grand conspiracy, which we propose, if we are permitted, to put in evidence. The question objected to is, who was Edmund Cooper? That was all the question. I suppose my friends do not mean seriously to object to that.

Mr. STANBERY—We asked what you expected to prove in reference to it?

Mr. BUTLER—I have replied to that. I propose to prove that Edmund Cooper took possession of the office of Assistant Secretary of the Treasury before the 30th of November, showing that the President gave a commission illegally and in violation of the Tenure of Office act, to which I wish to call attention.

The sixth section of that act declares that the making, signing and sealing, countersigning or issuing any commission or letter of authority in place of an officer whose removal has not been sent to the Senate, shall be deemed a high misdemeanor; therefore, the very signing of this letter of authority to Mr. Cooper, the signing, if he did not issue it, and the issuing, if he did not sign it, there being no vacancy in the office, is a crime, and is a part of the great conspiracy. The question therefore will be, whether we will be allowed to go into that matter?

Mr. STANBERY said:—We do not object so much to the question as to who Edmund Cooper is, but we want to know what it has to do with this case, and what even the illegal appointment of Edmund Cooper to the office of Assistant Secretary has to do with this case? We want to know what the appointment of Edmund Cooper for the purpose of controlling the moneys of the Treasury has to do with the case? I understand the learned manager to say that the proof he intends to make in regard to Edmund Cooper is, in the first place, that there was an illegal appointment of Mr. Cooper, and that the President violated the Constitution of the United States and violated the Tenure of Office act.

Have they given us notice to come here and defend any such delinquency as that? Has the House of Representatives impeached the President for anything done in the removal of Mr. Chandler, if he were removed, or in the appointment of Mr. Cooper in his place, if he were appointed. The managers select one instance of what they claim to be a violation of the Constitution and of the Tenure of Office act, and in reference to a temporary appointment of an officer during the recess of the Senate. That was the case of General Thomas, and of General Thomas alone.

As to that, of course, we have no objection to its being given in evidence, because we have notice of it, and are here ready to meet it; but as to any high crime or misdemeanor in reference to the appointment of Mr. Cooper, certainly the managers have no authority to make such a charge, because they come here with a delegated authority; they come here only to make charges that have been found good by the House, and not to make charges which they choose to manufacture here.

The managers have no right to amend these articles; they must go to the House for that right. If they choose to go to the House to get a new article founded upon the illegal act of the President in appointing Mr. Cooper, let them do so, and let us have time to answer it and to meet it.

So much as to the admissibility of testimony in regard to the illegal appointment of Mr. Cooper, it is a matter not charged; that is enough; it is a matter which the managers are not authorized to charge. They have no such delegated authority here. What is the ground on which they seek to prove anything in relation to Mr. Cooper? They say they expect to prove that Mr. Cooper was put into that office of Assistant Secretary of the Treasury by the President in order to control the disbursements of money in that department.

Now, if it were necessary to have an article charging the President with the appointment of General Thomas as a means used by him, to get control of the public moneys, of course, it would be equally necessary to have an article founded on the same line of conduct in regard to Mr. Cooper.

Mr. BINGHAM said:—Mr. President, we consider the law to be well settled and accepted everywhere in this country and in England, that every independent act on the part of the accused, looking to the subject matter of the inquiry, may be given in evidence, and we go no further than that we undertake to say on very high and commanding authority, that it is settled that such other and independent acts, showing the purposes of the accused to bring about the same general results, although they may be the subject matter of a separate indictment, may, nevertheless, be given in evidence. If a person is charged with having counterfeit notes in his possession of a certain denomination, it is competent to show that he was in possession of other counterfeit notes of a different denomination, and the rule of the books is, that whatever is competent to prove the general charge is competent to prove the intent. What is the allegation in the eleventh article? That the President, for the purpose of setting aside and defeating this law—

Mr. STANBERY—What law?

Mr. BINGHAM—The Tenure of Office act. I undertake to say that, by the existing law, the appropriation made for the support of the army can only be reached in the Treasury through a requisition drawn by the Secretary of War. Here is an independent act done by the accused for the purpose of aiding this result. How? By appointing an Assistant Secretary of the Treasury, who, under the law and regulations, is authorized to sign warrants that may be drawn on the Treasury; in other words, by appointing a person to discharge the very duty which would enable him to carry out the design with which we charge him.

If the appointment of such an officer throws no light on that subject, of course it has nothing to do with the matter. If it does, of course it has a great deal to do with the matter. If the question stops with the simple inquiry, who Edmund Cooper is, of course it throws no light on the subject, but if the testimony disclosed such relations to the President, and an appointment under such circumstances as to indicate the intention of Cooper to co-operate with the President in this general design, I apprehend it throws a great deal of light on the subject.

In case of the removal of the Secretary of the Treasury, then this Assistant Secretary of the Treasury would have control of the whole question. I am free to say, that if nothing further be shown than the appointment of Mr. Cooper, it will not throw any light upon the subject; but I do not so understand the matter.

Mr. BUTLER—In order that there may be a distinct proposition before the Senate, we offer to prove that there being no vacancy in the office of Assistant Secretary of the Treasury, the President unlawfully appointed his friend and his heretofore private secretary, Edmund Cooper, to that position, as one of the means by which he intended to defeat the Tenure of Office act and other laws of Congress.

Mr. EVARTS suggested that a date should be inserted.

Mr. BUTLER said he would insert a date satisfactory to himself. He then modified his proposition so as to read, "We offer to prove that, after the President determined on the removal of Mr. Stanton, Secretary of War, in spite of the action of the Senate, there being no vacancy in the office of Assistant Secretary" of the Treasury, &c.

Mr. EVARTS suggested that that did not indicate the date sufficiently.

Mr. BUTLER—I think if the learned gentleman will allow me I will make my offer as I like it myself. (Laughter).

Mr. EVARTS—Of course; I only ask you to name a date.

Mr. BUTLER repeated the offer.

The Chief Justice asked the counsel for the President if they desired to be heard in support of the objection?

Mr. EVARTS replied—No; we simply object to it. It ought not to need any argument.

The Chief Justice said he would submit the question to the Senate whether the testimony would be admitted.

Senator SHERMAN requested the managers to read the particular part of the eighth and eleventh articles to prove which the testimony is offered.

Mr. BUTLER replied by reading that part of the eighth article which charges the President with intending unlawfully to control the disbursements of the moneys appropriated for military service and for the Department of War, and also by reading that part of the eleventh article which charges the President with unlawfully devising and contriving, and attempting to devise and contrive, means then and there to prevent the execution of an act entitled an act making appropriations for the support of the army. He also read that part of the eleventh article, which charges the President with unlawfully devising and contriving, and attempting to devise and contrive means by which he should prevent Edwin M. Stanton from forthwith resuming the functions of the office of Secretary for the Department of War, notwithstanding the refusal of the Senate to concur in the suspension theretofore made.

He said that in that connection the managers claimed that the appointment of Mr. Cooper was part of the machinery to carry out the designs of the President. The question was, he said, whether Mr. McCulloch would answer to requisitions of General Thomas, or of any one else whom the President might put in the office of Secretary of War, if Mr. Stanton should hold out. It was clear that the President knew he would not do so, and, therefore, the President's design was to get somebody in the Treasury who would sign warrants on the requisition of General Thomas. In this way the President would have got the whole army and Treasury of the United States in his control, and it was with that intent that he made the appointment of Mr. Cooper.

Senator JOHNSON put the following question to the managers, in writing:—The managers are requested to say whether they propose to show that Mr. Cooper was appointed by the President in November, 1867, as a means to obtain the unlawful possession of the public money other than by the appointment itself.

Mr. BUTLER—We certainly do; we propose to show that he appointed him, and that thereupon Cooper went in to exercise the duties of the office before his appointment could, by any possibility, be legal; and we hope and believe that we will show that he has been controlling other public moneys since.

Senator HENDERSON requested that the testimony of the witness in reference to the mode and manner of obtaining money on the requisitions of the Secretary of War should be read.

The Chief Justice remarked that the witness might be asked to repeat his statement.

Senator HENDERSON said that his object was, to know whether money could be obtained on the signature of an Assistant Secretary instead of the Secretary.

Mr. BUTLER proceeded to examine the witness on that point.—Q. State whether the Assistant Secretary of the Treasury can sign warrants for payment of moneys?

Mr. EVARTS—That is not the question.

Mr. BUTLER—Q. State whether on requisition of any department of the government the Assistant Secretary of the Treasury can sign warrants on the Treasury, for the payment of money? A. Until the passage of the late statute, whenever the Secretary of the Treasury was present and acting, money could not be drawn from the Treasury on the signature of the Assistant Secretary; an act has been passed within a year allowing the Assistant Secretary to sign warrants for the payment of money into the Treasury; covering in warrants, and warrants for the payment of money on accounts stated; but the practice still continues of honoring all customary warrants by the signature of the Secretary of the Treasury. The warrants are prepared and the initials of the Assistant Secretary put on them, and then are signed by the Secretary of the Treasury, when they are presented.

Senator FESSENDEN asked that the law to which witness referred might be read.

While the messenger was gone for the statutes, the Chief Justice said he would ask the witness whether, before the passage of the act to which he referred, any warrant could be drawn by the Assistant Secretary unless he was Acting Secretary in the absence of the Secretary?

Witness—There could not. No money can be drawn from the Treasury on the signature of the Assistant Secretary unless when he is acting as Secretary.

Mr. BUTLER—When the Assistant Secretary acts for the Secretary does he sign all warrants for the payment of moneys? A. When he is acting Secretary of course he signs all warrants for the payment of moneys.

Senator CAMERON said that he desired to ask the witness a question.

The Chief Justice reminded him that the rules required questions by Senators to be reduced to writing.

While Senator Cameron was writing out his question,

Mr. BUTLER read the act referred to by Mr. Chandler. The act declared that the Secretary of the Treasury shall have power by appointment to delegate one Assistant Secretary to sign in his stead all warrants for the payment of money into the public Treasury, and all warrants for the disbursement of public moneys certified to be due on accounts duly audited and settled, and all warrants signed are to have the same validity as if signed by the Secretary himself.

Mr. EVARTS—What is the date of this law?

Mr. BUTLER—March 2, 1867. To witness—In case of the removal or absence of the Secretary of the Treasury the Assistant Secretary performs all the acts of the Secretary? A. That is the law.

Mr. BUTLER—I was only asking about the practice. Is that the practice? A. I am not certain that it is, without an appointment as Acting Secretary, signed by the President.

Senator CAMERON sent up his question in writing, as follows:—

Q. Can the Assistant Secretary of the Treasury, under the law, draw warrants for the payment of money by the Treasurer, without the direction of the Secretary of the Treasury? A. Since the passage of the act I understand that the Assistant Secretary can sign warrants for the payment of money in the cases specified, which is presumed, however, to be with the consent and approval of the Secretary of the Treasury.

Senator CAMERON desired to ask the witness another question, without reducing it to writing.

The Chief Justice said he could do so if there was no objection.

Senator WILLIAMS objected.

Senator CAMERON said he had merely desired to ask what had been the practice.

The Chief Justice said that the Senator was not in order.

Mr. BUTLER asked the question suggested, whether it has been the practice of the Assistant Secretary to sign warrants.

Answer by witness—Since the passage of the act in question it has been.

Senator FESSENDEN submitted the following question in writing:—

Q. Has it been the practice, since the passage of the law, for the Assistant Secretary of the Treasury to sign warrants unless he was specially appointed and authorized by the Secretary of the Treasury? Has any Assistant Secretary been authorized to sign any warrants unless such as are specified in the act? A. It has not been the practice of an Assistant Secretary since the passage of the act, to sign warrants unless on appointment by the Secretary for that purpose, in accordance with the provision of the act. A. Immediately on the passage of the act, the Secretary authorized one of his Assistant Secretaries to sign warrants of the character described in the act, and they have been customarily signed by that Assistant Secretary in all cases.

Q. Since that time has any Assistant Secretary been authorized to sign any warrants except such as are specified in the act? A. No Assistant Secretary has been authorized to sign warrants, except such as are specified in that act, unless when he is acting Secretary.

The Chief Justice put the question, whether the proof proposed by Mr. Butler should be admitted? The vote resulted. Yeas, 22; nays, 27, as follows:—

YEAS—Messrs. Anthony, Cameron, Cattell, Chandler, Cole, Conkling, Corbett, Cragin, Drake, Howard, Howe, Morrill (Vt.), Nye, Ramsey, Ross, Sprague, Sumner, Thayer, Tipton, Wilson.

NAYS.—Messrs. Bayard, Buckalew, Conness, Davis, Dixon, Doolittle, Edmunds, Ferry, Fessenden, Fowler, Frelinghuysen, Grimes, Henderson, Hendricks, Johnson, McCreery, Morrill (Me.), Norton, Patterson (N. H.), Patterson (Tenn.), Sherman, Stewart, Trumbull, Van Winkle, Vickers, Willey, Williams.

So the testimony was not permitted to be offered.

Examination of Charles A. Tinker.

Charles A. Tinker, sworn and examined by Mr. Boutwell.

Q. What is your business? A. Telegrapher.

Q. Are you in charge of any office? A. I am in charge of the Western Union Telegraph office, in this city.

Q. Were you at any time in charge of the military telegraph office, in the War Department? A. I was.

Q. From what time to what time? A. I can hardly tell from what time I was in charge of it up to August, 1867; I think I was in charge of it something like a year; I was connected with the office for something like five years.

Q. While in charge of this office, state whether a despatch from Lewis E. Parsons, of Montgomery, came to Andrew Johnson, President, and if so, at what date? A. I think while I was in that office I saw a good many such despatches.

Q. What paper have you now in your hand? A. I have what purports to be the copy of a telegram from Lewis E. Parsons, of Montgomery, Ala., addressed to His Excellency Andrew Johnson, President.

Q. Do you know whether that telegram came through the office. A. I recognize this as being the character of a despatch which was received at the Military Telegraph Office.

Q. Were duplicates of telegrams received kept at the military telegraph office? A. What is called a press copy is taken of every despatch before it is delivered.

Q. Is a copy taken of a despatch before it is sent? A. Not before being sent; the originals are kept on file at the office.

Q. State whether, at my request, you examined these press copies? A. I did.

Q. Did you find such a despatch as I have described among these press copies? A. I did.

Q. Did you make a copy of it? A. I made a copy of it.

Q. Have you got one on hand? A. No, I have not; I made a copy of the despatch, and answered the summons of the managers; I placed a copy in your hands, and heard you order your clerk to make a copy; afterwards the clerk returned with this copy, and gave me back the copy I had made; this is the copy which the clerk made.

Q. Have you the original despatch? A. I have.

Q. Produce the original despatch and the copy of both.

Mr. EVARTS—What is meant by the original despatch?

Witness—I mean that I have the press copy.

Mr. STANBERY (to the witness)—Did you make this copy yourself? A. The press copy is made by a clerk.

Mr. EVARTS objected to putting in evidence the copy from the press book.

Mr. BUTLER said he would pass from that for a moment, and would ask the witness this question:—Do you recollect whether such a telegram as this passed through the office? A. I do not remember this despatch having passed through the office.

Q. State whether on the same day, you have an original despatch signed "Andrew Johnson?" A. I have the despatch in full.

Q. Are you familiar enough with the signature of Andrew Johnson, to tell whether that is his signature or not? A. I believe it to be his signature; I am familiar with his handwriting.

Q. Have you any doubt of this in your own mind? A. None whatever.

Q. Is that book which you hold in your hand the record book of the United States Military Telegraph, in the executive office, where the original despatches are put on record? A. It is the book in which original despatches are filed.

Q. Do you know whether the despatch to Lewis C. Parsons passed through the office? I do know it from the marks it bears. It is marked as having been sent.

Mr. STANBERY—Let us see the despatch.

Mr. BUTLER was handing the book to Mr. Stanbery, when he suddenly remarked, "I will give you a copy of it." (Laughter.) He subsequently, however, handed the book to Mr. Stanbery, who inquired what was the object of the proof.

Mr. BUTLER—Do you object to the document, whatever is the object of the proof?

Mr. STANBERY—We want to know what it is.

Mr. BUTLER—The question which I ask is, whether you object to the vehicle of proof.

Mr. STANBERY—Oh, no.

Mr. BUTLER to witness—What is the date of that despatch? A. January 17, 1867.

Mr. STANBERY to Mr. BUTLER—Now what is the object of it.

Mr. BUTLER—Not yet sir. To the witness—On the same day that this is dated, do you find in the records of the department a press copy of a despatch from Lewis C. Parsons of which this is an answer? A. I find the press copy of a despatch to which that was an answer.

C. Was this telegraph office under the control of the War Department. A. It was.

Q. And the officers were employees of the War Department? A. They were.

Q. Were the records kept at that time in the War Department? A. They were.

Q. And are those books and papers produced from the War Department? A. No, sir, they are not.

Q. Where do they come from now? A. They come from the War Department to the telegraph office.

Mr. BUTLER said he now proposed to give in evidence the despatch of Lewis C. Parsons, to which Andrew Johnson made answer, and asked was there any objection as to the vehicle.

Mr. EVARTS said on that point, although we regard the proof of Mr. Parsons' despatch as insufficient, yet we will waive any objection of that kind, and the question we now stand upon is, as to the competency of the proof. We have had no notice to produce the original despatch of Mr. Parsons, but we care nothing about that. We waive that, and now we inquire in what views and under what article, these despatches, dated prior to the Tenure of Office act, are introduced.

Mr. BUTLER—In order that we may understand whether those papers are admissible in evidence, it becomes necessary, with permission of the President and of the Senate, to read them de bene esse.

Mr. CURTIS—We do not object to your reading them de bene esse.

Mr. BUTLER thereupon read the despatch, as follows:—

MONTGOMERY, Ala., Jan. 17, 1867.—His Excellency, Andrew Johnson, President:—Legislature in session; efforts made to consider vote on Constitutional Amendment; report from Washington says it is probable an enabling act will pass; we do not know what to believe.

LEWIS C. PARSONS, Exchange Hotel.

UNITED STATES MILITARY TELEGRAPH, EXECUTIVE OFFICE, WASHINGTON, D. C., Jan. 17, 1867.—Hon. Lewis C. Parsons, Montgomery, Ala.:—What possible good can be obtained by reconsidering the Constitutional Amendment? I know of none. In the present posture of affairs, I do not believe the people of the whole country will sustain any set of individuals in the attempt to change the whole character of our government by enabling acts.

In this way I believe, on the contrary, that they will eventually uphold all who have the patriotism and courage to stand by the Constitution, and who place their confidence in the people. There should be no faltering on the part of those who are earnest in determination to sustain the several co-ordinate departments of the government in accordance with its original design.

ANDREW JOHNSON.

Mr. BUTLER said he did not desire to argue the question as to the admissibility of the evidence. He claimed that it was competent, either under the tenth or eleventh articles.

Mr. CURTIS—The tenth article sets out speeches and not telegrams.

Mr. BUTLER—I am reminded by the learned counsel that these are speeches, not telegrams, that the tenth article refers to; I know they are, but with what intent were these speeches made; for what purpose were they made?

They were made for the purpose of carrying out the conspiracy against the Congress and its lawful acts, and to bring Congress into ridicule and contempt; but now I am on a point where an attempt is made to array the people against the lawful acts of Congress; to destroy the regard and respect of all good people for Congress, and to excite the odium and resentment of all the good people of the United States against Congress and a law which it had enacted. The President went through the country in September, 1866, declaring that Congress had no power to do what it was proposing to do.

Congress had proposed the Constitutional Amendment to the people of the States, and for the purpose of preventing that Constitutional Amendment being accepted every possible contumely was thrown at Congress and every possible step taken to prevent the adoption of the amendment. This telegram from the President is one of those steps. He found that while that amendment was being considered in the Southern States the President of the United States, stepped down from his high position and telegraphing to the Legislature of Alabama not to accept the proposed amendment. I do not care to argue the question further.

Mr. EVARTS—If the honorable managers are right, this evidence is proposed to be relevant and competent only in reference to the crimes charged in the tenth and eleventh articles. Is that your proposition?

The proposition is that it is relevant to them. I made no proposition as to the others.

Mr. EVARTS—You did not name any of the others.

Mr. BUTLER—I did not think it necessary.

Mr. EVARTS—Then I shall not think it necessary to consider the others. The article here charges that the President of the United States devised and intended to retard the rightful authority and power of the Congress of the United States, and devised and intended and attempted to bring into disgrace, ridicule, and contempt and reproach the Congress of the United States, or to destroy the respect and regard of all good people of the United States for the legislative power of Congress, and to excite the odium and resentment of all good people against Congress and the laws constitutionally enacted by them.

Now the acts charged to be done by the President with this intent are, first, a speech delivered by him in the Executive mansion, in August, 1866; second, a speech delivered by him at St. Louis, and in a speech delivered in Cleveland in September, 1866; and the article concludes that by means of these utterances Andrew Johnson brought the high office of President of the United States into ridicule, contempt and disgrace, and thereby committed high crimes and misdemeanors.

Now, Senators will judge, from the reading of the telegram dated July, 1867, whether it in any way supports the principal charge of intent. Article 11 sets forth that, in those speeches, he affirmed in substance that the Thirty-ninth Congress was not the Congress of the United States, authorized by the Constitution to exercise legislative authority; but, on the contrary, that it was a Congress only of a portion of the United States, and thereby denying that the legislation of that Congress was valid or obligatory on him, except so far as he thought proper to admit or recognize the same, thereby intending to deny the authority of Congress to pass amendments to the Constitution of the United States; and in further pursuance of that intent he, in disregard of the requirements of the Constitution of the United States, did, on the 23d day of February, 1868, attempt to prevent the execution of an act entitled "An act to regulate the Tenure of Office," passed March, 1867, after the date of this despatch, by attempting to contrive means to prevent Edwin M. Stanton from executing the office of Secretary of War, and by further contriving to prevent the execution of an act making appropriations for the support of the army for the fiscal year 1868, passed March 2, 1867; and also for contriving to prevent the execution of an act for the more efficient government of the United States, also referred to in this despatch.

Mr. Evarts then read the despatch to Lewis E. Parsons. and continued:—There is nothing in this despatch pertinent to the charge; nothing that tends to raise a scandal on the Presidential office; nothing that has the slightest relation to defeat the law; nothing that can be claimed to be a proper subject of an allegation of high crimes and misdemeanors on the part of the President, and we say that the testimony, spread over the widest field of inquiry, fails to support any charge of crime, or any intent, or any purpose mentioned in the article.

Mr. BOUTWELL. for the managers, contended that the evidence of the telegraphic despatches was admissible in support of the charges contained in the eleventh article. If attention be given to the eleventh article, it will be seen that it charges that on August 18, 1866, the President, in the city of Washington, in a public speech, delivered by him, affirmed in substance that the Thirty-ninth Congress

was not a Congress authorized by the Constitution, to execute legislative power; that it was not a Congress of the United States, but a Congress of only a portion of the States, thereby denying that the legislation of said Congress was valid or obligatory on him, except in so far as he thought fit to recognize or admit it. thereby denying the right of said Congress to pass articles of amendment to the Constitution of the United States.

This is the very substance of this telegraphic despatch, and in pursuance of it, said declaration. the President afterwards to wit, on February 21, 1868, which we understand to include all these dates; besides, the declaration, which is the basis of the article. is open to us for the introduction of testimony tending to show the acts of the President on this point; that at the city of Washington, he, in disregard of the requirements of the Constitution, attempted to prevent the execution of an act entitled an act to regulate the tenure of office, and by devising and contriving, and attempting to devise and contrive means then and there, to prevent the execution of an act providing for the support of the army; and also, to prevent the execution of an act to provide for the more efficient government of the Southern States, and thereby to properly see and understand the nature and extent of the influence of the President in sending this telegram. Here is Mr. Parsons, known to be Provisional Governor of Alabama in 1865 and 1866, and possessing immense influence in that part of the country, and who asks the President's opinion on the subject of the reconstruction of the Rebel States.

He, Governor Parsons, says that the Legislature is in session and about to take up the question of the Constitutional Amendment. The reports from Washington say that probably an enabling act would be passed, relating to the act known as an act for the more efficient government of the Rebel States, through which these States were to be restored to the Union, and he (Parsons) asks the opinion of the President as to what he shall do.

What does the President reply to this? "What good can be obtained by reconsidering the Constitutional Amendment? I do not believe the people will support any set of individuals." Here is the whole gist of the telegraphic despatch as it applies to the charge in the eleventh article. There we set forth that, in September, 1866, the President declared that the Thirty-ninth Congress was not a constitutional body, representing the whole Union, and in this despatch he speaks of Congress in the same way. He says:—"I do not believe that the people of the country will sustain any set of individuals," thus describing and characterizing the Thirty-ninth Congress as a set of individuals, eager in an attempt to change the whole character of our government by passing enabling acts, or otherwise. We say he is, we have evidence of the intent of the President to defeat the will of Congress, in regard to the enforcement of an act, and that proves the offense charged against him in the eleventh article. I am reminded that the Reconstruction act provided for the adoption of the Constitutional Amendment, under the Constitution and coincident as to the right of a State under an enabling act, to be restored to the Union.

The despatches were again read, and cries of "Question, question."

Mr. BUTLER—Let me first call attention to the fifth section of the act of March 2, 1867, known as the Reconstruction act:—"And when said State, by a vote of its Legislature, elected under said Constitution, shall have adopted the amendment to the Constitution of the United States, proposed by the Thirty-ninth Congress, and known as article fourteen, and when said article shall become part of the Constitution of the United States, the said State shall be entitled to representation in Congress, and Senators and Representatives shall be admitted therefrom on their taking the oath prescribed by law:" so that the adoption of the amendment is a part of the Reconstruction act.

Cries of question.

Mr. HOWARD—Mr. President, I offer a question. It was read as follows:—What amendment to the Constitution is referred to in Mr. Parson's despatch?

Mr. BUTLER—There was but one at that time before the country, and that was known as the fourteenth article, and is the one I have just read, and which is required to be adopted by every State Legislature before the State can be admitted to representation in Congress.

The Chief Justice again stated the question to be, whether the evidence offered by the managers is admissible.

Senator DRAKE called for the yeas and nays on seconding the call. Several Senators held up their hands, but the Chief Justice said the Senators will rise.

The call was ordered and resulted as follows:—

YEAS.—Messrs. Anthony, Cameron, Cattell, Chandler, Cole, Conkling, Conness, Corbett, Cragin. Drake, Henderson, Howard, Morgan, Morrill (Vt.), Nye, Patterson (N.H.), Pomeroy, Ramsey, Ross, Sherman, Sprague, Stewart, Sumner, Thayer, Tipton, Willey and Wilson—27.

NAYS—Messrs. Buckalew, Davis, Dixon, Doolittle, Edmunds, Ferry, Fessenden, Fowler, Frelinghuysen. McCreery, Morrill (Me.), Norton. Patterson (Tenn.), Trumbull, Van Winkle, Vickers, Williams—17.

So the evidence was admitted.

Mr. DOOLITTLE moved that the court now adjourn until to-morrow at noon.

Mr. SUMNER—I hope not.

The Chief Justice put the question, and declared it lost. Several Senators called for a division.

Senator RAMSEY—The question was not understood.

The Chief Justice put the question again, and said the yeas seemed to have it.

The question was agreed to, and the Chief Justice vacated the Chair, and the Senate adjourned.

PROCEEDINGS OF FRIDAY, APRIL 3.

Preliminaries.

The Chaplain prayed that the issue of this trial would restore peace to the country and establish our government on its only true basis—liberty and equality.

As usual, no legislative business was transacted, but the chair was, immediately after the opening, assumed by the Chief Justice, and proclamation made in due form. The managers were announced and took their seats, and directly thereafter the House of Representatives, in Committee of the Whole, appeared, in number about equal to the managers.

The journal was then read.

In the meantime the galleries had become tolerably filled. To-day, for the first time, a fair sprinkling of sable faces appeared among the spectators.

The Seventh Rule.

When the reading of the journal was concluded Senator DRAKE rose and said:—Mr. President, I move that the Senate take up the proposition which I offered yesterday to amend the seventh rule.

The Chief Justice—It will be considered before the Senate, if not objected to.

It was read, as follows:—Amend rule 7 by adding the following:—Upon all such questions the vote shall be without a division, unless the yeas and nays be demanded by one-fifth of the members present, or requested by the presiding officer, when the same shall be taken.

Senator EDMUNDS—Mr. President, I move to strike out that part of it relating to the yeas and nays being taken by the request of the presiding officer.

Senator CONKLING—Mr. President, not having heard the motion of the Senator (Edmunds), I ask for the reading of the seventh rule.

It was read as proposed to be amended.

Senator DRAKE—I have no objection to the amendment of the Senator from Vermont.

The rule, as amended, was adopted.

On motion of Senator DRAKE, the rules were ordered to be printed as amended.

Mr. Tinker's Testimony.

Charles A. Tinker recalled:—

Mr. BUTLER—Before interrogating Mr. Tinker, I will read a single paper. The paper is the message of the President of the United States, communicating to the Senate the report of the Secretary of State, showing the proceedings under the concurrent resolution of the two Houses of Congress of the 18th of June, in submitting to the Legislatures of the several States an additional article to the Constitution of the United States.

Senator THAYER—What article?

Mr. BUTLER—The fourteenth article. It is dated June 22, 1866. It is the same one to which the despatch related. An executive document of the first session of the Thirty-ninth Congress.

In order to show to what despatch he referred, the message was handed to the President's counsel for inspection, after which it was read by the Secretary. The examination of the witness was then proceeded with.

Q. You said you were manager of the Western Union Telegraph Office in this city? A. Yes, sir.

Q. Have you taken from the records of that office what purports to be a copy of a speech which was telegraphed through by the company, or any portion of it, as made by Andrew Johnson on the 18th day of August, 1866. If so, produce it? A. I have, sir; I have taken from the files what purports to be a copy of the speech in question. (Producing the document.)

Q. From the course of the business of the office are you enabled to say whether this was sent? A. It has the "sent" marks put on all the despatches sent from the office.

Q. And this is the original manuscript? A. This is the original manuscript.

Q. When was this paper sent, to what parts of the country, and, first place, by what association was this speech telegraphed? A. By the Associated Press; by their agents in the city of Washington.

Mr. CURTIS, of counsel, was understood to object to the paper.

Q. By Mr. BUTLER—Can you tell me, sir, to what extent through the country the telegraph messages sent to the Associated Press go? A. I suppose they go to all parts of the country; I state positively to New York, Philadelphia and Baltimore; they are addressed to the agents of the Associated Press; from New York they are distributed through the country.

Cross-examination waived.

Mr. BUTLER—You may step down for the present.

Examination of J. B. Sheridan.

James B. Sheridan, sworn and examined by Mr. BUTLER—

Q. What is your business? A. I am a stenographer; employed at present in New York city; on the 18th of August, 1866, I was a stenographer; I reported a speech of the President made on the 18th of August, 1866, in the east room of the Presidential Mansion; I have the notes taken at the time of that speech; took the speech down correctly as it was given; I did it to the best of my ability; I have been a reporter some fourteen years; I wrote out that speech at the time; I wrote out a part of it at the President's mansion; there were several reporters present; there was Mr. James O. Clephane and Mr. Francis H. Smith, reporters.

Q. Do you mean Mr. Smith, the official reporter to the House? A. I believe he was at that time connected with the House.

Q. Who else were there? A. I think Colonel Moore was in the room part of the time.

Q. What Colonel Moore? A. The President's favorite Secretary, William G. Moore.

Q. After it was written, what, if anything, was done with it? A. I do not know; I think Mr. Moore took it out; I was very sick at the time, and did not pay much attention; either he or Mr. Smith took it out; I did my share of it; we divided among us, Clephane, Smith and I.

Q. Look at this file of manuscript (placing before the witness manuscript furnished from the telegraph office as sent to the Associated Press), and see whether you find any of your handwriting? A. I recognize some of the writing as mine.

Q. Have you since written out any portion of the speech as you reported it? A. I wrote out a couple of extracts from it.

Q. Is this your handwriting? (Handing a paper to witness.) A. It is; what I hold in my hand is a correct transcript of that speech, made from my notes. It was written when I appeared before the board of managers.

(Witness, by direction of Mr. Butler, placed his initials on the paper.)

Cross-examined by Mr. EVARTS—Q. You have produced a note-book of a lengthy stenographic report of a speech of the President. Is it of the whole speech? A. It is of the whole speech; the report was wholly made by me; the speech occupied in the delivery, I suppose, some twenty or twenty-five minutes.

Q. By what method of stenographic reporting did you proceed on that occasion? A. By Pitman's system of phonography.

Q. Which is, I understand, reporting by sound, and not by sense? A. We report the sense by the sound.

Q. I understand you; you report by sound only? A. Yes.

Q. And not by memory or of attention to sense? A. No good reporter can report unless he pays attention to the sense and understands what he is reporting.

Q. State whether you were attending to sound, and setting down in your notation, or attending to sense, and setting it down from your memory and from your attention to sense? A. Both.

Q. Your characters are arbitrary, are they not? That is, they are peculiar to your art? A. Yes, sir.

Q. They are not letters? A. No, sir; nor words; we have some word signs; this transcript, which I made of a portion of the report for the use of the committee, was made recently a few weeks ago.

Q. What, in the practice of your art, is the experience as to the accuracy of transcribing by stenographic notes after the lapse of a considerable period of time? A. I will give you an illustration; when I was called before the managers I did not know what was wanted with me, and when they told me to turn to my report of the President's speech, I found it in my book, and read out, at their request, the extract which they desired me to copy.

Q. You read from your stenographic notes? A. Yes; the reporter for the managers took it down, and I afterwards wrote it out.

Q. Do you make a sign for every word? A. Almost every word, except that we sometimes drop particles.

Q. You have signs which belong to every word, excepting when you drop the particles? A. Yes sir; but not, as a matter of course, a sign which is the representative of a whole word; we have some signs representing whole words.

Q. For the word "jurisprudence" you have no one sign that represents it? A. No sir; I should write J R S P, and that is an illustration of the proceeding.

Counsel examined attentively the notes of the witness, and seemed to be apparently satisfied.

Mr. Clephane's Testimony.

James O. Clephane, sworn and examined by Mr. BUTLER—Q. What is your business? A. I am at present a deputy clerk of the Supreme Court of the District of Columbia.

Q. What was your employment on the 18th of August, 1866? A. I was then secretary to Mr. Seward, Secretary of State.

Q. Are you a phonographic reporter? A. I am.

Q. How considerable has been your experience? A. Eight or nine years.

Q. Were you employed on the 18th of August, 1866, to make a report of the President's speech in reply to Mr. Reverdy Johnson? A. I was; I was engaged, in connection with Mr. Smith, for the Associated Press, and also for the *Daily Chronicle*, of Washington.

Q. Did you make that report? A. I did.

Q. Where was the speech made? A. In the east room of the White House.

Q. Who were present? A. I noticed a good many persons present; I noticed General Grant and several other distinguished gentlemen.

Q. Were any other of the Cabinet officers present? A. I do not recollect.

Q. Did you report that speech? A. I did.

Q. What was done with that report? A. Colonel Moore, the President's private secretary, desired the privilege of revising it before publication, and, in order to expedite matters, Mr. Smith, Mr. Sheridan and myself united in the labor of transcribing it; Mr. Sheridan transcribed one portion, Mr. Smith one, and I a third; after it was revised by Colonel Moore it was then taken and handed to the agent of the Associated Press, who took it and telegraphed it over the country.

Q. Look at that roll of manuscript before you, and say if it is a speech of which you transcribed a portion. A. I do not recognize any of my handwriting; it is possible that I may have dictated my portion to a longhand writer.

Q. Who was present at the time writing? A. Mr. Smith, Mr. Sheridan and Colonel Moore, as I recollect.

Q. Do you know Colonel Moore's handwriting? A. I do not.

Q. Did you send your report to the *Chronicle?* A. Mr. Macfarlan, who had engaged me to report for the *Chronicle*, was unwilling to take the revised speech, and decided to have the speech as delivered, as he stated, with all the imperfections, and, as he insisted on my re-writing the speech, I did so; it was published in the *Sunday Morning Chronicle* of the 9th.

Q. Have you a copy of that paper? A. I have not.

Q. After that report was published in the *Chronicle* on Sunday morning did you see it? A. I did, and examined it very carefully; I had a curiosity to know how it would read under the circumstances, being a literal report, except of a word changed here and there.

Q. How do you mean? A. Where the word used would evidently obscure the meaning, I made the change; although, perhaps, I would not be able to point it out just now.

Q. With what certainty can you speak with reference to the *Chronicle's* report being accurate? A. I think I could speak with certainty as to its being an accurate, literal report, with the exception I have named; perhaps there is a word or two changed here and there.

Q. Give us an illustration of this change. A. My attention was called to the matter by some correspondent, who, learning that the *Chronicle* had published a *verbatim* report, had carefully scrutinized it, and he wrote to the *Chronicle* to say that in one instance there was no expression used by the President of "You and I have sought," or something of that kind; that expression was corrected in the report I wrote out.

Mr. BUTLER here stated that he was informed that there are two manuscript copies in the telegraph office, and that Mr. Tinker had given the one, that which was written out at length as a duplicate, and not the original manuscript as he had supposed. He would, therefore, have to bring him again, and he would send for him.

Cross-examination by Mr. EVARTS.—Q. You were acting in the employment of the Associated Press? A. Yes, sir, in connection with Mr. Smith.

Q. You were jointly to make a report? No; we were to report the entire speech—each of us—and we then divided to save labor of transcribing

Q. Did you take phonographic notes of the whole speech? A. I did.

Q. Where are your phonographic notes? A. I have searched for them and cannot find them.

Q. At any time after you had completed the phonographic notes, did you translate or write them out? A. I did.

Q. The whole? A. Yes; the whole speech.

Q. Where is that translation or written transcript? A. I do not know. The manuscript, of course, was left at the *Chronicle* office; I wrote it for the *Chronicle* in full.

Q. You have never seen it since? A. I have not.

Q. Have you made search for it? A. I have not.

Q. And these two acts of yours, the phonographic report and the translation or writing out, is all that you had to do with the speech? A. That is all.

Q. You say that subsequently you read a newspaper copy of the speech in the Washington *Chronicle?* A. I did.

Q. When was it that you read that newspaper copy? A. The morning of the publication—Sunday morning, August 19.

Q. Where were you when you read it? A. I read it at my room.

Q. It was from that curiosity that you read it? A. I read it more carefully because of that.

Q. Had you before you your phonographic notes, or your writing transcribed from them? A. I had not.

Q. And have you never seen them in comparison with the newspaper copy of the report? A. No, sir.

Re-direct examination by Mr. BUTLER—Q. Have you before you a copy of the *Sunday Morning Chronicle* of the 19th of August? A. I have.

Q. Look on the page before you, and see if you can find the speech as you reported it? A. I find it here.

Q. Looking at that speech, tell me whether you have any doubt that that is an accurate verbatim report of the speech of Andrew Johnson on that occasion, and if so, what ground have you for the doubt.

Objections.

Mr. EVARTS.—We object to that. It is apparent that the witness took notes of this speech, and that the notes have been written out.

They are the best and most trustworthy evidence of the actual speech made. In all public proceedings we are entitled to that degree of accuracy and trustworthiness which the nature of the case demands, and whenever papers of that degree of authenticity are presented, then, for the first time, the question will arise whether the evidence is competent. It is impossible to contend, on the evidence of this witness as it now stands, that he remembers the speech of the President so that he can produce it by recital, or so that he can say from memory that this is the speech. What is offered here?

The same kind of evidence, and that alone which would grow out of some person who heard the President deliver the speech, and when he subsequently read in the *Chronicle* a report of it. He would say that he thinks the report was a true statement of the speech. This witness has told us distinctly, that in reading this speech from curiosity, to see how it would appear when reproduced without the ordinary guarantees of accuracy, he had neither his original notes nor his written transcript, and that he read the newspaper as others would read it, but with more care from that degree of curiosity that he had. Now, if this matter is to be regarded as important, we insist that that kind of evidence, giving a newspaper report of it is not admissible.

Stenography.

Mr. BUTLER—There is no question of degrees of evidence. We must take the business of the world as we find it, and must not busy ourselves and insist that we have wakened up a hundred years ago. The art of stenographic writing has progressed to a point where men must rely upon it in all the business of life. There is not a gentleman in this Senate who does not rely upon it every day. There is not more than one member of the Senate who, in this trial, is taking any notes of it. Why? Because Senators rely on the fingers of the reporter who sits by my side, to give you a transcript of it, on which you must judge. Therefore, in every business of the court we rely on the stenographer. This gentleman says that he has made a stenographic report of that speech; that it was jointly made by himself, Mr. Sheridan and Mr. Smith; that his employer not being satisfied with that joint report, which was the President's utterances distilled through the alembic of Colonel Moore's critical discrimination, he wrote out with care an exact literal transcript under the guiding of his employer, and for a given purpose, and that the next day, having the curiosity to see how the President of the United States would appear if put to paper, literally, he examined that speech in the *Chronicle*, and that then, with the matter fresh in his mind, and only a few hours intervening, and with his attention freshly called to it, recognized it as a correct copy.

Now the learned counsel says that the manuscript is the best evidence. If there were any evidence that the manuscript had been preserved, perhaps we might be called upon to produce it, in some technicality of law as administered in a very technical manner; but who does not know that in the ordinary course of business in newspaper offices, that after such manuscript has been got through with it is thrown into the newspaper basket; therefore, I add, upon that usual and common incident of the business of life, this is a question for the witness. The question we are discussing is this. Looking at that report, from your knowledge of the reporter having twice written it out, and having seen it the next morning with your curiosity awakened, can you tell the Senate whether that is a correct copy? Thereupon the counsel for the President excepts, and says he cannot. How does the learned counsel for the President know that? How does he know that Mr. Clephane is not one of those gentlemen who having once read his speech can repeat it next day? The question is a plain one. I say, sir, there is a transcript of that speech. From your knowledge of it, having heard it, having written it down in shorthand, having re-written it once for correction by the President's Private Secretary, and having again re-written it from your notes for publication, then having examined it immediately after it was published, from all these sources of knowledge, can you say that this is a correct copy?

Thereupon, the counsel for the President says he cannot. How does he know that? How does he know that he cannot repeat every word of it? The difficulty is that the objection does not apply, and I would content myself with that statement of it, except that, once for all, I propose to put before the Senate an argument as to the evidence of stenographic reporting. Allow me to state, once for all, two authorities on this point. I do not intend to argue the point hereafter, because I know that, in doing so, I should be playing into the hands of that delay which has been so often attempted here.

Precedents.

In the O'Connell case, to prove his speeches on that great trial—and no trial was ever brought with more sharpness or bitterness—the newspapers were introduced, containing what purported to be Mr. O'Connell's speeches, and the only proof adduced was, that the papers had been properly stamped and issued from the office, the court holding that Mr. O'Connell, allowing these speeches to go for months without contradiction, must be held responsible for them.

In the trial of James Watson, for high treason, the question arose whether a copy might be used, which was made from partially obliterated short hand notes, and after argument, the witness was allowed to produce a transcript. Now, while this authority is not exactly to the point raised here, I desire to put it once for all for these questions, because I heard the cross-examination as to the merits of Pitman's system of writing, and as to the whole system of stenography being an available means of furnishing information.

Reportorial Accuracy.

Mr. EVARTS—The learned manager is quite correct in saying that I do not know but that this witness can repeat verbatim the President's speech, and when he offers himself as a witness so to do, I shall not object. It is entirely competent for this person who has heard a speech, to repeat it under oath, he asserting that he remembers it and can do so, and whenever Mr. Clephane undertakes that feat, it is within the competency of evidence. Another form of trustworthy evidence, is the reporter's notes.

Whenever that form is admitted, and when the witness swears that he believes in his accuracy and competency as a reporter, we shall make no objections to that as not trustworthy; but when the learned managers seek to evade responsibility and accuracy through the oath of the witness applying in either form, and seek to put it neither upon his present memory nor upon his own memorandum, but upon the accuracy with which he has failed to detect inaccuracies in the newspaper report published the subsequent day, and thereupon to give credit and authenticity to the newspaper report upon his wholesale and general approval of it, then you must contend that the sacred right of the freedom of speech is sought to be invaded by overthrowing certainly one of the most responsible and most important protections of it, and that the oath of somebody who heard and can remember it, or who has preserved the aids and assistances by which he can repeat it, must adhere in a court of justice; and we are not to be told that it is technical to maintain, in defense of what has been regarded as one of the commonest and surest rights in any free country—freedom of speech—that whenever it is drawn in question, it shall be drawn in question on the surest and most faithful evidence.

The learned manager has said that you are familiar, as a part of the daily routine of your Congressional duties, with the habit of stenographic reporting and reproduction in the newspapers, and that you rely upon it habitually, and, I may add, to be habitually correcting it. Correction is the first demand of every public speaker; correction and revision when with those reports, dependant upon the ear, upon the sudden strokes of the ready writer, may not be the formed judgment against a man as to what is said by him; and now when seditiously this newspaper has undertaken that no such considerations of accuracy should be afforded to the President of the United States in order that that speech should be spread before the country with all its imperfections—

Mr. BUTLER, interrupting—I pray correction, sir. I have not said that I said that the speech of the President's Private Secretary should not go to the public.

Mr. EVARTS—The instructions of the editor were that the speech should be reported with all its imperfections as caught by the shorthand writer, without the opportunity for that revision which every public speaker at the hustings or in the halls of debate demands, as a primary and important right. Whenever, therefore, Mr. Clephane shall rise and speak from memory, swearing to his accuracy, or when he shall produce his notes and transcribe—as in the Watson case—some foundation for the proof of his word in this case, will then have been made.

Mr. Tinker was again called by Mr. BUTLER, and made the following statement:—Yesterday when I was called upon the stand I was attending to my duties in the telegraph office, in the gallery; I hadn't a moment's notice that I was to be called; I then telegraphed to the office for the manuscripts contained in the package that was there, that I had been previously examined about before the managers; These documents were brought to me by a boy from the office, and I brought them with me to the stand, and last night I deposited them in the office of the Sergeant-at-Arms, and this morning I brought one of those packages on the stand and opened it here, supposing it to be the one on which I was to be examined; but when I saw the reporters were put to trouble about it, I went to my office while Mr. Clephane was on the stand, and I have now got the speech telegraphed by the Associated Press on the 18th of August, 1866.

Mr. STANBERY—What document was that which Mr. Butler handed to you?

Witness—That was one of the documents on which I was examined.

Mr. STANBERY—If that is not the speech of 18th August—

Mr. BUTLER—That is the 22d of February speech. (Laughter.) You will find out what that document is in

good time, gentlemen. (Laughter.) To the witness—Now, sir, will you give me the document I asked for? (Document produced). Is this the document that you supposed you were testifying about, then? A. Yes, sir.

Q. Do you give the same testimony about that?

Mr. STANBERY—That won't do.

Mr. BUTLER—We will give you all the delay possible. (Laughter.) To the witness—Now, sir, will you tell us whether this was sent through the Associated Press? It bears the marks of having been sent. It is taken from the files of that day. From the course of business in your office have you any doubt of its having been sent? A. None whatever.

Mr. CARTER, of the counsel, objected to the witness' opinions.

Q. After that speech was sent out, did you see it published by the papers as the Associated Press report? A. I can't say positively; I think I did.

Q. Was that brought to your office for the purpose of being transmitted, whether it was or not? A. I did not personally receive it, but it is among the Associated Press despatches sent on that day.

James B. Sheridan recalled.

Mr. BUTLER—Will you examine that manuscript and say if you see any of your handwriting in it? A. I see my writing here.

Q. What is that you have got there? A. It is a report of the speech made by the President on the 18th of August.

Q. What year? A. 1865.

Q. Have you ever seen Mr. Moore write? A. A good many years ago when he used to report for the *National Intelligencer*, and I was a reporter for the Washington *Union.*

Q. He was a reporter also? A. Yes, sir.

Q. Are there any corrections made in that report? A. Yes, sir.

Q. Did you see any of them made? A. No, sir.

Q. Is that the manuscript that was prepared in the President's office? A. I think it is; I am pretty certain that it is.

Q. No doubt in your mind? A. Not the least.

Q. Was the President there to correct it? A. No, sir.

Q. Then he did not exercise that great constitutional right of revision to your knowledge? A. Didn't see the President after he left the east room.

Q. Do you know whether Colonel Moore took any memoranda of that speech? A. I do not; there was quite a crowd there.

You pick out and lay aside, sir, the portions that are in your handwriting.

[Witness selects a portion of the manuscript.]

Q. Do you think you have all that is in your handwriting? A. No, sir.

Cross-examined by Mr. EVARTS.—Q. You have selected the pages that are in your handwriting? you have them before you? A. Yes, sir.

Q. How large a proportion do they make of the whole manuscript? A. I could hardly tell.

Q. Now was this whole manuscript made as a transcript from your notes? A. This part that I wrote out.

Q. The whole was not? A. No, sir.

Q. Then it is only the part that you now hold in your hands that was produced from the stenographic original notes which you have brought in evidence here? A. Yes, sir.

Q. Did you write it in yourself, from your stenographic notes, following the latter with your ears, or were your notes read to you by any other person? A. I wrote it from my own notes, reading my notes while I wrote.

Q. Have you made any subsequent comparison of the manuscript now in your hands with your stenographic notes? A. I have not.

Q. When was this completed on your part? A. A very few minutes after the speech was delivered.

Q. What did you do with the manuscript after you went from the Executive Mansion? A. I hardly know; it went from the table just as I wrote it. I am not certain about it.

Q. And that ended your connection with it? A. Yes, sir.

Mr. EVARTS—It is desired that you should have your original stenographic notes here.

Mr. BUTLER—Put your initials on them. One of my associates desires me to put this question which I suppose you answered before:—Whether that manuscript, which you have produced in your handwriting, was a true transcript of your notes of that speech? A. It was sir; I won't say it was written out exactly as it was delivered.

Q. What was the change, sir, if any? A. I don't know that there were any changes, but frequently in writing we exercise a little judgment; we don't always write out a speech just as it is delivered.

Q. Is that a substantially true version of what the President said? A. It is.

Examination of Francis H. Smith.

Francis H. Smith, sworn and examined by Mr. BUTLER—Q. Mr. Smith, are you the official reporter of the House? A. I am, sir.

Q. How long have you been so engaged? A. In the position I now hold, since the fifth of January, 1865.

Q. How long have you been in the business of reporting? A. Something over eighteen years.

Q. Were you employed, and if so, by whom, to make a report of the President's speech, in August, 1866? A. I was employed at the instance of the Agent of the Associated Press—one of the agents.

Q. Who aided in that report? A. Mr. James O. Clephane and Mr. James B. Sheridan.

Q. Did you make such a report. A. I did.

Q. Have you got your notes? A. I have.

Q. Here? A. Yes, sir.

Q. Produce them?

[Witness produces notes.]

Q. After you had made your shorthand report, what did you do then? A. In company with Mr. Clephane and Mr. Sheridan, I retired to one of the offices in the Executive Mansion, and wrote out a portion of my notes.

Q. What did the others do? A. The others wrote out other portions of the same speech.

Q. What was done with the portion that you wrote? A. It was delivered to Colonel Moore, Private Secretary of the President, sheet by sheet, as written by me, for revision.

Q. How came you to deliver it to Colonel Moore? A. I did it at his request.

Q. What did he do with it? A. Read it over and made certain alterations.

Q. Was the President present while this was being done? A. He was not.

Q. Had Colonel Moore taken any memoranda of the speech to your knowledge? A. I am not aware whether he had or not.

Q. Did Colonel Moore show you any signs by which he knew what the President meant to say, so that he could correct his speech? A. He did not; he stated to me, prior to the delivery of the speech, that he desired permission to revise the manuscript, simply to correct the phraseology, not to make any change in any substatial matter.

Q. Will you look, and see if you can find any portion of your manuscript as you wrote it there? A. After examining it I recognize some of it, sir.

Q. Separate it as well you can?

Witness disengages a portion of the manuscript.

Q. Have you now got the portions occurring in two different portions of the speech which you wrote out? A. Yes, sir.

Q. Are there any corrections in that manuscript? A. There are, sir, quite a number.

Q. In whose handwriting, if you know? A. In the handwriting of Colonel Moore, so far as I see.

Q. Have you written out from your notes since the speech? A. I have.

Q. Is that it as it is written out? [Showing manuscript to witness.] A. It is.

Q. Is that a correct transcript of your notes? A. It is, with two unimportant corrections.

Q. Do you remember what they were? A. In the sentence, "I could embrace more by means of silence by letting silence speak, what I should and what I ought to say," should have been "letting silence speak and you infer." The words "and you infer" had been omitted, and there was the word "overruling" omitted between the words "under Providence."

Cross-examined by Mr. EVARTS.—Q. This last paper which has been shown you is a transcript of the whole speech—of the entire speech? A. Yes, sir.

Q. From your notes exclusively? A. From my notes exclusively.

Q. Have you any doubt that the transcript which you made at the Executive Mansion from your notes was correctly made? A. I have no doubt the transcript made from my notes at the Executive Mansion was substantially and correctly made; I remember that, having learned that the manuscript was to be revised, I took the liberty of making certain revisions myself in the language, correcting ungrammatical expressions (laughter), changing the order of words in sentences, in certain cases, and corrections of that sort.

Q. Those are liberties then you took in writing out your own notes? Yes, sir.

Q. Have you ever made any examination to see what changes you have made? A. I have not and cannot now point them out.

Q. Well, you have made a more recent transcript from your notes, did you allow yourself the same liberty now? A. I did not.

Q. That, then, you consider a true transcript of your notes? A. It is, sir.

Q. Do you report by the same system of sound phonography, as it is called? A. I hardly know, sir, what system I do report with; I studied shorthand when I was a boy, going to school; the system of phonography as then published by Andrews & Boyle; I have included some changes of my own since then, and made various changes.

Q. Can any phonographic reporters write out from one another's report? A. I don't think any one could write out my notes, sir, except myself.

Q. Could you write out anybody else's? A. Probably not, unless written with a very great degree of accuracy and care.

Mr. Clephane Recalled.

James O. Clephane recalled, and examined by Mr. BUTLER. [Manuscript shown.]

Q. You have already told us that you took the speech and wrote it out, whether that is the manuscript of your writing out? A. It is, sir.

Q. Has it any corrections? Yes, in the first line.

Q. Who made those? A. I presume they were made by Colonel Moore. He took the manuscript as I wrote it.

Q. Was that manuscript, as you wrote it, a correct copy of the speech as made, sir? A. I can't say that I adhered as perfectly to the notes in the report as I did in that of the Chronicle.

Q. Was it substantially accurate? A. It was, sir.

Q. Did you, in any case, change the sense? A. Not at all, sir, only the form of expression.

Q. The form of expression, why, sir? A. Oftentimes when it obscured the meaning, to make it more readable.

Cross-examined by Mr. EVARTS—What rules of change did you prescribe to yourself in the deviations you made from your stenographic notes? A. As I said, sir, I made changes in the form of expression.

Q. When the meaning did not present itself to you, as it should, you made it clear. A. I will say, sir, that Mr. Johnson is in the habit of speaking—

Mr. EVARTS, interrupting—Well, sir, was that it that when the meaning did not present itself to you as it should, you made it clear? A. Yes, sir.

Q. What other rule of change did you allow yourself? A. No other, sir.

Q. No grammatical improvement? A. Yes, sir; I may have—very often the singular verb was used where, perhaps, the plural ought to be.

Q. You corrected, then, the grammar? A. Yes, sir.

Q. Can you suggest any other rule that you followed? A. I cannot, sir.

Mr. William G. Moore examined.

William G. Moore, sworn.—Examined by Mr. BUTLER.

Q. What is your rank, sir? A. I am a paymaster in the army, sir, with the rank of Colonel.

Q. When were you appointed, sir? On the 14th day of November, 1866.

Q. Did you ever pay anybody? (Laughter.) A. No, sir, not with government funds, sir. (Laughter.)

Q. What has been your duty? A. I have been on duty at the Executive Mansion.

Q. What kind of duty? A. I have been in the capacity of Secretary for the President.

Q. Were you so acting before you were appointed? A. I was, sir.

Q. How long had you acted as Secretary before you were appointed? A. I was directed to attend the President in the month of November, 1865.

Q. Had you been in the army prior to that time. A. I had been a major and assistant adjutant-general.

Q. In the War Deartment? A. Yes, sir.

Q. Did you hear the President's speech of the 18th of August, 1866? A. I did, sir.

Q. Did you take any notes of it? A. I did not, sir.

Q. Look at the manuscript which lies there before you, and see whether you corrected it? I don't care whether you examined it at all. Did you correct any portion of it? A. Yes, sir.

Q. Where were the corrections made? A. In an apartment of the Executive Mansion.

Q. Who were in the appartment when you made the corrections? A. Francis H. Smith, James B. Sheridan, and James O. Clephane, and, I think, Mr. Hatland, of the Associated Press.

Q. Had you any memorandum from the President by which to correct it? A. None, sir.

Q. Do you claim to have the power of remembering, after hearing a speech, what a man says? A. I do not, sir.

Q. Didn't you know that the President, on that occasion, had been exercising his greater constitutional right of "freedom of speech."

Mr. CURTIS—That puts a question of law to the witness. (Laughter.)

Q. Didn't you so understand it, sir? A. I so understood it, sir.

Mr. STANBERY—We are to understand, then, that it is constitutional to exercise freedom of speech.

Mr. BUTLER—That it is constitutional to exercise it in this way, it may be constitutional, I think, not decent.

Q. How dare you correct the President's great constitutional right of freedom of speech, without any memoranda to do it? (Laughter.) A. The authority I assumed.

Q. How came you to assume the authority to correct this great constitutional right? A. It is a difficult question to answer.

Q. Why should you assume the authority to correct his speech? A. My object was as the speech was extemporaneous, simply to correct the language and not to change the substance.

Q. Did you change the substance in any way? A. Not that I'm aware of.

Q. Are there not pages there where your corrections comprise the most of it? A. I am not aware, sir, that there is, from a hasty examination I have made any one change, perhaps there may be a single exception where my writing predominates, there are places where there are erasures, but whether or not I erased them I don't know.

Q. Do you know whether anybody else did so? A' No, sir.

Q. Did you do that revision by direction of the President? A. I did not, sir, so far as I recollect.

Q. He did not direct you? No, sir?

Q. Did you say to Mr. Smith, then and there, that you did it by the direction of the President? A. Not that I remember, sir.

Q. You mean to say that you made these alterations and corrections upon the very solemn occasion of this speech, without any authority whatever? A. That is my impression.

Q. After you made the revision, did you show it to the President? A. No, sir.

Q. Did you ever tell him that you had taken that liberty with his constitutional rights? (Laughter.) A. I can't recollect that I did.

Q. As you corrected the paper what did you do with the manuscript? A. The manuscript as it was revised was handed to the agent of the Associated Press, who sent it to the office that it might be published in the afternoon papers.

Q. Was it published in the afternoon papers? A. I have no doubt of it.

Q. Was that speech purporting to come from the President published from the Associated Press despatches? A. I don't know, sir; it reached the Associated Press.

Q. Was the same speech published in the *Intelligencer?* A. The speech was published in the *Intelligencer*.

Q. Is that the paper taken in the Executive Mansion? A. Yes, sir.

Q. Was it at that time? A. It was at that time.

Q. And seen by the President? A. I presume it was, sir.

Q. Did he ever chide you or say you had done wrong, or misrepresented him in this speech at all? A. He did not, sir.

Q. Never down to this day? A. He has never done so, sir.

Q. Has he ever said there was anything wrong about it? A. I have never heard him say so.

Cross-examination waved.

Mr. BUTLER—I now propose, with your Honor's leave and that of the Senate, to read the speech as corrected by Colonel Moore, unless that is objected to: I propose to put in evidence the report of Mr. Smith, the Associated Press report, and the report of the *Chronicle*. You are aware, sir, that the President complains in his answer that we do not give the whole speech. We have now all the versions that we can conveniently give of the whole speech. If not objected to, we will put them all in, otherwise I will only put in the extracts.

Mr. EVARTS—Which do you now offer?

Mr. BUTLER—All; I guess we will get through with the whole of it.

Mr. EVARTS—You have proved by a number of witnesses the version which passed under Colonel Moore's eye.

Mr. BUTLER, interrupting—I think I must ask that the objection must be made in writing.

Mr. EVARTS—Before it is made?

Mr. BUTLER—No, sir; as it is made.

Mr. EVARTS, continuing—And the speech, as it is proved in Mr. Smith's copy and Mr. Sheridan's copy, we regard as in the shape of evidence—the accuracy of the report to be judged of as being competent evidence on the subject. The speech in the *Chronicle* we do not understand to be supported by any such evidence. We shall object to that as not being authentically proved. The speech in the *Intelligencer* seems to have been overlooked by the honorable manager, as it is not produced. The *Chronicle's* speech we consider as not being proved by authentic evidence submitted to the court. The stenographic reports of the former, with proper proof to support them, and which is competent, may be considered accurate, their accuracy to be subject of remark, of course, and without desiring here to anticipate the discussion as to whether any of the evidence that is offered here with reference to the eleventh article is admissible, and saving that for the purpose of discussion in the body of the case, we will make no other objection to the reading of the speeches.

Mr. BUTLER—Do you want the whole of them read?

Mr. EVARTS—Whichever version you wish.

Mr. BUTLER—We will put them all in evidence—we will read one.

Mr. TIPTON moved to take a recess of fifteen minutes.

Mr. TRUMBULL suggested the motion be modified to an adjournment until three o'clock, so as to take up the order in regard to the ticket system. He made a motion accordingly, which was lost.

The question was put on taking the recess, which was agreed to.

Adjournment.

After the recess, Senator GRIMES moved that when the Senate, sitting as a court, adjourn to-day, it adjourn to meet on Monday next.

Senator DRAKE called for the yeas and nays.

The vote was taken, and resulted yeas, 19; nays, 28, as follows:—

YEAS.—Messrs. Buckalew, Corbett, Davis, Dixon, Fessenden, Fowler, Grimes, Henderson, Hendricks, Johnson, McCreery, Norton, Patterson (Tenn.), Ramsey, Saulsbury, Trumbull, Van Winkle, Vickersa and Wilson—19.

NAYS.—Messrs. Anthony, Cameron, Cattell, Chandler, Cole, Conkling, Conness, Cragin, Drake, Edmunds, Ferry, Frelinghuysen, Howard, Howe, Morgan, Morrill (Me.), Morrill (Vt.), Nye, Patterson (N. H.), Pomeroy, Ross, Sprague, Stewart, Thayer, Tipton, Willey and Williams—28.

The August Speech.

Mr. BUTLER proceeded to read the manuscript of the President's speech of 17th August speech, 1866, as reported by Mr. Smith, and without the corrections made in the report by Colonel Moore.

Senator ANTHONY proposed to call up the order which he had previously offered in legislative session in reference to the admission of a reporter for the Associated Press on the floor of the Senate.

The Chief Justice ruled that it was not in order.

Senator Conkling offered it originally.

Mr. ANTHONY—Then I move that the presiding officer be authorized to assign a place on the floor of the Senate to the reporter of the Associated Press.

Mr. CONKLING—One single reporter.

The Chief Justice ruled that the proposition was not in order.

Mr. EVARTS asked Mr. Butler what copies or versions of the President's speech he considered in evidence.

Mr. BUTLER said he considered two copies in evidence; the one made by Mr. Smith and the one which had been corrected by the President's private secretary.

Mr. EVARTS—And no other?

Mr. BUTLER—I do not offer the *Chronicle*, not because it is not evidence, but I have the same things in Mr. Smith's report.

Mr. EVARTS—Then it is those two reports you offer?

Mr. BUTLER—Yes; and they will be both printed as part of the evidence.

The Cleveland Oration.

William N. Hudson, sworn and examined by Mr. BUTLER.—Q. What is your business? A. I am a journalist by occupation.

Q. Where is your home? A. In Cleveland, Ohio.

Q. What paper are you in charge of, or do you edit? A. The Cleveland *Leader*.

Q. Where were you about the 3d or 4th of September, 1866? A. In Cleveland.

Q. What was your business then? A. I was then one of the editors of the *Leader*.

Q. Did you hear a speech by President Johnson from the balcony of the hotel there? A. I did.

Q. Did you report it? A. I did, with the assistance of another reporter.

Q. Who is he? A. His name is Johnson.

Q. Was your report published in the paper the next day? A. It was.

Q. Have you a copy of it? A. I have.

[Witness produced it.]

Q. Have you your original notes? A. I have not.

Q. Where are they? A. I cannot tell; they are probably destroyed.

Q. What can you show as to the accuracy of your report? A. It was a verbatim report, except in portions; a part was verbatim and a part substantial.

Q. Does the report distinguish the parts which are not verbatim from the parts which are? A. It does.

Q. State whether anything that Mr. Johnson said is left out?

Mr. EVARTS—Which Johnson—the President or the reporter Johnson?

Mr. BUTLER—I mean Andrew last aforesaid. (Laughter.)

Witness—The report leaves out some portions of Mr. Johnson's speech, and states them in a synoptical form.

Q. Was anything of it there which is not said? A. There are words used which he did not use. In stating the substance of what was said there is nothing substantially stated which was not said.

Q. When was that report prepared? A. It was prepared on the evening of the delivery of the speech.

Q. Did you see it after it was printed? A. I did.

Q. Did you ever examine it? A. I did.

Q. What can you say as to the accuracy of the report whenever the words are purported to be given? A. To the best of my recollection it was accurate.

Q. How far is it accurate when the substance purports to be given? A. It gives substance—the sense without the words.

Q. Taking the synoptical part and the verbatim part of the report, does the whole together give the substance of what he said on that occasion? By way of illustration take this part:—"Haven't you got the court? Haven't you got the Attorney-General? Who is your Chief Justice?" Is that the synoptical part, or is that verbatim report? A. It is part of the verbatim report.

Cross-examined by Mr. EVARTS—This newspaper which you edit, and for which you report, was it of the politics of the President, or of opposite opinion in politics? A. It was Republican in politics.

Q. Opposite to the views of the President as you understand them? A. Yes.

Q. At what time was this speech made? A. On the 3d of September, about nine o'clock in the evening.

Q. When did it conclude? A. I think about a quarter before ten o'clock.

Q. Was there a large crowd there? A. There was.

Q. Consisting of the people of Cleveland? A. Of the people of Cleveland and of the surrounding towns.

Q. This balcony from which the President spoke, was that also crowded? It was.

Q. Where were you? I was on the balcony.

Q. Were you in sight of the President? A. Yes.

Q. And what conveniences or arrangements had you for taking notes? A. I took notes on my knees.

Q. Where did you get the light from? A. From the gas above.

Q. At what time that evening did you begin to write out your notes? A. About eleven o'clock.

Q. When did you finish? A. Between twelve and one o'clock.

Q. When did the paper go to press? A. Between three and four o'clock in the morning.

Q. Did you write the synoptical parts from your notes, or from your recollection of the drift of the speech? A. From my notes.

Q. You added nothing, you think, to your notes? A. Nothing.

Q. But you did not produce all that was in the notes? A. I did not; I endeavored to copy the substance of what the President said.

Q. You mean the meaning, do you not; that is the drift of it? A. Yes.

Q. What you mean exactly is that, that you meant to give the drift of the whole when you did not report *verbatim?* A. Yes.

Q. Did you not leave out any other drift? A. Not to my recollection.

Q. Have you ever looked to see? A. I have not compared the speech with any full report of it.

Q. Or with your own notes? A. I did subsequently compare the speech with notes.

Q. This drift part? A. I mean to say that I compared this report with my notes.

Q. The part that is synoptical, did you compare that with your notes? A. Yes.

Q. When? A. The next day.

Q. When did your notes disappear? In the course of two weeks? A. They were not preserved at all.

Q. Are you sure that you compared the report of your notes the following day? A. I am.

Q. Did you destroy your notes intentionally? A. I did not.

Q. Then where are they? A. I cannot tell.

Q. Now, in reference to the part of the speech which you say you reported *verbatim*, did you at any time, after writing them out that night, compare the transcript with the notes? A. I did.

Q. For the purpose of seeing that it was accurate? A. Yes.

Q. When was that? A. Next day.

Q. With what assistance? A. Without any assistance, to the best of my memory.

Q. Did you find any change? A. There were some typographical errors in the reading of the proof; there were no material errors.

Q. Were there no errors in the transcript from your notes? A. I did not compare the transcript with my notes; I compared it as printed.

Q. With what? With my notes.

Q. That was not my question; but you did compare the speech as printed with your notes, and not with the transcript? A. Yes, with my notes; not with the transcript.

Q. Did you find that there were any errors in the printed report as compared with the original notes? A. There were some typographical errors.

Q. And no others? A. Not that I remember.

Q. Are you prepared to say that you compared the printed paper next morning with your phonographic notes, and the report in the printed paper was absolutely correct? A. They were not phonographic notes.

Q. What were they? Common writing, written out in long hand? A. Yes, sir.

Q. Now, do you mean to say that you can write out in long hand, word for word, a speech as it comes from the mouth of a speaker? A. In this instance I did write out portions of the speech.

Q. Then you did not even have notes that were worth making except of a part of the speech? A. That is all.

Q. And you made the synopsis of the drift as it went along? A. Yes.

Q. How did you select the parts where you should report accurately and the parts where you should give the drift? A. Whenever it was possible to report correctly and full I did so, and when I was unable to keep up I gave the substance. There were times during the speech, owing to the slowness with which the speaker spoke when a reporter writing in longhand was able to keep up with the remarks of the President.

Q. Then this report was not made by the aid of stenography or shorthand? A. No, sir.

Q. Did you abbreviate or write out the words in full when you did write? A. I abbreviated in many instances.

Q. Do you recollect them? A. I do.

Q. Can you give an instance of one of your abbreviations? A. I cannot.

Q. Without any printed paper before you, how much of the President's speech, as made at Cleveland on the 3d of September, can you repeat? A. None of it.

Q. None of it? A. None whatever; verbatim, none.

Q. Do you think you could give the drift of some of it? A. I think I might.

Q. As you understand it and recollect it? A. Yes.

Q. Do you mean it to be understood that you wrote down one single sentence of the President's speech, word for word, as it came from his mouth? A. Yes.

Q. Point out any such sentence? A. The sentence that was read by the manager was written out word for word.

Q. Do you mean to say that any ten consecutive lines of your report printed in your newspaper, you wrote down in long hand, word for word, as they came from the President's mouth? A. I cannot tell how much of it I wrote down at this distance of time; I have the impression, however, that there was as much of it as that.

Q. Can you say anything more than that you intended to report, as nearly as you could and as well, under the circumstances, without the aid of short-hand faculty, what the President said? A. I can say in addition to that that there are parts of the speech which are reported as he said it.

Q. Do you say so from your present memory? A. From my memory of the method with which the notes were taken.

Q. What parts can you so state to be verbatim? A. I cannot swear that they are his absolute words in all cases. I will swear that it is an accurate report.

Q. What do you mean by accurate? But not absolute; I mean to say that it is a report which gives the general form of each sentence as it was uttered, perhaps varying in one or two words.

Q. You mean to say you intended to report as well as you could, without the aid of shorthand facilities? A. I say, in addition, that there are portions which are reported verbatim.

Q. Now, I want you to tell me whether that which purports to be verbatim is, to your memory and knowledge, accurately reported? A. It is accurately reported; I cannot say it is absolutely accurate.

Q. The whole of it? A. Yes.

Q. In reference to the part of the speech of which you did not profess to report *verbatim*, what assurance have you that you did not omit part of the speech? A. I endeavored to report the substance and meaning of the speech; I cannot say that I did give it all?

Q. What assurance have you that some portions of the speech were not omitted entirely from your *synoptical* view? A. I was able to report nearly every sentence, and am confident that I did not fail to take notes of any paragraph of his speech.

Q. That is to say you are confident that nothing which would have been a paragraph after it was printed was left out by you? A. He did not speak in paragraphs.

Q. You say you are sure you did not leave out what would be a paragraph; did you leave out what would be half a paragraph? A. I endeavored to give the substance of the President's remarks in every subject that the President took up.

Q. This synoptical report which is made out, was it anything but your original notes? A. It was condensed from them.

Q. That is to say, your original synoptical views as written down were again reduced in a shorter compend by you that night? A. Partly so.

Q. Still you think that in that last analysis you had the whole of the President's speech? A. I endeavored to give the meaning of it.

Q. Can you pretend to say that, in reference to any of that portion of your report, it is presented in a shape in which any man should be judged as coming from his own mouth?

Mr. BUTLER—I object to the question.

Mr. EVARTS—I ask of the witness if he professes to state that in this synoptical portion of the printed speech made by him it is so *produced* as to be properly judged as having come from the mouth of the speaker.

Mr. BUTLER—No objections to that.

Witness—I can only say that, to the best of my belief, this is a fair report of what was said.

Q. In your estimation and belief? A. In my estimation and belief.

Q. You speak of a reporter named Johnson, who took part, as I understand you, in that business. What part did he take? A. He, also, took notes of what Mr. Johnson said.

Q. Wholly independent of you? A. Wholly independent of me.

Q. And the speech, as printed in your paper, was not from his notes? A. It was made up from mine, with the assistance of his.

Q. Then you condensed and mingled the reporter, Johnson's, report and your own, and produced this printed result? A. Yes.

Q. What plan did Johnson proceed on in getting the draft of effect of the President's speech? A. Johnson took as full notes as possible.

Q. You mean possible for him? A. Yes.

Q. How much of that report and how much of that analysis or estimation of what the President said was made out of your notes and how much of Johnson's? A. Whenever Johnson's notes were fuller than mine I used his to correct mine.

Q. Was that so in many instances? A. It was not so in a majority of instances but in the minority—in a considerable minority.

Q. Did Johnson write longhand too? A. Yes.

Q. What connection has Johnson with you on the paper? A. He is the reporter of the paper.

Q. Was there no phonographic reporter to take down the speech? A. There was no one for our paper; there were reporters present, I believe, for other papers.

Re-direct by Mr, BUTLER—Q. You have been asked about the manner in which you took the speech; were there considerable interruptions? A. There were.

Q. Was there considerable bawling for the President? A. There was necessary bawling.

Q. Why necessary? A. Because of the interruptions of the crowd.

Q. Was the crowd a noisy one? It was.

Q. Were the crowd and the President bandying epithets?

Mr. EVARTS—The question is what was said.

Mr. BUTLER—I do not adopt the language of the counsel. I will repeat my question whether epithets were thrown back and forth between the President and the crowd?

Mr. EVARTS—We object to the question. The question is, what was said. Every one does not know what bandying epithets is.

Mr. BUTLER, to the witness—Do you know what bandying epithets it?

Mr. EVARTS—I suppose our objection will be first disposed of.

Mr. BUTLER—I beg your pardon. However, I will withdraw the question. My proposition is this—.

Mr. EVARTS—(Interrupting)—There is no objection to your withdrawing the question.

Mr. BUTLER—I only withdraw my question as to the meaning of a word which one of the counsel did not understand. (Laughter.) In Lord George Gordon's case the cries of the crowd were allowed to be put in evidence, but that question precisely is not raised here, because I am on the point of showing what was said there by way of interruptions. It was asked whether there were interruptions, and whether there was a crowd, and if the President stopped in his speech to throw back epithets at the crowd.

Mr. EVARTS—The questions which we object to were those about the bandying of epithets back and forth between the President and the crowd.

Mr. BUTLER—I will put it in another form. Q. What was said by the crowd to the President and by the President to the crowd? A. The President was frequently interrupted by cheers, hisses and cries from those opposed to him.

Mr. BUTLER—You have a right to refresh your memory by any memorandum or copy of a memorandum made by you at the time.

Mr. EVARTS—No. Not by any copy of memorandum.

Mr. BUTLER—Yes. Any copy of memorandum which you know to be a copy made at the time.

Mr. EVARTS—We do not regard a newspaper as a memorandum.

Mr. BUTLER—Well, we may as well have that settled, because when a man says I wrote down as best I could, and put it in type within four hours from that time, and I know it to be correct, I insist that as a rule of law that is a memorandum, from which the witness may refresh his recollection.

Mr. EVARTS—This witness is to speak from his recollection, if he can. If he cannot, he is allowed accordingly to refresh his memory by the memorandum which he made at the time.

Mr. BUTLER—I deny that to be the rule of law. He may refresh his memory by any memorandum which he knows to be correct.

The Chief Justice required Mr. Butler to reduce his question to writing.

Mr. BUTLER having reduced the question to writing, put it to the witness in this form:—I desire you to refresh your recollection from any memorandum made by you at or near the time, and then state what was said by the crowd to the President, and by the President to the crowd.

Mr. EVARTS—That question we have objected to.

The Chief Justice asked the witness whether that was a memorandum made by him at the time?

Witness—It is a copy of a memorandum made at the time.

The Chief Justice—The witness has a right to look at a paper which he knew to be a true copy of a memorandum made at the time.

Mr. BUTLER, to witness—Go on.

Witness, reading from the paper—The first interruption to the President was —

Mr. EVARTS—We understand the ruling of the Chair to be that the witness is allowed to refresh his memory by looking a memorandum made at the time, or what is the equivalent, and thereupon to state from his memory: thus refreshed, what the facts are, that he might state it from his memory, but not read from the memorandum.

Mr. BUTLER to witness—Read it.

Witness—The first interruption to the President occurred when he referred to the name of General Grant, and said he knew that a large number of the crowd desired to see General Grant, and to hear what he had to say, whereupon there were cheers for General Grant, and the President went in; the next interruption occurred when he referred to the object of his visit, and alluded to the name of Stephen A. Douglas; there were then cheers; the next cries of interruption occurred at the time the President used this language:—"I was placed on the ticket (meaning the ticket for the Presidency) with the distinguished citizen now no more," whereupon there were cries of, "It's a pity," "too bad," "unfortunate;" the President proceeded, "Yes, I know some of you say 'unfortunate.'"

Q. What was then said by the crowd? A. The President went on to say "It was unfortunate for some that God was on high—"

Mr. EVARTS—(Interrupting)—asked if the point made by the learned manager was this, that in following the examination of this witness he could show there were interruptions for spaces; that is the whole matter as I understand it. Now the witness is reading the President's speech, which is not yet in evidence.

Mr. BUTLER—And as I understand it, he is not reading the President's speech, but giving such portions of it only as to show where the interruption came in; now when he compares the interruptions with the portions of the speech where he took notes you will see why there was time to take portions *verbatim.*

The Chief Justice, to witness—Look at the memorandum and then testify from memory at the present time.

Witness—The next interruption that occurred was when the President remarked that if his predecessor had lived—

Mr. EVARTS—The question was, if the interruption, their duration and their cause——

Mr. BUTLER—I beg your pardon; I put the question, and there was no objection to it—What did the President say to the crowd, and what did the crowd say to the President? Now, I want that. (Laughter.) To witness—Go on and answer.

Witness—When this remark was made the crowd responded, "Never, never," and gave three cheers for Congress; the President went on to say "I came here as I was passing along and being called on for the purpose of exchanging views——"

The Chief Justice, interrupting—Mr. Manager, do you understand that the witness is to read the speech?

Mr. BUTLER—No, sir; he is skipping whole paragraphs, and he is only reading where the interruption came in. To witness—Just use the latter words of the President.

Witness—When the President remarked that he came here for the purpose of ascertaining what was wrong, there were cries "You are," long continued cheers.

The President inquired, later in his speech, who could put his finger on any acf of the President's deviating from the right, whereupon there were cheers and counter cheers, long continued. That cry was repeated, often

breaking the sentences of the President's into paragraphs. Then there were cries of "Why not hang Jeff Davis?" The President responded, "Why not hang Jeff Davis." Then there were shouts of "Down with him," and other cries of "Hang Wendell Phillips." The President said:—"Why not you hang him?" The answers "Won't give us an opportunity"—the President then went on to ask, "Have you not a court and an a torney general? who is the Chief Justice, and who is to sit on his trial?" (Laughter in court). There were then interruptions by groans and cheers; he then said, "Call upon your Congress that is trying to break up our government; then there cries of "Liar" among the crowd; then there was a voice of "Don't get so mad?" the President said "I am not mad;" then there were hisses and two or three more cheers were given for Congress; after another sentence of his, a voice cried out, "What about Moses?" (Laughter in court.) The next interruption I recollect was, when the President inquired, "Will you hear me?" then the cries were taken up and continued for some minutes; all this time there was great confusion—cheers by the friends of the President, and counter cheers by those apparently opposed to him; the President repeated his question, asking for the people to hear him for his cause and for the Constitution of his country;" there were then cries of "Yes, yes! Go on;" the next sentence he inquired when, under any circumstances, he had violated the Constitution of his country, to which there were cries, in response, of "Never, never," and counter cheers; the next interruption was when Mr. Seward's name was mentioned, and there were cheers for Mr. Seward; the President said he would bring Mr. Seward before the people; he asked who was a traitor; there were cries of "Thad. Stevens;" the President asked, "Why don't you hang Thad. Stevens and Wendell Phillips;" then there were cheers and hisses; the President proceeded to say that "having fought traitors at the South, he would fight them at the North," then there were cheers and hisses; there were also cries when the President said he would "do this by the help of the people;" there were cries of "we won't give it;" the interruption continued in the shape of cheers, hisses and cries of the same sort throughout the speech.

Mr. BUTLER—State whether these cries, cheers and hisses would be continued so as to make interruption last for some time? A. Yes, frequently, for several minutes.

Q. In that time would you be able to get up your report? A. I was able to make during the most of them a verbatim report of what the President said.

Re-cross-examination by Mr. EVARTS.

Q. You made a memorandum of the time of these interruptions? A. I did.

Q. Of those cries and hisses? A. I did.

Q. While you were doing that you could catch up with the President's speech, could you. (Laughter.) Now, have you not, in each statement you have made of these interruptions, read from the newspaper before you? A. I have read from the newspaper; I think that every one of them was in the newspaper.

Q. Are you not quite sure of it? A. I am not positive.

Q. Without that newspaper, did you recollect any of those interruptions? A. I do.

Q. All of them? A. I should not have been able to give them all without the aid of the memorandum.

Q. You made a report of those interruptions on your notes? A. Yes.

Q. Of all that the crowd said? A. Not of all.

R Why not of all? A. I made notes of all that I was able to catch.

Q. You made notes of all that you were able to catch and put down, and yet you say you were able to catch up with the President? A. I gave my first attention to keeping up with the President; whenever there was time to put the interruptions down and the cries, I did so.

Senator GRIMES put the following question to the witness in writing:—

I desire the witness to specify the particular part of the report, as published, which was supplied by the reporter Johnson.

Witness—It is impossible for me to do that at this time.

Mr. BUTLER—State whether any special part of it was supplied by him, or whether it was only connected by Mr. Johnson's notes. A. The report was made out from my notes and corrected by Mr. Johnson; I cannot say whether there were any other sentences on Mr. Johnson's notes or not.

Q. State whether long practice in reporting would enable a person, by long hand, to make out a substantially accurate report?

Mr. EVARTS—Ask whether this witness can do it?

Witness—I have had considerable practice in reporting in that way, and can make out a substantially accurate report.

Examination of Daniel C. McEwen.

Daniel C. McEwen sworn and examined by Mr. BUTLER—Q. What is your profession? A. A short-hand reporter.

Q. How long has that been your profession? A. About four or five years.

Q. Were you employed in September, 1866, in reporting for any paper? A. I was.

Q. What paper? A. The New York *World.*

Q. Did you accompany Mr. Johnson and the Presidential party when they went to lay the corner-stone of the monument in honor of Mr. Douglas? A. I did.

Q. Where did you join the party? A. At West Point, New York.

Q. How long did you continue with the party? A. I continued until it arrived at Cincinnati on its return.

Q. Did you go professionally as a reporter? A. I did.

Q. Had you accommodations as such? A. I had.

Q. Had you the *entree* of the Presidential car? A. I had.

Q. Were you at Cleveland? A. I was.

Q. Did you make a report of the President's speech at Cleveland from the balcony? A. I did.

Q. How? A. Stenographically.

Q. Have you your notes here? A. I have.

[Witnesses produced them.]

Q. Have you, at my request, copied them out since you have been here? A. I have.

Q. Is this (handing a paper to the witness) a copy of them? A. It is.

Q. Is it an accurate copy from your notes? A. It is.

Q. How accurately are your notes a representation of the speech? A. My notes I consider very accurate so far as I took them; some few sentences in the speech were left out by confusion in the crowd, but I have in those cases in my transcript inclosed in brackets the parts about which I am uncertain.

Q. Where they are not inclosed in brackets, how are they? A. They are correct.

Q. Was your report published? A. I cannot say; I took notes of the speech, and knowing the lateness of the hour, eleven o'clock or after, and that it was impossible for me to write out a report of the speech and send it to the paper I represented, therefore I went to the telegraph office after the speech was given. and dictated some of my notes to other reporters and correspondents, and we made a report which was given to the Agent of the Associated Press, Mr. Gobright.

Q. Did the agent of the Associated Press accompany the Presidential party for the purpose? A. Yes.

Q. Was it his business and duty to forward reports of the speeches? A. I supposed it to be.

Q. Did you so deal with him? A. I did.

Q. Have you put down the cheers and interruptions of the crowd, or any portion of them? A. I have put down a portion of them; it was impossible to get all.

Q. Was there not a great deal of confusion and noise there? A. A great deal.

Q. Were there expressions of ill feeling and temper? A. I think there was.

Q. On the part of the crowd? A. Yes, sir.

Q. How on the part of the President? A. I consider that he was a little excited.

Q. Was anything said there to him by the crowd about his keeping his dignity? A. I have it not in my notes.

Q. Do you recollect it? A. I do not recollect it.

Q. Was there anything said about his not getting mad? A. Yes, sir.

Q. Did the crowd caution him about not getting mad? A. The words used were—"Don't get mad, Andy."

Q. Did he appear considerably excited at that moment when they told him not to get mad?

Mr. EVARTS said that was not a part of the present inquiry.

Mr. BUTLER remarked—I want to get as much as I can from this witness' memory, and as much as I can from his notes, so with both together we may have a perfect transcript of the proceedings. The allegation denied is that there was a scandalous and disgraceful scene, the conditions being that the counsel for the President claim freedom of speech, and we claim decency of speech. We are now trying to show the indecency of the occasion.

Mr. EVARTS—I understand freedom of speech in this country to mean liberty to speak properly and discreetly.

Mr. BUTLER—I regard freedom of speech in this country as freedom of the private citizen to say anything in a decent manner.

Mr. EVARTS—Yes, it is the same thing, and who is to judge of the decency.

Mr. BUTLER—The court before which a man is tried for violating the laws.

Mr. EVARTS—Did you ever hear of a man being tried for freedom of speech.

Mr. BUTLER—No, but I saw two or three who ought to have been. (Laughter in the court.)

To the witness—I was asking you whether there was considerable excitement in the manner of the President at the time he was cautioned by the crowd not to get mad. A. I was not standing where I could see the President; I could not know his manner; I only heard the tone of his voice.

Q Judging from what you heard he seemed excited? A. I do not know what his manner is, from personal acquaintance, when he is angry.

Cross-examined by Mr. EVARTS.—Q. Did you report the whole of the President's speech? A. The hour was late and I left shortly before he closed; I do not know how long before the close of his speech.

Q. So that your report does not purport to give the whole speech? A. No, sir.

Q. From the time that he commenced until this point at which you left, did you report the whole of his speech? A. No, sir; certain sentences were broken off by the interruptions of the crowd.

Q. But aside from the interruptions did you continue through the whole of the speech to the point at which you left? A. I did.

Q. Did you make a report of it word for word as you supposed? A. Yes, sir, as I understood it.

Q. And did you not take word for word the interruptions of the assembly? A. I did not; I took the principle exclamations; I could not hear all of them.

Q. And this copy, or transcript, which you produce, when did you make it? A. I made that about two weeks

since; after I was summoned before the managers of impeachment.

Q. Can you be as accurate or as confident in the transcript taken after the lapse of two years, as if it had been made recently, when the speech was delivered? A. I generally find, that when a speech is fresh on my mind, I write my notes with more readiness than when they have become old; but as to the correctness of the report, I think I can make as accurate a transcript of the notes now as I could have done then.

Q. You have nothing to help you when you transcribe after the lapse of time but the notes before you? A. That is all.

Q. And are you not aware that in phonographic writing there is often obscurity, from the haste and brevity of the notation? A. There sometimes is.

Re-direct by Mr. BUTLER—The counsel on the other side asked the politics of the Cleveland *Leader*. May I ask you the politics of the New York *World?* I have always understood them to be Democratic.

Examination of Edwin B. Stark.

Edwin B. Stark, sworn and examined by Mr. BUTLER—

Q. What is your profession? A. I practice the law now.

Q. What was your profession in September, 1866? A. I was an editor in Cleveland, and I do more or less of it now.

Q. Did you report the speech of Andrew Johnson, President of the United States, from the balcony of the Cleveland Hotel on the night of the 3d of September, 1866? A. Yes.

Q. For what paper? A. The Cleveland *Herald*.

Q. Did you take short-hand notes of it? A. Yes, I did.

Q. Was it written out by you and published as written out by you? A. I have; it was.

Q. Have you your short-hand notes? I have not.

Q. Are they in existence? A. I suppose not; I paid no attention to them, but I suppose they were thrown into waste basket?

Q. Did you ever compare the printed speech in the *Herald* with your notes or with the manuscript? A. I did with the manuscript that night; I compared the printed slips with the copy taken from my original notes.

Q. How did it compare? A. It was the same.

Q. Were they slips of the paper that was published next day? A. They were just the same, with such typographical corrections as were made then.

Q. Have you a copy of the paper? A. A. I have [producing it.]

Q. Can you now state whether this is a substantially accurate report in this paper of what Andrew Johnson said? A. Yes, sir, it is generally; there are some portions which were cut down, and I can point out just where these places are.

Q. By being cut down, you mean the substance given instead of the words? A. Yes, sir.

Q. Does it appear in the report what part is substantially and what part is verbatim? A. Not to any person but myself.

To witness—Point out what part is substituted and what part is accurate in the report.

Witness—Do you wish me to go over the whole speech or that purpose?

Mr. BUTLER—I will for the present confine myself to such portions as are in the article. If my learned friends wish you to go over the rest they will ask you.

The witness commenced a little before where the specification commences in the article of impeachment—I will read just what Mr. Johnson said on that point.

Mr. BUTLER—Do so.

Witness—He said, "Where is the man living, or the woman, or the community whom I have wronged; or where is the person who can place his finger on one single pledge that I have violated, or one single violation of the Constitution of my country; what tongue do s he speak; what religion does he profess? let him come forward and put his finger upon one pledge I have violated;" there were several interruptions, and various remarks were made, of which I have noted one, because it was the only one that Mr. Johnson paid any attention to—that was a voice said, "Hang Jeff. Davis! hang Jeff. Davis!" The President—"Hang Jeff. Davis!—why don't you?" There were then some applause and interruptions, and he replied, "Why don't you?" There was again applauses and interruptions, and the President went on; have you not got the courts?—have you not got the attorney-general?—who is your chief justice?—who has refused to set at the trial? There were then some interruptions and applause, and he said:—I am not the prosecuting attorney; I am not the jury, but I will tell you what I did do—I called on your Congress, which is trying to break up the government; at that point there were interruptions and confusion, and there may have been words uttered there by the President which I did not hear, but I think not; then the President went on to say —but let the prejudices pass —.

Mr. BUTLER—Go on to the conclusion where you reported accurately.

Witness commencing—He said, "In bidding you farewell, here to-night, I would ask you with all the pains that Congress has taken to calumniate me, what has Congress done? Has it done anything to restore the Union of the States? On the contrary, has it not done everything to prevent it?—and, because I stand now, as I did when the Rebellion commenced, I have been denounced as a traitor. My countrymen here to-night, who has suffered more than I? Who has run greater risks than I? Who has borne more than I? But Congress, factious, domineering, tyrannical Congress, has undertaken to poison the minds of the American people and create a feeling against me."

So far were Mr. Johnson's words; I have completed the sentence here in this fashion:—"In consequence of the manner in which I have distributed the public patronage;" those were not Mr. Johnson's words, but a condensation in a summary way of the reasons which he gave, just at that point, for the maligning—

Mr. EVARTS to Mr. Butler—Do you propose to put hem in?

Mr. BUTLER—We do. I observe in the answer of the President that objection is made that we did not put in all he said, and I mean to give all.

Mr. EVARTS cross-examined the witness as follows:—

Q. What is the date of that newspaper you have? A. September 4, 1866.

Q. Did you make a stenographic report of the whole of the President's speech? A. I did with one exception.

Q. What exception was that? A. It was a part of the speech in which he spoke about the Freedmen's Bureau; it was in the latter half of the speech, somewhat in the details and figures which I omitted to take down.

Q. Did you write down your notes in full? A. No, sir.

Q. And you have not now either the notes or any transcript of them? A. Only this in the newspaper.

Q. Did you prepare for the newspapers the report that was published? A. I did.

Q. And you prepared it on the plan of some part verbatim and some part condensed? A. Yes, sir.

Q. What was your rule of condensation and the motive? A. I had no definite rule; but I can give the reason why I left out a part of what was said about the Freedman's Bureau.

Mr. EVARTS—That is not condensed at all.

Witness—Yes, sir; a part of it was not taken, and what I did take of it was somewhat condensed.

Q. What was your rule in relation to what you put verbatim into the report, and what you condensed? How did you determine what part you would give one way and what part another? A. Perhaps I was influenced somewhat by what I considered would be a little more spicy or entertaining to the reader.

Q. In which interest—in the interest of the President or his opponents? A. I do not know that.

Q. On which side were you? A. I was opposed to the President.

Q. But you did not know where you thought the interest was when you selected the spicy part? A. I was very careful in all those parts where there was considerable excitement in the crowd, to take down carefully what the President said.

Q. The part which the crowd was most interested in you took down carefully? A. Yes.

Q. And the part which the crowd seemed to have the most interest was the part in which they made the most outcry? A. Yes, sir.

Q. Are you able to say that there is a single expression in that part of your report given substantially which was used by the President, so that they are the words as they fell from his lips? A. No, sir. I think it is not the case in those particular parts which I condensed, I did so by the use in some parts of my own words.

Q. Was not your rule of condensation partly when you got tired of writing out? No, sir. As it was getting on between three and four o'clock in the morning, I was directed to cut down, and towards the last I did so.

Q. More towards the last than in the early part of the speech, so as to be ready to go to press? A. Yes, sir.

Mr. EVARTS—We object to this report as no report of the President's speech.

Witness was directed to mark the paper with his initials.

Mr. BUTLER—Q. What are the politics of the Cleveland Herald? A. At that time it was what was called Johnson-Republican. The editor of the Herald had the Post Office at the time.

Mr. BUTLER said he proposed to offer the Leader's report of Mr. Johnson's speech, as sworn to by Mr. Hudson.

Mr. EVARTS—That we object to. The grounds of the objection are made manifest, doubtless, to the observation of the Chief Justice and of the Senators, and are greatly enhanced when we find that the managers are in possession of the original notes of the short-hand writer of the whole speech, and of his transcript made therefrom, sworn to by him. We submit that the substitution for that evidence of the whole speech thus authenticated, the statement of Mr. Hudson, as testified to by him, is against the first principles of justice or of evidence.

He has not testified how much of the report is his and how much of it is the reporter, Johnson's. Besides, it is for the great part a condensed statement, directed by circumstances. The same objection may be made to the second Herald report.

Mr. BUTLER said—I do not propose to argue the question, but if we were trying any other case for substantive words, would not this be sufficient proof? I do not propose to withdraw the other report of Mr. McEwen.

I propose to put it in, subject to be read and commented upon by the gentleman on the other side, and propose to put the other reports in also, so that we can have all three reports the Post office report, the Republican report and the Democratic report. My natural leaning will lead me to this particular report as the one on which I mean to rely, because it is sworn to expressly by the party as having been written down by him himself, published by himself and corrected by himself; and I am surprised at the objection.

Mr. EVARTS—Nothing can better manifest the soundness of the objection than the statement of the manager. He selected by preference a report made by and through the agency of political hostility, and on a plan of condensation, and on a method of condensing another man's notes, instead of a sworn report by a phonographer who took every word, who brings his original notes and a transcript of them, and swears to their accuracy; and here, deliberately in the face of this testimony as to what was said there authentically proved, and brought into court to be; related, the honorable manager proposes to present a speech, with notes made and published on the motive and with the feelings, and under the influence, and on the method which has been stated. We object to it as evidence of the words spoken.

Mr. BUTLER—If, Mr. President and Senators, I had not lived too long to be astonished at anything, I should be surprised at the tone in which this proposition is put. Do I keep back from these gentlemen anybody's report. Do I not give them all I can lay my hands on. Shall I not use the reports of my friends and not those of my enemies, when I gave them the report of my enemies to cancel those of my friends? Is all virtue and propriety confined to Democratic reports? At one time, I think, President Johnson, if I recollect aright, would not have liked me very well to look in the World's report for him, and when the change took place, exactly, I do not know, therefore, I have this report. Why? Because it is the fullest and completest report.

The reason I did not rely upon Mr. McEwen's report is, that he testified on the stand that he got tired and went away, and did not report the whole speech. Mr. Stark and Mr. McEwen both swear that they left out portions. I could not, therefore, put these in. If I did I might be met by the objection that it was not the whole report. Here are three reports, representing three degrees of opinion, and we offer them all.

Mr. EVARTS—Discredit is now thrown on the most authentic report, on account of omissions, and because it is a Democratic report. I did not know before that the question of the authenticity of a stenographic report depends upon the political opinions of the stenographer. We submit that there is no such evidence; no living witness who from memory can repeat the President's speech, and there is no such authentication of notes in any case but Mr. McEwen's, which makes the public speech evidence.

Mr. BUTLER—I shall not debate the matter further than simply to say that I have not made any such proposition. I think this is an accurate report so far as we have put it into the article. It is an accurate report, a sworn report, and made by a man whom we can trust, and do trust. The other we think is just as accurate, perhaps. That question we do not go into, we simply put them in so that if there is a choice the President can have the benefit of it.

The President comes in here and says in his answer that we will not give him the full benefit of all he said, and when we take great pains to bring everybody here who made a report, and when we offer all the reports, then he says, "You must take a given one." So that we answer, "We take the one, but we take the one which has the whole speech," and now to test the question, if the gentlemen will agree not to object to McEwen's report because it is not a report of the whole speech, I will take that.

Mr. EVARTS—We will not make that objection.

Mr. BUTLER—We want it fully understood we put in Mr. McEwen's report of the speech as the standard report, and we put in the other two, so that if the President come with witnesses to deny the accuracy of the report, then we shall have the additional authentication of the other two reports.

Mr. EVARTS—The learned manager is familiar enough with the course of trials to know that it is time enough for him to bring in additional proof to contradict proof of ours when we make it.

Mr. BUTLER—Will you allow this report to be received? Do you make any objection?

Mr. EVARTS—We object to the two copies from newspapers

Mr. BUTLER—Very good. I asked that this question should be decided. I want all to go in, and I offered the whole three at once.

The Chief Justice said he could not put the question in all three at once.

Mr. BUTLER—Then I will first offer the Leader report.

The Chief Justice—The managers offer the report made in the Leader newspaper as evidence in this case. It appears from the statement of the witness that the report was not made by him, but was made by him with the assistance of another person, whose notes were not produced, and who is not himself produced as a witness.

The Chief Justice thinks that that paper is inadmissible.

The yeas and nays were demanded upon the question as to the admissibility of the report in the Cleveland Leader.

The vote was then taken and resulted, yeas, 35; nays, 11, ag follows:—

YEAS—Messrs. Anthony, Cameron, Cattell, Chandler, Cole, Conkling, Conness, Corbett, Cragin, Drake, Edmunds, Ferry, Fessenden, Frelinghuysen, Henderson, Howard, Johnson, Morgan, Morrill (Me.), Morrill (Vt.), Norton, Nye, Patterson (N. H.), Pomeroy, Ramsey, Ross, Sherman, Sprague, Stewart, Sumner, Thayer, Tipton, Van Winkle Willey and Williams—35.

NAYS—Messrs. Buckalew, Davis, Dixon, Doolittle, Fowler, Hendricks, Howe, McCreery, Patterson (Tenn.), Trumbull, and Vickers—11.

So the report was admitted as evidence.

Mr. BUTLER—I now offer the report prepared by Mr. McEwen.

Mr. EVARTS—We make no additional objection.

Mr. BUTLER—We now offer the report in the Cleveland *Herald.* Is there objection to that?

Mr. EVARTS—It is on the same principle.

Mr. Butler was proceeding to read the report when it was agreed that they should be all considered as read.

On motion of Mr. EDMUNDS, the Senate, sitting as a court of impeachment, adjourned until to-morrow at twelve o'clock.

PROCEEDINGS OF SATURDAY, APRIL 4.

Opening of the Court.

At twelve o'clock the Chair was vacated for the Chief Justice.

Proclamation was made, and the managers and members of the House were announced as usual, the former being all present, as well as the President's counsel.

L. L. Waldridge's Testimony.

After the Journal had been read, L. L. Waldridge was sworn and examined by Mr. BUTLER, and testified as follows:—

I am a short-hand writer; have been engaged in that business nearly ten years; have had during that time considerable experience in that business; I have had experience during the whole of that time, including newspaper and outside reporting; I have been lately connected with the Missouri *Democrat,* previous to that time the Missouri *Republican.*

Q. Do the names of those papers indicate their party proclivities, or are they reversed? A. They are reversed; the *Democrat* means Republican, and the *Republican* means Democrat; I was attached on or about the 8th of September, 1866, to the Missouri *Democrat;* I reported a speech delivered from the balcony of the hotel in St. Louis by Andrew Johnson; the speech was delivered between eight and nine o'clock in the evening; there was a crowd in the streets, and also on the balcony; also where I was; I was within two or three feet of the President while he was speaking; I don't know where the President's party was; I have no recollection of seeing one of the party on the balcony; I believe the President came to answer a call from the crowd in the street apparently; I know there was a very large crowd on the street, and continual cries for the President; in response to these cries I suppose he came out; he had, sir, been received in the afternoon by the municipal authorities; the Mayor made him an address; he answered that address; I reported that speech; I took every word.

Q. How soon was it written out after it was taken? A. Immediately, by my dictation; the first part of the speech previous to the banquet was written out in the rooms of the Southern Hotel; that occupied about half an hour, I should think; we then attended the banquet, at which speeches were made; immediately after the close of the banquet I went to the *Republican* office, and there I dictated the speech to Mr. Monaghan and Mr. McHenry, two of the attaches of the *Republican* office.

Q. There was a banquet given to the President by the city? A. Yes, sir; immediately after speaking from the balcony, at that banquet, the President made a very short address.

Q. After that speech was written out, was it published? A. On the next morning in the *Sunday Republican;* after it was published I revised the republication by my notes; immediately after the speech was published in the *Sunday Morning Republican,* I went down to the *Democrat* office in company with my associate, Mr. Edwin F. Adams, and we very carefully revised the speech for the Monday morning *Democrat;* it was on the same day; on the same Sunday that I made the revision; when I made the revision I had my notes; I compared the speech as printed with those notes at that time and since; my recollection is that there was one or two simple corrections of errors in transcribing, on the part of the printer; that is all I remember in the way of corrections; it was a little over a year ago; I was summoned here by the Committee on the New Orleans Riot, I think; it was a little after receiving the summons I hunted up my notes and again made a comparison with the speech; the second comparison verified my correctness.

Q. In regard to the particularity of the report whether you were unable to report so correctly as to give inaccuracy pronunciation? A. Yes, sir, I did so in many instances; I can't tell where my original notes are now; I searched for them a little after I was summoned here, but I failed to find them; I had them at the time I was examined before the Committee on the New Orleans Riots; I have no recollection of them since that time; I have a copy of that paper. (Witness produces printed paper.) This is it.

Q. From your knowledge of the manner in which you took speeches, from your knowledge of the manner in which you corrected it, state whether you are enabled to say the paper which I hold in my hand contains an accurate report of the speech of the President delivered on that occasion. A. I am able to say it is an accurate report.

Mr. BUTLER said he proposed, if there was no objection, to offer the paper in evidence, and he proposed to do so, also, if there were objections. (Laughter.)

Cross-examined by Mr. EVARTS.—Took down the entire speech from the President's mouth, word for word, as he delivered it; in the transcript from my notes and in this publication I preserved that form and degree of accuracy and completeness; it is all of the speech; no part of it is condensed or paraphrased; it is all of the speech; besides the revision of the speech which I made on the Sunday following the delivery of the speech, I made a revision of it a year ago, at the time that I was summoned before the committee of Congress on the New Orleans riot, at Washington; I can't say when that was; it was over a year ago; I cannot fix the date precisely; I was then inquired of in relation to the speech, and produced them to that committee; I was not examined before any other committee than that; my testimony was reduced to writing.

Mr. BUTLER—Was your testimony before the New Orleans Riot Committee published? A. I am not aware whether it was or not.

Mr. BUTLER then put in a copy of the St. Louis *Democrat's* report of the President's speech in St. Louis, made on September 8, 1866. The speech was read in full by the Clerk. The most offensive portions are set out in the third specification of the tenth article. It contains a paragraph predicting that the Fortieth Congress, constituted as the Thirty-seventh Congress, would try to impeach and remove him from office on some pretense of violating the Constitution or refusing to enforce some laws.

Testimony of J. A. Dean.

Joseph A. Dean, sworn and examined by Mr. BUTLEY—I am a reporter; I have been in the business five years; I am a short-hand writer; I joined the President's party when it went to St. Louis, via Cleveland; I joined it in Chicago; I was in the President's party at St. Louis; I reported all the speeches made there; I was with the party as correspondent for the Chicago *Republican;* I made the report for the St. Louis *Times;* I have a part of my notes; there was speaking on the steamboat; I reported that speech; I think it was a speech in answer to an address of welcome, by Captain Leeds, who represented a committee of citizens which met at Afton; I made that report in short-hand writing, and wrote it out; that evening the report was made for the St. Louis *Times;* and reported for a paper of strong Democratic politics; I corrected the inaccuracies of grammar; that is all; I have since written out from my notes so far as I have notes; this paper is in my hand writing from my notes; it is an exact transcript so far as it goes; it is an accurate report of the speech as made by Andrew Johnson, with the exceptions I have mentioned.

Mr. STANBERY to Mr. Butler—Is that the steamboat speech?

Mr. BUTLER—No, it is the speech from the balcony of the Southern Hotel.

Witness—The first speech is the speech at the Lindell Hotel; the other is the speech at the Southern Hotel.

Mr. BUTLER to witness—Take the one at the Southern Hotel. So far as that report goes, is this an accurate report of the speech? A. It is, but it is not all here, because I have lost part of my notes.

Q. Whereabouts did it commence? A. The speech commences in the middle of a sentence; the first words are:—"Who has shackles on their limbs and who are as much under the control and will of their masters as the colored men who are emancipated."

Witness (to a Senator)—This speech was made at the Southern Hotel in St, Louis; the speech then goes through as printed to the end; I have not compared the transcript with this paper (the St. Louis *Democrat*).

Mr. BUTLER offered the transcript as evidence.

Cross-examined by Mr. STANBERY—My report was published in the St. Louis *Times* on the Sunday following; I think the 9th of September.

Q. How much more time does it require a short-hand writer to write out his notes in long-hand than is required in taking the notes? A. We generally recken the difference in the rates between long and short-hand about six or seven to one.

A. J.'s Oratorical Powers.

Re-direct by Mr. BUTLER—Do I understand you to say that the whole of the speech was published in the *Times*? A. No, sir, not the whole of it; it was condensed for publication; it was considerably condensed; Mr. Johnson is a fluent speaker, but a very incoherent one; he frequently repeats his words; he is tautological; very verbose; that enables him to be taken with more ease; it is so in my experience that there are men who, by practice of long-hand and by abbreviations, can follow a speaker pretty accurately who speaks as Andrew Johnson speaks; I think they can give the sense of his speech without doing him any injustice.

Q. How is it when taking into consideration interruptions? A. The reporter would have to indicate the interruption; he would not write them out.

Q. But could he get the sense of the speaker; A. Yes he could.

By Mr. STANBERY—A long-hand writer, you say, may take the sense and substance of a speech; that is, he may take the sense and substances as to his ideas of what they are? A. Yes, his own view of what the speaker is saying.

To Mr. Butler—By dictating a report from the notes to another person it can be written out much more rapidly.

R. T. Chew Examined.

Robert T. Chew, sworn, and examined by Mr. BUTLER.—I am employed in the State Department; I am Chief Clerk in the State Department.

Q. It is a part of your duty to supervise commissions that are issued? A. A commission is first written out by a person who is called the Commission Clerk of the department; it is brought to me and by me sent to the President; when it is returned with the President's signature it is submitted by me to the Secretary of State, who countersigns it; then it goes to the Commission Clerk for the seal to be affixed to it; when a commission does not belong to my department, if it is for the Treasury it goes to the Treasury; that is to say the commissions of officers of the Treasury are prepared at my department; for Comptroller, Auditor, Treasurer, Assistant Treasurer, Auditors of the Mint, Collectors of the Revenue, etc.; for Secretary and Assistant Secretary also; after they are prepared they are sent to the Treasury; these belong to my office; are issued from my office, from the Department of State.

Q. Have the kindness to tell us whether, after the passage of the Civil Tenure of Office act, any change was made in the commission of officers of your department to conform to that act? A. There was.

Q. What was that change; tell us how the commission ran in that respect before, and how it ran afterwards? A. The form of the old commission was "during the pleasure of the President of the United States for the time being." These words have been stricken out, and the words substituted "subject to the conditions prescribed by law."

Q. Does that apply to all commissions? A. It applies to all commissions.

Q. When was that change made? A. Shortly after the passage of the civil Tenure of Office act; I cannot exactly say when the first came up making it necessary for the Commission Clerk to prepare a commission; he applied for instructions under that act; the subject was then examined at the department; that change was made after the examination; the case was submitted by the Secretary to the examiner, and on his opinion the change was made, I think, by order of the Secretary; we print our commissions on parchment from a copper-plate form; the copper-plate was changed to conform; we have blank forms of the various kinds of commissions issued by our department; prior to the passage of the act of March 2, 1867, being the Civil Tenure of Office act, the commission to hold office for or during the pleasure of the President for the time being, were all issued in that form; after the change all commissions have been issued in the changed form; such changed commissions have been signed by the President; there have been no other changes than what I have mentioned down to this day; no commission whatever to any officer has been

sent out from the department since the passage of the act except in that changed form, that I am aware of; there could not have been any except by accident without my knowing it.

Mr. BUTLER put the forms of commission in evidence.

Cross-examination by Mr. STANBERY—Q. The old forms contained this clause, as I understand it:—"The said officer to hold office during the pleasure of the President of the United States for the time being?" A. Yes, sir.

Q. These words, you say, are left out? A. Yes, sir, and these other words are inserted—"Subject to the conditions prescribed by law."

Q. Have you ever changed one of your plates or forms so as to introduce in place of what was there before these words—"To hold until removed by the President, with the consent of the Senate?" A. No, sir; no commission has been issued to the heads of departments different from those which were issued before the Tenure of Office act that I am aware of.

Q. Have you a separate plate for the commissions of heads of departments? A. I cannot answer that question; I recollect no instance in which any change has been made there.

Mr. BUTLER—Has any commission been issued to the head of a department since March 2, 1867? A. I do not recollect it.

Mr. BUTLER—Then of course there is no change.

Mr. STANBERY—Of course not.

To the witness—Q. How long have you been chief clerk? A. Since July, 1866; I have been in the office since July, 1833; that is thirty-three years.; in all that time, before this change, all commissions ran in this way:—"During the pleasure of the President for the time being."

Mr. BUTLER—Do you know Mr. Seward's handwriting? A. Yes, sir; this letter is signed by him.

Appointments and Removals.

Mr. BUTLER—I now offer in evidence a list prepared by the Secretary of State, and sent to the managers, of all the appointments and removals of officers, as they appear in the State Department, from the beginning of the government.

Mr. STANBERY—Of all officers?

Mr. BUTLER—No; of all heads of departments. It is accompanied with a letter simply describing the list, and which I will read. The letter is as follows:—

"Hon. John A. Bingham, Chairman, &c.—Sir:—In reply to the note address d to me on the 23d inst., on the part of the House of Representatives, in the matter of the impeachment of the President, I have the honor to submit herewith two schedules, A and B. Schedule A presents a statement of all removals of heads of departments made by the President of the United States during this session of the Senate. so far as the same can be ascertained from the records of the department. Schedule B contains a list of all appointments of heads of departments at any time made by the President with the advice and consent of the Senate, and while the Senate was in session, so far as the same appear on the records of the State Department. I have the honor to be, &c..

"WILLIAM H. SEWARD."

Mr. BUTLER then put in evidence Schedule As being the list of removals of heads of department, made by the President at any time during the session of the Senate, the only one being that of Timothy Pickering, Secretary of State, removed May 18, 1800.

Mr. BUTLER also put in evidence schedule B, being a list of appointments of heads of departments made by the President at any time during the session of the Senate. The list contains thirty appointments, extending from 1794 down to 1866, and are principally the appointments of chief clerks to act temporarily as heads of departments.

Mr. BUTLER to the witness—There are in this list thirty acting appointments like those of Mr. Hunter, Mr. Appleton and Mr. Frederick W. Seward. I do not ask the authority under which they were made, but I ask the circumstances under which they were, and what was the necessity for making them, whether it was the absence of the Secretary or otherwise? A. The absence of the Secretary.

Q. Has there been in the thirty-four years that you have been in the department any appointment of an Acting Secretary except on account of the temporary absence of the Secretary? A. I do not recollect any at this time.

Q. By whom were these acting appointments made? A. They were made by the President, or by his order.

Q. Did the letters of authority proceed in most of these cases from the President, or from the heads of departments?

Legal Sparring.

Mr. EVARTS objected, and stated that the papers themselves were the best evidence, and must be produced.

Mr. BUTLER said that he was merely asking from whence the papers were issued; whether they came directly from the head of a department to the chief clerk, or came from the President to him.

Mr. EVARTS—That is the very objection we make; the letters of the authority are themselves the best evidence.

Mr. BUTLER—Suppose there were no letters of authority.

Mr. EVARTS—Then you would have to prove the fact by other evidence.

Mr. BUTLER—I am asking whence the authority proceeded, because I cannot know now to whom to send to produce them.

The Chief Justice (to the witness)—Is the authority in writing?

Witness—It is always in writing.

Mr. BUTLER—I put this question to the witness:—From whom did those letters of which you speak come?

Mr. EVARTS objected.

The Chief Justice directed the question to be reduced to writing.

Mr. BUTLER then modified it so as to read:—State whether any of the letters of authority which you have mentioned came from the Secretary of State, or from what other officer?

Mr. BUTLER said—My object in putting the question is, that if he says that they all came from the President, that will end the inquiry: and if he says that they all came from the Secretary of State, then I want to send for them.

Mr. EVARTS—We object to proof of authority other than by the production of the writing, which, as the witness has stated, exists in all cases.

Mr. BUTLER—I am not now proving the authority. I am endeavoring to find out from what source these letters came, and am following the usual course of examination.

Mr. CURTIS (to Mr. Butler)—Do you mean to inquire who signed the letters of authority?

Mr. BUTLER—I mean to inquire precisely whether the letters came from the Secretary of State or from the President.

Mr. CURTIS—Do you mean by that who signed the letter; or do you mean from whose manual possession it came?

Mr. BUTLER—I mean who signed the letter?

Mr. CURTIS—That we object to.

Mr. BUTLER—I do not do it for the purpose of proving the contents of the letter, but for the purpose of its identification.

Mr. EVARTS—We say that the paper itself will show who signed it.

Mr. BUTLER—The difficulty with me is that unless I take an hour in my argument, these gentlemen are determined that I shall never have the reply on my proposition. My proposition is not to prove the authority, nor to prove the signature, but it is to prove the identity of the paper. It is not to prove that it was a letter of authority, because Mr. Seward signed it, but it is to prove whether I am to look for my evidence in a given direction or in another direction.

The Chief Justice decided that the question in the form in which it was put was not objectionable, and that the question whether these documents were signed by the President would be also competent.

Mr. BUTLER—State whether any of the letters or authority which you have mentioned, came from the Secretary of State, or from what other officer?

Mr. CURTIS—I understand that the witness is not to answer by whom they were sent.

Mr. BUTLER (Tartly)—I believe I have this witness.

The Chief Justice—The Chief Justice will instruct the witness not to answer at present by whom they were signed.

Witness—They came from the President.

Mr. BUTLER—All of them? A. Such is the usual rule; I know of no exception; I know of no letter of authority to a chief clerk to act as Secretary of State that did not come from the President; I will, on my return to the office, examine and see if there is any.

Mr. STANBERY—I see by this list only one instance of the removal by the President of the head of a department, and that was during the session of the Senate, and that was an early one, May 13, 1800. You know nothing of the circumstances of that re-

moval? A. Not at all: I do not know whether that officer had refused to resign when requested.

Q. In your knowledge, since you have been in the department, do you know of any instance in which the head of a department, when requested by the President to resign, has refused to resign?

Mr. BUTLER (to the witness)—Stop a moment; I object.

The objection was either sustained or the question withdrawn.

Mr. STANBERY—Have you ever examined the records to ascertain under what circumstances it was that President Adams removed Mr. Pickering from the head of the State Department in 1800, when the Senate was in session? A. I have not.

Mr. BUTLER—Do you know that he was removed when the Senate was in session of your own knowledge? A. I do not.

Mr. BUTLER—I now offer, sir, from the ninth volume of the works of John Adams, "The Little & Brown edition by his grandson, Charles Francis Adams," what purports to be official letters from Timothy Pickering, Secretary of State, to John Adams, and from Mr. Adams to him. Any objection? (To Mr. Stanbery.)

Mr. STANBERY—Not the least.

Mr. BUTLER—The first one is dated the 10th of May, 1808, pages 53, 54 and 55. I offer them as the best evidence of the official letters of that date. I have not been able to find any record of them thus far. Any objection, gentlemen?

Mr. STANBERY—Not at all, sir.

Timothy Pickering's Removal.

Mr. BUTLER read a letter from President Adams to Timothy Pickering, Secretary of State, dated 10th May, 1800, which he said was Saturday, announcing that the Administration deemed a change in the office of Secretary of State necessary, and stating that the announcement was made in order to give Mr. Pickering an opportunity to resign. He next read the reply of Mr. Pickering, dated "Department of State, May 12, 1800," stating that he had contemplated a continuance in office until the 4th of March following after the election of Mr. Jefferson, which was considered certain, and refusing, from various personal considerations, to resign. He then read the letter of President Adams of the same date, and removing Mr. Pickering from office.

Mr. BUTLER—Now, will the Senate have the goodness to send for the executive journal of May 13, 1800, to be brought here? I propose to show that at the same hour, on the same day, Mr. Adams, the President, sent the nomination to the Senate.

Mr. STANBERY—Do I understand the honorable member to say at the same hour? Do you expect to prove it?—to Mr. Butler.

Mr. BUTLER—When I come to look at the correspondence I think I am wrong. I think the action of the Senate was a little precarious. (Laughter.)

Mr. STANBERY—You do?

Mr. BUTLER—Yes, sir.

On motion of Mr. SHERMAN it was ordered that the Journal in question be furnished.

Mr. Creecy Called.

Mr. C. Eaton Creecy recalled and examined by Mr. BUTLER.— You have been sworn, I believe? A. Yes, sir. (Paper shown to witness.)

Q. You told us that you were appointed Clerk in the Treasury. Are you familiar with the handwriting of Andrew Johnson? A. I am; that is his handwriting; I procured this letter from the archives of the Treasury to-day.

The Removal of Mr. Stanton.

Mr. BUTLER—Just step down a moment. Mr. President and Senators:—It will be remembered that the answer of the President to the first article says in words:—"And this has ever since remained, and was the opinion of this respondent at the time when he was forced as aforesaid to consider and decide what act or acts should and might lawfully be done by this respondent as President of the United States to cause the said Stanton to surrender the said office." This respondent was also aware that this act (the Tenure of Office act) was understood and intended to be an expression of the opinion of the Congress by which that act was passed; that the power to remove executive officers for cause might by law be taken from the President, and vested in him and the Senate jointly.

Mr. Butler read further from the articles the President's claim that he had removed Stanton under the Constitution.

He then read the 2d section of the Tenure of Office act empowering the President, during a recess of the Senate, to suspend civil officers, except United States Judges, for incapacity, misconduct, &c., authorizing him to designate a temporary successor to hold until acted upon by the Senate, and requiring him to report such action within twenty days from the next meeting of the Senate, with the reasons therefor, &c. He also read the eighth section, requiring the President to notify the Secretary of the Treasury of such temporary appointments made without the consent of the Senate. He continued :—It will be seen that the President of the United States says, in his answer, that he suspended Mr. Stanton under the Constitution, suspended him indefinitely, and at his pleasure.

We propose now, unless it is objected to, to show that is false under his own hand. I offer his letter to that effect, which, if there is no objection, I will read.

Mr. STANBERY, after examining the letter—We see no inconsistency in that nor falsehood.

Mr. BUTLER—That is not the question I put to you; I asked you if you had any objection.

Mr. STANBERY—I have no objection.

Mr. BUTLER—The falsehood is not in the letter; it is in the answer.

He then read the letter, dated Washington, D. C., Aug. 14, 1867, as follows :—

Sir:—In compliance with the requirements of the eighth section of the act of Congress of March 2, 1867, entitled an act to regulate the tenure of certain civil offices, you are hereby notified that, on the 12th inst., the Hon. Edwin M. Stanton was suspended from his office as Secretary of War. General U. S. Grant is authorized and empowered to act as Secretary of War *ad interim.* I am, sir, very respectfully, yours,   ANDREW JOHNSON.
To the Hon. Hugh McCulloch, Secretary of the Treasury.

Mr. BUTLER—I wish to call attention to this again, because it may have escaped the attention of Senators.

Mr. CURTIS—We object. We wish to know what all this discussion means. What question is now before the Senate. How it is that this statement is made?

Mr. BUTLER—I am endeavoring to show that when the President said that he did not suspend Mr. Stanton under the Tenure of Office act, and that he had come to the conclusion that he had the right to suspend before August 12, 1867, without leave of the Tenure of Office act, he sent a letter, saying that he did under that act, to the Secretary of the Treasury, under the eighth section of the act to which he refers. He expressly says in that letter that he did suspend him under this act.

Mr. CURTIS—We do not object to the honorable manager offering his evidence. We do object to his argument.

Ancient Precedent.

Mr. BUTLER—I am arguing nothing, sir. I read the law.

The Journal asked for arrived at this point, and was delivered to Mr. Butler. He read the proceedings of Monday, May 12, 1800, and the subsequent action of the Senate on the following day, as follows :—

"On Tuesday, May 13, 1800, the Senate proceeded to consider the message of the President of the United States of the 12th inst., and the nomination contained therein of John Marshall, of Virginia, to be Secretary of State, whereupon it was

"*Resolved,* That they do advise and consent to the appointment according to the nomination.

Mr. STANBERY—Please to read when it appeared there at what hour this was done.

Mr. BUTLER—I will not undertake to state the hour, sir. I state directly to the Senate in answer to you that the nomination went to the Senate, as it will appear from an examination of the whole case, prior to the letters giving to Mr. Pickering—

Mr. STANBERY—Will the honorable manager allow me to add that he said he expected to prove it.

Mr. BUTLER—I expected it would appear from the whole case. He sent it first, I am quite sure; now, then, as it was the duty of Mr. Adams to send it first to the Senate, I presume he did his duty and sent it to the Senate first before he sent it to Mr. Pickering. (Laughter.) I want to say for them that, being all on the same day, it must be taken to be done at the same time in law; but another piece of evidence is that he asked Mr. Pickering to send in his resignation, because it was necessary to send the suspension to the Senate as soon as they sat, which he did.

Mr. STANBERY requested a certified copy of the Executive document in question.

C. Eaton Creecy, Recalled.

Mr. BUTLER—Q. Upon receipt of that notification by the President of the United States that he had suspended Mr. Stanton according to the provisions of the Civil Tenure act, what was done? A. A copy of the Executive communication was sent to the First Comptroller, the First Auditor, Second Auditor and Third Auditor.

Q. Have you the letters of transmissal there? A. Witness produces and reads one of the letters promulgating the information by the Secretary of the Treasury to the First Comptroller; he stated that the others were similar.

C. Are those officers the proper accounting and disbusing officers of the department? A. They are for the War Department.

Q. Then I understand you all the disbursing officers and accounting officers of the Treasury for the War Department were notified in pursuance of that act? Objection by Mr. CURTIS.

Mr. BUTLER—Q. Were thereupon notified? A. Yes, sir.

Q. Were you there to know of this transmission? A. Yes, sir.

Q. Did you prepare the papers? A. Yes, sir, but not in pursuance of any other act of Congress except the Civil Tenure.

Recess.

On motion of Mr. CONNESS the Senate took a recess of fifteen minutes from half-past two.

An Appeal for Time.

After the recess Mr. CONNESS suggested an adjournment, whereupon

Mr. CURTIS said:—Mr. Chief Justice, it is suggested to me by my colleagues that I should make known at this time to the Senate that it is our intention, if the testimony on the part of the prosecution should be closed to-day, as we suppose it will, to ask the Senators to grant to the President's counsel three days in which to prepare and arrange their proofs, and enable themselves to proceed with the defense. We find ourselves in a condition in which it is absolutely necessary to make this request, and I hope the Senators will agree to it.

In response to an intimation from the Chief Justice that the request be postponed until the Senate was fuller, Mr. CURTIS said he had merely suggested it lest it should not be in order at another time.

Argument of Mr. Boutwell.

Mr. BOUTWELL called the attention of counsel to the statutes as explaining the nature of the proceedings in the case of the appointment of Mr. Pickering. He said the only appointment of the head of a department which appeared on the record to have been made during a session of the Senate, was in 1st Statutes of September, 1789, in which it is provided that there shall be a Postmaster-General with powers and compensation to the assistant clerks and deputies whom he may appoint, and the regulations of the Post Office shall be the same as they were under the resolution and ordinances of the last Congress. It was provided in the second section that this act shall continue in force until the end of the next session of Congress, and no longer, showing that it was merely the continuance of the Post Office Department that war contemplated.

On the 4th of August, 1790, Congress passed a supplementary act, in which it was provided, that the act of last session, entitled "An act for the Establishment of a Post Office Department," be and the same is hereby continued in force until the end of the next session of Congress, which was a continuance of the Continental system of post office management. On the 9th day of March, 1791, Congress passed another act, continuing the act for the temporary establishment of a post office department in full force and effect until the end of the next session of Congress and no longer. On the 20th of February, 1792, Congress passed an act making various arrangements in regard to the administration of the Post Office Department and to establish certain postal routes; that act provided, that the act of the preceding session be continued in full force for two years and no longer. This act did not provide for the establishment of a post office department as a branch of the government, so that the act of the previous session was continued by it until 1794. On May 8, 1794, Congress passed an act covering the whole ground of the post office system, providing for a General Post Office, and meet the wants of the counsel for the respondent.

Mr. WILSON called attention to several entries in the Journal of 1800, showing that the Senate met before noon.

Mr. BINGHAM offered in evidence the Executive messages to the Senate, of December 16 and December 19, 1867, and January 18, 1868, in which the President gives his reasons for the suspension from office of several officers. Also, a communication from the Secretary of State accompanying one of the messages, in which he reports the action under the Tenure of Office laws.

Mr. BUTLER then informed the Senate that the case, on the part of the House of Representatives, was substantially closed, although they might call a few more witnesses, whose testimony would be only cumulative.

The Question of Time.

Mr. CURTIS, on behalf of the President's counsel, then made a motion that when the court adjourned it should be to Thursday next, in order to afford them three working days in which to prepare their testimony.

Mr. CONNESS (Cal.) moved that the court adjourn until Wednesday next.

Senator JOHNSON—If it is in order, I move to amend the motion made by the honorable Senator from California, by inserting Thursday instead of Wednesday.

The question was put on the amendment of Mr. Johnson, and agreed to, with only one dissenting voice.

The Chief Justice stated the question to be on the motion as amended.

Senator CAMERON—Mr. President—

The Chief Justice—No debate is in order.

Senator CONKLING—I wish to inquire whether the managers want to submit some remarks on the motion for delay.

The Chief Justice—The question is on the motion to adjourn.

Mr. CONKLING—My purpose was to ascertain whether they desire to make some remarks or not.

Mr. BUTLER—We want to have it understood—

In reply to an inquiry from Senator Anthony, the Chief Justice restated the question.

Mr. CONNESS said the motion to amend had been submitted before he was aware of it. He had desired to accept it.

Mr. CAMERON—I was going to ask the honorable managers whether they will not be prepared to go on with this case on Monday. I can see no reason why the other side will not be as well prepared.

Mr. BUTLER—We are ready.

Senators CAMERON and SUMNER simultaneously—Mr. President—

The Chief Justice—No debate is in order.

Senator CAMERON—I am not going to debate the the question, your Honor. I have just arisen to ask the question, whether the managers will be ready to go on with this case on Monday?

Senator SUMNER—I wish to ask a question also. I want to know if the honorable managers have any views to present to the Senate, sitting now on the trial of this impeachment, to aid the Senate in determining this question of time? On that I wish to know the views of the honorable managers.

The Chief Justice—The Chief Justice is of opinion that pending the motion of adjournment no debate is in order.

The motion as amended was then agreed to by the following vote:—

YEAS.—Messrs. Anthony, Bayard, Buckalew, Cattell, Conness, Corbett, Cragin, Davis, Dixon, Edmunds, Ferry, Fowler, Frelinghuysen, Grimes, Henderson, Hendricks, Howard, Howe, Johnson, McCreery, Morrill (Me.). Morrill (Vt.). Norton, Nye, Patterson (N. H.), Patterson (Tenn.), Ramsey, Ross, Saulsbury, Sherman. Sprague, Tipton, Trumbull, Van Winkle, Vickers, Willey, and Williams—37.

NAYS.—Messrs. Cameron, Chandler, Cole, Conkling, Drake, Morgan, Pomeroy, Stewart, Sumner, and Thayer —10.

The Chair was vacated, and was immediately resumed by the President pro tem., whereupon, without transacting any legislative business,

On motion of Mr. GRIMES, the Senate adjourned.

PROCEEDINGS OF THURSDAY, APRIL 9.

The Opening.

The doors were opened to the crowd at eleven o'clock this morning, and the galleries were considerably filled by an audience of the usual well-dressed order at the opening of the Senate, at twelve o'clock.

Prayer.

After prayer, by a stranger, in which all the departments of the government were remembered, the President pro tem. relinquished the chair for the Chief Justice, and the court was opened by the usual proclamation.

Entering of the Managers.

At ten minutes past twelve the managers were announced, and all appeared but Mr. Stevens.

The counsel for the President were all promptly present. The members of the House were announced at quarter past twelve, and a rather larger proportion than on recent occasions put in their appearance.

The Chief Justice asked—Have the managers on the part of the House of Representatives any further evidence to bring in?

Mr. BUTLER—We have.

On motion of Senator JOHNSON, the further reading of the journal was dispensed with when but little progress had been made.

Examination of W. H. Wood.

Mr. BUTLER, on the part of the managers, then called in W. H. Wood, of Alabama, who was sworn.

Q. Where is your place of residence? A. Tuscaloosa, Alabama; I served in the Union army during the war; from July, 1861, to July, 1865; some time in September, 1866, I called upon President Johnson, and presented him testimonials for employment in the government service; it was on the 21st day of September, 1866; I fix the time partly from memory, and partly from the journal of the Ebbitt House.

Q. How long before that had he returned from Chicago from his trip to the tomb of Douglas? A. My recollection is that he returned on the 15th or 16th; I awaited his return; I presented my testomonials to him, when he examined part of them.

Q. What then took place between you?

Mr. STANBERY—What do you propose to prove? Has it anything to do with this case?

Mr. BUTLER—Yes, sir.

Mr. STANBERY—What articles?

Mr. BUTLER—As to the intent of the President; in several of the articles.

Mr. STANBERY—What to do?

Mr. BUTLER—To oppose Congress.

Q. What did he say? A. He said my claims for government employment were good, or worthy of attention; he inquired about my political principles; I told him I wasn't a political man; I told him I was a Union man, a loyal man, and in favor of the administration; I had confidence in Congress and in the Chief Executive; he asked me if I knew of any differences between himself and Congress; I told him I did; I knew of some differences on minor points; then he said, "They are not minor points; the influence of patronage" (I don't know which) "shall be in my favor; that's the meaning.

Q. Were those the words? A. I will not swear that they were the words.

Q. What did you say to that? A. I remarked that under those conditions I could not accept an appointment of any kind if my influence was to be used for him in contradistinction to Congress, and retired.

Cross-examined by Mr. Stanbery—Q. Do you know a gentleman in this city by the name of Koppel? A. I do.

Q. Have you talked with him since you have been in the city? A. I have; I called on him when I first came to the city; I did not tell him yesterday morning that all you could say was more in his favor than against him; I did not tell Mr. Koppel that when I was brought up to be examined, since I arrived in this city, there was an attempt made to make me say things which I would not say; I might, in explanation of that question, say that there was a misunderstanding between the managers and a gentleman in

Boston, in regard to an expression that they supposed I could testify to, which I could not.

Q. Have you been examined before this time by any one? A. I have, sir.

Q. Under oath? A. Yes, sir; by the managers first; my testimony was taken down; I was not examined nor talked to by any one of them under oath; I had informal interviews with two of them before I was examined; I could hardly call it an examination; they were Governor Boutwell and General Butler; it was on Monday of this week.

Q. Did you say to Mr. Koppel that since you had been in this city a proposition was made to you that in case you would give certain testimony it would be to your benefit? A. I did not, sir.

Re-direct examination by Mr. BUTLER—Q. Who is Mr. Koppel? (emphasizing the name so as to provoke laughter in the galleries.) A. Mr. Koppel, sir, is an acquaintance of mine on the avenue; a merchant; he is a manufacturer of garments—a tailor. (Laughter).

Q. Do you know of any sympathy between him and the President? A. I have always supposed that Mr. Koppel was a northern man in spirit; he came from South Carolina here; he ran the blockade.

Q. Do you mean that to be an answer to my question of sympathy between the President and him? (Laughter). A. Yes, sir. (Laughter).

Q. Now, sir, the counsel for the President has asked you if you told Mr. Koppel that you had been asked to say things which you could not say, or words to that effect. You answered in explanation, as I understand, that there was a misunderstanding which you explained to Mr. Koppel. Will you have the goodness to tell us what that misunderstanding was?

Mr. STANBERY rose to object.

Mr. BUTLER—If you give a part of the conversation I have a right to the whole of it.

Q. I will ask, in the first place, did you explain the matter to him? A. I did.

Q. Very well, tell us what that understanding was that you explained to him in that conversation? A. I think, sir, a gentleman in Boston wrote you that the President asked me if I would give twenty-five per cent. of the proceeds of my office for political purposes. I told you that I did not say so. The gentleman from Boston misunderstood me. The President said nothing of the kind to me, and I explained that to Mr. Koppel.

Q. Did you explain when the misunderstanding arose? A. I told him it must have occurred in a conversation between a gentleman from Boston and myself.

Q. In regard to what? A. In regard to twenty-five per cent.

Q. Did you explain to Mr. Koppel where the idea came from that you were to give twenty-five per cent.? A. I did, sir.

Mr. EVARTS—We object. The witness has told us distinctly that nothing else occurred between the President and himself. It is certainly quite unimportant what occurred between this gentleman and another in Boston.

Butler and Evarts have a Tilt.

Mr. BUTLER—I pray judgment on this. You have put in a conversation between a tailor down on Pennsylvania avenue, or somebody else, and this witness. I want the whole of the conversation. I suppose from evidence of the gentleman that the conversation between Mr. Koppel, the tailor, and this witness, was put in for some good purpose. If it was, I want the whole of it.

Mr. EVARTS—Mr. Chief Justice, the fact is not exactly as stated. In the privileged cross-examination, counsel for the President asked the witness distinctly whether he had said so and so to a Mr. Koppel. The witness said he had not, and then volunteered a statement that there might have been some misunderstanding between Mr. Koppel and himself on that subject, or some misunderstanding somewhere. Our inquiry had not reached, or asked for, or brought out the misunderstanding. We hold virtually that everything that relates to any conversation or interview between the President and this witness, whether as understood or misunderstood, has been gone through, and the present point of inquiry and the further testimony as to the grounds of the misunderstanding between this witness and some interlocutor in Boston, we object to.

Mr. BUTLER—Having put in a part of this testimony in regard to Mr. Koppel, whether voluntary or not, I have a right to the whole of it. I will explain. I want to show that the misunderstanding was not

that the President said that twenty-five per cent. was to be given to him, but to one of his friends. That is where the misunderstanding was. Do the gentlemen still object?

Mr. EVARTS—Certainly.

Mr. BUTLER—That's all.

Testimony of Foster Blodgett.

Foster Blodgett, sworn, and examined by Mr. BUTLER.—Q. Were you an officer of the United States at any time? A. Yes; in Augusta, Ga., holding the office of Postmaster of the city; I was appointed on the 25th of July, 1865, and went into the office in the following September.

[Witness produced his commission, which is exhibited by Mr. Butler to the counsel for the President.]

Q. Where you confirmed by the Senate? A. I was, and I was suspended from office; I have not a copy of the letter of suspension here; it was dated the 3d of January, 1868.

Q. Have you examined to see whether your suspension, and the reasons therefor have been sent to the Senate? A. I have been told by the Chairman of the Post Office Committee that they have not been sent.

Mr. BUTLER—I suppose that Senators can ascertain for themselves how that is.

Senator JOHNSON—Of course, we know all about it.

Mr. BUTLER—I supposed you did know all about it.

To the witness. Has any action been taken on your suspension? A. None that I know of.

The witness was not cross-examined.

Mr. BUTLER called upon counsel for the President to present the original of the suspension.

Mr. BUTLER then put in evidence the letter of Adjutant-General Thomas, dated War Department, February 21, 1868, acknowledging his appointment as Secretary of War ad interim.

Mr. BUTLER stated he was instructed by the managers to say that they would ask leave to put in a proper certificate from the records of the Senate, to show that no report of the suspension of Foster Blodget has ever been made to the Senate.

The Chief Justice remarked that that could be put in at any time.

The Managers' Close.

Mr. BUTLER then said, on the part of the managers, "We close."

Mr. STANBERY—I ask the honorable manager under what article this case of Mr. Blodget comes?

Mr. BUTLER—In the final discussion I have no doubt that the gentleman who closes the case for the President will answer that question to your satisfaction.

Mr. STANBERY—I have no doubt of that myself. The question is why we are to be put to the trouble of answering it.

The Chief Justice remarked that the case was closed on the part of the managers, and that there was no question before the court which this discussion could continue.

Mr. STANBERRY—The question is that we merely want to know under what article this case of Mr. Blodgett comes.

The Chief Justice—The managers state that they have concluded their evidence. Gentlemen, counsel for the President, you will proceed with your defense.

Mr. CURTIS rose to open the case on the part of the President.

Mr. Curtis' Speech.

Mr. Chief Justice and Senators:—I am here to speak to the Senate of the United States, sitting in its judicial capacity as a Court of Judicial Impeachment, presided over by the Chief Justice of the United States, for the trial of the President of the United States. (Here one or two sentences were entirely inaudible.)

Inasmuch as the Constitution requires that there shall be a trial, and inasmuch as in that trial the oath which each one of you has taken is to administer impartial justice according to the Constitution and laws, the only appeal that I can make here in behalf of the President, is an appeal to the conscience and to the reason of each judge who sits in this court, on the law and the facts in the case upon its judicial merits on the duties incumbent on that high office. By virtue of his office, and on his honest endeavor to discharge those duties, the President rests his case; and I pray each of you, to listen with that patience which belongs to a judge, for his own sake, but which I cannot expect by any efforts of mine to elicit, while I open to you what that defense is. The honorable managers, through their associate who has addressed you, have informed you that this is not a court—that whatever may be the character of this body, it is bound by no law. On that subject I shall have something hereafter to say.

The honorable managers did not tell you, in such terms, at least, that there are no articles before you, because a statement to that effect would be in substance to say that there are no honorable managers before you, inasmuch as the only power by which the honorable managers are clothed by the House of Representatives is an authority to present here at your bar certain articles, and within the limits of them to conduct this prosecution; therefore, I shall make no apology for asking your close attention to these articles, in manner and form as they appear presented. to ascertain, in the first place, what the substantial allegations in each of them are; what is to be the legal proof and effect of these allegations, and what proof is necessary to be adduced in order to sustain them.

Here is a section, a part of which applies to all civil officers as well as to those being in office as to those who should thereafter be appointed, and the body of this section contains a declaration that every such officer is, that is, if he is now in office and shall, that is, if he shall be hereafter appointed to office, entitled to hold until another is appointed and qualified in his place; that is in the body of section, but out of that body of section it is explicitly declared that there is to be excepted a particular class of officers as to whom something is otherwise provided, that a different rule is to be made for them. Now, the Senate will perceive that in the body of the section, every officer, as well as those holding office as those hereafter to be appointed included, the language is, every person holding civil office, to which he has been appointed by and with the advice and consent of the Senate. and every person who shall be hereafter appointed is and shall be entitled to hold, &c.

It affects the President—it sweeps over all who are in office. It includes them all by its terms, as well as those who may hereafter be appointed; but when you come to proviso, the first noticeable thing is that that language is not used. It is not that every Secretary of State, of the Treasury, of War, is to hold his office. It is a rule for the future only, and the question whether any particular Secretary comes within that rule, is a question whether he comes within the general description contained in the proviso. There is nothing to bring him within the proviso. There is no express declaration, as in the body of the section, that he is and hereafter shall be entitled to hold his office, &c.; nothing to bring him within 'the body of the proviso, except the description. and the question is whether the proviso contains, applies to and includes this case. Now let us see if it does.

The Secretary of State, the Secretary of the Treasury, etc., shall hold their offices respectively for and during the term of the President by whom they may have been appointed, and one month thereafter. The first inquiry which arises on this language is this, as to what is meant by "for and during the term of the President by whom they may have been appointed." Mr. Stanton appears, by the construction which has been put on the case by the honorable managers, to have been appointed during the first term of President Lincoln, in January, 1862. Is this part of the language, "during the term of the President by whom they may have been appointed," applicable to Mr. Stanton's case. That depends whether a person expounding that law judicially has any right to add to it any other term for which he may afterwards be elected.

I shall begin with the first article, not merely because the House of Representatives, in arranging these articles, has placed it first in order, but because the subject matter in that article is of such a character that it forms the foundation of the eight first articles in the series, and enters materially into the body of the remaining eleven. What, then, is the substance of this first article? What are what the lawyers call the *gravar vima* contained in it? There is a good deal of verbiage. I do not mean unnecessary verbiage in the description of the substantial thing set down in that article. Stripped of that, it amounts to exactly these things:—First, that the order set out in the article for the removal of Mr. Stanton, if executed, would have been a violation of the Tenure of Office act. Second. That it was a violation of the Tenure of Office act. Third. That it was an intentional violation of the Tenure of Office act. Fourth. That it was a violation of the Constitution of the United States; and fifth. That it was by the President intended to be so; or to draw all these into one sentence, which I hope may be intelligible and clear enough, I suppose the substance of this first article is that the order for the removal of Mr. Stanton was, and was intended to be, a violation of the Tenure of Office act; and was, and was intended to be, a violation of the Constitution of the United States.

These are the allegations which it is necessary for the honorable managers to make out in order to support that article. Now, there is a question involved here which enters deeply, as I have already intimated, into the first eight articles of this series, and materially touches two others, and to that question I desire, in the first instance, to invite the attention of the court. That question is, whether Mr. Stanton's case comes under the Tenure of Office act? If it does not; if the true construction and effect of the Tenure of Office act, when applied to the facts in this case, include it, then it will be found by honorable Senators, when they come to examine this and the other articles, that a deep, indisputable and material wound has attempted to be inflicted on the Constitution.

[The Reporter will not vouch for the accuracy of this sentence, on account of the impossibility of hearing.]

I must ask your attention, therefore, to the question of the consideration and application of the first section of the Tenure of Office act. It is, as Senators know, but dry work, but it requires close and careful attention, and no doubt will receive it. Allow me, in the first place, to read it:—

"That every person holding any civil office, to which he

has been appointed by and with the advice and consent of the Senate, and every person who shall hereafter be appointed to any such office, and shall become duly qualified to act therein, is and shall be entitled to hold such office until a successor shall have been in like manner appointed and duly qualified, except as herein otherwise provided."

Then comes what is otherwise provided:—

"*Provided*, That the Secretaries of State, of the Treasury, of War, of the Navy and of the Interior, the Postmaster-General and the Attorney-General, shall hold their offices respectively for and during the term of the President by whom they may have been appointed, and one month thereafter, subject to removal by and with the advice and consent of the Senate."

By what authority short of the legislative power can these words be added to the statute, during the term of the President? Does it mean any other term or terms for which the President may be re-elected? I respectfully submit that no such judicial interpretation can be put upon the text. At the time when this order was issued for the removal of Mr. Stanton, was he holding during the term of the President by whom he was appointed? The honorable managers say yes; because, as they say, Mr. Johnson is merely serving out the residue of Mr. Lincoln's term. But is that so under the provisions of the Constitution of the United States? I pray you to allow me to read one or two sentences that are exactly applicable to this question.

The first is the first section of the second article of the Constitution, which says:—"The Executive power shall be vested in a President of the United States of America. He shall hold his office during a term of four years, and, together with the Vice President, chosen for the same period, be elected as follows." There is a declaration that the President and the Vice President is each respectively to hold his office for the term of four years. But that does not stand alone. Here is a qualification of that statement:—"In case of removal of the President from office, or of his death, resignation or inability to discharge the duties of the said office, the same shall devolve on the Vice President." So that, although the President, like the Vice President, is elected for the term of four years, and each elected for the same term, the President is not to hold his office absolutely during four years.

The limit of four years is not an absolute limit. There is a conditional limit as lawyers term it, imposed, and when, according to the second passage which I have read, the first dies or is removed, then his term of four years for which he was elected and during which he was to hold provided he should so long live, terminates, and the office devolves on the Vice President. For what period of time? For the remainder of the term for which the Vice President was elected. There is no more propriety under this provision of the Constitution of the United States in calling the time during which Mr. Johnson holds the office of President, as it was devolved on him as part of Mr. Lincoln's term, than would be propriety in saying that one sovereign who succeeds to another sovereign by death, holds a part of his predecessor's term. The term assigned by the Constitution was a conditional assignment. It was to last four years, if not sooner ended, but if sooner ended by death, then the office was to devolve on the Vice President, and the term of the Vice President to hold the office then began,

I submit, then, that on this language it is equally apparent that Mr. Stanton's case cannot be considered as within this act. This law, however, as Senators very well know, had a purpose. There was a practical object in view, and however clear it may seem the language of the law, when applied to Mr. Stanton, will exclude that case. However clear that may seem on the mere words of the law, if the purpose can be discerned, and that purpose plainly required a different interpretation, that different interpretation should be given; but, on the other hand, if the purpose that was in view is one which requires this interpretation for which I have been drawing your attention, then it greatly strengthens the argument; but shows that not only the language of the act itself, but the practical object which the legislation had in view in using that language, requires this interpretation.

Now there can be no dispute concerning what that purpose was, as I suppose. Here is a peculiar class of officers singled from all others and brought within this purpose. Why is it? It is because the Constitution has provided that those principal officers in the several executive departments may be called upon by the President for advice respecting the language of the Constitution, but not respecting their several duties. As I read the Constitution the President may call upon the Secretary of War for advice concerning questions arising in the Department of War; that he may call upon him for advice concerning questions which are a part of the duty of the President, and which touch his duties as well as questions that belong to the Department of War. Allow me to see if that is not a true interpretation.

The language of the Constitution is that the President may require the opinion in writing of the principal officer of each of the Executive Departments on any subject relating to the duties of their respective offices. As I read it, it is relating to the duties of the office of those principal officers, or relating to the duties of the President himself. At all events such was the practical interpretation put upon the Constitution from the beginning, and every gentleman who listens to me, and who is familiar, as all are with the political history of the country, knows that from an early period of the country, in the administration of General Washington. his secretaries were called upon for their advice concerning matters not within their respective departments, and so the practice has continued from that time to this.

This is what distinguished this class of officials in one particular from any other officers embraced within the body of this law. But there is another distinction: the Constitution undoubtedly contemplated that there should be executive departments organized, the heads of which were to assist the President in the administration of the laws, as well as by their advice. They were to be the hands and the voice of the President, and accordingly that has been so practiced from the beginning, and is countenanced directly and explicitly by the legislation of Congress in the organization of the departments and in the act which constitutes the Department of War. That act provides, as Senators will remember, in so many words, that the Secretary of War is to discharge the duties, within a certain general description there given, as shall be assigned to him by the President, and that he is to do it under the President's instructions and directions.

Let me repeat. The Secretary of War and the other Secretaries, the Postmaster-General and the Attorney-General are deemed to be the assistants of the President in the performance of his great duties, to take care that the laws are faithfully executed, and they are to speak and to act for him. Now, do not these suggestions or views show that this class of officers was excepted out of the Tenure of Office act? They were to be the advisers of the President; they were to be the immediate confidential assistants of the President, for whom he was to be responsible, and in whom he was expected to repose the gravest honor, trust and confidence. Therefore it was that this act has connected the tenure of office of these officers with that of the President by whom they were appointed.

It says, in fact, that as to the secretaries who were appointed by some particular President:—They shall continue to hold their office during the term of that President; but that as to secretaries who are in office, and who are not appointed by any President now in office, Congress has nothing to say, and leaves them as they stand. I submit, Senators, that that is the natural, and, having regard to the character of these officers, the necessary interpretation of the Tenure of Office act; so that it was the intention of Congress to compel the President to continue in office a Secretary not appointed by himself.

Fortunately, however, we have not only those means of interpreting this law which I have alluded to, namely, the language of the act and the evident object and purposes of the act—but we have decisive evidence of what was intended and understood by the law in each branch of Congress at the time it was passed. In order to make this more apparent and its just weight more evident, allow me to state what is very familiar, undoubtedly to Senators, but which I wish to recall to their minds—the history of this proviso. The bill, as Senators will recollect, originally excluded those officers altogether. It made no attempt—indeed, it rejected all attempts—to prescribe the Tenure of Office for them; so the bill went to the House of Representatives. It was there amended by putting the Secretaries on the same footing as other civil officers appointed with the advice and consent of the Senate, and, thus amended, it came back to this body.

This body disagreed to the amendment. Thereupon a committee of conference was appointed. That committee on the part of the House had for its chairman the Hon. Mr. Schenck, of Ohio, and on the part of this body it had the Hon. Mr. Williams and the Hon. Mr. Sherman. That committee of conference came to an agreement to alter the House bill, by striking those Secretaries out of the body of the bill, and inserting therein the proviso containing the matter now under consideration. Of course, when this report was made to the House of Representatives it was incumbent on the committee appointed by that body to explain what was done, or agreed to be done, so that the House itself might understand and act intelligently on the matter. Now I wish to read to the Senate the explanation given by the Hon. Mr. Schenck, the chairman of the committee on the part of the House, when he made the conference report to the House. After reading the report, Mr. Schenck said:—

I propose to demand the previous question on agreeing to the report of the Committee of Conference, but before doing so, I will explain to the House the conditions of the bill, and the decisions of the Committee of Conference upon it. It will be recollected that the bill, as it passed the Senate, was to provide that the concurrence of the Senate should be required in all removals from office, except in the case of heads of departments. The House amended the bill of the Senate, so as to extend this requirement to the heads of department as well as to other officers. The Committee of Conference has agreed that the Senate shall accept the amendment of the House, but inasmuch as this would compel the President to keep around him heads of departments until the end of his term, and who would hold over to the next term, a compromise was made, by which a further amendment is added to this portion of the bill, so that the term of office of heads of departments shall expire with the term of the President who appointed them, allowing these heads of departments one month longer, in which, in case of death or otherwise, other appointments can be made. That is the whole effect of the proposition reported by the Committee of Conference.

It is, in fact, an acceptance by the Senate of the position of the House. When, then, these questions were put to Mr. Schenck, he went on to say:—Their terms of office, "that is, the terms of office of the Secretary, &c., are limited as they are." so that they expire with the term of service of the President who appoints them, and one month after, in case of death or accident, until others can be substituted for them. Allow me to repeat that sentence. "They

expire with the term of service of the President who appoints them, and one month after, in case of death or accident." Now, in this body, when the report of the Committee of Conference was made, Mr. Williams made an explanation of it, and that explanation was "in substance the same as that made by Mr. Schenck in the House."

Thereupon a considerable debate sprung up. No debate had sprung up in the House, for the explanation of Mr. Schenck was accepted by the House as correct, and was unquestionably voted by the House as giving the true tone, meaning and effect of the bill in this body. However, a considerable debate sprung up. It would take too much of your time and too much of my strength to undertake to read this debate, but I think the whole of it may fairly be summed up in this statement; that it was charged by one of the honorable Senators from Wisconsin (Mr. Doolittle), that it was the intention of those who favored this bill to keep in office Mr. Stanton and some other Secretaries; (that that was directly met by the honorable Senator from Ohio (Mr. Sherman), one of the members of the Conference Committee, by this statement, "I do not understand the language of the Senator from Wisconsin. He first attributes a purpose to the Conference Committee, which I say is not true. I say that the Senate has not legislated with a view to any person or to any President, and, therefore, he commences by asserting what is not true. We do not legislate to keep in the Secretary of War, the Secretary of the Navy, or the Secretary of State." Then a conversation arose between the honorable Senator from Ohio and the honorable Senator from Wisconsin, and the honorable Senator from Ohio continued thus:—

"That the Senate has no such purpose is shown by its vote since to make this exception. That this provision does not apply to the present case is shown by the fact that its language is so framed as not to apply to the present President. The Senator shows that himself, and argues truly that it would not prevent the present President from removing the Secretary of War, the Secretary of the Navy or the Secretary of State; and if I supposed that either of these gentlemen were so wanting in manhood, or in honor, as to hold his place after the politest intimation from the President of the United States that his services were no longer needed, I certainly, as Senator, would consent to his removal at any time, and so would we all. I read this, Senators, not as expressing the opinion of an individual Senator concerning the meaning of a law that is under discussion and that is about to pass into legislation. I read it as the explanation of the report of the Committee of Conference, appointed by this body to see whether it could agree with the House of Representatives in the terms of this bill. And now I ask the Senate, if, looking at the language of this bill, looking at its purpose, looking at the circumstances under which it was passed, looking at the meaning attached to it by each of the bodies who assented to it, it is possible to hold that Mr. Stanton's case is within the scope of this Tenure of Office act?

I submit that it is not. I now return to the allegations of this article. The first, as Senators will remember, is that the issuing of the order which is set out in the article, was a violation of the Tenure of Office act. It is perfectly clear that this is not true. The Tenure of Office act, in its sixth section, enacts that every removal, appointment and emolument that may have been exercised contrary to the provisions of this act shall be deemed a high misdemeanor. Well, in the first place, no removal has been proved. They set out the order of removal; if Mr. Stanton had obeyed that order it would have been a removal, but inasmuch as Mr. Stanton did not obey it, there was no removal, so that it is quite clear that, looking at this sixth section of the act, they have made out no case of removal within the statute, and, therefore, no case of violation by any removal.

It must not only be a removal, but it must be contrary to the provisions of the Tenure of Office act; and, therefore, if you hold the order to be in effect a removal, unless Mr. Stanton's case was within this act, and unless this act gave Mr. Stanton a tenure of office, his removal would not have been contrary to the provisions of the act. But this article, as Senators will perceive on looking at it, does not allege simply that the order for the removal of Mr. Stanton was a violation of the Tenure of Office act.

The honorable House of Representatives has not, by its articles, attempted, in other words to erect a mistake into a crime. I have been arguing to you at considerable length, and, no doubt, tiring your patience, the construction of this law. I have a clear idea of what its construction ought to be. Senators who have listened to me may have a different idea about it, but I think they will, in all candor, admit that there is a question of construction here, and a question as to what the meaning of this law was, a question whether it is applicable to Mr. Stanton's case—A very honest and solid question which any man may entertain, and therefore I repeat it is important to observe that the honorable House of Representatives has not by this article endeavored to charge the President with a high misdemeanor, because he had failed in construing that law.

The House charges him with intentionally misconstruing it so that, in order to maintain the substance of this article, without which it was not designed by the House of Representatives to stand, and could not stand, it is necessary for the managers to show that the President wilfully misconstrued this bill; that having reason to believe, and actually believing, after the use of due inquiry, that Mr. Stanton's case was within the law, he acted as if it was not within it; that is the substance of the charge of this article.

Well, what is the proof in support of it? Not a particle of evidence. Senators must undoubtedly be familiar with the fact that the office of President of the United States, as well as many other executive offices, and, to some extent, judicial offices, call upon those who hold them for the exercise of judgment and skill in the construction and application of laws, and on their judgment and skill in the application of the Constitution itself. It is true the judicial power of the country, so to speak—technically speaking—is all vested in the Supreme Court, and in such inferior courts as Congress from time to time has established or may establish; but then there is a great mass of judicial work to be performed by executive officers in the discharge of their duties which is of a judicial character.

Take for instance, all that is done in the auditing of accounts, that is judicial, whether it be done by an auditor or comptroller, or whether it be done by a chancellor, it is of the same character when done by one as when done by the other. They must construe and apply the laws; they must investigate and ascertain the facts; they must come to some results founded on the law and on the facts. Now this class of duties the President of the United States has to perform. A case is brought before him which, in his judgment, calls for action.

His first inquiry must be, what is the law on the subject? and he encounters among other things this Tenure of Office act in the course of that inquiry. His first duty is to construe that law to see whether it applies to the case and to use, of course, in doing so, all those means and appliances which the Constitution and laws of the country have put into his hands to enable him to come to a correct decision. But, after all, he must decide in order either to act or refrain from acting.

That process the President was obliged to go through in this case, and did go through, and he came to the conclusion that the case of Mr. Stanton was not within this law. He came to that conclusion, not merely by examination into this law himself, but by resorting to the advice which the Constitution and laws of the country enable him to call for in order to assist him in coming to a correct conclusion. Having done so, will the Senate be prepared to say that this must have been a wilful misconstruction of the law—so wilful, so wrong that it can justly and properly, and for the purpose of this prosecution effectively be termed a high misdemeanor.

How does the law read? What are its purposes and objects? How was it understood here at the time it was passed, and how is it possible for this body to convict the President of the United States of a high crime and misdemeanor for construing the law as those who made it construed it at the time of its passage. I submit to the Senate that thus far no great advance has been made towards the conclusion of either of the allegations in this article, that this order was a violation of the Tenure of Office act, or that there was an intent on the part of the President thus to violate it; and yet, although we have not yet gone over all the allegations in this article, we have met its head's front, and what remains will be found to be nothing but incidental and circumstantial, and not the principal subjects.

If Mr. Stanton was not within this law; if he held, during the pleasure of President Johnson, as he had held during the pleasure of Mr. Lincoln, and if he was bound to obey that order, to quit the place instead of being sustained in resisting it, I think that the honorable managers will find it extremely difficult to construct out of the broken fragments of this article anything that will amount to a higher misdemeanor. What are they? They are, in the first place, that the President did violate, and intend to violate the Constitution of the United States by giving this order. How? They say, as I understand it, that the order of removal was made during the session of the Senate, and that for that reason the order was a violation of the Constitution of the United States. Now, if I can make our ideas of it plain, I think there is nothing left of that article. Now, in the first place, as Senators will observe this is the case of a Secretary of War, holding by the terms of his commission during the pleasure of the President, and holding under the act of 1789, which created that department, and which, although it does not directly confer on the President the power of removing the Secretary, does clearly imply that he had that power, by making a provision for what shall happen in case he exercises it.

That is the case which is under consideration. The question is this, whether under the law of 1789, and the tenure of office created by that law, created after great debate, the President could have removed such a Secretary during the session of the Senate? Why not? Certainly there is nothing in the Constitution of the United States to prohibit it. The Constitution has made two distinct provisions for filling offices. One is by a nomination to the Senate, a confirmation by that body and a commission by the President on that confirmation. The other is the commission of an officer, when a vacancy happens during a recess of the Senate.

But the question now before you is not a question as to how vacancies shall be filled, for that the Constitution has provided for, but a question how vacancies may be created, which is a totally distinct question. Whatever may be thought of the soundness of the Constitution—arrived at after a lengthy debate, in 1789—concerning the tenure of office, or concerning the power of removal from office, no one, I suppose, will question the fact that a conclusion was arrived at, and that that conclusion was that the Constitution of the United States had lodged with the President this power of removal, independently of the Senate.

This may be a decision which ought to be reversed. It may have been now reversed. On that I say nothing at present; but that it was made the legislation of Congress in 1789, and on down to 1867, proceeded on the assumption,

express or implied, that that decision had been made, nobody who understands the history of the legislation of the country will deny. Consider, if you please, what that decision was; that the Constitution had lodged this power in the President, that he was to exercise it, and that the Senate had not and could not have any control whatever over it. If that be so, what materiality is it whether the Senate is in session or not? If the Senate is not in session, and the President has this power, a vacancy is created, and the Constitution has made provision for filling the vacancy by commissioning until the end of the next session of the Senate.

If the Senate is in session, then the Constitution has made provision for filling the vacancy thus created by nomination, and the laws of the country made provision for filling it ad interim, so that if this be the case within the scope of the decision made by Congress in 1789, and within the scope of the legislation which followed on that decision, then it is a case where, either by force of the Constitution the President had the power of removal without consulting the Senate, or else the legislation of Congress had given it to him, and in either way, neither the Constitution nor the legislation of Congress had made it incumbent on him to consult the Senate on the subject.

I submit, therefore, that if you look at this case as it has been presented on a decision made in 1789 on the legislation of Congress following that decision, are the terms of the commission under which Mr. Stanton holds, you must come to this conclusion without any further reference to the subject, that the Senate had nothing whatever to do with the removal of Mr. Stanton, either whether the Senate was in session or not; that his removal was made either under the constitutional power of the President as it had been interpreted in 1789; or if that be considered reversed under the grant made by the Legislature to the President in reference to all those secretaries not included within the Tenure of Office act.

This, however, does not rest simply on this application of the Constitution and legislation of Congress. There has been, and I shall bring it before you, a practice on the part of the government, going back to a very early day, and coming down to a recent period, for the President to make removals from the office, when the case called for them, without regard to the fact whether the Senate was in session or not. The instances, of course, would not be numerous where, if the Senate was in session, he would not send a nomination to the Senate, saying "I appoint A. B. instead of C. D., removed:" but there were occasions, not of frequent occurrence, where the President had not time to select a person whom he would nominate; where he would not trust the officer then in possession of the office to continue in it, and where it was necessary for him, by a special order, to remove him from the office wholly independent of the nomination of his successors.

Let me bring before your attention a case which happened recently within the knowledge of the Senate. We were on the eve of a civil war; the War Department was in the hands of a man who was disloyal and unfaithful to his trust. His chief clerk, who, on his removal or resignation, would come to the place, was in the same category with his master. Under these circumstances, the President of the United States said—"Mr. Floyd, I must have possession of the office." Mr. Floyd had too much good good sense or good something else to do anything but immediately resign, and instantly the President put in the office General Holt, the Postmaster-General, without the delay of an hour, when a delay of twenty-four hours would have been of most practical consequences.

There are several of this class of cases arising in all the departments, and followed by this action, and we shall bring before you evidence showing what those cases were, so that it will appear that as long as offices were held during the pleasure of the President, and wholly independent of the advice which he might receive from the Senate with reference to their removal, whenever there was an occasion for it, the President used the power, whether the Senate was in session or not.

I have now given the considerations applicable to the Tenure of Office act, and to those allegations that the President violated, knowingly violated the Constitution of the United States in the order for the removal of Mr. Stanton from office while the Senate was in session.

The counsel for the President deem that it is not essential in order to his vindication from this charge, to go farther into the subject. The President, nevertheless, takes a broader view of the matter, and it is due to the President that it should be brought into court, and that I now propose to open to your consideration. The Constitution requires the President of the United States to take care that the laws be faithfully executed. It also requires of him, before he is qualified for his office, to swear that he will faithfully execute the laws and that, to the best of his ability he will preserve, protect and defend the Constitution of the United States.

I suppose that every man will agree that as long as the President in good faith is endeavoring to take care that the laws be faithfully executed, and is in good faith, to the best of his ability, preserving, protecting, and defending the Constitution of the United States, although he may be mistaken, he has not committed high crimes and misdemeanors. In the execution of these duties the President found various reasons, which it is not my province at this time to state, but which will be exhibited to you hereafter, that it was impossible for him to allow Mr. Stanton to continue to hold the office of Secretary of War while he was responsible for his conduct in the manner in which he is required by the Constitution and laws to be responsible. This was intimated to Mr. Stanton, and did not produce the effect which in the opinion of well-informed men, such an intimation usually produces. Thereupon the President first suspended Mr. Stanton, and reported that fact to the Senate. Certain proceedings took place here, which will be adverted to more particularly presently.

They resulted in the return of Mr. Stanton to the occupation by him of his office.

Then it was necessary for the President of the United States to consider first whether this Tenure of Office act applied to the case of Mr. Stanton; and, second, whether, if it applied to the case of Mr. Stanton, the law itself was a law of the land, or inoperative, because conflicting with the Constitution. Now, I am aware that it is insisted that it is the civil and moral duty of all men to obey these laws that have been passed through all the forms of legislation until they shall have been declared by the judicial authority not to be binding; but it is evident that that is too broad a statement of the civil and moral duty, incumbent either upon private citizens or upon public officers, because, if this be the measure of the duty, there never could be a decision, there never could be a decree that the law is unconstitutional, inasmuch as it is only by disregarding the law that any question can be raised upon it.

I submit to Senators that not only is there no such rule of civil or moral duty, but that it may be and has been a high and patriotic duty in a citizen to raise a question whether the law is within the Constitution of his country. Will any question the patriotism or the propriety of John Hampden's act when he brought the question before the courts of England, whether ship money was within the Constitution of England. Not only is there no such rule incumbent upon private citizens, which forbids them to raise such questions, but let me repeat, there may be, and there often have been instances in which the highest patriotism and the purest civil and moral liberty required it. Let me ask any of you if you were a trustee for the rights of third persons, and if those rights of third persons which they could not defend, themselves, by reason perhaps, of sex or age, should be attacked by an unconstitutional law, should you not deem it your sacred duty to resist that law and have the question tried? And if a private trustee may be subject to such duty, and impelled by it to such action, how is it possible to maintain that he who is a trustee for the people, with powers confided to him for their protection, for their security, for their benefit, may not, in that character of trustee, defend what has been thus committed to him?

Do not let me be misunderstood upon this. I am not intending to advance upon or to occupy any extreme ground, because no such extreme ground has been advanced upon, or is occupied by the President of the United States. He is to take care that the laws are faithfully executed. When a law has been passed through the forms of legislation, either with his assent or without his assent, it is his duty to see that the law be faithfully executed, so long as nothing is required of him in his ministerial action. He is not to erect himself in a judicial court, and decide that the law is unconstitutional, and that therefore, he will not execute it.

If that was done, there manifestly never could be a judicial decision. The President would not only veto the law, but would refuse all action under the law after it was passed, and would thus prevent any judicial decision being made upon it. He asserts no such power, he has no such idea of his duty; his idea of his duty is that, if a law is passed over his veto which he believes to be unconstitutional, and, if that law affects the interests of third parties, those whose interests are affected must take care of them, and must raise questions concerning them.

If such a law affects the interests of the people, the people must take care of them at the polls, in a constitutional and proper way; but when a question arises whether a particular law has cut off a power confided to him, and when he alone can raise that question, and when he alone can cause a judicial decision to come between the two branches of the government to see which of them is right, and when, after due deliberation, with the advice of those who are his proper advisers, he settles down firmly in the opinion that such is the character of the law, it remains to be decided by you whether there is any violation of his duty in doing so.

Suppose a law should declare or provide that the President of the United States shall not make a treaty with England or with any other power. That would be a plain infraction of his constitutional power, and if an occasion arose when such a treaty was expedient, desirable or necessary, in his judgment, it would be his duty to disobey the law, and the fact that it would be declared a high misdemeanor if he disobeyed, it no more releases him from the responsibility through the motive of fear of that law than he would be relieved from that responsibility by a bribe.

Suppose a law is passed that he shall not be the commander-in-chief; that is a plain case of an infraction of that provision of the Constitution which has confided to him that command in order that he be the head of all the military power of the country shall be its highest civil magistrate, and that the law may always be superior to arms. Suppose the President shall resist a law of that kind in the manner which I have spoken of, by bringing it to a judicial decision. It may be said that these are plain cases of express infraction of the Constitution. But what is the difference between a power conferred upon the President by the express words of the Constitution and the power conferred upon him by a clear implication of the Constitution? Where is the power in the Constitution to levy taxes? Where does the power come from to limit Congress in assigning original jurisdiction to the Supreme Court of the United States? Where do a multitude of powers on which Congress acts, come from in the Consti-

tution, except by fair implication? Whence do you derive power to confer on the Senate the right to prevent removals from office without its consent? Is it expressly given in the Constitution, or is it an implication from some of its provisions?

I submit that it is impossible to draw any line to limit the duty of the President simply because a power is derived from an implication of the Constitution instead of from an express provision of it. One thing, unquestionably, is to be expected from the President on all such occasions, and that is that he shall carefully consider the question, and if he shall be of opinion that it is necessary for the public service that the question shall be decided, he shall take all competent and proper advice on the subject, and, when he has done that, if he finds that he cannot follow the law in a particular case without abandoning the powers which he believes to have been confided to him by the people, it is his solemn conviction that it is his duty to assert the power and to obtain a judicial decision thereon; and although the President does not perceive, nor do his counsel perceive that, it is essential to his defense in this case, to maintain this part of the argument. Nevertheless, if this tribunal should be of that opinion, then before this tribunal, before all the people of the United States, and before the civilized world, he asserts the truth of that position.

I am compelled now to ask your attention, quite briefly however, to some considerations which weighed on the mind of the President, and led him to conclude that the power of removal was one of the powers of his office, and that it was his duty in the manner I have indicated to endeavor to protect it.

It is a rule long settled, existing I suppose in the laws of all civilized countries, certainly existing in the laws of every system of government which I have consulted, that a cotemporary exposition made by those who are competent to give it a construction, is of very great weight, and that when such a cotemporary exposition of the law has been made and has been followed by an actual and practical construction of it, has been continued during periods of time, and applied to great numbers of cases, it is afterwards too late to call in question the correctness of such a decision.

The rule is laid down in the quaint language of Lord Coke, as follows:—"Great regard ought, in construing a law, to be paid to the construction which the sages who lived about the time, or soon after it was made, put upon it, because they were best able to judge of the intention of the makers at the time when the law was made. *Cotemporanea expositis est fortissima in lege.*

Mr. Curtis then read from Chief Justice Marshall's "Life of Washington" in regard to the action by the House of Representatives on a bill on the subject in 1789, when Mr. Benson offered an amendment, to the effect that the power of removal is solely in the President, and said that if that prevailed he would move to strike out certain words conveying the implication that it was a subject of legislative power. That motion was seconded by Mr. Madison, and both amendments were adopted, and the bill passing into a law, had ever since been considered as the sense of the legislative department on this subject.

Mr. CURTIS continued—Some allusion has been made to the fact that this law was passed only by the action of the Vice President. Upon that subject I beg leave to read from the Life of Vice President Adams, by his grandson, vol. I, pages 448 and 450. He here gives an account, so far as can be ascertained, of what that debate was.

He terminates the subject in this way:—"These reasons" (he says), that is, the Vice President's reasons, "were not committed to paper, however, and can, therefore, never be known, but in their substance it is certain that he never had the shadow of a doubt." I refer, also, to 1st Story's Commentaries on the Constitution, section 448. It will there be found that the learned commentator considered a contemporary construction of the Constitution, which he there describes, as of very great weight in determining his reasons.

Mr. CURTIS read the extract to the effect that the exposition of various departments of government upon particular questions approach in their nature and have the same recommendation that belongs to a law. He continued.—In comparing the decision made in 1789 with the tests which are here suggested by the writer, it will be found in the first place that the precise question was under discussion; secondly, that there was a deep sense of its importance, for it was seen that the decision was not to affect the few cases arising here and there in the course of the government, but that it would enter deeply into its practical and daily administration.

In the next place the determine was, so far as such a determination could be entertained and carried into effect, thereby to fix the system for the future. And in the last place, the men who participated in it must be admitted to have been exceedingly well qualified for their task. There is another rule to be added to this, which is also of very frequent application, and that is, that a long continued practical application of a decision of this character by those to whom the execution of a law is confided is of decisive weight. I will borrow again from Lord Cote, "*optimus legum interpres consuetudo*" practice is the last interpretation of the law. Now, what followed this original decision?

From 1789 down to 1867 every Senator, every President and every Congress participated in and acted under the construction of the government in 1789. Not only was the government so conducted, but it was a subject sufficiently discussed among the people to bring to their consideration that such a question had existed, had been settled in this manner, had been raised again from time to time, and yet, as everybody knows, they were so far from interfering with this decision, so far from expressing in any manner their disapprobation of the practice which had grown up under it. It is well known that all parties favored and acted upon this system.

At this point, 2'20, on motion of Mr. EDMUNDS, a recess of fifteen minutes was ordered.

After the recess the court was, as usual, slow in reassembling. At a quarter before three Senator MORRILL (Me.) moved to adjourn and called the yeas and nays, which proved effectual in drawing in the absentees. Senators McCreery and Patterson (Tenn.) only voted yea; Senator Morrill himself voting nay.

Mr. CURTIS continued, after recapitulating the point he was discussing before the recess, as follows:—

This is a subject which has heretofore been examined and passed upon judicially in very numerous cases. I do not speak now, of course, of judicial decisions of this particular question which is under consideration, whether the Constitution has lodged the power of removal in the President alone, or in the President and the Senate, or has left it in part to the Legislative power, but I speak of the judicial exposition of such a practical construction of the Constitution of the United States, originating in the way in which this was originated, continued in the way in which this was continued, and sanctioned in the way in which this has been sanctioned.

There was a very early case which arose soon after the organization of the government, and reported under the name of Stewart against ——, 1st Cranch's Reports, 299. It involved a question concerning the interpretation of the Constitution as to the power which the Legislature had to assign to the Judges of the Supreme Court certain duties. From that time down to the decision of the case of —— against the Port Wardens of Philadelphia, reported in the 12th Howard, 315, a period of more than half a century, there has been a series of judicial decisions on the fact of such a cotemporaneous construction of the Constitution, followed by such a practice in accordance with it; and it is now a fixed and settled rule, which I think no lawyer will undertake to controvert, that the effect of such a construction is not merely to give weight to an argument, but to fix an interpretation, and, accordingly, it will be found, by looking into the books written by those who were cognizant of the subject, that they have so considered and held.

I beg leave to refer to the most eminent of all commentators on American laws, and will read from Chancellor Kent's lectures, found in the first volume, page 310, marginal paging. After considering this subject—and it should be noted in reference to this very learned and experienced jurist—considering it in an unfavorable light, because he himself thought that, as an original question that had better have been settled the other way, that it would have been more logical, more in conformity with his views of what the practical heads of the government were, that the Senate should participate with the President in the power of removal. Nevertheless, he sums it up in this wise:—

This amounted to a legislative construction of the Constitution, and it has ever since been acquiesced in and acted upon as of decisive authority of the case, and it applies equally to every other officer of the government appointed by the President and the Senate, whose time of duration is not specially declared. It is supported by the written reason that the subordinate officers in the Executive departments ought to hold at the pleasure of the head of that department, because he is interested generally with the Executive authority, and every participation in that authority by the Senate is an exception to the general principle sought to be taken strictly. The President is the great responsible officer for the faithful execution of the laws, and the power of removal was incidental to that duty, and might often be requisite to fulfil it.

This, I believe, will be found to be a fair expression of the opinion of those who had occasion to examine this subject in their researches, or as a matter of speculation. In this case, however, the President of the United States had to construe, not merely the general question where this power was lodged—not merely the effect of this decision, made in 1789, in the practice of the government under it—but he had to construe a particular law, the provisions of which were before him, and might have an application to the case upon which he felt called upon to act; and it is necessary, in order to do justice to the President in reference to this matter, to examine what the theory of the law is, and what its operation is or must be, if any, upon the law which he had before him—namely, the case of Mr. Stanton.

During the debate in 1789 there were three distinct theories, by different persons in the House of Representatives. The one was that the Constitution had lodged the powers of removal with the President alone; the other was that the Constitution had lodged the power with the President, acting only by and with the consent of the Senate; the third was that the Constitution had lodged it nowhere, but had left it to the legislative powers, to be acted upon in connection with the prescription of the tenure of office.

The last of these theories was, at that day, held by but comparatively few persons. The first two received not only the greater number of votes, but much the greater weight of reason in the course of that debate, so much so that when this subject came under the consideration of the Supreme Court of the United States, in an *ex parte* case, Mr. Justice Townsend, who delivered the opinion of the court in that case, says that it has never been doubted that the Constitution had lodged the power either in the President alone or in the Senate. Certainly an inaccuracy; but, then, it required a very close scrutiny, and a careful examination of the individual opinion expressed in that debate, to ascertain that it had been determined in one way or the other.

The Constitution settled the question. Nevertheless, as I understand—and I may be mistaken in this, but as I understand—it is the theory of this law which the President had before him that both of these opinions were wrong; that the Constitution has not lodged the power anywhere, except that it has left it, as I understand, a legacy which may be controlled. of course, by the Legislature itself, according to its will; because, as Chief Justice Marshall somewhere remarks—and it is one of those pertinent remarks which will be found to have been carried by him into many of his decisions—when it come to a question whether a power exists, the peculiar mode in which it must be exercised must be left to the will of the body that possesses it. And, therefore, if this be a legislative power, it was very apparent to the President of the United States, as it would have been very apparent to Mr. Madison, and as declared by him in the course of his correspondence—which is no doubt familiar to the Senators—that if this be a legislative power, the Legislature may lodge it in the Senate, may retain it in the two Houses of Congress, or may give it to the House of Representatives.

I repeat, the President has to construe this particular law. As I understand the theory of law, I do not undertake to say it is an unfounded claim; I do not undertake to say that it may not be maintained successfully, but I do undertake to say that it was originally questioned by the ablest minds that had this subject under consideration in 1789; that whenever the question has been started since, it has had, through a recent period, a few advocates, and that no fair, candid mind can deny or doubt at this day that it is capable of being doubted and disbelieved after examination. It may be the truth, after all, but it is not a truth which shines with such a clear and certain light that a man is guilty of a crime because he does not perceive it.

The President had not only to construe this particular law, but he had to construe its application, its constitutional ability to apply to this particular case, supposing the case of Mr. Stanton to be what I have endeavored to show, which was not within its terms. Let us assume that the case is within its application; let us assume that the proviso, in describing the case of the Secretary, described the case of Mr. Stanton. Did Mr. Stanton, having been appointed by President Lincoln, under the act of 1862, and commissioned to hold during the pleasure of the President, by force of this law acquire a right to hold this office against the will of the President until April 1869.

Now, there is one thing certain that has been doubted—under the Constitution it is not capable of being doubted—and that is, that the President is to make the choice of officers. Whether, having made the choice, and being inducted into office, they can be removed, is another question; to the President alone is confided the power of choice. In the first place, he alone can nominate. When the Senate has consented to the nomination he is not bound to commission the officers. He has a second opportunity for the consideration and acceptance or rejection of the choice he originally made. Upon this subject allow me to read from the opinion of Chief Justice Marshall, in the case of —— against ——, where it is expressed more clearly than I can do.

Mr. CURTIS read from the opinions which enunciate the clauses of the Constitution bearing upon the subject, and said these seem to contemplate three distinct operations:—The nomination, which is the sole voluntary act of the President, and the appointment, which is also his voluntary act, by and with the advice and consent of the Senate; then the commission, to grant which might perhaps be deemed a duty enjoined by the Constitution.

The opinion, however, holds that it is optional with the President to commission after appointment,

He continued:—All this shows that the choice is with the President, that the action of the Senate upon the choice is an advisory action only at a particular stage after the nomination, and defers the appointment or commission.

Now, as I have said before, Mr. Stanton was appointed under the law of 1789 constituting the War Department, in accordance with that law. He was commissioned to hold during the pleasure of the President. He (President Lincoln) has said to the Senate—"I nominate Mr. Stanton to hold the office of Secretary for the Department of War during my pleasure." The Senate has said:—"We assent to Mr. Stanton holding the office of Secretary for the Department of War during the pleasure of the President."

What was this for? If it operates in the case of Mr. Stanton so that Mr. Stanton can hold office against the will of the President, contrary to the terms of his commission, contrary to the law under which he was appointed, down to the 9th of April, 1869—for this new law fixed and extended the term—where is Mr. Stanton's commission? Who made the appointment? Who has assented to it? It is a legislative act; it is a legislate appointment; it is assented to by the two branches of Congress, acting in their legislative capacity, and no other. The President has had no voice in the matter; the Senate, as the advisers of the President, have had no voice in the matter. If he holds it all, he holds it by force of legislation, and not by any choice made by the President or assented to by the Senate.

This was the case, and the only case, which the President had before him, and on which he was to consider whether, for having formed an opinion on the Constitution of the United States—an opinion which he shares with every President who has preceded him, with every Congress which has preceded the last; an opinion formed on the grounds which I have imperfectly indicated; an opinion which, when applied to this particular case, raises the doubts which I have indicated here arising out of the fact that this law does not pursue either of the opinions which were originally held on this subject, and have occasionally been stated and maintained by those who were restless under its operation; an opinion justified by the practice of the government from its origin down to the present time.

If he might properly and honestly form such an opinion under the lights which he had, and with the aid of this advice which we shall show you he received, then is he to be impeached for acting upon it to the extent of obtaining a judicial decision whether this department of the Executive Department of the government was right in its opinion, or whether the Legislative Department was right in its opinion? Well, strangely enough, the honorable managers themselves say, "No, he is not to be impeached for that."

I beg leave to read from the argument of the honorable manager, by whom the case for the prosecution was opened, "If the President had really desired solely to test the constitutionality of the law or his legal right to remove Mr. Stanton, instead of his defiant message to the Senate, of February 21, informing them of his removal, but not suggesting the purpose, which is thus shown to be an afterthought, he would have said in substance, 'Gentlemen of the Senate, in order to test the constitutionality of the law entitled an act regulating the tenure of certain civil offices, which I verily believe to be unconstitutional and void, I have issued an order for the removal of Edwin M. Stanton from the office of Secretary for the Department of War. I felt myself constrained to make this removal, lest Mr. Stanton should answer the information in the nature of a *quo warranto*, which I intend the Attorney-General shall file at an early day, by saying that he holds the office of Secretary of War by the appointment and authority of Mr. Lincoln, which has never been revoked. Anxious that there shall be no collision or disagreement between the several departments of the government and the Executive, I lay before the Senate the message, as the reason of my action, as well as the action itself, for the purpose indicated, may meet your consideration."

Thus far the quotation shows the communication which the President should have obtained from the managers and sent to the Senate in order to make the matter exactly right. Then follows this:—"Had the Senate received such a message the representatives of the people might never have deemed it necessary to impeach the President for such an act, to insure the safety of the country, even if they had denied the accuracy of the legal position," so that it seems that it is, after all, not the removal of Mr. Stanton, but the manner in which the President communicated the fact of that removal, after it was made public, the President is to be impeached for.

That message is called here "the defendant's message of the 21st of February." I have read that message as you all have read it. If you can find anything in it but what is decorous and respectful to the Senate and to all concerned, your tastes are different from mine. But whether it be a point of the managers, well or ill conceived, one thing seems to be quite clear, that the President is not impeached here because he entertained an opinion that the law was unconstitutional; he is not impeached here because he acted on that opinion, and removed Mr. Stanton; but he is impeached here because the House of Representatives considers that this honorable body was addressed by a defiant message, when it should have been addressed in the terms which the honorable manager has dictated.

I now come, Mr. Chief Justice and Senators, to another topic connected with this matter of the removal of Mr. Stanton, and the action of the President under it. The honorable managers take the ground, among others, that whether, upon a construction of this Tenure of Office act, Mr. Stanton is not legally Secretary of War, or even if you should believe the President thought it unconstitutional and had a right in some way to construe it, by his own conduct and declaration the President is estopped; he is not to be permitted to assert the true interpretation of this law; he is not to be permitted to allege that his purpose was to test the question concerning its constitutionality; and the reason is that he has done and said such and such things.

Well we all know that there is at common law a doctrine called rules of *estoppel*, founded undoubtedly on good reason, although they were called in the time of Lord Coke, and have been down to the present day, odious, because they shut out the truth, nevertheless there are circumstances when it is proper the truth should be shut out. What are these circumstances? They are, where a question of private right is involved, where, in a matter of fact the private right accrues, and wherein the party to the controversy does himself what he ought not in good conscience to be allowed after to assert or deny. But did any one ever hear of estoppel in a matter of law? Did any one ever hear that a party had put himself into such a condition, that when he came into a court of justice upon a claim of private right, he could not ask a judge to construe an estoppel and insist on such a construction? Did anybody ever hear, least of all, that a man was affected by reason of an estoppel, under any system of jurisprudence that ever prevailed in the civilized world—that the President of the United States should be impeached and removed from office, not by reason of the truth of his case, but because he is estopped from appealing. It would be a spectacle for God and man.

There is no matter of fact here. They have themselves put in Mr. Stanton's commission, which shows the date of the commission, and the terms of the commission, and that is the whole matter of fact involved. The rest is the construction of this Tenure of Office act, and the application of it to the case, which they have thus made for themselves, and also the construction of the Constitution of the United States in the abstract question, whether that was lodged the power of removal with the President, with the Senate, or with both.

I respectfully submit, therefore, in reply to this ground, which is taken here, that no conduct of the President, who endeavors to assert, not a private right, but a great public right, confided to his office by the people, in which, if any body is estopped, the people may be estopped, that nothing that the President could do or say, could put this great public right into that extraordinary position. What has he done? what are the facts which they rely upon, out of which to work this estoppel as they call it? Why, in the first place he sent a message to the Senate, on December 12, 1867, informing the Senate that he had suspended Mr. Stanton by a certain order, a copy of which he gave; that he had appointed General Grant to exercise the duties of that office, *ad interim*, by a certain order, a copy of which he gave, and then entered into a discussion, in which he showed the existence of this question, whether Mr. Stanton was in the Tenure of Office bill, and the existence of the other question, whether this was or was not a constitutional law. Then he revoked the action of the Senate.

There was nothing misrepresented; there was nothing concealed, which he was bound to state. It is complained by the honorable managers that he did not tell the Senate that if their action should be such as to restore Mr. Stanton practically to the position of the office he should go to law. It may have been, possibly, an omission; but I rather think that that good taste which is so prevalent among the managers, and which they so insist upon here, would hardly insist that the President should have held out to the Senate something which might possibly have been rejected. They said he made a case for their action, in which he was the defendant to the Senate, both by reason of their conduct and his, and also other conduct too deferential.

Senators, there is no inconsistency in the President's position or conduct in this instance. Suppose a party who has a private right in question, submit to the sole tribunal in the same proceeding, these questions:—First, I deny the constitutionality under which the right is claimed against me; secondly, I assert that the interpretation of that law will not affect the case; thirdly, I insist that even if it is within the laws, I have made a case within the laws.

Is there any inconsistency in that? Is it not seen every day, or something analogous to it, in courts of justice? Suppose the President had summed up his message in this way:—"I insist, in the first place, that the law is unconstitutional; I insist, in the second place, that Mr. Stanton is not within the law; and I respectfully submit, in the third place, whether, if it be a constitutional law and Mr. Stanton be within it, the facts that I present to you be not made such a case that you will not ask me to receive him back?" He has questioned whether the law was constitutional and whether Mr. Stanton was within it, and then he submits that he had reason to believe and did think that the law was unconstitutional; that he had no reason to believe that they thought Mr. Stanton was within it; he submitted to their consideration the facts that he acted upon and within it. Well, the President, it seems, has not only been thus anxious to avoid, but has taken measures to avoid a collision with the Senate, but he has actually, in some things else, obeyed it.

Mr. Curtis went on to refer to the commission of acts on which charges have been made by the President, and with his sanction, and to the removal and suspension of collectors, etc., said it had doubtless been done under the law, and when an emergency arose, as in case of Mr. Stanton, when he must either act or abandon the power that he holds, it was insisted upon that he must run against the law, and take every possible opportunity to give it a blow. On questions of administrative duty merely, the President felt bound to obey it. When this emergency, however, arose, so that this department of the government could not be carried on, he must meet it. He did not fear embarrassment or difficulty in the public service because of the suspension or removal of a fraudulent collector.

These changes in the commissions issued had nothing to do with the subject. They were made subject to conditions prescribed by law, one of which was the Senate must consent to a removal. Not only the law of Congress, but the Constitution was the law of the land. The changes in the Treasury Department, also, had nothing to do with the subject of his removal. Wherever it was vested, all officers are held subject to the power of removal which is vested somewhere.

He saw nothing in this subject of estoppel growing out of the action of the President, either in the message to the Senate of December 12, or in the changes in the commissions, or in the sending to the Senate notices of suspension of different officers, that has any bearing on the construction of the Tenure of Office act, as affecting the case of Mr. Stanton. The law might be constitutional, the President might have acted, and might have been bound to act under it; still, if Mr. Stanton was not within it the case remains as it was originally, and the case not being within that law the first article was entirely without foundation.

At this point Mr. Curtis plead fatigue, and, on motion of Mr. JOHNSON, the court adjourned until noon to-morrow; and at 3·50 P. M., the Senate went into Executive Session, and soon after, adjourned.

PROCEEDINGS OF FRIDAY, APRIL 10.

The President *pro tem* called the Senate to order. Prayer was offered by the Chaplain.

The chair was then vacated for the Chief Justice, and the Court was opened by proclamation in due form.

The managers and members of the House of Representatives were successively announced, and took their places.

The journal of yesterday was read, and in the meantime the galleries had become about half filled.

General Sherman again occupied a seat on the floor.

Mr. CURTIS, of the President's counsel, resumed his argument at 12·15.

What with the buzzing conversation of uninterested newspaper correspondents and other sources, and the reporters' remote positions, occasional imperfections may be found in the report.

Mr. Curtis Resumes his Argument.

Mr. CURTIS said:—Mr. Chief Justice—Among the points which I omitted to notice yesterday is one which seems to me of specific importance, and which induces me to return to it for a few moments. If you will indulge me, I will read a short passage from Saturday's proceedings. In the course of those proceedings, Mr. Manager Butler said:—

"It will be seen, therefore, Mr. President and Senators, that the President of the United States says in this answer that he suspended Mr. Stanton under the Constitution indefinitely, and at his pleasure, and I propose now, unless it be objected to, to show that that is false under his own hand, and I have his letter to that effect, which if there is no objection, I will read, the signature of which was identified by C. E. Creecy:—

Then followed the reading of the letter, which is as follows:—

"EXECUTIVE MANSION, WASHINGTON, D. C., Aug. 14, 1867.—Sir:—In compliance with the eighth section of the act of Congress of March 2, 1867, entitled 'an act regulating the tenure of certain civil offices,' you are hereby notified that on the 12th inst. Hon. Edwin M. Stanton was suspended from office as Secretary of War, and General Ulysses S. Grant authorized and empowered to act as Secretary of War *ad interim*.

"I am, sir, very respectfully, yours,
"ANDREW JOHNSON.
"To Hon. Hugh McCulloch, Secretary of the Treasury."

This letter was read to show, under the hand of the President, that when he says in his answer that he has removed Mr. Stanton by virtue of the Tenure of Office act, that statement was a falsehood. Allow me now to read the 8th section of that act:—

"That whenever the President shall, without the advice and consent of the Senate, designate, authorize or employ any person to perform the duties of any office, he shall forthwith notify the Secretary of the Treasury thereof, and it shall be the duty of the Secretary of the Treasury thereupon to communicate such notice to all the proper accounting and disbursing officers in his department."

The Senate will perceive that this section has nothing to do with the suspension of an officer, but the purport of the section is that in case the President, without the advice and consent of the Senate, shall, under any circumstances, designate a third person to perform, temporarily, the duties of the office, he is to make a report of that designation to the Secretary of the Treasury, who is to give the necessary information to the accounting officers. The section applies in terms to, and includes all cases it applies to, and includes the designation on account of sickness, or absence, or resignation, or any cause of vacancy, whether temporary or permanent, whether occurring by reason of a suspension or a removal; and, therefore, when the President says to the Secretary of the Treasury, "I give you notice that I have designated General Thomas to perform the duties *ad interim* of Secretary of War," he makes no allusion, by force of that letter, to the manner in which that vacancy occurred; and, therefore, instead of showing, under the President's own hand, that he has repeated a falsehood, it has no reference whatever to the matter.

Mr. BUTLER—Will you read the second section, if you please. The first clause of the second section?

Mr. CURTIS (reading)—"That when any officer appointed as aforesaid, excepting judges of the United States courts, shall, during the recess of the Senate, be shown by evidence satisfactory to the President," &c.

The President is allowed to suspend such officers. Now, the President states in his answer that he did not act under it.

Mr. BUTLER—That is not reading the section.

Mr. CURTIS—I am aware that it is not reading the section. It is a very long section.

Mr. BUTLER—The first clause of the section is all I want.

Mr. CURTIS—It allows the President, because of crime or other occasion designated in it, to suspend the officer. The section applies to all occasions. Whether suspensions

under this second section—whether temporary disqualification, sickness, death, resignation—no matter what that cause may be, if for any reason there is a vacancy, he is authorized to designate a person to supply the office *ad interim*, of which notice is to be given to the Secretary of the Treasury. Therefore, I repeat, sir, that the subject matter of this eighth section, and the letter which the President wrote in consequence of it, has no reference to the subject of the authority upon which he removed or suspended Mr. Stanton.

I now ask the attention of the Senate to the second article, and I will begin as I began before by stating what is the substance of this article. I hope the Senate will be able to see now every one of these allegations is controverted by what is already in the case, and that I shall be enabled to state what we propose to offer by way of proof in respect to each of them. The first substantial allegation in this article is the delivery of the letter of authority to General Thomas without authority of law; that it was an intentional violation of the Tenure of Office act; that it was an intentional violation of the Constitution of the United States, and the delivery of the order to General Thomas was made with intent to violate that act and the Constitution of the United States. That is the substance of the second article.

Now, the Senate will at once perceive that if the suspension of Mr. Stanton was not a violation of the act in point of fact—or, to state it in other terms, if the case of Mr. Stanton is not within the act, then his suspension or his removal, if he has been actually removed, or a removal which did actually take place, would not be a violation of the act; because if his case is not within the act at all which does not apply to the case of Mr. Stanton, of course his removal is not in violation of this act.

If Mr. Stanton continued to hold under the commission which he received from President Lincoln, and has continued to hold under the act of 1789, it was no violation of the Tenure of Office act that Mr. Johnson removed or intended to remove Mr. Stanton; and, therefore, the Senate will perceive that it is necessary to come back again, to recur under this article, because it will be found necessary to recur under the whole of the first eight articles, to the inquiry whether Mr. Stanton's case was within the Tenure of Office act; secondly, whether it was so clearly and plainly within that act that it can be attributed to the President as a high misdemeanor, that he considered it as not including that case. But, suppose the case of Mr. Stanton is within the Tenure of Office act, still the inquiry arises whether the delivering of this letter of authority to General Thomas was a violation of the act. I shall necessarily ask your careful attention to the general subject matter of this act and the particular provisions contained in it. Senators will remember undoubtedly that this act, as it finally passed, differed in many particulars from the bill as it was originally introduced.

The law related to two distinct subjects—the one to the subject of removal, the other to the subject of appointments to office. It seems that a practice had grown up under the government, that where a person was nominated to the Senate for an office, and when the Senate either did not act upon his nomination or rejected it, it was considered competent for the President, after the adjournment of the Senate, by a temporary commission to appoint that same person to the same office. That was deemed by a large majority of Senators to be an abuse of power—not an intentional abuse of power. It was a practice that had prevailed under the government to a very considerable extent. It was not limited to recent years. It had been supported by the opinions of the Attorney-Generals; but still it was esteemed by Senators to be a departure from the spirit of the Constitution, and in derogation of the just powers of the Senate in reference to nominations to office. That being so, it will be found on examination of this law that the first and second sections of the act related exclusively to removals from office and to temporary suspensions during a recess of the Senate; whereas, the other sections, to which I shall particularly ask your attention, related exclusively to that other subject of temporary appointments—appointments made to office after the Senate had refused to concur in the nomination of the person appointed.

This law provides that the President shall have power to fill all vacancies which may happen during a recess of the Senate, by reason of death or resignation. It will be remarked that this does not include all cases. It does not include the case of the expiration of a commission, but it includes simply death and resignation during the recess of the Senate. Why this was so I do not know. It is manifest that the law does not affect them. In point of fact it does not cover all cases that may arise, even belonging to this general class, to which the section was designed to refer. It provides that the President shall have power to fill all vacancies which may happen during the recess of the Senate, by reason of death or resignation, by granting commissions which shall expire at the end of the next session thereafter; and if no appointment by and with the advice and consent of the Senate shall be made to such office, during such next session, then such office shall remain in abeyance without any salary, fees or emoluments attached thereto, until the same shall be filled by appointment, by and with the advice and consent of the Senate; and during such time all powers and duties belonging to such office shall be exercised by such other officer as may by law exercise such powers and duties. In case of vacancy in such office, all the offices brought within the provision of a vacancy occurring during the recess of the Senate, and all the filling of that vacancy by the President, are treated as going into abeyance unless the Senate shall have assented to some nomination before its adjournment, and that applies, as I have said, to the two classes of cases, namely, vacancies happening by reason of death or resignation, but it does not apply to any other vacancy. The next section does not relate to that subject, but to the subject of removal:—"Nothing in this act shall be construed to extend the term of any officer," &c.

The fifth section is "that if any person shall, contrary to the provisions of this act, accept any appointment to or employment in any office, or shall otherwise attempt to hold or exercise any such office or employment, they shall be deemed and declared to be guilty of a high misdemeanor, and upon trial and conviction therefore, shall be punished by a fine not exceeding $10,000 and by imprisonment." What are the provisions of this act in relation to accepting any appointment? They are found in the third section of the act putting some offices into abeyance under similar circumstances, which are described in that section.

If any person does accept an office which is thus put into abeyance, or any emolument or authority in reference to such office, he comes within the penal provisions of the fifth section; but outside of that there is no such thing as accepting an office contrary to the provisions of the act, because the provisions of the act extend no further than to those cases. And so of the next section. Every removal, appointment or employment made, had or exercised contrary to the provisions of this act, &c., shall be deemed and is hereby declared to be a high misdemeanor. The stress of this article does not seem to me to depend at all upon this question of the construction of the law, but upon a totally different matter, which I agree should be fairly and carefully considered.

The allegation in the article is that this letter of authority was given to General Thomas, enabling him to perform the duties of Secretary of War ad interim, without authority of law. That I conceive to be the main inquiry which arises under this article, provided the case of Mr. Stanton and his removal comes under the Tenure of Office act at all. I wish first to bring to the attention of the Senate the act of 1795, which is found in 1 Statutes at Large, p. 450. It is a short act, and I will read the whole of it:—

"Be it enacted, &c., That in case of a vacancy in the office of Secretary of State, Secretary of the Treasury, or Secretary of the Department of War, of any officer in either of said departments who is not appointed by the head of a department, whereby they cannot perform their duties in the said office, it shall be lawful for the President of the United States, in case he shall think it necessary, to authorize any person or persons, at his discretion, to perform the duties of the said respective offices, until a successor be appointed or each vacancy be filled. Provided, No one vacancy shall be supplied in the manner aforesaid for a longer term than six months."

This act, it has been suggested, may have been repealed by the act of February 20, 1863, which is found in 12 Statutes at Large, page 656. This, also, is a short act, and I will read it:—

Be it enacted, &c., That in case of the death, resignation, absence from the seat of government or sickness of the head of any executive department of the government, or of any officer in either of said departments, whose appointment is not in the head of the office, whereby they cannot perform the duties of their respective offices, it shall be lawful for the President of the United States, in case he shall think it necessary, to authorize any other officer of the department, whose appointment is vested in the President, at his discretion, to perform the duties of said respective offices until a successor is appointed, or until such absence or inability by sickness shall cease; Provided, that no one vacancy shall be supplied in the manner aforesaid for a longer term than six months."

Now these acts, as the Senate will perceive, although they may be said in some sense to relate to the same general subject matter, are very different in their provisions, and the latter law contains no express repeal of the earlier law. If, therefore, the latter law operates as a repeal of the older law, it is only by implication. It says, in terms that all acts or parts of acts inconsistent with it are repealed; but the addition of these words adds nothing to its meaning at all. The same inquiry would arise if they were not contained in it, namely: how far is that latter law inconsistent with the provisions of the earlier law?

There are certain rules on the subject which I shall not fatigue the Senate by citing cases to prove, because every lawyer will recognize them. In the first place, there is a rule as to the repeal by implication. As I understand it, the courts go upon the assumption of the principle that if the legislature really intended to repeal the law it would have said so—not that it should necessarily say so, because there are repeals by implication, but the presumption is that if the legislature entertains a clear and fixed intention to repeal a law, it will be likely at least to say so; therefore, the rule is a settled one that repeals by implication are not favored by the court. Another rule is, that the repugnancy between the two subjects must be clear. It is not enough that under some circumstances one law may possibly be repugnant to the other; the repugnance must be clear, and if the two laws can stand together, the latter does not operate as a repeal of the former.

If Senators have any desire to refer to the authorities on this subject, they will find a sufficient number of them collected in Sedgwick on statute laws, page 156. Now, there is no repugnance whatsoever, that I can perceive, between these two laws. The act of 1795 applies to all vacancies, however created. The act of 1863 applies only to vacancies temporarily, or otherwise, occasioned by

death or resignation, removals from office, &c.; expirations of commission are not included in it.

The act of 1795 applies only to vacancies; the act of 1863 applies to temporary absence or sickness. The subject matter, therefore, of the two laws is different. There is no inconsistency between them; they may stand together, each operating on the case to which it applies, and, therefore, I submit that, in the strictest view that can be taken of this subject, and which may be ultimately taken of it, it is not practicable to maintain that the law of 1863 repeals altogether the act of 1795; but whether it did or not, I state here what I have so frequently had occasion to state before, that it is a fair question:—Is it a crime to be on one side of this question, and not on the other? Is it a high misdemeanor to believe that a certain view, taken as to the repeal of the earlier view by the latter one, is a sound view? I submit that that would be altogether too stringent a rule even for the honorable managers themselves, and they do not, and the House of Representatives does not contend, for any such rule. The House puts it on the ground that there was a wilful intention to give this letter with authority of law. Not that it was a mistaken one; not that it was one which, after due consideration, lawyers might differ about, but that it was a wilful intention to act without authority. That I submit from the nature of the case, cannot be made to appear.

The next allegation to which I desire to call attention as contained in this article, is that the giving of this letter to General Thomas during the session of the Senate was a violation of the Constitution of the United States, and to that I will desire your attentive consideration. The Constitution, as you are well aware, has provided for two modes of filling offices. The one is a temporary commission during the recess of the Senate, when a vacancy happens during the recess, and the other is by appointment, with and by the advice and consent of the Senate, followed by a commission by the President; but it very early became apparent to those who administered the government that cases might and would occur to which neither of the modes provided by the Constitution could be promptly and conveniently applied.

Cases, for instance, of the temporary absence of the heads of a department, which department, especially during the recess of Congress, must, for the public interest, continue to be administered; cases of sickness, or cases of resignation or removal, where the President was not in the condition immediately to make a nomination to fill the office, or even to issue a commission, and, therefore, it became necessary, by legislation, to supply those defects which existed, notwithstanding those two provisions of the Constitution.

Accordingly, beginning in 1792, there will be found to be a series of acts on that subject, the filling of vacancies by temporary appointment, or by ad interim appointment. The counsel in this connection referred to several acts, from the act of 1792 to the act of February 20, 1863, and continued:—The Senate will perceive what difficulties these laws were designed to meet. The difficulty was the occurrence of some sudden vacancies in office, or of some sudden inability, on the part of the officer to perform his duties, and the intention of each of these laws was to make provision so that, notwithstanding this vacancy, or this temporary disability, the duties of the office would still be discharged. That was the purpose of these laws. It is apparent that these temporary vacancies are not as liable to occur during the session of the Senate as they are during the vacations, and that it is just as necessary to have a set of legislative provisions to enable the President to carry on the public service during the session of the Senate as it is to have the same set of provisions during the vacation.

Accordingly, it will be found, by looking into these laws, that they make no distinction whatsoever between the sessions of the Senate and the vacations of the Senate in reference to these temporary appointments whenever the vacancy shall occur. Is the language of the statute "whenever there shall be a death or a resignation or an absence or a sickness?" The law applies when the occurrence takes place which gives rise to the event which the law contemplates; and the particular time when it occurs is of no particular consequence in itself, and is admitted by the law as of no consequence.

In accordance with that, it has been the uniform, certain and frequent practice of the government from its very earliest days, as I am instructed we shall be able to prove, not in one or two instances, but in a great number of instances; the honorable managers themselves produced, the other day, a schedule of temporary appointments, during the sessions of the Senate, of inferior officers of departments, to perform temporarily the duties of heads of departments, and those instances run on all fours with the cases of removals or suspensions of officers.

Take the case, for instance, of Mr. Floyd, whom I alluded to yesterday. Mr. Floyd went out of office; his chief clerk was a person in sympathy with him, and under his control. If the third section of the act of 1789 was allowed to operate, the control of the War Department went into the hands of that chief clerk. The Senate was in session; it would not answer to have the War Department in that condition one hour, and Mr. Buchanan sent to the post office and took the Postmaster-General into the War Department, and put it into his charge.

There were then in this body a sufficient number of persons to look after a matter of that sort if they felt an interest in it; and accordingly they passed a resolve inquiring of President Buchanan by what authority he had made an appointment of a person to take charge of the War Department without the consent of the Senate.

In answer to that, a message was sent in containing the facts, and showing to the Senate of that day the propriety and necessity of the step, and the long-continued practice under which similar authority was exercised, giving a schedule running through the time of General Jackson, and of his two immediate successors, and showing a great number of *ad interim* appointments of that kind. There can be no ground, then, whatever, for the allegation that this *ad interim* appointment was a violation of the Constitution of the United States.

I pass, therefore, to the next article which I wish to consider; and that is not the next in number, but the eighth article. I take it in that order because the eighth I have analyzed. It differs from the second only in one particular, and, therefore, taking it in connection with the subject of which I have been just speaking, it will be necessary for me to say but a very few words in relation to it. It charges an intent unlawfully to control the appropriations made by Congress for the military service, and that is all there is of it, except what is in the second article, and on that certainly, at this stage of the case, I do not deem it necessary to make any observations.

The Senate will remember the offer of proof on the part of the managers, designed, as it was stated, to connect the President of the United States, through his Private Secretary, with the Treasury, and thus to enable him to control the appropriations made for the military service. The evidence, however, was not received, and therefore it seems quite unnecessary for me to make any comment upon it. The allegations are:—First, that the President appointed General Thomas; second, that he did it without the advice and consent of the Senate; third, that he did it when no vacancy had happened during a recess of the Senate; fourth, that he did it while there was no vacancy at the time, and fifth, that he committed a high misdemeanor by thus intentionally violating the Constitution of the United States.

I desire to say a word or two on this subject; and first, we deny that he ever appointed General Thomas to the office of Secretary of War. An appointment can be made to an office only by the advice and consent of the Senate, and through a commission signed by the President, and bearing the great seal. That is the only mode in which an appointment can be made. The President, as I have said, may temporarily commission officers when vacancies occur during the recess of the Senate; but that is not an appointment; is not so considered in the Constitution. The President may also, under the acts of 1795 and 1863, grant authority to persons to perform temporarily the duties of a certain office, when there is a vacancy. All that the President did in this case was, to issue a letter of authority to General Thomas, authorizing him *ad interim*, to perform the duties of Secretary of War.

In no sense was this an appointment. But it is said that it was made without the advice and consent of the Senate. Certainly it was. How could the advice and consent of the Senate be obtained to an *ad interim* authority of that kind? This was an appointment to supply, temporarily, a defect in the administrative machinery of the government.

If the President had gone to the Senate for its advice and consent, he must have gone under a nomination made by him of General Thomas for that office—a thing which he certainly never intended to do, and never made any attempt to carry out.

If Mr. Stanton's case is not within the Tenure of Office act; if, as I so frequently have repeated, he held his office under the act of 1789, and during the pleasure of the President, the moment he received that order which General Thomas carried to him, that moment there was a vacancy. In point of law, however, he may have refused to obey the order in point of fact, The Senate will observe that two letters were delivered to General Thomas at the same time, one of them an order to Mr. Stanton to vacate the office, and the other a direction to General Thomas to take possession of the office.

When Mr. Stanton obeys the order just given, may not the President issue a letter of authority, in contemplation that a vacancy is about to occur? Is he bound to take a technical view of the subject, and to have the order which creates the vacancy first sent and delivered, and then to sit down to his table, and afterwards sign a letter to another to hold the office? If the President expects a vacancy; if he has done an act which in his judgment is sufficient to create a vacancy, may he not sign the necessary paper appointing another to carry on the duties of the office? If I have been successful in the argument which I have already addressed to you, you must be of the opinion that, in point of fact, there was no violation of the Constitution of the United States in delivering this letter of authority, because the Constitution makes no provision for this temporary authority, and the law of Congress has made no provision for it.

Here, also, I beg leave to remind the Senate that the case does not fall within the Tenure of Office act. If the order which the President gave to Mr. Stanton to vacate the office was a lawful order, and one which he was bound to obey, everything contained in this article, as well as the preceding articles, falls. It is impossible, I submit, for the honorable managers to construct a case of an intention on the part of the President to violate the Constitution of the United States by anything which he did in reference to the appointment of General Thomas, provided that the order to Mr. Stanton was a lawful order, and he was bound to obey it.

I advance now, Senators, to a different class of articles, which may be called the conspiracy articles, because they rest upon a charge of a conspiracy between the President and General Thomas.

There are four of them.

The fourth, fifth, sixth and seventh in number as they stand. The fourth and sixth are found under the act of July 31, 1861, which is found in the 12th vol. of Statutes at Large, page 286. The fifth and seventh are found under no act of Congress. They allege an unlawful conspiracy, but they refer to no law by which the acts charged are made unlawful. The acts charged are called unlawful, but there is no law referred to, and no case made by the articles within any law of the United States; and I therefore shall treat these articles, the fourth and sixth, and the fifth and seventh together, because I think they belong in that order. The fourth and sixth charge a conspiracy within the Conspiracy act.

It is necessary for me to state the substance of the law in order that you may see whether it can have any possible application to the case. It was passed on the 31st of July, 1861, and is entitled "an act to define and punish certain conspiracies." It enacts that if two or more persons within the States or Territories of the United States shall conspire together to overthrow, or put down, or destroy by force, the Government of the United States; or to levy war upon the United States; or to oppose by force the authority of the Government of the United States, or by force to prevent, hinder or delay the execution of any law of the United States; or by force to seize, take or possess any property of the United States, against the will and contrary to the authority of the United States; or by force, or intimidation, or threats to prevent any person from occupying or holding any office of trust or place of confidence under the United States—they shall be guilty of conspiracy.

The fourth and sixth articles contain allegations that the President and General Thomas conspired together, by force, intimidation and threats, to prevent Mr. Stanton from continuing to hold the office of Secretary for the Department of War, and also that they conspired together, by force, to obtain possession of property belonging to the United States. These are the two articles which I suppose are designed to be drawn under this act, and these are the allegations which are intended to be sustained by it. Now, it does seem to me that the power to wrest this law to any bearing whatsoever upon this case, is one of the most extraordinary attempts ever made.

In the first place, so far from its having been designed to apply to the President of the United States, or to any act which he might do in the course of the execution of what he believed to be his duty, or to apply to any man or anything in the District of Columbia at all, the words of the act are that, "If two or more persons within any State or Territory of the United States not within the District of Columbia" shall do so and so. Now this is a highly penal law, and an indictment charging things done under this law within the District of Columbia would, I undertake to say, be quashed on demurrer, because the act is made applicable to certain portions of the country, and is not made applicable to the District of Columbia. We are not, however, standing upon that point, which is a technical point, nor do I refer to it with any such intention, but let us see what is this case.

The President is of opinion that Mr. Stanton holds the office of Secretary for the Department of War at his pleasure. He thinks so, first, because Mr. Stanton is not provided for in the Tenure of Office act, and that no tenure of office is secured to him. He thinks so, second, because he believes that it would be judicially decided, if the question could be raised, that the law depriving him of the power of removing an officer at his pleasure, is not a constitutional law. He is of opinion that in this case he can not allow this officer to continue to act as his adviser and his agent to execute the laws. If he has the lawful power to remove him, under those circumstances, he gives this order to General Thomas.

Now I do not view this as a purely military order. The service there invoked was a civil service, but at the same time Senators will observe, that the person who gave the order is Commander-in-Chief of the Army. The person to whom the order was given is the Adjutant-General of the Army. That the subject-matter of the order relates to the performance of service essential to carry on the military service, and therefore when such an order was given by the Commander-in-Chief to the Adjutant-General respecting a subject of this kind, is it too much to say that there was invoked that spirit of military obedience which constitutes the strength of the service?

I do not mean to say that it was a mere military order, or that General Thomas would have been subject to court-martial for disobeying it, but I do say that the Adjutant-General of the Army of the United States was, in the interest of the service, bound to accept the appointment, unless he saw or knew that it was unlawful. I do not know how the fact is, certainly there is no proof on the subject, but when the distinguished General of the Army of the United States, on a previous occasion, accepted a similar appointment, it was under views of propriety and duty, such as those which I have now alluded to; and how and why is it to be attributed to General Thomas that he was guilty of designing to overthrow the laws of the country, when he simply did what the General of the Army had done before?

Take a case in private life, if you please, and put it as strongly as you please, in order to test the question of conspiracy; suppose one of you had a claim which he considers to be a just and legal claim to property, and he says to A B, go to C D, who is in possession of this property, and deliver to him this order to get possession of the property from him, would anybody ever imagine that that was a conspiracy? Does not every lawyer know that the moment you introduce any transaction of this kind, the element of a claim, if right, every criminal intention ceases.

This was a case of public duty, of public right; claimed upon constitutional grounds and upon an interpretation of the law which had been given to it by the law-makers themselves. How then, I again ask, can the President of the United States, under such circumstances, be looked upon by anybody as guilty of conspiracy under this act. These articles say that the conspiracy between the President and General Thomas was to employ force, threats and intimidations. What they prove against the President is that he issued this order. They prove that and that alone.

Now, in the face of these orders, there is no apology for the assertion that it was the design of the President that anybody, at any time, should use force, threats, or intimidation. The order is to Mr. Stanton to deliver up possession; the order is to General Thomas to receive possession from Mr. Stanton when delivered up. No force is assigned to him; no authority is given him to apply force in any direction whatever; there is not only no express authority, but there is no implication of authority to apply for or obtain or use anything but the order which was given to him; and we shall offer proof that the President, from the first, had indicated simply a desire to test the question by law, and this was the whole of it.

We shall show you what advice the President received on this subject; what views he entertained; what views his counsel and advisers entertained. But, of course, it is not my province now to comment upon the evidence. The evidence must be first adduced, and then it will be time to comment upon it. The other two conspiracy articles will require very little observation from me, because they make no new allegations of facts which are not in the fourth and sixth articles, to which I at first adverted, the only distinction between them and the others being that they are not founded upon the Conspiracy act of 1861. They simply allege an unlawful conspiracy, and leave the matter there. They do not allege sufficient facts to bring the case within the act of 1861. In other words, they do not allege force, threats or intimidation.

I shall detain the Senate for a few moments on the ninth article, which is the one relating to the conversation with General Emory. The meaning of that article as I read it is, that the President brought General Thomas before himself as Commander-in-Chief of the Army, for the purpose of instructing him to destroy the law, with an intent to induce General Emory to disobey, and with an intent to enable himself unlawfully, and by the use of military force, through General Emory, to prevent Mr. Stanton from continuing to hold the office. Now, I submit that not only does this article fail of proof in its substance as thus stated, but that it is disproved by the witness, who has been introduced to prove it.

In the first place, it appears clear, from General Emory's statement, that the President did not bring him there for any purpose connected with the Reconstruction bill, affecting the command of the army, or the issuing of orders relating to the army. It is a subject which General Emory introduced himself, and when the conversation was broken off he again recurred to it himself, asking the President's permission to bring it to his attention. Whatsoever was said on that subject was not because the President of the United States had brought the commander of troops in Washington there for that purpose, but because having brought him there for another purpose, the commanding general introduced the subject, and conversed upon it, and gave the President his views.

In the next place, having had his attention called to the act of Congress, and the order under it, the President expressed personally the same opinion to General Emory as he had previously publicly expressed to Congress itself, at the time when the act was signed by him. It is found in his answer on the thirty-second page of the official report of these proceedings what that opinion was. He considered that that provision of the law interfered with his constitutional right as the Commander-in-Chief of the Army, and that is what he said to General Emory. There is not even a probable cause to believe that he said it for any other than the natural and evident reason that Gen. Emory had introduced the subject. He asked leave to call the President's attention to it, evidently expecting and desiring that the President should say something on the subject, and if he said anything was he not to say the truth?

That is exactly what he did say. I mean the truth as he approved it. It will appear, in proof, as I am instructed, that the reason why the President sent for General Emory was not that he might endeavor to seduce that distinguished officer from his allegiance to the laws and Constitution of the country, but because he wished to obtain information about military movements which he was informed, on authority on which he had a right to rely, and which he was bound to respect, might require his personal attention. I pass, then, from the article as being one on which I ought not to detain Senators, and I come to the last one—concerning which I shall have much to say—and that is the tenth article, which is of and concerning the speeches. In the front of this inquiry the question presents itself. What constitutes an offense against the Constitution of the United States? On this question dissertations have been written and printed. One of them is annexed to the argument of the honorable manager who opened this case for the prosecution, and another was written by one of the honorable managers on the proceedings in the House of Representatives on the occasion of the first attempt to impeach the President, and there have been others written and published by learned parties touching this subject.

I do not propose to detain the Senate with any of these precedents drawn from the middle ages.

The framers of our Constitution were equally as familiar with them as the persons who drew up these dissertations, and the framers of our Constitution, as I conceive, had drawn from them a lesson which they embodied in their work, and I propose therefore, instead of the research from the precedents, which were made in the times of the Plantagenets, the Tudors, and the Stuarts, and which have been repeated since to come, much nearer home, and see what the provisions of the Constitution of the United States are bearing upon this question.

My first proposition is that when the Constitution speaks of treason and bribery, and other high crimes and misdemeanors, it refers to and includes only high criminal offenses against the United States—against some law of the United States existing when the acts complained of were committed—and I say that that is plainly to be inferred from each and every provision of the Constitution on the subject. Nobody will deny that treason and bribery are high crimes against the United States, made such by the laws of the United States, and which the framers of the Constitution knew must be provided for in the laws, because these are high crimes which strike at the existence of the government.

Now, what is meant by "other high crimes and misdemeanors?" *Noscitur a sociis.* They are high crimes and misdemeanors, so high that they belong in the same company with treason and bribery. That is clear in the face of the Constitution. There can be no crime, no misdemeanor, without a law of some kind, written or unwritten, expressed or implied. There must be some law, otherwise there is no crime. My impression of it is that high crimes and misdemeanors mean offenses against the laws of the United States.

Let me see if the Constitution has not in substance stated so. The first clause of the second section of the second article of the Constitution says that the President shall have power to grant reprieves and pardons for offenses against the United States, except in cases of impeachment. Offenses against it would include cases of impeachment, and might be pardoned by the President if they were not excepted by the Constitution. These cases of impeachment, according to the expressed declaration of the Constitution itself, are cases of offense against the United States. Still the learned manager says that this is a court, and that whatever may be the character of the prosecution, it is bound by no law. What, then, was the understanding of the fathers on this subject?

Mr. BUTLER—Pardon me, sir. I said bound by no common or statute law.

Mr. CURTIS proceeded to read some authorities from law books, and then said:—Another position to which I desire the attention of the Senate, is that there is enough written in the Constitution to prove that this is a court in which a trial is now being carried on. The Senate of the United States, says the Constitution, shall have the sole power to try all impeachments. Where the President is tried the Chief justice shall preside. It also provides that the trial of all crimes, except in cases of impeachment, shall be by a jury. This, then, is the trial of a crime. You are the triers, presided over by the Chief Justice of the United States, and on the express word of the Constitution.

There is also, according to its express word, to be an acquittal or conviction on this trial for a crime. No person shall be convicted on impeachment without the concurrence of two-thirds of the members present. There is also to be a judgment in case there shall be a conviction. A judgment in case of a conviction shall not extend further than removal from office, and disqualification to hold any office of honor, trust or profit under the United States.

Here, then, there is to be a trial of a crime—a trial by a tribunal designated by the Constitution, in the place of a court and jury. There is to be a conviction if guilt is proved, a judgment on that conviction, and a punishment inflicted by the judgment of the court, and this, too, by the express term of the Constitution.

I say, then, that it is impossible to come to the conclusion that the Constitution of the United States has not designated impeachment offenses as offenses against the United States. It has provided for the trial of these offenses; it has established a tribunal for the purpose of trying them; it has directed the tribunal, in case of conviction, to pronounce a judgment and to inflict a punishment, and yet the honorable manager tells us that this is not a court, and that it is bound by no law. But the argument does not rest mainly, I think, on the provisions of the Constitution, or the direct subject of impeachment.

It is, at any rate, vastly strengthened by the additional prohibition that Congress shall pass no bill of attainder or *ex post facto* law. According to that prohibition of the Constitution, if every member of this body, sitting in a legislative capacity, and if every member of the other House, also sitting in a legislative capacity, should unite in passing an act to punish an offense after it was committed, that law would be of no account. Yet what is here claimed by the honorable manager on behalf of the House of Representatives?

It is claimed that, as Congress can make a law to punish those acts, if no law existed at the time they were committed, the members of the Senate may, sitting here as judges, not only after the fact, but when the case is brought to trial, create, each individual for himself, a law on the subject. The claim on the part of the honorable manager would clothe each of you with imperial power. It would enable you to say, *sic volo, sic jubeo stat pro ratione voluntas*—I make a law unto myself, by which law I propose to govern others. Each one of you has taken an oath that he will administer justice impartially in this case, according to the Constitution and the laws; but according to the view of the honorable manager, that oath would mean according to such laws as the individual Senator might himself make for his own government,

I respectfully submit that this view cannot consistently and properly be taken of the nature of this trial, or of the duties and powers incumbent on this body. Look for a moment, if you please, at the other provision of the Constitution, that Congress shall not pass a bill of attainder. What is a bill of attainder? It is a law made by Parliament to apply to facts already existing, and where every legislator is to use the phrase of the honorable manager, a law unto himself, and is to act according to his discretion. Is this view what is proper and politic under the circumstances. Of what use would be prohibition in the Constitution against passing bills of attainder if it is only necessary for the House of Representatives, by a majority, to vote articles of impeachment, and for two-thirds of the Senate to sustain these articles? An act of attainder is thus effected by the same process, and depends on identically the same principles as a bill of attainder in the English Parliament. It is the individual wills of the legislators, instead of the conscientious discharge of the duty of the judges. I submit, then, Senators, that this view of the duties and powers of this body cannot be entertained; but the attempt made by the honorable managers to obtain conviction on this tenth article is admitted with so much peculiarity that I think it is the duty of the counsel for the President to advert to it. The first eight articles are framed upon the allegation that the President broke a law. I suppose the honorable manager did not intend to carry this so far as to say that unless you find that the President did intentionally break a law, those articles are sustained; therefore, there must be a law, and the very gist of the charge is, that he broke a law. You must find that a law existed—you must construe it and apply it to this case; you must find a criminal intention on his part to break a law, before he can be found guilty on these articles. But when we come to this tenth article, we find that it stands on no law at all, but is attended with some extraordinary peculiarities.

The complaint is that the President made speeches against Congress. The true statement could be much more restricted than that; for, although in those speeches the President used the word "Congress," undoubtedly he did not mean the entire constitutional body, organized under the Constitution of the United States. He meant the dominant majority. Everybody so understood it; everybody must have so understood it. But the complaint is that he made speeches against this whole government, against Congress. Well, who are the grand jurors in this case? One of the parties, the complainants. And who are triers? The other complainant.

Now, I think there is some incongruity in this. I think there is some reason for pausing before taking any further strides in this direction. The honorable House of Representatives send the managers here to take notice of what? That the House of Reprentatives has erected itself into a school of manners and, selecting from its ranks these gentlemen, whom it deems most competent, by precept and example, to teach decorum of speech, it desires the judgment of this body as to whether the President of the United States has not been guilty of indecorum; whether he has spoken improperly, for that is the phrase of the honorable managers.

Now, there used to be an old-fashioned notion that there ought to be a difference of opinion about speeches that a very important test in reference to them was whether they were true or false—whether what was said was true or false, but it seems that in this case that is no test at all. The honorable manager (Mr. Butler), in opening the case, finding, I suppose, that it was necessary in some manner to advert to this subject, has done it in these terms. The words are not alleged to be either false or defamatory, because it is not within the power of any man, however high his official position in effect, to stand in the Congress of the United States, in the ordinary sense of that word, so as to call upon Congress to answer as to the truth of the accusation.

Considering the nature of our government; considering the experience which we have gone through on that subject, that is a pretty lofty claim. If you go back to the time of the Plantagenets and seek for precedents there, you will not find that so lofty a claim as that was made. I beg leave to read from two statutes, one from III Edward, chap. 1, 34, and the other from II Richard, chap. 2, 1. The statute of Edward the First, after a preamble, enacts that "from henceforth no one be so hardy to tell or publish any false news or tales whereby discord or occasion of discord or slander may grow between the King and his people, or the great men of the realm, and he that doeth shall be taken and kept in till he he shall have been brought into court. The statute of Richard II refers to "dealers" in false news and in horrible and false lies against dukes, princes, earls and other nobles and great men of the realm, and also the chancellor, treasurer, clerk of the privy seals, the judges and other great officers of the realm, so that the Senators will see, even in those distant times, those high officers and bodies were not safe against horrible and false lies. And it will be remembered that in the course of our own experience, during the war with France, and under the Administration of Mr. Adams, an attempt was made to check, not freedom of speech, but freedom of writing—an attempt which is stamped in the opinion of posterity with the name of the Sedition law.

Senators will find that although it applied only to written libels, it contained an express section that the truth of the libel might be given in evidence. That was a law, as Senators know, making it penal, by written publications, to excite hatred or contempt of the government or of Congress. I will read the second section. It enacts that if any person shall write, print, utter or publish, or shall cause or procure to be written, uttered or published, or shall knowingly and willingly assist or aid in writing, printing, uttering, or publishing any false, scandalous writing against the Government of the United States, or either House of the Congress of the United States, or the President of the United States, with intent to defame the said government, or either House of said Congress, or the said President, or to bring them, or either of them, into contempt or disrepute, or to excite against them, or either of them, the hatred of the good people of the United States, or to start up sedition within the United States, or to incite unlawful combination therein, etc., etc.

The third section enacts that if any person shall be prosecuted under this act for the printing or publishing of any libel, it shall be lawful for the defendant, on the trial of the case, to give, in evidence on his defense, the truth of the matter contained in the published charge, and that the jury who shall try the case shall have the right to determine the law and the facts, under the direction of the court, as in other cases.

I desire now to read from the fourth volume of Madison's works, pages 542-547, a short passage, which, in my judgment, is as masterly as anything which Mr. Madison ever wrote on the subject of the relations of the Congress of the United States in contrast with the relations of the Government of Great Britain and the people of that island. The essential difference between the British Government and the American Constitution will place this subject in the clearest light in the British Government.

The danger of encroachments on the rights of the people is understood to be confined to the Executive magistrate. The representatives of the people in the Legislature are not only exempt themselves from distrust, but are considered as sufficient guardians of the rights of their constituents against the danger from the Executive. Hence, it is a principle that the Parliament is unlimited in its power, or, in their own language, is omnipotent; hence, too, all the ramparts for protecting the rights of the people, such as their Magna Charta, their bill of rights, &c., are not reared against the royal prerogative.

They are merely legislative precautions against Executive usurpations. Under such a government as this, an exemption of the press from previous restraint, by licenses appointed by the king, is all the freedom that can be secured to it. In the United States the case is altogether different. The people, not the government, possess the absolute sovereignty. The Legislature, no less than the Executive, is under limitations of power. Encroachments are regarded as possible from the one as well as from the other; hence, in the United States, the great and essential rights of the people are secured against legislative as well as against Executive ambition.

They are secured not by laws paramount to a prerogative, but by constitutions paramount to laws. This security of the freedom of the press requires that it should be exempt not only from previous restraint from the Executive, but from legislative restraint also; and this exemption to be effectual must be an exemption not only from the previous inspection of licensers, but from the subsequent penalty of laws.

The next passage which I shall read, from page 547 of the same volume, has an extraordinary application to the subject-matter now before us. It is as follows:—"The Constitution supposes that the President, the Congress and each of its houses, may not discharge their trusts either from defect of judgment or other causes. Hence they are all made responsible to their constituents at the returning periods of election, and the President, who is singly intrusted with very great powers, is, as a further guard, subjected to an intermediate impeachment.

"Second. Should it happen, as the Constitution supposes it may happen, that either of these branches of the government may not have duly discharged its trust, it is natural and proper that according to the cause and degree of their faults they should be brought into contempt or dispute, and incur the hatred of the people.

"Third. Whether it has in any case happened that the proceedings of either or all of those franchises evince such a violation of duty as to justify a contempt, a disrepute, or hatred among the people, can only be determined by a free examination thereof, and a free communication among the people thereon.

"Fourth. Whenever it may have actually happened that proceedings of this sort are chargable on all or either of the branches of the government it is the duty, as well as the right of intelligent and faithful citizens, to discuss and promulgate them freely, as well as to control them by the censorship of the public opinion, as to promote a remedy, according to the rules of the Constitution; and it cannot be avoided, that those who are to apply the remedy must feel in some degree a contempt or hatred against the transgressing party."

These observations of Mr. Madison were made in reference to the freedom of the press. There were two views entertained at the time when the Sedition laws were passed concerning the powers of Congress on that subject. One view was that when the Constitution spoke of the freedom of the press, it referred to the common law definition to ascertain what that freedom might be. That was the feeling in part which Mr. Madison was controverting in one of the passages which I have read.

The other view was, that the common law definition

should not be followed, and that the freedom provided for by the Constitution, so far as the action of Congress was concerned, was an absolute freedom; but no one ever imagined that freedom of speech, in contradistinction to written libel, could be constrained by law of Congress, for whether you treated the prohibition in the Constitution as absolute in itself, or whether you refer to the common law for the definition of its limits and meaning, the result will be the same.

Under the common law no man was ever punished criminally for spoken words. If he slander his neighbor he must make good the injury to his neighbor in damages, but there is no such thing at common law as an indictment for spoken words; so that this prohibition in the Constitution against any legislation by Congress, in restraint of the freedom of speech, is necessarily an absolute prohibition. Therefore this is a case not only where there is no law made prior to the act to punish the act, but it is a case where Congress is expressly prohibited from making any law to operate on the future.

What is the law to be? Is it to be derived, as the manager imagined it should be, from the will or sense of propriety or expediency of each Senator? The only rule, he says, which can be properly applied is, that we must require the speaker to speak properly. Now, who are to be the judges whether he speaks properly? In this case they are to be the Senate of the United States, on presentation of the House of Representatives of the United States, and that is supposed to be the freedom of the speech secured by the absolute prohibition of the Constitution.

That is the same freedom of speech, Senators, in consequence of which thousands of men were brought to the scaffold under Tudors and Stuarts. That is the same freedom of speech which caused thousands of heads of men and women to fall from the guillotine in France. That is the same freedom of speech which has caused in our day more than once "order to reign in Warsaw." Is that the freedom of speech intended to be secured by our Constitution, that a man must speak properly in the opinion of his judges?

Mr. Chief Justice and Senators, I will detain you but a very short time with a few observations concerning the eleventh article. They will be very few, for the reason that the eleventh article, as I understand it, contains nothing new that needs notice from me. It appears by the official copy of the articles, which is before us, that the tenth and eleventh articles were drafted at a later period than the preceding nine articles. I suppose that the honorable managers, looking over the work they had already performed, and not feeling perfectly satisfied to leave the matter in the shape in which it then stood, came to the conclusion to adopt this eleventh article, and they have compounded it out of the materials which they had previously worked up into others.

In the first place they said:—Here are speeches, we must have something about them. Accordingly they begin with the allegation that the President, at the Executive Mansion, on a certain occasion, made a speech, and without giving his words, they attribute to him a certain intention to declare that this was not a Congress within the meaning of the Constitution. All of which is denied in his answer, and there is no proof to support the allegation. The President, by his whole course of conduct, has shown that he could entertain no such intention. He has sustained that fully in the answer, and I do not think it necessary to go into it here.

Then they come to the old subject of the removal of Mr. Stanton. They say that the President made this speech denying the competency of Congress to legislate with an intent, and following up his intent, endeavored to remove Mr. Stanton. I have frequently discussed that, and I will not weary the attention of the Senate by doing so any further. Then they say that he made this speech and followed up its intent by endeavoring to get possession of the money appropriated for the military service of the United States. On that too, I have said all that I desire to say.

Then they say he made it with the intent to obstruct what is called the law for the better government of the Rebel States, passed March 2, 1867, and in support of that they have offered a telegram from Governor Parsons to him, and an answer to that telegram, from the President, on the subject of an amendment to the Constitution of the United States, which telegrams were sent in January, before the March when this law came into existence; and, so far as I know, this is the only proof they have offered on this subject.

I leave, therefore, with this remark, that article to the consideration of the Senate of the United States; it must be unnecessary for me to say anything concerning the importance of this case, not only now, but in the future; it must be apparent to any one in any way concerned in or connected with this trial, that it is and will be, the most conspicuous instance that ever has been or can ever be expected to be found of American justice or of American injustice; of that justice which Mr. Burke says is the great policy of all civilized States; of that injustice which is certain to be condemned, which makes even the wisest man mad, and which, in the fixed and unalterable order of God's providence, is sure to return to plague the inventor.

Mr. Curtis here resumed his seat, and the Senate, at 2·30, took a recess for fifteen minutes.

After the recess Major-General L. Thomas was called, and took the stand in military costume. He spoke very fluently and readily, but at the same time with indistinctness, so that the following report of his testimony is imperfect in many instances:—

Q. By Mr. STANBERY. General Thomas, will you state how long you have been in the service? The answer, which was lengthy, was inaudible in the gallery, save the concluding words:—"And have been in the army since that date."

Q. What is your present rank? A. I am brigadier-general—major-general by brevet.

Q. What date does your brevet bear? A. I really forget.

Q. Do you recollect the year? A. It was after I returned from one of my southern trips in 1863.

Q. During the war? A. Yes, sir; towards the close of it.

Q. When were you first appointed Adjutant-General? A. The 7th of March, 1867.

Q. On what service were you during the war generally? Give us an idea of your service? A. During the organization of the War Department by Mr. Cameron I was nominated as Adjutant-General; I accompanied him on his Western tour to Missouri and Kentucky; he then returned, and after making the report he left and Mr. Stanton was appointed; I remained in the Department some time after Mr. Stanton was appointed; the first duty, I think, he placed me on from the office, that is, one of the duties, he sent me down on James river to make an exchange of prisoners of war, under the arrangement made by General Dix.

Mr. BUTLER—What is the object of that?

Mr. STANBERY—To bring round the reasons why there was an interruption in the Adjutant-General's position.

Q. What was the next service? A. I went twice or three times to Harrisburg to organize volunteers and to correct some erroneous—not erroneous exactly—but in order to put skeleton regiments together—once to Philadelphia and twice to Harrisburg; I was sent to Harrisburg also at the time that Lee was invading Maryland and Pennsylvania; afterwards I was sent down on the Mississippi river.

Q. What was your duty there? A. My duty was threefold:—First, to inspect the army in that part of the country. Second—

Mr. BUTLER—Would not that appear better by the order?

Witness—I have it.

Mr. STANBERY suggested that such a course would tend to delay.

Mr. BUTLER—Very well; we don't want to spend time.

Q. By Mr. STANBERY—What was your other duty? A. To take charge of negro regiments and organize them.

Q. Were you the first officer who organized those negro regiments? A. No, sir.

Q. Who was prior to you? A. I think General Butler organized them before me.

Q. What number of regiments were organized under your care? A. I organized upwards of eighty thousand colored men; the particular number of regiments I don't recollect.

Q. After this service was performed, what was the next special duty you were detailed on? A. I returned when I heard of the surrender of Lee; I then came to Washington; the next duty I entered upon was to make an inspection of the Provost Marshal-General's office throughout the country—first at Washington, and then at other cities.

Q. What next? A. Then I was ordered to my last service; I was ordered throughout the United States to examine the national cemeteries, under the law passed by Congress; that duty I have performed, but my report is not yet in; it is very voluminous.

Q. These duties fall under your proper duties as Adjutant-General? A. Perfectly, and as inspector of the army.

Q. This last duty, the inspection of the cemeteries, was the last special duty you have been called upon to perform? A. Yes, sir.

Q. When did you return from having performed that last special duty? A. I came to Washington on three different occasions the last time.

Q. When your last service was performed—the last detail upon the national cemeteries—when did you return from that duty? A. I don't think I am able to state the day, but it was towards the close of that year.

Q. You say you had then completed this last detail or duty? A. Yes, sir; I had visited every State where cemeteries were made; there are only one or two small ones I have not visited.

Q. You were then ready to make your report? A. Yes, sir; I am ready now, and had it not been for interruptions of this sort I should have made it.

Q. You have not since been detailed upon any other special service except about the War Department? A. No, sir; I was returned to the office.

Q. At what time were you returned to your Adjutant-General's office? A. The President gave me a note to General Grant, dated 11th of February, and I received a note from General Grant; I think it was on the 13th.

Q. Who had occupied your office during your absence? A. General Townsend, the Assistant Adjutant-General, with the rank of colonel.

Q. Then you never lost your rank as Adjutant-General? A. No, sir. I spoke to the President about a month ago, stating that when I got through with this business, I would like to have charge of my office.

Mr. BUTLER—I wish to object to any conversation between this person and the President.

Mr. STANBERY—This is simply his application to the President to restore him to his duties.

Q. You applied once or twice for restoration? A. Yes, sir.

Q. On the 13th of April you received the order which you requested? A. It was not a note to me but to General Grant.

Q. To restore you to your position? A. Yes, sir.

Q. When after that, did you see the President, and what did he say to you? Or did you see him between that time

IMPEACHMENT OF ANDREW JOHNSON. 113

and the time you received your order on the 21st? A. Yes, sir; on one occasion I went over to tender my resignation.

Q. After you had been restored to your office? A. Yes, sir; the resignation Mr. Stanton gave me.

Q. Was that the first time he spoke to you about taking possession of the War Office?

Mr. BUTLER—I object to that as leading, grossly leading.

Q. Was that the first time that he spoke, assuming that he had spoken?

Mr. STANBERY—We will come to it in another way.

Q. Do you recollect what occurred on the 21st of February? A. Yes, sir; I thought your question was anterior to that.

Q. It was. What happened at the War Office on the 21st of February in regard to closing the office on the succeding day, the 22d? A. About twelve o'clock I went up myself, and asked Mr. Stanton, then Secretary of War, if I should close the office the next day, the 22d of February. He directed me to do it, and I sent a circular round to the different departments.

Q. Was not that order made my you as Adjutant-General? A. Yes, sir, by his order.

Q. Was that before you had seen the President that day? A. Yes, sir.

Q. What took place after you had issued that order? A. Very soon after I issued it, I received a note from Col. Moore, Private Secretary of the President, that the President wished to see me; I immediately went over to the White House; saw the President; he came out of his library; he had two communications in his hand.

Q. He came out with two papers in his hand? A. Yes, sir; he handed them to Colonel Moore to read; they were read to me; one was addressed to Mr. Stanton dismissing him from office, and directing him to turn over to me the books, papers, &c., pertaining to the War Department; the other was addressed to myself, appointing me Secretary of War ad interim, and stating that Mr. Stanton had been directed to transfer his office to me.

Q. Was that the first time you saw those papers or either of them? A. The first time.

Q. You had no hand at all in writing those papers or dictating them? A. Nothing whatever.

Mr. BUTLER—That is rather leading again.

Mr. STANBERY—What was said by the President at that time to you, or by you to the President?

Mr. BUTLER—A single word, sir. Do you propose to put in evidence a conversation with the President?

Mr. STANBERY—I do.

Mr. BUTLER—Between this party and the President?

Mr. STANBERY—I do. It was at the time the letters were handed him by the President.

Mr. BUTLER—I have no objections.

Mr. STANBERY—What did he say? A. He said he was determined to support the Constitution and the laws; he desired me to do the same; (great laughter); I told him I would; (laughter).

Q. What further took place? A. He then directed me to deliver this paper, addressed to Mr. Stanton, to him.

Q. Did you then leave? A. Then I told him that I was going to take somebody out of my department with me to see that I had delivered them; and I stated that I would take General Williams, Assistant Adjutant-General in my department.

Q. You told the President you would take him along to witness the transaction? A. Yes, sir.

Q. What did you do then? A. I then went over to the War Department and went into one of my rooms and told General Williams I wished him to go with me; I did not tell him for what purpose; I did not tell him what for, but I told him to note what occurred; I then went to the Secretary's room and handed him the first paper, which was that, "the paper addressed to him—"

Q. What took place then; did he read it? A. He got up and said, "good morning." and I handed him that paper and he put it down on the corner of his table and sat down, and presently he took it up and read it. He said, "do you wish me to vacate the office at once, or will you give me time to get my private property together?" I said, "act your pleasure."

Q. Did he say what time he would require? A. No, sir; I didn't ask him; I then handed him the paper addressed to me, which he read; he asked me to give him a copy.

Q. What did you say? A. In the meantime General Grant came in, and I handed it to him; he asked if it was for him; I said no, merely for his information; then I went down to my own room.

Q. It is below that of the Secretary? A. Below General Schriver's room.

Q. On the lower floor? A. Yes, sir; a copy was made which I certified as Secretary of War, ad interim. (Laughter). I took that up and handed it to him; he then said—"I don't know whether I will obey your instructions;" he stood there; nothing more passed, and I left.

Q. Was General Grant there at the second interview? A. No, sir.

Q. Did General Williams go up with you the second time? A. No, sir.

Q. What time of the day was this? A. I think it was about twelve when I went to see the Secretary, and after that I came down to the President, about one o'clock, I suppose.

Q. Immediately after you had written the order to close the office? A. Yes, sir.

Q. Was that all that occurred between you and the Secretary on the 21st? A. I think it was; oh, no! no; I was thinking of the 22d.

Q. What followed? A. I went into the other room, and

I said that I should issue orders as Secretary of War; he said that I should not, or that he would countermand them, and he turned round to Generals Schriver and Townsend, who were in the room, and directed them not to obey my orders as Secretary of War.

Q. Was that on the 21st or 22d? A. The 22d; he wrote a note and handed it to me.

Q. Have you got that note? A. I gave it to you, I think; (Witness searches his pockets); the note was dated the 21st.

Mr. STANBERY produces a paper. Q. See if that is the paper. A. That is it, sir; the body of it is not in Mr. Stanton's handwriting; he took it out to General Townsend, a copy was made, and Mr. Stanton signed it and handed it to me.

Q. Will you read it, if you please?

Mr. BUTLER said, "Wait a moment if you please." But so rapid was the witness that he had read the date, &c., and had got as far as "Sir" before the hon. manager could stop him, amid general laughter.

After examination, Mr. BUTLER made no objection, and the witness read the letter dated February 21, commanding him to abstain from issuing any order other than in his capacity as Adjutant-General of the Army, signed by Edwin M. Stanton, Secretary of War.

Q. Did you see the President after that interview? A. I did.

Q. What took place?

Mr. BUTLER——Stop a moment; I object now, Mr. President and Senators, to the conversation between the President and General Thomas after this time. I would not object, as you will observe, to any orders or directions which the President gave or any conversation had between the President and General Thomas at the time of issuing the commission; but now the commission has been issued, the demand has been made, it has been refused; the peremptory order to General Thomas, to mind his own business and to keep out of the War Office, has been put in evidence.

Now, suppose the President by talking to General Thomas, or General Thomas by talking to the President, confirms his own declarations for the purpose of making evidence in favor of himself. The Senate has already ruled by solemn vote, in consequence, I believe, of a dicision of the presiding officer, that there was such evidence of criminal intent between these parties as to allow us to put in the acts of either to bear on the other, but I challenge any authority, that can be shown anywhere, that where we are trying a man for an act before any tribunal, whether a judicial court or any other body of trial, I challenge anybody, I say, to show that testimony can be given of what the respondent said in his own behalf, especially to his servant, or a fortiori to his co-conspirators, the conspiracy being presumed. Can it be that the President can call up any officer of the army, and, by talking to him after the act he has done, justify the act? The act that we complain of, was the removal of Stanton, and the appointment of Thomas, that has been done—that is, if he can be removed at all.

I understand the argument, just presented to us by the learned counsel to be that, "even after having delivered his argument," there was no removal at all, and no appointment at all. If that is the case, there has not been anything at all done, and we may as well stop here. But the point of his argument, to wit., that the only power of removal remained in the President, or in the President and the Senate. If that be true, then all that it wanted to be quite right depended on Mr. Stanton's legs in walking out, because everything had been done but that.

We insist that there was a removal; that there was an appointment, and that is the act which is being inquired about, whatever the character of that act is, be it better or worse. But after that act I say that General Thomas cannot make evidence by talking to the President, nor can the President by talking to Thomas.

Even suppose that the act was as innocent a thing as a conspiracy to get up a lawsuit, then, after the conspiracy had taken place, and had eventuated in the act they could not put in their declarations. There is not much evidence of such a conspiracy, because I suppose if the President conspired with anybody to get up a lawsuit, he conspired with his Attorney-General, and not with his Adjutant-General.

But even a thing so innocent as that could not, after it was done, have been ameliorated, the time altered or changed by the declarations of the parties, one for the other; therefore, a limine, I must object, and I need not go any further now than objecting to any evidence of what the President says, which is not a part of the thing done, a part of the "resgestæ," or any conversation which took place after the act took place.

Mr. STANBERY—Mr. Chief Justice, if I understand the case, the gentleman supposes it to be now the whole case depends on the removal of Stanton.

Mr. BUTLER—I have not said any such thing; I don't know what you understand.

Mr. STANBERY—You say it stands between Stanton's commission and the order for his removal, and does your understanding stop there? Does your case stop there? I agree that your case stops with the order, because I agree with the view taken by the honorable manager that that did, in fact, remove Stanton. If it did, it was a law that gave it that effect.

There is no question about a removal, merely, in effect – no question about an ouster by force here, but a question about a legal removal. I understand the manager to say that that order, in his judgment, effected a legal removal, and it was not necessary for Mr. Stanton's legs to remove him out of office. He was already out. If Stanton is out by the order, then it must be a legal order, making a legal removal, not a forcible illegal ouster.

But, says the learned manager, the transaction ended in giving the order and receiving the order. You are to have no testimony of what was said by the President or General Thomas, except of what was said just then, because that was the transaction—that was the *resgestæ*. Does the learned gentleman forget his testimony?—does he forget how he attempted to make a case?—does he forget what took place on all the evidence between the President and General Thomas?—not what we are going into, but what took place at night? Does he forget the sort of race against the President, not at the time when that order was given, not at the period of which we are now talking, but at night, under his conspiracy counts?

The gentleman has undertaken to give in evidence, that on the night of the 21st General Thomas declared that he was going to enter that office by force. That is the matter to which our evidence is now addressed; that the conspiracy between Thomas and the President should be executed by force, intimidation and threats; and to prove that, what has he got? The declarations of General Thomas not made under oath as we propose to have them made now, but his declarations not made under oath, when the President was present, and could contradict him.

He has gone into all that to make a case against the President, of this conspiracy, and not merely that, but on the 22d again, and as far back as the 9th of March, at the President's levee, brings a witness here with the eyes of all Maryland upon him.

Mr. BUTLER and Senator JOHNSON, simultaneously —Delaware.

He proves by that witness, or thinks he proves, that on that night, General Thomas also made a declaration involving the President as a party to a conspiracy to keep Mr. Stanton out of office.

Well, now, how are we to defend ourselves against these charges? How is the President ro defend himself against it but by calling General Thomas? Is General Thomas impeached here as a conspirator, so that his mouth is shut in regard to the transaction? Not at all. He is brought here as a witness. What better evidence can we have to contradict this conspiracy than one of the conspirators? For if Thomas did not conspire the President did not combine.

I wish to show that when he received that order he gave no orders and gave no instructions to use, and that at the subsequent day after Thomas returned and told him that Stanton refused to give up, that the President gave no directions and entered into no conspiracy; and that, consequently, on the night of the 21st, when General Thomas spoke of his own intentions he had no authority to speak for the President

Mr. BUTLER—I think I must have made myself very nearly understood if what I said has been fairly met or attempted to be met by the learned counsel. This is my objection—not that he shall not prove by General Thomas that he did not say what he did say to Mr. Burleigh. He will be a bold man to say that. He did not say it, however; not that they shall not prove that he did not say what he did say to Mr. Karsener, but the proposition I make is a legal proposition, and it has not been met or touched by the argument.

The counsel do not pretend to show that Gen. Thomas did not say to Mr. Burleigh:—"We are about to use force," by proving what was said between General Thomas and the President. We say that the President cannot put in his declaration, and I shall challenge a law-book—common, parliamentary, statutory or constitutional law, or a law unto yourselves—any law. We meet no such proposition.

Tell me of a case where, after we show that a man has done an act, which act is complained of, and where he is on trial for that act, can bring his servant or his co-conspirator and show what he said to him, in order to his justification. What thief could not defend himself by that means? Showing conversations the one for the other, and the other for the one, after the act was done.

Now it is said—and I hope this case will not be carried on by some little snapcatch of a word—that I said that there was a removal, and therefore I must have said that it was a legal removal. I say this—there never was a legal removal of Mr. Stanton. There was an act of removal, so far as the President of the United States could exercise the power—so far as he could do it—so far as he is criminally responsible for it—so far as he must be held to every intendment of the consequences of it as much as though Stanton had gone out in obedience to it; because, Mr. President, he is the Chief Executive, he has the army and navy, he has issued an order to an officer of the army to take possession.

But I am now upon this proposition—not that the President should ask General Thomas, "Sir do you conspire," and I will ask him in return, "Do you conspire with the President." Do you do this, or do you do that. But my proposition is that they cannot put in what the President said to General Thomas, and what General Thomas said to the President after he had given the order.

The learned counsel says:—Why, these gentlemen managers have put in what General Thomas said all along; we understand that so we can; and what the President said all along. It is the commonest thing in all courts of justice where I have seen cases tried, and where I have not—the books are one way—it is the commonest thing in the world to put in the conversation of a criminal made down to the day of trial, made the moment the officer brings him and puts him into the dock; but who ever heard of a case of bringing what he said to his accomplice after the act was done, be the act what it may.

It is said we must allow him to put this act in because

the President cannot defend himself otherwise. He has all the facts to defend himself. What I mean to say is that he shan't defend himself by word of mouth; I do not claim that the conspiracy was made between the 21st of February and the 7th of March. I claim that it was made before that time. I expect to be able before we get through to convince everybody else of it. I say I find certain testimony of it between these two dates, and I do not object to their asking General Thomas what he said to Mr. Burleigh, or what he said to anybody.

I have put in what he said about it, but as to putting in the President's declaration after the time, I do not want any more of these exceptions. We have simple orders given by the President to his subordinate. It is a very harmless thing, quite in the common course, given to him with a flourish of trumpets—"I want you to sustain the Constitution and the laws," and the officer says, "I shall sustain the Constitution and the laws." Don't we understand what that is? It is a declaration made for the purpose of evidence. Does he ever say to any officer as he commissions him, "Now, I want you to sustain the Constitution and the laws," and then solemnly that officer says, "I will sustain the Constitution and the laws."

Why was it done in this case? Done for the purpose of blinding whatever court that should try the case, in order that it might be put in as an exemplification. Oh, I don't mean to do anything but to sustain the Constitution and the laws, and I said so at the time. Put him out of the usual and ordinary course of things, and it is to prove any number of these declarations, got up and manufactured by this criminal at the time when he was going to commit the crime; and after the crime was committed, then to give him the opportunity of manufacturing testimony, never was heard of in any court of justice.

Mr. EVARTS—Mr. Chief Justice, if the crime, as it is called, of the President of the United States, was complete when this written order was handed by him to General Thomas, and received by General Thomas, why have the managers occupied your attention with other and later proceedings, in this belief. In the removal of Mr. Stanton, the first, the only act in regard to that removal which the managers introduce, was of the twenty-second, and the presentation of General Thomas, there and then, with the purpose, as it was said, of forcibly ejecting Mr. Stanton from the office of Secretary of War.

That is the act; that is the fact; that is the *resgestæ* on which they stand, and it was by the combination of the Delegate from Dacota invited to attend and take part in that act that the force was sought to be brought into this case of the intention of the President of the United States, and then the evidence connecting the intention of the President of the United States with this act. This fact, this *resgestæ* of the 22d, was drawn from the hearsay evidence of what General Thomas had said and by pledge of the managers that they would convict the President with it. And now, in the presence of this court of justice, and in the Senate of the United States, the managers of the House of Representatives, speaking in the name of all the people of the United States, say that when we seek to show what did occur between the President and General Thomas, up to the time of the only act and fact, they introduce by hearsay evidence of General Thomas' statements of what he meant to do.

They have sought to implicate the President in the intent to cause force to be used, by the pledge that they would connect the President with it. And we offer the evidence that we said in the first instance should have been brought here, under oath of this agent or actor himself, to prove in what connection the President was, when it has been let in as secondary evidence; and we are undertaking to show by the oath of the actor, the agent, the officer, what really occurred between the President of the United States and himself. They say that is of no consequence; that is no part of the *res gestæ*; that is no part of the evidence showing what the relation between the parties was.

Why, Mr. Chief Justice and Senators, if the learned managers had objected that General Thomas was not to be received as a witness because he was a co-conspirator, some of these observations of the learned managers might have some application. But that is not the topic, that is not the claim which the learned managers have presented to your notice. It is that General Thomas, being a competent witness to speak the truth here as to whatever is pertinent to this case, is not to be permitted to say what was the agency, what was the instruction, what was the concomitant observation of the President of the United States at every interview which they have given as evidence.

The managers have given evidence as to what General Thomas had been empowered to do or to say by the President, which makes his statement pertinent to commit the President. Now if they can show through General Thomas, by hearsay, what they claim is to implicate the President in intent, then we can certainly prove by General Thomas up to any date in reference to which evidence has been offered, all that did occur between the President and himself.

Mr. BINGHAM replied, on the part of the managers— The Senators will notice that an attempt is now made, for the first time in this trial, and, I may say, the first time in any tribunal of justice in this country, by respectable counsel, to introduce in the defense of an accused criminal his own declarations, made after the fact. The time has not yet come, Senators, for the full discussion of the question whether it was a crime for Andrew Johnson, with intent to violate the Tenure of Office Act, to issue an order for the removal of Mr. Stanton from the War Department, not only in contravention of the act, but in defiance of the act of the Senate, then had on the suspension under the same law, by the same Secretary.

For myself, I stand ready to make the challenge in this stage of the case, to say that if the Tenure of Office act is to be considered a valid act, the attempt to remove Mr. Stanton is itself a misdemeanor, not simply at the common law, but by the laws of the United States. I am not surprised that that utterance was made here at this stage of the case, after the counsel for the defense had closed his argument, and ventured to declare that an attempt to commit a misdemeanor, made such by the law, was not itself a crime consummated by the very attempt, and was not of itself a misdemeanor.

The only question before the Senate is, whether it is competent for an accused criminal, high or low, after the fact charged, to make evidence for himself by his own declarations to a co-conspirator, or to anybody else. The rule has been settled in every case that ever has been tried heretofore, that in the general law of evidence appointed for a common law proceeding cover these proceedings. If there is an exception to be found to that, in trials of this kind. I challenge its production.

The Chief Justice said he would submit the question to the Senate, and the yeas and nays having been ordered the question was taken upon allowing the question to be put, and decided in the affirmative. Yeas, 41; nays, 10—as follows:—

YEAS.—Messrs. Anthony, Bayard, Buckalew, Cattell, Cole, Conkling, Corbett, Davis, Dixon, Doolittle, Edwards, Ferry, Fessenden, Fowler, Frelinghuysen, Grimes, Henderson, Hendricks, Howe, Johnson, McCreery, Morgan, Morrill (Me.), Morrill (Vt.), Morton, Norton, Patterson (N. H.), Patterson (Tenn.), Pomeroy, Ross, Sherman, Sprague, Stewart, Sumner, Tipton, Trumbull, Van Winkle, Vickers, Willey, Williams, Wilson and Yates—42.

NAYS.—Messrs. Cameron, Chandler, Conness, Cragin, Drake, Harlan, Howard, Nye, Ramsey and Thayer—10.

So the question was put to the witness as follows:—

Q. What occurred between the President and yourself on the 21st of February? A. I stated to the President that I had delivered the communication, and that he gave this answer.

Q. What answer? A. The answer, "Do you wish me to vacate at once, or will you give me time to take away my private property?" and that I answered "at your pleasure;" I then stated, that after delivering the copy of the letter to him, he said, "I do not know whether I will obey your instructions or resist them;" the President's answer was, "Very, well, go on and take charge of the office, and perform the duty;" that was all that passed; this was immediately after giving the second letter to Mr. Stanton; the next morning I was arrested before I had my breakfast; the officer, at my request, accompanied me to see the President; I went to the room where the President was, and stated that I had been arrested, at whose suit I did not know.

Mr. BUTLER (to the witness)—Stop a moment.

To the Chief Justice—Does the presiding officer understand the ruling of the Senate to apply to what took place the next day?

The Chief Justice—The Chief Justice so understands it.

Mr. STANBERY (to witness)—Go on.

Witness—The President said, "Very well; that is the place I want it, in the event;" he advised me then to go to you (meaning Mr. Stanbery), and the Marshal permitted me to go to your quarters at the hotel; I told you I had been arrested, and asked you what I should do.

Mr. BUTLER again interrupted the witness, and asked the Chief Justice whether that was within the rules.

Mr. STANBERY—It is a part of the conspiracy. (Laughter.)

Mr. BUTLER—I have no doubt of it. (Laughter.)

Mr. STANBERY, to the witness—Did you go into the court? A. I presented myself to Judge Cartter.

Q. What happened then?

Mr. BUTLER—I object.

Mr. STANBERY, to witness—Were you admitted to bail in $5000? A. I was then discharged from custody; but there is one point which I wish to state, if admisible; I asked the judge distinctly what that bail meant.

Mr. BUTLER to witness—"Stop a minute."

To the Chief Justice—"Does your honor allow that?"

Mr. STANTON to witness—"That is another part of the case." Q. How long did you remain there? A. I suppose I was there altogether about an hour; my friends came in to give bail; I had nobody with me, not even my wife.

Q. After you were admitted to bail, did you go to the War Department that day, the 22d? A. I did; I think the other matter I was going to mention, is material to me.

Mr. BUTLER—I will withdraw the objection, if the witness thinks it material to him.

Mr. STANBERY (to witness)—Very well; what is the explanation you wish to make?

Witness—I asked the Judge what it meant, and he said it was simply to present myself at ten o'clock the following Wednesday; I then asked if it suspended me from any of my functions; he said it had nothing to do with them; that is the point I wanted to make. (Laughter in the court.)

Q. State when you next went to the War Department that day? A. I went immediately to the President's after giving bail, and stated the facts to him. He made the same answer—"Very well, I wanted to get it into the courts." I then went to the War Office, and found the eastern door locked; this was on the 22d; I asked the messenger for the key, and he told me that he hadn't it; I then went to Mr. Stanton's room—the one which he occupies as an office—and found him there with some six or eight gentlemen; some of them I recognized, and I understood

that they were all members of Congress; they were all sitting; I told the Secretary of War that I came to demand the office; he refused to give it to me and ordered me to my room as Adjutant-General; I refused to obey; I made the demand a second and third time, and was still refused, and induced to go to my own room; he then said, "you can stand there as long as you please;" I left the room and went into the office of General Schriver, and had a chat with him, as he is an old friend; Mr. Stanton followed me in there, and Governor Moorhead, a member of Congress from Pittsburg, Pa., came in; Mr. Stanton told Governor Moorhead to note the conversation, and I think he took notes of it at a side table; he asked me pretty much the same questions as before, whether I insisted on acting as Secretary of War, and whether I claimed the office; I gave the direct answer, and there was some little chat between the Secretary of War and myself.

Q. Did other members of Congress withdraw then? Tell us what happened between you and the Secretary of War after they withdrew. A. I do not recollect what first occurred, but I said to him, "the next time you have me arrested (for I found it was at his suit I was arrested)—

Mr. BUTLER—I object to the conversation between the Secretary of War and General Thomas at a time which we have not put in, because we put in only the time when the other gentlemen were there, and this was something which took place after they had withdrawn.

The Chief Justice—If it was immediately afterwards, it was a part of the same conversation.

Mr. BUTLER—Does General Thomas say it was the same conversation?

Witness—Mr. Stanton listened to me, and got talking in a very familiar manner to me; I said the next time you have me arrested, please don't do it until I get something to eat (Laughter); I have had nothing to eat or drink to-day (continued laughter); he put his arm around my neck, as he used to do, in a familiar manner, and ran his hand through my hair, and turned around to General Schriver and said, "Schriver, have you got a bottle here? bring it out" (Roars of laughter); Schriver unlocked his desk and took out a small vial; the Secretary then proposed we should have a spoonful of whisky; I said I would like a little; General Schriver poured it out into a tumbler and divided it equally.

Mr. STANBERY—Q. He shared it then? A. He took the glasses up this way (indicating), and measured them with his eye; presently a messenger came in with a full bottle of whisky, and the cork was drawn and he and I took a drink together.

Q. Was that all the force exhibited that day? A. That was all.

Q. Have you at any time attempted to use force to get into that office? A. At no time.

A. Have you ever had instructions from the President to use force, intimidations or threats?

Mr. BUTLER—"Stop a moment. At any time; that brings it down to to-day; but suppose the ruling does not come down so far as that. Ask the witness what occurred prior to the 21st or 22d of February. I am content.

Mr. STANBERY—Well, we will say up to the 9th of March.

Mr. BUTLER—The 9th of March is past, as decided as it would be; say till the day the President was impeached on the 22d of February; but suppose he had got up his case then?

Mr. EVARTS—We have a right to negative up to the point for which you have given any positive evidence, which is the 9th of March.

Mr. BUTLER—We have given no evidence as to what instructions were given by the President. We have given the evidence of what Mr. Thomas said, but if there is anything in any rule of law, this testimony cannot be admitted.

Mr. EVARTS—The point, if anything, Mr. Chief Justice, on which Mr. Karsener was allowed to state the interview between General Thomas and himself, on the 9th of March was that General Thomas' statement then made might be held to, either from something that had been proved on the part of the managers, or from something that would be proved on the part of the managers, a committal of the President. Now, certainly, under the ruling, as well as under the necessary principles of law and of justice, the President is entitled to a negative through the witness who knows anything that has been proved as to what occurred between the President and this witness.

Mr. BUTLER—I do not propose to argue any further, for if the point is not sufficiently clear to everybody, no argument can make it plainer. I simply object to the question as to what had been the directions of the President down to the 7th of March, after he was impeached.

Mr. EVARTS said, the point is that we negatively can show up to and including the date which they have given in evidence what they claim to implicate the President, that the President had not given any instructions to use force.

Mr. BUTLER—How does that prove that Gen. Thomas did not say so?

Mr. EVARTS—It only proves that he said it without the authority of the President, which is the main point.

The Chief Justice directed Mr. Stanbery to reduce his question to writing.

Mr. STEVENS remarked in a low tone, "Oh, it is not worth while to appeal to the Senate after that decision."

The question was read—Did the President at any time prior to or including the 9th of March, authorize you to use force, intimidation or threats to get possession of the War Office?

The question was put to the Senate, and decided in the affirmative, without a division. The witness then replied—He did not. He also said in conversation with Mr. Burleigh or Mr. Wilkson, he could not tell which, he had said, that if I found my door locked, I would break it open; and to the officer I said that I would call on General Grant for forces; I have got this conversation mixed up, and cannot separate them; he then described the interview with Mr. Karsener at the President's levee on the 9th of March, when Karsener claimed acquaintance; witness said. I tried to get away from him, but he then said he was a Delawarian, and said the eyes of all Delaware are on you, and they expect you to stand fast; I said certainly, I will stand firm; he put the same question a second time, and then said:—Are you going to kick this fellow out? and I said, "Oh! we'll kick him out by and by."

Q. Are you certain the kicking out came from him first? A. Certainly, sir; but I did not mean any disrespect to Mr. Stanton at all; I said it smilingly, and I was very glad to get away from him.

In cross-examination witness disclaimed any unkind feeling towards Mr. Stanton; General Grant had recommended his being retired, but the President did not set him aside.

Q. Did you ever ask Mr. Stanton to restore you to office? A. No, I did not.

Q. With the kind feeling you had to him all the time did you not ask Mr. Stanton to restore you to office? A. No, I did not.

Q. With the kind feeling you had to him all the time, why did you not ask him? A. I knew perfectly well that my services on special business was very important; I knew that Mr. Stanton said himself that I was the only one that could do the work, and that he, therefore, sent me; I did not ask Mr. Stanton to restore me, because I did not suppose he wanted me in the office, although there was no unkind feeling; the President sent for me on the 18th of February, three days before I received the order; I never had an intimation before the 18th that the President had any idea of making me Secretary of War.

Mr. BUTLER—Did you not swear before the committee that you had a previous intimation? A. I afterwards made a correction in that paper.

Mr. BUTLER—Excuse me, I did not ask you about corrections, but what you swore to? A. I swore that I had received an intimation, but I found that it was not so, when I came to look at my testimony; the intimation that I received was about the Adjutant-General's office, which was made some few weeks before the occurrence; I swore that I received an intimation from Colonel Moore; I cannot give the time, it was in the course of two or three weeks; when I swore, the restoration of Adjutant-General and the appointment of Secretary of War *ad interim* was on my mind; when I was examined, I thought the appointment as Secretary would cease, because it had been intimated to me by the President; I told him I would obey his orders, because he was Commander-in-Chief; I did not make this response on receiving other commissions, as they were ordinary ones, and this was an extraordinary one, as I never had one of that kind before. (Laughter.)

Q. Did you go to Mr. Stanton between the 18th and 21st, and tell him you were going to take his place? A. No, sir; I was at the War Department every day in the meantime; on the 21st the President sent for me again, but I had no suspicion as to what he wanted me for, and after giving me the two papers, the notice to Mr. Stanton and the appointment of myself as Secretary *ad interim*, they being first read by Colonel Moore, the President said, "I shall uphold the Constitution and the laws, and I expect you to do the same;" I said, "Certainly I shall do so, and shall obey your orders."

Q. Let me see if I have got this. The President, you say, came out with two papers, which he handed to Colonel Moore; Colonel Moore read them, and the President then said:—"I am going to uphold the Constitution and the law, and I want you to do the same." and you said, "I will obey your orders." Why did you put in that about obeying his orders? A. I suppose it was very natural.

Q. What next was said? A. He told me to go to Mr. Stanton, and deliver the papers to him.

Q. Which you did? A. Yes.

Q. At that first interview, before you left the building, Mr. Stanton gave you a letter. A. Yes, sir.

Q. Then you knew that he did not intend to give up the office? A. I did.

Q. You so understood fully? A. Yes.

Q. You went back and reported that to the President? A. Yes.

Q. Did you report to him that Mr. Stanton did not mean to give up the office? A. I reported to him exactly what Mr. Stanton had said.

Q. Did he not ask you what you thought about it? A. He did not.

Q. Did you tell him? A. I did not.

Q. You reported the same facts to him which made the impression on your own mind that Mr. Stanton was not going to give up the office? A. I did; I reported the facts of the conversation.

Q. Did you tell him about the letter? A. No.

Q. Why did you not? A. I did not suppose it necessary.

Mr BUTLER—Why here was a letter ordering you to desist.

Mr. STANBERY—I object to your arguing to the witness. Ask him the question.

Mr. BUTLER—Please wait till the question is asked before you object.

To the Witness—Q. You had a letter which showed that your acts were illegal, and which convinced you, as you say.

Mr. STANBERY—(Interrupting)—Reduce the question to writing.

Mr. BUTLER—I shall not be able to reduce it to writing if you don't stop interrupting me. To the witness—Q. You had a letter from Mr. Stanton, which, together with other facts convinced you that Mr. Stanton did not intend to give up the office; now with that letter in your pocket, why did you not report it to your chief? A. I did not think it was necessary; I reported the conversation.

Q. Did you tell the President that Mr. Stanton had given orders to General Schriver and General Townsend not to obey you? A. I think I did.

Q. Have you any doubt about it in your own mind? A. I don't think I have any doubt about it.

Q. So that I understand you to say the President replied, "Very well; go on and take possession of the office?" A. I think so.

Q. Was there anything more said? A. I think not, at that time.

Q. You went away? A. Yes.

Q. About what time of the day was that? A. About one or two o'clock.

Q. You told Mr. Wilkeson that you meant to call on General Grant for a military force to take possession of the office; did you mean that, or was it mere rhodomontade? A. I suppose I did not mean it; I have never had it in my head to use force.

Q. You did not mean it? A. No.

Q. Was it merely boast and brag? A. Yes.

Q. Did you again tell him that you intended to use force to get into the office? A. That I do not recollect; I stated it to him once, I know.

Q. Can you not tell whether you bragged to him again that evening? A. I did not brag to him.

Q. Did you not tell him at Willard's that you meant to use force? A. I told him either at Willard's or at my own house; I do not think I told him more than once.

Q. You saw Mr. Burleigh that evening? A. Yes, sir.

Q. Did you tell him that you meant to use force? A. The expression that I used was, that if I found my doors locked, I would break them open.

Q. Did he not put the question to you in this form—What would you do if Stanton did not go out? and did you not say you would put him out? A. I suppose I did, but I am not certain.

Q. Did he not then say—Suppose he bars the door? and did not you say you would break the door down, and was that brag? A. No, that was not brag; I meant it then.

Q. You had got over the brag at that time? A. When I had this conversation with Mr. Burleigh I felt it.

Q. And at that time you really meant to go on and break down the doors. A. Yes, if they were locked.

Q. And you really meant to use force? A. I meant what I said.

Q. What you said to him you meant in good, solemn earnest? A. Yes.

Q. There was no rhodomontade then? A. No.

Q. And having got over the playful part of it, and thinking the matter over, you come to the conclusion to use force, and having come to that conclusion, why did not you use it? A. Because I reflected that it would not answer; I might produce difficulty.

Q. What kind of difficulty? A. I suppose bloodshed.

Q. What else? A. Nothing else.

Q. Then by difficulty you mean bloodshed? A. If I used force I supposed I would be resisted by force, and blood might have been issued; that is my answer.

Q. What time did you leave Mr. Burleigh, or Burleigh leave you? A. It was after night when he came there; his visit was a very short one.

Q. About what time did he leave? A. About nine o'clock, I suppose.

Q. How long was it after Mr. Burleigh left; was it before you left to go to the masquerade ball? A. I went there, I think, about half-past nine o'clock.

Q. Did you see anybody of your own family between the time that Mr. Burleigh left and the time you started for the ball? A. Yes.

Q. Who? A. A little girl next door was going with my young daughter to a masquerade ball, and I went with them.

Q. You did not discuss this matter with them? A. I did not.

Q. Did you discuss it with anybody after you left Mr. Burleigh? A. I did not.

Q. A masquerade ball is not a good place to discuss high ministerial duties, is it? A. I should think not; I went there solely to take charge of my little girl and to throw off care; I had promised her two days before.

Q. Did you consult anybody after you left Mr. Burleigh? A. I did not.

Q. The last that you told anybody on this question was when you told Burleigh in solemn earnest that you were going to use force, and then you went to the ball, and from thence to bed, and saw nobody the next morning until the Marshal came, why did you change your mind from your solemn determination to use force? A. I changed it soon after, but cannot say when I had changed before I was arrested, and had determined not to use force.

Q. Did you tell Mr. Burleigh that the reason you did not use force was because you had been arrested? A. I do not think that I did; I had no doubt that Mr. Stanton would resist any attempt to take possession by force, and that to obtain possession, force would have to be used.

Q. Did you report this conclusion to the President? A. I did not think it necessary; I never asked the President for advice or for orders; I had four interviews with Mr. Stanton, and every time, Mr. Stanton refused; I suggested to the President that the true plan would be in order to get possession of the papers, to call upon Gen. Grant; I wrote a draft of an order on General Grant and left it with the President.

Q. Did you sign it? A. Yes; the letter is dated the 10th of March; I had spoken to the President before about the matter, and the letter was to be issued as my order, and it was left for the consideration of the President; it was a peaceable order, and I had no idea any bloodshed would grow out of it; I have attended Cabinet meetings, and been recognized continually as Secretary *ad interim* by the President and Heads of Department down to the present hour.

Q. And all your action as Secretary *ad interim* has been confined to attending Cabinet meetings? A. I joined in the ordinary conversation that took place at the meetings, but I don't know that I gave him any particular advice; he asked me several times if I had any business to lay before him, but I never had any. (Laughter.)

Q. The President did not agree to send that notice to General Grant, did he? A. When I first spoke to him about it, I told him that the mode of getting possession of the paper was to write a note to General Grant, asking him to issue an order calling upon the heads of bureaus, as they were military men, to send him communications designed for the President or for the Secretary of War; that was one mode.

Q. What was the other mode that you suggested? A. The other mode was to require the mails to be delivered from the post office to me.

Q. And he told you to draw up the order? A. No; he did not.

Q. But you did so? A. I did it of myself after having this conversation.

Q. And did he agree to that suggestion of yours? A. He said he would take it and think about it, and he put the paper upon his desk.

Q. When was that? That was on the 10th.

Q. Has he ever spoken to you about that order since? A. I think I may have mentioned it.

Q. Did he ever ask you to know where the troops were about Washington? A. He never did.

Q. Or who had charge of them? A. He never did.

Q. Did you tell Colonel Moore that you were going to the ball? A. I think not; he may have known that I was going, for I had secured tickets for my children some days before.

Q. Did the President, in any of those interviews with you as his Cabinet counselor or Cabinet adviser, suggest to you that he had not removed Mr. Stanton? A. Never; he always said that Mr. Stanton was out of office.

Q. Did he ever tell you you were not appointed? A. No sir.

Q. Have you not always known you were appointed? A. Yes, sir.

Q. Has he not over and over again told you that you were appointed? A. Not over and over again; I do not know that that came up at all.

Q. Will you tell what you meant when you told the President that you were going to uphold the Constitution and the laws? A. I meant that I would be governed by the Constitution and the laws made in pursuance thereof.

Q. And did you include in that the Tenure of Office act? A. Yes, so far as it applied to me.

Q. You had that in your mind at the time? A. Not particularly in my mind.

Q. Did the President at any time when you have seen him give you any directions, other than those about taking possession of the War office? A. He has told me on several occasions that he wanted to get some nominations sent up which are lying on Mr. Stanton's table, and he could not get them; he did not get them.

Q. What did he tell you about them? A. I could not get them.

Q. And he could not so far as you know? A. So far as I know.

Q. And he complained to you? A. No; he died not complain; he said he wanted them as some of them were going over; I twice said to Mr. Stanton that the President wanted these nominations, and he said he would see to it; this was while acting as Adjutant-General; the testimony given by Mr. Karsener was read to me, and I was asked if it was correct, and I did not object to any words as incorrect; I objected to manner, and said that I did not use the word "kicking," but that it was Karsener said it; Mr. Karsener was called up at that time and asked by the tye managers whether his manner was playful, and he said it seemed serious.

The cross-examination was continued for some time longer, and being closed, the court adjourned.

PROCEEDINGS OF SATURDAY, APRIL 11.

The managers and some eight or ten members of the House were in attendance this morning. After the reading of the journal,

The Twenty-first Rule.

Mr. BINGHAM rose and made a motion on the part of the managers, speaking in an inaudible tone, to which fact Senator CONKLING called attention. By the direction of the Chief Justice, he then reduced it to writing, as follows:—

The managers move the Senate to so amend rule twenty-first as to allow such of the managers as desire to be heard, and also such of the counsel of the President as desire to be heard, to speak on the final arguments, and objecting to the provision of the rule that the final argument shall be opened and closed by the managers on the part of the House.

The Chief Justice stated the question,

Senator POMEROY—If that is in the nature of a resolution, under our general rules it should lie over one day for consideration.

The Chief Justice was understood to coincide in the opinion.

Mr. BUCKALEW moved that it be laid over until Monday.

Mr. EDMUNDS inquired of the Chair whether the twenty-first rule does not now provide by its terms that this privilege may be extended to the managers and counsel, and whether, therefore, any amendment of the rule is necessary?

The Chief Justice replied in the affirmative, and said he had heard no motion to that effect.

Mr. FRELINGHUYSEN moved that such an order be adopted.

Mr. POMEROY—I have no objection to taking the vote now.

The Chief Justice—The Senator will reduce his motion to writing.

Mr. SHERMAN—If it is in order, I will move that the twenty-first rule be relaxed, so as to allow persons on each side to speak on the final argument.

The Chief Justice decided the motion out of order for the present, and Mr. Frelinghuysen having reduced his motion to writing, it was read, as follows:—

Ordered, That as many of the managers and counsel for the President be permitted to speak on the final argument as shall desire to do so.

Mr. HOWARD hoped it would lie over until Monday.

Several Senators—No! no! let us vote on it.

Mr. HOWARD—I object to it.

Mr. TRUMBULL said it did not change the rule, and therefore could not be required to lie over.

The Chief Justice decided that, objection having been made, it must lie over.

Mr. CONKLING—May I inquire under what rule it is that this must lie over upon the objection of a single Senator?

The Chief Justice—The Chief Justice, in conducting the business of the Court, adopts for his general guidance the rules of this Senate sitting in legislative session, as far as they are applicable. That is the reason.

Mr. CONKLING called attention to the fact that the very rule under discussion provided for the case by the use of the words "unless otherwise ordered."

The Chief Justice—It is competent for the Senator to appeal from the decision of the Chair.

Mr. CONKLING—Oh, no, sir; that is not my purpose.

Mr. JOHNSON said he did not desire to debate the question, and was proceeding to make a remark about the order, when he was cut short by the Chief Justice directing the counsel for the President to proceed.

General Thomas Makes Corrections.

Mr. STANBERY said that General Thomas desired to make some corrections in his testimony, and General Thomas took the stand and said:—I wish to correct my testimony yesterday; I read a letter signed by Mr. Stanton and addressed to me on the 21st of February; I didn't receive the copy of that letter until the next day after I had made the demand for the office; the Secretary came in and handed me the original; my impression is that I noted in that original the receipt; I then handed it to General Townsend to make the copy that I read here; I had it not until the 22d of February.

Q. Then when you saw the President on the afternoon of the 21st you had not read that letter from Mr. Stanton? A. I had not. The next correction I want to make is this: I said that the President told me to take possession of the office; he expressed it "take charge" of the office.

Q. Are you certain that was the expression? A. I

am positive; I was asked if I could give the date of my brevet commission; don't know whether it is important or not; I have it here; the date is 12th of March, 1865; Mr. Stanton gave it to me; he had more than once intended to give it to me, but on this occasion, when I returned from my duty, I said the time had arrived when I ought to have the commission, and he gave it to me. Here is another point: I stated when I was before the committee of the House managers. General Butler asked the clerk, I think it was, for the testimony of Dr. Burleigh; he said he had it not; that it was at home; I don't know whether he said or I said "It makes no difference;" he asked me a number of questions in reference to that; I assented to them all; I never heard that testimony read; I never heard Dr. Burleigh's testimony, nor do I recollect the questions, except that they were asked me, and I said Dr. Burleigh no doubt would recollect the conversation better than I.

His Cross-examination.

Cross-examined by Mr. BUTLER—Q. General Thomas, how many times did you answer yesterday that the President told you at that time to "take possession of the office?" A. Well, I have not read over my testimony; I have not read over any testimony, and I don't know how many times.

Q. Was that untrue each time? A. If I said so, it was; "take charge" were the words used.

Q. Have you any memorandum by which you can correct that expression? If so, produce it. A. I have no memorandum with me here; I don't know that I have any; I have not looked at one since I was on the stand; I can state it better to-day than I did yesterday, because I saw and read that evidence as reported; I gave it yesterday myself, and I know better what it was by reading it than when I testified to it; and I am sure the words were "take charge of," and the three times when I reported to him that Mr. Stanton would not go out or refused to go out, each time he said "take charge of the office;" my attention, at the time he said that, was not called to the difference between the words "take charge of the office" and "take possession of the office;" but I recollect it distinctly now, because I know that was the expression; I have always known that that was the expression; I made the mistake, because I think the words were put into my mouth.

Q. Just as Mr. Karsner did? (Laughter.) A. Yes, sir; I don't know that I am in the habit when anybody puts words into my mouth, of taking them; after I and Karsner were summoned here as witnesses, I went and quarreled with him; I had some words with him in the room here adjoining (indicating the door behind him); I called him a liar and a perjurer. (Laughter.) Liar and perjurer! Both; I did certainly call him a liar and a perjurer; I knew that he and I were both in the witness-room waiting to be called, and I knew he was here for that purpose; while he was there I undertook to talk with him about his testimony; I stated to him in two instances; I will give them to you.

Q. Answer my question. I asked you this question: whether you undertook to talk to him about the testimony? A. I don't know who introduced the conversation; certainly not I, I don't think, for he was there for some time before I spoke to him.

Q. Did you speak first or he? A. That I don't recall.

Q. Did you tell him that he was a liar and perjurer at that time? A. I did tell him that he was a liar, and may have said he was a perjurer.

Q. Did you offer violence to him except in that way? A. I was then in full uniform, as I am now—major-general's uniform.

Q. Another question I want to ask you which was omitted: Do you still intend to take charge or possession of the office of Secretary of War? A. Firmly —I do; I have never said to any person within a few days that we will have that fellow (meaning Mr. Stanton) out of it or sink the ship.—never.

Q. Did you say to Mr. Johnson anything to that effect? A. Not that I have any recollection of.

Q. Do you know whether you did or not? A. What Mr. Johnson do you mean?

Q. I mean D. B. Johnson. A. There was a Mr. Johnson came to see me at my house in reference to another matter; we may have had some conversation about this.

Q. When was that that Mr. Johnson came to your house? A. I hardly recollect.

Q. About how long ago? A. I am trying to recollect now. He came to me about the business of—

Q. Never mind what the business was; what was said? A. I want to call it to mind; I have a right to do that, I think.

Q. But not to state it? A. (After a pause) I can hardly state, but recently; not very long ago.

Q. Within two or three days? A. No, sir, before that; I think it is more than a week.

Q. Let me give you a date, as far back as Friday week? A. I don't know about that.

Thomas in a Joking Mood.

Q. Was it longer than that? A. I did not charge my memory with it; it was a private conversation that we had; I was joking then. (Laughter.)

Q. Did you, joking or otherwise, use these words:— "We will have Stanton out if we have to sink the ship?" A. I have no recollection of using any such expression.

R. Did you make use of any expression equivalent to it? A. I have no recollection of it.

Q. Have you such recollection of what you did say as to know what you did not say? A. I have not; I would rather Mr. Johnson would testify himself as to the conversation.

Q. Do you deny that you said so? A. Well, I won't deny it, because I do not know that I did. (Laughter.)

Q. You say you would rather he would testify; we will try and oblige you in that respect; but if you did say so, was it true, or was it merely brag? A. You may call it what you please.

Q. What do you call it? A. I do not call it brag.

Q. What was it? A. It was a mere conversation whatever was said; I didn't mean to use any influence against Mr. Stanton to get him out of office.

Q. What did you mean by the expression that "you would have him out if you sink the sink the ship. A. I say that I do not know that I used that expression.

Q. We will show that by Mr. Johnson; but I am assuming that you did use it, and I ask you what meaning did you have?

Mr. EVARTS—You have no right to assume that Mr. Johnson will testify that; he has not said so yet.

Witness—I cannot say what the conversation was; Mr. Johnson was there on official business connected with the dismissal of an officer from the army.

Mr. BUTLER—Then you were joking on that subject? A. Certainly.

Q. Did you ever see Mr. Johnson before? A. I do not recollect, possibly I may have seen him.

Q. Have you ever seen him since? A. Not to my knowlege.

Q. Here was a stranger who called upon you upon official business connected with the army, and did you go to joking in that way with him, a total stranger? A. I knew him as the lawyer employed by Colonel Belger to get him reinstated.

Q. Who was a stranger to you? A. I think he was.

Q. And did you go to joking with a stranger on such a subject? A. Certainly; we had quite a familiar talk.

Q. And that is the only explanation you can give of the conversation? A. It is sufficient, I think.

Q. Sufficient or not, is it the only one you can give? A. It is the only one I do give.

Q. And is it the only one you can give? A. Yes.

Q. Did anybody talk to you about your testimony since you left the stand yesterday? A. I suppose I have talked with a dozen persons; several persons met me and said they were very glad to hear my testimony; I was met to-day by several, who spoke to me jocularly about my taking an equal drink with the Secretary of War; I have talked with my own family about it.

Q. Has anybody talked with you about this point when you changed your testimony? A. I came here this morning and saw the managers, and told them.

Mr. BUTLER—You don't mean the managers?

Mr. EVARTS suggested that he meant the counsel for the President.

Witness—I meant the counsel for the President.

Mr. BUTLER—Did you talk with anybody before that on these points? A. Yes, with General Townsend this morning.

Q. The Assistant Adjutant-General, but with nobody else? A. I have said no, and I am sure, (laughter); I did not receive a letter, a copy, or note from Mr. Stanton on the 21st of February; I said yesterday that he gave me the original; I have not seen that original since; the date was noted on that original; the one I read here was given on the 22d of February; it was handed to General Townsend, and he made a copy; that was on the 22d; it was dated the 21st; it was prepared the day before, I believe.

Q. Dou you mean to take all back that was said in General Schriver's room about your not going on with the office, or about their not obeying you on the afternoon of the 21st? A. Oh, yes, it was the 22d, I think; General Townsend was there on the 21st.

Q. Then on the 21st there was nothing said about any one obeying you? A. I think not; I think there was not anything said about not obeying me; there was nothing said about not obeying me on the 21st at all, I think.

Q. And you never reported to the President that Mr. Stanton said on the 21st he would not obey you? A. I reported to the President the two conversations I had with him; on the 21st there was no such conversation as I testified to, that is, not in reference to that; there was no conversation at all as to General Townsend not obeying me on the 21st.

Q. Then when you told us yesterday that you reported that to the President, and that you got his answer to it, all that was not so? A. (With emphasis) That was not so.

Q. Now for another matter. When were you examined before the committee?

Witness—What committee? I have been examined twice.

Thomas Bothered.

Q. You were examined before the Committee of the House, not the managers, and in answer to this question, "Did you make any report on Friday of what transpired? did you not use these words:—'Yes, sir; I saw the President and told him what had occurred;' he said, 'Well, go along and administer the department.' A. When I stated what had occurred with Mr. Stanton, he said to me:—'You must just take possession of the department and carry on the business.'"

Q. Did you swear that before the committee? A. I say, as I said before, that I was mistaken then.

Q. That is not the question. The question is did you swear it? A. If that is there I suppose I swore it.

Q. Was it true? A. No; I never used the words together; I wish to make one statement in reference to that very thing; I was called there hastily; a great many events had transpired; I requested on two occasions that the committee would let me wait and consider; the committee refused, and would not let me, and pressed me with questions.

Mr. BUTLER—Q. When was that? A. When I was called before that committee, on the evening of the trial.

Q. February 26? A. Yes; I went there after getting through that trial, and on two occasions I requested the committee to postpone the examination until the next morning, until I could go over the matter, but that was not allowed me.

Q. Did you make any such request? A. I did, twice.

Q. From whom? A. From those who were there; the committee, I think, was pretty full; I do not know whether Mr. Stevens was there; he was there a portion of the time, but I do not know whether he was there at that particular time.

Lorenzo Wants Time to Consult his Mind.

Q. Do you tell the Senate, on your oath, that you requested the committee to give you time to answer a question, and that the committee refused. A. I requested that the examination might be deferred until the next morning, when I could have an opportunity to go over the matter in my own mind; that was not granted; there was no refusal made, but I was pressed with questions; then there is another matter I want to say; I came in to correct that testimony because there are two things confounded in it, in reference to the date of my appointment as Adjutant-General and the date of my appointment as Secretary of War ad interim; I supposed the committee was asking in reference to the first and that is the reason why these two things got mixed up; when I went there to correct the testimony I was told to read it over; I found this mistake, and I found that some of it was not English; I thought something was taken down too that I did not say; the committee would not permit me to correct the manuscript, but I put the corrections at the bottom, just in a hasty way, and I suppose it is on that paper that you hold in your hand.

Mr. BUTLER—We will come to that. Q. Have you got through with your statement? A. I have.

Q. Very well. Did you not come and ask to see your testimony as it was taken down before the committee? A. I went to the clerk and saw him.

Q. Did he give you the report which I hold in my hand? A. He was not in the first time, and I came the next day; that day he handed it to me, and he went twice, I think, to some member of the committee, I do not know who, for instructions; I said I wanted to make the report decent English, and I wanted to know whether I could not correct the manuscript, and he reported that I might make my corrections in writing; I think I read the whole testimony over; I am not certain; I do not know that I did; I came to correct this first portion it particularly; that was the reason I went there.

Q. Did you want to correct any other portion of it? A. The first part only; it referred to a mistake as to the time about my mixing up the appointment of Adjutant-General and Secretary of War ad interim; it had reference to a notification given to me by the President to be Secretary of War or of Adjutant-General; that was mixed up; I stated that I received that notification from Colonel Moore; Colonel Moore did give me a notification that I would probably be put back as Adjutant-General, but he did not give me a notification that I would probably be appointed Secretary of War, and it was that that I wished to correct; that was the principal correction; I did not want to correct anything else, but if anything else was wrong I did; I wished to correct any errors, whatever they might be; I then went over my testimony and corrected such portions as I pleased; I had the privilege to do that, of course, and I wrote out here on portions of two sheets my corrections; this is my handwriting; it is my own handwriting, and I signed it "Lorenzo Thomas, Adjutant-General."

Q. Now having read over your testimony, did you correct anything in that portion of it where you are reported as saying that the President ordered you to go forthwith and take possession and administer the office? A. I do not think I made any such correction as that.

Q. You swear that that was not true? A. I have said so.

Q. Why didn't you correct it? A. I have thought the matter over since.

Stanbery Asks a Question.

Re-direct examination by Mr. STANBERY. Q. I found in the report of your testimony, given yesterday, that in your original examination you were asked this question:—What occurred between the President and yourself at the second interview, on the 21st of February?" Your answer given is this:—"I stated to the President that I had delivered the communication and that he gave this answer, 'Do you wish me to vacate at once, or will you give me time to take away my private property?' and that I answered, 'at your pleasure;' I then stated that, after delivering the copy of the letter to him, he said, 'I do not know whether I will obey your instructions or resist them;' this I mentioned to the President; his answer was, 'Very well; go on and take charge of the office; perform the duty.'" Now, did the President say that? A. Yes, sir.

Ad Interim in a Muddle.

Mr. BUTLER—Q. Then you mean to say, in answer to Mr. Stanbery, that you got it all right, and that in answer to me you got it all wrong? A. Yes, in reference to your examination.

Mr. BUTLER—That is all.

Mr. STANBERY intimated that counsel would again call General Thomas after they got in some record evidence.

Mr. BUTLER said they might call him any time.

Lieutenant-General Sherman Sworn.

Lieutenant-General William T. Sherman, who appeared in the undress uniform of his rank, was next sworn and examined by Mr. STANBERY—I was in Washington last winter; I arrived here about the 4th of December; remained here two months, until about the 3d or 4th of February; I came here as a member of the Indian Peace Commission; I had no other business here at that time; subsequently I was assigned to a board of officers, organized under a law of Congress, to make articles of war and regulations for the army; as to the date of that assignment I can procure the order, which will be perfect evidence as to the date; it was written within ten days of my arrival here; I think it was about the middle of December that the order was issued; I had a double duty for a few days; during that time, from the 4th of December to the 3d or 4th of February, I had several interviews with the President; I saw him alone, when there was no persons present but the President and myself; I saw him, also, in company with General Grant once, and I think twice; I had several interviews with him in reference to the case of Mr. Stanton.

Mr. BINGHAM—We desire, without delay, to respectfully submit our objections to this, declining, however, to argue it. We submit our objections, believing it our duty as Representatives of the House to do so.

Mr. STANBERY—Objections to what?

Mr. BINGHAM—To the declarations of the President touching any matter involved in this issue not made at the time when we have called them out ourselves. They are not competent evidence.

Mr. STANBERY—Allow me to come to some question that we can start upon. This is merely introductory. You will soon see the object of the examination of General Sherman.

Mr. BINGHAM—I understand the object to be to prove his conversation with the President.

The Chief Justice—No question of that kind has been asked yet.

Mr. BINGHAM—We understand it.

Mr. STANBERY—We will come to that point. [To the witness.] Q. While you were here, did the President ask you if you would take charge of the office of the Department of War on the removal of Mr. Stanton?

Mr. BUTLER— Stop a moment. I object, and ask that that question be reduced to writing.

Mr. STANBERY—Do you object to the question because it is leading, or do you object to it in substance?

Mr. BUTLER—I object to it for every reason. Please put your question in writing.

Mr. STANBERY to witness—At what time were those interviews?

[Witness referred to some memoranda to find the dates.]

Mr. STANBERY—Had you an interview with him before Mr. Stanton came back into the office, and while General Grant was still in it? A. Yes, sir.

Q. Of a social nature? A. Entirely so, before that time.

Q. Had you an interview with him before that? A. I had. The day following Mr. Stanton's return, I think; General Grant was also present.

Q. What did that interview relate to?

Mr. BUTLER—Stop a moment. Put the question in writing.

Mr. STANBERY—The question is what did it relate to?

Mr. BUTLER—I object to that.

Mr. STANBERY to witness—Well, then, did it relate to the occupation of the War Department by Mr. Stanton? A. It did.

Q. Now, what was it?

Mr. BUTLER—stop a moment. I object to that. Put your motion in writing.

Q. By Mr. STANBERY.—What conversation passed between you and the President?

Mr. BUTLER—Excuse me. I asked to have the question in writing.

The Chief Justice—The counsel will please put the question in writing.

The question was reduced to writing, as follows:—

Q. At that interview what conversation took place between the President and you in reference to the removal of Mr. Stanton?

Mr. BUTLER—To that we object. I suppose we can agree as to the date. It was the 14th of January. On the 13th Mr. Stanton was reinstated, and the 14th was the day after.

Mr. STANBERY, to witness—Can you give us the date of that conversation? Witness referring to a memorandum which he held—Mr. Stanton was reinstated in possession of his office as Secretary of War on Tuesday, the 13th of January, and the conversation occurred on Wednesday, the 14th.

The Chief Justice—The Chief Justice thinks the question admissible within the principle of the decision already made by the Senate, but he will be pleased to put the question to the Senators.

Senator CONNESS demanded the yeas and nays on the admission of the question.

Mr. STANBERY rose to argue the point. He said the counsel for the President ask merely to state the ground on which they claim to put the question. We expect to prove by General Sherman—

Mr. BUTLER—Interrupting. I object to your stating that, I did not ask that. That is an attempt to get before the court, I mean before the Senate the testimony by the statement of counsel. The question solely is whether the declaration of the President can be given in evidence--what the declarations are it would be improper to state because that would be begging the whole question and attempting to get them in that way by a recital by the counsel. The whole question is whether any declaration of the President can be competent evidence. Therefore there is no occasion to state what the conversation was.

Mr. STANBERY—Do you propose to argue it?

Mr. BUTLER—We do not wish to argue it.

Mr. STANBERY—Then I will:—

Stanbury's Argument.

Mr. Chief Justice and Senators:—The testimony which we expect to elicit from General Sherman I look upon as vital, as admissible, and as testimony which we are entitled to have, upon legal grounds well understood and perfectly unanswerable. I presume I can say in argument what we expect to prove. First of all, what is shown here? What is the point which the gentlemen assume to make against the President? Let these gentlemen speak for themselves.

First. I read from the honorable manager who opened the case, on page 94 of his argument:—

"Having shown that the President wilfully violated the act of Congress without justification, both in the removal of Mr. Stanton and the appointment of Mr. Thomas, for the purpose of obtaining wrongfully possession of the War Office by force, if need be, and certainly by threats and intimidations, for the purpose of controlling its appropriations through its ad interim chief, who shall say that Andrew Johnson is not guilty of the high crime and misdemeanors charged against him in the first eight articles?"

Then, on page 109, speaking of the orders of removal, he says:—"These and his concurrent acts show conclusively that his attempt to get the control of the military force of the government by the seizing of the Department of War was done in pursuance of his general design, if it were possible, to overthrow the Congress of the United States, and he now claims by his answer the right to control, at his own will, for the execution of this very design, every officer of the army, navy, civil and diplomatic service of the United States." Then, on page 99, he says:—"Failing in his attempt to get full possession of the office through the Senate, he had determined, as he admits, to remove Stanton at all hazards, and endeavored to prevail on the General to aid him in so doing. He declines. For that the respondent quarrels with him, denounces him in the newspapers, and accuses him of bad faith and untruthfulness. Thereupon asserting his prerogatives as Commander-in-Chief, he creates a new military department of the Atlantic.

"He attempted to bribe Lieutenant-General Sherman to take command of it by promotion to the rank of General by brevet, trusting that his military services would compel the the Senate to confirm him. If the respondent can get a General by brevet appointed, he can then, by simple order, put him on duty according to his brevet rank, and thus have a General of the Army in command at Washington, through whom he can transmit his orders and comply with the act which he did not dare transgress, as he had approved it, and get rid of the hated General Grant. Sherman spurned the bribe.

"The respondent, not discouraged, appointed Major-General George H. Thomas to the same brevet rank, but Thomas declined. What stimulated the ardor of the President just at that time, almost three years after the war closed, but just after the Senate had reinstated Mr. Stanton, to reward military service by the appointment of generals by brevet? Why did his zeal of promotion take that form and no other? There were many other meritorious officers of lower rank desirous of promotion. The purpose is evident to every thinking mind. He had determined to set aside Grant, with whom he had quarreled, either by force or fraud, either in conformity with or in spite of the act of Congress, and control the military power of the country. On the 21st of February (for all these events cluster nearly about the same point of time), he appoints Lorenzo Thomas Secretary of War, and orders Mr. Stanton out of the office. Mr. Stanton refuses to go. General Thomas is about the streets, declaring that he will put him out by force (kick him out); he has caught his master's words."

Still more clearly to the point is the argument in reference to the admission of Mr. Chandler's testimony, which we find on page 251. They had called Mr. Cooper to show the intent of the President to get Mr. Chandler into the Treasury Department, in the carry ing out of his alleged conspiracy by controlling the requisitions of the Treasury Department, and thus controlling the purse as well as the sword of the nation. The only question is, says the learned manager, is this competent if we can show it was one of the ways and means?

The difficulty that rests in the minds of my learned friends on the other side is, that they cluster everything about the 21st of February, 1868. They seem to forget that the act of the 21st of February, 1868, was only the culmination of a purpose formed long before, as in the President's answer he sets forth to-wit:—"As early as the 12th of August, 1867 * * *

"To carry it out there are various things to do. He must get control of the War Office, but what good does that do if he cannot get somebody who shall be his servant, his slave, dependent on his breath to answer the requisitions of his pseudo officer whom he may appoint, and, therefore, he began when Stanton was suspended, and as early as the 12th of December he had got to put this suspension and the reasons for it before the Senate, and he knew it would not live there one moment after it got fairly considered. Now he begins; what is the first thing he does? To get somebody in the Treasury Department that will mind me precisely as Thomas will if I can get him in the War Department? That is the first thing, and thereupon, without any vacancy, he must make an appointment. The difficulty that we find is, that we are obliged to argue our case step by step on a single point of evidence. It is one of the infelicities always of putting in a case that sharp, keen, ingenious counsel can insist at all steps, on impaling you upon a point of evidence, and, therefore, I have got to proceed a little further.

"Now, our evidence, if you allow it to come in, is:— First, that he made this appointment; that, this failing, he sent it to the Senate, and Cooper was rejected. Still determined to have Cooper in, he appointed him *ad interim*, precisely as this *ad interim* Thomas was appointed, without law and against right. We put it as a part of the whole machinery by which to get, if he could, his hand into the Treasury of the United States, although Mr. Chandler has just stated there was no way to get it except by a requisition through the War Department—and at the same moment, to show that this was a part of the same illegal means, we show you that although Mr. McCulloch, the Secretary of the Treasury, must have known that Thomas was appointed, yet the President took pains, as will be seen by the paper we have put in, to serve on Mr. McCulloch an attested copy of the appointment of Thomas *ad interim*, in order than he and Cooper might recognize his warrants."

This is to show that the intention of the President began as early as the 12th of August, 1867; that it was progressed in by the appointment of Mr. Cooper in the fall of 1867, going through all the subsequent time, until it at last culminated, say the gentlemen, on the 21st of February, by the President finding the proper tool to put in the War Office. According to this argument, he was looking for a proper tool for a servant—for one who would do his bidding—and after that search they say he found the proper man in a person whom they have called a "disgraced officer."

Now, Mr. Chief Justice and Senators, especially those of you who are lawyers, what case are they attempting to make against the President? Not simply that he did certain acts—that does not make him guilty—but that he did those acts *mala fida*, with an unlawful intent and criminal purpose. They do not prove, or attempt to prove, that purpose by any positive testimony, but they say we have certain facts which raise a presumption of criminal intent. This being so, what is the rule to rebut this presumption? When a prosecution is allowed to raise presumption of the intent of the accused by proving circumstances, may not that presumption be rebutted by proof of other circumstances, to show that the accused had no such intention? Was anything ever plainer than that?

Consider in what attitude the person charged with a crime of passing counterfeit money, if you must prove his intent, is placed; you must prove circumstances from which the presumption arises that he knew that the bill was a counterfeit bill; that he had been told so; that he had seen other money of the same kind; and you must in this way raise the presumption of a criminal intent. How may he rebut that presumption? In the first place, he may do it by proving a good character, and that is allowed to rebut a presumption of guilt; not that he did what was right in that transaction; not that he did certain things, or

made declarations about the same time which explain that his intent was honest; but, going beyond that and through the whole field of presmption, he may rebut the presumption of guilt by proof of general good character.

Mr. BUTLER—I have no objection to your proving good character.

Mr. STANBERY—You would admit such general proof as that, and yet you object to this. Now, what evidence can be given against a person charged with a crime, where it is necessary to make out an intent against him, and where the intent is not positively proved by his own declarations, but is to be gathered by proof of other facts, of what was allowed against him, to raise the presumption of his guilt, a proof of facts from which the mind itself infers the guilt intended.

But when the prosecution may make such a case against him by such testimony, why may he not rebut the case by exactly the same sort of testimony. If it is a declaration on which they rely as made by him at one time may he not meet it by declarations about the same time in reference to the same transaction. They cannot be too remote I admit, but if they are about the time, if they are connected with the transaction then the declaration of the defendants from which the influence of innocence is to be presumed are just as admissible as his declarations from which the prosecution has attempted to deduce the inference of the guilt.

In this connection, Mr. Stanbery read from First State Trials, in case of Lord Hardy, quoting the remarks of Mr. Erskine, who, defending Hardy, and in which reference was made to other celebrated cases, including those of Lord George Gordon and Lord William Russell. Having finished his citations, Mr. Stanbery proceeded to say:—We propose to prove that so far from there being any intent on the part of the President to select a tool to take possession of the War office, that he asked the General of the Army, General Grant, to take possession of it, and the next most honored soldier of the Army, General Sherman.

The manager who opened the case charged that the President was looking out for a tool; that he was looking to find a man who could take a bribe, by a brevet rank, and that he did find such a tool in the person of General Thomas, a disgraced officer. Well, if that was his intent, then it must have been with the same intent that the President would put General Sherman in the office before he thought of Thomas or of any other subordinate. It must have been with the same intent that he would take one of the most honored officers in the land and ask him to come in and take the office, not to carry it on as he had carried on the war, a trusted and honored man, but to become his tool and subordinate. Will the managers dare to say that? Would the President, in the first place, have dared to make such a proposition to such a man as General Sherman? If they raise a presumption that he intended to carry out an unlawful act by appointing General Thomas, how does it happen that they will not give him the benefit of presumption arising from his intent to get such a man as General Sherman to take the office, a man who would not be made a tool of; take the case, for instance, of Lord George Gordon, who was indicted for a treasonable speech made upon a certain day before a certain association. He was allowed to go into proof, running through a period of two years before, to show that in meetings of that same association, instead of encouraging and raising an insurrection, he had set his face against it. Lord George Gordon went back two years, but we propose to start from the very time that the managers fixed.

We do not ask to give any testimony as to the President's declarations, or the President's intent, except as to acts which the managers have brought forward to raise a presumption of his guilt. These acts began, they say, in the fall of 1867, with the appointment of Cooper. The conversation we propose to prove took place on the subsequent winter night in the middle of this transaction. We want to show by the fact of his declarations to General Sherman at that time that he was seeking for an honorable high-minded soldier, to do what? What was unlawful?—no; but to do that which the President believed to be lawful. We will show you that he asked General Sherman to take that office on the removal of Mr. Stanton.

Mr. BUTLER rose to object to Mr. Stanbery's stating what he intended to prove.

Mr. STANBERY, refusing to yield, said, I insist upon it as a right. If the Senate choose to stop me I shall stop; but I hope I shall be allowed to state what we expect to prove. I have been too long at the bar not to know that I have a perfect right to do it. The manager may answer my argument, but I hope he will not stop it.

Mr. BUTLER—If you look at the book of State Trials which you hold in your hand, you will find that Mr. Erskine stopped an advocate in the same case, who was proceeding to state what he intended to prove.

Mr. STANBERY—I have been saying what I shall expect to prove, but the gentleman in taking me up does not know what he says; he puts an intent in my mind which I have not got, as he has a very good faculty for putting intents into other men's minds. We expect to show that the President not only asked General Sherman to take this office, and that he told him distinctly what his purpose was, and that it was to put the office in such a situation as to drive Mr. Stanton into the courts of law. It is not necessary to argue the case. I ask any lawyer who ever tried a case where the question was one of intention, and where the case against his client was to prove the fact on which a presumption was sought to be raised by the prosecution, whether he may not show cotemporaneous facts, covering the same time as those used against him, and declarations within the same time as those used against him, and whether he will not be allowed to rebut the general presumption of guilt, and to show that the intent was fair, honest and lawful.

General Butler's Reply.

Mr. BUTLER—Mr. President and Senators, I was quite willing to leave this case to the judgment of both lawyers and laymen of the Senate without a word of argument, and I only speak now to lawyers because the learned counsel for the President emphasized that word, as though he had expected some peculiar advantage in speaking to lawyers. All the rules of evidence are founded on the good sense of mankind, as experience in courts of law has shown what is most likely or most unlikely to be true, and to elicit the truth. They address themselves just as much to laymen as they do to lawyers, because there are no gentlemen in the Senate, nay, there are no gentlemen anywhere, who cannot understand the rules of evidence.

I agree that I labor not under any great difficulty in the argument just made, but I do labor under great difficulty in the opinion of the presiding officer, and in his deciding, without argument, that in his opinion the question comes within the ruling of yesterday. If it did I should not have troubled the Senate, because I have long since learned to bow to all decisions of the tribunal before which I act; but this is entirely another and a different case. What is the exact question? It is, "In the interview, to wit, on the 14th January, what conversation took place between the President and you in reference to the removal of Mr. Stanton?" What conversation? They do not ask for acts. How is this offer of evidence to be supported? I agree that the first part of the argument made by the learned Attorney-General was the very best one he ever made in his life, because it consisted merely of his reading what I had said. (Laughter.) I have a right to say so without any immodesty, because he adopted all that I said, which is one of the highest compliments ever paid to me. (Laughter.) I thought it was a good argument at the time I made it, and I hoped to convince the Senate that I was right in it, but I failed.

If the argument can do any better now in the mouth of the Attorney-General, I desire to see the result. I was arguing about putting the President's acts before the Senate in his appointing Mr. Cooper, and I tried in every way to convince the Senate that it ought to admit them; but the Senate decided by an almost solid vote that it would not; my argument failed to convince you. Will it do any better when read by the musical voice of my friend from Ohio? (Laughter.) I think not; the point then was that I was trying to prove not a declaration of Mr. Johnson, but an act. Here they offer his declaration.

The Senate decided that we could not put in any act except such as were charged in the articles. We do not charge in the articles any attempt on the part of Mr. Johnson to bribe or to find a tool in the gentleman now on the stand, for whom we all have such high respect. I do not think that we have that appreciation of him. What do we charge? We charge that he used the man who was on the same stand an hour before as a tool, and judge ye whether he is not on his appearance here a fit instrument. Judge ye! judge ye!! You saw him a weak, vacillating, vain old man,

just fit to be pampered by a little bribe to do the thing which no brave man would dare to do.

Let me call your attention for a moment to him, as he appeared on the stand yesterday. He was going on to say that the conversation with Karsner was playful; but when he saw that did not put him in a dignified position, he swung back and told us that he meant to have the office.

Mr. EVARTS—He stated exactly the contrary.

Mr. BUTLER—He said that he had made up his mind to use force.

Mr. EVARTS—No, but to break the door; and when he thought of shedding blood he retracted.

Mr. BUTLER—And he remained of that mind till the next morning. What he found to change his mind in the masquerade ball or elsewhere he has not told us, nor can he tell us. When did he change his mind—but I pass from that.

Now, how is the attempt to be supported? The learned gentleman from Ohio says that in a counterfeit case you have to prove the *scienter*. Yes; but how? By showing the passage of other counterfeit bills? Yes. But, gentlemen, did you ever hear, in the case of a counterfeiter, the defendant prove that he did not know the bill was bad by proving that at some other time he passed a good bill? We try the counterfeit bill which we nailed to the counter on the 21st of January, and in order to prove that Mr. Johnson did not issue it, he wants to show that he passed a good bill on the 24th of January.

It does not take any lawyer to understand that that is the exact proposition. What is the next ground that it is put upon? But before I pass from that, I will say further we proved that the counterfeiter passed a bad bill (and I am following the illustration of the learned counsel before me), and he proposes to prove that at some other time he told somebody else, a good man, that he would not pass bad money, and you are asked to admit that evidence. Is there any authority for it? No. What is the next ground which is put? The next ground is, that it is competent in order to show Andrew Johnson's good character. If they put that in testimony I will open the door wide. I have no objection whatever that they shall offer it. (Laughter.) I will take evidence of his character, as to his loyalty, patriotism, or any other matter that they may wish to prove to you. But how do they propose to prove good character? By showing what he said to another gentleman. Did you ever have a character proved in that way?

Lawyers of the Senate, a man's character is at issue, and he calls upon his neighbor and asks him to state what he himself told him of his character. That is not the way to prove a character. Character is proved by general repute in the community. The learned counsel for the President then went on to quote from Lord Hardy's case. Now, I have never before seen cited in the course of a trial the argument of the counsel. I thought that that was never part of the record. Am I not right in that, lawyers of the Senate? and yet, for page after page the counsel read the argument of Mr. Erskine, who was going as far as he could to save the life of his client. He cites that as a precedent. So unprofessional an act I never knew.

Mr. STANBERY, interrupting—I read, and I wish the gentleman to attend to what I now say, I read only so much of the argument of Mr. Erskine as showed the application of the case.

Mr. BUTLER—I attended with care. I had the book in my hands, and followed the gentleman, and the argument of the counsel in the case only was read by him. Now, what was the question there? It was, what were the public declarations of Hardy? He was accused of having made a series of speeches which were held to be treasonable, and then the question was, what was his character as a loyal man, and after argument it came down to this—after all that you have seen of him, what is his character for sincerity and truth? A. I had every reason to believe him a simple, sincere, honest man. If this had been stated at first, I do not see what possible objection there could have been to it, and so, if counsel will ask General Sherman, or anybody else, what is Andrew Johnson's character for sincerity and truth, I will not object, I assure you. (Laughter.) Now, what was Lord George Gordon's case? Lord George Gordon was accused of treason in leading a mob of Protestants against the House of Parliament, and the cries of the mob made publicly and openly, were allowed to be put in evidence against him as a proof of the *res gestœ*. The defense was the insanity of Lord George Gordon, and on the whole case they went in for the worst possible range of evidence. Let the counsel in this case come in and plead that Andrew Johnson is insane, and we shall go into all the conversation to see if they were the acts of a sane man, not otherwise.

The counsel then went into the Lord William Russell case. That case was one of those so eloquently-denounced by the gentleman who opened for the President yesterday, as one of the cases of the Plantagenets and Tudors, which he would appeal to for authority, and they have to prick into these cases, which yesterday they were to lay aside. The question then was, what was Lord William Russell's character for loyalty? The answer was, good. How long have you known him? A. I have known him for a long time. Did you ever hear him express himself against the King and against the government? A. No. Did you ever hear him express himself in favor of insurrection? No. Just precisely as evidence, and the man's character is given. They are not arguing as to what Lord Russell said, but they were often told that the he did not say anything treasonable. Again, let me call your attention to another point on which this is pressed, and it seems to be the strong point in the case, because my friend says it is vital, hoping, I suppose, to affright you from your propriety. While it is a very important matter, you must pardon me for arguing it at some length.

Mr. STANBERY—The gentleman has fallen into error in referring to my citation.

Mr. BUTLER—I cannot allow you to interpolate any remarks.

Mr. STANBERY—One moment, if you please.

Mr. BUTLER—I cannot spare a moment for that purpose.

Now, then, Senators, what is the other point? and that is the only one I feel any trouble about. It is that some gentleman may think that this question comes within the ruling of the Senate yesterday. Yesterday we objected to the President's declaration after he said the conspiracy had culminated, but the Senate decided that it should be put in. Now, however, they propose to go a month prior to that time. We offered to prove who Mr. Cooper is, and what Mr. Cooper was doing in December, in order to show the President had intent at that time, but the Senate of the United States rules it out; and now the counsel for the President propose to show what he said to General Sherman in December.

It has been remarked that I have said that the President was seeking for a tool, I have said so. At the same time I said he never found one in General Sherman. What I do say is this, and what I will say to you and the country, that Mr. Johnson was seeking for somebody by whom he might get Mr. Stanton out. First he tried General Grant; then he wanted to get General Sherman, knowing that General Sherman, not wishing to have the cares of office, would be ready to get rid of them at any time, and then the President should get in somebody else. He began with General Grant, and went down through Grant and Sherman, and from Sherman to General G. H. Thomas—anything, down, down, down, until he got to General Lorenzo Thomas.

Now they want to prove that because the President did not find a tool in General Sherman, he therefore did not find one in General Thomas. These two things do not hold together. Does it convince you that because he did not find a proper man to be made _ad interim_ Secretary, and to sit in his Cabinet _ad interim_, in General Sherman, that therefore he did not find the proper man in General Thomas. Then as to the vehicle of proof. They do not propose to prove this by his acts. I am willing that they should put in any act of the President about that time, or prior to it, or since, although the Senate ruled out an act which I offered to prove. But how do they propose to prove it? By a conversation between the President and General Sherman. I know, Senators, that you are a law unto yourselves, and that you have a right to admit or reject any testimony; but you have no right to override the principles of justice and equity, and to allow the case of the people of the United States to be prejudiced by the proof of the criminal made in his own defense before the acts done which the people complain of. If they have a right to put in evidence a conversation with General Sherman, have they not a right to put in evidence of the conversations of the President with reporters and correspondents, and call Mack, and John, and Joe, and J. B. S. as witnesses. I think there is no law which makes the President's conversations with General Sherman any more competent than his conversations with any other man; and where are you going to stop, if you admit it? They will get the

forty, the sixty, the ninety, or a hundred days that they asked for, by simply reporting the President's conversations, for I think I may say, without offense, that he was a great conversationalist.

He will have reporters and everybody else to tell us about what he said. Allow me to say one thing further; I stated that I did not think it right for the learned counsel to state what he expected to prove; and in order to prevent his statement I said he might imagine any possible conversation. I thought it an unprofessional thing that he should go on and state what he expected to prove, and I said if he would examine the book he held in his hand he would find that in Hardy's case the Attorney-General of England offered to read a letter found in Hardy's possession, and began to read it, when Mr. Erskine objected, and said, "You must not read it until it is allowed and given in evidence." The Attorney-General said he wished the court to understand what the letter was. Mr. Erskine said it could not be read for that purpose.

The counsel for the President stated in the case that he wanted to show that the President had tried to get this officer of the army to take possession of the War Department so that he could get Mr. Stanton out. That is what we charge. We charge that he would take anybody or do anything to get Mr. Stanton out. That is the very thing we charge. He would be glad to get General Sherman in, or glad to get General Grant in, and failing in both, and failing in Major-General George H. Thomas, the hero of Nashville, he took Lorenzo Thomas to get Mr. Stanton out. What for? In order, says the Attorney-General, to drive Mr. Stanton into the courts. He knew what his counsel knew, that Mr. Stanton would not go into the courts to get back the office. There is no process by which Mr. Stanton could be, through the courts, reinstated in his office. I think they will find it difficult to show that where a general law applies to States and territories of the United States, it does not also apply to the District of Columbia.

Now, then, the simple question, and the only one on which you are expected to rule, is whether the conversations of the President with General Sherman are evidence, and if they are evidence, why are not all the conversations which he had at any time, with anybody, evidence? Where is the distinction to be drawn?

Mr. EVARTS—Mr. Chief Justice and Senators:—As questions of ordinary propriety have been raised and been discussed at some length by the learned manager, allow me to read from page 165 of the record of this trial, on the question of stating what is intended to be proved.

Mr. Manager BUTLER—The object is to show the intent and purpose with which General Thomas went to the War Department on the morning of the 22d of February; that he went with the intent and purpose of taking possession by force; that he alleged that intent and purpose; that, in consequence of that allegation, Mr. Burleigh invited General Moorhead and went up to the War Office. The conversation which I expect to prove is this:—After the President of the United States had appointed General Thomas and given him directions to take the War Office, and after he had made a quiet visit there on the 21st, on the evening of the 21st he told Mr. Burleigh that the next day he was going to take possession by force. Mr. Burleigh said to him—

Mr. STANBERY—No matter about that; we object to that testimony.

Mr. Manager BUTLER—You do not know what you object to, if you don't hear what I offer.

Mr. BUTLER made some remark to the effect that Mr. Evarts was misrepresenting him.

Mr. EVARTS—In the case of Hardy, stated by my learned associate, I understand the question related exclusively to introduction of conversations between the accused and the witness, professedly antecedent to the period of the alleged treason, and even that was allowed. And now, Mr. Chief Justice and Senators, as to the merits of this question of evidence, this is a very peculiar case. Whenever evidence is stated to be made applicable to it, then it is a crime of the narrowest dimensions and of the most puny proportions. It consists for its completeness, for its guilt, in the delivery of a written paper by the President to General Thomas, to be communicated to the Secretary of War, and that offense, in these faded proportions, if contrary to a valid law, and if done with intent to violate that law, may be punished by a fine of six cents. That is the naked dimensions of a mere technical statutory offense, and if it concluded within the mere act of the delivery of paper, unattended by grave public consequences which should bring it into judgment here. But when we come to magnificence of accusation, as of the accusation as founded on page 77, we will see what it is:— "We suggest, therefore, that we are in the presence of the Senate of the United States, convened as a constitutional tribunal, to inquire into and determine whether Andrew Johnson, because of malversation in office, is longer fit to retain the office of President of the United States, or hereafter to hold any office of honor or profit." On page 97 we come a little nearer, and I beg the attention of Senators to what is said there bearing upon this question:—"However, it may be said that the President removed Mr. Stanton for the very purpose of testing the constitutionality of this law before the courts, and the question is asked, will you condemn him as for a crime for so doing? If this plea were a true one, it ought not to avail, but it is a subterfuge.

We shall show you that he has taken no step to submit the question to any court, although more than a year has elapsed since the passage of the act." Then on page 108 we are told:—"Upon the first reading of the articles of impeachment the question might have arisen in the minds of some Senators—Why are these acts of the President only presented by the House when history informs us that others equally dangerous to the liberties of the people, if not more so, and others of equal usurpation of powers, if not greater, are passed by in silence! To such possible inquiry we reply, that the acts set out in the first eight articles are but the culmination of a series of wrongs, malfeasances and usurpations committed by the respondent, and therefore, need to be examined in the light of his precedent and concomitant acts to grasp their scope and design." Then common fame and history are referred to, confirmed by citations of two hundred and forty years old from the British courts to show that there are good grounds to proceed upon.

Then, bringing this to a head, he says:—"Who does not know that from the hour he began these, his usurpations of power, he everywhere denounced Congress, the legality and constitutionality of its action, and defied its legitimate powers, and for that purpose announced his intentions and carried out his purpose as far as he was able, of removing every true man from office who sustained the Congress of the United State; and it is to carry out this plan of action that he claims this ultimate power of removal, for the illegal exercise of which he stands before you this day."

Now these are the intentions of public inculpation of the Chief Magistrate of the nation, which are, of such great import from their intent and design, and from their involving the public interests and the principles of government, that they are worthy of the attention of this great tribunal. If this evidence be pertinent under any one of the eleven articles, it is pertinent and admissible now.

The speech of August 18, 1866, is alleged as laying the foundation of the illegal purpose which culminated in 1868. The point of criminality which is made the subject of the accusation in these articles is the speech of 1868.

So, too, a telegram to Governor Parsons, in January, 1868, is supposed to be evidence as bearing upon the guilt completed in the year 1868. So, too, an interview between Mr. Wood, an office-seeker, and the President in September, 1866, is supposed to bear in evidence upon the question of intent in the consummation of a crime alleged to have been committed in 1868, and I apprehend that in the question of time this interview between General Sherman and the President of the United States on a matter of public transaction of the President, changing the head of the War Department, which was actually completed in February, 1868, is near enough to that intent, and to show the purposes of the transaction.

There remains, then, but one consideration as to whether this evidence is open to the imputation that it is a mere proof of declaration on the part of the President concerning his intentions and objects in regard to the removal of Mr. Stanton. It certainly is not limited to that force or effect. Whenever evidence of that character is offered that question will arise, to be disposed of on the very point as to what the President's object was. What we propose to show is a consultation with the Lieutenant-General of the Army of the United States to induce him to take the place.

On the other question, as to whether his efforts were to create violence, civil war, or bloodshed, or even a breach of the peace in the removal of the Secretary of War, we propose to show that in that same consulta-

tion it was the desire of the President that the Lieutenant-General should take the place, in order that by that change the Judiciary might be got to decide between the Executive and Congress as to the constitutional powers of the former.

If the conduct of the President in reference to the matters which are made the subject of inculpation, and, if the efforts and means which he used in the selection of agents, are not to rebut the intentions of presumption sought to be raised, well was my learned associate justified in saying that this is a vital question—vital in the interest of justice at least, if not vital to any important consideration of the case.

It is vital on the merest principles of common justice that the Chief Magistrate of the nation is brought under inculpation, and when motives are assigned for his action, and presumptions raised and inuendoes urged, we should be permitted, in the presence of this great council sitting this day and doing justice to him as an individual, but more particularly doing justice in reference to the office of the President of the United States, and doing justice to the great public questions proposed to be affected by your judgment, to have this question properly decided.

I apprehend that this learned court of lawyers and of laymen will not permit this fast and loose game of limited crime for purposes of proof, and of unlimited crime for purposes of accusation.

The Senate here, at 2·40, took a recess of fifteen minutes.

After the recess, Mr. WILSON, of the managers, took the floor and said, I will claim the attention of the Senate for but a few minutes. My present purpose is to get before the minds of Senators the truth in the Hardy case as it fell from the lips of the Lord Chief Justice who passed upon the question which had been propounded by Mr. Erskine, and objected to by the Attorney-General.

Mr. Wilson's Argument.

Mr. WILSON read from the State Trials the decision by the Lord Chief Justice to the effect that declarations applying even to the particular case charged, though the intent should make a part of the charge, are evidence against the accused, but are not evidence for him, because the principle upon which declarations are evidence, is that no man would declare anything against himself unless it were true, but any man would, if he were in difficulty, make declarations for himself.

He also read the subsequent proceedings affected by that decision and continued:—Now, what is the question which has been propounded by the counsel for the President to General Sherman? It is this:—In that interview what conversation took place between the President and you in regard to the removal of Mr. Stanton?. Now I contend that calls for just such declarations on the part of the President as fall within the limitation of the first branch of the rules laid down by the Lord Chief Justice in the Hardy case, and therefore must be excluded. If this conversation can be admitted, where are we to stop? Who may not be put on the stand and asked for conversations had between him and the President, as my associate suggests, at any time since the President entered upon possession of the Presidential office, showing the general intent and drift of his mind and conduct during the whole period of his official career? and why, if this be competent and may be introduced, may it not be followed by an attempt here to introduce conversations occurring between the President and his Cabinet and General Grant, by way of inducing the Senate, under pretense of trying the President, to try a question between the General of the Army and the President of the United States?

That interview occurred about the same time, and I suppose the next offer will be the conversations occurring between the President, his several Secretaries and the General of the Army in order that the weight, the preponderance of testimony submitted thereon, this trial may weigh down the General of the Army. I say that that may occur because it was a conversation which transpired about that time.

Mr. BUTLER—Only the day before.

Mr. WILSON—Yes, only the day before. We certainly must insist upon this well-known rule being applied to this particular objection for the purpose of ending forever, so far as this case is concerned, the introduction of the declarations of the President, made, it may be, for the purpose of meeting this impeachment.

It is offered to be proved, as the counsel inform us, that the President told General Sherman that he desired him to take possession of the War Department in order that Mr. Stanton might be driven to the courts of law for the purpose of testing his title to that office, and inasmuch as the counsel have referred to the closing argument of my associate manager, seemed to delight in reading therefrom, let me read a brief paragraph or two from that opening applying to this pretended purpose of the President of driving the Secretary of War to the courts to test his title on that occasion. The manager said:—"The President knew or ought to have known his official adviser who now appears as his counsel could and did tell him, doubtless, that he alone as Attorney-General could file an information in the nature of a *quo warranto*, to determine this question of the validity of the law."

Mr. Stanton, if ejected from office, was without remedy,

because a series of decisions has settled the law to be that an ejected officer cannot reinstate himself either by *quo warranto*, *mandamus* or other appropriate remedy in the courts. Then the purpose was not the harmless one of getting the Lieutenant-General of the Army in the position of Secretary of War to the additional end of having a judicial decision of this question, but the purpose was to get possession, as we have charged, of that department for his own purposes, and putting the Secretary of War in a position where he could not secure a judgment of the courts upon his title to that office. Now, I beg counsel to remember, not that we charge that the President expected that he could make a tool of General Sherman, but that he might oust Mr. Stanton from that office by getting General Sherman to accept it, thereby putting Mr. Stanton in a position where he could not have returned to office, expecting and believing that the Lieutenant-General of the Army would not long desire to occupy the position and would retire, and that then the Adjutant-General of the Army or some other person equally pliant could be put into the place vacated by the Lieutenant-General.

Now, the President did not succeed in that, and as it has been said, he appointed on down until he came to Adjutant-General Thomas. Then he found the person who was willing to undertake this work; who was willing to use force, as he declared, to 'get possession of that office. And now, with that proof of the President's own declarations and acts before the Senate, it is offered to make his innocence apparent by giving in evidence, his own declarations at another time. If a case can be defended in this way, no officer of the United States can ever be convicted on impeachment, and if the same rule is to apply in courts of justice, no criminal can ever be convicted for any offense therein, for the officer or the criminal may make his own defense by his own declarations. He will always have one to meet his case. I do not desire to detain the attention of the Senate. I am willing to let the case rest upon the authority shown by the learned counsel for the President, for under it and by force of it this matter must be decided.

The Vote.

The Chief Justice—Senators, the Chief Justice has expressed the opinion that the question now proposed is admissible within the vote of the Senate of yesterday. He will state briefly the grounds of that opinion. The question decided yesterday had reference to a conversation between the President and General Thomas after the note addressed to Mr. Stanton was written and delivered, and the Senate decided it admissible. The question to-day has reference to a conversation relating to the same subject matter between the President and General Sherman, which occurred before the note of removal was written. Both questions are asked for the purpose of proving the intent of the President in the attempt to remove Mr. Stanton. The Chief Justice thinks that proof of a conversation occurring before the transaction is better evidence of the intent of an act than proof of a conversation occurring after the transaction.

The yeas and nays were taken on the question, and the Senate excluded the question by the following vote:—

YEAS.—Messrs. Anthony, Bayard, Buckalew, Cole, Davis, Dixon, Doolittle, Fessenden, Fowler, Grimes, Hendricks, Johnson, McCreey, Morgan, Norton, Patterson (Tenn.), Ross, Sprague, Sumner, Trumbull, Van Winkle, Vickers, Willey—23.

NAYS.—Messrs. Cameron, Cattell, Chandler, Conkling, Conness, Corbett, Cragin, Drake, Edmunds, Ferry, Frelinghuysen, Harlan, Henderson, Howard, Morrill (Me.), Morrill (Vt.), Morton, Nye, Patterson (N. H.), Pomeroy, Ramsey, Sherman, Stewart, Thayer, Tipton, Williams, Wilson, Yates—28.

Examination Resumed.

Mr. STANBERY—Q. General Sherman in any conversations with the President, while you were here, what was said about the Department of the Atlantic?

Mr. BUTLER—Stop a moment. I submit that that falls within the rule just made. You cannot put in the declarations about the fact.

The Chief Justice—The counsel will reduce it to writing.

Mr. STANBERY—I will vary it.

Q. What do you know about the creation of the Department of the Atlantic?

Mr. BUTLER—We have no objection to what General Sherman knows about the Department of the Atlantic, provided he speaks from his own knowledge and not from the declarations of the President. All orders, papers, his own knowledge, if he has any, do not amount to a declaration. We do not object to it, although we do not see how this is in issue and the Chief Justice will instruct the witness, as in the other case, to separate knowledge from hearsay. I have no doubt the General knows himself. These gentlemen ask for the President's declarations, not his acts.

The Chief Justice—Does the counsel for the President ask for the President's declarations?

Mr. STANBERY—I may misunderstand the honorable managers, but I understand them to claim that the President created the Department of the Atlantic as a part of his intent, by military force, to oust Congress. Do I understand the managers to abandon that claim?

Mr. BUTLER—I am not on the stand, Mr. President, when I am I will answer the question to the best of my ability. The presiding officer asks the counsel a question which he doesn't seem to want to answer. The question put to him was, do you ask for the President's declarations?

The Chief Justice—The counsel for the President are asked whether they ask for the statements made by the President.

Mr. STANBERY—We expect to prove in what manner the Department of the Atlantic was created; who prescribed its boundaries, and what was the purpose for which it was created.

The Chief Justice—Was it subsequent to the time of removal or before it?

Mr. STANBERY—I do not know whether it was subsequent; it was prior I believe.

The Secretary read the question by direction of the Chief Justice.

Mr. BUTLER—That department can only be created by an order.

The Chief Justice—Do you object?

Mr. BUTLER—I object to it in every aspect; but first I object to any declarations by the President.

The Chief Justice put the question on the admission of the question, and it was excluded.

Mr. STANBERY—Q. I will ask you this question. Did the President make any application to you respecting your acceptance of the office of Secretary of War, *ad interim*? Did he make a proposition to you; did he make an offer to you?

Mr. BUTLER—Is that question in writing?

Mr. STANBERY—Yes, sir (handing a paper to the manager). It is to prove an act, not a declaration.

Mr. BUTLER—After consultation, I am instructed, Mr. President, to object to this, because indirectly, in explanation an application can be made in writing or conversation, and then they would be the written or oral declaration of the President, and it is immaterial to this case.

Mr. EVARTS—Mr. Chief Justice, the grounds of the understanding upon which the evidence in the form and the extent in which our question, which was overruled, sought to introduce it, was overruled because it put in evidence declarations of the President, several statements of what he was to do or what he done. We offer this present evidence as Executive action of the President at the time, and in the direct power of a proposed investment with office of General Sherman.

Mr. BUTLER—To that we simply say, that that is not the way to prove Executive action. To anything done by the Executive, we do not object, but applications made in a closet cannot be put in, whether upon declaration or otherwise.

Mr. STANBERY—Of course, Mr. Chief Justice and Senators, if we were about to prove the actual appointment of General Sherman to be Secretary *ad interim*, we must produce the paper. The order—the Executive order—that is not what we are about to show. The offer was not accepted. What we offer is not a declaration, but an act which was proposed by the President to General Sherman, unconnected if you please with any declaration of any intention. Let the act speak for itself.

Mr. BUTLER—Very well; put in the letter.

Mr. STANBERY—Is it a question under the Statute of Frauds, that you must have it in writing; that a thing that must be made in writing is not good in parole? What we are about now is what we have not discussed as yet. It is an act, a thing proposed, an office, tender to a party. Gen. Sherman, will you take the position of Secretary of War, *ad interim?* Is not that an act? Is that a declaration merely of intent? Is it not the offer of the office? We claim it is not a declaration at all. It is not declaring anything about what his intention is, but it is doing an act. Will you take the office? I offer it. Let that act speak for itself.

Mr. BUTLER—Mr. President, I do not claim any right to close the discussion, but I will just call the attention of the Senator to this:—Suppose he did offer it, what does that prove? Suppose he did not, what does that prove? If you mean to deal fairly with the Senate, and not get in a conversation under the guise of putting in an act, what does it prove? If he was trying to get General Sherman to take that office, it was an attempt to get Mr. Stanton out. If it was a mere act I would not object. The difficulty is while it is not within the Statue of Frauds, it is an attempt under the guise of an act to get in a conversation by direction of the Chief Justice.

The Clerk read the question, which had been reduced to writing, as follows:—

Q. "Did the President make any application to you respecting your acceptance of the duties of the War Department *ad interim?*"

The Chief Justice submitted the point to the Senate, and the question was admitted.

Sherman Offered the War Office.

Mr. STANBERY to witness.—Q. Answer the question, if you please? A. The President tendered me the office of Secretary of War *ad interim* on two occasions; the first was on the afternoon of January 25 and the second on Thursday, the 30th of January, in his own usual office between the library and the clerk's room, in the Executive Mansion; Mr. Stanton was then in office, as now.

Q. Was any one else present then? A. I think not; Mr. Moore may have been called in to show some papers, but I think he was not present when the President made me the tender; both of them were in writing; I answered the first one on the 27th of January; I did not receive any communication in writing from the President on that subject; the date of my first letter was the 27th of January.

(Another question was answered here inaudibly to the reporters.)

Another Question Objected To.

Q. Now referring to the time when the offer was first

made to you by the President, did anything further take place between you, in reference to that matter, the tender by him or the acceptance by you consummate?

Mr. BUTLER—That we object to. This is now getting into the conversations again. Senators, I call your attention to the manner in which the case is conducted. I warned you that if you let in the act, then the declaration would come after it. Now they say, they have got the act, and they want to see if by this means they canuot get around the declaration.

Mr. EVARTS—What is the proposition of the manager?

Mr. BUTLER—My proposition is, that the evidence is incompetent, and based upon evasion, getting in the act which looked to be immaterial. It was quite liberal in the Senators to vote to let in the act, but that liberality is taken advantage of, to endeavor to get by the ruling of the Senate, and put in the declarations which the Senate has ruled out.

Mr. EVARTS—The tender by the Chief Executive of the United States to a General in the position of General Sherman, of the War Office, is an Executive act, and as such has been admitted in evidence by the Senate, like every other act which is admitted in evidence as an act it is competent to attend it by whatever was expressed from one to the other, in the course of that act and the termination of it, and on that proposition the learned manager shakes his finger of warning at the Senators of the United States against the malpractices of counsel for the President. Now, Senators, if there be anything clearer, anything plainer in the law of evidence, without which truth is shut out, and the form and features of the fact permitted to be proved, excluded, it is this rule, that a spoken act is a part containing the qualifying trait and part of the act itself.

Mr. BUTLER—To that I answer, Senators, that of an immaterial act, an act wholly immaterial, the only qualification that could be put in would be the answer, perhaps, of General Sherman; that is not offered, but then the offer is to put in an incompetent conversation as explaining an immaterial act. What is the proposition put forward? It is Executive offers of offices to any man in the country; and they would put in the fact that he made the offer of the office, and as illustrative of that fact put in everything he said about it. That is the proposition. I did think there was a little malpractice about that proposition, but it is a most remarkable one. He does an act himself, and now he says, "I have got the act in, you must put the declaration in;" that is the proposition. It is not worthy of words. A criminal puts in his account, presses it in. "Now close," he says; "I have got the account in, now I want, also what I said about it in order to explain it." Why it is an argument itself.

By direction of the Chief Justice, the Clerk read the question which had been reduced to writing, as follows:—

"At the first interview at which the tender of duties of Secretary of War ad interim was made to you by the President, did anything further pass between you and the President in reference to the tender or your acceptance of it?"

The Chief Justice submitted the question to the Senate on which the yeas and nays were demanded by Messrs. Drake and Howard, and the question was excluded by the following vote:—

YEAS.—Messrs. Anthony, Bayard, Buckalew, Cole, Davis, Dixon, Doolittle, Fessenden, Fowler, Grimes, Hendricks, Johnson, McCreery, Morgan Norton, Patterson (Tenn.), Ross, Sprague, Sumner, Trumbull, Van Winkle, Vickers, Willey.—23.

NAYS.—Messrs. Cameron, Cattell, Chandler, Conkling, Conness, Corbett, Cragin, Drake, Edmunds, Ferry, Frelinghuysen, Harlan, Henderson, Howard, Howe, Morrill (Me.), Morrill (Vt.), Morton, Nye, Patterson (N. H.), Pomeroy, Ramsey, Sherman, Stewart, Thayer, Tipton, Williams, Wilson, Yates—29.

Mr. STANBERY—Q. In the second interview did he again make an offer to you to be Secretary of War ad interim? A. Very distinctly.

Q. At that interview was anything said in explanation of that offer?

Mr. BUTLER—We ask the presiding officer whether that does not fall exactly within the rule?

The Chief Justice was understood to reply in the affirmative.

Still Another Refused.

Mr. STANBERY—Q. In these conversations did the President state to you that his object was to make a question before the court?

Mr. BINGHAM and Mr. BUTLER objected simultaneously.

Mr. STANBERY—We have a right to offer it.

Mr. BUTLER—We have a right to object. Mr. President, courts sometimes say that after they have ruled upon a question, it is not within the proprieties of a trial to offer the same thing over and over again. It is sometimes done in courts for the purpose of making bills of exceptions, or writs of error on the ruling. If the counsel say that that is the present object, we shall not object, because they ought to preserve their rights in all forms, but supposing this to be the court of last resort, if a court at all, there can be no occasion—at least, no proper occasion—to throw themselves against the rules.

Mr. STANBERY—Mr. Chief Justice, I do not understand that the ruling was upon the specific question. It was the general question of what was said that was ruled out. I want to make the specific question now to indicate what the point was.

Mr. BUTLER—I would call attention to the distinct admission of the counsel that question was within ruling.

He expected it to be ruled out, but now he goes on to make the offer.

Mr. EVARTS—That was the previous question.

Mr. BUTLER—No, sir; the last one.

Mr. EVARTS said that though there was to be no review of the proceedings of this court, it was entirely competent to bring to the notice of the court, which was to pass on questions of final judgment, the evidence supposed to be admissible, in order that it might be made a question of argument. He claimed that counsel had a right to do that, and that the difference between the specific question now asked and the general question which was overruled was, that while a general conversation could not be admitted, the witness might be permitted to testify upon the specific point.

The Chief Justice directed that the question be reduced to writing.

The question having been reduced to writing, was handed to Mr. BUTLER, who said:—I object to the question, as both outrageously leading in form, and as incompetent under the rule.

The question was, "In either of those conversations did the President say to you that his object in appointing you was that he might then get the question of Mr. Stanton's right to the office before the Supreme Court?"

Senator HOWARD demanded the yeas and nays upon admitting the question.

The yeas and nays were ordered, and

Senator DOOLITTLE asked Mr. Butler again to state his objection.

Mr. BUTLER said he objected to the question as outrageously leading, and as being against the ruling of the Senate.

The vote was taken and resulted, yeas, 7; nays, 44, as follows:—

YEAS.—Messrs. Anthony, Bayard, Fowler, McCreery, Patterson (Tenn.), Ross, Vickers.

NAYS.—Messrs. Buckalew, Cameron, Cattell, Chandler, Cole, Conkling, Conness, Corbett, Cragin, Davis, Dixon, Doolittle, Drake, Edmunds, Ferry, Fessenden, Frelinghuysen, Grimes, Harlan, Henderson, Hendricks, Howard, Howe, Johnson, Morgan, Morrill (Me.), Morrill (Vt.), Morton, Norton, Nye, Patterson (N. H.), Pomeroy, Ramsey, Sherman, Sprague, Stewart, Thayer, Tipton, Trumbull, Van Winkle, Willey, Williams, Wilson and Yates—44.

During the call Senator JOHNSON asked for the reading of the question. The question being partly read, Senator JOHNSON said that will do, I vote no.

Senator DAVIS, having already voted, said that as the question was leading, he would vote no.

Mr. STANBERY—Mr. Chief Justice, this question was undoubtedly overruled on a matter of form, and I propose to change the form.

The Question in a New Shape.

The question, in a new form, having been handed to Mr. Butler,

Mr. BUTLER said, the question as presented to me, Mr. President and Senators is, "Was anything said at that conversation by the President, as to any purpose of getting the question of Mr. Stanton's right to the office before the courts?"

Now Mr. President and Senators, this is the last question without its leading part of it. I so understand it. I understand it to be a very well settled rule when counsel deliberately produce a question, leading in form, and has it passed upon, he cannot afterwards withdraw the leading part and put the same question, without it. Sometimes this rule has been relaxed in favor of a very young counsel (laughter), who did not know what the question meant. I have seen very young men so offending, but the court let them up. Now, I call the attention of the presiding officer and of the Senate to the fact, that I three times over objected to the question as being outrageously leading, and I said it, so that there might be no mistake about it; yet the counsel for the President went on and insisted not only in not withdrawing it, but in having it put to a vote of the Senate by yeas and nays.

If I had not called their attention to it, I agree that perhaps the rule might not be enforced, but I called their attention to it. There are five gentlemen, of the oldest men in the profession, to whom this rule was well known, they chose to submit to the Senate a tentative question, and now they propose to try it over again, and keep the Senate voting on forms of questions until its patience is wearied out. Now, I have had the honor to state to the Senate, a little while ago, that all rules of evidence are founded on good sense, and this rule, too, is founded on good sense. It is founded on the proposition that counsel shall not put a leading question to a witness to instruct him what they want to prove, and then, after the question is overruled, to put the same question, without its leading form. Of course, that was not meant here, but I think that the Senate should not allow itself to be played with in this way. If you choose to sit here and have the yeas and nays called, I can stay here as long as anybody.

Mr. STANBERY—Mr. Chief Justice and Senators:—This is too grave and serious and responsible an issue and too important in its results to allow us to descend to such a form of controversy. The gentleman again says I am an old lawyer, long at the bar, and I hope I am not in the habit of making factious opposition before any court, high or low, and especially not before this body; but the learned manager intimates here that I have deliberately asked a leading question, resorting to the low tactics of the Old Bailey Court for the purpose of getting time, making factious opposition. I scorn any such intimation. He says it is a leading question. Undoubtedly it is a leading question; but was it intended to be a leading qustion? Was it intended to draw General Sherman to say something which he would otherwise not have said?

The learned manager says:—Oh, no; it was not intended so far as General Sherman was concerned; but that so far as counsel was concerned the purpose was to put it in that form so that counsel might have another opportunity of putting it in a legal form. He charges that it was deliberately manufactured, in a leading form, knowing that it would be rejected, for the purpose of getting ten or fifteen minutes time. A leading question, sir; will the honorable manager read over the record of this case and see hundreds of leading questions, put by him, until we got tired of objecting to them? I may, of course, be permitted to disclaim any intention; this is a matter of great importance; the interests of our client are in our hands, and we are to defend them in the best way we can.

The question was modified at Mr. EVARTS suggestion so to read as follows:—"Was anything said at either of these interviews by the President as to any purpose of getting the question of Mr. Stanton's right to the office before the courts?"

The Chief Justice put it to the vote of the Senate, and the question was overruled without a division, and Senator HENDERSON sent up in writing the following question to be put to the witness? –

"Did the President, in tendering you the appointment of Secretary of War *ad interim*, express the object or purpose for so doing?"

Mr. BINGHAM—I object to that question as being within the ruling. It is both leading and incompetent.

The Chief Justice said he would submit the question to the Senate.

Senator DOOLITTLE arose and said—Mr. Chief Justice, I arose for the purpose of moving that the Senate should go into consultation on this question, (cries of "no! no!"), but there might not be time to-night to go into consultation, and I, therefore, move that the court adjourn.

The motion was rejected without a division.

The vote was then taken on admitting Senator Henderson's question, and it was rejected. Yeas, 25; nays, 27, as follows:—

YEAS.—Messrs. Anthony, Bayard, Buckalew, Davis, Dixon, Doolittle, Fessenden, Fowler, Grimes, Henderson, Hendricks, Johnson, McCreery, Morrill (Me.), Morton, Norton, Patterson (Tenn.), Ross, Sherman, Sprague, Sumner, Trumbull, Van Winkle, Vickers, Willey—25.

NAYS.—Messrs. Cameron, Cattell, Chandler, Cole, Conkling, Conness, Corbett, Cragin, Drake, Edmunds, Ferry, Frelinghuysen, Harlan, Howard, Harris, Morgan, Morrill (Vt.), Nye, Patterson (N. H.), Pomeroy, Ramsey, Stewart, Thayer, Tipton, Williams, Wilson and Yates—27.

Senator TRUMBULL, at half-past three, moved that the court adjourn. The question was taken by yeas and nays, and resulted—yeas, 25; nays, 27.

Mr. STANBERY sent to Mr. Butler another form of question.

After reading it, Mr. BUTLER said:—We object to this, both as a leading question and for substance. It has been voted on three times already.

The question was read, as follows:—"At either of those interviews was anything said in reference to the use of threats, intimidation or force, to get possession of the War Office, or the contrary?"

The Chief Justice submitted to the Senate the admissibility of the question, and without a division it was ruled to be inadmissible.

The Chief Justice asked the counsel for the President whether they had any other question to put to the witness.

Mr. STANBERY replied that counsel were considering that point.

Senator ANTHONY moved that the court adjourn.

Senator CONKLING inquired whether the managers meant to cross-examine the witness?

Mr. BUTLER replied that they did not.

The vote was again taken by yeas and nays on the question of adjournment, and it resulted—yeas, 20; nays, 32.

So the court refused to adjourn.

Stanbery Discomfited.

Mr. STANBERY then arose and said:—Mr. Chief Justice and Senators:—I desire to state that under these rulings we are not prepared to say that we have any further questions to put to General Sherman, but it is a matter of so much importance that we desire to be allowed to recall General Sherman on Monday if we deem it proper to do so.

Mr BUTLER rose and commenced to object, saying, we are very desirous that the examination of this witness should be concluded, but before he could conclude the sentence,

Mr. BINGHAM rose and said:—We have no objection.

The court then, at a quarter of five, adjourned, and the Senate immediately afterwards adjourned.

PROCEEDINGS OF MONDAY, APRIL 13.

The court was opened in due form, and the managers were announced at 12·05, Messrs. Bingham, Butler and Williams only appearing. Mr. Stevens was in his chair before the court was opened. The other managers entered shortly afterward.

The Twenty-first Rule.

The Chief Justice stated that the first business in order was the consideration of the order offered by Senator Frelinghuysen, amendatory of Rule 21. as follows:—Ordered, That as many of the managers of this court and the counsel for the President be permitted to speak on the final argument as shall choose to do so.

Mr. SUMNER—I send to the chair an amendment to that order to come in at the end.

It was read as follows:—

"Provided, That the trial shall proceed without any further delay or postponement on this account."

Mr. FRELINGHUYSEN accepted the amendment.

Mr. Manager WILSON rose and asked the indulgence of the Senate for a moment. He said he did not propose to contest the right of the Senate to adopt a rule reasonably limiting debate on the final argument of this question, in conformity with the universal rule in the trial of civil actions and criminal indictments. He was not here to oppose such a reasonable limitation as the interests of justice may require, as may be necessary to facilitate a just decision. He thought, however that the rule was calculated in some degree to embarrass the gentlemen sent here to conduct this case on the part of the people.

The House having devolved the duty upon seven of its members, in which they had not departed from the ordinary course, the effect of the rule would be to exclude from the final debate on the articles submitted by them at least four of the managers. He was not opposed to a reasonable limit. It would have been in accordance with the rule in regard to interlocutory questions, and would have avoided diffuseness.

The Senate had said that the public convenience and the interests of the people required that a certain limit of time should be divided among the managers. The rule did not meet with the approbation of the managers in the first instance. They thought it unusual, and they had directed their chairman to make this application. There had been five cases of impeachment before the Senate of the United States.

Mr. WILSON recited the circumstances attending each of the impeachments of Blount, Pickering, Chase, Peck and Humphreys, claiming that all these cases were analagous to the present. All the managers were allowed to speak on the final argument, save in one instance, where there were seven managers, and one of them failing to speak, Mr. Randolph, their chairman, spoke twice. He (Mr. Wilson) might be mistaken, but thought the right of the House of Representatives to be heard through all its managers had never been questioned. One case in British history was familiar to the school-boy recollections of every man in this nation, or who is familiar with the English language—a case made memorable not as much by the great interests involved as by this fact, that it was illustrated by the genius of the greatest men that England had ever produced, and that it continued for seven years.

In the latter respect he hoped this would not resemble it; but it would be remembered that the labor in that case was distributed amongst all the managers. The present case was not an ordinary one. Nothing in our history compared with it. They were making history to-day, and they should show that they appreciated the magnitude of the interest involved. He felt the difficulty of realizing the magnitude rising to the height of this great argument. It was not the case of a district judge or custom-house officer, but the Chief Magistrate of a great people, and its importance was felt from sea to sea, with millions of people watching for the verdict. Such a limitation should be accounted for in only one way, namely, that the case was of small consequence, or that it was so plain that the judge required no research and no argument from any-body. He had not in what he said been moved by any consideration personal to himself. He had lived to a time of life when the ambition to be heard did not rest heavily upon him, or at all events he had lived too long to attempt to press an argument upon an un-willing audience. If they allowed an extension of time, he did not know whether he would speak on the final argument or not. It would depend on his strength, and upon what was said by others. He con-cluded by warning the Senate that if they placed such a limit upon a case of such magnitude, it might here-after be used as a precedent in less important cases for reducing the number of counsel to one, or perhaps dispensing with them altogether.

Mr. STEVENS, one of the managers, rose and said:— I have but a few words to say, and that is of very little importance. I do not expect, if the rule be relaxed, to say many words in the closing argument. There is one single article which I am held somewhat re-sponsible for introducing, on which I wish to address the Senate for a very brief space, but I do desire that my colleagues may have full opportunity to exercise such liberty as they deem proper in the argument. I do not speak for my colleagues. If the Senate should limit the time that the managers may have, let them divide it among themselves—however, this is a mere suggestion. I merely wish to say that I trust that some further time will be given, as I am some-what anxious to give the reasons why I so pertina-ciously insisted upon the adoption of an article that the managers had reported, leaving that article out. I confess I feel in that awful condition that I owe it to myself and to the country to give the reasons why I insisted, with what is called obstinacy, on having that article introduced, but I am willing to be confined to any length of time which the Senate may deem proper.

What I have to say I can say very briefly. Indeed, I cannot, as a matter of fact, speak at any length if I would. I merely make this suggestion, and beg par-don of the Senate for having intruded so long upon its time.

Senator SHERMAN moved to amend the order sub-mitted by Senator Frelinghuysen by striking out the last proviso, and inserting in lieu of it another, which he sent to the Clerk's desk.

Senator FRELINGHUYSEN desired to modify his own resolution by adding another proviso that only one counsel on the part of the managers shall be heard at the close. He said it was not his purpose to change the rule excepting as to the number who should speak.

The Chief Justice directed the order, as modified by Senator Frelinghuysen, to be read, as follows:—

Ordered, That as many managers and of the counsel for the President be permitted to speak upon the final argument as shall chose to do so; provided, that the trial shall proceed without any further delay or post-ponement; and provided further, that only one mana-ger shall be heard in the close.

Senator SHERMAN'S amendment was to add to the order the following:—"But any additional time allowed by this order to each side shall not exceed three hours."

Precedents.

Mr. BOUTWELL, one of the managers, rose and said:—

Mr. Chief Justice and Senators:—I would not have risen to speak on this occasion, had it not been for the qualifi-cation made by the honorable Senator from New Jersey. I ask the Senate to consider that in the case of Judge Peck, after the testimony was submitted to the Senate, it was first summed up by two managers on the part of the House; that then the counsel for the respondent argued the case for the respondent by two of their number, and that then the case was closed on the part of the House of Representatives by two arguments made by the managers. I ask the Senate to consider that in the trial of Judge Chase the argument on the part of the House of Repre-sentatives and of the people of the United States was closed by three managers, after the testimony had been submitted, and the arguments on behalf of the respondent had been closed.

I also ask the Senate to consider that in the trial of Judge Prescott, in Massachusetts, which I venture to say in this presence was one of the most ably conducted trials in the history of impeachments, either in this country or Great Britain, on the part of the managers, assisted by Chief Jus-tice Shaw, and on the part of the respondent by Mr. Web-ster, that two arguments were made by the managers on the part of the House and on the part of the people of the Commonwealth, after the case of the respondent had been absolutely closed, both upon the evidence and upon the arguments. I think the matter needs no further illus-tration to satisfy this tribunal that the case of the people, the case of the House of Representatives, if this trial is to be opened to full debate by gentlemen who represent the respondent here, ought not to be left, after the close of the

respondent, to a single counsel on the part of the House of Representatives.

Mr. Stanbery's Opinion.

Mr. STANBERY rose and said that the counsel for the President neither asked for nor refused the order pro-posed. They had no objection to all the seven of the managers on the other side arguing the case, but he un-derstood the amendment of the Senator from Ohio to fix a limit, whereas in the rule in the time allowed for the clos-ing up was unlimited. The rule only spoke of the number of the counsel, not of the time they should occupy. He de-sired to call the attention of the Senate to the amendment, so that there might be no misunderstanding. He hoped that not one of the counsel for the President had any idea of lengthening out the trial. He spoke as one competent to know, and he knew that when the counsel were through they would stop, and would only take as much time as they needed. They knew that if they went be-yond that they would not have the attention of the Senate. He could say that he spoke for his associates in saying that they would not take a moment longer in the case than they considered necessary. They would take every moment that was necessary, but not a moment that was unnecessary.

He referred to the fact that in the Supreme Court of the United States when arguments are limited to two hours, that limit is frequently, in important cases, removed, and he mentioned one case where he, himself, had spoken for two days. If counsel were limited to an exact time, they would generally be embarrassed, because they were look-ing continually at the clock instead of their case, and were afraid to begin an argument for fear they would exhaust too much time upon it, and be cut off from the more im-portant matters in the case. In conclusion he begged the Senate not to limit the time of counsel.

Senator SHERMAN, after hearing the remarks of Mr. Stanbery, withdrew his amendment.

Mr. Butler's Views.

Mr. BUTLER desired the counsel for the President to say whether they wished this rule adopted, because if they did not wish it, that fact would have its impression upon the mind as to what time should be granted. He wanted to say, however—and he stated it without preju-dice to anybody—that from the kind attention he had re-ceived from the Senate in his opening argument he did not intend, in any event, to trespass a single moment in the closing argument, but to leave it to the very much better argumentation of his assistants. He only wished, without any word on his part, that such argumentation should be had as should convince the country that the case had been as fully stated on the one side as on the other.

Senator SUMNER moved to strike out the last proviso in the order, and to insert in lieu of it the following:—

"And provided further, That according to practice in cases of impeachment, all the managers who speak shall close."

Senator CONKLING begged to ask the counsel for the President to answer the question asked by Mr. Manager Butler.

Fair Play.

Mr. EVARTS rose and said, Mr. Chief Justice and Sena-tors, I was about to say a word in reference to the ques-tion, when the Senator from Massachusetts arose to offer his amendment. It will not be in the power of the coun-sel of the President, if the rules should now be enlarged, to contribute the aid of more than two additional advo-cates on the part of the President. The rule was early adopted and known to us, and the arrangement of the number of counsel was accommodated to the rules. If the rule shall be enlarged, all of us would with pleasure take advantage of the liberality of the Senate. In regard, however, to the arguments of six against four, as then would be the odds, we naturally must feel some interest, particularly if all our opponents are to speak after we shall have concluded. The last speech hitherto has been made in behalf of the President.

If there is any value in debate, it is that, when it begins and is a controversy between two sides, each, as fairly as may be, shall have an opportunity to know and reply to the arguments of the other. Now the present rule very properly, as it seems to me, and wholly in accordance with the precedents in all matters of forensic debate, re-quires that the managers shall close by one of their num-ber, and that the counsel for the President shall be al-lowed to speak, and that the second manager, appearing in their behalf, shall close. So, if the rule shall be en-larged, it would seem especially proper, if there is to be such a disparity as that of six against four, that an equally just arrangement should be made in the distribution of the arguments of the managers and for the President.

Senator WILLIAMS moved to lay the order and the amendment on the table, in order, he said, to have a test vote as to whether the rule should be enlarged.

Senator DRAKE raised a question of order, that in the Senate, sitting for the trial of an impeachment, there is no authority to move to lay a proposition on the table.

The Chief Justice said he could not undertake to limit the Senate in its mode of determining questions, and that he conceived the motion to lay on the table to be in order.

Senator WILLIAMS called for the yeas and nays, which were ordered.

The Vote.

The vote was taken, and resulted—Yeas, 38; nays, 10—as follows:—

YEAS.—Messrs. Buckalew, Cameron, Cattell, Chandler, Cole, Conkling, Conness, Corbett, Cragin, Drake, Edmunds, Ferry, Fessenden, Harlan, Henderson, Hendricks, Howard, Howe, Johnson, Morrill (Me.), Morgan, Morrill (Vt.), Morton, Norton, Patterson (N. H.), Pomeroy, Ramsey, Ross, Sherman, Stewart, Sumner, Thayer, Tipton, Van Winkle, Williams, Wilson and Yates—38.

NAYS.—Messrs. Anthony, Davis, Dixon, Doolittle, Fowler, Grimes, McCreery, Patterson (Tenn.), Trumbull and Willey—10.

So the order and amendment were laid on the table.

During the vote, Senator ANTHONY stated that his colleague, Mr. Sprague, was called away by telegraph to attend the death-bed of a friend.

General Sherman Recalled.

Lieutenant-General W. T. Sherman was then recalled to the stand.

Question by Mr. STANBERY—After the restoration of Mr. Stanton to the War Office, did you form an opinion as to whether the good of the service required another man in that office than Mr. Stanton?

Mr. BUTLER—Stay a moment. We object. We want the question reduced to writing.

Mr. STANBERY said—I am perfectly willing to reduce the question to writing, but I do not want to be compelled to do so at the demand of the learned manager. I made a similar request of him more than once, which he never complied with.

Mr. BUTLER—I ask a thousand pardons.

The Chief Justice said that the rules required questions to be reduced to writing.

Mr. STANBERY said that his impression was that that was a request to be made by a Senator, and not by one of the managers or one of the counsel.

The Chief Justice directed that the fifteenth rule he read, and it was read as follows:—

"All motions made by the parties or their counsel shall be addressed to the presiding officer, and if he or any Senator shall require, they shall be committed to writing and read at the Secretary's table."

The question having been reduced to writing by Mr. Stanbery, was read as follows:—

"After the restoration of Mr. Stanton to office, did you form an opinion whether the good of the service required a Secretary of War other than Mr. Stanton, and if so, did you communicate that opinion to the President?"

Mr. Bingham Objects.

Mr. BINGHAM objected to the question, and stated the grounds of his objection, the first few sentences of which were inaudible to the reporters. When he did become audible, he was understood to say:—It is not to be supposed for a moment that there is a member of the Senate who can entertain the opinion that questions of this kind, now presented, under any possible circumstances could be admitted in any criminal prosecution. It must occur to the Senate that the ordinary test of truth cannot be applied to it at all; and in saying that, it has no relation at all to the truthfulness or veracity of the witness. But there is nothing on which the Senate can pronounce any judgment whatever. Is the Senate to decide questions on the opinions of forty or fifty thousand men as to what might be for the good of the service.

The question involved here is a violation of a law of the land. It is a question of fact which is to be dealt with by witnesses, and it is a question of law and fact which is to be dealt with by the Senate. After giving his opinion, as is proposed by the question, the next thing in order would be his opinion as to the application of the law, the restrictions of the law, the prohibitions of the law. Who can suppose that the Senate would entertain such questions for a moment? It must occur to the Senate that by adopting such a rule as this, it would be impossible to limit inquiry or to end the investigation. If it be competent for this witness to give his opinion, it is equally competent for forty thousand other men in the country to give their opinions to the Senate, and where is the inquiry to end? We object to it as utterly incompetent.

Speech of Mr. Stanbery.

Mr. STANBERY—Mr. Chief Justice and Senators:—If ever there was a case involving the question of intent, and how far acts which might be criminal or indifferent, or might be proper and actuated by intent, this is that case and it is on the question of intent that we propose to put this inquiry to the witness. [Mr. Stanbery's habit of speaking with his back to the court added much to the other inconveniences of the reporters and prevented his being properly reported]. With what intent, said he, did the President remove Mr. Stanton? The managers say the intent was against the public good, and in the way of usurpation to get possession of the war office, and to drive out a meritorious officer, and put in a tool and a slave in his place.

On that question what do we propose to offer? We propose to show that the second officer of the army feeling the complications and difficulties in which that office was surrounded by the restoration of Mr. Stanton, formed an opinion that the good of the service required it to be filled by some other man. Who could be a better judge than that distinguished officer now upon the stand? The managers asked what are his opinions more than any other man's opinion, if given, merely as abstract opinions. We do not intend to give them as mere abstract opinions.

The gentleman did not read the whole question, or he would not have asked that. It is not merely what opinion had you, General Sherman; but, having formed an opinion, did you communicate to the President that the good of the service required Mr. Stanton to leave the office, and re-

quired some other man to be put in his place. This is a communication made by General Sherman to the President to regulate the President's conduct, and to justify it; indeed, to call upon him, looking at the good of the service to get rid of in some way, if possible, of this confessed obstacle to the good of the service.

Look what appears in Mr. Stanton's own statement, that from the 12th of August, 1867, he has never seen the President; has never visited the Executive Mansion; has never sat at the board the President's legal advisers, the heads of departments, are supposed to be. It may be said the differences between him and the President had got to the point that Mr. Stanton was unwilling to go there, lest he might not be admitted. Why, he never made that attempt. Mr. Stanton says in his communication to the House of Representatives on the 4th of March, when the House sent the correspondence between the President and General Grant, that he not only had not seen the President, but had had no official communication with him since the 12th of August.

How was the army to get along, and how was the service to be benefited in that way. Certainly it is for the benefit of the service that the President should have in that office some one with whom to advise. What has the Secretary of War become? One of two things is inevitable:—He is either to run the War Department without any advice of the Secretary, or he is to be removed from office. The President could not get out of the difficulty unless by humiliating himself before Mr. Stanton, and sending a note of apology to him for having suspended him. Would you ask him, Senators, to do that? Now, when you are inquiring into motives; when you consider the provocation that the President has had; when, beyond that, you see the necessities of the public service; when you see that no longer could there be any communication between the Secretary of War and the President; is it fit, I ask, that the service shall be carried on in that way which is to enable the Secretary of War to hold on to his office, and become there a mere *locum tenens?*

Then when you are considering the conduct and intention, and the matter in the mind of the President in the removal of Mr. Stanton; and when you find that he has not only been advised by General Sherman that the good of the service required Mr. Stanton to be suspended, and that General Sherman undertook to communicate also to him the opinion of General Grant to the same purport; and when we shall follow that up by the agreement of those two distinguished generals to go to Mr. Stanton and tell him that for the good of the service he ought to resign, does it not show a reason why this evidence bearing upon the question of intent should be admitted?

Now, when you are trying the President for motive, for intention, whether he acted in good faith or in bad faith, will you, Senators, shut out the views of those two distinguished generals, and declare that his motive was to remove a faithful officer, and to get some tool in his place?

Speech of General Butler.

Mr. BUTLER—Mr. President and Senators:—I foresaw that if we had remained in session on Saturday evening long enough to have finished this witness, we would have got rid of all these questions. I foresaw that the effort would be renewed again in some form to-day, with the intent to get in the declarations of the President, or to the President; and now the proposition is to ask General Sherman whether he did not form an opinion that it was necessary that Mr. Stanton should be removed; whether the good of the service did not require a Secretary of War other than Mr. Stanton, and, if so, whether he did not communicate that opinion to the President. Well, of course, there could not be any other Secretary than Mr. Stanton, unless Mr. Stanton resigned or was removed. It will be necessary, then, to ask him whether he indicated his opinion to Mr. Stanton, if his opinion is to be put in at all, because—

Mr. STANBERY—How is that?

Mr. BUTLER—How long is our patience to be tried in this way? I am very glad that the Senate has been told that these tentative experiments are to go on, for what purpose, Senators themselves will judge; certainly for no legal purpose. Now it is is said that it is necessary to put this in, or else that counsel cannot defend the President. Well, if they cannot defend the President without another breach of the law added to his breach of the law, then I do not see the necessity of his being defended. They are breaking a law in defending him, because they are attempting to put in testimony which has no relevancy, no cogency, no competency. Under the law it is easy to test it, very easy, after you have let this question go in. Senators, if you were to do so, will you allow me to ask General Sherman whether he had not come to an equally firm opinion that it was for the good of the service and the good of the country that Mr. Johnson should be removed. The learned Attorney-General says that General Sherman came to the opinion that the "complications," as he called them, in the War Department, required that some other person than Mr. Stanton should occupy the office. I should like to ask him whether he did not think that these complications required the removal of Mr. Johnson?

The House of Representatives have thought that these complications could be got over by the removal of Mr. Johnson. Are you now going to put in General Sherman, to counterbalance the weight of the opinion of the House of Representatives? Is the President to be relieved of a wrong intent because General Sherman thought that Mr. Stanton was a bad man, and that, therefore, it was for the good of the service to put Mr. Stanton out? Is the President, I say, to be held innocent, therefore, in putting him out? Can we go into this origin of his opinion—I speak wholly without reference to the witness, and upon general principles—we would have to ask General Sherman as to his relations with Mr. Stanton; whether he quarreled with him, and whether those relations did not make him think that it would be for the good of the service to get rid of him?

We would have to ask him, Is there not an unfortunate difficulty between you? If the Senate will allow opinions to go in, it cannot prevent our going into the various considerations which produced these opinions. It is a kind of inquiry into which I have no desire to enter, and I pray the Senate not to enter into it, for the good of the country and for the integrity of the law.

Another question would be, what were the grounds of General Sherman's opinions? We should have to go further. We should have to call as many men upon the other side as we could. If General Sherman is put in as an expert, we would have to call General Sheridan and General George H. Thomas and General Meade, and other men of equal expertness to say whether, on the whole, they did not think it would be better to keep Mr. Stanton in?

I think that nothing can more clearly demonstrate the fact that this evidence cannot be put in than the ground that General Sherman is an expert as an army officer. If it is, we will have army officers, who, if not quite so expert, are just as much experts in the eye of the law as he, and the struggle will be on which side the weight of evidence would be. The counsel for the President say that they offer this to show that the President had not a wrong intent.

There has been a good deal said about intent—as though intent had got to be proved by somebody swearing that the President told him he had a wrong intent. That seems to be the proposition here; that you must bring some man who heard the President say he had a bad intent, or something equivalent to that. The question before you is, did Mr. Johnson break the law of the land by the removal of Mr. Stanton? Then the law supplies the intent, and says that no man can do wrong intending to do right.

If it were a fact that Mr. Stanton should have been put out, would that justify the President in breaking the law of the land in putting him out? Shall you do evil that good may come? The question is, not whether it were better to have Mr. Stanton out. On that question Senators may be divided in opinion. There are, for aught I know, and for aught I care, many Senators here who think it would be better to have Mr. Stanton out, but that is not the question. Is it right that the law of the land should be broken by the chief executive officer in order to get Mr. Stanton out?

See where you are going. It would be admitting justification for the President, or any other executive officer, to break the law of the land, if he could show that he did what he thought was a good thing, but a wicked one.

I am aware that executive officers have often acted upon that idea. Let me illustrate:—You Senators and the House of Representatives agreeing together as the Congress of the United States, passed a law that no man should hold office in the Southern States who could not take the oath of loyalty.

I am aware that the President of the United States put men into office who could not take that oath, and attempted to justify that before the Senate and before the House, on the ground that he thought he was doing the best thing for the service. That was a breach of the law, and if we had time to follow out the innumerable things he has done in that way and brought them before the Senate, we could have sustained articles of impeachment upon them. One other thing I desire to call your attention to. We have heard how, over and over again, that Mr. Stanton would not have a seat in the Cabinet Council since August 12, 1867.

Whose fault was that? He attended every meeting up to within a week of August 12. He did his duty up to within a week of the 12th of August, and he was then suspended until the 13th of January, and when he came back into office it was not for the President to humble himself, but it was for the President to notify Mr. Stanton, at the head of the War Department, to come and take his seat in the Cabinet, but that notification never came. It was not for Mr. Stanton to thrust himself upon the President, but it was for him to go when he understood that his presence would be welcome; but it is put forward, as if the country could not go on without a Cabinet Board, and the learned counsel has just told us that it was a constitutional board.

On that I want to take issue once for all. Senators, it is an unconstitutional board. There is not a word in the Constitution about a Cabinet or about a board. The learned gentlemen have told us that a board was almost a shield for the President, and there has been an attempt by some of the late President's friends to get this board around them to shield them from the consequences of their acts. The Constitution says that the heads of departments may be called upon in reference to their respective offices, to give opinions in writing to the President, and the rule of the early Presidents was to call upon Cabinet officers for their opinions in writing.

I have on my table here an opinion in writing, given by Thomas Jefferson to Washington, about his right to appoint ambassadors. Heads of departments are not to sit down and consult with the the President; they are not to have Cabinet counsels; that is an assumption of executive power, which has grown up little by little, formed upon the cabinets of the old world. The framers of the Constitution well knew that from the Cabinet counsels in England came that celebrated word "cabal," which has been the synonym of all that is evil in political combinations from that time to this, and it was not mere capri-

ciousness on their part that they required, not that there should be verbal consultations semi-weekly, and that secret conclaves might be held, but that there should be written opinions asked and given.

Think of it. Picture to yourselves, Senators, President Johnson and Lorenzo Thomas in Cabinet consultation to shield the President, and of Lorenzo Thomas stating to him that it was for the good of the service that he should be appointed. If they have a right to put in one Cabinet officer they have a right to put in another. If they have a right to put in the opinion of one Attorney-General, who is not, by the way, a Cabinet officer, or if they have a right to put in the opinion of one head of a department, they have a right to put in another. If permanent, then temporary. If temporary, then *ad interim*. Therefore, I find no dereliction of duty on the part of Mr. Stanton in not attending the Cabinet councils.

Let them show that the President has ever asked from Mr. Stanton an opinion, in writing, as to the duties of his department, or that he has ever sent an order to him which he has disobeyed, and that will show a reason; but I pray the Senate not to let us go into the regions of opinion. I have taken this much time, Senators, because I think it will save time to come to a right decision on this question.

This case is to be tried by your opinion, not by the opinion of anybody whether Mr. Stanton was a good or a bad officer. It is to be tried upon the opinion whether the President broke the law in removing Mr. Stanton, and he must take the consequences of that breach of the law.

It is said that he broke the law in order to get the matter into court. I agree in that, and if his counsel is correct as to the character of the Senate, the President has got the matter into court, where he will have the benefit of law.

Proposition from Senator Conkling.

Senator CONKLING submitted the following proposition in writing:—Do the counsel for the respondent offer at this point to show by the witness that he advised the President to remove Mr. Stanton in the manner adopted by the President, or merely that he advised the President to designate for the action of the Senate some person other than Mr. Stanton?

Why the Lieutenant-General is Introduced.

Mr. EVARTS rose and said:—Mr. Chief Justice and Senators:—I do not propose to discuss the constitutional relations of the President of the United States with his Cabinet, nor do I propose to enter into the consideration of the merits of the case, as it shall be presented on final argument. If the accusations against the President of the United States on which he is on trial here, and the conviction on which must result in his deposition from his great office, turned only on the mere question of whether the President has been guilty of a formal violation of a statute law, which might subject him, if indicted for it, to a fine of six cents or imprisonment for ten days, there might be some reason for those technical objections, but I think that the honorable manager (Mr. Williams) who so eloquently and warmly pressed upon your consideration to-day that the case of Warren Hastings was nothing compared to this, was rather a little out of place, if the trial is to turn on the mere formal technical infraction of the Tenure of Office act.

Now, Mr. Chief Justice and Senators, you cannot fail to see that General Sherman is not called here as an expert to give an opinion whether Mr. Stanton is a good Secretary of War or not. He is not called here as an expert to assist your judgment in determining whether or not it was for the public interests that Mr. Stanton should be removed, in the sense of determining whether this form of removal was legal or not. He is introduced here as the second in command of the armies of the United States, to show an opinion on his part as a military man, and in that position, that the military service required that a Secretary should take the place of Mr. Stanton whose relations to the service and to the Commander-in-Chief were not such as those of Mr. Stanton were, and that that opinion was communicated to the President; and we shall enlarge the area by showing that the opinion was concurred in by other competent military authorities. And now, if the President of the United States, when brought on trial before a court of impeachment, is not at liberty to show that the acts which are brought in question as against the public interest, and as being done with a bad motive, to obstruct the law and disturb the public peace, if I say he cannot show, in his defense, that in the judgment of those most competent to think, most competent to advise, most responsible to the country, in every sense, for their opinion, and their advice, how is he to defend himself? We propose to show that he was furnished with those opinions and supported by those opinions. Now, Senators, reflect; you are taking part in a solemn transaction, which is to effect, if your judgment be unfavorable, a removal of the Chief Magistrate of the nation for some attempts which he has made against the public welfare, with bad motives and for improper purposes.

We offer to show you that on consultation, and deliberation, and advice from those who, unconnected with any matters of personal or political controversy, occupied solely by their position, their duty and of that to their country enacted and desired to accomplish the change. We cannot prove everything at once; nor is it a criticism upon the testimony just excluded that it does not itself prove all; but if it should be followed, as it would be, by evidence of equal authority and weight, and by efforts of the President or authority to make efforts given by the President, to secure a change in the control of that office, which the service of the country then demanded, we shall show you, by an absolute negator, that this intention, this motive—the public injury, so vehemently and so pertinaciously imputed in the course of the argument—did not exist at all.

Equal Justice.

Mr. BINGHAM arose to reply, and was, as usual, for the first sentence, entirely inaudible in the reporters' gallery. He went on to say, the suggestion made by the honorable Senator from New York (Mr. Conkling) shows the utter incompetency and absurdity of the proposition. It was whether counsel for the President propose to ask a witness whether he advised the removal of the Secretary of War in the mode and manner in which the President did remove him, or attempted to remove him? Is there any one here bold enough to say that if the witness had formed an opinion against the legality of the proposition, and had so expressed himself to the President, it would be competent for us to introduce such matter in evidence?

The reason, Mr. Chief Justice, why I arose now, is that I might notice the reply in the utterances of the gentleman, who has just taken his seat (Mr. Evarts), and who has enunciated here the extraordinary opinion that the rules of evidence which would govern in a court of justice, in the prosecution of a beggar arrested in your streets for a crime, punishable with fine or five hours of imprisonment, are not the rules of evidence which would hold good when you come to prosecute the Chief Magistrate of the nation. The American people will entertain no opinions of that sort, nor will the Senate. We have the same rules of justice and the same rules of guidance for the trial of the President of the United States, as we have for the trial of the most defenseless or weakest of our citizens.

Mr. EVARTS—The honorable managers will allow me to say that the only illustration I used, was that of an indictment against the Chief Magistrate on trial before a police court.

Mr. BINGHAM—I supposed myself that when the gentleman made use of the remark, he intended, certainly, to have the Senate understand that there was a different rule of evidence and of administration—of justice, in the prosecution of an indictment where the penalty was six cents, from that which should prevail in the prosecution of the President.

Mr. EVARTS—When the issues are different, the evidence will be different. It does not depend on the dignity of the defendant.

Mr. BINGHAM—It is very difficult to see how the gentleman can escape from the difficulty by making the remark that he supposed the President to be under prosecution. It is a very grave question whether the President of the United States can be prosecuted for an indictable offense before his impeachment; but I do not stop to argue that question now; I do not care who is prosecuted on an indictment, whether the President or a beggar, the same rule of evidence applies to each. I do not care who is impeached, whether it be the President of the United States or the lowest civil officer in the service of the United States, the same rule of evidence obtains. Only the common law maxim, that where an offense is charged which is unlawful in itself and which is proved to have been committed, as I venture to say, have been proved in respect to all of these articles. The law itself declares that the intent was criminal, and it is for the accused to show justification. That is the language of the books; I so read it in the volume before me. The legality of the President's conduct is not to be solved by opinions of the witnesses but by the judgment of the Senate, to the exclusion of any other tribunal of earth, for so it is written in the Constitution. The law and the judges of the law will determine whether the act was unlawful. Opinions of third parties, although ever so often offered and expressed, cannot make an unlawful act lawful, and cannot ged rid of the intention, which the law itself necessarily attaches to the commission of an unlawful act. Well, say the gentlemen again, the President has taken the advice of an honored and honorable general. The Constitution, as the Senate well knows, indicates who shall be the President's advisers in such a case as this, the removal of the head of a department. That Constitution expressly declares that he may appoint and thereby necessarily remove an incumbent by and with the advice and consent of the Senate. The tenure of office act following the Constitution, provides further that he may for sufficient reasons to him appearing, suspend an incumbent and take the advice of the Senate, laying the facts before the Senate, and the evidence on which he acted, whether the suspension should be made absolute. The President did take the advice of the Senate, and did suspend this officer, whose removal he now undertakes to prove the public service required. He sent it to the Senate and the Senate, as his constitutional adviser, acted upon it, and gave him notice that it advised him not to attempt any further interference with the Secretary for the Department of War. The Senate gave him notice that under the law he must not go a step further, and thereupon he falls back upon his reserved rights, and undertakes to defy the Constitution, to defy the Tenure of Office act, to defy the Senate and to remove the Secretary of War, and make an appointment of another in his place without the advice and consent of the Senate. Except such outsiders as he choses to call into his counsel now, he undertakes to justify his acts by having witnesses to swear to their opinions. We protest against it in the name of the Constitution; we protest against it in the name of the laws enacted in pursuance of the Constitution; and we protest against it in the name of that great people whom we this day represent, whose rights have been outrageously betrayed, and who are now being audaciously defied before this tribunal.

The Senate proceeded to vote by yeas and nays upon the admission of the question, as follows:—

"After the restoration of Mr. Stanton to office, did you form an opinion whether the good of the service required a Secretary of War other than Mr. Stanton, and if so, did you communicate that opinion to the President?"

The Final Vote.

The vote resulted, yeas, 15; nays, 35, as follows:—

YEAS.—Messrs. Anthony, Bayard, Buckalew, Dixon, Doolittle, Fowler, Grimes, Hendricks, Johnson, McCreery, Patterson (Tenn.), Ross, Trumbull, Van Winkle, Vickers—15.

NAYS.—Messrs. Cameron, Cattell, Chandler, Cole, Conkling, Conness, Corbett, Cragin, Davis, Drake, Edmunds, Ferry, Fessenden, Frelinghuysen, Harlan, Henderson, Howard, Harris, Morgan, Morrill (Me.), Morrill (Vt.), Morton, Norton, Nye, Patterson (N. H.), Pomeroy, Ramsey, Sherman, Stewart, Thayer, Tipton, Willey, Williams, Wilson and Yates—35.

So the question was not admitted.

Another Mooted Question.

Senator JOHNSON proposed to ask the witness the following question:—

"Did you at any time, and when, before the President gave the order for the removal of Mr. Stanton, as Secretary of War, advise the President to appoint some other person than Mr. Stanton?"

Mr. BUTLER—I have the honor to object to the question, as being leading in form, and as being covered by the decision just made.

Mr. EVARTS—An objection to a question as leading in form cannot be made when the question is put by a member of the court.

Senator DAVIS inquired whether one of the managers or of the counsel for the defense could interpose an objection to a question put by a member of the court.

Mr. Butler Sustained.

The Chief Justice ruled that the objection must be made by a member of the court.

Senator DRAKE renewed the objection.

The Chief Justice said the only mode in which the question can be decided is to rule whether it is admissible or inadmissible. The question of the Senator from Maryland has been proposed unquestionably in good faith, and it is for the Senate to determine whether the question shall be addressed to the witness or not. The vote was taken by yeas and nays, and resulted—yeas, 18; nays, 32, as follows:—

YEAS.—Messrs. Anthony, Bayard, Buckalew, Dixon, Doolittle, Edmunds, Fessenden, Fowler, Grimes, Henderson, Hendricks, Johnson, McCreery, Patterson (Tenn.), Ross, Trumbull, Van Winkle, Vickers—18.

NAYS.—Messrs. Cameron, Cattell, Chandler, Cole, Conkling, Conness, Corbett, Cragin, Davis, Drake, Ferry, Frelinghuysen, Harlan, Howard, Howe, Morgan, Morrill (Me.), Morrill (Vt.), Morton, Norton, Nye, Patterson (N. H.), Pomeroy, Ramsey, Sherman, Stewart, Thayer, Tipton, Willey, Williams, Wilson, Yates—32.

So the question was excluded.

Senator Sumner, though in his seat, did not vote on either of the last two questions.

The Chief Justice asked the President's counsel whether they had any further questions to propose to the witness.

Mr. STANBERY replied that they had not.

The Chief Justice then inquired of the managers whether they proposed to cross-examine General Sherman.

Mr. BINGHAM replied that they had no questions to ask the witness.

The Chief Justice inquired whether the counsel for the President would require General Sherman to be again called.

Exit Sherman.

Mr. Stanbery stepped up to General Sherman and had a brief conversation with him, and Mr. Butler also stepped up and had a conversation with General Sherman. While they were conversing, the Senate, on motion of Senator Cole, at five minutes past two o'clock, took a recess for fifteen minutes.

Testimony of R. J. Meigs.

After the recess, R. J. Meigs was called and sworn on behalf of the President, and examined by Mr. STANBERY.

Q. What office do you hold? A. Clerk of the Supreme Court of the District of Columbia.

Q. Clerk of that court in February last? A. Yes, sir.

Q. Have you with you the affidavit and warrant under which Lorenzo Thomas was arrested? A. Yes, sir (producing papers).

Q. The original paper? A. The original paper.

Q. Did you affix the seal of the court to the appointment? A. I did.

Q. On what day? A. On the 22d of February last.

Q. At what hour of the day? A. It was between two and three o'clock on the morning of that day.

Q. At what place? A. At the Clerk's office.

Q. Who brought that warrant to you? A. I don't know the gentleman who brought it to me; he said he was a member of Congress.

Mr. PILE (Mo.)—Q. He brought it to your house at that hour of the morning? A. Yes, sir.

Q. And you went then to the Clerk's office? A. I went to the Clerk's office and affixed the seal.

Q. To whom did you deliver the warrant.
Mr. PILE—Q. The Marshal was not there at that time?
A. No, Sir.
Q. Have you got the warrant there? A. Yes, sir.
Q. Did you bring the affidavit upon which it was founded, or did you get that afterwards? A. I believe I have got all the papers.
Q. Is that the affidavit (showing paper)? A. That is the affidavit.
Mr. BUTLER. [After examining the paper.] Mr. President, before the counsel for the President offer the affidavit and warrant in evidence, I would like to ask the witness a question, if it is in order. [To the witness.]—Q. You say you affixed the seal about two o'clock in the morning, if I understand you? A. Between two and three o'clock in the morning.
Q. You were called upon to get up and do that. A. I was.
Q. And in a case where a great crime is committed, and when it is necessary to stop the further progress of the crime, that is not unusual. A. Where it was necessary to prevent a crime, I have done the same thing, in habeas corpus cases and in one replevin case, I think.
Q. Where it is a matter of consequence, do you do that? A. Yes, sir.
Q. It is nothing unusual for you to do that in each case? A. It is unusual; I have done it.
By Mr. STANBERY—Have you been often called upon to do it? A. Only in extreme cases.
Mr. BUTLER—I have the honor to object to the warrant and affidavit of Mr. Stanton. I do not think that Mr. Stanton can make testimony against the President or for him by any affidavit he can put in any proceeding between him and Lorenzo Thomas. I do not think the warrant is relevant to this case in any form. The fact that Thomas was arrested can be shown, and that is all. The affidavit upon which he was arrested is certainly *res inter alias.* That is a matter between Thomas and the President, and this is between Thomas and Stanton; and in no view is it pertinent or relevant to this case, or competent in any form, so far as I am instructed.

Another Legal Discussion.

Mr. EVARTS—Mr. Chief Justice, the arrest of General Thomas has been shown in the testimony, and they argue, I think, in their opening, the intention to use force to take possession of the War Office. We now propose to show what that arrest was in the form and substance by the authentic documents of it, through the warrant and the affidavit on which it was based. The affidavit, of course, does not prove the facts stated in it, but the proof of the affidavit shows the fact upon which, as a judicial foundation, the warrant proceeded. We then propose to follow this opening by showing how it took place, and how the efforts were made in behalf of General Thomas, by habeas corpus, to force the question to a determination in the Supreme Court of the United States.
Mr. BUTLER—I understand, if this affidavit goes in at all, it is then evidence of all that is stated, if they have a right to put it in.
Mr. EVARTS—You have a right to your own conclusions from it.
Mr. BUTLER—Not from the conclusions; but I think nothing more clearly shows that it cannot be evidence than that fact. Now this was not an attempt of the President to get this matter before the court; it was an attempt of Mr. Stanton to protect himself from violence which had been threatened before. This was made at night, if we may judge from the evidence of the threats made to Wilkeson and Burleigh, and the threats made at Willard's Hotel; being informed of it, he did not know at what hour this man might bring his masqueraders upon him, and thereupon he tried to protect himself. How that relieves the President from crime, because Stanton arrested Thomas, or Thomas arrested Stanton, is more than I can see. Suppose Stanton had not arrested Thomas, would it show that the President is not guilty here? Suppose he did arrest him, does it show that he is guilty? Is it not *res inter alias*—acts done by other parties? We only adverted to the arrest to show what effect it had upon his crime.
Mr. EVARTS—It has already been put in proof by General Thomas that he went to the court upon this arrest. He saw the President, and he told him of his arrest, and that the President immediately replied that that was as he wished it to be. The question in the court now. I propose to show that this is the question that was in the court, to wit, the question of the criminality of a person accused under this Civil Tenure act, and I then propose to sustain the answer of the President, and also the sincerity and substance of this statement, already in evidence, that this proceeding, having been commenced, as it was, by Mr. Stanton against General Thomas, was immediately taken hold of as the speediest and most rapid mode through a habeas corpus, in which the President or General Thomas, acting in that behalf, would be the actor, in order to bring at once before the Supreme Court of the district the question of the validity of his arrest and confinement under an act claimed to be unconstitutional, with an immediate opportunity of appealing to the Supreme Court of the United States then in session, from which at once there could have been obtained a determination of the question.
Mr. BUTLER—Whenever that is proposed to be shown, I propose to show that Thomas was discharged from arrest upon motion by his own counsel, and, therefore, the Senate will be traveling into the question of various facts taking place in another court. I have not yet heard any of the learned counsel say that this does not come within the rule of *res inter alias* facts done between other parties.

Mr. EVARTS—I did not think it necessary.
Mr. BUTLER—Perhaps that would be a good answer; but whether it is necessary or not, is it not so? Is there a lawyer anywhere that does not understand and does not know that proceedings between two other persons, after a crime was committed, were never yet brought into a case to show that the crime was not committed? Did he see that affidavit? Never. Did he know what was in it? No. All he knew was that this man was carried into court under a process. He never saw a paper. He did not know what was the evidence, but Thomas went and told him "They have arrested me." He said, "That's where I want it to be—in the courts."
This affidavit of Mr. Stanton is excellent reading. It shows the terror and alarm in this good District of Columbia, when, at night, men well known to be men of continency and sobriety, representing important districts in Congress, saw it was their duty to call upon the Judges of the Supreme Court, to call the venerable Clerk of the Court, out at night to get a warrant and take immediate means to prevent the consummation of this crime. It shows the terror and alarm that the unauthorized, illegal and criminal acts of this respondent created. That is all in it. Undoubtedly that is all in the affidavit.
Undoubtedly all that can be shown; and then we have before the Senate this appeal to the laws by Mr. Stanton, which this respondent never asked either before or since, although furnished with all the panoply of attack or defense in his Attorney-General, he never brought a writ of *quo warranto* or any process. All that might appear; we should be compelled to have it in, provided it does not open up into regions of unexplored, uncertain, diffuse, improper evidence upon collateral issues. If you are ready to go into it, I am, but I say it does not belong to this case. I think we can make quite as much of it as they can, but it is no portion of this case. It is not the act of the President; it has nothing to do with the President. The President never saw these papers; it is not evidence. What Stanton and Thomas did, they themselves must answer.
Mr. STANBERY—Mr. Chief Justice and Senators:—There are two grounds upon which we ask the admission of this evidence. First of all, it is claimed by the managers from what is already in evidence—mark, that already in evidence of the declaration of the President—that he made the removal to bring the question of that law to the consideration of the courts. That is already in evidence; but as to that the managers say, that is all a pretense—a subterfuge.
Mr. BUTLER—Where in evidence?
Mr. STANBERY—In the speech of the honorable manager who opened this case.
Mr. BUTLER—If you put my speech in evidence I have no objection.
Mr. STANBERY—And here the gentleman has repeated that this is all a pretense, that it is a subterfuge, an afterthought, a mere scheme on the part of the President to avoid the consequences of an act done with another intent. Again upon his intention with regard to the occupation of that office by General Thomas, they have sought to prove that the intentions of the President were not to appeal to the law, but to use threats, intimidations and force; and now all the declarations of General Thomas as to this purpose of intimidation or force the Senate has admitted in evidence against the President, on the mere declarations of Thomas of his intentions to enter that office by force or intimidation, and they are to be considered as declarations of the President.
If the gentlemen think that was sought by the respondent, the prompt arrest of General Thomas the next morning was the only thing that prevented the accomplishment of the purpose that was in the mind of the President and General Thomas. Who calls that a subterfuge? Now we wish to show by this proceeding, got up at midnight, as the learned manager says, in view of a great crime just committed, or about to be committed, got up under the most pressing necessity, with a judge, as we will show, summoned from his bed at an early hour on the morning of the 22d of February, as though it was an urgent and pressing necessity, either pretended or real on the part of Mr. Stanton to avoid the use of force and intimidation in his removal from that office. We shall show that when they had got him arrested they fixed the time of the trial of the great criminal for the next Wednesday—all this being done on Saturday; that when they got there they had got no criminal and the counsel of General Thomas say:— "He is in custody—we surrender him—we do this for the purpose of getting a habeas corpus."
It was not until that was announced that they act. The counsel for Mr. Stanton say that this great criminal had been kept in bond for good behavior. We expressly consent not that he should give bonds for his good behavior, but that he should be absolutely discharged and go free; not bound over to keep the peace, but wholly discharged; and, as we shall show you, discharged for the very purpose of preventing the prompt action of the habeas corpus, that the case might be got immediately to the Supreme Court of the United States, the only body in which a decision could be reached. Senators, is not that admissible?
Mr. BUTLER—Mr. President, I do not mean to trouble the Senate with more than one or two statements. First, it is said that Mr. Thomas was discharged wholly. That depended upon the Chief Justice of that court. If we are going to try him by impeachment, wait until after we get through with this case. One trial at a time is sufficient, because he did his duty under the circumstances, and Mr. Stanton, nor you, nor anybody else, has any right to condemn the act of that judge until he is here to defend him-

self, and the Chief Justice of the Supreme Court is amply able to do it.

Then there is another point which I wish you to take into consideration. "As to the claim that Thomas had become a good citizen." I have not agreed to that, and I do not believe that anybody else has. He himself says that on the next morning he agreed to remain neutral until they took a drink together. That next morning he agreed to stop and take a drink and remain neutral. (Laughter.)

Mr. STANBERY—Then Stanton took a drink with the "great criminal?"

Mr. BUTLER—He took a drink with the President's "tool," that's all. The thing was settled. The "poor old man" came and complained that he hadn't had anything to eat or drink, and in tender mercy, Mr. Secretary Stanton gave him something to drink. He says from that hour he never had any idea of force. Now I want to call the attention of the Senate to another fact, and that is, that they did not tell him to keep the peace. He said he was not told to keep the peace. He said it was necessary for him to make that point, and he said that the judge told him, "This don't interfere in any way with your duties as Secretary of War." But there is still another point. This unconstitutional law has been on the statute books since a year ago last month, and the learned Attorney-General, who sits before me, has never put in a *quo warranto*.

Mr. STANBERY attempted to say he had prepared a *quo warranto*.

Mr. BUTLER.—I have never heard of it, but it will be the first exhibition that was ever made before a court of the United States. Where is there a *quo warranto* filed in any court? Where is the proceedings taken under it? And I put it to him as a lawyer, did he ever take one? He is the only man in the United States that could file a *quo warranto*, and he knows it. He is the only man that could initiate this proceeding, and yet it was not done, and he comes and talks about putting in the quarrels of Mr. Stanton and General Thomas, which are *res inter alias* in this matter.

They have nothing more to do with this case than the fact which the President, with the excellent taste of his counsel, put in evidence against my objection that Mr. Stanton had, when this man was suffering from want of his breakfast, given him a drink. The offer of the affidavit, &c., was put in writing, and read by the Clerk, and the Chief Justice was understood to decide that it was admissible.

Mr. BUTLER.—Does your Honor understand that the affidavit is admitted?

The Chief Justice—Yes.

Mr. BUTLER—I heard one Senator ask for the question.

The Chief Justice inquired if any Senators asked for the question, and

Senator CONNESS replied in the affirmative.

The Chief Justice stated the question to be on the admission of the affidavit and warrant, and they were admitted by the following vote:—

YEAS.—Messrs. Anthony, Buckalew, Cattell, Cole, Corbett, Cragin, Davis, Dixon, Doolittle, Fessenden, Fowler, Frelinghuysen, Grimes, Henderson, Hendricks, Johnson, McCreery, Morrill (Me.), Morrill (Vt.), Morton, Norton, Patterson (N. H.), Patterson (Tenn.), Pomeroy, Ross, Sherman, Sumner, Trumbull, Van Winkle, Vickers, Willey, Williams, Yates—33.

NAYS.—Messrs. Cameron, Chandler, Conkling, Conness, Drake, Edmunds, Ferry, Harlan, Howard, Howe, Morgan, Nye, Ramsey, Stewart, Thayer, Tipton, Wilson—17.

The papers were then read in evidence.

Mr. STANBERY—Q. I see this is the Judge's warrant at Chambers? A. Yes, sir.

Q. Are you in the habit of keeping any records other than filing the papers or did you make any records further than filing the papers on that proceeding?

Witness was understood to reply in the negative.

Q. Has this defendant been discharged?

Mr. BUTLER—That appears from the record.

Witness—The record shows that; the docket shows that—the docket of the court; the recognizance of the court shows it.

Q. Do you make no record of those papers? A. No, sir; they are filed.

Q. Have you got your docket with you? A. No, sir; the subpœna did not require it.

Mr. STANBERY—(as the witness was leaving the stand.)

Q. Will you bring this docket that contains this evidence? A. Yes, sir.

Mr. BUTLER—Q. Will you not extend the record as far as you can, and bring up a certified copy of this case? A. Yes, sir.

Reverdy Johnson Puts a Question.

Mr. STANBERY then called Mr. James O. Clephane, but Senator JOHNSON sent to the Chair the following question to be put to General Sherman, who then resumed the stand:—

Q. When the President tendered to you the office of Secretary of War *ad interim*, on the 27th day of January, 1868, and on the 31st of the same month and year, did he, at the very time of making such tender, state to you what his purpose in so doing was?

Mr. BINGHAM objected to the question as being incompetent within the ruling of the Senate.

The Chief Justice put the question to the Senate on the admission, and it was admitted by the following vote:—

YEAS—Messrs. Anthony, Bayard Buckalew, Cole, Davis, Dixon, Doolittle, Fessenden, Fowler, Frelinghusen, Grimes, Henderson, Johnson, McCreery, Morrill (Me.), Morrill (Vt.), Morton, Norton, Patterson (Tenn.), Ross,

Sherman, Sumner, Trumbull, Van Winkle, Vickers, Willey—20.

NAYS—Messrs. Cattell, Chandler, Conkling, Conness, Corbett, Cragin, Drake, Edmunds, Ferry, Harlan, Howard, Howe, Morgan, Nye, Pomeroy, Ramsey, Stewart, Thayer, Tipton, Williams, Wilson, Yates—22.

The Secretary read the question put by Senator Johnson? A. He stated to me that his purpose—

Mr. BUTLER—Wait a moment; the question is whether he did state it, not what he said.

Witness—He did.

Mr. STANBERY—What purpose did he state?

Mr. BUTLER—We object.

Mr. President—The counsel had dismissed this witness.

The Chief Justice decided that it was competent to recall the witness.

Senator JOHNSON—I propose to add to the question:—If he did, what did he state his purpose was?

Mr. BINGHAM.—Mr. President, we object. We ask the Senate to answer that. The last clause—what did the President say?—is the very question upon which the Senate solemnly decided adversely. The last clause, now put to the witness by the honorable Senator from Maryland, is, What did the President say?—making the President's declarations evidence for himself. It was said by my associate, in the argument on Saturday, that if that method were pursued in the administration of justice. and the declarations of the accused were made evidence for himself at his pleasure, the administration of justice would be impossible.

Senator DAVIS—I rise to a question of order. It is that the learned manager has no right to object to question pronounced by a member of the court,

Mr. BINGHAM was proceeding to discuss the point, when he was interrupted by

The Chief Justice, who said that, while it was not competent for the managers to object to a member of the court asking a question, it was, in his opinion, clearly competent to object to a question when asked.

Mr. DRAKE inquired whether it was competent for a Senator to object to the question being put.

The Chief Justice thought not, but said that after it was put it must necessarily depend on the judgment of the court.

Mr. BINGHAM—Mr. President, I hope I may be pardoned for saying that my only purpose is to object to the question, not to object to the right of the honorable Senator from Maryland to offer the question. The point we raise before the Senate is, that it is incompetent for the accused to make his own declarations evidence for himself.

The Chief Justice—Senators:—The Chief Justice has already said upon a former occasion that for the purpose of proof of the intent this question is admissible, and he thinks also, that it comes within the rule which has been adopted by the Senate as a court for its proceedings. This is not an ordinary court, but it is a court composed largely of lawyers and gentlemen engaged in business transactions, who are quite competent to weigh the questions submitted to them. The Chief Justice thinks it in accordance with the rule which the Senate has adopted for themselves, and which he has adopted for his guidance.

Mr. BUTLER—Do I understand the Chief Justice to say that this is precisely the same question that was ruled upon last night?

The Chief Justice—The Chief Justice does not undertake to say that. What he does say is, that it is a question of the same general import, tending to show the intent of the President in this transaction. I wish, if there is any regular mode of doing so, to ascertain another point, and that is, whether the fact that this offer was made by the witness on the stand was first put in by the defense or the prosecution.

The Chief Justice—The Chief Justice will remind the Senate that the question is not debateable.

Mr. EVARTS—I may be permitted to state that it is put in by the defense

Mr. HOWE—I wish the Chief Justice to understand that it is not debating to ask a question.

The Chief Justice—It may be.

Mr. HOWE—It may not be.

The question as modified was again read.

The Chief Justice submitted it to the Senate, and it was admitted by the following vote:—

YEAS.—Messrs. Anthony, Bayard, Buckalew, Cole, Corbett, Davis, Dixon, Doolittle, Fessenden, Fowler, Frelinghuysen, Grimes, Henderson, Hendricks, Johnson, McCreery, Morton, Norton, Patterson (Tenn.), Ross, Sherman, Sumner, Trumbull, Van Winkle, Vickers, Willey—26.

NAYS.—Messrs. Cameron, Chandler, Cattell, Conkling, Conness, Cragin, Drake, Edmunds, Ferry, Harlan, Howard, Howe, Morgan, Morrill (Me.), Morrill (Vt.), Nye, Patterson (N. H.), Pomeroy, Ramsey, Stewart, Tipton, Williams, Wilson and Yates—24.

The question having been put to the witness, General Sherman replied as follows:—The conversations were long and covered a great deal of ground, but I will endeavor to be as precise upon the point as possible. The President stated to me that the relations which had grown up between the Secretary of War (Mr. Stanton) and himself—

Mr. BUTLER—I must again interpose an objection. The question is for the witness simply to state what the President said his purpose was, and not to introduce his whole declarations. I pray that the point may be submitted to the Senate whether we will have the whole of the long conversation between the President and the witness, or whether we shall have nothing but the purpose expressed by the President?

Witness—I intended to be very precise in my statement of the conversation, but it appeared to me necessary to state what I began to state—the President told me that the relations between himself and Mr. Stanton and between Mr. Stanton and other members of the Cabinet were such that he could not execute the duties of the office which he filled as President of the United States without making nominations, *ad interim*, for the office of Secretary of War, and that he had the right under the law, and that his purpose was to have the office administered in the interests of the army and of the country, and he offered me the office in that view; he did not state to me then that his purpose was to bring it into the courts directly, but for the purpose of having the office administered properly in the interests of the country and of the whole country. (Sensation in the court.) I asked him why the lawyers could not make the case? I did not wish to be brought, as an officer of the army, into the controversy.

Senator CONKLING—Please repeat that last answer, General.

Witness—I asked him why lawyers could not make a case, and not bring me as an officer into the controversy; his answer was that it was found impossible, or that a case could not be made up, but, said he, "If we could bring the case into the courts it would not stand for an hour."

Mr. STANBERY—Have you answered as to both occasions?

Witness—The conversation was very long, and covered a good deal of ground.

Mr. BUTLER—I object to this examination being renewed by the counsel for the President, whatever may be the pretense under which it is renewed. I hold with due order that this cannot be allowed. See how it is attempted. Counsel had dismissed the witness. He was gone, and was brought back at the request of one of the judges.

Mr. STANBERY—I must interrupt the learned gentleman to say that we did not dismiss the witness. On the contrary both sides asked to retain him, the learned manager (Mr. Butler) saying at the time that he wanted to give him a private examination. (Laughter.)

Mr. BUTLER—I must deny that. I want no private examination. I say the witness was dismissed from the stand, and that he was called back by one of the judges. It is not in any court wherein I ever practiced, allowed, after the question is put by the judge, for the counsel on either side to resume the examination of the witness after having dismissed him.

Senator JOHNSON asked for the reading of the questions as proposed by himself, and they were read by the Clerk.

The Chief Justice—Nothing is more usual in courts of justice than to recall witnesses for further examination, especially at the instance of any member of the court. It is frequently done at the instance of counsel. It is, however, one of those questions properly within the discretion of the court. If the Senate desire I shall put the question to the Senate whether the witness shall be further examined.

Mr. EVARTS—May we be heard upon the question?

The Chief Justice—Certainly.

Mr. EVARTS—The question Mr. Chief Justice and Senators, whether a witness may be recalled, is always a question within the discretion of the court, and it is always allowed, unless there be suspicion of bad faith, or unless there be special circumstances where collusion is suspected. Courts frequently may lay down a rule that neither party shall call a witness who has been once dismissed from the stand, and of course we will obey whatever rule the Senate may adopt in this case, but we are not aware that anything has occurred showing a necessity for the adoption of such a rule.

Mr. BUTLER—When the witness was on the stand on Saturday, this question was asked of him:—"At that interview what conversation took place between the President and you in relation to the removal of Mr. Stanton?" That question was objected to, and after argument the Senate solemnly decided that it should not be put. That was exactly the same question as this. Then other proceedings were had, and after considerable delay the counsel for the President got up and asked permission to recall this witness this morning. The Senate gave that permission. This morning they recalled the witness, and put to him such questions as they pleased. Then the witness was sent away, and then one of the judges desired to put a question to satisfy his own mind. Of course he was not acting as counsel for the President; that cannot be supposed.

Senator JOHNSON, rising—What does the honorable manager mean?

Mr. BUTLER—I mean precisely what I say, that it cannot be supposed that the Senator was acting for the President.

Senator JOHNSON—Mr. Chief Justice, if the honorable manager means to impute that in anything I have done in this trial I have been acting as counsel, or in the spirit of counsel, he does not know the man of whom he speaks. I am here to discharge a duty, and that duty I purpose to discharge. I know the law as well as he does.

Mr. BUTLER—Again I repeat, so that my language may not be misunderstood, that it cannot be supposed that he was acting as counsel for the President. Having put his question to satisfy his mind upon something which he wanted to know, how can it be that that opens the case so as to allow the President's counsel to go on to a new examination? How do we know that he is not acting as counsel for the President, and that there is not some understanding between them, which I do not charge? How can the President's counsel know what satisfied the Senator's mind? He recalls a witness for the purpose of satisfying his own mind.

I agree that it is common to recall witnesses for some-

thing overlooked or forgotten, but I have never known that, where a member of the court wants to satisfy himself by putting some question that opens up the case to the counsel on the other side, who puts other questions. The court is allowed to put questions, because a judge may want to satisfy his mind on a particular point; but having satisfied himself on that particular point, there is an end of the matter, and it does not open the case. I trust that I have answered the honorable Senator from Maryland that I make no imputation on him, but am putting it right the other way.

Senator JOHNSON—I am satisfied. Mr. Chief Justice, I rise to say that I did not know that the counsel proposed to ask any question of the witness, and I agree with the honorable manager that they have no right to do any such thing. (Sensation in the court.)

Mr. BINGHAM—I desire, on behalf of the managers, to say that there shall be no possible misunderstanding, to disclaim once for all that there was no intent by my associate who has just taken his seat, or any intent by the managers at any time, or in any way to question the right and the entire propriety of Senators calling on any witness, and putting any question which they may see fit. We impute no improper motive to any Senator in doing so, but recognize his perfect right to do so, and the entire propriety of it.

Mr. EVARTS—A moment's consideration, I think, will satisfy the Senate and the Chief Justice that the question is not precisely as to the right to recall a witness, but as to whether a witness having been recalled to answer the question of one of the judges, the counsel on the other side is obliged to leave that portion of the evidence incomplete. Some evidence might be brought out, which, as it stood noted, might be prejudicial to one side or the other, and certainly it would be competent under the ordinary rules of examination, that the counsel should be permitted to place the matter before the court within the proper rules of evidence.

Reverdy Johnson's Services.

Mr. STANBERY—The honorable Senator from Maryland having put his question to the witness, a new door has been opened which was closed upon us before. New evidence has been gone into which was a concealed book to us, and about which we could neither examine or cross-examine. It was closed to us by a decision of the court on Saturday, but it is now opened to us by the question of the Senator. Now, is it possible, that we must take an answer for better for worse to a question which we did not put. If in that answer the matter had been condemnatory to the President; if the answer had been that the President told the witness expressly that he intended to violate the law; that he was acting in bad faith; that he meant to use force, are we to be told that because the fact was brought out by a Senator and not by ourselves, we cannot put one question to elicit the whole truth?

This is not testimony of our seeking. Suppose it has been brought out by the Senator. Is the Secretary of War sacred against the pursuit of the true and sacred right of examination? Does the doctrine of "estoppel" come in here, that whenever a question is answered on the prerogative of a Senator we must take the answer without any opportunity of testing it further? If so, then we are estopped, not by our act, not by the testimony which we called out ourself, but by the act of another, and we are shut out from the truth because a Senator has chosen to put a question. We hold that the door has been opened, that new testimony has been introduced into the case, and that we have a right to cross-examine the witness to explain the testimony, to controvert it, if we can, to impeach the very witness who testifies to it, if we can. We are entitled to use every weapon which a defendant has put into his hands.

Mr. BINGHAM—Although the Senate cannot fail to have observed the extraordinary remarks which have just fallen from the lips of the honorable counsel for the President, it is perfectly apparent to intelligent men, whether on the floor of the Senate or in those galleries, that the counsel for the President have attempted to obtain, through this witness, the mere naked declarations of the accused to rebut the legal presumption of his guilt, arising from his having done an unlawful act.

I am not surprised at the feeling with which the honorable gentleman has discussed this question. If I heard aright the testimony which fell from the witness, it is testimony which utterly disappointed and confounded the counsel for the accused. What was it? "Nothing was said," said the witness, "in the first conversation about an appeal to the courts, and finally it was said by the President that it was impossible to make up a case by which to appeal to the courts."

These declarations of the President, standing in due form, yet not satisfactory to the counsel, are brought up, to be sure, on a question from the honorable Senator from Maryland; but there is no satisfaction to the counsel, and now they tell the Senate that they have a right to cross-examine. To cross-examine whom? To cross-examine their own witnesses. For what purpose? In search of the truth, they say. Well, it is in pursuit of the truth under difficulties. (Laughter.) The witness has already sworn to matters of fact. That shows the naked falsity of the defense interposed here by the President—that his only purpose in violating the law was to test the validity of the law in the courts. Why did he not test the validity of the law in the courts?

It will not do to say to the Senate of the United States that he has accounted for it by telling this witness that a case could not be made up. The learned gentleman who has just taken his seat is too familiar with the law of the country, too familiar with the able adjudications in this very case in the Supreme Court, to venture to indorse for a moment these utterances of his client made to the Lieutenant-General, that it was impossible to make up a case. I stand here to assert what the learned gentleman knows right well, that all that was needful to make up a case was for the President of the United States to do what he did do in the first instance, issue an order directing Mr. Stanton to surrender the office of Secretary of War to Lorenzo Thomas, to surrender all the records and property of the office to him, and on the Secretary of War's refusal to obey that order, to exercise the authority which is vested in the President alone, through his Attorney-General, who now appears as his attorney in the trial in the defense in this case, and to issue out this writ of *quo warranto.*

That is the law which we undertake to say is settled in the case of Wallace, 5 Wheaton, the opinions of the Court being delivered by Chief Justice Marshall, and no member of the court dissenting. It was declared by the Chief Justice as the opinion of the court that a writ *quo warranto* could not be maintained except at the instance of government. That power, therefore, was vested in the Attorney-General. Let the President's counsel in some other way than by this declaration, obtain what is sought to be reached by cross-examination of their own witness. But, Senators, there is something more than that in this case, and I desire simply to refer to it here in passing.

The question which arises here in argument now is, in substance and in fact, whether having violated the Constitution and laws of the United States in the manner shown here. They cannot at last strip the people of the power which they retain to themselves by impeachment, to hold such malefactors to answer before the Senate of the United States, to the exclusion of the interposition of every tribunal of justice on God's footstool. What has this question to do with the final decision in this case. I say that if your Supreme Court was sitting to-day in judgment on this question it would have no influence over the action of this Senate. The question belongs to the Senate exclusively. The words of the Constitution are that "the Senate shall have sole power to try impeachments."

The sole or only power to try impeachments includes the power to determine the law and the facts arising in the case. It is in vain that the decision of the Supreme Court, or of the Circuit Courts, or of the District Court, or of any other court outside of this high tribunal, is invoked for the decision of any question arising between all the people and their guilty President. We protest against the speech that has been made here; we protest, also, against the attempt to cross-examine this witness to get rid of the matter already stated so truthfully by the witness, which clearly makes against their client, strips him naked for the avenging hands of justice to reach him without let or hindrance.

Mr. EVARTS—Mr. Chief Justice and Senators, I cannot consent to leave matters so misrepresented. My learned associate, arguing on a hypothetical case, asked whether, if evidence elicited on the question of a judge should be injurious to a party, the party would be restricted from cross-examination. It had not the remotest application to, and as must have been apparent to every Senator, was not connected in the least with the evidence given.

The evidence given is agreeable to the managers—is extremely satisfactory to us. On inquiry of the President by the Lieutenant-General, whether lawyers could not make up a case without an *ad interim* appointment, the President said it could not be done; but that when there was an *ad interim* appointment the case could not stand half an hour.

Mr. BINGHAM—I desire in response to remark very briefly that instead of the counsel for the President bettering his client's case, he has made it worse by the attempt to explain the positions of the President to the witness, as to its being impossible to make up a case without an *ad interim* appointment. But how does the case stand? Has not the President made an *ad interim* appointment three months before this conversation with the Lieutenant-General? Has he not made an *ad interim* appointment of General Grant in August, 1867? "Ah!" say the gentlemen, "he only suspended Mr. Stanton then under the Tenure of Office act, and therefore, the question could not be very well raised." I have no doubt that that will be the answer of the counsel, and it is all the answer they can make.

But, gentlemen, Senators, how does such an answer put in here by the President, that he did not make that suspension under the Tenure of Office act, but under the Constitution of the United States, and by virtue of the power vested in him by that Constitution? He cannot play fast and loose in that way in the presence of the Senate, and of the people of the country. Why did he not sue out his writ of *quo warranto*, in August last, when he made his appointment of Secretary of War *ad interim?*

Why did he not go into the courts forestalling the power of the people to try him by impeachment for violation of law, for this unlawful act, which by the law of every country where the common law obtains, carries the criminal intent with it and on its face, which he cannot drive from the records by any false statement, nor swear from the record in any shape or form by any mere declarations of his own. Now one word more and I have done with this matter.

He tells General Thomas. They got that evidence in, and now they want to contradict that evidence too. That after Mr. Stanton refused to obey General Thomas' orders, and after he had ordered Thomas to go to his own place, and Thomas refused to obey his orders, he tells Thomas, I say, not that he was going into the courts; not that he

should apply to the Attorney-General for a *quo warranto.* There was no intimation of that sort, but there was a declaration of the accused to Lorenzo Thomas on the night of the 21st of February, after he had committed this crime against the laws and the Constitution of his country, that Thomas should go and take possession of his office and discharge his functions as Secretary of War *ad interim.*

Senator DAVIS inquired of the Chief Justice whether the questions proposed by Senator Johnson had been fully answered.

The Chief Justice said it was impossible for him to reply to that question. The witness only could reply to that.

Mr. DAVIS asked that the questions of Senator Johnson be read.

(They were accordingly read).

The Chief Justice ruled only the objection of the question proposed by Mr. Stanbery, that it was not a matter fairly within the discretion of the court, but it was usual under such circumstances to allow counsel to continue the inquiry to the same subject matter.

The questions and answers were read by the reporter, and then Mr. Stanbery's question was put to the witness, as follows:—

"Have you answered as to both occasions?"

Witness—The question first asked me seemed to restrict me so closely to the purpose that I endeavored to confine myself to that point alone. The first day, or the first interview in which the President offered me the appointment *ad interim;* he confined himself to general terms, and I gave him no definite answer. The second interview, on the afternoon of the 30th, not the 31st as the question puts it, was the interview during which he made the point which I have testified to, and in speaking or referring to the constitutionality of the bill known as the Tenure of Office act; it was the constitutionality of that bill which he seemed desirous of having decided when he said, "If it could be brought before the Supreme Court properly, it would not stand half an hour;" I said, that if Mr. Stanton would simply resign, although it was against my interest, against my desire and against my personal wishes and my official wishes, I might be willing to undertake to administer the office *ad interim;* then he supposed that the point was yielded, and I made this point, "supposing Mr. Stanton will not yield?" he answered, "Oh, he will make no opposition. You present the order and he will retire;" I expressed my doubt, and he remarked, "I know him better than you do; he is cowardly" (laughter in court); I then begged to be excused from an answer; I gave the subject more reflection, and gave him my final answer in writing; I think that letter, if you insist on knowing my views, should come in evidence, and not parole testimony taken of it.

But my reasons for declining the office were mostly personal in their nature.

Senator HENDERSON submitted in writing the following question:—Did the President, on either of the occasions alluded to, express to you a conviction, resolution or determination to remove Mr. Stanton from his office?

Witness—If by removal by force, he never conveyed to my mind such an impression; but he did most unmistakably say that he could have no more intercourse with him on the relations of President and Secretary of War.

Senator HOWARD proposed the following question in writing:—You say the President spoke of force. What did he say about force?

A. I inquired, "supposing Mr. Stanton does not yield, what then was to be done?" "Oh, said he, there is no necessity of considering that question; on the presentation of an order he will retire."

Senator HOWARD—Is that a full answer to the question?

Witness—I think it is.

Senator HENDERSON proposed the following question in writing:—Did you give any opinion or advice to the President on either of these occasions in reference to the legality or principle of an *ad interim* appointment, and if so, what advice did you give, or what opinions did you express to him?

Mr. BINGHAM—That we must object to.

Mr. BUTLER—That question has been overruled once to-day.

The Chief Justice put the question to the Senate and the Senate refused to admit it.

Mr. STANBERY stated that he had no further question to ask the witness.

Mr. BUTLER remarked that he did not know that the counsel for the President had anything to do with the examination.

The Chief Justice asked the managers whether they desired to cross-examine the witness?

Mr. BINGHAM said they did not at present desire to ask him any questions, but they would probable call him to-morrow.

General Sherman remarked, I am summoned before your committee to-morrow.

Mr. EVARTS insisted that the cross-examination should proceed before the witness was allowed to leave the stand.

Mr. BINGHAM said, we do not propose to cross-examine him at present.

Mr. EVARTS insisted that the cross-examination should proceed.

Mr. BINGHAM remarked that the counsel for the President had asked on Saturday for leave to recall the witness, and that the managers made no objection. It was for the Senate to determine whether the managers might call him to-morrow.

Mr. EVARTS said, we have no desire to be restrictive in

these rules, but we desire that the rules be equally strict on both sides.

The Chief Justice remarked that under the rules the witness should be cross-examined, but that it was a matter for the Senate to say whether they would allow him to be re-called by the managers to-morrow.

Mr. BUTLER said this witness has not been called by the counsel for the President, and therefore we do not cross-examine him; we take our own course in our own way.

R. J. Meigs Re-called.

Mr. STANBERY asked the witness to read from his books the records of the case of the United States vs. Lorenzo Thomas.

Mr. BUTLER objected that the docket entry of a court until the record is made up, is nothing more than the minutes from which the record is to be extended, and is not evidence.

The Chief Justice asked the managers whether they objected?

Mr. BUTLER—I have objected.

The Chief Justice directed the question to be educed to writing.

Being reduced to writing it was read as follows:—

Have you got the docket entries as to the disposition of the case of the United States vs. Lorenzo Thomas; if so, will you produce and read them?

The Chief Justice—The Chief Justice thinks that this is a part of the same transaction. He will put the question to the Senate if any one desires it.

No vote having been called for, the Chief Justice directed the witness to answer the question.

The witness handed the record to the reading clerk, who read as follows:—

No. 5711. United States vs. Lorenzo Thomas, Warrant for his arrest issued by Hon. Chief Justice Cartter, on the oath of E. M. Stanton, to answer a charge of high misdemeanor, in that he did unlawfully accept an appointment to the office of Secretary of War *ad interim*. Warrant served by the Marshal; recognizance for his appearance on Monday, the 26th inst.; discharged by Chief Justice Cartter on motion of defendant's counsel.

The witness was not cross-examined.

Senator JOHNSON moved that the court do now adjourn.

Senator HENDERSON called for the yeas and nays, but they were not ordered.

The question was taken by division, and the motion was carried by 24 to 18, so the court, at quarter of five o'clock adjourned, and the Senate immediately after adjourned.

PROCEEDINGS OF TUESDAY, APRIL 14.

The court was opened in due form. On motion, the reading of the journal was dispensed with.

Mr. STANBERY was absent at the opening.

Mr. SUMNER offered and sent to the Chair the following order:—

Arguments of Counsel.

Ordered, That in answer to the motion of the managers in reference to the limiting of the final argument, unless otherwise ordered, such other managers and counsel as choose may print and file their remarks at any time on the closing argument.

The Chief Justice—If there be no objection, it will be so ordered.

Mr. CONNESS—I object, Mr. President.

Mr. SUMNER—I would respectfully ask under what rule such objection can be made?

The Chief Justice replied that on several occasions he had decided the rules of the Senate to be the rules of the court as far as applicable.

Mr. SUMNER—Of course, it is not for me to argue the question, but I beg leave to remind the chair of the rule under which this order was made.

The Chief Justice—It will lie over.

To the Counsel—The counsel for the President will proceed with the defense.

Illness of Mr. Stanbery.

Mr. EVARTS rose and said it was the misfortune of the President's counsel to be obliged to state to the court that since the adjournment yesterday Mr. Stanbery had been seized with an illness which prevented his attendance this morning. He (Mr. Evarts) had seen Mr. Stanbery this morning, and had learned that in the opinion of the physician he would undoubtedly be able to resume his duties within forty-eight hours.

There might be some hope that he could not do so to-morrow. In view of the suddenness of the occurrence and of their arrangements in regard to proofs, it would be difficult and almost impossible with any propriety, with proper attention to the case, to proceed to-day, and they supposed that an indulgence at least for to-day would lessen the chances of longer procrastination. The Senate would bear in mind that much of their proposed evidence was within the personal knowledge of Mr. Stanbery, and not within that of his associates. It was, of course, unpleasant to them to introduce these personal considerations, but in their best judgment it was necessary to submit the motion to the discretion of the Senate, whether the indulgence should be limited to this day, or extended to the time necessary for the restoration of Mr. Stanbery, whom he had seen last evening, and supposed that he would be able to go on this morning, as usual, as had Mr. Stanbery, and had only learned this morning that Mr. Stanbery would be confined by direction of his physician.

Mr. DRAKE sent the following to the Chair, and it was read:—Cannot this day be occupied by the counsel for the respondent in giving in documentary evidence?

Mr. EVARTS—It cannot, as we understand the nature and condition of the proofs.

Adjournment until To-day.

On motion of Mr. HOWE, the Senate, sitting as a court, adjourned until to-morrow at twelve o'clock, Messrs. Sumner and Pomeroy only voting nay.

PROCEEDINGS OF WEDNESDAY, APRIL 15.

The court was opened in due form, and the managers and members of the House were announced and took their places.

Messrs. Stevens and Williams were absent at the opening, but appeared shortly afterward. Mr. Stanbery was also absent.

The Managers' Speeches.

After the journal was read,

The Chief Justice stated the question to be on the order of Senator Sumner, submitted yesterday, which was read, as follows:—

Ordered, That in answer to the motion of the managers, under the rule limiting the argument on a side unless otherwise ordered, such other managers and counsel for the President as choose may print and file arguments at any time before the closing argument on the part of the managers.

Senator EDMUNDS—I move to amend the order so it will read, "may print and file arguments at any time before the argument of the opening manager should be concluded, in order that the counsel for the defense may see it and reply to it."

Senator SUMNER—I have no objection to that.

The order as amended was read.

Mr. EVARTS—Mr. Chief Justice, may I be allowed to ask a question? The amendment offered and accepted places, I suppose, the proper restrictions upon the arguments to be filed on the part of the managers?

Several Senators—We cannot hear.

Mr. EVARTS, in a louder tone—The restriction proposed to be placed on this liberty by the amendment puts the matter on a proper basis, I suppose, as regards the printed briefs, that may be put in on the part of the managers; that is, that they shall be filed before we make our reply. On our part, it would be proper that we should have the opportunity to file the brief at any time before the closing manager makes his reply, so we may have an opportunity of replying in our brief to that of the managers.

Mr. BINGHAM—Mr. President:—I desire to say that it would seem, if the order be made as it is suggested, that additional arguments made by the counsel in behalf of the President need not be filed till the close of the arguments made orally to the Senate, the managers on behalf of the people would have no opportunity to see the arguments. I would ask the Senate to consider whether it is right to give the counsel for the President an opportunity to review and reply to arguments of the counsel for the people before any argument whatever may be filed here on behalf of the President.

Mr. EVARTS—Undoubtedly there are inconveniences in this enlargement of the rule, however applied; but there seems to be a propriety in requiring the managers to file their argument before the reply of counsel for the President. The same rule would be applied to us that, by the present amendment, would be applied to the managers of the impeachment, for they are not required to file theirs, except at the very moment that they close their oral argument, and then we are obliged to commence our oral argument.

Charge of Delay.

Mr. NELSON, after making some remarks in an inaudible tone, until admonished by Senators to speak louder, proceeded as follows:—

In consequence of the imputation made by the managers that we desired unnecessarily to consume the time of the Senate, those of us who, under this arrangement, had not intended to argue the case, did not yield, either by ourselves or by others, to make any application to the Senate for an enlargement of the rule; but since that application has been made on the part of the managers, I desire to say to the Senate that, if we are permitted to argue at all, I think it would be more fair to the two counsel who did not expect to argue the case, to permit us to make an extemporaneous argument before the Senate. We have not made any preparation in view of written arguments whatever. We suppose that the managers on the part of the House, who have had this subject before them for a much longer period than we have, are more familiar with it, and are better prepared to make written arguments; so that, if the rule be extended, we respectfully ask the Senate to allow us to address the Senate in such mode, either oral or written, as we may desire.

I do not expect to be able to interest the Senate as much as the learned gentleman to whom the management of the case has hitherto been confided on the part of the President, yet, as a resident of the President's own State, and I have practiced my profession in the town of his own domicile for the last thirty years, and as he has thought proper to ask my services in his behalf, and as I fully concur with him in the leading measures of his administration, I desire I may be allowed to be heard in the manner in which I have suggested.

An Amendment to the Amendment Proposed

Senator CONNESS made a motion, in writing, to strike out all after the word "ordered," and insert the following as a substitute:—

That the twenty-first rule shall be so amended to allow as many of the managers and of the counsel for the President to speak on the final argument as shall chose so to do, provided that not more than four days on each side shall be allowed, but the managers shall make the opening and closing argument.

Senator DRAKE asked the yeas and nays, and the substitute was lost by the following vote:—

YEAS.—Messrs. Cameron, Conness, Cragin, Dixon, Doolittle, Fowler, Harlan, Henderson, Hendricks, McCreery, Patterson (Tenn.), Ramsey, Sherman, Stewart, Trumbull, Van Winkle, Willey, Wilson, and Yates—19.

NAYS.—Messrs. Anthony, Buckalew, Cattell, Chandler, Cole, Conkling, Davis, Drake, Edmunds, Ferry, Frelinghuysen, Howard, Howe, Johnson, Morgan, Morrill (Me.), Morrill (Vt.), Morton, Patterson (N. H.), Pomeroy, Ross, Saulsbury, Sumner, Thayer, Tipton, Vickers, and Williams—27.

The question was then stated to be on the order of Senator Doolittle—Mr. Chief Justice, I prefer oral argument to printed ones; and I submit the following, notwithstanding there are but four cries of "order--order" of the counsel for the President, and six of the managers of the House. (Order—order.) I have sent to the chair an order which I will ask to have read. It was read, as follows:—

Strike out all after the word order, and insert "on the final argument two managers of the House shall open, two of the counsel for the respondent reply; then two of the managers speak, and they to be followed by the two other counsel for the respondent; and they in turn to be followed by the two other managers of the House, who shall conclude the argument."

Mr. DRAKE—Mr. President, I move the indefinite

postponement of the whole proposition, together with the subject.

Mr. SUMNER called for the yeas and nays, and the motion was carried by the following vote:—

YEAS.—Messrs. Anthony, Buckalew, Chandler, Cole, Conkling, Conness, Corbett, Davis, Dixon, Drake, Edmunds, Ferry, Fessenden, Grimes, Harlan, Henderson, Hendricks, Howard, Howe, Johnson, Morgan, Morrill (Me.), Morrill (Vt.), Patterson (N. H.), Pomeroy, Ross, Saulsbury, Sherman, Stewart, Thayer, Tipton, Williams and Yates—24.

NAYS.—Messrs. Cameron, Cattell, Cragin, Doolittle, Fowler, Frelinghuysen, McCreery, Patterson (Tenn.), Ramsey, Sumner, Trumbull, Van Winkle, Vickers, Willey and Wilson—14.

So the subject was indefinitely postponed.

Mr. FERRY offered the following:—

Ordered, That the twelfth rule be so amended as that the hour of the day at which the Senate shall sit upon the trial now pending, shall be, unless otherwise ordered, eleven o'clock A. M., and that there shall be a recess of thirty minutes each day, commencing at two o'clock P. M.

The order was rejected by the following vote:—

YEAS.—Messrs. Cameron, Cattell, Chandler, Cole, Conkling, Conness, Corbett, Cragin, Drake, Ferry, Frelinghuysen, Harlan, Howard, Howe, Morgan, Morrill (Me.), Morrill (Vt.), Ramsey, Sherman, Stewart, Sumner, Thayer, Williams, and Wilson—24.

NAYS.—Messrs. Anthony, Bayard, Buckalew, Davis, Dixon, Doolittle, Edmunds, Fessenden, Fowler, Grimes, Henderson, Hendricks, Johnson, McCreery, Morton, Patterson (N. H.), Patterson (Tenn.), Pomeroy, Ross, Saulsbury, Tipton, Trumbull, Van Winkle, Vickers, Willey and Yates—26.

Resumption of Business.

The Chief Justice directed the counsel to proceed with the case.

Mr. EVARTS—Mr. President and Senators, although I am not able to announce as I should be very glad to do, that our associate, Mr. Stanbery, according to the hope we entertained, has not been able to come out to-day. Yet I am happy to say that he is quite convalescent, and cannot be long kept from giving the case his attention. Under these circumstances and from a desire to do whatever we may properly do in advancing the trial of this cause, we propose to proceed to put in documentary evidence, hoping that we will not be called upon to put in any oral testimony until to-morrow.

Nomination of Ewing.

Mr. CURTIS said he would have to call upon the Executive Clerk of the Senate to produce the nomination of Thomas Ewing, Sr., of Ohio, to the office of Secretary of War, on the 21st of February, 1868.

The Chief Justice was understood to express a doubt as to whether, under the rules of the Senate, nominations were not under the injunction of secrecy.

Senator EDMUNDS asked the unanimous consent of the Senate to show that the fact of a nomination being made was considered not subject to the injunction of secrecy.

Mr. CURTIS said he was so instructed, and therefore he had supposed that no motion to remove the injunction of secrecy was necessary.

Senator SHERMAN said that, if a motion was considered necessary, he would move that the Executive Clerk of the Senate be sworn as a witness in the case.

The motion was agreed to, and the Executive Clerk of the Senate, Mr. Dewitt Clark, was sworn, and examined by Mr. Curtis, as follows:—

Mr. Clark's Testimony.

Q. State what document you have before you? A. I have the original nomination, by the President, of Thomas Ewing, Sr., as Secretary of the Department of War.

Q. Please to read it? A. Witness reads as follows:—"To the Senate of the United States:—I nominate Thomas Ewing, Sr., of Ohio, to be Secretary for the Department of War.   ANDREW JOHNSON.

"Washington, D. C., Feb. 21, 1868."

Q. On what day was this actually received by you. A. On the 22d of February.

An Executive Message.

Mr. CURTIS said—I now desire to put in evidence a message from the President of the United States to the Senate of the United States, which bears date February 24, 1868. I have a printed copy, which is an authorized copy, and I suppose it will not be objected to.

Mr. BUTLER—The vehicle of proof is not objected to, but the proof is objected to for a very plain reason. This message was sent after the President was impeached by the House, and of course his declarations put in, or attempted to be put in after his impeachment, whether directed to the Senate or any body else, can't be given in evidence. The exact order of time may not be in the mind of Senators, and I will therefore state it. On the 21st of February, a resolution was offered in the House looking to the impeachment of the President, and it was referred to a committee on the 22d of February, the committee reported, and the impeachment was actually voted, then intervened Sunday, the 23d. Any message sent on the 24th of February must have been known to the President to be after his impeachment.

Mr. CURTIS—It will be recollected that the honorable manager put in evidence a resolution of the Senate to which this message is a response, so that the question is whether the honorable managers can put in evidence a resolve of the Senate transmitted to the President of the United States with reference to the removal of Mr. Stanton, and refuse to receive a reply which the President made to that resolve.

Mr. BUTLER.—I have only to say that this is an argument of prejudice and not of law. Will my learned friends opposite dare to say that they have read of a case where, after the indictment of a criminal, the respondent was allowed to put in evidence his statement of his own defense? If so, where does that right cease? We put in the resolve referred to because it is a part of the transaction of the removal of Mr. Stanton. It was made before impeachment was determined upon, and now we are asked to admit the criminal's declarations made after that day. I only ask the Senate to consider of it as a precedent hereafter, as well as being a great wrong upon the people, that after indictment, after impeachment, the President can send in a message which shall be taken as evidence.

Mr. EVARTS—The learned managers ask wheeher we dare to do something. We have not been in the habit of considering the measure for the conducting of forensic disputations to be a question of daring. We are not in the habit of applying such epithets to opponents; nor hitherto in the habit o receiving them from them. The measure of duty of counsel is the measure which we shall strive to obey, and not the measure of daring. If for no ether reason thau this—that on rules of law, of fact and evidence, we may perhaps expect some superiority, but on measures of daring, never. (Laughter.) Is the learned manager entirely right in saying that the impeachment was voted on the 22d of February? The 22d was on Saturday, and unless I am mistaken, a vote was not taken until the following Monday.

Mr. BUTLER—The vote was taken on Saturday, the 22d of February.

Mr. EVARTS—That is that articles of impeachment shall be brought in.

Mr. BUTLER—Yes, sir.

Mr. EVARTS—The articles, however, were not voted until the 24th. Now, it is said that because the vote that the impeachment should proceed was taken on the 22d of February, that impugns the admissibility of the evidence proposed to be laid before the Senate. My learned associate has distinctly stated the situation of the matter. Perhaps both of these transactions—the vote in the Senate and this message—may be within the range of argument. But the managers have put in evidence this transaction of the Senate, and exactly what bearing this has as a part of the res gestæ, the removal of Mr. Stanton, which took place before the resolution was passed by the Senate. It was not easy to see. It was, however, received as proper evidence, and the reason why we did not consider it objectionable was because we supposed, as a matter of course of right, that this message, which is an answer to that resolution on the introduction of the topic before offered in evidence, would be admissible in testimony. We submit, therefore, that in every principle of law and of discussion in reference to the completeness of the record on the point, this message of the President should be allowed to be read and given in evidence.

Mr. BUTLER—I simply desire to call the attention of the Senate to the fact, whether that is a matter of daring or of professional knowledge. Neither counsel have stated any possible reason which is proper should be received in evidence. We put in the resolve of the Senate to show that, notwithstanding that resolve was served on the President on the night of the 21st of February, he still went on and treated this Lorenzo Thomas as Secretary of War ad interim; that Lorenzo Thomas was thus recognized by him after that as the Secretary ad interim, and that after that Lorenzo Thomas was carrying out his design to take possession of the office by force. We offered it in order to show that the President of the United States was determined on disobeying the law of the land, and that notice was served upon him for the purpose of having him know the action of the Senate, so that he might stay his hand. Now, can a prepared argument, made after that, and after he was impeached by the House of Representatives, be put in evidence? One ounce of action in obedience to the law and the resolution of the Senate would have been a great deal better than pages of argument. I will not use the word "dare," for I know that counsel would dare to do all that good lawyers would dare to do in favor of their client, but I will say that the gentlemen have not shown any sound reason on which this can be done.

The Chief Justice directed the counsel for the President to put in writing what they proposed to prove. While they were engaged in doing so,

Mr. BUTLER stated that, for fear there might be some mistake, he had sent the Clerk of the House for the record of the proceedings on impeachment.

Mr. McPherson, Clerk of the House, having come in soon afterwards, and handed the House Journal to Mr. Butler, the latter said—I find upon examination that the state of the record is this:—On the 21st of February the resolution of impeachment was prepared and referred to a committee; on the 22d the committee reported, and that report was debated through the 22d and into Monday, the 24th, and the actual vote was taken on Monday. the 24th.

Mr. EVARTS—Late in the afternoon; five o'clock; so that I was correct.

Argument of Mr. Bingham.

Mr. BINGHAM—I rise to state a further reason why we insist upon this objection. The House of Representatives, as appears by the journal now furnished, voted on the 22d of February that Andrew Johnson be impeached of high crimes and misdemeanors. On the day preceding the 22d of February it appears that the Senate of the United States proceeded to consider another message of the President, in which he had reported to the Senate that he had removed from the Department of War Edward M. Stanton, then Secretary of War by previous action of the Senate. The Senate refused to concur in the suspension—refused to acquiesce in the reasons assigned by the President under the Tenure of Office act, having given the President notice thereof. The President proceeds thereupon to remove him, and to appoint Lorenzo Thomas as Secretary of War ad interim, in direct contravention of the express words of the act itself and of the action of the Senate.

The record shows that on the 21st of February, 1868, the Senate of the United States passed a resolution reciting the action of the President in the premises, to wit:—The removal of the Secretary of War, and his appointment of Secretary ad interim, and declaring that under the Constitution and laws of the United States the President had no power to make the removal or to make the appointment of Secretary ad interim. That was the action of the Senate, and notice of that action was served on the President on the night of the 21st of February. Now what takes place? Here is a presentment made on the 21st or 22d of February, 1868, against the President before the grand inquest of the nation. After that presentment he was within the power of the people, although he had fled to the remotest end of the earth.

He could not have stopped for a moment the proper course of this inquiry to final judgment, even though personal process had never been served upon him. It is so provided in the text of the Constitution. It is to be challenged by no man. After these proceedings thus instituted, and two days after the effect of the action of the Senate being made known to him, and three days after the effect of the commission of his crime, the President enters deliberately on the task of justifying himself before the nation for a violation of its laws; for a violation of its Constitution; for a violation of his oath of office; for his defiance of the Senate; for his defiance of the people—by sending a message to the Senate of the United States, on the 24th day of February, 1868

What is it, Senators, any more than the voluntary declaration of the criminal after the fact, made in his own behalf? Does it alter the case in law? Does it alter the case in the reason or the judgment of any man living, either within the Senate or outside of the Senate, that he chooses to put his declaration in his own defense in writing? The law makes no such distinction. I undertake to assert here, regardless of any attempt to contradict my statement, that there is no law by which anybody accused criminally, after the fact, can make declarations, either oral or in writing, either by a message to the Senate or a speech to a mob, that can be given as evidence to acquit himself, or to affect in any manner his criminality within a tribunal of justice; or to make evidence which should be admitted upon any form of law, upon his motioh, to justify his own criminal conduct. I do not hesitate to say that every authority which the gentleman can bring into court relating to rules of evidence in proceedings of this sort, is directly against the proposition, and for the simple reason that this is a written declaration, made by the accused voluntarily after the fact, in his own behalf.

I read for the information of the Senate the testimony touching this fact of the service of the notice of the action had by the Senate, and of the conduct of the President, whereof he stands accused. Mr. William H. McDonald, Chief Clerk of the Senate, testifies, on page 148:—

"An attested copy of the foregoing resolutions was delivered by me into the hands of the President, at his office in the Executive Mansion, about ten o'clock P. M., on the 21st of February, 1868."

And on the 24th of February, three days afterwards, the President volunteers a written declaration, which his counsel now propose to make evidence in his behalf before this tribunal of justice. Of course, it is evidence for no purpose whatever, except for the purpose of exculpating him of the criminal accusations preferred against him.

Senators will bear with me while I make one further remark. The proposition is to introduce this whole message, not simply what the President says for himself, not simply the argument which he chooses to present in the form of a written declaration in vindication of his criminal conduct, but the declaration of third persons. The Senate is asked to accept this, too, as evidence on the trial of the accused; the declarations of third persons, whom he calls his constitutional advisers. He states their opinions without giving their language. He gives their conclusions, and those conclusions are to be thrown before the Senate as part of the evidence.

I beg leave to say here, in the presence of the Senate, that there is no colorable excuse for the President or his counsel coming before the Senate to say that he has any right to attempt to shelter himself from a violation of the laws of his country under the opinion of any member of his Cabinet. The Constitution never vested his Cabinet counsellors with any such authority, as it never vested the President with authority to suspend the laws, or to violate the laws, or to make appointments in direct contravention to the laws, and in defiance of the fiat of the Senate acting in express obedience to the law.

There is no tolerable excuse for these proceedings; I say it with all respect for the learned counsel, and I challenge now the production of authority in any respectable court that ever allowed any man, high or low, officially or unofficially, to introduce his own declarations, written or unwritten, made after the fact in his defense. That is the point I take here. I beg pardon of the Senate for having detained them so long in the statement of a proposition so simple, and the law of which is so clearly settled, running through centuries. I submit the question to the Senate.

Mr. Evarts States His Views.

Mr. EVARTS—Mr. Chief Justice and Senators:—The only apology which the learned manager has made for the course of his remarks is an apology for the consumption of your time, and yet he has not hesitated to say, and again to repeat that there is no color of justification for the attempt of the President of the United States to defend himself, or for the effort that his counsel make to defend him. We do not receive our law from the learned manager.

Mr. BINGHAM, rising—Will the gentleman allow me?

Mr. Evarts was proceeding with his remarks.

Mr. BINGHAM—The gentleman misrepresents me.

Mr. EVARTS—I do not misrepresent the honorable manager.

Mr. BINGHAM—I did not say that there was no color of excuse for the President's attempt to defend himself, or for the counsel's attempt to defend him, but that there was no color of excuse for offering this testimony.

Mr. EVARTS—It all comes to the same thing. Everything that is admitted on our view or line of the subject in controversy, except it conform to the preliminary view which the learned managers choose to throw down, is regarded as wholly outside of the color of law and of right on the part of the President and his counsel, and is so repeatedly charged. Now, if the crime was completed on the 21st, which is not only the whole bases of this argument of the learned manager, but of every other argument on the evidence which I had the honor of hearing from him, I should like to know what application and relevancy the resolution had which was passed by the Senate on the 21st of February, after the act of the President had been completed, and after the act had been communicated to the Senate?

There can be no single principle of the law of evidence on which that view can be proved on behalf of the managers, and on which the reply of the President can be excluded. What would be thought in a criminal prosecution of the prosecutor giving in evidence what a magistrate or a sheriff had said to the accused concerning the deed, and then shut the mouth of the accused as to what he had said then and there in reply. The only possible argument by which what was said to him could be given in evidence, is that, unreplied to, it might be construed into an admission or submission.

If the sheriff were to say to the prisoner, "You stole that watch," and if that could be given in evidence, and the prisoner's reply, "It was my watch, and I took it because it was mine," could not be given in evidence, that would be precisely the same proposition which is being applied here by the learned managers to this action had between the President and the Senate.

Mr. BUTLER—If the thief did not make a reply until four days afterwards, and then sent in a written statement "as to who owned the watch," was putting also in what his neighbor said would be a more appropriate illustration. I take the illustration as a good and excellent one. The sheriff says to the prisoner, "Where did you get that watch?" Four days afterwards the prisoner sends to the sheriff, after he had been in jail, after an indictment had been found against him, a written answer, and claims in his defense that that answer may be read; not only that, but he goes on to put in that which everybody else said, or what four or five other men said, and claims that that may be given in evidence.

If it is desirous to know what the Cabinet said, let the members of the Cabinet be brought here, and let us cross-examine them, and find out what they meant when they gave this advice, and how they came to give it, and under what pressure. But at present we do not want the President to put in the advice of the Cabinet.

Mr. EVARTS—Mr. Chief Justice and Senators:—Every case is to be regarded according to its circumstances, and you will judge whether a communication from the Senate to the President on the 22d of February could well have been answered sooner than the 24th of February.

Mr. BUTLER—It was communicated on the 21st of February

Mr. EVARTS—I understood you to say that you could not state whether it was the 21st or the 22d.

Mr. BUTLER—It was at ten o'clock on the night of the 21st.

Mr. EVARTS—Very well; it was communicated at ten o'clock on the night of the 21st of February. The Senate was not in session on the 22d more than an hour, it being a holiday. Then Sunday intervening I ask whether an answer to that communication, sent on Monday, the 24th, is not an answer, according to the ordinary course of prompt and candid dealing between the President and the Senate, concerning the matter in difficulty? As far as the simile about the President being in prison goes, I will remove that by saying that he was not impeached until five o'clock P. M. of Monday, the 24th, but we need not pursue these trivial illustrations. The matter is in the hands of the court, and must be disposed of by the court.

Mr. Bingham Resumes.

Mr. BINGHAM—I desire to say once for all that I have said no word, and intend to say no word during the progress of the trial that would justify the assertion of the counsel for the President in saying that we deny them the right to make defenses of the President. What I insist upon here, what I ask the Senate to act upon is, that he shall make a defense precisely as an unofficial citizen of the United States makes defense—according to the law of the land, and not otherwise. That he shall not, after the commission of a crime, manufacture evidence in his own behalf, either orally or in writing, by his own declarations, and incorporate into them the declarations of third persons. It has never been allowed in any respectable court in this country. When men stand on trial for their lives they never are permitted, after the fact, to manufacture testimony by their own declarations, either written or unwritten, and on their own motion introduced them into a court of justice. I have another word to say in the light of what has dropped from the lips of the counsel, that he has evaded most skillfully the point which I took occasion to make in the hearing of the Senate, that here is an attempt to introduce not only written declarations of the accused in his own behalf after the fact, but declarations of third persons not under oath. I venture to say that a proposition to the extent of this never was made before in any tribunal of justice in the United States where any man was accused of crime—a proposition not merely to give his own declaration, but to report the declarations of third persons in his own behalf and throw them before a court as evidence. The gentleman seems to think that the President had a right to send a message to the Senate of the United States, which should operate as evidence. I concede that the President of the United States has a right under the Constitution to communicate from time to time to the two Houses of Congress such matter as he thinks pertain to the public interest, and if he thinks this matter pertained to the public interest, he might send a message, but I deny that there is any tolerable excuse. I repeat my words here for intimating that the President of the United States, being charged with the commission of a crime on the 21st of February, 1858—being proved guilty, I undertake to say proved guilty, by his written confession, to the satisfaction of every intelligent and unprejudiced mind in or out of the Senate in this country—can proceed to manufacture evidence in his own behalf, in the form of message, three days after the fact. That is the point that I make here. We are asked, what importance then do we attach to the action of the Senate? I answer, that we attach precisely this importance to it, that the law of the land enjoins upon the President of the United States the duty to notify the Senate of the suspension of an officer, and the reason therefor, and the evidence on which he made the suspension, and the law of the land enjoins upon the Senate the duty to act upon the report of the President, so made, and to come to a decision upon that report, and upon the evidence accompanying it, in pursuance of the requirement of the second section of the Tenure of Office act. The Senate of the United States, by an almost unanimous decision, came to the conclusion that the reasons furnished by the President and the evidence adduced by him for the suspension of the Secretary of War were unsatisfactory. In accordance with the law, the Senate non-concurred in the suspension. The law expressly provides that if the Senate concur, they shall notify the President. The law, by every intendment, provides that if the Senate non-concur they shall notify the Secretary of War that he may, in obedience to the express requirements of the act, forthwith, resume the functions of his office from which he was suspended. The Senate in this case did give that notice. Why should it not also notify the Executive that he might know with whom to communicate, and that he might not be longer communicating with a Secretary of War *ad interim?* The gentleman, I trust, is answered as to the importance and propriety of our introducing this evidence. But there was another reason for it. It was to leave the President without an excuse before the Senate and before the people for persisting in his unlawful attempt in violating a law of the land, by executing the duties of the office of Secretary of War through another person than Edwin M. Stanton. It was his business to submit to the final decision of the Senate, whether the suspension should become absolute or should be rejected. But here is a man defying the action of the Senate; defying the express letter of the law that the Secretary of War, in whose suspension the Senate had refused to concur, should forthwith resume his functions; proceeding with his conspiracy with General Thomas to confer the functions of that office on another, regardless of the law regulating the tenure of office, regardless of the Constitution, regardless of his oath and regardless of the rights of the American people; and he winds up the farce by coming before the Senate with his written declaration, which is of no higher authority than his oral declarations made three days after the fact, and he asks the Senate to consider that as evidence.

Chief Justice Chase Decides.

The Chief Justice—Senators:—There is no branch of the law where there is more difficulty to lay precise rules than that which regards the intent with which an act is done. In the present case it appears that the Senate on the 21st of February passed a resolution which I will take the liberty of reading:—"*Whereas*, The Senate have received and considered the communication of the President, stating that he had removed Edwin M. Stanton, Secretary of War, and had designated the Adjutant-General of the Army to act as Secretary of war, *ad interim;* therefore, *Resolved*, By the Senate of the United States, under the Constitution and laws of the United States, the President has no power to remove the Secretary of War and to designate any other officer to perform the duties of that office *ad interim*." That resolution was adopted on 21st of February, and was served on the evening of the same day. The message now proposed to be offered in evidence was sent to the Senate on the 24th of February. It does not appear to the Chief Justice that the resolution of the Senate called for an answer, and, therefore, the Chief Justice must regard the message of the 24th of February as a vindication of the President's act, addressed to the Senate. It does not appear to the Chief Justice that that comes within any of the rules of evicence which would justify its being received in evidence on this trial. The Chief Justice, however, will take the views of the Senate in regard to it.

No vote being called for, the Chief Justice ruled the evidence inadmissible.

Tenure of Office,

Mr. CURTIS then offered to put in evidence a tabular statement compiled at the office of the Attorney-General, containing a list of Executive officers of the United States, with their statutory tenures or act of Congress creating the office, the name or title of the office, showing whether the tenure was for a definite time, at the pleasure of the President, or for a term indefinite. He said that of course, it was not strictly evidence, but it had been compiled as a matter of convenience, and he desired to have it printed, so that it might be used in argument by counsel on both sides.

After some objection and interlocutory remarks by Mr. BUTLER, the paper was, on motion of Mr. TRUMBULL, ordered to be printed, as a part of the proceeding.

Mr. CURTIS then offered in evidence, papers in the case of the removal of Mr. Pickering, by President Adams, remarking that it was substantially the same as had been put in evidence by Mr. Butler, except that it was more formal.

A Correction.

The witness, Mr. Dewitt C. Clark, here desired to make a correction of his testimony to the effect that the message of the President was not delivered to him on the 22d of February, but on the 24th of February; that it was brought up by Mr. Moore, the President's Private Secretary, on the 22d of February, but that the Senate not being in session. Mr. Moore returned it to the Executive Mansion, and brought it back on the 24th.

Mr. CURTIS—Q. Do I understand your statement now to be that Colonel Moore brought it and delivered it to you on the 22d of February? A. He brought it up on the 21st; he did not deliver it to me as the Senate was not in session.

Q. He took it away and brought back on the 24th? A. Yes.

Mr. BUTLER—Q. How did you know that he brought it here on the 22d? A. Only by information from Colonel Moore.

Q. Then you have been telling us what Colonel Moore told you? A. That is all.

Then we don't want any more of what Colonel Moore told you.

Secretary Moore Recalled.

William G. Moore, the President's Private Secretary, was recalled and examined as follows:—

Q. By Mr. CURTIS.—What is the document that you hold in your hand? A. The nomination of Thomas Ewing, Sr., of Ohio, as Secretary for the Department of War.

Q. Did you receive that from the President of the United States? A. I did.

Q. On what date? A. On the 22d of February, 1868.

Q. About what hour? A. I think it was about twelve o'clock.

Q. And before what hour? A. Before one o'clock.

Q. Then it was between twelve and one o'clock? A. It was.

Q. What did you do with it? A. By direction of the President I brought it to the Capitol to present it to the Senate.

Q. About what time did you arrive here? A. I cannot state definitely, but I presume it was about a quarter-past one.

Q. Was the Senate then in session, or had it adjourned? A. It had, after a very brief session, adjourned.

Q. What did you do with the document in consequence? A. I returned with it to the Executive Mansion.

Q. Were you apprised before you reached the Capitol, that the Senate had adjourned? A. I was not.

Q. What did you do with the document in consequence? A. I returned with it to the Executive Mansion, after having visited the House of Representatives.

Q. Was anything more done with the document by you, and if so, when and what did you do? A. I was directed by the President on Monday, the 24th of February, 1868, to deliver it to the Senate.

Q. What did you do in consequence? A. I obeyed the orders.

Cross-examined by Mr. BUTLER.

Q. Was that as it is now, or was it in a sealed envelope? A. It was in a sealed envelope.

Q. Did you put it in yourself? A. I did not.

Q. Did you see it put in? A. I did not.

Q. How do you know what was in the envelope? A. It was the only message that was to go that day; I gave it to the clerk, who sealed and handed it to me.

Q. Did you unseal it or examine it till you delivered it on the 24th? A. Not to my recollection.

Q. Did you show it to anybody here on the 22d? A. No, sir; it was sealed.

Q. Have you spoken this morning with Mr. Clarke on the subject? A. He asked me on what date I had delivered the message, and I told him it was the 24th.

Mr. BUTLER—That is all.

President Tyler's Appointments.

Mr. CURTIS then put in evidence, without objection, certified copies of the appointment by President Tyler, on the 29th of February, 1844, of John Nelson, Attorney-General, to discharge the duties of Secretary of State ad interim, until a successor to Mr. Ushur should be appointed, and of the subsequent confirmation by the Senate, on March 6, 1844, of John C. Calhoun to that office. Also, the appointment by President Fillmore, on July 23, 1850, of Winfield Scott as Secretary of War, ad interim, in place of George W Crawford, and of the confirmation by the Senate, on August 25, 1850, of Charles M. Conrad as Secretary of War.

Buchanan's Cabinet.

Mr. CURTIS also offered in evidence the appointment by Mr. Buchanan, in January, 1861, of Moses Kelley as acting Secretary of the Interior.

Mr. BUTLER inquired whether counsel had any record of what had become of the Secretary of the Interior at that time, whether he had resigned or had run away, or what? (Laughter.)

Mr. CURTIS said he was not informed, and could not speak either from the record or from recollection.

Miscellaneous Removals and Appointments.

Mr. CURTIS also offered in evidence the appointment by President Lincoln of Caleb B. Smith as Secretary of the Interior.

Mr. CURTIS also offered in evidence a document relating to the removal from office of the Collector and Appraiser of Merchandise in Philadelphia.

Mr. BUTLER objected to putting in evidence the letter of removal signed by McClintock Young, Acting Secretary of the Treasury.

Mr. CURTIS inquired whether the manager wanted evidence that McClintock Young was Acting Secretary of the Treasury?

Mr. BUTLER replied that he did not.

Mr. CURTIS remarked that the documents were certified by the Secretary of the Treasury as coming from the records of that department. They were offered in evidence to show the fact of the removal by Mr. Young, who stated that it was by direction of the President.

Mr. BUTLER—The difficulty is not removed. It is an attempt by Mr. McClintock Young, admitted to have been Acting Secretary of the Treasury, to remove officers by reciting that he is directed by the President so to do. If this is evidence we have got to go into the question of the right of Mr. Young to do this act, and whether an appraiser is one of the inferior officers whom the Secretary of the Treasury may remove, or whom the President may remove without the advice and consent of the Senate. It is not an act of the President in removing the head of a department, and it is remarkable as the only case to be found to warrant any such removal. If it is evidence at all, it only proves that rule by the exception.

Mr. CURTIS—I understand the manager to admit that Mr. Young was acting Secretary of the Treasury.

Mr. BUTLER—Yes, sir.

Mr. CURTIS—I take this act of his, therefore, as having been done by the Secretary of the Treasury. He says that he proceeded by order of the President. I take it to be well settled, judicially especially, that whenever the head of a department says he acts by order of the President, he is presumed to tell the truth. It requires no evidence to show that he acts by order of the President. No such evidence was ever given. No record is ever made of the direction which the President gives to one of the heads of departments to proceed in a transaction of this kind. But when the head of a department says that he acts by order of the President, all courts and all bodies presume that he tells the truth.

The Chief Justice ruled that the act of the Secretary of the Treasury was the act of the President, but said he would put the question to the Senate if any Senator desired it.

No vote being called for, the testimony was admitted.

Mr. CURTIS—I now offer in evidence a document from the Navy Department.

While the document was being examined by Mr. Butler Senator CONKLING moved that the court take a recess for fifteen minutes.

Senator SUMNER moved, as an amendment, that business shall be resumed forthwith after the expiration of the fifteen minutes.

The question was put on Senator Sumner's amendment, and it was rejected. The court then, at a quarter past two, took a recess for fifteen minutes.

Mr. Butler Resumes.

After the recess, Mr. BUTLER proceeded to state the grounds of his objections. He said the certificate was not that the paper was not a copy of a record from the Navy Department, but simply that the annexed is a mere statement from the records of this department, under the head of memoranda. It was a statement made up by the chief clerk of the Navy Department of matters that he had been asked to, or volunteered to furnish, leaving out many things that would be necessary in order to show the bearing of the paper on the case. He read one of the cases enumerated, the appointment of Mr. Morton as Navy Agent at Pensacola, and said the paper did not show what the consequent action was, nor whether the Senate was then in session, nor whether the President sent another appointment to the Senate at the same moment. It was merely a statement verified as being made from the record by somebody not under oath, and on it there were occa sional memoranda in pencil, apparently made by other persons.

Mr. CURTIS—Apply India rubber to that.

Mr. BUTLER—Yes, sir; but it is not so much what is stated as what is left out. Everything that is of value is left out. There are memorandas made up from the records, that A. B. was removed: but the circumstances under which he was removed; who was nominated in his place, and when that person was nominated, does not appear. It only appears that somebody was appointed at Pensacola.

Mr. JOHNSON—Are the dates given?

Mr. BUTLER—The dates are given in this way. On the 19th of December such a person is removed. Then, on the 5th of January, Johnson was informed that he was appointed. He must have been nominated to the Senate before that. *Non constat.* He was nominated. Then Johnson was lost on the voyage, and on the 29th another man was appointed. But the whole of the value is gone, because they have not given us the record. Who has any commission to make memoranda from the record as evidence before the Senate? And then the certificate says:—The word "copy" stricken out and written is a true statement from the record—a statement such as Mr. Edgar Welles or somebody else was chosen to make.

I never heard that anybody had a right to come in and certify a memorandum from a record and put it in evidence. That is one paper. Then, again, in the next paper, although it alleges they are true copies of record from the office, they are letters about the appointment and removal of officers—navy agents again. But, being so removed and appointed, only a portion of the correspondence is given when the nominations were sent in. I do not mean to say that my friends on the other side chose to leave them out, but whoever prepared this for them has chosen to leave out the material facts, whether the Senate was in session or whether others were sent.

I want to call the attention of the Senate still further. All these appointments contained in these papers, all they have offered are by the act of the 15th of May, 1820, appointed under the laws of the United States, for four years, all lists of attorneys and collectors of customs, and providing that they shall be removable from office at pleasure, so enacted by the laws that created them, and the counsel are going to show that under that law, in some particular instances, were removed at pleasure, but not the manner of their removal, and then they attempted to show that by memoranda, made up by young Welles, certified by Gideon Welles. Is that evidence?

Mr. CURTIS—I understand the substance of the objection made to these documents to be two. The first objection is that these are only memoranda from the records, and it is said that it is not proper to adduce in evidence such statements of results made from the records; that instead of giving a paper containing the name of the officer, the office that he holds, the date when he was removed, and the person by whose orders he was removed, there should be an extended copy of the entire act, and all the papers relating to it. Now, in the first place, I wish the Senate to call to mind that the only document of this character, relating to removals from office, which has been put in by the honorable managers is a document from the Department of State, which contains exactly those memoranda of facts:—"Schedule B—List of appointments of heads of departments made by the President at any time during the session of the Senate—Timothy Pickering, Postmaster-General, June 1, 1794," etc. This is a list extracted out of the records of the Department of the Secretary of State, containing the names of officers, the office they held, the date when they were removed, and the authority by which they were removed. It is simply certified by the Secretary of State.

This is a copy which I hold in my hands, and I am not prepared to say how it was certified. It is in evidence, and I think it will be found to be simply a letter from the Secretary of State, saying there were found from the records of his department these facts, and not any formal certificate. If, however, the Senate should think that it is absolutely necessary, or under the circumstances of these cases, proper to require their certificate of the copies of the entire acts instead of taking the names, dates and other particulars from the records, in the form in which we have thought most convenient, which certainly takes up less time and space than the other would, we must apply for and obtain them. If there is a technical difficulty of that sort, it is one which we must remove. We propose, when we have closed the offer of this species of proof, to ask the Senate to direct its proper officer to make a certificate from its records from the beginning to the end of all sessions of the Senate, from the origin down to the present time. That is what we shall call for at the proper time, and that will supply that part of the difficulty which the gentleman suggests. The other part is, that it does not appear that the President did not follow these removals by the proper nominations. Well, it does not appear, but if the gentleman proposes to argue that the President did follow them up by immediate nominations, he will find undoubtedly that the records of the Navy Department, from which this statement comes, can furnish no such thing. Therefore that objection is groundless.

Mr. BUTLER said the President's counsel had judged well; that when the managers had taken any particular course, that must be the right one, the one which they ought to follow, the managers would accept as being the last exposition, so far as they were concerned. But the difficulty was that he (Mr. Butler) had asked them if they objected to the testimony in question, and they made no objection. If they had, he might have been more formal.

They went to the wrong sources for evidence. These things were to be sought for only in the State Department, where appeared all the circumstances connected with the removal or appointment of any officer, by and with the advice and consent of the Senate, and they could have got all these particulars there, precisely as given in the case of Mr. Pickering.

Mr. CURTIS—Does the honorable manager understand that under the laws of the United States all of these officers must be commissioned by the Secretary of State, and the fact appear in his department, including the officers of the Interior, the Treasury, the War and the Navy Departments?

Documentary Evidence.

Mr. BUTLER—With the single exception of the Treasury, I do, and it will so appear. Mr. BUTLER proceeded to say that the commissions of the persons named in the memoranda as appointed, could have been found in the State Department. If it were a mere matter of form, he would care nothing about it, and if the counsel would say that they would put in the exact dates of the nominations, he would have no objection. Instead of that they sought to put in part of a transaction, leaving the prosecution to look up the rest of it. He quoted from Brightley's Digest, that all books, papers, and documents of the War, Navy, Treasury, and Post Office Departments, and the Attorney-General's office, may be copied and certified under seal, as in the State Department and with the same force and effect. This law of February 22, 1849, referred to that in regard to the Secretary of State, which was dated February 15, 1789, and which made such copies of records, when properly certified, legal evidence equally with the original paper. It gave no right to make extracts like these, which were the gloss, the interpretation, the collation, the diagnosis of the record to the clerk of that department.

The Chief Justice stated that he would submit the question to the Senate.

Senator HENDRICKS asked whether the managers objected on the ground that the papers should be given in full, so far as they relate to any particular question.

Mr. BUTLER replied in the affirmative.

Mr. CONKLING sent the following question to the Chair:—Do the counsel for the respondent rely upon any statute other than that referred to?

Mr. CURTIS did not mean to state what he pleased as evidence. They did not offer these documents as copies of records relating to the cases named in the documents themselves; they were documents of the same character as that which the managers had put in.

Mr. EDMUNDS asked whether the evidence was offered as touching any question or final conclusion of fact, or merely as giving the Senate the history of the practice under consideration.

Mr. CURTIS—Entirely for the last purpose.

Mr. BUTLER said if this evidence did not go to any issue of fact, the managers would have no objection.

Mr. CURTIS—I would say, lest there should be a misapprehension, that it went to matters of practice under the law.

Mr. BUTLER—Well, if it goes to matters of fact, we object that it is not proper evidence.

Mr. EVARTS thought it might be of service to call attention to the record in regard to the letter of the Secretary of State, put in evidence by the managers. He read the letter heretofore published in regard to the appointments of heads of departments.

Mr. HOWARD submitted the following question:—Do the counsel regard these memoranda as legal evidence of this practice of the government, and are they offered as such?

Mr. CURTIS replied that the documents were not full copies of any record, and were not, therefore, strictly and especially legal evidence for any purpose; they were extracts of evidence from the records. By way of illustration he read as follows:—Isaac Henderson was, by direction of the President, removed from the office of Navy Agent at New York, and instructed to transfer to Paymaster John D. Gibson, of the United States Navy, all the public funds and other property in his charge. That was not offered to prove the merits and causes of the removal, but simply to show the practice of the government under the laws, instead of putting in the whole of the documents in the case. They had taken the only fact of any importance to the inquiry. Should the Senate decide to adhere to the technical rule of evidence, the counsel for the President must go to the records and have them copied in full.

Mr. BOUTWELL said if the counsel did not prove the document, it did not prove any record. The first thing to prove a practice was to prove one or more cases under it. The vital objection to this evidence was that it related to a class of officers—navy agents—who were then and are now appointed under a special provision of the law creating the offices, and which takes them entirely out of the line of precedents for the purposes of this trial. Naval officers were created under a statute of the year 1850, in which a tenure of office was established for the office so created of four years, removable at pleasure. It was unnecessary to go into the circumstances that led to that provision being made, but the practice under it could not in any degree enlighten this tribunal upon the issue on which it is called upon to pass. The counsel could see that it was no evidence in regard to the practice relative to removals not made under that statute.

Mr. CURTIS said the counsel might have been under a misapprehension respecting the views of the managers in conducting this prosecution, but they had supposed that the managers meant to attempt to maintain that, even if Mr. Stanton, at the time when he was removed, held at the pleasure of the President, even if he was not within the tenure of Office act, inasmuch as the Senate was in session; it was not competent for the Senate to remove him, and that although Mr. Stanton might have been removed, by the President not being within the Tenure of Office act, his place could not be even temporarily supplied by an order to General Thomas, the Senate being in session. It was offered with a view to show that whether the Senate was in session or not, the President could make an *ad interim* appointment. If the managers would agree that if Mr. Stanton's case was not within the Tenure of Office act, the President might remove him during the session of the Senate, and might lawfully make an *ad interim* appointment. They (the counsel) did not desire to put this in evidence.

Senator SHERMAN—I would like to ask the counsel whether the papers now offered in evidence contain the date of the appointment and the character of the offices?

Mr. BUTLER—To that we say that they only contain the date of the removals, but do not give us the date of the nomination.

Mr. CURTIS again read the case of the removal of Isaac Henderson, by way of illustration, stating that it contained the date of the removals.

The Chief Justice put the question to the Senate, stating that, in his opinion, the evidence was competent in substance; whether it was so in form was for the Senate to decide.

The evidence was admitted by the following vote:—

YEAS.—Messrs. Anthony, Bayard, Buckalew, Cole, Corbett, Conkling, Davis, Dixon, Doolittle, Edmunds, Fessenden, Ferry, Fowler, Frelinghuysen, Grimes, Henderson, Hendricks, Howe, Johnson, McCreery, Morrill (Me.), Morrill (Vt.), Morton, Patterson (N.H.), Patterson (Tenn.), Ross, Saulsbury, Sherman, Stewart, Sumner, Trumbull, Van Winkle, Vickers, Willey, Wilson, Yates—36.

NAYS.—Messrs. Cameron, Cattell, Chandler, Conness, Cragin, Drake, Harlan, Howard, Morgan, Nye, Pomeroy, Ramsey, Thayer, Tipton, Williams—15.

By consent, the documents were considered as read,

Mr. CURTIS—There is another document from the Navy Department which, I suppose, is not distinguished from those which have been just admitted. It purports to be a list of civil officers appointed for four years under the statute of the 15th of May, 1820, and removable from office at pleasure, with their removals so indicated, the term of office not having expired. Then comes a list giving the name of the officer, the date of his general appointment, the date of his removal, and by whom removed, in a tabular form.

Mr. BUTLER called attention to the fact that it did not contain the statement whether the Senate was in session.

Mr. CURTIS We shall get that in another form.

No objection being made the paper was admitted in evidence.

Mr. CURTIS, producing other documents—Here are documents from the Department of State, showing the removal of heads of departments, not only during the session of the Senate, but during the recess, and covering all causes. The purpose being to show a practice of the government, so extensive with the necessity that arose out of the different cases of death, resignation, sickness, absence or removal. It differs from the schedule which has been put by the manager to cover the heads of departments only, because that applies only to removals during the session of the Senate. It includes them, but it includes a great deal more matter.

Mr. BUTLER read several of the records, being temporary appointments during the absence of incumbents. All, he said, were of that character with two exceptions. One was that frequently such appointments were made to cover possible contingencies, as when Asbury Dickens was appointed to act as Secretary of the Treasury when that officer shall be absent. There were three cases. One in President Monroe's time, one in President Adams' time, and one in President Jackson's time, all reciting that the appointment was under the act of 1792. All the others were temporary. Would the Senate admit a series of acts done exactly in conformity with the law of 1792 and 1795 as evidence in a case in violation of the acts of March 2, 1867, and February 20, 1868? Would that throw any light upon what was admitted in the answer to be a breach of the law, if it comes within it?

Mr. CURTIS did not wish to reply, taking it for granted that the Senate would not settle any question as to the merits of the case when they were public in the evidence.

The evidence was admitted, no objection being made, and was considered as read.

Mr. CURTIS then offered documents from Postmaster-General's office, showing the removal of postmasters during the session of the Senate, and the *ad interim* appointments to fill such places.

No objection being made, they were read.

A Message of President Buchanan.

Mr. CURTIS—I now offer in evidence from the Journal of the Senate, vol. 4, second session, Thirty-sixth Congress, page 1, the message of President Buchanan to the Senate in reference to the office of Secretary for the Department of War, and to the manner in which he had filled that office in place of Mr. Floyd; accompanying that message is a list of the names of persons, as shown by the records of the State Department, who discharged the duties of Cabinet officers, whether by appointments made during the recess of the Senate, or as *ad interim* appointments, and his list is furnished as an appendix to the message, and I wish the message to be read.

Mr. BUTLER—The difficulty I find in the message is this:—It is the message of Mr. Buchanan, and can't be put in evidence in this case any more than the declarations of any one else. We should like to have Mr. Buchanan brought here on oath and cross-examined as to this. There are a good many questions that I should like to ask him—for instance, as to his state of mind at that time, and whether he had any clear perception of his duties at the time. (Laughter.) But a still further objection to it is that most of the message consists of statements of Mr. Jeremiah S. Black, who concluded that he would not have anything to do with this case anyhow. (Laughter.)

I do not think that the statements of that gentleman, however respectable, are to be taken here as evidence. They might be referred to, perhaps, as public documents, but I do not believe they can be put in as evidence. How do we know how correctly Mr. Black and his clerks make up this list. Are you going to put in his statements of what was done, and put it upon us, or upon yourselves, to examine and see whether they are not all illusory and calculated to mislead. I do not care to argue the question any further.

Mr. CURTIS—I offer it to show the practice of the government.

Mr. BUTLER. I object, once for all, to the practice of the government being shown by the acts of James Buchanan, alias Jeremiah Black.

The Chief Justice put the question to the Senate, and the testimony was admitted without a division.

The Clerk then read Mr. Buchanan's message in reference to filling the office of Secretary of War, caused by the resignation of Mr. Floyd.

Mr. CURTIS—I now desire to move for an order on the proper officer of the Senate to furnish, so that we may put into the case, a statement of the dates of the beginning and end of each session of the Senate, including its Executive as well as its legislative sessions, from the origin of the government down to the present time. That will enable us, by comparing the dates with those facts which we have put into the case, to see what was done within, and also done without the sessions of the Senate.

The Chief Justice was understood to say that that order would be required to be made in legislative session.

Mr. CURTIS then said, we have concluded our documentary evidence as at present advised. We may possibly desire, perhaps, to offer some additional evidence of that character, but as we now understand it we shall have no more to offer.

The court then, on motion of Senator JOHNSON, adjourned till noon to-morrow.

PROCEEDINGS OF THURSDAY, APRIL 16.

The court was opened in due form, all the managers being present. Mr. Stanbery was again absent. On motion, the reading of the journal was dispensed with,

Mr. Sumner's Paper.

Senator SUMNER rose and said:—Mr. Chief Justice:—I sent to the Chair a declaration of opinions to be adopted by the Senate, as an answer to the constantly recurring questions on the admissibility of testimony. The paper was read by the Clerk, expressing the opinion that, considering the character of this proceeding, being a trial of impeachment before the Senate of the United States, and not a proceeding by indictment in an inferior court, and that members are judges of the law as well as of fact, from whose decision there is no appeal, and that, therefore, the ordinary reasons for the exclusion of evidence do not exist, and, therefore, it is deemed advisable that all evidence, not trivial or obviously irrelevant, shall be admitted, it being understood that in order to decide its value it shall be carefully considered on its final judgment.

Mr. CONNESS moved to lay the paper on the table, which was agreed to by the following vote:—

YEAS.—Messrs. Buckalew, Cameron, Cattell, Chandler, Cole, Conkling, Conness, Corbett, Cragin, Davis, Dixon, Doolittle, Drake, Edmunds, Ferry, Fessenden, Frelinghuysen, Harlan, Howard, Howe, Johnson, Morgan, Morrill (Me.), Morrill (Vt.), Patterson (N. H.), Pomeroy, Ramsey, Saulsbury, Stewart, Thayer, Tipton, Williams, Yates—33.

NAYS.—Messrs. Anthony, Fowler, Grimes, Morton, Patterson (Tenn.), Sherman, Sumner, Van Winkle, Vickers, Willey, Wilson—11.

The Chief Justice directed the court to proceed.

Mr. Evart's Remarks.

Mr. EVARTS said:—Mr. Chief Justice and Senators, I am not able to announce the recovery of Mr. Stanbery, but I think, had not the weather been so entirely unfavorable he would have been able to appear, perhaps, to-day. He is, however, convalescent, but nevertheless the situation of his health and proper care for its restoration prevents us from having much opportunity for consultation during this session of the court. We shall desire to proceed to-day with such evidence as may be properly produced in his absence, and may occupy the session of the court with that evidence. We shall not desire to protract the examination with any such object or view, and if before the close of the ordinary period of the session we shall come to the end of that testimony, we shall ask for an adjournment.

Mr. Curtis Offers Documentary Evidence.

Mr. CURTIS said—Mr. Chief Justice, I offer two documents received this morning, coming from the Department of State, in character precisely similar to some of those received yesterday. They are continuations of what was put in yesterday, so as to bring the evidence of the practice of the government down to a more recent period.

Mr. CURTIS—I will now put in evidence, so that they will be printed in connection with this documentary evidence, two statements furnished by the Secretary of the Senate, under the order of the Senate, one showing the beginning and ending of each legislative session of Congress from 1798 to 1868, the other being a statement of the beginning and ending of each special session of the Senate from 1789 to 1868. They were considered as read.

W. S. Cox on the Stand.

Walter S. Cox, sworn in behalf of the respondent, and examined by Mr. CURTIS—I reside in Georgetown: I am a lawyer by profession; I have been engaged in the practice of law ten years in this city, in the courts of the District; I was connected professionally with the matter of General Thomas before the Criminal Court of this District; my connection with that matter began on Saturday, the 22d of February.

Mr. BUTLER—If I have heard the question correctly, the question put was:—When and under what circumstances did your connection with the case of General Thomas before the Supreme Court of this District commence? To that we object. It is impossible to see how the employment of Mr. Cox to defend General Thomas could have anything to do with this case. We put in that Mr. Thomas said that if it had not been for the arrest he should have taken possession by force of the War Office. They then produced the record—the affidavit. Now, I do not propose to argue, but I ask the attention of the Senate to the question whether the employment of Mr. Cox by Mr. Thomas, as counsel, the circumstances under which he was employed, and the declarations of Mr. Thomas to his counsel, can be put in evidence under any rule? The circumstances are too trivial, if it was legally competent.

Mr. CURTIS—I understand the question to be that we cannot show that General Thomas employed Mr. Cox as his counsel, and that we cannot show the declarations made by General Thomas to Mr. Cox as his counsel. We do not propose to prove either of these facts. If the gentleman will wait long enough to see what we do propose, he will see that this objection is not relevant. To the witness—Now, state when and by whom, and under what circumstances, you were employed in this matter?

Mr. BUTLER—Stop a moment. I object to the why and the by whom and under what circumstances this gentleman was employed. If he was employed by the President, that is worse in my judgment than if he was employed by the other. I desire the question to be put in writing.

The Chief Justice—The Chief Justice sees no objection to the question as an introductory question, but he will put it to the Senate if any Senator desires it.

No vote being called for, the Chief Justice directed the witness to answer the question.

Witness—On Saturday, February 22d, a messenger called at my house and stated to me that Mr. Seward desired to see me immediately.

Mr. BUTLER—I object to the declarations of anybody.

The Chief Justice intimated to the witness that he need not state what Mr. Seward said.

Witness—The message stated further that he was to take me immediately to the President's house; I accompanied him to the President's house, and found the President and General Thomas alone there.

Q. About what hour was this? A. About five o'clock in the afternoon; after I was seated the President stated—

Mr. BUTLER—Stop a moment; I object to statements of the President at five o'clock P. M. (A titter in the court, some Senators laughing outright.)

Senator EDMUNDS asked that the offer of evidence be put in writing, so that Senators might understand it precisely.

The proposition was reduced so writing, as follows:—

"We offer to prove that Mr. Cox was employed professionally by the President, in the presence of General Thomas, to take such legal proceedings in the case that had been commenced against General Thomas as would be effectual to raise judicially the question of Mr. Stanton's right to have and hold the office of Secretary for the Department of War against the authority of the President, and also an order to obtain a writ of *quo warranto* for the same purpose, and we shall expect to follow up this proof by evidence of what was done by the witness in pursuance of the above employment."

Senator EDMUNDS asked what was the date of this interview?

Mr. CURTIS replied that it was the 22d of February.

Mr. BUTLER—This testimony has two objections, Mr. President and Senators. The first is, that after the act done and after the impeachment proceedings were agreed upon before the House, and after Mr. Stanton had sought to protect himself from being turned out of office by force, the President then sends, as it is proposed to prove, for Mr. Cox, the witness, and gives him certain directions. It is alleged that those directions were that he should sue out a *quo warranto*. I had supposed that a writ of *quo warranto* was to be filed, if at all, by the President; but as that writ has gone out of use, an information in the nature of a *quo warranto* is a proper proceeding. Now, let us see, just here, how the case stands. The President had told General Sherman that the reason why he did not reply to the lawyers was that it was impossible to make up a case. One of the Senators asked him to repeat his answer, and he repeated it; he says:—"The President said:—'I am told by the lawyers that it is impossible to make up a case.'"

Now, after he had been told that, and after he had been convinced of that, he still undertakes to show you here that he made the removal of Mr. Stanton in order to make up a case which he himself had declared it was impossible to make up. He was convinced that no case could by possibility be brought into court except from the declarations and threats of his officer (Mr. Thomas) to turn by force Mr. Stanton out of the War Department. He then sends for a very proper counsel—as I have no doubt the Senate will be quite convinced before we get through—and having got him there, he undertakes to make up a case for the Senate, before which he was about to be tried.

Now they say they expect to prove that the President wanted a case made up to go into court, and that in pursuance of that Mr. Cox so acted. Mr. Cox cannot be permitted to testify to that, for another person in the counsel themselves have put in the record what imports absolute verity, an what cannot be contradicted by parole or other evidence, that General Thomas was dismissed; on motion of his counsel, the case was dismissed, and, therefore, we object in the first place that these declarations of the President to his lawyer, after the fact and after he was in process of being impeached, shall be put in evidence. We object, then, that what was done in court may not be proved except by the record: then we object further that this whole proceeding is between other parties in the court.

There is no evidence so far as it is put in here, and the whole record is put in to show that the President went into that court and asked to have that case carried on, or that he made himself apparent in it. He does not appear on the record; he does not appear as employing counsel. It looks on the record as though it was a case against General Thomas, and the court dealt with it as against General Thomas. If the President had decided to have the case decided as a great constitutional *non obsta*, the court would have decided it. All that appears was that this witness appeared as counsel for General Thomas, and the question was as to whether General Thomas should be held under bond, or whether, under the circumstances, he was likely to appear and answer when the grand jury sat, it being then found out that there was no danger from his personal action, by silence.

Mr. EVARTS—Mr. Chief Justice and Senators, I trust that I may be excused for saying that none of the suggestions by the learned and honorable manager appear to us to have any bearing on the question of evidence now before us. He says that the Attorney-General has, by law, no official function in any court except in the Supreme Court of the United States, and no *quo warranto* proceedings can be commenced there, as has heretofore been contended on the part of the managers, and in reference to which no dispute has arisen, can only be made by issuing on the part of the government, on the part of the officer who has been excluded from office; and it may appear that if this adhesion of the Attorney-General, or his approval, that the proceeding should be taken by General Thomas' professional adviser, is required, we shall be able to produce that proof.

Now it is said that because the President told General Sherman that it was impossible to make up a case, it is therefore impossible for us to show that he did attempt to make a case. This, I assume, is a new application of the doctrine of estoppel; but the fact is simply this, that in advance of the official action of the President towards the removal of Mr. Stanton, and when General Sherman had been asked to receive from the Chief Executive authority for the discharge of the duties of that office *ad interim*, and while he (General Sherman) was revolving in his own mind what his duty as a citizen, and a friend and a servant of the government was, he asked the President whether the question could not be decided by lawyers alone, without making a deposit of the *ad interim* authority in an army officer, and the President replied that it was impossible to make up a case except by such executive action as to lay a basis for judicial interference and determination.

Then, in advance, the President did not anticipate the necessity of being driven to this judicial controversy, because, in the alternative of General Sherman's accepting the trust reposed in him, the President expected the retirement of Mr. Stanton, and that, by his acquiescence, no need would arise for further controversy in court or elsewhere. That is the condition of the proof as it now stands before the Senate, or as we shall contend that it now stands, in reference to what occurred between the President and General Sherman.

We have already seen in the proof that General Thomas received from the President on the 21st of February this designation to take charge of the office from Mr. Stanton if he retired, and his report to the President in the first instance of what was regarded as equivalent to an acquiescence by Mr. Stanton in that demand for the office, and its surrender to the charge of General Thomas. It is there shown in evidence that General Thomas was arrested on the morning of February 22, and that before he went to the court he communicated the fact of his arrest to the President, and received the President's response that that was as he wished it should be—to have the matter in court.

Now we propose to show that on the evening of the same day, the matter being thus in court, the President did take it up as his controversy to be determined by the highest judicial tribunal of the country, by the most rapid method which the law and the competent advisers as to the law could afford. But we are met by the objection that the matter to be proved is in the state of the record between the United States and General Thomas in that criminal complement, not in the state of facts as regards the action and purposes of the President of the United States in attempting to produce before the tribunals of the country for solemn judicial determination of the matter in controversary.

That because the record of the criminal charge against General Thomas does not contain the matter or action of the President of the United States, we cannot show, therefore, what the action of the President was. The learned managers say it does not appear by the record that the President made this his controversy. Certainly it does not. No lawyer can say how and by what possible method the President could appear on the record in a prosecution against General Thomas.

But this is wholly aside from the point of inquiry here. Now, Mr. Chief Justice and Senators, we are not to be judged by the measure we are able to offer through this witness as regards the effect and value of the entire evidence bearing on this point as it shall be drawn from this witness and from other witnesses, and from other forms of testimony. We state here, distinctly, so as not to be misunderstood, that by the unexpected resistance of Mr. Stanton to this form of retirement, the President was obliged to find resources in the law, which he had contemplated as a thing impossible without antecedent proceedings on which a proper footing could be had in court, and that thence he did, with such promptness and such decision, and such clear and unequivocal purpose as will be indicated in the evidence, assume immediately that duty.

It will appear that a method thus presented to him for a more speedy determination of the matter than a *quo warranto*, or information in the nature of a *quo warranto* would present, was provided by the action of Mr. Stanton, the prosecutor of the court, on the movement of the prosecution to get the case out of court, as frivolous and unimportant in its proceedings against General Thomas, and becoming formidable and offensive when it gave an opportunity to the President of the United States, by habeas corpus, to get an instant decision in the Supreme Court of the United States. We then propose to show that this opportunity being thus avoided, the President proceeded to adopt the only other resource of judicial determination, by information in the nature of a *quo warranto*.

Mr. BUTLER—I am very glad to have an opportunity afforded me by the remarks of the learned counsel for the President, to deal a moment with the doctrine of estoppel. I deny that an argument has been founded to the prejudice of my case by the use of the argument which I made in the opening of the case, and to which I wish to call the attention of the Senate, as bearing on the doctrine of estoppel. I will not be long, and I pray you, Senators, to bear in mind that I never have referred to that argument. While I was discussing the obliquy thrown upon Mr. Stanton, I used these words:—"To desert it now, therefore, would be to imitate the treachery of his accidental chief. But, whatever may be the construction of the Tenure of Civil Office act by others, or as regards others, and Mr. Johnson, the respondent, is concluded upon it, he permitted Mr. Stanton to exercise the duties of his office in spite of it. If that office were affected by it, he suspended him under its provisions. He reported that suspension to the Senate, with his reasons therefor, in accordance with its provisions, and the Senate, acting under it, declined to concur with him, whereby Mr. Stanton was reinstated. In the well-known language of the law, is not the respondent stopped by his solemn official acts from denying the legality and constitutional propriety of Mr. Stanton's position?"

That is all I said. I never said, nor intended to say, nor would any word of mine honestly bear out any man in assuming that I said that the President was estopped from trying this case before the Senate of the United States, and

showing the unconstitutionality of the law, as was argued in the opening of his side, and has been more than once referred to since. I said that, as between him and Mr. Stanton, his position was such that he was estopped from denying the constitutional and legal effect of the provision. Thereupon it was argued that I claimed, on the part of the managers of the House of Representatives, that the President was estopped from denying the constitutionality of the law here, and the learned counsel, running back to Coke, and coming down to the present time, have endeavored to show that the doctrine of estoppel did not apply to law. Whoever thought that it did? I think there is only one point where the doctrine of estoppel applied in this case, and that is, that counsel should be estopped from misrepresenting the arguments of their opponents, and thus making an argument to the prejudice of them.

That is an application of the doctrine of estoppel which I want carried out throughout this trial. I have not said that the President was estopped, by his declarations to General Sherman, from showing that he attempted to put this man forward as his counsel. I have only said that the fact that he spoke to General Sherman, and said to him that it was impossible to make up a case, shows that he shall not be allowed, after the fact, to attempt to get up a defense for himself by calling in this counsel.

Now, it is said, what lawyer would suppose that it would appear upon the record in the case against General Thomas, that the President of the United States was in the controversy? I say that fair dealing, honesty of purpose, uprightness of action and frankness of official position would have made him appear in that case. The President of the United States, if he had employed counsel for General Thomas in the case, should have sent his counsel into court, who should then have stated:—"Mr. Chief Justice:—We are here appearing at the instance of the President of the United States for the purpose of trying the great constitutional question which he has endeavored to raise here, and for that purpose we want to get it into the Supreme Court of the United States;" and then, if the Chief Justice of this District had refused to hear that case, there might have been some ground for the use of the harsh word of "evasion," which the counsel has applied.

The counsel has said that that question was evaded. By whom? It must have been by the Chief Justice of the District, for he alone made the decision. He said that Mr. Stanton had this case conducted so as to evade a decision. The record of the court shows that this man Thomas was discharged on motion of his own counsel. If his counsel had not moved his discharge, I venture to say he would not have been discharged. Certainly there is no evidence that he would have been. Now, therefore, in that view that Thomas was discharged on the motion of his counsel, could they go back to-day and tell us what they thought, in order to show, through Mr. Cox, that the Chief Justice evaded the point?

If you allow Mr. Cox to come in here and put in declarations made to him by the President, then I suppose we must enter into the merits of Mr. A. B, and all sorts of counsel whom the President brings about him, and we will have to bring before you the Chief Justice, to get his account of the matter, thus getting up a side-door issue, and try whether the proceedings in the Supreme Court of the District of Columbia were regular or otherwise. I will not say that this is designedly, but I say it is artistically contrived for the purpose of leading us away from the real issue. I never heard such a proposition in any court. A single word as to this matter of *quo warranto*. I have had a reasonable degree of practice on this question, and I undertake to say that every lawyer knows that an information in the nature of a *quo warranto* cannot be prosecuted except in the name of the Attorney-General for any public office.

If any such case can be found and shown in this country where it has been prosecuted differently, I would beg my friend's pardon—a thing which I do not like to do. (Laughter.) Do they say that a *quo warranto*, whether by Mr. Cox or Mr. Stanbery, has ever been presented to any court in this case? Not at all. Has anybody ever heard of this *quo warranto* until they came to the necessity of the defense—aye, and until I put it in the opening speech, which has taught my friends so much? (Laughter.) Never, never!

I will not object to evidence of any writ of *quo warranto*, or to evidence in the nature of information of a *quo warranto* filed in any court, from that of a justice of the peace up to the Supreme Court, if they will show that it was filed before the 21st of February, or prepared before that time; but I want it to come from the records, and not from the memory of Mr. Cox.

You may say, Senators, that I am taking too much time in this, but really it is aiding you, because if you open this door to the declarations of the President he can keep you going on from now until next July; aye, until next March, precisely as his friends in the House of Representatives threatened they would do if the impeachment was carried here. To be forewarned is to be forearmed. Senators, his defenders in the House of Representatives, when arguing against this impeachment, said:—"If you bring it to the Senate we will make you follow all the forms, and his official life will be ended before you can get through the trial of impeachment." That was the threat, and when your summons required the President, as every summons does, to come in and file his answer, he asked for forty days to do so. He got ten, and he then asked for further delay, so that forty three days have been expended since he filed his answer, or rather since he ought to have filed his answer, and thirty-three days since he actually filed it

Of that time but six days have been expended on the part of the managers in the trial, and about six days have been expended by the counsel for the defense. The other twenty odd working days, while the whole country is calling for action, and while murder is stalking through the country unrebuked, have been used in lenity to him and his counsel, and we are now asked to go into an entirely side-door issue, which is neither relevant nor competent under any legal rule and which, if it was, could have no effect.

Senator FERRY sent up in writing the following question to the President's counsel:—

"Do the counsel for the President undertake to contradict or vary the statement of the docket entry produced by them, to the effect that General Thomas was discharged by Chief Justice Cartter on the motion of the defendant's counsel?"

Mr. CURTIS—Mr. Chief Justice, I respond to the question of the Senator, that counsel do not expect or desire to contradict anything which appears upon docket evidence. The evidence which we offer of the employment of this professional gentleman for the purpose indicated, is entirely consistent with everything which appears on the docket. It is evidence, not of declarations, as the Senators may perceive, but of acts, because it is well settled, as all lawyers know, that there may be verbal acts as well as other acts, and that the verbal act is as much capable of proof as a physical act is. Now, the employment for a particular purpose of an agent, whether professional or otherwise, is an act, and it may be always proved by the necessary evidence of which it is susceptible, namely:— What was said by the party in order to create that employment.

That is what we desire to prove on this occasion. The dismissal of General Thomas, which has been referred to, and which appears on the docket, was entirely subsequent to all these proceedings. It took place after it had become certain in the mind of Mr. Cox and of his associate counsel that it was of no use to endeavor to follow the proceedings farther. As to the argument or remarks addressed by the honorable manager to the Senate, I have nothing to say. They do not appear to me to require any answer.

Mr. WILSON, one of the managers, said:—I beg the indulgence of the Senate for a few moments. I ask the members of this body to pass upon what we declare to be the real question involved in the objection interposed to the testimony now offered by the counsel for the respondent. On the 21st of February the President of the United States issued an order removing Edwin M. Stanton from the office of Secretary of the Department of War. On that same day he issued a letter of authority to Lorenzo Thomas, directing him to take charge of the Department of War, and to discharge the duties of the office of Secretary of War *ad interim*.

The articles based upon the violation of the Tenure of Office act are founded upon those two acts of the President on the 21st day of February. Counsel for the respondent now proposed to break the force of these acts, and of that violation of the law, by showing that on the 22d day of February the President employed counsel to raise in the courts the question of the constitutionality of the Tenure of Office act. Now, I submit to this honorable body that no act, no declaration of the President made after the fact, can be introduced for the purpose of explaining his intent; and on that question of intent let me direct your minds to this consideration:—that the issuing of the orders of the President state the body of the crime with which the President stands charged.

Did he purposely and willfully issue an order to remove the Secretary of War? Did he purposely and willingly issue the order appointing Thomas as Secretary of War *ad interim*? If he did thus issue the order, the law raises the presumption of guilty intent, and no act done by the President after those orders were issued can be introduced for the purpose of rebutting that intent. The orders themselves were in violation of the Tenure of Office act, and being a violation of that act, they constitute an offense under and by virtue of its provisions, and the offense being thus established, must stand upon the intent which controlled the action of the President at the time he issued the order.

If, after this subject was introduced into the House of Representatives, the President became alarmed at the state of affairs, and concluded that it was better to attempt by some means to secure a decision in the courts, upon the question of the constitutionality or unconstitutionality of the Tenure of Office act, it cannot avail this case. We are inquiring as to the intent which controlled and directed the action of the President at the time the act was done, and if we succeed in establishing that intent either by the fact or by the presumptions of law, no subsequent act can interfere with it or relieve him of the responsibility which the law places on him, because of the act done.

Mr. EVARTS replied to the argument of Mr. Wilson, and contended for the legality of the proof offered. The implication, he said, which alone gave character to the trial, was that there was a purpose in the mind of the President injurious to the public interest and to the public safety. The President's counsel ask to put the prosecution in its proper place on that point, and to say that the President intended no violation and no interruption of the public service; that he intended no seizure of military appropriations, and that he had no purpose in his mind but to secure Mr. Stanton's retirement. If this evidence were eluded, then when counsel came to the summing up of the case they must take the crime in the dimensions and in the consequences here avowed, and he (Mr. Evarts) should be entitled before this court and before the country to treat the accusation as if the article had read that the President had issued that order for Mr. Stanton's retirement, and for General Thomas to take charge *ad interim* of the War Department, with the intent and purpose of raising a case for the decision of the Supreme Court of the United States to test the constitutionality of an act of Congress.

If such an article had been produced by the House of Representatives, and submitted to the Senate, it would have been the laughing stock of the whole country. He offered this evidence to prove that the whole purpose and intent of the President, in his action with reference to the occupancy of the office of Secretary of War, had this extent and no more—to obtain a peaceable delivery of that trust, and, in case of its being refused, to have the case for the decision of the Supreme Court of the United States. If that evidence was excluded, they must treat every one of the articles as if they were limited to an open averment that the intent of the President was such as he proposes to prove it.

Mr. BUTLER referred the court to 5th Wheaten on the subject of the writ of *quo warranto*, to the fact that that writ can only be maintained at the instance of the government.

Mr. CURTIS admitted that that was undoubtedly the law in reference to *quo warranto* in all the States with whose laws he was acquainted. He admitted that there could be no writ of *quo warranto* or information in the nature of the writ, except on behalf of the public. But the question as to what officer was to represent the public, and in what name the information was to be tried, depended upon the particular statutes applicable to the case. Those statutes differ in the different States. Under the laws of the United States, all proceedings in behalf of the United States in the Circuit and District Courts were taken by District Attorneys in their own names, and all proceedings in behalf of the United States in the Supreme Court were taken by the Attorney-General in his name.

In reference to Mr. Cox, he expected to show an application by Mr. Cox to the Attorney-General to obtain his signature to the proper information and the obtaining of that signature.

The Chief Justice—Senators, the counsel for the President offer the proof that the witness, Mr. Cox, was employed professionally by the President, in the presence of General Thomas, to take such legal proceedings in the case which had been commenced against General Thomas as would be effectual to raise judicially the question of Mr. Stanton's legal right to continue to hold the office of Secretary for the Department of War against the authority of the President, and also in reference to obtaining a writ of *quo warranto* for the same purpose; and they state that they expect to follow up this proof by evidence as to what was done by the witness in pursuance of that employment. The first article of impeachment, after charging that Andrew Johnson, President of the United States, in violation of the Constitution, issued orders (which have been frequently read) for the removal of Mr. Stanton, and proceeds to say such orders were unlawfully issued, with intent then and there to violate the act entitled "An Act Regulating the Tenure of Office," &c. The article charges, first, that the act done was done unlawfully; and then it charges that the act was done with intent to accomplish a certain result. That intent the President denies, and it is to establish the truth of that denial that the Chief Justice understands this evidence now to be offered. It is evidence of an attempt to employ counsel in the presence of the President and General Thomas, and it is evidence so far of the fact. It may be evidence, also, of declarations connected with that fact. This fact and those declarations, which the Chief Justice understands to be in the nature of facts, he thinks are admissible in evidence. The Senate has already on former occasions decided by a solemn vote that evidence of declarations of the President to General Thomas, and by General Thomas to the President, after this order was issued to Mr. Stanton, was admissible. It has also admitted evidence to the same effect averred by the honorable managers

It seems to me that this evidence now offered comes within the principles of this decision, and as the Chief Justice has already had occasion to say, he thinks that the principles of this decision are right. It is a decision proper to be made by the Senate sitting in its high capacity as a court of impeachment, and composed as it is of lawyers and of gentlemen thoroughly acquainted with the business transactions of life, and entirely competent to weigh any evidence which may be submitted.

Senator DRAKE called for the yeas and nays on admitting the evidence.

The vote was taken, and resulted—yeas, 29; nays, 21, as follows:—

YEAS.—Messrs. Anthony, Bayard, Buckalew, Corbett, Davis, Dixon, Doolittle, Fessenden, Fowler, Frelinghuysen, Grimes, Henderson, Howe, Johnson, McCreery, Morrill (Me.), Morton, Norton, Patterson (N. H.), Patterson (Tenn.), Ross, Saulsbury, Sherman, Sprague, Sumner, Trumbull, Van Winkle, Vickers and Willey—29.

NAYS.—Messrs. Cameron, Cattell, Chandler, Conkling, Cragin, Drake, Edmunds, Ferry, Harlan, Howard, Morgan, Morrill (Vt.), Nye, Pomeroy, Ramsey, Stewart, Thayer, Tipton, Williams, Wilson and Yates—21.

Mr. CURTIS then resumed the examination of the witnesses, as follows:—

Q. Now state what occurred between General Thomas and the President and yourself on that occasion? A. After referring to the appointment of General Thomas as Secretary of War *ad interim*, the President stated that Mr. Stanton had refused to surrender possession of the department to General Thomas, and that he desired the necessary legal proceedings, to be instituted without delay to test General Thomas' right to office, and to put him in possession; I inquired if the Attorney-General was to act in the matter, and whether I could consult with him; the President stated that the Attorney-General had been so much occupied in the Supreme Court that he had not time to look into the authorities, but he would be glad if I would confer with him; I promised to do so, and stated that I would examine the subject immediately, and soon after I took my leave.

Q. When you left, did you leave General Thomas and the President there? A. I did; I do not suppose I was there more than twenty minutes; I left my own house in a carriage at five o'clock.

Q. State now anything that you did subsequently in consequence of that employment?

Mr. BUTLER, to the Chief Justice—Does the President decide that anything which Mr. Cox did afterwards tend to show the President's intent?

The Chief Justice remarked that the witness could proceed under the ruling of the Senate.

Witness, after reflecting on the subject—Supposing that the—

Mr. BUTLER, interposing—I think that suppositions can hardly come in. I never heard of a witness' suppositions being put in evidence.

Witness—I came to the conclusion—

Mr. BUTLER, again interposing—We don't want your conclusion; we want your acts.

Mr. CURTIS—It is a pretty important act for a lawyer to come to a conclusion.

Mr. BUTLER—It may or it may not be.

Witness—I will be instructed by the court what course to pursue.

Mr. BUTLER—Let the witness state what he did; I want him to be restricted to that.

Mr. CURTIS—He came to a conclusion, and I want to know what that was.

Mr. BUTLER—I object to conclusions of his own mind.

The Chief Justice said that the witness might proceed.

Witness—Knowing that a writ of *quo warranto* was a very tedious one, and that it could not be brought to a conclusion within even a year, and General Thomas having been arrested for a violation of the Tenure of Office act, I thought that the best mode of proceeding was

Mr. BUTLER, again interposing—I object to the witness' thoughts. (Laughter.) We must stop somewhere.

The Chief Justice, to the witness—Give your conclusions.

Witness—I determined then to proceed, in the first instance, in the case case of General Thomas.

Q. Proceed how? A. Before examining the justice of the case, and if the case was in a condition for it, to bring my client before the Supreme Court of the United States by a writ of habeas corpus, so that the Supreme Court, on the return of the writ, would examine the case.

Mr. BUTLER, interposing—These are not acts; they are thoughts, conclusions and reasonings of the witness—what he would do if something else was done.

The Chief Justice—Suppose that the counsel employed by the President may state what course he pursued, and why he pursued it.

Mr. BUTLER—Do you think that he can put in his own determinations and reasonings?

The Chief Justice—In relation to this matter, yes.

Mr. BUTLER—I should like to hear the judgment of the Senate upon this.

The Chief Justice—Counsel will please put the question in writing if any Senator desires it. If not, the witness will proceed.

Senator HOWARD asked that the question might be reduced to writing.

The question having been reduced to writing, was read, as follows:—"State what conclusion you arrived at as to the proper course to be taken to accomplish the instructions given you by the President?"

Mr. BUTLER—I do not object to that. What I objected to, was the witness putting in his thoughts and his reasoning, by which he came to a conclusion. What he did, was one thing; what he thought, what he determined, what he wished and what he hoped, depended as much upon his state of mind, and upon whether he was loyal or disloyal in his disposition; that we do not want.

The Chief Justice—The Chief Justice will direct the witness to confine himself to the conclusions to which he came, and to the steps which he took.

Witness—Having come to the conclusion that the most expeditious way of bringing the question in controversy before the Supreme Court, was to apply for writ of habeas corpus in the case of General Thomas. The case was in proper shape for it; I had a brief interview with the Attorney-General on Monday morning, and this course met his approval; I then proceeded to act with counsel whom General Thomas had engaged to act in his behalf in the first instance.; in order, however, to procure a writ of habeas corpus it was necessary that the commitment should be made by a court, not by a justice in chambers, or by a justice of the peace: General Thomas had been arrested and previously examined before one of the Justices of the Supreme Court of the District at chambers, and had been held to appear for further examination on Wednesday, the 26th; on Wednesday, the 26th, the Criminal Court was opened, Chief Justice Cartter presiding, and he announced that he would then proceed to the examination of the case against General Thomas.

Mr. BUTLER—We object to any proceeding in court being proved, other than by the records of the court.

Mr. CURTIS—We wish the witness to state what he did in court. It may have resulted in a record and it may not. Until we know what he did we cannot tell whether it resulted in a record or not. There may have been an ineffectual attempt to get into court.

Mr. BUTLER—I call your attention, Mr. President and Senators, to the ingeniousness of that speech. The witness testified that the court had opened, and he was going on to say what the Chief Justice, Cartter, announced in a criminal court.

Mr. CURTIS, interposing—Will the honorable manager give me one moment. I said, and intended to be so understood, that there was a Chief Justice sitting in a magisterial capacity, and also, as Mr. Cox stated, he was sitting there holding the criminal court. What we desire to prove is that there was an effort made by Mr. Cox to get this case transferred from the Chief Justice, in his capacity as magistrate, into and before the Criminal Court, and we wish to show what Mr. Cox did in order to obtain that.

Mr. BUTLER—If the Senate were to try Chief Justice Cartter as to whether he did right or wrong, I only desire that he shall have counsel here and be allowed to defend himself. I never heard of the proceedings of a court, or of a magistrate, attempted to be proved in a tribunal where he was not on trial, by the declarations of the counsel for the criminal.

The Chief Justice—The counsel will reduce the question to writing, and the Chief Justice will submit it to the Senate.

The question being reduced to writing, was read, as follows:—"What did you do toward getting out a writ of habeas corpus under the employment of the President?"

Mr. BUTLER—That is not the question that we have been debating about. I made an objection, Mr. President, that the witness should not state what took place at court, and now counsel puts a general question which evades that.

Mr. EVARTS—Our general question is intended to draw out what took place in court.

Mr. BUTLER—Then we object.

Mr. EVARTS—Then we understand you, but I do not want to be catechised about it.

The Chief Justice put the question to the court, as to whether the testimony would be admitted.

Mr. BUTLER—I ask that there be added to the question these words:—"This being intended to cover what the witness heard in court."

Mr. EVARTS—The question needs no change whatever. It is intended to call out what the witness did towards getting out a writ of habeas corpus, and it covers what he did in court, the very place to do it.

Mr. CURTIS—If any change or addition is to be made to the question, I should like to alter the word "court," because there may be a double meaning to that. What was done or intended to be done was before a magistrate.

Mr. BUTLER—Sitting as a judge?

Mr. CURTIS—Sitting as a magistrate.

The question was then modified so as to read, "What did you do towards getting out a habeas corpus under the employment of the President?"

The yeas and nays were taken and resulted—Yeas, 27; nays, 23, as follows:—

YEAS.—Messrs. Anthony, Bayard, Buckalew, Davis, Dixon, Doolittle, Fessenden, Fowler, Frelinghuysen, Grimes, Hendricks, Johnson, McCreery, Morrill (Me.), Morton, Norton, Patterson (N. H.), Patterson (Tenn.), Ross, Saulsbury, Sherman, Sprague, Sumner, Trumbull, Van Winkle, Vickers, Willey—27.

NAYS.—Messrs. Cameron, Cattell, Chandler, Conkling, Conness, Cragin, Drake, Edmunds, Ferry, Harlan, Howard, Howe, Morgan, Morrill (Vt.), Nye, Pomeroy, Ramsey, Stewart, Thayer, Tipton, Williams, Wilson and Yates—23.

So the question was admitted.

Witness—When the Chief Justice announced that he would proceed as an examining justice to investigate the case of General Thomas, not as holding court, our first application to him was to adjourn the investigation to the Criminal Court, in order to have the action of that court; after some little discussion the application was refused; our next effort was to have General Thomas committed to prison, in order that we might apply to that court for a writ of habeas corpus, and upon his being remanded by that court, if it should be done, we might follow up the application by one to the Supreme Court of the United States; the counsel who represented the government, Messrs. Carpenter and Riddle, applied to the court then for a postponement.

Mr. BUTLER (to the witness)—Stop a moment.

To the Chief Justice—Does this ruling apply to what was done by others?

The Chief Justice—If it is a part of the same transaction, the Chief Justice conceives that it comes within the ruling.

The witness then proceeded:—The Chief Justice having indicated the intention to postpone the examination, we directed General Thomas to decline giving bail for his appearance, and to surrender himself into custody, and we announced to the Judge that he was in custody, and then presented to the Criminal Court an application for the writ of habeas corpus; the counsel on the other side objected that General Thomas could not put himself into custody, and that they did not desire that he should be detained in custody; the Chief Justice also declared that he would not restrain General Thomas of his liberty, nor hold him, nor allow him to be held in custody; supposing that he must either be committed or finally discharged; we then claimed that he should be discharged, not supposing that the counsel on the other side would consent to it, but supposing that that would bring about his commitment, and that thus we would have an opportunity of getting the habeas corpus; they made no objection, however, to his final discharge, and accordingly the Chief Justice did discharge him; immediately after that I went in company with the counsel whom he employed, Mr. Merrick, to the President's house, and reported our proceedings and the result to the President; he then urged us to proceed.

Mr. BUTLER to the witness—Wait a moment.

To the Chief Justice- Shall we have another interview with the President put in?

The Chief Justice to the witness—What date was that? A. It was the 26th of February, immediately after the court adjourned.

Mr. CURTIS—We propose to show that having made his report to the President of the failure of the attempt, he then received from the President other instructions on that subject to follow up the attempt in another way.

Mr. BINGHAM—Do I understand that this interview with the President was on the 26th?

Mr. CURTIS—It was.

Mr. BINGHAM—Two days after he had been impeached by the House of Representatives?

Mr. CURTIS—Yes.

Mr. BINGHAM—Two days after he was presented, and you are asking the President's declarations to prove his own innocence?

Mr. CURTIS—We do not ask for his declarations, we ask for his acts.

Mr. BUTLER—Two days after his arraignment at this bar? We ask for a vote of the Senate.

The Chief Justice—The Chief Justice may have misunderstood the ruling of the Senate, but he understands it to be this:—That facts in relation to the intention of the President to obtain a legal remedy, commencing on the 22d, may be pursued to the legitimate termination of that particular transaction, and, therefore, the Senate has ruled that the witness may go on and testify until that particular transaction comes to a close. Now the offer is to prove the conversation after the termination of that effort in the District Court. The Chief Justice does not think that that is the view of the Senate, but he will submit the question to the Senate.

The question was submitted, and the evidence was ruled out without a division.

By Mr. CURTIS—Q. After you had reported to the President, as you have stated, did you take any further step, or do any further act, in reference to raising the question of the constitutionality of the law, or the Tenure of Office act?

Mr. BUTLER—If what the President did himself after he was impeached after the 22d of February cannot be given in evidence, I do not see that what his counsel did for him can be. It is only one step further.

Mr. EVARTS—We may, at least, put the question, I suppose.

Mr. BUTLER—The question was put, and I objected to it.

Mr. EVARTS—It was not reduced to writing.

By direction of the Chief Justice, the question was put in writing, as follows:—After you had reported to the President the result of your efforts to obtain a writ of habeas corpus, did you do any other act in pursuance of the original instructions you had received from the President on Saturday to contest the right of Mr. Stanton to continue in the office? If so, state what the acts were?

The Chief Justice thinks the question inadmissible, within the last vote of the Senate, but will put it to the Senate, if any Senator desires it.

Mr. DOOLITTLE asked a vote.

By request of Mr. SHERMAN, the fifth article was read by the Secretary.

Mr. EVARTS said it was proposed to show a lawful intent.

Mr. HOWE—If it is proper, I would like the first question addressed to the witness read again.

The Chief Justice—On which the ruling took place?

Mr. HOWE—No.

Mr. EVARTS—The offer to prove?

Mr. HOWE—The offer to prove.

The offer to prove was again read.

The Chief Justice decided that under the fifth article on the question of intent, the question was admissible.

Mr. HOWARD asked that the question be put to the Senate, and the question was admitted by the following vote:

YEAS.—Messrs. Anthony, Bayard, Buckalew, Davis, Dixon, Doolittle, Fessenden, Fowler, Grimes, Hendricks, Howe, Johnson, McCreery, Morrill (Me.), Morton, Norton, Patterson (N. H.), Patterson (Tenn.), Ross, Saulsbury, Sherman, Sprague, Sumner, Trumbull, Van Winkle, Vickers and Willey—27.

NAYS.—Messrs. Cameron, Cattell, Chandler, Conkling, Conness, Cragin, Drake, Edmunds, Ferry, Frelinghuysen, Harlan, Howard, Morgan, Morrill (Vt.), Nye, Pomeroy, Ramsey, Stewart, Thayer, Tipton, Williams, Wilson and Yates—23.

Witness—On the same day or the next, the 21st, I filed an information in the nature of a *quo warranto*; I think a delay of one day occurred in the effort to procure certified copies of General Thomas' commission as secretary of War *ad interim;* I then applied to the District Attorney to sign the information in the nature of a *quo warranto*, and he declined to do so without instructions from the President or Attorney-General; this fact was communicated to the Attorney-General, and the papers were sent to him, and we also gave it as our opinion that it would not be—

Mr. BUTLER—Stop a moment; we object to the opinion given to the Attorney General.

Mr. EVARTS—We don't insist upon it.

Mr. CURTIS—You can now proceed to state what was done after this time. A. Nothing was done after that time by me.

On motion of Mr. CONNESS, the Senate took a recess of fifteen minutes, at half-past two.

After the recess the witness was cross-examined by Mr. BUTLER.

Q. Have you practiced in Washington always? A. Yes, sir.

Q. Were any other counsel associated with you by the President? A. No, sir, not to my knowledge.

Q. Were you counsel in that case for the President, or for General Thomas? A. I considered myself counsel for the President.

Q. Did you so announce yourself to Chief Justice Cartter? A. I did not.

Q. Then you appeared before him as counsel for Gen. Thomas? A. I did in that proceeding.

Q. And he did not understand in any way so far as you knew that you were desiring to do anything there in behalf of the President? A. I had mentioned the fact that I had been sent for to take charge of some proceedings.

Q. As counsel for the President? A. Yes, sir; that I had been sent for by the President.

Q. But did you tell him that you were coming into this court as counsel for the President? A. No, I did not.

Q. In any of your discussions of questions before the court, did you inform the court or counsel that you desired to have the case put in frame so that you could get the decision of the Supreme Court? A. I don't think I did.

Q. Had they any means, either court or counsel, of knowing that that was the President's purpose or yours, so far as you were concerned? A. Only by the habeas corpus spoken of in General Thomas' answer.

Q. Nothing, only what they might infer? A. Yes, sir; I had no conversation with them whatever.

Q. I am not speaking of conversations with counsel outside of the court, but I am speaking of the proceedings in court? A. No, sir.

Q. And, so far as the proceeding in court were concerned, there was no intimation, direct or indirect, that there was any wish on the part of the President or the Attorney-General to make a case to test the constitutionality or the propriety of any law? A. There was none that I remember in the presence of the Judge on the bench at that time other than private intimations.

Q. Your private intimations I have not asked for; were there any to the counsel that appeared on the other side? A. No, sir.

Q. Then, so far as you know, the counsel on the other side would only treat this as a question of the rights of personal liberty of Mr. Thomas? A. Yes, sir.

Q. Well, sir, it being your desire to have that question tested, and as you appeared for Mr. Thomas, and as it must have been done by consent of the other side, the prosecutor, why didn't you speak to the opposite counsel, and ask to have it put in frame for that? A. Because I didn't think they would consent to it; we didn't want to let them know what our object was.

Q. Then you meant to conceal your object? A. We rather did; they seemed to divine it from the course they took.

Q. You say you prepared papers for an information in the nature of a *quo warranto?* A. Yes, sir.

Q. What day was that? A. That was either on Wednesday the 26th or on the next day.

Q. 26th or 27th of February? A. I think it was on the 27th.

Q. And that was after the President was impeached? A. Yes, sir.

Q. Did you see the President between the time that you reported to him and the time when you got this paper? A. I did not, sir; I have never seen him since.

Q. You prepared that paper? A. Yes, sir, and carried it to the Attorney-General, to the District Attorney; I spoke to him, and he said he must have some order from the Attorney-General, or the President.

Q. Yes, sir; and then you went to the Attorney-General? A. I sent the papers.

Q. Did you send a note with them? A. I don't recollect; I sent the information, either verbal or written.

Q. Who did you send it by? A. By Mr. Merrick or Mr. Bradley.

Q. What Bradley? A. The elder.

Q. Was he concerned in the matter? A. He appeared in court with us, merely as adviser to General Thomas.

Q. Joseph R. Bradley appeared in the District Court as attorney? A. He appeared in person, but not in the character of attorney.

Q. Did he say anything? A. Nothing to the court.

Q. Is that the man that was disbarred? A. The same; so that he could not appear.

Q. Well, after you sent these papers to the Attorney-General, did you ever get them back? A. I did.

Q. When? A. A few days ago.

Q. By a few days ago, when do you mean; since you have been summoned as a witness? A. I think not.

Q. Just before, I believe, preparatory to your being summoned as a witness? A. No, not that I'm aware of.

Q. After this case was opened? A. After.

Q. How long after? A. I couldn't say; I think it was four or five days ago.

Q. Have you had any communication with the Attorney-General about them between the time when you sent them and the time when you read them? A. None in person.

Q. Had you in writing? A. No, sir.

Q. Then you had none in any way? A. Yes, sir; Mr. Merrick did; it was more convenient for him to see him.

Q. Of which you only know from what he said? A. Yes, sir.

Q. They were returned to you; where are they now? A. I have them in my pocket.

Q. Were they not returned to you for the purpose of your having them when you were called as a witness? A. No, sir; they came with a message.

Q. How soon before you were summoned? A. Not more than a day or two.

Q. On the same day? A. I think a day or two before.

Q. To your knowledge have those papers ever been presented to any judge of any court? A. They have not.

Q. Up to the hour that we are speaking, have you been directed, either by the Attorney-General or by the President, to present them to any judge of any court? A. The papers came to me with the direction to use them as Mr. Merrick or myself chose in our discretion.

Q. Verbal or written? A. Verbal, to Mr. Merrick.

Q. But Mr. Merrick was not associated with you as counsel for the President? A. He was not, as I understood; he was counsel for General Thomas.

Q. Was this movement on the part of General Thomas, for the information, made as a *quo warranto?* A. No, sir; it was filed on the relation of General Thomas.

Q. Have you received, in writing or verbally, to yourself, any direction either from the President or the Attorney-General, to file those papers? A. No positive orders.

Q. Any positive or impositive from them to you? A. Not immediately,

Q. I don't mean through Mr. Merrick? A. The only communication I received was through him.

Q. From whom did he bring you a direction or communication? A. From the Attorney-General.

Q. Who? A. The Attorney-General.

Q. Who is that? Q. Mr. Stanbery.

Q. And this was five days ago—why, he resigned as Attorney-General some fortnight ago!—How did he come as Attorney-General to speak by order of the President? A. I meant Mr. Stanbery.

Q. Have you ever received any directions through Mr. Merrick from the Attorney-General officially, as a direction for the President's counsel through Mr. Merrick? A. All that I received was—

Eexcuse me. Q. Have you received any communication through Mr. Merrick or anybody else from the Attorney-General of the United States—not the resigned Attorney-General of the United States? A. I have not, sir, from any other.

Q. And you have not received any from him, either verbal or otherwise, while he was Attorney-General of the United States? A. I have not.

Q. When you handed him the papers was he the Attorney-General? A. I believe so, sir.

Q. Could you not be certain on that point? A. I don't know when he resigned.

Q. And the resignation made no difference in your action? A. I don't think he had resigned at that time; I am very sure the papers were sent to him within two or three days after the discharge of General Thomas.

Q. And were returned by him to you within four or five days? A. Yes, sir.

Q. Four or five days from when? after he resigned? A. I think it was; yes, sir.

Q. So that when you told us Mr. Merrick had brought it from the Attorney-General it was from Mr. Stanbery? A. Yes, sir.

Q. You have received no communication from the President or Attorney-General as to what should be done with this proceeding? A. No, sir.

Q. Then, so far as you know, there has not been any direction or any effort from the Attorney-General or the President, leaving out Mr. Stanbery, who is not Attorney-General now, to have anything done with these papers? A. There has been no direction, I know.

Q. No communication? A. No communication since the paper was forwarded to me, to go to the court for a moment.

Q. Did Mr. Merrick or yourself make a motion to have Mr. Thomas discharged? A. Yes, sir.

Q. Was he not in custody, under his recognizance, up to the time of making that motion? A. He claimed that he was, but the other side denied it.

Q. And to settle that question you moved a discharge? A. Yes, sir.

Q. And that was granted? A. It was.

Q. Did you make that motion? A. Yes, sir.

Q. So that, in fact, General Thomas was discharged from custody on the motion of the President's counsel?

Mr. CURTIS—He has not said that.

Mr. BUTLER—Excuse me.

Q. If he was not discharged from custody what was he discharged from? A. Discharged from any further detention or examination.

Q. He could not be detained without being in custody, could he? A. Not very well.

Q. Then, I will repeat the question upon which I was interrupted, whether, in fact, Mr. Cox, Mr. Thomas was not discharged from custody, from detention, from further being held to answer on that complaint upon the motion of the President's counsel? A. He was, sir.

Q. Now, then, sir, was that information signed by any Attorney-General, past, present or to come, so far as you know? A. No, sir.

Richard T. Merrick, sworn on behalf of respondent—Examined by Mr. CURTIS—Q. Where do you reside? A. I reside in this city.

Q. What is your profession? A. I am a lawyer, sir.

Q. How long have you been in that profession? A. Nineteen or twenty years, sir.

Q. Were you employed professsonally in any way in connection with the matter of General Thomas before Chief Justice Cartter? A. I was employed by General Thomas on the morning of the 22d of February to appear in the proceeding about being brought before Chief Justice Cartter.

Q. In the course of that day, the 22d of February, did you have an interview, in company with General Thomas or otherwise, with the President of the United States? A. I went to the President's house for the purpose of taking to the President the affidavit, &c., filed by General Thomas, and communicating to the President what had transpired in regard to the case.

Q. Did you communicate to him what had transpired in regard to the case?

Mr. BUTLER—I submit, Mr. President, that that is wholly immaterial; the Senate ruled in the President's acts in employing Mr. Cox as his counsel. But what communication took place between the President and Mr. Merrick, who very frankly tells us that he was employed by General Thomas as his counsel, I think cannot be evidence.

The Chief Justice was understood to rule the question admissible.

Mr. CURTIS—Q. State whether you communicated to the President, in the presence of General Thomas, what had transpired in reference to the case. A. My recollection is, that I communicated what had transpired to the President, in the absence of General Thomas; that he was not at the Executive Mansion when I called; that during the interview General Thomas arrived, and the same communication was then made in a general conversation, in which the Attorney-General, Mr. Stanbery, the President, General Thomas and myself participated.

Q. Please state whether, either from the President himself or from the Attorney-General, in his presence, you received afterwards any instructions or suggestions as to the course to be pursued by you in General Thomas' case? In the first place you may fix, if you please, the hour of the day when this occurred on the 22d? A. I think the proceedings before Chief Justice Cartter at chambers, took place between ten and half-past ten, to the best of my recollection, about half-past, and immediately after they concluded, and they extended over a very short period; I ordered copies of the papers to be made, and as soon as they were made, I took them to the Executive mansion; I think I occupied probably from thirty minutes to an hour to make the copies, and my impression is I reached the Executive mansion about noon.

Q. Now you can answer the residue of the question, whether you received either from the President himself or the Attorney-General in the presence of the President, any directions or suggestions as to the course to be taken by you as counsel in the case?

Mr. BUTLER to Mr. CURTIS—Q. Do you ask now for the conversations?

Mr. CURTIS—I ask for directions to this gentleman. I do not care how far it goes.

Mr. BUTLER—I think, sir, these conversations cannot be put in. This is not the employing and sending there of his counsel to do anything, but giving directions as to how General Thomas' counsel are to try this case.

Mr. CURTIS—I suppose it depends upon what was said. They might amount to "verbal acts," as they are called in the books, if this gentleman so received and acted upon them. I suppose they then passed out of the range of declarations. The question is whether he received directions or suggestions from the President or the Attorney-General.

Mr. BUTLER—The difficulty is this. It is not the mere question of the difference between acts and declarations, although declarations make it one degree farther off. My proposition is that the President's acts, in giving directions to General Thomas' counsel to defend General Thomas, that counsel not being employed by the President, cannot be evidence, whether acts or declarations.

Mr. EVARTS—It does not follow that these instructions were to defend General Thomas. The first of the inquiry is, that the instructions were to make investigations, that this proceeding being such as could be taken on behalf of the President, you cannot anticipate what the answer may be. An offer to show that the Attorney-General, in the presence of the President, as soon as the report of the situation of this case of General Thomas was made, gave certain instructions to this gentleman of the profession, in reference to grafting upon that case the act of having a habeas corpus.

Mr. BUTLER—I do not propose to argue it; the statement of it is enough. The President has no more right to direct General Thomas' lawyer than to direct me, and thereupon they do not offer the declarations of the President, but they offer the declarations of the President's lawyer—Attorney-General Stanbery, now his counsel—to be put into the case; there is no fact on earth that to them is any good in that way.

The offer of evidence was reduced to writing, as follows:—

"We offer to prove that at the hour of twelve o'clock, noon, on the 22d of February, on the first communication with the President as to the situation of General Thomas' case, the President, or the Attorney-General in his presence, gave the witness certain directions as to obtaining a writ of habeas corpus for the purpose of testing, judicially, the right of Mr. Stanton to continue to hold the office of Secretary of War against the authority of the President."

The Chief Justice decided that the proof was admissible

within the rule adopted by the Senate, but said that he would put the question to the Senate if any Senator desired it.

No vote being called for, the examination was resumed.

Mr. CURTIS—The question is, whether the President, or the Attorney-General in his presence, gave you any instructions in reference to the proceedings to obtain a writ of habeas corpus to test the right of Mr. Stanton to hold the office contrary to the will of the President? A. The Attorney-General, on learning from me the situation of the case, asked if it was possible in any way to get it into the Supreme Court immediately; I told him I was not prepared to answer that question. He then said:—"Look at it, and see whether or not you can take it up to the Supreme Court immediately on habeas corpus, and have the decision of that tribunal." And I told him I would.

Q. Subsequent to that time, had you come into communication with any gentlemen acting as counsel for the President, in relation to that matter? A. I examined the question as requested by the Attorney-General, and on the evening or afternoon of the 22d, and I think, within two or three hours after I had seen him, I wrote him a note.

Mr. BUTLER—We object to the contents of the note being given as evidence.

Mr. CURTIS to the witness—Stating the result? Witness. Stating the result of that examination.

Mr. BUTLER—Whatever is in that note, you must not state.

Mr. CURTIS to the witness—You wrote him a note on that subject? Witness—I wrote him a note on that subject, the following Monday or Tuesday, this being Saturday; I met Mr. Cox, who was the counsel for the President, as I understood, and in consultation with him I communicated to him the conclusion I had arrived at in the course of the examination on the Saturday previous; we having come to the same conclusion, agreed to conduct the case together in harmony, with a view to accomplish the contemplated result of taking it to the Supreme Court by a habeas corpus.

Q. State now anything which you and Mr. Cox did for the purpose of accomplishing that result? A. Having formed our plan of proceeding we went into court on the day on which, according to the bond, General Thomas was to appear before Judge Cartter, in chambers. That was, I think, on Wednesday, the 26th, if I am not mistaken. Can I state what transpired?

Mr. CURTIS—Yes, so far as regards your acts.

Mr. BUTLER—I respectfully submit once again, Mr. President, that the acts of General Thomas's counsel, under the direction of the Attorney-General after the President was impeached, cannot be put in evidence.

Witness—Will you allow me to make a correction?

Mr. CURTIS—Certainly.

Witness—You asked when I next came in contact with any one representing the President. I should have stated that on Tuesday night, by appointment, I had an interview with the President on the subject of this case, and of the proceedings to be taken on the following day.

Mr. BUTLER—I don't see that that alters the question, which I request may be reduced to writing before I argue it, because I have argued one or two questions to-day, and then found other questions put in their place.

The Chief Justice—Counsel will please reduce the question to writing.

The question being reduced to writing, read as follows:—
"What, if anything, did you and Mr. Cox do in relation to accomplishing the result you have spoken of?"

Mr. BUTLER—Does that include what was done in court?

Mr. CURTIS—It includes what was done before Chief Justice Cartter.

The Chief Justice—The Chief Justice thinks it competent, but he will put it to the Senate if any Senator desires it.

No vote having been called for, the question was allowed to be put to the witness.

Witness—To answer that question, it is necessary I should state what transpired before the Judge in chambers and in court on Wednesday, when all that we did was done to accomplish that result; we went into the room in the City Hall in which the Criminal Court held its session in the morning; Judge Cartter was then holding the term of the Criminal Court, and the Criminal Court was regularly adjourned; after some business of the Criminal Court was discharged, the Chief Justice announced that he was ready to hear the case of General Thomas.

The question was then suggested whether it should be heard in chambers or before the court. The Chief Justice said he would hear it as in chambers. The Criminal Court not having been then adjourned, the case was thereupon called up. The counsel appearing for Mr. Stanton, or for the government, Messrs. Carpenter and Riddell, moved that the case be continued or postponed until the following day, on the grounds of the absence of one or two of the witnesses, I think, and on the additional plea of Mr. Carpenter's indisposition; to that motion, after a consultation with my associates, Mr. Cox and Mr. Joseph H. Bradley, who appeared as advisory counsel for General Thomas, I arose and objected to a postponement, stating that I was constrained to object, notwithstanding the plea of personal indisposition, to which I always yielded, and that I objected now for the reason that this was a case involving a question of great public interest and which the harmonious action of the government rendered necessary to be speedily determined. I elaborated that view, and Mr. Carpenter replied, representing that there could be no detriment to the public service, and he earnestly urged the court for a postponement.

The Chief Justice thereupon remarked, I think, that it was the first time he knew a case in which the plea of personal indisposition of counsel was not acceded to by the other side; that it was generally sufficient; and, he went on to remark on the motion further, insomuch that I concluded that he would continue the case till the following day. As soon as he said that he would continue the case, we brought forward a motion that it be then adjourned from before the Chief Justice at Chambers to the Chief Justice holding the Criminal Court. That motion was argued by counsel and overruled by the Judge at Chambers, not in court. We then submitted to the Judge.

Mr. BUTLER interposing—Mr. President, I wish simply to be understood, so that I may clear my skirts of the matter, that this all comes in under our objection, and under the ruling of the presiding officer.

The Chief Justice (with severe dignity in his tone).—It comes in under the direction of the Senate of the United States. To the witness—Proceed, sir.

Witness—We then announced to the Judge that General Thomas' bail had surrendered him, or that he was in the custody of the Marshal, and the Marshal was advancing towards him at the time; I think that Mr. Bradley or Mr. Cox handed me, while on my feet and while making that announcement, the petition for the habeas corpus, which I then presented to the Criminal Court, which, having opened in the morning, had not yet adjourned, and over which the Chief Justice was presiding; I presented the petition for the habeas corpus to the Criminal Court, representing that General Thomas was in the custody of the Marshal, and I asked that I should be heard.

Mr. BUTLER—Was that petition in writing?

Witness—That petition was in writing. I believe I said it was handed to me by one of my associates; and, if my recollection serves me right, I have seen the petition since; it was not signed when handed to me; General Thomas and Mr. Bradley were sitting immediately behind me; I laid it down, and it was taken up by some of the reporters; it was not regained for half an hour.

Mr. CURTIS—After you had read it, what occurred?

Witness—After I read it, a discussion arose on the propriety of the petition, and the legality of the time of its presentation; counsel on the other side contended that General Thomas was not in custody, and that it was a remarkable case; I remember that expression of Mr. Carpenter's, for the accused party to insist upon putting himself in custody; we contended that he was in custody, and that he did not propose to put himself in custody; counsel on the other side stated that they desired neither that he should be put in custody nor that he give bonds, because they were certain, from his character and position, that he would be present to answer any charge that might be brought against him.

The Chief Justice replied that in view of the statement of counsel he would neither put him in custody nor demand bond for his appearance; he was himself satisfied that there was no necessity for pursuing either course; we then remarked that if General Thomas was not in custody nor under bond he was discharged, and I think some one stated he is discharged; thereupon, in order that there should be a decision in reference to the alternatives presented of his being placed in custody or discharged on the record, we moved for his discharge in order to bring up the question officially of his commitment; he was thereupon discharged.

Mr. CURTIS—I believe that is all we desire to ask this witness.

Cross-examined by Mr. BUTLER—Q. Were you counsel for Surratt? A. I was.

Q. Was Mr. Cox? A. He was not.

Q. Was Mr. Bradley, who was advising counsel in these proceedings? A. He was.

Q. When you got to the Executive Mansion that morning, you say Thomas was not there? A. I think not; that is my recollection.

Q. Did you learn when he had been there? A. I do not recollect whether I did or not; had I so learned I probably should have recollected it.

Q. Did you not learn that Thomas was then over at the War Department? A. I do not recollect that I did, and I think I did not.

Q. Did you learn when he returned that he had been there? A. I do not recollect.

Mr. BUTLER—I will not tax your want of recollection any further. (Laughter.)

Edwin O. Perrine sworn and examined by Mr. EVARTS.

Q. Where do you reside? A. I reside in Long Island, near Jamaica.

Q. How long have you been a resident of that region? A. I have been a resident of Long Island over ten years.

Q. Previous to that time where did you reside? A. In Memphis, Tennessee.

Q. Are you personally acquainted with the President of the United States? A. I am.

Q. For how long a time have you been so personally acquainted? A. I knew Mr. Johnson in Tennessee for several years before he left the State, having met him more particularly on the stump in political campaigns; I being a Whig and he being a Democrat.

Q. Has that acquaintance continued to the present time? A. It has.

Q. Were you in the city of Washington in the month of February? A. I was.

Q. For what period of time? A. I came here about the 1st of February, or near that time, and remained until the 1st of March or last of February.

Q. During that time were you at a hotel or at a private house? A. I was at a private boarding house.

Q. Did you have any interview with the President of the United States on the 21st of February? A. I did.

Q. Alone, or in company with whom? A. In company with a member of the House of Representatives.

Q. Who was he? A. Mr. Selye, of Rochester, N. Y.

Q. How did it happen that you made this visit?

Mr. BUTLER, interposing—I pray judgment.

Mr. EVARTS—This is simply introductory, nothing material.

Witness—Mr. Selye said that while he knew the President he never had been formally presented to him, and understanding that I was a friend of the President, and well acquainted with him, he asked me if I would not go up with him to the President's and then introduce him.

Q. When did this occur? A. On the 20th, or the day before.

Q. And your visit then on the 21st was on this appointment? A. I made the appointment for the next day; I informed Mr. Selye that it was Cabinet day, and that it was of no use to go till two o'clock, as we probably would not be permitted to enter, and he appointed two o'clock at his room, in Twelfth street, to meet him for that purpose.

Q. You went there? A. I went to Mr. Selye's room; he called a carriage, and we drove to the President's house a little after two o'clock.

Q. Did you have any difficulty in getting in? A. We had; Mr. Cushan, the usher at the door, when I handed him Mr. Selye's card and mine, said that the President had some of his Cabinet with him yet, and that no one would be admitted; I told him that I wished him to go in and say to the President or to Colonel Moore with my compliments—

Mr. BUTLER—Interrupted the witness.

Mr. EVARTS—Was the fact that Mr. Selve was a member of Congress mentioned? Witness—Yes.

Q. So that you got in? A. Yes.

Q. Then you went up stairs? A. We were up stairs when this took place; we were in the ante-room.

Q. Then you went into the President's after awhile? A. Yes.

Q. Was the President alone when you went in? A. He was alone.

Q. Did you introduce Mr. Selye? A. I introduced Mr. Selye as a member of Congress from the Rochester District.

Q. Without reference to any other conversation that occurred between you and the President, or between Mr. Selye and you and the President, I come now to what I suppose to be pertinent to this case. Before this time, had you heard that any order for the removal of Mr. Stanton had been made? A. I had heard nothing of it.

Q. Had Mr. Selye heard of it, so far as you know? A. So far as I know, he had not; I found him lying down when I got to his room, at two o'clock.

Q. Did he then hear from the President of the removal of Mr. Stanton.

Mr. BUTLER—I object to the statement of the President to this witness, or to Mr. Selye, or to anybody else. If his declarations made to all the persons in the country are to be given in evidence, there would be no end to this case. Everybody would be brought here, and where are we to stop? If there is to be any stop, it is now.

Mr. EVARTS—The evidence is proper. The time to consider about the public interest was when the trial commenced. Of course it would be more convenient to stop the case at the end of the prosecution; it would save the time of the country.

Mr. BUTLER—The question is simply what was said between the President and Mr. Selye, and Mr. Perrine. I have the honor to object to it.

Mr. EVARTS—I am reducing the question to form.

The offer of proof being reduced to writing, and handed over to Mr. Butler for his examination, was read by the clerk, as follows:—

"We offer to prove that the President then stated that he had issued an order for the removal of Mr. Stanton, and the employment of General Thomas to perform the duties ad interim; that thereupon Mr. Perrine said:— 'Supposing Mr. Stanton shall oppose the order;' and the President replied:— 'There is no danger.' He then added:—'It is only a temporary arrangement. I shall send into the Senate at once a good name for the office.'"

Mr. BUTLER objected. He said that this was mere narration, mere statement of what the President had done and what he intended to do; that it never was evidence and never would be evidence in any organized court. He did not see where any limit was to be put if such testimony were received. If Mr. Perrine, who had been heretofore on the stand, could go to the President and ask questions and be answered, and then come to give evidence of his conversation with the President, why do so. If Mr. Selye could go there, why could not everybody else go? Why could not the President make declarations to every man, aye, and every woman, too·(laughter), of what he intended to do, and what he had done, and bring them in here to testify and to instruct the Senate of the United States in its duty as a High Court of Impeachment?

Mr. EVARTS said he was not aware the credit of the testimony was at all effected by the fact that Mr. Perrine had been engaged in politics. Nor did he suppose that that fact would assist the court in determining what was evidence. The question was whether declarations at the time and under those circumstances of the President's intent, and if what he had done was proper to be given in evidence. It would be observed that this was an interview between the President and a member of Congress, one of the grand inquests of the nation. That at that hour the President supposed, from the statement of General Thomas, that Mr. Stanton was ready to leave the office,

desiring time to accommodate his private occasion, and that the President stated to those gentlemen that he had removed Mr. Stanton, and appointed General Thomas ad interim, which was their first intelligence of its occurrence.

As to the motive and purpose then entertained by the President, this conversation shows that the President was not intending, as charged by the managers, to place a slave or a tool in the War Department, to the detriment of the public interest; but, on the contrary, that the appointment of General Thomas was a mere temporary arrangement, and that he should at once send in a good name for the office to the Senate. This bore upon the question of purpose, and the fact had already been shown that a nomination for the office of Secretary of War was sent to the Senate on the following day, before one o'clock.

Mr. WILSON, one of the managers, objected to the evidence as being outside of any former ruling of the Senate, and as being perfectly within the rule laid down in Hardy's case, and to which he called the attention of the Senate. If this offer of proof did not come perfectly within the rule in that case, then he never met with a case in all his experience which came within it. He would leave the objection on that point to the decision of the Senate.

Mr. EVARTS argued for the admission of the evidence. He admitted that the question now proposed was not entirely covered by any ruling of the Senate, because there were circumstances attending the first offer of evidence which were not precisely reproduced here, but Senators would observe that before the controversy arose, and at a time, when, in the President's opinion, there was to be no controversy, he had made this statement in the course of this intercourse with a member of Congress, thus introduced to him, concerning his public action. The evidence had a bearing also upon the question whether the President was using or justifying force. It also had a bearing upon the fact, that the next day the President actually did send in the name of Mr. Ewing, of Ohio, for the place of Secretary of War.

Mr. BUTLER said there were one or two new facts on which this evidence was pressed, the first and most material being that the conversation had occurred before any controversy had arisen between the President and Congress on the subject of Mr. Stanton. If that were so, then there might be same color or shadow of a claim to admit this evidence. But had there not been a controversy going on; had not the President known that the Senate had restored Mr. Stanton; had not the President put Mr. Stanton out, and had not the Senate put him back.

Had not the President been then besieging General Sherman to take the office on the Monday before, yet the President's counsel were attempting to put this evidence before the Senate, because it was the President's declaration made before any controversy arose, or was likely to arise. Another proposition was that it might be evidence because it was said to a member of Congress.

He was aware that members of Congress had rights and privileges belonging to their position, but he never was aware before that one of those rights was that was said to members was evidence. There were a good many things said to him which he should be very unwilling to have admitted as evidence. For instance, a written declaration had been sent to him to-day, "Come prepared to meet your God." (Laughter). "The adversary is on your track. Hell is your portion." (Continuous laughter).

He trusted that that was not evidence, because it was said to a member of Congress—(laughter)—and yet it was just as pertinent and just as competent as the evidence here proposed. He did not mean, by any remark before, to suggest that the fact of the declaration being made to a gentleman who had been on the stump made it more or less competent; he had only meant to say the evidence was utterly outside the case. He objected to it, foreseeing what might come quite as properly as it. He foresaw that some of the lady friends of the President—(he begged pardon; he meant some of the women friends)—might go to the White House and be told by the President what his purpose was, and then come and testify to it here, which would be just as good evidence, in his judgment, as what was now offered.

Mr. EVARTS made a few remarks in support of the offering of the testimony.

The Chief Justice said—Senators:—The Chief Justice is unable to determine the precise extent to which the Senate applies its own decision. He has understood the decision to be that evidence may be given for the purpose of showing the conversations of the President at or near the time of the transaction. It is said that this evidence is distinguishable from that just introduced. The Chief Justice is not able to distinguish it, and will submit the question to the Senate whether the testimony shall be admitted.

The vote of the Senate was taken, and resulted—Yeas, 9; nays, 37, as follows:—

YEAS.—Messrs. Bayard, Buckalew, Davis, Dixon, Doolittle, Hendricks, McCreery, Patterson (Tenn.), and Vickers—9.

NAYS.—Messrs. Cameron, Cattell, Chandler, Conkling, Conness, Corbett, Cragin, Drake, Ferry, Fessenden, Fowler, Frelinghuysen, Grimes, Harlan, Howard, Howe, Johnson, Morgan, Morrill (Me.), Morrill (Vt.), Morton, Nye, Patterson (N. H.), Pomeroy, Ramsey, Ross, Sherman, Sprague, Stewart, Thayer, Tipton, Trumbull, Van Winkle, Willey, Williams, Wilson, and Yates—37.

So the evidence was overruled.

Mr. EVARTS then said, this evidence having been excluded, we have no other questions to ask the witness.

Mr. BUTLER said they did not wish to cross-examine him.

Mr. EVARTS then submitted that the counsel had reached a point where the Senate might conveniently adjourn, as they would have no other witness to-day.

Mr. BUTLER opposed the adjournment and asked that the counsel for the President be called upon to go on with their case. He had only to apply to them the argument made by Mr. Merrick in the case before Chief Justice Cartter, that although it was always an ungracious thing to object to postponement on account of the sickness of the counsel, still, as the case involved a matter of so much public interest, it should not be postponed on that account. On that point he would say, "I thank thee, Jew, for teaching me that word." Mr. Thomas could not wait on account of the sickness of a counsel, and so the managers now could not wait on account of the sickness of the Attorney-General. Why should they? Why should not this President be called upon to go on with his case. There had been thirty-three working days since the President was required to file his answer.

The managers had used six of those, and the counsel for the President had used a portion of the six, the other twenty-one having been given to delays. The legislation of the country was standing still. The House of Representatives were here at the bar of the Senate, day after day. The appropriations for carrying on the government could not be passed because the trial was in the way. Nothing could be done, and the whole country was waiting for its close.

Far be it from him not to desire to have his friend the Attorney-General here, but public interests were greater than the interests of any individual. Two hundred thousand men had laid down their lives in the war, and were they now to stop for the sickness of one man. He had in his hand testimony of what was going on this day, and this promised the South—

Mr. CURTIS (jocularly)—"We object to the introduction of that testimony."

Mr. EVARTS (in the same temper) challenged its relevancy.

Mr. BUTLER said that its relevancy was this:—That while they were waiting for the Attorney-General to get well, a number of their fellow-citizens were being murdered in the South, and there was not a man in the Senate Chamber who did not know that the moment justice was done to this great criminal, these murders would cease. (Stamping of feet in the galleries, and attempted manifestations of applause, which were suppressed). That was the way things stood here, and they were being asked by every true man of the country, why they sat here idle. In Alabama, a register in bankruptcy was to-day driven from his duties and his home by the Kuk-Klux Klan (laughter), and the evidence of that laid upon his table. Should they then delay longer in this case, knowing their responsibilities to their countrymen, to their consciences and to their God?

The true Union men of the country were being murdered, and on the skirts of Congress their blood was if they remained here longer idle. He also reminded the Senators that since the 20th day of February last, ten millions of gold had been sold out of the Treasury at a sacrifice, and $12,000 paid in commissions to a man whom the Senate had refused to continue in office. This gold was sold at from one-and-a-half to two per cent. lower than the market rates. More than that, he had, from the same source, the fact that there had been bought, in the city of New York, since this trial had been begun, United States bonds to the amount of $27,058,100, which had been sold at from one-half to five-eighths and three-quarters above the market rates.

Some Senator remarked in an under tone that he meant below the market rates.

Mr. BUTLER repeated that it was above the market prices. He knew what he said, and he never was mistaken. (Laughter.) He demanded safety for the finances of the people, for the progress of legislation, for the safety of the true and loyal men of the North, who had perilled their lives for four years for the good of the country, for all that was dear to any patriot, that no further delay should be allowed, but the case should be brought to a decision.

If the President of the United States were to go free and unwhipped of justice, then they might as well have that state of facts; but if he was guilty, as the House of Representatives had charged, and if he was an obstruction to the peace of the country, then that obstruction should be removed, and all those murders and corruptions would cease. In the name of Heaven, said he, let us have an end of this, and say to-day that we sit at least four hours a day, and attend to this great business of the people. He called the attention of the Senate to one of the great State trials in England, where the court sat from nine o'clock in the morning until one o'clock at night, and where the court refused Lord Erskine to meet one hour later in the morning in order that he might have a chance for preparing his summing up, the doing of which occupied nine hours. That was the way that cases of great consequence were tried in England. He was not complaining of the Senate, but was merely contrasting the delay in this case, and kindness shown to the President, the courtesies extended to him in this greatest of all cases, with cases tried elsewhere. The managers had been ready at all hazards, and only asked that now the counsel for the President should be ready, and should go on, instead of having these interminable delays. He reminded the Senate, also, of the threat made by Mr. Brooks, in the House of Representatives, that if the impeachment was carried into the Senate, they would require all forms to be observed, and would keep it going on until the end of Mr. Johnson's term.

He appealed to the Senators not to allow that threat to be carried out, as it has been attempted to be carried out by these continual delays. He never opened his mails in the morning without taking up some case of murder in the South—of the murder of men whom he had known as standing by the side of the Union, and whom he now heard of as laying in their cold graves. It was the feeling for the loss of those who stood by their country that perhaps stirred his heart very much, so that he was not able, with that coolness with which judicial proceedings should be characterized, to address the Senate on this subject. He would say nothing of the daily and hourly threats made against the managers, and against every great officer of the Senate. He would say nothing of that, as they were all safe. There was an old Scotch proverb in their favor. "A threatened dog lives the longest." He had not the slightest fear on that account, and these threats of those unseemly libels, in their forms of government, would all go away when that man (meaning Mr. Johnson) went out of the White House.

Senator CONKLING offered the following order:—

That each day hereafter the Senate, sitting as a Court of Impeachment, shall meet at eleven A. M.

Senator SUMNER offered the following as a substitute:—

Ordered, That considering the public interests that suffer from the delay of this trial, and in pursuance of the order already to proceed with all convenient despatch, the Senate will sit from ten o'clock in the forenoon till five o'clock in the afternoon, with such brief recess as may be ordered.

Senator TRUMBULL inquired from the Chief Justice whether these resolutions were in order. The Chief Justice replied that they were not, if any Senator objected.

Senator TRUMBULL—I object.

Mr. EVARTS rose and said:—Mr. Chief Justice and Senators, I am not aware how much of the address of the manager is appropriate to anything which has come from me. At the opening of the court this morning, I stated how we might be situated, and I remarked that when that point of time arrived, I should submit the matter to the Senate for consideration. I never heard such an harangue before as I have just heard, though I cannot say that I may not hear it again in this court. All these delays and evil consequences seem to press upon the managers exactly at the precise time when some of their mouths are open, occupying your attention with their long harangues.

If you will look to the reports of the discussions of questions of evidence as they appear in the newspapers, you will see that all we have to say is embraced within a paragraph, while columns are taken up with the views of the learned managers. Hour after hour is taken up in debates on the production of our evidence, by their prolonging the discussion, and now twenty minutes by the watch have been consumed in this harangue of the able manager about the Kuk-Klux-Klan.

Senator CAMERON inquired if the word "harangue" was in order.

Senator DOOLITTLE suggested the inquiry whether the harangue itself was in order.

Senator FERRY moved to adjourn.

Senator SUMNER moved that the adjournment be until ten A. M. to-morrow.

The Chief Justice ruled that Senator Sumner's motion was not in order, as the motion to adjourn must be to adjourn to the usual time.

Senator SUMNER called for the yeas and nays on the motion to adjourn, but they were not ordered and the court, at 4.45 P. M., adjourned until noon to-morrow.

PROCEEDINGS OF FRIDAY, APRIL 17.

The court was opened in due form. There was a rather larger attendance of members of the House than usual this morning. On motion, the reading of the Journal was dispensed with.

The Chief Justice stated the first business in order to be the order offered by Mr. Conness, yesterday, that on each day hereafter the Senate, sitting as a Court of Impeachment, shall meet at eleven o'clock A. M., to which Senator SUMNER offered the following amendment:—

Ordered, That, considering the public interests, which suffer from the delay of this trial, and in pursuance of the order already to proceed with all convenient despatch, the Senate will sit from ten o'clock in the forenoon till six o'clock in the afternoon, with such brief recess as may be ordered.

Senator Sumner's amendment was rejected. Yeas, 12; nays, 30; as follows:—

YEAS.—Messrs. Chandler, Cameron, Cole, Corbett, Harlan, Morrill (Me.), Pomeroy, Ramsey, Stewart, Thayer, Tipton and Yates—12.

NAYS.—Messrs. Anthony, Cattell, Conness, Davis, Dixon, Doolittle, Drake, Ferry, Fessenden, Fowler, Frelinghuysen, Grimes, Hendricks, Howard, Howe, Johnson, Morgan, Morrill (Vt.), Morton, Patterson (Tenn.), Patterson (N. H.), Ross, Saulsbury, Sherman, Trumbull, Van Winkle, Vickers, Willey, Williams and Wilson—30.

The order offered by Mr. Conness was adopted by the following vote:—

YEAS.—Messrs. Cameron, Cattell, Chandler, Cole, Conkling, Conness, Corbett, Cragin, Drake, Ferry, Frelinghuysen, Harlan, Howard, Howe, Morgan, Morrill (Me.), Morrill (Vt.), Patterson (N. H.), Pomeroy, Ramsey, Sherman, Stewart, Sumner, Thayer, Tipton, Williams, Willey, Wilson and Yates—29.

NAYS.—Messrs. Anthony, Doolittle, Fowler, Grimes, Hendricks, Johnson, Patterson (Tennessee.), Ross, Saulsbury, Trumbull, Van Winkle and Vickerss.—12.

A Correction.

Mr. FERRY offered the following order:—

Whereas, There appears in the proceedings of the Senate yesterday, as published in the *Globe* of this morning, certain tabular statements incorporated in the remarks of Mr. Manager Butler, on the question of adjournment, which tabular statements were neither spoken in the discussion nor offered, nor received in evidence; therefore,

Ordered, That said tabular statements be omitted from the proceedings of the trial, as published in the proceedings of the Senate.

Mr. BUTLER—I desire to say that I stated the effect of the tabular statement to the Senate, and I did not read them at length because it would take too much time.

Mr. HENDRICKS—I rise to a question of order and propriety. I wish to know whether it would be right for any Senator to defend the Secretary of the Treasury against the attacks made, or whether our mouths are closed while these attacks are made; and if it is not proper and right for a Senator, whether it is the right of a manager to make the attack upon him?

The Chief Justice—An amendment can be made to the resolution proposed by the Senator from Connecticut (Mr. Ferry). If the Senate thinks it proper, the Senate can retire for consultation. If no Senator makes that motion, the Chair thinks it proper that the honorable manager should be heard in explanation.

Mr. BUTLER—I wish to say that I did not read them because I thought them voluminous. I had them in my hand, and made them part of my argument. I read the conclusions and inferences to be drawn from them, and thought it was due to myself and the Senate that they should be put exactly as they were, and I therefore incorporated them in the *Globe.* To the remarks of the Honorable Senator (Mr. Hendricks) I simply say that I made no attack on the Secretary of the Treasury. I said nothing of him. I did not know that he was here at all to be discussed, but I dealt with the acts as the acts of the Executive simply, and whenever called upon I can show the reason why I dealt with that act.

The Chief Justice stated the question.

Mr. ANTHONY understood the Senator from Indiana (Mr. Hendricks) to ask if, under the rules, he could be permitted to make a defense of the Secretary of the Treasury.

The Chief Justice—The rules positively prohibit debate.

Mr. ANTHONY—By unanimous consent it might be made.

Some Senator objected, and the order was then adopted, with but few dissenting voices.

Testimony of William W. Armstrong.

William W. Armstrong sworn, and examined by Mr. CURTIS. Q. Where do you reside? A. At Cleveland, Ohio.

Senator DRAKE called the attention of the Chief Justice to to impossibility, on his side of the Chamber of hearing the witness.

Mr. EVARTS suggested that there was not so much silence in the Camber as there might be, and that they must take witnesses with such natural powers as they possessed.

The Chief Justice remarked that conversation was going on at the back of the Senators, and that it must be stopped.

The examination of the witness was resumed.

Q. What is your occupation or business? A. I am one of the editors and proprietors of the Cleveland *Plaindealer.*

Q. Were you at Cleveland at the time of the visit made to that city by President Johnson, in the summer of 1866? A. I was.

Q. Were you present at the formal reception of the President by any committee or body of men? A. I was.

Q. State by whom he was received, and where? A. The President and his party arrived about half past eight o'clock in the evening, and were escorted to the Kennard House; after taking his supper the President was escorted on to the balcony of the Kennard House, and there he was formally welcomed to the city of Cleveland in behalf of the municipal authorities and citizens by the President of the City Councils.

Q. Did the President respond to that address of welcome? A. He did.

Q. What was the situation of that balcony, in reference to the street, in reference to its exposure? state, also, whether there was not a large crowd of persons present? A. There was a large crowd of persons present, and there was a crowd of persons on the balcony.

Q. How did it proceed after the President had began his response? A. For a few moments there were no interruptions, and I judged from what the President said that he intended—

Mr. BUTLER—Excuse me; stop a moment. I object to what the witness supposes was the President's intention.

Mr. CURTIS, to the witness—Q. From what you heard and saw, was the President in the act of making a continuing address to the assembly, or was he interrupted by the crowd? Describe how the affair proceeded. A. The President commenced his speech by saying he did not intend to make a speech; I think, to the best of my recollection, he had come there simply to make the acquaintance of the people, and bid them good-by; I think that was the subject of the first paragraph of his speech; he apologized for the non-appearance of General Grant, and then proceeded with his speech.

Q. How did he proceed; was it a part of his address, or was it in response to the calls made upon him by the people; describe? A. I did not hear all the speech.

Q. Did you hear calls made upon him from the crowd, and interruptions? A. I did; quite a number of them.

Q. From what you saw and heard the President say, and from all that occurred, was the President closing his remarks at the time these interruptions began? A. That, I cannot say.

Q. Can you say whether these interruptions and calls upon the President were responded to by his remarks? A. Some of them were.

Q. Were the interruptions kept up during the continuance of the address, or was he allowed to proceed without interruption? A. They were kept up very nearly to the conclusion of the President's speech.

Q. What was the character of the crowd, orderly or disorderly? A. The large majority of the crowd was orderly, as to the rest there was a good deal of disorder.

Q. Was that disorder confined to one or two persons, or did it affect enough to give character to the interruptions? A. I have no means of ascertaining how many were engaged in the interruptions.

Q. That is not what I asked you; I asked you whether there were enough to give general character to the interruptions?

Cross-examination by Mr. BUTLER.—Q. Was Mr. F. W. Belton President of the City Councils? A. I believe so.

Q. Was not his address on the balcony to the President simply in the hearing of those who were on the balcony? and did not the President, after he received that welcome, then step forward to address the multitude? A. I believe that after Mr. Belton's address several of the distinguished gentlemen who accompanied the party were presented, and then, in response to the calls of the people, the President presented himself.

Q. Would you say that this was a correct or an incorrect report:—"About ten o'clock, the supper being over, the party repaired to the balcony, where the President was formally welcomed by Mr. F. W. Belton, President of the City Council, as follows," &c.; would that be about the substance? A. That would be about the substance.

Mr. BUTLER, continuing to read—"Then the President and several members of the party appeared at the front of the balcony, and were introduced to the people. Then the vast multitude which filled the streets became most boisterous, and sometimes bitter, and sarcastic." A. I did not hear any interruptions to the President's speech until after he had proceeded five or ten minutes.

Q. But whenever they did come, would that be a fair representation of them? A. To some extent.

Senator JOHNSON here remarked that the Senators had not heard a word of the two or three last answers.

The Chief Justice—That conversation behind the Senators made it very difficult to hear the witness.

Mr. BUTLER, continuing to read—"They listened with attention a part of the time, and at other times completely drowned the President's voice with vociferations."

Q. Is that so? A. That is so.

Mr. BUTLER continuing to read after the presentation was made.

"Loud calls were made for the President to appear, and he spoke as follows:—"

I will read the first part of that speech:—"Fellow citizens:—It is not for the purpose of making a speech that I now appear before you. I am aware of the great curiosity which prevails to see strangers who have notoriety and distinction in the country. I know a large number of you desire to see General Grant and to hear what he has to say. (A voice—three cheers for Grant)."

Q. Was not that the first interruption? A. I believe so.

Q. Was there any interruption after that until he spoke of Stephen A. Douglas, and was that simply the interruption of applause? A. There were three cheers given, I believe, for Stephen A. Douglas; then he went on without interruption until this phrase came in:—"I come before you as an American citizen simply, and not as the Chief Magistrate clothed in the insignia and paraphernalia of state, being an inhabitant of a State in the Union; I know it has been said that I was an alien."

Q. Then came in laughter; was not that the next interruption? A. I do not recollect that paragraph in his speech.

Q. Do you recollect any other interruption until he came to the paragraph:—"There was two years ago a ticket before you for the Presidency; I was placed upon that ticket with a distinguished citizen now no more." Voices—It's a pity; (too bad); (unfortunate). A. I did not hear those words.

Q. Do you know whether they were or not said? A. I do not know.

Mr. BUTLER—I will not trouble you any further,

Testimony of Barton Able.

Barton Able, sworn, and examined by Mr. CURTIS—
Q. Where do you reside? A. In St. Louis.

Q. What is your business? A. I am engaged in the mercantile business, and am Collector of Internal Revenue for the First District of Missouri.

Q. Were you at St. Louis in the summer of 1866, at the time President Johnson visited that city? A. Yes, sir.

Q. Were you on any committee connected with the President's reception? A. I was on the Committee of Reception—the Merchants' Union Committee.

Q. Where did the reception take place? A. Citizens of St. Louis met the President's party at Alton, Ill., some twenty miles above St. Louis; the Mayor, I recollect, received him at the Lindell Hotel, in St. Louis.

Q. You speak of being on a committee of some mercantile association; what was that association? A. It was composed of the merchants and business men of the city.

Q. Not a political association? A. No, sir.

Q. Did the President make a public address, or an address to the people of St. Louis while he was there? A. He made a speech in the evening, to the citizens, at the Southern Hotel.

Q. Were you present at the hotel before the speech was made? A. Yes sir.

Q. As one of the committee of which you have spoken? A. Yes sir.

Q. State under what circumstances the President was called upon to speak? A. I was in one of the parlors of the hotel with the committee and the President, when some of the citizens came in and asked him to go out and respond to the calls of the citizens; he declined, or rather said that he did not care to make any speech; the same thing was repeated two or three times by other citizens who came in, and he finally said that he was in the hands of his friends, the committee, and if they said so he would go out and respond to the calls, which he did do.

Q. What did the committee say? A. A portion of the committee, two or three of them—stated, after some consultation, that they presumed he might as well do it, as there was a large crowd outside in front of the hotel.

Q. Did the President say anything before he went out as to whether he wanted to make a long speech or a short speech, or anything to characterize the speech which he proposed to make? A. My understanding was that he did not care to make any speech at all.

Mr. CURTIS—You have already explained that he manifested reluctance. Now, if he said anything as to his purpose on going out I should like to have you state it? A. I understood from his acceptance that his intention was to make a short speech when he went out.

Q. Did you or not hear what he said, or were you in a position so that you could hear what he said? A. I heard his conversation with the committee.

Q. I mean after he went out? A. I heard very little of it.

Q. Was it a large crowd or a small one? A. A large crowd.

Q. Were you present near enough on the balcony to be able to state what the demeanor of the crowd was towards the President? A. I heard from the inside; I was not on the balcony of the hotel at all; but I heard from the parlor one or two interruptions.

Q. You remained in the parlor all the time? A. Between the parlor and the dining-room; I was not on the balcony.

Cross-examination by Mr. BUTLER—Q. You met the President at Alton, and you, yourself, as one of the committee made him an address, on board the steamer? A. I introduced him to the Committee on Reception from St. Louis?

Q. That was made on board the steamer? A. Yes, sir.

Q. Then Captain Eades, who was the chairman of the citizens, made him an address of welcome? A. Yes, sir.

Q. And after that the President made a response? A. Yes, sir.

Q. And in that address he was listened to with particular attention, as became his place as President. A. I observed nothing to the contrary.

Q. Then you went to the Lindell Hotel? A. I did not go to the Lindell Hotel.

Q. Well, the President went? A. I think the carriage of the President went to the Lindell Hotel.

Q. And en route to the Lindell Hotel he was escorted by a procession, was he not, from the landing? A. Yes.

Q. By a procession of benevolent societies? A. I do not recollect what societies they were; it was a very large turn-out, and perhaps most of the societies in the city were represented.

Q. Were you at the Lindell Hotel at all? A. Yes; I was not there when he arrived at the Lindell Hotel.

Q. Were you there when he was received by the Mayor? A. No, sir.

Q. You do not know whether the Mayor made him an address of welcome? A. Only from what I saw in the press.

Q. Now, do you know that the President responded? A. I was not present.

Q. What time of the day was it when he got to the Lindell Hotel? A. It was in the afternoon.

Q. When he left the steamboat landing? A. I do not know what time he got to the hotel, for I was not present at his arrival.

Q. Cannot you tell nearly the time? A. It was probably between one and five o'clock.

Q. After that did you go with the President from the Lindell Hotel to the Southern Hotel? A. I do not recollect whether I accompanied them from the one hotel to the other or not.

Q. He did go from the one to the other? A. Yes.

Q. There was to be a banquet for him and his suite at the Southern Hotel that night? A. Yes.

Q. At which there was intended to be speaking to him and by him? A. There were to be toasts and responses.

Q. What time was that banquet to come off? A. I do not recollect the exact hour; I think somewhere about nine o'clock.

Q. At the time the President was called upon by the crowd, were you waiting for the banquet? A. I do not think the banquet was ready; he was in the parlor with the committee and citizens.

Q. The citizens being introduced to him? A. Yes.

Q. Did you hear any portion of his speech on the balcony? A. Only such portions of it as I could catch occasionally from the inside; I did not get on the balcony at all.

Q. Could you see on the balcony from where you were? A. I could see on the balcony, but I do not know whether I could see precisely where he stood or not.

Q. While he was making that speech, and when he got to the sentence—"I will neither be bullied by my enemies, nor overawed by my friends," was there anybody on the balcony trying to get him back? A. I can hardly answer that question, as I was not there to see.

Q. You might have seen persons trying to get him off? A. I did not.

Q. Can you tell whether it was so or not? A. I should think that if I could not see it I could not tell.

Mr. BUTLER—I only want to make sure on that point.

Witness—I am positive on that point. (Laughter.)

Q. Who was on the balcony besides him? A. I suppose the balcony would hold perhaps two hundred people; there were a great many people there.

Q. Give me the name of some one of the two hundred, if you can name anybody who was there? A. I think Mr. Howe was there; my recollection is that the President walked out with Mr. Howe.

Q. Was General Frank Blair there at any time? A. I do not recollect it if he was.

Q. Did the President afterwards make a speech at the banquet? A. A short one.

Q. Was the crowd a noisy and boisterous one? A. I heard a good deal of noise from the crowd while I was moving about inside.

George Knapp, Examined.

George Knapp sworn, and examined by Mr. CURTIS.
Q. Where do you reside? A. In St. Louis.

Q. What is your business? A. I am one of the publishers and proprietors of the St. Louis *Republican*.

Q. Were you in St. Louis at the time of President Johnson's visit to that city, in the summer of 1866? A. I was.

Q. Were you in the room where the President was? A. I was.

Q. Please state what occurred between the President and citizens, or a committee of citizens, in reference to his going out to make a speech? A. The crowd on the outside had called repeatedly for the President. I recollect that Captain Abel, Captain Taylor and myself were together; the crowd continued to call, and some one suggested, I think it was I, that the President ought to go out; some further conversation occurred, I think, between him and Captain Able.

Q. You mean the gentleman who has just left the stand? A. Yes, sir; I think I said to the President that he ought to go out and show himself to the people and say a few words, at any rate; he seemed reluctant to go out; we walked out together on the balcony and he addressed the assembled multitude.

Q. What was the character of the crowd? Was there a large number of people there? A. I do not think I got far enough on the balcony to look upon the magnitude of the crowd; I think I stayed back some distance.

Q. About what number of people were on the balcony itself? A. I suppose there was probably from fifteen to twenty; there may have been twenty-five.

Q. Could you hear from the crowd? A. I could.

Q. What was the character of the proceedings so far as the crowd was concerned? A. I do not recollect distinctly; my impressions are that occasional or repeated questions were apparently put to the President; I do not recollect exactly what they were.

Q. Was the crowd orderly or otherwise, so far as you could see? A. At times they seemed to be somewhat disorderly, but of that I am not very certain.

Cross-examination by Mr. BUTLER—Q. Did you go out on the balcony at all? A. Yes, I stepped out; it is a wide balcony; perhaps twelve or fifteen feet; it covers the whole of the sidewalk; I stepped out; it was probably one, two or three feet back of the President; part of the time he was talking; there were a number of doors and windows leading to the balcony; you could stand in a window or door and hear every word he said.

Q. Did you listen to this speech so that you could hear every word he said? A. I listened pretty attentively to the speech while I stayed there, but whether I stayed there during the whole of the time I do not now recollect.

Q. You have told us there were fifteen to twenty persons on the balcony? A. That is my impression; I am not certain about that.

Q. How many persons would the balcony hold? A. I suppose the balcony would hold a hundred people.

Q. Then it was not at all crowded on the balcony? A. I do not recollect whether it was or not; I did not change my mind, nor do I now recollect that the parlors were full, and I think it very likely that a large number of the people crowded on the balcony to hear the speech, but whether the balcony was crowded or not I do not recollect.

Q. Were you present at the time, so as to remember distinctly when he said "I will neither be bullied by my enemies nor overawed by my friends?" A. I do not recollect that phrase.

Q. Did this confusion in the crowd sometimes prevent him going on, or did it not? A. I think it likely that it did, but I am only speaking from my present impression, as I do not recollect.

Q. Did you hear him say anything about Judas? A. No, sir; I do not recollect.

Q. Did you hear him say anything about attending to John Bull after a while? A. I have no recollection of the points of his speech.

Q. So far as you know, and all that you know which would be of advantage to us to us to hear is, that you were present when some citizens asked the President to go out and answer the call of the crowd? A. I cannot say that some citizens; those present in the parlor asked him.

Q. While the banquet was waiting? A. Yes, sir.

Q. What time was the banquet to take place? A. I think at eight o'clock.

Q. What time had this got to be? A. I do not recollect.

Q. Was it not near eight o'clock at that time? I think when the President went out it was near the time for the banquet to take place; I think also—I know, in fact—that while the President was speaking, several persons stated it was time for the banquet to commence, or something of that sort.

Q. Then the banquet had to wait while the crowd outside was spoken to? A. I do not know; I think that probably the hour had passed, but it often happens that banquets do not take place exactly at the hour fixed.

Mr. BUTLER—Q. It appears that this did not; was that because it waited for the President, or because the banquet was not ready? A. I think it was because it waited for the President.

Q. Did you publish that speech next morning in your paper? A. Yes, sir, it was published.

Q. Did you again republish it on Monday morning? A. Yes.

Q. While your paper is called the *Republican*, it is is really a Democratic paper, and the *Democrat* is the Republican paper? A. The *Republican* was commenced in early times, for I have been connected with it over forty years myself and at the time—

Mr. BUTLER, interrupting—Excuse me, I do not want to go back forty years. (Laughter.)

Q. Was it in fact a Democratic newspaper at the time the President was there? A. Yes.

Q. And the St. Louis *Democrat*, so-called, was really the Republican paper? A. Yes.

Q. In the Democratic paper called the *Republican*, the speech was published on Sunday and Monday. A. Yes.

Q. Was it ever republished since? A. No, sir, not to my knowledge.

Q. State why you caused an edition of the speech to be corrected for Monday morning's publication? A. I met our principal reporter.

Q. Please not state what took place between your reporter and yourself; I want the facts, not the conversation? A. I gave directions to Mr. Ziber, on reading the speech, to have it corrected.

Q. Were your directions followed, so far as you know? A. I do not recollect as to the extent of the corrections; I never read the speech carefully.

Q. Did you ever complain afterwards to any man that the speech, as published in the Monday morning's *Republican*, was not as it ought to be? A. I cannot draw the distinction between Monday's and Sunday's papers; I have repeatedly spoken of the imperfect manner in which I conceived the speech was reported and published in the *Republican* on Sunday; whether I spoke of it in reference to Monday or not, I do not recollect.

Q. You say that you directed a revised publication for Monday, and that it was published, now did you ever complain to any body within the next three months after that revised publication was made, that that publication was not a true one? A. It is possible that I may have complained on Monday morning if the corrections were not made, but I do not recollect.

Q. And it is possible you did not? A. That, I say, I cannot recollect.

Q. Nor will you say that in any important particular this speech, as published in your paper, differed from the speech as put in evidence here? A. I cannot point out a solitary particular, because I have not read the speech as put in evidence here, nor have I read the speech since the morning after it was delivered.

Mr. BUTLER—I will not trouble you any further.

A Reporter on the Stand.

Henry F. Ziber, sworn and examined.—Before the examination commenced, the witness intimated to Mr. Curtis that he was somewhat deaf.

Mr. CURTIS.—Where did you reside in the summer of 1866, when the President visited St. Louis? A. In St. Louis, Missouri.

Q. What was then your business? A. I was then engaged as a short-hand writer for the *Missouri Republican*, a paper published in St. Louis.

Q. Had you anything to do with making a report of the speech which the President delivered from the balcony of the Southern Hotel? A. I made a short-hand report of the speech, and was authorized to employ what assistance I needed; I employed Mr. Walbridge to assist me; Mr. Walbridge wrote out the speech for the Sunday morning *Republican*; I went over the speech the same afternoon, and made several alterations for the Monday morning *Republican*; I made the corrections from my own notes.

Q. Did you make any corrections except those which you found were required by your own notes? A. There were three or four corrections, which I did not then make, but I marked them on the proof-sheet in the counting room.

Q. With those exceptions, did you make any corrections except what were called for by your own notes? A. Those were called for by my own notes, but they were not in fact made.

Q. Were the other corrections called for by your notes? A. Oh, yes, all of them

Q. Have you compared the report which you made and which was published in the *Republican*, of Monday, with the report published in the St. Louis *Democrat*? A. I more particularly compared the report published in the Monday *Democrat* with the Sunday *Republican*.

Q. You compared those two? A. Yes, there are about sixty changes.

Q. Differences? A. Yes, sir.

Describe the character of those differences.

Mr. BUTLER—I object to his describing the character; let him state the differences.

Mr. CURTIS.—Do you want him to repeat the sixty differences?

Mr. BUTLER—Certainly, if he can.

Mr. CURTIS, to witness—Have you a memorandum of these differences? A. I have.

Read them, if you please.

Mr. BUTLER—Before he reads I should like to know when it was made.

Mr. CURTIS, to witness—When did you make this comparison? A. Last Saturday, the 11th of April.

Q. When did you make the memorandum? A. I made the memorandum on the Sunday following.

Mr. BUTLER—Last Sunday? A. Yes, sir.

Mr. CURTIS—Q. For whom did you make the memorandum? A. I was brought here by the managers, and discharged after being here twenty-four days. I had just returned to St. Louis, when I got a telegraphic despatch that I was summoned again to appear before the Senate I then went to the *Republican* office and took the bound files of the *Republican* and the bound files of the *Democrat*, and, in company with Mr. Joseph Monaghan, one of the assistant editors, made a comparison of the two papers, and noted the differences, and compared the differences twice afterwards, to see that they were correct; that was Saturday last; I started for Washington Sunday afternoon, at three o'clock.

Q. This paper which contains those differences, when was it made? A. Last Saturday.

Q. Was it made at the same time when you made this comparison, or at different times? A. It was made at the same time.

Mr. CURTIS—Now, if the honorable managers wishes to have all these differences, you can read them.

Mr. BUTLER—Stay a moment; any on which you rely we wish to have read.

Mr. CURTIS—We rely upon all of them, more or less.

Mr. BUTLER—Then all of them, more or less, must be read.

Mr. CURTIS—We should prefer, in order to save time, to give specimens of the differences, but if you desire to have all read you can have them read.

Mr. BUTLER—There is a question back of this; that is, we have not the standard of comparison. This witness goes to the *Republican* office and there takes a copy of the paper, but we cannot tell whether it was the true paper or not, or what edition it was; and he compares it with a copy of the *Democrat*, and having made that comparison, he now proposes to put in the result of it. I do not see how that can be evidence. He may state anything which he has any recollection of, but to make the memorandum evidence, and to read the memorandum, is something I never heard of. Let me restate it. This witness goes to the *Republican* office to get the *Republican*. What *Republican*—how genuine—what edition it was, except that it was in a bound volume, is not identified. He takes the *Democrat*—of what edition we do not know—and he compares the two. He then comes here and attempts to put in the results of a comparison made in which Monaghan held one end of the matter and he held the other. Can that be evidence?

Mr. CURTIS—I want to ask the witness a question, and then I will make an observation. To the witness—Q. Who made the report that was in the *Republican* which you examined, and compared with the report in the *Democrat*? Witness—Mr. Walbridge on Saturday, September 8, 1866; it was published in the Sunday morning *Republican*, September 9.

Q. Have you looked at the proceedings in this case to see whether that report has been put in evidence? A. The Sunday *Republican* mentions Mr. Walbridge's testimony, in which he states that he made one or two simple corrections for the Monday morning *Democrat*.

Q. Now, I wish to inquire whether the report which you read in the files of the *Republican*, and which you compared with the report in the *Democrat*, was the report which Mr. Walbridge made. A. Undoubtedly it was.

Mr. CURTIS—It is suggested by the learned manager, Mr. Chief Justice—

Mr. BUTLER, interrupting—I will save you all trouble; put it in as much as you choose; I don't care if you leave it unread.

Mr. CURTIS—We simply want to have it put in the case to save time, and to have it printed.

Mr. BUTLER—There cannot be anything printed that is not read.

Mr. CURTIS—We understand; you wish to dispense with the reading.

The Chief Justice—Let it be read if the manager desires it.

Mr. BUTLER—I do not desire it.

Mr. EVARTS—Is it to go in evidence, Mr. Chief Justice, or is it not?

The Chief Justice—Certainly, it is.

Mr. BUTLER—It may go in for all I care, sir.

Cross-examined by Mr. BUTLER—Q. How long have you been troubled with your unfortunate affliction? A. To what do you refer?

Q. I understand you are a little deaf; is that so? A. I have been sick a great part of this year, and was compelled to come here a month ago, almost before I was able to come, and I have not got well yet.

Q. Did you hear my question—How long have you been deaf, if you are deaf at all? A. I have been deaf for the last two years.

Q. About what time did it commence? A. I do not recollect.

Q. You know when you became deaf, do you not? A. I know I was not deaf when you made your St. Louis speech in 1866.

Q. That is a very good date to refer to, but suppose you try it by the almanac? A. That was in October, 1866.

Q. How soon did you become deaf after that? A. Probably about a month. (Laughter.)

Q. You are quite sure you were not deaf at that time? A. I am quite certain, because I know I heard some remarks which the crowd made, and which you did not hear. (Laughter.)

Q. I have no doubt you heard much better than I did, but suppose we confine ourselves to this matter; you say that about a month after that you became deaf? A. Partially; I recovered from that again and took sick again.

Q. Have you your notes of the President's speech? A. No, sir.

Q. When did you see them last? A. The last recollection I have of them was when Mr. Walbridge was summoned to give his testimony before the Reconstruction Committee on the New Orleans riots.

Q. Did you or he then go over that speech together? A. We went over only a part of it.

Q. The part that referred to New Orleans? A. Yes.

Q. Was there any material difference between you and him when you had your notes there together, in that part of the speech? if so, state what? A. There was.

Q. What was it? A. He asked me to compare notes with him.

Mr. BUTLER—Excuse me; I am not asking what he said. I am asking what difference there was between that report and his report on that comparison, and what the material difference was?

Mr. EVARTS—I submit, Mr. Chief Justice, that as the manager has asked a precise question what the difference was in that comparison, the witness should be permitted to state what it was and how it arose.

Mr. BUTLER—I have not asked any difference that arose between the witness and Mr. Walbridge. Far be it from me to go into that. I have asked what difference there was between the reports of the speech.

Mr. CURTIS—As it appeared from that comparison?

Mr. BUTLER—As found at that time.

Witness—I was going on to answer, and if the gentleman will have patience a few moments I will answer.

The Chief Justice—The witness will confine himself entirely to what is asked and make no remarks.

Witness—We proceeded to compare the speech relating to the New Orleans riots; Mr. Walbridge read over his notes, and I looked over mine; when he came to this passage, "When you read the speeches that were made or packed up the facts you will find the speeches were made," I called Mr. Walbridge's attention to those words qualifying the sentence, "If the facts are as stated;" he replied to me, "Oh, you are mistaken; I know I am right," and he went on; as he was summoned to swear to his notes and not to mine, I did not argue the question further, but let him go on.

Y. What other difference were there? A. In the New Orleans matter?

Mr. BUTLER—Yes. Witness—The President referred to the Convention which had been called in New Orleans and which was extinct by reason of its power having expired; the words, "by reason of its power having expired," were in my report and were not in Mr. Walbridge's.

Q. Was there any other difference? A. No other; Mr. Walbridge proceeded with his report of the matter with reference to the New Orleans riots; the latter part of the report was not compared at all nor was the first part.

Q. Have you the report as it appeared in the *Republican* of Monday before you? A. I have.

Q. Let me read a few sentences, and tell me how many errors there are in this that was put in evidence here?—"Fellow citizens, of St. Louis:—In being introduced to you, to-night, it is not for the purpose of making a speech. It is true I am proud to meet so many of my fellow citizens here on this occasion, and under the favorable circumstances that I do." Cry—"How about British subjects?"

"We will attend to John Bull after a while, so far as that is concerned. (Laughter and cheers.) I have just stated that I was not here for the purpose of making a speech."

Witness, interrupting—The President said, "I am not here."

Mr. BUTLER—Q. Then the difference is between the word "was" and the word "am?" Do you know that the President used the word "am," instead of "was?" A. Of course I do.

Mr. BUTLER, continuing to read—"But after being introduced, simply to tender my cordial thanks for the welcome you have given me in your midst"—(a voice, "Ten thousand welcomes!"—hurrahs and cheers)—Thank you, sir, I wish it was in my power to address you under favorable circumstances upon some of the questions that agitate and distract the public mind at this time."

Witness, interrupting—The word was "which agitate, &c."

Mr. BUTLER, continuing to read—"Questions that have grown out of a fiery ordeal we have just passed through, and which I think as important as those we have just passed by. The time has come when it seems to me that all ought to be prepared for peace. The Rebellion being suppressed, and the shedding of blood being stopped, the sacrifice of life being suspended and stayed, it seems that the time has arrived when we should have peace, when the bleeding arteries should be tied up. (A voice—'New Orleans.' 'Go on.')" Q. So far all is right except the two corrections you have made? A. Yes, sir; I wish to make a correction at the New Orleans part.

Mr. BUTLER—Q. Why should you wish anything about it?

Witness—You were proceeding to make a correction, and when you came to the New Orleans part you stopped.

Mr. BUTLER—I will take this portion of the speech:—"Judas, Judas Iscariot, Judas. There was a Judas once."

Witness interrupting—There is one Judas too much there. (Laughter).

Mr. BUTLER—Q. You are sure that he did not speak Judas four times? A. Yes, sir.

Q. How many times did he speak Judas? A. Three times.

Witness to Mr. Butler—In the report that is in evidence, those words are italicised, are they not, and stretched out?

Mr. BUTLER—Two of the Judases are spelled with the last syllable, a-a-s; do you mean to say that the President spoke that part with emphasis? A. I mean to say that he did not speak them in that way.

Mr. BUTLER (continuing to read)—"There was a Judas once: one of the twelve Apostles; oh! yes, and these twelve Apostles had a Christ. (A voice—And a Moses too. Great laughter) The twelve Apostles had a Christ, and he could not have had a Judas unless he had had twelve Apostles." So far it is right? A. Yes; not stretched out.

Mr. BUTLER—Yes, sir, stretched out. Is there any other question you would like to ask me? (Laughter.)

Now, sir, will you attend to your business, and say what differences there are?

Continuing to read—"The twelve Apostles had a Christ, and he could not have had a Judas unless he had twelve Apostles. If I have played the Judas who has been my Christ that I have played the Judas with? Was it Thad. Stevens? was it Wendell Phillips? Was it Charles Sumner? (Hisses and cheers.) Are these the men that set up and compare themselves with the Savior of men."?

Witness—The word "that" should be "who."

Mr. BUTLER—Q. Is that a fair specimen of the sixty corrections you have made? A. There are four in the next three lines.

Mr. BUTLER—Q. Answer the question; is that a fair specimen of the sixty corrections?

Mr. EVARTS—Mr. Chief Justice:—I suppose the corrections, the whole of which are put in evidence, will show all this.

Mr. BUTLER—I am cross-examining the witness, and I prefer that the witness shall not be instructed.

Mr. EVARTS—It is not instructing the witness. We thought it would save time by putting in the memorandum; whether this is a fair specimen or not as compared with the whole paper, will appear from a comparison by the court.

Mr. BUTLER—I am testing the witness's credibility, and I do not care to have him instructed.

The Chief Justice—If the question is objected to the honorable manager will please put it in writing.

Mr. EVARTS—It is not a question of credibility; it is a matter of judgment between the two papers, whether one correction is a fair specimen of all?

Mr. BUTLER to the witness—I ask whether the corrections you have made in answer to my questions are of the same average character as the other sixty corrections?

Mr. EVARTS.—We object to the question. It requires a re-examination of the whole subject.

Mr. BUTLER—Well. I will pass from that rather than take up the time. Mr. Witness, you told us that in the next three lines there were corrections. I will read the next four lines. "In the days when there ware twelve Apostles, and when there ware a Christ, while there ware Judases there ware unbelievers too. Yas, while there were Judases there were unbelievers—(Voices, 'hear.' "Three groans for Fletcher.' Yes, oh yes, unbelievers in Christ."

Witness—The word "were" is spelled four times "ware," and the first time it should be "was."

Mr. BUTLER—Q. Then your corrections are all on questions of pronunciation and grammar? A. The President did not use those words.

Q. You say the President did not pronounce the word

"were" broadly, as is sometimes the Southern fashion? A. I say he did not use the word as used in that paper.

Q. Did he not speak broadly the word "were" when he used it? A. Not so that it could not be distinguished from "ware."

Q. Then it is a question of how you spell and pronounce that you corrected? A. The tone of voice could not be represented in print.

Q. And you think that "were" better represents his tone of voice? A. Yes, sir.

Q. Although it cannot be represented in print? A. Yes.

Q. Now, sir, with the exception of corrections in pronunciation and in grammar, is there any correction of the report as printed in the *Democrat* on Monday compared with the report of the *Republican?* A. Of what day?

Mr. BUTLER—The *Republican* of Sunday or Monday? I repeat, with the exception of corrections in grammar and punctuation, is there any other correction in substance between the two reports as printed that morning between the Monday *Republican* and the Monday *Democrat?* A. Yes, sir.

Q. What are they? A. One is:—"Let the government be restored; I have labored for it; I am for it now." The words, "I am for it now," are omitted in the *Democrat,* and there is a change in the punctuation in the commencement of the next sentence.

Q. What else is there? A. Speaking of the neutrality law, he says, "I am sworn to support the Constitution, and to execute the laws." Some cried out, "Why did you not do it?" He answered, "The law was executed; the law was executed." These words, "Why did you not do it?" and "The law was executed" are omitted in the *Democrat.*

Q. What else, in substance, is omitted? A. I do not know that I can point out any other without the memorandum.

Q. Use the memorandum, and point out any difference in substance—not grammar, not punctuation, not pronunciation. The witness, after examining the memorandum, stated that in one sentence the word "sacrifice" was used in the *Democrat's* report, the proper word being "battled."

Mr. BUTLER to the witness—Well, I will not trouble you further.

Witness—I will point out more.

Mr. BUTLER—That is all, sir.

Novel Evidence.

Mr. CURTIS—We offer in evidence this document. It is the commission issued by President Adams to General Washington, constituting him Lieutenant-General of the Army of the United States. The purpose is to show the form in which commissions were issued at that day to military officers. It is the most conspicuous instance in our history as regards the practice.

Mr. BUTLER—There were two appointments to General Washington. Was this the one accepted by him, or the one rejected?

Mr. EVARTS—We understand it is the one actually issued to him.

Mr. BUTLER—And accepted?

Mr. EVARTS—We understand so.

Mr. BUTLER—We have no objections.

The paper was read.

Mr. CURTIS—We next offer a document from the Department of the Interior, showing removals of Superintendents of Indian Affairs, Indian Agents, land officers, receivers of public moneys, surveyor-generals, and certain miscellaneous officers. It shows the date of the removal, and of the name of the officer and the offices held; and it also contains memoranda, showing whether removed during the recess, or during the session of the Senate.

Mr. BUTLER—Mr. President, I have one objection to this species of evidence without anybody being here to testify to it; and that is this:—I have learned that in the case of the Treasury Department, which I allowed to go in without objection, there are other cases not reported where the power was refused to be exercised, and I do not know whether it is so in the Interior Department or not; but most of those examined by us are simply under the law, fixing their tenure during the pleasure of the President for the time being, and some of them are inferior officers originally made by the War Department, but if the counsel for the President thinks they have any bearing, we have no objection.

Mr. CURTIS said he had not had an opportunity to examine them minutely, but he understood a large number of them held office under a fixed tenure. It might be a matter of argument hereafter.

Mr. BUTLER—What class of officers do you speak of?

Mr. CURTIS—Receiver of Public Moneys is one of the classes.

Senator JOHNSON—What is the first date of removal?

Mr. CURTIS—I think they extend through the whole period of the existence of that department. I do not mean the date when the department was established, but I think they run through the whole of it.

Evidence by F. W. Seward.

Frederick W. Seward sworn on behalf of respondent, examined by Mr. Curtis.

Mr. CURTIS—Mr. Seward, will you please to state the office you hold under the government? A. Assistant Secretary of State.

Q. How long have you held that office? A. Since March, 1861.

Q. In whose charge in that department is the subject of consular and vice consular appointments? A. Under my charge.

A. Please to state the practice of making appointment

of vice consuls in the case of death, resignation, incapacity or absence of consuls, usually consuls?

Mr. BUTLER—Is not that regulated by law?

Mr. CURTIS—That is a matter of argument; we think it is.

Mr. BUTLER—So do we.

Mr. CURTIS—I want to show the practice under the law, just as we have done in other cases. I have the document here, but it requires some explanation to make it intelligible to the witness. When a vacancy has not been foreseen, the consul nominates a vice consul who enters upon the discharge of his duties at once, at the time the nomination is sent to the Department of State. The department approves or disapproves of the nomination, in case the vacancy has not been foreseen. If the consul is dead, absent, sick, or unable to discharge the duties, then the minister of the country may make a nomination to the Department of State, or if no minister, the naval commander not unfrequently makes a nomination and sends it to the Department of State, and the vice consul so designated acts until the department approve or disapprove. In other cases the department has often designated a vice consul without any previous nomination from either consul, minister, or naval commander, and he enters upon the discharge of his duties in the same manner.

Q. How is he authorized or commissioned? A. He receives the certificate of his appointment, signed by the Secretary of State.

Q. Running for a definite period, or how? A. Running subject to the restrictions provided by law.

Q. Is this appointment of vice consul made temporarily to fill a vacancy, or how otherwise? A. It is made to fill the office during the period which elapses between the time it takes for the information to reach the department and a successor to be appointed.

Q. That is, for a succeeding consul to be appointed? A. Yes; sometimes weeks or months may elapse before a newly-appointed successor can reach this place.

Q. It is then in its character an *ad interim* appointment to fill the vacancy? A. Yes, sir.

Mr. BUTLER—Is there anything said in the commissions about their being *ad interim,* or in the letter or appointment?

Witness—The letter of appointments say, "Subject to the conditions made by law."

Q. Is that the only limitation there is? A. Yes, sir.

Q. Are not the appointments made under the fifteenth section of the act of August 11, 1856? A. August 18, isn't it?

Mr. BUTLER—I think you are right, sir; August 18, 1856.

Witness—I think the act of 1856 does not create the office or give the power of appointment, but it recognizes the office as already in existence, and the power as already in the President.

Mr. BUTLER—We will see that in a moment, sir.

Mr. BUTLER read from 11 Statutes at Large, sections 14 and 15. He continued:—

Q. Now, sir, have they ever, in the State Department, undertaken to make a vice consul against the provisions of this act? A. I am not aware that they ever have.

Q. Nor ever attempted to do it? A. No, sir; not that I am aware of.

Mr. CURTIS—I now offer from the Department of State, this document, which contains a list of the consular officers appointed during the session of the Senate, when vacancies existed at the time such appointments were made. The earliest instance was in 1803, and they come down to about 1862, if I remember right.

Mr. BOUTWELL—I wish to call the counsel for the respondent to the fact that it does not appear, from these papers that these vacancies happened during the recess of the Senate. It merely states that they were filled during the session of the Senate.

Mr. CURTIS—It does not appear when the vacancies happened. The purpose is to show that these temporary appointments were made to fill vacancies during the session of the Senate. * * * * I give notice that we propose to consider these as cases happening during the recess of the Senate.

Mr. EVARTS—During the session.

Mr. BOUTWELL—We don't know anything about that.

Mr. EVARTS—The certificate is to that effect, filed during the session of the Senate.

Mr. BOUTWELL—We do not object to the paper. I only give notice how we propose to consider it.

Testimony of Gideon Welles.

Gideon Welles, sworn on behalf of the respondent. Examined by Mr. EVARTS.

Q. Mr. Welles, you are now Secretary of the Navy? A. Yes, sir.

Q. At what time, and from whom did you receive that appointment? A. I was appointed in March, 1861, by President Lincoln, and have held the office continually until now from that date.

Q. Do you remember on the 21st of February last your attention being drawn to some movements of troops or military officers? A. On the evening of the 21st of February my attention was called to some movements that were made then.

Q. How was that brought to your attention? A. My son brought them to my attention. He had been attending a party, when an order came requiring all officers under the command of General Emory to report forthwith to headquarters.

Q. Did you, in consequence of that seek to have an interview with the President of the United States? A. I requested my son to go over that evening or the following day.

Mr. BUTLER—Stop a moment.

Mr. EVARTS—You attempted to find a messenger at that time? A. I did. On Saturday, the 22d, I went myself about noon to see the President on this subject; I told him what I had heard, and asked him what he meant.

Mr. BUTLER—We object to that conversation, and before we go to the objection, I would ask the witness to fix the time a little more carefully.

Witness—About 12 o'clock on the 22d of February.

Q. How close to 12; before or after? A. I should think it was a little before 12; I will state a circumstance or two; the Attorney-General was there when I went in, and while I was there the nomination of Mr. Ewing was made as Secretary of War, and was delivered to the Private Secretary to be carried to the Capitol.

Mr. BUTLER—Stop a moment.

Mr. EVARTS—It is not the time for cross-examination now.

Mr. BUTLER—It is in order to ascertain whether it is admissible.

Mr. EVARTS—It is quite immaterial.

Mr. BUTLER to witness—You think it was very near twelve? A. About twelve o'clock.

Q. Could it have been as early as half-past eleven? A. No, sir. I don't think it was.

Q. Between that time and half-past twelve sometime? A. Yes, sir.

Mr. EVARTS.—What passed between you and the President after you had made that statement to him with reference to that communication?

Mr. BUTLER asked to have the question put in writing, which was done.

Mr. EVARTS.—I will state that this evidence is offered in reference to the article that relates to the conversation between the President and General Emory.

Mr. BUTLER—That is precisely as we understand it; but we also understand the fact to be that Gen. Emory was sent for before Mr. Welles appeared on the scene. I am instructed by my associates to say that we are endeavoring to get the matter settled that General Emory received a note to come to the President at ten o'clock in the morning. That he got there before the Secretary of the Navy we cannot at this moment ascertain, but it does not appear that this conversation was before Emory was sent for.

Mr. EVARTS—That is a matter of proof which is to be considered when it is all in, as to which is right on our side, and which on theirs.

Mr. BUTLER—The proof of what was said in the conversation is not to be considered as proof of which was right on the facts, for I suppose my learned opponent would not claim that if this was after Emory came there they could put in the testimony.

The Chief Justice considered the evidence competent, and no Senator raising a question it was admitted.

The question was again read.

Witness—I cannot repeat the words; I should think the words of the President were, "I don't know what Emory means," or "I don't know what Emory is about;" I remarked that I thought he ought to know that when he was sending for his officers at such a time it must be for some reason; he hesitated somewhat; we had a little conversation; I think he said he would send for him; either that, or that he would send and inquire into it; I think he said he would send for him.

Mr. EVARTS—Q. I will call your attention to the 21st of February, at the time of the close of the Cabinet meeting that day, at what hour was the Cabinet meeting held on that day, Friday? A. At twelve o'clock, the regular hour.

Q. That is the usual hour, and that is the usual day of the Cabinet meeting? A. Yes, sir.

Q. Did you at that time have any interview with the President of the United States at which the subject of Mr. Stanton's removal was mentioned? Answer, yes or no? A. I did.

Q. At about what hour of the day was that? A. About two o'clock.

Q. Had you up to that time heard of the removal of Mr. Stanton? A. I had not; I was told before I left.

Q. And after the Cabinet meeting was closed this interview took place, at which this subject was mentioned? A. The President remarked—

Q. No matter; state whether it was? A. It was.

Q. What passed between you and the President at that time?

Mr. BUTLER objected.

On motion, the Senate here took a recess of fifteen minutes, after which the cross-examination of Secretary Welles was continued by Mr. EVARTS.

Q. Did the President make any communication to you on this occasion concerning the removal of Mr. Stanton—yes or no? A. Yes; he did.

Q. Was this before this Cabinet meeting had broken up, or at what step of your meeting was it? A. We had got through with our departmental business, and were about separating, when the President remarked—

Mr. EVARTS, interrupting—Q. Who were present? A. I believe all were present, unless it was Mr. Stanton.

Mr. EVARTS—Now, I offer to prove that on this occasion the President communicated to Mr. Welles and the other members of the Cabinet, before the meeting broke up, that he had removed Mr. Stanton and appointed General Thomas Secretary of War *ad interim*, and that upon the inquiry by Mr. Welles whether General Thomas was in possession of the office, the President replied that he was; and, upon further question of Mr. Welles whether Mr. Stanton acquiesced, the President replied

that he did; all that he required was time to remove his papers.

Mr. BUTLER—I want to call the attention of the counsel to this question:—"I understand Mr. Welles that it was after the Cabinet meeting broke up."

Mr. EVARTS—No; I have put that according to the fact, that it was when they had got through with what he calls their department business, and before the act of breaking up, that the President made that communication.

Mr. BUTLER objected that it could not be evidence. He said it was now made certain that this act was done without any consultation of his Cabinet by the President either verbally or otherwise. The President had no right to consult his Cabinet except by the constitutional method. Jefferson had taken the same view on this question which he (Mr. Butler) had heretofore taken before the Senate. The Constitution, for good purposes, required the President when he wished the advice of his Cabinet to ask it in writing, so that it could appear for all time what that advice was.

That was because there had been attempts made on the various trials of impeachment of members of the Cabinet, to put in the fact of the advice, by order of the King; to the Cabinet, or the advice of the various members of the Cabinet to each other. That was exploded in the Earl of Danbury's case. That question had been settled then, so that it might not arise thereafter. He was glad to learn that the President was solely responsible, and acted upon his sole responsibility, without the advice of his Cabinet. Could the President then, by his narration of what he had done, and what he had intended to do, defend himself before this tribunal for the consequences of his acts?

It was exactly the same question almost unanimously decided yesterday in the case of Mr. Perrine and Mr. Selye, where a conversation a few minutes earlier or later, was ruled out. This was not an attempt to take the advice of Mr. Welles, but to inform him and the rest of the Cabinet of what had been done, and that after the Cabinet meeting, while they were talking together as any other citizens might do, it would be as if a question should be attempted to be put into this case after the court adjourned.

Mr. EVARTS denied that the witness had said anything to show that the act of removal or appointment took place without previous advice by the Cabinet. However that fact appeared, the fact was that Mr. Welles had not then heard of the fact that had taken place. The managers had, perhaps, not heard what the witness said, but the fact stood that in a Cabinet meeting on Friday, the 21st of February, when the routine business of the different departments was over, or when it was in order for the President to communicate to his Cabinet whatever he designed to lays before them, the President did communicate this fact.

Here they got rid of the suggestion that it was a mere communication to a casual visitor, which was the argument in the case of Perrin and Selye. Here it was got in, and, being in, they were entitled to have it brought in as a part of the *res gestæ* in its sense as a "governmental act" with all the benefit that came from it, as to the intent of the President to place the office in a proper condition for public service, and as announced by him to General Sherman, the preceding January. It negatived the idea that the President was responsible for the statements of General Thomas to Wilkeson or Burleigh, and presented the matter in its true light as a peaceful movement of the President of the United States.

Mr. CURTIS wished it to be remembered that they did not base their argument that this was admissible upon the ground that it was advice from the Cabinet to the President, but because it was an official act, done by the President himself, in a proper manner, The subject matter of the information being such as they were all interested in, though somewhat in advance of the question which must presently arise, he would take up the matter of the advice and opinions of the Cabinet officers referred to by the manager.

Mr. CURTIS then quoted the *Federalist*, and other authorities on the subject, to show that from the time of Jefferson down to the present day the Cabinet had acted and voted as a council, of which the President was a member, he having the power to decide a question independently of them, if he choose. He held that any communication made to the Cabinet by the President, respecting an official act then in *fieri*, was competent evidence. He reminded them that in England the ministers of the Crown are responsible themselves for their acts, and not as in this country the sovereign power, and that, therefore, the English precedents were not applicable.

Mr. BUTLER, in reply, said he would not pursue the discussion of the matter of the advice, since it was argued by the counsel that none was either given or asked. He supposed that no act could be called an official one that was an act required by some law or some duty. Frequently acts done by an officer were officious and official. Could the counsel inform him under what law, what practice or what constitutional provision the President was required to inform his Cabinet at any time of an act of removal?

The only law on the subject was the act of March 2, 1867, requiring him to inform the Secretary of the Treasury, for the purpose of notifying the accounting officers, in order that the person removed could not get his salary, and the President had informed the Secretary of the Treasury especially in conformity with that act. Mr. Butler called attention to the fact that while the counsel excepted to his statement that it was in evidence that this was not a consultation of the Cabinet, they had not stated that the Cabinet was ever consulted about the matter; that being waived by the counsel, and this not being an official act, how could it be evidence?

He (Mr. Butler) was willing to admit that at the time the President had no idea of using force, because he though Stanton was already out quietly, but what had he meant to do in case Stanton should resist. General Sherman had let out that something was said between him and the President about force, though he could not remember what it was. They might admit this as of little moment but if so, they must admit all declarations of other members of the Cabinet, or involve themselves in inconsistency. He was still unable to distinguish any difference between the declarations of Perrine and those to Secretary Welles, other than that one was a Cabinet officer and the other was not. While it was admitted that this was not made for the purpose of asking advice, they preferred to put what the President thought he would then do.

Mr. EVARTS could not consent that the testimony of General Sherman should be misinterpreted or misconceived. It was that, when something was said about force, the President said there will be no force, Stanton will retire, and that all the allusion to force was originated by the witness himself, the President having conveyed to his mind that force was to be used.

The Chief Justice expressed the opinion that the evidence was admissible as a part of a transaction that forms the basis of several of the articles, and that it was proper to aid in forming an enlightened judgment in regard to the intent of the President.

Some Senators called for a vote.

Mr. CONNESS called for the reading of the written offer of the counsel in relation to the testimony of Parrine yesterday, and it was read.

Senator SUMNER—What was the vote of the Senate on that?

The Secretary read the vote as yeas, 9; nays, 37.

Senator TRUMBULL—I would like to know how the Senator from Massachusetts (Mr. Sumner) voted upon it. (Laughter.)

Senator HOWARD put the following question in writing to the counsel for the President:—

"In what way does the evidence which the counsel for the accused now offer meet any of the allegations contained in the articles of impeachment? How doth it affect the gravamen of any one of the charges?"

Mr. EVARTS said—It is enough to say, probably, in answer to the question, that it bears upon the question of the intent with which the act charged was done. It bears upon the conspiracy articles, and it bears upon the eleventh article.

Mr. WILSON, one of the managers—The question was asked by a member of the Senate as to the date of the conversation between the President and Mr. Perrine. It was the twenty-first.

The Chief Justice—The Chief Justice will state how the question presents itself to his mind. The question on which the Senate ruled yesterday was in reference to the removal of Mr. Stanton, as the Chief Justice understood it, but in reference to the immediate appointment of a successor, by the President sending the name of Mr. Ewing. The question to-day relates to the intention of the President in the removal of Mr. Stanton, and it relates to a communication made to his Cabinet after the departmental business had closed, and before the Cabinet had separated. The Chief Justice is clearly (speaking with emphasis) of opinion that that is a part of the transaction, and that it is entirely proper to take this evidence into consideration, as showing the intent in the President's mind.

The Senate proceeded to vote upon the question of admitting the testimony, and the vote resulted—yeas, 26; nays, 23, as follows:—

YEAS.—Messrs. Anthony, Bayard, Buckalew, Cole, Conkling, Corbett, Davis, Dixon, Doolittle, Fessenden, Fowler, Grimes, Hendricks, Johnson, McCreery, Morton, Patterson (Tenn.), Ross, Saulsbury, Sherman, Sprague, Sumner, Trumbull, Van Winkle, Vickers, Willey—26.

NAYS.—Messrs. Cameron, Cattell, Conness, Cragin, Drake, Edmunds, Ferry, Frelinghuysen, Harlan, Howard, Howe, Morgan, Morrill (Me.), Morril (Vt.), Patterson (N. H.), Pomeroy, Ramsey, Stewart, Thayer, Tipton, Williams, Wilson, and Yates—23.

So the evidence was admitted, and the examination of witness was continued.

Mr. EVARTS to the witness—Please state what communication was made by the President to the Cabinet on the subject of the removal of Mr. Stanton and of the appointment of General Thomas, and what passed at that time? Witness—After the departmental duties had been disposed of, the President remarked that before the Cabinet separated it was proper for him to say that he had removed Mr. Stanton and appointed the Adjutant-General, Lorenzo Thomas, Secretary of War *ad interim;* I asked him whether General Thomas was in possession, and the President said he was; I inquired whether—

Senator HOWARD rose and complained that it was impossible to hear the witness.

The Chief Justice remarked that there was too much conversation in the Chamber.

Witness continued—I inquired whether General Thomas was in possession; the President said he was, but that Mr. Stanton required some little time to remove his writings and his papers; I said, or perhaps I asked, "Does Mr. Stanton, then, acquiesce in it?" he said he did as he understood it.

Mr. EVARTS—Q. Was it a part of the President's answer that all Mr. Stanton required was time to remove his

papers? A. The President made that remark when I inquired if General Thomas was in possession.

Q. Was the time at which this announcement of the President was made in accordance with the ordinary routine of your meetings as to such subjects? A. It was; the President usually communicated after the Secretaries had got through with the several department duties.

Q. Now, as to a matter which he spoke of incidentally, You were there the next meeting? A. I was.

Q. While there did you see the appointment of Mr. Ewing? A. I did.

Q. Was it made out before you came there or after you came there, or while you were there? A. While I was there.

Q. And you then saw it? A. I then saw it; the Attorney-General was there, and said he must be at the Supreme Court.

Q. Does not the Supreme Court meet at eleven o'clock? A. I think his business was at twelve o'clock.

Q. Did you become aware of the passage of the Civil Tenure of Office act, as it is called, at the time it passed Congress? A. I was aware of it.

Q. Were you present at any Cabinet meeting at which, after the passage of that act, the act became the subject of consideration? A. I was there on two occasions.

Q. Who were present and what was done on the first occasion? A. The first occasion was, I think, on Friday, the 15th day of February, 1867, at the Cabinet meeting

Q. Who were present? A. I think all the Cabinet were

Q. Was Mr. Stanton there? A. Mr. Stanton was there, I think, on that occasion; the President said that he had two bills about which he wanted to be advised; one of these was—

Mr. BUTLER (interrupting)—We object to the evidence of what took place there.

Mr. EVARTS (o the witness—This Civil Tenure of Office act was the subject of consideration the?n A. It was submitted then.

Q. How was it brought to the attention of the Cabinet? A. By the President.

Q. As a matter of consideratian for the Cabinet? A. For consultation and for the advice of members of the Cabinet.

Q. How did he submit the matter to your consideration?

Mr. BUTLER, interrupting—If that involves anything he said, we object.

Mr. EVARTS—Yes, it does.

Mr. BUTLER—We object to anything which took place in the Cabinet consultation; and in order to have this brought to a point we should like the offer of proof to be in writing.

The Chief Justice directed the counsel for the President to put their offer in writing.

Mr. EVARTS—We will present the whole matter in writing.

Some fifteen minutes were occupied by the counsel in considering and preparing the offering of evidence, during which time the Senators and members on the floor and the spectators in the gallery kept up quite a noisy conversation.

The offer being completed was handed to Mr. Butler for examination, and was then read as follows:—

"We offer to prove that the President, at a meeting of the Cabinet, while the bill was before the President for his approval, laid before the Cabinet the Tenure of Civil Office bill for their consideration and advice to the President, respecting his approval of the bill, and that thereupon the members of the Cabinet then present gave their advice to the President that the bill was unconstitutional, and should be returned to Congress with his objections, and that the duty of preparing a message, setting forth the objections to the constitutionality of the bill, was devolved upon Mr. Seward and Mr. Stanton. This to be followed by proof as to what was done by the President and Cabinet up to the time of sending the message by the President.

Senator SHERMAN—Does that offer give the date?

Mr. EVARTS—It gives the date as during the time when the bill was before the President.

Senator CONKLING—During the ten (10) days?

Mr. EVARTS—We omitted the precise date, because there were two occasions.

Mr. BUTLER—I assume, Mr. President and Senators, for the purpose of this objection, that the time to which this offer of proof refers is during the ten days between the first passage of the bill by the two Houses, and the time of its return with the objections of the President for reconsideration. I only propose to open the debate in order that my learned friends may be possessed, so far as I may be able to possess them, of the grounds of our objection.

The question is whether, after a law has been passed, under the due forms of law, the President can show what his opinions were and what the opinions of his Cabinet were before it was passed, as a justification for refusing to obey it and execute it.

I venture to say to you, Senators, that heretofore the struggle has been on the trial of impeachment whether the king's order should sustain the minister; and I was somewhat sharply reminded how familiar it was to everybody that the king can do no wrong in the eye of the British Constitution, and that, therefore, the minister was responsible. But the question which I brought to your attention in the struggle in impeachments in former times, was whether a king, not being considered able to do any wrong, when he gave an express order or advice to a minister, could shield the minister in the British Parliament.

In Earl Danby's case it was decided that it could not. He produced for his justification the order of the king.

That decision was thought to be a great point. Now, the proposition is, we have got a king, who is responsible if we can have the ministers to shield him? That is the proposition, whether the advice of the cabinet can shield the king. In other words, whether the Constitution has placed these heads of the departments around him as aids or shields—that is the question? Because if that can be done, then the question of impeachment is ended in this country for any breach of law, for no President there will be who cannot find subservient Cabinet Ministers to advise him as he wants to be advised, especially so if the Senate settle the proposition here, that these Cabinet Ministers are dependent upon his will, and that he cannot be restrained by law from removing them. He told the Senate in his message, that if Mr. Stanton had told him that he thought the law was constitutional, he would have removed him before it went into effect. If the President has that power, any President can find a Cabinet subservient enough to give him advice, and if that advice can shield him, there is the end of impeachment.

Mr. CURTIS—We would like to understand to what message the honorable manager is referring.

Mr. BUTLER—I was referring to the message of December 12, 1868, in which this language is used in substance, but I will take care that the exact quotation appears in my remarks:—That if Mr. Stanton informed him that he believed the law constitutional, he would have taken care to have removed him before its going into operation; or words to that effect. I say that if that unlimited power can be held by the President, then he will always defend himself by his Cabinet.

Let us look at it in the light of another great tribunal, whom you, Mr. President, may be called upon to try some time or another (alluding to Jefferson Davis.) I have no doubt that he had a Cabinet around him by whose advice he could defend himself for most of the treason he has committed. Let us take another view. I have had gentlemen say to me on this question, "would you not allow a military commander who should either give battle or forbear a battle to show that he called a council of his officers, and to show what their advice was, so as to justify him in the case of his refusal to give battle or his giving battle imprudently?" To that, I mean to answer that I would do so, but I would make a wide distinction; I would not let any general call around him his staff officers and those depending upon his breath for their offical existence, and allow him to show their opinions as the authority for his acts; I do not, as I have stated, propose by any means to argue this case; I proposed simply, when I arose to open the proposition, and I desire now to put in a single authority as a justification for what I have had the honor to say, that Jefferson thought it the better opinion that the constitutional right of the Cabinet was to give opinion in writing; I read on this subject from note 3, section 1498, of the second volume of "Story on the Constitution."

The note is, in substance, that Mr. Jefferson has informed us that, in Washington's administration, on measures of difficulty a consultation was held with the heads of the departments, either assembled or taking their opinions separately in conversation or in writing; that in his own Administration he follows the practice of assembling the heads of the departments in Cabinet council, but that he thinks the course of requiring separate opinions in writing from the respective heads of departments as more strictly within the spirit of the Constitution.

I have here, in the third volume of Adams' Works, with an appendix, an opinion of Mr. Jefferson, furnished to General Washington, on the question of Washington's right to appoint ambassadors, or rather to fix the grade of ambassadors, the right to appoint being in the Constitution, or whether the Senate had a right to negative that grade so fixed by the President. There is an example of one of the opinions that President Washington required of his Secretary of State as early as April 24, 1790, on this very question to appoint to office. We have it now, to be seen and read, whereas, if it had not been for trial, we never should have known the opinion of the Secretary of the Navy was on this great constitutional question.

In conclusion, Mr. Butler referred to the President's message of December 12, 1867, containing the following clause:—"If any of the gentlemen (meaning his Cabinet ministers) had then stated to me that he would avail himself of the provisions of that bill, in case it became a law, I should not have hesitated a moment as to his removal."

Mr. EVARTS—The point of the President's statement was that there was a concurrence of all the Secretaries who were appointed by Mr. Lincoln that they were not within the law, or otherwise he would have had Cabinet ministers of his own appointment. The question, as stated by the honorable manager, is whether the President can show his opinion and the advice of his Cabinet as to the constitutionality of a law as a justification of his refusal to obey the law. This is the manager's proposition.

Now, Mr. Chief Justice and Senators, this involves, more or less, the general merits of the case, as they have been necessarily anticipated somewhat by incidental arguments but we did not propose to occupy your time with preliminary discussions of what must form a very large and important part of the final considerations to be disposed of in this case. It is enough, in reference to questions of evidence when it is introduced in a trial, that it shall be apparent that the premises, both of fact and of law, are necessary to the introduction of evidence trustworthy, and to be used and applied according to the theory of law and facts.

Now, the proposition in this matter on behalf of the managers may be stated briefly thus:—If what was done

by the President on the 21st of February in reference to the Civil Tenure of Office act, in the writing out and delivery of these two orders, one calling on Mr. Stanton to surrender the office, and the other directing General Thomas to take charge of the surrendered office—if these two papers were a consummate crime, then the law imparts an intent to do the thing done, and so to commit the crime, and that all else is inapplicable within the law of an impeachment.

That is one view put forward by the managers. It will be for you to determine hereafter whether the violation of a statute, however complete, is necessarily a high crime and misdemeanor, within the meaning of the Constitution, for which this remedy of impeachment may be sought and may carry its punishment. So, too, is not to be forgotten that in the matter of defense, all the circumstances of intent, and deliberation, and inquiry, and pursuit of duty on the part of a great official, to arrive at a determination as to what is his official duty in an apparent conflict between the Constitution and the law, form a part of the general issues of impeachment and defense.

Now, the answer undoubtedly does set forth and claim that whatever we have done in the premises has been done on the President's judgment of duty under the Constitution of the United States, and after due deliberation, responsibility, upright and sincere effort to get all the aid and law on the subject of his duty which was accessible and within his power. One of the most important—one of his recognized as among the most important—of the aids and guides, supports and defenses which the Chief Magistrate of this country is to have in the opinions of the people at large, in the opinions of the two Houses of Congress, in the opinion even of judicial consideration when a case shall properly come before a court of whether he has followed his duty, or attempted to pursue his duty, is the view that those chief officers of the government under his constitutional right to call upon them for opinions, and under the practice of this government, convened in council for the purpose of arriving at opinions, have given them in reference to the matter of conflict and difficulty.

This offer of evidence here touches that part of the case, and is to supply that portion of the evidence as to what care, what deliberation, what advice attended the step of the President as he proceeded in the stress in which he was placed, and in the very matter in which he was called upon to proceed, not by a voluntary case assumed by himself, but in a matter pressing upon his duty as President, in reference to the conduct of one of the chief departments of the government. That is the range of the issue, and that is the application of this evidence. That it bears upon the issue, and is authentic testimony within the range of the President's right and duty to aid and support himself in the performance of his office, cannot be doubted.

But it is said that this involves matters of grave constitutional difficulty, and that if this kind of evidence is to be adduced that will be the end of all impeachment trials, for it will be equivalent to the authority claimed under the British Constitution, which denies that the king's order can shield the minister. Whenever any such pretension as that is set forth here—that the order of the Cabinet in council, as to any act of the President, is to shield him from his amenability under the Constitution to trial and judgment for his acts before this constitutional tribunal—it will be time enough to insist on the argument or to attempt an answer. Is there any fear that any such privilege or any such right, as we call it, shall interfere with the due power of this tribunal, and the proper responsibility of all other great officers of the government to it, on questions which make up the sum and catalogue of crimes against the State within the general proposition of impeachable offenses?

It is impossible that matters of this kind should come into play. In cases of treason or bribery, or offenses involving turpitude and sinning against the country's welfare, no such matter can properly come in play. Of course, in some matters of the conduct of foreign affairs, which might by an implication come within the range of treason, it may be supposed that the constitutional advisers of the President might, by their opinions, support him in the conduct which was made the subject of accusation. But here it will be perceived that the very matter in controversy must be regarded by the court in determining whether this species of evidence is applicable, and in determining its applicability, I need not plead before so learned a court, that the question of its weight and force is not to be anticipated.

Senator CONNESS moved that the court do now adjourn.

Several Senators—"Oh, no! Let us vote on this proposition."

Senator Conness was understood to say that he made the motion at the request of the managers.

The motion was agreed to, and the court, at 4.45, adjourned until eleven o'clock to-morrow.

PROCEEDINGS OF SATURDAY, APRIL 18.

The Tenure of Office Act.

The first business in court was the offer of the President's counsel to prove that, while the Tenure of Office bill was before the President for approval, he submitted it to his Cabinet, and was advised by them that it was unconstitutional; that Secretaries Seward and Stanton were delegated to prepare a message setting forth his objections to it.

Speech of Manager Wilson.

Mr. Manager WILSON rose and said:—As this objection confronts one of the most important questions involved in this case, I wish to present the views of the managers respecting it with such care and exactness as I may be able to command. The respondent now offers to prove, doubtless as a foundation for other Cabinet advice of more recent date, that he was advised by the members of his Cabinet that the act of Congress, upon which rest several of the articles to which he has made answer, to wit: "An act regulating the tenure of certain civil officers," passed March 2, 1867, was and is unconstitutional, and therefore void. That he was so advised he has alleged in his answer. Whether he was so advised or not we hold to be immaterial to this case and irrelevant to the issue joined. The House of Representatives were not to be entrapped in the preparation of their replication by any such cunning device, nor by the kindred one whereby the respondent affirms that he was not bound to execute said act because he believed it to be unconstitutional. The replication says that the House of Representatives do deny each and every averment in said several answers, or either of them, which denies or traverses the acts, intents, crimes or misdemeanors charged against the said Andrew Johnson in the said articles of impeachment, or either of them, and for replication to said answer do say that said Andrew Johnson, President of the United States, is guilty of the high crimes and misdemeanors mentioned in the said articles, &c.

There is no acceptance here of the issue tendered by the respondent, and in support of which he offers the immaterial, incompetent and irrelevant testimony, to which we object. The advice which he may have received, and the belief which he may have formed touching the constitutionality of such act, cannot be allowed to shield him from the consequences of his criminal acts. Nor can his mistaken view of the Constitution relative to his right to require the opinions of the heads of the several executive departments upon certain questions aid his efforts to escape from the just demands of law. In his answer to the first article, he alleges this respondent had, in pursuance of the Constitution, required the opinion of each principal officer of the executive departments upon this question of constitutional power, and daily had been advised by each of them, including said Mr. Stanton, Secretary for the Department of War, and under the Constitution of the United States this power of removal was lodged by the Constitution in the President of the United States, and that consequently it could be lawfully exercised by him, and the Congress could not deprive him thereof. The respondent found no provision in the Constitution authorizing him to pursue any such course.

The Constitution says the President may require the opinion in writing of the principal officer in each of the Executive departments upon any subject relating to the duties of their respective offices—Article 2, Section 2. Not of his office, nor of the legislative department, nor of the judicial department. But when did he require the opinions and receive the advice under cover of which he now seeks to escape? His answer informs us that this all transpired prior to his veto of the bill. Upon those unwritten opinions and that advice he based his message. He communicated his objections to Congress; they were overruled by both Houses, and the bill was enacted into a law in manner and form as prescribed by the Constitution. He does not say that since the final passage of the act he has been further advised by the principal officer of each of the Executive departments; that he is not bound to enforce it, and if he had done so he would have achieved a result of no possible benefit to himself, but dangerous to his advisers, for it will be borne in mind that the articles charge that he "did unlawfully conspire with one Lorenzo Thomas and with other persons to the House of Representatives unknown." He might have disclosed that the unknown persons were the members of his Cabinet.

This disclosure must have placed them in jeopardy without diminishing the peril which attends upon his own predicament. It is not difficult to see that the line of defense to which we have directed the present objection involves the great question of this case, it tends to matters more weighty than a mere resolution of the technical offenses which float on the surface of this presentation. Whoever attempts to measure the magnitude of the case by the comparatively insignificant acts which constitute the technical crimes and misdemeanors with which the respondent stands charged will attain a result far short of its true character and be rewarded with a beggardly appreciation of the immensity of its real proportions, for above and below and beyond these mere technical offenses, grave as they undoubtedly are, the great question which you are to settle is to be found. It envelopes the whole case and everything pertaining thereto. It is the great circle which bounds the sphere composed of the multitude of questions and is presented for your determination.

The respondent is arraigned for a violation of and a refusal to execute the law. He offers to prove that his Cabinet advised him that a certain bill, presented for his approval, was in violation of the Constitution; that he accepted their advice and vetoed the bill. And upon that and such additional advice as they may have given him, claims the right to resist and defy the provisions of the bill, notwithstanding its enactment into a law by two-thirds of both Houses over his objections. In other words, he claims, substantially, that he may determine for himself what laws he will obey and execute, and what laws he will disregard and refuse to enforce. In support of this claim he offers the testimony which, for the time being, is excluded by the objection now under discussion. If I am correct in this, then I was not mistaken when I asserted that this objection confronts one of the most important questions involved in this case. It may be said that this testimony is offered merely to disprove the intent alleged and charged in the articles, but it goes beyond this, and reaches the main question, as will clearly appear to the mind of any one who will read with care the answer to the first article. The testimony is improper for any purpose and in every view of the case.

The Executive Power.

The Constitution of the United States, Article II, section 1, provides that "The executive power should be vested in a President of the United States of America." The person at present exercising the functions of the executive office is the respondent, who stands at your bar to-day charged with the commission of high crimes and misdemeanors in office. Before he entered upon the discharge of the duties devolved on him as President, he took and subscribed the constitutionally prescribed oath of office in words, as follows:—"I do solemnly swear that I will faithfully execute the office of President of the United States, and will, to the best of my ability, preserve, protect and defend the Constitution of the United States."

The oath covers every part of the Constitution, imposes the duty of observing every action and clause thereof, and includes the distribution of powers therein made. The powers embraced and distributed are legislative, executive and judicial. Of the first, the Constitution declares that all legislative power herein granted, shall be vested in a Congress of the United States, which shall consist of a Senate and House of Representatives (Article one, section one). This includes the entire range of legislative action. The will of the Legislative Department is made known by the terms of the bills which it may pass. Of these expressions of the legislative will, the Constitution says:—"Every bill which shall have passed the House of Representatives and the Senate shall, before it becomes a law, be presented to the President of the United States, and if he approve he shall sign it, but if not, he shall return it to that House in which it shall have originated, who shall enter the objections at large on their journal, and proceed to reconsider it." "If, after such reconsideration, two-thirds of that House shall agree to pass the bill, it shall be sent, together with the objections, to the other House, by which it shall be likewise reconsidered; and if approved by two-thirds of that House, it shall become a law."—Article 1, section 7. Thus laws are made, but laws cannot execute themselves. However wise, just and necessary they may be, they are lifeless declarations of the legislative will until clothed with the power of action by other departments of the government. The builders of our Constitution understood with great exactness the philosophy of government, and provided for every contingency. They knew that laws, to be effective, must be executed; that the best and purest law could not perform its proper office in the absence of executive power; therefore, they created that power, and vested it in a President of the United States. To insure due execution of the power, they imposed the duty of taking and subscribing the oath above quoted on every person elected to the Presidential office, and declared he should comply with the conditions before he enters on the execution of his office. Chief among the executive duties imposed by the Constitution and secured by the oath is the one contained in the injunction that the President shall take care that the laws be faithfully executed— Act 2, section 3. What laws? Those which may have been passed by the Legislative Department in manner and form as declared by that section of the Constitution heretofore recited. The President is clothed with no discretion in this regard. Whatever is declared by the legislative power to be the law the President is bound to execute. By his power to veto a bill passed by both houses of Congress he may challenge the legislative will, but if he be overruled by the two-thirds voice of the houses, he must respect the decision and execute the law which that constitutional voice has spoken into existence. If this be not true then the Executive power is superior to the legislative power.

If the Executive will may declare what is and what is not law, why is a legislative department established at all? Only to impose on the President the constitutional obligation to take care that the laws be faithfully executed. If he may determine what acts are and what are not law; it is absurd to say that he has any discretion in this regard; he must execute the law. The great object of the Executive Department is to accomplish this purpose, and without it, be the form of government whatever it may, it will be utterly worthless for offense or defense; for the redress of grievances, or the protection of rights for the happiness or good order, or safety of the people— Story on the Constitution, vol. 2, 6419; De Tocqueville, in his work on Democracy in America, in opening the chapter on Executive power, very truly remarks, that "the American Legislature undertook a difficult task in attempting to create an executive power dependent on a majority of the people, and nevertheless sufficiently strong to act without restraint in its own power.

"It was indispensable to the maintenance of the republican form of government that the representation of the Executive power should be subject to the will of the nation." Vol. 1, p. 128.

The task was a difficult one, but the great minds from which our Constitution sprung were equal to its severest demands. They created an executive power strong enough to execute the will of the nation, and yet sufficiently weak to be controlled by that will. They knew that power will intoxicate the best of hearts as wine the strongest heads, and, therefore, they surrounded the Executive agent with such proper restraint and limitation as would confine him to the boundaries prescribed by the national will, or crush him by its power if he stepped beyond. The plan adopted was most perfect. It created the Executive power, provided for the selection of the person to be intrusted with its exercise, determined the restraints and limitations which should rest upon, guide and control him, and out of abundant caution decreed that the President * * * * of the United States shall be removed from office on impeachment for and conviction of treason, bribery or other high crimes and misdemeanors.

It is preposterous for the respondent to attempt to defend himself against the corrective power of this grand remedy by interposing the opinions or advice of the principal officers of the Executive Department, either as to the body of his offense or the intent with which he committed it. His highest duty is to "take care that the laws be faithfully executed," and if he fail in this particular he must fail in all, and anarchy will usurp the throne of order. The laws are but expressions of the national will, which can be made known only through the enactments of the Legislative Department of the government. A criminal failure to execute that will, and every wilful failure, no matter what its inducement may be, is criminal; may justly call into action the remedial power of impeachment. This power is, by the express terms of the Constitution, confided to one branch of the Legislative Department, in these words:—

"The House of Representatives * * * shall have the sole power of impeachment." Article 1, section 2. This lodgment of the most delicate power known to the Constitution is most wise and proper, because of the frequency with which those who may exercise, are called to account for their conduct at the bar of the people, and this is the check balanced against a possible abuse of the power, and it has been most effectual; but the wisdom which fashioned our Constitution did not stop here.

It next declared that the Senate shall have the power to try all impeachments.—Article I. section 3. In the theory of our Constitution, the Senate represents the States, and, its members being removed from accountability to the people, are supposed to be beyond the reach of those excitements of passion which so frequently change the complexion of the House of Representatives, and this is the more immediate check provided to balance the possible hasty action of the representatives. Wise, considerate and safe to the perfect work of demonstration is this admirable adjustment of the powers with which we are now dealing. The Executive power was created to enforce the will of the nation. The will of the nation appears in the law. Two houses of Congress are intrusted with the power to enact laws, the objections of the Executive to the contrary notwithstanding. Laws thus enacted, as well as those which receive the Executive sanction are the voice of the people. If the person clothed for the time being with the Executive power—the only power which can

give effect to the people's will—refuses or neglects to enforce the legislative decrees of the nation or wilfully violates the same, what constituent elements of governmental form could be more properly charged with the right to present, and the means to try and remove the contumacious Secretary than those intrusted with the power to enact the laws of the people, guided by the checks and balances to which I have directed the attention of the Senate? What other constituent part of the government could so well understand and adjudge of a perverse and criminal refusal to obey, or wilful declination to execute the national will, than those joining in its expression? There can be but one answer to these questions.

Wisdom and Justice of the Constitution.

The provisions of the Constitution are wise and just beyond the power of disputation, in leaving the entire subject of the responsibility of the Executive to faithfully execute his office and enforce the laws to the charge, trial and judgment of the two several branches of the Legislative Department, regardless of the opinions of Cabinet officers, or of the decisions of the Judicial Department. The respondent has placed himself within this power of impeachment by trampling on the constitutional duty of the Executive, and violating the penal laws of the land. I readily admit that the Constitution of United States is in almost every respect different from the Constitution of Great Britain. The latter is, to a great extent, unwritten, and is, in all regards, subject to such changes as Parliament enact. An act of Parliament may change the Constitution of England. In this country the rule is different. The Congress may enact no law in conflict with the Constitution. The enactments of the Parliament become a part of the British Constitution. The will of Parliament is supreme. The will of Congress is subordinate to the written Constitution of the United States, but not to judged of by the Executive Department. But the theory upon which the two Constitutions rest at the present time are almost identical. In both the Executive is made subordinate to the legislative power. The Commons of England tolerate no encroachment on their powers from any other estate of the realm.

British Precedent.

The Parliament is the supreme power of the kingdom. In spite of the doctrine that "the King can do no wrong," and in support of the assertion that the exercise of the sovereignty rest in the several States, the kindred character of the theories permeating the Constitution may be illustrated by certain parliamentary and ministerial action connected with the American Revolution, and which will well serve the purposes of my argument. On the 27th day of February, 1782, General Conway moved, in the House of Commons. the following resolution:—"That it is the opinion of this House that the further prosecution of offensive war on the continent of North America, for the purpose of reducing the revolted colonies to obedience, for the better means of weakening the efforts of this country against her European enemies, dangerously to increase the mutual enmity so fatal to the interests both of Great Britain and America, and by preventing our happy reconciliation with that country, to frustrate the earnest desire graciously expressed by his Majesty, to restore the blessings of public tranquility."—Hanseard, vol. 22, page 1071.

The Commons passed the resolutions; the Ministry did not seem to catch its true spirit, and, therefore, on March the next following, General Conway moved another resolution in these more express and emphatic terms, to wit:— "That after the solemn declaration of the opinion of the House in their humble address presented to his Majesty on Friday last, and his Majesty's assurance of his gracious intention in pursuance of their advice to take such measures as shall appear to his Majesty to be most conclusive to the restoration of harmony between Great Britain and the revolted colonies so essential to the prosperity of both, this House will consider as enemies to his Majesty and this country all those who shall endeavor to frustrate his Majesty's paternal care for the care and happiness of his people, by advising or by any means attempting the farther prosecution of offensive war on the continent of North America, for the purpose of reducing the revolted colonies to obedience by force."—Ibid, page 1089.

This resolution led to an animated debate, the temper of the Commons was equal to the directness of the revolution. The Ministry saw this, and understood exactly its meaning. They were disposed to avoid the implied censure, and attempted to show by expressions of a determination to observe and respect the opinion of the House as declared in the first resolution that necessity existed for the adoption of the second to effectuate this end. Lord North, the Premier, in the course of his remarks, said:— "The majority of that House had resolved that peace should be made with America, and the answer given from the Throne was so satisfactory that the House had just concurred in a motion to return thanks to his Majesty for making it. Therefore where there could be no ground for coming to a resolution which seemed to doubt the propriety or sincerity of that answer? He was not of the disposition of those who condemned them, and by factious and seditious misrepresentations held them out to the public. In the most odious colors a majority of that House was in parliamentary language the House itself.

"It could never make him change a single opinion, yet he bowed to that opinion which was sanctioned by the majority. Though he might not be a convert to such opinion, still he held it to be his indispensable duty to obey it, and never once to lose sight of it in the advice which, as a servant of the Crown, he should have occasion to give his Sovereign. It was the right of that House to command;

it was the duty of a Minister to obey its resolutions. Parliament had already expressed its desires or its orders, and as it was scarcely possible that a Minister should be found daring and infamous enough to advise his Sovereign to differ in opinion from his Parliament, so he could not think the present motion, which must suppose the existence of such a Minister, could be at all necessary."—Ibid, p. 1090. And again he said:—"To the policy of that resolution he could not subscribe, but as Parliament had thought proper to pass it, and as Ministers were bound to obey the orders of Parliament, so he should make that resolution the standard of his future conduct."—P. 1107. These protestations of Lord North did not arrest the action of the Commons; the resolution passed, and peace followed.

It will be observed that these proceedings on the part of the Commons trenched on ground covered by the prerogatives of the Crown, and affected, to some extent, the powers of declaring war, making peace and entering into treaties. Still the minister bowed in obedience to the command of the House, and declared that it was scarcely possible that a minister should be found hardy, daring and infamous enough to advise his sovereign to differ in opinion from his Parliament. This grand action of the Commons and its results disclosed the sublimest feature of the British Constitution. It was made to appear how thoroughly under that Constitution the executive power was dependant on the legislative will of the nation. The doctrine that the king can do no wrong, while it protected his person, was resolved into an almost perfect subordination of the ministers, through whom the powers of the Crown are exerted to the acts and resolutions of the Parliament, until at last the roar of the lion of England is no more than the voice of the Commons of the realm. So completely had this principle asserted itself in the British Constitution that the veto power had passed into disuse for nearly a century, and it has not been exercised since.

The last instance of its use was in April, 1696, when William III refused the royal assent to a "bill to regulate elections of members to serve in Parliament."—Hansard, vol. 5, p. 993.

The men who framed our Constitution in 1789 were not untaught of these facts in English history, and they fashioned our government on the plan of the subordination of the executive power to the written law of the land. They did not deny the veto power of the President, but they did declare that it should be subject to a legislative limitation, under the operation of which it might in any given case be overruled by the Congress; and when this happens, and the vetoed bill becomes law, the President must yield the convictions of his own judgment as an individual to the demands of the higher duty of the office and execute the law.

His oath binds him to this, and he cannot pursue any other course of action without endangering the public weal. The Constitution regards him in a double capacity as a citizen and public officer. In the first, it leaves him to the same accountability to the law in its ordinary process as would attach to and apply in case he were a mere civilian or the humblest citizen, while in the latter it subjects him to the power of the House of Representatives to impeach, and that of the Senate to remove him from office if he be guilty of "treason, bribery, or other high crimes and misdemeanors." If the citizen disobey the law, and be convicted thereof, he may be relieved by pardon; but the officer who brings upon himself a conviction or impeachment, cannot receive the Executive clemency, for while it is provided that the President "shall have power to grant reprieves and pardons for offenses against the United States," it is also expressly declared that this power shall not extend to "cases of impeachment."—Article 2, section 2. The same person, if he be a civil officer, may be indicted for a violation of law, and impeached for the same act. If convicted in both cases, he may be pardoned in the former, but in the latter he is beyond the reach of forgiveness. The relief provided for the disobedient citizen is denied to the offending officer.

The Law-Making Power.

I have already observed that the Constitution of the United States distributes the powers of the government among three departments. First in the order of constitutional arrangement is the Legislative Department, and this, doubtless, because the law-making power is the supreme power of the land, through which the will of the nation is expressed. The legislative power, in other words the law-making power, is "vested in a Congress of the United States." The acts of Congress constitute the municipal power of the Republic. Municipal law is a rule of action prescribed by the supreme power of a State, commanding what is right and prohibiting what is wrong.—Blackstone, page 44. The supreme power of a State is that which is the highest in authority; and, therefore, it was proper that the Constitution should name first the legislative department in the distribution of powers, as through it alone the State can speak. Its voice is the law; the rule of action to be respected and obeyed by every person subject to its direction or amenable to its requirements.

Executive Department.

Next in the order of its distribution of powers the Constitution names the Executive Department. This is proper and logical for the will, the law of the nation, cannot act except through agents or instrumentalities charged with its execution. The Congress can enact a law, but cannot execute it; it can express the will of the nation, but some other agencies are required to give it effect. The Constitution resolves those agencies and instrumentalities

into an Executive Department. At the head of this department, charged imperatively with the due execution of its great power, appears the President of the United States, duly enjoined to take care that the laws be faithfully executed. If the law which he is to execute does not vest him with discretionary powers, he has no election. He must execute the will of the nation as expressed by Congress. In no case can he indulge the uncertainties and take the responsibilities of official discretion unless it be conceded to him by express enactment. In all other cases he must follow and enforce the Legislative will.

The office of executing a law excludes the right to judge of it, and as the Constitution charges the President with the execution of the laws. It thereby declares what is his duty, and gives him no power beyond.—Rowle on the Constitution, p. 136. Undoubtedly he possesses the right to recommend the enactment and to advise the repeal of laws. He may also, as I have before remarked, obstruct the passage of laws by interposing his veto, but beyond these means of changing, directing or obstructing the national will he may not go. When the law-making power has resolved, his opposition must be at an end. That resolution is a law, and resistance to it is punishable.—Federalist, No. 70.

The judgment of the individual intrusted for the time being with the executive power of the republic may reject as utterly erroneous the conclusion arrived at by those invested with the legislative power, but the officer must submit and execute the law. He has no discretion in the premises, except such as the particular statute confers on on him, and even this, he must exercise in obedience to the rules which the act provides. A high officer of the government once gave to the President of the United States an opinion relative to this doctrine in these words, "To the Chief Executive Magistrate of the Union is confided the solemn duty of seeing the laws faithfully executed, that he may be able to meet this duty with a power equal to its performance, he nominates his own subordinates and removes them at his pleasure."

This opinion was given prior to the passage of the act of March 2, 1867, which requires the concurrence of the Senate in removals from office, which, while denying to the Senate the power of absolute removal, concedes to him the power to suspend officers, and to supply their places temporarily. For the same reason the land and naval forces are under his orders, as their commander-in-chief; but his power is to be used only in the manner prescribed by the Legislative Department. He cannot accomplish a legal purpose by illegal means, or break the laws himself to prevent them from being violated by others. The acts of Congress sometimes give the President a broad discretion in the use of the means by which they are to be executed, and sometimes limit his power, so that he can exercise it only in a certain prescribed manner. Where the law directs a thing to be done without saying how, that implies the power to use such means as may be necessary and proper to accomplish the end of the Legislature; but where the means of performing a duty is pointed out by statute, the exclusive mode and no other can be followed.

No Common Law.

The United States have no common law to fall back upon when the written law is defective. If, therefore, an act of Congress declares that a certain thing shall be done by a particular officer, it cannot be done by a different officer. The agency which the law furnishes for its own execution must be used to the exclusion of all others.—Opinion of Attorney-General Black, November 20, 1860.

This is a very clear statement of the doctrine which I have been endeavoring to enforce, and on which the peculiar branch of this case now commanding our attention rests. If we drift away from it we unsettle the very foundation of the government and endanger their stability to a degree which may well alarm the most peaceful mind and appal the most courageous. A departure from this view of the character of the Executive power, and from the nature of the duty and obligation resting upon the officer charged therewith, would surround this nation with its most fearful proportions and of unparalleled magnitude. Such a departure would not only justify the respondent in his refusal to obey and execute the law, but also approve his usurpation of the judicial powers. When he resolved that he would not observe the Legislature's will, because, in his judgment it did not conform to the provisions of the Constitution of the United States touching the subjects embraced in the articles of impeachment on which he is now being tried at your bar. Concede to him, and when and where may we look for the end? to what result shall we arrive? Will it naturally and inevitably lead to a consolidation of the several powers of the government in the Executive Department, and would this be the end? Would it not rather be the beginning? If the President may defy and usurp the powers of the Legislative and Judicial Departments of the government, as his caprices or the advices of his Cabinet may incline him, why may not his subordinate, each for himself, and touching his own sphere of action determined how far the directions of his superior accord with the Constitution of the United States, and reject and refuse to obey all that comes short of the standard erected by his judgment. It was remarked by the Supreme Court of the United States, in the case of Martin vs. Mott, 12 Wheaton, 19, that "if a superior officer has a right to contest the orders of the President upon his order, doubt as to the exigency referred to by the statute having arisen, it must be equally the right of every inferior soldier, and any act done by any person in furtherance of such orders would subject him to responsibility in a civil suit, in which his defense must finally rest upon his ability to establish the facts by competent proofs. Such a course would be subversive of all discipline, and expose the best disposed officers to the chances of the ruinous litigation. * * * * * *

The power itself is confined to the Executive of the Union; to him who is by the Constitution the commander of the militia when called into the actual service of the United States; whose duty is to take care that the laws be faithfully executed, and whose responsibility for an honest discharge of his official obligation is secured by the highest sanction. He is necessarily constituted the judge of the existence of the exigency in the first instance, and is bound to call for the militia. His orders for this purpose are in strict conformity with the provisions of the law, and it would seem to follow as a necessary consequence that every act done by a subordinate officer in obedience to such orders is equally justifiable.

The law contemplates that under such circumstances orders will be given to carry the power into effect, and it cannot, therefore, be a correct inference that any other person has a just right to disobey them. Apply the principles here enunciated to the case at the bar, and they become perfect support. If the President has a right to control and refuse to obey the laws enacted by Congress, his subordinates may exercise the same right and refuse to obey his orders. If he may exercise it in one case, they may assert it in any other. If he may challenge the laws of Congress, they may question the orders of the President. It is his duty to carry out the laws of the nation, and their duty to obey his orders. He may be allowed to defy the legislative will, they may be allowed to disregard the Executive order. This brings confusion, and the affairs of the public are made the sport of the contending factions and conflicting agents.

No such power belongs to either. To Congress is given the power to enact laws, and while they remain on the statute book it is the constitutional duty of the President to see their faithful execution. This duty rests upon all of his subordinates. Its observance by all, the President included, makes the Executive Department, through ten thousand agents, a unit. Unity produces harmony. Harmony effects direction of action, and thus secures a due execution of the laws; but if the President may disregard the law because he has been advised by his Cabinet, and believes that the Congress violated the Constitution in its enactments, and his subordinates may follow any example, disobey his orders and directions, the object and end of an Executive unity is defeated, anarchy succeeds order; force, irresponsible and vicious, supplants law, and ruin envelopes the republic and its institutions.

If the views which I have imperfectly presented are correct—and such I believe them to be—the testimony to which we object must be excluded from your consideration, and thus will be determined one of the most important questions encircled by this case. If I have been able to arrest your attention, and to centre it upon the question which I have imperfectly discussed, the time occupied by me will not be without profit to the nation. I have endeavored to show that the royal fiction, which asserts that "the king can do no wrong," cannot be applied to the President of the United States in such manner as to shield him from the just condemnation of violated law. The king's crimes may be expiated by the vicarious atonement of his minister, but the President is held personally amenable to the impeaching power of the House of Representatives. Concede to the President immunity through the advice of his Cabinet officers, and you reverse by your decision the theory of our Constitution. Let those who will assume this responsibility. I leave it to the decision of the Senate.

Rejoinder of Mr. Curtis.

Mr. CURTIS said:—I have no intention, Senators, to make a reply to the elaborate argument, which has now been introduced here by the honorable manager, touching the merits of this case. The time for that has not come, and the testimony is not before you. The case is not in a condition for you to consider and pass upon its merits whether they be based on law or the facts.

The simple question now before the Senate is, whether a certain offer of proof may be carried out in evidence. Of course that involves another. That other inquiry is, whether the evidence which is offered is pertinent to any matter involved in this case; and when it is ascertained the matter is pertinent, I suppose it is to be received. Its credit, ability, its wealth, its effect finally upon the merits of the case, or any question, cannot be considered and acted upon preliminarily to the reception of the evidence, and leaving on one side the whole of this elaborate argument which is now addressed to you, I propose to make a few observations to show that this evidence is pertinent to issues in this case.

The honorable manager has read a portion of the answer of the President, and has stated that the House of Representatives has taken no issue upon that part of the answer. As to the effect of that admission by the managers, I shall have a word or two to say presently. But the honorable manager has not told you that the House of Representatives, when they brought to your bar these articles, did not intend to assert and prove the allegations contained in them, which are matters of fact. One of these allegations, Mr. Chief Justice, as you will find by referring to the first article, and to the second article, and to the third article, is that the President of the United States in removing Mr. Stanton and appointing General Thomas intentionally violated the Constitution of the United States; that he did these acts with the intention of violating the Constitution

the United States. Instead of favoring that, it is wholly immaterial what intention the President had; it is imma-

terial whether he honestly believed that the act of Congress was unconstitutional; it is wholly immaterial whether he believed that he was acting in accordance with his oath of office, to preserve, protect and defend the Constitution when he did this act.

Now, then, we offer to introduce evidence here bearing upon this question of intent, evidence that before offering any opinion upon this subject, he resorted to proper advice to enable him to form a correct judgment, and that when he did form a fixed opinion on this subject, it was under the influence of this proper advice, and that when he did this act, whether it was lawful or unlawful, it was not done with an intention to violate the Constitution. The honorable manager gets up here, and addresses you for an hour by the clock, that it is wholly immaterial what his opinion was, or what advice he had received in conformity with which he acted in this matter. The honorable manager's argument may be a sound one. The Senate may ultimately come to that conclusion after they have heard this clause. This is a discussion into which I shall not enter. But before the Senate can come to the consideration of these questions, they must pass over this allegation; they must either say, as the honorable manager says, that it is wholly immaterial what opinion the President formed, and under what advice or under what circumstances he formed it, or else it must be admitted by Senators that it is material, and the evidence must be considered. Now, how is it possible at this stage of the inquiry to determine which of these courses is to be taken by the honorable Senate?

If the Senate should finally come to the conclusion that it is wholly immaterial, this evidence will do no harm. If, on the other hand, the Senate should finally come to the conclusion that it is material what the intention of the President was in doing these acts, and that they will examine to see whether it was or not a wilfull violation of the Constitution, what then? It would have excluded the evidence upon which it could have determined that question. I respectfully submit, therefore, that whether the argument of the honorable managers is sound or unsound, whether it will finally appear in the judgment of the Senate that this evidence is material or not, this is not the time to exclude it. Upon the ground that an examination of the merits hereafter, and a decision upon those merits will show that it is immaterial, when that is shown the evidence can be laid aside. If the other conclusion should be arrived at by any one Senator, or by the body, then they will be in want of this evidence which we now offer. In reference to this question, Senators, it is not pertinent.

I do not intend to enter into the constitutional inquiry which was started yesterday by the honorable manager, Mr. Butler, as to the particular character of the Cabinet council. One thing is certain, that every President from the origin of the government, has assented to oral discussion in his presence, questions of public importance arising in the course of his official duty. Another thing is apparent; that is, although the written letter remains and therefore it would appear with some certainty what the advice of a Cabinet council was if it were put in, yet every practical man who has had connection with the business affairs of life, every lawyer, every legislator knows that there is no satisfactory mode of bringing out the truth as an oral discussion face to face of those who are interested in the subject, that it is the most satisfactory mode of arriving at a conclusion, and that solitary written opinions, composed in a closet, away from the collision between men, which brings out new thoughts, new conceptions, more accurate views, is not the best method of arriving at a conclusion; and under the influence of this the practical consideration undoubtedly is, that this habit, beginning with General Washington, not becoming universal by any means until Mr. Jefferson's time, but from that day to this this habit has been formed, President Johnson found it in existence when he went into office.

He continued it, and I therefore say that when the question of his intention comes to be considered by the Senate, when the question arises in their minds whether the President honestly believed that this was an unconstitutional law, when the particular exigencies arises, when, if he carried out or obeyed that law, he must quit the powers which he believed were conferred upon him by the Constitution, and not be able to carry on the departments of the government in the manner the public interests required. When these questions arise for the consideration of the Senate, then they ought to have before them the fact that he acted by the advice of the usual and proper advisors, that he resorted to the last means within his reach to form a full opinion upon this subject, and that therefore it is a fair conclusion that when he did form that opinion, it was an honest and fixed opinion, which he felt he must carry out into practice if the proper occasion should arise. It is in this point of view, and this point of view only, that we offer this evidence.

The honorable Senator from Michigan (Mr. Howard) has proposed a question to the counsel for the President. It is this:—"Do the counsel for the accused not consider that the validity of the Tenure of Office bill was purely a question of law?" I shall answer that part of the question first. The constitutional validity of any law is of course purely a question of law. It depends upon a comparison of the provisions of the bill. With a law enacted by the people for the government of their agents it depends upon whether these agents have transcended the authority which the people gave; and that comparison of the Constitution with the law is in the sense in which it was intended by the Senator. The next branch of the question is:—"Whether that question is to be determined in the trial by the Senate?" That is a question I cannot answer. That is a question that can be determined only by the

Senate themselves. If the Senate should find that Mr. Stanton's case was not within this law, then no such question arises. Then there is no question in this particular case of a conflict between this law and the Constitution.

If the Senate should find that in these articles charged against the President that it is necessary for the Senate to believe that there was some act of turpitude on his part, connected with this matter, some *mala fides*, some bad intent, and that he did honestly believe, as he states in his answer, that this was an unconstitutional law; that a case having arisen when he must act accordingly, under his oath of office, if the Senate comes to that conclusion, it is immaterial whether this was a constitutional or unconstitutional law. Be it one or be it the other; be it true or false that the President has committed an offense by his interpretation of the law, he has not committed an impeachable offense, as charged by the House of Representatives, and as we must advance beyond this question before we reach the third question that the Senator propounds, there is no necessity for the Senate to determine that question.

The residue of the question is—"Do they consider that the opinions of Cabinet officers touching that question—that is, the constitutionality of the law—"is competent evidence, by which the judgment of the Senate ought to be influenced?" Certainly not. We do not put them on the stand as experts on questions of constitutional law. The judges will determine that out of their own breasts. We put them on the stand as advisers of the President, to state what advice, in point of fact, they gave him, with a view to show that he was guilty of no improper intent to violate the Constitution.

In reply to the question of the honorable Senator from Michigan (Mr. Howard), as to why we should put members of the Cabinet on the stand, I would say that we put them on the stand for the same purpose as the Senator when practicing law, has frequently put lawyers on the stand. A man is proceeded against by another for an improper arrest, or for a malicious prosecution, and it is necessary to prove malice. If no proper cause is proved, malice is inferable; but it is perfectly well settled, that when the defendant can show that he fairly laid his case before counsel, and that counsel advised him that there was probable cause, the inference of malice is overthrown. We wish to show here that the President called the opinions of his advisers, and acted upon that advice.

In response to the question of the honorable Senator from Maryland, (Mr. Johnson,) he will allow me to say that this is a question which the managers could answer much better than the President's counsel. The question is, "do the counsel for the President understand that the managers deny the statement made by the President in his message of December 12, 1867, as given in evidence by the managers, (page 45, Official Report,) that the members of the Cabinet gave in the opinion there stated as to the Tenure of Office act, and as the evidence offered and corroborated that statement, or for what other object is it offered?"

We now understand, from what the honorable manager has said this morning, that the House of Representatives has taken no issue on that part of our answer. The honorable manager does not understand that that now controverts or denies that part of our argument. We do also understand that the honorable managers themselves put in evidence the message of the President to the Senate of the 12th of December, in which he states that he was advised by the members of his Cabinet unanimously, including Mr. Stanton, that that law was unconstitutional. Nevertheless, Senators, this is an affair of the utmost gravity in any respect or in any possible view of it, and we do not feel at liberty to evade or abstain from offering the members of the President's Cabinet, so that they might state to you, under the sanction of their oaths, what advice was given to the President by them on the subject.

Question from Senator Wilson.

Senator WILSON submitted the following question to the counsel:—"Is the advice given to the President by his Cabinet with a view of preparing a veto message pertinent to prove the right of the President to disregard the law after it was passed over his veto?"

Mr. CURTIS—I consider it strictly pertinent. It is not enough that the President received such advice, but he must show that an occasion arose for him to act upon it which, in the judgment of the Senate, was such occasion that any wrong intention could be imputed to him; but the first step is to show that he honestly believed that it was an unconstitutional law.

I wish, in closing, simply to say that Senators will perceive how entirely aside this view which I have presented to the Senate is from any claim on the part of the President. He may disregard a law simply because he thinks it unconstitutional! He makes no such claim. He must make a case beyond that, a case such as is stated in his answer, but in order to make a case beyond that it is necessary for him to begin by satisfying the Senate that he honestly believed the law unconstitutional, and it is with that view that we now offer this evidence.

The Chief Justice States the Question.

The Chief Justice—Senators, the only question which the Chief Justice considers as before the Senate, respects not the weight but the admissibility of the evidence offered, to determine the question. It is necessary to show what is charged in the articles of impeachment. The first article charges that on the 21st of February the President issued an order for the removal of Mr. Stanton from the office of Secretary of War; that that order was made unlawfully, and that it was made with intent then and there to violate the Constitution of the United States. The same charge is

repeated in the articles which relate to the appointment of Mr. Thomas, and which are necessarily connected with this transaction. The intent, then, is the subject to which much of the evidence on both sides has been directed, and the Chief Justice conceives that this testimony is admissible for the purpose of showing the intent with which the President has acted in this transaction. He will submit the question to the Senate, if any Senator desires it.

The Vote.

Senator HOWARD called for the yeas and nays. The vote was taken and resulted—yeas, 20; nays, 29, as follows:—

YEAS.—Messrs. Anthony, Bayard, Buckalew, Davis, Dixon, Doolittle, Fessenden, Fowler, Grimes, Henderson, Hendricks, Johnson, McCreery, Patterson (Tenn.), Ross, Saulsbury, Trumbull, Van Winkle, Vickers and Willey—20.

NAYS.—Messrs. Cameron, Cattell, Chandler, Cole, Conkling, Conness, Corbett, Cragin, Drake, Edmunds, Ferry, Frelinghuysen, Harlan, Howard, Howe, Morgan, Morrill (Me.), Morrill (Vt.), Patterson (N. H.), Pomeroy, Ramsey, Sherman, Sprague, Stewart, Thayer, Tipton, Williams, Wilson and Yates—29.

So the evidence was excluded.

Secretary Welles Recalled.

Secretary Welles was then called to the stand, and his examination was resumed, as follows:—

Mr. EVARTS—Q. At the Cabinet meeting held during the period from the presentation of the bill to the President till his message sending in his objections was completed, was the question whether Mr. Stanton was within the operation of the Civil Tenure act the subject of consideration and determination?

Mr. BUTLER—We object.

The Chief Justice directed the counsel to put their offer in writing.

The offer was reduced to writing, as follows:—"We offer to prove that at the meetings of the Cabinet at which Mr. Stanton was present, held while the Tenure of Office act was before the President for approval, the advice of the Cabinet in reference to the same was asked by the President and given by the Cabinet, and thereupon the question whether Mr. Stanton and the other Secretaries who had received their appointments from Mr. Lincoln were within the restrictions, or the President's power of removal from office, created by said act, was considered, and the opinion expressed that the Secretaries appointed by Mr. Lincoln were not within the restrictions."

Mr. BUTLER objected, stating that the question came within the ruling already made by the Senate.

Mr. EVARTS replied to that objection, stating that he did not regard the question as coming within the ruling. The ruling already made might have turned on one of several considerations quite outside of the present inquiry. The present evidence sought to be introduced presented questions of another complication. In the first place it presented the question as to the law itself, whether it had in any way or ways pleaded, to have any application to Secretaries whom the President had never selected or appointed.

This point had formed the subject of much consideration and opinion in the Senate and in the House of Representatives, and was made a subject of inquiry and of opinion by the President himself, and his action concerning it was what brought the question here. The removal of Mr. Stanton was based on the President's opinion, after proper and diligent efforts to get a correct opinion, that Mr. Stanton was not within the law, and therefore the evidence would show that the President's conduct and action in removing Mr. Stanton was not to the intent of violating the law. The purpose now was to show that he did not do it with intent of violating the law, but with intent of exercising a well-known perfectly established constitutional power, deemed by him, on the advice of his Cabinet, not to be effected by the law.

If the question of intent, or purpose of motive and object in the removal of Mr. Stanton were the subject of inquiry here, then it was proper to show that he acted within obedience to the Constitution and the law as he was advised. The question, too, had a bearing upon the presence of Mr. Stanton, and his assent to the opinions of the Cabinet, and had a bearing in reference to the President's right to expect from Mr. Stanton's acquiesence in the exercise of the power of removal.

Mr. Butler's Argument.

Mr. BUTLER said that without desiring to enter upon debate, he wished to call the attention of the Senate to the fact that the question sought to show whether the Cabinet, including Mr. Stanton, had not advised the President that the bill did not apply to Mr. Stanton. In that connection he would refer the Senate to the President's message of the 12th of December, in which he made use of the following language:—"To the Senate of the United States:—I have carefully examined the bill to regulate the tenure of certain civil offices; the material portion of the bill is contained in the first section, and is of the effect following, namely:—"That every person holding any civil office to which he has been appointed by and with the advice and consent of the Senate, and every person who shall hereafter be appointed to any such office, and shall become duly qualified to act therein, is and shall be entitled to hold such office until his successor shall have been appointed by the President, with the advice and consent of the Senate, and duly qualified, and that the Secretaries of State, of the Treasury, of War, of the Navy, and of the Interior, the Postmaster-General and the Attorney-General shall hold their offices respectively for and during the term of the

President by whom they may have been appointed, and for one month thereafter, subject to removal by and with the advice and consent of the Senate." These provisions are qualified by a reservation in the fourth section, that nothing contained in the bill shall be construed to extend the term of any office the duration of which is limited by law. In effect the bill provides that the President shall not remove from their places any of the civil officers whose terms of service are not limited by law, without the advice and consent of the Senate of the United States. The question, as Congress is well aware, is by no means a new one. The President, in that same message, went on to argue upon the debate in 1789, which wholly applied to Cabinet officers, and the Senate would find that that was the gist of the argument on page 41. The President, after having exhausted the argument as to Cabinet officers, went on to say:—It applies equally to every other officer of the government appointed by the President whose term of duration is not specially declared.

It is supported by the weighty reason that the subordinate officers in the Executive Department ought to hold at the pleasure of the head of the department, because he is invested generally with the executive authority, and the participation in that authority by the Senate was an exception to a general principle, and ought to be taken strictly. The President is the great responsible officer for the execution of the law, and the power of removal was incidental to that duty, and might often be requisite to fulfill it.

Mr. Butler went on to call the attention of the Senate to the constitutional reason suggested by Mr. Evarts in reference to Mr. Stanton giving consideration to the law; the proof was offered to show that the President, when he removed Mr. Stanton, he supposed that Mr. Stanton did not believe himself within the law. But Mr. Stanton had just been reinstated under the law, and had refused to resign, because the law could not touch him. He had put the President's power at defiance, "as the President himself stated in his message," and now he (Mr. Butler) asked whether any sane man believed that the President thought on the 21st of February that Mr. Stanton would yield the office on the ground that he was not governed by the law.

The President had not put it upon any such ground. He had not only put it on the ground that Mr. Stanton was a coward and would not dare to resist; his reliance had been upon the nerve of the man, and not upon his construction of the law. He reminded the Senate that the solemn decision declared that the advice of the Cabinet officers are not the legal vehicle of truth by which facts are to be shown to the Senate.

Mr. EVARTS followed in an argument in support of the proof offered. He said that the line of consideration whether or not the law applied to Secretaries appointed by Mr. Lincoln could not possibly have been the subject of the President's decision in his veto message.

The President had sent in his objections to the bill on constitutional grounds, and had not discussed the question whether the bill included the officers who had received their commissions from President Lincoln or did not include them. The learned manager seemed equally unfortunate in his reference to the conduct of Mr. Stanton on the preliminary proceedings of his suspension under the Tenure of Office act, for no construction could be put on Mr. Stanton's conduct there except that he did not think he was under the act, because he had stated to General Grant that he did not yield to the act, but that he did yield to force. It would be observed that the President had a perfect right to suppose that Mr. Stanton would not attempt to oppose him in the exercise of an accustomed authority as the Chief Executive, unless he (Mr. Stanton) believed it to be unlawful.

If the Executive had been advised by Mr. Stanton on that very point, that he (Mr. Stanton) was not protected by the restrictions of the Civil Tenure bill, then the President had a right to suppose that while the Executive authority given by the Constitution, as it was understood by Mr. Stanton, was not impeded by the operation of the special act of Congress; so Mr. Stanton would, of course, yield to that unimpeded constitutional power.

The Chief Justice—The Chief Justice is of opinion that the testimony is proper to be taken in consideration by the Senate, sitting as a Court of Impeachment, but he is unable to determine to what extent the Senate propose to give to its previous ruling, or how far the principle of that ruling is applicable to the present question. I will, therefore, submit the question to the Senate.

The Vote.

The vote was taken and resulted—yeas, 22; nays, 26, as follows:—

YEAS,—Messrs. Anthony, Bayard, Buckalew, Davis, Dixon, Doolittle, Fessenden, Fowler, Grimes, Henderson, Hendricks, Johnson, McCreery, Patterson (Tenn), Ross, Saulsbury, Sherman, Sprague, Trumbull, Van Winkle, Vickers and Wiley—22.

NAYS.—Messrs. Cameron, Cattell, Chandler, Cole, Conness, Corbett, Cragin, Drake, Edmunds, Ferry, Frelinghuysen, Harlan, Howard, Howe, Morgan, Morrill (Me.), Morrill (Vt.), Patterson (N. H.), Pomeroy, Ramsey, Stewart, Thayer, Tipton, Williams, Wilson and Yates—26.

So the testimony was rejected. Senators Sumner and Conkling were in their seats, and neither voted.

Secretary Welles' Examination Resumed.

The examination of Secretary Welles was again resumed.

Mr. EVARTS—Q. At any of the Cabinet meetings held between the time of the passage of the Civil Tenure act and the removal of Mr. Stanton, did the subject of the public service, as affected by the operations of that act, come up for the consideration of the Cabinet?

Mr. BUTLER—We object.

Mr. EVARTS—It is merely introductory.

Mr. BUTLER—To be answered by yes or no?

Mr. EVARTS—Yes.

Witness (in reply to the question)—Yes.

Mr. EVARTS—Did it come up repeatedly on some two occasions during these considerations and discussions? Was the question of the importance of having some determination, judicial in its character, of the constitutionality of that law considered?

Mr. BUTLER—We object.

Mr. EVARTS—Only to be answered yes or no.

Mr. BUTLER—If it means only to get in yes or no.

Mr. EVARTS—That is all.

Mr. BUTLER—By asking a series of well-contrived questions one may get pretty well at what occurred in the Cabinet, and, therefore, we object as immaterial: and now, we may perhaps as well have the question settled at once. If this line of testimony is immaterial then it is immaterial whether it was considered in the Cabinet. If the determination of the Senate is that what was done in the Cabinet must not come in then these questions are entirely immaterial.

Mr. EVARTS.—Yes, but the honorable manager will be so good as to recollect that the ruling of the Senate has determined that all that properly bears on the question of the intent of the President in making the removal of Mr. Stanton and appointing a Secretary *ad interim*, with a view of raising a judicial question, is admissible, and has been admitted.

Mr. BUTLER—We never have heard that ruling.

Mr. EVARTS—By examining the record you will find it.

Mr. BUTLER—We have examined the record with great care, and we cannot find that in it.

Mr. EVARTS—It's within the memory of the court.

The Chief Justice directed the counsel to reduce the offer of proof in writing. The offer was reduced to writing as follows:—"We offer to prove that at the Cabinet meeting between the passage of the Tenure of Office bill and the order of the 21st of February, 1868, for the removal of Mr. Stanton, on occasions when the condition of the public service, as affected by the operation of that law, came up for the consideration and advice of the Cabinet, that it was considered by the President and Cabinet that a proper regard for the public service made it desirable that, on some proper case, a judicial determination of the constitutionality of the law should be obtained."

Mr. BUTLER objected, and said that the managers understood that the Senate had determined that Cabinet discussions should not be a shield to the President. This was understood to be the broad principle on which the question stood; therefore those attempts to get around that decision, to get in by detail and by retail efforts, which, in their wholesale character, could not be given in, was simply tiring and wearing out the patience of the Senate. He would like to have the thing settled, once for all, whether Cabinet consultations on any subject were to be given in evidence. This particular offer of proof, however, he would leave to the Senate, with a single suggestion. It was offered to show that the Cabinet consulted on the desirability of getting up a case to test the constitutionality of the law; that was either material or immaterial; it might possibly be material in one view, if it was meant to say that the Cabinet consulted upon getting up this case in the mode and manner in which it was brought here. (Laughter.) It was only in that view that it could possibly be material.

The first passage of the Tenure of Office act might possibly have been inadvertence on the part of the Senate. The President then presented it for their opinion, and the Senate passed it again in spite of any constitutional argument against it. The President then removed Mr. Stanton, and again presented the unconstitutionality of the act, and presented also the question whether Mr. Stanton was within it, and the Senate, after argument and deliberation, had solemnly decided that Mr. Stanton was within its provisions, and that the law was constitutional, and now the offer was to show the discussions in the Cabinet upon the constitutionality of the act, and thus to overrule the quadruple opinion solemnly expressed by the Senate on this question. Was such testimony to be admitted?

Mr. EVARTS said that he must be allowed to remark, that if the patience of the Senate, so often referred to by the learned manager, was being taxed, it seemed to be a sort of unilateral patience; the Senate had already ruled that evidence might be admitted to show that the President's action was governed by a desire to raise a question for judicial determination.

About the admission of that evidence there could be no question. The present inquiry was to show that within the period covered by that decision it became apparent to the President, in consultation with the heads of departments, that the operation of that law raised impediments in the public service, and rendered it important as a practical matter that there should be a determination concerning its constitutionality, and that it was desirable that a proper case for such determination should be had. He submitted to the Senate that that was proper testimony.

Senator HENDERSON suggested the following question to the managers:—If the President should be convicted and must be removed from office, if his case shall be deemed to demand such punishment, he may be disqualified to hold and enjoy office under the United States, is not the evidence now offered competent to go before the court in mitigation?

Mr. BUTLER—Mr. President and Senators, I am instructed to answer that, while we do not believe this can be evidence in any event, all evidence in mitigation of punishment must be submitted after verdict and before judgment. Evidence in mitigation is never put in to influence the verdict, but after the verdict is rendered then the subject matter of mitigation, such as good character, or inadvertence, or anything which goes to mitigate the punishment, may be given.

Senator CONKLING asked whether that rule would be applicable before this tribunal?

Mr. BUTLER replied that under the general rule judgment is never given by the House of Peers until demanded by the House of Commons. Whether that rule were applicable here he did not propose now to consider. There was always an appreciable time, in this tribunal and in all others, between the conviction and the giving of judgment, and if any such evidence as that offered could be given at all, it must be given then. He had already stated that he did not believe it to be competent at all, and he was so instructed by his associate managers; but even if it were competent, it would not be competent at this time.

The Evidence Rejected.

The Chief Justice submitted the question to the Senate upon the admissibility of the evidence.

The vote was taken, and resulted—yeas, 19; nays, 30, as follows:—

YEAS.—Messrs. Anthony, Bayard, Buckalew, Davis, Dixon, Doolittle, Fessenden, Fowler, Grimes, Henderson, Hendricks, Johnson, McCreery, Patterson (Tenn.), Ross, Saulsbury, Trumbull, Van Winkle, and Vickers—19.

NAYS.—Messrs. Cameron, Cattell, Chandler, Cole, Conkling, Conness, Corbett, Cragin, Drake, Edmunds, Ferry, Frelinghuysen, Harlan, Howard, Howe, Morgan, Morrill (Me.), Morrill (Vt.), Patterson (N. H.), Pomeroy, Ramsey, Sherman, Sprague, Stewart, Thayer, Tipton, Willey, Williams, Wilson and Yates—30.

So the testimony was excluded.

The Senate then, at five minutes before two o'clock, took a recess for fifteen minutes.

After the recess the examination of Secretary Welles was resumed.

Mr. EVARTS—Mr. Welles, was there within the period embraced in the inquiry in the last question, and at any discussion or deliberations of the Cabinet concerning the operations of the Tenure of Civil Office act, and the requirement of the public service in regard to the same, any suggestion or intimation whatever touching or looking to the vacation of any office by force, or taking possession of the same by force?

Mr. BUTLER objected to the question as immaterial, and it was excluded by the following vote:—

NAYS.—Messrs. Anthony, Bayard, Buckalew, Davis, Dixon, Edmunds, Fessenden, Fowler, Grimes, Hendricks, Johnson, McCreery, Patterson (Tenn.), Ross, Saulsbury, Trumbull, Van Winkle and Vickers—18.

YEAS.—Messrs. Cattell, Chandler, Cole, Conkling, Conness, Corbett, Cragin, Ferry, Frelinghuysen, Harlan, Howard, Howe, Morgan, Morrill (Me.), Morrill (Vt.), Patterson (N. H.), Pomeroy, Ramsey, Sherman, Stewart, Thayer, Tipton, Willey, Williams, Wilson and Yates—26.

Mr. Sumner was present but did not vote.

Mr. FERRY stated that Senator Drake had been called away by illness in his family.

Mr. EVARTS to Mr. Butler—You can cross-examine.

After a few moments consultation among the managers, Mr. Butler proceeded with the cross-examination.

Q. You were asked if you were Secretary of the Navy, if you held under a regular commission, and you gave the date of the commission; you have had no other? A. No, sir, and I am Secretary of the Navy down to to-day.

Q. Has Lorenzo Thomas acted as a member of the Cabinet down to to-day? A. From the time he was appointed he has met with the Cabinet.

Q. Did he meet as a member or an outsider?

Mr. EVARTS—I submit, Mr. Chief Justice, that this is no cross-examination on any matter that the witness has been asked about.

Mr. BUTLER—I will waive it. I won't have a word upon that sir (to the witness). Q. Now I believe you told us something was said between you and the President about the movement of troops; I want to get a little more accurately when that was. In the first place, what day was it? A. It was on the 22d of February: there is no doubt about that; it was not far from twelve o'clock.

Q. I understand you to fix that time of day by something that happened with the Attorney-General; what was that? A. I called on the President on the 22d, about twelve o'clock; the reception of our official business was from eleven to twelve; I left as soon as that was over, and therefore it was a little after twelve o'clock, I suppose; when I called on the President, the Attorney-General was there; while there, the nomination of Mr. Ewing was made out.

Mr. BUTLER, interrupting—Never mind about that.

Witness continuing—The Private Secretary went to take it up, and Mr. Stanbery remarked he must go about twelve o'clock, or had some appointment about twelve o'clock, and it got to be near that time.

Q. I understand you to say he had some appointment in the Supreme Court? A. I wouldn't say what it was.

Q. Did you say so yesterday? A. Perhaps I inferred that it was.

Q. Didn't you so testify yesterday? A. Perhaps I did.

Q. How did you remember to testify on that point yesterday? A. I presumed he had gone to the Supreme Court, as it was twelve o'clock.

Q. Haven't you heard since yesterday that the Supreme Court did not sit on that day? A. No, sir.

Q. Do you know whether they sit on Saturdays or not? A. I do not know, sir.

Q. Did you learn that there were any other movements of troops, except an order to the officers of a regiment to meet General Emory? A. I had heard of two or three things.

Q. I am now speaking of the officers of a regiment. A. I understand.

Q. Any move? A. I heard that the officers of regiments were required to meet General Emory at headquarters on the evening of the 21st, and the officers were called to headquarters. I did not learn whether it was to give them directions about keeping away from a masquerade or going to it. (Laughter.) I did not hear the reason. I heard the facts that they were called that evening at an unusual hour, and called from a party that was on G street—I think G street—for reception.

Q. Now, sir, that was all the movements of troops you spoke of yesterday, was it not? A. I don't recollect what I spoke of.

Q. Had you any other in your mind but that yesterday? A. There were some other movements in my mind, but they were not in connection with General Emory; none were communicated to me whatever; I heard the War Department was lighted up in an unusual manner; I don't know that I stated that to President Johnson, but that was an instance that I had heard of the evening before, and then the movement was to call the officers of one regiment to meet General Emory.

Q. How many officers did you hear were called? A. I didn't hear the number of officers; I heard that General Emory's son and one or two orderlies had been sent to the party, requesting that any officers belonging to the Fifth Regiment should repair forthwith to headquarters; it was thought to be a very unusual movement.

Q. I didn't ask you that; and that was all you stated to the President about the movements of troops? A. I wouldn't say that that was all.

Q. Is it all you remember you did? A. I won't be sure whether I stated to him the fact of the lighting up of the War Department at night, or whether I alluded to the fact of a company or a part of a company.

Mr. BUTLER—I am only asking what you stated, not what you didn't state.

Mr. EVARTS—Your question was whether that was all he stated.

Mr. BUTLER—I am asking him not for what he didn't state, but for what he did state.

Witness—I state what I know.

Mr. BULER—Well, stop there.

Witness—Very well; I stated to him in relation to Gen. Emory; whether I alluded to other facts in my mind I cannot say; the 22d was to be kept as a holiday; it's a half holiday, I believe; the War Department closed the office, but I suppose that is a violation of the law; the law is that the departments are to be kept open every day of the year save the 4th of July and the 25th of December; I am not stating a legal opinion; it is a fact; we didn't keep it as a holiday, such as the 4th of July; I understood that the War Department was closed on that day, but the law is—

Q. I do not want any comparisons between the Navy and the War Departments. I only want the fact that it was closed on that day. Did you inquire whether the officers were called together to inform them that it was to be a holiday? A. I made no inquiry on the subject further than to communicate to the President what I had heard.

Testimony of Edgar T. Welles.

Edgar T. Welles, sworn, on behalf of respondent, and examined by Mr. EVARTS.—Q. You are a son of Mr. Secretary Welles? A. Yes, sir; I am employed in that department as chief clerk.

(Papers shown.) Q. Please look at this paper and say if that is a blank form of the navy agent's commission? A. Yes, sir; the blank form newly issued.

Q. Do you remember that on Friday, the 21st of February, your attention was drawn to some movement or supposed movement connected with the military organization here? A. Yes, sir; it was about five o'clock; I was attending a small reception, and the lady of the house informed me.

Mr. BUTLER—Excuse me. You needn't tell what the lady of the house said.

Mr. EVARTS—It does not prove the truth of the lady's statement.

Mr. BUTLER—As nothing but the truth is put in evidence, we don't want to know what she stated.

Mr. EVARTS—The truth is that he came to this knowledge and she stated it.

Mr. BUTLER—The answer to that is that it is not the proper way to prove the truth of the case by putting in what the lady said to this man; no matter how he got the information, let him give it.

Mr. EVARTS—What information did you get?

Mr. BUTLER—No, sir; what did he give?

Mr. EVARTS—I want to prove that he gave the same that he got.

Mr. BUTLER—I will not object.

Witness—It was that General Emory's son had come there with a message that certain officers who were named should report to headquarters immediately, and also that he had sent his son, requesting that certain officers of the cavalry and artillery should report at headquarters immediately.

Q. After this did you communicate this to your father? A. Yes, sir, I suppose about 10 o'clock the same evening I was sent on a message to the President concerning this by my father, and I went in the evening shortly afterwards;

I couldn't give the time; the President was engaged at dinner, and I did not see him, and reported to my father; nothing further was done that night, that I know of, on the subject.

The managers waived cross-examination.

Mr. EVARTS—We have other evidence by the Secretary of State, Secretry of the Treasury, Secretary of the Interior and the Postmaster-Generhl. We offer them as witnesses to the same points that have been inquired of from Mr. Welles, and that have been covered by the ruling of the court. If objection is made to their examination, then of course they will be covered by the ruling already made.

Senator WILLIAMS—I did not fully understand the last witness. I would like to have him recalled.

The witness was recalled, and took the stand.

Q. I would like to know whether this was told you by this lady or by the officers? A. By the lady.

Mr. EVARTS—We tender these witnesses for examination upon the point that Secretary Welles has been interrogated concerning, and that the rulings of the Senate have covered, if objection is made it must be so considered.

Testimony of the Postmaster-General.

Alexander W. Randall, sworn on behalf of respondent. Examined by Mr. Evarts.

Q. You are now Postmaster-General? A. I am; I was appointed in July, 1866; before that time I was First Assistant Postmaster-General; since the passage of the Civil Tenure act cases have arisen in the postal service in which officers came in question for appointment to duty in the service; I remember the case of Foster Blodgett; he was Postmaster of Augusta, Georgia.

Q. Was there any suspicion of Mr. Blodgett in his office, or in its duties?

Mr. BUTLER—That suspension must be put in evidence by some writing.

Mr. EVARTS—I am asking the question whether there was one. I expect to produce it.

Witness—He was; it was made by me as Postmaster-General; the President had nothing to do with it; he did not know it, not that I am aware of.

Q. Please look at these papers and see whether they are the official papers in the case? They are: I received a complaint against Mr. Blodgett, and it was on that complaint that I acted in suspending him.

Q. The complaint came to you and upon what fact?

Mr. BUTLER, interrupting.—The complaint will speak for itself, let it be produced.

Mr. EVARTS—We ask in what form the complaint came to the witness; is that objected to?

Mr. BUTLER—No; if you mean whether it was in writing or verbal.

Witness—It came in writing and verbally, too.

Mr. EVARTS—Q. On the complaint, verbally and in writing, this action was taken? A. Yes, sir.

Mr. EVARTS—We propose to put these papers in evidence.

Mr. BUTLER asked for the papers and after examining them he inquired from Mr. Evarts whether counsel had the copy of the indictment referred to in the papers.

Mr. EVARTS replied that he presumed the witness had.

Mr. BUTLER—The indictment is all that there is of it. We object to those papers because, very carefully, somebody has left out the only thing that is of any consequence.

Mr. EVARTS (tartly)—Whose case do you refer to?

Mr. BUTLER—Of the man who did it.

Mr. EVARTS—Who is that?

Mr. BUTLER—I don't know.

Mr. EVARTS—Very well.

Mr. BUTLER—This Mr. Blodgett is now attempted to be affected in his character and business, and I feel bound to take care of him. Those papers refer to the evidence of his misconduct, but the evidence itself is not produced. There is not even a recital of it; it is therefore unjust to Mr. Blodgett to put in Mr. Randall's statement, when he has in his department the fact itself—the indictment, which has been by somebody to me unknown carefully kept away.

Mr. EVARTS—Mr. Chief Justice and Senators:—The learned—(correcting himself)—the honorable managers choose sor some reason best known to themselves, to offer in evidence as a part of this examination an act of the President of the United States in the removal of Foster Blodgett. I propose to show what that act was.

Mr. BUTLER—I have not objected, if you will show what that act was in the inculpation of Mr. Blodgett, but I object to these papers.

Mr. EVARTS—I am not inculpating Mr. Blodgett. I am merely proving the act of the executive officer, which you have put in as oral testimony.

Mr. BUTLER—You have put in the fact that he was removed on a complaint verbally and in writing.

Mr. EVARTS—And you say that we must produce the papers, and we do produce them.

Mr. BUTLER.—You do not produce the complaint.

Mr. EVARTS—We will not wrangle about that. I present the official papers connected with the removal of Mr. Blodgett.

Mr. BUTLER—And I object.

Mr. EVARTS—The learned manager treats this as if it affected Mr. Blodgett. I put it in as simply showing an official act on the part of the executive officer. We want to prove what that act was.

Mr. BUTLER—Then produce the whole thing on which it was done.

Mr. EVARTS—If you want the indictment produced, it

certainly may be produced, but that is no legal objection to these papers.

The Chief Justice asked the counsel to put their offer of evidence in writing.

Mr. EVARTS—We offer in evidence the official action of the Post Office Department in the removal of Foster Blodgett, which removal was put in evidence by the managers.

Senator SHERMAN asked for the reading of the papers, so that the Senate might know on what to vote.

The Chief Justice replied that it was not usual to read papers on their simply being offered in evidence until they are actually received.

The offer of evidence was reduced to writing, as follows:—

We offer in evidence the official action of the Post Office Department in the removal of Mr. Blodgett, which removal was put in evidence by oral testimony, by the managers.

The Chief Justice said that he considered the evidence competent.

Mr. BUTLER said that the managers would not object any further, and the papers were thereupon read. The first paper, marked "A," dated January 3, 1868, was a paper from the Post Office Department to the effect that, it appearing from an exemplified copy of a bill of indictment now on file in the department that Foster Blodgett, Postmaster of Augusta, Ga., had been indicted in the United States District Court for the Southern District of Georgia for perjury, he be suspended from office, and that George W. Somers be designated special agent to take charge of the post office at that place. The paper marked "B" is a notification to Mr. Somers of the change in the post office; the paper marked "C" was a letter inclosing blank forms of the bond to be entered into by Mr. Somers; and the paper marked "D" was a copy of a communication to Mr. Blodgett, announcing his suspension for the cause named.

Cross-examined by Mr. BUTLER.—Q. Is the post office at Augusta, Ga., one that is within the appointment of the President, under the law. A. It is; and Mr. Blodgett was appointed by the President some time ago, and his appointment was confirmed by the Senate.

Q. Under what law did you as Postmaster-General suspend him? A. Under the law of necessity, and under a law authorizing me to put a special agent in charge of an office where I am satisfied injustice is being done by the postmaster, and under the practice of the department.

Q. I am asking you about the law now; we will come to the practice by and by. Can you tell us whereabouts that law is to be found? A. No, sir, not without referring to my notes.

Mr. BUTLER—Well, sir, I refer to your notes; of course I do not mean the unwritten law of necessity.

Witness.—The question was whether I should close up the office or remove him; here is a letter which I wrote.

Mr. BUTLER.—I do not care about your letter; I am asking you to refer me to the law?

Witness.—I can make no further inference than I have done, except to give my authority to appoint special agents.

Q. Under what statute did you do this act? A. I do not justify myself under any particular statute, nor under any general statute; I communicated this case to the President; I do not recollect when; sometime after it was done; perhaps a week; I did not take any advice of the President, or consent or order before I made this removal; the verbal complaint was the same as the written complaint against Foster Blodgett; it was the statement that he had been indicted by the district attorney.

Q. Was there any other complaints? A. There was a copy of the indictment.

Q. Was there any other complaints than that? I do not recollect now whether there was or not. The complaint was made to me by the district attorney of the district. He stated to me fact that an indictment was found against Blodgett, but did not ask him to forward me a copy of the indictment: somebody did so; I cannot tell who, unless he did.

Q. Why is not the copy of the indictment here? A. It was not inquired for, and I did not think of it.

Q. Who made the inquiry for the papers? A. One of the attorneys asked me about the case.

Q. You mean one of the counsel for the President? A. Yes; he asked me what was the condition of the case, or what the testimony of Mr. Blodgett meant; I told him, and said that I would furnish all the orders made in the case; I volunteered to furnish the orders; I did not think of the indictment; I would have furnished it to you if you had asked me for it; you did not ask me for any copies.

Q. Had you any other complaint against Foster Blodgett except the fact that he was indicted? A. I do not recollect any now.

Q. Have you any recollection of acting on any other? A. I do not recollect anything else; the papers are quite voluminous.

Q. Was not that an indictment brought by the grand jury of that county against Mr. Blodgett for taking the test oath? A. Yes, sir.

Q. Was there anything else except that he was supposed to have sworn falsely when he took the test oath. A. Not that I remember.

Q. It was for taking the test oath as an officer of the United States, he having been in the Rebellion? A. Yes.

Q. And you removed him for that? A. I did not remove him.

Q. You suspended him. Did you give him a notice that you were going to suspend him? A. No; I directed a notice to be sent to him that he was suspended.

Q. You did not give him any means of defending himself or showing what had happened to him, or how it came in? A. No, sir.

Q. But you suspended him at once? A. I did.

Q. Is there any complaint on your books that he had not properly administered his office? A. I do not recollect any; certainly none on which I acted, that I remember.

Q. He was a competent officer, and was acting properly, and because somebody found an indictment against him for taking the test oath, you suspended him without trial? A. I did not make any such statement.

Q. What part of it is incorrect? A. I cannot tell you about that; if you ask me what there is about the case, I shall be very glad to tell you; ask your questions, and I will answer them.

Q. Did you not suspend an officer, without investigation or trial, simply on the fact that an indictment being found against him of having taken the test oath to qualify himself for that office, and against whom no other complaint was made in your office. A. I do not recollect any now.

Q. And therefore, if you answer the whole question, you will have to answer that you did suspend him. A. I did so suspend him; if there had been a conviction, I should have had him removed.

Q. Did you suspend him under the civil Tenure of Office act? A. No, sir.

Q. You took no notice of it? A. Yes, sir; I took notice of it.

Q. You took no notice of it to act under it? A. I could not act under it.

Q. How many hundreds of men have you appointed who could not take the test oath? A. I do not know of any.

Q. Do you not know that there are men appointed to office who have not taken the test oath? A. As postmaster?

Mr. BUTLER—Yes. A. No, sir; I do not know of one; never one with my consent.

Q. Did you learn who the prosecutors were under this indictment? A. No, sir.

Q. Did you inquire? A. I did not.

Q. Whether they were Rebels or Union men? A. I did not; I did not ask whether it was a prosecution by Rebels; it was none of my business; I simply inquired as to the fact of his having been indicted for perjury.

Q. Will you have the kindness to furnish me with a copy of the indictment, duly certified? A. I will, and of any other complaint I can find in my department against Foster Blodgett.

Mr. CURTIS—We should prefer that the witness furnish it to the court. I suppose that will answer your purpose. (To Mr. Butler.)

Mr. BUTLER—I do not know, sir, that it will.

Mr. CURTIS—It was a mere inadvertance that the indictment was not produced. I wish it now produced.

To the Witness—Will you furnish to the Secretary of the Senate a copy of the indictment?

Mr. BUTLER—I desire to have it furnished to me. I object to anything else being put on the file without my seeing it.

Mr. EVARTS—The only object of having it here is as evidence?

Mr. BUTLER—I cannot tell that it will be. We shall want the Postmaster-General with it.

Mr. EVARTS—You can call him if you want him.

Witness—There is another case.

Mr. BUTLER, interrupting him—Never mind about the other case.

Mr. EVARTS to the witness—Q. I understand from you that your judgment as Postmaster-General was that this suspension should be made? A. Yes, sir.

Q. It occurred not during a recess of the Senate? A. No, sir, it was during a session of the Senate.

Q. So that it is within the Civil Office act? A. So I understand it.

Mr. EVARTS—Q. It was not in a recess, and the Civil Tenure act does not apply to the case. The perjury for which he was indicted as you were informed was in taking the oath for the office which he held. A. Yes, sir.

Mr. BUTLER—I object until we have the indictment.

Mr. EVARTS—You have asked the question whether it was not for taking a false oath that Blodgett was indicted. I ask the witness whether it was not for taking the oath qualifying himself for the office from which he was suspended?

Witness—I so understood.

Senator Sherman Submits a Question.

Senator SHERMAN—I desire to submit this question to this witness, or any other member of the Cabinet. State if after the 2d of March, 1867, the date of the passage of the Tenure of Office act, the question whether the Secretaries appointed by President Lincoln were included within the provisions of that act, came before the Cabinet for discussion, and if so, what opinion was given on that question by members of the Cabinet to the President?

Mr. BINGHAM—I desire to object to that on the ground of incompetency, and because the question comes directly within the ruling of the Senate two or three times made this day.

Mr. BUTLER—The very same question?

Mr. BINGHAM—The same question?

Senator SHERMAN, without noticing the interruption—I should like to have the question put to the Senate.

Senator HOWARD raised a question of order, that the question had been once decided.

The Chief Justice said he thought it undoubtedly a proper question to be put to the witness, but whether it should be answered was for the Senate to judge.

Mr. BUTLER desired to have read the offer of evidence which had been already excluded, and which he held covered exactly the same ground.

Senator SHERMAN—If the Senate will allow me, I will state in a word what the difference is.

Senator CONNESS and others objected.

The offer of proof referred to was as follows:—

"We offer to prove that at the meeting of the Cabinet at which Mr. Stanton was present that while the Tenure of Office bill was before the President for approval, the advice of the Cabinet in reference to the same was asked by the President and given by the Cabinet, and thereupon the question whether Mr. Stanton and the other Secretaries who had received their appointments from Mr. Lincoln were within the restrictions of the President's power of removing from office created by said act was considered, and the opinion was expressed that those Secretaries appointed by Mr. Lincoln were not within such restrictions."

The vote was taken, and resulted—yeas, 20; nays, 26, as follows:—

YEAS.—Messrs. Anthony, Bayard, Buckalew, Davis, Dixon, Doolittle, Fessenden, Fowler, Grimes, Hendricks, Johnson, McCreery, Patterson (Tenn.), Ross, Saulsbury, Sherman, Trumbull, Van Winkle, Vickers and Willey—20.

NAYS.—Messrs. Cameron, Cattell, Chandler, Cole, Conkling, Conness, Corbett, Cragin, Edmunds, Ferry, Frelinghuysen, Harlan, Howard, Howe, Morgan, Morrill (Me.), Morrill (Vt.), Patterson (N. H.), Pomeroy, Ramsey, Stewart, Thayer, Tipton, Williams, Wilson, Yates—26.

So the question was excluded.

Mr. EVARTS then rose and said:—Mr. Chief Justice and Senators:—The counsel for the President are now able to state that evidence on his part is closed as they understand their duty in the case.

The conduct of the proofs, however, have been mainly intrusted to Mr. Stanbery, both on the part of counsel and for personal reasons in reference to his previous knowledge of the controversy, and of the matters to be put in evidence from his official familiarity with the question. Mr. Stanbery's health, we are sorry to say, is still such as to have precluded anything like a serious conference with him since he was taken ill. We submit, therefore, to the Senate that on such consideration it is possible some other proof may need to be offered, but we do not, at present, expect that it will be so.

Senator JOHNSON asked the managers whether they had any proof to offer.

Mr. BUTLER was understood to say that they had none to offer until the defense was through.

Mr. EVARTS—We suppose ourselves to be through. I have only stated that in the absence of Mr. Stanbery some further evidence may need to be offered which we do not at all expect.

The court thereupon at 3·40 adjourned till Monday, at eleven o'clock, and the Senate immediately afterward adjourned till the same time.

PROCEEDINGS OF MONDAY, APRIL 20.

The court was opened in due form at eleven o'clock. All the managers were present.

The Defense Finish their Testimony.

In response to an inquiry from the Chief Justice, Mr. CURTIS stated that the counsel for the President considered their evidence as closed.

Mr. BINGHAM said the managers might desire to place on the stand one or two witnesses who had been subpœnaed early in the trial, but who had not appeared hitherto.

The Chief Justice was understood to say it would be proper to first obtain an order from the Senate.

Mr. BINGHAM—I wish it to be understood that I desire to consult my associates about it first. So far as the order is concerned, I take it for granted that the suggestion made at the time the evidence was closed on the part of the managers, that it would be competent for us, without further order, if those witnesses should appear, to introduce them on the stand, is sufficient, because the Senate will recollect, although I have not myself referred to the journal, that it was stated by my associate manager, Mr. Butler, in the hearing of the Senate, that he considered our case closed, reserving, however, the right of calling some other witnesses, or offering some documentary testimony that might be obtained afterwards.

Senator JOHNSON—I am not sure that I heard correctly the honorable manager. I rise merely for the purpose of inquiring whether the managers desire to have the privilege of offering any evidence after the argument begins?

Mr. BINGHAM—As at present advised, although on that subject, as doubtless known to the honorable Senator, though I am prepared to say that it has happened in this country, I am sure that it did in the case of Justice Chase, such orders have been made. I am not aware that the managers have any desire of that sort. I wish to be understood only by the Senate that there are one or two witnesses, who are deemed important on the part of the managers, who were early subpœnaed on this trial, and although we have not been able yet to find them, we have been advised that they have been in the Capitol for the last forty-eight hours.

Mr. YATES repeated the inquiry whether the managers intended to offer testimony after the argument was commenced.

Mr. BINGHAM—As at present advised, we have no purpose of the sort, since we do not know what may occur in the progress of this trial.

Manager Butler Offers Additional Evidence.

Mr. BUTLER, having come into the Chamber, put in evidence from the journal of Congress of 1774-75, (the first Congress) the commission issued to General Washington, as Commander-in-Chief of the armies of the United Colonies, directing him, among other things, to observe and follow such directions as he should from time to time receive from that Congress, or from a committee of Congress—the commission to continue in force until revoked by that or a future Congress.

Mr. BUTLER said that the point on which he offered it was to show that that was the only form of commission ever prescribed by law in this country to a military officer, and that the commission was "to be held during the pleasure of Congress," instead of, as has since been inserted in commissions, "during the pleasure of the President."

Mr. BUTLER then offered in evidence a letter from the Treasury Department, to show the practice of the government as to the appointing of officers during a recess of the Senate. He said it was one of a series of letters which had not been brought to the attention of the Senate in the schedule already put in evidence.

Mr. EVARTS asked Mr. Butler whether he considered that letter as referring to any point which the counsel for the President had made, either in argument or in evidence, and whether he regarded it simply as the expression of opinion on the part of the Secretary of the Treasury. It was simply an immaterial piece of evidence, and he didn't consider it worth while to discuss it.

Mr. BUTLER—I ask whether you object to it?

Mr. EVARTS—We do not.

Mr. BUTLER—Very well.

Mr. Butler then put in evidence the letter which is dated "Treasury Department, August 23, 1855," signed by James Guthrie, Secretary of the Treasury, acknowledging the receipt of a letter recommending somebody for surveyor of some district in South Carolina, stating that the office not having been filled before the adjournment of the Senate, it must necessarily remain vacant until the next session, but that the recommendation of the writer would receive the respectful consideration of the President.

Mr. BUTLER then stated that the Postmaster-General had not brought to him until this moment the papers which he had called for last Saturday, and he asked some moments to examine them.

After a short interval of time, Postmaster General Randall was again called to the stand, and cross-examined by Mr. BUTLER, as follows:—

Q. Have you a copy of the indictment against Foster Blodgett on file in your office? A. Yes.

Q. When was it made? A. I cannot tell you; I suppose about the time that the original copy was filed.

Q. Have you produced it here? A. No, sir.

Q. What did you do with it? A. It is in the office.

Q. Is the copy of it here? A. Yes.

Q. From where does it come? A. From the Treasury Department.

Q. Why did you not produce the copy from your own office? A. Because that would not prove anything; I could not certify that it was a true copy without having the original.

Q. Have you the original? A. I understand it is here.

Q. Where? A. With some committee; the letter of Mr. McCulloch explains that.

Mr. BUTLER—The letter of Mr. McCulloch explains about the Hopkins case, which I do not want to go into.

Witness—Copies of the indictments in the two cases are fastened together, and the originals are there, as I understand.

Mr. BUTLER then proceeded to read a copy of the indictment found against Foster Blodgett, at the November term, 1867, of the United States District Court for the Southern District of Georgia. It recites that on the 27th

of July, 1866, Foster Blodgett was appointed by the President of the United States to the office of Postmaster of Augusta, Georgia; that after said appointment, and before entering upon the duties of the office, and before being entitled to any salary or emolument therefor, he was required by law to take and subscribe an oath which is set forth in the indictment, to the effect that he had never borne arms against the United States, or given aid or encouragement to the enemies of the United States, and that he took that oath before a magistrate, on the 5th of September, 1866; whereas, in truth and in fact, he had voluntarily borne arms against the United States, and had given aid and encouragement to its enemies, and had accepted and held the office of captain in an artillery company, and that, therefore, Foster Blodgett was guilty of wilfull and corrupt perjury, contrary to the statute, &c.

The cross-examination of Mr. Randall was resumed by Mr. BUTLER. Q. On the notice which you have put in being sent to Mr. Blodgett, did he return an answer, and is this paper the answer or a copy of it? A. These are copies of the papers on file; I can only swear to them as such copies; I believe it is a copy of this answer.

Q. The notice of his suspension is dated the 3d of January? A. Yes, sir, I think so.

Q. On the 10th he returned this answer? A. Yes, sir.

Mr. BUTLER—I propose to offer it in evidence.

Mr. EVARTS objected. He said that the counsel for the President had put in evidence nothing but the official action of the Post Office Department in the suspension of Mr. Blodgett, and that only in answer to an oral statement concerning it, which Mr. Blodgett had himself given. Now the manager brought in the indictment, and having got that in, he claimed the right to repel it. He (Mr. Evarts) submitted to the Senate that the proof was irrelevant.

Mr. BUTLER—Mr. President, the case stands thus. Mr. Foster Blodgett, who is Mayor of the city of Augusta, appointed by General Pope, and is a member of the Constitutional Convention of Georgia—

Mr. EVARTS, interrupting—What does the manager propose?

Mr. BUTLER—I am proposing to put in evidence, and am stating the case. He was a member, I say, of the Constitutional Convention, and an active Union man.

The Chief Justice, interrupting—The honorable manager will please reduce to writing what he proposes to prove.

Mr. BUTLER—I will after I state the grounds of it.

The Chief Justice required the offer of proof to be reduced to writing before argument. He said that the managers must state the nature of the evidence which they proposed to offer, and the Senate would then pass upon the question whether it desired to hear that class of evidence.

Senator JOHNSON to Mr. Butler—Does the manager propose to offer that paper in evidence?

Mr. BUTLER—I do.

Senator JOHNSON—Nothing else?

Mr. BUTLER assented, and said this is the first time in this trial that any counsel has been stopped. It seems, Mr. President, that the same rule should have been applied yesterday as to-day.

The Chief Justice—The honorable manager appears to the Chief Justice to be making a statement of matters which are not in proof, and of which the Senate has as yet heard nothing. The manager states that he intends to put them in evidence. The Chief Justice, therefore, requests that the nature of the evidence which the manager proposes to put before the Senate shall be reduced to writing, as the ordinary offers of proof have been, and then the Senate will judge whether it will receive that class of evidence or not.

Mr. BUTLER—I am trying to state that this was a part of the record produced by the counsel for the President, and I have a right to say that this is the first time that any counsel has been interrupted in this way.

The Chief Justice—Does the honorable manager decline to put his statements in writing?

Mr. BUTLER—I am not declining to put the statement in writing.

The Chief Justice—Then the honorable manager will have the goodness to put it in writing.

Mr. BUTLER—I will do it if I can take sufficient time.

The Chief Justice—Yes, sir.

After some time spent in fixing the form of offer, Mr. BUTLER read it, as follows:—

We offer to show that Foster Blodgett, Mayor of the city of Augusta, Georgia, appointed by General Pope, a member of the Constitutional Convention of Georgia, being, because of his loyalty, obnoxious to some portion of the citizens lately in rebellion against the United States, by the testimony of such citizens was indicted; that said indictment was sent to the Postmaster-General, and that thereupon, without authority of law, he, the Postmaster-General, suspended said Blodgett from office, without any other complaint against him, and without any hearing, and did not send to the Senate the report of his suspension, the office being one within the appointment of the President, with the advice and consent of the Senate. This proof in part by the answer of Mr. Blodgett to the Postmaster-General being a portion of the papers on file in the Post Office Department, on which the action of the Postmaster-General was taken, a portion of which has been put in evidence by the counsel for the President, is to show that Mr. Blodgett has always been friendly and loyal to the United States Government.

Mr. EVARTS—We object to the evidence as being foreign and alien to the case. Foster Blodgett and the evidence concerning him were produced on the part of the managers. On their part the evidence was confined to his oral testimony that he had received a certain commission, under which he held the office of Postmaster in Augusta; that he had been suspended from office by the Executive of the United States, and there was a superadded conclusion that his case had not been sent to the Senate.

In taking up that case the defense offered nothing but the official action of the Post Office Department, coupled with the evidence of the head of the department, that this was his own act, without the previous notice to or subsequent direction of the President of the United States. It appears that the ground of the action was the indictment against Mr. Blodgett. The complaint was made last Saturday that the indictment had not been produced. The managers having now procured it, have put it in evidence, and they now propose to put in evidence Mr. Blodgett's answer to that indictment, or to the accusation made before the Postmaster-General.

Mr. BUTLER—His answer? No; the Postmaster-General's notice; not the indictment.

Mr. EVARTS—His answer to the accusation and the evidence concerning the accusation as placed before the Postmaster-General, I understand.

Mr. BUTLER—Not his answer to the indictment.

Mr. EVARTS—His answer to the indictment, so far as it was the accusation before the Postmaster-General, I understood you to say so, to prove that he was friendly to the United States and that he always had been, notwithstanding he had been a captain in the Rebel army. The honorable manager states that paper is a part of the evidence to sustain Mr. Blodgett's loyalty, and to defeat the accusation against him. Part of it is a letter written by him ten days after his removal, and the honorable manager states to you that that letter is a part of the papers on which the Postmaster-General acted in suspending him from office. How that can be, in the nature of things, it is difficult for me to see. Now, the honorable court can see that this is not evidence introduced by us in disparagement of Foster Blodgett. It is evidence introduced by us to show the action of the Post Office Department in his removal, which removal the managers have put in by oral testimony; and under cover of that the learned manager (Mr. Butler) first asks the introduction of the accusation against Blodgett, and then asks to refute it. If this evidence be rightfully put in on their part, we, of course, will meet it on ours, and we will have an interesting excursion from the impeachment trial of the President to the trial of Mr. Blodgett on a question of loyalty. I am instructed to say that there is a witness in the city who can testify that he was a captain in the Rebel army, and we are ready to go on with that proof if it is deemed desirable.

Mr. BUTLER—Mr. President and Senators, I think now that it will not be out of any order made either to-day or yesterday, or the day before, for me to state the grounds on which I offer this evidence. Foster Blodgett was called here to show that, without this case being referred to the Senate, he had been suspended by the President of the United States, as he supposed and as we supposed, on the 3d of January, 1868, without any violation of his duty so far as his official duties were concerned, and without any justification or conviction of any crime, and that a man was placed in the office as special agent with the same salary and a little more, so that it amounts to a removal and putting another man in the office. Mr. Blodgett testified that up to the time that he testified he had not any knowledge that his case was before the Senate, and he could get no redress. We thought that on the proposition that the President desired to obey the law, except where he wanted to make a case to test the constitutionality of it this was quite pertinent evidence.

The President put forward broadly in his answer that he was exceedingly desirous to obey the laws, especially the Civil Tenure act, except where he wanted to make a case to decide its constitutionality. These facts were put in, and these facts were not in dispute. They call Mr. Postmaster-General Randall on the stand; he produces, and they put in a letter of appointment to one Summers as special agent, with a salary therein set out. And they also put in a letter informing Mr. Blodgett that he had been suspended from office. That letter states precisely that it was on that indictment for perjury—not setting the indictment, so as to leave us to infer that Mr. Foster Blodgett had in some controversy between neighbor and neighbor, or between citizen and citizen, committed wilful and corrupt perjury, and that it was so.

Here was a case in which the Postmaster-General felt compelled instantly to suspend him. It was a case, he said, where the great law of necessity compelled suspension at once. In order to meet that we ask for the indictment, and get at last a copy of it from the Treasury Department. Mr. Foster Blodgett being notified of his suspension on the 3d of January, sends this answer to the Postmaster-General on the 10th, seven days afterwards, not ten days, as the counsel said.

Mr. EVARTS—It is entirely immaterial.

Mr. BUTLER—I do not consider it material, only as a matter of correction. A week afterwards he sent and put on file in the department his justification, saying that this was all a Rebel plot and treason against the United States. Having put that on file it is a part of the case. Now I have not said to the Senate that this paper was one on which Mr. Randall acted in suspending Blodgett, but I do say that it is a paper on which Mr. Randall is acting, in not returning the suspension through the President to the Senate. It may be said that Mr. Randall had no business to return it to the Senate. He had as much business to return it to the Senate as he had to suspend him. We are answered to that that the counsel for the President only put in the official act of the defendant. I had the honor to explain to the Senate,

some days ago, that I understood an official act to be that which it is made a man's duty by law to do. I never understood there was any other official act. I always understood that the acts which the law does not empower a man to do, are officious acts, not official; and I think this the most officious act I have ever known. The case affects the President because he was informed of this suspension after it was made, and he has taken no action upon it; and when we put Mr. Blodgett on the stand to testify that he has been suspended, and that he could not get his case before the Senate, the answer is what? They put in the fact that he was indicted in order to blacken his reputation and to send it out to the country.

Now, gentlemen of the Senate, I never saw Foster Blodgett until the day he was brought to the stand, and I have no interest in him any more than in any other gentlemen of position in the South, but I put it to you if you had been treated in that way, called here as a witness under a summons of the Senate, by the managers of the House of Representative, and if then the President, after refusing you any hearing before the constitutional and legal tribunal, had put in a fact to blacken your character, you would not like to have the privilege of putting in at last your answer? It is part of the record in the case. It is said to be a letter from Mr. Blodgett. True, it is, but it also contains certificates and other papers to establish the facts claimed by him beyond controversy. It is said with a slur, by the counsel for the President, that they have a witness to prove that Blodgett was in the Rebel army.

I do not doubt it; plenty of them, whether he was or not. But what I say is this, that while he was only a captain of a military company, and was called into the service and bound to obey the powers, that he is indicted because he yielded to the powers of the State of Georgia, which compelled him to hold the commission, and he had either got to go into service or lose his life. He may well swear, though he went in as a military captain into the service of the Confederacy, that he did not voluntarily go. He has a right to have his defense placed before the country where he has been traduced. He is a man so well known among his neighbors, that they select him to make constitutional law for them; a man among his neighbors so well known that when the State of Georgia comes in here and demands a place in this Chamber, I have no doubt Foster Blodgett will come and take his place by the side of the noblest of you. Under these circumstances, I feel it my duty to put this testimony before you, and if the objection is merely as to its relevancy, I put it as a matter of justice to the witness, whom the summons of this body has brought here, and who is now being oppressed with the entire Executive power of the United States, and who has been, confessedly, without law, and against right, removed from this office, and being so removed, can get no hearing before this tribunal or any other, because the President controls the District Attorney, and he cannot get a trial down there, nor can he get a trial here.

It appeals to justice. I do not propose to go into any discussion about trying the case of Foster Blodgett. I only propose to put in all the papers that are on file in the Post Office Department, about this case, to bear on my side of the case. The counsel for the President put in such part of the papers as they choose to bear on their side, and I propose to put in such papers as bear on my side of the case, out of the same bundle. They shall not pick out such as please them, without my being permitted to pick out from the same bundle such as please us.

Mr. EVARTS—We put in nothing from the bundle. We put in merely the action of the department; we have as little care for Foster Blodgett as you have. You brought him here, and if his case is to be tried by this court we are ready to try.

Mr. BUTLER asked leave to withdraw the offer of evidence, and to substitute for it the following:—"The defendant's counsel having produced from files of the Post Office Department a part of the record showing the alleged reasons for the suspension of Foster Blodgett as Postmaster of Augusta, Ga., we now propose to give in evidence the residue of said record, including the papers on file in the said case, for the purpose of showing the whole of the case as the same was presented to the Postmaster-General, before and at the time of the suspension of said Blodgett.

Mr. EVARTS renewed his objection to the offer on account of irrelevancy.

The Chief Justice put the question to the Senate whether the evidence should be received, and it was declared without a division that the testimony was excluded.

Mr. BUTLER—Mr. Randall I have been informed that you desire to make some statement. If it does not include anything that the President said or that anybody else said, I have no objection.

Witness—I wish to explain the circumstances under which I made this suspension. A copy of this indictment was brought to me by the District Attorney at or about the same time; soon after it was found he came to me and made a statement of the circumstances under which this was found. Under the office tenure law, as I understood it, the President could have no power to suspend any officer during the session of the Senate. The only thing he could do would be to send up the name of some man in his place, and remove Mr. Blodgett. It occurred to me that this violation of the law by Mr. Blodgett might be merely a technical one, and if it was merely a technical violation of law, if it was true that he was forced into the Rebel service and got out of it as soon as he could, and this violation of the law was merely a technical violation, I did not want him turned out, and for that reason I took the responsibility of doing this thing and putting a temporary agent in until I should ascertain more fully what action to take.

Mr. BUTLER—Why did you not report it to the President for his action? A. I told the President what I had done afterwards.

Q. Why didn't you report it before you undertook to take the responsibility? A. Because the only thing he could do if he did take action was to send in another name and turn this man out.

Q. And you thought you would break the law, as you could do nothing better? A. I did not consider that case at all; I thought if he was an honest man I would take this course, and try to ascertain; I know it is a technical violation of the law, but I did it for the purpose of having an act of justice done him, if he was an honest man.

Q. Was the Senate in session the third day of January? A. I can't tell you whether it was on that day or not.

Q. Hadn't it then adjourned over? A. It might be; I don't remember.

Q. Then the reason that the Senate was in session did not apply? A. I considered that the Senate was in session; I don't recollect whether it was in session on that day.

Q. You deemed it to be in session? A. Yes sir; one explanation I had forgotten; the reason why something further has not been done in the case was I was trying to get some further information on the subject, and then this trouble began, and so the case has lain since.

Q. By trouble you mean the impeachment? (Laughter.) A. Yes sir.

Senator CONNESS submitted the following question to to the witness:—Have you ever taken any step since your act suspending Foster Blodgett in further investigation of his case? A. Yes, sir, in trying to secure further information; there is considerable further information beyond what has been offered and put in.

The witness then left the stand.

Mr. BUTLER—I now offer, Mr. President, an official copy of the order creating the Military Division of the Atlantic and putting General Sherman in charge.

Mr. EVARTS—What does that rebut? We are not aware of any evidence that that rebuts.

Mr. BUTLER—Do you object?

Mr. EVARTS—We do. It is not relevant. I do not recall any evidence that we have given concerning the department.

Mr. BUTLER—It is put in to show the action of the President at the same time that he restored Mr. Thomas. On the same day that he restored General Thomas he took this action, and that date was not fixed until after General Thomas was on the stand. It is to show what was done militarily on the same day.

Mr. EVARTS—We do not still see any connection with General Thomas' testimony. The only connection the honorable manager suggests is, that he learned from Gen. Thomas when he was restored. If he did learn that, it does not connect itself at all with any evidence that we have produced. If it is put in on the ground that it was overlooked, that is another matter. If it is put in in rebuttal, it has no relevancy that we can see.

Mr. BUTLER—When I spoke of learning a thing in the trial of a cause, I meant learning in the course of judicial evidence on the trial, not ascertaining it from the newspapers. They are not always the best source of knowledge. I say that General Thomas testified that on the 13th the President gave the order that he should be restored. Now, then, that was fixed, a thing that was not known, either in the court or in the country, because that was an order given on the 13th to General Grant which was not published. I want to show that on the day before this new military division was made here, and General Sherman ordered here in command, showing the acts of the President at or about the some time, and as the presiding officer has very well told us heretofore, the competency of the acts of a party about the same time being a part of the *resgestœ*, and the Senate has so allowed testimony to come in. It is a part of the thing done by the President on the very day, the 12th of February being the very day before Thomas was restored. I don't mean to say a word on the question of rebutting. I don't understand that that rule belongs here.

The Chief Justice stated that he would put the question to the Senate.

Mr. ANTHONY called for the yeas and nays.

Mr. BUCKALEW asked for the reading of the question put to General Sherman on this question some days since.

Mr. BUTLER—Being a matter that we can refer to in the argument, we withdrew it. I have now, Mr. President and Senators, a list prepared as carefully as we were able in the time given us from the law of the various offices in the United States, who would be affected by the President's claim here, of a right to remove at pleasure; that is to say, if he can remove at pleasure and appoint, *ad interim*. This is a list of officers taken from the law, with their salaries, being a correlative list to that one put in by the counsel, showing the number of officers and the amount of salaries which would be affected by the power of the President.

In order to bring it before the Senate I will read the recapitulation only in the Navy, War, State, Interior, Post Office, Attorney-General's, Treasury, Agricultural and Educational Departments; 41,558 officers; the amount of their emoluments, $31,188,736'87 a year. I suppose that the same course will be taken with this as with the like schedule printed as a part of the case.

The Chief Justice (to the counsel)—Any objection?

Mr. EVARTS (after examination)—We have no objection.

Mr. BUTLER—I have the honor to offer now, from the files of the Senate, the message of Andrew Johnson, nominating Lieutenant-General William T. Sherman to be General by brevet in the Army of the United States, on the 13th of February, 1868.

Mr. EVARTS—Under what article is that?

Mr. BUTLER—That is under the eleventh article and under the tenth.

Mr. EVARTS—The tenth is the speeches.

Mr. BUTLER—I would say the ninth.

Mr. EVARTS—Do you offer this in evidence, on the ground that conferring the brevet on General Sherman was intended to obstruct the Reconstruction acts?

Mr. BUTLER—I have already, in the argument, stated my views on that question, and was replied to, I think, by yourself. I was, I am certain, by Mr. Curtis.

Mr. EVARTS—It does not seem to us to be relevant—it certainly is not rebutting. We have offered no evidence bearing upon the only evidence you offered—the telegrams between Governor Parsons and the President. We have offered no evidence on that subject, and we do not see that this appointment is relevant.

Mr. BUTLER—I offer also the appointment by brevet of Major-General George H. Thomas, first to be Lieutenant-General by brevet, and then General by brevet, and that was done on the same day that Stanton was removed—the 21st of February.

Mr. EVARTS—It is apparent that this does not rebut any evidence that we have offered. It is then offered as evidence in chief. The conferring of brevets upon these two officers is somewhere within the evil intents that are alleged in these articles. In that question there is nothing in this evidence that controverts any such evil intent.

Mr. BUTLER—I wish only to say upon this that we do not understand that this case is to be tried on the question of whether evidence is rebutting or original. We understand that to-day the House of Representatives can bring in new articles, if they choose; but we have a right to put in new evidence anywhere in the case.

Mr. EVARTS—When does our right to give in evidence end?

Mr. BUTLER—When you get through with competent evidence.

Mr. EVARTS—I supposed there was a different rule for us.

Mr. BUTLER—No, sir; when you get through with competent evidence. In many of the States—I know in the State of New Hampshire—the rule of rebutting evidence does not obtain in their courts at all; each party calls such evidence as he chooses up to the hour when he says he has got through, and no injustice is done to anybody.

The Chief Justice put the question to the Senate, and the evidence was rejected by the following vote:—

YEAS,—Messrs. Anthony, Cole, Fessenden, Fowler, Grimes, Henderson, Morton, Ross, Sumner, Tipton, Trumbull, Van Winkle, Willey and Yates—22.

NAYS.—Messrs. Buckalew, Cameron, Cattell, Chandler, Conkling, Conness, Corbett, Cragin, Davis, Dixon, Doolittle, Drake, Edmunds, Ferry, Frelinghuysen, Harlan, Hendricks, Howard, Howe, Johnson, McCreery, Morgan, Morrill (Me.), Morrill (Vt.), Patterson (N. H.), Patterson (Tenn), Pomeroy, Ramsey, Sherman, Sprague, Stewart, Thayer, Vickers, Williams and Wilson—25.

Mr. BUTLER—I have the honor to say that the case on the part of the managers is closed, and all witnesses here subpœnaed at the instance of the managers, may be discharged.

Mr. EVARTS—We are able to make the same announcement in regard to witnesses attending on the part of the defense by subpœna; and this announcement on both sides, we assume to close necessarily any attempt to proceed with evidence.

The Chief Justice—The honorable managers will please proceed with their argument.

Mr. BOUTWELL—I have had the honor to be chosen by the managers to make the first argument on the part of the House of Representatives, and it is very likely that I shall be obliged to occupy the larger part of the day in presenting to the honorable Senate the views that I shall deem it my duty to offer. Under these circumstances I shall have to ask the Senate to do me the favor of adjourning the court until to-morrow morning.

Senator JOHNSON—Mr. Chief Justice, I move that the Senate, sitting as a court, adjourn until to-morrow.

Mr. EVARTS—May I be heard?

Chief Justice—On the motion to adjourn there is no debate allowed.

Mr. JOHNSON withdrew the motion to adjourn.

Mr. EVARTS—I do not rise for the purpose of making the least objection to the request of the honorable managers, but to make a statement to which I beg leave to call the attention of the Senate. Our learned associate, Mr. Stanbery, has, from the outset, been relied upon by the President and by the associate counsel to make the final argument in this cause, and there are many reasons, professional and other, why we should all wish that that purpose should be carried out.

It has been his misfortune, in the midst of this trial, to be taken suddenly ill. This illness, of no great gravity, is yielding to the remedies and to the progress of time, and he is convalescent, so that he now occupies his parlor. The summing up of a cause of this weight, in many respects, considering the amount of testimony and the subject, is, of course, a labor of no ordinary magnitude, physically and otherwise, and Mr. Stanbery is of opinion that he will need an interval of two days, which, added to what he has had in the course of the trial, would probably bring him in condition for the argument, with adequate strength for that purpose.

This might have been left until the day on which he should appear, and then a request made for a day or two's relief in this regard, but it occurred to us to be much fairer to the managers than the interval we propose should be interposed at a time when it would be useful and valuable to them; also, as the proofs are not entirely printed in the proper form of evidence and the voluminous evidence on the subject of appointments, and on the practice of the government are such as to require considerable investigation in order to point out to the Senate the efficacy of what is to be proved, it is therefore our duty now to suggest and accompany it with the suggestion of the managers that until to-morrow should be given for the introduction of the argument on their part, that you would consider this statement that I have made to you, and see whether it is not better in all respects that the matter should be now disposed of, in which the managers will concur, and consider the Providential interference with the President's counsel and his confidential friend and adviser. The suggestion is that an interval of two days should be given, and, as I understand, the managers believe that it is better that it should occur now than later.

Mr. BOUTWELL said he would express no opinion upon the request made by the learned counsel, but he desired that whatever time was given should be granted at once, as he wished to make further and a more careful examination of papers than he had yet been able to do. Under the circumstances, however, he did not feel at liberty to ask the favor on his own account.

Mr. EVARTS made an additional remark that if Mr. Stanbery's expectation to be able to speak should be disappointed, it was a matter of some importance to the defense to be able properly to supply his place.

Mr. JOHNSON moved that when the Senate, sitting as a court, adjourn, it be until Thursday morning next.

Several Senators—"Wednesday."

Mr. JOHNSON—I modify the motion, Mr. Chief Justice, by making it Wednesday.

Mr. DOOLITTLE suggested at twelve o'clock.

Several Senators—"No," "No."

Mr. LOGAN—I wish to make a request. Is this the proper time to do it?

Chief Justice—Yes.

Mr. LOGAN—I desire to make a request of the Senate before it adjourns. Doubtless the adjournment will proceed on the statement of the managers and the counsel. It is this, I had not presumption enough to ask leave of the Senate to speak on the issue presented to the Senate, but I ask that I may be permitted to file to-day a printed argument that I have made as part of the record, without taking up the time of the Senate, inasmuch as the evidence is all in.

Senator STEWART—I move that leave be granted.

Chief Justice—As that would involve a change of the rule, it cannot be done if there is any objection.

Senator BUCKALEW—I object.

Senator JOHNSON—May I ask the Hon. manager if the speech is now in print.

Mr. LOGAN—It is.

Senator WILSON called for the reading of the rule in question. The twenty-first rule was read.

Mr. LOGAN added that his reason for making this request to file it to-day was so that the counsel for the respondent, if they thought it worthy of it, might reply.

The Chief Justice again said that under the rule it could not be considered except by unanimous consent.

Mr. BUTLER—There is no objection.

Mr. DOOLITTLE—I object.

Mr. BUTLER—Before the adjournment of the Senate, I beg to call the attention of the counsel for the respondent to one feature. It so happens that the managers, under the construction given to the rule, are to proceed first. A large mass of testimony has been introduced upon the subject of removals and appointments. I am not informed whether these are special cases on which the counsel for the respondent rely. I think it may be proper for me at this time to ask them whether these are cases on which they purpose to rely as furnishing precedents for the course pursued by the President on the 21st of January.

Mr. ANTHONY—I will make a motion to lie over until to-morrow, that the twenty-first rule be so modified as to allow the honorable manager to present his views in writing.

Ordered, That the honorable manager, Mr. Logan, have leave to file his written argument to-day, and furnish a copy to each of the counsel for the respondent.

Mr. SHERMAN offered the following as an amendment:—

Ordered, That the managers on the part of the House of Representatives, and the counsel for the respondent have leave to file written arguments before the oral argument commences.

Mr. SHERMAN accepted the amendment.

Mr. BUCKALEW again objected, and the rule went over.

Senator Johnson's motion, that when the court adjourn it be to meet on Wednesday next, was agreed to.

The court then, on motion, adjourned,

PROCEEDINGS OF WEDNESDAY, APRIL 22.

The court was opened with the usual formalities at eleven o'clock A. M.

Filing of Written or Printed Arguments.

The Chief Justice stated the first business in order was the consideration of the following order, offered by Senator Sumner:—

Ordered, That the managers on the part of the House of Representatives have leave to file written or printed arguments before the oral argument commences.

Senator VICKERS offered an amendment proposing to allow such of the managers as are not authorized to speak to file written or printed arguments, or make oral addresses, and the counsel for the President to alternate with them in so doing,

Mr. CURTIS—Mr. Chief Justice:—It may have some bearing upon the decision of this proposition if I state what I am now authorized to state, that of the counsel for the President. Mr. Stanbery's indisposition is such that it will be impracticable for him to take any further part in the proceedings.

The substitute was agreed to by the following vote:—

YEAS—Messrs. Buckalew, Cragin, Davis, Doolittle, Edmunds, Fessenden, Frelinghuysen, Grimes, Hendricks, Johnson, McCreery, Morrill (Me.), Morton, Norton, Patterson (N. H.), Patterson (Tenn.), Saulsbury, Sprague, Tipton, Trumbull, Van Winkle, Vickers, Willey, Wilson and Yates—26.

NAYS.—Messrs. Cameron, Cattell, Chandler, Conness, Corbett, Drake, Ferry, Henderson, Howard, Howe, Morgan, Morrill (Vt.), Pomeroy, Ramsey, Ross, Sherman, Stewart, Sumner, Thayer and Williams—20.

The question recurring on the order as amended, it was lost by the following vote:—

YEAS.—Messrs. Buckalew, Cragin, Davis, Doolittle, Fowler, Hendricks, Johnson, McCreery, Morton, Norton, Patterson (N. H.), Patterson (Tenn.), Saulsbury, Sumner, Tipton, Trumbull, Van Winkle, Vickers, Willey, Wilson and Yates—20.

NAYS.—Messrs. Cameron, Cattell, Chandler, Conness, Corbett, Drake, Edmunds, Ferry, Fessenden, Frelinghuysen, Grimes, Henderson, Howard, Howe, Morgan, Morrill (Me.), Morrill (Vt.), Pomeroy, Ramsey, Ross, Sherman, Sprague, Stewart, Thayer and Williams—26.

Mr. STEVENS—Mr. President, I desire to make an inquiry, and that is, whether there is any impropriety in the managers publishing short arguments? After the motion made here on Saturday, some few of us, I among the rest, commenced to write out a short argument, which I expect to finish by to-night, which, if the first order had passed, I should have filed. I do not know that there is any impropriety in it except that it will not go into the proceedings. I do not like to do anything improper, and hence I make the inquiry.

Senator FERRY—Mr. President, I would inquire whether it would be in order to move the original order, on which we have taken no vote.

The Chief Justice—It would not, as the Chief Justice understands the matter has been disposed of.

The reading of the order submitted by Senator Stewart some days ago, was called for, and it was read, as follows:—

That one of the managers on the part of the House be permitted to file his printed argument before the adjournment to-day, and that after an oral opening by a manager, and the reply of one of the President's counsel, shall have the privilege of filing a written or of making an oral address, to be followed by the closing speech of one of the President's counsel, and the final reply of a manager, under the existing rule.

The Chief Justice said it could be considered by unanimous consent.

No objection was made.

Mr. CONNESS offered the following as a substitute: That such of the managers and counsel of the President as may chose to do so may file their arguments on or before April 24.

Mr. SUMNER—That is right.

Mr. BUCKALEW moved to lay the order and the amendment on the table.

Rejected without a division.

Senator Conness' amendment was rejected by the following vote.

YEAS—Messrs. Cameron, Cattell, Chandler, Conkling, Conness, Corbett, Cragin, Drake, Ferry, Henderson, Howard, Morrill (Vt.), Patterson (N. H.), Pomeroy, Ramsey, Sherman, Stewart, Sumner, Thayer, Tipton, Willey, Williams, Wilson and Yates—24.

NAYS—Messrs. Anthony, Bayard, Buckalew, Davis, Dixon, Doolittle, Edmunds, Fessenden, Fowler, Frelinghuysen, Grimes, Hendricks, Howe, Johnson, McCreery, Morgan, Morton, Norton, Patterson (Tenn.), Ross, Saulsbury, Sprague, Trumbull, Van Winkle and Vickers—25.

The question recurred on the order offered by Senator Stewart, and

On motion of Senator JOHNSON, it was amended by striking out the word "one" in the first line and inserting "two."

Mr. Manager WILLIAMS suggested that the order would leave the matter substantially as it stood before, as but one of the managers was prepared with a printed argument. If it was amended so as to allow them to file written or printed arguments, it would be satisfactory.

On motion of Senator SHERMAN, the order was so modified.

Senator GRIMES inquired how it was possible for the counsel for the respondent, if the printed or written arguments were filed to-day, to examine them so as to reply to-morrow morning.

Senator HOWARD—It is not necessary.

Mr. CORBETT moved to strike out the word "another" and insert the word "two" before the words "of the President's counsel."

Mr. EVARTS—Mr. Chief Justice and Senators:— Will you allow me to say one word on this question? As the rule now stands, two of the President's counsel are permitted to make oral arguments. By the amendment, without the modification of inserting "two" instead of "another," we understand that three of the President's counsel will be enabled to make oral arguments to the Senate. That is as many as under the circumstances could wish, or be enabled to do so.

At the suggestion of Mr. Trumbull, Senator CORBETT withdrew his amendment.

Mr. STEVENS—Mr. President, this would embarrass the managers very much. Would it not do so that the managers and counsel of the President may file written or printed arguments between this time and the meeting of the court to-morrow? That would relieve us from the difficulty.

Senator CONNESS, at the instance, he said, of one of the managers, moved to amend by striking out the words, "before the adjournment to-day," and inserting, "before noon to-morrow." Agreed to.

Senator HENDERSON offered the following substitute:—Provided, That all the managers not delivering oral arguments, may be permitted to file written arguments at any time before the 24th instant, and the counsel for the President not making oral arguments may file written arguments at any time before eleven o'clock on Monday, the 27th instant.

Senator THAYER moved to lay the whole subject on the table. Rejected. Yeas, 13; nays, 37.

Mr. NELSON, of the President's counsel, said he had felt an irresistible repugnance to say anything to the Senate on this subject. He was averse to addressing an unwilling audience—the Senate having indicated by rule that they were unwilling to allow any further argument thereof. The President's counsel's, by consent of the rest, had assumed the direction of the case, and to them had been committed the task of arguing it. As the probabilities were now, however, it was not likely that Mr. Stanbery would be able to make the final argument, and he (Mr. Nelson) would ask permission to address the Senate on the side of the President.

He thought the rule should be so enlarged as to allow the privilege to all of the President's counsel who chose to exercise it. Under the circumstances, they had not prepared written arguments, and it was too late now to do so. He was prepared from memoranda, however, to make an oral argument, and hoped he would be allowed to do so. He had lived too long to be animated by any spirit of idle vanity in making this request. He was aware that sometimes more was gained by silence than by speech. He was satisfied that the President desired that the case should be argued by all the counsel, and he had no objections that the same privileges should be extended to all the managers. In the case of the impeachment of Judge Chase, six managers and five counsel were heard. He trusted that in such a momentous case, no limit would be placed on the argument.

Senator HOWARD inquired whether the proper construction of the amendment of the Senator from Missouri (Mr. Henderson), would not leave the door open and repeal the twenty-first rule; in short, whether it would not allow all the counsel on the part of the accused and all the managers, should they see fit, to make oral arguments on the final summing up.

Senator CONNESS proposed, in order to make it entirely clear, to insert in the amendment the words, "subject to the twenty-first rule."

The proposition was agreed to.

Senator TRUMBULL moved the following as a substitute:—

Ordered, That as many managers and of counsel for the President as desire to do so be permitted to file arguments or to address the Senate orally.

The substitute was agreed to. Yeas, 29; nays, 20, as follows:—

YEAS.—Messrs. Anthony, Buckalew, Conkling, Cragin, Davis, Doolittle, Edmunds, Ferry, Fessenden, Fowler, Grimes, Henderson, Johnson, McCreery, Morrill (Me.), Norton, Patterson (N. H.), Patterson (Tenn.), Ramsey, Saulsbury, Sherman, Sprague, Tipton, Trumbull, Van Winkle, Vickers, Willey and Yates—29.

NAYS.—Messrs. Cameron, Cattell, Chandler, Conness, Corbett, Dixon, Drake, Frelinghuysen, Harlan, Howard, Howe, Morgan, Morrill (Vt.), Morton, Pomeroy, Ross, Stewart, Sumner, Thayer, and Williams—20.

Senator BUCKALEW moved to amend the substitute by adding to it the following words:—"But the concluding oral argument shall be made by one manager, as provided by the twenty-first rule."

Various other amendments were offered and voted down, and finally, after nearly two hours spent in attempts to settle the question, the substitute offered by Senator Trumbull, as amended on motion of Senator Buckalew was adopted instead of the original order.

Mr. Manager BOUTWELL, then, at ten minutes before one o'clock, proceeded to make his argument to the Senate.

Manager Boutwell's Argument.

Mr. President, Senators:—The importance of this occasion is due to the unexampled circumstance that the Chief Magistrate of the principal republic of the world is on trial upon the charge that he is guilty of high crimes and misdemeanors in office. The solemnity of this occasion is due to the circumstance that this trial is a new test of our public national virtue and also of the strength and vigor of popular government. The trial of a great criminal is not an extraordinary event—even when followed by conviction and the severest penalty known to the laws. This respondent is not to be deprived of life, liberty, or property. The object of this proceeding is not the punishment of the offender but the safety of the State. As the daily life of the wise and just magistrate is an example for good, cheering, encouraging, and strengthening all others, so the trial and conviction of a dishonest or an unfaithful officer is a warning to all men, especially to such as occupy places of public trust.

The issues of record between the House of Representatives and Andrew Johnson, President of the United States, are technical and limited. We have met the issues, and, as we believe, maintained the cause of the House of Representatives by evidence, direct, clear and conclusive. Those issues require you to ascertain and declare whether Andrew Johnson, President of the United States, is guilty of high crimes and misdemeanors as set forth in the several articles of impeachment exhibited against him, and especially whether he has violated the laws or the Constitution of the country in the attempt which he made on the 21st of February last, to remove Edwin M. Stanton from the office of Secretary for the Department of War, and to appoint Lorenzo Thomas Secretary of War ad interim.

These are the issues disclosed by the record. They appear in the statement to be limited in their nature and character; but your final action thereon involves and settles questions of public policy of greater magnitude than any considered in the political or judicial proceedings of the country since the adoption of the Constitution.

Mr. Johnson attempts to defend his conduct in the matter of the removal of Mr. Stanton by an assertion of "the power at any and all times of removing from office all executive officers for cause to be judged of by the President alone."

This claim manifestly extends to the officers of the army and of the navy, of the civil and the diplomatic service. In this claim he assumes and demands for himself and for all his successors absolute control over the vast and yearly increasing patronage of this government. This claim has never before been asserted, and surely it has never been sanctioned; nor is there a law or usage which furnishes any ground for justification, even the least.

Heretofore the Senate has always been consulted in regard to appointments, and during the sessions of the Senate it has always been consulted in regard to removals from office. The claim now made, if sanctioned, strips the Senate of all practical power in the premises, and leaves the patronage of office, the revenues and expenditures of the country in the hands of the President alone. Who does not see that the powers of the Senate to act upon and confirm a nomination is a barren power, as a means of protecting the public interests, if the person so confirmed may be removed from his office at once or without the advice and consent of the Senate? If this claim shall be conceded the President is clothed with power to remove every person who refuses to become his instrument.

An evil-minded President may remove all loyal and patriotic officers from the army, the navy, the civil and the diplomatic service, and nominate only his adherents and friends. None but his friends can remain in office; none but his friends can be appointed to office. What security remains for the fidelity of the army and the navy? What security for the collection of the public revenues? What accountability remains in any branch of the public service? Every public officer is henceforth a mere dependent upon the Executive. Heretofore the Senate could say to the President you shall not remove a faithful, honest public officer. This power the Senate has possessed and exercised for nearly eighty years, under and by virtue of express authority granted in the Constitution. Is this authority to be surrendered? Is this power of the Senate, this prerogative we may almost call it, to be abandoned? Has the country, has the Senate, in the exercise of its legislative, executive, or judicial functions, fully considered these broader and graver issues touching and affecting vitally our institutions and system of government?

The House of Representatives has brought Andrew Johnson, President of the United States, to the bar of this august tribunal, and has here charged him with high crimes and misdemeanors in office. He meets the charge by denying and assailing the ancient, undoubted, constitutional powers of the Senate. This is the grave, national, historical, constitutional issue. When you decide the issues of record, which appear narrow and technical, you decide these greater issues also.

The managers on the part of the House of Representatives, as time and their abilities may permit, intend to deal with their criminal and with these, his crimes, and also to examine the constitutional powers of the President and of the Senate. I shall first invite your attention, Senators, to the last-mentioned topics.

It is necessary, in this discussion, to consider the character of the government, and especially the distribution of powers and the limitations placed by the Constitution upon the executive, judicial, and legislative departments.

The tenth amendment to the Constitution provides that "the powers not delegated to the United States by the Constitution, nor prohibited by it to the States, are reserved to the States respectively, or to the people."

This provision is not to be so construed as to defeat the objects for which the Constitution itself was established; and it follows, necessarily, that the three departments of the government possess sufficient power, collectively, to accomplish those objects.

It will be seen from an examination of the grants of power made to the several departments of the government that there is a difference in the phraseology employed, and that the legislative branch alone is intrusted with discretionary authority. The first section of the first article provides that "all legislative powers *herein granted* shall be vested in a Congress of the United States, which shall consist of a Senate and House of Representatives."

The first section of the second article provides that "the executive power shall be vested in a President of the United States of America;" and the first section of the third article provides that "the judicial power of the United States shall be vested in one Supreme Court, and in such inferior courts as the Congress may, from time to time, ordain and establish." The words "herein granted," as used in the first section of the first article of the Constitution, are of themselves words of limitation upon the legislative powers of Congress, confining those powers within the authority expressed in the Constitution. The absence of those words in the provisions relating to the executive and judicial departments do not, as might at first be supposed, justify the inference that unlimited authority is conferred upon those departments. An examination of the Constitution shows that the executive and judicial departments have no inherent vigor by which, under the Constitution, they are enabled to perform the functions delegated to them, while the legislative department, in noticeable contrast, is clothed with authority "to make all laws which shall be necessary and proper for carrying into execution the forogoing powers, *and all other powers vested by this Constitution in the government of the United Statts, or any department or officer thereof.*"

By virtue of this provision the Constitution devolves upon Congress the duty of providing by legislation for the full execution, not only of the powers vested in Congress, but also of providing by legislation for the execution of those powers which, by the Constitution are vested in the executive and judicial departments. The legislative department has original power derived from the Constitution, by which it can set and keep itself in motion as a branch of the government, while the executive and judicial departments have no self-executing constitutional capacity, but are constantly dependent upon the legislative department. Nor does it follow, as might upon slight attention be assumed, that the executive power given to the President is an unlimited power, or that it answers or corresponds to the powers which have been or may be exercised by the executive of any other government. The President of the United States is not endowed by the Constitution with the executive power which was possessed by Henry VIII or Queen Elizabeth, or by any ruler in any other country or time, but only with the power expressly granted to him by the Constitution, and with such other powers as have been conferred upon him by Congress, for the purpose of carrying into effect the powers which are granted to the President by the Constitution. Hence it may be asserted that whenever the President attempts to exercise any power, he must, if his right be questioned, find a specific authority in the Constitution or laws. By the Constitution he is Commander-in-Chief of the army and navy; but it is for Congress to decide, in the first place, whether there shall be an army or navy, and the President must command the army or navy as it is created by Congress, and subject, as is every other officer of the army, to such rules and regulations as Congress may from time to time establish.

The President "may require the opinion in writing of the principal officer in each of the executive departments upon any subject relating to the duties of their respective offices," but the executive offices themselves are created by Congress, and the duties of each officer are prescribed by law. In fine, the power to set the government in motion, and to keep it in motion is lodged exclusively in Congress, under the provisions of the Constitution.

By our system of government the sovereignty is, in the people of the United States, and that sovereignty is fully expressed in the preamble to the Constitution. By the Constitution the people have vested discretionary power—limited, it is true—in the Congress of the United States, while they have denied to the executive and judicial departments all discretionary or implied power whatever.

The nature and extent of the powers conferred by the Constitution upon Congress have been clearly and fully set forth by the Supreme Court. (McCulloch vs. the State of Maryland, 4th Wheaton, pp. 409 and 420.) The court, in speaking of the power of Congress, says:—"The government which has a right to do an act, and has imposed on it the duty of performing that act, must, according to the dictates of reason, be allowed to select the means." Again, they say:—"We admit, as all must admit, that the powers of the government are limited, and that these limits are not to be transcended; but we think the sound construction of the Constitution must allow to the *National Legislature* that discretion, with respect to the means by which the powers it confers are to be carried into execution, which will enable that body to perform the high duties assigned to it in the manner most beneficial to the people.

If the thing be legitimate, let it be within the scope of the Constitution, and all means which are appropriate, which are plainly adapted to the end, which are not prohibited, and consistent with the letter and spirit of the Constitution, are constitutional."

It is also worthy of remark, in this connection, that the article which confers legislative powers upon the Congress of the United States declares that *all* legislative powers herein granted, that is, granted in the Constitution, shall be vested in the Congress of the United States; while in the section relating to the powers of the President it is declared that *the* executive power shall be vested in a President of the United States of America. The inference from this distinction is in harmony with what has been previously stated. "The executive power" spoken of is that which is conferred upon the President by the Constitution, and is limited by the terms of the Constitution, and it must be exercised in the manner prescribed by the Constitution. The words used are to be interpreted according to their ordinary meaning.

It is also worthy of remark that the Constitution, in terms, denies to Congress various legislative powers specified. It denies also to the United States various powers, and various powers enumerated are likewise denied to the States. There is but one denial of power to the President, and that is a limitation of an express power granted. The single instance of a denial of power to the President is in that provision of the Constitution wherein he is authorized "to grant reprieves and pardons for offenses against the United States, except in cases of impeachment." As the powers granted to the President are specified, and as he takes nothing by implication or inference, there was no occasion to enumerate or recite powers not delegated to him. As the Constitution clothes Congress with powers of legislation which are ample for all the necessities of national life, wherein there is opportunity for the exercise of a wide discretion, it was necessary to specify such powers as are prohibited to Congress. The powers of Congress are ascertained by considering as well what is prohibited and what is granted: while the powers of the Executive are to be ascertained clearly and fully by what is granted. Where there is nothing left to inference, implication, or discretion, there is no necessity for clauses or provisions of inhibition. In the single case of the grant of the full power of pardon to the President, a power unlimited in its very nature, the denial of the power to pardon in case of impeachment became necessary. This example fully illustrates and establishes the position to which I now ask your assent. If this view be correct it follows necessarily, as has been before stated, that the President, acting under the Constitution, can exercise those powers only which are specifically conferred upon him, and can take nothing by construction, by implication, or by what is sometimes termed the necessity of the case.

But in every government there should be in its Constitution capacity to adapt the administration of affairs to the changing conditions of national life. In the Government of the United States this capacity is found in Congress, in virtue of the provision already quoted, by which Congress is authorized "to make all laws which shall be necessary and proper for carrying into execution the foregoing powers, (*i. e.*, the powers given to Congress), and all other powers vested by this Constitution in the Government of the United States, or in any department or officer thereof."

It is made the duty of the President, "from time to time, to give to the Congress information of the state of the Union, and recommend to their consideration such measures as he shall judge necessary and expedient."

Provision is also made in the Constitution for his co-operation in the enactment of laws. Thus it is in his power to lay before Congress the reasons which, in his opinion, may at any time exist for legislative action in aid of the executive powers conferred by the Constitution upon the President; and under the ample legislative powers secured to Congress by the provision already quoted, there is no reason in the nature of the government why the constitutional and lawful powers of the Executive may not be made adequate to every emergency of the country. In fine, the President may be said to be governed by the principles which govern the judge in a court of law. He must take the law and administer it as he finds it, without any inquiry on his part as to the wisdom of the legislation. So the President, with reference to the measure of his own powers, must take the Constitution and the laws of the country as they are, and be governed strictly by them. If, in any particular, by implication or construction, he assumes and exercises authority not granted to him by the Constitution or the laws, he violates his oath of office, by which, under the Constitution, it is made his duty "to take care that the laws be faithfully executed," which implies necessarily that he can go into no inquiry as to whether the laws are expedient or otherwise; nor is it within his province, in the execution of the law, to consider whether it is constitutional. In his communications to Congress he may consider and discuss the constitutionality of existing or proposed legislation, and when a bill is passed by the two Houses and submitted to him for approval, he may, if in his opinion the same is unconstitutional, return it to the House in which it originated, with his reasons. In the performance of these duties he exhausts his constitutional power in the work of legislation. If, notwithstanding his objections, Congress, by a two-thirds majority in each House, shall pass the bill, it is then the duty of the President to obey and execute it, as it is his duty to obey and execute all laws which he or his predecessors may have approved.

If a law be in fact unconstitutional it may be repealed by Congress, or it may, when a case duly arises, be annulled in its unconstitutional features by the Supreme Court of the United States. The repeal of the law is a legislative act; the declaration by the court that it is unconstitutional is a judicial act; but the power to repeal, or to annul, or to set aside a law of the United States, is in no aspect of the case an executive power. It is made the duty of the Executive to take care that the laws be faithfully executed—an injunction wholly inconsistent with the theory that it is in the power of the executive to repeal, or annul, or dispense with the laws of the land. To the President in the performance of his executive duties all laws are alike. He can enter into no inquiry as to their expediency or constitutionality. All laws are presumed to be constitutional, and whether in fact constitutional or not, it is the duty of the Executive so to regard them while they have the form of law. When a statute is repealed for its unconstitutionality, or for any other reason, it ceases to be a law in form and in fact. When a statute is annulled in whole or in part by the opinion of a competent judicial tribunal, from that moment it ceases to be law. But the respondent and the counsel for the respondent will seek in vain for any authority or color of authority in the Constitution or the laws of the country by which the President is clothed with the power to make any distinction upon his own judgment, or upon the judgment of any friends or advisers, whether private or official persons, between the several statutes of the country, each and every one of which he is, by the Constitution and by his oath of office, required faithfully to execute. Hence it follows that the crime of the President is not, either in fact or as set forth in the articles of impeachment, that he has violated a constitutional law; but his crime is that he has violated a law, and in his defense no inquiry can be made whether the law is constitutional; for inasmuch as he has no constitutional power to inquire for himself whether the law was constitutional or not, so it is no excuse for him that he did unlawfully so inquire and came to the conclusion that the law was unconstitutional.

It follows, from the authorities already quoted, and the positions founded thereon, that there can be no inquiry here and now by this tribunal whether the act in question —the act entitled "An act regulating the tenure of certain civil offices"—is in fact constitutional or not. It was and is the law of the land. It was enacted by a strict adherence to constitutional forms. It was, and is, binding upon all the officers and departments of the government. The Senate, for the purpose of deciding whether the respondent is innocent or guilty, can enter into no inquiry as to the constitutionality of the act, which it was the President's duty to execute, and which, upon his own answer, and by repeated official confessions and admissions, he intentionally, wilfully, deliberately set aside and violated.

If the President, in the discharge of his duty "to take care that the laws be faithfully executed," may inquire whether the laws are constitutional, and execute those only which he believes to be so, then, for the purposes of government, his will or opinion is substituted for the action of the law-making power, and the government is no longer a government of laws, but the government of one man. This is also true, if, when arraigned, he may justify by showing that he has acted upon advice that the law was unconstitutional. Further, if the Senate, sitting for the trial of the President, may inquire and decide whether the law is in fact constitutional, and convict the President if he has violated an act believed to be constitutional, and acquit him if the Senate think the law unconstitutional, then the President is in fact tried for his judgment, to be acquitted if, in the opinion of the Senate it

was a correct judgment, and convicted if, in the opinion of the Senate, his judgment was erroneous. This doctrine offends every principle of justice. His offense is, that he intentionally violated a law. Knowing its terms and requirements, he disregarded them.

With deference I maintain still further, that it is not the right of any Senator in this trial to be governed by any opinion he may entertain of the constitutionality or expediency of the law in question. For the purposes of this trial the statute which the President, upon his own confession, has repeatedly violated is the law of the land. His crime is, that he has violated the law. It has not been repealed by Congress; it has not been annulled by the Supreme Court; it stands upon the statute-book as the law; and for the purposes of this trial it is to be treated by every Senator as a constitutional law. Otherwise it follows that the President of the United States, supported by a minority exceeding by one a third of this Senate, may set aside, disregard, and violate all the laws of the land. It is nothing to this respondent, it is nothing to this Senate, sitting here as a tribunal to try and judge this respondent, that the Senators participated in the passage of the act, or that the respondent, in the exercise of a constitutional power, returned the bill to the Senate with his objections thereto. The act itself is as binding, is as constitutional, is as sacred in the eye of the Constitution as the acts that were passed at the first session of the first Congress. If the President may refuse to execute a law because in his opinion it is unconstitutional, or for the reason that, in the judgment of his friends and advisers, it is, unconstitutional, then he and his successors in office may refuse to execute any statute the constitutionality of which has not been affirmatively settled by the Supreme Court of the United States. If a minority, exceeding one-third of this Senate by one, may relieve the President from all responsibility for this violation of his oath of office, because they concur with him in the opinion that this legislation is either unconstitutional or of doubtful constitutionality, then there is no security for the execution of the laws. The constitutional injunction upon the President is to take care that the laws be faithfully executed; and upon him no power whatsoever is conferred by the Constitution to inquire whether the law that he is charged to execute is or is not constitutional. The constitutional injunction upon you, in your present capacity, is to hold the respondent faithfully to the execution of the constitutional trusts and duties imposed upon him. If he wilfully disregards the obligation resting upon him, to take care that the laws be faithfully executed, then the constitutional duty imposed upon you is to convict him of the crime of wilfully disregarding the laws of the land and violating his oath of office.

I indulge, Senators, in great plainness of speech, and pursue a line of remark which, were the subject less important or the duty resting upon us less solemn, I should studiously avoid. But I speak with every feeling and sentiment of respect for this body and this place of which my nature is capable. In my boyhood, from the gallery of the old Chamber of the Senate, I looked, not with admiration merely, but with something of awe upon the men of that generation who were then in the seats which you now fill. Time and experience may have modified and chastened those impressions, but they are not, they can not, be obliterated. They will remain with me while life remains. But, with my convictions of my own duty, with my convictions of your duty, with my convictions of the danger, the imminent peril to our country if you should not render a judgment of guilty against this respondent, I have no alternative but to speak with all the plainness and directness which the most earnest convictions of the truth of what I utter can inspire.

Nor can the President prove or plead the motive by which he professes to have been governed in his violation of the laws of the country. Where a positive specific duty is imposed upon a public officer, his motives cannot be good if he wilfully neglects or refuses to discharge his duty in the manner in which it is imposed upon him. In other words, it is not possible for a public officer, and especially the President of the United States, who is under a special constitutional injunction to discharge his duty faithfully, to have any motive except a bad motive, if he wilfully violates his duty. A judge, to be sure, in the exercise of a discretionary power, as in imposing a sentence upon a criminal where the penalty is not specific, may err in the exercise of that discretion and plead properly his good motives in the discharge of his duty. That is, he may say that he intended, under the law, to impose a proper penalty; and inasmuch as that was his intention, though all other men may think that the penalty was either insufficient or excessive, he is fully justified by his motives.

So, the President, having vested in him discretionary power in regard to granting pardons, might, if arraigned for the improper exercise of that power in a particular case, plead and prove his good motives, although his action might be universally condemned as improper or unwise in that particular case. But the circumstances of this respondent are wholly different. The law which, as he admits, he has intentionally and deliberately violated, was mandatory upon him, and left in his hands no discretion as to whether he would, in a given case, execute it or not.

A public officer can neither plead nor prove good motives to refute or control his own admission that he has intentionally violated a public law.

Take the case of the President; his oath is: "I do solemnly swear that I will faithfully execute the office of President of the United States, and will, to the best of my ability, preserve, protect and defend the Constitution of the

United States." One of the provisions of that Constitution is, that the President shall "take care that the laws be faithfully executed." In this injunction there are no qualifying words. It is made his duty to take care that the *laws, the laws*, be faithfully executed. A law is well defined to be "a rule laid, set, or established by the law-making power of the country." It is of such rules that the Constitution speaks in this injunction to the President; and in obedience to that injunction, and with reference to his duty under his oath to take care that the laws be faithfully executed, he can enter into no inquiry as to whether those laws are expedient, or constitutional, or otherwise. And inasmuch as it is not possible for him, under the Constitution, to enter lawfully into such inquiry, it is alike impossible for him to plead or to prove that, having entered into such inquiry, which was in itself unlawful, he was governed by a good motive in the result which he reached, and in his action thereupon. Having no right to inquire whether the laws were expedient or constitutional, or otherwise, if he did so inquire, and if upon such inquiry he came to the conclusion that, for any reason, he would not execute the law, according to the terms of the law, then he wilfully violates his oath of office and the Constitution of the United States. The necessary, the inevitable presumption in law is, that he acted under the influence of bad motives in so doing, and no evidence can be introduced controlling or coloring in any degree this necessary presumption of the law.

Having, therefore, no right to entertain any motive contrary to his constitutional obligation to execute the laws, he cannot plead his motive. Inasmuch as he can neither plead nor prove his motive, the presumption of the law must remain that in violating his oath of office and the Constitution of the United States he was influenced by a bad motive. The magistrate who wilfully breaks the laws, in violation of his oath to execute them, insults and outrages the common sense and the common nature of his countrymen when he asserts that their laws are so bad that they deserve to be broken. This is the language of a defiant usurper, of a man who has surrendered himself to the counsel and control of the enemies of his country.

If a President, believing a law to be unconstitutional, may refuse to execute it, then your laws for the reconstruction of the Southern States, your laws for the collection of the internal revenue, your laws for the collection of custom house duties are dependent, for their execution, upon the individual opinion of the President as to whether they are constitutional or not; and if these laws are so dependent, all other laws are equally dependent upon the opinion of the Executive. Hence it follows, that whatever the legislation of Congress may be, the laws of the country are to be executed only so far as the President believes them to be constitutional. The respondent avers that his sole object in violating the Tenure of Office act was to obtain the opinion of the Supreme Court upon the question of the constitutionality of that law. In other words, he deliberately violated the law, which was in him a crime, for the purpose of ascertaining judicially whether the law could be violated with impunity or not. At that very time, he had resting upon him the obligations of a citizen to obey the laws, and the higher and more solemn obligation, imposed by the Constitution upon the first magistrate of the country, to execute the laws. If a private citizen violates a law, he does so at his peril. If the President, or Vice President, or any other civil officer, violates a law, his peril is that he may be impeached by the House of Representatives and convicted by the Senate. This is precisely the responsibility which the respondent has incurred; and it would be no relief to him for his wilfull violation of the law, in the circumstances in which he is now placed, if the court itself had pronounced the same to be unconstitutional. But it is not easy to comprehend the audacity, the criminal character of a proceeding by which the President of the United States attempts systematically to undermine the government itself by drawing purposely into controversy, in the courts and elsewhere, the validity of the laws enacted by the constituted authorities of the country, who, as much as himself, are individually under an obligation to obey the Constitution in all their public acts. With the same reason, and for the same object, he might violate the Reconstruction laws, Tax laws, Tariff acts, or the Neutrality laws of the country; and thus, in a single day of his official life, raise questions which could not be disposed of for years in the courts of the country. The evidence discloses the fact that he has taken no step for the purpose of testing the constitutionality of the law. He suspended numerous officers under, or if not under, at least, as he himself admits, in conformity with the Tenure of Office law, showing that it was not his sole object to test its constitutionality. He has had opportunity to make application through the Attorney-General for a writ of *quo warranto*, which would have tested the validity of the law in the courts. This writ is the writ of the government, and it can never be granted upon the application of a private person. The President never attempted to test the law in the courts. Since his attempted removal of Mr. Stanton on the 21st of February last, he might have instituted proceedings by a writ of *quo warranto*, and by this time have obtained, probably, a judicial opinion covering all the points of the case. But he shrinks from the test he says he sought. Thus is the pretext of the President fully exposed. The evidence shows that he never designed to test his rights in the courts. His object was to seize the offices of the government for purposes of corruption, and by their influence to enable him to reconstruct the Union in the interest of the rebellious States. In short he resorted to this usurpation as an efficient and necessary means of usurping all power, and of restoring the government to rebel hands.

No criminal was ever arraigned who offerad a more unsatisfactory excuse for his crimes. The President had no right to do what he says he designed to do, and the evidence shows that he never has attempted to do what he now assigns as his purpose when he trampled the laws of the country under his feet.

These considerations have prepared the way in some degree, I trust, for an examination of the provisions of the Constitution relating to the appointment of ambassadors and other public ministers and consuls, judges of the Supreme Court, and other officers of the United States, for whose appointment provision is made in the second section of the second article of the Constitution. It is there declared that the President "shall nominate," and, by and with the consent of the Senate, shall "appoint ambassadors and other public ministers and consuls, judges of the Supreme Court, and all other officers of the United States whose appointments are not herein provided for and which shall be established by law." The phrase, "are not herein otherwise provided for," is understood to refer to Senators, who, under the Constitution, in case of vacancy, and may be appointed by the governors of the several States, and to those appointments which might be confided by law to the courts or the heads of departments. It is essential to notice the fact that neither in this provision of the Constitution nor in any other is power given to the President to remove any officer. The only power of removal specified in the Constitution is that of the Senate, by its verdict of guilty, to remove the President, Vice President, or other civil officer who may be impeached by the House of Representatives and presented to the Senate for trial.

Upon the premises already laid down it is clear that the power of removal from office is not vested in the President alone, but only in the President by and with the advice and consent of the Senate. Applying the provision of the Constitution already cited to the condition of affairs existing at the time the government was organized, we find that the course pursued by the first Congress and by the first President was the inevitable result of the operation of this provision of the organic law. In the first instance, several executive departments were established by acts of Congress, and in those departments offices of various grades were created. The conduct of foreign affairs required the appointment of ambassadors, ministers and consuls, and consequently those necessary offices were established by law. The President, in conformity with this provision of the Constitution, made nominations to the Senate of persons to fill the various offices so established. These nominations were considered and acted upon by the Senate, and when confirmed by the Senate the persons so nominated were appointed and authorized by commissions under the hand of the President to enter upon the discharge of their respective duties. In the nature of the case it was not possible for the President, during a session of the Senate, to assign to duty in any of the offices so created by any person who had not been by him nominated to the Senate, and by that body confirmed, and there is no evidence that any such attempt was made. The persons thus nominated and confirmed were in their offices under the Constitution, and by virtue of the concurrent action of the President and the Senate. There is not to be found in the Constitution any provision contemplating the removal of such persons from office. But inasmuch as it is essential to the proper administration of affairs that there should be a power of removal, and inasmuch as the power of nomination and confirmation vested in the President and in the Senate is a continuing power, not exhausted either by a single exercise or by a repeated exercise in reference to a particular office, it follows legitimately and properly that the President might at any time nominate to the Senate a person to fill a particular office, and the Senate, in the exercise of its constitutional power, could confirm that nomination, that the person so nominated and confirmed would have a right to take and enjoy the office to which he had so appointed, and thus to dispossess the previous inumbent. It is apparent that no removal can be made unless the President takes the initiative, and hence the expression "removal by the President."

As by a common and universally recognized principle of construction, the most recent statute is obligatory and controlling wherever it contravenes a previous statute, so a recent commission, issued under an appointment made by and with the advice and consent of the Senate, supersedes a previous appointment although made in the same manner. It is thus apparent that there is, under and by virtue of the clause of the Constitution quoted, no power of removal vested either in the President or in the Senate, or in both of them together as an independent power; but it is rather a consequence of the power of appoinment. And as the power of appointment is not vested in the President, but only the right to make a nomination, which becomes an appointment only when the nomination has been confirmed by the Senate, the power of removing a public officer cannot be deemed an executive power solely within the meaning of this provision of the Constitution.

This view of the subject is in harmony with the opinion expressed in the seventy-sixth number of the *Federalist*. After stating with great force the objections whic exist to the "exercise of the power of appointing to office by an assembly of men," the writer proceeds to say:

The truth of the principles here advanced seems to have been felt by the most intelligent of those who have found fault with the provision made in this respect by the convention. They contend that the President ought solely to have been authorized to make the appointments under the Federal Government. But it is easy to show that every advantage to be expected from such an arrangement would in substance be derived from the power of *nomination*, which is proposed to be conferred upon him, while several disadvantages which might attend the absolute power of appointment in the hands of that officer would be avoided. In the act of nominating his judgment alone would be exercised, and as it would be his sole duty to point out the man who with the approbation of the Senate should fill an office, his responsibility would be as complete as if he were to make the final appointment. There can, in this view, be no difference between nominating and appointing. The same motives which would influence a proper discharge of his duty in one case would exist in the other; and as no man could be appointed but upon his previous nomination, every man who might be appointed would be in fact his choice.

But his nomination may be overruled. This it certainly may, yet it can only be to make place for another nomination by himself. The person ultimately appointed must be the object of his preference, though, perhaps not in the highest degree. It is also not very probable that his nomination would often be overruled. The Senate could not be tempted by the preference they might feel to another to reject the one proposed, because they could not assure themselves that the person they might wish would be brought forward by a second, or by any subsequent nomination. They could not even be certain that a future nomination would present a candidate in any degree more acceptable to them. And as their dissent might cast a kind of stigma upon the individual rejected, and might have the appearance of a reflection upon the judgment of the Chief Magistrate, it is not likely that their sanction would often be refused, where there were not special and strong reasons for the refusal.

To what purpose, then, require the co-operation of the Senate? I answer that the necessity of their concurrence would have a powerful, though in general, a silent operation. It would be an excellent check upon the spirit of favoritism in the President, and would tend greatly to preventing the appointment of unfit characters, from State prejudice, from family connection, from personal attachment, or from a view to popularity. And, in addition to this, it would be an efficacious source of stability in the administration.

It will be readily comprehended that a man who had himself the sole disposition of office would be governed much more by his private inclinations and interests than when he was bound to submit the propriety of his choice to the dictation and determination of a different and independent body, and that body an entire branch of the Legislature. The possibility of rejection would be a strong motive to care in proposing. The danger of his own reputation, and, in case of an elective magistrate, to his political existence, from betraying a spirit of favoritism, or an unbecoming pursuit of popularity, to the observation of a body whose opinion would have great weight in forming that of the public, could not fail to operate as a barrier to one and to the other. He would be both ashamed and afraid to bring forward for the most distinguished or lucrative stations candidates who had no other merit than that of coming from the same State to which he particularly belonged, or of being in some way or other personally allied to him, and possessing the necessary insignificance and pliancy to render them the obsequious instruments of his pleasure.

When the President has made a nomination for a particular office, and that nomination has been confirmed by the Senate, the constitutional power of the President is exhausted with reference to that officer. All that he can do under the Constitution is, in the same manner to nominate a successor, who may be either confirmed or rejected by the Senate. Considering the powers of the President exclusively with reference to the removal and appointment of civil officers during the session of the Senate, it is clear that he can only act in concurrence with the Senate. An office being filled, he can only nominate a successor, who, when confirmed by the Senate, is, by operation of the Constitution, appointed to the office, and it is the duty of the President to issue his commission accordingly. This commission operates as a *supersedeas*, and the previous occupant is thereby removed.

No legislation has attempted to enlarge or diminish the constitutional powers of the President, and no legislation can enlarge or diminish his constitutional powers in this respect, as I shall hereafter show. It is here and now in the presence of this provision of the Constitution concerning the true meaning, of which there neither is nor has ever been any serious doubt in the mind of any lawyer or statesman, that we strip the defense of the President of all the questions and technicalities which the intellects of men, sharpened but not enlarged by the practice of the law, have wrung from the legislation of the country covering three-fourths of a century.

On the 21st day of February last, Mr. Stanton was *de facto* and *de jure* Secretary for the Department of War. The President's letter to Mr. Stanton, of that date, is evidence of this fact:—

EXECUTIVE MANSION, WASHINGTON, D. C., Feb. 21, 1868.—Sir;—By virtue of the power and authority vested in me as President by the Constitution and laws of the United States, you are hereby removed from office as Secretary for the Department of War, and your functions as such will terminate upon receipt of this communication.

You will transfer to Brevet Major-General Lorenzo Thomas, Adjutant-General of the army, who has this day been authorized and empowered to act as Secretary of War *ad interim*, all records, books, papers, and other public property now in your custody and charge.

Respectfully, yours, ANDREW JOHNSON.
Hon. Edwin M. Stanton, Washington, D. C.

This letter is an admission, not only that Mr. Stanton was Secretary of War on the 21st of February, 1868, but also that the suspension of that officer of the 12th of August, A. D. 1867, whether made under the Tenure of Office act or not, was abrogated by the action of the Senate of the 13th of January, 1868, and that then Mr. Stanton thereby was restored lawfully to the office of Secretary for the Department of War.

On the 21st day of February the Senate was in session. There was then but one constitutional way for the removal of Mr. Stanton:—a nomination by the President to the Senate of a successor, and his confirmation by that body. The President attempted to remove Mr. Stanton in a way not known to the Constitution, and in violation thereof, by issuing the said order for his removal. In the first of the articles it is set forth that this order was issued "in violation of the Constitution and the laws of the United States." If we show that he has violated the Constitution of the United States, we show also that he has violated his oath of office which pledged him to support the Constitution. Thus is the guilt of the President, under the Constitution and upon admitted facts, established beyond a reasonable doubt. This view is sufficient to justify and require at your hands a verdict of guilty under the first article, and this without any reference to the legislation of the country, and without reference to the constitutionality of the Tenure of Office act or to the question whether the Secretary of War is included within its provisions or not. But I intend in the course of my argument to deal with all these questions of law, and to apply the law as it shall appear to the facts proved or admitted. To be sure, in my judgment the case presented by the House of Representatives in the name of all the people of the United States might safely be rested here; but the cause of justice, the cause of the country, requires us to expose and demonstrate the guilt of the President in all the particulars set forth in the articles of impeachment. We have no alternative but to proceed. In this connection I refer to a view presented by the counsel for the President in his opening argument. He insists, or suggests, that inasmuch as the letter to Stanton of the 21st of February did not, in fact, accomplish a removal of the Secretary, that therefore no offense was committed. The technicalities of the law have fallen into disrepute among the people, and sometimes even in the courts. The technicalities proper of the law are the rules developed by human experience, and justly denominated, as is the law itself, the perfection of human reason. These rules, wise though subtle, aid in the administration of justice in all tribunals where the laws are judicially administered. But it often happens that attorneys seek to confuse the minds of men, and thwart the administration of justice, by the suggestion of nice distinctions which have no foundation in reason, and find no support in general principles of right.

The President cannot assume to exercise a power, as a power belonging to the office he holds, there being no warrant in law for such exercise, and then plead that he is not guilty because the act undertaken was not fully accomplished. The President is as guilty, in contemplation of law, as he would have been if Mr. Stanton had submitted to his demand and retired from the office of Secretary for the Department of War.

If these views are correct, the President is wholly without power, under and by virtue of the Constitution, to suspend a public officer. And most assuredly nothing is found in the Constitution to sustain the arrogant claim which he now makes, that he may, during a session of the Senate, suspend a public officer indefinitely, and make an appointment to the vacancy thus created, without asking the advice and consent of the Senate either upon the suspension or the appointment.

I pass now to the consideration of the third clause of the second section of the second article of the Constitution:—

The President shall have power to fill up all vacancies that may happen during the recess of the Senate, by granting commissions which shall expire at the end of their next session.

The phrase, "may happen," construed according to the proper and well-understood meaning of the words when the Constitution was framed, referred to those vacancies which might occur independently of the will of the government—vacancies arising from death, from resignation, from circumstances not produced by the act of the appointing power. The words "happen" and "happened" are of frequent use in the Bible, "that well of pure English undefiled," and always in the sense of accident, fortuity, chance, without previous expectation, as to befall, to light, to fall, or to come unexpectedly. This clause of the Constitution contains a grant of power to the President, and under and by virtue of it he may take and exercise the power granted, but nothing by construction or by implication. He then, by virtue of his office, may, during the recess of the Senate, grant commissions which shall expire at the end of the next session, and thus fill up any vacancies that may happen, that is, that may come by chance, by accident, without any agency on his part.

If, then, if it be necessary and proper, as undoubtedly it is necessary and proper, that provision should be made for the suspension or temporary removal of officers who, in the recess of the Senate, have proved to be incapable or dishonest, or who in the judgment of the President are disqualified for the further discharge of the duties of their offices, it is clearly a legislative right and duty, under the clause of the Constitution which authorizes Congress "to make all laws which shall be necessary and proper to carry into execution the foregoing powers, and all other powers vested in the Government of the United States, or in any department or officer thereof," to provide for the contingency. It is no answer to this view of the case to say that until the second of March, 1867, Congress neglected to legislate upon this subject, and that during the long period of such neglect, by the advice of Attorneys-General, the practice was introduced and continued, by which the President, during the recess of the Senate, removed from office persons who had been nominated by the President and confirmed by the Senate. This practice having originated in the neglect of Congress to legislate upon a subject clearly within its jurisdiction, and only tolerated by Congress, has, at most, the force of a practice or usage, which can at any time be annulled or controlled by statute.

This view is also sustained by the reasoning of Hamilton, in the 67th number of the *Federalist*, in which he says:—

The last of these two clauses, it is equally clear, cannot be understood to comprehend the power of filling vacancies in the Senate, for the following reasons:—First, the relation in which that clause stands to the other, which declares the general mode of appointing officers of the United States, denotes it to be nothing more than a supplement to the other, for the purpose of establishing an auxiliary method of appointment in cases to which the general method was inadequate. The ordinary power of appointment is confided to the President and Senate *jointly*, and can therefore only be exercised during the session of the Senate; but as it would have been improper to oblige this body to be continually in session for the appointment of officers, and as vacancies might happen *in their recess*, which it might be necessary for the public service to fill without delay, the succeeding clause is evidently intended to authorize the President, *singly*, to make temporary appointments "during the recess of the Senate, by granting commissions which should expire at the end of their next session."

The arguments which I have thus offered and the authorities quoted show that the President had not the power during the session of the Senate to remove either the Secretary of War or any civil officer from office by virtue of the Constitution. The power of removal during the recess of the Senate was recognized by the act of 1789, and tolerated by the country upon the opinions of Attorneys-General till 1867. The President claims, however, and as an incident of the power of removal, the power to suspend from office indefinitely any officer of the government; but inasmuch as his claim to the power of removal is not supported by the Constitution, he cannot sustain any other claim as an incident of that power. But if the power to remove were admitted, it would by no means follows that the President has the power to suspend indefinitely. The power to suspend indefinitely is a different power from that of removal, and it is in no proper sense necessarily an incident. It might be very well conceived that if the framers of the Constitution had though fit to confer upon the President the power to remove a public officer absolutely, his removal to be followed by the nomination of a successor to the Senate, they might yet have denied to the President the power to suspend public officers indefinitely and to supply their places by his appointees without the advice and consent of the Senate. But, inasmuch as the power to suspend indefinitely is not a power claimed as a specific grant under the Constitution, and as the claim by the President of the power of removal is not sustained by the text of the Constitution or by any good authority under it, it is not important to consider whether, if the power of removal were admitted to exist, the power to suspend indefinitely could be considered as an incident of that power. It is sufficient to say that neither power, in the sense claimed by the President, exists under the Constitution or by any provision of law.

I respectfully submit, Senators, that there can be no reasonable doubt of the soundness of the view I have presented, both of the language and meaning of the Constitution in regard to appointments to office. But, if there were any doubt, it is competent and proper to consider the effects of the claim, if recognized, as set up by the President. And in a matter of doubt as to the construction of the phraseology of the Constitution, it would be conclusive of its true interpretation that the claim asserted by the President is fraught with evils of the gravest character. He claims the right, as well when the Senate is in session as when it is not in session, to remove absolutely, or to suspend for an indefinite period of time, according to his own discretion, every officer of the army, of the navy, and of the civil service, and to supply their places with creatures and partisans of his own. To be sure, he has asserted, in direct form, his right to remove and suspend indefinitely officers of the army and navy; but when you consider that the Constitution maks no distinction in the tenure of office between military, naval and civil officers; that all are nominated originally by the President, and receive their appointments upon the confirmation of the Senate, and hold their offices under the Constitution by no other title than that which secures to a cabinet officer or to a revenue collector the office to which he has been appointed, there can be no misunderstanding as to the nature, extent, and dangerous character of the claim which the President makes. The statement of this arrogant and dangerous assumption is a sufficient answer to any doubt which might exist in the mind of any patriot as to the true intent and meaning of the Constitution. It cannot be conceived that the men who framed that instrument, who were devoted to liberty, who had themselves suffered by the exercise of illegal and irresponsible power, would have vested in the President of the United States an authority, to be exercised without the restraint or control of any other branch or department of the government, which would enable him to corrupt the civil, military and and naval officers of the country by rendering them absolutely dependent for their positions and emoluments upon his will. Moreover, this claim was never asserted by any President, or by any public man, from the beginning of the government until the present time. The history of the career of Andrew Johnson shows that he has been driven to the assertion of this claim by circumstances and events connected with his criminal design to break down the power of Congress, to subvert the institutions of the country, and thereby to restore the Union in the interest of those who participated in the Rebellion. Having entered upon this career of crime, he soon found it essential to the accomplishment of his purpose to secure the support of the immense retinue of public officers of every grade and description in the country. This he could not do without making them entirely dependent upon his will; and in order that they might realize their dependence, and thus be made subservient to his purposes, he determined to assert an authority over them unauthorized by the Constitution, and theretofore not attempted by any Chief Magistrate. His conversation with Mr. Wood, in the autumn of 1866, fully discloses this purpose.

Previous to the passage of the Tenure of Office act he had removed hundreds of faithful and patriotic public officers, to the great detriment of the public service, and followed by an immense loss of the public revenues. At the time of the passage of the act he was so far involved in his mad schemes—schemes of ambition and revenge—that it was, in his view, impossible for him to retrace his steps. He consequently determined, by various artifices and plans, to undermine that law and secure to himself, in defiance of the will of Congress and of the country, entire control of the officers in the civil service, and in the army and in the navy. He thus became gradually involved in an unlawful undertaking, from which he could not retreat. In the presence of the proceedings against him by the House of Representatives he had no alternative but to assert that under the Constitution power was vested in the President exclusively, without the advice and consent of the Senate, to remove from office every person in the service of the country. This policy, as yet acted upon in part, and developed chiefly in the civil service, has already produced evils which threaten the overthrow of the government. When he removed faithful public officers, and appointed others whose only claim to consideration was their unreasoning devotion to his interest and unhesitating obedience to his will, they compensated themselves for this devotion and this obedience by fraud upon the revenues, and by crimes against the laws of the land. Hence it has happened that in the internal revenue service alone, chiefly through the corruption of men whom he has thus appointed, the losses have amounted to not less than twenty-five, and probably to more than fifty millions of dollars a year during the last two years.

In the presence of these evils, which were then only partially realized, the Congress of the United States passed the Tenure of Office act, as a barrier to their further progress. This act thus far has proved ineffectual as a complete remedy; and now the President, by his answer to the articles of impeachment, asserts his right to violate it altogether, and by an interpretation of the Constitution which is alike hostile to its letter and to the peace and welfare of the country, he assumes to himself absolute and unqualified power over all the offices and officers of the country. The removal of Mr. Stanton, contrary to the Constitution and the laws, is the particular crime of the President for which we now demand his conviction. The extent, the evil character, and the dangerous nature of the claims by which he seeks to justify his conduct, are controlling considerations. By his conviction you purify the government and restore it to its original character. By his acquittal you surrender the government into the hands of a usurping and unscrupulous man, who will use all the vast power he now claims for the corruption of every branch of the public service and the final overthrow of the public liberties.

Nor is it any excuse for the President that he has taken the advice of his Cabinet officers in support of his claim. In the first place, he had no right under the Constitution to the advice of the head of a department, except upon subjects relating to the duties of his department. If the President has chosen to seek the advice of his Cabinet upon other matters, and they have seen fit to give it upon subjects not relating to their respective departments, it is advice which he had no constitutional authority to ask, advice which they were not bound to give, and that advice is to him, and for all the purposes of this investigation and trial, as the advice of private persons merely. But of what value can be the advice of men who, in the first instance, admit that they hold their offices by the will of the person who seeks their advice, and who understand most clearly that if the advice they give should be contrary to the wishes of their master, they would be at once, and in conformity with their own theory of the rights of the President, deprived of the offices which they hold? Having first made these men entirely dependent upon his will, he then solicits their advice as to the application of the principle by which they admit that they hold their places to all the other officers of the government. Could it have been expected that they, under such circumstances, would have given advice in any particular disagreeable to the will of him who sought it?

It was the advice of serfs to their lord, of servants to their master, of slaves to their owner.

The Cabinet respond to Mr. Johnson as old Polonious to Hamlet:—

Hamlet says:—Do you see yonder cloud that's almost in shape of a camel?

Polonius—And by the mass, and 'tis like a camel, indeed.

Hamlet—Methinks it is like a weasel.

Polonius—It is backed like a weasel.

Hamlet —Or like a whale?

Polonius—Very like a whale.

The gentlemen of the Cabinet understood the position that they occupied. The President, in his message to the Senate upon the suspension of Mr. Stanton, in which he says that he took the advice of the Cabinet in reference to his action upon the bill regulating the tenure of civil offices, speaks thus:—

"The bill had then not become a law. The limitation upon the power of removal was not yet imposed, and there was yet time to make any changes. If any one of these gentlemen had then said to me that he would avail himself of the provisions of that bill in case it became a law, I should not have hesitated a moment as to his removal."

Having indulged his Cabinet in such freedom of opinion when he consulted them in reference to the constitutionality of the bill, and having covered himself and them with public odium by his announcement, he now vaunts their opinions, extorted by power and given in subserviency, that the law itself may be violated with impunity. This, says the President, is the exercise of my constitutional right to the opinion of my Cabinet. I, says the President, am responsible for my Cabinet. Yes, the President is responsible for the opinions and conduct of men who give such advice as is demanded, and give it in fear and trembling lest they be at once deprived of their places. This is the President's idea of a Cabinet, but it is an idea not in harmony with the theory of the Constitution.

The President is a man of strong will, of violent passions, of unlimited ambition, with capacity to employ and use timid men, adhesive men, subservient men, and corrupt men, as the instruments of his designs. It is the truth of history that he has injured every person with whom he has had confidential relations, and many have escaped ruin only by withdrawing from his society altogether. He has one rule of life: he attempts to use every man of power, capacity, or influence within his reach. Succeeding in his attempts, they are in time, and usually in a short time, utterly ruined. If the considerate flee from him, if the brave and patriotic resist his schemes or expose his plans, he attacks them with all the enginery and patronage of his office, and pursues them with all the violence of his personal hatred. He attacks to destroy all who will not become his instruments, and all who become his instruments are destroyed in the use. He spares no one. Already this purpose of his life is illustrated in the treatment of a gentleman who was of counsel for the respondent, but who has never appeared in his behalf.

The thanks of the country are due to those distinguished soldiers who, tempted by the President by offers of kingdoms which were not his to give, refused to fall down and worship the tempter. And the thanks of the country are not less due to General Emory, who, when brought into the presence of the President by a request which he could not disobey, at once sought to protect himself against his machinations by presenting to him the law upon the subject of military orders.

The experience and the fate of Mr. Johnson's eminent adherents are lessons of warning to the country and to mankind; and the more eminent and distinguished of his adherents have furnished the most melancholy lessons for this and for succeeding generations.

It is not that men are ruined when they abandon a party; but in periods of national trial and peril the people will not tolerate those who, in any degree or under any circumstances, falter in their devotion to the rights and interests of the republic. In the public judgment, which is seldom erroneous in regard to public duty, devotion to the country, and adherence to Mr. Johnson are and have been wholly inconsistent.

Carpenter's historical painting of Emancipation is a fit representation of an event the most illustrious of any in the annals of America since the adoption of the Constitution. Indeed, it is second to the ratification of the Constitution, only in the fact that that instrument, as a means of organizing and preserving the nation, rendered emancipation possible. The principal figure of the scene is the immortal Lincoln, whose great virtues endear his name and memory to all mankind, and whose untimely and violent death, then the saddest event in our national experience, but now not deemed so great a calamity to the people who loved him and mourned for him as no public man was ever before loved or lamented, as is the shame, humiliation, disgrace and suffering caused by the misconduct and crimes of his successor. It was natural and necessary that the artist should arrange the personages of the group on the right hand and on the left of the principal figure. Whether the particular assignment was by chance, by the taste of the artist, or by the influence of a mysterious Providence which works through human agency, we know not. But on the right of Lincoln are two statesmen and patriots, who, in all the trials and vicissitudes of these eventful years, have remained steadfast to liberty, to justice, to the principles of Constitutional government. Senators and Mr. Chief Justice, in this presence I venture not to pronounce their names.

On the left of Lincoln are five figures representing the other members of his Cabinet. One of these is no longer among the living; he died before the evil days came, and we may indulge in the hope that he would have escaped the fate of his associates. Of the other four, three have been active in counseling and supporting the President in his attempts to subvert the government. They are already ruined men. Upon the canvass they are elevated to the summit of virtuous ambition. Yielding to the seductions of power, they have fallen. Their example and fate may warn us, but their advice and counsel, whether given to this tribunal or to him who is on trial before this tribunal, cannot be accepted as the judgment of wise or of patriotic men.

Leaving the discussion of the provisions of the Constitution, I am now prepared to ask your attention to the character and history of the act of 1789, on which stress has been laid by the President in his answer, and by the learned counsel who opened the case for the respondent. The discussion in the House of Representatives in 1789 related to the bill establishing a Department of Foreign Affairs. The first section of that bill, as it originally passed the House of Representatives, after recapitulating the title of the officer who was to take charge of the department, and setting forth his duties, contained these words in reference to the Secretary of the Department:—"To be removable from office by the President of the United States." The House, in Committee of the Whole, discussed this provision during several days, and all the leading members of the body appear to have taken part in the debate. As is well known, there was a difference of opinion at the time as to the meaning of the Constitution. Some contended that the power of removing civil officers was vested in the President, absolutely, to be exercised by him, without consultation with the Senate, and this as well when the Senate was in session as during vacations. Others maintained that the initiative in the removal of a public officer must be taken by the President, but that there could be no actual removal except by the advice and consent of the Senate, and that this rule was applicable to the powers of the President, as well during the vacation as during the session of the Senate. Others maintained that during the session of the Senate, while the initiative was in the President, the actual removal of a civil officer could be effected only upon the advice and consent of the Senate, but that during the vacations the President might remove such officers and fill their places temporarily, under commissions, to expire at the end of the next session of the Senate. Mr. Madison maintained the first of these propositions, and he may be said to be the only person of historical reputation at the present day who expressed corresponding opinions, although undoubtedly his views were sustained by a considerable number of members. It is evident from an examination of the debate that Mr. Madison's views were gradually and, finally, successfully undermined by the discussion on that occasion.

As is well known, Roger Sherman was then one of the most eminent members of that body. He was a signer of the Declaration of Independence, a member of the convention which framed the Constitution of the United States, and a member of the House of Representatives of the First Congress. He was undoubtedly one of the most illustrious men of the constitutional period of American history; and in each succeeding generation there have eminent persons of his blood and name; but at no period has his family been more distinguished than at the present time. Mr. Sherman took a leading part in the discussion, and there is no doubt that the views which he entertained and expressed had a large influence in producing the result which was finally reached. The report of the debate is found in the first volume of the Annals of Congress; and I quote from the remarks made by Mr. Sherman, preserved on pages 510 and 511 of that volume:—

"Mr. Sherman—I consider this a very important subject in every point of view, and therefore worthy of full discussion. In my mind it involves three question. First. Whether the President has, by the Constitution, the right to remove an officer appointed by and with the advice and consent of the Senate. No gentleman contends but that the advice and consent of the Senate are necessary to make the appointment in all cases, unless in inferior officers where the contrary is established by law; but then they allege that although the consent of the Senate be necessary to the appointment, the President alone, by the nature of his office, has the power of removal. Now it appears to me that this opinion is ill-founded, because this provision was intened for some useful purpose, and by that construction would answer none at all. I think the concurrence of the Senate as necessary to appoint an officer as the nomination of the President; they are constituted as mutual checks, each having a negative upon the other.

"I consider it as an established principle that the power which appoints can also remove, unless there are express exceptions made. Now the power which appoints the judges cannot displace them, because there is a constitutional restriction in their favor; otherwise the President, by and with the advice and consent of the Senate, being the power which appointed them, would be sufficient to remove them. This is the construction in England, where the King has the power of appointing judges; it was declared to be during pleasure, and they might be removed when the monarch thought proper. It is a general principle in law, as well as reason, that there shall be the same authority to remove as to establish. It is so in legislation, where the several branches, whose concurrence is necessary to pass a law, must concur in repealing it. Just so I take it to be in cases of appointment, and the President alone may remove, when he alone appoints, as in the case of inferior offices to be established by law.

* * * * * * *

"As the office is the mere creature of the Legislature we may form it under such regulations as we please, with such powers and duration as we think good policy requires. We may say he shall hold his office during good behavior, or that he shall be annually elected. We may say he shall be displaced for neglect of duty, and point out how he shall be convicted of it without calling upon the President or Senate.

"The third question is, if the Legislature has the power to authorize the President alone to remove this officer, whether it is expedient to invest him with it? I do not believe it absolutely necessary that he should have such power, because the power of suspending would answer all the purposes which gentlemen have in view by giving the power of removal. I do not think that the officer is only to be removed by impeachment, as is argued by the gentleman from South Carolina (Mr. Smith), because he is the mere creature of the law, and we can direct him to be removed on conviction of mismanagement or inability, without calling upon the Senate for their concurrence. But I believe, if we make no such provision, he may constitutionally be removed by the President, by and with the advice and consent of the Senate; and I believe it would be most expedient for us to say nothing in the clause on this subject."

I may be pardoned if I turn aside for a moment, and, addressing myself to the learned gentleman of counsel for the respondent who is to follow me in argument, I request him to refute, to overthrow the constitutional argument of his illustrious ancestor, Roger Sherman. Doing this he will have overcome the first, but only the first, of a series of obstacles in the path of the President.

In harmony with the views of Mr. Sherman was the opinion expressed by Mr. Jackson, of Georgia, found on page 508 of the same volume. He says:

"I shall agree to give him (that is the President) the same power in cases of removal that he has in appointing, but nothing more. Upon this principle, I would agree to give him the power of suspension during the recess of the Senate. This, in my opinion, would effectually provide against those inconveniences which have been apprehended, and not expose the Government to those abuses we have to dread from the wanton and uncontrollable authority of removing officers at pleasure."

It may be well to observe that Mr. Madison, in maintaining the absolute power of the President to remove civil officers—coupled with his opinions upon that point—states doctrines concerning the power of impeachment which would be wholly unacceptable to this respondent. And, indeed, it is perfectly apparent that without the existence of the power to impeach and remove the President of the United States from office, in the manner maintained, Mr. Madison in that debate, said:

"The danger to liberty, the danger of maladministration, has not yet been found to lie so much in the facility of introducing improper persons into office as in the difficulty of displacing those who are unworthy of the public trust. (Page 515, vol. 1, Annals of Congress.)"

Again he says:

"Perhaps the great danger, as has been observed, of abuse in the executive power lies in the improper continuance of bad men in office. But the power we contend for will not enable him to do this; for if an unworthy man be continued in office by an unworthy President, the House of Representatives can at any time impeach him, and the Senate can remove him, whether the President chooses or not. The danger, then, consists merely in this:—The President can displace from office a man whose merits require that he should be continued in it. What will be the motives which the President can feel for such abuse of his power and the restraints that operate to prevent it? In the first place, he will be impeachable by this House before the Senate for such an act of maladministration; for I contend that the wanton removal of meritorious officers would subject him to impeachment and removal from his high trust. (Page 517, vol. 1, Annals of Congress.)"

It is thus seen that Mr. Madison took great care to connect his opinions of the power of removal in the President with a distinct declaration that if this power was improperly exercised by the President he would himself be liable to impeachment and removal from office. If Mr. Madison's opinions were to be accepted by the President as a whole, he would be as defenceless as he is at the present time if arraigned upon articles of impeachment based upon acts of maladministration in the removal of public officers. The result of the debate upon the bill for establishing the Executive Department of Foreign Affairs was that the phrase in question which made the head of the department "removable from office by the President of the United States" was stricken out by a vote of 31 in the affirmative to 19 in the negative, and another form of expression was introduced into the second section, which is manifestly in harmony with the views expressed by Mr. Sherman, and those who entertained corresponding opinions.

The second section is in these words:—

"Section 2. *And be it further enacted*, That there shall be in the said department an inferior officer, to be appointed by the said principal officer, and to be employed therein as he shall deem proper, and to be called the chief clerk of the Department of Foreign Affairs, and who, whenever the said principal officer shall be removed from office by the President of the United States, or in other case of vacancy, shall, during such vacancy, have the charge and custody of all records, books and papers appertaining to said department." (United States Statutes at Large, vol. 1, p. 29.)

It will be seen that the phrase here employed, "whenever the said principal officer shall be removed from office by the President of the United States," is not a grant of power to the President; nor is it, as was asserted by the

counsel for the respondent, a legislative interpretation of a constitutional power. But it is merely a recognition of a power in the Constitution to be exercised by the President, at some time, under some circumstances, and subject to certain limitations. But there is no statement or declaration of the time when such power could be exercised, the circumstances under which it might be exercised, or the limitations imposed upon its exercise.

All these matters are left subject to the operation of the Constitution. This is in entire harmony with the declaration made by Mr. White, of North Carolina, in the debate of 1789. He says:—

"Let us then leave the Constitution to a free operation, and let the President, with or without the consent of the Senate, carry it into execution. Then, if any one supposes himself injured by the determination let him have recourse to the law, and its decision will establish the true construction of the Constitution."

Mr. Gerry, of Massachusetts, also said:—

"Hence all construction of the meaning of the Constitution is dangerous or unnatural, and therefore ought to be avoided. This is our doctrine, that no power of this kind ought to be exercised by the Legislature. But we say, if we must give a construction to the Constitution it is more natural to give the construction in favor of the power of removal vesting in the President, by and with the advice and consent of the Senate; because it is in the nature of things that the power which appoints removes also."

Again, Mr. Sherman said, speaking of the words which were introduced into the first section and finally stricken out:—

"I wish, Mr. Chairman, that the words may be left out of the bill, without giving up the question either way as to the propriety of the measure."

The debate upon the bill relating to the Department for Foreign Affairs occurred in the month of June, 1798; in the following month of August Congress was engaged in considering the bill establishing the Treasury Department. This bill originated in the House, and contained the phrase now found in it, being the same as that contained in the bill establishing the State Department.

The Senate was so far satisfied of the impolicy of making any declaration whatever upon the subject of removal, that the clause was struck out by an amendment. The House refused to concur, however, and the Senate, by the casting vote of the Vice President, receded from the amendment.

All this shows that the doctrine of the right of removal by the President survived the debate only as a limited and doubtful right at most.

The results reached by the Congress of 1789 are conclusive upon the following points:—That that body was of opinion that the power of removal was not in the President absolutely, to be exercised at all times and under all circumstances; and secondly, that during the sessions of the Senate the power of removal was vested in the President and Senate, to be exercised by their concurrent action; while the debate and the votes indicate that the power of the President to remove from office, during the vacation of the Senate, was, at best, a doubtful power under the Constitution.

It becomes us next to consider the practice of the Government, under the Constitution, and in the presence of the action of the first Congress, by virtue of which the President now claims an absolute, unqualified, irresponsible power over all public officers, and this without the advice and consent of the Senate, or the concurrence of any other branch of the Government. In the early years of the Government the removal of a public officer by the President was a rare occurrence, and it was usually resorted to during the session of the Senate, for misconduct in office only, and accomplished by the appointment of a successor, through the advice and consent of the Senate. Gradually a practice was introduced, largely through the example of Mr. Jefferson, of removing officers during the recess of the Senate, and filling their places under commissions to expire at the end of the next session. But it cannot be said that this practice became common until the election of General Jackson, in 1828. During his administration the practice of removing officers during the recesses of the Senate was largely increased, and in the year 1832, on the 18th of September, General Jackson removed Mr. Duane from the office of Secretary of the Treasury. This act on his part gave rise to a heated debate in Congress, and an ardent controversy throughout the country, many of the most eminent men contending that there was no power in the President to remove a civil officer, even during the recess of the Senate. The triumph of General Jackson on that controversy gave a full interpretation to the words which had been employed in the statute of 1789.

But, at the same time, the limitations of that power in the President were clearly settled, both upon the law and the Constitution, that whatever might be his power of removal during a recess of the Senate, he had no right to make a removal during a session of the Senate except upon the advice and consent of that body to the appointment of a successor. This was the opinion of Mr. Johnson himself, as stated by him in a speech made in the Senate on the 10th of January, 1861:—

"I meant that the true way to fight the battle was for us to remain here and occupy the places assigned to us by the Constitution of the country. Why did I make that statement? It was because on the 4th day of March next we shall have six majority in this body, and if, as some apprehended, the incoming administration shall show any disposition to make encroachments upon the institution of slavery, encroachments upon the rights of the States, or any other violation of the Constitution, we, by remaining in the Union and standing at our places, will have the power to resist all these encroachments. How? We have the power even to reject the appointment of the Cabinet officers of the incoming President. Then, should we not be fighting the battle in the Union by resisting even the organization of the administration in a constitutional mode, and thus, at the very start, disable an administration which was likely to encroach on our rights and to violate the Constitution of the country? So far as appointing even a minister abroad is concerned, the incoming administration will have no power without our consent if we remain here. It comes into office handcuffed, powerless to do harm. We, standing here, hold the balance of power in our hands; we can resist it at the very threshhold effectually, and do it inside of the Union and in our House. The incoming administration has not even the power to appoint a postmaster, whose salary exceeds $1000 a year, without consultation with, and the acquiescence of, the Senate of the United States. The President has not even the power to draw his salary, his $25,000 per annum, unless we appropriate it."—(*Congressional Globe*, vol. —, page —.)

It may be well observed, that for the purpose of this trial, and upon the question whether the President is or is not guilty under the first three articles exhibited against him by the House of Representatives, it is of no consequence whether the President of the United States has power to remove a civil officer during a recess of the Senate. The fact charged and proved against the President, and on which, as one fact proved against him, we demand his conviction is, that he attempted to remove Mr. Stanton from the office of Secretary of War during a session of the Senate. It cannot be claimed with any propriety that the act of 1789 can be construed as a grant of power to the President to an extent beyond the practice of the government for three-quarters of a century under the Constitution, and under the provisions of the law of 1789. None of the predecessors of Mr. Johnson, from General Washington to Mr. Lincoln, although the act of 1789 was in existence during all that period, had ever ventured to claim that either under that act, or by virtue of the Constitution, the President of the United States had power to remove a civil officer during a session of the Senate, without its consent and advice. The utmost that can be said is, that for the last forty years it had been the practice of the Executive to remove civil officers at pleasure during the recess of the Senate. While it may be urged that this practice, in the absence of any direct legislation upon the subject had become the common law of the country, protecting the Executive in a policy corresponding to that practice. It is also true, for stronger reasons, that Mr. Johnson was bound by his oath of office to adhere to the practice of his predecessors in other particulars, none of whom had ever ventured to remove a civil officer from his office during the session of the Senate, and appoint a successor, either permanent or *ad interim*, and authorize that successor to enter upon the discharge of the duties of such office.

Hence it is that the act of 1789 is no security to this respondent, and hence it is that we hold him guilty of a violation of the Constitution and of his oath of office, under the first and third articles of impeachment, exhibited against him by the House of Representatives, and this without availing ourselves of the provisions of the Tenure of Office act of March 2, 1867.

I respectfully ask that the views now submitted in reference to the act of 1789 may be considered in connection with the argument I have already offered, upon the true meaning of the provisions of the Constitution relating to the appointment of civil officers.

I pass now to the consideration of the act of the 13th of February, 1795, on which the President relies as a justification for his appointment of Lorenzo Thomas as Secretary of War *ad interim*. By this act it is provided:—

"In case of vacancy in the office of Secretary of State, the Secretary of the Treasury, or of the Secretary of the Department of War, or of any other officer of either of the said departments, whose department is not in the head thereof, whereby they cannot perform the duties of their said respective offices, it shall be lawful for the President of the United States, in case he shall think it necessary, to authorize any person or persons, at his discretion, to perform the duties of the said respective offices until a successor be appointed, or such vacancy be filled. *Provided*, That no one vacancy shall be supplied, in manner aforesaid, for a longer term than six months." (1 Stat. at Large, p. 415).

The ingenuity of the President and his counsel has led them to maintain that the phrase "in case of vacancy," used in this statute, relates to any and every vacancy however produced. But the reading of the entire section, whether casually or carefully, shows that the purpose of the law was to provide a substitute temporarily in case of vacancy, whereby the person in office *could not perform the duties of his office*, and necessarily applied only to those contingencies of official life which put it out of the power of the person in office to discharge the duties of the place; such as sickness, absence, or inability of any sort. And yet the President and his counsel contend that a removal by the President is a case of vacancy contemplated by the law, notwithstanding the limitation of the President in his power of appointing an officer temporarily, is to those cases which render it impossible for the duly commissioned officer to perform the duties of his office. When it is considered, as I have shown, that the President has no power—and this without considering the Tenure of Office act of March 2, 1867—to create a vacancy during a session of the Senate, the act of 1795,

even upon his construction, furnishes no defense whatever. But we submit that if he had possessed the power which he claims by virtue of the act of 1789, that the vacancy referred to in the act of 1795 is not such a vacancy as is caused by the removal of a public officer, but that that act is limited to those vacancies which arise unavoidably in the public service, and without the agency of the President. But there is in the section of the act of 1795 on which the President relies, a proviso which nullifies absolutely the defense which he has set up. This proviso is, that no one vacancy shall be supplied in manner aforesaid (that is, by a temporary appointment) for a longer term than six months. Mr. Johnson maintains that he suspended Mr. Stanton from the office of Secretary of War on the 12th of August last, not by virtue of the Tenure of Office act of March 2, 1867, but under a power incident to the general and unlimited power of removal. which, as he claims, is vested in the President of the United States, and that, from the 12th of August last, Mr. Stanton has not been entitled to the office of Secretary for the Department of War. If he suspended Mr. Stanton as an incident of his general power of removal, then his suspension, upon the President's theory, created a vacancy such as is claimed by the President under the statute of 1795. The suspension of Mr. Stanton put him in such a condition that he "could not perform the duties of the office." The President claims also to have appointed General Grant Secretary of War *ad interim* on the 12th of August last, by virtue of the statute of 1795. The proviso of that statute declares that no one vacancy shall be shall be supplied in manner aforesaid (that is, by temporary appointment) for a longer term than six months. If the act of 1795 were in force, and if the President's theory of his rights under the Constitution, and under that act were a valid theory, the six months during which the vacancy might have been supplied temporarily expired by limitation on the 12th day of February, 1868, and yet on the 21st day of February, 1868, the President appointed Lorenzo Thomas Secretary of War *ad interim* to the same vacancy, and this in violation of the statute which he pleads his own defense. It is too clear for argument that if Mr. Stanton was lawfully suspended, as the President now claims, but not suspended under the Tenure of Office act, then the so-called restoration of Mr. Stanton on the 13th of January was wholly illegal. But if the statute of 1795 is applicable to a vacancy created by suspension or removal then the President has violated it by the appointment of General Thomas Secretary of War *ad interim*. And if the statute of 1795 is not applicable to a vacancy occasioned by a removal, then the appointment of General Thomas Secretary of War *ad interim* is without authority or the color of authority of law.

The fact is, however, that the statute of 1795 is repealed by the operation of the statute of the 20th of February, 1863. (Statutes at Large, vol. 12, p. 656).

If Senators will consider the provisions of the statute of 1863 in connection with the power of removal under the Constitution during a session of the Senate, by and with the advice and consent of the Senate, and the then recognized power of removal by the President during a recess of the Senate to be filled by temporary appointments, as was the practice previous to March 2, 1867, they will find that provision is made for every vacancy, which could possibly arise in the public service.

The act of February 20, 1863, provides:—

"That in case of the death, *resignation*, absence from the seat of government, or sickness of the head of an executive department of the government, or of any officer of either of said departments whose appointment is not in the head thereof, *whereby they cannot perform the duties of their respective offices*, it shall be lawful for the President of the United States, in case he shall think it necessary, to authorize the head of any other executive department or other officer in either of said departments whose appointment is vested in the President, at his discretion to perform the duties of the said respective offices until a successor be appointed, or until such absence or inability shall cease? *Provided*, That no one vacancy shall be supplied in manner aforesaid for a longer term than six months."

Provision was thus made by the act of 1863 for filling all vacancies which could occur under any circumstances. It is a necessary rule of construction that all previous statutes making other and different provisions for the filling of vacancies are repealed by the operation of more recent statutes; and for the plain reason that it is inconsistent with any theory of government that there should be two legal modes in existence at the same time for doing the same thing.

If the view I have presented be a sound one, it is apparent that the President's conduct finds no support either in the Constitution, in the act of 1789, or in the legislation of 1795, on which he chiefly relies as a justification for the appointment of Thomas as Secretary of War *ad interim*. It follows, also, that if the Tenure of Office act had not been passed the President would not have been guilty of a high misdemeanor, in that he issued an order for the removal of Mr. Stanton from office during the session of the Senate, in violation of the Constitution and of his own oath of office ; that he was guilty of a high misdemeanor in the appointment of Lorenzo Thomas as Secretary of War *ad interim*, and this whether the act of the 13th of February, 1795, is in force, or whether the same has been repealed by the statute of 1863, or annulled and rendered obsolete by the intervening legislation of the country, His guilt is thus fully proved and established as charged in the first, second, and third articles of impeachment exhibited against him by the House of Representatives, and this without considering the requirments or constitutionality of the act regulating the tenure of certain civil offices.

I pass now to the consideration of the Tenure of Office act. I preface what I have to say by calling your attention to that part of my argument already addressed to you in which I have set forth and maintained, as I was able, the opinion that the President had no right to make any inquiry whether an act of Congress is or is not constitutional. That, having no right to make such inquiry he could not plead that he had so inquired, and reached the conclusion that the act inquired about was unconstitutional. You will also bear in mind the views presented, that this tribunal can take no notice of any argument or suggestion that a wilfull violation by the President is unconstitutional. The gist of his crime is, that he intentionally disregarded a law, and, in the nature of the case, it can be no excuse or defense that such law, in his opinion, or in the opinion of others, was not in conformity with the Constitution.

In this connection, I desire to call your attention to suggestions made by the President, and by the President's counsel—by the President in his message of December, 1867, and by the President's counsel in his opening argument—that if Congress were by legislation to abolish a department of the government, or to declare that the President should not be Commander-in-Chief of the army or the navy, that it would be the duty of the President to disregard such legislation. These are extreme cases, and not within the range of possibility. Members of Congress are individually bound by an oath to support the Constitution of the United States, and it is not to be presumed, even for the purpose of argument, that they would wantonly disregard the obligations of their oath, and enact in the form of law rules or proceedings in plain violation of the Constitution. Such is not the course of legislation, and such is not the character of the act we are now to consider. The bill regulating the tenure of certain civil offices was passed by a constitutional majority in each of the two Houses, and it is to be presumed that each Senator and Representative who gave it his support did so in the belief that its provisions were in harmony with the provisions of the Constitution. We are now dealing with practical affairs, and conducting the government within the Constitution; and in reference to measures passed by Congress under such circumstances, it is wholly indefensible for the President to suggest the course that, in his opinion, he would be justified in pursuing if Congress were openly and wantonly to disregard the Constitution and inaugurate revolution in the government.

It is asserted by the counsel for the President, that he took advice as to the constitutionality of the Tenure of Office act, and being of opinion that it was unconstitutional, or so much of it at least as attempted to deprive him of the power of removing the members of the Cabinet, he felt it to be his duty to disregard its provisions; and the question is now put with feeling and emphasis, whether the President is to be impeached, convicted and removed from office for a mere difference of opinion. True, the President is not to be removed for a *mere* difference of opinion. If he had contented himself with the opinion that the law was unconstitutional, or even with the expression of such an opinion privately or officially to Congress, no exception could have been taken to his conduct. But he has attempted to act in accordance with that opinion, and in that action he has disregarded the requirements of the statute. It is for this action that he is to be arraigned, and is to be convicted. But it is not necessary for us to rest upon the doctrine that it was the duty of the President to accept the law as constitutional and govern himself accordingly in all his official doings. We are prepared to show that the law is in truth in harmony with the Constitution, and that its provisions apply to Mr. Stanton as Secretary for the Department of War.

The Tenure of Office act makes no change in the powers of the President and the Senate, during the session of the Senate, to remove a civil officer upon a nomination by the President, and confirmation by the Senate, of a successor. This was an admitted constitutional power from the very organization of the government, while the right now claimed by the President to remove a civil officer during a session of the Senate, without the advice and consent of the Senate, was never asserted by any of his predecessors, and certainly never recognized by any law or by any practice. This rule applied to heads of departments as well as to other civil officers. Indeed, it may be said, once for all, that the tenure by which members of the Cabinet have held their places corresponds in every particular to the tenure by which other civil officers have held theirs. It is undoubtedly true that, in practice, members of the Cabinet have been accustomed to tender their resignations upon a suggestion from the President that such a course would be acceptable to him. But this practice has never changed their legal relations to the President or to the country.

There was never a moment of time, since the adoption of the Constitution, when the law or the opinion of the Senate recognized the right of the President to remove a Cabinet officer during a session of the Senate, without the consent of the Senate given through the confirmation of a successor. Hence, in this particular, the Tenure of Office act merely enacted and gave form to a practice existing from the foundation of the government—a practice in entire harmony with the provisions of the Constitution upon the subject. The chief change produced by the Tenure of Office act had reference to removals during the recess of the Senate. Previous to the 2d of March, 1867, as has been already shown, it was the practice of the President during the recess of the Senate to remove civil officers and to grant commissions to other persons, under the third clause of the second section of the second article of the Constitution. This power, as has been seen, was a doubtful one in the beginning. The practice grew up under the act of 1789, but the right of Congress by legislation to regulate the exercise of that power was not questioned in the great debate of that year, nor can it reasonably be drawn into controversy now.

The act of March 2, 1867, declares that the President shall not exercise the power of removal, absolutely, during the recess of the Senate, but that if any officer shall be shown, by evidence satisfactory to the President, to be guilty of misconduct in office, or of crime, or for any reason shall become incapable or legally disqualified to perform his duties, the President may suspend him from office and designate some suitable person to perform temporarily the duties of such office until the next meeting of the Senate and the action of the Senate thereon.

By this legislation the removal is qualified, and is made subject to the final action of the Senate, instead of being absolute, as was the fact under the practice theretofore prevailing. It is to be observed, however, that this feature of the act regulating the tenure of certain civil offices is not drawn into controversy by these proceedings; and therefore, it is entirely unimportant to the President whether that provision of the act is constitutional or not. I can, however, entertain no doubt of its constitutionality. The record of the case, however, shows that Mr. Stanton was suspended from office during the recess, but was removed from office, as far as an order of the President could effect his removal, during a session of the Senate. It is also wholly immaterial to the present inquiry whether the suspension of Mr. Stanton on the 12th of August, 1867, was made under the Tenure of Office act, or in disregard to it, as the President asserts.

It being thus clear, that so much of the act as relates to appointments and removals from office during the session of the Senate is in harmony with the practice of the government from the first, and in harmony with the provisions of the Constitution on which that practice was based, and it being admitted that the order of the President for the removal of Mr. Stanton was issued during a session of the Senate, it is unnecessary to inquire whether the other parts of the act are constitutional or not, and also unnecessary to inquire what the provisions of the act are in reference to the heads of the several executive departments. I presume authorities are not needed to show that a law may be unconstitutional and void in some of its parts, and the remaining portions continue in full force.

The body of the first section of the act regulating the tenure of certain civil offices is in these words:—

"Every person holding any civil office to which he has been appointed by and with the advice and consent of the Senate, and every person who shall hereafter be appointed to any such office, and shall become duly qualified to act therein, is, and shall be entitled to hold such office until a successor shall have been in like manner appointed and duly qualified, except as herein otherwise provided."

Omitting for the moment to notice the exception, there can be no doubt that this provision would have applied to the Secretary of War, and to every other civil officer under the government; nor can there be any doubt that the removal of Mr. Stanton during a session of the Senate is a misdemeanor by the law, and punishable as such under the sixth section of the act, unless the body of the section quoted is so controlled by the proviso as to take the Secretary of War out of its grasp. The proviso is in these words:—

"That the Secretaries of State, of War, of the Navy, and of the Interior, the Postmaster General and the Attorney-General shall hold their offices respectively for and during the term of the President by whom they may have been appointed, and one month thereafter, subject to removal by and with the advice and consent of the Senate."

We maintain that Mr. Stanton, as Secretary of War, was, on the second day of March, 1867, within and included under the language of the proviso, and was to hold his office for and during the term of the President by whom he had been appointed, and one month thereafter, subject to removal, however, by and with the advice and consent of the Senate. We maintain that Mr. Stanton was then holding the office of Secretary of War, for and in the term of President Lincoln, by whom he had been appointed; that the term commenced on the fourth of March, 1865, and would end on the fourth of March, 1869. The Constitution defines the meaning of the word "term." When speaking of the President, it says:—"He shall hold his office during the term of four years, and, together with the Vice President, chosen for the same term, be elected as follows. Now, then, although the President first elected may die during his term, the office and the term of the office still remain. Having been established by the Constitution, it is not in any degree dependent upon the circumstance whether the person elected to the term shall survive to the end or not. It is still a Presidential term. It is still in law the term of the President who was elected to the office. The Vice President was chosen at the same time and elected for the same term. But it is the term of a different office from that of President—the term of the office of Vice President. Mr. Johnson was elected to the office of Vice President for the term of four years. Mr. Lincoln was elected to the office of President for the term of four years. Mr. Lincoln died in the second month of his term, and Mr. Johnson succeeded to the office.

It was not a new office, it was not a new term. He succeeded to Mr. Lincoln's office, and for the remainder of Mr. Lincoln's term of office. He is serving out Mr. Lincoln's term as President. The law says that the Secretaries shall hold their offices respectively for and during the term of the President by whom they may have been appointed. Mr. Lincoln's term commenced on the 4th of March, 1865. Mr. Stanton was appointed by Mr. Lincoln; he was in office in Mr. Lincoln's term, when the act regulating the tenure of certain civil offices was passed; and by the proviso of that act he was entitled to hold that office until one month after the 4th of March, 1869, unless he should be sooner removed therefrom, by and with the advice and consent of the Senate.

The act of March 1, 1792, concerning the succession, in case the office of President and Vice President both became vacant, recognizes the presidential term of four years as the constitutional term. Any one can understand that in case of vacancy in the office of President and Vice President, and in case of a new election by the people, that it would be desirable to make the election for the remainder of the term. But the act of 1792 recognizes the impossibility of this course in the section which provides that the term of four years for which a President and Vice President shall be elected (that is, in case of a new election, as stated,) shall in all cases commence on the fourth day of March next succeeding the day on which the votes of the electors shall have been given.

It is thus seen that by an election to fill a vacancy the government would be so far changed in its practical working that the subsequent elections of President, except by an amendment to the Constitution, could never again occur in the years divisible by four, as at present, and might not answer to the election of members of the House of Representatives, for the Presidential elections might occur in the years not divisible by two. The Congress of 1792 acted upon the constitutional doctrine that the Presidential term is four years and cannot be changed by law.

On the 21st of February, 1868, while the Senate of the United States was in session, Mr. Johnson, in violation of the law—which, as we have already seen, is in strict harmony in this particular with the Constitution and with the practice of every government—issued an order for the removal of Mr. Stanton from his office as Secretary for the Department of War. If, however, it be claimed that the proviso does not apply to the Secretary of War, then he does not come within the only exception made in the statute to the general provision in the body of the first section already quoted; and Mr. Stanton having been appointed to office originally by and with the advice and consent of the Senate, could only be removed by the nomination and appointment of a successor, by and with the advice and consent of the Senate. Hence, upon either theory it is plain that the President violated the Tenure of Office act in the order which he issued on the 21st day of February, A. D. 1868, for the removal of Mr. Stanton from the office of Secretary for the Department of War, the Senate of the United States being then in session.

In support of the view I have presented, I refer to the official record of the amendments made to the first section of the tenure of office act. On the 18th of January, 1867, the bill passed the Senate, and the first section thereof was in these words:

"That every person [excepting the Secretaries of State, of the Treasury, of War, of the Navy, and of the Interior, the Postmaster General, and the Attorney General] holding any civil office to which he has been appointed by and with the advice and consent of the Senate, and every person who shall hereafter be appointed to any such office, and shall become duly qualified to act therein, is and shall be entitled to hold such office until a successor shall have been in like manner appointed and duly qualified, except as herein otherwise provided."

On the second day of February, the House passed the bill with an amendment striking out the words included in brackets. This action shows that it was the purpose of the House to include heads of departments in the body of the bill, and subject them to its provisions as civil officers who were to hold their places by and with the advice and consent of the Senate, and subject, during the session of the Senate, to removal by and with the advice and consent of the Senate only; but subject to suspension under the second section during a recess of the Senate as other civil officers, by virtue of the words at the close of the section, "except as herein otherwise provided." At the time the bill was pending between the two Houses, there was no proviso to the first section, and the phrase "except as otherwise herein provided," related necessarily to the second and to the subsequent sections of the bill. On the 6th of February the Senate refused to agree to the House amendment, and by the action of the two Houses the bill was referred to a committee of conference. The conference committee agreed to strike out the words in brackets, agreeably to a vote of the House, but as a recognition of the opinion of the Senate, the proviso was inserted which modified in substance the effect of the words stricken out, under the lead of the House only in this, that the Cabinet officers referred to in the body of the section as it passed the House were to hold their offices as they would have held them if the House amendment had been agreed to, without condition, with this exception, that they were to retire from their offices in one month after the end of the term of the President by whom they might have been appointed to office. The object and effect of this qualification of the provision for which the House contended was to avoid fastening, by operation of law, upon an incoming President the Cabinet of his predecessor, with no means of relieving himself from them unless the Senate of the United States was disposed to concur in their removal.

In short, they were to retire by operation of law, at the end of one month after the expiration of the term of the President by whom they had been appointed, and in this particular their tenure of office was distinguished by the proviso, from the tenure by which other civil officers mentioned in the body of the section were to hold their offices, and their tenure of office is distinguished in no other particular.

The counsel who opened the cause for the President was pleased to read from the *Globe* the remarks made by Mr. Schenck, in the House of Representatives when the report of the Conference Committee was under discussion. But he read only a portion of the remarks of Mr. Schenck, and connected with them observations of his own, by which he may have led the Senate into the error that Mr. Schenck entertained the opinion as to the effect of the proviso which is now urged by the respondent; but so far from this being the case, the statement made by Mr. Schenck to the House is exactly in accordance with the doctrine now maintained by the managers on the part of the House of Representatives. After Mr. Schenck had made the remarks quoted by the counsel for the respondent, Mr. Le Blond, of Ohio, rose and said:—

"I would like to inquire of the gentleman who has charge of this report whether it becomes necessary that the Senate shall concur in all appointments of executive officers, and that none of them can be removed after appointment without the concurrence of the Senate?"

Mr. Schenck says, in reply:—

'"That is the case; but their terms of office are limited (as they are not now limited by law), so that they expire with the term of service of the President who appoints them, and one month after, in case of death or other accident, until others can be substituted for them by the incoming President."

Mr. Le Blond, continuing, said:—

"I understand, then this is to be the effect of the report of the Committee of Conference; in the event of the President finding himself with a Cabinet officer who does not agree with him, and whom he desires to remove, he cannot do so, and have a Cabinet in keeping with his own views, unless the Senate shall concur."

To this Mr. Schenck replies:—

The gentleman certainly does not need that information from me, as this subject has been fully debated in this House.

Mr. Le Blond said, finally:—

"Then I hope the House will not agree to the report of the Committee of Conference,

This debate in the House shows that there was there and then no difference of opinion between Mr. Schenck, who represented the friends of the bill, and Mr. Le Blond, who represented the opponents of the bill, that its effect was to confirm the Secretaries who were then in office, in their places, until one month after the expiration of Mr. Lincoln's term of office, to wit, the 4th day of March, 1869, unless, upon the nomination of successors, they should be removed by and with the advice and consent of the Senate. Nor does the language used by the honorable Senator from Ohio, who reported the result of the conference to the Senate, justify the inference which has been drawn from it by the counsel for the respondent. The charge made by the honorable Senator from Wisconsin, which the honorable Senator from Ohio was refuting, seems to me to have been in substance, that the first section of the bill and the proviso to the first section of the bill had been framed with special reference to Mr. Johnson as President, and to the existing condition of affairs. In response to this, the honorable Senator from Ohio said:—

"I say that the Senate have not legislated with a view to any persons or any President, and therefore he commences by asserting what is not true. We do not legislate in order to keep in the Secretary of War, the Secretary of the Navy, or the Secretary of State."

It will be observed that this language does not indicate the opinion of the honorable Senator as to the effect of the bill; but it is only a declaration that the object of the legislation was not that which had been intimated or alleged by the honorable Senator from Wisconsin. This view of the remarks of the honorable Senator from Ohio is confirmed by what he afterwards said in reply to the suggestion that the members of the Cabinet would hold their places against the wishes of the President, when he declares that under such circumstances, he, as a Senator, would consent to their removal at any time, showing most clearly that he did not entertain the idea that, under the Tenure of Office act, it would be in the power of the President to remove a Cabinet officer without the advice and consent of the Senate. And we all agree that, in ordinary times and under ordinary circumstances, it would be just and proper for a Cabinet officer to tender his resignation at once, upon the suggestion of the President that it would be acceptable, but that it would be the height of personal and official indecorum if he were to hesitate for a moment as to his duty in that particular. But the justification of Mr. Stanton, and his claim to the gratitude and the encomiums of his countrymen, is, that when the nation was imperilled by the usurpations of a criminally-minded Chief Magistrate, he asserted his constitutional and legal rights to the office of Secretary for the Department of War, and thus, by his devotion to principle, and at great personal sacrifices, he has done more than any other man since the close of the Rebellion to protect the interests and maintain the rights of the people of the country.

But the strength of the view we entertain of the meaning and scope of the Tenure of Office act is nowhere more satisfactorily demonstrated than in the inconsistencies of the argument which has been presented by the learned counsel for the respondent in support of the President's positions. He says, speaking of the first section of the act regulating the tenure of certain civil offices:—"Here is a section, then, the body of which applies to all civil officers, as well to those then in office as to those who should thereafter be appointed. The body of this section contains a a declaration that every such officer 'is,' that is, if he is now in office, and 'shall be,' that is, if he shall hereafter be appointed to office, entitled to hold until a successor is appointed and qualified in his place. This is the body of the section." This language of the eminent counsel is not only an admission, but it is a declaration that the Secretary for the Department of War, being a civil officer, as is elsewhere admitted in the argument of the counsel for the respondent, is included in and covered and controlled by the language of the body of this section. It is a further admission that in the absence of the proviso, the power of the President over the Secretary for the Department of War would correspond exactly to his power over any other civil officer, which would be merely the power to nominate a successor, whose confirmation by the Senate, and appointment, would work the removal of the person in office. When the counsel for the respondent, proceeding in his argument, enters upon an examination of the proviso, he maintains that the language of that proviso does not include the Secretary for the Department of War. If he is not included in the language of the proviso, then, upon the admission of the counsel, he is included in the body of the bill, so that for the purposes or this investigation and trial it is wholly immaterial whether the proviso applies to him or not. If the proviso does not apply to the Secretary for the Department of War, then he holds his office, as in the body of the section expressed, until removed therefrom by and with the advice and consent of the Senate. If he is covered by the language of the proviso, then a limitation is fixed to his office, to wit:—That it is to expire one month after the close of the term of the President by whom he has been appointed, subject, however, to previous removal by and with the advice and consent of the Senate.

I have already considered the question of intent on the part of the President and maintained that in the willful violation of the law he discloses a criminal intent which cannot be controlled or qualified by any testimony on the part of the respondent.

The counsel for the respondent, however, has dwelt so much at length on the question of intent, and such efforts have been made during the trial to introduce testimony upon this point, that I am justified in recurring to it for a brief consideration of the arguments and views bearing upon and relating to that question. If a law passed by Congress be equivocal or ambiguous in its terms, the Executive, being called upon to administer it, may apply his own best judgment to the difficulties before him, or he may seek counsel from his official advisers or other proper persons; and acting thereupon, without evil intent or purpose, he would be fully justified, and upon no principle of right could he be held to answer as for a misdemeanor in office. But that is not this case. The question considered by Mr. Johnson did not relate to the meaning of the Tenure of Office act. He understood perfectly well the intention of Congress, and he admitted in his veto message that the intention was expressed with sufficient clearness to enable him to comprehend and state it. In his veto message of the 2d of March, 1867, after quoting the first section of the bill to regulate the tenure of certain civil offices, he says:—

"In effect the bill provides that the President shall not remove from their places *any civil officers* whose terms of service are not limited by law without the advice and consent of the Senate of the United states. The bill, in this respect, conflicts, in my judgment, with the Constitution of the United States."

His statement of the meaning of the bill relates to all civil officers, to the members of his Cabinet as well as to others, and is a declaration that, under that bill if it became a law, none of these officers could be removed without the advice and consent of the Senate. He was, therefore, in no doubt as to the intention of Congress as expressed in the bill submitted to him for his consideration, and which afterwards became the law of the land. He said to the Senate, "If you pass this bill I cannot remove the members of my Cabinet." The Senate and House in effect said, "We do so intend," and passed the bill by a two-thirds majority.

There was then no misunderstanding as to the meaning or intention of the act. His offense, then, is not that upon an examination of the statute he misunderstood its meaning and acted upon a misinterpretation of its true import, but that understanding its meaning precisely as it is understood by the Congress that passed the law; precisely as it is understood by the House of Representatives to-day; precisely as it is presented in the articles of impeachment, and by the managers before this Senate, he, upon his own opinion that the same was unconstitutional, deliberately, wilfully and intentionally disregarded it. The learned counsel say that he had a right to violate this law for the purpose of obtaining a judicial determination. This we deny. The constitutional duty of the President is to obey and execute the laws. He has no authority under the Constitution, or by any law, to enter into any schemes or plans for the purpose of testing the validity of the laws of the country, either judicially or otherwise. Every law of Congress may be decided in the courts, but it is not made the duty of any person to so test the law. It is not specially the right of any person to so test the laws, and the effort is especially offensive in the Chief Magistrate of the country to attempt by any process to annul, set aside, or defeat the laws which by his oath he is bound to execute.

Nor is it any answer to say, as is suggested by the counsel for the respondent, that " there never could be a judicial decision that a law is unconstitutional, inasmuch as it is only by disregarding a law that any question can be raised judicially under it." If this be true, it is no misfortune. But the opposite theory, that it is the duty or the right of the President to disregard a law for the purpose of ascertaining judicially whether he has a right to violate a law is abhorrent to every just principle of government, and dangerous to the highest degree to the existence of free institutions.

But his alleged purpose to test the law in the courts is shown to be a pretext merely. Upon this theory of his rights, he could have instituted proceedings by information in the nature of a *quo warranto* against Mr. Stanton on the 13th of January, 1868. More than three months have passed, and he has done nothing whatever. When by Mr. Stanton's action Lorenzo Thomas was under arrest, and proceedings were instituted which might have tested the legality of the tenure of office act, Mr. Cox, the President's special counsel, moved to have the proceedings dismissed, although Thomas was at large upon his own recognizance. Can anybody believe that it was Mr. Johnson's purpose to test the act in the courts? But the respondent's insincerity, his duplicity, is shown by the statement which he made to Gen. Sherman in January last. Sherman says:

"I asked him why lawyers could not make a case, and not bring me, or any officer, into the controversy? His answer was 'that it was found impossible, or a case could not be made up;' 'but,' said he, 'if we can bring the case to the courts, it would not stand half an hour.' " He now says his object was to test the case in the courts. To Sherman he declares that a case could not be made up, but if one could be made up the law would not stand half an hour. When a case was made up which might have tested the law, he makes haste to get it dismissed. Did ever audacity and duplicity more clearly appear in the excuses of a criminal?

This brief argument upon the question of intent seems to me conclusive, but I shall incidentally refer to the evidence on this point in the further progress of my remarks.

The House of Representatives does not demand the conviction of Andrew Johnson unless he is guilty in the manner charged in the articles of impeachment; nor does the House expect the managers to seek a conviction except upon the law and facts considered with judicial impartiality. But I am obliged to declare that I have no capacity to understand those processes of the human mind by which this tribunal, or any member of this tribunal, can doubt, can entertain a reasonable doubt, that Andrew Johnson is guilty of high misdemeanor in office, as charged in each of the first three articles exhibited against him by the House of Representatives.

We have charged and proved that Andrew Johnson President of the United States, issued an order, in writing, for the removal of Edwin M. Stanton from the office of Secretary for the Department of War while the Senate of the United States was in session, and without the advice and consent of the Senate, in violation of the Constitution of the United States and of his oath of office, and of the provisions of an act passed March 2, 1867, entitled, "an act regulating the tenure of certain civil offices," and that he did this with intent so to do; and thereupon, we demand his conviction under the first of the articles of impeachment exhibited against him by the House of Representatives.

We have charged and proved that Andrew Johnson, President of the United States, violated the Constitution and his oath of office, in issuing an order for the removal of Edwin M. Stanton from the office of Secretary for the Department of War, during the session of the Senate, and without the advice and consent of the Senate, and this without reference to the Tenure of Office act; and thereupon we demand his conviction under the first articles of impeachment exhibited against him by the House of Representatives.

We have charged and proved that Andrew Johnson, President of the United States, did issue and deliver to one Lorenzo Thomas, a letter of authority in writing, authorizing and empowering said Thomas to act as Secretary of War *ad interim*, there being no vacancy in said office, and this while the Senate of the United States was in session, and without the advice and consent of the Senate, in violation of the Constitution of the United States, of his oath of office, and of the provisions of an act entitled "An act regulating the tenure of certain civil offices," and all this with the intent so to do; and, thereupon, we demand his conviction under the second of the articles of impeachment exhibited against him by the House of Representatives.

We have charged and proved that Andrew Johnson, President of the United States, in the appointment of Lorenzo Thomas to the office of Secretary of War *ad interim* acted without authority of law, and in violation of the Constitution and of his oath of office; and this without reference to the Tenure of Office act; and thereupon we demand his conviction under the third of the articles of impeachment exhibited against him by the House of Representatives.

At four o'clock Mr. Boutwell, at the suggestion of Mr. CONKLING, yielded to a motion to adjourn the court stating that he would occupy about an hour and a half to-morrow, and accordingly the court adjourned.

PROCEEDINGS OF THURSDAY, APRIL 23.

The Senate reassembled at 11 o'clock, and the court was opened in the usual form.

Mr. GRIMES submitted the following:—

Ordered, That hereafter the hour for the meeting of the Senate, sitting on the trial of the impeachment of Andrew Johnson, President of the United States, shall be 12 o'clock meridian each day, except Sunday.

Mr. SUMNER and several others objected, and the order was laid over.

At 11·20 o'clock Mr. BOUTWELL resumed his address.

The learned counsel for the respondent seems to have involved himself in some difficulty concerning the articles which he terms the conspiracy articles, being articles four, five, six and seven. The allegations contained in articles four and six are laid under the act of July 31, 1861, known as the conspiracy act. The remarks of the learned counsel seem to imply that articles five and seven were not based upon any law whatever. In this he greatly errs. An examination of articles four and five shows that the substantive allegation is the same in each article, the differences being that article four charges the conspiracy with intent, by intimidation and threats, unlawfully to hinder and prevent Edwin M. Stanton from holding the office of Secretary for the Department of War. The persons charged are the respondent and Lorenzo Thomas. And it is alleged that this conspiracy, for the purpose set forth, was in violation of the Constitution of the United States, and of the provisions of an act entitled "An act to punish certain conspiracies," approved July 31, 1861.

The fifth article charges that the respondent did unlawfully conspire with one Lorenzo Thomas, and with other persons, to prevent the execution of the act entitled " An act regulating the tenure of certain civil offices," and that in pursuance of that conspiracy, they did unlawfully attempt to prevent Edwin M. Stanton from holding the office of Secretary for the Department of War. It is not alleged in the article that this conspiracy is against any particular law, but it is alleged that the parties charged did unlawfully conspire. It is very well known that conspiracies are of two kinds. Two or more persons may conspire to do a *lawful* act by *unlawful* means; or two or more persons may conspire to do an *unlawful* act by *lawful* means. By the common law of England such conspiracies have always been indictable and punishable as misdemeanors.

The State of Maryland was one of the original thirteen States of the Union, and the common law of England has always prevailed in that State, except so far as it has been modified by statute. The city of Washington was originally within the State of Maryland, but it was ceded to the United States under the provisions of the Constitution. By a statute of the United States, passed February 27, 1801 (Statutes at Large, vol. 2, p. 103), it is provided:—

"That the laws of the State of Maryland, as they now exist, shall be and continue in force in that part of the said District which was ceded by that State to the United States, and by them accepted as aforesaid."

By force of this statute, although probably the law would have been the same without legislation, the English common law of crimes prevails in the city of Washington. By another statute, entitled "An act for the punishment of crimes in the District of Columbia," 'Statutes at Large, vol. 4. page 450), approved March 2, 1831, special punishments are affixed to various crimes enumerated, when committed in the District of Columbia. But conspiracy is not one of the crimes mentioned. The fifteenth section of that act provides:—

"That every other felony, misdemeanor, or offense, not provided for by this act, may, and shall be punished as heretofore, except that in all cases where whipping is part or the whole of the punishment, except in the cases of slaves, the court shall substitute for imprisonment in the county jail, for a period not exceeding six months."

And the sixteenth section declares:—

"That all definitions and descriptions of crimes, all fines, forfeitures, and incapacities, the restitution of property, or the payment of the value thereof, and every other matter not provided for in this act, be and the same shall remain as heretofore."

There can then be no doubt that, under the English common law of crimes, sanctioned and continued by the statutes of the United States in the District of Columbia, the fifth and seventh articles set forth offenses which are punishable as misdemeanors by the laws of the District.

Article sixth is laid under the statute of 1861, and charges that the respondent did unlawfully conspire with Lorenzo Thomas, by force to seize, take and possess the property of the United States in the Department of War, and this with intent to violate and disregard the act entitled "An act regulating the tenure of certain civil offices." The words used in the Conspiracy act of 1861 leave room for argument upon the point raised by the learned counsel for the respondent. I admit that the District of Columbia is not included by specific designation, but the reasons for the law and the natural interpretation of the language justify the view that the act applies to the District. I shall refer to a single authority upon that point.

The internal duties act of August 2, 1813, (Stat., vol. 3, p. 82) subjects, in express terms, the "several Territories of the United States and the District of Columbia," to the payment of taxes imposed; upon which the question arose whether Congress has power to impose a direct tax on the District of Columbia, in view of the fact that by the Constitution "representation and direct taxes shall be apportioned among the several States which may be included within the Union, according to their respective numbers.'

In the case of Loughborough vs. Blake, the Supreme Court of the United States unanimously decided, in a brief but well written opinion by Chief Justice Marshall, that although the language of the Constitution apparently excepts the District of Columbia from the imposition of direct taxes, yet the reason of the thing requires us to consider the District as being comprehended, in this respect within the intention of the Constitution. (Lough. vs. Blake, 5 Wheaton, p. 317.

The reasoning of the Supreme Court and its conclusion in this case were satisfactory to the bar and the country, and no person has deemed it worth while to raise the question anew under the direct tax act of August 5, 1861 (Sts. xii., 296), which also comprehends the Territories and the District of Columbia.

But the logical rules of construction applicable to an act of Congress are the same as those applicable to the Constitution. An act of Congress and the Constitution are both laws, nothing more, nothing less, except that the latter is of superior authority. And, if in the construction of the Constitution, it may be satisfactorily maintained that the District of Columbia is to be deemed, because of the reason of things, to be comprehended by a provision of the Constitution, which in words, and in their superficial construction, excludes it, must not the same rule of construction produce the same result in the determination of the legal intent and import of an act of Congress, when an obscurity exists in the latter for the same cause?

The seventh article is laid upon the common law, and charges substantially the same offenses as those charged in the sixth article. The result, then, is that the fifth and seventh articles, which are based upon the common law, set forth substantially the same offenses which are set forth in the fourth and sixth articles, which are laid upon the statute of July 31, 1861; and as there can be no doubt of the validity of the fifth and seventh articles, it is practically immaterial whether the suggestion made by the counsel for the respondent, that the conspiracy act of 1861 does not include the District of Columbia, as a valid objection or not. Not doubting that the Senate will find that the charge of conspiracy is sufficiently laid under existing laws, I proceed to an examination of the evidence by which the charge is supported.

It should always be borne in mind that the evidence in proof of conspiracy will generally, from the nature of the crime, be circumstantial; and this case in this particular is no exception to the usual experience in criminal trials. We find, in the first place, if the allegations in the first, second and third articles have been established, that the President was engaged in an unlawful act. If we find Lorenzo Thomas or any other person co-operating with him upon an agreement or an understanding, or an assent on the part of such other person to the prosecution of such unlawful undertaking, an actual conspiracy is proved. The existence of the conspiracy being established, it is then competent to introduce the statements of the parties to the conspiracy, made and done while the conspiracy was pending, and in furtherance of the design; and it is upon this ground that testimony has been offered and received of the declarations made by Lorenzo Thomas, one of the parties to the conspiracy, subsequent to the 18th day of January, 1868, or perhaps the 13th of January, 1868, the day on which he was restored to the office of Adjutant-General of the Army of the United States by the action of the President, and which appears to have been an initial proceeding on his part for the purpose of accomplishing his unlawful design—the removal of Mr. Stanton from the office of the Secretary for the Department of War. The evidence of agreement between the respondent and Thomas is found in the order of the 21st of Febuary, 1868, appointing Thomas, and in the conversation which took place at the time the order was placed in Thomas' hands. The counsel for the respondent at this point was involved in a very serious difficulty. If he had admitted (which he took care not to do) that the order was a military one, he saw that his client would be involved in the crime of having issued a military order which did not pass through the General of the Army, and thus would be liable to impeachment and removal from office for the crime of violating the law of the 2d of March, 1867, entitled " an act making appropriations for the support of the army for the fiscal year ending June 30, 1868, and for other purposes." If he had declared that it was not a military order, then the transaction confessedly was in the nature of an agreement between the President and Lorenzo Thomas; and if the act contemplated by that agreement was an unlawful act, or if the act were lawful, and the means employed for accomplishing it were unlawful, then clearly the charge of conspiracy would be maintained. Hence he was careful to say, in denying that the order was a military order, that it nevertheless "invoked that spirit of military obedience which constitutes the strength of the service."

And, further, he says of Thomas, that as a faithful Adjutant-General of the Army of the United States, interested personally, professionally, and patriotically to have the office of Secretary of the Dpartment of War performed in a temporary vacancy, was it not his duty to accept the appointment unless he knew that it was unlawful to accept it? The admissions and statements of the learned counsel are to the effect, on the whole, that the order was not a military order, nor do we claim that it was a military order, but it was a letter addressed to General Thomas, which he could have declined altogether, without subjecting himself to any punishment by a military tribunal.

This is the crucial test of the character of the paper which he received, and on which he proceeded to act. Ignorance of the law, according to the old maxim, excuses no man; and whether General Thomas, at the first interview he had with the President, on the 18th of January, 1868, or at his interview with him on the day when he received the letter of appointment, knew that the President was then engaged in an unlawful act, is not material to this inquiry. The President knew that his purpose was an unlawful one, and he then and there induced General Thomas to co-operate with him in the prosecution of the unlawful design. If General Thomas was ignorant of the illegal nature of the transaction, that fact furnishes no legal defense for him, though morally it might be an excuse for his conduct. But certainly the President, who did know the illegal nature of the proceeding, cannot excuse himself by asserting that his co-conspirator was at the time ignorant of the illegal nature of the business in which they were engaged.

It being proved that the respondent was engaged in an unlawful undertaking in his attempt to remove Mr. Stanton from the office of Secretary for the Department of War, that by an agreement or understanding between General Thomas and himself they were to co-operate in carrying this purpose into execution, and it being proved, also, that the purpose itself was unlawful, all the elements of a conspiracy are fully established; and it only remains to examine the testimony in order that the nature of the conspiracy may more clearly appear, and the means by which the purpose was to be accomplished may be more fully understood.

The statement of the President in his message to the Senate under date of 12th of December, 1867, discloses the depth of his feeling and the intensity of his purpose in regard to the removal of Mr. Stanton. In that message he speaks of the bill regulating the tenure of certain civil offices at the time it was before him for consideration. He says:—"The bill had not then become a law; the limitation upon the power of removal was not yet imposed, and there was yet time to make any changes. If any of those gentlemen (meaning the members of his Cabinet) had then said to me that he would avail himself of the provisions of that bill in case it became a law. I should not have hesitated a moment as to his removal."

When, in the summer of 1867, the respondent became satisfied that Mr. Stanton not only did not enter into the President's schemes, but was opposed to them, and he determined upon his suspension and final removal from the office of Secretary for the Department of War, he knew that the confidence of the people in Mr. Stanton was very great, and that they would not accept his removal and an appointment to that important place of any person of doubtful position, or whose qualifiations were not known to the country. Hence he sought, through the suspension of Mr. Stanton and the appointment of General Grant as Secretary of War ad interim, to satisfy the country for the moment, but with the design to prepare the way thereby for the introduction into the War Department of one of his own creatures.

At that time it was supposed that the suspension of Mr. Stanton and the appointment of General Grant were made under and by virtue of the act regulating the tenure of certain civil offices; and although the conduct of the President during a period of nearly six months in reference to that office was in conformity to the provisions of that act, it was finally declared by him that what he had done had been done in conformity to the general power which he claims, under the Constitution, and that he did not in any way recognize the act as constitutional or binding upon him. His message to the Senate of the 12th of December was framed apparently in obedience to the Tenure of Office act. He charged Mr. Stanton with misconduct in office, which, by the act, had been made a ground for the suspension of a civil officer; he furnished reasons and evidence of misconduct which, as he alleged, had been satisfactory to him, and he furnished such reasons and evidence within twenty days after the meeting of the Senate next following the day of suspension.

All this was in conformity to the statute of March 2, 1867. The Senate proceeded to consider the evidence and, reasons furnished by the President, and in conformity to that act passed a resolution, adopted on the 13th of January, 1868, declaring that the reasons were unsatisfactory to the Senate, and that Mr. Stanton was restored to the office of Secretary for the Department of War. Up to that time there had been no official statement or declaration by the President that he had not acted under the Tenure of Office act; but he now assumed that that act had no binding force, and that Mr. Stanton was not lawfully restored to the office of Secretary for the Department of War.

Upon the adoption of the resolution by the Senate, General Grant at once surrendered the office to Mr. Stanton. This act upon his part filled the President with indignation both towards General Grant and Mr. Stanton, and from that day he seems to have been under the influence of a settled and criminal purpose to destroy General Grant and to secure the removal of Mr. Stanton. During the month following the restoration of Mr. Stanton the President attempted to carry out his purpose by various and tortuous methods. First, he endeavored to secure the support of General Sherman. On two occasions, as is testified by General Sherman—on the 27th and 31st of

January, tendered him the position of Secretary of War ad interim.

It occurred very naturally to General Sherman to inquire of the President whether Mr. Stanton would retire voluntarily from the office; and also to ask the President what he was to do, and whether he would resort to force if Mr. Stanton would not yield. The President answered, "Oh, he will make no objection; you present the order and he will retire." Upon a doubt being expressed by General Sherman, the President remarked, "I know him better than you do; he is cowardly." The President knew Mr. Stanton too well to entertain any such opinion of his courage as he gave in his answer to General Sherman; the secret of the proceeding, undoubtedly was this:—

He desired, in the first place, to induce General Sherman to accept the office of Secretary of War ad interim upon the assurance on his part that Mr. Stanton would retire willingly from his position, trusting that when General Sherman was appointed to and had accepted the place of Secretary of War ad interim, he could be induced, either upon the suggestion of the President or under the influence of a natural disinclination on his part to fail in the accomplishment of anything which he had undertaken, to seize the War Department by force. The President very well knew that if General Sherman accepted the office of Secretary of War ad interim he would be ready at the earliest moment to relinquish it into the hands of the President, and thus he hoped through the agency of General Sherman to secure the possession of the department for one of his favorites.

During the period from the 13th day of January to the 21st of February he made an attempt to enlist General George H. Thomas in the same unlawful undertaking. Here, also, he was disappointed. Thus it is seen that from August last, the time when he entered systematically upon his purpose to remove Mr. Stanton from the office of Secretary for the Department of War, he has attempted to secure the purpose he had in view through the personal influence and services of the three principal officers of the army; and that he has met with disappointment in each case. Under these circumstances nothing remained for the respondent but to seize the office by an open, wilfull, defiant violation of law; and as it was necessary for the accomplishment of his purpose that he should obtain the support of some one, and as his experience had satisfied him that no person of capacity, or respectability, or patriotism would unite with him in his unlawful enterprise, he sought the assistance and aid of Lorenzo Thomas.

This man, as you have seen him, is an old man, a broken man, a vain man, a weak man, utterly incapable of performing any public service whatever in a manner creditable to the country; but possessing, nevertheless, all the qualities and characteristics of a subservient instrument and tool of an ambitious, unscrupulous criminal. He readily accepted the place which the President offered him, and there is no doubt that the declarations which he made to Wilkeson, Burleigh and Karsner, were made when he entertained the purpose of executing them, and made also in the belief that they were entirely justified by the orders which he had received from the President, and that the execution of his purpose to seize the War Department by force would be acceptable to the President. That he threatens to use force there is no doubt from the testimony, for he has himself confessed substantially the truth of the statements made by all the witnesses for the prosecution who have testified to that fact.

These statements were made by Thomas on or after the 21st of February, when he received his letter of authority, in writing, to take possession of the War Department. The agreement between the President and Thomas was consummated on that day. With one mind they were then, and on subsequent days, engaged, and up to the present time, they are engaged in the attempt to get possession of the War Department. Mr. Stanton, as the Senate by its resolution has declared, being the lawful Secretary of War, this proceeding on their part was an unlawful proceeding. It had in view an unlawful purpose; it was therefore in contemplation of the law a conspiracy, and the President is consequently bound by the declarations made by Thomas in regard to taking possession of the War Department by force.

Thomas admits that on the night of the 21st it was his purpose to use force; that on the morning of the 22d his mind had undergone a change, and he then resolved not to use force. We do not know precisely the hour when his mind underwent this change, but the evidence disclosed that upon his return from the Supreme Court of the District, where he had been arraigned upon a complaint made by Mr. Stanton, which, according to the testimony, was twelve o'clock, or thereabouts, he had an interview with the President; and it is also in evidence, that at or about the same time the President had an interview with General Emory, from whom he learned that the officer would not obey a command of the President unless it passed through General Grant, as required by law.

The President understood perfectly well that he could neither obtain force from General Grant nor transmit an order through General Grant for the accomplishment of a purpose manifestly unlawful; and inasmuch as General Emory had indicated to him in the most distinct and emphatic manner his opinion that the law requiring all orders to pass through the headquarters of the General commanding, was constitutional, indicating, also, his purpose to obey the law, it was apparent that at that moment the President could have had no hope of obtaining possession of the Department of War by force. It is a singular coincidence in the history of this case that at or about the same time, General Thomas had an interview with the

President, and came to the conclusion that it would not be wise to resort to force.

The President has sought to show his good intention by the fact that, on the 22d or the 24th of February, he nominated the Hon. Thomas Ewing, Sr., as Secretary for the Department of War. Mr. Ewing is not an unknown man. He has been a member of the Senate and the head of the Treasury Department. His abilities are undoubted, but at the time of his nomination he was in the seventy-ninth year of his age, and there was no probability that he would hold the office a moment longer than his sense of public duty required. It was the old game of the President—the office in the hands of his own tool, or in the hands of a man who would gladly vacate it at any moment. This was the necessity of his position, and throws light upon that part of his crime which is set forth in the eleventh article.

For, in fact, his crime is one—the subversion of the government. From the nature of the case we are compelled to deal with minor acts of criminality by which he hoped to consummate this greatest of crimes.

In obedience to this necessity he appointed Grant, hoping to use him and his influence with the army, and failing in this, to get possession of the place and fill it with one of his own satellites; foiled and disappointed in this scheme, he sought to use, first, General Sherman, then General George H. Thomas, then Hon. Thomas Ewing, Sr., knowing that neither of these gentlemen would retain the office for any length of time. There were men in the country who would have accepted the office and continued in it, and obeyed the Constitution and the laws. Has he named any such person? Has he suggested any such person? His appointments and suggestions of appointment have been of two sorts—honorable men, who would not continue in the office, or dishonorable, worthless men, who were not fit to hold the office.

The name of General Cox, of Ohio, was named in the public journals; it was mentioned, probably, to the President. Did it meet with favor? Did he send his name to the Senate? No.

General Cox, if he had accepted the office at all, would have done so with the expectation of holding it till March, 1869, and with the purpose of executing the duties of the trust according to the laws and the Constitution. These were purposes wholly inconsistent with the President's schemes of usurpation. But is it to be presumed or imagined that when the President issued his order for the removal of Stanton, and his letter of authority to Lorenzo Thomas, on the 21st of February, he had any purpose of appointing Mr. Ewing Secretary of War? Certainly not. On the afternoon of the 21st he informs his Cabinet that Stanton is removed, and that Thomas has possession of the office. He then so believed. Thomas had deceived or misled him. On the 22d inst. he had discovered that Stanton held on to the place, and that Emory could not be relied upon for force.

What was now his necessity? Simply a resort to his old policy. He saw that it was necessary to avoid impeachment if possible, and also to obtain the sanction of the Senate to a nomination which would work the removal of Mr. Stanton, and thus he would triumph over his enemies and obtain condonation for his crimes of the 21st of February. A well laid scheme, but destined to fail and to furnish evidence of his own guilty purposes. With the office in the possession of Mr. Ewing, he foresaw that for the prosecution of his own plans the place would always be vacant.

Thus has this artful and criminal man pursued the great purpose of his life. Consider the other circumstances. On the 1st of September last General Emory was appointed to the command of the Department of Washington. He has exhibited such sterling honesty and vigorous patriotism in these recent troubles and during the war, that he can bear a reference to his previous history. He was born in Maryland, and in the early part of the war the public mind of the North questioned his fidelity to the Union. His great services and untarnished record during the war are a complete defense against all suspicion; but it is too much to believe that Mr. Johnson entertained the hope that General Emory might be made an instrument of his ambition.

Nobly has General Emory undeceived the President, and gained additional renown in the country. In General Lorenzo Thomas the President was not deceived. His complicity in recent unlawful proceedings justifies the suspicions entertained by the country in 1861 and 1862 touching his loyalty. Thomas and the President are in accord. In case of the acquittal of the President they are to issue an order to General Grant putting Thomas in possession of the reports of the army to the War Department.

Is there not in all this evidence of the President's criminal intention? Is not his whole course marked by duplicity, deception, and fraud? "All things are construed against the wrong-doer," is the wise and just maxim of the law. Has he not trifled with and deceived the Senate? Has he not attempted to accomplish an unlawful purpose by disingenuous, tortuous, criminal means?

His criminal intent is in his wilfull violation of the law, and his criminal intent is moreover abundantly proved by all the circumstances attending the violation of the law.

His final resort for safety was to the Senate, praying for the confirmation of Mr. Ewing. On the 21st of February he hoped that Stanton would yield willingly, or that Emory could be used to remove him. On the 22d he knew that Stanton was determined to remain, that Emory would not furnish assistance, that it was useless to appeal to Grant. He returns to his old plan of filling the War Office by the appointment of a man who would yield the

place at any moment; and now he asks you to accept as his justification an act which was the last resort of a criminal attempting to escape the judgment due to his crimes. Upon this view of the law and the facts, we demand a conviction of the respondent upon articles four, five, six and seven exhibited against him by the House of Representatives.

The evidence introduced tending to show a conspiracy between Johnson and Thomas to get possession of the War Department tends also, connected with other facts, to show the purpose of the President to obtain possession of the Treasury Department. Bearing in mind his claim that he can suspend or remove from office, without the advice and consent of the Senate, any civil officer, and bearing in mind also that the present Secretary of the Treasury supports this claim, and every obstacle to the possession of the Treasury Department is removed.

There is no reason to suppose the present Secretary of the Treasury would not yield a cordial support to any scheme which Mr. Johnson might undertake; but if the Secretary should decline to co-operate it would only be necessary for the President to remove him from office and place the Treasury Department in the hands of one of his own creatures.

Upon the appointment of Thomas as Secretary of War ad interim, the President caused notice to be given thereof to the Secretary of the Treasury, accompanied with the direction, under the President's own hand, to that officer to govern himself accordingly. It also proved that on the 22d day of December Mr. Johnson appointed Mr. Cooper, who had been his private secretary and intimate friend, Assistant Secretary of the Treasury.

The evidence fully sustains the statements made in the opening argument of Manager Butler, in support of article nine. The facts in regard to General Emory's interview with the President were then well known to the managers, and the argument and view presented in the opening count in all that is necessary to be said upon that article. It may be added, however, that although the President on the 22d had obtained from General Emory what he now says was the purpose of this interview, a knowledge of the number and assignment of troops in the city of Washington, yet on the following day, Sunday, the 23d of February, he had an interview with General Wallace, apparently for no other purpose than to get from him the same information which, on the preceding day, he had received from General Emory.

The learned counsel who opened the case for the President seems not to have comprehended the nature of the offense set forth in the tenth article. His remarks upon that article proceeded upon the idea that the House of Representatives arraign the President for slandering or libelling the Congress of the United States. No such offense is charged; nor is it claimed by the managers that it would be possible for Mr. Johnson or any other person, to libel or slander the government. It is for no purpose of protection or indemnity of punishment that we arraign Mr. Johnson for words spoken in Washington, Cleveland and St. Louis. We do not arraign him for the words spoken; but the charge in substance is, that a man who could utter the words which, as is proven, were uttered by him, is unfit for the office he holds. We claim that the common law of crimes, as understood and enforced by Parliament in cases of impeachment, is in substance this:—That no person in office shall do any act contrary to the good morals of the office; and that, when any officer is guilty of any act contrary to the good morals of the office which he holds, that act is a misdemeanor for the purpose of impeachment and removal from office.

Judge Chase was impeached, and escaped conviction by four votes only, for words spoken from the bench of the Circuit Court, sitting in Baltimore; words which are decorous and reputable when compared with the utterances of Mr. Johnson. Judge Humphries was convicted and removed from office for words spoken, treasonable in character, but not more calculated to weaken and bring the government of the United States into contempt than were the words uttered by Mr. Johnson in his speech of the 18th of August, 1866. Judge Humphries was convicted by the unanimous vote of the Senators, nineteen of whom sit on this trial. If a magistrate can ever be guilty, for words spoken, of an impeachable misdemeanor, there can be no doubt that Mr. Johnson is so guilty.

I ask you to consider in comparison, or in contrast, the nature of the language used by Chase, Humphreys and Johnson, as set forth in the articles of impeachment preferred in the several cases.

The eighth article in the case of Chase, is in these words:—

"And whereas, mutual respect and confidence between the Government of the United States and those of the individual States, and between the people and those governments, respectively, are highly conducive to that public harmony, without which there can be no public happiness, yet the said Samuel Chase, disregarding the duties and dignity of his judicial character, did, at the Circuit Court for the District of Maryland, held at Baltimore, in the month of May, 1803, pervert his official right and duty to address the Grand Jury then and there assembled, on matters coming within the province of the said jury, for the purpose of delivering to the said Grand Jury an intemperate and inflammatory harangue, with intent to excite the fears and resentment of the said Grand Jury, and of the good people of Maryland, against their State government and Constitution, a conduct highly censurable in any, but peculiarly indecent and unbecoming in a judge of the Supreme Court of the United States; and, moreover, that the said Samuel Chase, then and there, under pretense of exercising his judicial right to address the said grand jury as aforesaid, did, in a manner highly unwarrantable, endeavor to excite the odium of the said Grand Jury, and of the good people of Maryland, against the Government of the United States, by delivering opinions which, even if the judiciary were competent to their expression, on a suitable occasion and in a proper manner, were, at that time, and as delivered by him, highly indecent, extra-judicial, and tending to prostitute the high judicial character with which he was invested to the low purpose of an electioneering partisan."

The first article against Humphreys was as follows:—

"That, regardless of his duties as a citizen of the United States, and unmindful of the duties of his said office, and in violation of the sacred obligation of his official oath, 'to administer justice without respect to persons.' 'and faithfully and impartially discharge all the duties incumbent upon him as Judge of the District Court of the United States for the several di-tricts of the State of Tennessee, agreeable to the Constitution and laws of the United States,' the said West H. Humphreys, then being a citizen of the United States, and owing allegiance thereto, and then and there being Judge of the District Court of the United States for the several districts of said State, at a public meeting, on the day and year last aforesaid, held in said city of Nashville, and in the hearing of divers persons then and there present, did endeavor, by public speech, to incite revolt and rebellion within said State against the Constitution and Government of the United States, and did then and there publicly declare that it was the right of the people of said State, by an ordinance of Secession, to absolve themselves from all allegiance to the Government of the United States, the Constitution and laws thereof."

The offense with which Humphreys is charged in this article was committed on the 29th of December, 1860, before the fall of Sumter, and when only one State had passed an ordinance of secession. The declaration was merely a declaration in a public speech that the State of Tennessee had the right to secede from the Union.

The President, in his speech of the 18th of August, 1866, at Washington, says:—

"We have witnessed in one department of the government every effort, as it were, to prevent the restoration of peace, harmony and union; we have seen, as it were, hanging upon the verge of the government, as it were, a body calling or assuming to be the Congress of the United States, when it was but a Congress of a part of the States; we have seen Congress assuming to be for the Union when every step they took was to perpetuate dissolution, and make dissolution permanent. We have seen every step that has been taken, instead of bringing about reconciliation and harmony, has been legislation that took the character of penalties, retaliation and revenge. This has been the course; this has been the policy of one department of your government."

These words have been repeated so frequently, and the public ear is so much accustomed to them, that they have apparently lost their influence upon the public mind. But it should be observed that these words, as has been proved by the experience of two years, were but the expression of a fixed purpose of the President. His design was to impair, to undermine, and, if possible, to destroy the influence of Congress in the country. Having accomplished this result, the way would then have been open to him for the prosecution of his criminal design to reconstruct the government in the interest of the Rebels, and, through his influence with them, to secure his own election to the Presidency in 1868. It must, however, be apparent that the words in the speech of Mr. Johnson are of graver import than the words which were spoken by Judge Chase to the Grand Jury at Baltimore, or those uttered by Judge Humphreys to the people of Tennessee.

And yet the latter was convicted by a unanimous vote of this Senate; and the former escaped conviction by four votes only. These words are of graver import, not merely in the circumstance that they assail a department of the government, but in the circumstance that they were uttered by the President of the United States in the Executive Mansion, and in his capacity as President of the United States, when receiving the congratulations and support of a portion of the people of the country, tendered to him in his office as Chief Magistrate. Judge Chase, although a high officer of the government, was without political influence and without patronage; his personal and official relations were limited, and his remarks were addressed to the grand jury of a judicial district of the country merely.

Judge Humphreys was comparatively unknown; and although his words were calculated to excite the citizens of Tennessee, and induce them to engage in unconstitutional undertakings, his influence was limited measurably to the people of that State.

Mr. Johnson addressed the whole country; and holding in his hands the immense patronage and influence belonging to the office of President, he was able to give practical effect to the declarations he made.

Moreover, in the case of Judge Chase, as is stated by Mr. Dana in his "Abridgement," (vol. 7, chap. 232):—

"On the whole evidence, it remained in doubt what words he did utter. The proof of seditious intent rested solely on the words themselves; and as the words were not clearly proved, the intent was in doubt."

In the case of Mr. Johnson there is no doubt about the words uttered: they have been fully and explicitly proved. Indeed, they are not denied by the respondent. The unlawful intent with which he uttered the words not only appears from the character of the language employed, but it is proved by the history of his administration. In his message of the 22d of June, 1866, relating to the Constitu-

tional Amendment, in his annual message of December, 1866, and numerous other declarations, he has questioned, and substantially denied, the legality of the Congress of the United States.

In the trial of Judge Chase it was admitted by the respondent "that for a judge to utter seditious sentiments with intent to excite sedition, would be an impeachable offense." (Dana's Abridgement, vol. 7, c. 222). And this, not under the act known as "the sedition act;" for that had been previously repealed; but upon the general principle that an officer, whose duty it is to administer the law, has no right to use language calculated to stir up resistance to the law. If this be true of a judge, with stronger reason it is true of the President of the United States, that he should set an example of respect for all the departments of the government, and of reverence for and obedience to the laws of the land.

The speeches made by the President at Cleveland and St. Louis, which have been proved and are found in the record of the case, contain numerous passages similar in character to that extracted from his speech of the 18th of August, 1866, and all calculated and designed to impair the just authority of Congress. While these declarations have not been made the basis of substantive charges in the articles of impeachment, they furnish evidence of the unlawful intent of the President in his utterance of the 18th of August, and also of the fact that that utterance was not due to any temporary excitement or transient purpose which passed away with the occasion that had called it forth. It was a declaration made in accordance with a fixed design, which had obtained such entire control of his nature that whenever he addressed public assemblies he gave expression to it.

The evidence which has been submitted by the respondent bearing upon the tenth article, indicates a purpose, in argument, to excuse the President upon the ground that the remarks of the people stimulated, irritated and excited him to such an extent that he was not wholly responsible for what he said. If this were true, it would exhibit great weakness of character; but as a matter of fact it is not true. The taunts and gibes of the people whom he insulted served only to draw from him those declarations which were in accord with the purpose of his life. This is shown by the fact that all his political declarations made at Cleveland and St. Louis, though made under excitement, are in entire harmony with the declarations made by him in the East Room of the Executive Mansion, on the 18th of August, 1866, when he was free from any disturbing influence, and expressed himself with freedom and without excitement.

The blasphemous utterances at St. Louis cannot be aggravated by me, nor can they be extenuated by anything which counsel for the respondent can offer. They exhibit the character of the speaker.

Upon these facts, thus proved, and the views presented, we demand the conviction of the respondent of the misdemeanors set forth in article ten.

Article eleven sets forth that the object of the President in most of the offenses alleged in the preceding articles was to prevent the execution of the act passed March 2, 1867, entitled, "An act for the more efficient government of the Rebel States." It is well known, officially and publicly, that on the 29th of May, 1865, Mr. Johnson issued a proclamation for the reorganization of the Government of North Carolina, and that that proclamation was followed by other proclamations, issued, during the next four months, for the government of the several States which had been engaged in the Rebellion. Upon the death of Mr. Lincoln Mr. Johnson entered upon the office of President in a manner which indicated that, in his judgment, he had been long destined to fill the place, and that the powers of the office were to be exercised by him without regard to the other departments of the government. In his proclamation of the 29th of May, and in all the proclamations relating to the same subject, he had assumed that in his office as President, he was the "United States," for the purpose of deciding whether under the Constitution the government of a State was republican in form or not; although by a decision of the Supreme Court it is declared that this power is specially vested in the two Houses of Congress. In these proclamations he assumed, without authority of law, to appoint, and he did appoint, Governors of the several States, thus organized. In fine, between the 29th of May, 1865, and the assembling of Congress in December of that year, he exercised sovereign power over the territory and people of the eleven States which have been engaged in rebellion.

On the assembling of Congress, in the month of December, he informed the Senate and House of Representatives that the Union was restored, and that nothing remained for the two Houses but severally to accept as Senators and Representatives such loyal men as had been elected by the Legislatures and people of the several States. Congress refused to ratify or to recognize those proceedings upon the part of the President as legal or proper proceedings, and from that time forward he has been engaged in various projects for the purpose of preventing the reconstruction of the Union on any other plan than that which he had inaugurated. In the execution of this design he attempted to deprive Congress of the confidence of the people of the country; hence it was that, among other things, on the 18th day of August, 1866, at the city of Washington, as set forth in the tenth and eleventh articles, he did, in a public speech, declare and affirm in substance that the Thirty-ninth Congress of the United States was not a Congress authorized by the Constitution to exercise legislative power under the same; but, on the contrary, was a Congress of only a part of the States.

In the further execution of his purpose to prevent the reconstruction of the Union upon any plan except that which he had inaugurated, he attempted to prevent the ratification by the several States of the amendment to the Constitution-known as article fourteen. By the Constitution the President has no power to participate in amendments or in propositions for amendments thereto; yet, availing himself of the circumstance of the passage of a resolution by the House of Representatives on the 13th day of June, 1866, requesting the President to submit to the Legislatures of the several States the said additional article to the Constitution of the United States he sent to the Senate and House of Representatives a message in writing, in which he says:—

"Even in ordinary times any question of amending the Constitution must be justly regarded as of paramount importance. This importance is at the present time enhanced by the fact that the joint resolution was not submitted by the two houses for the approval of the President; and that of the thirty-six States which constitute the Union eleven are excluded from representation in either House of Congress, although, with the single exception of Texas, they have been entirely restored to all their functions as States, in conformity with the organic law of the land, and have appeared at the national capital by Senators and Representatives, who have applied for and have been refused admission to the vacant seats. Nor have the sovereign people of the nation been afforded an opportunity of expressing their views upon the important question which the amendment involves. Grave doubts, therefore, may naturally and justly arise as to whether the action of Congress is in harmony with the sentiments of the people, and whether the State Legislatures, elected without reference to such an issue, should be called upon by Congress to decide respecting the ratification of the proposed amendment."

He also says:—

"A proper appreciation of the letter and spirit of the Constitution, as well as of the interests of national order, harmony and union, and a due deference for an enlightened public judgment, may at this time well suggest a doubt whether any amendment to the Constitution ought to be proposed by Congress and pressed upon the Legislatures of the several States for final decision, until after the admission of such loyal Senators and Representatives of the now unrepresented States as have been, or as may hereafter be, chosen in conformity with the Constitution and laws of the United States."

This message was an extra-official proceeding, inasmuch as his agency in the work of amending the Constitution is not required; and it was also a very clear indication of an opinion on his part that, inasmuch as the eleven States were not represented, the Congress of the United States had no power to act in the matter of amending the Constitution.

The proposed amendment to the Constitution contained provisions which were to be made the basis of reconstruction. The laws subsequently passed by Congress recognize the amendment as essential to the welfare and safety of the Union. It is alleged in the eleventh article that one of the purposes in the various unlawful acts charged in the several articles of impeachments, and proved against him, was to prevent the execution of the act entitled "An act for the more efficient government of the Rebel States," passed March 2, 1867. In the nature of the case it has not been easy to obtain testimony upon this point, nor upon any other point touching the misconduct and crimes of the President. His declarations and his usurpations of power have rendered a large portion of the office-holders of the country, for the time being, subservient to his purposes; they have been ready to conceal, and reluctant to communicate, any evidence calculated to implicate the President.

His communications with the South have been generally, and it may be said almost exclusively, with the men who had participated in the Rebellion, and who are now hoping for final success through his aid. They have looked to him as their leader, by whose efforts and agency in the office of President of the United States they were either to accomplish the objects for which the war was undertaken, or at least to secure a restoration to the Union under such circumstances that, as a section of the country and an interest in the country, they should possess and exercise that power which the slaveholders of the South possessed and exercised previous to the Rebellion. These men have been bound to him by strong bonds of hope, fear and ambition. The corruptions of the public service have enriched multitudes of his adherents and quickened and strengthened the passion of avarice in multitudes more. These classes of men, possessing wealth and influence in many cases, have exerted their power to close up every avenue of information.

Hence the efforts of the committee of the House of Representatives and the efforts of the managers to ascertain the truth and to procure testimony which they were satisfied was in existence, have been defeated often by the devices and machinations of those who in the North and in the South are allied to the President. There can, however, be no doubt that the President in every way open to him, used his personal and official influence to defeat the ratification of the Constitutional Amendment. Evidence of such disposition and of the fact is also found in the telegraphic correspondence of January, 1867, between Mr. Johnson and Lewis E. Parsons, who had been previously appointed Governor of Alabama by the President. It is as follows:—

MONTGOMERY, Ala., January 17, 1867.—Legislature in session. Efforts making to reconsider vote on Constitutional Amendment. Reports from Washington say it is

probable an enabling act will pass. We do not know what to believe. I find nothing here.

LEWIS E. PARSONS,
Exchange Hotel.

His Excellency ANDREW JOHNSON, President.

UNITED STATES MILITARY TELEGRAPH, EXECUTIVE OFFICE, WASHINGTON, D. C., January 17, 1867.—What possible good can be obtained by reconsidering the Constitutional Amendment? I know of none in the present posture of affairs; and I do not believe the people of the whole country will sustain any set of individuals in attempts to change the whole character of our government by enabling acts or otherwise. I believe, on the contrary, that they will eventually uphold all who have patriotism and courage to stand by the Constitution, and who place their confidence in the people. There should be no faltering on the part of those who are honest in their determination to sustain the several co-ordinate departments of the government in accordance with its original design.

Hon. LEWIS E. PARSONS, Montgomery, Ala.

ANDREW JOHNSON.

This correspondence shows his fixed purpose to defeat the Congressional plan of reconstruction. Pursuing the subject further, it is easy to discover and comprehend his entire scheme of criminal ambition. It was no less than this:—To obtain command of the War Department and of the army, and by their combined power to control the elections of 1866 in the ten States not yet restored to the Union. The Congressional plan of reconstruction contained as an essential condition, the extension of the elective franchise to all loyal male citizens, and the exclusion from the franchise of a portion of those who had been most active in originating and carrying on the Rebellion. The purpose of Mr. Johnson was to limit the elective franchise to white male citizens, and to permit the exercise of it by all such persons, without regard to their disloyalty.

If he could secure the control of the War Department and of the army it would be entirely practicable, and not only practicable but easy for him in the coming elections quietly to inaugurate a policy throughout the ten States by which the former Rebels, strengthened by the military support of the Executive here, and by the military forces distributed over the South, would exclude from the polls every colored man, and to permit the exercise of the elective franchise by every white Rebel. By these means he would be able to control the entire vote of the ten Rebel States; by the same means, or indeed by the force of the facts, he would be able to secure the election to the Democratic National Convention, of delegates favorable to his own nomination to the Presidency.

The vote of these ten States in the Convention, considered in connection with the fact that he and his friends could assure delegates from other sections of the country that, if he were nominated, he could control beyond peradventure the electoral vote of these ten States, would have secured his nomination. This he confidently anticipated. Nor, indeed, can there be much doubt that this scheme would have been successful; but it was apparent that there was no possibility of his obtaining the control of the War Department and of the army unless he could disregard and break down the act regulating the tenure of certain civil offices, passed March 2, 1867. If, however, he could annul, or disregard, or set aside the provisions of that act, then the way was open for the successful consummation of his plan. With thousands and tens of thousands of office-holders, scattered all over the country, depending upon him for their offices and for the emoluments of their offices, he would be able to exert a large influence, if not absolutely to control the nominations of the Democratic party in every State of the Union. With the War Department in his hands, and the Tenure of Office act broken down, he would be able to remove Gen. Grant, General Sherman, General Sheridan, or any other officer, high or low, who, in his opinion, or upon the facts, might be an obstacle in the way. With the army thus corrupted and humiliated, its trusted leaders either driven from the service or sent into exile in distant parts of the country, he would be able to wield the power of that vast organization for his own personal advantage.

Under these circumstances it was not probable merely, but it was as certain as anything in the future could be, that he would secure, first, the nomination of the Democratic party in the national nominating convention, and, secondly, that he would secure the electoral votes of these ten States. This being done, he had only to obtain enough votes from the States now represented in Congress to make a majority of electoral votes, and he would defy the House and Senate should they attempt to reject the votes of the ten States, and this whether those States had been previously restored to the Union or not. In a contest with the two Houses he and his friends and supporters, including the War Department, the Treasury Department and the army and navy, would insist that he had been duly elected President, and by the support of the War Department, the Treasury Department, the army and the navy, he would have been inaugurated on the 4th of March next President of the United States for four years.

That the President was and is hostile to Mr. Stanton, and that he desired his removal from office, there is no doubt; but he has not assumed the responsibility which now rests upon him, he has not incurred the hazard of his present position, for the mere purpose of gratifying his personal feelings towards Mr. Stanton. He disregarded the Tenure of Office act; he first suspended and then removed Mr. Stanton from the office of Secretary for the Department of War; he defied the judgment of and the advice and authority of the Senate; he incurred the risk of impeachment by the House of Representatives, and trial and conviction by this tribunal, under the influence of an ambition unlimited and unscrupulous, which dares anything and everything necessary to its gratification. For the purpose of defeating the Congressional plan of reconstruction, he has advised and encouraged the people of the South in the idea that he would restore them to their former privileges and power; that he would establish a white man's government; that he would exclude the negroes from all participation in political affairs; and, finally, that he would accomplish in their behalf what they had sought by rebellion, but by rebellion had failed to secure.

Hence, it is through his agency and by his influence the South has been given up to disorder, rapine, and bloodshed; hence it is that since the surrender of Lee and Johnston thousands of loyal men, black and white, have been murdered in cold blood or subjected to cruelties and tortures such as in modern times could have been perpetrated only in savage nations and in remote parts of the world; hence it is that 12,000,000 of people are without law, without order, unprotected in their industry or their rights; hence it is that ten States are without government and unrepresented in Congress; hence it is that the people of the North are even now uncertain whether the rebellion, vanquished in the field, is not finally to be victorious in the councils and in the Cabinet of the country; hence it is that the loyal people of the entire Union look upon Andrew Johnson as their worst enemy; hence it is that those who participated in the Rebellion, and still hope that its power may once more be established in the country, look upon Andrew Johnson as their best friend, and as the last and chief supporter of the views which they entertain.

The House of Representatives has brought this great criminal to your bar for trial, for conviction, and for judgment; but the House of Representatives, as a branch of the legislative department of the government, has no special interest in these proceedings. It entered upon them with great reluctance, after laborious and continued investigation, and only upon a conviction that the interests of the country were in peril, and that there was no way of relief except through the exercise of the highest constitutional power vested in that body. We do not appeal to this tribunal because any special right of the House of Representatives has been infringed, or because the just powers of the existence of the House are in danger, except as that body must always participate in the good or ill fortune of the country. They have brought this great criminal to your bar, and here demand his conviction in the belief, as the result of much investigation, of much deliberation, that the interests of this country are no longer safe in his hands.

But the House of Representatives, representing the people of the country, may very properly appeal to this tribunal, constituted, as it is, exclusively of Senators representing the different States of this Union, to maintain the constitutional powers of the Senate. To be sure, nothing can injuriously affect the powers and rights of the Senate which does not affect injuriously the rights of the House of Representatives and of the people of the whole country; but it may be said, with great truth, that this contest is first for the preservation of the constitutional powers of this branch of the government. By your votes and action in concurrence with the House of Representatives, the bill "regulating the tenure of certain civil offices" was passed, and became a law, and this notwithstanding the objections of the President thereto, and his argument against its passage. On a subsequent occasion when you considered the suspension of Mr. Stanton and the message of the President, in which by arguments and by statements he assailed the law in question, you asserted its validity and its constitutionality, by refusing to concur in the suspension of Mr. Stanton. On a more recent occasion, when he attempted to remove Mr. Stanton from office, you, by solemn resolution, declared that his action therein was contrary to the laws and to the Constitution of the country.

From the beginning of the government this body has participated under the Constitution, and by virtue of the Constitution, in all matters pertaining to appointments to office; and, by the universal practice of the country, as well before the passage of the Tenure of Office act as since, no removal of any officer whose appointment was by and with the advice and consent of the Senate, has been made during a session of the Senate, with your knowledge and sanction, except by the nomination of a successor, whose nomination was confirmed by and with the advice and consent of the Senate. Mr. Johnson, in presence of this uniform practice of three-quarters of a century, and against the express provisions of the Tenure of Office act, made in this particular in entire harmony with that practice, asserts now, absolutely, the unqualified power to remove every officer in the country, without the advice or consent of the Senate.

Never in the history of any free government has there been so base, so gross, so unjustifiable an attempt upon the part of any executive, whether Emperor, King, or President, to destroy the just authority of another department of the government.

The House of Representatives has not been indifferent to this assault; it has not been unmindful of the danger to which you have been exposed; it has seen, what you must admit, that without its agency and support you were powerless to resist these aggressions, or to thwart, in any degree, the purposes of this usurper. In the exercise of their constitutional power of impeachment they have brought him to your bar; they have laid before you the evidence showing conclusively the nature, the extent and the depth of his guilt. You hold this great power in trust, not for yourselves merely, but for all your successors in these high places, and for all the people of this country. You cannot fail to discharge your duty; that duty is clear.

On the one hand it is your duty to protect, to preserve, and to defend your own constitutional rights, but it is equally your duty to preserve the laws and the institutions of the country. It is your duty to protect and defend the Constitution of the United States, and the rights of the people under it; it is your duty to preserve and to transmit unimpaired to your successors in these places all the constitutional rights and privileges guaranteed to this body by the form of government under which we live. On the other hand it is your duty to try, to convict, to pronounce judgment upon this criminal, that all his successors, and all men who aspire to the office of President, in time to come, may understand that the House of Representatives and the Senate will demand the strictest observance of the Constitution; that they will hold every man in the Presidential office responsible for a rigid performance of his public duties.

Nothing, literally nothing, can be said in defense of this criminal. Upon his own admissions he is guilty in substance of the gravest charges contained in the articles of impeachment exhibited against him by the House of Representatives. In his personal conduct and character he presents no quality or attribute which enlists the sympathy or the regard of men. The exhibition which he made in this Chamber on the 4th of March, 1865, by which the nation was humiliated and republican institutions disgraced, in the presence of the representatives of the civilized nations of the earth, is a truthful exhibition of his character. His violent, denunciatory, blasphemous declarations made to the people on various occasions, and proved by the testimony submitted to the Senate, illustrate other qualities of his nature. His cold indifference to the desolation, disorder and crimes in the ten States of the South exhibit yet other and darker features.

Can any one entertain the opinion that Mr. Johnson is not guilty of such crimes as justify his removal from office and his disqualification to hold any office of trust or profit under the Government of the United States? William Blount, Senator of the United States, was impeached by the House of Representatives and declared guilty of a high misdemeanor, and though not tried by the Senate, the Senate did, nevertheless, expel him from his seat by a vote of twenty-five to one, and in the resolution of expulsion declared that he had been guilty of a high misdemeanor. The crime of William Blount was, that he wrote a letter and participated in conversations, from which it appeared probable that he was engaged in an immature scheme to alienate the Indians of the Southwest from the President and the Congress of the United States; and also, incidentally, to disturb the friendly relations between this government and the Governments of Spain and Great Britain. This, at most, was but an arrangement, never consummated into any overt act, by which he contemplated, under possible circumstances which never occurred, that he would violate the neutrality laws of the United States.

Andrew Johnson is guilty, upon the proof in part and upon his own admissions, of having intentionally violated a public law, of usurping and exercising powers not exercised nor even asserted by any of his predecessors in office.

Judge Pickering, of the District Court of New Hampshire, was impeached by the House of Representatives, convicted by the Senate, and removed from office, for the crime of having appeared upon the bench in a state of intoxication. I need not draw any parallel between Judge Pickering and this respondent.

Judge Prescott, of Massachusetts, was impeached and removed from office for receiving illegal fees in his office to the amount of ten dollars and seventy cents ($10.70) only. Judge Prescott belonged to one of the oldest and most eminent families of the State, and he was himself a distinguished lawyer. But such was the respect of the Senate of that State for the law, and such the public opinion that it was the duty of the magistrates to obey the law, that they did not hesitate to convict him and remove him from office.

The Earl of Macclesfield was impeached and convicted for the misuse of his official powers in regard to trust funds, an offense in itself of a grave character, but a trivial crime compared with the open, wanton and defiant violation of law by a Chief Magistrate whose highest duty is the execution of the laws.

If the charges preferred against Warren Hastings had been fully sustained by the testimony, he would be regarded in history as an unimportant criminal when compared with the respondent. Warren Hastings, as Governor-General of Bengal, extended the territory of the British empire, and brought millions of the natives of India under British rule. If he exercised power in India for which there was no authority in British laws or British customs—if in the exercise of that power he acquired wealth for himself or permitted others to accumulate fortunes by outrages and wrongs perpetrated upon that distant people, he still acted in his public policy in the interest of the British empire and in harmony with the ideas and purposes of the British people.

Andrew Johnson has disregarded and violated the laws and Constitution of his own country. Under his administration the government has not been strengthened, but weakened. Its reputation and influence at home and abroad have been injured and diminished. He has not outraged a distant people, bound to us by no ties but those which result from conquest and the exercise of arbitrary power on our part; but through his violation of the laws and the influence of his evil example upon the men of the South, in whose hearts the purposes and passions of the war yet linger, he has brought disorder, confusion and bloodshed to the homes of twelve millions of people, many of whom are of our own blood, and all of whom are our own countrymen. Ten States of this Union are without law, without security, without safety; public order everywhere violated, public justice nowhere respected; and all in consequence of the evil purposes and machinations of the President. Forty millions of people have been rendered anxious and uncertain as to the preservation of public peace and the perpetuity of the institutions of freedom in this country.

There is no limits to the consequences of this man's evil example. A member of his Cabinet, in your presence, avows, proclaims indeed, that he suspended from office, indefinitely, a faithful public officer who was appointed by your advice and consent; an act which he does not attempt to justify by any law or usage, except what he is pleased to call the law of necessity. Is it strange that in the presence of these examples the ignorant, the vicious and the criminal are everywhere swift to violate the laws? Is it strange that the loyal people of the South, most of them poor, dependent, not yet confident of their newly acquired rights, exercising their just privileges in fear and trembling, should thus be made the victims of the worst passions of men who have freed themselves from all the restraints of civil governments? Under the influence of these examples good men in the South have everything to fear, and bad men have everything to hope.

Caius Verres is the great political criminal of history. For two years he was prætor and the scurge of Sicily. The area of that country does not much exceed ten thousand square miles, and in modern times it has had a population of about two million souls. The criminal at your bar has been the scourge of a country many times the area of Sicily, and containing a population six times as great. Verres enriched himself and his friends; he seized the public paintings and statues and carried them to Rome. But at the end of his brief rule of two years he left Sicily as he had found it—in comparative peace, and in the possession of its industries and its laws. This respondent has not ravaged States nor enriched himself by the plunder of their treasures; but he has inaugurated and adhered to a policy which has deprived the people of the blessings of peace, of the protection of law, of the just rewards of honest industry.

A vast and important portion of the Republic, a portion whose prosperity is essential to the prosperity of the country at large, is prostrate and helpless under the evils which his administration has brought upon it. When Verres was arraigned before his judges at Rome, and the exposure of his crimes began, his counsel abandoned his cause and the criminal fled from the city. Yet Verree had friends in Sicily, and they erected a gilded statue to his name in the streets of Syracuse. This respondent will look in vain, even in the South, for any testimonials to his virtues or to his public conduct. All classes are oppressed by the private and public calamities which he has brought upon them. They appeal to you for relief. The nation waits in anxiety for the conclusion of these proceedings. Forty millions of people, whose interest in public affairs is in the wise and just administration of the laws, look to this tribunal as a sure defense against the encroachments of a criminal Chief Magistrate.

Will any one say that the heaviest judgment which you can give is any adequate punishment for these crimes? Your office is not punishment, but to secure the safety of the Republic. But human tribunals are inadequate to punish those criminals who, as rulers or magistrates, by their example, conduct, policy and crimes, become the scourge of communities and nations. No picture, no power of the imagination, can illustrate or conceive the suffering of the poor but loyal people of the South. A patriotic, virtuous, law-abiding Chief Magistrate would have healed the wounds of war, soothed private and public sorrows, protected the weak, encouraged the strong, and lifted from the Southern people the burdens which are now greater than they can bear.

Travelers and astronomers inform us that in the Southern heavens, near the Southern Cross, there is a vast space which the uneducated call the hole in the sky, where the eye of man, with the aid of the powers of the telescope has been unable to discover nebulæ, or asteroid, or comet or, planet, or star, or sun. In that dreary, cold, dark region of space, which is only known to be less than infinite by the evidences of creation elsewhere, the Great Author of celestial mechanism has left the chaos which was in the beginning. If this earth were capable of the sentiments and emotions of justice and virtue, which in human mortal beings are the evidences and the pledge of our Divine, origin and immortal destiny, she would heave and throw, with the energy of the combined forces of air, fire, and water, and project this enemy of two races of men into that vast region, there forever to exist in a solitude eternal as life, emblematical of, if not really, that "outer darkness of which the Savior of man spoke in warning to those who are the enemies of themselves, of their race and of their God. But it is yours to relieve, not to punish. This done and our country is again advanced in the intelligent opinion of mankind. In other governments an unfaithful ruler can be removed only by revolution, violence or force. The proceeding here is judicial, and according to the forms of law. Your judgment will be enforced without the aid of a policeman or a soldier. What other evidence will be needed of the value of republican institutions? What other test of the strength and vigor of our government? What other assurance that the virtue of the people is equal to any emergency of national life?

The contest which we carry on at your bar is a contest in defense of the constitutional rights of the Congress of the United States; representing the people of the United States, against the arbitrary, unjust, illegal claims of the Executive.

This is the old contest of Europe revived in America. England, France and Spain have each been the theatre of this strife. In France and Spain the Executive triumphed. In England the people were victorious. The people of France gradually but slowly regain their rights. But even yet there is no freedom of the press in France; there is no freedom of the legislative will—the Emperor is supreme.

Spain is wholly unregenerated. England alone has a free Parliament and a government of laws emanating fram the people who are entitled to vote. These laws are everywhere executed, and a sovereign who should wilfully interpose any obstacle would be dethroned without delay. In England the law is more mighty than the king. In America a President claims to be mightier than the law.

This result in England was reached by slow movements, and after a struggle which lasted through many centuries. John Hamden was not the first nor the last of the patriots who resisted executive usurpation, but nothing could have been more inapplicable to the present circumstances than the introduction of his name as an apology for the usurpations of Andrew Johnson.

"No man will question John Hampden's patriotism, or the propriety of his acts, when he brought the question whether ship-money was within the Constitution of England, before the courts;" but no man will admit that there is any parallel between Andrew Johnson and John Hampden. Andrew Johnson takes the place of Charles I, and seeks to substitute his own will for the laws of the land. In 1636 John Hampden resisted the demands of a usurping and unprincipled King, as does Edwin M. Stanton to-day resist the claims and demands of an unprincipled and usurping President.

The people of England have successfully resisted an executive encroachment upon their rights. Let their example be not lost upon us. We suppressed the Rebellion in arms, and we are now to expel it from the Executive Councils. This done, republican institutions need no further illustration. All things relating to the national welfare and life are made as secure as can be by any future events.

The freedom, prosperity and power of America are assured. The friends of constitutional liberty throughout Europe will hail with joy the assured greatness and glory of the new republic. Our internal difficulties will rapidly disappear. Peace and prosperity will return to every portion of the country. In a few weeks or months we shall celebrate a restored union upon the basis of the equal rights of the States, in each of which equality of the people will be recognized and established. This respondent is not to be convicted that these things may come, but justice being done these things are to come.

At your bar the House of Representatives demands justice—justice for the people, justice to the accused. Justice is of God, and it cannot perish. By and through justice comes obedience to the law by all magistrates and people; by and through justice comes the liberty of the law, which is freedom without license.

Senators, as far as I am concerned, the case is now in your hands, and it is soon to be closed by my associate. The House of Representatives has presented this criminal at your bar with equal confidence in his guilt and in your disposition to administer exact justice between him and the people of the United States.

His conviction is the triumph of law, of order, of justice. I do not contemplate his acquittal—it is impossible. Therefore, I do not look beyond. But, Senators, the people of America will never permit an usurping Executive to break down the securities for liberties provided by the Constitution. The cause of the country is in your hands. Your verdict of *guilty* is *peace* to our beloved land.

When Mr. BOUTWELL had concluded, at 1·05 P.M., on motion of Senator JOHNSON, the court took a recess of fifteen minutes.

Judge Nelson's Address.

At twenty minutes before two, Mr. NELSON took the floor on behalf of the President. His opening words were rather indistinct, but he spoke substantially as follows:—

Mr. Chief Justice and Senators:—I have been engaged in the practice of my profession as a lawyer for the last twenty years, and I have, in the course of my somewhat diversified professional life, argued cases involving liberty, property and character; I have prosecuted and defended every species of crime known to the law, from murder in the first degree down to a simple assault, but in rising to address you to-day, I feel that all the cases in which I was ever concerned, sink into comparative insignificance when compared to this, and a painful sense of the magnitude of the case in which I am now engaged, and of my inability to meet and to defend, as it should be defended, oppresses me as I rise to address you; but I would humbly invoke the Great Dispenser of events to give me a mind to conceive, a heart to feel, and a tongue to express those words which should be proper and fitting on this great occasion.

I would humbly invoke the assistance which cometh from on high, for when I look at the results which may follow from this great trial; when I endeavor to contemplate in imagination how it will affect our country and the world, I stand back, feeling that I am utterly incapable of comprehending its results, and that I cannot look into the future and foretell it. I feel, somehow, that it will be necessary upon this occasion for me to notice many things which, as I suppose, have but little bearing upon the specific articles of impeachment which have been presented, and in doing so, to follow the language of Mr. Wirt upon the trial of Judge Chase. If I follow the argument of the honorable manager more closely than would seem necessary to some of the court, it will be remembered that it would seem presumptuous to slight any topic which the learned and honorable managers have deemed it proper to press upon the consideration of the court.

It has been charged that the President was trifling with the Senate. Scarcely had he entered upon this trial before charges were made against him of seeking improperly to gain time, to effect an unworthy and improper procrastination. I shall dwell but a moment upon that. We supposed that there was nothing improper in our asking at the hands of the Senate a reasonable indulgence to prepare our defense.

When the subject of impeachment had been before the House of Representatives in some form for more than a twelvemonth, and when the House or the managers were armed at all points, and ready to contest the case on the one hand, and we, upon the other, were suddenly summoned from our professional pursuits; we, who are not politicians, but lawyers, engaged in the practice of our profession, to measure arms with gentlemen who are skilled in political affairs, and who are well posted upon all the subjects that may be involved in this discussion.

But it is not merely the complaint as to delaying and trifling with the Senate that it will become my duty to notice. A great many things have been said, and among the rest an attempt has been made to stigmatize the President as a traitor to his party, as disgracing the position held by some of the most illustrious in the land, as a dangerous person, "a criminal, but not an ordinary one," and as encouraging murder, assassination and robbery all over the Southern States, and finally, by way of proving that there is but one step between the sublime and the ridiculous, as bandying ribald epithets with a jeering mob. My excuse for noticing these charges, which have been made here in the progress of the investigation is, that nothing has been said in vindication of the President from them.

It will be my duty, Senators, to pay some attention to them to-day. We have borne it long enough, and I propose, before I enter upon the investigation of the articles of impeachment, to pay some attention to those accusations which have been heaped upon us almost every day from the commencement of the trial, and which have been passed unanswered and unnoticed on the part of the President of the United States.

If it is true, as is alleged, that the President is guilty of all these things; if he be guilty of one tithe of the offenses which have been imputed to him in the opening argument of yesterday and to-day, then I am willing to confess that he is a monster of such frightful mien "that to be hated needs but to be seen."

I am willing to admit that if he was guilty of any of the charges which have been made against him, he is not only worthy of the censure of this Senate, but you should
    "Place a whip in every honest hand,
    To lash the scoundrel naked through the land."
He should be pointed at everywhere as a monster to be banished from society, and his name should become a word to frighten children with throughout the land, from one end to the other, and when any one should meet him or see him, "Each particular hair should stand on end, like quills on the fretful porcupine.

If he was, then I agree that neither I nor those associated with me can defend him. But who is Andrew Johnson? Who is this man that you have on trial now, in regard to whom the gaze, not "of little Delaware," but of the whole Union and of the civilized world is directed at the present moment; who is Andrew Johnson?

That is a question which but a few short years ago many of those I now address could have answered with pleasure. Who be Andrew Johnson? Go to the town of Greenville, but a few short years ago, a little village in the mountains of East Tennessee, and you will see a poor boy entering that village—a stranger, without acquaintances or friends, following an humble mechanical pursuit, scarcely able to read, unable to write, but yet industrious in his profession, honest and faithful in his dealings, and having a mind such as the God of Heaven implanted in him, and which was designed to be called into exercise and play before the American people.

He enters the State of Tennessee, arriving poor, penniless, without the favor of the great, but scarce had he set his foot upon her soil, when he was seized and caressed with parental fondness, embraced as though he had been a favorite child, and patronized with liberal and fond beneficence. In the first place, the people of his county honor him by giving him a seat in the lower Legislature; next he ascends to a seat in the Senate, then to the House of Representatives of the American Congress; then, by the voice of the people, he was elected Governor of the State; then he was sent to the Senate of the United States, and his whole career thus far has been a career in which he has been honored and respected by the people, and it has only been within two or three years that charges have been preferred against him, such as those which are presented now. Never since the charges of Warren Hastings, never since the charges of Sir Walter Raleigh, has any man been stigmatized with more severe reprobation than the President of the United States.

All the powers of invective which the able and ingenious managers can command have been brought into requisition to fire your hearts and to prejudice your minds against him. A perfect storm has been raised around him. All the elements have been agitated.

    "From peak to peak, the rattling crags along,
    Leaps the live thunder.
    Not from one lone crowd,
    But every mountain now hath found a tongue.
    And Jura answers through her misty shroud,
    Back to the joyous Alps, who call to her aloud."

This storm is playing around him, the pitiless rain is beating upon him, the lightnings are flashing upon him, and I have the pleasure to state to you, Senators, to-day, and I hope my voice will reach the whole country, that he still stands firm, unbroken, unawed, unterrified. No words of menace at the Senate of the United States, threatening no civil war to deluge the country with blood, but feeling a proud consciousness of his own integrity, appealing to Heaven to witness the purity of his motives in his public administration, and calling upon you, Senators, in the name of the living God, to whom you have made a pledge that you will do equal and impartial justice in this case according to the Constitution and the laws, to pronounce him innocent of the offenses charged against him. Are there not Senators here whose minds go back to the stirring times of 1860 and 1861, when treason was rife in this Capital—when men's faces turned pale—when despatch after despatch was sent from this Chamber to fire the heart of the Southern people and prepare the Southern mind for that revolution which agitated our country, and which cost the lives and treasures of the nation to such an alarming extent?

Where was Andrew Johnson then? Standing here almost within ten feet of the place at which I now stand, solitary and alone in this magnificent Chamber, when bloody treason flourished o'er us, his voice was heard arousing the nation. Some of you heard its notes as they rolled from one end of the land to the other, arousing the patriotism of our country—the only man from the South who was disposed to battle against treason then, and who now is called a traitor himself. He who has periled his life in a thousand forms to put down treason; he who has been reckless of danger; he who has periled his life, his fortune and his sacred honor to save its life from destruction and ruin, now is stigmatized and denounced as a traitor, and from one end of the land to the other that accusation has rung until the echoes even come back to the capital here, intending if possible to influence the judgment of the Senate.

Is Andrew Johnson a man who is disposed to betray any trust reposed in him? A man who has on all occasions been found standing by his neighbors, standing by his friends, standing by his country; who has been found on all occasions worthy of the high confidence and trust that has been reposed in him. I know, Senators, that when I state these things in your presence and in your hearing, I may extort but a smile of derision among some of those who differ with him in opinion. I know that an unfortunate difference of opinion exists between the Congress of the United States and the President; and in attempting to address you upon some of the very questions through which this difficulty arose, I pray Almighty God to direct me and lead me aright, for I believe in this presence to-day that my distinguished client is innocent of the charges preferred against him, and I hope that God's blessing, which has followed him so far in life, will follow him now, and that he will come out of the fiery furnace unscathed.

Who is Andrew Johnson? Why, Senators, when the battle of Manassas—as we call it at the South, or of Bull Run, as I believe it is called in the North, was fought—when our troops were driven back defeated, and were pursued in haste and confusion to the capital—when men's faces turned pale and their hearts faltered—where was Andrew Johnson then? With a resolution undismayed, and unfaltering believing in the justice of the great cause in which the country was engaged, his voice was heard here, proclaiming to the whole country and to the whole world the objects and purposes of the war. Then it was that his voice was heard among the boldest of those who declared it the purpose of Congress to stand by and defend the Constitution, and to maintain and uphold the government.

One word more Senators, in regard to the President of the United States. It is urged upon all hands, that we are addressing gentlemen of the highest intelligence and position in the land, many of whom, as has been repeatedly said, are judges and lawyers well versed in the law. What has been your rule of conduct heretofore as judges or lawyers, when you came to pronounce judgment upon the conduct of a fellow-man? You have endeavored to place yourselves in his position, and to judge from his standpoint, and when you thus acted, you were enabled, understandingly, to determine in regard to a man's conduct, whether it was right or wrong. I may ask you if it is possible for you to do it; to place yourselves in Andrew Johnson's place and judge a little from his standpoint, and in the manner in which he would judge.

I know that this is asking a great deal at your hands. It is asking a great deal of men who have fixed opinions like those which you hold, to ask them to review their opinions, and especially where they differ from those of the man whom they are to judge. But I know I am not addressing such a Senate as the honorable managers spoke of the other day. I am not addressing politicians. I feel that I am addressing judges—the most eminent judges known to law and the Constitution of the country—judges sitting upon the greatest trial known to the Constitution; and though we all know and feel what is the power of passions and prejudices and preconceived opinion, and how difficult it is to lay their influence aside, yet, Senators, I would respectfully and most humbly invoke you, in the name of that God before whom you have sworn to judge impartially, to endeavor to banish, as far as possible, all preconceived opinions and all politics, and rise to the dignity of judges and the high dignity of this great occasion. I would even ask you to rise to that superhuman Godlike effort which shall enable you to banish these opinions, and perform that impartial justice which you have sworn to do. Some people think it is impossible that we can close our eyes to what is at our very doors.

It is impossible not to know that the newspaper press, the greatest and most tremendous power in the country, greater than Senators or Representatives, and it is impossible to close our eyes to the fact that this case has been discussed and decided over and over again by those who favor impeachment and those opposed to it. All manner of opinions have been expressed, and some have made their calculations on the result of the trial. Senators, I have made no such calculations; I declare to you and to the country most solemnly that I make no such calculations—no such unworthy investigation has for a moment agitated my mind. No, Senators, I would not do a thing so manifestly improper to the position I occupy. Whatever others may say, I tell you that I do not regard impeachment as a foregone conclusion. If I thought so, humble as I am. and exalted as you are, I would scorn the idea of addressing myself to this honorable body.

But I do not believe it, and no force, and nothing but the result which I trust in God may never happen, will bring my mind to the conclusion that any such state of things exists, or can be brought about, for we all know enough about the history of our country to know that it requires no ordinary talent, no ordinary character, no ordinary experiment, to get this Chamber, in which you are acting as representatives of your respective States. For it requires talent and character to enable men to come here and occupy the positions which you occupy now; and when I think that the honor of the Senate, the honor of our noble ancestry, who framed this tribunal to do equal and impartial justice, is at stake, I cannot for a moment credit such things as are reported, and I would say now as ever to the American people, place no confidence in these things, believe that the Senate of the American nation are honest and honorable men, and in every time of trial and danger, when the billows of excitement roll high, when men's passions are aroused and agitated to the highest degree, look to the Senate with hope and confidence; to those men who are in some degree elevated above dependence upon mere popular clamor, look to the Senate with confidence, and thus looking, your hope shall not be in vain.

Thus it is that I shall endeavor to address you on this occasion. It is with this hope and influenced by the considerations that I now approach some of the other topics which claim our attention. I ask you again, if possible, to place yourselves in the condition of the President of the United States, and divest yourselves, as far you can—and I agree that it requires an almost superhuman effort to do it—of all preconceived opinions, and place yourselves in his condition and place, Then as to this life as a politician. Who is the President of the United States? Why, a Democrat of the strictest sect and most strict construction; an old Jackson, Jeffersonian Democrat; a man who proclaimed his democracy in the very teeth of acceptance which he wrote at the time when nominated for the office of Vice President of the United States, and you and the whole country were told that he was a Democrat, and he endeavored to rouse the old Democratic party to what he called the pure and correct doctrines of democracy, and to stand by the country in the great conflict in which it was engaged.

When we look at this, and examine the records of Congress and the debates, and look at his record on every question in which the Constitution of the United States was involved, where do you find the President? You find him under all circumstances, as a strict constructionist of the Constitution, adhering with strict tenacity to the principles and spirit of the Constitution, and of that party faith in which he had been trained; and when you look at the great difference between him and the House of Representatives upon the great questions which agitate the country yet, Senators, I ask you if he may not entertain an opinion different from your own without blame? Do accord to him something of that freedom of opinion which you accord to every man on trial. Accord to him something of the privilege which is accorded to the meanest criminal. Accord to him the presumption that he is innocent until he is declared guilty.

Look at his motives. Look at the manner in which he has acted, and if there has been an unfortunate difference between him and the Congress of the United States upon great constitutional questions, why attribute that difference, if you please, to the training, to the education, to the habits of thought of his whole life, but do not attribute it, in the absence of proof, to unworthy, base, dishonorable, mean motives, as you are asked to do upon the other side. I beg leave, Senators, to remind you of the resolution to which I adverted a moment ago; for in the view which I take of this case, that resolution furnishes a key to the whole conduct of the President in the controversy out of which this unfortunate proceeding has arisen.

That resolution adopted in 1861 declares that Congress, in the prosecution of the war for the suppression of the Rebellion, will recollect only its duty to the whole country; that the war is prosecuted in no spirit of revenge, nor for the purpose of overthrowing any of the institutions of the country, but to defend the Constitution and all laws made in pursuance thereof, and to preserve the dignity, equality and rights of all the States impartially, and that as soon as the ends were accomplished the war should cease. There is the chart which has guided the President of the United States in the discharge of his official duty. There is the platform upon which he has stood, and if he has not viewed it in the light in which others have regarded it, still I ask if it is not capable of being regarded in the light in which he has viewed it?

If it is, then I claim that we shall remove from this prosecution all idea of improper motives, and I declare that, in view of the testimony offered on the other side; in view of all that is known to the country, with the exception of one single instance, the President of the United States has stood up, in letter and in spirit, to what he believes to be the doctrine of this resolution, which was adopted with all but perfect unanimity by the two houses of Congress in 1861. In the progress of the war he felt it necessary for him to yield the question of slavery so far as he had any influence in the section of country in which he resided, and that he did yield.

He went as far as the farthest in proclaiming emancipation in the State over which he was placed as Military Governor, and in other respects he has endeavored to carry out that resolution in the spirit in which it was introduced by the venerable Crittenden, whose memory will be respected by those of you who know them, and as long as America shall have a name, so long as talent, genius and independence, faithfulness and firmness shall be venerated, so long will the name of that great and good man be honored in our own and other lands—who declared in the resolution which he offered, that the war was not prosecuted for the purpose of conquest or subjugation, but that the dignity and equality and rights of all the States should be impartially maintained.

Do not misunderstand, Senators. It is not my purpose to enter into any discussion on the difference of opinion between the President and Congress in regard to the reconstruction policy which has been pursued by them. I only advert to it for the purpose of showing that there was a pledge of equality of rights to be preserved in 1860 and 1861, when the galleries of the Senate Chamber rang with the applause of the multitude; "when fair women and brave men" were not ashamed to express their admiration and gratitude for him who is now on trial before you for the course he then took, while he had advocated a doctrine which was exceedingly obnoxious to the Southern people. What was it? It was that the Congress of the United States had the power to compel obedience to the Constitution and laws of the United States. He denounced the docrine of secession, and denied that any State had the right to withdraw from the Union without the consent of all the States.

He insisted that the great power of the government should be brought into requisition to keep these States within the Union. And when the war was over; when Lee had surrendered; when the government of the United States was cast upon him suddenly and unexpectedly; in the sudden emergency in which he was called upon to act hastily and speedily, so as to bring the war to a termination as soon as possible, what did he do? There was no time to call Congress together; no time to assemble the Representatives of the nation; and such was the state of the country as to demand immediate and prompt action. What did the President of the United States do? The President undertook to carry out what he believed to be the policy of his lamented predecessor. He undertook this in good faith. He manifested no desire to segregate himself from the party by whom he had been elevated to power. He endeavored faithfully to carry out the resolution of 1861, to preserve the dignity, equality and rights of the States, and not impair them in the slightest degree. And now the question is, suppose he is wrong; suppose the Congress is right; in the name of all that is great and good I ask any one of you to say if he is a traitor to his principles, or a traitor to the party that elected him?

It is a mere difference of opinion, an unfortunate difference; a very unfortunate difference between him and the Congress of the United States. But who can say, in the spirit of candor and truth, that he was not endeavoring and did not try, in all his acts, to carry out what he believed to be the policy of the party by whom he was elevated to power; and after he had taken his stand he did all he could to have the policy of the lamented Lincoln carried out in regard to Arkansas and Louisiana, believing that when Mr. Lincoln made his proclamation in regard to the restoration of the States, he designed to restore the States to which they were before the war commenced. I ask, who can say there was guilt in that? You may differ in opinion, you may think he was wrong—undoubtedly a large majority of this Senate believe conscientiously that he was wrong—but still do you believe you can deprive him of the claim of honesty and integrity.

Is a judge to be tried because he mistakes the law in a charge to a jury? I need not turn to authority, I need not read law books to satisfy you that any man acting in a judicial capacity, from a simple justice of the peace to the chief justice of the highest court in the United States, is protected by the laws while in the faithful and honest exercise of the judgment which is conferred upon him. You hear a great deal about the doctrine of implied power, and I shall have occasion to speak of that more in another part of my remarks, but let me put one plain, simple question to this Senate, and to the whole country.

Can any one put his finger upon any sentence or clause in the Constitution of our country which says who is to restore the relation of peace in the land when they have been disturbed by a civil war? You have the power to suppress rebellion, but the moment you go beyond the language of the Constitution you make use of an implied power; and the moment you admit the doctrine of implication, then I maintain that that doctrine is just as applicable to the President of the United States as to any Senator or Representative.

I ask this question again; I know whom I am addressing; I know the intelligence and the high respectability of character of this great tribunal, and I put the question with fearless confidence to every Senator:—Where does he find the power in the Constitution to pass your Reconstruction laws unless under the power to suppress insurrection? where, unless under those general powers by which the war was carried on and under which it is declared that the government has the inherent right to protect itself against dissolution, and in the name of law and justice that you inaugurate here in this Chamber, and inscribe over the doors that are the entrance here; I ask you in the name of law and order and justice, where do you get this power if not from implication?

The Constitution is silent; it does not say that Congress shall pass laws to reconstruct States that have been in rebellion; it does not say that the President of the United St tes shall do this. You are obliged to resort to implication. He is the commander-in-chief of the army and navy in time of war. Peace had not been declared when these measures of his were undertaken. It was necessary to protect the country against the ruin that was likely to follow in the wake of hundreds and thousands of soldiers turned loose upon the country. There was no time to ask the judgment of the Congress of the United States. He was forced to act in construing the powers and duties that belonged to him upon his own judgment, as commander-in-chief of the army and navy, and if he misconceived his duty or his power; if he fell into an error, into which you may say Mr. Lincoln, his lamented predecessor, had fallen, let me ask you, gentlemen, is there to be no charity, no toleration, no liberality for a difference of opinion?

Are we to judge in the spirit that governed the world two hundred years ago? Are we like those who burned heretics at the stake to introduce in this nineteenth century such a standard of judgment, and forget that the spirit of the gospel has been spread abroad and that a spirit of liberality is infused into the minds of the people of this age? I ask Senators if the President is to be judged in the spirit of the dark ages, or of the middle ages, or in an enlightened, patriotic and Christian spirit? Now, I maintain upon this great question that the President, in his position of the chief executive officer of the nation, is entitled to the credit of having acted honestly, and being governed by upright and correct motives. And I maintain also, that in this court, or in any court under heaven honesty and integrity of motive is a shield and protection to him against all the darts that may be leveled at him from any quarter, high or low.

It is a protection to him. The servant who knew his master's will but did it not, was punished, but never the servant who did not know his master's will, or who erred in an honest exercise of his judgment and reason. Now, Senators, I maintain that this cursory glance at the history of the country, and at the difference of opinion that exists between Congress and the President, is sufficient to show that he was animated by correct and upright motives, and that he ought not to be judged in the spirit in which the honorable managers ask that he shall be judged. His acts ought not to be taken as an evidence that he intended contrary to what he deemed to be his duty under the circumstances.

Now, without discussing the question further, but merely for the purpose of calling the attentions of Senators to the subject, I beg leave to remind them, as I have already done, that according to Mr. Stanton's own testimony, in another investigation which has been published under the authority and sanction of Congress, the President of the United States endeavored to carry out what he believed to be the policy of Mr. Lincoln. I will refer you to some few dates and circumstances in connection with this, and I shall then pass from it without undertaking to discuss the merits of differences of opinion between the Senate and the President. I only do so for the purpose of relieving him from the charge of being a usurper, a traitor, a tyrant, and a man guilty of every crime known under heaven.

Now, Mr. Lincoln, in his proclamation of the 8th of July 1864, stated that while he had failed to oppose the first Reconstruction bill passed by Congress, yet he expressed an unwillingness to set aside the Constitutions of Arkansas and Louisiana. And in his Emancipation Proclamation of 1863 he invited the Rebel States to form new constitutions, to be adopted by not less than one-tenth in number of the votes cast in each State at the Presidential election of 1860, each having taken the oath prescribed by his proclamation.

Mr, Johnson, as you know, when he came into power, recognized Governor Peirpoint as the Governor of West Virginia, which the Congress of the United States thought (and rightly) was sufficiently well organized to justify them in consenting to the formation of a new State. Senators will pardon me if I fall into errors on the e subjects, because I am no politician, and it is like carrying coals to Newcastle for any of us to argue these questions before Senators and the House of Representatives, who are more familiar with them than we are—and if I fall into errors, they are errors of ignorance and not of design. I know the great superiority that the honorable managers have in this respect over us, and I acknowledge it because each member of the House of Representatives and every Senator, in reference to these subjects, have been concerned in them. But still, Senators, I beg leave to remind you that Mr. Johnson recognized her Governor.

That State was recognized as a State under an election held by the people. Under that election West Virginia was formed into a new State, and all this was done, if I am not misinformed, without any act of reconstruction being passed by the Congress of the United States. Now when the President came into power; when he saw that the Congress of the United States had recognized and accepted West Virginia as a State, was he not justified in the belief that he was pursuing not only the policy of Mr. Lincoln and the party that elected him to power, but the policy of the Senate and the House of Representatives of the United States? and if he committed an error, I repeat it was an error, I repeat it was an error of the head and not of the heart, and ought not to be made a matter of accusation against him. Let me now call your attention to the fact that between the 29th of May and the 13th of July, 1865, he appointed Provisional Governors for North Carolina, Mississippi, Georgia, Texas, Alabama, South Carolina and Florida,

Now let me pause a moment, and ask you a question here. Up to the time of the assembling of the Congress of the United States in December, 1865, who was there in all this broad land, from one end of it to the other, that dared to point the slow, unmoving finger of scorn at Andrew Johnson, and say that he was a traitor to his party, or that he had betrayed any trust that had been reposed in him. He was faithfully carrying out what he believed to be the policy of the Congress and his predecessor, who was anxious that the Union should be restored.

He was anxious to pour oil upon the troubled waters and to heal the living wounds of his distracted and divided country, and if he erred it was an error which intended to restore peace and harmony to our bleeding country. If it was an error, it was designed to banish the recollection of war, and which was intended to bring in a fraternal embrace the brother and sister, the husband and wife, who had been separated during the awful calamity which overshadowed our country in that terrible civil war that drenched the land in human gore; I say, if he committed an error, in these things, it is not an error that should be imputed a crime. However you may differ with him, if you pronounce on his conduct that judgment which I invoke elevated judges to pronounce—if you will pronounce that cool, dispassionate judgment, which must be exercised by every one of you who intends faithfully to redeem the pledge which he has made to God and the country—I think, Senators, that you will acquit him of this accusation that has been made against him.

Now one other thought, and I leave this branch of the subject. On the 20th of August, 1866, the President of the United States proclaimed the Rebellion at an end, and on the 2d of March, 1867, an act was approved entitled, "An act to provide for a temporary increase of the pay of officers in the army of the United States, and for other purposes." By the second section of that act it is enacted that Section 1 of the act entitled "An act to increase the pay of soldiers in the United States army, and for other purposes, approved June 20, 1864, be and the same is hereby continued in full force and effect for three years from and after the close of the Rebellion, as announced by the President of the United States by proclamation bearing date the 20th day of August, 1866.

There is a legislative recognitition of the fact that the war is at an end. There is a recognition of the President's power so to proclaim it, and without discussing these questions, for I have said I will not enter upon the discussion of them, I advert to it, and my reason for alluding to it is, by the remarks, I might say repeated remarks that have been made by the honorable managers that this did not show that this legislative recognition of the President's proclamation announcing the termination of the civil war, and the close of the rebellion was a recognition of the facts that the Southern States were not out of the Union, and that it goes far to extenuate, if not to justify the view which the President took in reference to the restoration of the States to their harmonious relations with the government of the country.

And now, Senators, having disposed to some extent, but not entirely, of these personal charges made against the President, and having reviewed briefly and imperfectly something of his personal and political history, I invite you to look back upon the record of his whole life and his name.

I ask you—I ask the country to-day to remember his course. We appeal with proud confidence to the whole country to attest the purity and integrity of his motives; and while we do not claim that his judgment is infallible or that he may not have committed error—and who, in his position, may not commit great and grievous errors—while we claim no such attributes as these, we do claim, before the Senate and before the world, that he is an hon. st man; that he is a man of integrity, of pure and upright motives, and notwithstanding the clamor that has been raised against him, he appeals to the judgment of this Senate and the world to vindicate him.

Mr. Chief Justice and Senators:—One of the first and most important questions in my view, is a question which I have barely touched in passing along, but have not attempted to notice at length. That question is, what sort of a tribunal this is? Is it a court or not? Some votes have been taken on this question, but it has not been discussed, according to my recollection, by any of the counsel for the President. At an early period of the trial you deliberated upon it in your Chamber. What debates you had there I know not. Whether they have been published or not I know not. Your votes were announced by the Chief Justice, but whether the discussions in secret session have been published I know not. All I have to say is that I have not seen them if they have been published.

While I do not know to what extent the opinions of Senators may be fixed and confirmed on this question, I ask you as a matter of right, whether you consider yourselves as having decided it or not, that you will allow me to address myself for a short time to the consideration of this question, which I regard as one of the greatest questions which has been presented since the formation of our government. I think I am not asking too much at the hands of the Senate, when I ask to be heard on this subject. It was argued by the honorable manager who opened the case that this is a mere Senate. It is a court. I will call your attention to a single paragraph or two in the argument of the learned manager, who has managed this case with such consumate tact and ability on the side of the prosecution, and from whom we have had so many fine examples of the decency and propriety of speech.

He says:—"We claim and respectfully insist that this tribunal has none of the attributes of a judicial court as they are commonly received and ununderstood. Of course this question must be largely determined by the express provisions of the Constitution, and in it there is no word, as is well known to you, Senators, which gives the slightest coloring to the idea that this is a court, save that in the trial of this particular respondent that the Chief Justice of the Supreme Court must preside." That question has been confirmed again in argument by others, and pamphlets. I had almost said volumes, have been written on this subject in the learned arguments which have been presented to the Senate and through the newspapers to the public. Gentlemen, in their research, have gone back to the black-letter learning of the English law books to search for precedents and authorities in reference to this question, and have assumed this as the result—that this is a High Court of Impeachment, possessing all the powers of a court of impeachment in England; that it is to be governed by the same rules and regulations; that you are not to go to common law for precedents to guide your judgment, but that you are, in the language of the gentleman on the other side, "a law unto yourself."

Let us consider this argument a moment. I have but one answer to make to it. It is not my purpose, Senators, to follow the careful, industrious, vigilant and learned managers (and these are not mere words, for they have shown talents in the highest degree creditable to them), into all their carefully prepared precedents, and argue them at length, but I submit one or two arguments which seem to me pertinent and appropriate.

My first position is this:—I deny, out and out, that you are to go according to a law of Parliament, because I maintain that this tribunal is different from any other that has ever existed—no such tribunal is known in history. It never had a parallel. You are to interpret the Constitution, not in the light of English history alone, but in the light of the circumstances under which it was adopted. I do not say that you are to ignore history, nor the precedents given us by the English Parliament, or that have been made in English courts of justice.

What I do say is this, that upon some subjects it is perfectly right and proper to go to English history and English law books, with a view to interpret those phrases and terms known to English law which have been incorporated into our Constitution, but it never will afford any clue to this investigation, or throw any light on the subject. Why? Because this tribunal has no exemplar in the history of the world. It is a tribunal of the American Constitution, and we must look to the language of that Constitution in order to ascertain what it means.

I ask (and I hope the Chief Justice will not take offense at my phraseology) whether it was the intention of the framers of the Constitution that the Chief Justice of the United States should be called down from the most elevated tribunal on the face of the earth to preside over your deliberations and when he comes here, he shall have no more power than an ordinary Speaker of an ordinary House of Representatives, and hardly so much—a machine through which the votes of the Senate are to pass to the records of the country. I insist that there was a high object and purpose intended by the framers of the Constitution when they called the Chief Justice from his elevated position to preside over the deliberations of the Senate.

There was an object and a purpose such as never was attained in English history, an object such as was unknown to the British Constitution, and I contend, therefore, that it it was not intended by the framers of the Constitution that the Chief Justice was to be a mere cipher in this trial. I beg leave to remind you of some facts relating to the history of this subject, and I do consider in doing so to bring in the volumes and read page after page to you. I take it for granted that the Senators are a great deal better informed upon it than I am. All that I deem important or material for me to do is to refresh your recollection in relation to some of the subjects connected with the incorporation of that provision in the Constitution of the United States.

You will recollect, Senators, that when the Constitution was about to be formed there were various plans of government submitted. Colonel Hamilton introduced a plan of government, the ninth section of which provided that the Governor, Senators and all officers of the United States should be liable to impeachment for malfeasance and corrupt conduct, and that on impeachment the person convicted should be removed from office and disqualified from holding any office of trust or profit under the United States—all impeachments were to be tried by a court to consist of the chief or senior judge of the Superior Court of law in each State; provided that such judge held his place during good behavior and had a permanent salary. That plan was introduced in the Convention on the 18th of June, 1787, and it is found in the first volume of Elliott's Debates on the Federal Constitution, page 108.

Mr. Randolph had a plan of government, the thirteenth proposition of which was that the jurisdiction of the national judiciary should extend to cases of impeachment of any national officer, and to questions involving the national peace and harmony. This was introduced on the 19th of June, 1787, and is set out in first Elliott's Debates, page 182. In Mr. Charles Pinckney's plan, introduced first of May, 1787, it was provided that the jurisdiction of the

court, to be termed the Supreme Court, should extend to the trial or impeachment of officers of the United States. Mr. Madison preferred the Supreme Court for the trial of impeachments, or rather a tribunal of which that court should form a part.

Mr. Jefferson, in his letter of 22d February, 1798, to Mr. Madison, alludes to an attempt to have a jury trial of impeachments (fourth volume of Jefferson's Works, 215), and Mr. Hamilton, in the *Federalist* (No. 65, page 335), asks whether it would have been an improvement on the plan to have united the Supreme Court to the Senate in the form of a Court of Impeachment. He says it would certainly have been attended with certain advantages, but he asks whether they would not have been overbalanced by the disadvantages arising from the same judges having again to try the defendant, in case of a double prosecution. He adds that, to a certain extent, the benefits of that union would be obtained by making the Chief Justice of the Supreme Court, President of the Court of Impeachment, as was proposed.

Madison, Mason, Morris, Pinckney, Williamson, and Sherman discussed the impeachment question. A committee on style and arrangement was appointed, consisting of Johnson, Hamilton, Morris, and King. On Wednesday, 12th of September, 1787, Doctor Johnson reported a digest of the plan, and on Tuesday, 17th of September, 1788, the Engrossed Constitution was read and signed. So far as we have examined this question, it does not appear when nor how these words—"when the President of the United States is tried the Chief Justice shall preside"—were inserted in the Constitution. No doubt you are much better informed on the subject than myself.

I have read and seen it stated that they must have been introduced by a conference committee, and that that fact is shown by Mr. Madison's writings; but in the searches which I have been able to make in the short time during which this investigation has been going on, I have not been able to ascertain whether that is so or not. So far as I do comprehend or understand it, I maintain the following proposition, to which I respectfully ask the attention of the Chief Justice himself, and also the attention of the Senate.

I shall not dwell upon it at any great length, but leave it to you, Senators, and to the Chief Justice, to judge for yourselves whether it is founded on sound reason. First, I hold that the law of Parliament furnishes no satisfactory explanation of the union of the Chief Justice with the Senate on impeachment trials. That explanation must be found in the circumstances under which the Constitution was formed. I think it is one of the most important considerations in the investigation of this great question. You have seen that one of the plans was to have impeachments tried by a court to be composed of judges from each of the States; another plan was to have them tried by the Supreme Court of the United States.

Another plan was to have the Supreme Court of the United States associated with the Senate in the trial. Every one of these plans, you will perceive looked to judicial assistance in the trial of the cause, and when it was determined that the Chief Justice should preside, I imagined that it was determined that he should come here as a judge, that he should come here clothed as he is in his robes of office that he should declare the law and pronounce a judicial opinion upon every question arising in the case. While I know that it is for your honor to determine what course you will pursue, while I do not presume to dictate to this honorable court or to the Chief Justice who presides over it, for it is my province to argue, and it is your province to decide and determine.

I do respectfully insist, before the Senate and before the world, that I have a right as one of the counsel for the President, to call, as I do call, upon the venerable Chief Justice, who presides over your deliberations, for an expression of his judgment and opinion on any question of law that may arise, and now, in the name of common sense, does this doctrine of mine trench in the slightest degree upon any right of the American Senate? Does it conflict with any duty, or with any power imposed upon you by the Constitution of our common country.

Why, Senators, learned as you are, respectable as is your standing at home, high as is your position which your States have conferred upon you in placing you here, you still may derive instruction from the opinion of a gentleman learned in the law, and holding the highest judicial office in the land; does it invade any privilege, any prerogative—I do not like that word—or any power of the American Senate, to say that we ask the deliberation and the prudent and dispassionate judgment of one who is presumed to hold the scales of justice in an unfaltering and untrembling hand of one who holds his office independent of popular excitement and popular commotion, who has been elevated to his high position because of his learning, his integrity, his talents and his character.

Is it, I ask, any disparagement even to the American Senate, to respectfully request of him that he shall deliver an opinion to you upon any question that may arise in this case? And then, Senators, it will be for you to judge and determine for yourselves, under such an opinion. Whatever may be the opinion you have formed, I insist that so far from being an argument in disparagement either of the power or of the intelligence of the Senate, it is an argument which, in its nature, is calculated to aid the Senate as a court in arriving at a correct conclusion; and I hold that no man who regards the Constitution and the law of the law—no man who is in search of justice—no man who is willing to see the law faithfully and honestly and impartially administered, can for one moment deny the right of this great Civil Magistrate, clothed in his judicial robes, and armed with all the power and authority of the Constitution, to declare what he believes to be the law on questions arising in this case When you look at the clause of the Constitution under which this power is conferred, you see that every word in it is a technical word. The Senate shall try the impeachment, and on this trial they shall be on oath or affirmation, and the Chief Justice shall preside. I do not quote the words literally, but they are familiar to you all.

What is the meaning of the word "trial?" It is not necessary for me to enter into any elaborate definition of it. It is enough for me to say that it is not used in the Constitution in the sense of suffering, nor in the sense in which it is used in common parlance, but it is used in the sense of a judicial proceeding. The word "trial" is a word dear to every Englishman; it is a word dear to every American; it conveys the idea of a judicial trial, or trial in which a judge is to preside; a trial, in which a man skilled and learned in the law, and supposed to be a man of independence, is to preside

It is a proceeding dear to every Englishman, and dear to every American; because, for centuries in England, and since the formation of the government here, it has been regarded as essential to the preservation of the liberty of the citizen that a trial shall be thus conducted, with all the aid of judicial interpretation that can be obtained. Worcester defines presiding as being placed over others, having authority over others; presiding over an assembly. So the word "trial," as i have said, is not used in the sense of the manager, but to convey the idea of judicial proceedings similar to those before court and jury. So the word "Chief Justice," as used in that phrase in the Constitution, is a technical word. What does it mean? It means a judicial officer. The Constitution does not say in so many words that a judicial tribunal shall be created in which there shall be a Chief Justice.

It authorized Congress to create judicial tribunals; it took for granted that there would be a court; it assumed that in that court there would be a Chief Justice, and that he should be a Judge; and when it assumed that he should act in that capacity, which I insist upon, without dwelling on the argument further I can only say that in the views which I entertain of the question, I conceive it to be one of the most important questions ever presented to the consideration of this or any other country. We all know, Senators, that so far, this is the first case under the American Constitution in which the Senate has been called upon as a Court of Impeachment to try the Chief Magistrate of the land. The precedent which you are to form in this case, if our government survives the throes of revolution, and continues undiminished and unimpaired to remote posterity. It is one which will last for a thousand years.

The decision made now is one which will be quoted in after ages, and will be of the very highest importance. I maintain, therefore, that in the view which has just been presented, we have a right to call upon the Chief Justice to act not merely as a presiding officer, but to act as a judge on the conduct and management of this trial. I have already noticed some startling and extraordinary propositions made by the managers. Mr. Manager Bingham says that "You are a rule and a law unto yourself." Mr. Manager Butler claims, that as a constitutional tribunal, you are bound by no law, either statute or common. He states further, that common fame and current history may be relied upon to prove facts, that is to prove the President's course of administration, and further, that the momentous question is raised whether the Presidential office ought in fact to exist.

Senators, in the whole course of American history I have never heard or seen there such startling propositions as those which are insisted upon by the honorable managers. They are dangerous to liberty; they are dangerous to the perpetuity of the American Constitution and the American Government. They would overthrow every principle of justice and of law that is known in the civilized world, if they were carried out to the extent which the honorable managers insist upon. I never heard or dreamed that in this land of liberty, this land of law, this land where we have a written Constitution, such doctrines would be asserted here. If I do not misunderstand the language used, the learned managers think that this Senate has the power to set aside the Constitution itself.

Many of the most eminent and learned writers in England and in our country, when treating on the subject of the distribution of powers between the executive, legislative and judicial branches of the government, have sounded the note of warning, that the danger is not to be apprehended from the executive, not to be apprehended from the judicial department, but is to be apprehended from the encroachments of the House of Commons, of the popular branch of the government, and now we hear learned, and able, and distinguished leaders of the House of Representatives, the chief men of this impeachment trial, arguing that the Senate has the right to judge and determine for itself whether the provisions of the Constitution shall be maintained. Senators, that is not in conformity with the healthful doctrine of the American Constitution.

The sovereignty of the land is not in you, it is not in the President, it is not in the Chief Justice. It is in the American people, and they only can alter their Constitution. No Senate, no House of Representatives, no Judiciary, no Congress can alter the American Constitution. I noticed during the trial that when one of the witnesses spoke of the President of the United States saying that he intended to support the Constitution of the country, it caused a universal smile in the Senate and galleries. That venerable instrument, established by the wisdom of some of the bravest and most distinguished men the world ever saw;

that noble instrument which was purchased with the blood and treasure of the Revolution, and which we have been accustomed to regard with sacred reverence, seems to have been so often trampled upon and violated in this land, that when somebody dares to mention it with some of the reverence of ancient times,

It excites smiles of derision and laughter; God grant that a more faithful sentiment may animate and inspire the hearts of the American people, and that we will return—now that the war has passed away, back to something of the veneration and respect for the American Constitution, and that we will teach our children, who are to come after us, to love, and venerate, and respect it as the popular safeguard of the country, which is not to be treated with anything short of that respect and veneration, and high reverence with which we have been accustomed to regard it. But you are told that you are to act on common fame. Is it possible that we have come to that?

It is possible that this great impeachment trial has reached so lame and impotent a conclusion as that the honorable managers are driven to the necessity of insisting before you that common fame is to be regarded as evidence by Senators? I hope it will not grate harshly on your ears when I repeat the old and familiar adage that "comman fame is a common liar." Are Senators of the United States to try the chief executive magistrate on rumor the most vague, the most uncertain, the most unreliable. The glory and boast of English law and of the American Constitution are that we have certain fixed principles of law, fixed principles of evidence, which are to guide and govern a trial on the investigation of cases. One of the boasts of the system of American independence, and one of its greatest perfections is this, that when you go into a court of justice there is nothing taken of rumor or fame.

There sits the judge. There the jury, and here, are the witnesses. They are called on to testify; they are not allowed to give in evidence any rumor. They are compelled to speak of facts within their own knowledge. The case is investigated slowly, cautiously and deliberately. The truth is arrived at, not by any hasty conclusions, but upon solemn trial, and upon patient and faithful investigation; and, when the result is found, it commands the confidence of the country, it secures the approbation of the world, and it is acquiesced in; if it be in the highest court, it passes in the history of law, and goes down to posterity, as a precedent to follow in all time to come; and herein, Senators, is the greatest of liberties of American people.

I hope you will pardon my giving utterance to one thought, I will not say that it is original, but it is a thought which I have frequently cherished and indulged in—that the liberty of the American people is not that liberty which is defended in a written Constitution; is not that liberty which is enforced by Congressional enactment. But what do the American people think of it? I would to God that they would think of it a thousand times more intensely than they do. The only liberty which we now have, or ever have had, so far as American citizens is concerned, is that liberty which is enforced and secured in the judicial tribunals of the country. We talk about our social equality, about our all being free and equal—it is an idle song, it is a faithless tale, it is a vain and empty expression, unless that liberty and that equality is enforced in a court of justice. I have seen a thousand times a poor and humble man come into court, either as a plaintiff or as a defendant, and I have seen an impartial judge sit, blind to all external emotions, and declaring the law, trying the case, and administering the justice to that poor and unfortunate man against the richest and the most powerful of the land.

There is your law, there is your justice, there is only liberty which is worth enjoyment, and to admit common fame and common rumor before the highest tribunal known to the Constitution as a criterion of judgment, would be to overthrow the Constitution itself, and to destroy that liberty which has thus far been enjoyed in the land. You are told that you are to be "a law unto yourselves." Why, Senators, if this be so, then your Constitution has been written in vain; if this be so, then all the volumes which swell the public libraries of the country and the private libraries of lawyers and statesmen have been written and published in vain. Then we would be brought back, in imagination, to the days of the Spanish Inquisition, to some of those dark, secret, unknown tribunals in England, in Venice, in the Old World, where the proceedings were hidden from mankind, and whose judgments were most awful, and terrible, and fearful in their results.

No, Senators, I deny that you are a "law unto yourselves." I maintain that you have a Constitution. I insist that you must look to parliamentary history, and to common law, not as an authoritative exposition of the duties incumbent upon you, but as a guide to enlighten your judgment and understanding, and that you must be governed by those great, eternal principles of justice and reason which have grown up with the growth of centuries, and which lie at the very foundation of all the liberties which we enjoy. This, Senators, is what I insist is the true doctrine of the American Constitution, and I insist that the wide latitudinarian, unauthorized interpretation of the honorable managers, can find no justification anywhere, in view of the correct and eternal principles of justice incorporated in the American Constitution, and which form part of the law of the land in every State.

If this be so, if you are governed by no law, if you are a "law unto yourselves," if the Constitution has nothing to do with it, if common fame and common rumor are to govern and control here, then the very oath which you took here is an extra-judicial oath, not binding on the conscience, and not binding according to the law of the land. This would invest the Senate of the United States with the most dangerous power that ever was invested in any tribunal on the face of the earth.

It would enable the Senate of the United States, under the pretext of being a law unto itself, to defeat the will of the American people, and remove from office any man who might be displeasing to it; to set at naught elections and to engross into its own hands all the powers of the country. Senators, I can conceive of no despotism worse than that—I can conceive of no dangers menacing the liberty of the American people more awful and fearful than the dangers which menace them now, if this doctrine finds any sort of favor in the mind or heart of any Senator to whom it is addressed.

I do not believe that the American Senate will, for one moment, cherish any such doctrine, or act upon it in th slightest degree. It would prostrate all the ramparts of the Constitution, despoil the will of the American people, and engross in the hands of the Congress of the United States all the powers that were intended to be limited and distributed among the different departments of the government.

Another question, Mr. Chief Justice, and it is a question of very considerable interest, is as to what are crimes and misdemeanors under the Constitution. I desire to remind the Senate and the Chief Justice of a proposition which was asserted at an early period in this trial, by one of the learned managers. I regretted at the moment that I had not answered it, but it is in the record and it is not too late to give a passing remark to it now. The honorable manager made use of the expression, that "The great pulse of the nation beats perturbedly, fitfully, pauses when we pause, and goes forward when we go forward."

And we have been told time and time again, that the honorable managers are acting for all the people of the United States. I may have something to say about that, Senators, before I close my remarks which I have to make, but I shall postpone the consideration of that for the present. The honorable managers told you that "The public pulse beats perturbedly, that it pauses when you pause, and goes forward when you go forward." And you have been told, time and time again, that the people out of doors are anxious for the conviction of the President of the United States. Permit me, Mr. Senators, to be guilty of the indecorum almost of saying one word about myself, and I am only doing so by the way of stating my argument.

In the whole course of my professional career, from the time I came first a young man to practice law till the present moment, I never had the impudence or the presumption to talk to a judge out of court about any case in which I was concerned. My arguments before him have always been made in court. I have had sufficient respect for the independence of the judges before whom I had the honor to practice my profession to take it for granted that they were men of honor, men of intelligence, and that they would not hear any remark which I should make to them out of doors, and not in the presence of my adversary.

But the doctrine here is that the "public pulse beats"— Ah! have we come to that? Is this case to be tried before the greatest court in Christendom, not upon the law, not upon the evidence, not under the instruction of the Chief Justice of the United States, but to be tried on common rumor; and is it to become interesting, or to cease to be interesting, just according to the beating of the public pulse. Why. Senators, if it were not that I do not intend to say one word designed to be offensive to any gentleman on the other side, or to the Senate, I would say that I almost regard this as an insulting argument. But I do not make use of that expression. It is not my intention in anything that I have said or may say to wound the sensibilities of any one, or to give just offense to anybody connected with this case.

But you are told that you are to try the case according to the public pulse. What an argument to advance to the American Senate! What an argument put forward in the American nation! Why, all history teems with examples of the gross, outrageous injustice which has been done in criminal trials. Trials in Parliament, and trials in courts of justice—aye, and our own country has not been exempt from some notable instances of it, where public clamor was allowed to influence the judgment of the judges. Those instances that are recorded in history, those instances of blood and of murder, of outrage and wrong perpetrated in the name of justice, are admonitions to us that the public pulse should have nothing to do with this trial.

Senators, regarding every man whom I address as a judge, as a sworn judge, allow me for one moment to call your attention to one great trial in this country, which I hope in some of its principles will be applied by you in this. There was a case which occurred in the early history of the American nation where there was a great political trial, and where the waves of political excitement ran high. It was understood that the President of the United Stated himself desired the conviction of the offender. The public pulse beat fitfully then. It went forward as the judge went forward, and it went backward as the judge went backward.

It was a great occasion. It was one of the most illustrious trials that ever occurred in English or American jurisprudence. There was a great criminal who was morally guilty indeed, for so he has been held in the judgment of posterity. There sat the judge, one of the illustrious predecessors of the illustrious and distinguised gentleman who presides over your deliberations now. There he sat, calm, unmoved, unawed by the public pulse, the very impersonation of justice, having no motive under heaven except to administer the law and administer it faithfully,

and he had nerve and firmness to declarre the law in the fear of God rather than in the fear of man.

Although the criminal was acquitted, and although there was some popular clamor in reference to the acquittal, yet the judgment of posterity has sanctioned the correctness of the judicial determination, and every American citizen who has any regard for his country, every judge and every lawyer who has any respect for judicial independence and integrity will look back with veneration and respect to the name and to the conduct of John Marshall; and so long as judicial independence shall be admired, so long as judicial integrity shall be respected, the name of John Marshall will be esteemed in our own country, and throughout the civilized world, as one of the brightest luminaries of the law, and one of the most faithful judges that ever presided in a court.

It is true that clouds of darkness gathered around him for the moment, but they soon passed away, and were forgotten,

"Like some tall cliff that lifts its awful form,
 Swells to the gale, and midway meets the storm,
 Though around its breast the rolling clouds are spread,
 Eternal sunshine settles on its head."

Such was the name and such the fame of John Marshall, and God grant that his spirit may fall like the mantle of Elijah on the illustrious magistrate who presides, and on every judge who sits here, so that you may catch its inspirations and throw to the owls and to the bats all those appeals to your prejudice, and so that you may discharge your whole duty in the fear of that God to whom you appeal. If I might press such a low, contemptible consideration on the minds of Senators, if I might be pardoned for the very thought which makes me shrink back almost with horror for myself, I would say to Senators that, if you rise above those prejudices cast this clamor away from your thoughts, do your duty like impartial men in the fear of God and in no pitiful political point of view, it would make you stand higher with your own party and with the whole world. Forgive me for such a dissertation, for really it is beneath the dignity of the Senate to entertain such a thought for a moment. No, Senators, I entreat you as judges, I entreat you as honorable men, I entreat you as sworn officers of the law, and thus entreating you, I say that I banish all such thoughts from my mind, and come before you as an impartial tribunal, believing before God and my country that you will try to do your duty in this case, irrespective of popular clamor and regardless of opinions from without; and when you, and I, and all of us shall pass away from the scene of human actions, and when the memory of the stirring events which now agitate the public mind shall almost be forgotten, I trust that future ages will look back with wonder and admiration, and with love, and respect, and honor, to the American Senate for the manner in which it shall have discharged its duty in this case. I trust, Senators, that the result will be such as to command the approbation, not only of your own consciences, not only of the State which you have the honor to represent, but the approbation of Him who is a greater judge than you are, and the approbation of posterity.

A most excellent rule of interpreting was adverted to by Chief Justice Marshall, in the trial to which I have referred, Burr's trial, speaking of the words "levying war," as used in the Constitution, said that it was a technical term, and that it must be considered as being employed in the Constitution as it was employed in England, unless the contrary was proved by the contract, or unless it was incompatible with other parts of the Constitution. He held that it was used in the same sense in which it was used in England, in the statute of Edward the Third, from which it was borrowed. Now the words treason, bribery, and crimes and misdemeanors, were words just as familiar to the framers of the Constitution as they are to us.

One of the honorable managers made an argument here to show that because Dr. Franklin was in London at the time of Warren Hastings' trial, that had a good deal to do with the proper mode of construing the American Constitution on the subject of the power of the Chief Justice. Those words were almost as familiar to the lawyers at the time of the formation of the Constitution as they are to the lawyers and judges of the present day.

In one passage of Burke, he says that crimes and misdemeanors are almost synonymous words, but, in another and further expression of it, he undertakes to show, and does show, that the word "crimes" is used in the sense of charges such as usually fall within the denomination of felony, and that the word "misdemeanor" is used in the sense of those trivial and lighter offenses, which are not punished with death, but with fine or imprisonment.

Now, what is the rule of interpretation? It is not necessary for me to turn to authorities on the subject. Words are to be construed in the connection in which they are used and the sense of those being of the same kind. If I correctly apprehend the law at the date of the forming of the Constitution, treason, by the law of England, was a felony, punishable with death; bribery was misdemeanor not punishable with death, but punishable with fine and imprisonment. When the word "crimes," therefore, is used in the Constitution, it is to be construed in the same sense as the word "treason."

It is to be understood as a felonious offense; an offense punishable with death or imprisonment in the penitentiary. The word "misdemeanor" has reference to other offenses. It does not mean simple assault, for the expression in the Constitution is "high crimes and misdemeanors"—high crimes referring, of course, to such crimes as are punishable with death, and high misdemeanors referring to such misdemeanors as were punishable by fine and imprisonment, not to such simple misdemeanors as an assault.

What then is the argument upon that? What is the true meaning of the words "crimes and misdemeanors" as embodied in the Constitution of the United States? One set of constitutionists hold that you are not to look at the common law to ascertain the meaning of the words "crimes and misdemeanors," but that you are to look at the parliamentary law to ascertain. Now, so far as I have any knowledge on the subject, the parliamentary does not define or did never undertake to define what is the meaning of "crimes and misdemeanors."

What did the parliamentary law undertake to do? It undertook to punish not only its members, but citizens, for offenses which were regarded as offenses against the government. Often without turning the offender over to the courts, the parliament impeached him, or proceeded against him in a manner similar to impeachment. But there was no definition, as far as I know, of "crimes and misdemeanors."

The language of the honorable manager is in great part a law unto itself; but when framers of the Constitution incorporated these words in our charter, did they borrow them from parliamentary law, or did they get them from Blackstone and Hall and from the other writers on criminal law in England? They got them from the common law of England, and not from the law of parliament. Then what proposition follows as a corollary from the premises? I have laid down, if the premises be correct, why it follows inevitably that the words crimes and misdemeanors received in the sense in which they are employed by writers on criminal law in England.

I doubt whether the laws of the United States within the meaning of the American Constitution has a right to create a new crime and a new misdemeanor from something which was not known 'as a crime or as a misdemeanor at the date of the adoption of the American Constitution. I think it is a matter of great doubt, to say the least of it.

It is, Mr. Chief Justice, on these and on kindred questions, that I respectfully submit that we have a right respectfully to demand at the hands of your honor a judicial exposition of the meaning of the Constitution. It will be for you, under your own sense of duty, under your own construction of the powers conferred upon you by the Constitution of our common country, to decide for yourself whether this respectful question will be answered or not.

Senator YATES, at 4 o'clock, suggested that if counsel desired the Court might now adjourn.

Mr. NELSON intimated that he did feel somewhat fatigued, but would proceed if the court did not now desire to adjourn.

Senator YATES submitted his motion and the court thereupon adjourned.

PROCEEDINGS OF FRIDAY, APRIL 24.

At the opening of the court, this morning, the Chief Justice stated that the first business in order was the consideration of the following order, offered yesterday by Mr. Grimes:—

Hour for Assembling.

Ordered, That hereafter the hour for the meeting of the Senate, sitting for the trial of impeachment of Andrew Johnson, President of the United States, shall be 12 o'clock M. of each day, except Sunday.

The order was adopted by the following vote:—

YEAS—Messrs. Anthony, Davis, Doolittle, Fessenden, Fowler, Grimes, Henderson, Hendricks, Johnson, McCreery, Morgan, Morrill (Vt.), Morton, Patterson (Tenn.), Ramsey, Saulsbury, Trumbull, Van Winkle, Vickers, Willey, Yates—21.

NAYS—Messrs. Conkling, Conness, Cragin, Edmunds, Harlan, Howe, Pomeroy, Sprague, Stewart, Sumner, Thayer, Tipton, Wilson—13.

Reporters and the Final Deliberations.

Mr. EDMUNDS then offered an amendment to admit the official reporters to report the speeches on the final deliberation of the Senate, which was objected to by a number, and went over under the rules.

Mr. Nelson's Argument Continued.

Mr. NELSON then proceeded with his argument as follows:—

Mr. Chief Justice and Senators:—In the course of my argument of yesterday, I alluded to certain opinions expressed by one of the managers in a report, to which his name is affixed, made to the House of Representatives. Lest any misunderstanding should arise, I desire to state, in regard to that portion which I adopt as my argument, that I do not consider that there is any inconsistency in the position which the honorable manager assumed in his report to the House of Representatives and the position which he has assumed here in argument. If I understand the honorable manager's position, while he insists, as I understood yesterday, that you are to look to the common law, and not merely the law of Parliament, in order to ascertain the use of the words crime and misdemeanor in the Constitution, yet if I correctly comprehend his argument, he insists that it is competent for Congress to make a crime or misdemeanor under the Constitution, and that such crime or misdemeanor is an impeachable offense. If I correctly understand the gentleman's position, I hope neither he nor the court will misunderstand me when I call attention to those parts of the gentleman's argument which I rely upon, because the arguments he makes are much more forcible than any I can hope to make.

Mr. Nelson quoted from the minority report of Mr. Wilson, now one of the managers, made in November, 1867, on a former impeachment investigation, and continued:—I come to a point now which I have already endeavored to make my argument, namely, that the definition given by the honorable manager who opened the argument is not a correct definition. That opening, as the Senate will remember, was accompanied by a very carefully prepared and learned argument on the part of Mr. Lawrence, to which reference was made by the honorable manager. It is this—"We define, therefore, an impeachable high crime or misdemeanor to be one in its nature or consequences subversive of some fundamental or essential principle of government, or highly prejudicial to the public interest, and this may consist of a violation of the Constitution, of law, and official oath, or of duty by an act committed or omitted, or without violating positive law by the abuse of revolutionary powers from improper motives, or for any improper purpose." Now, if you go to the law of Parliament for a definition of treason or other high crimes, as I have already said, you will not find it. If you will not find it if you go to to the law of Parliament for the purpose of ascertaining what is an impeachable offense, then you go to a law that is not in force in this country at all. Every species of offense which Parliament chooses to consider as such, was declared by statute or was the subject matter of impeachment by Commons or the House of Lords. Their form of government is different from ours. Persons were tried in England for very slight and very trivial offenses, and severe punishments, were inflicted on various occasions in the progress of English history, upon persons who were supposed to have been guilty of such offenses. This process of impeachment is one of which we have not any account in history so far as I have been able to examine the subject. It is true, as the gentleman has said, that five hundred years ago the subject was introduced into the English Parliament, and they considered it then, and claimed that the House of Commons had jurisdiction over this subject in consequence of the law of Parliament, but how that law of Parliament arose, where it originated, neither the House of Lords nor Mr. ———, in his elaborate report and argument, in the House of Commons undertook to state. It arose from what they assumed to be usage, and if you go to Parliament in order to determine that in this country then you would be obliged to punish anything as an offense, without any authority whatever.

Mr. Nelson read from the history of the British Constitution, instances of punishment in England, by the pillory and by whipping at the cart's tail, for trifling offenses, which, he said, if the declaration of the managers were correct, would be impeachable offenses. He continued, you can only look to the common law for the purpose of ascertaining the definition of high crimes and misdemeanors. Mr Story, I know, says, in his work on the Constitution, that in one case it was settled in this country that the term "crimes and misdemeanors" did not have the signification which I insist upon, but at the same time he asserts that there is a contrariety of opinion on this subject among interpreters of the Constitution, and that distinguished gentlemen, as I understand him, does not regard the question as being by any means finally and authoritatively settled, so that in order to ascertain what are impeachable crimes and misdemeanors, it is necessary to go to the common law for a definition of what is an impeachable offense in this country, within the meaning of the Constitution as a crime or misdemeanor. You must show that it was known as such at the time when the Constitution was adopted; in other words, I respectfully maintain that Congress has no power to create a crime different in its nature from crimes and misdemeanors known and understood to be such at the time of the adoption of the Constitution. Briefly and imperfectly as this argument has been presented, I will not undertake to dwell upon it further. I desire, although it is not exactly in the order which I had prescribed for my remarks, to call the attention of the Senate to some observations made by the honorable manager who addressed the Senate yesterday; and in order that there may be no misunderstanding as to the observations to which I wish to call your attention, I will read a paragraph from that gentleman's speech of yesterday.

Mr. Nelson quoted a portion of Mr. Boutwell's argument charging that the President is a man of violent passions and unlimited ambition, and that he seeks to use subservient and corrupt men for his own purposes, and then abandons them. And alluding to his treatment of Judge Black, saying that, though announced as the President's counsel, he had never appeared, he continued:—It is true, Senators, a source of much embarrassment how to speak in reply to the accusations which have thus been preferred against the President of the United States. It would seem, from the description given by the honorable manager, that the very presence of the President would breed a contagion, as if almost the very atmosphere of his presence would produce death, but I very respectfully insist on the statement of a fact, which I will make to you in a moment, and which, I think, is called for by a reference which has been made to Judge Black, to show that injustice has been done, unintentionally, by the manager in the language he has used. I regret that this topic has been introduced.

I am not aware that I ever saw Judge Black in my life until I met him in consultation in the President's Council Chamber, and in all the interviews we had our intercourse was very pleasant and agreeable, and it is with feelings of embarrassment that under these circumstances I deem it necessary to say anything upon this subject at all; but in order that you may understand what I have to say about it, I desire to refer the Senate to a brief statement which I have prepared, and which, on account of the delicacy of the subject, I choose to put in writing, and, although I have no had the time which I could have desired to prepare it, it will comprehend all the material facts of the case. You will understand that I do not propose to give a full statement, but a synopsis of what may be called the Alta Vela case. A mere outline will be sufficient.

Having given this outline of the facts in relation to the case, Judge Nelson proceeded to say that after the action in the matter which he had recited, while Judge Black was one of the counsel for the President, he had an interview with the respondent in this case, urging upon him to take action in reference to the rights of citizens of the United States upon that island and the sending of an armed vessel to take possession of it. The President having declined to do so, Judge Black declined to appear further as counsel in this case. Such, said he, are the facts in relation to the withdrawal of Judge Black, and so far as the President of the United States is concerned, the "head and front of his offending hath this extent, no more."

It is not necessary that I should censure Judge Black, or make any imputation upon him or any of the honorable managers. I have no reasons to charge that any of the managers are engaged or interested in it. The presumption is, that the letter which I read, which was signed by him, was signed as such letters often are, by members of Congress without any personal interest in the matter to which they relate. Judge Black thought it his duty to press this claim, and now Senators, I ask you to put yourselves in the place of the President of the United States, if his action in this matter is made a subject of accusation against him. Ask yourselves how the President must feel in relation to it. I am willing that this subject should be spread before the country, and that even his enemies should understand what has been his conduct and his motives in this matter.

I wish to call your attention particularly to the fact, that all these transactions took place before the impeachment proceedings were commenced, and that the charges have been made since. Another fact in favor of the President is, that while I do not make any implications against the honorable managers, these recommendations to which I have referred, were signed by the honorable gentlemen whom the House of Representatives have intrusted with the duty of managing the impeachment against him. Let me suggest a single idea with regard to the impeachment. If the President went to war with a weak and feeble power and gained an island it would seem that he did so in fear of the managers, and in fear of losing the high and valuable services of Judge Black.

If he refused to do what they called upon him to do, there was danger that he would exasperate Judge Black, and it was under these delicate circumstances that this question was presented to the President. He was between Scylla and Charbydis. In forming his determination in regard to the matter, no matter which way he might determine, his integrity might be assailed. But the honorable managers must know the President less familiarly than I do, if they supposed that he could be driven or forced by any consideration to do what he thought wrong. He is a man of a peculiar disposition.

By careful management he may perhaps be led, but it is a delicate and difficult matter to do that which, with his peculiar disposition, no man under Heaven can compel him to do; go one inch beyond what he believes right; and although he knew that by rejecting this claim he might raise up enemies; and although he was well aware that a powerful influence might be brought to bear against him on his trial, and it might be trumpeted over the land, from one end to the other, that Judge Black had abandoned him on account of his belief in his guilt. Although the President knew that a black cloud would be raised against him, he was prepared to say that "though in that cloud were thunders charged with lightning, let them burst."

He placed himself upon the principles of the Constitution, faithful to the rights of the people who had exalted him to that high position, unmindful of self and regardless of consequences, and he was determined not to be driven to any act which he believed to be wrong; determined not to use the whole power of the United States against a little feeble power that had no capacity to resist. He was determined not to be used as an instrument in the hands of anybody, or any set of men under Heaven, to carry on a speculation which he believed might be carried on with dishonor to the government or disgrace to himself, if he consented to be concerned in it. I ask you, then, to weigh his conduct, to allow an impartial judgment, and look this statement of facts in the face, and pronounce upon it as you have to pronounce upon this impeachment, when you come to look over the whole of the President's conduct. I

think you will find that, like the grave charges presented by the honorable manager yesterday, they will vanish away, and "like the baseless fabric of a vision, leave not a wreck behind."

I trust that the conclusion of this trial will be such that, although the President is now passing through the fiery furnace, and although he is for every act being called to an account, he fears not the investigation; he challenges the utmost scrutiny that can be made into his conduct. While, as I have said, he hurls no defiance at the Senate, and does not desire his counsel to say a word that shall be offensive to this body, yet he defies his enemies as he always has done, and appeals to his own motives of purity and honesty to vindicate him in this case, as in every other. Instead of being a matter for accusation against the President of the United States, in the view that I entertain of it, and in the view which I think every high-minded man will entertain, his conduct will elevate him a head and shoulders taller in the estimation of every high-minded man, and it will be regarded as one of the most worthy acts of his life, that he could not be coaxed nor driven into a wrong act.

This "Alta Vela" affair is referred to, as though the President had done something wrong. What wrong did he do? How did any failure result from Judge Black's refusal to act as counsel? Did the President discard Judge Black, and tell him he did not want him to appear any more in his case? No, sir; it was upon his own voluntary motion that he withdrew from the case. If the President has done him any injury, he knows it, but his counsel know it not. I leave it for the judgment of the world to determine how much justice there is in the accusations which are so strongly made against him.

Senators—Allow me to call your attention to another paragraph in the speech of the honorable manager who last addressed you (Mr. Boutwell). It is not my purpose or intention to endeavor to answer at length that able and carefully-prepared argument which the honorable manager has made. I must leave notice of that to those who are to follow me on the side of the President, but there is another paragraph, which reads in these words: "Having indulged his Cabinet in such freedom of opinion when he consulted them in reference to the constitutionality of the bill, and having covered himself and them with public odium by its announcement, he now vaunts their opinions, extorted by power and given in subserviency, that the law itself may be violated with impunity."

"This," says the President, "is the exercise of my constitutional right to the opinion of my Cabinet." "I," says the President, "am responsible for my Cabinet." Yes, the President is responsible for the opinions and conduct of men who give such advice as is demanded, and give it in fear and trembling, lest they be at once deprived of their places. "This is the President's idea of a Cabinet, but it is an idea not in harmony with the theory of the Constitution." In another place the gentleman speaks of the members of the Cabinet as being serfs. "It was the advice of serfs to their lord, of servants to their masters, of slaves to their owners."

I desire, Senators, to refresh your recollection, by calling your attention to the extract from the President's message, which was put in evidence upon the part of the prosecution, dated December 12, 1867, and I wish to state in reference to this message, as well as all other documents signed by the President, that if any rule of law is to obtain in this high and honorable tribunal, it is that when we put these documents before the Senate they may be permitted to speak as witnesses.

They do not try to discredit this document. I regretted that we were not permitted to introduce certain members of the Cabinet to prove certain statements of the President; yet, upon sober, second thought, I am inclined to the opinion that probably the Senate had settled the question exactly right—that it was unnecessary for us to introduce members of the Cabinet or introduce their testimony to sustain these statements so long as they are not impugned on the other side. I will read the extract from page 138 of the reported proceedings:—

"This was not the first occasion on which Mr. Stanton, in discharge of a public duty, was called upon to consider the provisions of that law. The Tenure of Office act did not pass without notice. Like other acts, it was sent to the President for approval. As is our custom, I submitted its consideration to my Cabinet for their advice upon the question whether I should approve it or not. It was a grave question of constitutional law, in which I would, of course, rely most upon the opinion of the Attorney-General and Mr. Stanton, who had once been Attorney-General."

Nor can such words be unnoticed as the honorable manager has used—"he calls his serfs around him." The President says:—"Every member of my Cabinet advised me that the proposed law was unconstitutional. All spoke without doubt or reservation, but Mr. Stanton's condemnation of the law was the most elaborate and emphatic. He referred to the constitutional provisions, the debates in Congress, especially to the speech of Mr. Buchanan when a Senator; to decisions of the Supreme Court, and to the usage from the beginning of the government, through every successive administration, all concurring to establish the right of removal as vested by the Constitution in the President.

"To all these he added the weight of his own deliberate judgment, and advised me that it was my duty to defend the power of the President from usurpation, and to veto the law." There is the plain, unvarnished statement of the President of the United States, uncontradicted by any one at all, a statement that we offered to verify by the introduction of members of the Cabinet as witnesses. We offered to prove that every word—at least the substance of every word—contained in that paragraph of the message was correct, had we been permitted to introduce the members of the Cabinet, but our testimony was not admitted; and inasmuch as it was not admitted, since this message was introduced by the prosecution and we offered to prove it, I assume as an indisputable fact on this occasion, that Mr. Stanton, about whom the world is to be set on fire now, advised the President that this Tenure of Office act, about which such a great cry has been raised in the land was unconstitutional, and that it was his duty to veto it I never saw Mr. Stanton to my knowledge, but if I were in his place, I think I would say, as some one else has said, "Save me from my friends, and I will take care of my enemies." I think if any man ever had reason to exclaim, "Save me from my friends," Mr. Stanton has had reason to do so, and to exclaim, "Save me from the disgrace to any independent officer of the low, mean, debased, mercenary motives by which such an officer may be influenced. But as it is a sort of a family quarrel, I will not interfere any further," One other thing in regard to Mr. Stanton; I will show you that before he advised the President that this law was unconstitutional, he advised him on another matter which does not stand in the category of his opinions as a member of President Johnson's Cabinet.

On the 3d of March, 1865, Mr. Stanton addressed a letter to his Excellency, Andrew Johnson, Vice President elect, in which he says that the War Department had learned with admiration the firmness and faithfulness with which he had discharged his duties as Military Governor of Tennessee, and that his noble and patriotic services were duly appreciated, and congratulating him on being called from the arduous and trying duties which he had so honorably performed, to the safe and easy duties of civil life, assuring him that he was about to assume the duties of Vice President at the close of a period of unparalleled trial, after having brought peace and safety to his own State.

Three short years have elapsed since the letter by Mr. Stanton indorsing the President of the United States was written. I have referred to it for the purpose of showing you that when I spoke of the services of the President, I was only speaking in regard to matters for which at that time he received the high encomium of Mr. Stanton—for services in behalf of the Union for which he had not hesitated to expose even his own life.

It is hardly conceivable that in the short period of three years a gentleman of whom the Secretary of War spoke in high terms of commendation, which I have read to you, should become the monster, the tyrant, the usurper, the wicked man, whom he is represented to be upon the other side. Mr. Stanton runs through this whole trial. He is, I believe, in eight of the eleven articles of impeachment. His name is almost everywhere, and you have him in two relations. First, as indorsing the President, in the words which I have read to you, and also indorsing the President's action when the Civil Tenure bill was passed, in March, 1867, and if a difference of opinion grew up afterwards, and unkind feelings existed between them, and if there was a loss of confidence on the part of the President, and if their relations towards each other became less harmonious than they had been before, all I have to say about it is, that it furnishes no ground of impeachment; none in the world; nor should it, in the slightest degree, affect his character or motives.

There is one other thing, before I resume the consideration of the various articles of impeachment, that I desire, Senators, to call your attention to, and that is this same proceeding which was had in the House of Representatives upon the subject of impeachment. I know not how it strikes the minds of Senators, nor how it impresses the minds of the people of the country; but one of the strangest of things in the history of our government is that these articles of impeachment should be gotten up against the President after twelve months' examination of this matter, and that charges against him, of which I will speak after a while, should be founded upon acts that were done in reference to the Thirty-ninth Congress.

Is it not passing strange that if the President was guilty of the acts charged against him, and if he has done acts worthy of impeachment, that the Thirty-ninth Congress took no notice of it; and that after that Congress is defunct, passed out of existence, its memory and name gone into history, is it not strange that another Congress should take up offenses against that Congress and make them matters of grave accusation against the President? One of the charges presented against him by the House of Representatives is, that he has been guilty of an intent to subvert the government of the United States. [Reading the first article of impeachment.] The fact is, if my memory serves me aright, and I have not been misinformed, the House of Representatives, when they considered these articles referred to—

The Chief Justice was compelled to call the Senate to order, as it was impossible to hear the speaker on account of the conversation in the hall and galleries.

Mr. NELSON, resumed:—The House of Representatives refused to entertain these articles of impeachment against the President by a solemn vote, and if there were any law in this tribunal, as the gentlemen say there is, not unless it be that law of Parliament which they rely upon, and which amounts to no law at all. If there was law here, or any application of law by analogy of the law, I would avail myself of the doctrine of estoppel, which was so learnedly expounded by one of the learned managers, and I would insist that the House of Representatives, with all due reference and respect, after having voted down this charge that the President had slandered and maligned the Congress of the United States were stopped making any accusation of that kind against the President now.

But I hope I may say, without offense, that still the Senate of the United States, sitting here as a judicial tribunal, can look to the circumstances under which these charges were preferred, without any disrespect whatever to the House of Representatives; and when you go to the circumstances under which these charges of impeachment were preferred, you have, at least, evidence that they were done without any great amount of deliberation in the House, and possibly under the influence of that excitement which great assemblies, as well as private individuals, are liable to experience, and which this assembly of grave, reverend signors, who are impanelled here under the Constitution, may look upon and must regard in considering the facts in the case.

When articles of impeachment were presented against Warren Hastings, in England, they were the subject of long and anxious debate in the Parliament before they were presented; and Senators, I maintain that it is your province and your duty to look to this fact, and not to give the same importance to accusations made under more careful deliberation, especially when the House of Representatives had a short time before acquitted the President of a large number of the charges presented against him. In the unanimous report, presented by the committee under these circumstances, it will be no disparagement to the House, no disparagement to ourselves to look at the fact that these charges were hastily drawn up, and if upon a sober view of the facts you should believe that these charges came to you in at least a questionable shape, so far as the circumstances under which they were adopted are concerned, it will be no reflection upon the House should you so decide, any more than it would were a private individual only concerned. As the House of Representatives is composed of men of flesh and blood like yourselves, I trust they will consider it no disparagement to say that they were acting under the impulse of feeling, and what, upon second sober thought, they would not do over again.

We all know human nature well enough, at least in our own persons and characters, to know that when we act in passion, in hate or in excitement, we are apt to do things which, upon reflection, we have reason to regret. And these actions, while they are in a great measure excusable on account of the haste and passion in which they are committed, yet they are actions which do not command the same power and influence in society that they would do if they were the result of grave and careful consideration.

Now, Senators, I will have to call your attention to these different articles of impeachment, though it is rather a disagreeable thing to treat this mill-horse round, and take them up one by one, and make brief comments upon them, as it is my purpose to do, though I know the subject is becoming stale and weary, not only to the Senate but to those who gather around to hear this investigation. Yet I cannot, in accordance with my sense of duty in this case, take my seat until I offer some consideration to the Senate on each one of the articles of impeachment, although it must necessarily become, to some extent, a tedious business, yet I do so because, Senators, if you follow the precedents of other cases, you will be required to vote upon each one of these articles separately, and will have to form your judgments and opinions on each in a separate way. Now, in regard to the first article of impeachment, it may not be out of place to look to that article as it is presented, and to state very briefly the article itself. I do not propose to go through all the verbiage of that article, nor to repeat all that is said in the answer, but the principal features of it are these:—

The Speaker here quoted the article in substance, and the answer of the President thereto, and then continued:—

Now, one word or one thought, Senators, before entering upon the consideration of this first article, which I conceive is applicable to all the articles. Indeed, much of what we have to say on the first article applies to all the other articles, and involves, to some extent, a necessary repetition, but I shall endeavor, as far as I can, to avoid such repetition. Now all these articles of impeachment, or nearly all of them, charge a removal.

If you follow the precedents of trials of impeachment which we have already had in the United States, and especially if you follow the decisions on the British Parliament, there ought to be something substantial in the articles that are preferred against a man. Now, what is it that is provided for by the Civil Tenure bill? Why, it is removal of a person, and that is what is charged in each one of what I may, for want of better work, call the "counts" of this indictment.

Now, Senators, if you follow the law, and the rules of law that have been adopted in other cases, and look to them as being a precedent to some extent, although not binding and obligatory to all intents and purposes as judicial procedures, what is the familiar rule of the law? There is not a judge or lawyer in this Senate who does not know that in every law book that has been written for two hundred years, a distinction is taken between a crime and an attempt to commit a crime. The distinction is just as broad and wide as Pennsylvania avenue?

Why, according to statutory regulations almost everywhere, and even according to the common law, murder is one thing, and an attempt to commit murder is another and a different thing. Burglary is one thing, and an attempt to commit that offense is another and a different thing. Now I ask with all earnestness of this Senate, as lawyers and judges, that the doctrine contended for by the learned managers be the true doctrine, that the civil Tenure bill is constitutional, and that the President has no power to remove except with the advice and consent of the Senate, then, Senators, I ask you how is it that the President can be found guilty of removing Mr. Stanton from office?

Taking the premises of the honorable gentleman to be correct, when there was no removal at all, but there was an attempt to remove; there is no sort of doubt but there was no removal from office at all; and you do not bring it within the Civil Tenure bill unless you have a case of removal. It is not a case of removal, but, if their construction be true, it is a case of an attempt to remove a person from office; so that it is impossible for the honorable managers to escape the dilemma which the nature of their case places them in on the first count.

I desire to maintain briefly three propositions. First, that the Tenure of Office bill is unconstitutional and void. Second, that if the civil Tenure of Office bill is not unconstitutional, it does not embrace such a case as the removal of Mr. Stanton; and third, if both these propositions are erroneous, that the President acted with a laudable and honest motive, and is therefore not guilty of any crime or misdemeanor.

On the first proposition as to the unconstitutionality of the Civil Tenure of Office bill, as it has not been done already in behalf of the President, I avail myself of the occasion to remind you of certain things which occurred in the debates of 1789, although I know they are familiar, probably, to every Senator I address, yet I regard these things as material and important to our line of defense, and at the risk of wearying the patience of the Senate, I must ask the privilege of presenting briefly the views I entertain on that subject.

In the House debate which occurred on the 16th of June, 1779, on the bill for establishing an Executive Department, to be denominated the Department of Foreign Affairs, Mr. White moved to strike out the words "to be removable from office by the President of the United States." He advocated this because the Senate had the joint power of appointment. His views were sustained by Mr. Smith, of South Carolina; Mr. Huntington, Mr. Sherman, Mr. Jackson, Mr. Gerry and Mr. Livermore, and were opposed by Messrs. Benson, Ames and others, as is shown in Seaton's Debates, vol. 1, pp. 473 to 608.

Mr. Madison said, in that debate, it was evidently the intention of the Constitution that the first magistrate should be responsible for the Executive Department, and that so far, therefore, as we do not make the officers who are to aid him in the duties of that department responsible to him, he is not responsible to the country, basing his argument mainly on the constitutional provision that the Executive power shall be vested in the President.

Mr. Sedgwick said if expediency is at all to be considered, gentlemen will perceive that this man is as much an instrument in the hands of the President as the pen is the instrument of the Secretary in corresponding with foreign courts. If, then, the Secretary of Foreign Affairs is the mere instrument of the President, we would suppose, on the principle of expediency, this officer should be dependent upon him.

I say it would be absurd in the highest degree to continue such a person in office contrary to the will of the President, who is responsible that the business be conducted with propriety and for the general interest of the nation. Upon that debate I merely suggest that it states plainly the affair as it exists between the President and Mr. Stanton, and as this debate occurred soon after the adoption of the Constitution, and that several gentlemen who had participated in the formation of the Constitution—among them Mr. Madison, one of the ablest men who ever wrote on this subject, not even excepting Alexander Hamilton—also took part in this debate. We must give it the highest consideration, and if there is to be anything in the doctrine of the law, which is applied to every other case, that when a decision of a legal question is made, that decision should stand; and if there be anything in the doctrine of State decisions, I maintain, Senators, that an opinion which, so far as I know, has never been controverted at any time except during the time of Andrew Jackson, and an opinion which has stood for nearly eighty years, is not an authority, then I can conceive of nothing that is sufficient to be taken as a precedent.

If, according to the English law, a man is protected in his real estate after sixty years' possession, and if, as in my own State, seven years' adverse possession gives a good title, why may we not argue, and argue with propriety, before the American Senate, that this question was settled eighty years ago, and when the decision has never been controverted until the present time, except on the occasion to which I have referred, I do maintain, Senators, as earnestly as I am capable of maintaining, any proposition, that that decision is an authoritative conclusion, and is on principle binding and obligatory on this Senate, and that you must follow it on the same principle that judges are in the habit of following judicial determinations in reference to the rights of property which have been long acquiesced it, and have become principles of law.

Mr. Nelson then went on to quote the argument made by Mr. Sedgwick, in the debate in the House of Representatives, in 1789, when the subject of the President's power to remove civil officers was under discussion, in which argument Mr. Sedgwick had stated many of the reasons why the power of removal must be left in the President. Among those reasons were the following:—That the President might be fully convinced of the moral or mental unfitness of the person to hold his position, but could not in one case out of ten bring sufficient evidence thereof, before the Senate; that under those circumstances it would be wrong to saddle such an officer upon the Presi-

dent against his will, and that the President could not be held responsible unless he had control over the officer.

Never, said Mr. Nelson, had more sensible remarks fallen from the lips of mortal man than those observations of Mr. Sedgwick, and they are as descriptive as it is possible for language to be, of the circumstances under which the removal of Mr. Stanton occurred.

Mr. Nelson went on to quote still further from the same debate, and then referred the Senate to the remarks of Chancellor Kent and of Judge Story on the same subject.

Thus we see, said he, that although the *Federalist* opposed the power of removal, Mr. Madison and Judges Kent and Story regarded it as firmly settled and established. If authority is worth anything, if the opinions of two of the ablest judges of this country are worth anything, I maintain that it follows inevitably that the Civil Tenure bill is unconstitutional, and that the President was justified in exercising his veto power against it. Whether or not that view of the case be correct, there is still another view of it.

If the President was wrong, if he was erroneously advised by his Cabinet, if he came to an improper conclusion, if the view taken by counsel on the subject be incorrect, still the argument is pertinent and appropriate as to the question of intention.

I respectfully ask whether the Senate, sitting as judge, cannot rely with the greatest confidence on the opinion of the two most eminent jurists whom our country has produced—Kent and Story. They are names as familiar to every judge and every lawyer in the United States as household words. And not here alone are those names distinguished. In Westminster Hall, in that country from which we borrowed our law, the names of Kent and Story are almost as familiar as they are in the chamber where your Honor presides as Chief Justice of the United States.

Their words are quoted by British judges, by British lawyers, by text writers, and no two names in English or American jurisprudence stand higher than the names of those two distinguished men. If they are not sufficient authority to satisfy the minds of the Senate, as they probably could not be in view of its action hitherto on the subject that the Civil Tenure law is unconstitutional, yet I ask you, Senators, if the views of two such distinguished men as these, might not well guide the action of the President of the United States, and relieve him from the criminality imputed to him in these articles of impeachment? I hope you will allow me, Senators, to call your attention to some other opinions on this subject. Appointments to and removals from office have been the subject of investigation in various forms by the Attorney-General of the United States. I know that the learned manager (Mr. Butler), when he came to speak of the opinion of the Attorney-General, said that after the office became political, he did not consider it a matter of any great importance to quote these opinions. No one is more skilled than that gentleman in the management of a case. I will do him the justice to say, although I do not exactly agree with him in his notions about the decency and propriety of speech, that I have hardly ever seen a gentleman who managed a case with more skill and art and ability that he had done for the prosecution.

With that astuteness which distinguished him, he passed over the opinions of the Attorney-General with the remark I have referred to. I had a slight suspicion that possibly the authority of the Attorney-General might not be just exactly the kind of authority which gentlemen wanted, and so, although I did not know much on the subject, I concluded I would look at those opinions of the Attorney-General, and I will state to you what I have learned from the slight examination I have given them; I maintain that in the proper construction of the act of 1789 it is a matter of perfect indifference whether the President is advised by the particular Attorney-General who may belong to the Cabinet in reference to any particular act. I maintain that the opinions delivered by the Attorney-General are in the nature of the judicial decisions.

I do not say they are to all intents and purposes judicial decisions, but in the view which I entertain of the act of 1789, I insist that they should be as operative and effectual in this high and honorable court as judicial decisions are in the court over which your Honor presides. Why do I say so? Unless I have misread the Constitution of the United States, there is no provision there declaring that the decision of the Supreme Court of the United States shall be final, and conclusive, and authoritative in questions of law. The framers of the Constitution assumed that there was a certain state of things in existence at the time they made it; they assumed that the history of English jurisprudence would be known to the American Senators. In other words they assumed that there was and would continue to be a certain amount of knowledge, and information, and reformation in the world.

It was, therefore, unnecessary for them to put in the Constitution that the decision made by the Supreme Court of the United States would be binding. They knew that the practices of English judges had been for years to regard a decision by a judicial tribunal in a case carefully considered, and especially where it had stood for any length of time unreversed, as an authority from which it was not safe in administration of the law to depart.

Now the argument that I make is, that while the Constitution of the United States does not specify that the decision of judges shall have all the force of authority in the land, any more than it does in reference to the opinions of the Attorney-General, yet on any fair construction, or any fair legal intendment, I argue that under the act of 1789, the opinions of the Attorney-General may be regarded by the President, and by all others who have anything to do with that opinion as a valid authority, and should be sufficient to justify his action in any given case that might be covered by that opinion.

The act of September 24, 1788, provides that there shall be appointed an Attorney-General of the United States, whose duty it shall be to prosecute and conduct all cases in the Supreme Court in which the United States are concerned, and to give his advice and opinion of questions of law, when required by the head of any of the departments touching matters connected with their respective departments.

Take the two provisions together—the provision in the Constitution that the President may call on these officers for advice and information, and the provision in the act of 1789, that he may call on the Attorney-General for advice and opinion—then I maintain, Senators, that, when opinions have been given in cases like the one under consideration, those opinions are in the nature of judicial opinions, and are a perfect shield and protection to the President, if he can bring his act in that particular case within the spirit and meaning of them.

Mr. Nelson referred to the opinions of Attorney-General Wirt, Attorney-General Berry, Attorney-General Legare, Attorney-General Nelson, Attorney-General Crittenden, and Attorney-General Speed, on several points having more or less affinity with the question of the power of removal and appointments. In reference to Mr. Speed, he said that gentlemen stood very high in some quarters of the United States, and his opinion was entitled to much weight in those quarters.

Senator CONKLING asked whether the opinion of Mr. Speed was published in the volumes of opinions of the Attorny-General?

Mr. NELSON said it was not, but that he had a certified copy of it, and proceeded to read an extract from the opinion, as follows:—

"It is his duty (meaning the President) to do all that he has the power to do when occasion requires the exercise of authority. To do less on such an occasion would be *pro lanto* to abdicate his high office. The Constitution is the supreme law—a law superior and paramount to any other. If any law be repugnant to the Constitution it is void."

This, said Mr. Nelson, bears not only upon the Civil Tenure bill, but it is square up to all the questions which the gentlemen on the other side have argued in connection with it. Here is advice given to the President by a man on whose judgment he had a right to rely; for, be it known to you, the President of the United States is not himself a lawyer. He never studied the legal profession, and has no claim or pretensions to know anything about it. In the discharge of his official duties he has a right to consult the legal advisers who are given to guide and direct him on questions of law by the Constitution of the country and by the act of 1789, and when he finds an opinion on file in his office, or recorded in any reported volume of the opinions of the Attorney-General's, and when he acts upon that opinion it must protect him against the imputation of unlawful or improper motives. And now, Mr. Chief Justice, if you see fit, in the discharge of your duty, to comply with the respectful request of you to deliver an opinion upon any legal question involved in this case, I most respectfully ask you to consider this opinion of Attorney-General Speed, and to say that it is sound law. Allow me to call attention to the closing sentence of that opinion, which, I think, is the very essence of the law itself. It is as follows:—

"But before such a case arises, and in the absence of an unauthoritative exposition of the law by the Judicial Department, it is equally the duty of the officer holding the executive powers of the government to determine for the purpose of his conduct and action as well as the operation of conflicting laws the unconstitutionality of any law."

This, continued Mr. Nelson, is the opinion of an Attorney-General who is not a member of Mr. Johnson Cabinet, not a serf of the President's, who gave his opinion before the present incumbent came into office.

There is his opinion, placed on record in one of the departments of the government, to stand there and to stand forever, so far as the opinion of any one will go, to guide the highest executive officer of the government. It declares that if a law is unconstitutional in the view of the President it is no law at all, and he is not bound to follow it. It declares that the President has the right, in the absence of any judicial exposition, to construe the law for himself. I need not tell the Senate that that is no new doctrine. Why, Senators, within your day and mine, we all recollect an executive officer of the United States—a man of strong will, a man not possessing any great advantages of education or of mental culture, but still a man of strong intellect, and of a determination just as strong as his intellect; we all recollect Andrew Jackson, a name which was once potent in the United States. No name was ever more powerful in this government from the time of its foundation to the present than the name of Andrew Jackson. "There were giants in those days." When Andrew Jackson was at the head of the United States he exercised his powers of removal. His right to do so was called in question by some of the ablest men that ever stood within the Senate of the United States. It was discussed, and learnedly discussed, yet he persevered in his determination of the power and authority of the President of the United States to remove from office, and to make appointments. A resolution was introduced into the Senate, I believe, in reference to the removal of Mr. Duane, to the effect that the President of the United States, in his late proceedings, had violated the Constitution. That resolution passed the Senate. A gentleman who is now no more, but whose name is well known in the political history of the United States (Mr. Benton), took up the subject. I have not referred to the history of the debate with

sufficient accuracy to tell you how long it was that he continued to agitate the question. My own recollection is, that it was for several years, and I remember, as the Senators will remember, the remarkable expression which Mr. Benton used:—"Solitary and alone," said he, "I set this ball in motion."

He determined that that resolution censuring the action of the President should be expunged from the records of the Senate. He debated it time and again with tremedous energy and fervor until at last the resolution was expunged from the records of the Senate of the United States, and that is the latest record we have in favor of the power removal. So far as that action of the Senate of the United States goes, it is in favor of the power and authority for which I have argued. There are two other subjects to which I desire to bring your attention in this connection. But let us see first how far we have progressed in the argument. I have shown you the opinions of Mr. Madison and Mr. Sedgwick, and others in the debate of 1789. I have shown you the opinions of Judges Kent and Story, two of our ablest American commentators.

I have shown you the opinions of Attorney-Generals eminent in their profession, and standing high in the confidence of the country. I have shown you the action of the American Senate in the expunging resolution. I thus present to you what I may call in the language of Judge Story, an unbroken current of authority in favor of the proposition, that not only is the Civil Tenure bill unconstitutional, but that the President has the right to remove from office, which he claims in his answer; and I maintain, Senators, that, whether he was right or wrong, this current of authority for eighty years is sufficient to throw protection around him.

When I show, as I have done, from the opinion of Mr. Speed, that in the absence of any judicial determination, it is the sworn and bounden duty of the President of the United States to judge of a constitutional question for himself, I do not present to this Senate any novel doctrine. It is not for me to say whether the doctrine is right or wrong. My opinions are of no sort of consequence in this Senate. If my arguments are well founded and well supported, they will have influence, and if not, they will be rejected. So it is not necessary for me to say what I think, but I maintain that that is no novel doctrine in the United States.

I told you yesterday that the President is a Democrat of the strictest sect. I told you that he was really nominated as a Democrat in the Convention which nominated Mr. Lincoln and himself for President and Vice President of the United States. That was not a Democratic convention; it was a convention composed of Union men, without any reference to the old lines of demarcation between Whigs and Democrats; it was a convention which assembled together for the purpose of sustaining Mr. Lincoln, and whose view and opinion was, that by sustaining Mr. Lincoln and the measures of his administration, it would be sustaining the strong arm of the government in putting down the Rebellion, which had not then been brought to a conclusion.

In the reply which he made when he was informed of his nomination, he remarked that he was a Democrat; and now, Senators, I will read you the two opinions of Mr. Jefferson and General Jackson on the subject of appointments to office, and before I do so, let me call your attention to one fact. Keep the political training of the President of the United States ever in your minds. Go to his standpoint; look at things as he looked at them —judge of them as he judged of them—for you are now in search of motive; that is what you are trying to determine in this case.

You are in search of the question of intention, and when you judge of his conduct, recollect that he is a Democrat of the Jefferson and Jackson school, if I can show you, as I will presently show you, that Mr. Jefferson and General Jackson undertook to construe the Constitution for themselves and claimed that as Executive officers they had a right to do so: when I will show you that, according to the political training and education of Mr. Johnson, he might well believe that they had, and especially when he had Mr. Speed's opinion confirmatory of that doctrine, it furnishes us a satisfactory vindication and protection of the President as to the exercise of his judgment.

Mr. Nelson referred to a letter written by Mr. Jefferson, and found in the sixth volume of Jefferson's works, page 461, and said that the Senate would see that Mr. Jefferson went far beyond Mr. Johnson in the views which he entertained. Mr. Johnson had said that he was anxious to have this question between him and Congress settled by the judicial department, but Mr. Jefferson claimed that he had a right to decide for himself, irrespective both of Congress and of the Judiciary.

Mr. Nelson also referred to another letter of Mr. Jefferson, to be found in the seventh volume of his works, page 135, in which he says that his construction of the Constitution is that each department is truly independent of the other, and has an equal right to decide for itself what is the meaning of the Constitution, or the cases submitted to its action, and especially where it is to act ultimately and without appeal. If that doctrine be correct, the President of the United States had a right to decide this question for himself, independent of any intention or design to have a case made and prepared for the adjudication of the judicial tribunal of the country; but if that be not correct, then, Senators, it certainly goes far to explain if not to justify, the action of the President in the removal of Mr. Stanton. Mr. Nelson also referred to General Jackson's veto of the United States Bank bill, wherein he declared that if the opinion of the Supreme Court covered the whole ground of that act, it ought not to control a co-ordinate authority of the government. I want you, continued Mr. Nelson, to notice these assertions, for you will see that such great men as Jefferson and Jackson went beyond the present President of the United States in their assertions, because they denied the right of the Supreme Court even to adjudicate the question.

Mr. Nelson went on to quote from General Jackson's veto on the Bank bill, to the effect that the lawyers, the Executive and the Supreme Court must each for itself be guided by its opinion of the Constitution; that every public officer who takes an oath to support the Constitution swears to support it as he understands it, and not as it is understood by others; that it is as much the duty of the House of Representatives, of the Senate, and of the President, to decide upon the constitutionality of a bill or resolution that may be presented to them for passage or approval as it is for the Supreme Judges when the case is brought before them for judicial decision.

That the opinion of the judges has no more authority upon Congress than the opinion of Congress has upon the judges; that upon that point the President is independent of both, and that the Supreme Court must not, therefore, undertake to control either Congress or the President. We have had a good deal of talk here about prerogative. That was the prerogative which General Jackson asserted, that he had a right to construe the Constitution of the United States for himself, independent of the judicial tribunals of the country.

If General Jackson and Mr. Jefferson asserted such executive power, how much more might Andrew Johnson, the present President? He says, here is a question about which there is some difference of opinion between the Congress of the United States and myself; here is a question which has distracted and divided the country. I desire to have this question settled. I do not wish to settle it by my own right. I desire to submit to the judicial tribunals of the country, and in order to do that, I will exercise power which has been exercised from the foundation of the government. I will remove Mr. Stanton, and I will put this case in a condition in which it can be settled by the judicial tribunals of the country. I will invoke the action of the highest judicial tribunal of the country, and if the Supreme Court of the United States decides this question in favor of the views which Congress has presented, I will acquiesce in and submit to the decision. If the Supreme Court of the United States decides the question in the other way, I will persevere in the determination to appoint some one in the place of an officer of my Cabinet who is obnoxious to me.

Now, I maintain, Senators, that there was nothing wrong or illegal in that. But it is argued on the other side that after the President of the United States has vetoed a bill, and after it has been passed over his veto by two-thirds of both Houses, it is then placed in such a situation that he has no right to put any construction upon it different from that which Congress has put upon it. I cannot see the logic of the argument; a law passed by Congress and approved by the President and put upon the statute book, is nothing more than a law. If the President of the United States exercises his veto power, and attempts to prevent the passage of the law, by refusing that assent which the Constitution empowers him to give, or withhold, and if the Congress of the United States passes it over his veto, and it comes on the statute book, is it anything more than a law?

Has it any greater or more binding force in the one case than the other? If the President of the United States has any power or judgment at all, may he not exert it in the one case just as much as he may exercise it in the other? I cannot, for the life of me, see the force of the definition which the honorable managers are attempting to make. No, Senators, there are questions peculiarly belonging to the Executive Department which the President must, of necessity, have the right to determine for himself, and specious and ingenious as the argument of the honorable manager (Mr. Boutwell) was, that there may be an implication in favor of Congress as to the right of powers enumerated in the Constitution, and that there is no implication in favor of the President as to the duties which are imposed upon him by the same instrument, that argument has no foundation in sound reasoning, or in any authority known to the law. The very term "executive power," like most of the other terms employed in the Constitution, is technical. I have shown you how Mr. Madison understood it, in the debate of 1789. I have shown you what a wide latitude he took in dealing with the words "executive power," and in arguing that the President was responsible for the action of the Cabinet, which he called around him.

Well, if you can get from the Constitution an implication to be derived from the words "Executive power," or from the words that "he shall take care that the laws be faithfully executed," or from some other words in his oath, or from some other words in the Constitution, relating to that power; if, I say, you can derive any power in the one case, then the doctrine of implication arises as to all the other powers that may be conferred upon him, and I can see no reason why you may not imply anything that is necessary to be done as much in favor of the President as you may imply it in favor of Congress. By the Constitution Congress may create a navy, declare war, may levy taxes; but the Constitution does not say whether it is to do that particular act by taxation or not; it does not prescribe whether the vessels are to be iron-clad or wooden-clad, whether they are to be steam vessels or sailing vessels; it does not pre-

scribe how much tonnage they shall have; all these and a thousand other things are left to the discretion of Congress.

Congress derives the power, as a necessary incident, under the general provisions of the Constitution, to do anything that may be necessary and proper to carry all the foregoing powers into effect. If this doctrine of implication, which is absolutely necessary and essential to the legitimate and proper exercise of the powers conferred by the Constitution upon Congress, has been acquiesced in from the foundation of the government by Congress, why may it not be acquiesced in as well for the President of the United States? There is no force, as I contend, in the distinction which the honorable manager insists upon.

The court here, at a quarter before two o'clock, took a recess for fifteen minutes.

After the recess Mr. NELSON continued his argument, and referred again to the debate on the removal of Mr. Duane by General Jackson, and to the part which Mr. Clay and Mr. Webster took in the debate. He also referred to a letter written by Mr. Madison, and to be found in the fourth volume of Madison's Works. The argument on the other side, he continued, is that the President of the United States is, under the Constitution, a mere man in buckram; that he has no power or authority to decide anything; that he can do nothing on the face of the earth except it is nominated in the bond; that he must be the passive instrument of Congress, and that he must be subject to the government and control of the other departments.

The argument which we make is, that under the Constitution there are many powers and duties vested in and imposed on the President of the United States, and that he must of necessity have a right, in cases appropriately belonging to his department, to exercise something like judicial opinion; that he must act upon his own authority and upon his own construction of the Constitution; and whether he does that in reference to the removal of an officer, or in reference to anything else, I maintain that it is different from the action of a private individual. A private individual, if he violates the law of the land, is amenable for its violation under the principle that ignorance of the law excuses no man; but the President of the United States, having the Executive power vested in him by the Constitution, has a right to exercise his best judgment in the situation in which he is placed; and if he exercises that judgment honestly and faithfully, and not from corrupt motives, then his action cannot be reviewed by Congress or any other tribunal except the tribunal of the people in the Presidential election, should he be a candidate before them again. That is the only place where it can be reviewed.

Mr. NELSON proceeded to quote from another speech of Mr. Madison, to the effect that the co-ordinate departments of the government have a right, each for itself and each within its appropriate sphere, and in reference to its own appropriate duties, to construe the Constitution. If this view be right, then the President of the United States had the right to construe the Constitution for himself, notwithstanding the passage of the Civil Tenure act, and he had the right to act upon it in the manner in which he did and you cannot make a crime, you cannot make an offense out of such an action, you cannot justify it in the view of the American people, you cannot justify it to the civilized world. Senators, I maintain that you cannot justify it to your own consciences, to put such a construction as that upon the act of the President and to deny him the power which he has attempted to exercise in this case.

Mr. Nelson then referred to the famous protest of General Jackson, claiming the rights of the President to remove officers, and said:—You will see that General Jackson, with characteristic energy and courage, stood up faithfully in vindication of the executive power, while he was President of the United States. Now, Senators, at the risk of some repetition, allow me at this point, to sum up as far as I have gone. I have shown you that in the debate in 1789, some of the ablest men whom this country has ever produced, and some of the very men who had an agency in forming the Constitution, conceded the power of removal as claimed by the President. I have shown you that for eighty years, with the single exception of the struggle which took place in General Jackson's time, that power has been acquiesced in.

I have shown you that two of the most eminent writers in American jurisprudence, Kent and Story, have regarded the question as settled. I have shown you, from the opinions of some of the ablest attorney-generals who have ever been in office in this country, that the power of removal exists in the manner in which it was exercised by the President. I have shown you that during the long period of time to which I have adverted, it was conceded that the power of removal belonged to the President, in virtue of the Constitution, and that the Senate had no constitutional right or power to interfere with it. Having shown you all that, I have now a few words to say in relation to the President's action in removing Mr. Stanton, and in further answer to the first article against him.

Yes, you have observed the first proposition that I have endeavored to demonstrate is, that the Civil Tenure bill is unconstitutional and void, for if the doctrines be correct, which I have endeavored to maintain before you, and if this long chain of authority is entitled to the slightest degree of respect, then it follows inevitably that Congress had no power to pass the law, and it follows, furthermore, that the President had the right to exercise a judgment in reference to retaining or removing one of the counsellors. whom the Constitution had placed around him for the purpose of aiding him in the administration of public affairs. But the other view in which I wish to argue the case is this. It has already been indicated in various statements from time to time made by me in the progress of my remarks. Suppose that the proposition which I have endeavored to maintain before you is erroneous; suppose that Congress is right and the President is wrong; suppose that Congress had the power to pass the Civil Tenure bill; suppose that the President had no right to act contrary to it—again the question comes up whether or not he is guilty on any of these articles of impeachment.

The first eight articles charge in different forms an intent to violate the Constitution, or violate the Civil Tenure bill, or violate the act of 1862; every one of them containing a charge of an unlawful intention. Now, referring to what I have already said on the subject, I desire to sustain what I have already said, by reference to some of the opinions contained in law books, and to ask the question, how can any unlawful intent be predicated on this act of the President? According to Foster, Hall and other writers on the subject of criminal law, every crime must have these marked characteristics, it must be an act forbidden by the law, and must be intentional.

That is as applicable to high misdemeanors as it is to high crimes. The act is innocent or guilty, just as there was or was not an intention to commit crime. For example, a man embarks on board a ship in New York for the purpose of going to New Orleans; if he went with the intention to perform a legal act he is perfectly innocent, but if his intentions were to levy war against the United States, then he is guilty of an overt act of treason.

Chitty says that "intent is not always inferrable from the act done," and I maintain that if there was intention, there can be crime or misdemeanor.

In continuation of this line of argument Mr. Nelson referred to Wharton, Roscoe, and other writers on criminal law, and continued:—How can it be said that the President had any wrong or unlawful intent, when the Constitution gives him the power to judge for himself in reference to the particular act charged? How can it be said that he had any wrong or unlawful intent, when the practice of the government for all the periods of time of which I have referred was sufficient to justify him in exercising the powers which he attempted to exercise?

How can it be said that he had any wrong or unlawful intent, when he had all these opinions of the Attorney-General to guide, lead and direct him? How can it be said that there was any unlawful intent on his part, when he had the opinions of the very Senators and Representatives, at the time when the law was passed, as a guide to lead and direct him in the performance of his duty? It does seem to me that it beggars all belief, to say that the President intended anything wrong. It outrages all our ideas of common justice and of common sense, to say that there was any purpose or intent on his part either to violate the Constitution, or to violate the Civil Tenure bill.

If Chitty's view is correct, and if the other writers are correct, and the President believed the law was unconstitutional then, at least until the question was adjudicated in the highest court in the United States, the President has a right to exercise his judgment, and you cannot hold that he was guilty of any criminal intent. Was there ever such a case presented? How bold how naked does this charge appear when you look at the principle involved. I will not take up time to turn to the evidence of the witnesses which you all have fresh in your recollection. Was there ever such a scene in the history of the world, among men claiming to have intelligence, among persons in the exercise of ordinary reason and judgment as the scene which occurred in reference to Mr. Stanton's removal, and the attempt to bring this question before a court of justice.

There was old General Thomas, who has been stigmatized a good deal on the other side, but whom I take to be a plain, simple-hearted, honest old man. He has been forty years in the military service of the country. I have no suspicions such as the gentleman (Mr. Boutwell) alluded to yesterday, as to whether he was in favor of the Rebellion or against it. If he was in favor of it, it was very extraordinary in Mr. Stanton to send him into the Southern States, and that he should organize seventy or eighty thousand negroes to fight the battles of the country.

He appears to be a plain, simple-hearted old man, whose very countenance is a recommendation of him. Perhaps he was a little vain at the idea of being appointed Secretary of War ad interim, but who that heard his testimony here in this court doubts for a moment his intention to speak the truth in everything he said. He goes there, and you have that wonderful scene that takes place when he attempts to get possession of the office of Secretary of War.

Was there ever such a thing seen since the world began? Was there ever such an act of force as that which took place between Mr. Thomas and Mr. Stanton while this proceeding was going on? They meet together like twin brothers, they almost embrace each other. I believe he said that Mr. Stanton did hug him, or something like that. (Laughter.) If he did not hug him he came very near it. (Laughter.) And in the fullness of his heart, Mr. Stanton became exceedingly kind and liberal, and called for liquor, and had it brought out. The little vial contained only about a spoonful, but it was fairly, honestly and equally divided between these two aspiring Secretaries. (Laughter.)

It was done in a spirit of fraternity and love such as I suppose was never before witnessed in any forcible contest. (Loud laughter.) Mr. Stanton says to him in effect, "This is neutral ground, Thomas, between you and me; there is no war here while we have this liquor on hand." (Laughter.) Not only did Mr. Stanton divide

that spoonful, but he felt so good that he sent out and got a bottle full more; and I suspect, Senators, that our old friend General Thomas not only felt a little elevated about the idea of being appointed Secretary of War ad interim, after having served the country in inferior positions, for a considerable length of time, but I imagine that the old man took so much of that good liquor on that occasion that he felt his spirits very much elevated, and that he was disposed to talk to Mr. Karsener and the other men as he did. But they tell you he was to take the office by force. Oh yes, force! He was forcibly to eject Mr. Stanton from the office of Secretary of War by drinking a spoonful of liquor with him, and then dividing a bottle. (Laughter.)

Was there ever such a farce before? Was there ever such a lame and incompetent conclusion as the testimony on the other side? and then Mr. Stanton goes out that night, or somebody else for him, and awakens up Mr. Meigs in the dark hours of the night; they go and arouse up Mr. Meigs as if felony was about to be committed; they go there as if they were attempting to raise a hue and cry. They awaken him from his slumbers and require him to go to his office and make out a warrent against the old man Thomas, for trying to violate the Civil Tenure Bill. Mr. Meigs arises and goes to his office in hot haste, with something like the haste with which these impeachment proceeding were gotten up.

He goes to his office and issues a warrant with all proper gravity and decorum; it is put in the hands of an officer, and poor old Thomas is seized before he had got his whisky in the morning (laughter), and is to be tried for this great offense of violating the Civil Tenure bill. But lo and behold, when the old man gets counsel to defend him, and goes before the judge, and lawyers get to discussing the question, this terrible offense, which it took the midnight warrant to meet—this terrible offense which it required a sheriff with his tip-staff, to take care should not be committed, begins to sink into insignificance.

When the lawyers got up and argued it before the judge they began to find out that there was some idea of taking the thing up to the Supreme Court, and then, all at once, the offense which two hours before was so terrible, sunk into insignificance, and the old man Thomas was discharged on his own recognizance. No cause is to be made out for settlement or adjudication in the Supreme Court of the United States. It reminds me of an anecdote which I used to hear in Tennessee about two Irishmen who came to this country. They were walking along one day, when they saw a little ground squirrel run up a stump and run down the hollow of the stump.

One of the Irishmen concluded that he would catch him to see what kind of a baste it was; so he put his hand down in the hole. "Have you got him, Pat?" said the one. "No," says Pat; "but by the powers he has got me." (Laughter.) That was just exactly the way in which Mr. Stanton and his friends waged war upon General Thomas. Instead of catching General Thomas, they found that he was likely to catch them, and therefore he was discharged on his own recognizance. Whoever did hear of such proceedings as that intended to be converted into a great and terrible charge against the President of the United States —or any other man? (Laughter.)

I shall not repeat what I esteem to be the unanswerable argument of Judge Curtis, that the case of Mr. Stanton is not embraced, or intended to be embraced, within the Tenure of Office bill. It is enough for me to refer to that argument, without attempting to repeat it. Having concluded the third proposition, with which I set out; having endeavored to demonstrate, first, that the law was unconstitutional; second, that the removal of Mr. Stanton was not a violation of the Tenure of Office bill, because it is manifest from the discussion that took place, that it was not intended to embrace the Secretary of War; and third, that if both of these proposition be incorrect, still there was no intent, so as to maintain the accusation made in the first article.

Mr. Nelson then proceeded to recapitulate briefly the charges made in the second, third, fourth, fifth, sixth and seventh articles, and the answers of the President to each of them.

Mr. NELSON read a portion of the eighth article of the answer, and continued:—

I remark that there is nothing in the Tenure of Civil Office act against the intent lawfully to control the disbursement of the moneys appropriated for the military service in the War Department, and no pretense can be lawfully imputed of such an intent. Under the Constitution the President is to take care that the laws shall be faithfully executed. The President is to make army rules and regulations, there being no limitation on the subject, He may lawfully exercise control over the acts of his subordinates, as was determined by the Supreme Court of the United States in the case of the United States against Ellis."—(16 Peters, 291; 14 Curtis, 304.)

The precedents have been declared by the Supreme Court of the United States to be such as we maintain—that no offense can be predicated from such acts. Wilcox vs. Jackson, J. B. Peters, 498—where it is said that the President acts in many cases through the heads of departments, and the Secretary of War having directed the sale of a section of land reserved for military purposes, the court assumed it to be done by direction of the President, and held it to be by law his act; which, by the way, would be a very good authority in answer to the honorable managers, that no implication results in favor of the powers claimed by the President under the Constitution.

here is a case where the Supreme Court of the United States enforced the doctrine of implication in his favor, and held that it would be presumed that the Secretary had acted by direction of the President of the United States, and that that would be sufficient.

Mr. NELSON read the ninth article, charging the President with endeavoring to induce General Emory to violate the provisions of the Tenure of Office act, &c., and also the President's answer thereto, and continued:—You will see that there is no substantial difference, as I understand it, between the conversation as set out in the President's answer and the conversation as stated by General Emory himself. He says that he did not request General Emory to disobey any law; that he merely expressed the opinion that the law was in conflict with the Constitution, and General Emory sustained that to all intents and purposes, for when the subject was introduced General Emory interrupted the President and called his attention to this Appropriation act.

Now, I have to say, in reference to this ninth article, that the Constitution, article two, section two, with which you are all familiar, provides that the President shall be Commander-in-Chief of the Army of the United States. The object of this was as stated in 1 Kent, 283; 3 Elliot's debates, 103; Story on the Constitution, section 1491: 92 Marshall, 583–8. The object was to give the exercise of power to a single hand. In the Meigs' case, Mr. Attorney-General Black (and I presume, from the eulogy passed on Attorney-General Black by the honorable member yesterday, his opinion ought to be a very authorative opinion) — in Captain Meigs' case, Attorney-General Black says:—"As Commander-in-Chief of the Army it is your right to decide according to your own judgment what officers shall perform any particular duties, and as the supreme Executive magistrate you have the power of appointment, and no one can take away from the President, or in anywise diminish the authority conferred on him by the Constitution."

Mr. Nelson quoted from Story's Commentaries, vol. 3, 1485, and from the commentaries of Chancellor Kent to the same effect. He proceeded:—Now, in the case of The United States against Ellis, 16 Peters, 291, it is said that the President has unquestioned power to establish rules for the government of the army, and the Secretary of War is his regular organ to administer the military establishment of the government, and rules and orders promulgated through him must be made as the acts of the Executive, and as such are binding on all within the sphere of his authority; and now, I ask, is there any proof shown here, in the first place, that there was any unlawful or improper conversations between the President and General Emory?

Mr. Manager Butler, with that fertility of invention which he has so eminently displayed at every stage of this proceeding, argues that it was either to bring about a civil war, by resisting a law of Congress by force, or to recognize a Congress composed of Rebels and Northern sympathizers, that this conversation was had. Let us look at the circumstances under which it took place. The correspondence with General Grant occurred between the 25th of January and the 11th of February, 1868, and the President had either charged or intimated in the course of that correspondence that he regarded General Grant as having manifested a spirit of insubordination.

The suspension or removal of Stanton took place on the 21st of February. The Senate's resolution of the 21st February disapproved of the removal of Stanton, and the President's protest occurred on the 22d of February. I have not brought any newspapers here, Senators, and I do not intend to bring any, because these facts, which I am about to state, are so fresh in your recollection, that without going into the minutiæ or detail, it is enough for me to state in general terms, that when this unfortunate difference of opinion, for no matter who is right or who is wrong about it, it is an unfortunate thing that there is a difference of opinion between the Chief Executive of the nation and the Congress, or any part of the Congress of the United States, it is a matter of regret that such a difference of opinion exists; but when this correspondence occurred, when these resolutions were offered in the Senate and in the House within the short period of time that had elapsed, there was telegram upon telegram, offer upon offer, made on the one side to Congress to support them, and on the other side to support the Preside....

The Grand Army of the Republic—the G. A. R.—seemed to be figuring upon a large scale, and but for the exercise of very great prudence on the part of Congress, and very great prudence on the part of the President of the United States himself, we would have had this country lit up with the flames of civil war; but I do hope, Senators, that no matter what opinion you may entertain on that subject, and no matter who you may think was the strongest, and God forbid that the country should ever have any occasion to discover which has the greatest military power at command, the Congress of the United States or the President of the United States, I say, without entering upon such a question, which we all ought to view with horror, to give the President of the United States the credit of believing that he has some friends in this country, he has persons in the different States who would have been willing to rally around him. How, if an unfortunate military contest had taken place in the country, it would have resulted, God in his wisdom only knows. All that I have claimed for him is that, whether he had few or many forces at his command your President has not told you. From the first day of your session here your President has manifested a degree of patriotic forbearance for which the worst enemy he has on the face of the earth ought to give him credit. If he is a tyrant or usurper, if he has the spirit of a Cæsar or Napoleon, if his object if to wrest the liberties from this country, why your President could very easily have sounded the tocsin of war, and he could have had some kind of a force, great or small, to rally around him, but instead of doing that, he comes in here through his counsel before the Senate of the United States. Although he and his counsel (or at least I, for one of them, would not undertake to speak for the others) honestly and sincerely believe that under the Constitution of the United States organizing the Senate and the House of Representatives, the House of Representatives as at present constituted, with fifty representatives from the Southern States absent, have no power to present articles of impeachment, and although he believes that the Senate, as at present constituted, with twenty Senators absent from this Chamber who have a right to be here, have no right to try this impeachment, yet I shall not argue this question, for, in view of the almost unanimous vote cast against the resolution of Senator Davis, recently, I think it would be an idle consumption of time to do it, and I only advert to it so as to place it on the record. I say that the President, and at least one of his counsel, entertain this opinion. We think it has no right to present these charges and try them under the Constitution, which says that no State shall be deprived of equal representation in the Senate, yet the President, instead of resorting to war or arbitrary tyranny, which was resorted to by the ambitions men that have been described in this Chamber, he submits this question in a peaceful and quiet manner, to be adjudged and determined by the Senate of the United States of its present organization; and now will you not at least give him credit for some degree of forbearance? When gentlemen talk of his trying to turn usurper, and his having a purpose in sending for General Emory, do they prove any improper design on his part? None on the face of the earth. Was it not natural in this state of things, when the whole country was agitated and excited, when men's minds were aroused everywhere in the unfortunate condition of parties in the United States to such an extent as that they were offering troops, on the one hand, to sustain Congress, and on the other to sustain the President, and when the Lieutenant-General of the Army and the President had differed in their opinions.

I maintain that the very fact that he has done nothing of a military character, shows that he had no intention to do the acts which are imputed to him. But it was right. It was natural when he saw these despatches; when he knew that there was a difficulty between General Grant and himself; when he knew that there were persons sending despatches through the newspaper governors, and prominent men in various States in the Union; sending despatches stating how they were to stand up for the Congress of the United States. In that controversy, it was natural and right, and within the legitimate scope of the powers conferred upon him by the Constitution, that he should send for this officer, that he should inquire what was the meaning of these new troops that were brought into the Department of Washington. He had a right to do it, and the fact that he did it is no evidence of an unlawful design on his part, but it proves that he was endeavoring to understand, as it was his duty to understand as the Commander-in-Chief of the Army and Navy of the United States, what was the meaning of the introduction of these forces. What did he know but what General Grant in the progress of this quarrel might assume the power of a military dictator? How did he know but what General Grant might be endeavoring to surround him with troops to have him arrested? Had not he a right to send for an officer and inquire if he knew of the introduction of these military forces here, and when he found that it was only a trivial force; when he found that there was no expressed design on the part of anybody to violate the Constitution of the United States, didn't he stop? No effort was made on his part to manage the army or to persuade the army to go to war with the Congress of the United States, but he retained his counsel, and, in a peaceful manner, submits himself to the judgment of the Senate; and I stand here in the face of this Senate and say that the history of the whole world does not furnish anything in moral sublimity and grandeur surpassing the triumphant spectacle which we now behold. I was delighted and rejoiced to see that this unfortunate controversy was taking this turn. I regretted that any such controversy had originated—that any such difference of opinion had occurred between Congress and the President; but in view of those red-hot despatches which were pouring in on both sides, from every quarter of the United States, I felicitated my country and you upon the thought that the President of the United States had come here through his counsel and was willing to abide the arbitrament of the American Senate, and as one man at least let them judge of their own constitutional power—judge as does every other court of justice does in determining the question of jurisdiction— to let you judge for yourselves whether you had the constitutional power to try it.

He comes in this peaceful and quiet mode, and I maintain that he is not justly chargeable with the imputations that are made against him and his conduct in the arguments that are made by gentlemen on the other side. They may impute motives as much as they please by the conversation with General Emory or anybody else. The President has brought no force here; he has not attempted, in any manner whatever, to overawe Congress or to plunge this country into a revolution. He has acted peaceably and quietly, and the charges that are made against him are wholly without foundation. In fact, all the testimony shows that the President of the United States had it in view to have this question settled in a peaceful and amicable mode, intending that it should go before the Supreme Court.

Mr. Nelson quoted the tenth article in regard to the President's speeches at the Executive Mansion, at Cleveland, and at St. Louis, and continued:—A great deal of testimony has been taken about this. I might make an argument as to whether they are faithful representations of what the President said or not, but I shall not worry your patience, after having delayed you so long with my argument, on that point. Mr. Nelson then quoted from the answer. He proceeded:—We say, therefore, that this is a personal right in the President and in the citizen. I say, further, that these speeches were not official like his communications to Congress, but were private and personal, and in answer to the call of his fellow-citizens.

Why, ten years ago, it would have struck the American people with astonishment that such a charge should be preferred against the President of the United States. Why, almost from my boyhood, down to the commencement of the war, I had talked time and again about what was known as the old seldition laws, and if there was anything that stunk in the nostrils of the American people, it was that. The object of that was to prevent the publication of matter that might affect the President or the Government of the United States. We, in this country, like to exercise the freedom of speech which our fathers guaranteed to us in the Constitution, and like the liberty of the press, which is also another cherished right of every American citizen.

We look to have the largest liberty in the exercise of that right. The American people have been accustomed to it ever since they were a nation, and it is a great deal better to tolerate even impropriety and indecency of speech, and to tolerate the licentiousness of the press, than it is to impose such restrictions as are imposed in other countries upon these things. Public opinion, as a general rule, will regulate the indecency of speech, as it will regulate and control the licentiousness of the press. If public opinion does not do it, why, as a general rule in a great many cases, the arm of the law is long enough and strong enough to apply any corrective that may be necessary, but the American people will suffer no restriction of the freedom of speech.

Let it be known and remembered always that powerful as Congress may be, great as the powers of the President of the United States are, in a technical sense, it has always been admitted by all politicians and public men in the United States that there is a power in which is the sovereign and master of both: that is the people. They are the constituency of Congress and the President.

Members of Congress have the right to speak, and to speak with perfect freedom of the conduct of the President; and the President, in turn, has a right to carry the war into Africa, and speak about Congress when he is assailed. And, if he does this, he has just the same right to do it as any other citizen in our government. And, when you destroy the right of the President of the United States to defend himself against charges made against him, either in Congress or out of Congress, why then you put the President at the feet of Congress, and you destroy that independence which was intended by the Constitution to be secured to each of the co-ordinate departments of the government in their appropriate spheres.

It was intended that the legislative department should be independent in its sphere and within the circle of its appropriate duty; and that the judicial department in a like manner should be independent in the function appropriately belonging to it, and that the President should be equally independent both of the judiciary and of Congress, and to hold otherwise, if you had Congress to be able to monopolize all the powers of the Constitution, it becomes ultimately a despotism, such as was never contemplated by the fathers nor Senators.

I do not intend to go further into this discussion, and I shall close my remarks very soon. I do not intend to go minutely into the discussion of this question, but I have to say in regard to the President of the United States, just as I have said in regard to the House of Representatives, he is a mortal man—he is made of flesh and blood. The President has a temper and passion, just any other man, and when he is attacked in Congress, or anywhere else, why may he not defend himself?

We all know when the venerable leader of the House of Representatives, who had opposed the President's nomination at Baltimore, and who, if I am not much mistaken, just a few days before the President made one of his speeches which he has made in the cause of this controversy, spoke in the House of Representatives about Charles I. The President made a speech in the Executive Mansion on the 22d of February, in which he noticed that speech, treating it as a sort of irritation to assassination.

That irritation, so far as I know, was never noticed by the managers of the House of Representatives; he had a perfect right to say anything he pleased about the President of the United States, but when these things were done by members of Congress, and circulated all over the land, published broadcast in the newspapers, what is there in the situation of the President of the United States that prevents him from exercising the ordinary right of self-defense that belongs to every citizen of the land. I admit that the President of the United States in a communication to you officially as members of Congress, ought to preserve a proper decorum; but amenity of expression—if I may use such a term—which should be employed in the intercourse between one department and the other.

But I mention that when Andrew Johnson took his tour from Washington City to Chicago, and St. Louis, and Cleveland, and Cincinnati, and returned to the City of Washington, he was nothing but a private citizen; to be sure he is President of the United States, but nothing in the Constitution, nothing in the laws authorizes any one to regulate his movements. He goes as a private citizen, and if he is called to make a speech and he chooses to respond to it, and some severe phillippics have been hurled against him by members of Congress, and he chooses to answer them, and members of Congress have insisted in the strongest terms on their right to hold this, that or the other doctrine, cannot the President answer the charges in the same way

Appealing, as he does, to the people to judge between them, who would deny to any Senator or Representative either, in what is ordinarily called a stump speech, or in any other mode of communication, to assail the conduct of the President of the United States? Why, Senators, it is the very life and salvation of our republic, although party spirit seems to have culminated in an extraordinary degree within the last four or five years. It is the preservation of the liberties of the American citizen. When parties are equally balanced they watch each other, and they are sedulously cautious in regard to anything that might violate the Constitution of the United States.

I believe it has been proved in regard to every one of those occasions that it was sought, not by the President, but by others; as when Senator Johnson and others called upon the President at the Executive Mansion, they called upon him in their character as citizens, and he replied to them as he had a right to reply to them. When he went to Cleveland it is shown that he did not desire to do anything more than to make a salutation to the people, but he was urged by his friends to do more, and I think it very likely, from the circumstances which were detailed here in evidence, that in all probability there was a mob there in Cleveland, ready, cut and dried to insult and abuse the President in the manner they did, so as to prevent him, if possible, from speaking, and when there, gave him provocation. He replied just as any other man should do, and had a right to do; and if he used strong expressions in regard to Congress, they were not stronger than he had a right to use.

I tell you, Senators, he has a right to speak of any act of Congress, in any mode that he sees proper—there is no law and nothing in the Constitution to prevent it. One of the greatest rights secured to the people under the Constitution would be invaded if this privilege was denied.

Mr. Nelson then quoted from the eleventh article and from the President's answer, and continued:—Time and time again the President in his veto messages has asserted these views and opinions as to the rights of the Southern States, now excluded from representation; and although the phraseology is a little more courtly and elegant in the messages than in the speeches, yet substantially the President has in almost every one of these communications insisted that these States are entitled to representation in Congress.

The gentleman who last addressed you (Mr. Boutwell) said that the President wished to obtain control of the army and navy, and to control the elections of 1868-69, allowing Rebels to exercise the elective franchise, and excluding negroes from voting. What authority did the honorable manager get in this case to make that assertion? He says that the South has been given up to bloodshed. I live in the South, and have not the slightest doubt that although there has been a bad state of things in some portions of the South, nine-tenths of the murders and assassinations were sensation stories, made with a view to excite men. As to the President assuming powers not warranted by the Constitution, I have endeavored in a feeble way to show you that he is not guilty.

I say to you, Senators, that you have a solemn responsibility. I have the same faith now that I have had ever since I undertook this case; the same confidence which ought to be reposed in the American Senate. I do believe that men of your character, of your position in the world, have the ability to decide this cause impartially, and to set aside all party consideration in its determination. Every lawyer knows of cases where men, especially upon circumstantial evidence, have been tried and executed, when it afterwards appeared upon more careful investigation that they were not guilty. I think that even the Senate of the United States may look at the history of the world for the purpose of deriving the lesson intended to be impressed upon courts and juries by the books.

So, without going over these things again, I can say that I think even the Senate of the United States may look back to the history of the world for the purpose of deriving some instructive lessons. Without undertaking to travel along the whole course of history, some three or four examples have occurred in the history of the world that are not unworthy of a passing notice. The account which has been transmitted to us of the murder of Cæsar by Brutus, has raised the question for nearly twenty centuries whether that act was an act of patriotism, and whether it was justified or not. The execution of Charles I is another of the historical problems which has never been, and never will be settled. In the opinion of mankind, some regard Cromwell as a patriot, animated by the purest motives, others as an ambitious man craving for power and property.

That question still remains open, but the deeds of violence committed in the world have not always been followed by peace and quiet to those who have done them. A few short years after the execution of Charles I, and the bodies of Cromwell and Bradshaw, and one or two others who were concerned in his execution, were, in consequence of a change in public opinion, taken from their graves and hung by the party that came into power. Louis XVI was executed by the people of France. Did that act give peace and quiet to the French Kingdom?

No! It was soon followed by deeds of bloodshed such as the world has never seen. The guillotine was put in motion, and the streets of Paris ran with human gore.

Those deeds that are done in times of high party and political excitement are deeds that should admonish you as to the manner in which you discharge the duty that devolves upon you. I have no idea that consequences such as I have described will result, but yet deeds that are done in excitement often come back in after years and cause a degree of feeling. I will not attempt to describe; that has been done a great deal better than I can do by a master hand, who tells us "Forever and anon of griefs subdued. There comes a token like a scorpion's sting, scarce seen but with fresh bitterness imbued, and slight withal may be the thoughts which bring back to the heart, the weight of which it would fling away forever."

"It may be a sound, a line of music, summer eve or spring, the wind of the ocean which shall sound striking the electric chain wherewith we are darkly bound, and how or why we know not, nor can trace home to its cloud this lightning of the mind, nor can efface the blight and blackening it leaves behind." God grant that the American Senate may never have such feelings as these. God grant that you may so act in the discharge of your duty that there shall be no painful remembrance, Senators, to come back upon you in a dying hour. God grant that you may so act that you will not only be able to look death and eternity in the face, but feel that you have discharged your duty and your whole duty to God and your country. If so, you will receive the approbation of men and angels and the admiration of posterity.

I do not know, Mr. Chief Justice and Senators, that it is exactly in accordance with the etiquette of the court of justice for me to do what I propose to do now, but I trust the Senate will take the will for the deed, and if there is anything improper in it you will overlook it. I cannot close the remarks I have made in this case without stating my profound thanks to the Chief Justice and the Senators for the very kind and patient attention with which you have listened to me on this occasion, imperfect and lengthy as has been the argument I have offered. You have submitted with a patient attention which I had little reason to expect, and I cannot take my seat without extending to you my thanks, whether it be in accordance with the usage or not.

Mr. NELSON having concluded his argument at fifteen minutes past four o'clock, the court adjourned until twelve o'clock to-morrow.

PROCEEDINGS OF SATURDAY, APRIL 25.

Admission of Official Reporters.

After the opening of the court, the Chief Justice stated that the first business in order was the order offered by Senator Edmunds yesterday to admit the official reporters to report the proceedings in secret session on the final question.

Mr. EDMUNDS, at the suggestion, he said, of several Senators, moved to postpone the consideration until Monday.

Senator DRAKE—I move that that order be indefinitely postponed, and on that I call the yeas and nays.

Senator EDMUNDS—Mr. President, so do I.

The motion of Mr. Drake was voted down by the following vote:—

YEAS.—Messrs. Cameron, Chandler, Conkling, Corbett, Drake, Ferry, Harlan, Howard, Morrill (Me.), Morrill (Vt.), Morton, Nye, Pomeroy, Ramsey, Ross, Stewart, Sumner, Thayer, Tipton and Yates—20.

NAYS.—Messrs. Anthony, Buckalew, Cragin, Davis, Dixon, Doolittle, Edmunds, Fessenden, Fowler, Frelinghuysen, Grimes, Henderson, Hendricks, Howe, Johnson, McCreery, Morgan, Norton, Patterson (Tenn.), Saulsbury, Sherman, Trumbull, Van Winkle, Vickers, Willey, Williams and Wilson—27.

The motion to postpone till Monday was agreed to.

Mr. Sumner's Order.

Mr. SUMNER offered the following order:—

Ordered, That the Senate, sitting for the trial of Andrew Johnson, President of the United States, will proceed to vote on the several articles of impeachment at twelve o'clock on the day after the close of the argument.

Senator JOHNSON objected, and it was laid over.

Senator SUMNER—I send to the Chair two additional rules, the first of which is derived from the practice of the Senate in the trials of Judge Chase and Judge Peck.

They were read as follows:—

Rule 25.—In taking the votes of the Senate on the articles of impeachment, the presiding officer shall call each Senator by name, and upon such article propose the following question in the manner following:—

Mr. ——, how say you, is the respondent guilty or not guilty, as charged in the — article of impeachment? Whereupon each Senator shall rise in his place and answer "Guilty" or "Not Guilty."

Rule 24.—On a conviction by the Senate, it shall be the duty of the presiding officer forthwith to pronounce the removal from office of the convicted person, according to the requirements of the Constitution, and any further judgment shall be on the order of the Senate.

Senator JOHNSON again objected, and the rules went over.

The Chief Justice then directed the counsel for the President to proceed with the argument.

Mr. Groesbeck's Argument.

Mr. GROESBECK said:—Mr. Chief Justice and Senators:—I am sorry that I am not so well to-day as I should like to be, but I know the desire of the Senate to get on with this argument, and have, therefore, preferred to come here this morning and attempt to present an outline, at least, of the views I have formed of the respondent's case. Since the organization of our government we have had five trials on impeachment, one of a Senator and four of judges, who have held their office by appointment, and for a tenure during life and good behavior. It has not been the practice, nor is it the wise policy of a republic to avail itself of the remedy of impeachment for the regulation of its elective officers. Impeachment was not invented for that purpose, but rather to lay hold of offices that were held by inheritance and for life, and the true policy of a republican government, according to my apprehension, is to leave these matters to the people, who are the great and supreme tribunal to try just such questions, and they assemble statedly for that purpose with the single object of deciding whether an officer shall be continued or whether he shall be removed from office. I may be allowed, Senators, to express my regret that such a case as this is before you, but it is here, and it must be tried, and therefore I proceed as I promised at the outstart, to say what I may be able to say on behalf of the respondent.

In the argument of one of the managers the question was propounded, "Is this body now sitting to determine the accusation of the House of Representatives against the President of the United States, the Senate of the United States or a court?" The argument goes on to admit if this body is a court in any manner as contra-distinguished from the Senate, then we agree that the accused may claim the benefit of the rules of criminal cases, although he can only be convicted when the evidence makes the case clear beyond a reasonable doubt, and in view of this statement, and in view of the labored effort which has been made by the managers in this cause, I ask, Senators, your attention to the question, In what character you proceed to this trial? We have heard protracted and elaborate discussion to show that you do not sit as a court. The managers have even taken offense at any such recognition of your character. For some reason that I will not allude to, they have done even more, and claimed for this body the most extraordinary jurisdiction. Admitting that it was a constitutional tribunal they have yet claimed that it knew no law, either statute or common; that it consulted no precedents save those of parliamentary bodies; that it was a law in itself; in a word, that its jurisdiction was without bounds, and could impeach from any cause and there was no appeal from its judgment.

The Constitution would appear to give it somewhat its jurisdiction, but everything it may deem impeachable becomes such at once, and when the phrase "high crimes and misdemeanors" are used in that instrument they are without significance, and intended merely to give solemnity to the tribunal to sustain this extraordinary view of the character of this tribunal. We have been referred to English precedents, and especially to early English precedents, when, according to my recollection, impeachment and attainder, and bills of pains and penalties have labored together in the work of murder and confiscation.

Senators, I do not propose to linger about these English cases. We have cases of our own upon this subject. We have teachings of our own. We know our fathers, in framing the Constitution, were jealous of delegating powers, and tried to make a limited constitutional government; tried to enumerate all the powers they were willing to intrust to any department of it. The Executive Department is limited; the Judicial Department is limited, and the Legislative Department we have supposed was also limited; but according to the argument made here in this trial, it is otherwise, and it has in its service and at its command an institution that is above all law and acknowledges no restraint—an institution worse than a court-martial, in that it has a broader and more dangerous jurisdiction.

Senators, I cannot believe for one moment that there is lying in the heart of the Constitution any such tribunal as this, and I invite your attention to a brief examination of our own authorities and of our own teachings on this subject. It was with much doubt and hesitation that the jurisdiction to try impeachment at all was intrusted to the Senate of the United States. The grant of jurisdiction to the Senate was deferred to the last moment of time; nor was your jurisdiction overlooked. Allow me to call your attention to the proceedings in the Journal of the Federal Convention upon this subject. In the first report that was presented they proposed to allow impeachment for malpractice or neglect of duty. It will be observed that this is very English-like and very broad. There is not necessarily any crime in the jurisdiction here proposed to be conferred. In the next report they proposed to allow the tribunal jurisdiction over treason, bribery and corruption. It will be observed that they began to get away from English precedent and to approach the final result at which they arrived. The jurisdiction is partly criminal and partly broad and open, not necessarily involving criminality. In the next report on this very question of jurisdiction they reported to the Senate, or rather to the Supreme Court of the United States, to which body up to the very last moment they confided the jurisdiction.

In the next report they proposed to allow jurisdiction for treason or bribery and nothing else. It will be observed that here was nothing but a gross flagrant crime, and that gives the jurisdiction that we have in the present Constitution—treason, bribery, and other high crimes and misdemeanors, not malpractices, not neglect of duty, nothing that left jurisdiction open; the jurisdiction is short and limited by any fair construction of this language, and it was intended to be short. It is impossible to observe the progress of the deliberations of that Convention upon this single question, beginning with the briefest and most open jurisdiction, and ending in a jurisdiction confined in its terms, without coming to the conclusion that it was their determination that the jurisdiction should be circumscribed and limited. In what character Senators do you sit here? You have heard the argument of the managers, you have heard the discussion of the subject all through the progress of the case; you have been referred to English precedents by the managers to support their theory that you sit here, not as a court, but as an inquest of office, or as a nameless tribunal with unfixed and illimitable jurisdiction. We have our own precedents on this subject, and I will call your attention to them.

It has been heard in this trial for the first time, that this tribunal now sitting as you are sitting, is anything else than a court. I challenge the gentlemen, after their investigations of the action of the Constitutional Convention, to show anything that has been said or done, calculated to make the impression that the tribunal to try impeachment is anything else than a court. Let us look, Senators, at our own history. We have had four trials of impeachment in the United States. The first was the case of Blount. What was the language of the tribunal in that trial? When it came to make a final decision, it did so in this language:—"The court is of opinion that the matter alleged is not sufficient in law to show that this court ought to hold jurisdiction of the said impeachment." That is good authority—that is good American precedent on this question. It is the deliberate opinion of the Senate of the United States in the first trial in which it sat in that capacity, declaring itself in the most solemn language, which it uttered during the trial as its final decision, that it was a court and not an inquest of office, or some nameless thing, calculated only to frighten the timid.

What is the next case? The Pickering case. Throughout its progress the Senate styled itself "The Senate sitting in the capacity of a Court of Impeachment," and the last action of the body, its decision, was on a question in this form:—"Is the court of opinion that John Pickering be removed." So too in the next case, the case of Chase. The President in that case styled the body "a court," and was more fortunate than the Chief Justice, in that he escaped all censure from the managers of the House of Representatives. How in the next case, the Peck case, the tribunal itself put the final point in this language—"Resolved, That this court will now pronounce judgment in the case of William H. Peck, Justice of the United States for the District of Missouri." Now Senators, I have gone over every precedent that we have in our own history on this question, and they show that in every instance the Senate solemnly declared itself to be a court. If we are to go by precedent, let us take our own precedents rather than those which have been so liberally quoted from abroad, by the managers on this occasion. In what spirit, Senators, shall you try this case? Allow me to refer you on that subject, to the language of Story in his Commentaries on the Constitution. He says, "The great objects to be attained in the selection of a tribunal for the trial of impeachments, are impartiality, integrity, intelligence and independence. If either of these be wanting, the trial must be radically imperfect.

To secure integrity there must be a deep sense of duty and a deep responsibility to future times and to God; to secure intelligence there must be a "high intelligence—powers as well as attainments—necessary to secure independence; there must be numbers as well as talents, and a confidence resulting at once from permanency of place, dignity of station and enlightened patriotism." On the next page Story adds:—"Strictly speaking, the power, that is, the power of impeachment, is partly of a political character, and on this account it requires to be guarded in its exercise against the spirit of faction, the intolerance of party and the sudden movements in peculiar feeling." Senators, this is not my language, it is the language of a distinguished jurist whom you all respect, but I may affirm by all our own authorities and by all our teachings on the subject, that it is a true and faithful portraiture of what is meant in the Constitution by the tribunal to try impeachment.

For that purpose you have been sworn anew as it were to prepare you for this occasion. The oath which you took when you entered this Senate Chamber, as Senators, was a political, a legislative oath. The oath which is now upon you is purely a judicial oath to do impartial justice. We are then, Senators, in a court. What are you to try? You are to try the charges contained in those articles of

impeachment, and nothing else. On what are you to try them? Not on common fame, not on presumption of guilt, not on any views of party politics. You are to try them on the evidence offered here, and on nothing else. By the obligation of your oaths, what is the issue before you? Senators, allow me to say that it is not a question whether this or that thing was done. You are not here to try a mere issue of fact. By the very terms of the Constitution you can only try in this tribunal, crime. Let me repeat the jurisdiction:—"Treason, bribery, or other high crimes or misdemeanors."

The jurisdiction is comprised within that language. The only issue which this court can try, is the issue of crime. What is crime? In every crime there must be unlawful purpose or intention, and when this is wanting there can be no crime. There must be an unlawful purpose prompting its commission, otherwise there can be no crime. Let me illustrate:—Suppose a crazy man should burst into this Chamber and kill one of us; he has committed the act of homicide, but he has not committed a crime. Suppose the President should become deranged, and should, while in that condition, attempt to bribe and to break law upon law, you have no jurisdiction to try him on impeachment. Let me put another case that is not suppositious. Mr. Lincoln claimed and exercised the power to organize a military commission under which he arrested and imprisoned citizens within the loyal States. He had no act of Congress warranting it, and the Supreme Court of the United States has declared that the act was against the express provisions of the Constitution, Suppose he did violate the express provisions of the Constitution, then, according to the argument of the managers, he might be impeached and convicted.

I beg to read from the argument of one of the managers on that subject. The honorable manager who addressed us the day before yesterday referred to the motives of the President, and declared that the necessary inference of the law is, that he acted under the influence of bad motives; whereby the gentleman seems to acknowledge that, in order to constitute a crime there must be a motive. There can be no crime without a motive; but now, when the President comes forward, and offers to prove his good motive, you will not allow him to make that proof. When he comes forward and offers to prove this from his warm and living heart, the answer is, "we make up the motive out of the presumptions of the law, and conclude you on that point; we will not hear you; you must be silent."

Now, Senators, the jurisdiction of this body is to try crime, and there is no crime without unlawful intention and purpose. You cannot get a crime without showing the unlawful intent or purpose behind the act itself. What is your verdict? Not that the President did this or that act. That is not it. But was he guilty of high misdemeanor, it being his purpose to commit it?

With these preliminary observations, I propose to proceed to a brief examination of the case presented. You are now, all of you, familiar with the arguments which have been presented thus far in this case, and I need not attempt to go over them. I have this to say, and you will all concur with me, that the first eight articles are built upon two acts of the President; the one being the removal of Edwin M. Stanton, the other the letter of authority given to Lorenzo Thomas. Now, if you will take those eight articles, and notice the substantial argument around which they are bound, with all their assertions of good or bad intent, and all their arguments of every kind, you will find that there are but those two acts—the removal of Mr. Stanton and the letter of authority to General Thomas. To do that, we have only to inquire in reference to these two acts in order to ascertain the merits of this case. If the President of the United States had the right to remove Edwin M. Stanton, then these eight articles are without support. If, in addition to that, he had the right to give the letter of authority to Lorenzo Thomas, then these articles fall to ruin.

Now, there is no Senator who has studied this case who will not see the application of this statement at once, and it relieves us from the necessity of going over article by article, step by step, in our progress. Give me those two proposition—the right to remove Stanton and the right to issue the letter of authority to Thomas—and the articles fall instantly, and there is nothing left of them, so that we have, in asking your consideration of these articles, but two inquiries to make. Had the President the right to remove Mr. Stanton, and had he the right to issue the letter of authority to Thomas? I propose now, as well as I am able, to examine this question. Had the President the right to remove Edwin M. Stanton? I propose to examine that question first, in connection with the act regulating the Tenure of Civil Offices. It is claimed on the one side that, by the operation of this law, Mr. Stanton was withdrawn from his previous position, and is covered and protected here. It is claimed upon the other side that the law does not apply to his case at all. I think it will be readily acknowledged by Senators that the President has the right to remove him.

Allow me to call your attention to one question of this law in which the question seems to be involved. It provides, "That every person holding any civil office to which he has been appointed by and with the advice and consent of the Senate, and every person who shall hereafter be appointed to any such office and become duly qualified to act therein, is entitled to hold such office until his successor shall have been appointed and duly qualified, except as herein otherwise provided. Provided, That the Secretary of State, the Secretary of the Treasury, the Secretary of War, the Secretary of the Navy, and the Secretary of the Interior, the Postmaster-General, and the Attorney-General shall hold their offices respectively for and during the term of the President by whom they were appointed, and for one month thereafter, subject to removal by and with the advice and consent of the Senate."

Now, gentlemen, let me state a few facts before we proceed to the consideration of this act. The first fact is, that the act was passed on the 2d of March, 1867. I further call your attention to the fact that Mr. Stanton's commission is dated on the 15th of January, 1862. It is a commission given to him by President Lincoln, by which he is to hold the office of Secretary for the Department of War, during the pleasure of the President for the time being. Mr. Johnson became President on the 15th day of April, 1865, and he has not, in any manner, commissioned Mr. Stanton. Now, upon these facts, Senators, I claim that it is clear that Mr. Stanton is not protected by this Civil Tenure act. Let us inquire. The law proposes to grant to the Cabinet officers, as they are called, a term that shall last during the term of the President by whom they are appointed, and one month thereafter. Mr. Johnson has not appointed Mr. Stanton. He was appointed during the first term of Mr. Lincoln. He was not appointed at all during the term of President Johnson. He holds his office by a commission, if at all, that would send him through administration after administration indefinitely, or until he is removed.

Now, what is the meaning of this language—"He shall hold his office during the term of the President by whom he is appointed?" He was not appointed during the present term. I think that is plain. It does seem to me that that simple statement settles this question. The gentleman has said this is Mr. Lincoln's term. The dead has ownership in no office or estate of any kind. Mr. Johnson is the President of the United States with a term, and this is his term. But if Mr. Lincoln were living to-day; if Mr. Lincoln were President to-day, he could remove Mr. Stanton. Mr. Lincoln would not have appointed him during this term. It was during the last term that Mr. Stanton was appointed and not this. And an appointment by the President during one term, by the operation of this law, will not extend the term of one President through that of another because that same person happened to be re-elected to the Presidency. Mr. Stanton holds the office, therefore, under the commission given him, and not under the law. But, Senators, his tenure of office cannot be changed or extended from his commission to the law. What is the proposition of this law?

Mr. Stanton held his office during the pleasure of the President, for the time being. This law proposes to give him a term of four years, and one month thereafter. By what authority can the Congress of the United States extend the term in this manner? An office can only be held by the appointment of the President. His nomination and his appointment must cover the whole term which the appointee claims. On any other theory the Congress of the United States might extend the office of the persons who has been appointed, indefinitely through years and years, and thus defeat the constitutional provision that the President shall nominate and shall appoint for office for the whole term for which he was appointed. Thus, practically, Senators, it appears that the law cannot be made to apply to any offices which were occupied at the time of its passage.

Take the case of an officer who holds his commission at the pleasure of the President, What is the character of that tenure? It is no tenure known to the law, it is a tenure at pleasure, at sufferance at will. To convert that to a tenure for a fixed time is to enlarge it, to extend it, to increase it, to make it of larger estate than it was before; and if the office be one that cannot be filled without a Presidential nomination and appointment, it seems to me that, whatever may be the office, it cannot be extended and controlled in this way. This appears to be the construction of the act of March 3, 1867. But I am compelled to leave it with this brief examination. Mr. Stanton is, in my opinion, left where he was before its passage. It is further to be shown that the act of March 2, 1867, has no repealing clause. We are, therefore, remitted to the previous laws applicable to this case, to the averments of the Constitution, and to the act of 1789.

By the provisions of this law, it is provided, among other things, that there shall be an Executive Department, denominated the Department of War, and that there shall be a principal officer therein, to be called the Secretary for the Department of War, who shall perform and execute such duties as shall from time to time be enjoined upon him, and who shall conduct the business of such department in such manner as the President of the United States shall from time to time order and instruct, and there shall be in the said department an inferior officer to be appointed by said principal officer, to be employed therein as he shall deem proper, to be called the Chief Clerk of the Department of War. But whenever the said principal officer shall be removed from office by the President of the United States, or in any other case of vacancy, he shall have charge of the records, books, &c. That is the law to which we are referred, unless the act regulating the tenure of civil offices, covers the case of Mr. Stanton. By the terms of that law, by the commission that was issued to Mr. Stanton to run during the pleasure of the President for the time being, framed upon this law, the President had the right to remove Mr. Stanton according to his pleasure.

[At this point the offer of the counsel to speak was with so much apparent effort, Senator FESSENDEN proposed that the counsel should have permission to suspend his argument for the present, or until after another argument had been presented on the part of the managers.]

Mr. GROESBECK returned his thanks to the Senator for his kindly suggestion, but saying he would be very thankful for the attention of the Senate to what he might say, in the condition of voice in which he found himself, he thought he would prefer to go on with his argument to its conclusion. He then said:—

We are told, Senators, by the gentleman who argued this case, that there has been no such case as the removal of the head of a department without the co-operation of the Senate, and that this construction, which we claim as applicable to this law, does not apply. Let me call your attention to the documents, as found on pages 357 to 359 of these proceedings. I refer to the letters of John Adams, written under one of the extreme laws that were passed by the First Congress under the Constitution. I give you the letter of the 12th of May, 1800, which is as follows:—

"Sir—Divers causes and considerations, essential to the administration of the government, in my judgment, requiring a change in the Department of State, you are hereby discharged from any further service as Secretary of State. (Signed) "JOHN ADAMS, "President of the United States.

"To Timothy Pickering."

That was the act of John Adams, by whose casting vote in the Senate, this bill was passed. That act was done according to the construction that was given to the bill, and is an act of outright removal during the session of the Senate, without the co-operation of the Senate. The act is done in May. The letter is addressed to the Secretary in his office, declaring him removed; and when Mr. Adams comes to send his nomination of a successor, he nominates John Marshall, not "in place of Mr. Pickering, to be removed, with their assent, but in place of Mr. Pickering removed, by my will, or in accordance with the law" now existing.

Why Senators, there is no doubt about it. If John-Adams, who passed this law in the Senate by his casting vote, had the least idea that the power of removal was not as granted in the law, in his own hands, do the gentleman suppose that he would have taken the course he did that he would not have taken some such course as this: "Senators, I propose for your consideration the removal of Mr. Pickering, if that was not the construction of that law." His acts, the true construction according to his own interpretation and according to the interpretation given from that day to this, down to the act of March 2, 1867, done while the Senate was in session, done by himself without consultation with or the co-operation of the Senate, and that was the form which he adopted when he did remove him, as a distinct and independent act, and which has been adopted from that day to this.

While upon this subject let me call your attention, Senators, to the language of John Marshall in the case of Marbury vs. Madison. He was discussing the question when an appointment was made, or when it was complete, so that it was withdrawn from the control of the President. He held that it was complete when the commission was made out; but in the course of the discussion he goes on to say:—"When the officer is removable by the President at the will of the Executive," &c.; so it has always been understood "removable by the President," that is the language. So the the commission ran, "removable at the pleasure of the President for the time being." When? In session? At his pleasure? In term, in session? "At his pleasure" is the language of the commission, and the authority that controls the commission and the law. So it has always been construed. Now, Senators, if I am right in the view I have here taken, Mr. Stanton was not covered by the law, and was subject to removal under the commission which he received from Mr. Lincoln, and under the law of 1789.

I beg you to observe that that law is in full force. There is no attempt to repeal it in the act of March 2, 1867. That act, in fact, has not a repealing clause. What then? What becomes of the first eight articles of this case? Let us stand at this point for a moment. It is an excellent point of observation from which to look at these acts. We have removed one difficulty, we have ascertained one fact, then; Mr. Stanton can be removed by the President. I should like to linger longer on this question, and if I had voice sufficient, I should like to call your attention to some other points. I should like to read the language of one of your Senators, especially the pertinent language of the Senator on the committee that reported this bill. I should like to read his language which was the last utterance in this Chamber before the bill was passed. But I pass on, and I ask your attention, Senators, to pause here a moment at this point of observation and look over this case. We have borne down the main structure of this great argument.

Take out the single question of the power of the removal of Mr. Stanton from these eight articles, and you are without support, and all you have left to consider is the single question of the right to confer the letter of authority upon Lorenzo Thomas. Why, Senators, we shall see more than that if this be so. All through these questions which have occupied so much of the attention of the court, vanish out of sight; for if we had this power we had the right to remove, and we were not bound to come to court to ascertain that fact. Senators, allow me to ask you to consider one other question. Suppose Mr. Stanton is within the Tenure of Office act, what then? The question then comes for your consideration, whether the President is criminal in acting upon the supposition that he was not within the act. Now, this inquiry does not challenge the constitutionality of the law. It is a question of interpretation or construction of a doubtful law.

Is there a Senator in this Chamber who will not admit, whatever his view may be upon this subject, that it was not a law upon which any one might not attempt this construction? Why, I believe that a majority of the Senate in this Chamber are of the opinion that it does not apply to the case of Mr. Stanton, and even if they did think that it does, there would be a very small majority certainly, who would say there was not room for doubt, as to the constitutionality of the law. Let me then refer you to the act creating the office of Attorney-General:—

"There shall be also a person learned in the law appointed Attorney-General of the United States, who shall be sworn, and whose duty shall be to prosecute all suits in the Supreme Court of the United States in which the United States shall be concerned, and to give his advice and opinion upon questions of law when required by the President of the United States." I need not read further. There was a law construe it as you will, in reference to the question of the operation of which there might be a difference of opinion. No Senator will differ as to the fact that it might be interpreted as not covering Mr. Stanton's case by its provisions. Now suppose the President of the United States, upon consulting upon the subject, did construe the law in that way, is there a Senator in this chamber who will say that there was any blame to attach to him on account of such an interpretation?

I am assuming here that this law was a law of doubtful construction as it is, and if the President availed himself of the counsels of his Cabinet officer, who is designated to do this special duty, then he is acquitted of the charge of wilfully misinterpreting it; and, now, what is the testimony on that subject? It shows that consultations were held between the President and his Cabinet. Not idle consultations, but consultations for the purpose of deciding upon this great and important question, and which, if you undertake to investigate the question of motive, you cannot pass by. It appears that this subject came up for consideration and it was taken for granted that these Cabinet officers, who had been appointed by Mr. Lincoln, were not affected by the provisions of the Tenure of Office act. I do not remember that the point was thus stated, but I recollect that it was suggested by one member of the Cabinet who was appointed by Mr. Lincoln, and that no dissent was expressed. The Attorney-General, Mr. Stanbery, was there—the entire Cabinet was there—and this subject was considered, and this very question of construction came up, and the opinion was expressed that he (Mr. Stanton) was not included in the provisions of the act.

(The speaker's voice, which had gradually become fainter, here became almost inaudible to the reporters.)

He considered this the most important point in this case, but should this view not be correct and the law did apply to Mr. Stanton, the next inquiry was whether the conduct of the President in removing Mr. Stanton was criminal. Senators who participated as legislators in the passage of this very law and had affirmed its constitutionality, in the unfortunate condition of this case, became the judges, and, therefore, they must not be understood as arguing the point with a view to change their opinions or to show that the law was unconstitutional. That was not his object. It was to present the inquiry whether, in the condition of the question and in the condition of the President, he had a right to take the steps he did take without incurring the charge of criminality. Our government is composed of three departments. Power has been distributed among them, and they are each independent of the other; no one responsible to the other. They are responsible to the people, and they are enjoined each to take care of its own prerogatives, and to protect itself against all possible encroachment from the other.

This they do, each and every department, by observing with the utmost fidelity the instruction of the written Constitution. At the head of one of these departments, the executive, stands the President of the United States; he is sworn by an oath, the most solemn obligation that could be administered, faithfully to execute the office of President, and to preserve, protect and defend the Constitution. It is not an oath merely to execute the laws, but also to the best of his ability to preserve, protect and defend the Constitution. It would seem that such an oath would impress him with the idea that the first and paramount duty of the executive was to act according to the terms of the Constitution, and that in all trial and doubts he should take shelter under it. The learned managers contended that the President should simply execute the laws passed by Congress and no more. That was not the interpretation that should be given to the language of the Constitution. He was the Chief Magistrate of the nation and in charge of one of the great departments of the government, and must maintain the powers conferred by the Constitution on that department; but shall he disregard a law, "never."

He should never in mere wantonness disregard any act of Congress in any manner. Shall he execute all laws? He took issue with the learned manager on this point in toto. According to the theory of the managers, the President should be convicted of a crime even though the law was not constitutional. He denied this. If a law be declared by the Supreme Court, the third department of the government, and by the very terms of the Constitution itself the highest and final arbiter of the constitutionality of Congressional enactment, if that court should declare a law to be unconstitutional the President would be false to his oath of office if he should execute that law. He would tell the gentleman, in answer to his long argument, that if a law be unconstitutional it was no law; it never was a law and never had a particle of validity although it might be in the form of a Congressional enactment. From the beginning ab initio it is no law, and is void, and to execute it is a violation of the Constitution. Therefore he should not execute such a law.

Again, if a law be upon its very face in blank contradiction to the plainly expressed provisions of the Constitution, as, for instance, a law declaring that the President should

not be Commander-in-Chief of the Army and Navy, or declaring that he had no power to make treaties, the President should, without going to the Supreme Court, maintain the integrity of his department, which, for the time being, is intrusted to him, and is bound to execute no such law. He would be untrue to his high official position if he should execute that law. But the difficulty was not here; the difficulty arises in doubtful cases, in cases which are not plainly stated in the Constitution, and this was the question of inquiry in the present case. The law of interpretation to be observed in doubtful cases was a point to which he called the attention of the Senate. He would not question the constitutionality of the Tenure of Office act. He did not challenge its constitutionality here, because the Senate had affirmed it. He would therefore simply read a few opinions of the Supreme Court and quote from other standard authorities in regard to this question.

The counsel here read at length several decisions on this point, and then proceeded with the argument.

Now, Senators, I have called your attention to the decision of the question by the court. I have given you the utterance from the bench. I have given you the opinions of Marshall, and of Kent, and now let me refer you to the Executive Department. From the beginning of the government down to March 2, 1867, it has been the uniform construction and practice of every administration that it had the power of removal. Washington approved of the bill; Adams voted for it; Jefferson maintained it; Madison drew it up; Monroe and Jackson maintained the same construction of it. Every President, including President Lincoln, through all our history of eighty years, and of twenty administrations, maintained this construction on the question of where is the power of removal lodge.

The Judicial Department has concurred in the construction that the power of removal is lodged by the Constitution in the President. The Executive Department, from Washington down, through all the Presidents, has acted on this construction and affirmed this practice. Washington called the attention of the First Congress to the fact that the Executive Departments under the old Confederation had ceased to exist, and that it was necessary to organize new and corresponding ones under the new government, and he suggested that, before Congress legislated on the subject, it should, in debate, fix the principles and determine the number of departments necessary. Congress at once entered on the subject, and agreed to establish three departments.

At this point of the argument the court, at quarter past two, took a recess for a quarter of an hour.

Mr. GROESBECK resumed his argument, commencing by reminding the court of the points he had been calling its attention to before the recess. He expressed his astonishment at Mr. Boutwell's summing up of the debate of 1789, and declared, with all respect to the honorable manager, that the statement was not authorized by anything that occurred in that debate. The only question that was discussed and settled in that debate, was whether the power of removal was lodged in the President alone, or lodged in the President and Senate, and it was decided that the power was in the President alone. The phraseology of the bills was changed so that all appearance of a grant of the power from the Legislature might be avoided, ane that Congress might appear as simply recognizing the fact that the power was vested by the Constitution in the President. He had stated accurately the substance of the debate, and challenged all contradiction.

What had followed? That Congress had passed three bills establishing three Executive Departments, and in the language of Chief Justice Marshall, it had, in order to avoid legislative instability on that question, framed those bills so that they should not take the form of a grant from the Legislature, but should appear as a constitutional interpretation. These laws were in force to this day; they were professedly an interpretation of the Constitution; were so declared by the Supreme Court; were so declared and treated be the Congress which passed them, and were so regarded by every subsequent Congress down to the Thirty-ninth Congress.

He would pass on for nine years, and come down to 1798. Another executive department was then formed, called the Navy Department, and in the law creating it, the power of removal was recognized in the phraseology, "in case of vacancy by removal or otherwise." The words were not "removal by the President;" the idea being conveyed that it was a power lodged by the Constitution in the President. He passed on for twenty years—to the creation of the Post Office Department, the law creating which contained this provision:—"In case of the resignation or removal from office of the Postmaster-General. It did not say by whom the removal was to be made, but it adopted the preceding laws in reference to which it was distinctly understood that they were interpretations of the Constitution, acknowledging that the power of removal was lodged in the President, and therefore not necessary to be conferred by express grant.

Then he came to the act of March, 1849, creating the Interior Department, and providing that the Secretary of the Interior was to hold his office by the same tenure, and to receive the same salary as the secretaries of the other departments. Under that law the Secretary of the Interior was removable at pleasure. Then he came to the law establishing the seventh department, that of the Attorney General. In the law establishing that office there was not one word said on the subject of removal or vacancy, but the Attorney General had taken his commission during the pleasure of the President for the time being, and had been subject to removal by the President just as any other of the heads of the departments.

He had thus gone through the legislation establishing the executive departments ranging from 1789 to 1849, a period of sixty years, and showing the principle that the power of removal was recognized as being lodged by the Constitution in the President. But that was not all. He might cite a large number of laws on the subject of other officers, such as postmasters, &c., and bearing out the same idea. He stated, not from his own examination, but from information on which he could rely that if all the laws of Congress were collected from 1789 to 1867 which affirmed this construction, they would average two or three to each Congress.

The law of March, 1867, came into work on the concurrent chain of constitutional interpretation, but he would ask Senators whether human reason might not pause here and human judgment doubt on this question. All the Presidents had affirmed the Constitution had acted on it for eighty years; the Supreme Court had affirmed it; thirty-eight Co..gresses had concurred in it. All this was on the one side o. the question, and on the other side there was the action of one Congress. Might not, therefore, human reason pause and human judgment doubt? Was it criminal in the President to stand by that great mass of precedent and to believe as thirty-eight Congresses had believed; as all Administrations had believed, and as the Supreme Court had affirmed, that the power of removal from office was vested by the Constitution in the President? That was the question this court was to decide.

Did Senators believe that at the time Andrew Johnson honestly thought that the Constitution lodged the power of removal in the hands of the President? What should be the effect of this long line of interpretation by every department of the government? What rule should be applied? Stability was as much needed in regard to powers not expressed in the Constitution as in regard to those as are expres.ed. If it was to be fixed by interpretation and decision. When was it to be regarded as fixed? In five hundred years? They would all agree to that. In four hundred years? He thought they would all agree to that. In two hundred years? Yes, in one hundred years? Yes! Well, here was a construction and interpretation existing for seventy-eight years. If this government was ever to have stability in its institutions it must adopt and adhere to the rule of *State decisus*. The Thirty-ninth Congress alone had given a different interpretation of the Constitution. He did not propose to institute any comparison between that Congress and any preceding one.

He would not say that it was not just as able and in just as good condition as any other to offer a correct opinion, but he would say that it was no better. This brought him to the question. whether the Senate was prepared to drive the President from his office and convict him of crime because he had believed as every other President before him had believed, as the Supreme Court had believed, and as the Thirty-eighth Congress had believed? Was Mr. Johnson to lie down with his hand upon his mouth, and his mouth in the dust, before Congress? or was he to stand up as the Chief Magistrate of the nation in the great contest to defend the integrity of his department? It was for the President to execute the laws, to execute even doubtful laws; but when he was called upon to execute a law against which all precedents were arrayed, against which all the voices of the past were sounding in his ears, was he not justified in seeking to get a judicial interpretation of the question, and was the Senate to undertake to brand him with criminality because he proposed to go to the Supreme Court and have a decision on the question.

He (counsel) should have referred also to the President's conduct in reference to his consulting those who are by law his advisers and counsellors. The Senate had shut out many of these facts and would not hear the evidence upon them. Suppose it had been brought to the attention of Senators that on a serious and important question like this the President had disregarded the advice of his Cabinet, had turned his back upon his counsellors, had held no consultation with them, but had in wilfulness and disregard of their wishes acted in the manner he had done.

The managers would probably have put that in evidence against him, but yet the fact that he could prove just the contrary was excluded from testimony. What was Mr. Johnson's condition? He had Cabinet officers who were unfriendly to him personally and politically. All confidential relations between them had been broken off. That officer himself had told the Senate, in a letter dated as lately as the 4th of February, 1868, that he had no correspondence with the President since the 12th of August last, and had received no orders from him. It thus appears that that Cabinet officer was merely a non-executive repudiating the President, having no official communication with him, and proposing to have none, and proposing to carry on his department without recognizing even the President's name.

This was the condition of President Johnson when he communicated with General Sherman, and counsel would read to the Senate what General Sherman's testimony on that point was. General Sherman said:—"I intend to be very precise and very short, but it appeared to me necessary to state what I began to state, that the President told me that the relations between him and Mr. Stanton, and between Mr. Stanton and the other members of the Cabinet, were such that he could not execute the office which he filled, as President of the United States, without making provision *ad interim* for that office, and that he had the right under the law. He claimed to have the right, and his purpose was to have the office administered in the interest of the army and the country, and he offered me the office in that view. He did not state to me then that it was his purpose to bring it to the courts directly, but for the purpose of having the office administered properly in the interest of the army and of the whole country."

That was the condition of things with a Cabinet officer who refused all intercourse. Counsel did not intend to go into any inquiry as to who was right or wrong; he merely stated the naked fact. This Cabinet officer had refused all intercourse, and was proposing to carry on his department without communicating with the President, and as a sort of secondary executive. In that condition of things, was it not the duty of the Chief Magistrate to make a change? There was not a Senator before him who would not have made the change. It was impossible to administer the department while there were wranglings and controversies, and want of confidence between the head of the department and the President. In that necessity it was that Mr. Johnson had moved to procure a change in the department. If he had sued out a writ of *quo warranto*, as the manager suggested, he would have been laughed at and ridiculed, because a determination of it could not have been reached before a year, and because it was reported at the time that he would be impeached and removed in ten, twenty, or thirty days.

But Mr. Stanton had brought a suit against General Thomas, and had had him arrested. There was the President's opportunity; by reason of that he could reach a nice decision instantly. The President snatched at it, but it was anxiously snatched away from him. The managers had talked of force—where was the force? Where was there one single bitter, personal interview in all that transaction? There was not a quarrelsome word with anybody. The only force exhibited was in the cordial embrace between General Thomas and Mr. Stanton, with the one putting his arm around the other and running his fingers affectionately through his silver locks. That was the "force, intimidation and threat" that was used, and that was about all there was of it. Counsel for the President had offered to bring here the members of the Cabinet to testify as to what their advice was to the President on the subject. They had consulted on that very question, but yet the Senate would not hear them; it shut their mouths and remanded the defense to the man from Delaware.

The Senate was asked to find the employment or the intimation to employ force from the utterances of that man from Delaware, and from the conversation, or at midnight masquerades of a man dressed in a little brief authority, and yet the Senate would not hear the deliberations of the Cabinet, the consultations which were held on that very question when the transaction was warm in the minds of the parties; there was no rescuing this trial from the manifest imperfection of the testimony on that point. Now, what was the President's course? Why did he give this letter of authority to Lorenzo Thomas? He had to do it. There was no other way he could adopt by which he could put the case in a condition to test the law. If the President had nominated to the Senate the office would have remained in the exact condition it was without nomination, and, therefore, it was necessary by an arrangement of this kind to get into the office one who could represent the government on that question.

The President's intention in all the movement was simply to get rid of that defiant, friendly Secretary. Counsel used this expression without conveying any personal sentiment. What had the President done in the first place? He had selected General Grant, a man whom the country delighted to honor, in whom it had the utmost confidence, and for whom probably the honorable manager, Mr. Butler, intended to express still greater confidence. The President had selected such a man as that, and yet this was to be regarded as a mischievous transaction. What next did the President do? The very next step that the President took was, not to get a dangerous man, not to get a man in whom the Senate had no confidence, but the next man to whom he offered the place was General Sherman—would any one charge wickedness upon that high officer? But.General Sherman would not take the office. To whom did he next offer it? To Major General George H. Thomas. It seemed that the President had picked out the three men of all others in the nation who could command the respect and confidence of the nation in reference to the purpose he had in view in the matter. You cannot make crime out of this, Senators.

The President had one purpose in view, and that was to change the head of the War Department, and it would have delighted him to make the change, and put there permanently any competent man, and thus get rid of the condition of his Cabinet. What then, gentlemen? He executed this law in other respects. He changed the forms of his commissions: he reported suspensions under this law, and, Senators, it is one of the strongest facts in this case. He did not take up this law and tear it to pieces; he did not take this law and trample it under foot; and in all other respects he tried to obey it without the surrender of his own convictions. It is said that in the suspension of Mr. Stanton he acted under the law. I cannot adjust it to your law; and instead of seizing upon that as a subject of censure, I tell you it was an overture from the President to get out of this difficulty and to conciliate you. Take that suspension—take the act. In the very letter of the message of suspension he tells you my Cabinet, and Mr. Stanton the most emphatic of all, believe this law is unconstitutional.

Mr. Stanton was the one that was selected to draw up these objections. But the President tells you in that act of suspension what his views were about the law. He goes on and tells you further in that very message:—"We had this matter up in the Cabinet meeting, when the Secretaries said it did not apply to him or to any other of Mr. Lincoln's Cabinet." All these opinions were in his mind. He communicated them in the very message where you say he surrendered himself to the terms of the Civil Office bill. He did all that, and it is to his credit that he has not gone about everywhere violating the law, instructing its violation or forbidding it to be exercised until it was ascertained as to its constitutionality in some way or another. Well, now, I have been sitting here listening to the evidence presented in this case for a long time, and reading more or less about it, and I have never been able to come to the conclusion that, when all these matters were placed before the Senate, and understood, they could convict the President of criminality for doing what was done.

There is no force—where is it? Where is the threat? Where is the intimidation? Nowhere. He did to get into the courts; that we know. He did his best to get it there; ran after a case by which he could have got it there. Where is his criminality? Is he criminal because he did not surrender the convictions of his mind on the constitutionality, according to your interpretation of the act of 1867? Why, so was General Washington criminal; so was Adams criminal. But the precedent in the whole history of the government is at his back in the position which he has taken. How are we going to try criminality upon this single question of the constitutionality of the act of 1867, having the opinion of every Congress at his back, the opinion of the administrations, and the opinion of the Supreme Court, as far as it goes?

Let us go back a moment to that brief examination which I made of the right construction of the civil office act. I told you then that if Stanton were not included, the first eight articles of this case substantially fell, and even if he were included, and we were advised as we were, there could be no criminality in acting upon a question of law under the advice of the Attorney-General, who was officially designated for the very purpose of giving us that advice. So that from that point of view, suppose Stanton were under the law, and we had no excuse for what he did, then the question is, where in the condition of this question was the power of removal lodged?

You may have your own opinion about the constitutionality, but there is another question which I present. It is this:—It is a question of construction. Will you condemn as criminal a President who stood on the side where every decision of the government had been up to that time? I come now, gentlemen, to the next question about the *ad interim* appointment, and I beg you to observe that, if you shall come to the conclusion that the President had the right to make an *ad interim* appointment, then there is great shipwreck in his case. It nearly all tumbles into ruin. I beg you again, when you come to examine these articles, to see how many of them are built upon the two facts—the removal of Stanton and the *ad interim* appointment of Thomas. He made the appointment, Senators, under the act of February 13, 1795.

Mr. Groesbeck read the law which authorizes the President, in case of a vacancy in the offices of the Secretary of State and of War, to authorize a person to perform the duties of such office until a successor shall be appointed, and continued:—You will observe that all possible conditions of the department are expressed under the single word, "vacancy." It covers the removal, the expiration of the term of office, resignation, absence, sickness—every possible condition of the department in which it would be necessary *ad interim* to supply the place. That law was passed on February 13, 1795. There has been another act passed partially covering the same ground, under the date of February 20, 1863. Now, does that act repeal the act of February 13, 1795? Allow me to draw your attention to a few rules of interpretation of statutes before I compare them:—

First, The law does not favor repeals by implication. Again, if statutes are to be construed together they are to stand. Still another, a better statute in order to repeal a former one must fully embrace the whole subject matter. Still again, to effect an entire repeal of all of the provisions of the previous statute the whole subject matter must be covered. Let me illustrate. Suppose, for illustration, there was a statute extending from myself to yonder door; then if another statute were passed which would reach half way, it would repeal so much of the former statute as it overlay, and leave the balance in force. What lies beyond is the legislative will, and just as binding as the original statute.

Now we come to a comparison of these statutes. The statute of February 20, 1862, provides for the occasion of death, resignation, absent from the seat of government, or sickness. There are two cases that are not provided for by this statute, and they are covered by the statute of 1795—removal and expiration of term; so that we are advised by that simple statement that the reach of the statute of 1795 was beyond that of the statute of February, 1863, and so much of it as lies beyond the latter statute is still in force.

With these few remarks upon the repeal of statutes I come to the consideration of the *ad interim* letter. From the foundation of the government, as you have been advised by my colleague (Mr. Curtis) and others, it has been the policy of the government to provide for filling offices *ad interim*. They are not appointments. There is no commission under seal. It is a mere letter of appointment, and they are not considered as filling the office.

When Mr. Upshur was killed, in 1844, an *ad interim* appointment was made to supply the vacancy occasioned by that accident, and soon afterwards the President nominated to the Senate Mr. Calhoun to fill the office permanently. That illustrates the condition of an *ad interim* in the office. It has been the policy of the government from the beginning to thus supply vacancies in the department from sickness, absence, resignation, or any of those causes,

and this occurs both when the Senate is in session and when it is in recess. The law of 1863 makes no difference. It may be at any time.

Now, Senators, I will dismiss this part of the subject by calling your attention to *ad interim* appointments that were made during the session, of heads of departments. In the first place I give you Mr. Nelson, who was appointed, during the session of the Senate, Secretary of the State. I give you General Scott, who was appointed *ad interim* Secretary of War during the session of the Senate. I give you Mr. Moses Kelley, who was appointed *ad interim* during the session of the Senate to the Department of the Interior. I give you Mr. Holt, who was appointed *ad interim*, during the session of the Senate, Secretary of War. But I intend to linger a little at the case of Mr. Holt, which deserves especial consideration and attention.

Mr. Groesbeck read from the message of President Buchanan of January 1, 1868, in reply to a resolution of inquiry by the Senate in regard to the appointment of Mr. Holt to succeed John B. Floyd, and continued:—There was a case where the Senate took the matter under consideration and inquired of the President what he had done, and by what authority he had done it. Why did you not do that? Why did you not report upon it? A full inquiry was made by the Senate into that case of this *ad interim* question, and Mr. Buchanan replied that he had supplied the vacancy by an *ad interim* appointment under the law of 1795. He communicated that fact to the Senate. The Senate received that communication, and were satisfied that it was *res adjudicata* on his part.

The Senate, on that occasion, investigated thoroughly this identical question of *ad interim* appointments during the session, and received Mr. Buchanan's reply that he did it under the very law under which we acted, and the Senate did not censure that act, while they bring us forward as a criminal and brand us with crime for ours. You cannot discriminate between them. Both were done under the same law, both done during the session.

I shall glance now at the next article. I do not intend to linger upon such charges as are contained in it. It makes a great noise in the articles, but it is very hard to see through it. What is the proof to sustain this article? The President had an interview with General Emory, and in the course of that interview General Emory informed him of the passage of a certain law. They had a conversation about it, and the President said, in the course of that conversation, that the law was unconstitutional. He did not say anything more; and that is the enormous crime committed under article nine. He said it was unconstitutional. What about that? Is it not in evidence before you and uncontradicted that the President had been informed that there were unusual military movements going on in the city the night before; and Secretary Welles called upon him to inform him of that fact, and the President said he would inquire about it?

He sent a note to General Emory, and General Emory waited upon him with the information. That is all. Is that not an explanation? Does anybody contradict it? No! The time the occasion, everything in the transaction adjusts itself to that explanation, and no other. Here was a President whom you has subordinated to an inferior—I mean to the extent of requiring him to send orders through an inferior—groping in the dark, as it were, called upon by one of his Cabinet to inquire about it.

I now come to article ten. I shall leave the elaborate discussion of this article to my colleague, but I wish to say just a few words about it. I refer you to the provision of the Constitution bearing upon this subject, which denies to Congress the power to deny freedom of speech. Are there any limitations of this provision? Does this privilege belong only to the private citizen? Is it denied to officers of the government? Cannot the Executive discuss the measures of any department? May Congress set itself up as the standard of good taste? Is it for Congress to prescribe the rules of Presidential decorum? Will it not be quite enough for Congress to preserve its own dignity? Can it prescribe the forms of expression which may be used, and punish by impeachment what Congress cannot forbid in the form of a law? But I do not propose to discuss it. In 1798 some of the good people of the country, who had been operated upon very much as the House of Representatives were in this instance, took it into their heads to make a sedition law. It was very like article ten. I propose to read it.

Mr. Groesbeck read the law punishing libellous publications or utterances against the President or Congress by fine and imprisonment, and proceeded:—This was the most offensive that has ever been passed since the government was started. So obnoxious was it that the people would not rest under it, and they started, as it were, a hue and cry against everybody who was concerned in it, and they devoted a great many, for their connection with this law, to a political death. But it was a great law compared with article ten. So unpopular was it that since then no law punishing libel, from that day to this, has been passed. It has been reserved for the House of Representatives, through its managers, to renew this questionable proposition; but I take it upon myself to suggest that before we are condemned in a court of impeachment, we shall have some law upon the subject.

Mr. Groesbeck then read a burlesque law, with a number of preambles, which created considerable laughter, reciting the duty of the President to observe official decorum and to avoid the use of unintelligible phrases, such as calling Congress "a body hanging on the verge of the government," and recognizing the right of Congress, and especially the House of Representatives, to lay down rules of decorum to be observed, punishing the President by fine and imprisonment for any breach of such decorum. "That," he said, "is article ten." (Laughter.)

He then took up article two, saying there was no testimony to support it, except the telegram between Governor Parsons, of Alabama, and the President, dated on the 15th day of January preceding the March in which the law was passed. They had heard the magnificent oration of one of the managers about it, sounding, and sonorous, and sensational, but would they uphold that article upon such proof as that? He had now gone as far as he need go, since he was to be followed by a gentleman who would take it up, step by step, article by article.

Looking back over the case, he was glad to be able to say there were no political questions involved in it. The questions were, where is the power of removal lodged by the Constitution? Is that covered by the Civil Tenure act? Could the President make an *ad interim* appointment? Did he do anything mischievous in his interview with General Emory? and then the matter of freedom of speech which he apprehended nobody would carry on his back as a heavy load for the remainder of his life, stripped of all verbiage. That was the case upon which their judgment was asked. It shocked him to think it possible that the President could be dragged from his office on such questions as whether he could make an *ad interim* appointment for a single day. Was this a matter justifying the disturbing the quiet of the people, shaking their confidence in the President, and driving him from office? How meagre, he said, how miserable is this case—an *ad interim* appointment for a single day, an attempt to remove Edwin M. Stanton, who stood defiantly and poisoned all the channels of intercourse with the President. I do not speak this in censure of Mr. Stanton, but such is the fact.

We have been referred to many precedents in the past history of England; but those precedents should be to you, Senators, not matters for imitation, but the beacon lights to warn you from the dangerous rocks on which they stand. What is to be the judgment, Senators? Removal from office and perpetual disqualification? If the President has done anything for which he should be removed from office, he should also be disqualified from holding office hereafter. What is his crime? He tried to pluck a thorn out of his heart, for it had become a thorn there, and the Senate had fastened it there. What more had he done? He had made an *ad interim* appointment, to last for a single day, which you could have terminated whenever you saw fit. You had only to take the nomination which he sent to the Senate, and which was a good nomination, and the *ad interim* would have vanished like smoke. The thing was in your hands. You had only to act on the nomination, and the matter was settled. That was no crime.

I can point you to cases that have occurred, and I point especially to that case of Floyd's, where the Senate, in its legislative capacity, weighed the question, decided upon it, heard the report of the President, and received it as satisfactory. For the purpose of this trial, that is *res adjudicata*. What else did the President do? He talked with an officer about the law. That is the Emory article. What else did he do? He made intemperate speeches. When reviled, he should not have reviled again. When smitten on the one cheek, he should have turned the other, then he would have escaped impeachment. "But," said the gentleman who addressed you the day before yesterday—Mr. Boutwell—"He was eager for pacification, and to restore the South." I deny it in the sense in which the gentleman presented it as being criminal. Here, too, the President followed reason, and trod the path on which were the foot-prints of Lincoln, and which was lightened by the radiance of that divine utterance of Lincoln's, "Charity towards all, malice towards none."

He was eager for pacification. He knew that the war was ended; the drums were all silent; the arsenals were all shut; the noise of the cannon had died, and the army had disbanded. Not a single enemy confronted us in the field, and he was eager for pacification. The hand of reconciliation was stretched out to him, and he took it. Was this kindness—this forgiveness—a crime? Kindness a crime! Kindness is omnipotent for good; more powerful than gunpowder or cannon. Kindness is statesmanship, Kindness is the high statesmanship of heaven itself. The thunder of Sinai did but terrify and distract. It is the kindness of Calvary that subdues and pacifies. What shall I say of that man? He has only walked in the path and by the light of the Constitution. The mariner, tempest-tossed on the seas, is not more sure to turn to the stars for guidance than this man in the trials of public life to look to the star of the Constitution. He does look to the Constitution; it has been the study of his life. He is not learned or scholarly like many of you. He is not a man of many ideas, or of much speculation. He is a man of intelligence. He is a patriot second to no one of you in the measure of his patriotism. He may be full of errors. I will not canvass how he views his love to his country, but I believe he would die for it if need be. His courage and his patriotism are not without illustration.

My colleague referred, the other day, to the scene which occurred in this chamber when he alone, of all the Senators from his section, remained, and even when his own State had seceded. That was a trial of which many of you, by reason of your locality and of your lifelong associations, know nothing. How his voice rang out in this hall on that occasion, in the hour of alarm, and in denunciation of the Rebellion! But he did not remain here. This was a pleasant and easy position. He chose a more difficult, and arduous and perilous service. That was a trial of his courage and patriotism of which some of you who now sit in judgment upon him know nothing.

I have thought that those who dwell at the North at a

safe distance from the collision of war, know but little of its actual trying dangers. We who lived upon the border know it. Our homes were always surrounded with red flame, and it sometimes came so near that we felt the heat on the outstretched hands. Mr. Johnson went into the very borders of the war, and there he served his country long and well. Which of you has done more? Not one. There is one among you whose services, as I well know, cannot be over estimated, and I withdraw all comparison; but it is enough to say that his services were greatly needed, and it seems hard, it seems cruel that he should be struck here upon these miserable technicalities, or that anybody who had served his country and borne himself well and bravely, should be treated as a criminal, and condemned upon these miserable charges. Even if he had committed a crime against the laws, his services to the country entitle him to some consideration.

But he has precedent for everything he has done. Excellent precedents! The voices of the great dead come to us from their graves sanctioning his course. All our past history approves it. Can you single out this man now in this condition of things and brand him before the country? Will you put your brand upon him because he made an *ad interim* appointment and attempted to remove Edwin M. Stanton? I can at a single glance, Senators, fix my eye on many of you who would not endure the position the President occupied. You do not think it right yourselves. You framed this very Civil Tenure act to give every President his own Cabinet, and then the President's whole crime is that he wants an officer in the War Department with whom he can communicate on public business and entertain friendly relations.

Senators, I am too tired, and no doubt you are. There is a great deal crowding on me for utterance, but it is not from my head, it is rather from my heart, and would be but a repetition of what I have been saying this last half hour. Andrew Johnson, administrator of the Presidential office, is to me as nothing in comparison with the possible consequences of your action in the government of the country. No good can come of conviction on the articles of impeachment. But how much will the heart of the country rejoice if it learns that the United States Senate was not unmindful amid the storm, and passion, and strife, of this power of the Constitution, and of its country, and of its own dignity.

Mr. Groesbeck was, throughout the whole argument, but particularly at the close, listened to with marked attention by the Senate, and with straining eagerness by the spectators. It was to be regretted that, on account of indisposition, he could not make himself heard distinctly. The reporters for the Associated Press, anxious as they were to give a verbatim report of the speech, were unable to do so from the difficulty of hearing it in the gallery, and had, therefore, to put much of it in the third person, and in other parts to construct the sentences out of the portions which they did happen to hear distinctly.

The court, at half-past four, adjourned till Monday, at noon.

PROCEEDINGS OF MONDAY, APRIL 27.

The floor of the Senate Chamber was filled early to-day, a large number of members of the House being present.

Senator Nye appeared in his seat for the first time since his illness.

The first business was Senator Edmunds' motion to admit the official reporters after the arguments are concluded and while the doors are closed for final deliberation.

Senator WILLIAMS proposed an amendment that no Senator shall speak more than once, and not to exceed fifteen minutes, during such deliberation. Agreed to.

Senator HOWARD then moved a further amendment, that each Senator should speak but fifteen minutes upon one question, when the decision was demanded, and it was lost by 19 to 30.

The Republicans voting in the affirmative were Messrs. Fessenden, Fowler, Frelinghuysen, Grimes, Howard, Trumbull and Willey.

Senator ANTHONY moved to allow each Senator to speak thirty, instead of fifteen minutes. This also was lost by a vote of 16 to 34.

Republicans voting in the affirmative—Messrs. Corbett, Fessenden, Fowler and Grimes.

On motion of Senator MORTON, the further consideration of the subject was postponed till after the arguments are concluded.

Senator Sumner's motion and his amendments to the rules were also postponed until after the arguments, at his own request.

Manager STEVENS then took the floor at 12·30 P. M., and commenced reading his speech, standing at the clerk's desk.

Mr. Stevens had not spoken more than half an hour when he was compelled to sit down, and soon after had to give up reading entirely.

General BUTLER then stepped up and volunteered to read for him.

Mr. STEVENS thanked him.

Mr. BUTLER proceeded in a clear, loud voice to read the remainder of the speech.

Argument of Manager Stevens.

May it please the court:—I trust to be able to be brief in my remarks, unless I should find myself less master of the subject which I propose to discuss than I hope, experience having taught that nothing is so prolix as ignorance. I fear I may prove thus ignorant, as I had not expected to take part in this debate until very lately.

I shall discuss but a single article, the one that was finally adopted upon my earnest solicitation, and which, if proved, I considered then and still consider, as quite sufficient for the ample conviction of the distinguished respondent, and for his removal from office, which is the only legitimate object for which this impeachment could be instituted.

During the very brief period which I shall occupy, I desire to discuss the charges against the respondent in no mean spirit of malignity or vituperation, but to argue them in a manner worthy of the high tribunal before which I appear, and of the exalted position of the accused. Whatever may be thought of his character or condition he has been made respectable and his condition has been dignified by the action of his fellow-citizens. Railing accusation, therefore, would ill-become this occasion, this tribunal, or a proper sense of the position of those who discuss this question on the one side or the other.

To see the chief servant of a trusting community arraigned before the bar of public justice, charged with high delinquencies, is interesting. To behold the Chief Executive Magistrate of a powerful people charged with the betrayal of his trust, and arraigned for high crimes and misdemeanors, is always a most interesting spectacle. When the charges against such public servant accuse him of an attempt to betray the high trust confided in him and usurp the power of a whole people, that he may become their ruler, it is intensely interesting to millions of men, and should be discussed with a calm determination, which nothing can divert and nothing can reduce to mockery. Such is the condition of this great republic as looked upon by an astonished and wondering world.

The offices of impeachment in England and America are very different from each other, in the uses made of them for the punishment of offenses; and he will greatly err who undertakes to make out an analogy between them, either in the mode of trial or the final result.

In England the highest crimes may be tried before the High Court of Impeachment, and the severest punishments, even to imprisonment, fine and death, may be inflicted.

When our Constitution was framed, all those personal punishments were excluded from the judgment, and the defendant was to be dealt with just so far as the public safety required, and no further. Hence, it was made to apply simply to political offenses—to persons holding political positions, either by appointment or election by the people.

Thus it is apparent that no crime containing malignant or indictable offenses, higher than misdemeanors, was necessary either to be alleged or proved. If the respondent was shown to be abusing his official trust to the injury of the people for whom he was discharging public duties, and perservered in such abuse to the injury of his constituents, the true mode of dealing with him was to impeach him for crimes and misdemeanors (and only the latter is necessary), and thus remove him from the office which he was abusing. Nor does it make a particle of difference whether such abuse arose from malignity, from unwarranted negligence or from depravity, so repeated as to make his continuance in office injurious to the people and dangerous to the public welfare.

The punishment which the law under our Constitution authorizes to be inflicted fully demonstrates this argument:—That punishment upon conviction extends only to removal from office, and if the crime or misdemeanor charged be one of a deep and wicked dye, the culprit is allowed to run at large, unless he should be pursued by a new prosecution in the ordinary courts. What does it matter, then, what the motive of the respondent might be in his repeated acts of malfeasance in office? Mere mistake in intention, if so persevered in after proper warning as to bring mischief upon the community, is quite sufficient to warrant the removal of the officer from the place where he is working mischief by his continuance in power.

The only question to be considered is:—Is the respondent violating the law? His perseverance in such a violation, although it shows a perseverance, is not absolutely necessary to his conviction. The great object is the removal from office and the arrest of the public injuries which he is inflicting upon those with whose interests he is intrusted.

The single charge which I had the honor to suggest, I am

expected to maintain. That duty is a light one, easily performed, and which, I apprehend, it will be found impossible for the respondent to answer or evade.

When Andrew Johnson took upon himself the duties of his high office, he swore to obey the Constitution and take care that the laws be faithfully executed. That, indeed, is and has always been the chief duty of the President of the United States. The duties of legislation and adjudicating the laws of his country fall in no way to his lot. To obey the commands of the sovereign power of the nation, and to see that others should obey them, was his whole duty—a duty which he could not escape, and any attempt to do so would be in direct violation of his official oath; in other words, a *misprision of perjury*.

I accuse him, in the name of the House of Representatives, of having perpetrated that foul offense against the laws and interests of his country.

On the 2d day of March, 1867, Congress passed a law, over the veto of the President, entitled "An act to regulate the tenure of certain civil offices," the first section of which is as follows:—

"*Be it enacted by the Senate and House of Representatives of the United States of America in Congress assembled*, That every person holding any civil office to which he has been appointed by and with the advice and consent of the Senate, and every person who may hereafter be appointed to any such office and shall become duly qualified to act therein, is and shall be entitled to hold such office until a successor shall have been in like manner appointed and duly qualified, except as herein otherwise provided: *Provided*, That the Secretaries of State, of the Treasury, of War, of the Navy, and of the Interior, the Postmaster-General, and the Attorney-General, shall hold their offices respectively for and during the term of the President by whom they may have been appointed, and for one month thereafter, subject to removal by and with the advice and consent of the Senate."

The second section provides that when the Senate is not in session, if the President shall deem the officer guilty of acts which require his removal or suspension, he may be suspended until the next meeting of the Senate; and that within twenty days after the meeting of the Senate the reasons for such suspension shall be reported to that body; and, if the Senate shall deem such reasons sufficient for such suspension or removal, the officer shall be considered removed from his office; but if the Senate shall not deem the reasons sufficient for such suspension or removal, the officer shall forthwith resume the functions of his office, and the person appointed in his place shall cease to discharge such duties.

On the 12th day of August, 1867, the Senate then not being in session, the President suspended Edwin M. Stanton, Secretary of the Department of War, and appointed U. S. Grant, General, Secretary of War *ad interim*. On the 12th day of December, 1867, the Senate being then in session, he reported, according to the requirements of the act, the causes of such suspension to the Senate, which duly took the same into consideration. Before the Senate had concluded its examination of the question of the sufficiency of such reasons, he attempted to enter into arrangements by which he might obstruct the due execution of the law, and thus prevent Edwin M. Stanton from forthwith resuming the functions of his office as Secretary of War, according to the provisions of the act, even if the Senate should decide in his favor.

And in furtherance of said attempt, on the 21st day of February, 1868, he appointed one Lorenzo Thomas, by letter of authority or commission, Secretary of War *ad interim*, without the advice or consent of the Senate, although the same was then in session, and ordered him (the said Thomas) to take possession of the Department of War and the public property appertaining thereto, and to discharge the duties thereof.

We charge that, in defiance of frequent warnings, he has since repeatedly attempted to carry those orders into execution, and to prevent Edwin M. Stanton from executing the laws appertaining to the Department of War, and from discharging the duties of the office.

The very able gentleman who argued this case for the respondent has contended that Mr. Stanton's case is not within the provisions of the act "regulating the tenure of certain civil offices," and that therefore the President cannot be convicted of violating that act. His argument in demonstrating that position was not, I think, quite equal to his sagacity in discovering where the great strength of the prosecution was lodged. He contended that the proviso which embraced the Secretary of War did not include Mr. Stanton, because he was not appointed by the President in whose term the acts charged as misdemeanors were perpetrated; and in order to show that, he contended that the *term* of office mentioned during which he was entitled to hold meant the time during which the President who appointed him actually did hold, whether dead or alive; that Mr. Lincoln, who appointed Mr. Stanton, and under whose commission he was holding indefinitely, being dead, his *term* of office referred to had expired, and that Mr. Johnson was not holding during a part of that *term*. That depends upon the Constitution, and the laws made under it. By the Constitution, the whole time from the adoption of the government was intended to be divided into equal Presidential periods, and the word "*term*" was technically used to designate the time of each. The first section of the second article of the Constitution provides "that the executive power shall be vested in a President of the United States of America. He shall hold his office during the *term* of four years, and together, with the Vice President, chosen for the same *term*, be elected as follows," &c. Then it provides that "in case of removal from office, or of his death, resignation, or inability to discharge the duties of said office, the same shall devolve on the Vice President, and Congress may by law provide for the case of removal, death, resignation, or inability both of the President and Vice President, designating what officer shall then act as President, and such officer shall then act accordingly until the disability is removed or a President shall be elected."

The learned counsel contends that the Vice President, who accidentally accedes to the duties of President, is serving out a new Presidential term of his own, and that, unless Mr. Stanton was appointed by him, he is not within the provisions of the act. It happened that Mr. Stanton was appointed by Mr. Lincoln in 1862 for an indefinite period of time, and was still serving as *his* appointee, by and with the advice and consent of the Senate. Mr. Johnson never appointed him, and, unless he held a valid commission by virtue of Mr. Lincoln's appointment, he was acting for three years, during which time he expended billions of money and raised hundreds of thousands of men, without any commission at all. To permit this to be done without any valid commission would have been a misdemeanor in itself. But if he held a valid commission, whose commission was it? Not Andrew Johnson's. Then in whose term was he serving, for he must have been in somebody's term? Even if it was in Johnson's term, he would hold for four years unless sooner removed, for there is no term spoken of in the Constitution of a shorter period for a Presidential term than four years. But it makes no difference in the operation of the law whether he was holding in Lincoln's or Johnson's term. Was it not in Mr. Lincoln's term? Lincoln had been elected and re-elected, the second term to commence in 1865, and the Constitution expressly declared that that term should be four years.

By virtue of his previous commission and the uniform custom of the country, Mr. Stanton continued to hold during the term of Mr. Lincoln, unless sooner removed. Now, does any one pretend that from the 4th of March, 1865, a new Presidential term did not commence? For it will be seen upon close examination that the word "*term*" alone marks the time of the Presidential existence, so that it may divide the different periods of office by a well-recognized rule. Instead of saying that the Vice President shall become President upon his death, the Constitution says:—"In case of the removal of the President from office, or of his death, resignation, or inability to discharge the *powers and duties* of the said office, the same shall devolve on the Vice President." What is to devolve on the Vice President? Not the Presidential commission held by his predecessor, but the "duties" which were incumbent on him. If he were to take Mr. Lincoln's term he would serve four years, for term is the only limitation to that office defined in the Constitution, as I have said before. But the learned counsel has contended that the word "*term*" of the Presidential office means the death of the President. Then it would have been better expressed by saying that the President shall hold his office during the *term* between two assassinations, and then the assassination of the President would mark the period of the operation of this law.

If, then, Mr. Johnson was serving out one of Mr. Lincoln's terms, there seems to be no argument against including Mr. Stanton within the meaning of the law. He was so included by the President in his notice of removal, in his reasons therefore given to the Senate and in his notification to the Secretary of the Treasury; and it is too late when he is caught violating the very law under which he professes to act, to turn round and deny that that law affects the case. The gentleman treats lightly the question of estoppel; and yet really nothing is more powerful, for it is an argument by the party himself against himself, and although not pleadable in the same way, is just as potential in a case *in pais* as when pleaded in *record*.

But there is a still more conclusive answer. The first section provides that *every* person holding civil office who has been appointed with the advice and consent of the Senate, and every person that hereafter shall be appointed to any such office, shall be entitled to hold such office until a successor shall have been in like manner appointed and duly qualified, except as herein otherwise provided. Then comes the proviso which the defendant's counsel say does not embrace Mr. Stanton, because he was not appointed by the President in whose term he was removed. If he was not embraced in the proviso, then he was now here specially provided for, and was consequently embraced in the first clause of the first section, which declares that every person holding any civil office not otherwise provided for comes within the provision of this act.

The respondent, in violation of this law, appointed General Thomas to office, whereby, according to the express terms of the act, he was guilty of a high misdemeanor. But whatever may have been his views with regard to the Tenure of Office act, he knew it was a law, and so recorded upon the statutes. I disclaim all necessity, in a trial of impeachment, to prove the wicked or unlawful intention of the respondent, and it is unwise ever to aver it.

In impeachments more than in indictments, the averring of the fact charged carries with it all that it is necessary to say about intent. In indictments you charge that the defendant, "instigated by the devil," and so on; and you might as well call on the prosecution to prove the presence, shape and color of his majesty, as to call upon the managers in impeachment to prove intention. I go further than some, and contend that no corrupt or wicked motive need instigate the acts for which impeachment is brought. It is enough that they were official violations of law. The counsel has placed great stress upon the necessity of proving that they were wilfully done. If by that he means that they were voluntarily done, I agree with him. A mere accidental trespass would not be sufficient to convict. But that which is *voluntarily* done is *wilfully* done, according to every honest definition; and whatever malfeasance is willingly perpetrated by an office-holder is a misdemeanor in office, whatever he may allege was his intention.

The President justifies himself by asserting that all previous Presidents had exercised the same right of removing officers, for cause to be judged of by the President alone. Had there been no law to prohibit it when Mr. Stanton was removed, the cases would have been parallel, and the one might be adduced as an argument in favor of the other. But, since the action of any of the Presidents to which he refers, a law had been passed by Congress, after a stubborn controversy with the Executive, denying that right and prohibiting it in future, and imposing a severe penalty upon any executive officer who should exercise it. And that, too, after the President had himself made issue on its constitutionality and been defeated. No pretext, therefore, any longer existed that such right was vested in the President by virtue of his office. Hence the attempt to shield himself under such practice is a most lame evasion of the question at issue. Did he "take care that this law should be faithfully" executed? He answers that acts, that would have violated the law had it existed, were practiced by his predecessors. How does that justify his own malfeasance?

The President says that he removed Mr. Stanton simply to test the constitutionality of the Tenure of Office law by a judicial decision. He has already seen it tested and decided by the votes, twice given, of two-thirds of the Senators and of the House of Representatives. It stood as a law upon the statute books. No case had arisen under that law, or is referred to by the President, which required any judicial interposition. If there had been, or should be, the courts were open to any one who felt aggrieved by the action of Mr. Stanton. But instead of inforcing that law, he takes advantage of the name and the funds of the United States to resist it, and to induce others to resist it. Instead of attempting, as the Executive of the United States, to see that that law was faithfully executed, he took great pains and perpetrated the acts alleged in this article, not only to resist it himself, but to seduce others to do the same. He sought to induce the General-in-Chief of the Army to aid him in an open avowed obstruction of the law, as it stood unrepealed upon the statute book. He could find no one to unite with him in perpetrating such an act, until he sunk down upon the unfortunate individual bearing the title of Adjutant-General of the army. Is this taking care that the laws shall be faithfully executed? Is this attempting to carry them into effect, by upholding their validity, according to his oath? On the other hand, was it not a high and bold attempt to obstruct the laws and take care that they should not be executed? He must not excuse himself by saying that he had doubts of its constitutionality and wished to test it. What right had he to be hunting up excuses for others, as well as himself, to violate this law? Is not this confession a misdemeanor in itself?

The President asserts that he did not remove Mr. Stanton under the Tenure of Office law. This is a direct contradiction of his own letter to the Secretary of the Treasury, in which, as he was bound by law, he communicated to that officer the fact of the removal. This portion of the answer may, therefore, be considdred as disposed of by the non-existence of the fact, as well as by his subsequent report to the Senate.

The following is the letter just alluded to, dated August 14, 1867:—

"Sir:—In compliance with the requirements of the act entitled "An act to regulate the tenure of certain civil offices," you are hereby notified that, on the 10th instant, the Hon. Edwin M. Stanton was suspended from his office as Secretary of War, and General U. S. Grant authorized and empowered to act as Secretary *ad interim*.

"Hon. Secretary of the Treasury."

Wretched man! a direct contradiction of his solemn answer! How necessary that a man should have a good conscience or a good memory! Both would not be out of place. How lovely to contemplate what was so assiduously inculcated by a celebrated Pagan into the mind of his son: "Virtue is truth, and truth is virtue." And still more, virtue of every kind charms us, yet that virtue is strongest which is effected by justice and generosity. Good deeds will never be done, wise acts will never be executed, except by the virtuous and the conscientious.

May the people of this Republic remember this good old doctrine when they next meet to select their rulers, and may they select only the brave and the virtuous!

Has it been proved, as charged in this article, that Andrew Johnson in vacation suspended from office Edwin M. Stanton, who had been duly appointed and was then executing the duties of Secretary of the Department of War, without the advice and consent of the Senate; did he report the reasons for such supension to the Senate within twenty days from the meeting of the Senate; and did the Senate proceed to consider the sufficiency of such reasons? Did the Senate declare such reasons insufficient, whereby the said Edwin M. Stanton became authorized to forthwith resume and exercise the functions of Secretary of War, and displace the Secretary *ad interim*, whose duties were then to cease and terminate; did the said Andrew Johnson, in his official character of President of the United States, attempt to obstruct the return of the said Edwin M. Stanton and his resumption forthwith of the functions of his office as Secretary of the Department of War; and has he continued to attempt to prevent the discharge of the duties of said office by said Edwin M. Stanton, Secretary of War, notwithstanding the Senate decided in his favor? If he has, then the acts in violation of law, charged in this article, are full and complete.

The proof lies in a very narrow compass, and depends upon the credibility of one or two witnesses, who, upon this point, corroborate each other's evidence.

Andrew Johnson, in his letter of the 31st of January, 1868, not only declared that such was his intention, but reproached U. S. Grant, General, in the following language:—

"You had found in our first conference 'that the President was desirous of keeping Mr. Stanton out of office *whether sustained in the suspension or not.*' You knew what reasons had induced the President to ask from you a promise; you also knew that in case your views of duty did not accord with his own convictions it was his purpose to fill your place by another appointment. Even ignoring the existence of a positive understanding between us, these conclusions were plainly deducible from various conversations. It is certain, however, that even under these circumstances you did not offer to return the place to my possession, but, according to your own statement, placed yourself in a position where, could I have anticipated your action, I would have been compelled to ask of you, as I was compelled to ask of your predecessor in the War Department, a letter of resignation, or else to resort to the more disagreeable expedient of suspending you by a successor."

He thus distinctly alleges that the General had a full knowledge that such was his deliberate intention. Hard words and injurious epithets can do nothing to corroborate or to injure the character of a witness; but if Andrew Johnson be not wholly destitute of truth and a shameless falsifier, then this article and all its charges are clearly made out by his own evidence.

Whatever the respondent may say of the reply of U. S. Grant, General, only goes to confirm the fact of the President's lawless attempt to obstruct the execution of the act specified in the article.

If General Grant's recollection of his conversation with the President is correct, then it goes affirmatively to prove the same fact stated by the President, although it shows that the President persevered in his course of determined obstruction of the law, while the General refused to aid in its consummation. No differences as to the main fact of the attempt to violate and prevent the execution of the law exists in either statement; both compel the conviction of the respondent, unless he should escape through other means than the facts proving the article. He cannot hope to escape by asking this High Court to declare the "law for regulating the tenure of certain civil offices" unconstitutional and void; for it so happens, to the hopeless misfortune of the respondent, that almost every member of this high tribunal has more than once—twice, perhaps three times—declared, upon his official oath, that law constitutional and valid. The unhappy man is in this condition:—He has declared himself determined to obstruct that act; he has, by two several letters of authority, ordered Lorenzo Thomas to violate that law; and he has issued commissions during the session of the Senate, without the advice and consent of the Senate, in violation of law, to said Thomas. He must, therefore, either deny his own solemn declarations and falsify the testimony of General Grant and Lorenzo Thomas, or expect that verdict, whose least punishment is removal from office.

But the President denies in his answer to the first and the eleventh articles (which he intends as a joint answer to the two charges) that he had attempted to contrive means to prevent the due execution of the law regulating tenure of certain civil offices, or had violated his oath " to take care that the laws be faithfully executed." Yet, while he denies such attempt to defeat the execution of the laws, in his letter of the 31st of January, 1868, he asserts and reproaches General Grant by the assertion, that the General knew that his object was to prevent Edwin M. Stanton from forthwith resuming the functions of his office, notwithstanding that the Senate might decide in his favor; and the President and U. S. Grant, General, in their angry correspondence of the date heretofore referred to, made an issue of veracity—the President asserting that the General had promised to aid him in defeating the execution of the laws by preventing the immediate resumption of the functions of Secretary of War by Edwin M. Stanton, and that the General violated his promise; and U. S. Grant, General, denying ever having finally made such promise, although he agrees with the President that the President did attempt to induce him to make such promise and to enter into such an arrangement.

Now, which of these gentlemen may have lost his memory, and found in lieu of the truth a vision which issues from the Ivory Gate—though who can hesitate to choose between the words of a gallant soldier and the pettifogging of a political trickster—is wholly immaterial, so far as the charge against the President is concerned. That charge is, that the President did attempt to prevent the due execution of the Tenure of Office law by entangling the General in the arrangement; and unless both the President and the General have lost their memory and mistaken the truth with regard to the promises with each other, then this charge is made out. In short, if either of these gentlemen has correctly stated these facts of attempting the obstruction of the law, the President has been guilty of violating the law and of *misprision of official perjury.*

But, again, the President alleges his right to violate the act regulating the tenure of certain civil offices, because, he says, the same was inoperative and void, as being in violation of the Constitution of the United States. Does it lie in his mouth to interpose this plea? He had acted under that law, and issued letters of authority, both for the long and the short term, to several persons under it, and it

would hardly lie in his mouth after that to deny its validity, unless he confessed himself guilty of law-breaking by issuing such commissions.

Let us here look at Andrew Johnson accepting the oath "to take care that the laws be faithfully executed."

On the 2d of March, 1867, he returned to the Senate the Tenure of Office bill, where it originated and had passed by a majority of more than two-thirds, with reasons elaborately given why it should not pass finally. Among these was the allegation of its unconstitutionality. It passed by a vote of 35 yeas to 11 nays. In the House of Representatives it passed by more than a two-thirds majority; and when the vote was announced the Speaker, as was his custom, proclaimed the vote, and declared, in the language of the Constitution, "that two-thirds of each House having voted for it, notwithstanding the objections of the President, it has become a law."

I am supposing that Andrew Johnson was at this moment waiting to take the oath of office as President of the United States, "that he would obey the Constitution, and take care that the laws be faithfully executed." Having been sworn on the Holy Evangels to obey the Constitution, and being about to depart, he turned to the person administering the oath, and says, "Stop; I have a further oath. I do solemnly swear that I will not allow the act entitled 'An act regulating the tenure of certain civil offices,' just passed by Congress over the Presidential veto, to be executed; but I will prevent its execution by virtue of my own constitutional power."

How shocked Congress would have been. What would the country have said to a scene equaled only by the unparalleled action of this same official, when sworn into office on that fatal fifth day of March, which made him the successor of Abraham Lincoln! Certainly he would not have been permitted to be inaugurated as Vice President or President. Yet such in effect, has been his conduct, if not under oath, at least with less excuse, since the fatal day which inflicted him upon the people of the United States. Can the President hope to escape if the fact of his violating the law be proved or confessed by him, as has been done? Can he expect a sufficient number of his tryers to pronounce that law unconstitutional and void—those same tryers having passed upon its validity upon several occasions? The act was originally passed by a vote of 29 yeas to 9 nays. Those who voted in the affirmative were:—Messrs. Anthony, Brown, Cattell, Chandler, Conness, Cragin, Edmunds, Fogg, Foster, Frelinghuysen, Grimes, Harris, Henderson, Howard, Howe, Lane, Morgan, Morrill, Poland, Ramsey, Sherman, Sprague, Sumner, Van Winkle, Wade, Willey, Williams, Wilson, Yates—29.

Subsequently the House of Representatives passed the bill with amendments, which the Senate disagreed to and the bill was afterward referred to a Committee of Conference of the two Houses, whose agreement was reported to the Senate by the managers, and was adopted by a vote of 22 yeas to 10 nays. Those who voted in the affirmative were:—Messrs. Anthony Brown, Chandler, Conness, Fogg, Fowler, Henderson, Howard, Howe, Lane, Morgan, Morrill, Ramsey, Ross, Sherman, Stewart, Sumner, Trumbull, Wade, Williams, Wilson, and Yates—22.

After the vote, upon reconsideration of the bill in the Senate, and after all the arguments against its validity were spread before that body, it passed by a vote of 35 yeas to 11 nays. It was voted for by the following Senators:—Messrs. Anthony, Cattell, Chandler, Conness, Cragin, Edmunds, Fessenden, Fogg, Foster, Fowler, Frelinghuysen, Grimes, Harris, Henderson, Howard, Kirkwood, Lane, Morgan, Morrill, Nye, Poland, Pomeroy, Ramsey, Ross, Sherman, Sprague, Stewart, Sumner, Trumbull, Van Winkle, Wade, Willey, Williams, Wilson, and Yates—35.

The President contends that by virtue of the Constitution he had the right to remove heads of departments, and cites a large number of cases where his predecessor had done so. It must be observed that all those cases were before the passage of the Tenure of Office act, March 2, 1867. Will the respondent say how the having done an act when there was no law to forbid it justifies the repetition of the same act after a law has been passed expressly prohibiting the same. It is not the suspension or removal of Mr. Stanton that is complained of, but the manner of suspension. If the President thought he had good reasons for suspending or removing Mr. Stanton, and had done so, sending those reasons to the Senate, and then obeyed the decision of the Senate on their finding, there would have been no complaint; but instead of that he suspends him in direct defiance of the Tenure of Office law, and then enters into an arrangement, or attempts to do so, in which he thought he had succeeded, to prevent the due execution of the law after the decision of the Senate. And when the Senate ordered him to restore Mr. Stanton, he makes a second removal by virtue of what he calls the power vested in him by the Constitution.

The action of the Senate on the message of the President, communicating his reasons for the suspension of E. M. Stanton, Secretary of War, under the act entitled an act to regulate the tenure of certain civil offices, was as follows:—

IN EXECUTIVE SESSION, SENATE OF THE UNITED STATES, January 13, 1868.

Resolved, That having considered the evidence and reasons given by the President in his report of December 12, 1867, for the suspension from the office of Secretary of War of Edwin M. Stanton, the Senate do not concur in such suspension.

And the same was duly certified to the President, in the face of which he, with an impudence and brazen determination to usurp the powers of the Senate, again removed

Edwin M. Stanton, and appointed Lorenzo Thomas Secretary *ad interim* in his stead. The Senate, with calm manliness, rebuked the usurper by the following resolution:—

IN EXECUTIVE SESSION, SENATE OF THE UNITED STATES, February 21, 1868.

Whereas, The Senate has received and considered the communication of the President stating that he had removed Edwin M. Stanton, Secretary of War, and had designated the Adjutant-General of the Army to act as Secretary of War *ad interim;* therefore

Resolved, by the Senate of the United States, That under the Constitution and laws of the United States, the President has no power to remove the Secretary of War, and to designate any other officer to perform the duties of that office *ad interim.*

Yet he continued him in office. And now this offspring of assassination turns upon the Senate, who have thus rebuked him in a constitutional manner, and bids them defiance. How can he escape the just vengeance of the law? Wretched man, standing at bay, surrounded by a cordon of living men, each with the axe of an executioner uplifted for his just punishment. Every Senator now trying him, except such as had already adopted his policy, voted for this same resolution, pronouncing his solemn doom. Will any one of them vote for his acquittal on the ground of its unconstitutionality? I know that Senators would venture to do any necessary act if indorsed by an honest conscience and an enlightened public opinion; but neither for the sake of the President nor of any one else, would one of them suffer himself to be tortured on the gibbet of everlasting obloquy. How long and dark would be the track of infamy which must mark his name and that of his posterity! Nothing is therefore more certain than that it requires no gift of prophesy to predict the fate of this unhappy victim.

I have now discussed but one of the numerous articles, all of which I believe to be fully sustained, and few of the almost innumerable offenses charged to this wayward, unhappy official. I have alluded to two or three others which I could have wished to have had time to present and discuss, not for the sake of punishment, but for the benefit of the country. One of these was an article charging the President with usurping the legislative power of the nation, and attempting still his usurpations.

With regard to usurpation, one single word will explain my meaning. A civil war of gigantic proportions, covering sufficient territory to constitute many States and nations, broke out, and embraced more than ten millions of men, who formed an independent government, called the Confederate States of America. They rose to the dignity of an independent belligerent, and were so acknowledged by all civilized nations, as well as by ourselves. After expensive and bloody strife, we conquered them, and they submitted to our arms. By the law of nations, well understood and undisputed, the conquerors in this unjust war had the right to deal with the vanquished as to them might seem good, subject only to the laws of humanity. They had a right to confiscate their property to the extent of indemnifying themselves and their citizens; to annex them to the victorious nation, and pass just such laws for for their government as they might think proper. This doctrine is as old as Grotius, and as fresh as the Dorr rebellion. Neither the President nor the judiciary had any right to interfere, to dictate any terms, or to aid in reconstruction, further than they were directed by the sovereign power. That sovereign power in this Republic is the Congress of the United States.

Whoever, besides Congress, undertakes to create new States or to rebuild old ones, and fix the condition of their citizenship and union, usurps powers which do not belong to him, and is dangerous or not dangerous, according to the extent of his power and his pretensions. Andrew Johnson did usurp the legislative power of the nation by building new States, and reconstructing, as far as in him lay, this empire. He directed the defunct States to come forth and live by virtue of his breathing into their nostrils the breath of life. He directed them what constitutions to form, and fixed the qualifications of electors and of office-holders. He directed them to send forward members to each branch of Congress, and to aid him in representing the nation. When Congress passed a law declaring all these doings unconstitutional, and fixed a mode for the admission of this new territory into the nation, he proclaimed it unconstitutional, and advised the people not to submit to it, nor to obey the commands of Congress. I have not time to enumerate the particular acts which constitute his high-handed usurpations. Suffice it to say, that he seized all the powers of the government within these States, and, had he been permitted, would have become their absolute ruler. This he persevered in attempting, notwithstanding Congress declared more than once all the governments which he thus created to be void and of none effect.

But I promised to be brief, and must abide by the promise, although I should like the judgment of the Senate upon this, to me, seeming vital phase and real purpose of all his misdemeanors. To me this seems a sublime spectacle. A nation, not free, but as nearly approaching it as human institutions will permit of, consisting of thirty millions of people, had fallen into conflict, which among other people always ends in anarchy or despotism, and had laid down their arms the mutineers submitting to the conquerors. The laws were about to regain their accustomed sway, and again to govern the nation by the punishment of treason and the reward of virtue. Her old institutions were about to be reinstated so far as they were applicable, according to the judgment of the conquerors. Then one of their inferor servants, instigated by unholy ambition, sought to seize a portion of the territory according to the fashion of neighboring anarchies, and to convert a land of freedom into a land of slaves. This people spurned the traitors, and have put the chief of them upon his trial, and demand judgment upon his misconduct. He will be condemned, and his sentence inflicted without turmoil, tumult, or bloodshed, and the nation will continue its accustomed course of freedom and prosperity, without the shedding any further of human blood and with a milder punishment than the world has accustomed to see, or perhaps than ought now to be inflicted.

Now, even if the pretext of the President were true and not a mere subterfuge to justify the chief act of violation with which he stands charged, still that would be such an abuse of the patronage of the government as would demand his impeachment for a high misdemeanor. Let us again for a moment examine into some of the circumstances of that act. Mr. Stanton was appointed Secretary of War in 1862, and continued to hold under Mr. Johnson, which, by all usage, is considered a reappointment. Was he a faithful officer, or was he removed for corrupt purposes? After the death of Mr. Lincoln, Andrew Johnson had changed his whole code of politics and policy, and instead of obeying the will of those who put him into power, he determined to create a party for himself to carry out his own ambitious purposes. For every honest purpose of the government, and for every honest purpose for which Mr. Stanton was appointed by Mr. Lincoln, where could a better man be found? None ever organized an army of a million of men and provided for its subsistence and efficient action more rapidly than Mr. Stanton and his predecessor.

It might, with more propriety, be said of this officer than of the celebrated Frenchman, that he "organized victory." He raised, and by his requisitions distributed more than a billion of dollars annually, without ever having been charged or suspected with the malappropriation of a single dollar; and when victory crowned his efforts he disbanded that immense army as quietly and peacefully as if it had been a summer parade. He would not, I suppose, adopt the personal views of the President; and for this he was suspended until restored by the emphatic verdict of the Senate. Now, if we are right in our narrative of the conduct of these parties and of the motives of the President, the very effort at removal was a high handed usurpation as well as a corrupt misdemeanor, for which, of itself, he ought to be impeached and thrown from the place he was abusing. But he says that he did not remove Mr. Stanton for the purpose of defeating the Tenure of Office law. Then he forgot the truth in his controversy with the General of the Army. And because the General did not aid him and finally admit that he had agreed to aid him in resisting that law, he rallied upon him like a very drab.

The counsel for the respondent allege that no removal of Mr. Stanton ever took place, and that, therefore, the sixth section of the act was not violated. They admit that there was an order of removal and a recision of his commission; but as he did not obey it, say it was no removal. That suggests the old saying, that it used to be thought that "when the brains were out the man was dead." That idea is proved by learned counsel to be absolutely fallacious. The brain of Mr. Stanton's commission was taken out by the order of removal—the recision of his commission—and his head was absolutely cut off by that gallant soldier, General Thomas, the night after the masquerade. And yet, according to the learned and delicate counsel, until the mortal remains, everything which could putrify was shoveled out and hauled into the muck-yard, there was no removal. But it is said that this took place merely as an experiment to make a judicial case. Now, suppose there is anybody who, with the facts before him, can believe that this was not an afterthought, let us see if that palliates the offense.

The President is sworn to take care that the laws be faithfully executed. In what part of the Constitution or laws does he find it to be his duty to search out for defective laws that stand recorded upon the statutes, in order that he may advise their infraction? Who was aggrieved by the Tenure of Office bill that he was authorized to use the name and the funds of the government to relieve? Will he be so good as to tell us by what authority he became the obstructor of an unrepealed law instead of its executor, especially a law whose constitutionality he had twice tested? If there were nothing else than his own statement, he deserves the contempt of the American people, and the punishment of its highest tribunal. If he were not willing to execute the laws passed by the American Congress, and unrepealed, let him resign the office which was thrown upon him by a horrible convulsion, and retire to his village obscurity. Let him not be so swollen by pride and arrogance, which sprang from the deep misfortune of his country, as to attempt an entire revolution of its internal machinery, and the disgrace of the trusted servants of his lamented predecessor.

The gentleman has spoken of the great purity of the President in his transaction with Mr. Black and others. I admit that is a fair subject from which to infer general purity of conduct, and I will examine it a little. It was held by Socrates and Plato to be among the most atrocious of offenses to corrupt the youth, because that tended to overthrow the solid forms of government, and build up anarchy and despotism in their place. If it were so in an oligarchy, how much more would it be so in a government where the laws control, and where the laws should be pure, if that government is expected to be conducted with purity and to survive the temporary shocks of tyrants?

If it is proved or known that Andrew Johnson attempted at any time, to corrupt the loyal voters of the

United States, so as to change them from thier own true opinions, to those which he himself had adopted, there are few who will pretend that he was not guilty of a high misdemeanor. We need hardly call witnesses to prove a fact which everybody knows and nobody will deny. Does the sun shine at mid-day? It would hardly be thought necessary to answer that question by proof, and yet there is just as much necessity for it, as to prove that Andrew Johnson had changed his whole principles and policy and entered into the most dangerous and damaging contracts with aspirants for office, to induce them to aid him in changing the principles of those who sought office.

Who does not believe that the patronage was put into the hands of Doolittle, Cowan and that tribe of men, for distribution, on precisely such terms and conditions as they chose to make? Show me a more shameless perversion of patronage in any country or in any government, however corrupt and despotic, and I will admit that Andrew Johnson is as pure as the icicles that hung on Diana's Temple. Before that, Johnson appeared with Abraham Lincoln in the Senate Chamber, to take the oath of office, and they took it at the same time, in the same manner, with some small variation in the manner of the Vice President; but his friends hoped that such variations had not obliterated or obscured his consciousness of the oath he had taken, and that when he came to reflect, he would abide by all he had sworn to observe, notwithstanding his then condition.

Unfortunately the President was taken away, and left a temptation for the higher aspirations of Mr. Johnson. Instead of being content with the position the people had given him, and which, he said, he gladly accepted, he sought to become thereafter, as well as then, the chief of the nation. This he knew could only be done by changing principles and creating a new party to sustain him. After some little hesitancy he resolved upon that course, and perpetrated a betrayal of the party that had elected him and the principles he professed. Worse than the betrayal by Judas Iscariot, for he betrayed only a single individual, but Johnson sacrificed a whole nation and the holiest of principles.

In order to build up a party upon which he was to rely, it became necessary for him to proclaim entirely new principles and a new policy, and to bring about him an entirely new set of politicians, and as loose men enough already in the Republican party could not be found to carry him into power, corruption, therefore, became a necessity. That corruption was to be wrought by perverting the means which the Republican party had placed in his hands, and which he had solemnly sworn to execute according to their principles.

When he found that by an appeal to these principles he could rally but few followers, he did not hesitate to cast them off and seek recruits in the camp of the enemy. Instead of enforcing the provisions of the law and rendering treason odious, as he had so loudly proclaimed while Vice President, he proceeded to pardon all the influential traitors, and to restore to the conquered belligerents the property which had been confiscated by the act of Congress of July, 1862. He thus restored confiscated land and abandoned estates, sufficient had it all been honestly carried into the Treasury to have paid the national debt and all the damage done to loyal men by the Rebel raiders and by Rebel confiscation.

He set deliberately about corrupting the whole mass of those who aspired to office, and where he found an officeholder too virtuous to follow his treason, he offered his place to another, whose conscience was less scrupulous, or whose ambition was greater. The removals which he made were of Republicans who had been placed in office by Abraham Lincoln, upon Republican recommendation, because they held the same principles which he (Johnson) had professed. He did not hesitate, through his agents, to bargain for their support as the condition of their appointment or retention. He found a few men of respectable standing who had been indorsed by respectable States, such as Wisconsin and Pennsylvania. Look at the trusted agents of Pennsylvania and Wisconsin, who contracted to accept the office of recruiting sergeants for his shabby army to purchase the position of a commander of this band of pardoned traitors and corrupted renegades. They consented to lay down the Stars and Stripes and clothe themselves in the faded uniform of gray.

The gentleman (Mr. Groesbeck), in his peroration on Saturday, implored the sympathy of this Senate with all the eloquence and pathos of a Roman Senator pleading for virtue, and it is to be feared that his grace and eloquence turned the attention of the Senators upon the orator rather than upon the accused. Had he been pleading for innocence, his great powers would have been well exacted; had he been arguing with equal eloquence before a Roman Senate for such a delinquent, and Cato, the censor, had been one of the judges, his client would have soon found himself on the stocks in the middle of the Forum, instead of receiving the sympathy of a virtuous and patriotic audience.

[The above was telegraphed as manager Stevens had prepared and caused it to be printed; but in the form it was read to the Senate, several parts were omitted, namely:—"The list of yeas and nays in questions which had come before that body;" and near the close, the paragraph commencing, "The gentleman speaks of the great purity of the President," &c., down to the words "Uniform of gray."]

Speech of Hon. Thomas Williams.

Mr. WILLIAMS (Pa.), another of the managers, followed Mr. Stevens in a speech, which he read from manuscript, as follows:—

Mr. President and Senators of the United States:—Not used to the conflict of the forum, I appear in your presence to-day in obedience to command of the Representatives of the American people, under a sense of responsibility which I have never felt before.

The august tribunal where judges are the elect of mighty provinces, the presence at your bar of the representatives of a domain that rival in extent the dominions of the Cæsars, and of a civilization that transcends any that the world has ever seen—to demand judgment on the high delinquent whom they have arraigned in name of the American people for high crimes and misdemeanors against the State, the dignity of the delinquent, himself a king, in everything but the pomp paraphenalia and inheritance of royalty, to these crowded galleries, and, more than all, that greater world outside, which stands on tip-toe, as it strains its ears to catch from the electric messenger the first tidings of a verdict which is either to send a thrill of joy throughout an afflicted land, or to rack it over with the throes of anarchy and the convulsions of despair—all remind me of the colossal proportions of the issue you are assembled to try.

I cannot but remember too, that the scene before me is without an example or a parallel in human history. Kings, it is true, have been uncrowned, and royal heads have fallen upon the scaffold, but in two instances only, as I think, have the formalities of law been involved to give a coloring of order and justice to the bloody tragedy. It is only in a free land that a constitutional tribunal has been charged for the first time with the sublime task of vindicating an outraged law against the highest of its ministers, and passing judgment upon the question whether the ruler of a Union shall be strapped under the law and without shock or violence of the power which he has abused.

This great occasion was not sought by us. The world bear the representatives of the people witness that they did not come here for light and transient causes, but for the reason only that the issue has been forced upon them by a long series of bold assumptions of power on the part of the Executive, following each other with almost the blazing and blinding continuity of the lightning of the tropics, and culminating at last in mortal charge which, in the defense of their constitutional power as a branch of the American Congress, and as faithful sentinels over the liberties of the people, it was impossible for them to decline. With the open defiance of the legislative will they were left, of course, with no alternative but to abdicate, or rule and vindicate the right to make law and see that it was obeyed.

This imperious necessity the people, in whose name they speak, a branch of that race whose quick sensibility to public danger has ever kept a sleeping vigil over its liberties, have yielded at last with a reluctance which nothing but the weariness of civil strife, the natural longing for repose, the apprehensive sense that it is better, perhaps, "to bear the ills we have than fly to others that we know not of." The reflection that the administration must have an end, and above all, perhaps, the delusive hope that its law-defying head himself would ultimately submit to a necessity which was as strong as fate could have brought about or would have, perhaps, exercised. He has misunderstood their reason, as his counsel show they do now mistake their temper and presume upon their forbearance. He has forgotten that there was a point at which the conflict must end in the shock of two opposing forces and the overthrow of one or other of the antagonistic elements.

It was necessary, perhaps, in the order of Providence, that he should reach that point by striking such a blow at the public liberties as should awaken the people as with an earthquake shock to the consciousness that the toleration of usurping crime brings no security to nations. To show, however, how much they have borne and forborne, perhaps forgiven for the sake of peace, and how much they now pass over for the sake of a speedy solution of the impending trouble, which has impeded the onward and upward movement of this great government, and spread confusion and disorder throughout many of its departments, and what, moreover, is the true import and signification of the acts for which the President is now arraigned, I must be allowed, with your indulgence, to take for a moment the key which is required to unlock the mysteries of the position. The man who supposed that there is but a question of removal of an obnoxious officer, a mere private quarrel between two beligerents at either end of the avenue, wherein it is no great national consequence which of two opposing parties shall prevail, has no adequate apprehension of the gravity of the case, and greatly disparages the position and the motives of the high accusers. The House of Representatives espouses no man's quarrel, however considerable he may be. It has but singled out, from many others of equal weight, the facts here charged as facts both in the past, and recent occurrences, of great notoriety. The issue here is between two mightier antagonists, one the Chief Executive Magistrate of this nation, and the other the people of the United States, for whom the Secretary of War now holds almost the only strong position of which they have not been dispossessed.

It is but a renewal on American soil of the old battle between the royal prerogative and the privileges of the criminal, which was closed in England with the reign of the Stuarts—a struggle for the mastery between a temporary executive and the legislative power of a free State over the most momentous question that has ever challenged the attention of the people. The counsel for the President reflecting of course the views of their employer, would have you believe that the removal of a departmental head is an affair of State too small to be worthy of such an avenger as this. We propose standing alone, stripped o all the attendant circumstances that explain the act, and show the deadly *animus* by which it is inspired.

It is not improbable that there are some who might have been induced to think with them, that a remedy so extreme as this was more than adequate. It is only under the light upon the particular issue by antecedent facts which have passed into history that the giant proportions of this controversy can be fully seen, and they are not made sufficiently apparent now by the defiant tone of the President, and the formidable pretension set up by him in his thoughtfully considered and painfully elaborate plea.

The not irrelevant question, "Who is Andrew Johnson?" has been asked by one of his counsel, as it has often been by himself, and answered in the same way by himself by showing who he was and what he had done, before the people of the loyal States so generously intrusted him with that contingent power, which was made absolute only for the advantage of defeated and discomfitted treason by the murderous pistol of an assassin.

I will not stop now to inquire as to scenes enacted on this floor, and eloquently rehearsed by the counsel for the President, with two pictures of so opposite a character before me, or even to inquire whether his resistance to the hegira of the Southern Senators was not merely a question, himself being the witness as to the wisdom of such a step at that particular time.

The opportunity occurs just here to answer it as it is put, by showing who Andrew Johnson is, and what he has been since the hour of that improvident and unreflecting gift, *eheu quantum mutatus abille.* Alas! How changed! how fallen from that high estate that won for him the support of a too confiding people. Would that it could have been said of him, as of Lucifer, whose spirit was hurled in hideous ruin and combustion down from heaven's crystal battlements, that even in his fall he had not yet lost all his original brightness, nor appeared less than an archangel ruined.

The master key to the whole history of his administration, which has involved not a mere harmless difference of opinion, as one of his counsel seems to think, where gentlemen might afford to disagree without a quarrel, but one long and unseemly struggle by the executive against the legislative power, is to be found in the fact of an early and persistent purpose of forcing the Rebel States into the Union by means of his executive authority, in the interest of the men who had lifted their parricidal hand against it on terms dictated by himself, and in defiance of the will of the loyal people of the United States, as declared through their representatives.

To accomplish this object how much has he not done and how much has a long-suffering people not passed over, without punishment and almost without rebuke. Let history—let your public records, which are the only authentic materials of history—answer, and they will say that, for this, instead of convening the Congress in the most momentous crisis of the State, he has issued his royal proclamation for the assembling of conventions and the erection of State governments, prescribing the qualification of the voters and settling the conditions of their admission into the Union. For this, he had created offices unknown to the law, and filled them with men notoriously disqualified by law, at salaries fixed by his own mere will. For this he had paid these officers in contemptuous disregard of law, and paid them, too, out of the contingent fund of the departments of the government. For this he had supplied the expenses of his new governments by turning over to them the spoils of the dead Confederacy, and authorizing his satraps to levy taxes from the conquered people.

For this, he had passed away unnumbered millions of the public property to Rebel railroad companies without consideration, or sold it to them, in clear violation of law, on long credits, at a valuation of his own, and without any surety whatever. For this, he had stripped the Bureau of Freedmen and Refugees of its munificent endowment, by taking from it the land appropriated by Congress to the legal wards of the republic, and restoring to the Rebels their justly-forfeited estates, after the same had been vested by law in the Government of the United States. For this he had invaded, with a ruthless hand, the very penetralia of the Treasury, and plundered its sentinels for the benefit of favored Rebels, by ordering the restoration of the proceeds of sales of captured and abandoned property, which had been placed in its custody by law. For this, he had grossly abused the pardoning power conferred on him by the Constitution, in releasing the most active and formidable of the leaders of the Rebellion, with a view to their service in the furtherance of his policy, and even delegated that power for the same objects to men who were indebted to its exercise for their own escape from punishment.

For this, he had obstructed the course of public justice not only by refusing to enforce the laws enacted for the suppression of the rebellion and the punishment of treason, but by going into the courts and turning the greatest of the public malefactors loose, and surrendering all control over them by the restoration to them of their estates. For this, he had abused the appointing power by the removal on system of meritorious public officers for no other reason than because they would not assist him in his attempt to overthrow the Constitution and usurp the legislative power of the government. For this, he had invaded the rightful privileges of the Senate by refusing to send in nominations of officers appointed by him during the recess of that body, and, after their adjournment, reappointing others who had been rejected by them as unfit for the places for which they had been recommended.

For this, he had broken the privileges of and insulted the Congress of the United States, by instructing them that the work of reconstruction belonged to him only, and that they had no legislative right or duty in the premises, but only to register his will by throwing open their doors to such claimants as might come there with commissions from their pretended governments, that were substantially his own. For this, on their refusal to obey his imperial rescript, he had arraigned them publicly as a revolutionary assembly, and not a legal Congress, without the power to legislate for the States excluded, and as traitors at the other end of the line in actual rebellion against the people they had subdued. For this, he had grossly abused the veto power, by disapproving every important measure of legislation that concerned the Rebel States, in concordance with public declaration that he would veto all the measures of the law-making power whenever they came to him. For this, he had deliberately and confessedly exercised a dispensing power over the Test Oath law by appointing notorious Rebels to important places in the Revenue service, on the avowed ground that the policy of Congress in that regard was not in accordance with his opinions.

For this, he had obstructed the settlement of the nation by exerting all his influence to prevent the people of the Rebel States from accepting the Constitutional Amendment, or organizing under laws of Congress, and impressing them that Congress was blood-thirsty and implacable, and that their only refuge was with him. For this, he had brought the patronage of his office into conflict with the freedom of elections by allowing and encouraging his official retainers to travel over the country attending political conventions and addressing the people in support of his policy. For this, if he did not enact the part of a Cromwell, by striding into the halls of representatives of the people and saying to one man: "you are a hypocrite;" to another, "you are a whoremonger;" to a third, "you are an adulterer;" and to the whole, "you are no longer a parliament," he had rehearsed the same part substantially outside by traveling over the country and in indecent harangues, assailing the conduct and impeaching the motives of its Congress, inculcating disobedience to its authority by endeavoring to bring it into disrepute; declaring publicly of one of its members that he was a traitor; and of another that he was an assassin; and of the whole that they were no longer a Congress. For this, in addition to the oppression and bloodshed that had resulted from known partiality for traitors, he had pointed at efforts encouraging the murder of loyal citizens in New Orleans by a mob, by holding correspondence with its leaders; denouncing the exercise of the right of a political convention to assemble peacefully in that city as an act of treason to be suppressed by violence, and commanding the military to assist, instead of preventing the execution of the avowed purpose of disturbing them.

For this it is not too much to say, in view of the wrong and outrage, and the cry of suffering that has come up to us upon the Southern breeze, that he had in effect reopened the war, inaugurated anarchy, turned loose once more the incarnate devil of baffled treason and unappeaseable hate, when, as we fondly thought, our victories had overthrown and bound in chains, ordained rapine and murder from the Potomac to the Gulf, and deluged the streets of Memphis as well as those of New Orleans, and the green fields of the South already dotted with so many patriot graves, with the blood of martyred citizens; and because for all he has not been called to render an account, for the reasons that have been already named, it is now assumed and argued by his counsel that he stands acquitted by a judgment which disaffirmed its truth, although it rests for the most part on record evidence, in fact, that absolute verity which is, of course, not open to dispute,

The assumption is but another instance of that incorrigible blindness on the part of the President in regard to the feelings and motives of Congress that has helped to hurry him into his present humiliating predicament as a criminal at your bar. But all these things were not enough. It wanted one drop more to make a cup of forbearance overflow, one other act that should reach the sensorium of the nation, and make even those who might be slow to comprehend a principle, understand that further forbearance was ruin to us all, and that act was done in the attempt to seize by force or stratagem, that department of the government through which its armies were controlled. It was but a logical sequence of what had gone before the last of a series of usurpations, all looking to the same great purpose. It did not rise, perhaps, beyond the height of many of the crimes by which it was ushered in.

But its meanings could not be mistaken. It was an act that smote upon the ear of the nation in such a way as to render it impossible that it could be either concealed, disparaged or excused, as were the muffled blows of the pick-axe that had been silently undermining the bastions of the Republic. It has been heard and felt through all our wide domain like the reverbation of the guns that opened their iron throats upon our flag at Sumter, and it has stirred the loyal heart of the people again with the electric power that lifted it to the heighth of the sublimest issue that ever led a martyr to the stake or a patriot to the battle-field. That people is here to-day, through its representatives, on your floor, and in your galleries, in the persons alike of the veterans who have been scarred by the iron hail of battle, and of the mothers and wives and daughters of those who have died that the Republic might live, as well as of the commissioned exponents of the public will, to demand the reward of their toils, the consummation of their triumph—the award of a nation's justice upon the high offender.

And now as to the immediate issue which I propose to discuss only in its constitutional and legal aspect: The great crime of Andrew Johnson, as already remarked, running through all his administration, is that he has violated his oath of office and his constitutional duties, by obstruction and infraction of the Constution and the laws, and an endeavor to set up his own will against that of the law-making power with a view to a settled and persistent purpose of forcing the Rebel States into Congress on his own terms, in the interest of the traitors, and in defiance of the will of the loyal people of the United States. The specific offenses charged here, which are but the culminating facts, and only the last of a long series of usurpations, are of an unlawful attempt to remove the rightful Secretary of War, and substitute in his place a creature of his own, without the advice and consent of the Senate, although then in session; a conspiracy to hinder and prevent him from resuming or holding the said office after the refusal of the Senate to concur in his suspension; and to seize, take and possess the property of the United States in said department; an attempt to debauch an officer of the army from his allegiance, by inculcating insubordination to the law in furtherance of the same object; the attempt to set aside the rightful authority of Congress, and to bring it into public odium and contempt, and to encourage resistance to its laws by the open and public delivery of indecent harangues, impeaching its acts and purposes, and full of threats and menaces against it and and the laws enacted by it, to the great scandal and degradation of his own high office as President, and the devising and contriving of unlawful means to prevent the execution of the Tenure of Office, Army appropriation and Reconstruction acts of March 2, 1867. To allow these which relates to the attempted removal of the Secretary of War, the answer is:—

First, that the case of Mr. Stanton is not within the meaning of the first section of the Tenure of Office act; second, that if it be, the act is unconstitutional and void, so far as it undertakes to abridge the power claimed by him of removing, at any and all times, all executive officers, for causes to be judged of by himself alone, as well as of suspending them indefinitely, at his sovereign will and pleasure; and third, that whether the act be constitutional or otherwise, it was his right, as he claims it to have been his purpose, to disobey and violate it, with a view to the settlement of the question of its validity by the judiciary of the United States.

And first, as to the question whether the present Secretary of War was intended to be comprehended within the first section of the act referred to. The defendant insists that he was not, for the reason that he derived his commission from Mr. Lincoln, and not being removed on his accession, continued, by reason thereof, to hold the office and administer its duties at his pleasure only, without at any time having received any appointment from himself, assuming, as I understand, either that under the proviso to the first section of this act the case was not provided for, or that by force of its express language his office was determined by the expiration of the first term of the President who appointed him. The body or enacting clause of this section provides that every person then holding any civil office who had been appointed thereto by and with the advice and consent of the Senate, or who should be thereafter appointed to any such office, should be entitled to hold until a successor is appointed in the like manner.

It is therefore that its general object was to provide for all cases either then existing or to happen in the future. It is objected, however, that so much of the clause as referred to the heads of departments is substantially repealed by the saving clause, which is in the following words:— "*Provided*, That the Secretaries of State, of the Treasury, of War, of the Navy, and of the Interior, the Postmaster-General and the Attorney-General, shall hold their offices respectively for and during the term of the President by whom they may have been appointed, and for one month thereafter, subject to removal by and with the advice and consent of the Senate." This proviso was the result of a conference on the disagreeing votes on the amendment of the House, striking the exception in favor of the heads of departments, and was suggested, if he may be excused the egotism, by the individual who now addresses you and to whom, as the mover and advocate of the amendment, was very naturally assigned the duty of conducting the negotiation on the part of the House for the purpose of obviating the objection, taken in debate on this floor by one of the Senate managers, that the effect of the amendment would be to impose on an incoming President a Cabinet that was not of his own selection. I may be excused for speaking of its actual history, because that has been made the subject of comment by the learned counsel who opened this case on the part of the President. If it was intended or expected that it should so operate as to create exceptions in favor of an officer whose abuse of power was the proximate cause, if not the impeling motive for the enactment of the law, I did not know it. It will be judged, however, by itself, without reference either to the particular intent of him who penned it, or to any hasty opinion that may have been expressed in either house as to the construction of which it might be susceptible. The argument of the defendant rests upon the meaning of the word "appointed."

That word was both a technical and a popular one. In the former, which involves the idea of a nomination and confirmation in the constitutional way, there was no appointment, certainly, by Mr. Johnson. In the latter, which is the sense in which the people will read it, there unquestionably was. What then was meant by the employment of the word? It is a sound and well-accepted rule in all the courts, in exploring the meaning of the law given, especially in cases of remedial statutes, as I think this is, if it is not rather to be considered as only a declaratory one in this particular, to look to the old law for the mischief and the remedy, and to give a liberal construction to the language *in favorem libertatis*, in order to repress the mischief and advance the remedy, taking the words used in their ordinary and familiar sense, and varying the meaning as the intent, which is always the Polar star, may require.

Testing the case here by this, what is to be the construction here? The old law was not the Constitution, but a vicious practice that had gone out of a precedent involving an early and erroneous construction of that instrument, if it was intended so to operate. The mischief was, this practice had rendered the officers of the government, and among them the heads of departments, the most powerful and dangerous of all, from their assumed position of advisers of the President; by the very dependency of their tenure they were ministers of his pleasure and the slaves of his imperial will, that could at any moment, and as the reward of an honest and independent opinion, strip them of their employments and send them back into ranks of the people. The remedy would change them from minions and flatterers into men, by making them free, and to secure their loyalty to the law by protecting them from the power that might constrain their assent to its violation. To accomplish this it was necessary that the law should cover all of them, high and low, present and prospective.

That it could have been intended to except the most important and formidable of these functionaries either with a view to favor the present executive or for the purpose of subjecting the only head of department who had the confidence of Congress to his arbitrary will, is as unreasonable and improbable as it is at variance with the truth and with the obvious general purposes of the act. For the President of the United States to say, however, now, after having voluntarily retained Mr. Stanton for more than two years of his administration, that he was there only by sufferance, or as a mere movable, or heir-loom, or incumbrance that had passed to him with the estate, and not by virtue of his own special appointment, of not paltering with the people in a double sense, has very much the appearance of a not very respectable quibble.

The unlearned man who reads the proviso, as they for whose perusal it is intended, will read it, who is not accustomed to hand the metaphisic scissors of the professional casuists who are able "to divide a hair 'twixt west and northwest side," while he admits the ingenuity of the advocate will stand amazed if he does not scorn the officer who would stoop to the use of such a subterfuge. Assuming, however, for the sake of argument, that the technical sense is to prevent what is to be its effect. Why, only to make the law given enact a more unreasonable and impossible thing, by providing in words of the future sense, that the commission of the officer shall expire nearly two years before the passage of the law, which is a construction that the general rule of law forbids to test, let us substitute for the general denominative phrases of Secretary of War, of State, and of the Navy, the names of Messrs. Seward, Stanton, and Welles, and for that of the President who appointed them the name of Lincoln, and the clause will read, provided that Seward, Stanton, and Welles shall hold their offices respectively for and during the term of Abraham Lincoln and for one month thereafter. The effect will then be to put you in the position of having enacted, not only an absurdity, but an impossibility. But on this there are at least two rules of interpretation that start up in the way of solution. The first is, that it is not respectful to the Legislature to presume that it ever intended to enact an absurdity, if the case is susceptible of any other construction; and the second, that acts of Parliament that are impossible to be performed, are of no validity, and if there arise out of them collaterally any absurd consequences, manifestly contradictory to common reason, they are, with regard to these collateral consequences, void.

If the effect of the proviso, however, upon something analogous to the doctrine of *cypres*, or, in other words, of getting as near to the meaning as possible, was to determine the office at the time of the passage of the law, then, on the other hand, the retention of the officer by the President for five months afterwards, and through an intervening Congress, without a commission, or even a nomination, was a breach of the law, and therefore a misdemeanor in itself, which he could hardly plead, and could scarcely ask you to affirm against the general presumption of the performance of official duty, for the purpose of sheltering him from the consequences of another violation of law.

Assuming again, however, that, as is claimed by the defense, the case of Mr. Stanton does not fall within the proviso, what then is the result? Is it the predicament of a *casus omissus* altogether? Is he to be hung up, like Mahomet's coffin, between the body of the act and the proviso, the latter nullifying the former on pretext of an exception either repudiating the exception itself as to the particular case, or in the obvious and indisputable purpose of providing for all cases, whatever is to be carried out, by falling back on the general enacting clause, which would make him irremovable by the precedent alone, and leaving him outside of the provision as to tenure, which was the sole object of the exception?

There is nothing in the saving clause which is at all inconsistent with what goes before. The provision that takes every officer out of the power of the President, is not departed from it in that clause; all it enacts is, that the tenure shall be a determinate one in cases that fall within it. If Mr. Stanton was appointed by President Johnson, within the meaning of the proviso, he holds, of course, until the expiration of his term. If not, he holds subject to removal, like other officers under the enacting clause. It has been so often asserted publicly, as to have become a generally accredited truth, that the special purpose of the act was to protect him. I do not affirm this, and do not consider it necessary to say that I should—or important to the case whether he favored the passage of the law or not.

It will be hardly pretended, however, by anybody, that he was intended to be excluded entirely from its operation. Nor is the case helped by reference to the fourth section of the act, which provides that "nothing herein contained shall be construed to extend the term of any office, the duration of which is limited by law." The office in question was one of those which the tenure was indefinite. The construction insisted upon by me does not extend it. The only effect is to take away the power of removal from the President alone, and restore it to the parties by whom the Constitution intended that it should be exercised. Assuming then that the case of Mr. Stanton is within the law, the next question is as to the validity of the law itself.

And here we are met, for the first time in our history as a nation, by the assertion, on the part of the President, of the illimitable and uncontrollable power under the Constitution, in accordance, as he insists, with the judicial opinion, the professional sentiment and the settled practice under the government, of removing, at any and all times, all executive officers whatever, without responsibility to anybody, and as included therein the equally uncontrollable power of suspending them indefinitely, and supplying their places, from time to time, by appointments made by himself *ad interim*. If there be any case where the claim has heretofore extended, even in theory, beyond the mere power to create a vacancy by removal, during the recess of the Senate, I do not know it. If there be any wherein the power to suspend indefinitely, which goes even beyond what has been asserted, it is equally new to me.

This truly regal pretension has been fitly reserved for the first President who has ever claimed the imperial prerogative of founding governments by proclamation, of taxing without a Congress, of disposing of the public property by millions at his own will, and of exercising dispensing power over the laws. It is but a logical sequence of what he has already been permitted to do without absolute impunity and almost without complaint. If he could be tolerated thus far, why not consummate the work which was to render him supreme, and crown his victory over the legislative power by setting this body aside as an advisory council, and claiming himself to be the rightful interpreter of the laws?

The defense made here is a defiance, a challenge to the Senate and the nation that must be met and answered just now in such a way as shall determine which, if any, is to be the master. If the claim asserted is to be maintained by your decision, all that will remain for you will be only the formal abdication of your high trust as a part of the appointing power, because there will be then absolutely nothing left of it worth preserving.

But let us see what there is in the Constitution to warrant these extravagant pretensions, or to prevent the passage of a law to restore the practice of this government to the true theory of that instrument.

I do not propose to weary you with a protracted examination of this question. I could not add to what I have already said on the same subject, on the discussion in the House of the bill relating to removals from office. In December, 1866, to which I would have ventured to invite your attention if the same point had not been so fully elaborated here. You have already passed upon it in the enactment of the present law by a vote so decisive and overwhelming, and there is so little objection on the part of the counsel for the President by the validity of the law, that I may content myself with condensing the arguments on both sides into a few general propositions, which will comprehend their capital features.

The case may be stated, as I think, analytically and synoptically thus:—The first great fact to be observed is that, while the Constitution enumerates sundry offices, and provides the manner of appointment in those cases as well as in all others to be created by law, it prescribes no tenure except that of good behavior in the case of the judge, and is entirely silent on the subject of removal by any other process than that of impeachment.

From this the inferences are:—

First. That the tenure of good behavior being substantially equivalent to that for life, the office must, in all other cases be determinable at the will of some department of the government, unless limited by law, which is, however, but another name for the will of the law-maker himself, and this is settled by authority.

Second. That the power of removal at will being an implied one only is to be conferred to those cases where the tenure is not ascertained by law, the right of removal in any other form than by the process of impeachment depending entirely on the hypothesis of a will, of which the essential condition always is that it is free to act without responsibility.

Third. That the power of removal being implied as a necessity of State, to secure the dependence of the officer on the government is not to be extended by construction so as to take him out of the control of the Legislature, and make him dependent on the will of the Executive.

The next point is, that the President is, by the terms of the Constitution, to nominate, and by and with the advice and consent of the Senate "appoint" to all offices, and that without the concurrence he appoints to none, except when authorized by Congress; and this may be described as the rule of the Constitution. The exceptions are:—First, That in the cases of inferior officers, Congress may lodge this power with the President alone, or with the courts, or the heads of departments; and, Second, That in cases of vacancy happening during the recess of the Senate, he may

not appoint, but *fill* them up by granting commissions to expire at the end of the next session of that body, from which it appears:

First. That the President cannot, as already stated, in any case appoint alone, without the express authority of Congress, and then only in the case of *inferior* officers.

Second. That the power to supply even an accidental vacancy was only to continue until the Senate was in a condition to be consulted, and to advise and act upon the case; and

Third. As a *corollary* from these two propositions, that if the power to remove in cases where the tenure is indefinite, be as it is solemnly conceded by the Supreme Court of the United States—*In re Henan*, 13 Pet.—an incident to the power to appoint, it belongs to the President and Senate, and not to the President alone. As it was held in that case to be in the judge who made the appointment, the argument upon which this implied a merely infantile power, not of *filling up*, but of *making* a vacancy during the recess, which is now claimed to extend to the making of a vacancy at any time, has been defended, is,

First. The possible necessity for the exercise of such a power during the *recess* of the Senate, or, in other words, the argument *ab inconveniency*.

Second. That the power of removal is a purely executive function, which, passed by the general grant in the first section of the second article of the Constitution, would have carried the power to appoint if unprovided for, and is to be considered in him in all cases wherein it has not been expressly denied, or lodged in other hands; while the association of the Senate, the same not being an executive body, is an exception to the general principle, and seems to be taken strictly, so as not to extend thereto.

Third. That it is essential to the President, as the responsible head of the government, charged by his oath with the execution of the same, that he should control his own subordinates by making their tenure of office to depend upon his will, so as to make a unit of the Administration.

The answer to the first of these propositions is that there is no necessity for the exercise of the power during the recess, because the case supposed may be provided for by Congress, as it has been by the act now in question, under the express constitutional authority, to make all laws which shall be necessary or proper for carrying into execution all the powers vested in the government, or any department thereof. A power which, by the way, is very strongly claimed by one of the President's counsel to be *an implied one*.

To the second the answer is, that whether an executive power or not depends on the structure of the government, or, in other words, on what the Constitution makes it, that the clause in question is but a disturbance. That if all executive power is in the President, then by partly of reason all legislative power is in Congress without reference to the Constitution; that the Senate is not only associated with the President in the general appointing power, but that the power itself may be withdrawn by Congress almost entirely from both, under the provision in regard to inferior officers, which would involve a repugnancy to the general grant relied on, if the power be an executive one; that if the provision had been made for appointments in the Constitution the power to supply the omission would have resulted to the lawmaker under the authority just quoted to make all laws that might be necessary or proper for carrying into execution all power vested in the government or any department thereof, which carries with it the power to create all offices, and that moreover the power of removal in the only case wherein it is referred to, is made a *judicial* one.

To the third the answer is:—First, That however natural it may be for the President, after an unchecked career of usurpation for three long years, during which he has used his subordinates generally as the slavish ministers of his will, and dealt with the affairs of this nation as if he had been its master, also as well as their's, he greatly mistakes and magnifies his office, as has been already shown in the fact that, under the Constitution, he may be stripped at any time by Congress of nearly the whole of the appointing power; and second, that the responsibility of the President is to be graduated by, and can be only commensurate with the power that is assigned to him, that the obligation imposed on him is to take care that the *laws* are faithfully executed, and not his *will*, which is so strangely assumed to be the only law of the exalted functionaries who surround him, and that it is not only *not* essential to the performance of this duty, under the law that heads of departments should be the mere passive instruments of his will, but the very contrary. Upon this brief statement of the argument, it would seem as if there could be no reasonable doubt as to the meaning of the Constitution. But the high delinquent who is now on trial, feeling that he cannot safely rest his case here, and springing from the inexorable logic that rules against him, takes refuge in the past, and claims to have found a new Constitution that suits him better than the old one in the judicial authorities, in the opinion of the commentators, in the English professional and public sentiment of the nation, and in a legislative practice and construction that are coeval with the government, and have continued, without interruption, until the present time.

A little inquiry, however, will show that there is no altar or sanctuary, and no city of refuge there to shelter the greatest of the nation's malefactors from the just vengeance of a betrayed and indignant people. And first, as to judicial authority. There are but three cases, I think, wherein these questions have come up for adjudication before the Supreme Court of the United States, and in all of them the decisions have been directly in conflict with the theory and pretensions of the President. The first was the familiar one of Marbury vs. Madison (1st Cranch, 256), made doubly memorable from the fact that it arose out of one of the so-called midnight appointments made by the elder Adams—the same, by the way, whose casting vote as an executive officer turned the scale in favor of the power to which he was destined to succeed—in the First Congress of 1789, on the eve of his retirement, under a law which had been approved only the day before, authorizing the appointment of five justices of the peace for the District of Columbia, to serve respectively for the term of five years. The commission in question had been duly signed and registered, but was withheld by his successor, Jefferson, on the ground that the act was incomplete without a delivery. It was not claimed by him that the appointment was revocable if once consummated. If it had been revocable, resistance would have been unnecessary, and the assertion of the right of the office an idle one.

Chief Justice Marshall, in delivering the opinion of the court, holds this language:—"When an officer is removable at the will of the Executive, the circumstances which compelled his appointment is of no consequence, because the act is at any time revokable; but when the officer is not removable at the will of the Executive, the appointment is not revokable and cannot be annulled. Having once made the appointment, his power over the office is terminated in all cases when by the law the office is not removable by him.

Then, as the law creating the office gave the right to hold for five years, independent of the Executive, the appointment was not revocable, but rested in the officer. The point ruled here is precisely the same as that involved in the Tenure of Office act, to-wit:—That Congress may define the tenure of any office it creates, and that once fixed by law, it is no longer determinable at the will of anybody, the act being a mere substitution of the will of the nation for that of the Executive, by giving to that will the form of law which is indeed the only form that is consistently admissible in a government of law.

The present Executive insists, as Jefferson did not, that he has power under the Constitution to remove or suspend, at any and all times, any executive officer whatever, for causes to be judged of by himself alone, and that, in the opinion of his advisers, this power cannot be lawfully restrained, which is, in effect, to claim the power to appoint without the advice and consent of the Senate, as he has just now done, as well as to remove.

The next case in order is that ex parte Henan, reported in 13 Peters, which involved a question as to the right of the Judge of the District Court of Louisiana to remove, at his discretion, a clerk appointed by him indefinitely. Under the law the court said (then Thompson, Justice, delivering the opinion) that all offices, the tenure of which is not fixed by the Constitution or limited by law, must be held either during good behavior or at the will and discretion of some department of the government, and subject to removal at pleasure. And again, that, in the absence of all constitutional provisions or statutory regulations, it would seem to be a sound and necessary rule to consider the power of removal as an incident to the power to appoint. They add, however:—But it was very early adopted as the practical construction that the power was vested in the President alone, and that such would appear to have been the legislative construction, because, in establishing the three principal Departments of State, War, and Treasury, they recognized the power of removal in the President, although by the act of 1798 establishing the Navy Department, the reference was not by name to him.

The result was that upon the principles thus enunciated, involving the exception as to cases where the tenure was limited by law, as laid down in Marbury vs. Madison, they declared the power of removal to have been well exercised by the judge who made the appointment under the law, for the reason only that it was an incident thereto. It is well worthy of remark, however, in this connection, that, although what is thus gratuitously said as to the rule there recognized, it does not conflict in any way with the doctrine of Marbury vs. Madison. It is entirely at variance, as seems to be confessed with the decision itself, which, on the doctrine of Mr. Madison, in the debate of 1789, that the power of removal was a strictly executive one, and passed by the general grant of the Constitution, unless expressly denied, or elsewhere lodged, must have been inevitably the other way, because in that case it must have resulted not to the judge, but to the President, whether a mere permissive *sub silentio* exercise of a power like this, or even a temporary surrender on grounds of personal confidence or party favor, where it perhaps violated constitutional interest, and was in point of fact authorized as to all. But that superior officers can raise a proscription against a constitutional right, or how many laws it will require to abrogate the fundamental law, I will not stop now to inquire. It is sufficient for my purpose that the case decides that the power of removal is but an incident to the power of appointment, and that, of course, it can only be exercised by the same agencies as the Tenure of Office act exactly provides.

The next and last case is that of the United States vs. Guthrie, reported in 17 Howard, 284, which was an application for a mandamus to the Secretary of the Treasury to compel him to pay the salary of a territorial judge in Minnesota who had been removed by the President before the expiration of his term, which was fixed by law at four years. The case was dismissed upon the doctrine that the proceeding was not a proper one to try the title to an office, and thereupon the question of the power to remove was not disposed of or discussed, except by Justice McLean, who dissented on the main point and felt called upon, of course, to pass upon the other.

Here Mr. Williams read extracts from Judge McLean's opinion, and continued:—It will be said, perhaps, that all this is qualified by the remark that "this power of removal has been, perhaps, too long established and exercised to be now questioned." It is enough, however, to refer to the observation which follows that:—"The voluntary action of the Senate and the President would be necessary to change the practice." To show what was meant by him, such events as our eyes have witnessed, and such a conjuncture of affairs following fast upon their heels as would leave the Executive with all his formidable patronage and all the prestige of his place, without even the meagre support of a third in either House, were scarcely within the range of human probability when he remarks therefore that it was, perhaps, too late to question it.

He means, of course, to question it successfully, as the contest shows; if he had meant otherwise he would not have referred voluntarily to a change of practice as operating a corresponding change of the Constitution. He was too good a lawyer and too sage a statesman to affirm that the fundamental law of a great State could be wrested from its true construction either by the errors of the Legislature or the toleration of a mischievous practice and monster vice for less than eighty years. It is apparent, then, from all the cases, that the judicial opinion, so far from sustaining the views of the President, settles at least two points which are fatal to his pretensions:—First, that Congress may so limit the tenure of an office as to render the incumbent irremvoable, except by the process of impeachment; and second, that the power to remove, so far as it exists, is but an incident to power to appoint; nor is it any answer to say, as has been claimed in debate on this floor, that there were cases of inferior offices where, under the Constitution it was within the power of Congress to regulate them at its discretion. There is nothing in the provision as to inferior officers to distinguish them from others beyond the mere article of appointment. This is a question of tenure, and that is equally undefined as to both, except in the few cases specially enumerated therein. It was equally within the power of Congress to regulate in one case as in the other. The right to regulate is a necessary result of the right to create. When it establishes an office as it has established the department bureaus, by law, it has of necessity the right to prescribe its duties, and say how long it shall be held and when it shall determine. When it does say so, it can hardly be maintained, with any show of reason, that a power which is only implied from the fact that the tenure of office has been left indefinite in the Constitution, which has vested the establishment of offices in Congress, shall be held to operate to defeat its will and shorten the life of its own creature in cases were its legislation is express. And so, too, as to the doctrine that the power of removal is but an incident to the power to appoint. That is settled upon grounds of reason as a general principle, which has no more application to inferior officers than to superior ones. The idea is that the power of removal, whenever it exists, is, in the very nature of things, but part and parcel of the power to appoint, and that, as a consequence, the power that makes, and none other must unmake; and on this idea was ruled, in the particular case, that the power to remove was in the judge, because the authority to appoint was there. It equally rules, however, that where the appointment is in the head of a department the power of removal belongs to him; that where it is lodged by Congress in the President alone, it is him only; and where it is in the President and Senate conjointly, then it is in both which is precisely the doctrine maintained by the majority in Congress of 1789. It ought to be a sufficient answer, however, that no such distinction was taken by Justice Thompson in the Heenan case, although he referred to the departure from this rule in the practical construction which had assigned the power to the President at once.

The judicial opinions having thus signally failed to support the dangerous heresies of the President, the next resort is to that of the statements of lawyers and publicists who have from time to time illustrated our history; and here, too, it will be found that the great criminal who is at your bar, has not better support than he has found in higher quarters, I am not here to question the doctrine which has been so strongly urged upon the authority of Lord Coke. That cotemporaneous exposition is entitled to great weight in law. Taking it to be sound, however, it will hardly be pretended, I suppose, that there is anything of this description which will compare in value with the authoritative, I might also say, oracular utterance of the *Federalist*, which was the main agent, under Providence, in securing for the constitution the support of the people of the several States, and has since occupied the rank of a classic in the political literature of America. And yet, in the seventy-seventh number of that series, which is ascribed to the pen of Alexander Hamilton himself, perhaps the first among his peers in the convention which framed that instrument, it is assumed as an unquestionable proposition, and that, too, in the way of answer to the objection of instability arising from frequent changes of administration, that, inasmuch as the Senate was to participate in the business of appointment, its consent should therefore be necessary to displace as well as to appoint.

Nor was it considered even necessary to reason out a conclusion that is so obvious and inevitable. It does not seem to have been supposed by anybody that a power, so eminently social could ever be raised in the execution of a limited government out of the mere fact of the silence of the Constitution on that subject, and the failure to provide any other mode of removal than by the process of impeachment. If the conclusion, however, was not a sound one, then it was no better than a false pretense which these at least concur at present were morally estopped — estopped from controverting — and yet it is to one of the distinguished authors of these papers in his quality of a legislator that the nation is mainly indebted for the vote which inaugurated and fashioned so long upon it a mischievous and anti-republican principle.

It does not seem, however, to have affected any change in the opinion of the distinguished author, and we find him insisting in a letter written ten years afterwards, to James McHenry, then Secretary of War, that then the power to fill vacancies, happening during recess of the Senate, is to be confined to such offices as having been once filled, have become vacant by accidental circumstances. From the time of the settlement of the policy of the government on this subject by its first Congress down to the accession of the younger Adams, in 1826, a period of nearly forty years, the question does not seem to have been much agitated, for the very satisfactory reason, that the patronage was so circumscribed, and the cases of abuse so rare, as to attract no attention on the part of public men.

In the last named year, however, a committee was raised by the Senate, headed by Mr. Benton, and composed of some of the most eminent statesmen of that day, to consider the subject of restraining the power by legislation. That committee agreed in the opinion that the practice of dismissing from office was a dangerous violation of the Constitution, which had, in their view, been " changed in this regard," very constructive legislation, which was only another name for legislative construction, and reported sundry bills for its correction, not unlike, in some respects, to the present law.

These bills failed, of course, but with the public recognition of the new and alarming doctrine which followed the accession of the next Administration, that the public offices, like the plunder of a camp, were the legitimate spoils of the victorious party. The subject was revived in 1835 by the appointment of another committee, embracing the great names of Calhoun, Webster and Seaton, for the same subject. The result of their labor was the introduction of a bill requiring the President, in all cases of removal, to state the reason thereof, which passed the Senate by a vote of 31 to 16, or nearly two-thirds of that body. In the course of the debate on that bill Mr. Webster, whose unsurpassed, and, as I think, unequaled ability as a constitutional lawyer, will be contested by nobody held this emphatic language:—

"After considering the question again and again, within the last six years, I am willing to say that, in my deliberate judgment the original decision was wrong. I cannot but think that those who denied the power in 1789 had the best of the argument. It appears to me, after thorough, and repeated, and conscientious examination, that an erroneous interpretation was given to the Constitution, in this respect, by the decision of the first Congress. And again, I have the clearest conviction that they, the Convention, looked to no other mode of displacing an officer than by impeachment, or the regular appointment of another person. And further, I believe it to be within the just power of Congress to revise the decision of 1789, and I mean to hold myself at liberty to act hereafter upon that question, as the safety of the government and of the Constitution may require.

Mr. Calhoun was equally emphatic in his condemnation of the power, and speaks of previous cases of removal as rather exceptionable than as constituting a practice. A like opinion was obviously entertained by Kent and Story, the two most distinguished of the commentators on the Constitution, and certainly among the highest authorities in the country. The former, after referring to the construction of 1789 as but "a loose, incidental and declaratory opinion of Congress," was constrained to speak of it as a striking fact in the constitutional history of our government, that a power so transcendant as that which places at the disposal of the President alone the tenure of every executive officer appointed, and that the Senate should depend on inference merely, and should have been gratuitously declared by the 1st Congress in opposition to the high authority of the *Federalist*, and supposed or acquiesced in by some of those distinguished men who questioned or denied the power of Congress to incorporate a national bank. (Kent Com., Sec. 14, pp. 308, 309.) The latter speaks of it with equal emphasis, as "constituting the most extraordinary case in the history of the government of a power conferred by implication in the Executive, by the assent of a bare majority of Congress, which has not been questioned on many other occasions." (2 Com., Sec. 15, 43.) The same opinion, too, is already shown upon the testimony of Judge McLean, as cited above, to have been shared by the old Supreme Court, with Marshall at its head.

It seems, indeed, as though there had been an unbroken current of sentiment from sources such as these through all our history against the exercise of this power. If there be any apparently exceptional cases of any, with but the equivocal one of Mr. Madison, they will be found to rest only, as I think, upon the legislation of 1789, and the long practice that is supposed to have followed it. I make no account, however, of the opinions of Attorneys-General, although I might have quoted that of Mr. Wirt, in 1818, to the effect that it was only where a Congress had not undertaken to fix the tenure of office that the commission could run during the pleasure of the President. They belong to the same class as that of Cabinet officers.

It may not be amiss, however, to add just here, that, although this question was elaborately argued by myself upon the introduction of the bill to regulate removals from office in the House of Representatives, which was substantially the same as the present law which was pending at that time, no voice but one was lifted up, in the course of a protracted debate, against the constitutionality of the measure itself. What, then, is there in the legislation of 1789, which is claimed to be not only a cotemporary but an authoritative exposition of the Constitution, and has no value whatever, except as an expression of an opinion as to the policy of making the heads of the departments dependent on the President, unless the acts of that small and inexperienced Congress are to be taken as of binding force upon their successors, and upon the courts as a sort of oracular outgiving upon the meaning of the Constitution.

Whatever may have been the material provisions of the several acts passed at that session for the establishment of these departments, it is not to be supposed that it was intended to accomplish a result so clearly not within the province of the law-maker as the binding settlement of the sense of that instrument on so grave a question. The effect of these acts has, I think, been greatly misunderstood by those who rely on them for such a purpose. All that they amount to is the concession to the President, in such a form as was agreeable to his friends of a power of removal, which the majority was disposed to accord to him in cases where the tenure of the officer was left indefinite, and the office was, therefore, determinable at will, but which these friends declined to accept as a grant, because they claimed it as a right.

The result was but a compromise, which evaded the issue by substituting an implied grant for an express one, and left the question in dispute just where it found it. The record shows, however, that even in this shape the bill finally passed the House by a vote of only 29 to 22. In the Senate, however, where the debate does not appear, it was carried only by the casting vote of the Vice President, not properly himself a legislative but an executive officer, who had a very direct interest in the decision.

The case shows moreover, as already suggested, that there was no question involved as to the duration of the office. Whether it could be so limited as has been done in the Tenure of Office law, was not a point in controversy, and is not, of course, decided. That it might be so, is not disputed as to the inferior officer. The thing itself was done, and the right to do it acquiesced in and affirmed, as shown already in the case of Marbury against Madison, as early as 1801.

It cannot be shown, however that there is any difference between the case of inferior and superior officers in this respect? There is no word in the Constitution to require that the latter shall hold only at pleasure. Both are created by law, and Mr. Madison himself admits, in the debate of 1789, that the legislative power creates the office, defines the power, limits its duration, and annexes the compensation. All that the Constitution contains is the exception from the general power of appointment in the authority to Congress to vest that power, in inferior cases, in the President alone, in the courts of law or in the heads of departments.

But there is nothing as to the power of removal. Nothing but as to the privilege of dispensing with the Senate in the matter of appointments, and no limitation whatever upon the power over the office itself, in the one case more than in the other. And now, let me ask, what did the decision amount to, supposing it had even ruled the question at issue, but the act of a mere legislature, with no greater power than ourselves? Is there anything in the proceedings of the Congress of 1789 to indicate that it ever assumed to itself the prerogative of setting itself up as an interpreter of the fundamental law.

The men that composed it understood their functions better than to suppose that it had any jurisdiction over questions of this sort. If it had, so have we; and judgments may be reversed on a rehearing, as Constitutions cannot be; but it it did exist, whence was it derived? How was Congress to satisfy the people by altering the law to which it owed its own existence and all its power? It could not bind its successor by making even its own enactment unrepealable. If it had a right to give an opinion upon the meaning of the Constitution, why may not we do the same thing? The President obviously assumed that they were both wiser and better than ourselves.

If the respect which he professes for their opinions had animated him in regard to the Congresses which have sat under his administration, the nation would have been spared much tribulation, and we relieved of the painful necessity of arranging the Chief Magistrate of the Republic at your bar for his crimes against order and liberty, and his open defiance of law. However it may be with others, I am not one of those who think that all wisdom and virtue have perished with our fathers, or that they were better able to comprehend the import of our instruments, with whose practical working they were unfamiliar, than we who are sitting under the light of an experience of eighty years, and suffering from the mistakes which they made in regard to the future.

They made none greater than the illusion of supposing that it was impossible for our institutions to throw up to the surface a man like Andrew Johnson, and yet it was this mistake, and, perhaps, no other, that settled the first precedent which was so likely to be followed, in regard to the mischievous power of removal from office.

But if twenty-nine votes in the House at that day, making a meagre majority of only seven, and nine only in a Senate that was equally divided in the first of constitutional life, and with such a President as Washington, to fling a colored light over the future of the republic, had even intended to give, and did give a construction to our great charter of freedom, what is to be said of 133 votes to 3., constituting more than three-fourths of the House, and of 35 to 11, or nearly a like proportion of the other, in the maturity of our strength, with a population of nearly forty millions, and under the light of an experience that has proved that even the short period of eighty years was capable of producing what our progenitors supposed to be impossible, even in the long track of time.

But there is one other consideration that presented itself just here, and it is this:—It does not strike me by any means as clear that there was anything in the act of 1789, aside from any suppressed attempt to give it the force of an authoritative opposition to the Constitution, that was necessarily inconsistent with the view of that instrument which I have been endeavoring to maintain. Taking the authority lodged by it with the President as a mere general grant of power, there was nothing certainly in its terms to prevent it, so far, at least, as regarded the inferior officers. It resulted from the express authority of Congress to vest the power of appointment in the President alone, that they might have even left the power of removal in the same hands, also as an incident, and so too as to the superior ones.

The power to remove in any case was but an implied one. If it was necessary, as claimed, to enable the Executive to perform his proper functions under the Constitution, instead of raising the power in himself by the illogical conference that it must belong to him *qua executive*, it presented one of the very cases for which it is provided expressly that Congress shall "make all laws that shall be necessary and proper for carrying into execution all powers vested by the Constitution in the Government of the United States, or in any department or officer thereof." To infer, in the face of such a provision as this, that any or all powers necessary to either department of the government belong to them of course, because they are necessary, is a reflection on the understandings of the framers of the Constitution, and is, in effect, to nullify the provision itself by enabling the other departments of the government to dispense entirely with the action of the lawmaker.

But admitting the act of 1789 to impart in its extent all that it is claimed to have decided, it is further insisted that this untoward precedent has been ripened into unalterable law, by a long and uninterrupted practice in conformity with it. If it were even true as stated, there would be nothing marvelous in the fact that it has been followed by other legislation of a kindred character. It is not to be doubted that a general opinion did prevail for many years, that all the officers of the government not otherwise provided for in the Constitution, ought to be held at will, for the obvious reason among others, that it rendered the process of removal easy, by making an impeachment unnecessary. The only question in dispute was, in whose hands this power could be most appropriately lodged.

It so happened, however, that the first of our Presidents brought with him into the office an elevation of character that placed him above all suspicion, and assured to him a confidence so unbounded that it would have been considered entirely safe to vest him with unlimited command, and it was but natural, as it was certainly highly convenient, that the exercise of that will which was to determine the life of the officer, should be lodged with him. It is so lodged; but is there anything remarkable in the fact that the precedent, having been set, should have been followed up in the practice of the government? It would have been still more remarkable if it had been otherwise. It was a question of patronage and power, of rewarding friends and punishing enemies.

A successful candidate for the Presidency was always sure to bring in with him a majority in the popular branch at least, along with a host of hungry followers, flushed with their victory and hungering after spoils. Was it expected that they should abridge his power to reward his friends, or air their own virtue by self-denying ordinances? That would have been too much for men and politicians too. No! Though the wisest statesmen of the country had realized and deplored for forty years at least the great vice which had been gnawing into the very entrails of the State, and threatened to corrupt it in all its members, there was no remedy left but the intervention of that Providence which has purified the heart of the nation through the blood of its children, and cast down the man, who but yesterday might have stood against the world so low that with all his royal patronage there are none left—no, I think not one—so poor as to do him reverence.

It is true, however, that the precedent of the Congress of 1789 has been followed invariably and without interruption since that time. The history of our Legislature shows not only repeated instances where the Tenure of Office act has been so precisely defined, as to take the case entirely out of the control of the Executive, but some in which even the power of removal itself has been substantially exercised by Congress, as one would suppose it might reasonably be, where it creates and may destroy, makes and may make, even the subject of controversy itself.

The act of 1801, already referred to in connection with the case of Marbury vs. Madison, assigning a tenure of five years absolutely to the officer, involves a manifest departure from it. The several acts of August 14, 1848; March 3, 1849; September, 1850, and May 3, 1853, providing for the appointment of judges in the Territories of Oregon, Minnesota, New Mexico, Kansas and Nebraska, and fixing the term of office at four years absolutely, are all within the same category. The act of 25th February, 1863, followed by that of June 3, 1864, establishing the office of Controller of the Currency, defining his term and making him irremovable, except by and with the advice and consent of the

Senate, and upon reasons to be shown, is another of the same description

The act of March 3, 1865, which authorizes any military or naval officer who has been dismissed by the authority of the President, to demand a trial by court-martial, and which, in default of its allowance, within six months, of a sentence of dismissal or death, voids the order of the Executive, and the act of July 13, 1866, which provides that no officer, in time of peace, shall be dismissed, except in pursuance of a court-martial, or both.

Examples of the like deviation of the strongest kind, for the double reason that the President is, under the Constitution, the Commander-in-Chief of the Army and Navy of the United States, and none but civil officers are amenable to the process of impeachment, and that the officer dismissed is absolutely restored, awakened into new life, and raised to his feet by the omnipotent act of the legislative power. And lastly, the act of 15th of May, 1820, which dismissed by wholesale a very large and important class of officers, at periods specially indicated therein, not only fixed the tenure prospectively but involves a clear exercise of the power of removal itself on the part of the legislative.

Further development in the same direction would no doubt reward the diligence of the more pains taking inquirer. That, however, would only be a work of supererogation. Enough has been shown to demonstrate beyond denial that the practice relied on has been anything but uniform. To establish even a local custom or prescription, the element of continuity is as important as that of time. Any break in that continuity by an adverse entry, or even a continual chain, would arrest the flow of a statute of limitation against the rightful owner of a tenement.

An interruption of the enjoyment would be equally fatal to a prescription; but are we to be told that a case which, in this view, would not even be sufficient to establish composition for tithes, or a trifling easement between individuals, is sufficient to raise a prescription against a constitutional right, or to abrogate the fundamental law of a nation, and the inappreciable inheritance of its people. The very statement of the proposition would seem to furnish its own refutation.

Shortly after four o'clock Senator MORRILL (Vt.) moved to adjourn the court, prefacing the motion by saying that he was informed that Mr. Manager Williams was, from illness, unable to conclude his remarks this evening.

The motion was agreed to, and the court adjourned,

PROCEEDINGS OF TUESDAY, APRIL 28.

When the court had been opened in due form, Mr. SUMNER said:—I send to the Chair an amendment to the rules of the Senate upon the trial of impeachments. When that has been read, if there be any objection, I will ask that it go over until the close of the argument, and take its place with the other matters which will come up for consideration at the time. It was read, as follows:—

Whereas, It is provided in the Constitution of the United States that, on trials of impeachments by the Senate, no person shall be convicted without the concurrence of two-thirds of the members present; but this requirement of two-thirds is not extended to the judgment in such trials, which remains subject to the general law that a majority prevails; therefore, in order to remove any doubt thereupon,

Ordered, That any question which may arise with regard to the judgment shall be determined by a majority of the members present.

Senator DAVIS objected, and the Chief Justice said:—It will lie over.

To the managers—The honorable managers will proceed.

Mr. Williams Resumes his Argument.

Mr. Manager WILLIAMS, then, at 12·15, resumed his argument, and said:—

There is but one refuge left, and that is in the opinion of what is sometimes called his Cabinet, the trusted counsellors whom he is pleased to quote as the advisers whom the Constitution and the practice of the government have assigned to him. If all the world has forsaken him, they, at least, were still faithful to the chief whom they so long accompanied, and so largely comforted and encouraged through all his manifold usurpations. It is true that these gentlemen have not been allowed to prove, as they would have desired to do, that maugre, all the reasoning of judges, lawyers and publicists, they are implicitly of the opinion, and so advised the President, that the Tenure-of-Office law, not being in accordance with his will, was of course, unconstitutional. It may be guessed, I suppose, without danger to our cause, that if allowed, they would have proved it.

With large opportunities for information, I have not heard of any occasion where they have ever given any opinion to the President except the one that was wanted by him, or known to be agreeable to his will. If so, I should have been glad to have heard from some of these functionaries on that question. It would have been pleasant to have the witnesses on the stand, at least to discourse on constitutional law. If the public interest has not suffered, the public curiosity has. at least, been balked by the denial of the high privilege of testimony to the luminous exposition which some of them learned. The hand whose training has been so high as to warrant them in denouncing us all—the legislators of the nation—as no better than "Constitution tinkers," should have been able to help us with a large defense of the President, as set forth in his voluminous special plea, and elaborated by the argument of his opening counsel, not only that his Cabinet agreed with him in his views as to the law but that if he has erred, it was under the advice received from those whom the law had placed around him.

It is not shown, however, and was not attempted to be shown, that in regard to the particular offense for which he is now arraigned before you, they are never consulted by him. But to clear this part of the case of all possible cavil or exception, I feel that it will not be amiss to ask your attention to a few remarks upon the relations of the President with this illegitimate body—this excrescence; this mere fungus, born of decay, which has been compounded in process of time out of the heads of departments, and has shot up within the past four years into the formidable proportions of a directory for the general government of the State.

The first observation that suggests itself is, that this deference to the advice of others proceeds on the hypothesis that the President himself is not responsible, and it is, therefore, at war with the principal theory of the defense, which is that he is the sole responsible head of the Executive Department, and must, therefore, ex necessitate, in order to the performance of his appropriate duties, have the undisputed right to control and govern and remove them at his own mere will, as he has just done in the case of Mr. Stanton, a theory which precludes the idea of advice, in the fact that it makes the adviser a slave. But what, then, does the President intend? Does he propose to abandon this line of defense? He cannot do it without surrendering his case.

Is it his purpose, then, to divert us from the track by doubling on his pursuers, and leading them off on a false scent, or does he intend the offer of a vicarious sacrifice? Does he think to make mere scapegoats of his counsellors by laying all his multitudinous sins upon their backs? Does he propose to enact the part of another Charles, by surrendering another Strafford to the vengeance of the commons? We must decline to accept the offer. We want no ministerial heads. We do not choose, in the pursuit of fine game, to stop to any ignobler quarry, either on the land or on the sea. It would be anything but magnanimous in us to take, but would be ignoble in him to offer, the heads of those whom our past Legislature has degraded into slaves. When Cæsar falls his counsellors will disappear with him; perhaps he thinks, however, that nobody is responsible.

But shall we allow him to justify in one breath, the removal of Mr. Stanton, on the grounds that under the law he was Stanton's master, and then, in another, when arraigned for this, to say that he is not responsible for it because he took advice from those who are but mere automatons only in his hands and voice, in the language of his counsel, and no more than the mere creature of his imperial will. This would be a sad condition indeed for the people of a republic claiming to be free. We can all understand the theory of the British Constitution, "The King can do no wrong." The person of majesty is sacred, but the irresponsibility of the sovereign is beautifully reconsidered with the liberty of the subject, of holding the Ministry responsible, thus taking care he shall get no bad advice from them.

But what is to be our condition, with no recourse between the two. Either king or ministry will be not unlike what is said in the touching plaint of the Britons, "the barbarians drove us to the sea, and the sea drove us back again to the barbarians." But who made these men the advisers of the President. Not the Constitution, certainly not the laws, or they would have made them free. Still the Constitution has given him no advisers but the Senate, whose opinions he spurned, because he cannot get from it the advice he wants, and would obtain, no doubt, if it were reduced to the condition of that of Imperial Rome. All it proves in regard to the heads of department is that he may require the opinion in writing of each of them upon any subject relating to the duties of his own special office, and no more. He cannot require it as to the other matters, and by the strongest implication, it was not intended that he should not take it on any matter outside of their own respective offices and duties. He has undoubtedly the privilege which belongs to other men, of seeking for advice wherever he may want it; but if he is wise, and would be honestly as he does not wish to be advised, he will go to those who are in a condition to tell him the truth, without the risk of being turned out of office, as Mr. Stanton has been, for doing so. No tyrant who has held the lives of those around him in his hands has ever enjoyed the counsels of any but minions and sycophants. If it had been the purpose of the framers of the Constitution to provide a counsel for the President, they would have looked to it that he was not to be surrounded with creatures such as these.

But then it is said that the practice of holding Cabinet meetings was inaugurated by President Washington, and has since continued without interruption. It is unquestionable that he did not take the opinions in writing of the heads of departments on bills that were submitted to him in the constitutional way; and it is not unlikely that he may have consulted them as to appointments and other matters of Executive duty that involved anything like discretion. They may have met occasionally in after times upon the special invitation of the President. It was not, however, I think, until the period of the war, when the labors and responsibilities of the President as Commander-in-Chief of the Armies were so largely magnified as to make it necessary that he should take counsel from day to day, that they chrystalized into their fairest form as a sort of institution of State, and not till the accession of Andrew Johnson that they began to do the work of Congress, in a condition of peril, by legislating for the restoration of the Rebel States.

From that time forward, through all that long and unhappy interregnum of the law-making power, when the telegraph was waiting upon the "fiat" of those mysterious councils, that dark tribunal which was erecting States by proclamation, taxing the people, and surrendering up the public property to keep them on their feet, and exercising a supervisory power over the laws, had apparently taken the place of the Congress of the nation, with power. True, Congress has ever claimed to say that the acts of this cabal, which looked like some dark conclave, and conspirators plotting against the liberties of the people, were the results of free consultation, and comparison of views is to speak without knowledge. I, for one, mistrusted them from the beginning, and if I may be excused the egotism, it was under the inspiration of the conviction that they could not have held together so long under an imperious self-willed man like the present Executive, without a thorough submission to all his views, that I was moved to introduce and urge, as I did, through great discouragements, but, thank God, successfully, the amendment to the Tenure of Office bill that brings about this conflict. It has come sooner than I expected, but not too soon to vindicate, by its timely rescue of the most important of the departments of the government from the grasp of the President—the wisdom of a measure which, if it had been the law at the time of Mr. Johnson's accession, would, in my humble judgment, have set his policy aside, and made his resistance to the will of the people, and its project of governing the nation without a Congress impossible. The veil has been lifted since the passage of the law, and those who wish now read in letters of living light the great fact that, during the progress of all this usurpation that has convulsed the nation and kept the South in anarchy for four long years, there was scarce a ripple of dissent to move the stagnant surface of those law-making and law-breaking cabals—those mere beds of justice, who, in accordance with the theory of the President himself, had but one will, that reigned undisputed and supreme.

To insist, then, that any apology is to be found for the delinquincies of the President in the advice of a Cabinet where a difference of opinion was considered treason to the head and loyalty to law, instead of to the will of the President, punished by dismissal, is, it seems to me, on his part, the very climax of effrontery. What adequate cause does the President assign for the removal of Mr. Stanton? His counsel promised us in the opening that they would exhibit reasons to show that it was impossible to allow him to continue to hold the office. They have failed to do it. They have not even attempted it. Was it because he had failed to perform his duties, or in any way offended against the law? The President alleges nothing of the kind. Was it even a personal quarrel?

Nothing of this sort is pretended. Either all that we can hear of is that there was "a want of mutual confidence," that "his relations to Mr. Stanton were such as to preclude him for advice," (heaven save the mark!) or that he did not think he could be any longer safely responsible for him. His counsel say that Mr. Stanton is a thorn in his side. Well, so are Grant, Sherman and Sheridan, and so is Congress, and so is every loyal man in the country who questions and resists his will. The trouble is, as everybody knows, that Mr. Stanton does not indorse his policy and cannot be relied on to assist him in obstructing the laws of Congress; and that is just the reason why you want this thorn to stick, and, if need be, prick and fester a little, and it must remain there if you should be faithful to the nation and to yourselves. You cannot let Mr. Stanton go, by an acquittal of the President, without surrendering into his hands the very last fortress that you still hold, and now are holding only at the point of the bayonet.

But there is a point just here that seems to have been entirely overlooked by the counsel for the President, to which I desire especially to invite your attention. It seems to have been assumed by them throughout, if it is not, indeed, distinctly asserted in the defendant's pleas, that if they shall be able to succeed in establishing a power of removal in the President, either under the Constitution or the act of 1789 erecting the department now in question, he may exercise that power at his mere will and pleasure without responsibility, and having failed to show any adequate cause, or, indeed, any cause whatever for the act done, then he stands, of course, on this hypothesis. But is this the law?

Is there no such thing as an abuse of power, and a just responsibility as its attendants? Was it intended in either case, whether the power flowed from one source or from the other, that it should be exercisable without restraint? That doctrine would be proper in a monarchy, perhaps, but ill suited to the genius of institutions like our own. Nor was it the opinion of Mr. Madison, or those who voted and acted with him in the Congress of 1789. No man there, who asserted the power of removal to be in the President, or concurred in bestowing on him for the occasion, ever supposed that its exercise was to be a question of mere caprice or whim or will, to the objection that this would be the effect of the doctrine of removal.

It was answered by Mr. Madison himself, in these words:—"The danger consists merely in this, that the President can displace from office a man whose merits require that he should be continued in it; that will be the motive which the President can feel for such abuse of his power and the restraints that operate to prevent it." In the first place he is impeached by the House before the Senate for such an act of maladministion; for I contend that the wanton removal of a meritorious officer would subject him to impeachment and removal from his own high trust." And it was no doubt mainly on the argument that the power of removal was embodied in the law.

What then, have the President and his counsel to say in answer to this? Is the President impeachable in his own case, or does he expect to realize the points of the argument, and then repudiate the very grounds on which the alleged construction rests? Was Mr. Stanton a meritorious officer? Did his remits require that he should be continued in the place? No loyal man, I think, disputes that they did, and this Senate has already solemnly adjudged by their decision that, upon the reasons stated by the President, that there was no sufficient cause for his removal, while none others have since been shown by the accused himself? What, then, was the motive for the act of mal-administration, as Mr. Madison denominates it?

Nothing that we are aware of, except the fact that the President cannot control the War Office in the interests of his policy so long as he is there. Was this, then, a wanton removal? It was something more; it was a wicked one, and are we to be told now that he is bound to show no reasons, and cannot be compelled to answer to the nation by those who claim the power of removal for him on the footing that it alone would be impeachable? But it is further strenuously argued that, although the law may be constitutional and the case of Mr. Stanton within it, as it has already been held to be by this Senate, the case was not so clear a one as to authorize a charge of crime against the President unless it can be shown that he has willfully misconstrued it, and that, although whenever a law is passed through the forms of legislation it is his duty to see that it is faithfully executed, so long as it requires no more than ministerial action on his part: yet, where it is a question of cutting off a power confided to him by the Constitution—and he alone can bring about a judicial decision for the settlement—if, on deliberation and advice, he should be of the opinion that the law was unconstitutional, it would be no violation of duty to take the needful steps and raise that question so as to have it peacefully decided.

Allow me to say, in answer, that if ignorance of the law, which excuses nobody else, cannot be held to excuse the very last man in the nation, who ought to be allowed to plead it? The testimony shows, I think, that he did not misunderstand its meaning. This suspension of Mr. Stanton, which was an entirely new procedure, followed, as it was, by his report of the cause to the Senate within twenty days after its next meeting, is evidence that he did understand the law as comprehending that case, and did not intend to violate it if he could, but get rid of the obnoxious officer without resorting to so extreme and hazardous a remedy; but the question here is not so much whether he ignorantly and innocently mistook the law, as whether in the case referred to of an interference with the powers claimed by him under the Constitution, he may suspend the operation of a law by assuming it to be unconstitutional, and setting it aside until the courts shall have decided that it is a constitutional and valid one. In the case at issue it was not necessary to violate the law, either by contriving to prevent the incumbent from resuming his place under it, or turning him out by violence after he had been duly reinstated by the Senate. If he honestly desired to test its validity in the judicial forum, all that it was necessary for him to do was to issue his order of removal, and to give the officer a notice of that order and its object. If he refused to obey, the next obvious step would direct the Attorney-General to sue out a writ of quo warranto at his own relation.

This was not his course. This remedy was not summary enough for his uses, as his special counsel, employed after the arrest of his pseudo Secretary Thomas testifies, because I would have allowed the law to reign in the meantime, instead of creating an interregnum of mere will, by which he hoped to supersede it. His project was to seize the place by craft if possible, and by force if necessary, and for this purpose he claims to have made an arrangement with General Grant for its surrender to himself in case the judgment of the Senate should restore the officer, and now taxes him with bad faith to him individually for his obedience to the law. It stands, therefore, upon his own confession that he intended to prevent Mr. Stanton from resuming his position, in which case, as he well knew, and as his Attorney-General knew, and must have informed him, there was no remedy at law for the ejected officer.

Foiled and baffled by the integrity of Grant, after full deliberation he issued his order of removal on the 21st of February, and sends it by his lieutenant, Thomas, with a commission to himself to act as Secretary ad interim, and enter upon the duties of his office. He does not fail to suggest to him at the same time that Stanton is a coward and may be easily frightened out of the place with a proper show of energy on his part. He tells him also that he ex-

pects him to support the Constitution and the laws as he understands them.

Of course, Thomas is a martinet; he knows no law, as he confessed, but the order of his Commander-in-Chief. He has been taught no argument but arms, no logic, but the dialectics of hard knocks. Instructed by the President, he hoped to frighten Stanton by his looks, and he proceeds upon his warlike errand, in all the panoply of a brigadier, and loftily demands the keys of the fortress from the stern warder, who only stipulates for twenty-four hours to remove his camp equipage and baggage. The conquest is apparently an easy one, he reports forthwith to his chief, with the brevity of a Cæzar, "veni, vidi, vici;" and they rejoice no doubt together over the pusillanimity of the Secretary. The puissant Adjutant then unbends and pleads for relaxation, after his heroic and successful feat, to the delight and mysteries of the masquerade; not, however, until he had fought his battles o'er again, and invited his friends to be present at the surrender. On the following morning, which he advised them he intended to compel by force, if necessary. The masquerade opens:—

" Bright the lamps shone o'er fair women and brave men,
    Music ascends with its voluptuous swell,
And eyes looked love to eyes that spake again,
    And all went merry as a marriage bell."

The adjutant himself is there; the epaulette has modestly retired behind the domino; the gentleman from Tennessee, at least, will excuse me if, after his own example, I borrow from the celestial armory on which he draws so copiously. a little of light artillery, with which he blazes along his track. like a November midnight sky, with all its flaming asteroids.

" Grim-visaged war hath smoothed his wrinkled front."

And now, instead of mounting barbed steeds
To fight the souls of fearful adversaries,
He capers nimbly in a lady's chamber
To the lascivious pleasing of a lute."

But lo, a hand is laid, however, on his, which startles him in the midst of the festivities, like the summons to "Brunswick's fated chieftan" at the ball in Brussels, the night before the battle in which he fell. It is the messenger of the Senate, who comes to warn him that his enterprise is an unlawful one. On the following morning he is waited upon by another officer, with a warrant for his arrest, for threats which looked to a disturbance of the peace.

This double warning chills his martial ardor; visions of impending trouble pass before his eyes; he sees, or thinks he sees, the return of civil strife, the floors of the department daubed, perhaps, like those of the royal palace of Holyrood, with red spots of blood. But above all he feels that the hand of the law-maker and of the law itself, which is stronger than the sword, is on him, and he puts up his weapon and repairs in peaceful guise to take possession of his conquest. I do not propose, however, to describe the interview which followed. That will be the task of the dramatist; it will be sufficient to accompany him back to the White House, where he receives the order to "go on and take possession," which he was so unhappily called back to contradict, and which it was then well understood, of course, that he could not obtain, except by force, and he continues to be recognized as Secretary of War without a portfolio or a care, while he waits, under the direction of the President, not upon the laws, but only to see, like Micawber, what may turn up here, and to be inducted and installed, in proper form, as soon as your previous decision shall have been reversed, and his title affirmed by your votes in favor of an acquittal. The idea of a suit, in which direction no step was ever taken, is now abandoned, if it was ever seriously entertained.

The conversation, however, with General Sherman, who was called as a witness by the President himself, settles the fact conclusively, if not already demonstrated by all the attendant circumstances, that it was not his purpose at any time to bring the case into the courts for adjudication. He preferred the dextrous finesse or the strong hand, to a reference, which every sensible lawyer would have told him could be attended with only one result, and that a judgment in favor of the law.

But in this great strait, instead of a resort to the Attorney-General himself, his special counsel, Cox, employed only after the arrest of Thomas, is called to prove that he advised against the writ of quo warranto because of "the law's delays," and endeavors to seek a remedy more summary through a habeas corpus, in the event of the commitment of the Secretary ad interim. Supposing it all true, however, the movement came too late to help the employer's case, by showing a desire to put the issue in the way of a judicial decision upon the law.

Nor is it clear by any means, that such a process would have achieved the desired results, with a warrant good upon its face and charging a threatened disturbance of the peace, or an offense against a statute of the United States. I doubt whether any court would venture to declare the warrant void, or to discharge upon such a hearing, on the footing of the unconstitutionality of a law which had received nearly three-fourths of the votes of both houses, or indeed of any law whatever, while I do not see how even a decision against it could have had either the effect of ousting Stanton or putting Thomas in his place.

It is enough, however, for the present purpose, that the prisoner was discharged on the motion of his own attorney. The counsel for the President admits that he cannot, in ordinary cases, erect himself into a judicial tribunal, and decide that a law is unconstitutional, because the effect would be that there could never be any judicial decision upon it, but they insist, as already stated, that where a particular law has cut off a power confided to him by the Constitution, and he alone has the power to raise the questions for the courts; there is no objection to his doing so; and they instance the case of a law to prevent the making of a treaty, or to declare that he shall not exercise the functions of Commander-in-Chief.

It has been already very fully answered that there is no evidence here to show that there was any honest purpose whatever to bring this case into the courts, but that, on the contrary, there is very conclusive testimony to show that he intended to keep it out of them. But had he a right to hold this law a nullity until it was affirmed by another tribunal, whether it was constitutional or not? The Constitution gives to him the power of passing upon the acts of the two houses by returning a bill, with his objections thereto, but if it is afterwards enacted by two-thirds of both Houses, it is provided that "it shall become a law."

What is a law? It is a rule of civil conduct prescribed by the supreme power of a State? Is there any higher power than the Legislature? Is it essential to the operation of a law that it should have the approval of the judiciary as well as of the President? It is as obligatory on the President as upon the humblest citizen. Nay, it is, if possible, more so. He is its minister. The Constitution requires that he shall take care that it be faithfully executed. It is for others to controvert it if aggrieved in a legal way, but not for him. If they do, however, it is at their peril, as it would be at his, even in the cases put, where it is asked with great emphasis, whether he would be bound to obey?

These cases are extreme ones, but if hard cases are said to make bad precedents it may be equally remarked that extreme cases make bad illustrations. They are, moreover, of express persons. As this is not, it will be time enough to answer them when they arise.

It is not a supposable contingency that two-thirds of both Houses of Congress will flatly violate their oaths in a clear case. Thus far in their history they have passed no law, I believe, that has been adjudged invalid, whenever they shall be prepared to do what is now supposed, Constitutions will be useless; faith will have perished among men; limited and representative governments become impossible.

When it comes to this we shall have revolution, with bloody conflicts in our streets; with a Congress legislating behind bayonets, and that anarchy prevailing everywhere which is already foreshadowed by the aspect of a department of this great government beleaguered by the minions of despotism, with its head a prisoner, and armed sentinels pacing before its doors. Who shall say that the President shall be permitted to disobey even a doubtful law, in the assertion of a power that is only implied? If he may, why not also set aside the obnoxious section of the Appropriation bill upon which he has endeavored unsuccessfully to debauch the officers of the army by teaching them insubordination to the law?

Why not openly disregard your Reconstruction acts, as he will assuredly do if you shall teach him by your verdict here, that he can do it with impunity. The legal rule is that the presumption is, in every case, in favor of the law, and that is a violent one where none has ever been reversed. The President claims that this presumption shall not stand as against him. If it may not here, it cannot elsewhere. To allow this revolutionary pretension is to dethrone the law and substitute his will. To say that he may hold his office and disregard the law is to proclaim either anarchy or despotism. It is but a short step from one extreme to the other.

To be without law, and to leave the law dependent on a single will, are, in effect, but one and the same thing. The man who can declare what is law and what is not, is already the absolute master of the State. But who is to try this case? The President insists that it belongs to the jurisdiction of the Supreme Court, where, as he untruly says, he endeavored to bring it. So it would, if the question involved were one of merely private right; but in his executive efforts to get into one court, by turning his back upon it, he has stumbled unexpectedly in another.

It is not the one he sought, but it is the one the Constitution has provided just for such delinquencies as his, and he cannot decline its cognizance. I beg pardon, he does send you word through the special counsel, whom he sends here with his personal protest, that he might have declined it, on the opinion still entertained by both of them, that this is no Congress, and you are no court of competent jurisdiction to bring before you and try a President of the United States, by the logic of which argument he proves equally, of course, that he is no President.

To avoid a bloody conflict, however, although he has been tendered the necessary aid in men, and inasmuch, I suppose, as you have been so indulgent as not to put him to the humiliation of appearing in person at your bar, he waives his sufficient plea to the jurisdiction, and condescends, only out of the abundance of his grace and spirit of forbearance, for which he claims due credit at your hands, to make answer before a tribunal which he might rightfully have deferred; but he is here now by attorney in what his other counsel have taken great pains to prove to you to be a court indeed, although they insist, not very consistently, in almost the same breath, that it has only the functions of a jury. I shall not dispute that question with them.

I am willing to agree that the Senate *pro hac vice* is a court, and that too of extensive jurisdiction over the subject-matter in dispute, from which it follows by a necessary logic, as I think, that it is fully competent to try and decide the whole case for itself, taking such advice as it thinks proper as to the law, and then rejecting it if it is not satisfactory. If it cannot do this, it is but the shadow and mocking of what the defendant's counsel claim it to be in fact, but by what name soever it may be called, it will solve for the President the problem which he has desired to carry into another tribunal without waiting for any extraneous opinion.

It has already determined upon the constitutionality of the Tenure of Office law, by enacting it over his objections, as it has already passed upon its meaning by its condemnation of act for which he is now to answer at its bar. It will say, too, if I mistake not, that whether constitutional or not, it will allow no executive officer, and much less the Chief Magistrate of the nation, to assume that it is not so, and set up his own opinion in his place until its previous and well-considered judgment upon the same opinions has been judicially affirmed. But does it make any difference whether Mr. Stanton's case is within the Tenure of Office act or not? Had the Executive the power at any time, either during a session or a recess, to create a vacancy to be filled up by an appointment *ad interim*, to continue during his own pleasure; or, if he had could he prolong a vacancy so created beyond the period of six months?

The Constitution provides, and it requires such a provision, in view of the general clause which associates the Senate with the President, and makes their advice and consent necessary in all cases of appointment to authorize it; that he shall have power to fill all vacancies happening during the recess by temporary commissions, to expire at the end of the next session, and by a necessary implication. Of course he cannot do it in the same way or without their advice or consent while the Senate is at hand to afford it. The word "happen," as used here, imports accident or casualty only, according to the best authorities.

If this is a correct interpretation he cannot, of course, create a vacancy for that purpose during a recess under the Constitution, although he may claim to do so under the law establishing the department, which places the power of removal in his hands. If he does, however, the case then falls within the constitutional provision, and the vacancy thus created must be filled by a commission, to expire at the end of the next session. He did create a vacancy in this case, by the suspension, during the recess, which he proceeded to supply by the appointment of General Grant as Secretary of War, *ad interim*, at his pleasure, and this he now defends, not under the provisions of the Tenure of Office law, which would have authorized it, and which he expressly repudiates, but upon the footing, in the first place, of his constitutional powers. Nothing is clearer, however, than the proposition that there was no authority to do this thing, except what is to be found in the act which he repudiated. There are no laws, and no precedents, so far as I am advised, to justify or excuse it. If he may suspend indefinitely, and appoint at pleasure a Secretary *ad interim*, he may not only change terms of commission, but strip the Senate of all participation in the appointing power.

But then, he says again, that he did this under the authority also of the act of February 13, 1795, for filling temporary vacancies. The tenor of that act is that in case of a vacancy it shall be lawful for the President, if he deems it necessary, to authorize any person or persons to perform the duties until a successor is appointed, or such vacancy is filled, within the proviso, however, that no one vacancy shall be supplied in that manner for a longer term than six months, which proves, of course, that the exigency provided for was only to be a temporary one. We maintain that this act has been repealed by the more recent one of February 13, 1863, which confines the choice of the President to the heads of the other departments.

It is insisted, however, that while the former covers all cases of vacancy, the latter is confined to some particular instances, not including those of removal, or such as may be brought about by afflux of time, and it does not, therefore, operate as a repeal to that extent. Granting this for the sake of the argument to be tried, how is it to apply to a vacancy occurring during the recess without a repeal of the constitutional provision which is intended expressly for just such cases. Was it intended to supersede, and is it to be so interpreted? This will hardly be pretended, if it were even clear that the Legislature had such a power. The intent and meaning of the act are so transparent from the context, from the words of tenure, and from the six months limitation, that it is impossible to mistake them or even to doubt that it was designed for merely accidental and transient cases that were left unprovided for in the Constitution. The President's claim would perpetuate the vacancy by enabling him to refuse to fill or nominate a successor. If it is even true, however, that he might have appointed General Grant during the recess under the law of 1795, it is equally clear that he could not continue him in office or protract the vacancy beyond six months, and yet he insisted in his special pleas, in answer to the averment, of the absence of the condition of vacancy on the 21st of February, when he appointed General Thomas, which was more than six months after the appointment of General Grant, that there was a continuing vacancy at that time, intending, of course, that the act of the Senate in refusing to approve his suspension, and his resumption of the duties of the office, were to be treated as of no account whatever. From the premises of the President that the Civil Tenure act was invalid on constitutional grounds, and did not at all embrace that case; his inference of a continuing case is undeniable, and his appointment of General Thomas, therefore, entirely unauthorized by the act on which he relies.

But there is more in this aspect of the case than the mere failure of authority taken at that. Although he might possibly remove during the recess, he could not suspend and appoint a Secretary *ad interim* except by virtue of the Tenure of Office law, and that it may be well pleaded in his defense, even though he may have insisted that he did not refer to, or follow, or recognize it. I think it cannot be a question among lawyers, that all the acts of a public officer are to be conclusively presumed to have been done under the law which authorized them; but then it will be said, as it has been in regard to the proof of changes made in the forms of commissions to harmonize them with the now disputed law, and of other evidence cf a kindred character, and this only to set up the doctrine of estoppel, which, though not unreasonable, has been so often characterized as obvious in the civil courts against a defendant in a criminal proceeding. I am ready to admit that estoppels are obvious, because they exclude the truth; but I have never supposed that they were so when their effect was to shut out the false. It was not for this purpose, however, in my view at least, that such evidence was offered, but only to contradict the President's assertions by his acts, and to show that, when he pleads, through his counsel, if the law was valid, he honestly believed the contrary, and, if it embraced the case of Mr. Stanton, he innocently mistook its meaning, and did not intend wilfully to misconstrue it, he simply stated what was not true.

And now, a few words only upon the general question of intent itself, which has been made to figure so largely in this cause, under the shadow of the multiplied averments in regard to it. I do not look upon these averments as at all material, and if not material, then they are, as any lawyer knows, but mere surplusage, which never vitiates, and it is never necessary to prove. I do not speak as a criminal lawyer, but there is no professional man, I think, who reads these charges, that will not detect in them something more, perhaps by way of abundant cause, than even the technical nicety of the criminal pleaders can demand.

I do not know that even in the criminal courts, where an action charged in clear violation of a law forbidding it, and especially if it involves the case of a public officer, that it is any more necessary to allege that he violated the law with the intent to violate it, than to aver that he was not ignorant of the law, which every man is bound to know. The law presumes the intent from the act itself, which is a necessary inference if the law is to be observed, and its infraction punished, and the party committing it is responsible for all the consequences, whether he intended them or not. It makes no difference about the motive, for whenever the statute forbids the doing of a thing, the doing it wilfull, although without any corrupt motive, is indictable.—Swain's 677, 4, Tenn. Rep. 457.

So when the President is solemnly arraigned to answer here to the charge that he had infringed the Constitution, disobeyed the commands, or violates any of the provisions of the Tenure of Office or any other law, he cannot plead either that he did it ignorantly or by mistake, because ignorance of the law excuses nobody, or that he did it only from the best of motives, and for the purpose of bringing the question of its efficacy, or his obligation to conform to it to a legal test, even though he could prove the fact as he has most signally failed to do in the case before you. The motives of men, which are hidden away in their own breasts, cannot generally be scrutinized or taken into the account where there is a violation of the law.

An old Spanish proverb says that there is a place not to be named to ears polite, but which is "paved with good intentions." If they or even bad advices can be pleaded hereafter in excuse for either neglect or violation of duty, it will be something commendable at least, and few tyrants will ever suffer for their crimes. If Andrew Johnson could plead in apology of his own dispensation, with the test oath law, or any other feature of his law-defying policy, that his only aim was to conciliate the Rebels and facilitate the work of reconstruction, his great examplar, whom he has so closely copied, the ill-advised and headstrong James II, might equally have pleaded that he did the same things in the interests of universal tolerance.

The English monarch forfeited his throne and disinherited his heirs upon that case. It remains to be seen whether our king is to run out the parallel. I beg to say, however, in this connection, that I do not by any means admit that a case like this is to be tried or judged by the rigid rules and narrow interception of the criminal courts.

There is no question here of the life, or liberty, or property of the delinquent. It is a question only of official delinquencies, in violation, however, of the life of a great people. If the defendant is convicted he forfeits only his official place, and is, perhaps, disqualified from taking upon himself any other, which will be no severe infliction, I suppose, unless the Rebels themselves should be so fortunate as to come once more into the possession of the government, and so work it as to trust a man who had been untrue to them, and who had honored them so signally before.

The accusers here are forty millions of freemen; the accused but one, who claims to be their master, and the issue is whether he shall be allowed to defy their will, under the pretext that he can govern them more wisely than their Congress, and to take the sword, and, in effect, the purse of the nation into his own hands. On such an issue and before such a tribunal, I should not have hesitated to stand upon the plain, unvarnished, untechnical narrative of the facts, leaving the question as to their effect upon the interests of the nation and their bearing upon the fitness of Andrew Johnson to hold the helm of the great State to be

decided by statesmen instead of turning it over either to the quibbles of the lawyer or the subtleties of the casuist.

I have no patience for the disquisitions of the special pleader in a case like this. I take a broader view, one that I think is fully sustained by the authorities, and that is that in cases such as this the safety of the people which is the supreme law, is the rule. That is the true rule and the only rule that ought to govern the same question during the present Congress. I do not propose to argue that question now, because it seems to me something very like a self-evident proposition.

If Andrew Johnson, in the performance of the duties of his high office, has so demented himself as to show that he is no respecter of the laws; that he denies the will of those who make them, and has encouraged disobedience to their behests; that he has fostered disaffection and discontent throughout the lately revolted States; that he is a standing obstacle to the restoration of the peace and tranquility of this nation; that he claims and asserts the power of a dictator by holding one of your great departments in abeyance, and arrogates to himself the absolute and uncontrollable right to remove or suspend at his mere will every executive officer of the government on the land and on the seas, and to supply their places without your agency—if for any or all these reasons, the republic is not longer safe in his hands, then, before heaven and earth, as the conservators of the national weal, as the trusted guardians of its most valuable rights, as the depositaries of the most sacred and exalted trust that has ever been placed in the hands of man, it becomes your high and solemn duty to see that the republic shall take no detriment, and to speak peace to a disturbed and suffering land by removing him from the trusts he has abused, and the office he has disgraced?

There are other points in this case on which I would have decided to comment, if time and strength had been allowed me for the purpose. It is only within the last few days that I have entertained the hope that the Senate would so far relax its rule as to enable me to obtain what, under the the circumstances, is at best but an imperfect hearing; and I have felt it necessary, therefore, to confine myself to the leading arguments connected with the removal of the Secretary of War.

I wish it to be understood, however, that I do not underrate the value of such of the articles as I have been obliged to *pretermit*. There is nothing in the whole case, I think, of graver import than the means adopted by the President for overthrowing the legislative power by fostering disobedience to its enactments, and bringing its accredited organ into disrepute. To this charge there are three answers; the first is, the supposed constitutional right to the use of an unbridled tongue, which knows no difference between licentiousness and liberty; the second, the provocation supposed to have been offered in the language used by members of Congress in debate, in what seems to be forgotten to be its constitutional right, which not only protects it from challenge anywhere, but gives it the right freely to criticise the public conduct of the President, over whom the law has placed them, by making him amenable to them for all his errors, as they are not to him. The third is the harmless jest in the suggestion of a law to regulate the speech and manners of the President. If his counsel can find food for mirth in such a picture as the evidence has shown, I have no quarrel with their taste.

The President may enjoy the jest, perhaps, himself. I do not think he can afford it, but history informs us that "Nero fiddled while Rome was burning." Whether he does or not, however, I trust that he will find a censor such as Cato in the judicial opinion of this body, that the man who so outraged public decency, either in his public or private character, in the pursuit of an object so treasonable as this, has demonstrated his unfitness longer to hold the high place of a Chief Magistrate of a free, intelligent, and moral people.

I take leave of the unpalatable theme by remarking, that even the advocate of the people himself must feel, while he is compelled, as a child of the Republic, himself to say thus much, that he would rather turn his back, if it was possible, on such a spectacle, and throw a mantle over the nakedness that shames us all.

And now, American Senators, Representatives and judges, upon this mighty issue, joint heirs yourselves of that great inheritance of liberty that has descended to us all, and has just been ransomed and repurchased by a second baptism of blood, a few words more and I have done. If the responsibilities of the lawyer are such as to oppress him with their weight, how immeasurably greater are your own! The House of Representatives has done its duty; the rest is now with you.

While I have a trust in that God who went before our hosts as he did before the armies of Israel, through the fiery trials that led so many of the flower of our youth to distant graves in Southern battle-fields, which has never failed me in the darkest hour of the national agony, I cannot but realize that He has placed the destinies of the nation in your hands. Your decision here will either fall upon the public heart like a genial sunbeam, or shed a disastrous twilight, full of gloomiest portents of coming evil, over the land. Say not that I exaggerate the issue or overcolor the picture. This, if it were true, would be an error of much smaller consequence than the perilous mistake of underrating its importance.

It is, indeed, but the catastrophe of the great drama which began three years ago with murder, the denouement of the mortal struggle between the power that makes the law and that which executes it, between the people themselves and the chief of their servants, who now undertakes to defy their will. What is your verdict to decide? Go to the evidence and to the answer of the President himself, and they will give you the measure of the interests involved.

It is not a question only whether or not Andrew Johnson is to be allowed to serve as President of the United States for the remainder of his term. It is the greater question whether you shall hold as law the power that the Constitution gives you, by surrendering the higher one to him of suspending, dismissing and appointing, at his will and pleasure, every executive officer in the government, from the highest to the lowest, without your consent, and, if possible, the still higher one of disregarding your laws for the purpose of putting those laws on trial before they can be recognized.

He has made this issue with you voluntarily and defiantly. If you acquit him upon it, you affirm all his impartial pretentions, and decide that no amount of usurpation will ever bring a Chief Magistrate to justice, because you will have laid down at his feet your own high dignity along with your double functions of legislators and advisers, which will be followed, of course, by that of your other, I will not say greater, office as judges.

It will be a victory over you and us, which will gladden the heart of Rebellion with joy, while your dead soldiers will turn uneasily in their graves. A victory to be celebrated by the exultant ascent of Andrew Johnson, like the conqueror in a Roman triumph, dragging, not captive kings, but a captive Senate at his chariot wheels, and to be crowned by his re-entry into possession of that department of the government over which this great battle has been fought. It is shown in evidence that he has already intimated that he would wait on your action here for that purpose.

But is this all? I entreat you lay not to your bosoms the fond delusion that it was all to end there. It is but the beginning of the end. If his pretensions are sustained, the next head that will fall, as a propitiatory offering to the conquered Senate, will be that of the great chief who humbled the pride of chivalry by beating down its serried battalions in the field, and dragging its traitor standard to the dust, to be followed by the return of the Rebel officeholders, and a general convulsion of the States, which shall cast loose your Reconstruction laws, and deliver over the whole theatre of past disturbance to anarchy and ruin. Is this an exaggerated picture? Look to the history of the past, and judge. And now let me ask you, in conclusion, to turn your eyes to the other side of the question, and see what are to be the consequences of a conviction, if such a verdict as I think the loyal people of this nation, with one united voice, demand it at your hands. Do you shrink from the consequences? are your minds disturbed by visions of approaching trouble? The nation has already, within a few short years, been called to mourn the loss of a great Chief Magistrate, through the bloody catastrophy by which a Rebel hand has been unfortunately enabled to lift this man into his place, and the jar has not been felt, as the mighty machine of State, freighted with all the hopes of humanity, moved onward in its high career.

This nation is too great to be affected seriously by the loss of any one man. Are your hearts touched by the touching appeals of the defendant's counsel, who say to you that you are asked to punish this man only for his divine words, his exalted charity to others, to the murdered Dostie and his fellows, to the loyal men whose carcasses were piled in carts like swine, with gore dripping from the wheels, in that second holocaust of blood, that criminal murder which was enacted in New Orleans, to those who perished on that second Saint Bartholomew; at Memphis, when the streets were reddened with the lurid light of burning dwellings, and the loyal occupants who would have escaped were cast backward into the flames.

The Divine mercy itself is seasoned with justice, and waits only on contrition, and this is no place for such emotions; but if it is mercy to loyalty and innocence that cries aloud for the removal of this bold, bad man, if it is, remember that your loyal brethren are falling from day to day, in Southern cities, by the assassin's knife, and the reports of the Freedmen's Bureau are replete with horrors at which the face turns pale.

In your judgment stands no scaffold with the blood of the victim; no lictor waits at your doors to execute your stern decree; it is but the crown that falls, while none but the historian stands by to gibbet the delinquent for the ages that are to come; no weight of woe will disturb your slumbers, unless it comes up from the disaffected and disappointed South, which will have lost the foremost of its friends. Your act will be acceptable, and an example to the nations, that will eclipse even the triumph of your arms in the vindication of the public justice in the sublimer and more peaceful triumph of the law. The eyes of an expectant people are upon you; you have but to do your duty. The patriot will realize that the good genius of the nation, the angel of our deliverance, is about us and around us, as in the darkest hours of our trial.

Mr. WILLIAMS concluded his remarks at 1·40 P. M., when, on motion of Senator JOHNSON, the court took a recess of fifteen minutes, which, as usual, was spun out to half an hour.

After the recess Mr. BUTLER said, I ask leave, Mr. President and Senators, to make a short narration of facts, rendered necessary by what fell from Mr. NELSON, of the counsel for the President, in his speech on Friday last, which will be found on pages 888, 889, 890 of the Record.

The Chief Justice, interrupting—If there is no objection, the hon. manager may proceed.

Mr. BUTLER—And for certainty I have reduced what I have to say upon this matter to writing.

Speech of Manager Butler.

Mr. BUTLER then read as follows:—

I beg leave to make a narration of facts, rendered necessary by what was said by Mr. Nelson of the counsel for the President, in his argument on Friday last, contained on pages 888, 889, 890 of the record in relation to the Hon. J. S. Black and the supposed connection of some of the managers and members of the House in regard to the island of Alta Vela.

This explanation becomes necessary because of the very anomalous course taken by the learned counsel in introducing in his argument what he calls a statement of facts, not one of which would have been competent if offered in evidence, and upon which he founded an attack upon a gentleman, not present, and from which he deduces insinuations injurious to some of the managers and other gentlemen, members of the House of Representatives, who are not parties to the issue here, and who have no opportunity to be heard. The learned counsel was strenuous in the argument to prove that this was a court, and its proceedings were to be such only as are had in judicial tribunals, he, therefore, ought to have constrained himself, at least, to act in accordance with his theory.

The veriest tyro in the law in the most benighted position of the Southern country, ought to know, that in no court, however rude and humble, would an attack be allowed upon the absent, or counsel engaged in a cause, upon a statement of pretended facts, unsupported by oaths, unsifted by cross-examination, and which those to be affected by them had no opportunity to verify or to dispute. After extracting the detail of a document sent by his client to the Senate, the counsel proceeds in relation to a dispute concerning the island of Alta Vela as follows:—

According to the best information I can obtain, I state, that on the 9th of March, 1868, General B. F. Butler addressed a letter to J. W. Shaffer, in which he stated that he was clearly of opinion that under the claim of the United States, its citizens had the exclusive right to take guano there, and that he had never been able to understand why the Executive did not long since assert the rights of the government, and sustain the rightful claims of its citizens to the possession of the Island, in the most forcible manner consistent with the dignity and honor of the nation.

This letter was concurred in and approved of by John A. Logan, John A. Garfield, W. H. Koontz, J. K. Moorhead, Thaddeus Stevens, J. G. Blaine and John A. Bingham. On the same day of March, 1868, the letter expressing the opinion of Generals Butler, Logan and Garfield, was placed in the hands of the President by Chauncey F. Black, who, on the 16th of March, 1868, addressed a letter to him in which he inclosed a copy of the same with the concurrence of Thaddeus Stevens, John A. Bingham, J. G. Blaine, J. K. Moorhead and William H. Koontz.

After the date of this letter, and while Judge Black was counsel for the respondent in this cause, he had an interview with the President, in which he urged immediate action on his part, and the sending an armed vessel to take possession of the island; and because the President refused to do so, Judge Black, on the 19th of March, 1868, declined to appear further as his counsel in this case. Such are the facts in regard to the withdrawal of Judge Black, according to the best information I can obtain. So far as the President is concerned, "the head and front of his offending hath this extent, no more." It is not necessary to any purpose that I should censure Judge Black, or make any reflection upon or imputation against any of the honorable managers.

The Island of Alta Vela or the claim for damages, is said to amount in value to more than a million dollars, and it is quite likely that an extensive speculation is on foot. I have no reason to charge that any of the managers are engaged in it, and I presume that the letters were signed as such communications are often signed by members of Congress, through the importunity of friends. Judge Black, no doubt, thought it was his duty to other clients to press this claim, but how did the President view it?

There are two or three facts to which I desire to call the attention of the Senate and the country in connection with these recommendations. They are, first, that they were all gotten up after this impeachment proceeding was commenced against the President of the United States. Keep the dates in mind and you will see that such is the fact. Every one of them was gotten up after this impeachment proceeding was commenced. It cannot fail to be evident that, while the counsel disclaims any imputation either upon Judge Black or the managers, in words, he so states what he claims to be the facts as to convey the very imputation disclaimed. Therefore it is that I have felt called upon to notice the insinuated calumny.

My personal knowledge of matters connected with the Island of Alta Vela is very limited. Sometime in the summer of 1867, being in waiting on other business in the office of the Attorney-General (Mr. Stanbery), I was present at an argument by Judge Black in behalf of the American citizens claiming an interest in that island. I there, for the first time, learned the facts argued and in dispute concerning it, by listening to and incidentally taking a part, or being appealed to in the discussion. In February last, my attention was next drawn to the matter of the spoliation and imprisonment of American citizens upon the Island of Alta Vela, by inquiry of a personal friend, Colonel Shaffer, if I had any acquaintance with the question, and if so, would give him my opinion, as a lawyer, upon the merits of the controversy, to serve a friend. Simply upon recollection of the discussion with the Attorney-General I gave him such "opinion," the rough draft of which I hold in my hand, which is without date, and which, being copied, I signed and placed in his hand. This I believe to have been in the early part of February. Certainly before the act was committed by Andrew Johnson which brought on his impeachment.

From that time until I saw my "opinion" published in the New York *Herald*, purporting to come from President Johnson, I never saw or communicated with either of the gentlemen whose names appear in the counsel's statement attached thereto, in any manner, directly or indirectly, in regard to it, or the subject matter of it, or the Island of Alta Vela, or the claims of any person arising out of it or because of it.

Thus far I am able to speak of my own knowledge. Since the statement of the counsel, according to the best information he can obtain, I have made inquiry, and from the best information I can obtain, find the facts to be as follows:—That soon after the "opinion" was signed, Colonel Shaffer asked the Hon. John A. Logan to examine the same question presented him, his brief of the facts, and asked him if he could concur in the opinion, which, after examination, Mr. Logan consented to do, and signed the original paper, signed by myself. I may here remark, that the recollection of General Logan and Colonel Shaffer concur with my own, as to the time of these transactions. I have learned and believed, that my "opinion," with the signature of General Logan attached, was placed in the hands of Chauncey F. Black, Esq., and by him handed to the President of the United States, with other papers on the case.

Mr. Black made a copy of my "opinion," and afterwards, at his convenience, procured a member of Congress, a personal friend of his, one of the signers, to get the names of other members of Congress, two of whom happened to be managers of the impeachment. This was done by a separate application to each, without any concert of action whatever, or knowledge or belief that the papers were to be used in any way, or for any purpose other than the expression of their opinions on the subject-matter. This copy of my opinion, when so signed, was a very considerable time after the original given to the President.

I desire, further, to declare that I have no knowledge of or interest directly, or indirectly, in any claim whatever arising in any manner out of the island of Alta Vela, other than as above stated. In justice to the other gentlemen who signed the copy of the paper, I desire to annex here, to the affidavits of Chauncey F. Black, Esq., and Colonel J. W. Shaffer, showing that neither of the gentlemen signing the paper had any interest or concern in the subject-matter thereof, other than as above set forth.

While I acquit the learned counsel of any intentional falsity of statement, as he makes it to his "best information," which must have been obtained from and sent to Mr. Johnson, the statement itself contains every element of falsehood, being both the *suppressio veri* and the *suggestio falsi*, in that it says that on the 9th of March, General Benjamin F. Butler addressed a letter to J. W. Shaffer, and this letter was concurred in and approved of by John A. Logan, J. A. Garfield, W. H. Koontz, J. K. Moorhead, Thaddeus Stevens, and John A. Bingham, on the same day, 9th of March, 1868, when the President knew that the names of the five last mentioned gentlemen were procured on a copy of the letter long after the original was in his hands.

Again, there is another deliberate falsehood in the thrice reiterated statement that the signatures were procured and sent to him for the purpose of intimidating him into doing an act after he was impeached, the propriety and legality of which was contrary to his judgment, when, in truth and in fact, the signatures were procured and sent to him in order, as he averred, to sustain him in doing what he himself declared was just and legal in the premises, and which he intended to do. The use made of these papers is characteristic of Andrew Johnson, who usually raises questions of veracity with both friend and foe with whom he comes in contact.

"I, Chauncey F. Black, Attorney and Counseller at Law, do depose and say that the law firm of Black, Lamon & Co., have been counsellors for years on the behalf of Patterson & Marquendo, to recover their rights in the guano discovered by them in the Island of Alta Vela, of which they had been deprived by force, and the imprisonment of their agents by some of the inhabitants of Dominica; and as such counsel we have argued the cause to the Secretary of State and also the President, before whom the question has been pending since July 19, 1867.

"We have in various forms pressed the matter upon his attention, and he has expressed himself as fully and freely satisfied with the justice of the claims of our clients, and his conviction of his own duty to afford the desired relief, but had declined to ait because of the opposition of the Secretary of State. General J. W. Shaffer having become associated with the United States in the case, and having learned that General Butler had become acquainted with the merits of the case, procured his legal opinion upon it, and also a concurrence by General Logan. After receiving this opinion I inclosed it to the President The time when this opinion was read, and whether it was dated. I do not recollect. The time it was presented to the President by me, can be established by the date of my letter enclosing it.

"Learning from a mutual friend that it would be desirable for the President to receive the recommendations of other members of Congress, I carried a copy of the opinion to the House of Representatives and procured the signatures of some of my personal friends, and asked them to procure the signatures of others, which were attached to the copy. Some considerable time after I had forwarded the original I sent this copy, signed, to the President. These signatures

were procured upon personal application to the gentlemen severally, without any concert of action whatever on their part, and without any reference to any proceeding then pending, or the then present action of Congress in regard to the President whatever.

"From my relation to the case of Alta Vela I have knowledge of all the rights and interests in it, or in relation to it, so that I am certain that neither of the gentlemen who signed the paper or copy, have any interest in the claim or matter in dispute, or in any part thereof, or arising therefrom in any manner, directly or indirectly, or contingent, and that all averment to the contrary from any source whatever is untrue in fact.

(Signed)   "CHAUNCEY F. BLACK."

Sworn and subscribed before me this 28th day of April, A. D., 1868. (Signed)   N. CALLAN,
[Seal].   Notary Public.

"To the best of my knowledge and belief, the facts contained in the above affidavit are true in every particular.
(Signed)   "J. W. SHAFFER."

Sworn and subscribed before me, the 28th day of April, A. D., 1868. (Signed)   N. CALLAN,
(Stamp.)   Notary Public.

Mr. NELSON—Mr. Chief Justice and Senators:—You have heard the statement of the honorable manager addressed to you, which I deem will justify a statement from me. The honorable gentleman speaks—

The Chief Justice interrupting:—

The counsel can proceed by unanimous consent.

Mr. NELSON.—I beg pardon of the Chief Justice. I inferred from the silence the Senators were willing to hear me; the honorable gentleman speaks as to what he supposes to be the knowledge and duty of a tyro in the law, and animadverts with some severity upon the introduction of this foreign subject by me, in the course of this investigation.

I beg leave to remind the honorable Senators that, so far as I am concerned, I did not introduce that copy without having, as I believed, just cause and just reason to do it, and whatever may be the gentleman's views in regard to a tyro in the legal profession, I beg leave to say to him and the Senate, that I have never seen the day in my life, not from the earliest moment when my license was signed down to the present time, when a client was assailed, and as I believed, unjustly, that I did not feel it my very highest professional duty on the face of the earth, to vindicate and defend him against the assassin.

My views may be, and probably are, different from the views of the honorable manager and others, and if without casting any reflection upon my associates—if the duty had not devolved upon me to conduct the investigation of this case; if it had not devolved upon those of higher standing in the profession than myself, I would have met the gentleman in every case where he has made his assaults upon the President of the United States. I would have answered him from time to time as these charges were made, and I would not have permitted one of them to go unanswered, so far as an answer could be made on our side; and when the honorable gentleman who closed the argument, so far as it had progressed (Mr. Boutwell) at the time he addressed the Senate on the other side, saw fit to draw, in dark and gloomy colors, the pictures of the President of the United States under the influence which he had over his Cabinet; when he saw fit to represent them as serfs, obedient to the control of their master, and to make allusion to the withdrawal of Judge Black, I deemed that a fit and proper occasion—and so considering it, upon the most calm and mature reflection, I, as one of the counsel for the President, having the information in my possession—to meet and answer it and nail it to the counter, and think I have done so successfully.

You all know, and, if need be, I can hunt up the newspapers and furnish the testimony, that when Judge Black retired from the President's case, it was published in newspapers hostile to the President that Judge Black, seeing that the President's case was desperate, he had withdrawn from it in disgust; and the very highest professional duty devolved upon me, when this imputation was contained in the address of the honorable manager, and alluded to in the connection in which it was, to vindicate the President of the United State from the aspersions which had been made upon him, and it was for that reason, and for no other, and not with any desire to make any assaults upon the manager, and while I treated them with civility, with kindness, and, as I think, with very great forbearance, the honorable gentleman has made imputations upon me to-day which I hurl back with scorn, as undeserved imputations.

I treated him with courtesy and kindness, and he has rewarded me with outrage in the presence of the American Senate, and it will be for you, Senators, to judge whose demeanor has been proper, that of the honorable manager, who foully and falsely makes insinuations against me for my course in vindicating the President of the United States in the discharge of my professional duty here. So far as any question which the gentleman desires to make of a personal character with me is concerned, this is not the place to make it. Let him make it elsewhere if he desires to make it.

Senator YATES, at this point, rose and called the counsel to order.

Mr. NELSON—Mr. Chief Justice and Senators:—I will endeavor to comply with the suggestion of the Senator. I do not wish to make use of any improper language in this tribunal, but I hope the Senators will pardon me for answering the remarks of the honorable manager on the other side. What I desired to say to you, Senators, and which is much more important than anything else, is this:—When I made the statement which I did submit to the Senate, I made it with a full knowledge, as I believed, of what I was doing. It may be possible that I may have committed an error, as to the date of the paper which was signed by Messrs. Logan and the other managers. It may be possible I took it for granted that it bore the same date that it was signed, on the same day, the 9th of March, that was mentioned by the honorable gentleman; but that is an immaterial error, if it be one.

I had the letter in my possession on the day I addressed you, and if the gentleman had seen fit to deny any statement contained in those letters on that day, I had them here ready to read to the Senate. I had no expectation that this subject would be called up to-day, until the honorable gentleman told me during your adjournment of a few minutes. I have sent for the letters. I was fearful, however, that they would not be here in time to read them now, and if it becomes necessary, I shall ask leave to read them to-morrow, before my associate resumes his argument.

I shall ask leave of the Senate, as this topic is introduced by the gentleman in terms of censure of me, to allow me to read those letters. Why did I introduce those letters here at all in vindication of the imputation that was made against Judge Black? It was for the purpose of showing that the President of the United States had been placed in a dilemma such as no man under accusation has ever been placed in before, the purpose of showing that so far as that correspondence is concerned, it was a correspondence which arose after the articles of impeachment had been agreed upon, and published after they had been referred to the Senate.

It was for that purpose that I introduced the correspondence, and it has excited, and awakened, and aroused the attention of this whole nation, that the counsel for the President of the United States should abandon his cause, and that the true secret of that abandonment has not grown out of any insult that the President of the United States rendered to the counsel, out of any injury that he did to him, but out of the fact that a claim was pressed. As I believe stronger than I did the other day, and I will answer for it here or anywhere else. I believe that Judge Black acted improperly under the circumstances, in withdrawing his services from the President of the United States. Here is this accusation presented against him, and here is this astonishing claim presented to him, signed by four of the managers of the impeachment; presented at an extraordinary period of time; presented when this impeachment was hanging over him; and I maintain that I had a right—that it was my bounden duty to vindicate—

Mr. BUTLER—Does the gentleman know what he is saying—that a claim was signed by the managers?

Mr. NELSON—I meant to say letter, not claim. I may have used some word that I did not intend to use. What I meant to say is this:—That a letter was in the first instance signed by the honorable manager, General Butler; that there was an indorsement of that letter by three other members of the House of Representatives, who are managers in this case; that this letter and the indorsement of it had relation to the Alta Vela claim; that the subject was brought to the consideration of the President of the United States pending this impeachment, and that whether the letter was signed on the 9th of March, or at a later period, is wholly immaterial. It was signed after this impeachment proceeding was commenced, and Judge Black endeavored to get the attention of the President to the claim, and to have him decide upon it, as I am now informed and believe, though I have no written evidence of that fact, to decide this claim, and urged it upon him after this impeachment commenced, and after Judge Black had met some of the other counsel, not myself, in the council chamber of the President.

I was not present at that time, but I have it from the lips of the President, and I believe it to be true, that Judge Black urged upon him the decision of this claim, and his answer was, that he did not think it a proper time for him to act upon the claim, because Congress was in session, and asked if it was right and proper for a vessel to be sent down there for any act of public hostility? The President of the United States answered Judge Black, as I am informed and believe, by telling him that Congress was in session, and by asking him to call upon Congress to pass any law that might be necessary.

General BUTLER made a remark inaudible to the gallery.

Mr. NELSON—If the gentleman thinks I am carrying the matter too far, I will relieve him by saying I have said as much as I desire to say; I will ask permission, when I receive those letters, to read them.

Senator EDMUNDS then arose and asked that the rules be enforced, saying that the discussion was out of order.

Mr. LOGAN—Mr. President, I would like to say one word.

Chief Justice—If there is no objection the gentleman can proceed.

Mr. LOGAN—I merely wish to correct the statement of the counsel for the respondent, by saying that he is mistaken about this letter having been signed, after any of the impeachment proceedings had been commenced, by General Butler or myself. I know well when I signed. I hope the gentleman will make the correction.

Mr. NELSON—I will say with great pleasure that I had no design to misrepresent any gentleman concerned in the case. In order that the matter may be decided, I may have fallen into an error, but my understanding was that it was after the proceedings were commenced, but to obviate all difficulty I will produce the letter. No matter whether I am mistaken or not, I will bring it in fairness to the Senate. That is all the gentleman can ask, I am sure.

Speech of Mr. Evarts.

Mr. EVARTS then spoke as follows:—

Mr. Chief Justice and Senators:—I am sure that no conscientious man would wish to take any part in the solemn transactions which engage our attention to-day, unless held to it by something not inconsistent with his obligation of duty. Even if we were at liberty to confine our solicitudes within the horizon of politics; even if the interests of the country and of the party in power, duty to the country and duty to the party in power, as is sometimes the case, and as public men very easily persuade themselves is or may be the case in any juncture, were commensurate and equivalent, who will provide a chart or compass for the wide, uncertain sea which lies before us in the immediate future?

Who shall determine the currents which shall follow from the event of this stupendous political controversy? Who measure the force and who assume to control the storm? But if we enlarge the scope of our responsibilities and of our vision, and take in the great subjects that have been constantly pressing on our mind, who is there so sagacious in human affairs, who so confident of his capacity, who so circumspect of treading among grave responsibilities, and so assured of his circumspection, who so bold in his forecast of the future, and so approved in his judgment, as to see clearly the end of this great contest?

Let us be sure then that no man shall be here as a volunteer, or shall lift his finger to jostle the strugglers in the contest between the great forces of our government, of which contest we are witnesses, in which we take part, and which we, in our several vocations, are to assist in determining of the absolute and complete obligation which convenes the Chief Justice of the United States and the Senators in the court, for the trial of this impeachment. Of its authentic derivation from the Constitution there can be no doubt; so too of the authority of the honorable managers and their presence, and the attendance of the House of Representatives itself, in aid of their argument and of their appeal.

There is little doubt the President of the United States is here in submission to the same Constitution, and in obedience to it, and in obedience to the duty which he owes by the obligations which he has assumed to preserve, protect and defend the Constitution. The right of the President to appear by counsel of his choice, makes it as clear under the obligations of a member of the profession, and under the duty of a citizen of a free State, who has sworn fidelity to the Constitution and the laws, that he shall attend upon his defense.

No man can be familiar with the course of the struggle of law and liberty in the world, without knowing that the defense of the accused becomes the trial of the Constitution, and the protection of the common safety. It is neither by a careless nor capricious distribution of services to the State, that divides them among those who manage political candidacies, among those who defend the accused, and among those who, in the Senate, determine the grave issues of peace and war, and all the business of the State. It is from facts and instances that people are taught their constitution and the law, and it is by facts and instances, that these laws and constitutions are upheld and improved.

Constitutions are framed laws, established institutions built up, and the process of society goes on, until at length by some opposing, some competing, some contending forces in the States, an individual is brought to a point of collision, and the clouds, surcharged with the great forces of public welfare, burst over his head. It is then that he who defends the accused, in the language of Cicero, and in open recognition of the frequent instances in English and American history, is held to a distinguished public duty. As this duty has brought us all here to this august procedure, and has assigned to each his part in it, so through all its responsibilities to the end we must surrender ourselves to its guidance.

The constitutional procedure of impeachment, in our history as a nation, has really vouched none of the grave interests that are involved in the present trial. Starting from the first occasion in which it was moved, being against a member of the Senate, it decided nothing important, politically or judicially, except that a member of this body was not an officer under the United States. The next trial, against Judge Pickering, partook of no qualities except of personal delinquency or misfortune, and its result gave us nothing to be proud of, and gave to the constitutional law no precedent, except that an insane man may be convicted of crime by a party vote.

In the last trial, of Judge Humphreys, there was no defense, and the matters of accusation were so plain and clear that it was understood by the accused and the accusers and the court to be a mere formality. That leaves us no trials of interest except those of Judge Chase and Judge Peck.

Neither of those ever went beyond the gravity of a formal and solemn accusation of men holding dignified, valuable, eminent public judicial trusts, and their determination in favor of the accused, leaving nothing to be illustrated by their trials except that even when the matter in imputation and under investigation is a personal fault, and misconduct in office, politics will force themselves into the result.

What is the question here? Why, Mr. Chief Justice and Senators, all the political power of the United States of America is here; the House of Representatives is here as an accuser; the President of the United States is here as the accused, and the Senate of the United States is here as the court to try him, presided over by the Chief Justice, under a special constitutional provision. These powers of our government are not here for concord of action in any of the duties assigned to the government in the conduct of the affairs of the nation, but they are here in a struggle and contest as to which one of them shall be made to bow, by virtue of constitutional authority, to the other.

Crime and violence have put portions of our political government at some disadvantage; the crime and violence of the Rebellion has deprived this House of Representatives and this Senate of the full attendance of members, which will make up the body, under the Constitution of the United States, when it shall have been fully re-established over the whole country; the crime of violence and of assassination has put the Executive office in the last stage of constitutional authority; there is no constitutionally-elected successor of the President of the United States; and you have now before you a matter I shall call your attention to, not intending to exhibit here the discussion of constitutional views and doctrines, but simply the result to the government and the country which must follow from your judgment.

If you shall acquit the President of the United States of this accusation, all things will be as they were before; the House of Representatves will retire to discharge its usual duties in legislation, and you will remain to act with it in those duties, and to divide with the President the other associate duties of an executive character which the Constitution has confided to you.

The President, if freed from this accusation, will occupy through the constitutional term his place of authority, and, whatever course of politics may follow, the government and its Constitution will have received no shock; but if the President should be condemned, and if by the authority of the Constitution necessary to be exercised on condemnation, he shall be removed from office, there will be no President of the United States, for that name and title is conceded by the Constitution to no man who has not received the suffrage of the people for the primary and alternative gift of that office.

A new thing will occur, the duties of the office will attach to some other officer, and be discharged by him through the term which belongs to the first officer.

The presiding officer of the Senate will have to add to the office, conferred on him by the Senate, the performance of the duties of President of the United States, and and whatever there may be in the course of public affairs, it will result from the anomalous situation which is involved in the determination of this case; and therefore, you have directly proposed to you, as a necessary result of one determination, this novelty in our Constitution.

A great nation, whose whole form of government, whose whole scheme and theory of politics rests upon the suffrages of the people, will be without a President, and the office sequestered will be discharged by a member of the body whose judgment has sequestered it. I need not direct your attention—long since called to it, doubtless, and made more familiar, by your reflections, to you than it is to me—to the results that will follow from the exercise of these duties, and you will see at once that the situation, from circumstances for which no man is responsible, is such as to bring into the gravest possible consequences the act which you are to perform.

If the President of the United States, elected by the people, and having standing behind him the second officer of the people's choice, were on trial, no such disturbance or confusion of constitutional duties, and no such shock upon the feelings and traditions of the people would affect us, but as I have said, crime and violence, for which none of the agents of the government are responsible, have brought us to this situation.

Now it would seem that as this trial brings the legislative power of the government, confronted with the executive authority, and its result is to deprive the nation of a President of the United States, and to place the office in the Senate, it is a trial of the Constitution over the head and in the person of the Chief Magistrate who now fills the great office. The forces of this contest are gathered and this is the trial of the Constitution, and neither the dignity of the great office which he holds, nor any personal interest that may be felt in one so high in station, nor the great name and force of this exercise, the the House of Representatives speaking for all the people of the United States, nor the august composition of this tribunal, which brings together the Chief Justice of the great court of the country and the Senators who have States for their constituents—which recalls to us the combined splendors of Roman and English jurisprudence and power—not even this spectacle forms any important part of the watchful solicitude with which the people of the country are gazing on this procedure.

The sober thought of the people of the country is never affected by pageant, when they cover real issues and interests the people are thinking on far greater things than these. Why, Mr. Chief Justice, it is but a few days since the great tribunal in which you habitually preside, where the law speaks with authority for the whole United States, adjourned, embracing as it does, the great provinces of international law, the great responsibility of judging between the States and the General Government, the conflicting interests and passions belonging to our composite system, and of determining the limits of the co-ordinate branches of the government.

There is one other duty assigned to it in which the people of the country feel a nearer and deeper interest. It is as the guardians of the Bill of Rights of the Constitution, as the watchful protectors of the liberties of the people against the encroachments of law and government, that the people look to the Supreme Court with the greatest honor and greatest affection. That court having before it a subject touching the liberty of the citizens, finds the hamstrings of its endeavor and of its energy to interpose

the power of the Constitution in protection of the citizen, cut by the sharp edge of a Congressional enactment, and, in its breast, carries away from the judgment the Constitution and law, to be determined, if ever, at some future time and under some happier circumstances.

Now, in reference to this matter, the people of the United States give grave attention. They exercise their supervision of the conduct of all their agents, of whom, in any form and in any capacity, and in any majesty, they have not yet learned to be afraid. The people of this country have had nothing in their experience of the last six years to make them fear anybody, anybody's oppression, anybody's encroachment, anybody's assaults, anybody's violence, anybody's war. Masters of this country, and masters of every agent and agency in it, they bow to nothing but the Constitution, and they honor every public servant who bows to the Constitution.

At the same time, by the action of the same Congress, the people see the President of the United States brought as a criminal to your bar, accused by one branch of Congress, to be tried by the other; his office, as I have said, to be put in commission, and an election ordered. Now, he greatly mistakes who supposes that the attachment of the people of the United States to the office of President, and the great name and power which represents them in their collective capacity, in their united power and in their combined interests, is less than their attachment to any of the other departments of this government.

The President is, in the honor and in the custom of the the people of the United States, the Magistrate; the authority for which, they have that homage, that respect which belongs to the elective office. His oath of office is as familiar to the people in this country as it is to you, for they have heard it during the perilous period of the war from the lips which they revered; and they have seen its immense power under the resources of this Constitution, and supported by their fidelity to maintain the contest of this government against all our foes to sustain the Constitution and laws.

It has been spoken of here as if the President's oath was the oath to discharge faithfully the duties of his office, and as if the principal duty of the office was to execute the laws of Congress; but that is not the President's oath. That portion of it, that is the common oath of everybody in authority, is to discharge the duties of his office; but the peculiar oath of the President, the oath of the Constitution, is in the larger portion of it which makes him the sworn preserver, protector and defender of the Constitution itself—that is an office and that is an oath which the people of the United States have intrusted to and exacted from no other public servant than the President of the United States, and when they conferred that power and exacted that duty; they understood its tremendous responsibility, the tremendous opposition which it might encounter, and they understood their duty, implied in the suffrage which had conferred the authority and exacted the obligation to maintain him in it as against foreign aggression, as against domestic violence, as against encroachments from whatever quarter, under the guise of Congress or under whatever authority upon the true vigor of the Constitution.

President Lincoln's solemn declaration, on which he gained strength for himself, and by which he gave strength to the people, "I have a solemn vow registered in Heaven that I will preserve, protect and defend the Constitution of the United States," carried him and carried the people following him through the struggles, the changes, the vicissitudes of the Rebellion, and that vow as a legend now adorns the halls of legislation in more than one State of the Union.

This oath of the President, this duty of the President the people of this country do not in the least regard as personal to him; but it is an oath and a duty assumed and to be performed as their representative in their interests and for their honor, and they have determined, and will adhere to their determination, that that oath shall not be taken in vain. They understand that the literal phrase, "to the best of my ability," which is the modest form in which the President's obligation is assumed, means not only the ability of the President, but the ability of the country; and most magnificently have the people brought out its recourse in aid of that oath of President Lincoln's. And so, when the shock comes, not in the form of violence, of war, of rebellion, but of a struggle between foes of this government in relation to constitutional authority, the people of the United States regard the President as bound to the special fidelity of watching that all departments of this government obey the Constitution, as well as that he obeys it himself.

It gives him no assumption of authority beyond the laws and the Constitution; but all the authority and all the resources of the laws and of the Constitution are open to him, and they will see to it that he, the President of the United States, whoever he may be, in relation to the office and its duties, shall not take this oath in vain, if they have the power to maintain him in its performance. That, indeed, the Constitution is above him, as it is above all of the servants of the people; as it is above the people themselves, until their sovereignty shall change it they do not doubt, and thus all their servants, the President, the Congress, and whoever they may be, are watched by the people of the United States, in relation to the limitation of the Constitution. Not disputing the regularity, the complete authenticity the adequate authority of this entire procedure of accusation, through trial and down to sentence, the people yet claim the right to see and to know that it is duty to the Constitution, observed and followed throughout, which brings the result, whatever it may be.

Thus satisfied, they adhere to the Constitution, and they have no purpose to change it. They are converts to no theories of Congressional omnipotence; understand none of the nonsense of the Constitution being superior to the laws, except that the laws must be obeyed under the Constitution. They know their government and they mean to maintain it. And when they hear that this tremendous enginery of impeachment and trial and threatened conviction or sentence, "If the laws and facts will justify it," has been brought into play, that that power which has lain in the Constitution, like a sword in a sheath, is now drawn.

They wish to know what the crime is that the President is accused of. They understand that treason and bribery are made offenses; that those who are guilty of them should be brought into question and deposed. They are ready to believe that there may be other great crimes and misdemeanors touching the conduct of the government and the welfare of the State, which may equally fall within the jurisdiction and the duty, but they wish to know what the crimes are. They wish to know whether the President has betrayed our liberties or our possessions to a foreign State. They wish to know whether he has delivered up a fortress or surrendered a State. They wish to know whether he has made merchandise of the public trust or turned authority to private gain, and when informed that none of these things are charged or even declaimed about, they yet seek further information, and they are told that he has removed a member of his Cabinet. Now, the people of this country are so familiar with the removal of members of the Cabinet, and of all other persons in authority, that that mere statement does not strike them as a grave offense, needing the interposition of this special jurisdiction. Removal from office is not with the people, and especially those engaged in politics, a terror or a disagreeable subject.

Indeed, it may be said that it makes a great part of the political forces of the country; that removal from office is a thing in the Constitution and in the habit of its administration. I remember to have heard it said that an old lady once summed up an earnest defense of the seven dogmas of Calvinism by saying that if you took away her total depravity you took away all her religion. (Laughter.) And there are a good many people in this country of whom it may be said, if you took away removal from office, you took away all their politics. (Laughter.) So that on that mere statement it does not strike them either as an unprecedented occurrence or as one involving no great danger to the State.

Well, but how comes it to be a crime? they inquire. Why, Congress passed a law for the first time in the history of the government, understood to control this removal from office, and provided that if the President should violate it it should be a crime, or rather a misdemeanor; and that now he has removed, or undertaken to remove a member of his Cabinet, and is to be removed himself for that cause. He undertook to make an *ad interim* Secretary of War, and you are to have made for you an *ad interim* President in consequence.

Now, that seems the situation. Was the Secretary removed, they inquire. No, he was not removed, he is still Secretary, still in the possession of the department. Was force used, was violence meditated, attempted, or applied? No, it was all on paper, and all went no further than making the official attitude out of which a judgment of the Supreme Court could be got, and here Congress interrupting again, this great authority of the government is interposed the procedure of trial and impeachment of the President to settle by its own authority this question between it and the Executive. The people see and the people feel that under this attitude of Congress there seems to be a claim of right to the exercise of what is supposed to be a duty to prevent the Supreme Court of the United States from interposing the severe judgment in the collisions of the government and of the laws affecting either the framework of the government or the liberties of the citizen, and they are not slow to understand, without the aid of the arguments of the honorable managers, that it is a question between the omnipotence of Congress and the supremacy of the Constitution of the United States. That is an issue on which the people have no doubt. From the beginning of their liberties they have had had a clear opinion that tyranny was as likely to be exercised by the Parliament as by the King or any-body else. The honorable managers have directed your notice to the principles and the trials of the American Revolution as having shown a determination to overthrow the tyranny of the king, and they told us that this people will not bend their necks to the usurpations of the President. The people will not bend their necks to the usurpations of anybody. But they kno that their fathers went to war against the tyranny of Parliament, and that, under the necessity of finally securing their liberties, they severed their connections with the mother country. If any honorable member of either house will peruse the work in the convention which framed the Constitution of the United States, he will discover that, of all the powers which might grow up, the tyranny of Congress was more provided against than any other extravagance which the workings of our government might be supposed possible to produce.

Our people, then, are unwilling that our government should be changed. They are unwilling that the doctrine of Congressional supremacy should be fixed. They are unwilling that any department shall grow too strong or shall claim to be too strong for the restraints of the Constitution. And if men are wise they will attend to what was sagaciously said by an English statesman, which, if obeyed in England, might have saved great political shocks, and which is true for our guidance and for the

adoption by our people now as it was then for the people of England. Said Lord Bacon to Buckingham, the arbitrary minister of James I.:—"So far as it may be in you, let no arbitrary power be inaugurated. The people of this kingdom love the laws thereof, and nothing will oblige them more than a confidence in the free enjoyment of them."

What the nobles once said in Parliament, *volumus leges Angliæ mutari*, is imprinted in the hearts of all the people, and in the hands of all the people of this country. The supremacy of the Constitution, and obedience to it, are imprinted. Whatever progress new ideas of parliamentary government instead of executive authority dependent on the direct suffrage of the people, may have made with prophets and with statesmen, it has made no advance whatever in the hearts or in the heads of the people of this country

Now, I know there are a good many people who believe that a written Constitution for this country, as for every other nation, is only for the nascent state, and not for the prime and vigor of manhood. I know that it is spoken of as swathing bands, which may support and strengthen the puny limbs of infancy, but which shame and encumber the maturity of vigor. This I know, and in either House I imagine sentiments of that kind have been held during the debates of the past two Congresses.

But that is not the feeling or judgment of the people, and this is in their eyes, in the eyes of foreign nations, and in the eyes of the enlightened thinkers, a trial of the Constitution not merely in that inferior sense of a determination whether its powers accorded to one branch or other of the government have this or that scope, impression and force, but whether a government of a written Constitution can maintain itself in the forces prescribed and attributed to its various departments, or whether the immense passions of a wealthy and powerful and populous nation will force asunder all the bonds of the Constitution, and whether in a struggle of strength and wealth the natural forces, uncurbed by the supreme reason of the State, will determine the success of one and the subjection of the other.

Now, Senators, let us see to it that in this trial and in this controversy, that we understand wha is its extent and what is to be determined. Let us see to it that we play our part as it should be played, from the motives and interests which should control statesmen and judges. If it be that the guardian of liberty is at last to loosen her zone, and her stern monitor, law, debauched and drunken with that new wine of opinion which is crushed daily from ten thousand presses throughout this land, is to ignore its guardianship, let us at least be found among those who, with averted eye and reverend step backward, seek to veil the shameless rivalry and not with those who exult and jeer at its success.

Let us so act as that what we do, and what we propose, and what we wish, shall be to build up the States, to give new stability to the forces of the government, and curb the rash passions of the people. Thus acting, doubt not that the result shall be in accord with those high aspirations, and those noble impulses, and those exalted views. And whether or no the forces of this government shall feel the shock of this special jurisdiction, in obedience to law, to evidence, to justice, to duty, you will have built up the government, amplified its authority, and taught the people renewed homage to all branches of it.

And this brings me, Mr. Chief Justice and Senators, to an inquiry as to a theory of this case, which was discussed with emphasis, with force, and with learning, and that is, whether this is a court? I must admit that I have heard defenders argue that they were *coram non judice*, before somebody who was not a judge, but I never yet heard, until now, of a plaintiff or a prosecutor coming in and arguing that there was not any court, that this case was *coram non judice*.

Nobody is wiser than the intrepid manager who assumed the first assault on this court, and he knew the only way he could prevent his case from being turned out of court was to turn the court out of his case. (Laughter.) the expedient succeeds, his wisdom may be justified, I think, and yet it will be a novelty. Now, it is said there is no word in the Constitution which gives the slightest coloring to the ida that this is a court, except that in this case the Chief Justice must preside. So that the Chief Justice's gown is the only shred or patch of justice that there is within these halls. But it is only accidentally that that is here, owing to the character of the inculpated defender.

This, we are told, is a Senate to hold an inquest of office on Andrew Johnson. But we have not observed in your rules that each Senator is to rise in his place, and say:— "Office found," or "office not found." Probably every Senator does not expect to find it. [Laughter.] Your rules, your Constitution, your habit, your etiquette, all assume that there is a procedure here of judicial nature, and we found out finally on our side of the controversy that it was so much of a court at least that you could not put a leading question, and that is about the extreme exercise of the character of a court which we always habitually discover.

Now the Constitution, as has been pointed out to you, makes this a court. It makes this a trial, and it assigns a judgment; it accords a power of punishment to its procedure, and it provides that a jury in all judicial proceedings of a criminal nature shall be necessary, except in this court and under this form of procedure. We must assume, then, that so far as words go, it is a court, and nothing but a court. But it is a question, as the honorable manager says, of substance and not of form, and he concedes that if it be a count, you must find upon evidence something to make out the guilt of the offender to secure a judgment.

He argues against its being a court, not from any nice criticism of words, but, as he expresses it, for the substance. He has endeavored by many references, and by an interesting and learned brief appended to his opening speech, of English precedents and authorities to show that it is almost anything but a court. But, perhaps, during the hundreds of years in which the instrument of impeachment was used as a political engine, if you look only to the judgments and the reasons of the judgments you would not think it was really a very judicial proceeding, but that through all English history it was a proceeding in a court controlled by the rules of a court, as a court cannot be doubted.

Indeed, as we all know, though the learned manager has not insisted upon it, the trial, under the peculiar procedure and jurisdiction of impeachment in the House of Lords, was a part of the general jurisdiction of the House of Lords, as the great court of the Kingdom in all matters, civil and criminal. One of the favorite titles of the lords of Parliament in these early days was judges of Parliament; and now the House of Lords in England is the supreme court of that country as distinctly as ever the great tribunal of that name is in this country. But one page of British sound authority will put to flight all those dreamy, misty notions about a law and a procedure of Parliament in this country and in this trial that is to supersede the Constitution and the laws of our country. And now I will show you what Lord Thurlow thought of that suggestion, as prevalent or expected to prevail in England in the trial of Warren Hastings. Lord Thurlow said:—

"My lords, with reference to the laws and usages of Parliament, I utterly disclaim all knowledge of such laws; they have no existence. True, it is, in times of despotism and popular fury, when they impeached an individual and wished to crush him by the strong hand of power, of tumult or of violence, the laws and usages of Parliament were arre ted in order to justify the most iniquitous or atrocious acts; but in these days of light and of constitutional government, I trust that no man will be tried except by the law of the land, a system admirably calculated to protect innocence, and to punish crime." And after showing that in all the State trials under the Stuart reign, and even down to that of Sacheverell, were to be found the strongest marks of. tyranny, oppression, and injustice, lord Thurlow continued:—

"I trust your lordships will not depart from the recognized established law of the land. The Commons may impeach. Your lordships are to try the case, and the same rules of evidence, and the same legal forms that obtain in courts of law will, I am confident, be observed in this Assembly."

But the learned manager did not tell us what this was if it was not a court. It is true, he said it was a Senate, but that conveys no idea. It is not a Senate conducting legislative business; it is not a Senate acting on executive business; it is not a Senate acting in Congress on political forces; and the question remains, If it is not a Senate, what is it? If this is not an altar of justice; what is it if we are not all ministers of justice here to feel its sacred flame? What is the altar, and what is it that we do here about it? It is an altar of sacrifice, if it is not an altar of justice. and to what divinity is that altar erected but to to the divinity of party hate and party rage.

What, then, is the altar about which you are to minister? Now, our learned managers, representing the House of Representatives do not seem to have been at all at pains to conceal the party spirit and the party hate which displayed itself in the haste, record, and maintenance of this impeachment; and to show you what progress we may make in the course of thirty years in the true idea of the Constitution and of the nature of impeachment, let me read to you what the managers of the impeachment of Judge Peck had to say in that behalf. The managers on that occasion consisted of Judge Ambrose Spencer, of New York; Mr. Henry A. Stories, of New York; Mr. Mc-Duff and Mr. Pinckney, of South Carolina, and Mr. Wickliffe, of Kentucky, a pretty solid body of managers.

Ambrose Spencer, as stern a politician as he was an upright judge, upon the case, let me ask attention to what he said. "There is, however," said he, "one cheering and consolatory reflection—the House of Representatives, after a patient and full examination, came to the result to impeach Judge Peck by a very large majority, and the record will show the absence of all party feeling. Could I believe that that appeal for influence had mingled itself with a predominating power in that vote, no earthly consideration could prevail over me as one of the prosecutors of this impeachment. I have no words to express the abhorrence of my soul at the indulgence of such unhallowed feeling upon such a solemn procedure."

Now, Mr. Manager Butler talked to you many hours. Did he say anything wiser or juster or safer for the republic than that. Judge Spencer knew what it was to be a judge as well as a politician for twenty years. While on the bench in New York, a great judicial light in the common law jurisprudence of that State, he was the head and leader of a political party, and earnest, and unflinching in support of its measures and its discipline, and yet no lawyer, no suitor, no critic, ever ventured to say, to think, or to feel that Judge Spencer, on the bench, was the politician, or carried any trait or trace of party feeling on it.

Judge Spencer was a politician. In the House of Representatives Judge Spencer, in the management of an impeachment, could only say that, if party feeling mingled in it, he would have nothing to do with it; from his soul he abhorred it in reference to so solemn a procedure. Yes, indeed, this divinity of party hate, when it possesses a man,

throws him now into the fire and now into the water, and he is unsuitable to be a judge until he can come again clothed and in his right mind. But, to come down to the words of our English history and experience, if this is not a court it is a scaffold as the honorable manager (Mr. Stevens) yesterday told you. Each of you brandishes now, according to him, a cord and axe, having tried the offender on the night of the 21st of February last. Now, I would not introduce those bold words which should make this a scaffold in the eyes of the people of the country, and that should make your headsmen brandish your acts. The honorable manager has done so, and I have no difficulty in saying to you that if you are not a court, then you are that which he describes, and nothing else.

Is it true, that on the 21st of February, for a crime committed by the President at midday of that day, and on impeachment already moving forward to this Chamber from the House of Representatives, you did hold a court and did condemn him? If so, then you are here vindicating about the scaffold of execution, and the part which you are to play is only the part assigned you by the honorable manager, and he warned you to hold true fealty to your own judgment, and not to blanch at the sight of blood. Now, to what end is this precedent offered? To expel from this tribunal all ideas of a court and of justice? What is it but a bold, reckless, rash and foolish avowal that if it be a court, there is no case here which, upon judicial reason, or judicial scrutiny, or judicial weighing and balancing of facts and of law, could result in a judgment.

Alas! to what ends are the wisdom and the courage of civil prudence and the knowledge of history which our ancestors brought to the framing of the Constitution? Of what service those wise, those honest framers of the Constitution on ex post facto laws and bills of attainder? What is a bill of attainder? What is a bill of pains and penalties in the experience, the learning of English jurisprudence and Parliamentary history? Why, it is a proceeding by a Legislature as a Legislature—an act, trial, sentence and punishment all in one. Certainly, if you do not sit under the law to examine evidence, to be impartial, and to regard it as a question of personal guilt, to be followed by personal punishment and personal consequence to the alleged delinquent.

The counsel and the wisdom of our fathers all pass for nothing now. Our ancestors were brave and wise, but they were not indifferent to the dangers which attended this tribunal. They had no resources where they could so well fix this necessary duty in a free government, to servants amenable to public justice unless they devolved it on the Senate. But let me show you within the brief compass of the debate as it appears on the journal of the convention which framed the Constitution, how the fears and the doubts predominated. Mr. Madison objected to the trial of the President by the Senate, and especially as he was to be impeached by the other branch of the Legislature, and for any act which might be called a misdemeanor. The President, under these circumstances, was made, improperly, dependent upon Congress. He would prefer the Supreme Court for the trial of impeachment, or rather a tribunal of which that might form a part.

Mr. Gouverneur Morris thought that no other tribunal than the Senate could be trusted. The Supreme Court was too few in number, and might be warped or corrupted. He was against the dependence of the executive on the legislature, considering legislative tyranny the greatest danger to be apprehended; but there could be no danger that what the Senate would say on a trial, on their oaths, that the President was guilty of crimes of facts, especially as in four years he could be turned out. That was Gouverneur Morris's wisdom as to the extent to which the Senate might be trusted under the sanction and the obligations of their judicial oaths.

But Mr. Pinckney disapproved of making the Senate a Court of Impeachment, as rendering the President too dependent on the Legislature. If he opposes a primary law the two Houses would combine against him, and, under the influence of hate and faction, throw him out of office. Now, there is the sum and substance of the wisdom which our ancestors could bring to this subject, as to whether this was to be a court. Is is undoubtedly a very great burden, and a very exhaustive test on a political body, to turn it into a court for the trial of an Executive.

I may hereafter point out to you the very peculiar, the very comprehensive and aggressive concurrence and combination of circumstances combined in this trial, which require of you to brace yourselves on all the virtue that belongs to you, and to hold on to that oath for the Divine aid which may support you under these most extreme tests of human conduct to which our Constitution subjects you.

Now, what does the Constitution do for us? A few little words, that is all. Truth, justice, oath, duty; and what does the whole scope of our moral nature, and what support we may hope for; higher and extend to in any of our affairs of life than this. Truth, justice, oath, duty are the ideas which the Constitution has forced upon your souls to-day.

You receive them, or you neglect them; whichever way you turn you cannot be the same men afterwards that you were; accept them, embrace, obey, and you are noble, and stronger, and better. Spurn and reject them, and you are worse, and baser, and weaker, and wickeder than before. It is this, that a free government must be always held to the power of duty, to the maintenance of its authority, and to the prevalence of its own strength for its perpetual existence. They are little words, but they have a great power. Truth is to the moral world what gravitation is to the material world. It is the principle on which it is established and coheres. The adaptation of truth to the affairs of men is in human life what the mechanism of the heavens is to the principle which sustains the forces of the globe, duty is acceptance of obedience to those ideas, and this once gained secures the operation that was intended. When, then, you have been submissive to that oath, that faith among men which, as Burke says, holds the moral elements of the world together, and that faith in God which binds the world to His throne, subdues you to the service of truth and justice. The purity of the family and the sanctity of justice have ever been cared for and will ever be cared for by the ever-living guardian of human rights and interests, who does not neglect what is essential to the preservation of the human race and its advance.

The faries in old mythology had charge of the sanctity of an oath. The imaginations of the prophets of the world have sanctified the solemnity of an oath, and have peopled the places of punishment with oath-breakers. All the tortures and torments of history are applied to public servants, who, in betrayal of sworn trusts, have disobeyed this high, this necessitous obligation, without which the whole fabric of society falls into pieces. Now, I do not know why or how it is that we are so constituted, but so it is—the moral world has it laws as well as the material world—why a point of steel lifted over a temple or hut should draw the thunderbolt and speed it safely into the ground.

I know not how, in our moral constitution, an oath lifted to Heaven can draw from the great swollen cloud of passion, and of interest, and of hate, its charge; I know not, but so it is, and be sure that loud and long as these honorable managers may talk, although they speak in the voice of all the people of the United States, with their bold persuasions, that you shall not obey a judicial oath, I can bring against it but a single sentence and a single voice, but that sentence is a commandment, and that voice speaks with awe:—"Thou shalt not take the name of the Lord thy God in vain, for the Lord will not hold him guiltless that taketh His name in vain."

The moth may consume the ermine of that Supreme Court whose robes you wear, rust may corrode, Senators, the centre of your power, nay, Messrs. managers, time even shall devour the people whose presence, beating against the door of their Senate, you so much love to taunt and menace, but as to the word which I have spoken heaven and earth may pass away, but no jot or title of it will fail.

At this point Mr. Evarts yielded to a motion to adjourn, and the court, at 4½, adjourned until 12 o'clock to-morrow.

PROCEEDINGS OF WEDNESDAY, APRIL 29.

The court was opened in due form. Despite the unfavorable weather, the desire to hear Mr. Evarts had filled the galleries at an earlier hour than usual.

Mr. Nelson's Challenge.

Mr. SUMNER submitted an order reciting that Mr. Nelson, of the counsel for the President, having used disorderly words directed to one of the managers, namely:—"So far as any questions that the gentleman desires to make of a personal character with me is concerned, this is not the place to make them. Let him make it elsewhere, if he desires to do it;" and that language being discreditable to these proceedings, and apparently intended to provoke a duel, therefore that gentleman justly deserves the disapprobation of the Senate.

Mr. NELSON—Mr. Chief Justice and Senators—

Mr. SUMNER—I must object unless it is in direct explanation.

Mr. NELSON—All I desire to say this morning—

Mr. SHERMAN—I object to the consideration of the order.

Mr. NELSON—All that I desire to do is to read the letters as I suggested to the Senate on yesterday.

The Chief Justice—The order offered by the Senator from Massachusetts is not before the Senate if objected to.

Mr. BUTLER—I trust, so far as I am concerned, that on anything that arose yesterday—any language toward me—no further action will be taken. As to the reading of the letters, I object to them until they can be proved.

Mr. JOHNSON—I move to lay the resolution offered by the Senator from Massachusetts on the table.

The Chief Justice—It is not before the Senate.

Mr. NELSON again endeavored to get the attention of the Senate.

Mr. SUMNER—I must object to any person proceeding who has used the language in this Chamber used by that gentleman.

The Chief Justice—The Chief Justice thinks the Senate can undoubtedly give leave to the counsel to proceed if they see fit. If any objection is made, the question must be submitted to the Senate.

Mr. TRUMBULL—After what has occurred, and the statement having been received from them, I think it is proper that the counsel should also have permission to make a statement in explanation, and I move that he have leave.

Mr. SUMNER—I wish to understand the motion made by the Senator from Illinois. Is it that the counsel have leave to explain his language of yesterday?

Mr. JOHNSON—Debate is not in order.

The Chief Justice—No debate is in order.

Mr. TRUMBULL—My motion is, that he have leave to make his explanation. Inasmuch as one of the managers has made an explanation, I think it due to the counsel.

The motion was decided in the affirmative without a division.

Apology.

Mr. NELSON—Mr. Chief Justice and Senators, I hope you will allow me before I make an explanation to say a single word in answer to the resolution of the Senator. My remarks were made in the heat of what I esteemed to be very great provocation. I intended no offense to the Senate in what I said, and if anything is to be done with the resolution, I trust the Senate will permit me to defend myself against the imputation. As the honorable managers desire that this thing should end here, however, I meet it in the same way. So far as I am concerned I have nothing more to say of a personal nature. I will read the letters as part of my explanation.

Senator HOWE and others objected.

The Disputed Letters.

The Chief Justice—The Chief Justice is of the impression that the leave does not extend to the reading of the letters. If any Senator makes the motion it can be done.

Senator DAVIS—I rise to a point of order. After the Senate has permitted one of the counsel to make an explanation, I make the question whether a manager has any right to interpose an objection? I think a Senator may have such right, but I deny that the manager has any such right.

The Chief Justice—The Chief Justice understood the motion of the Senator from Illinois, Mr. Trumbull, to be confined to an explanation of the personal matter which arose yesterday, and as it did not extend to the reading of the letters, it is a question to be submitted to the Senate; leave can be given if the Senate sees fit.

Senator HOWARD—I beg leave respectfully to object to the reading of the letters proposed to be read by the counsel.

The Chief Justice—No debate is in order.

Senator HOWARD—I raise an objection to the letters being read until after they have been submitted to the managers for examination.

Senator HENDRICKS—I move that the counsel be allowed to read so much of the letters as will show what date they bear.

Senator TIPTON—I call for the regular order of of the morning, the defense of the President.

The Chief Justice—The regular order is the motion of the the Senator from Indiana, Mr Hendricks.

Senator HOWE called for a restatement of the motion.

Senator HENDRICKS—The motion I made is, that the attorneys for the President be allowed to read so much of the letter as will show its date and the place at which it was written.

The motion was agreed to.

Mr. NELSON—The first letter to which I alluded is the letter bearing date March 9th, 1868, addressed by Benj. F. Butler to Col. J. W. Shaffer, Washington, D. C.

Senator JOHNSON—Is that the original letter, or a copy?

Mr. NELSON—I understand it to be an original letter. My understanding is that these are the genuine signatures of Benj. F. Butler, Mr. Logan and Mr. Garfield. I am not acquainted with the handwriting and only speak from information. The Senate will allow me to read it. It is a very short one. I do not mean—

Senators HOWARD and HOWE objected.

The Chief Justice—The counsel cannot read it under the order made.

Mr. NELSON—The fact that I want to call attention to, is that this letter on the caption bears date on the 9th of March, 1868. It is signed by Benj. F. Butler. Below the signature, "I concur in the opinion above expressed by Mr. Butler," signed John A. Logan. Below that are the words, "and I," signed John. A. Garfield. There is no other date of that title except the 9th of March, 1868.

Senator JOHNSON—Is the handwriting of the date the same as the signature?

Mr. NELSON—The handwriting and the date are in precisely the same handwriting as the address. The body of the letter above the signature, as I take it, is in a different handwriting. On the 16th of March, 1868, Mr. Chauncey F. Black addressed a letter to the President stating that he inclosed the copy of the letter which I just referred to, and in order that the Senate may understand it, you will observe that the copy is, as I believe, identical with the original letter which I have produced here.

Senator HOWE objected to any argument, and the Chief Justice cautioned the counsel.

Mr. NELSON—If your Honor please, I cannot explain the matter without explaining this fact. I am not trying to make any argument.

Senator HENDRICKS—My motion was that the counsel should be permitted to read so much as would show the date, not to go further, except so far as may be in direct explanation to the argument of Manager Butler.

Mr. NELSON—I cannot explain about the date of this copy, unless I tell you the difference about those papers which I have read. It is impossible for me to explain the date. All that I can say is that this copy bears the same date as the original, and bears the additional signatures of Messrs. Koontz, Stevens, Moorhead, Blaine and Bingham, and that there is no other date to this letter except the caption of the letter, and you will see that the copy is precisely like the original down to the words, "And I, John A. Garfield," and then come the words, "I concur," signed by Messrs. Koontz, Stevens, Moorhead, Blaine and Bingham, and on that paper there is no date.

Senator TIPTON—I move that the gentleman be permitted to proceed for one hour.

The Chief Justice—The counsel for the President (Mr. Evarts) will proceed.

Mr. Butler, walking over to the desk of the President's counsel, extended his hand for the letters, and Mr. Nelson, after saying something in an inaudible tone, handed them to him, but Mr. Butler thereon turned away seemingly irritated by the accompanying remark.

Senator CAMERON offered the following:—

Ordered, That the Senate, sitting as a court of impeachment, shall hereafter hold night sessions, commencing at eight o'clock P. M. to-day, and continuing until eleven o'clock, until the arguments of the counsel for the President and the managers on the part of the House of Representatives shall be concluded.

Senator JOHNSON objected, and the order went over.

Mr. BUTLER—Mr. President, shall these orders which have been read be placed on the record.

The Chief Justice—The Chief Justice is unable to answer that question. He takes it for granted that no arrangement can be made without the consent of the Senate.

Mr. NELSON—All that I desire to do was this:—I told the honorable manager he could have them, provided he would return the original to me. I am perfectly willing that he should take them with that understanding.

The counsel then sent the letters to Mr. Butler by a page.

Mr. BUTLER—(Drawing back indignantly), No, sir.

Mr. NELSON—I will deposit them with the Secretary, sir, for the present.

Mr. BUTLER—Let the originals go on file.

Mr. Evarts Resumes his Argument.

Mr. EVARTS then took the floor in continuation of his argument. He said:—Mr. Chief Justice and Senators, if, indeed, we have arrived at a settlement or conclusion that this is a court; that it is governed by the law; that it is to confine its attention to facts applicable to the law, and regarded solely as supposed facts, to be embraced within the testimony of witnesses or documents produced in court, we have made some progress in separating, at least from your further consideration, much that has been pressed upon your attention heretofore. If the idea of power and will is driven from this assembly; if the President is here no longer exposed to attacks on the same principle that men claim to hunt the lion and harpoon the whale, then, indeed, much that has been said by the honorable managers, and much that has been urged upon your attention from so many quarters, falls harmless in your midst. It cannot be said in this Senate, *"fertur rumeris legis solutis,"* that it is caused by numbers and unrestrained by law.

On the contrary, right here is life and power, and as it is a servant in this investigation, you are here. It follows from this, that the President is to be tried on charges which are produced here, and not on common fame. Least of all, is he to be tried, in your judgment, as he has been arraigned, hour after hour in argument, upon charges which the impeaching authority, the House of Representatives, deliberately throw out as unworthy of impeachment, and unsuitable for trial. We at least, when we have an indictment brought into court, and another indictment ignored and thrown out, are to be tried on the former, and not on the latter. And if on the 9th of December last, the House of Representatives, with which by the Constitution rests the sole impeaching power under this government, by a vote of 107 to 57, threw out all the topics which make up the inflammatory addresses of the managers, it is enough for me to say that for reasons satisfactory to that authority, the House of Representatives, those charges were thrown out, so, too, if this be a trial on a public prosecution, and with the ends of public justice alone in view, the ordinary rules for the resisting of prosecuting authorities apply here; and I do not hesitate to say that this trial—to be in in our annals the most conspicuous in our history; to be scrutinized by more professional eyes; by the attention of more scholars at home and abroad; to be preserved in more libraries; to be judged of as a national trial, a national scale, and a national criterion forever—presents the

unexampled spectacle of a prosecution which overreaches judgment from the very beginning, and invades, impugns and oppresses, at every stage, the victim which it pursues. Now, the duty of constraint upon a prosecuting authority, under a government of law pursuing only public justice, is scarcely less strict and severe than that which rests upon the judge himself.

To select evidence that is not pertinent, to exclude evidence knowing that it bears upon the inquiry, to restrict evidence knowing that the field is thus closed against the true point of justice, is no part of a prosecuting authority's duty or power. Whatever may be permitted in the contest of the forum and the zeal of contending lawyers for contending clients, there is no such authority, no such duty, no such permission for a public prosecutor, much less when the proofs have been thus kept narrowed. When the charges are thus precise and technical, is it permissable for a prosecuting authority to enlarge the area of declamation and invective. Much less is it suitable for a public prosecutor to inspire in the minds of the court prejudice and extravagant jurisdiction.

Now it has usually been supposed, that on an actual trial, involving serious consequences, forensic discussion was the true method of dealing with the subject; and we lawyers appearing for the President, being, as Mr. Manager Butler has been polite enough to say, "attorneys whose practice in the law has sharpened but not enlarged their intellect," have confined ourselves to this method of forensic discussion. But we have learned here that there is another method of forensic controversy, which may be called the method of concussion. Now I understand the method of concussion to be to make a demonstration in the vicinity of the object of attack, whereas the method of discussion is to penetrate the position, and, if successful, capture it. The Chinese method of warfare is the method of concussion, and consists of a great braying of trumpets, sounding of gongs, and shouts and shrieks in the neighborhood of the opposing forces. When all this rolls away, and the air is freer, the effect is to be watched for. But it has been reserved to us in our modern warfare as illustrated here—in the Rebellion—to present a more singular and not able instance of the method of warfare by concussion than ever has been known before. A fort impregnable by the methods of discussion, "that is, penetrating and capturing it," has been, on a large scale, attempted to be captured by the method of concussion, and some hundreds of tons of gunpowder placed in a vessel near the walls of the fort, has been made the means to the concussion of this vast experiment.

Unsatisfied with that trial and its result, the honorable manager who opened this case seems to have repeated the experiment in the vicinity of the Senate. (Laughter). While the air was filled with epithets, the dome shook with invective. Wretchedness, misery, suffering and blood were made the means of this explosive mixture, and here we are surviving the concussion, and, after all, reduced to the humble and homely method of discussion which belongs to "attorneys whose intellects have been sharpened, not enlarged by the practice of law." (General and continuous laughter.) In approaching the consideration of what constitutes impeachable offenses within the true method and duty of this solemn and unusual procedure, and within the Constitution, we see that the effort of the managers was to make this an inquest of office, instead of a trial of personal and constitutional guilt. If it is an inquest of office, "Crowner's quest law" will do throughout for us, instead of the more solemn precedents and more dignified authorities and duties which belong to solemn trials. Mr. Manager Butler has given us a very thorough and well-considered suggestion of what constitutes an impeachable offense. Let me ask your attention to it. We define, therefore, an impeachable high crime or misdemeanor to be one, in its nature *or consequences, subversive of some fundamental or essential principle of government,* or highly prejudicial to the public interest, and they may consist of a violation of the Constitution, of law, of an official oath, or of duty, by an act committed or omitted, or without violating a positive law, by the abuse of discretionary powers, from improper motives, or for any improper purpose. Now, what large elements are included in that section?

The act must be subversive of some fundamental or essential principle of government, or highly prejudicial to the public interest, and must proceed from improper motives, or for an improper purpose. Now that was intended in the generality of its terms, to avoid the necessity of actual and positive crime. But it has given us in one regard everything that was needed to show what an impeachable offense must be. Now the fallacy of these general qualifying terms is in making them the substance of the crime, instead of the condition of the peccadility. You must have the crime defined under the law and Constitution, and even then it is not impeachable, unless you affect it with some of those public, general and important qualities which are indicated in this definition by the learned and honorable manager. Now let us look at a statement made by a committee of managers of the House of Representatives in the case of the impeachment of Judge Peck.

Mr. Evarts read an extract from the remarks of Mr. Buchanan, chairman of the managers in the case of Judge Peck, to the effect that the managers were bound to prove that the respondent had violated the Constitution or some known law of the land, and had committed misbehavior in office. He also read from Burke's invective in the case of Warren Hastings, to show that the charges against Hastings were not for errors or mistakes, such as wise and good men might fall into, and which might produce very pernicious effects without being, in fact, great offenses, and that a large allowance ought to be made for human infirmity and for human error, and that the crimes charged against him were not defects of judgment, or errors common to human frailty, which could be allowed for, but were offenses having their roots in avarice, insolence, treachery and criminality.

Mr. Evarts then continued:—I need not insist on the very definite, concise and effective argument of the learned counsel who opened the case for the respondent (Mr. Curtis), as to the clause in the Constitution prohibiting ex post facto laws and bills of attainder. But it is essential here that the act charged shall have what is crime against the Constitution and crime against the law, and then that that crime shall have those public propositions which are indicated in the definition of the opening manager, and those traits of freedom from errors which belongs, in the language of Mr. Burke, to an arduous public station. You will then perceive that under this necessary condition, either this judgment must be arrived at, that there is no impeachable offense here which carries with it these conditions, or else that the evidence offered in behalf of the respondent, which was to negative, which was to countervail, which was to refute all these qualifications, should have been admitted.

When a court like this has excluded the whole range of evidence relating to the public character of the accused, and to the difficulties of an arduous public station, it must have determined that the crime charged does not partake of that quality, or else the court would have regarded the charge to have been affirmatively supported by proof, and would have permitted the proofs to be refuted by a countervailing evidence. When a court sits only for a special trial, when its proceedings are incapable of review, when neither its law nor its facts can be subjected to reconsideration, the nceessary consequence is that when you come to make up your judgment, you must take into consideration all that offered to be proved, all that could fairly have been proved, or else it is your duty, before you reach the inevitable step of judgment and sentence, to resume the trial and call in the rejected evidence.

I submit it to you that a court without review, without new trial, without exception and without possible correction of errors, must deal with evidence in this rule; and that unless you arrive—as I suppose you must—at the conclusion that the determinations of this trial relate to a formal, technical infraction of a statute law that has been brought in evidence here, it will be your duty to reopen your doors, call the respondent again before you, and go into the field of inquiry, which has not been permitted to him, but has been occupied by passion and declamation on the part of the managers. When the powers of the Constitution put into it, as the necessary result of a trial of the President of the United States, and of his conviction, that his punishment should be deprivation of office, and that the public should suffer the necessity of an elec tion they showed you what they meant by high crimes and misdemeanors.

I know that soft words have been used by every manager here on the subject of the mercy of our Constitution in the smallness of the punishment—that it does not touch life, liberty or property. Is that the sum of the penalty? Is that the measure of punishment? Why, you might as well say that when the mother feels for the first time the newborn infant's breath, and it is snatched from her and destroyed before her eyes, that you have not deprived her of life, liberty or property; and, therefore, that the punishment is light in a Republic where public spirit is the life, and where public virtue is the glory of the State; and this in the presence of public men, possessing great public talents, high public passions and ambitions made up as this body of men, springing, many of them, from the ordinary conditions of American life, and by the force of their native talents and by the high qualities of endurance and devotion to the public service, who have elevated themselves into their eminent positions, if not the envy, the admiraion of all their countrymen. It is gravely proposed to you, holding this elevated position, and who still not disdains to look upon the Presidency of the United States as still a higher, a nobler, and a greater office, to say that it is a little thing to take a President from his public station and to strike him down, branded with high crimes and misdemeanors, to be a by-word and a reproach through the long vista of history forever and ever. In the great hall of Venice where long rows of doges cover the walls with their portraits, the one erased, the one defeatured canvas attracts to it, every eye; and yet we are to be told that one who, through his devotion to the public service, has reached the highest public eminence in the State, may be cast down forever into a pool, not of oblivion, but of infamy, and may carry with him to his posteriity, for generations, that infamy; and that is a trifling matter, and does not touch life, liberty or property. If these are the estimates of public character, of public fame, of public disgrace, with which you, the writers of this country are to record, you have indeed written for the youth of the country the solemn lesson that he is dust and ashes, indeed.

Why are the people of this country to be called to a Presidential election in the middle of a term, altering the whole calendar, it may be, of the government because there may have been an infraction of penal statute? It is accidental, to be sure, that the enforced and irregular election which must follow on your sentence at this time, concurs with the usual quadrennial elections, but it is simply accidental. The provision of that penal law limiting the scale of punishment is, that the fine shall not exceed ten thousand dollars, and that the imprisonment shall not exceed five years; but a fine of six cents and an imprisonment of one day, according to the nature of the offense, within the discretion of the court, may satisfy public justice under an indictment for violation of the law. Nor was this unrestricted mercy of the law unattended to in the debate on the bill. The honorable Senator from Massachusetts (Mr. Sumner) in the course of the discussion of that section of the bill, having suggested that it would be well at least to have a moderate minimum of punishment, and having suggested a thousand dollars or five hundred dollars as the lowest limit, the Senate acted on this wise intimation that some time or other there might come to be a trial under this section before a court which had a political virus.

Mr. Evarts read short extracts from the remarks of Senators Sumner, Edmunds and Williams, and continued: —That being the measure and that the reason of the law, there is clamped upon it a necessary and inevitable result which is to bring these vast consequences to the State and to the respondent. But even then you do not know or understand the full measure of the discretion unless you attend to the fact that such formal technical crimes as are made the subject of conviction and sentence are, according to the principles of our Constitution, and to the system of every other civilized government, made the subject of pardon; but under this process of impeachment there is but one punishment, and that the highest that can be inflicted upon the public fame and character of a man. The punishment is immitigable, immutable, irreversible, unpardonable, and no power whatever can lighten or relieve the load with which an impeached and convicted public servant goes forth from your chamber with a punishment heavier than he can bear. And now what answer is there to this but the answer that will take the load of punishment and infamy from him, and place it somewhere else. True it is that if he be unjustly convicted for technical and formal faults, then the judgment of this great nation of intelligent and independent men stamps upon his judges the consequences which they have failed to inflict upon the victim of their power. Then it is that the maxim is true—*Si innocens damnatur index quoque damnatur.* Then it is that the maxim finds its realization in the forum of public opinion, and in the recorded history of the country. I have introduced this consideration simply to show you that those notions that if you can prove that a man has stumbled over a statute, it is essential he must pay the penalty, find no support in reason, none in law, none in the good sense of this high tribunal, none in the habits and views of the great people whom we represent. Indeed, we should come under the condemnation of Cicero if we were to seek on this narrow view of law such consequences as I have pointed out. "*Summum jus sacpe, summa injuria est.*" The extremity of the law is often the extremity of wickedness.

And now I am prepared to consider the general traits and qualities of the offenses charged, and I shall endeavor to pursue in the course of my argument three propositions:—

First. That the alleged infractions of this penal statute are not in themselves, or in any quality or color that has been fastened upon them by the evidence in this case, impeachable offenses.

Second. That whatever else there is attendant, appurtenant, or in the neighborhood of the subjects thus presented for your consideration, is wholly political, not the subject of jurisdiction in this court, or in any court, but only in the great forum of political judgment, to be debated at the hustings and in the newspapers, by the orators and writers to whom we are always so much indebted for correct and accurate views of the subjects presented for such determinations. If I can accomplish this, I shall have accomplished everything.

Third. I shall ask your attention to the precise acts and facts as disclosed in the evidence, and charged in the articles, and shall bring you I think, to a safe and indisputable conclusion, that even the alleged infractions of penal law have none of them in fact, taken place.

We must separate, at least for the purpose of argument, the inuendoes, the imputations, the aggravation, which find their place only in the oratory of the managers, or only in your own minds, as conversant with the Constitution. Up to twelve o'clock on February 21, 1868, the President was innocent and unimpeachable, and at one o'clock on the same day he was guilty, and impeachable of the string of offenses which fill up all the articles.

Leaving out the Emory article, which relates to conversation on the morning of the 22d of February, what he did was all writing; what he did was all public and official what he did was all communicated to all the authorities of the government having relation to the subject.

Therefore you have at once proposed for your consideration, a fault, not of personal delinquency, not of morality, not of turpitude, not one which disparages in the judgment of mankind, not one which degrades or affects the position of the malefactor. It is, as Mr. Senator Williams truly said;—"A new offense under the laws, an offense not involving turpitude, and rather of a political character."

Now, too, on the proofs:—This offense carries no consequence beyond what its action indicates, to wit: a change in the head of a department. It is not a change of department; is is not an attempt to wrest a department or apply an office, against the law, contrary to the regulations of the government, or against the safety or the peace of the State. Not in the least. Whatever imagination may suggest, whatever invective may intimate, the fact is that it had no other object and no other plan, and would have had no other consequence, than the substitution for Mr. Stanton of some other citizen of the United States, who, by the advice and consent of the Senate, should be put in the vacant place of the Secretary of War, and to have, until that advice and consent were given, the office filled by some legal *ad interim* holder of it.

If, then, the removal had been effected; if the effort to

assert a constitutional authority by the President had been effectual, no pretense is made or can be made that anything was contemplated which could be considered as placing any branch of the government out of the authority of law. Whatever there might be of favor or support of public opinion in favor of Mr. Stanton for that post, and however well deserved all that may be, Senators cannot refuse to understand that there was nothing in his removal which should be exaggered into a crime against the safety of the State.

But I go a little further than that and say, that however great may have been the credit with the houses of Congress, and with the people of his own party, which Mr. Stanton enjoyed, it cannot be doubted that there was a general and substantial concurrence of view in Congress, among all the public men in the service of the government, and among the citizens generally, that the situation disclosed to public view and public criticism, an antagonism between a head of a department and the President of the United States, not suitable for the public service, and was not to be encouraged as a situation in the conduct of the executive government; and that there was a general opinion among thoughtful men and considerate people that, however much the politics of the Secretary of War might be regarded as better than the politics of the President, if they would uphold the form of government and recognize the official rights that belong to the two positions, it was a fair and just thing for the President to expect the retirement of the Secretary of War, rather than that his just and necessary powers should be crippled. It follows that the whole thing, in act, in purpose and in conduct, is a formal contravention of a statute. I will not say how criminal that may be; I will not say whether absolute, inflexible, personal obedience to every law of the land may not be exacted under penalty of death from everybody holding public station. That is a matter for the legislators. Now when you consider that this new law really reverses the whole action of the government; that, in the language of the Senators and Representatives who spoke in its behalf, it revolutionizes the practice of the government; and when you consider that the only person in the United States whom that law in relation to the holders of offices was intended to affect, or could, by its terms, affect, was the President of the United States; when you consider that nobody was subjected to it; that it was made a rule, a control, a restraint, a mandate, a diction, to nobody else in the United States except the President, just as distinctly as if it had said in it:—If the President shall remove from office, he shall be punished by fines and imprisonment, and when you know that it was claimed that the President, under the Constitution, had a right to remove from office, you at once see that, by a necessary exclusion and conclusion, it was an act political in its nature, and that its violation in support of, and in obedience to a higher obligation of the Constitution, should bring no such consequences as are attempted to be inflicted here now. Whenever anybody puts himself in that position it cannot be made a crime of in the moral judgment, or in the judicial determination of the sentence and measure of punishment.

But we are committed by the managers to the most extraordinary views on the subject of violating what is called an unconstitutional law. Why, nobody ever violates an unconstitutional law, because there never is any such obstacle to man's action, freedom, duty and right as an unconstitutional law. The question is whether he violates the law; not whether he violates a written paper published in a statute book, but whether he violates law; and the first lessons under a written constitution are and must be that a law unconstitutional is no law at all. The learned manager, Mr. Boutwell, speaks of law being annulled by the judgment of the Supreme Court, but the Supreme Court never annuls a law.

There is no difference in the binding force of a law, after the Supreme Court has annulled it, as he calls it, from what there was before. The Supreme Court has no political function; it has no authority or power to annul a law It has the faculty of judgment to discern what the law is, and what the law has been, and so to administer it. Apply this to an indictment for a violation of the Tenure of Office act, and, supposing that act to be unconstitutional, is a man to be punished because he has violated it, and because the Supreme Court has not yet declared it unconstitutional? No; he comes into court and says, "I have violated no law." The statute is read. The Constitution is read. The judges say you have violated no law, and that ends the matter. The man does not need to appeal to the decision of the court as to the measure of punishment, or to the mercy of the Executive. In the matter of pardons he has done what was right, and he needs to make no apology to Congress or to anybody else, but Congress owes an apology to him. I shall consider this matter more fully hereafter, and now allude to it only in view of fixing a necessarily reduced estimate of criminality in the act. Much has been said about the duty of the President to execute unconstitutional law. I claim that the President has no greater right in relation to a law which operates on him in his public duty, and upon him obviously to raise a question under the Constitution to determine to his right, and what his duty is, than any citizen has in private capacity, when a law infringes upon his constitutional rights, to say that Congress has no right to pass unconstitutional laws, and yet, that everybody is to obey them just as if they were constitutional, and to be punished for breaking them just as if they were constitutional; and to be prevented from raising the question whether they are constitutional, is, of course, trampling the Constitution, and those who obey it into the dust. Obey the Constitution as against an act

of Congress which invades it. If the act of Congress, with the sword of its justice, can cut off his head, and the Constitution has no power to save him, and there can be nothing but debate hereafter, whether he was properly punished or not, gentlemen neglect the first and necessary conditions of all constitutional government of this nature. But, again, the form of the alleged infraction of this law, whether it was constitutional or not, is not such as to bring any person within any imputation, I will not say of formal infraction of the law, but of any violent resistance to or contempt of the law. Nothing was done whatever but to issue a paper and have it delivered, which puts the posture of things in this condition, and nothing else. The Constitution, we will suppose says that the President has a right to remove the Secretary of War.

The act of Congress says that the President shall not remove the Secretary of War. The President says, "I will issue an official order which will raise the question between my conduct and the statute that the statute raises between itself and the Constitution." As there is and can be, and ever should be a reference of a law to the revision and determination of the Supreme Court, or of some other court, so when the Constitution and the law are, or are supposed to be at variance, or inconsistent, everybody upon whose rights are invaded has a right, under the usual condition of conduct, to put himself in a position to act under the Constitution and not under the law. The President of the United States has it all on paper thus far. The Constitution is on paper. The law is on paper, and he issued an order on paper, which is an assertion of the Constitution and a denial of the law. That paper has legal validity if the Constitution sustains it, and is illegal, invalid, and ineffectual,

If the law prohibits it, and if the law is conformed to the Constitution therefore, it appears that nothing was done but the mere course and process in the exercise of right, claimed under the Constitution, without force, without violence, and making nothing but the altitude of assertion, which, if questioned, might raise the point of judicial determination. Now, Senators, you are not, you cannot be unfamiliar with the principle of our criminal law, the good sense and common justice of which, "although it sometimes is pushed to extremes," approves itself to every honest mind, and that is that criminal punishments under any form of statute, or any definition of crime, shall never be made to operate upon acts, even of force and violence, which are or honestly may be believed to be done under claim of right.

It is for that purpose that the *animus*, the intent, the "*animus farani*," in cases of larceny; the malice prepense' in cases of murder, are made the very substance of the crime; and nothing is felt to be more oppressive, nothing has fewer precedents in the history of our legislation or of our judicial decisions, than any attempt to coerce the assertion that peaceful and civil claims of right by penal enactment. It is for that reason that our communities and our law-givers have always frowned upon any attempt to coerce the right of appeal under any restrictions or any penalties or costs. Civil rights are rights available and practical, just according as the people can avail themselves of them, and the moment you attach a punishment to the assertion of a claimed right, you infringe upon one of the necessary rights of the people.

Now, I ask your attention, at least I confess that I do it with reluctance, and contrary to my own tastes and judgment, very much to what is but a low level of illustration and of argument. But day after day it has been pressed upon you that a formal violation of a statute, although made under claim of a constitutional right and duty honestly felt by the President, is, nevertheless, a ground of impeachment, not to be impeded or prevented by any of those considerate inducements. I ask your attention to what is but an illustration of the general principle that penal laws shall not be enforced in reference to an intent governed by a claim of title. A poacher had set his wires, with the domain of the lord of a manor and had caught a pheasant in the wires; the gamester took possession of the wire and of the dead pheasant.

The poacher approached him with threats of force and violence, and took from him the wires and the dead pheasant. The poacher was arrested and tried for robbery. Vaughan, Baron, says:—"If the prisoner demanded the wires under the honest conviction that he had a right to them, though he may be liable for trespass in setting them, it is not robbery. The gamekeeper had a right to take them, and when so taken they never could have been recovered from him by the prisoner. Yet, still, if the prisoner acted under the honest belief that the property in them continued in himself, I think it is not a robbery. If, however, he used it simply as a pretense, it would be a robbery. The question for the jury is whether the prisoner did honestly believe that the property was in himself, or not." Thus does the criminal law of a free people distinguish between technical and actual faults. What mean the guarantees of the Constitution? What mean the practice and habits of English liberty, which will not allow anybody enjoying that liberty to be drawn into question criminally by any technical or formal view of law?

What mean those fundamental principles of our liberty, that no man shall be put on trial for accusation of crime, though formally committed, unless the grand jury shall choose to bring him under inculpation, and that, when he is brought under inculpation, he shall not be condemned by any judge or magistrate, but by the condemnation of his peers. Certainly, we have not so far forgotten our liberties and on what they rest, that we should bring a President of the United States under the formal apparatus of iron oppression, which, by necessity, if you set it a going shall, without crime, without fault, without turpitude, without the moral fault even of violating a statute which he believed to be binding upon him, bring about these monstrous consequences, monstrous in their condemnation of depriving him of his office and the people of the country of an executive head.

The court here, at two o'clock, took a recess for a quarter of an hour.

Mr. EVARTS continued.—I am quite amazed, Mr. Chief Justice and Senators, at the manner in which these learned managers are disposed to bear down upon people that obey the Constitution to the neglect or avoidance of a law.

It is the commonest duty of the profession to advise and maintain and advocate the violation of a law in obedience to the Constitution, and in the case of an officer whose duty is ministerial, whose whole obligation in his official capacity is to execute or give force to a law, even when the law does not bear upon him, his right then, in good faith and for the purpose of the public service, and with the view of ascertaining by the ultimate tribunal in season to prevent public mischief, whether the Constitution or the law is to be the rule of his conduct, and whether they be at variance, the officer should and does appeal to the court. I ask your attention to a case in third Seldon's reports, New York Court of Appeals, page 9, in the case of Newell, Auditor of the Canal Department, in error, against The People, State of New York The Constitution of the State of New York contains provisions restrictive upon the capacity or power of the Legislature to incur public debt.

The Legislature deeming it, however, within its right to raise money for the completion of the canals, upon a pledge of the canals and their revenue, not including what may be called the personal obligation of the State, undertook to raise a loan of six or ten millions of dollars, and Mr. Newell, the Canal Auditor, when a draft was drawn upon him, in his capacity as a ministerial officer, and obeyant to the law, refused to pay it, and raised the question whether this act was unconstitutional. Well, now, he ought to have been impeached; he ought to have had the Senate and the Court of Appeals convened on him, and been removed from office. The idea of a mere auditor setting himself up against what the learned manager calls law? He set himself up in favor of law, and against its contravention.

The question was carried to the Supreme Court of that State, and the court decided that the law was constitutional; but, upon an appeal to the Court of Appeals, that court held it unconstitutional, and the six million loan was rolled away as a scroll. Now, I would like to know if the President of the United States—who has taken an oath to preserve, protect and defend the Constitution of the United States—when a law is passed over his head, and he has appealed to the Constitution, this Constitution is to answer through the House of Representatives. We admit, for argument, that the law is unconstitutional; we admit it bears on you and your just rights, and on nothing else; and we admit that you have raised the constitutional question; yet such is the peril under which you do that, that we will cut off your head for questioning an unconstitutional law that bears upon your rights and contravenes that Constitution that you have sworn to protect and defend.

How will our learned managers dispose of this case of Newell, the auditor, against the people of the State of New York, where an upright and faithful officer acted in the common interest and for the maintenance of the Constitution? And are we such bad citizens when we advise that the Constitution of the United States may be defended, and that the President, without a breach of the peace, and with an honest purpose may make a case where the judgment of the court may be had and the Constitution sustained? Why, not long since the State of New York passed a law laying a tax on brokers' sales in the city of New York, at a half or three-quarters per cent. on all goods that should be sold by brokers, seeking to raise for the revenue purposes of the State of New York about ten millions of dollars on the brokers' sales of merchandise, which sales distributed, through the operations of that emporium, the commerce of the whole country for consumption through all the States of the Union.

Your sugar, your tea, your coffee that you consume in the valley of the Mississippi, was to be made to pay a tax in the city of New York to support the State of New York in this gigantic scheme, and they made it penal for any broker to sell them without giving a bond to pay it. Well, now, when all the brokers were in this distress, I advised some of them that the shortest way to settle that matter was, not to give the bonds, and when one of the most respectable citizens of the State was indicted by the grand jury for selling coffee without giving a bond, and it came before the courts, according to my advice, and I had the good fortune to be sustained in the Court of Appeals of the State of New York, in the proposition that the law was unconstitutional, and the indictment failed.

Was I a bad citizen for invoking the Constitution of the United States against these infractions of law? Was this defendant, in the indictment, a bad citizen for undertaking to obey the Constitution of the United States? Where are your constitutional decisions? Look at the case of Brown vs. Maryland, the Banks tax cases, all these instances by which a constitution is arrayed for the protection of the rights of the citizen; it is always by instances; it is always by big acts, and the only condition is, that it shall be done without a breach of the peace and in good faith. When Mr. Lincoln, before the insurrection had broken out, had issued the habeas corpus and undertook to arrest the mischief that was going on at Key West, where,

through the form of peace, an attack was made upon that fort and upon the government navy yard through the habeas corpus—an excellent way to take a fort— I do not know whether the honorable manager, who is so good a lawyer, tried that in any of his military experiences or not (laughter), but a habeas corpus was tried in order to strip that fort of all its soldiers, and it was succeeding admirably. The fort would have been taken by habeas corpus, but that President Lincoln suspended the habeas corpus, violating the law, violating the Constitution. Now, was it necessary that he should be impeached? What did he do? He suspended it by proclamation, on the 10th of May, 1861, and at the opening of the next session he referred to the fact of the illegality of the measures in question, saying they were ventured upon under public necessity, and committed them to the judgment of Congress. I will give you another act of this great, heroic President, the arrest of the members of the Legislature of Maryland, never justified by any law that I know of nor by the Constitution; and it so happens that the very statement there was, that "public action is to be judged by public men and public officers as private actions are to be judged by private men, according to the quality of the act," whether it shall be impeached or whether it shall be indemnified. I do not make this argument as going further than to meet the necessity which I understand the honorable managers to put forth that an infraction of a statute must carry out of office any President of the United States. Why the very next statute in this book, after the Civil Office Tenure act, on page 402, is an act to declare valid and conclusive certain proclamations of the President, and acts done in pursuance thereof in the supression of the late Rebellion. The military commissions had been declared invalid by the Supreme Court, and here we have an act of indemnity, covering a multitude of formal and technical sins, by indemnity and protection, to have the same effect as if the law had been passed.

If, therefore, this interpretation of law and duty, by their act unqualified, unscrutinized, unweighed, unmeasured, is to make the necessary occasion of a verdict of impeachment, it must be considered under the clear bright light on which true statesmanship sheds upon the subject. We, as conveniently at this point as afterwards, pay some attention to the astronomical punishment which the learned and honorable manager, Mr. Boutwell, thinks should be applied to the novel case of impeachment. Cicero, I think it is, who says that a lawyer should know everything, for sooner or later, there is no fact in history, in science, or in human knowledge, that will not come into play in his argument. Profoundly sensible of my ignorance, being devoted to a profession, "which sharpens and does not enlarge the mind," I can admire without envying the superior knowledge evinced by the honorable manager. But, nevertheless, while some of his colleagues were paying attention to an unoccupied and unappropriated island on the surface of the seas, Mr. Manager Boutwell, more ambitious, had discovered an untenanted and unappropriated region in the skies, (laughter) reserved, he would have us think in the final councils of the Almighty, as a place of punishment for convicted and deposed American Presidents. (Laughter.)

Now, at first, I thought that his mind had become so enlarged that it was not sharp enough to observe that the Constitution had limited the punishment (laughter), but on reflection, I saw that he was as legal and logical as he was ambitious and astronomical, for the Constitution has said, "removal from office," and has put no limit to the distance of removal. (Great laughter.) So, without shedding a drop of his blood, or taking a penny of his property, or ironing his limbs, he is sentenced to removal from office and transportation to the skies. (Laughter.) This is the great undertaking, and if the learned manager can only get over the obstacle of the laws of nature, the Constitution won't stand in the way. (Laughter.)

I can think of no method but that of a convulsion of the earth that should project the deposed President to this infinitely distant space; but a shock of nature of so vast an energy and so great a result might unsettle even the so firm members of Congress. (Laughter.) How shall we accomplish it? Why, in the first place, nobody knows where that space is but the learned manager himself (laughter), and he is the necessary deputy to execute the judgment of the court.

Let it then be provided, that in case of your sentence of deposition and removal from office, the honorable astronomical manager shall take into his own hands the execution of the sentence. With the President made fast to his broad and strong shoulders, and having already essayed the flight, by imagination, better prepared to execute it in form, taking advantage of ladders, as far as ladders would go, to the top of this high Capitol, and, spurning them with his feet, from the Goddess of Liberty let him set out upon his flight (laughter), while the Houses of Congress and all the people of the United States shall shout "Sicitur ad astra." (Laughter, loud and long continued.)

Here an oppressive doubt strikes me; how will the manager get back? How when he gets beyond the power of gravitation to restore him, will he get back? And so ambitious a wing as he could never stoop to a downward flight. No doubt as he passes through the expanse, that famous question of Carlyle, by which he points out the littleness of human affairs:—"What thinks Bootis of them as he leads his hunting dogs over the zenith in their leash of sideral fire," will occur to the managers. What indeed would Bootis think of this new constellation (laughter) looming through space, beyond the power of Congress to send for persons and papers? (Laughter.)

Who shall return and how decide in the contest there

begun in this new revolution thus established? Who shall decide which is the sun and which is the moon? Who shall determine the only scientific test, which reflects hardest upon the other? (Laughter). I wish to draw your attention to what I regard as an important part of my argument, a matter of great concernment and influence for all statesmen and all lovers of the Constitution—to the particular circumstances under which the two departments of the government now brought in controversy are placed. I speak not of persons, but of the actual, constant division of the two parties.

Now, the office of President of the United States, in the view of the framers of the Constitution, the experience of our national history, and in the estimation of the people, is an office of great trust and power. It is not dependent on any tenure of office, because the tenure of office is a source of original commission; yet it is, and is intended to be, an office of great authority, and the government, in its co-ordinate departments, cannot be sustained without maintaining all the authority that the Constitution has intended for this Executive office; but it depends for its place in the Constitution upon the fact that its authority is committed to the suffrage of the people, and that when this authority is exerted, it is not by individual purpose or will. Why the mere strength that a single individual can oppose to the corrective power of the Congress of the United States? It is because the people, who, by their suffrage have raised the President to his place, are behind him, holding up his hands, speaking with his voice, sustaining him in his high duties, that the President has his voice under the Constitution.

Its great power is safe thus to the people for the reasons I have stated, and it is safe to the President because the people are behind him, and have exhibited their confidence in him by their suffrage, but when one is lifted to the Presidential office who has not received the suffrage of the people for that office, then at once discord; dislocation begins; then at once the great powers of the office which are consonant with a free Constitution and with the popular will, and owes the very breath of life to the continuing power of the people; then it is that in the criticisms of the press, in the views of the people, these great powers, strictly within the Constitution, seem to be despotic and personal; and then you are subject to another difficulty that our vicious system of politics has introduced, and that is that in our nominations for the two offices, selecting always the true leader of the popular sentiment of the time for the place of President, we look about for a candidate for the Vice President to attract the minority and to assuage difficulty and to bring in consistent supporters.

Coupled with this phase in our politics, when the Vice President becomes President of the United States, not only is he in the attitude of not having the popular support for the great powers of the Constitution, but of not having the authoritative support for the fidelity and maintenance of his authority. Then, adhering to the original opinion and political attitudes which form the argument for placing him in the second place, he is denounced as a traitor to his party, and insulted and criticised by all the leaders of that party.

I speak not particularly in reference to the present incumbent, and the actual condition of parties here, but all the public men, all the ambitious men, all the men engaged in the public service, and in carrying on the government in their own views and the interests and duties of the party, all have formed these views and established their relations with the President, who has disappeared, and they, then, are not in the attitude and support, personal or political, that should properly be maintained among the leaders of a party.

Then it is that ambitious men who had formed the purpose both for the present and for the future, upon the faith of Presidential nomination, find their calculations disturbed Then it is, that prudence and wisdom find that terrible evils threaten the conduct of the government and the nation.

This we all know by looking back at the party differences in times past, as in the time of the Presidency of Mr. Tyler, when an impeachment was moved against him in the House of Representatives and had more than a hundred supporters, and it was found after it was all over that there was nothing in the conduct of Mr. Tyler to justify it. So, too, a similar imputation will be remembered in the conduct of Mr. Fillmore.

Then the opposition seize upon this opportunity, enter into the controversy, urged on the quarrel, but do not espouse it, and thus it ended in the President being left without the support of the guarantees of authority which underlie and vivify the Constitution of the United States, namely, the favor of the people; and so, when this unfortunate, this irregular condition of the Executive office concurs, with a time of great national conjointure, then, at once, you have at work the special or peculiar operation of forces upon the Executive office, which the Constitution left unprotected and undefended with the full measure of support which every department of the government should have in order to resist the others, pressing on to dangers and difficulties which may shake and bring down the pillars of the Constitution itself. I suggest then to you, as wise men, that you understand how out of circumstances for which, as man is responsible, attributable to the workings of the Constitution itself, there is a weakness, and a special weakness, in the Presidency of the United States, which is, as it were, an undefended fort, and to see to it that an invasion is not urged and made successful, by the temptation that is presented.

This exceptional weakness of the President, under our Constitution, is accompanied, in the present state of affairs, by the extraordinary development of party strength in Congress. There are, in the Constitution, but three barriers against the will of a majority in Congress. One is that which requires a two-thirds vote to expel a member of either House; another is that a two-thirds vote is necessary to pass a law over the objections of the President, and the third is that a two-thirds vote of the Senate, sitting as a court for the trial of impeachment, is necessary for conviction. And now these last two protections of the Executive office have disappeared from the Constitution, in its practical working, by the condition of parties, which has given to one the firm possession, by three-fourths, I think, in both houses, of the control of the government, of each of the other branches of the government. Reflect upon this.

I do not touch upon the particular circumstance that the non-restoration of the States has left the members in both Houses less than they might under other circumstances be. I do not calculate on whether that absence increases or diminishes the proportion that there would be in parties. Possibly their presence might even aggravate the political majority which overrides practically, on the calculations of the President's protection, in the guarantees of the Constitution. What did the two-thirds mean? It meant that in a free country where intelligence is diffused it was impossible to suppose that there would not be a somewhat equal division of parties. It was impossible to suppose that the excitement and zeal of party would carry all the members of it into any extravagancies. I do not call them extravagancies in any sense of reproach. I merely speak as to the extreme measures which parties may be disposed to adopt.

Certainly, then, there is ground to reflect before bringing to the determination this great struggle between the co-ordinate branches of the government, whether the co-ordination in the Constitution can be preserved, or whether it is better to urge a test which may operate upon the framework of the Constitution and upon its future, unattended by any exception of a peculiar nature which governs the actual situation. Ah, that is the misery of human affairs—that distresses come when the system is least prepared to receive it. It is misery that disease invades the form when health is depressed and the powers of the constitution to resist it are at the lowest ebb; it is misery that the gale rises and sweeps the ship to destruction when there is no sea room for it, and when it is on a lee shore, and if concurrently with these dangers to the good ship her crew be short, and her helm unsettled, and disorder begins to prevail, and there comes to be a final struggle for the maintenance of mastery against the elements, how wretched is the condition of that people whose fortunes are embarked in that ship of State. What other protection is there for the Presidential office but these two-third guarantees of the Constitution and the Supreme Court, placed there to determine the lines of separation, and of duty, and of power under our Constitution, between the Legislature and the President. Under the evidence proposed and rejected, the effort of the President was, when the two-thirds majority had urged the contest against him, to raise a case for the Supreme Court to decide, and then the Legislature, coming in by its special jurisdiction of impeachment, intercepts his efforts, and brings his head again within the mere power of Congress, where the two-thirds rule is equally ineffectual as between the parties to the contest.

This is a matter of grave import, of grave consideration, and is to be in the eye of history one of the determining evidences of this great controversy; for, great as is the question in the wisdom of the managers and of ourselves, and in the public intelligence of the people, as to how great the power shall be on one side or the other—with Congress or with the President—that question sinks into absolute insignificance compared with the greater and higher question—the question which has been in the minds of officers, and publicists and statesmen since our Constitution was founded—whether it was in the power of a written Constitution to draw lines of separation, and to put up buttresses of defense between co-ordinate branches of the government—

With that question settled adversely. with the determination that one can devour, and, having the power, will devour the other—then the balances of the American Constitution are lost, and lost for ever. No one can reinstate in paper what has once been struck down in fact. Mankind is governed by instances, not by resolutions. Then there is placed before the people of the country an attempt to establish new balances of power, by which the powers of the different departments, being more firmly fixed, one can be safe against the other, but who can be wiser than our fathers; who greater, who juster than they; who more considerate and more disinterested than they, and if their descendants had not the virtue to maintain what they so wisely and so nobly established, how can these same descendants hope to have the virtue or the wisdom to make a better establishment for their posterity? Now, Senators, I urge upon you to consider whether you will not recoil from settling so tremendous a subject, under so special, so disadvantageous, so disastrous circumstances as I have portrayed to you? A strong Executive, an absolute veto, with a longer term, with more permanent possession and control of official patronage will be necessary, if the wise, and just, and considerate measures of our ancestors shall not be allowed to prevail in your judgments. Or, if that be distasteful, unacceptable, inadmissable. then we will swing out all to the omnipotence of Congress, and return to the exploded experiment of the Confederation, where Congress was Executive and Legislative all at once.

There is one other general topic which is not to be left

unnoticed, on account of the very serious impression it brings upon the political situation which forms a staple of pressure on the part of the managers. I mean the very peculiar political situation of the country itself. The suppression of the armed rebellion, and the reduction of the revolted States to the power of the government, left a problem of as great difficulty in human affairs as was ever proposed to the action of any government.

The work of pacification after so great a struggle, where so great passions were enlisted, so great wounds had been inflicted; where so great discontents had originated controversies, and so much bitterness prevailed, its formal settlement presented a work of great difficulty, but there concurred with it a special circumstance, which by itself would have taken all the resources of statesmanship—I mean the emancipation of the slaves—which had thrown four millions of men, not by the process of peace, but by the sudden blow of war, into the possession of their freedom; which had placed at once, and against their will, all the rest of the population under those who had been their slaves.

Now, the process of adaptation of society and of law to so great a social change as that, even when accomplished in peace, and when not disturbed by the processes of war and by the discontent of a suppressed rebellion, was so much as any courage or any property as is given to any government can expect to carry through successfully. When these two great political facts concur and press upon a government, how vast, how difficult, how impracticable and unmanageable seems the posture of affairs. But this does not represent the measure, or even the principal feature of the difficulty.

When the government, whose arms had triumphed and suppressed resistance, is itself, by the theory and action of the Constitution, the government which by positive law is to maintain its authority, the process is simple; but under our complete government the restored Constitution surrenders their domestic affairs at once to the local governments of the people who have been in Rebellion. And then arises the question—What has formed the staple of our politics for the last four years—what has tried the wisdom, the courage, the patriotism of all? The question is, how far, under the Constitution as it stands, the General Government can exercise absolute control in the transition period between war and peace, and how much found to be thus manageable should be committed to the changes in the Constitution. When we understand that the great controversy in the formation of the Constitution itself, was how far the General Government should be intrusted with the domestic concerns, and that the people of the States were not willing to intrust the General Government with their domestic interests. We see at once how wide, how dangerous, how difficult is the arena of the controversy of constitutional law, and of differences of opinion as to what was or is constitutional, and as to what changes should be, or ought to be made in the Constitution to meet the practical situation. When you add that the people are divided on these questions, and as the parties of force on one side, and on the other are the loyal masses and the Rebel masses, and whoever divides from his neighbor, from his associates, from his party adherents in this line of constitutional opinion, and in this line of governmental action, which seems to press the least changes on the Constitution, and the least control on the masses lately in Rebellion, will be suspected and charged as an ally of traitors and Rebels. You have at once disclosed how the names of traitor and of Rebel, which belonged to the war, have been made the current phrases of political discussion. I do not question the rectitude, nor do I question the wisdom of any positions that have been taken as matter of argument, as matter of faith, or as matter of action in the disposition of this peculiar situation. I only attract your attention to the necessities and dangers of the situation itself, both in reference to public order and in reference to the changed condition of the slave. We were urged "stave super vias antiquae." It is not the question of standing upon ancient ways, for we are not on them. The problem of the situation is, as it was then, how to get on the ancient ways from those paths which disorder and violence and rebellion had forced us into, and here it was that the exasperations of politics came up, mingled with charges of infidelity to party, and of moral and political treason to the State. How many theories did we have in this Senate? If I am not mistaken, one very influential, and able and eloquent Senator was disposed to take the declaration of independence in the working forces of our Constitution as a sort of free constitution. In the other House a great leader was disposed to treat it on the trans-constitutional necessities which the situation itself imposed. And thus it was that minds trained in the old school, attached to the Constitution, were unable as orators and as reasoners, to adopt these learned phrases.

And now let me urge it, that all this is within the province of politics, and free governments would be unworthy of their freedom, and could not maintain it if their public servants, their public men, their chosen servants, were not able to draw the distinction between legal constitutional offenses and odious and abominable faults. When passions and struggles of force, in any form of violence, or of impeachment as an engine of power come into play, then freedom has become license, and then party has become faction. I hold in my hands an article from the *Tribune*, written in reference to this trial, and put with great force and skill. I do not propose to read it. I bring it here to show, and to say that it is an excellent series of articles of impeachment against the President of the United States, within the forum of politics, for political repugnance and obstruction, and as an honest conviction that the technical and formal crimes imputed in the articles before this court are of but paltry consideration.

Now, that is an excellent article of impeachment for the forum of politics, and for discussion at the hustings. There it belongs, there it must be taken. But this being a court, we are not to be tried for that of which we are not charged. How wretched the condition of him who is to be oppressed by vague, uncertain shadows, which he cannot resist. Our honorable managers must go back to the source of their authority if they would obtain what was once denied them—a general and open political charge. It must, I know, be maintainable in law, it must be maintainable in fact; but then it would be brought here, it would be written down, its dimensions would be known and understood, its weight would be estimated. The answer could be made, and then your leisure and that of the nation being occupied with hearing witnesses about political difficulties, and questions of political repugnance, and political obstruction on the part of the President, we should be heard in his defense in that political trial, and would at least have the opportunity of reducing the force of the testimony, and of bringing in the opposing and controverting proofs.

Then at least, if you would have a political trial, there would be something substantial to work upon. But the idea that the President of the United States is to be brought into the procedure of this court by a limited accusation, and be found not guilty under that, but be convicted under an indictment which the House refused to sustain, or under that wider indictment which the newspaper press present, and without an opportunity to bring proof and to make argument on the subject, seems to us too monstrous for any intelligence within or without this political circle, this arena of controversy, to maintain for a moment. My hope has been briefly to draw your attention to what lies at the basis of the discussion of the power and authority that may be rightfully exercised, or reasonably assumed to be exercised, by the President, between these two branches of the government.

The co-ordination of the powers of the government is not one of the greatest efforts in the frame of a paper constitution, but I think it must be conceded that as it occupies the main portion of the Constitution itself, so it has been regarded by all competent critics at home and abroad to have been a work most successfully accomplished by the framers of our government. Indeed if you will look at the Constitution, you will find that beyond that limit of defining what belongs to the government and what must be left to the liberties of the people, and then discriminating between what should be accorded to the General Government and what should be left to the domestic government of the States. The whole effort of the Constitution is to build up these three departments of the government, so that each should have strength to stand against the others, and not strength to encroach upon or overthrow the others.

Much has been said about Congress being the great depositor of power. Why, of course it is; it is the depositor of power and of will.

Congress must be intrusted with all the strings of power, and, therefore, the effort of the Constitution was to curb and restrain the exercise of that power by Congress, and so you find that almost all the additions to the Constitution are based upon Congress, restraining it from exercising power over the people, or over the States, or over the co-ordinate branches of the government. Nevertheless, there is an absolute and necessary deposit of authority in Congress. It is left master of the whole. To what purpose is it to provide that the judges of the Supreme Court shall hold their offices for life, and that their salaries shall not be diminished during their term of service, if Congress may omit or refuse to appropriate a dollar for the salary of that particular judge?

Nevertheless government is to be administered by men, and in an elective government the trust is that the elected agents of the people will be faithful to their interests. But simple as is the institution of the judiciary, when you come to the executive authority, then comes the problem which has puzzled, and which will puzzle all framers of government having no knowledge or idea of authority except what springs from the people. Under the British Constitution there is no difficulty in tracing up the Parliament, provided you leave standing the authority of the barons. But here the problem is, how is it without the support of the nobles? You can make an executive strong enough to maintain itself by the balance, as it is found in the Constitution. Our ancestors disposed of that question. It has served us till this time.

Sometimes in the heat of party the Executive has seemed too strong. Sometimes, in the heat of party, Congress has seemed too strong; yet every danger passes away, and the government is administered, controlled, protected by the great superior predominant interest and power of the people themselves. The essence of the Constitution is, that there is no period of authority granted by it in the six years' term to the Senate, in the four years' term to the President, and in the two years' term to the House of Representatives, that cannot be lived through in patience, subordinate and obedient, to the Constitution. As it was said in the debate in the Convention on a particular topic of impeachment, there will be no danger when a four years' occurring election restores to the common master of Congress and of the Executive the trust reposed in them. In connection with this part of his argument, Mr. Evarts read two extracts from speeches of Mr. Webster, and then, on motion of Senator Conkling, the court adjourned till twelve o'clock tomorrow.

PROCEEDINGS OF THURSDAY, APRIL 30.

The Chief Justice stated the first business to be the order offered by Senator Sumner, yesterday, censuring Mr. Nelson, of counsel, for words spoken in discussion, intended to provoke a duel, or signifying a willingness to fight a duel, and contrary to good morals.

Senator JOHNSON moved to lay the order on the table.

Sumner on Nelson.

Senator SUMNER said on that I ask the yeas and nays.

The yeas and nays were ordered. When Senator Anthony's name was called he said:—Mr. President, I would like to ask the counsel a question. I would ask him if in the remarks quoted in the resolution it was his intention to challenge the honorable manager to mortal combat. (Laughter.)

Nelson Belligerent.

Mr. NELSON—Mr. Chief Justice, it is a very difficult question for me to answer. During the recess of the Senate, the honorable gentleman remarked to me that he was going to say something on the subject of Alta Vela, and desired me to remain. He then directed his remarks to the Senate. I regarded them as charging me with dishonorable conduct before the Senate, and in the heat of the discussion, I made use of language which was intended to signify that I hurled back the gentleman's charge upon him, and that I would answer the charge in any way that he decided to call me to account for it. I cannot say that I had a duel in my mind; I am not a duelist by profession. Nevertheless, my idea was that I would answer the gentlemen in any way that he chose. I did not intend to claim any exemption on account of age, or anything else. I hope the Senate will recollect the circumstances. I have treated the gentleman with the utmost kindness and politeness, and gave marked attention to what he said, and to insult the Senate was an idea that never entered my mind. I entertain the kindest feeling towards the Senate, and would be as far as any man on the face of the earth, from insulting the gentlemen of the Senate, whom I was addressing.

The motion to lay on the table was agreed to by the following vote:—

The Vote.

YEAS.—Messrs. Anthony, Bayard, Buckalew, Cattell, Chandler, Corbet, Cragin, Davis, Dixon, Doolittle, Drake, Edmunds, Ferry, Fessenden, Fowler, Frelinguysen, Grimes, Harlan, Hendricks, Howe, Johnson, Morrill (Me.), Morton, Norton, Patterson (N. H.), Patterson (Tenn.), Ramsey, Ross, Saulsbury, Sherman, Tipton, Trumbull, Van Winkle, Vickers and Williams—35.

NAYS.—Messrs. Cameron, Howard, Morgan, Morrill (Vt.), Pomeroy, Stewart, Sumner, Thayer, Wilson and Yates—10.

So the order was laid on the table.

The Chief Justice then stated that the next business to the consideration of Mr. Cameron's order, offered yesterday, that the Senate hereafter hold sessions from 8 P. M. to 11 P. M.

Senator SUMNER offered the following as a substitute:—

Ordered, That the Senate will sit during the remainder of the trial from 10 o'clock in the forenoon till 3 o'clock in the afternoon, with such brief recess as may be ordered.

Senator TRUMBULL moved to lay the whole subject on the table, which was agreed to by the following vote:—

YEAS.—Messrs. Anthony, Bayard, Buckalew, Cattell, Corbet, Davis, Dixon, Doolittle, Drake, Ferry, Fessenden, Fowler, Frelinghuysen, Grimes, Hendricks, Howe, Johnson, McCreery, Morrill (Me.), Morrill (Vt.), Morton, Norton, Patterson (N. H.), Patterson (Tenn.), Ramsey, Ross, Saulsbury, Sprague, Trumbull, Van Winkle, Willey and Vickers—32.

NAYS.—Messrs. Cameron, Chandler, Conkling, Cragin, Edmunds, Harlan, Howard, Morgan, Ramsey, Sherman, Stewart, Sumner, Thayer, Tipton, Williams, Wilson and Yates—17.

And the subject was laid on the table.

Mr. Evarts Resumes.

Mr. EVARTS then proceeded with his argument, as follows:—

We perceive, then, Mr. Chief Justice and Senators, that the subject out of which this controversy has arisen between the two branches of the government—the executive and legislative—touches the very foundations of the balance of power in the Constitution; and in the arguments of the honorable managers it has to some extent been so pressed upon your attention. You have been made to believe, so mighty and important is this point in the controversy—the arrogation of the power of office included in the function of removal—that if it is carried to the credit of the Executive Department of government, it makes it a monarchy.

Why, Mr. Chief Justice and Senators, what a grave reproach is this upon the wisdom and foresight, the civil prudence of our ancestors, that has left unexamined and unexplored and unsatisfied, these doubts or measures of the strength of the Executive. Upon so severe a test or inquiry of being a monarchy, or a free republic, I ask, without reading the whole of it, your attention to a passage from the *Federalist*, one of the papers by Alexander Hamilton, who felt in advance these aspersions that are sought to be placed upon the establishment of the executive power in the President.

He then suggests in brief the solid discrimination and distinction between the President and a monarchy, and concludes by saying this, "What answer shall we give to those who would persuade that things unlike resemble each other? The same that ought to be given to those who tell us that a government, the whole power of which is to be in the hands of the executive and judicial servants of the people, is an aristocracy, a monarchy and a despotism." But a little closer attention to both the history of the framing of the Constitution, and to the opinions which maintained a contest in the body of the Convention—which should finally determine the general character and nature of the Constitution—will show us that this matter of the power of removal or the control of office as in dispute between the President and the Senate, touches more nearly one of the other great balances of the Constitution. I mean that that balance between the weight of numbers in the people and the equality of the States, irrespective of population, of wealth, and of size. Here it is, if I may be allowed to say so: that the opinions to which public attention was drawn by the honorable manager, Mr. Boutwell—the opinions of Mr. Sherman and their origin, one of the greatest statesmen of the last generation—said to me that it was to Mr. Sherman, and to his young colleague, Mr. Ellsworth, and to Judge Patterson, of New Jersey, that we owed it more than all else, in that Convention, that our government was made what that statesman pronounced the best government in the world—a Federal Republic; instead of being what it would have been but for these members of the Convention, as this statesman of the last generation expressed it—a consolidated empire, the worst government in the world.

And now between these two opinions it was the controversy whether the Senate should be admitted into a share of executive power of appointment. The great arm, the strength of the government came in play, and on this question of the equality of the States Mr. Sherman insisted that this participation should be reserved to the Senate, which others resisted as too great a subtraction from the sum of executive power to be safe. In this disintegration and frittering away, Mr. Adams, the first President under the Constitution, I am informed upon authority not doubted, bringing it to me from the opinions from his friends, did, in the opinion that participation in appointment, as construed and maintained in the practice of this government, would be the point upon which the Constitution would fail; that the allotting of power to a comparatively irresponsible administration in the Senate would ultimately so destroy the strength of the Executive with the people, and create so great a discontent among the people themselves with the Executive of their own choice; that they would not submit to the executive power thus bestowed, if given to a body that had its constitution without any popular election whatever, and where its basis and strength came, not by the strength and power of the people, but by the equality of the States. When you add to that this change which gave the Senate a voice in the removal from office, and then gave it the first hold upon the question of the weight of official power in the country, you change wholly the question of the Constitution, and instead of giving the Senate only the advisory course which that instrument commits to it, you change it into the absolute preliminary power of that body to say to the Executive of the United States that every administrative office under him shall remain as it is; that the officers shall be over him and against him, and that they will be with the Senate and for the Senate; and when you add to that the power of the Senate to say that "until we know and determine who the successor will be, we hold the reins of power, so that the office shall not be vacated," then you do indeed break down at once the balance between the Executive and the legislative power, and you break down the Federal election of the President at once, and commit to the equality of States the partition and distribution of the executive power of this country.

I would like to know how it is that the people of the country are to be made to adopt this principle of the Constitution, that the Executive power attributed to federal members, made up of Senators and Representatives added together from each State, that that executive power, which the people supposed was involved in its choice of President, is to be administered and controlled by a body made up of the equality of States.

I would like to know on what plan of politics it is to be carried out. How can you make the combination? How the forces; how the effects which are to clothe themselves into a popular election, and then to find that the executive power is already administered on the principle of the equality of States. I should like to know how it is that New York, and Pennsylvania, and Ohio, and Indiana, and Illinois, and Missouri, and the great and growing States are to carry the force of popular will into the executive chair, on federal members in the electoral college, and then find that Maryland and Delaware and the distant States unpeopled, are to control the whole possession and administration of the executive power.

I would like to know how long we are to keep up the form of electing a President, with the people behind him, and then bind him, stripped of the power that is committed to him in a partition of it between the States, without regard to numbers or popular opinion; there is the grave dislocation of the balances of the Constitution. There is the absolute destruction of the power of the people over Presidential authority, keeping up the form of the election while depriving it of all its results; and I would like to know if by what law or by what reason this body assumes to itself this derangement of the balances of the Constitution, as between the States and popular numbers, how long New England can maintain in its share of executive power as administered here as large a proportion as belongs to New York, to Pennsylvania, to Ohio, to Indiana, to Illinois and to Missouri together?

I must think, Mr. Chief Justice and Senators, that it has not been sufficiently considered how far these principles, thus debated, reach, and how the framers of the Constitution, when they came to debate, in the year 1789, in Congress, as to what was or should be the actual and practical allocation of that authority, understood the question in its bearing, and in its future necessities. True, indeed, that Mr. Sherman was always a stern and persistent advocate for the strength of the Senate, as against the power of the Executive. It was on that point that the Senate represented the equality of States, and he and Mr. Ellsworth, holding their places in the Convention as the representatives of Connecticut, a small State, between the powerful State of Massachusetts on the one side, and of New York on the other, and Judge Patterson, of New Jersey, a representative of that State, a small State, between the great State of New York on the one side, and the great State of Pennsylvania on the other, were the advocates of that distribution of power in the Senate, and it is well known in the history of the times that a correspondence of some importance took place between the elder Mr. Adams and Mr. Sherman, in the early days of the working of the government, as to whether the fears of Mr. Adams, that the Executive should prove too weak, or the purpose of Mr. Sherman that the Senate should be strong enough, were or were not most in accordance with the principles of the government. But all that was based upon the idea that the concurrence of the Senate, under the terms of the Constitution, in appointments, was the only detraction from the supremacy and independence of the Executive authority Now this question comes up in this form. The power of removal is and always has been claimed and exercised by the Executive of this government, separately and independently of the Senate, until the act of March 2, 1867. The actual power of removal by the Senate never has been claimed. Some construction on the affirmative exercise of the power of appointment by the Executive has at different times been suggested, and has received more or less support tending to the conclusion that then the Senate might have some hold upon the question of removal. Even this act of March 2, 1867, which we are to consider more definitely hereafter, does not assume, in terms, to give the Senate the participation in the distinct and separate act of removal from office.

Indeed, the manner in which the Congress has dealt with the subject, is quite peculiar. Unable, apparently, to find adequate support for a provision, that the Senate would claim a share in the distinct act of removal, of vacating of office, the scheme of law is to change the tenure of office, so that removability, as a separate and independent governmental act, by whomever to be exercised, is obliterated from the powers of this government. Look at that, now. That you do absolutely strike out of the capacity and the resources of this government, the power of removing an officer as a separate Executive act.

You have determined by law that there shall be no vacation of an office possible, except with the concurrence of the Senate; and so far have you carried out that principle that you do not make it even possible to vacate it by the concurrence of the Senate and the President; but you have deliberately determined that the office shall remain full as an estate and possession of the incumbent, from which he can be removed under no stress of the public necessity, unless by the fact occurring of a complete appointment for the permanent tenure of a successor, concurred in by the Senate, and made operative by the new appointee going there and qualifying himself in the office. Now this seems, at the first sight, a very extraordinary provision for all the exigencies of a government like ours, with its forty thousand officers, whose list is paraded here before you, with their twenty-one millions of emoluments, to show the magnitude of the great prize contended for between the Presidency and the Senate. It is a very singular provision, doubtless, that in a government which includes under it forty thousand officers, there should be no constitutional possibility of stopping a man in or removing him from an office, except by the deliberate succession of a permanent successor, approved by the Senate and concurred in by the appointee himself going to the place and qualifying and assuming his duty. I speak the language of the act:—"While the Senate is in session, there is not any power of temporary suspension or arrest of fraud, of violence, of danger, or of menace to the government by an officer: when the Senate is in recess there, is a power of suspension given to the Executive, and we are better off in that respect when the Senate is in recess than when it is in session, for the President can, by a definite and appropriate action, arrest the misconduct of an officer by his suspension. But, as I said before, I repeat it, under this act the incumbents of all those offices have a permanent estate in them till a successor, with your consent and his own, is inducted into the office. Now I do not propose to discuss, as quite unnecessary to any decision of any matter to be brought in on your judgment, at any great length the question of the unconstitutionality of that law. A very deliberate expression of opinion, after a very deliberate and thorough debate, conducted in this body, in which the reasons of each side were ably maintained by your most distinguished members, and after a very thorough consideration in the House of Representatives, where able and eminent lawyers, some of whom appear among the managers, gave the country the benefit of their knowledge and their acuteness, has placed this matter as the legislative judgment of its constitutionality; but I think all will agree that a legislative judgment of constitutionality does not conclude a court,; and that, while legislative judgments have differed, and while the practice of the Government for eighty years has been on one side, and the new ideas introduced are confessedly a reversal and a revolution of that practise. It is not saying too much to say, that after the expression of the legislative will, and after the opinion of the legislature in its action, there yet would remain for debate, among jurists and lawyers, among statesmen, among thoughtful citizens, and certainly properly within the province of the Supreme Court of the United States, the question whether the one or the other construction of the Constitution was vital in its influence on the government—was the safe and correct course for the conduct of the government. Let me ask your attention for a moment to the question, as presenting itself to the minds of Senators, as to whether this was or was not a reversal and revolution of the practice and theory of the government, and also as to the weight of a legislative opinion.

Mr. Evarts here quoted from the debate which took place in the Senate on the Civil Tenure act, the remarks of Senator Williams, of Oregon, to the effect that the bill undertook to reverse what had heretofore been the admitted practice of the government, and the President should at least have the selection of his Cabinet officers.

Mr. EVARTS then continued—This Senator touches the very marrow of the matter. that when you were passing this bill, which, in the whole official service of the country, reverses the practice of the government, you should at least leave the Executive all the Cabinet officers; the point was on leaving them in the bill as an exception. It was a reversal of the practice of the government as to all the rest of the officers, and the argument was that the Cabinet should be left as they were, because, as the Senator said wisely, "the country will hold the Executive responsible for what his Cabinet does," and the country will so hold him till the people find out that you have robbed the Executive of all responsibility by robbing it of what is the pith of responsibility—discretion.

Mr. EVARTS read some further extracts from the remarks of Senator Williams on that occasion, and also from the remarks of Senator Howard, who admitted the practice of the government in regard to appointments and removals, and reminded the Senate that that claim of power on the part of the Executive had been informally decided by some of the best minds of the country. Mr. Evarts continued:—And now as to the weight of mere legislative construction, even in the mind of the legislature itself, as compared with other sources of authoritative determination, let me ask your attention to some very pertinent observations of the honorable Senator from Oregon (Mr. Williams.) Those who advocate the Executive power of removal rely altogether on the legislative construction of the Constitution, sustained by the practice and opinions of individual men. I need not argue that a legislative construction of the Constitution has no binding force. It is to be treated with proper respect. But few constructions have been put on the Constitution at one time that have not been modified or overruled at another or subsequent time, so that, so far as the legislative construction of the Constitution on this question is concerned, it is entitled to very little consideration. Now the point in debate was that the legislative construction of 1789, as worked into the bones of the government, by the indurating process of practice and exercise, was a kind of powerful influence on the matter, and yet the honorable Senator from Oregon justly pushes the proposition that legislative construction per se is entitled to very little consideration—that it has no binding force. Well, shall we be told that a legislative construction of March 2, 1867, and the practice under it of one year, which has brought the Congress face to face with the Administration and introduced the sword of impeachment between the two branches on a removal from office, raising the precise question that an attempt by the President to remove a secretary and appoint an ad interim to discharge its duties, is to result in a removal by the Senate of the Executive itself, and in an appointment of one of its own members for the ad interim discharge of the duties of the Presidency? Now, that is the usual mode by recent legislative construction. But the honorable Senator from Oregon, with great force and wisdom, as it seems to me, proceeded in the debate to say that the courts of law, the Supreme Court of the United States, was the place to look for authoritative and permanent determination of the question at issue; and it will be found that in that he but followed the wisdom shown in the debate of 1789, and in the final result of it, in which Mr. Sherman concurred as much as any member of that Congress, that it was not for Congress to name or to assign the limits of Executive power by enactment, nor to appropriate and confer Executive power by endowment, through an act of Congress, but to leave it as Mr. White, of North Carolina, said, and as Mr. Gerry, of Massachusetts, said, and as Mr. Sherman, of Connecticut, said, to the Constitution itself to operate on the Foreign Secretary's act, and to let the action be made under it by virtue of a claim of right under the Constitution, and whoever was aggrieved let him raise the question in the courts of law on that resolution, and on that situation of things the final vote was taken, and the matter was disposed of in that Congress. But that it was then, and ever since, has been regarded as an authentic and *authoritative* determination, by that Congress, that the power was n the President; and that it has been so insisted upon, so acted upon ever since, and that nobody has been aggrieved, and that nobody has raised the question in the courts of law; that is the force and the weight of a resolution of that first Congress, and of the practice of the government under it.

In the House of Representatives, also, there was a debate on the contested point in the bill, and one of the best lawyers in that body, as I understand, by repute—Mr. Williams, one of the honorable managers—in his argument for the bill, said:—It aims at the reformation of a giant vice in the administration of this government, by bringing its practice back from the rule of its infancy and inexperience. He thought it was a faulty practice, but that it was a practice of the government from its infancy to the day of the passage of the bill; that it was a vice inherent in the system and exercising power over its action, he had no doubt.

He admits subsequently, in the same debate, that the Congress of 1789 decided, and that it successors for three-quarters of a century acquiesced in that doctrine. I will not weary the Senate with a thorough analysis of the debate of 1789. It is, I believe, decidedly the most important debate in the history of Congress. It is, I think, the best considered debate in the history of the government. I think it included among its debaters as many of the able, wise and learned men, the benefit of whose public service this nation has ever enjoyed, as any debate. or measure which this government has ever had or entertained. The premises in the Constitution were very narrow. The question of removal from office, as a distinct subject, had never occurred to the minds of the men of the Convention. The tenure of office was not to be made permanent except in the case of Judges of the Supreme Court. The periodicity of Congress, of the Senate, and of the Executive was fixed. Then there was an attribution of the whole interior administrative official powers of the government to the Executive, with the single qualification, exceptional in itself, that the advice and consent of the Senate should be required as a negative on the President's nomination.

Now, the point raised was exactly this—it may be very briefly stated—Those who, with Mr. Sherman, maintained that the concurrence of the Senate in removal was as necessary as it concurrence in appointment, supported themselves with the proposition that the same power which appointed should have the removal. That was a little begging of the question—speaking it with all respect—as to who the appointing power was really, under the terms and under the intent of the Constitution. But, concurring that the connection of the Senate with the matter really made it a part of the appointing power, the answer to the argument—triumphant as it seems to me—as it came from the distinguished speakers, Mr. Madison, Mr. Budinot, Mr. Fisher Ames, and others. was this: Primarily, the *whole* business of official, subordinate and executive action, is a part of the Executive functions, that being attributed in *solido* to the President, except that it is to be with the advice and consent of the Senate. With that limit the Executive power stands unimpeded. What then, is the rest of the consequence? Removal from office belongs to executive power, if the Constitution has not attributed it elsewhere. Then the question was, whether it was vital, whether its determination one way or other affected seriously the character of the government and its workings?

I think all agree that it was, and then what weight, what significance is there in the fact that the party which was defeated in the argument submitted to the conclusion and to the practice of the government under it, and did not raise a voice or take a vote in derogation of it during the whole course of the government. But it does not stand on this. After forty-five years' working of this system—between 1830 and 1835—there was great party exacerbation between the Democracy, under the lead of General Jackson, and the Whigs, under the mastery of the eminent men wno then filled this hall, and one of the most eminent of whom now does me the honor to listen to my remarks.

Under that antagonism there was renewed the great debate, and what was the measure which the contending parties, under the influence of party spirit, brought the matter to? Why, Mr. Webster said, when he led the forces in a victory, which, perhaps, for that single instance, combined the triumvirate of himself, Mr. Calhoun and Mr. Clay, that the contrary opinion and contrary practice was settled. He says:—"I regard it as a settled point—settled by construction, settled by precedent, settled by the practice of the government, settled by legislation"—and he did not seek to disturb it. He knew the force of forty-five years; the whole existence of the nation under its construction on questions of 'that kind, and he sought only to interpose a moral restraint upon the President by requiring him, when he removed an officer, to assign the reasons for removal.

General Jackson met the point firmly and promptly, and in his protest against the resolution which the Senate had adopted in 1834—I think to the effect that his action in the removal of Mr. Duane had been in der ogation of the Constitution and of the laws—met it with a defiance which brought two great topics up in debate, one, the independence of the Executive in his right to judge of constitutional questions, and the other, the great point that the concurring in the choice of a President by the people, through their representatives in federal members, was an important part of the Constitution, and that he was not a man of his own will, but renewed and reinforced by the will of the people.

That debate was carried on and determined by the Senate passing a resolution, declaring its opinion that General Jackson's conduct had been in derogation of the Constitution and the laws, and on that very point reference was made to the common master of us all, the people of the United States, and on the re-election of General Jackson the people themselves, in their primary capacity, sent to the Senate on this challenge a majority which expunged the resolution censuring the action of the Executive.

You talk about power to decide constitutional questions by Congress, power to decide them by the Supreme Court, power to decide them by the Executive. I show you the superior power of them all, and I say that the history of free countries, in the history of popular liberty, in the history of the power of the people, exercised not by passion or by violence, but by reason, the exercise of that power was never shown more distinctly and more definitely than on this very matter of whether the power of removal from office should reman in the Executive or be distributed among the Senators.

It was not my party that was pleased or was triumphant on that occasion; but as to fact of what the people thought, there was not any doubt, and there never has been any since, until the new situation has produced new interests and resulted in new conclusions.

Honorable Senators and Representatives will recollect how, in the debate which led to the passage of the Civil Tenure act, it was represented that the authority of the first lawyers of 1789 ought to be somewhat scrutinized because of influence on its debates and conclusions which the great character of the Chief Magistrate, General Washington, may have produced.

Well, Senators, why cannot we look at the present as we have at the past? Why can we not see in ourselves what we so easily discern as possible with others? Why can we not appreciate it, that perhaps the judgment of Senators and of Representatives now may have been warped or misled somewhat by their opinions and by their feelings towards the Executive? I apprehend, therefore, gentlemen, that this matter of party influence is one which it is quite as wise to consider, and that this matter of personal power and authority of character is quite as suitable to be weighed when we are acting, as when we are deciding upon the acts of others. Two passages I will be permitted to quote from that great debate as carried on in the Congress of 1789.

Mr. EVARTS here read from the remarks of Mr. Madison and of Mr. Boudinot in the Congress of 1789, those of the latter being to the effect that the President should not have officers imposed upon him who did not meet his approbation.

Mr. EVARTS continued:—In these words of Mr. Madison and Mr. Boudinot I find the marrow of the whole controversy. There is no escaping from it. If this body pursues the method now adopted, it must be responsible to the country for the action of the Executive Department, and if officers are to be maintained, as these wise statesmen say, over the head of the President, then that power in the Constitution, which allows him to have a choice in their selection is entirely void, for if his officers are to be dependent upon instantaneous selection, and if thereafter there can be no space for repentance or for change of purpose on the part of the Executive, it is idle to say that he has the power of appointment. It must be the power of appointment from day to day which is the power of appointment for which he is to be responsible, if he is to be responsible at all.

I now wish to ask attention to the opinions expressed by some of the statesmen who took part in this determination of what the effect and the important effect of the conclusion of the Congress of 1789 was. None of them overlooked its importance on one side or the other, and I beg leave to read from the Life and Works of the elder Adams, vol. 1, page 448.

Mr. EVARTS read from the work in question the paragraph giving the history of the question as to the President's power to appoint and remove officers. He also read from Mr. Fisher Ames to his correspondent, an intelligent lawyer in Boston, in reference to the same subject.

Mr. EVARTS then continued:—It will thus be seen, Senators, that the statesmen whom we most revere regarded this, so to speak, construction of the Constitution as important, as the framing of it itself had been, and now the question arises whether a law of Congress has introduced a revolution in the doctrine and in the practice of the government.

A legislative construction binding no one and being entitled to respect from the changeableness of legislative constructions, in the language of the honorable Senator from Oregon, and whether a doubt whether an act in relation to the constitutionality of that law on the part of the Exetive department is a ground of impeachment, the doctrine of unconstitutional law seems to be. I speak it with great respect, wholly misunderstood by the honorable managers in the propositions which they present.

Nobody can ever violate an unconstitutional law, for it is not a rule binding upon him or upon anybody else. His conduct in violating it, or in contravening it, may be at variance with ethical or civil conditions of duty, and for a violation of these ethical and civil conditions he may be responsible. If a marshal of the United States, executing an unconstitutional fugitive slave bill, enters with the process and the authority of law, it does not follow that resistance may be carried to the extent of shooting the marshal; but it is not because it is a violation of that law, for if it is unconstitutional there can be no violation of it.

It is because civil duty does not permit civil contests to be raised by force and violence. So, too, if a subordinate executive officer who has nothing but ministerial duty to perform as a United States marshal, in the service of process under an unconstitutional law, undertakes to deal with the question of its unconstitutionality, while the ethical and civil duty on his part is merely ministerial, and while he must either execute it in his ministerial capacity or resign his office, he cannot, under proper ethical rules, determine whether an execution of the law shall be defeated by the resistance of the officers provided for its execution.

But if the law bears upon his personal rights or official emoluments, then, without a violation of the peace, hemay raise a question with the law, consistent with all civil and ethical duties. Thus we see at once that we are brought face to face with the fundamental propositions in this case, and I ask your attention to a passage from the *Federalist*, at page 549. where there is very vigorous discussion by Mr. Hamilton of the question of unconstitutional law, and also to the case of Marbury against Madison (first Cranch, pp. 175), which I shall beg to include in the report of my remarks. The subject is old, but it is there discussed with a luminous wisdom which may well displace the more inconsiderate and loose views which have been presented in debate here. Undoubtedly, it is a question of very grave consideration, how far the different departments of government, legislative, judicial, and executive, are at liberty to act in relation to unconstitutional laws.

Judicial duty may perhaps be bound to wait for a case, to volunteer no advice, to exercise no supervision; but as between the legislature and the executive, where the Supreme Court has passed upon a question, it is one of the gravest constitutional points for public men to determine where and how the legislature may raise the question again by passing a law against the decision of the Supreme Court and against the determination of Congress, that we in this case have been accused of insisting on extravagant pretentions.

We have never suggested anything further than this, for the case only requires it, that whatever may be the doubtful or debatable region in the co-ordinate authority for the different departments of the government to judge for themselves of the constitutionality or unconstitutionality of laws, that when the President of the United States, in common with the humblest citizen, finds a law passed over his right, and binding on his action in the matter of his right, then all reasons of duty to self, to the public, to the Constitution, and to the law, require that the matter shall be put in the train of judicial decision, in order that the light of the serene wisdom of the Supreme Court may be shed upon it, to the end that Congress even may reconsider its action, and retract its encroachment on the Constitution.

But Senators will not have forgotten that Gen. Jackson, in his celebrated controversies with the Whig party, claimed that no department of the government should receive its final and necessary and perpetual exclusion and conclusion on constitutional questions, over the judgement even of the Supreme Court, and that under the obligation of one's oath, yourselves as Senators, yourselves as Representatives, and the President as Chief Executive, each must act in a new juncture or in reference to a new matter arising to raise again the question of constitutional authority. Now let me read a short passage in which Gen. Jackson in his protest sets this forth.

I read from the debate on the Fugitive Slave law, as conducted in this body in the year 1852, when the honorable Senator from Massachusetts (Mr. Sumner) was spokesman and champion of the right of each department of the government to judge of the constitutionality of law and of duty. But whatever may be the influence of this judgment, that is the judgment of the Supreme Court in the case of Prigg, as a rule for the judiciary, it cannot arrest our duty as legislators. Here I adopt with entire assent the language of President Jackson, in his memorable veto in 1832, of the Bank of the United States:—

"If the opinion of the Supreme Court covers the whole ground of this act, it ought not to control the co-ordinate authorities of the government. The Congress, the Executive and the court must each for itself be guided by its own opinion of the Constitution. Every public officer who takes an oath to support the Constitution, swears that he will support it as he understands it, and not as it is understood by others. It is as much the duty of the House of Representatives, of the Senate, and of the President to decide on the constitutionality of any bill or resolution which may be presented to them for passage and approval, as it is of the supreme judges when it may be brought before them for judicial decision. The authority of the Supreme Court must not, therefore, be permitted to control Congress or the Executive, but to have only such influence as the force of their reasoning may deserve."

With these authoritative words of Andrew Jackson, I dismiss the subject now. Times change, and we change with them. Nevertheless, principles remain; duties remain; the powers of the government remain; their co-ordination remains; the conscience of men remains, and everybody who has taken an oath; everybody who is subject to the Constitution, without taking an oath, in peaceful means, has a right to revere the Constitution in derogation of constitutional law; and any legislative law, or any judicial authority which shall deny the supremacy of the Constitution in its power to protect men, who thus conscientiously, thus peacefully raise questions for determination, in a conflict between the Constitution and the law, will not be consistent with the written Constitution or with the maintenance of the liberties of the people, as established by and dependent on the preservation of a written Constitution. Now let us see whether, on every ethical, constitutional and legal rule, the President of the United States was not the person on whom the civil tenure

act operated, not as an executive officer to carry out a law, but as one of the co-ordinate departments of the government, over whom, in that official relation to the authority of the act, was sought to be asserted. The language is general:—"Every removal from office contrary to the provisions of this act shall be a high misdemeanor." Who could remove from office but the President of the United States? Who had authority? Who could be governed by the laws but he? And it was not an official constitutional duty—not a personal right, not a matter of personal value, or choice, or interest with him that he acted.

When, therefore, it is sought and claimed that by force of the legislative enactment the President of the United States shall not remove from office whether the act of Congress was constitutional or not, he was absolutely prohibited from removing from office although the Constitution allowed him to do so, the Constitution could not protect him for the act, but that the act of Congress, seizing upon him, could draw him in here by impeachment and subject him to judgment for violations of the law, although maintaining the Constitution, and that the Constitution pronounces sentence of condemnation and infamy upon him for having worshipped its authority and sought to maintain it, and that the authority of Congress has that power and extent, then you practically tear asunder the Constitution.

If on these grounds you dismiss the President from this court, convicted and deposed. you dismiss him the victim of the Congress and the martyr of the Constitution, by the very terms of your judgement, and you throw open for the masters of us all. in the great debates of an intelligent, instructed, fearless, practical nation of freemen, a division of sentiment to shake this country to its centre—the omnipotence of Congress, as the rallying cry on one side and the supremacy of the Constttution on the other.

[The court, here, at two o'clock, took a recess.]

Mr. Evarts Continues.

After the recess, Mr, EVARTS continued:—There is but one other topic that I need to insist upon here as bearing upon that part of my argument which is intended to exhibit to the clear apprehension, and, I hope, the adoption of this court, the view that all here that possesses weight and dignity, that really presents the agitating contest that has been proceeding between the departments of our government is political, and not criminal, or suitable for judicial cognizance; and that is what seems to me to be decisive in your judgment and in your consciences, and that is the attitude that every one of you already, in your public action, occupies towards this subject.

Why the Constitution of the United States never intended so to coerce and constrain the consciences and duties of men as to bring them into the position of judges between themselves and another branch of the government. The eternal principles of justice are implied in the constitution of every country; and there are no more immutable, no more inevitable principles than these—that no man shall be a judge in his own case, and that no man shall be a judge in a matter in which he has already given judgment.

It is abhorrent to a natural sense of justice that men should judge in their own case. It is inconsistent with nature itself that man should assume an oath, and hope to perform it, of being impartial in his own judgment when he has already formed it. How many crimes that a President may have imputed to him, that may bring him to the judgment of a Senate, are crimes against the Constitution or the laws, involving turpitude or personal delinquency? They are crimes in which it is inadmissible to imagine that the Senate should be committed at all; they are crimes which, however much the necessary reflection of political opinions may bias, by personal judgment of this and that and all the members of the body, yet it must be possible only that they should give a color, or a turn, and not be themselves the very basis.

The substance of the judgment to be rendered, which therefore I show you, is from the records of this Senate; that yourselves have voted upon this law, whose constitutionality is to be determined, and that the question is upon constitutionality or judgment of constitutionality. When you have in your capacity of a Senate, undertook after the act was committed, as an act suitable in your judgment to be performed by you in your relation to the Executive authority, and your duty under this government to pronounce, as you did by resolution, that the removal of Mr. Stanton and the appointment of General Thomas was not authorized by the Constitution and the laws, you either did or did not regard that as a matter of political action; then you regarded it as a matter that could not possibly be brought before you in your judicial capacity for you to determine upon any personal consequences to the Executive.

How was it a matter for political action, unless it was a matter of his political action, and the controversy was wholly of a political nature? If you on the other hand, had in your minds a possibility of this extraordinary jurisdiction being brought into play by a complaint to be made by the House of Representatives against him, what an extraordinary spectacle should you present to yourselves and this country. No, the controlling, the necessary feeling, upon which you acted, must have been that it is a stage and a step in governmental action concerning which we made this suggestion and this reproof.

Why, in 1834, when the Senate of the United States was debating a resolution condemnatory of General Jackson's proceedings in reference to the deposits, the question was raised:—Have you, will you, should you pronounce an opinion upon a matter of this kind? It may be made the occasion for your views on a subject to be produced for judicial construction. It may be true that that resolution does not cover guilt; that it only expresses an opinion that the law and authority in the Constitution did not cover the action of the President.

But it does not impute violence, or design, or wickedness of purpose, or other than a justifiable difference of opinion, to resort to an arbiter between you. But even in that limited view, I take it, no Senator can think or feel that, as a preliminary part of the judgment of a court, that was the sentiment of the House, and the construction of the Senate showed it to be only a matter of political discussion, and absolutely set aside a motion of impeachment, and rendered, therefore, the debate a political debate, and the conclusion a political conclusion.

And now there is but one proposition that consists with the truth of the case, and with the situation of you, Senators, and that is, that you regard the acts as political action, and political decision, and not by possibility of matter of judgment a case of an impeachment, and the necessary trial. The answer of the great and trusted stateman of the Whig party of that day was, if there was in the atmosphere a whisper, if there was in the future a menace, if there was a hope or a fear, as some seem to think, that impeachment was to come, debate must be silenced, and the resolution suppressed; but they recognized the fact that it was mere political action that was being resorted to, and that was, or was to be possible, the complexion of the House to end in acquittal or conviction, this proceeding could be for a moment justified. Why, to two of the gravest articles of impeachment in the weightiest trial ever introduced into this court, and those in which as large a vote of condemnation was made as upon any others, were the two articles against Judge Chase, one of which brought him in question for coming to the trial in Pennsylvania with a formed and pronounced opinion; and in another, the third, was the following:—A juryman to enter the box on the trial of Callender at Richmond, who stated that he had formed an opinion, I would like to see a court of impeachment that regards this as a grave matter; that a judge should come to a trial and pronounce the condemnation of a prisoner before the counsel are heard, and that he allows a juryman to enter the box who had excused himself from having a free mind on the point to be discussed; and yet are we to be told that you, having formed and expressed an opinion, are to sit here the judges in such a matter as this. What is there but an answer of this kind necessary:—The Constitution never brings a Senate into an inculpation and a condemnation of a President upon matters in which, and of which, two departments of the government, in their political capacities, have formed and expressed political opinions.

It is of other matters and of other forms in which there are no parties and no discriminations of opinion; it is of offenses, of crime, in which the common rules of duty, of obligation, of excess, or of sin, are not determinable upon political opinions formed and expressed in debate; but here a principal is equally contravened, and this aids any argument, that it is political, and not personal or criminal. It is that you are to pass judgment of and concerning questions of the partition of the officers of this government between the President and yourselves. The matter of his fault is that he claims them; the very matter of his condemnation is that you had a right to them, and you, aided by the list furnished by the managers—of 41,000 in number, and $21,000,000 in annual emolument—are you to sit here, as judges, with this false claim, and is his appeal to a common arbiter, in a matter of this kind, to be imputed to him as personal guilt, and followed by personal punishment?

How would any of us like to be tried before a judge who, if he condemned us, would have our houses, and if he acquitted us we should have his? Why, so sensitive is the natural sense of justice on this point that the whole country was set in a blaze by a provision in the Fugitive Slave law that a Commissioner should have but five dollars if he set the slave free, and ten dollars if he remanded him. Have the judges of this court forgotten that crisis of the public mind as to allowing a judge to have an interest in the subject of his judgment? Have they forgotten that the honorable Senator from Massachusetts (Mr. Sumner), in the debate upon this Tenure of Office act, thought the political bias might effect a court so that it would not give judgment of more than nominal punishment for the commission of the act, and yet you are full of politics.

The whole point of my argument is an absolute demonstration that the Constitution of the United States never forces honorable men into a position where they are judges in their own causes, or where they come in contact with their opinions previously expressed, and have omitted from this consideration the fact that the great office itself, if by your judgment it shall be taken from elective control of this Republic, is to be put into the possession of a member of your own body chosen to-day, to-morrow, at any time by yourselves, and that you are taking the crown of the people's magistracy, of the people's glory, to decorate with honor an officer of the Senate, who, by virtue of your favor, holding the place of President *pro tem.*, adds the Presidency to its duties; and an officer, changeable from day to day by you as you choose to have a new President *pro tem.*, who, by the same title, assumes, day by day, the discharge of the duties of the President of the United States. Now, when the prize is that, but when the circumstances are as I explain them, Senators must decline a jurisdiction.

Upon this demonstration that human nature and human virtue cannot endure that men should be judges in such strife, I agree that your duty brings you here. You have no right to avoid it, but it is a duty consistent with judicial trials, and the subject itself, thus illustrated, snatches

from you at once the topics that you have been asked to examine. It suits my sense of the better construction of the separate articles to treat them at first somewhat generally, and then by such distribution as seems most to bring us finally to what, if it shall not before that time have appeared, shall appear to me the gravest matter for your consideration.

Now, let me ask you, at the outset, to see how little as matter of evidence this case is. Certainly the President of the United States has been placed under as trying and as hot a case of political opposition as ever man was or could be; certainly for two years there has been no partial construction of his conduct; certainly for two years he has been sifted by one of the most powerful winnowing machines that I have ever heard of, the House of Representatives of the United States of America. Certainly the wealth of the nation, certainly the exigencies of party, certainly the zeal of political ambition, have pressed into the service of imputation, of inculpation and of proof, all that this country affords, all that the power to send for persons and papers includes. They ran none of the risks that attend ordinary proceedings, of bringing their witnesses into court to stand the test of examination and cross-examination, but they can put them under the construction of an oath and an explanation in advance, and see what they can prove, and whom they can bring and whom they can reject.

They can take our witnesses from the stand, already under oath, and even those of so great and high a character as the Lieutenant-General of your armies, and out of court try him with a new examination, to see whether he shall help or hurt them by being cross-examined in court, using every arm and every art, stayed by no sense except of public duty to remove their power, or control its exercise, and yet here is the evidence. The people of this country have been made to believe that all sorts of personal vice and wickedness, that all sorts of official misconduct and folly, that all sorts of usurpation and oppression, practiced and executed on the part of this Executive, was to be explored and exposed by the prosecution, and certainly set down in the record of this court of public judgment.

Here you have it. For violence and oppression and usurpation—a telegram between the President and Governor Parsons, published two years ago; for the desire to repress the power of Congress—the testimony of a would-be office-seeker that the President said certain points were important, and he thought the patronage of the government should be in support of those principles. The would-be office-seeker went home and was supposed to have said that the President had made use of very violent and offensive words. Weights were the testimony upon the scale in which the nation weighs it, upon the scale that foreign nations look at it, upon the scale that history will apply to it, upon the scale that posterity will in retrospective guard it from.

It depends a good deal upon how large a selection a few specimens of the testimony came from. If I bring a handfull of wheat marked by the rust or weevel and show it to my neighbor, he would say, "Why, what a wretched crop of wheat you have made." But if I said to him, "These few kernels are what I have taken from the bins of my whole harvest," he would answer, "What a splendid crop of wheat you have had." Now, answer, answer, answer, if there is anything wrong in this.

Mr. Manager Wilson, from the Judiciary Committee, having examined this subject with all care, made a report, itself the wisest, the clearest and also one of the most entertaining reports on the subject of impeachment in the past and in the present that I have ever seen, or can ever expect to see. What is the result? That it is all political. All these thunder clouds are political, and it is only this little, petty pattering of rain conveying the infraction of the Constitution that is personal or criminal, and the grand inquest of the nation, before the final reverberation of the whole harangue, on the 9th of December, 1867, votes—107 to 57—no impeachment.

And now, I would like to know, if these honorable managers had limited their addresses to this court to matters which, in purpose, in character, in intent, and in effect occurred after that Bill of Impeachment was thrown out by us, how much would have been entertained of this case? I have not heard anything which had not occurred before that. The speeches were made eighteen months before the telegram was sent; a year before Wood, the office-seeker, came into play, long before. What is there, then? The honorable managers, too, do not seem to have been of one mind about these articles. The articles seem to have been originally discussed, and then assorted afterwards.

I understood the honorable manager (Mr. Butler) to say, that if there is not anything in the first article, you need not trouble yourselves to think of the eleventh, and Mr. Manager Stevens thinks if there is nothing in the eleventh article you had better not bother yourself for looking at anything in the first ten (renewed laughter), for he says, a county court lawyer could get rid of them.

Here is what Mr. Stevens says in the House:—"I wish it to be particularly noticed that which I intend to offer as an amendment. I wish gentlemen to examine and see that this charge is nowhere contained in any of the articles reported, and that unless it is inserted there can be no trial, and that if there be shrewd lawyers, as I know there will be, and caviling judges" (he did not state any certainty of that), "and without this article they do not acquit, they are greener than I was in any case I ever undertook before a court of quarter sessions." (Laughter.)

Well, now, it will not be very vain in us to think that perhaps we come up to that estimate on our side of the Quarter Sessions lawyer who would be adequate to dispose of these articles, and they were quite right about it. If you cannot get in what is political and nothing but political, you cannot get hold of anything that is criminal or personal.

Now, having passed from the general estimate of the lameness and feebleness of the addresses and charges, I begin with the consideration of the article in reference to it, and to the subject matter of which I am disposed to concede there is some proof, and that as to the speeches. Now, I think that it has been proved here that the speeches charged upon the President, in substance and in general, were made.

My first difficulty about them is, that they were made in 1866, and that they related to a Congress which has passed out of existence, and that they were the subject of a report of the Judiciary Committee to the House, and which the House voted that it would not impeach. My next difficulty is, that they are crimes against argument, against rhetoric, against taste, and perhaps against logic; but that the Constitution of the United States, neither in itself nor by any subsequent administration, has provided for the government of the people in this country in these regards.

Now, it is a new thing in this country to punish any man for making a speech. There is a great many speeches made in this country, and, therefore, cases would undoubtedly have arisen in eighty years of our history where men were punished for making speeches. Indeed, I believe if there is anything which more particularly marks us the approval of other nations, it is that every man in this country not only has a right to make a speech, but can make a speech, and a very good one, and that he does at some time or other actually do so.

The very lowest epithet for speech-making in the American republic adopted by the newspapers is "able and eloquent." (Laughter.) I have seen applied in the newspapers to the efforts of honorable managers here, the epithet in advance of "tremendous." (Laughter.) I have seen them spoken of before they were delivered as of tremendous force; and I saw once an accurate, authentical statement of the force of one, and that in advance, that it consisted of 33,000 words. (Laughter.)

Therefore a case must have arisen for a question if there was to be any punishment for speech-making. But now, for the first time, we begin with the President, and accuse him; we take him before no ordinary court, but we organize a court for the purpose, which court adjourns the moment it is over with the trial, furnishing no precedents, and must remove him from office and order a new election. Now that is a good deal to turn upon a speech. Only think of it—to be able to make a speech which would require a new election of President to be made. (Laughter.)

Well, if the trial is to take place, let the proclamation issue to this speech-making people. "Let him who is without sin among you cast the first stone," and see how the nation, on tip-toe, awaits to see who will answer that dainty challenge, who assumes that fastidious duty. We see, in addition, the necessary requirement. It must be one who, by long discipline, has learned to speak without bounds, one whose lips would stammer at an imputation, whose cheek would blush at a reproach, whose ears would tingle at an invective, and whose eyes would close at an indecorum. It must be one who, by strict continuance of speech, and by control over the tongue—that unruly member—has gained with all his countrymen the praise of ruling his own spirit, which is greater than one who taketh a city.

And now the challenge is answered, and it seems that the honorable manager to whom this duty is assigned, is one who would be recognized at once, in the judgment of all, as "First in war, first in peace, first in boldness of words, and first in the hearts of all his countrymen, who love this wordy intrepidity." (Unrepressed laughter.) Well, now, the champion being gained, we ask for the rules, and in an interlocutory inquiry, which I had the honor to address to him, he said the rule was the opinion of the court which was to try the case.

Now let us see whether we can get any guidance as to what your opinions are as to this subject of freedom of speech, for we are brought down to that, having no law or precedents, besides I find that the matter charged against the President is, that he has been unmindful of the harmony and courtesies which should prevail between the legislative and the executive.

If it should prevail from the Executive towards the legislative, it should also prevail from the legislative to the Executive. Except I am to be met with what I must regard as a most novel view presented by Mr. Manager Williams, in his argument the other day, that, as the Constitution of the United States prevents your being drawn in question anywhere for what you say, it is, therefore, a rule which does not work both ways. Well, that is an agreeable view of personal duty, that if I wear an impenetrable shirt of mail, it is just the thing for me to be drawing daggers against every one else.

Noblesse oblige seems to be a law which the honorable manager does not think applicable to the houses of Congress. If there were anything in that suggestion, how should you guard and regulate your use of freedom of speech? Now I have not gone outside of the debates which are connected with the Civil Tenure act.

My time has been sufficiently occupied with reading all that has been said in behalf of the House on that subject, but I find a well recorded precedent, not merely in the observation of a single Senator, but in the direct determination of the Senate itself, in passing on the question, which certainly points at least to freedom of speech as between two departments of the government.

The honorable Senator from Massachusetts, in the course of the debate, says, on the subject of this very law in reference to the President, "You may ask protection against whom? I answer plainly, protection against the President of the United States. There sir, is the duty of the hour. Ponder it well, and do not forget it. There was no such duty on our fathers. There was no such duty on our recent predecessors in this Chamber, because there was no President of the United States who had become the enemy of his country."

Well, now, the President had said that Congress was hanging on the verge of the government, but here is a direct charge that the President of the United States is the enemy of the country. Mr. Sumner being called to order for that expression, the honorable Senator from Rhode Island, Mr. Anthony, who not unfrequently presides with so much urbanity and so much control over your deliberations, gave this view as to what the common law of the tribunal is on the subject of the harmonies and courtesies which should prevail between the legislative and executive departments.

He said, "It is the impression of the chair that these words do not exceed the usual (laughter) latitude of debate which has been permitted here." (Laughter.) Now that is the custom of the tribunal established by the presiding officer.

Mr. Sherman, of Ohio, said, "I think the words objected to are clearly in order." (Loud Laughter.)

I have heard similar remarks fifty times (continued laughter) without any question of order being raised. And the Senate came to a vote, the opposing members of which remind me of some votes on evidence which we have had on this trial. The appeal was laid on the table by a vote of 29 yeas to 10 nays. But that is not all. Proceeding in the same debate, after being allowed to be in order, Mr. Sumner goes on with his speech, the eloquence of which I cannot sufficiently compliment, as it would be out of place to do so, but it certainly is of the highest order.

Of course, I make no criticism. He begins with the announcement of a very good principle.

He says:—

"I shall insist always on complete freedom of debate, and I shall exercise it. John Milton, in his glorious aspirations, said:—(Give me the liberty to know, to utter and to argue freely above all liberties.) "Thank God now that slave-masters have been driven from this court—such is the liberty of American Senators.

Of course, there can be no citizen of a republic too high for exposure, as there can be none too low for protection. These are not only invaluable liberties, but commanded duties. Now, is there anything in the President's answer that is nobler or more thorough-going than that? And if the President is not too high; if it a commanded, duty to call him an enemy of the country, is not the House of Representatives to be exposed to the imputation of a most intelligible aspersion upon them that they are hanging on the verge of the government. (Laughter.)

Then the honorable Senator proceeds in a style of observation, on which I shall make no criticism whatever, except that of Cicero against Cataline and against Verres does not contain more eloquence against the objects of his invective than that speech of the honorable Senator; and then it all ends in a wonderfully sensible and pithy observation, on the part of the honorable Senator from Michigan, Mr. Howard, who says, "the Senator from Massachusetts has advanced the idea that the President has become an enemy to his country," but I suppose that not only to be the condition of the sentiment in this Senate, touching the President of the United States, but I suppose we never had a President in regard to whom the opinion of the Senate was not divided on just that question—some thinking he was an enemy of the country, and others thinking that he was not; and I respectfully submit therefore that the Senator from Massachusetts will be as competent to try an impeachment if sent here against the President as I concede the Senator from Maryland, Mr. Johnson, will be competent to try it." Now that is good sense. Senatorial license may be made so wide as that.

We have also a report in the House of Representatives of a very brief debate between two of the most distinguished members of that body, who can as well as any others, for the purpose of this trial, furnish a standard of what is called by the honorable manager "propriety of speech." Mr. Bingham says, "I desire to say, Mr. Chairman, that it does not become a gentleman who recorded his vote fifty times for Jefferson Davis, the arch-traitor in this Rebellion (roars of laughter), as his candidate for the Presidency of the United States, to undertake to damage this cause by attempting to fasten an imputation either on my integrity or on my honor; I repel with scorn and contempt, any utterances of that sort, from any man, whether he be the hero of Fort Fisher *not* taken, or of Fort Fisher taken." (Continuous laughter.) Mr. Butler, after some remarks, said:—"But if, during the war, the gentleman from Ohio did as much as I did in that direction, I shall be glad to recognize that much.

"But the only victim of the gentlemen's prowess that I know of was an innocent woman hung upon the scaffold, one Mrs. Surratt; and I can sustain the memory of Fort Fisher, if he and his present associates can sustain him in shedding the blood of a woman who was tried by a military commission and convicted without sufficient evidence, in my judgment." Mr. Bingham replied with spirit:—"I challenge the gentleman; I dare him here, or anywhere in this tribunal, or any tribunal, to assert that I spoliated or mutilated any book. But such a charge, without one tittle of evidence, is only fit to come from a man who lives in a bottle, and is fed with a spoon." What that refers to I do not know.

[While the court and galleries were convulsed with laughter at the expense of the two managers referred to both these gentlemen sat at the table apparently unconcerned and uninterested spectators.]

Mr. EVARTS, continuing, said:—

This all comes within the common law of courtesy, in the judgment of the House of Representatives. We have attempted to show that in the President's addresses to the people there was something of irritation, something in the subject, something in the manner of the crowd which excused and explained, if it did not justify, the style of his speeches; and you might suppose that this interchange of debate which I have just read grew out of some subject which was irritating, which was in itself savage and ferocious. But what do you think the subject was that these honorable gentlemen were debating upon? Why it was charity.

A Senator—What?

Mr. EVARTS—Charity—a question of charity to the South; that was the whole staple of debate. "Charity which suffereth all things and is kind." (Laughter.) Charity which envieth not; charity which vaunteth not itself, is not puffed up, and doth not behave itself unseemly; seeketh not her own, is not easily provoked; thinketh no evil, rejoiceth not in iniquity, but rejoiceth in the truth; beareth all things, believeth all things, hopeth all things, endureth all things. "Charity never fails." But the apostle adds, what may not be exactly true in regard to the managers, "Tongues may fail." (Laughter.)

But now, now to be serious. In a free Republic who will tolerate this fanfaronade about speech-making. *Quis tolerit gracchos de seditione querentes?* Who will tolerate public orators prating about propriety of speech? Why can we not learn that their estimates of others must proceed on general views, and not vary according to particular passions and prejudice?

When Cromwell, in his career through Ireland in the name of the Parliament, had set himself down before the town of Ross, and summoned it to surrender, the Papist community, exhausted in its resistance, asked to surrender only on condition of freedom of conscience.

Cromwell replied:—"As to freedom of conscience, I meddle with no man's conscience, but if you mean by that liberty to celebrate the Mass, I would have you to understand that in no place where the power of the Parliament of England prevails, shall that be permitted." So the honorable managers do not complain of freedom of speech, but if any man says that the House of Representatives is "hanging on the verge of the government," we are to understand that in no place where the power of the two Houses of Congress prevails, shall that be permitted, although they meddle with no man's property or freedom of speech? (Laughter.) Now, Mr. Jefferson, who had occasion to give his views about infractions of the freedom of writing when the Sedition law was introduced into the legislation of this country, and, at the same time, to give some notions about the right of the Executive to have an opinion, says, in a letter to Mrs. President Adams, written in 1804:—"I discharged every person under punishment and prosecution under the Sedition law, because I considered and now consider that law to be a nullity as absolute and as palpable as if Congress had ordered us to fall down and worship the golden image, and that it was as much my duty to arrest its execution in every State as it would have been to have rescued from the fiery furnace those who should have been cast into it for refusing to worship the image." It was accordingly done in every instance, without asking what the offenders had done, or against whom they had offended, but whether the pains they were suffering were inflicted under the pretended sedition law, and in another letter he replies to some observation as to the freedom of the Executive about the constitutionality of laws:—"You seem to think it devolved on the judges to decide on the validity of the Sedition law, but nothing in the Constitution has given them a right to decide for the Executive more than for the Executive to decide for them. Both magistrates are equally independent in the sphere of action assigned to them; the judges believing the law constitutional had a right to pass sentence of fine or imprisonment, because the power is placed in their hands by the Constitution, but the Executive, believing the law to be unconstitutional, was bound to remit the execution of it, because that power had been confided to him by the Constitution, that its co-ordinate branches should be checks upon each other; but the opinion that gives the judges the right to administer what laws are constitutional and what are not, not only for themselves in their own sphere of action, but for the legislative and Executive also in their spheres, would render the judiciary despotic and tyrannical." Now, we have no occasion to assert, and we have not asserted, the right to resort to these extreme opinions, which, it is known Mr. Jefferson entertained. The opinions of Mr. Madison, more temperate but equally thorough, were to the same effect, and the co-ordinate branches of the government must surrender their co-ordination whenever they allow the past history to be a final bar from renewing or presenting constitutional questions for reconsideration and redetermination, if necessary, even by the Supreme Court; but we have here some questions of the courtesies of the different branches of the government in the severe expression of opinon which Mr. Manager Boutwell indulged in relation to the heads of departments.

What he said is as much severer and as much more degrading to that branch of the government than anything which was said by the President in relation to Congress, as can be imagined. Exception is here taken to the fact,

that the President called Congress, in a telegram, a set of individuals. Well, we have heard of an old lady, not very well instructed, who got very violent on being called an individual, but here we have an imputation in so many words on the heads of departments of this government, that they are serfs, the servants of a master, slaves of an owner, and yet, in this very presence, sits the eminent Chief Justice of the United States, and the eminent Senator from Maine (Mr. Fessenden), and the distinguished Senator from Pennsylvania (Mr. Cameron), all of whom have held Cabinet offices which are thus deprecated and derided, and if I were to estimate the Senators who aspire in the future to hold these degrading positions, I am afraid I should not have judges enough here to determine this case. (Laughter). I know this is all extravagance, *est modus in rebus, sunt certi denique fines.* There is some measure in things; there is some limit to the bounds of debate and discussion. Now, I agree that nothing can be more unfortunate than the language used by the President in the speech made in St. Louis.

The difficulty is undoubtedly that the President is not familiar with the graces; he has not been taught at school costly ornament and the studied contrivances of speech, but that he speaks right on, and when an article is presented in his path he steps right over it. Here is a rhetorical difficulty presented for a man who is not a rhetorician, as a sort of a metaphorical allusion was made to Judas. Well, now, if anybody attempts to become logical with a metaphor it will get him into trouble at once (laughter), and that is what the President did. If you look around with the eye of a logician you see that Judas was the betrayer of all goodness, and a man would naturally say, where is the goodness I have betrayed?

The moment, therefore, that you seek to be logical, by introducing the name of the divinity against whom Judas had thus sinned, there, of course, you produce that offense to our religious sentiment, which otherwise would not have been committed. I am not entirely sure that when you make allowance for the difference between the extempore speech of the President to a mob, and a written, prepared and printed speech to this court by the honorable managers, but there will be some little trace of the same impropriety of that figure of argument which presented Mr. Carpenter to your observation as an inspired painter, whose pencil was guided by the hand of Providence, and the appointment of Mr. Edwin M. Stanton to perpetual bliss and Governor Seward to eternal pain. (Laughter.)

But all that is matter of taste, matter of feeling; matter of distinction, matter of judgment. The serious views impressed upon you with so much force by the counsel for the President who opened this case (Mr. Curtis), and supported by the quotations from Mr. Madison, present this whole subject in its proper view to an American audience. I think that if our newspapers would find some more discriminating scale of comment on speeches than to make the lowest in the scale able and eloquent, we should have a better state of things in our orations.

Now, our position in reference to the speeches is that the subjects produced in proof should be considered; that words put into the speaker's mouth by the crowd, or called for by their unfriendly or impolite suggestions, are to have their weight and that without apologizing, for no man is bound to apologize before the laws before the court for the exercise of freedom of speech. It may be fairly admitted that it would be well if all men were accomplished rhetoricians and finished logicians, and had a bridle on their tongues. And now, without verging at all upon the eleventh article, which I leave to the observations of the honorable managers, and leave among themselves to dispose of, I will take up the Emory article.

The Emory article is an offense which began and ended on the 22d of February, and is comprised within a short conversation between the President and a general of our army. I dare say that in the rapid and heated course of events which took impeachment through the House of Representatives, it might have been understood by rumor, uncertain and implied, that there had occurred some kind of military purpose or communication on the part of the President which looked to the use of force. But under the proofs what can we say of it but that the President, under an intimation from Secretary Welles that all the officers were being called away from what, doubtless, is their proper occupation in time of peace, "attendance on levees," and were being summoned, as they were from the halls of revelry at Brussels to the battle of Waterloo, inquired, as it was natural to inquire, when and where this battle was to take place?

The President received it with great indifference; said he did not know about General Emory, and did not seem to care anything about it. But, finally, when Secretary Welles said that it would be better to look into it, the President did look into it, and it ended with a discussion of constitutional law between the President and General Emory, in which the General, reinforced by Mr. Reverdy Johnson, a lawyer, and Mr. Robert J. Walker, a lawyer, actually put down the President entirely. (Laughter.)

Now, if the President ought to be removed from office for that, and a new election ordered for that, you will so determine in judgment, and if any other President can go through four years without doing something worse than that we shall have to be more careful in our preliminary examinations, and in our nominating conventions. I understand this article to be hardly insisted on, then comes the conspiracy articles. Now, the conspiracy consists in this:—It was all commenced and accomplished in writing. "The documents were published; they were immediately promulgated, and that is the conspiracy," if it be one.

It is quite true that the honorable manager who conducted with so much force and skill the examination of the witnesses, did succeed in proving that besides the written order handed by the President to General Thomas, there were a few words of attendant conversation, and these were the words, "I wish to uphold the Constitution and the law," and there was an assent of General Thomas to the propriety of that course. But by the power of our profession the learned manager drew from General Thomas the fact that he had never heard these words before when a commission was delivered to him.

He argued that it was not ordinary, and that it carried infinite gravity of suspicion. But what expression is there so innocent that counsel cannot possibly fix suspicion upon? We recollect one very celebrated trial in which "chops and tomato sauce" were made the grounds of getting a verdict for breach of promise of marriage. Chops and mutton sauce do not import a promise of marriage.

There is not the least savor of courtship nor the least flavor of flirtation in chops and tomato sauce (laughter); and so we are told that these men, entering into the conspiracy at mid-day and in writing, meant bloodshed, civil commotion and war. Now, I cannot argue against that. Cardinal Woolsey once said that in political times you can get a jury that will bring in a verdict that Abel killed Cain. That may be, but an American Senate will hardly find in the allusion of the President to the Constitution and the law sufficient evidence to find him guilty of the purpose to produce commotion and civil war. But the conspiracy articles have but a trifling foundation to rest upon.

Here we have a statute passed at the eve of an insurrection, intended to guard the position of an officer of the United States from the intrusion, or intimidation, threats or force to disable the public service. It is, in fact, a reproduction of the first section of the Sedition act of 1798 amplified and extended. It is a law which is improper on its face, for it may include much more than might be called criminal, except in times of public danger; but the idea that a law intended to prevent the Rebels of the South, or the Rebel sympathizers, as they were called in the North, from intimidating officers in the discharge of their public duty, should be wrested to an indictment and trial of a President of the United States, and of an officer of the army on account of a written arrangement of orders to take possession of, and to administer one of the departments of the government against the law, is wresting the statute wholly from its application.

We are all familiar with the illustration which Blackstone gives us of the impropriety of following literally the words of a statute against the necessary implication, where he says that a statute against letting blood in the street, can properly support an indictment against a surgeon for tapping the vein of an apoplectic patient who happened to have fallen on the sidewalk; and there is no greater perversion and contrariety in the effort to make this statute applicable to ordinary and regular proceedings between recognized officers of the United States in the disposition of an office, than there would be in prosecuting the surgeon for relieving the apoplectic patient.

I cannot fully understand, though I carefully attended to it, the point of the argument of the learned manager. Mr. Boutwell, which brought into view the common law of Maryland, as adopted by Congress for the government of the domestic and ordinary affairs of life of the people of this district. It cannot be supposed that the President of the United States, in determining what his power and duties were in regard to giving office, should have looked into the common law of the District of Columbia, because the offices are exercised in the District. On these views presented in the conspiracy articles let us see what the evidence is. There was no preparation or application of force. There was no threat of force authorized on the part of the President, and there was no expectation of force, for he expected and desired nothing more nor nothing less, than that by the peaceful and regular exercise of authority on his part the office would be surrendered. If dissappointed in that, all that the President expected was, that, on that legal basis thus furnished by his official action, there should be an opportunity for taking the judgment of a court of law.

Now there seems to be left nothing but these articles which relate to the *ad interim* appointment of General Thomas and to the removal of Mr. Stanton. I will consider the *ad interim* appointment first, leaving it to be assumed for the purpose of examining the possible crime that the office had been vacated and was open to the action of the President.

If the office was full then there would be no appointment by the authority of the President or otherwise, and the whole action of the President was manifestly based on the idea that the office was to be vacated before an *ad interim* appointment could possibly be made, or was intended to take effect. The letter of appointment, or of authority, as it is called in the articles, accompanies the order of removal and was, of course, secondary to the order of removal.

General Thomas was only to take up the duties of the office and discharge them, if the Secretary of War should leave the office in need of such temporary charge. Now I think the only subject we have to consider before we look at the law governing *ad interim* appointments, is some suggestions as to any difference between *ad interim* appointments during the session of the Senate and during the recess. The honorable managers, perhaps all of them, (but certainly not the honorable manager, Mr. Boutwell), have contended that the practice of the government in regard to removals from office, covered only the case of removal during the recess of the Senate.

It will be part of my duty and labor, when I come to consider definitely the question of the removal of Mr. Stanton, to consider that point but for the purpose of Mr. Thomas' appointment. No such discrimination need to be made. The question of the right of the executive to vacate an office, to be discriminated between the recess of the Senate and its session, arises out of the constitutional distinction that is taken, to-wit, that the President can only fill offices during the session by the advice and consent of the Senate, and that he can, during the recess, commission by authority, to expire with the next session, but *ad interim* appointments do not rest upon the Constitution at all. They are not regarded, they never have been regarded, as an exercise of the appointing power in the sense of filling an office. They are regarded as falling within either the executive or the legislative duty of providing for the management of the duties of an office, before an appointment is or can properly be made.

Now in the absence of legislation it might be said that the power belonged to the executive; that part of his duty was when he saw that an accident had vacated an office, or that necessity required the removal of an incumbent so that the laws should be executed, and to provide that the laws should be executed, and to provide that the public service should be temporarily taken up and carried on, it might be fairly determined it was a *casus omissus*, for which the Constitution had provided a rule, and which the legislation of Congress might properly occupy.

As early, therefore, as 1792, provision was made for the temporary occupation of an office. The act of 1792, regulating three of the departments, provided that temporary absences and disabilities of the heads of departments might be met by appointments of a temporary character, to take charge of the office. The act of 1795 provides that in case of the vacancy in an office there should be power in the Executive which would not require him to fill the office by by the constitutional method, but temporarily to provide for the discharge of its duties.

Before considering the act of 1863, which, in terms, covers to a certain extent, but not fully, both of those points, I wish to ask your attention to some circumstances in regard to the passage of that act of 1863. I have said that the eighth section of the act of 1792 provided for the filling temporarily of vacancies. In January, 1863, the President sent to Congress this message, and Senators will perceive that it relates to this particular subject:—

"I submit to Congress the expediency of extending to other departments of the government the authority conferred on the President by the eighth section of the act of May 8, 1792, to appoint a person temporarily to discharge the duties of Secretary of State, Secretary of the Treasury and Secretary of War, in case of death, absence from the seat of government, or sickness."

That is to say, the temporary disability provision of the act of 1863, which covered all the departments then in existence, had never been extended by law to cover the other departments, and the President desired to have that act extended. This message having been referred to the Judiciary Committee, the honorable Senator from Illinois (Mr. Trumbull), chairman of the committee, made, I believe, a very brief report, in which he said:—

"There have been several statutes on the subject, and as the law now exists the President has authority temporarily to fill the offices of Secretary of State and Secretary of War from one of the other departments, by calling on somebody to discharge the duties. That other department was the Treasury. We have received a communication from the President of the United States, asking that the law may be extended to the other executive departments of the government, which seems to be proper, and we have framed a bill covering all of these cases, so that whenever there is a removal the President may temporarily devolve the office upon another cabinet officer, and appoint the chief officer of the department for the time being."

There does not seem to have been brought to the notice of the Senate or the honorable Senator the act of 1795. Nothing is said of it, and it would appear as if the whole of the legislation of 1863 proceeded upon the proposition of extending the act of 1792, of disabilities and not of vacancies, except that the honorable Senator uses the phrase "vacancy," and that he speaks of having provided for the occasions that might arise.

Now, the act of 1863 does not cover the case of vacancies, except by resignation. It does not add to the disability which the President had referred to in the case of the resignation which he did not ask to have covered, and which did not need to be covered by new legislation, because the act of 1795 covered it. But this act of 1863 does not cover all the cases of vacancy. It does not cover cases of vacancy by removal, and it does not cover the case of expiration of office, which is a case of vacancy.

Now, under that additional light, it seems as if the only question presented of guilt on the part of the President in respect to the appointments to office, *ad interim*, was a question of the final law. The Senators will remark the very limited form in which that question arises. It is not pretended that the appointment of Thomas, if the office was vacant, was a violation of the Civil Tenure act, although, perhaps, it may be so charged in the articles, because an examination of the articles shows that the only appointments, the infringement of which is made penal, is the appointment under the provisions of this act, as was pointed out by my colleague (Mr. Curtis), which seems to be a subject of argument on the other side. That appointment, prohibiting or attempting to prohibit, relates to the infraction of that act as an attempt to fill the offices. I believe that to be a sound construction of the law Very well, then, supposing that the appointment of General Thomas was not according to law, it is not against any law that prohibits it, nor against any law that has a penal clause or a criminal qualification upon the act. What would it be if attempted without the authority of the act of 1795? because that would be without the authority of the act of 1863. General Thomas was not an officer under that act.

It would seem that the President had appointed an officer, or attempted to appoint him *ad interim*, without authority of law. There are abundance of mandatory laws upon the President of the United States. It has never been customary to put a penal clause in them, as in the Civil Tenure act, but on this subject of penal appointment there is no penal clause, and no positive prohibition in any sense, but there would be a definite authority in the President to make the appointment.

What, then, would be the effect? Why General Thomas would not be entitled to discharge the duties. That is all that can be claimed in that regard, but we have insisted and we do now insist that the act of 1795 was in force, and that whether the act of 1795 was or was not, is one of those questions of dubious interpretation of a law upon which no officer, humble or high, can be brought into question for having an opinion one way or the other, and if you proceed upon these articles, if you execute a sentence of removal from office of a President of the United States, you proceed upon an infliction of the highest possible measure of civil condemnation and of the highest possible degree of interference with the constitutionally erected Executive, that it is possible for a court to commit, and you will set it either that the act of 1795 was repealed, or upon the basis that there was not a doubt, or a difficulty, or an interest upon which the President of the United States might make an *ad interim* appointment for a day, followed by the nomination of a permanent successor.

Truly, indeed, we are getting very nice in our measure and criticism of the absolute obligations and of the absolute duties of the President's functions when we seek to apply the process of impeachment and removal to a question whether an act of Congress requiring the head of a department to keep the place assigned to him or an act of Congress not repealed permitted him to be removed. You certainly do not, in the ordinary affairs of life, rig up a trip hammer to crack a walnut.

At this point, about half-past four, Mr. EVARTS said he would require about an hour to finish, but would yield to a motion to adjourn if desired; and on motion of Mr. HENDERSON, the court adjourned.

PROCEEDINGS OF FRIDAY, MAY 1.

The court was opened this morning with the usual formalities, in the presence of an audience that indicated an interest well sustained in the proceedings.

Mr. Evarts Resumes.

Mr. EVARTS proceeded at once to finish his task as follows:—

Mr. Chief Justice and Senators:—I cannot but feel that notwithstanding the unfailing courtesy, and the long-suffering patience which for myself and my associates, I have reason cheerfully to acknowledge on the part of the court in the progress of this trial, and in the long argument, you had at the adjournment yesterday reached somewhat of the condition of the feeling of the very celebrated Judge, Lord Ellenborough, who, when a celebrated lawyer, Mr. Curran, had conducted an argument on the subject of contingent remainder, to the ordinary hour of adjournment, and suggested that he would proceed whenever it should be his Lordship's pleasure to hear him, responded:—"The court will hear you, sir, to-morrow, but as to pleasure, that has been long out of the question." (Laughter.)

Be that as it may, duties must be done, however arduous, and certainly your kindness and encouragement relieves me from all unnecessary fatigue in the progress of the cause. We will look for a moment, under the light that I have sought to throw on the subject, a little more particularly at the two acts—the one of 1795, the other of 1863— that have relation to this subject of *ad interim* appointments. The act of 1795 provides that "in case of a vacancy in the offices of the Secretary of State, Secretary of the Treasury, or of the Secretary of the Department of War, or of any officer of either of the said departments whose appointment is not in the heads thereof whereby they cannot perform the duties of their said respective offices, it shall be lawful for the President of the United States, in case he should think it necessary, to authorize any persons or persons, at his discretion, to perform the duties of the said respective offices until a successor be appointed, or such vacancy be filled ; *provided*, that no one vacancy shall be supplied in the manner aforesaid for a longer term than six months."

The act of 1863, which was passed under the suggestion of the President of the United States, not for the extension of the Vacancy act (which I have read) to the other departments, but for the extension of the temporary disability provision of 1792, provides as follows:—"In case of

death, resignation, absence from the seat of government, or sickness of the head of any executive department, or of any officer of said department whose appointment is not in the head thereof, whereby they cannot perform the duties of their respective offices, it shall be lawful for the President of the United States, in case he should think it necessary, to authorize"—not any person or persons, as in the act of 1795, but to authorize—"any other of said departments, whose appointment is vested in the President, at his discretion, to perform the duties of the said respective offices until a successor be appointed, or until such absence or disability by sickness shall cease ; *provided*, that no one vacancy shall be supplied in manner aforesaid for a longer term than six months." Now, it will be observed that the eighth section of the act of 1792, to which I now call attention (being found on page (218), provides thus:—"That in case of the death, absence from the seat of government, or sickness of the Secretary of State, Secretary of the Treasury, or the Secretary of the War Department, or of any officer of either of the said departments, whose appointment is not in the head thereof, whereof they cannot perform the duties of their respective offices, it shall be lawful for the President of the United States, in case he should think it necessary, to authorize any person or persons, at his discretion, to perform the duties of the said respective office until a successor be appointed, or until the said disability, by absence or sickness, shall cease."

Now, I am told, or I understand from the argument, that if there was a vacancy in the office of Secretary of War by the competent and effective removal of Mr. Stanton, by the exercise of the President's authority in his paper order, which thus comes to be some infraction of law by reason of the President designating General Thomas to the *ad interim* charge of the office, because, it is said, that though under the act of 1790, or under the act of 1797, General Thomas, under the comprehension of "any person or persons," might be open to the President's choice and appointment ; yet, that he does not come within the limited and restricted right of selection for *ad interim* duties, which is proposed by the act of 1863.

It must be assumed in argument, that the whole range of selection permitted under that act was of the heads of departments ; but your attention is drawn to the fact that it permits the President to designate any person who is either the head of a department or holds any office in any department, the appointment of which is by the President ; and I would like to know why General Thomas, the Adjutant-General of the Armies of the United States, holding his position in that Department of War, is not a person appointed by the President, and open to his selection for this temporary duty ; and I would like to know upon what principle of ordinary succession or recourse any officer could be found better suited to assume for a day or a week the discharge of the *ad interim* duties than the Adjutant-General of the Armies of the United States, being the staff officer of the President, and the person who stands there as the principal directory and immediate agent of the War Department in the exercise of its ordinary functions. I cannot but think it is too absurd for me to argue to the Senate that the removal of the President of the United States would not depend upon the question whether an adjutant-general was a proper *locum tenens* or not ; or whether entangled between the boughs of repealed and unrepealed statutes, the President may have erred in that which he thought his rightful authority. Let me call your attention now to an exercise of this power of *ad interim* appointment as found in the administration of President Lincoln, page 582 in the record, before the enactment of the statute of 1863. Now, you will observe that before the passage of the act of 1863, there was in force no statutory authority for the *ad interim* discharge of the officers, except the acts of 1792 and 1795, which were limited in their terms to the Departments of War, of State and of the Treasury.

Now, you have directly in this action of President Lincoln, not an infraction of the prohibitory statute with a penalty, but of a technical appointment without the adequate support of an enabling act of Congress to cover it, for he proceeded on September 22, 1862, to appoint John B. Skinner, then acting First Assistant Postmaster-General, to be acting Postmaster-General *ad interim*, in place of Montgomery Blair, who was temporarily absent. That was in the Department of the Post Office, not covered by the acts of 1792 and 1795. Now, I would like to know whether, when Mr. Lincoln appointed Mr. Skinner to be Postmaster-General without an enabling and supporting act of Congress to justify him, he deserved to be impeached? Whether that is a crime against the Constitution and his oath of office, whether a duty due to the Constitution that he should be impeached and removed and a new election ordered? I cannot but insist upon always separating from these crimes alleged in the articles the guilt that is outside of the articles, and that has been perceived, and which their answer not even permitted to rebut by testimony.

I will take the question as it is, and I will read each article, including the whole compass of crime, the whole range of imputation, the whole scope of testimony and construction ; and unless there be some measure of guilt, some purpose, or some act of force, of violence, I cannot find in mistaken, erroneous acts of excess of authority, making no impression upon the fabric of the government, or giving either menace or injury to the public service, any foundation for this extraordinary proceeding of impeachment. Am I right in saying that you must give your judgment of guilty or not guilty, not of acts set forth in the articles, but as guilty or not guilty of high crime and misdemeanor.

as charged; that you will have the question as distinctly set as in the Peck and Chase trials, and not the questions as used in the Pickering trial, for the honorable manager (Mr. Wilson) denounces the latter as a mockery of justice and finding of the material facts, leaving no conclusion of law or judgment to be found by anybody.

There is another point of limitation of the President's authority, as contained in both the act of 1795 and the act of 1863, which has been made the subject of some comment by the learned and honorable manager, Mr. Boutwell. It is, that any how and any way, the President has been guilty of a high crime and misdemeanor, however innocent otherwise, because the six months' limit accorded to him by the act of 1795 or by the act of 1863 had already expired before he appointed General Thomas. Well, I do not exactly understand the reasoning of the honorable manager. But it is definitely written down, and words, I suppose, have their ordinary meaning. How it is that the President is chargeable with having filled a vacancy thus occurring on the 21st of February, 1868, if it occurred at all, by an appointment which he made *ad interim* on that day, because his six months' right had expired, I do not understand. It is an attempt to connect it in some way with the preceding suspension of Mr. Stanton, which certainly did not create a vacancy in the office; no matter, then, whether the suspension was under the Civil Tenure act or under the act of 1796, the office was not vacant until the removal. Now there remains nothing to be considered, except about an *ad interim* appointment as occurring during a session of the Senate or during the recess. An effort has been made to connect a discrimination between a session of the Senate and a recess of the Senate in its operation on the right of *ad interim* appointment with the discrimination which the Constitution makes between filling the office during the session, and the limited commission which is permitted during the recess. But sufficient, I imagine, for all purposes of convincing your judgment, has been shown to prove that a temporary appointment does not rest on constitutional provisions at all; that it not a filling of the office, but that the office remains just as vacant, so far as the constitutional right and duty remains, as if the temporary appointment had not been made.

When the final appointment is made it dates so as to supply the place of the persons whose vacancy led to the *ad interim* appointment, and in the very nature of things there can be no difference in that capacity between the recess and the session of the Senate. We have been able to present on the pages of this record cases enough applicable to the heads of departments to make it unnecessary for me to argue the matter any further upon general principles. Mr. Evarts, in this connection, referred to the *ad interim* appointments of Mr. Nelson, in the State Department, on the 29th of February, 1844; of General Scott, in the War Department, on the 23d of July, 1850; of Mr. Moses Kelley, in the Interior Department, June 10, 1861; and of General Holt, in the War Department, on the 1st of June, 1861.

Mr. EVARTS continued:—And now, having passed through all possible allegations of infractions of the statue, I come to the consideration of the removal of Mr. Stanton, which is charged as a high crime and misdemeanor in the first article, and which has to be passed upon by this court. Under that imputation, and under the President's defense, the crime, as charged, may be regarded as the only one on which judgment is to be passed. The necessary concession to this obvious suggestion will relieve me very much from the difficulty of any protracted discussion. Before taking up the form of the article and the consideration of the facts of the procedure, I ask attention now to some general lights to be thrown both on the construction of the act by the debates in Congress, and by the relations of the Cabinet, as proper witnesses in reference to the purpose or intent of the President.

Most extraordinary means have been presented in behalf of the House of Representatives in reference to Cabinet Ministers. The personal degradation fastened upon them by the honorable manager (Mr. Boutwell) I have sufficiently referred to; and I recollect that there are in your number two or three other honorable Senators—the honorable Senator from Maryland (Mr. Johnson), and the honorable Senator from Iowa (Mr. Harlan)—who must take their share of the opprobrium which I yesterday divided among three members of the court alone.

The ability of the President to receive aid and direction from these heads of departments, has been presented as a dangerous innovation, as a sort of Star Chamber council, which was to devour our liberties. Perhaps some members of this honorable Senate may have already had their views changed on that subject since the time when a representation was made to President Lincoln in reference to his Cabinet, to which I beg to call the attention of the Senate.

Mr. EVARTS read on this point the remonstrance, signed by twenty-five Senators, and addressed to Mr. Lincoln, on the subject of retaining Mr. Blair in his Cabinet, stating that the theory of the government is, and should be, that a Cabinet must agree with the President in political principles, and that such selection and choice should be made as to secure in the Cabinet unity of purpose and action; that the Cabinet should be exclusively composed of statesmen who are cordial, resolute and unvarying supporters of the principles and purposes of the Administration.

Senator JOHNSON inquired what the date of the paper was.

Mr. EVARTS said the paper has no date, but the re-marks, I think, were made some time in the year 1862 or 1863. It was a translation and a juncture which is familiar to the recollection of Senators who took part in it, and, doubtless, to all the public men whom I have now the honor to address. Now, the honorable managers on behalf of the House of Representatives do not hold to this idea at all; not at all; and I must think that the course of events accord in its administration of the laws of evidence as not enabling the President to produce the supporting aid of his Cabinet, which, as this paper says, he ought to have in all his measures and views has either proceeded on the ground that his action, in your judgment, did not need any explanation or support, or else on the ground that you have not sufficiently held to these useful views about the Cabinet, which were presented to the notice of Mr. Lincoln. Public rumor has said—and for the truth of which I do not vouch, as I have no knowledge of it—that Mr. Lincoln rather blunted the edge of that representation by suggesting that what the honorable Senators wanted was that "his Cabinet should agree with them rather than with him."

However that may be, the doctrines in that paper are true, and are accordant to the precedents of the country and the law of the government; and I find it, therefore, quite unnecessary to refute, by any very serious or prolonged argument, the imputations or invectives against the Cabinet because it agreed with the President, that have been urged upon your attention; but now, as bearing both upon the question of the right to doubt and deliberate on the power of the President, both as to the constitutionality of the Tenure of Office act, and as to the construction of its first section. I may be permitted to attract your attention to some points in the debates of Congress not yet alluded to.

I will not recall the history of the action of the House upon the general form and purpose of the bill, nor of the persistency with which the Senate, being still the advisers of the President in the matter of appointments, as members of the legislative branch of the government, insisted on the exclusion of Cabinet ministers from the purview of the bill altogether, but when it was found that the House was persistent in its view also, the Senate concurred with it, on a conference, in a measure of accommodation concerning this special matter of the Cabinet which is now to be found in the text of the first section of the act.

In the debate on the Tenure of Office bill, the honorable Senator from Oregon (Mr. Williams), who seems, with the Senator from Vermont (Mr. Edmunds), to have had some particular conduct of the debate, said; "I do not regard the exception as of any great practical consequence, because, I suppose, if the President and any head of a department should disagree so as to make their relations unpleasant, and if the President should signify that that head of department should retire from the Cabinet, would follow without any positive act of removal on the part of the President;" and Mr. Sherman, bearing on the same point, says, "Any gentleman fit to be a Cabinet minister, who receives an intimation from his Chief that his longer continuance in the office is unpleasant to him, would necessarily resign. If he did not resign, it would show that he was unfit to be there. I cannot imagine a case where a Cabinet officer would hold on to his place in defiance and against the wishes of his chief." But, nevertheless, this practical lack of importance in the measure which induced the Senate to yield their opinions of regulating any governmental proceedings, and to permit the modification of the bill, led to the enactment as it now appears.

And the question is how this matter was understood not by one man, not by one speaker, but, so far as the record shows, by the whole Senate, on the question of the construction of the act as inclusive of Mr. Stanton, or of any other incumbent of a Cabinet position. When the Conference Committee reported the section as it now reads—as the result of the compromise between the Senate, firm in its views, and the House, firm in its purpose—the honorable Senator from Michigan (Mr. Howard) asked that the proviso might be explained.

Now you are at the very point of finding out what it means, when the Senate got so far as to ask those who had charge of the matter and who were fully competent to advise about it. The honorable Senator, Mr. Williams, states that the tenure of office of the Cabinet ministers shall expire when the term of office of the President by whom they were appointed expires, and he went on to say, "I have, from the beginning of this controversy, regarded this as quite immaterial, for I have no doubt that any Cabinet officer who has a particle of self-respect, and I can hardly suppose that any man would occupy so responsible a position without it, would continue to remain in the Cabinet after the President had signified to him that his presence was no longer needed.

"As a matter of course the effect of the provision amounts to very little one way or the other, for I presume that whenever the President thinks proper to rid himself of an offensive Cabinet minister, he has only to signify that desire, and the minister will retire and the new appointment be made." Mr. Sherman said, "I agree to the report of the Committee of Conference with a great deal of reluctance. I think that no gentleman, no man of any sense, of honor, would hold a position as Cabinet officer after his chief desires his removal, and, therefore, the slightest intimation on the part of the President would always secure the resignation of the Cabinet officer, for that reason I do not wish to jeopard this bill about an unimportant and collateral question."

Mr. Sherman proceeds further, in answer to the demand of a Senator to know from the committee what it had done and what the operation of the law was to be, and says:—"The proposition now submitted by the Conference Committee is, that a Cabinet Minister shall hold his office during the life term of the President who appointed him. If the President dies the Cabinet goes out. If the President is removed for cause by impeachment, the Cabinet goes out; at the expiration of the term of the President's office the Cabinet goes out."

Now, how in the face of this can we with patience listen to long arguments to show that in reference to a Cabinet Minister, situated as Mr. Stanton is, the whole object of lamentation in the proviso and in the bill becomes nugatory and unprotective of the President's right, and forces upon him Cabinet officers whom he never appointed at all, and how shall we tolerate this argument that the term of a President lasts after he is dead, and that the term in which Mr. Stanton was appointed by Mr. Lincoln lasts through the succeeding term to which Mr. Lincoln was subsequently elected.

But that is not the point. You are asked to remove a President from office under the stigma of impeachment for crime, to strike down the only elective head of the government whom the actual circumstances permit the Constitution to have recourse to, and to assume to yourself the sequestration and administration of that office ad interim, because a President is guilty of thinking that Mr. Sherman, in behalf of the Conference Committee, was right in explaining to the Senate, what the Conference Committee had done. Nobody contradicted him; nobody wanted any further explanation. Nobody doubted that there was no vice or fault in that act. That in undertaking to recognize a limited right of that President, it was not intended to have Cabinet Ministers retained in office whom he had not had any voice in appointing.

I would like to know who it is in this honorable Senate who will bear the issue of the scrutiny of the revising people of the United States on the removal from office of the President for the removal of an officer whom the Senate has thus declared not to be within the protection of the Civil Tenure act. Agree that judicial decision may afterwards pronounce a different judgment, still, you must admit that the President might well act as he did in deference to the opinion of Mr. Sherman, even if judgment of an inferior court, to say nothing of the Supreme Court, or of the highest special judicature this court should determine otherwise.

But the matter was brought out a little more distinctly, Mr. Doolittle having said that the proviso would not keep in the Secretary of War, and that that had been asserted as the object of the bill. Mr. Sherman, still representing the Conference Committee, proceeds to say "That the Senate had no such purpose as was shown by its vote twice to make this general exception."

That this provisions does not apply to the present case is shown by the fact that its language is so framed as not to apply to the present President. Now, that was pretty definite on that subject. The Senator shows that himself, and argues truly that it would not prevent the present President from removing the Secretary of War, the Secretary of the Navy, and the Secretary of State, and he goes on to say:—"If I could suppose that either of those gentlemen were so wanting in manhood and in honor, as to hold his place under the politest intimation by the President of the United States, that his services were no longer needed, I would, certainly, as a Senator, consent to his removal, and so would we all."

And yet later, in continuation of his explanation, the same honorable Senator says:—"We provide that a Cabinet Minister shall hold his office not for a fixed term, not until the Senate shall consent to his removal, but as long as the power of appointing him holds office; if the principal office is vacated his Cabinet Ministers go out."

Now, Senators, I press upon your consideration the inevitable, the inestimable weight of this Senatorial discussion and conclusion. I do not press it upon the particular Senators who took part in it specially. I press it upon the concurring, unresisting, assenting, agreeing, confirming, corroborative silence of the whole Senate.

And I would ask if the President of the United States and his Cabinet, having before them the question for their own solution, of the ambiguities and difficulties, if there be any, as I think there are not, of this section, might not he repose upon the sense of the Senate that that body would not have agreed to a bill if it had any such efficacy as is now contended for, and might he not repose on the explanation of the Conference Committee, and of the acceptance of it by the Senate, that the bill had no such possible construction or force.

Nevertheless, if the President must be convicted of a high crime and misdemeanor for this concurrence with your united judgment, and if that sentence also proceeds on your united judgment, we shall have very great difficulty in knowing which of your united judgments is entitled to most regard.

In the House this matter was considered, and the result of the explanation there by Mr. Schenck was about the same as in the Senate, and the House came to the same conclusion. The whole great matter here is an impeachment by the House for making a removal, and a condemnation by the Senate on the same ground, and we are brought, therefore, to the consideration of the meaning of the act, of its constitutionality, of the right of the President to put its constitutionality in issue by proper and peaceful proceedings, or of his right to doubt and differ on the construction of the section, and to proceed honestly and peacefully, as he might feel himself best advised to do.

And now I may here at once dispose of what I may have to say definitely in answer to some propositions insisted upon by the honorable manager (Mr. Boutwell). He has

undertaken to disclose to you his views of the result of the debate of 1789, and of the doctrines of the government as they are developed, and he has not hesitated to claim that the limitation of those doctrines was confined to appointments during the session of the Senate. Nothing can be less supported by the debate or by the practice of the government.

In the whole of that debate, from the beginning to the end, there is not any suggestion of the distinction which the honorable managers have not hesitated to lay down in print for your guidance as to the result. The whole question was otherwise—whether the power of removal resided in the President absolutely? If it did, why should he not remove at one time as well as another? The power of removal would arise when the emergencies dictated instant action.

We understand that when the removal is political, or proceeds from the principle of rotation in office, as we call it, the whole notice of removal is the new appointment. The new appointment is the first thought and issue. There is no desire to get rid of the old officer except for the purpose of getting in the new one. The form of the notice, as in the last case on your table—the appointment of General Schofield—is that A. B. is appointed in place of C. D., not to be removed, but removed, meaning, "I, as the President, have no power to appoint unless there is a vacancy. I tell you, the Senate, that I have made a vacancy; or, I present to you the case of a vacancy created by my will, and I name to you A. B., to be appointed in the place of C. D., removed."

That is the meaning of that action of the government. Now, you will observe that there have been only two cases in the history of the government where there has been a separate act of removal, either during the session of the Senate or during the recess, of Cabinet officers. You can hardly suppose an instance in which a removal of a Cabinet officer could be possible, because, in the language of the honorable Senator, you can hardly conceive of the possibility of a Cabinet officer not resigning when it is intimated to him that his place is wanted.

Therefore all this pride of exultation that we have found no cases of removal of a Cabinet officer, save that of Timothy Pickering, rests upon Senator Sherman's proposition that you cannot conceive of the possibility of there being a Cabinet officer who would need to be removed.

The practice of our government has shown that those honorable Senators were right in their proposition, and that there never has been, from the beginning of the government to the present time, more than two cases where there were Cabinet ministers who, on the slightest intimation from their chief, did not resign. Therefore do not urge upon us the pancity of the case of removal of heads of departments, as that paucity rises on the fact of the retirement whenever the President desired it.

Mr. Pickering, having nothing but wild lands for his support, and having a family to provide for, frankly told Mr. Adams that he would not resign, because it would not be convenient for him to make any other arrangement for living till the end of his term; and the President, without that consideration of domestic reasons which perhaps Mr. Pickering hoped to obtain, immediately told him that he would remove him, and he did; and Mr. Pickering went back to his wild lands.

Now Mr. Stanton, under motives of public duty, as he says, took the position that the public interest would not allow him to retire; and these are the only two cases in our government in which the question has arisen. In the one case the Secretary was instantly removed, and in the other case an attempt was made to remove him; therefore the practice of the government could be expected to suggest only the peculiar cases where promptitude and necessity for the rough method of removal were demanded at the hands of the Executive.

I ask the attention of the honorable court to the cases we have presented in our previous arguments—instances of removals during the sessions of the Senate.

Mr. Evarts recapitulated these cases and continued:— Now I am sure that the honorable Senators will give their assent to the propositions I have submitted, that in reference to Cabinet officers it is almost impossible to expect removals; that in respect to subordinate officers, charged with any criminality, their resignation is generally procured by their sureties, or by their own sense of shame, or by their disposition to give no trouble. I think you will be satisfied, also, with the proposition assented to by every statesman, I think assented to by every debater on the passage of the Civil Tenure act, that the doctrine, and the action, and the practice of the government had been for the President to remove in session or in recess, although some discrimination of that kind was attempted. But I have already argued to show that there is no discrimination of the power of removal between the time during a session and a recess.

Look at it in this point of view. The Senate is in session, and a public officer is carrying on frauds either at San Francisco, or New York, or Hong Kong, or Liverpool, or wherever else you please, and the fact comes to the knowledge of the President; the session of the Senate is going on, but the fact of the President's knowledge does not put him in possession of a good man to succeed the officer, either in his own approval or in the approval of the Senate; and if it is necessary that the Consul at Hong Kong, or at Liverpool, or the Sub-Treasurer at New York, or the Master of the Mint at San Francisco, should go on with his frauds until the President finds a man and sends him out, and gets his assent, and gets him qualified, very well. It is not the kind of law adapted to the circumstances of the case. That is all I can venture to suggest.

No construction and no practice of the government

while the Executive Department was untrammelled by the legislative restriction has ever shown a discrimination between session and recess in regard to removals from office. Of course, a difference has been shown in regard to political appointments. And now that I come to consider the actual merits of the proceeding of the President, having given the precise construction to the first section of the bill, I need to ask your attention to a remarkable concession made by Mr. Manager Butler in his opening, that if the President had accomplished the removal of Mr. Stanton in a method, the precise terms of which the honorable manager was so good as to furnish, there would have been no occasion for impeachment.

It is not, then, after all, the *forbiter in re*, which the manager complains of, but the *suaviter in modo*, and you, as a court, and the honorable managers, under our arguments, are reduced to the necessity of removing the President of the United States, not for the act, but for the form and style in which it was done. But more definitely has the honorable manager, Mr. Boutwell, has laid down two firm and strong propositions bearing on the merits of the case, and I will ask your attention to them. We argue that if the Tenure of Office act is unconstitutional we had a right to obey the Constitution, at least in the intent and purpose of a peaceful submission of the matter to the court; and that our judgment in the matter, if deliberate and honest, and if supported by diligent application to the proper sources of information, is entitled to support us against an imputation of crime.

To meet that, and to protect the case from the inquiry which we proposed, the honorable manager (Mr. Boutwell) does not hesitate to say that the question of the constitutionality or unconstitutionality of the law does not make the least difference in the world; that the point is, that the law has been violated, and that for the President of the United States to violate an unconstitutional law is an act worthy of his removal from office.

Now mark the desperate result to which the reasoning of the honorable managers, under the pressure of our arguments, has reduced them; that is, their proposition, and the reason of this proposition is given in these terms:—"If that is not so, if the question of the constitutionality or unconstitutionality of the act is permitted to come into your consideration of crime, then you would be punishing the President for an error of judgment; releasing him or condemning him, according as he exercised it, right or wrong;" and that, the honorable manager tells us, is contrary to the first principles of justice.

The argument of the manager is in these words, to be found on page 815 of the record:—"If the President, in the discharge of his duty to take care that the laws be faithfully executed, may inquire whether the laws are constitutional, and execute those only which he believes to be so, then for the purposes of government his will or opinion is substituted for the action of the law-making power, and the government is no longer a government of law, but the government of one man. This is also true if, when arraigned, he may justify himself that he has acted upon advice that the law was unconstitutional.

"Further, if the Senate, sitting for the trial of the President, may inquire and decide whether the law is, in fact, constitutional, and convict the President if he has violated an act believed to be constitutional, and acquit him, if the Senate think the law unconstitutional, the President is, in fact, tried for his judgment; to be acquitted, if, in the opinion of the Senate, it was a correct judgment, and convicted, if, in the opinion of the Senate, his judgment was erroneous. This doctrine offends every principle of justice; his offense is, that he intentionally violated a law: knowing its terms and requirements, he disregarded them."

Well, that is what we say, it does offense to every principle of justice, to say that the President should be convicted because he honestly and peacefully sought to have a decision made between the Constitution and the law. And the honorable manager can escape from our argument on that point by no other mode than by the desperate recourse to this declaration, that constitutional laws and unconstitutional laws are all alike in this country of a written Constitution, and that every one who violates unconstitutional law meets with the same kind of punishment as he who violates constitutional laws.

This confusion of ideas as to a law being valid for any purpose, if unconstitutional, I have already sufficiently exposed in the general argument. No Senator, according to Mr. manager Boutwell, on page 815, has a right to be governed by his judgment, even if satisfied that the law is unconstitutional. You may all regard the law as unconstitutional, and yet you have got to remove the President. Now that is pretty hard upon us, that we cannot even go to the Supreme Court to find out if it is unconstitutional; that we cannot regard it in our own oath of office as unconstitutional, and that you cannot do it either.

Now, on the question of the construction of the law, what are the views of the honorable managers? We have claimed that if the President, in good faith, construed this law to not include Mr. Stanton under its protection, and if he went on under that opinion, he cannot be guilty. The honorable manager (Mr. Boutwell) takes up this question, and disposes of it in this very peculiar manner:—"If a law passed by Congress be equivocal or ambiguous in its terms, the Executive being called upon to administer it may apply his own best judgment to the difficulties before him, or he may seek counsel from his official advisers, or other proper persons, and acting thereupon without evil intent or purpose, he would be fully justified, and upon no principle of right could he be held to answer as for a misdemeanor in office."

We never contended for anything stronger than that.

On no principle of right can the President be held to answer as for a misdemeanor in office. Now, logic is a good thing—an excellent thing; it operates on the mind without altogether yielding to bias; but, if we press an argument, however narrow it may be, if it be logical the honorable managers are obliged to admit it in both the cases I have cited. They have thrown away their accusation.

Tell me, what more do we need than that? That when an ambiguous and equivocal law is presented to the President, and he is called upon to act under it, he may seek advice of his advisers and other persons, and may act thereupon without evil intent or purpose, and that he would be fully justified in doing so, and that on no principle of right can he be held to answer for a misdemeanor in office. And what is the answer which the honorable managers wish to that logical proposition? Why, that this act is not of that sort; that is as plain as the nose on a man's face, and that nothing but violent resistance to right could lead anybody outside of this Senate to doubt what the act meant. The honorable manager who follows me will have an opportunity to correct me in my statement of the proposition, and to furnish an adequate answer to the views which I have the honor now to present. And now for the act itself. It provides "that every person holding any civil office, to which he had been appointed by and with the advice and consent of the Senate, and every person who shall hereafter be appointed to any such office, is and shall be entitled to hold such office until his successor shall in like manner be appointed, and shall have qualified, except as herein otherwise provided."

Then the provision otherwise is "That the Secretary of State, of the Treasury, of War, and the Interior, the Postmaster-General, and the Attorney-General, shall hold their office respectively for and during the term of the President by whom they have been appointed, and one month thereafter, subject to removal by and with the advice and consent of the Senate." Now that is the operative section of this act. The section of crimination so far as relates to removals, I will read, and omit all that relates to any other matter.

The sixth section provides that every removal contrary to the provisions of the acts shall be deemed to be high misdemeanor, and shall be punished by a fine not exceeding ten thousand dollars, or by imprisonment not exceeding five years, or both, in the discretion of the court. You will observe that this act does not affix a penalty to anything but a removal—an accomplished removal—acts of a penal nature are to be construed strictly, and whenever we ask that necessary protection of the liberty, the property and life of a citizen of the United States under a penal statute, we are told that we are doing some very extraordinary thing for a lawyer in behalf of his client.

We are told in effect that when we have a President for a defendant, all the law writers die and wither, and politics and political constructions have a predominance, and that everything of law, of evidence, and of justice, is narrowed and not enlarged. Well, that may be; all that I can say is, that if the President had been indicted under this act, or if he shall be hereafter indicted under it, the law of the land would apply to his case as usually administered, and that if he has not removed Mr. Stanton, he cannot be punished for having done it. The act might have provided a punishment for an attempt to remove, but see what it has done; it has provided a punishment for any person who received any appointment or employment contrary to the provisions of the act, but it has not provided a punishment for any attempt at removal.

Now, what does the article charge in that behalf, for I believe it has not been claimed, as yet, that it is too narrow to insist that the crime as charged in the articles will be the one you ought to try. Removal is not charged in the articles anywhere. The allegation is that Andrew Johnson unlawfully, and in violation of the Constitution, issued an order in writing for the removal of Edwin M. Stanton, with intent to violate the act, and with intent to remove him, the Senate being in session.

Now, if you had a section in the statute which said that any removal, or the signing of any letter, or order or mandate of removal was a crime, then you would have an indictment and a crime on which you could proceed. But you have neither crime nor indictment, as appears in the first article. It is said that, in so small matter as the question of the removal of the President it does not do to insist on the usual rules of construction of criminal law. Now, what was the true attitude of Mr. Stanton and of the President towards this office and this officer at the time of the alleged infraction of the law?

Mr. Stanton held a perfectly good title to that office by the commission of a President of the United States—to hold it according to the terms of the commission, "during the pleasure of the President for the time being." He held a good title to that office. A *quo warranto* moved against him while he held that commission, unremoved, unannulled, and undetermined, would have been answered by the production of the commission. He would have answered, "I hold this office at the pleasure of the President of the United States for the time being, and I have not been removed by the President of the United States."

That was the only title he held up to the passage of the Civil Tenure act; but by the passage of that act it is said that a statutory title was vested in him—not proceeding from the executive power of the United States at all, not commissioned by the Executive of the United States at all—and superadded to the title from the executive authority which he held. This gave him a durable office, determinable only one month after the expiration of the Presidential term.

The first question to which I ask your attention is this

that the act is wholly unconstitutional and inoperative in conferring on Mr. Stanton, or anybody else, a durable office to which he has never been appointed. Appointments to all offices proceed from the President of the United States, or from such heads of departments, or such courts of law as your legislation may vest them in. You cannot administer appointments to office yourselves, for while the Constitution requires the President to have the control you cannot confer it anywhere else.

The appointment of the Secretary of War is one which cannot be taken from the President and conferred upon a court of law, or upon the heads of departments. That office is conferable only by the Executive, and when Mr. Stanton, or anybody else, holds an office during pleasure, which he has received by commission from the President of the United States, you can no more confer upon him by your authority an appointment and title, durable as against the President of the United States, than you can if he were out of office altogether. I challenge contradiction from the lawyers who oppose us, and from the judgment of honorable and intelligent lawyers here.

Where are you going to carry this doctrine of legislative appointment to office? If you can carry it the case of a man whom the President has never asked to hold an office, except from day to day, and you can enact him into a durable office for life, you may determine that an office shall be held for ten years, if you please. You may determine that an office shall be held for life. But the discretion and judgment of appointing to an office for life is very different from his appointing to an office during his pleasure and where he can change the incumbent at will.

You may sweep all the offices of the country, not only into the Senate, but into Congress, if you adopt this principle of enacting people into office; and if by an act of Congress, you can confer the tenure of an office which is held at suffrance or at will into estate for life for ten years, then you can appoint to office. Of that there can be no doubt. The next, and the only question of construction or of constitutionality, is whether the Secretary of War is within the first section of the act. The office of the Secretary of War is undoubtedly within the first section.

The question, therefore, is whether the provision concerning the office is of such force and effect as to put Mr. Stanton into office against the will of the President, by statutory terms. The argument that if Mr. Stanton is not within the proviso, then he is within the body of the section, stumbles over this fallacy. The question is, whether the office of Secretary of War is within the proviso or not.

You have not made a law about Mr. Stanton by name, and the question whether Mr. Stanton is in it, or whether Mr. Browning is in it or not, is not a question of Constitution or law.

Mr. Evarts proceeded to argue at some length on this point to prove that while the Tenure of Office act applied to the office of Secretary of War, it did not, or could not apply to the incumbent of the office for the time being.

Mr. Evarts resumed:—Let us now consider what the President did, assuming that the statute covers Mr. Stanton's case, and assuming that the removal of Mr. Stanton was prohibited by it. I have said to you that Mr. Stanton had an appointment to the office, dependent on the President's pleasure. He claimed, or others claimed for him, that he had a tenure depending on the statute. The question of dependency on the statute was a question to be weighed and determined as a novel one.

The question of tenure by appointment was undebatable. The President proposed to put himself in an attitude of reducing the tenure of Mr. Stanton to his statutory tenure, and, therefore, he issued a paper, which is a revocation of his commission and a recall of the officer. Without that question, whatever could be raised by any process on the statutory tenure, because tenure by commission from the President, would be an adequate answer to a *quo warranto*.

The President thus peaceably, in writing, and decorously issued a paper, which is served on Mr. Stanton, saying, in effect, "I, the President of the United States, by such authority as I have, relieve or remove you from the office of Secretary of War." That was a recall of the title derived from the Presidential appointment. Nobody can doubt Mr. Stanton refused to yield the office. Did the President then interpose force to terminate Mr. Stanton's statutory title; or did he, having thus reduced them to the condition his statutory title, propose to test that title? It is enough to say he did not do anything in the way of force; that he expected in advance, as it appears from his statement to General Sherman, that Mr. Stanton would yield the office.

But Mr. Stanton did not yield it. The grounds on which he put himself in August were, "that his duty required him to hold the office till Congress met." That is, to hold it so that the President's appointment could not take effect without the concurrence of the Senate. This public duty of Mr. Stanton, on his own statement, had expired. Mr. Stanton had told the President that the act was unconstitutional, and had aided him in writing the message which so disclosed the President's opinion, and had concurred in the opinion that he was not within the act submissive to those views; if not submissive to the views to which Senators here had expressed, "that no man could be supposed to refuse to give up his office after an intimation from his chief that his services were no longer needed, was to be expected from Mr. Stanton. If, when Mr. Stanton having said to General Thomas on the first presentation of his credentials, that he wished to know whether General Thomas desired him to vacate at once or would give him time to remove his private papers, the President regarded it as all settled, and so informed the Cabinet, as you have per-

mitted to be given in evidence; now, after that, after the 21st of February, what act was done by the President about the office of Secretary of War? Nothing whatever.

Mr. Stanton swore on the 21st, when he got out the warrant for General Thomas, that he was still in the possession of the office. And when General Thomas was taken into custody on that warrant, the President simply said, "Very well, the matter is in court" and counsel was consulted in order to have a habeas corpus carried into the Supreme Court. But Mr. Chief Justice Cartter, who everybody will admit, sees as far into a millstone as most people, let the matter drop out of his court by its own weight, and the habeas corpus fell with it. Now that is all the force there was. I submit to you, therefore, that a cause of resistance or violation of law does not at all arise.

He must then come either to intent, purpose, motion, or some force prepared, meditated, threatened or applied, or some invasion of the actual work of the department in order to give substance to this allegation of fault. No such fact, no such intent, no such purpose is shown. We are prevented from showing all attendant views, opinions and purposes on which the President proceeded; and if so, it must be on the ground that views, intent and purposes do not qualify the act.

Very well. Let the managers be held to the narrowness of their charges, when they ask for judgment, as they are when they exclude testimony; and let the case be determined on their reasoning, that an article framed on this plan that the President, well knowing an act to be unconstitutional, has, in virtue of his office, undertaken to make an appointment contrary to its provisions and conformable to the Constitution of the United States, with the intent that the Constitution of the United States shall prevail in relation to the office, in overthrowing the authority of an act of Congress, and that, thereupon and thereby, with an intent against which there can be no presumption; for he has presumed to have attempted to do what he did do. We ask that, for that purpose of obeying the Constitution, rather than of obeying an invalid law, he shall be removed from office.

This, assuredly, is no greater than that which the managers have committed, for it is but a statement of the proposition of law and of fact, to which the honorable managers have reduced themselves and their own theories, in this which excluded all evidence of intent or purpose, and of effect and conduct, and hold the President simply for an infraction of a statute, in saving that, under your judgment it does not make any difference whether the statute is unconstitutional or not. If that be so, then we have a right to claim that it is unconstitutional, and they agree. If you so treat it and find us guilty, then it would be against the first principles of justice to punish us for our erroneous or mistaken opinion concerning the unconstitutionality of an act.

Now, I do not propose to weary you with a review of the evidence which already lies within the grasp of a handful, and it would astonish you, if you have not already perused the record, to see how much depends on the argument and debates of counsel, and how little included in the testimony. As your attention has been turned by the simplicity and the folly, perhaps, of the conduct of General Thomas, all your attention must have fixed itself on the fact that to prove this they threaten a *coup d'etat* to overthrow the Government of the United States and get control of the Treasury and War Departments. The managers had to go to Delaware to prove a statement by Mr. Karsner, that twenty days afterwards General Thomas said he would kick Stanton out.

That is the fact; there is no getting over it. The *coup d'etat* in Washington, prepared on the 21st February, as proved by Mr. Karsner, who is brought on from Delaware to say that on the 9th of March, in the East Room of the White House, General Thomas said he meant to kick Mr. Stanton out. Well, that now is disrespectful, as undoubtedly intimating force rather of a personal than of a national act, I think. So it comes up to a breach of the peace, provided it had been perpetrated. (Laughter.) But it does not come to that kind of proceeding by which Louis Napoleon seized the liberties of the French Republic.

We expected, from the heat with which this impeachment was accompanied, we would find something of this character. The managers did not neglect little pieces of evidence, as shown by Mr. Karsner, and they found that, and produced it as a sharp point of their cause; then we may be sure there is nothing else; there is no bristling of bayonets under the hay-mow, you may be sure. Are there then, any limits of discrimination in transactions of State? Are there public prosecutions, public dangers, public fears, public menaces? Undoubtedly there may be; and undoubtedly many persons who voted for impeachment supposed there were, and undoubtedly the people of the United States, when they heard of impeachment, took it for granted that there was something to oppose. There was no defect of power or of will on the part of the managers to sift it all.

Every channel of public information was searched. The newspapers seem to be ardent and eager enough to aid this prosecution. All the people of the United States are united in it. They love their liberties and they love their government, and if anybody knew of anything which would bear upon the question of force and *coup d'etat*, we should have heard of it. We must, then, submit, with great respect, that on this evidence and on this allegation, there is no case made out of evil purpose, of large designs of any kind, and no act made which is an infraction of a law.

Now, what is the attitude which you must occupy towards each particular charge in those articles? You must say that the President is guilty or not guilty of a high crime or a misdemeanor, by reason of charges made and proved. Guilty of what the Constitution means as sufficient cause for removal of the President from office. You are not to reach over from one article to another; you are to say "guilty, or not guilty," upon each article, and you are to take it as it appears. You are to treat the President of the United States for the purpose of that determination, as if he was innocent of everything else—as if he was of good politics and of good conduct. You are to deal with him, under your oath to administer impartial justice, within the premises of the accusation and of the proof. You are to deal with him as if it were President Lincoln or General Grant who was charged with the same thing. If the proposition that political gratitude is a lively sense of benefit expected, leads men forward rather than backward in the list of Presidents, you are to treat it as if the respondent was innocent; as if he was your friend; as if you agreed in public sentiment and public policy with him; and, nevertheless, the crime charged and proved must be such as that you would remove General Washington or President Lincoln for the same offense.

Now, I will not be told that it was competent for the managers to prove that there was a *coup d'etat* hidden, and a purpose of evil to the State threatened in that innocent and formal act. Let them prove it; then let us disprove it, and then judge us within the compass of the testimony, and according to the law govern those considerations. But I ask you if I do not put it to you truly, that within the premises of the charge and proof, the same judgment must go against President Lincoln, with his good politics, and General Washington, with his majestic character, as against the respondent. And so, as you go along from the first article to the second, will you remove him for having committed an error in reference to a removal from office?

If the power of removing Mr. Stanton under the former practice of the government, unrestricted by this Civil Tenure act, existed, it existed during the session as well as during the recess. If that were debatable and disputable, the prevailing opinion was that it covered, and the practice of the government showed that it covered, removals during the session. At any rate, you must judge of him in that matter as you would have judged Mr. Lincoln if he had been charged with a high misdemeanor in appointing Mr. Skinner Postmaster-General when there was no authority to do so.

And this brings me very properly to consider, as I shall very briefly, in what attitude the President stands before you, when the discussion of vicious politics, or of repugnant politics—whichever may be right or wrong—is removed from the case. I do not hesitate to say that, if you separate your feelings and your conduct, and his feelings and his conduct from the aggravation of politics, as they have been bred since his elevation to the Presidency, under the peculiar circumstances which placed him there; and if your views are reduced to the ordinary standard and style of estimate which should prevail between the departments of the government, I do not hesitate to say that, on the impeachment investigation, and on the impeachment evidence, you have the general standing of the President unimpaired in his conduct and character, as a man or as a magistrate.

I hold that no man can find in his heart to say that evil has been proved against him here, and how much is there in his conduct towards and for his country, which, up to this period of division, commends itself to your and to the approval and applause of his countrymen. I do not insist on this topic, but I ask you to agree with me, in this that his personal traits of character, and the circumstances of his career, have made him in opinion, what he is without learning, as it is said by his biographer, "Never enjoying a day's schooling in his life, devoted always to such energetic pursuits in the service of his State as commended him to the favor of his fellow-citizens, and raised him, step by step, through all the gradations of the public service, in every trial of fidelity to his origin and to the common interest, proved faithful; struggling always in his public life against the aristocratic influences and oppressions which domineered so much in the section of the country from which he came; he was always faithful to the common interest of the common people, and carried, by his aid and efforts, as much as any one else, popular measures against the Southern policy of aristocratic government."

I ask you to notice that. That bred in a school of Tennessee Democratic politics, he had always learned to believe that the Constitution "must, and shall be preserved," and I ask you to recognize that when it was in peril, and when all men south of a certain line took up arms against it, and all men north of that line ought to have taken up arms in politics or in war for it, he loved the country and the Constitution more than he loved his section, and the glories which were promised by the evil spirits of rebellion. I ask you whether he was not as firm in his devotion to the Constitution when he said, in December, 1860, "Then let us stand by the Constitution, and, in saving the Union, we will save this the greatest country on earth." And whether, after the battle of Bull Run, he did not show as great adhesion to the Constitution when he said, "The Constitution, which is based upon principles immutable and on which rests the rights of man and the hopes and expectations of those who love freedom throughout the civilized world, must be maintained."

Now, he is no rhetoritician, no theorist, no sophist and no philosopher, the Constitution is to him the only political book that he reads; the Constitution is to him the only great authority which he obeys. His mind may not expand. His views may not be as plastic as those of many

of his countrymen. He may not think that we have outlived the Constitution, and he may not be able to embrace the Declaration of Independence as superior and predominant to it, but to the Constitution he adheres, for it and under it he has served the State from boyhood up—labored for, "loved it"—for it he has stood in arms against the frowns of the Senate, for it he has stood in arms against the rebellious forces of the enemy, and to it he has bowed three times a day with more than eastern devotion.

When I have heard drawn from the past of impeachments and attempts at deposition, and when five hundred years have been spoken of as furnishing the precedent explored by the honorable managers, I thought that they found no case where one was impeached for obeying a higher duty, rather than a written law regarded as repugnant to it, and yet familiar to every child in this country, as well as to every scholar. A precedent much older comes much nearer to this expected entanglement. When the princes came to King Darius, and asked that a law should be made, that whoever should ask any petition for thirty days, "save of thee, oh King," should be cast into the den of lions; and when the plea was made that "the law of the Medes and Persians alter not," and when the minister of that day, the great head and manager of the affairs of that empire, was found still to maintain his devotion to the superior law which made an infraction of the lower law, there was the case where the question was whether the power to which he had been obedient was adequate to his protection against the power which he had disobeyed; and now the question is whether the Constitution is adequate to the protection of the President for his obedience to it against the law which the province had obtained, and which seeks to assert itself against it.

The result of that impeachment we all know. The protection of the higher power was not withheld from the obedient servant. The honorable manager, Mr. Wilson, in that very interesting and valuable report of the minority of the Judiciary Committee, warned the House of the fate of impeachment, as turning always upon those who were ready with the axe and sword to destroy the victim. But you may remember the history of the fall of certain other impeachers:—"And they brought those men which had accused Daniel, and they cast them into the den of lions, them, their children and their wives; and the lions had the mastery of them, and brake all their bones in pieces, or even they come at the bottom of the den."

This, then, Senators, is the issue, not of politics, but of personal guilt, within the limits of the charge. Whoever decides it must so decide and must decide upon that responsibility which belongs to an infliction of actual and real punishment upon the respondent. We all hold one another in trust, and when the natural life is taken, He who framed it demands, "Where is thy brother?" And when under our frame of governments, whereby the creation of all departments proceed from the people, which breathes into these departments, executive and legislative, the breath of life, whose favor is yours as well as the President's, containing force and strength, and which asks of you, as your sentence is promulgated, "Where is thy brother?"

In this case no answer can be given that will satisfy them, or satisfy you, unless it be in truth and in fact, that for his guilt he was slain by the sword of the Constitution, upon the altar of justice. If that be the answer you are acquitted, he is condemned: the Constitution has triumphed, if he has disobeyed, and not obeyed it, and you have obeyed and not disobeyed it. Now, power does not always spread and spring from the same centre. I have seen great changes and great evils come from this matter of unconstitutional laws not attended to as unconstitutional, but assented to, and prevailing too, against the Constitution, till at last the power of the Constitution took another form than that of peaceful, judicial determination and execution.

I will repeat some instances of the effects of the disobedience of unconstitutional laws, and of the triumph of those who maintained it to be right and proper. I know a case where the State of Georgia undertook to make it penal for a Christian to preach the Gospel to the Indians, and I know by whose directions the missionary, determined that he would preach the Gospel, and not obey the law of Georgia, in the assurance that the Constitution of the United States would bear him out, and the missionary, as gentle as a woman, but as firm as every citizen of the United States ought to be, kept on with his teachings, and I know the great leader of the moral and religious sentiment of the United States, who, representing in this body the same State and bearing the same name as one of its distinguished Senators, viz:—the State of New Jersey, tried hard to save the country from the degradation of the oppression of the Indians by the haughty planters; and the Supreme Court of the United States held the law unconstitutional, and issued its mandate, and the State of Georgia laughed at it, and kept the missionary in prison, and Chief Justice Marshall and Judge Story and their colleagues hung their heads at the want of power in the Constitution to maintain itself.

But time rolled on, and from the clouds from Lookout Mountain, and sweeping down Missionary Ridge, came the thunders of the violated Constitution of the United States, and the lightnings of its power over the still home of the Missionary Wooster; and the grave of the Missionary Wooster, taught the State of Georgia what comes of violating the Constitution of the United States. I have seen an honored citizen of the State of Massachusetts, in behalf of its colored seamen, seek to make a case by visiting South Carolina to extend over these poor and feeble men the protection of the Constitution of the United States.

I have seen it attended by a daughter, a grandchild of a signer of the Declaration of Independence and a framer of the Constitution, who might be supposed to have a right to its protection, driven by the power of Charleston, and the power of South Carolina, and the mob and the gentleman alike—out of that State and prevented from making a case to take to the Supreme Court to assert the Constitution; and I have lived to see the case thus made up determined, that if the Massahusetts seamen, through the spirit of slavery, could not have a case made up, then slavery must cease; and I have lived to see a great captain, a gentleman of the name and of the blood of Sherman, sweeping his tempestuous war from the mountains to the sea, trampling the streets of South Carolina beneath the tread of his soldiery, and I have thought that the Constitution of the United States had some processes stronger than civil mandates that no resistance could overpower.

I do not think the people of Massachusetts supposed that efforts to set aside the unconstitutional laws, to make cases for the Supreme Court of the United States, are so wicked as is urged here by some of its Representatives; and I believe that, if we cannot be taught by the lessons we have learned of obedience to the Constitution in the peaceful methods of finding out its meaning, we shall yet meet with some other lessons on the subject. Now the strength of every system is to know its weakest parts, and allow for them; but when its weakest part breaks the whole is broken; the body fails and falls when the function is destroyed; and so with every structure, social and political, the weak point is the point of danger, and the weak point of the Constitution is now before you in the maintenance of the co-ordination of the departments of government.

If we cannot be kept from devouring one another, then the experiment of our ancestors will fail. They attempted to impose justice. If that fails, what can endure? We have come all at once to the great experience and trials of a full-grown nation, all of which we thought we should escape. We never dreamed that an instructed and equal people, with freedom in every form, with a government yielding to the touch of popular will so readily, ever would come to the trials of force against it.

We never thought that, whatever oppression existed in our system, a civil war would be our deliverance, from that oppression. We never thought that the remedy to get rid of a ruler, fixed by the Constitution, against the will of the people, would ever bring assassination into our political experience. We never thought that political difference, and under a created Presidency, would bring in any the departments of the government against one another, to anticipate our choice at the next Presidential election.

We have come to the full vigor of manhood, when the strong passions and interests that have disturbed other nations, composed of human nature like ourselves, have overthrown them. But we have put by the powers of the Constitution. These dangers prophesied when they should be likely to arise; as likely to be our doom, through the distraction of our powers; the intervention of irregular power through the influence of assassination.

We could summon from the people a million of men and inexhaustible treasure to help the Constitution in its time of need. Can we summon now, resources enough of civil prudence and of restraint of passion to carry us through this trial, here, so that whatever result may follow, in whatever form, the people may feel that the Constitution has received no wound through this court of last and best resort, in its determination here made; and if we—if you, could only carry yourselves back to the spirits, and the purpose, and the wisdom, and the courage of the framers of the government, how safe would it be in your hands? How safe is it now in your hands, if you were to enter into their labors and see and feel how your work compares in durability and excellency with theirs.

Indeed, so familiar has the course of this argument made us with the names of the great men of the convention and the first Congress, that I could sometimes seem to think that the presence even of the Chief Justice was replaced by the serene majesty of Washington, and that from Massachusetts we had Adams and Ames; and from Connecticut, Sherman and Ellsworth; and from New Jersey, Patterson and Boudinot; and from New York, Hamilton and Benson—that they were to determine the case for us. Act then, as if under this serene and majestic presence, your deliberations were to be conducted to their issue, and the Constitution was to come out from the watchful solicitudes of these great guardians of it, safe from their own judgment, in this high court of impeachment.

At five minutes before three, the Senate took a recess of fifteen minutes.

It was nearly half-past three before Mr. STANBERY commenced his remarks, the roll, in the meantime, having been called. Mr. Stanbery prefaced his remarks by saying, as nearly as, with his back to the gallery, he could be understood, that although in feeble health, an irresistible impulse urged him on, unseen but friendly hands sustained him, and voices inaudible to others he heard, whispering or seeming to say, "Feeble champion of the right, hold not back. Remember the race is not always to the swift, nor the battle to the strong. Remember a single pebble from the brook was enough to overthrow the giant that defied the armies of Israel." He proceeded as follows substantially, departing occasionally from the text of the prepared speech as given below.

Mr. Stanbery's Argument.

Mr. Chief Justice and Senators:—It is the habit of the advocate to magnify his case; but this case best speaks for itself. For the first time in our political existence, the three great departments of our government are brought upon the scene together—the House of Reprentatives as the accusers, the President of the United States as the accused; the Judiciary Department represented by its head, in the person of the Chief Justice, and the Senate of the United States as the tribunal to hear the accusation and the defense, and to render the final judgment. The Constitution has anticipated that so extreme a remedy as this might be necessary, even in the case of the highest officer of the government. It was seen that it was a dangerous power to give one department to be used against another department. Yet, it was anticipated that an emergency might arise in which nothing but such a power could be effectual to preserve the republic. Happily for the eighty years of our political existence which have passed, no such emergency has hitherto arisen. During that time we have witnessed the fiercest contests of party. Again and again the executive and legislative departments have been in open and bitter antagonism. A favorite legislative policy has more than once been defeated by the obstinate and determined resistance of the President. Upon some of the gravest and most important issues that we have ever had, or are ever likely to have, the Presidential policy and the legislative policy have stood in direct antagonism. During all that time this fearful power was in the hands of the legislative department, and more than once a resort to it has been advised by extreme party men as a sure remedy for party purposes; but, happily, that evil hitherto has not come upon us.

What new and unheard of conduct by a President has at last made a resort to this extreme remedy unavoidable? What Presidential acts have happened so flagrant, that all just men of all parties are ready to say, "the time has come when the mischief has been committed; the evil is at work so enormous and so pressing that in the last year of his term of office it is not safe to await the coming action of the people?" If such a case has happened, all honorable and just men of all parties will say amen; but if, on the contrary, it should appear that this fearful power has at last been degraded and perverted to the use of a party; if it appears that at last bad advice, often before given by the bad men of party, has found acceptance, this great tribunal of justice, now regarded with so much awe, will speedily come to be considered a monstrous sham. If it should be found to be the willing instrument to carry out the purposes of its party, then there remains for it and for every one of its members who participates in the great wrong, a day of awful retribution sure to come nor long to be delayed. But I will not anticipate nor speak further of the case itself, until its true features are fully developed.

I now proceed to a consideration of the articles of impeachment:—

They are eleven in number. Nine of them charge acts which are alleged to amount to a *high misdemeanor in office*. The other two, namely, the *fourth* and *sixth*, charge acts which are alleged to amount to a *high crime in office*. It seems to be taken for granted that, in the phrase used in the Constitution, "other high crimes and misdemeanors," the term *high* is properly applicable as well to misdemeanors as to crimes.

The acts alleged in the eleven articles as amounting to high misdemeanors or high crimes are as follows:—

In Article I, the issuing of the order of February 21, 1868, addressed to Stanton, "for the removal" of Stanton from office, with intent to violate the Tenure of office act and the Constitution of the United States, and to remove Stanton.

In Article II, the issuing and delivering to Thomas of the letter of authority of February 21, 1868, addressed to Thomas, with intent to violate the Constitution of the United States and the Tenure of office act.

In Article III, the appointing of Thomas by the letter addressed to him of the 21st of February, 1868, to be Secretary of War *ad interim*, with intent to violate the Constitution of the United States.

In Article IV, conspiring with Thomas with intent, by intimidation and threats, to hinder Stanton from holding his office, in violation of the Constitution of the United States and the Conspiracy act of July 31, 1861.

In Article V, conspiring with Thomas to hinder the execution of the Tenure of Office act, and in pursuance of the conspiracy, attempting to prevent Stanton from holding his office.

In Article VI, conspiring with Thomas to seize by force the property of the United States in the War Department, then in Stanton's custody, contrary to the Conspiracy act of 1861, and with intent to violate the Tenure of Office act.

In Article VII, conspiring with Thomas with intent to seize the property of the United States in Stanton's custody, with intent to violate the Tenure of Office act.

In Article VIII, issuing and delivering to Thomas the letter of authority of February 21, 1868, with intent to control the disbursements of the money appropriated for the military service and for the War Department, contrary to the Tenure of Office act and the Constitution of the United States, and with intent to violate the Tenure of Office act.

In Article IX, declaring to General Emory that the second section of the Army Appropriation act of March 2, 1867, providing that orders for military operations issued by the President or Secretary of War should be issued through the General of the Army, was unconstitutional and in contravention of Emory's commission, with intent to induce Emory to obey such orders as the President might give him directly and not through the General of the Army, with intent to enable the President to prevent the execution of the Tenure of Office act, and with intent to prevent Stanton from holding his office.

In Article X, that, with intent to bring in disgrace and contempt the Congress of the United States and the several branches thereof, and to excite the odium of the people against Congress and the laws by it enacted, he made three public addresses, one at the Executive Mansion on the 18th of August, 1866, one at Cleveland on the 3d of September, 1866, and one at St. Louis on the 8th of September, 1866, which speeches are alleged to be peculiarly indecent and unbecoming in the Chief Magistrate of the United States, and by means thereof the President brought his office into contempt, ridicule and disgrace, and thereby committed, and was guilty of a high misdemeanor in office,

In Article XI. that, by the same speech, made on the 18th of August, at the Executive Mansion, he did, in violation of the Constitution, attempt to prevent the execution of the Tenure of Office act, by unlawfully contriving means to prevent Stanton from resuming the office of Secretary for the Department of War, after the refusal of the Senate to concur in his suspension, and by unlawfully contriving and attempting to contrive means to prevent the execution of the *Act making appropriations for the support of the Army*, passed March 2, 1867, and to prevent the execution of the *Act to provide for the more efficient government of the Rebel States*, passed March 2, 1867.

It will be seen that all of these articles, except the tenth, charge violations either of the Constitution of the United States, of the Tenure of Office act, of the Conspiracy act of 1861, of the Military Appropriation act of 1867, or of the Reconstruction act of March 2, 1867. The tenth article, which is founded on the three speeches of the President, does not charge a violation either of the Constitution of the United States or of any act of Congress. Five of these articles charge a violation of the Constitution, to wit:—Articles I, II, III, IV and VIII. Seven of the articles charge violations of the Tenure of Office act, to wit:—Articles I, II, V, VI, VII, VIII, IX and XI. Two of the articles charge a violation of the Conspiracy act of 1861, to wit:—Articles IV and VI. Two of them charge violations of the Appropriation act of March 2, 1867, to wit:—Articles IX and XI. One only charges a violation of the Reconstruction act of March 2, 1867, and that is Article XI.

We see, then, that four statutes of the United States are alleged to have been violated. Three of these provide for penalties for their violation, that is to say, the Tenure of Office act, the Conspiracy act of 1861, and the Military Appropriation act of March 2, 1867. The violation of the Tenure of Office act is declared by the act itself to be a "high misdemeanor." The violation of the Conspiracy act is declared to be "a high crime." The violation of the second section of the Military Appropriation act is declared to be simply "a misdemeanor in office."

It will be observed that the first eight articles all relate to the War Department, and to that alone. Article one sets out an attempted removal of the head of that department. Three others relate to the *ad interim* appointment of Thomas to be acting Secretary of that Department. The four others relate to conspiracies to prevent Stanton from holding his office as Secretary for the Department of War, or to seize the public property in that department, or to control the disbursements of moneys appropriated for the services of that department.

Now, first of all, it must not escape notice that these articles are founded upon the express averment that from the moment of his reinstatement on the non-concurrence of the Senate, Mr. Stanton became the lawful Secretary for that department; that, upon such order of the Senate he at once entered into possession of the War Department and into the lawful exercise of its duties as Secretary, and that up to the date of the articles of impeachment that lawful right and actual possession had remained undisturbed; that all the acts charged in these eight articles were committed during that time; that, notwithstanding these acts, Stanton remains lawfully and actually in possession; and that the office has been at no time vacant.

We see, then, that, according to the case made in these eight articles, the President did not succeed in getting Mr. Stanton out of office, or of putting General Thomas in, either in law or in fact. We see, according to these articles, that the President did not succeed, either by force or otherwise, in preventing Mr. Stanton from holding his office, or in getting possession of the public property in that department, or in controlling the disbursements of public money appropriated for the use of that department. There has been, according to the very case made in these articles, no public mischief. The lawful officer has not been disturbed; the lawful custody of the public property and public money of the department has not been changed. No injury has been done either to the public service or the public officer. There has been no removal of Mr. Stanton —only an aborative attempt at removal. There has been no acting Secretary put in an office vacant by death, resignation, or disability—put there during the time of such actual vacancy or temporary absence. All the time the Secretary himself has been there in the actual performance of his duties. No *ad interim* officer has, in law or fact, been constituted; for, in law or fact, there has been no *ad interim* as to the Secretary himself. There has been no moment of time in which there could be an acting Secretary or an *ad interim* Secretary, either in law or fact; for it is impossible to conceive of an *ad interim* Secretary of War when there is no *interim*, that is, when the lawful Secretary is in his place and in the actual discharge of his duties.

Mark it, then, Senators that the acts charged as high crimes and misdemeanors in these eight articles, in respect to putting Mr. Stanton out and General Thomas in, are things *attempted* and *not* things *accomplished*. It is the attempt, and the unlawful intent with which it was formed, that the President is to be held responsible for. So that it comes to be a question of vital consequence in reference to this part of the case whether the high crimes and misdemeanors provided for in the Tenure of Office act and in the second section of the Military Appropriation act purport to punish, not only the commission of the acts, but to punish as well the abortive attempt to commit them.

I limit myself in what has been last said to the four articles touching the removal of Mr. Stanton and the appointment of General Thomas. As to the four conspiracy articles, there can be no question that the actual accomplishment of the thing intended is not made necessary to constitute the offense; for the statute against conspiracies expressly provides for the punishment of the unlawful intent, the unlawful conspiracy itself, without reference to any further act done in pursuance of it, or to the partial or complete accomplishment of the unlawful design. But, contrariwise, the other two acts do not punish the intent alone, but only the commission of the thing intended; and the offense provided for in these two acts, while it requires the unlawful intent to be a part of the crime, requires something else to supplement it, and that is the actual commission of the thing intended.

And here, Senators, before I proceed to consider these articles in detail, seems to me the proper time to bring your attention to another consideration, which I deem of very great moment. What is the subject-matter which constitutes these high crimes and misdemeanors? Under what legislation does it happen, that the President of the United States is brought under all this penal liability? What are these high crimes and misdemeanors? Has he committed treason or bribery? Has he been guilty of peculation or oppression in office? Has he appropriated the public funds or the public property unlawfully to his own use? Has he committed any crime of violence against any person, public officer, or private individual? Is he charged with any act which amounts to the *crimen falsi* or was done *causa lucri*? Nothing of the sort. These alleged high crimes and misdemeanors are all founded upon mere forms of executive administration; for the violation, they say, of the rules laid down by the Legislative Department to regulate the conduct of the Executive Department in the manner of the administration of Executive functions belonging to that department.

The regulations so made, purport to change what theretofore had been the established rule and order of administration. Before the passage of the second section of the Military Appropriation act, the President of the United States, as Commander-in-chief of the army, and head of the Executive Department, issued his orders for military operations, either directly to the officer who is charged with the execution of the order; or through any intermediate channel that he deemed necessary or convenient. No subordinate had a right to supervise his order before it was sent to its destination. He was not compelled to consult his Secretary of War who was merely his agent, nor the general next to himself in rank, as to that important thing, the subject matter of his order, or that merely formal thing, the manner of its transmission. But, by this second section, the mere matter of form is attempted to be changed. The great power of the President, as Commander-in-Chief, to issue orders to all his military subordinates is respected. The act tacitly admits that, over these great powers, Congress has no authority. The substance is not touched, but only the form is provided for; and it is a departure from this mere form that is to make the President guilty of a high crime and misdemeanor.

Then, again, as to the Tenure of Office act, that also purports to introduce a new rule in the administration of the Executive powers. It does not purport to take away the President's power of appointment or power of removal absolutely; but it purports to fix the mode in which he shall execute that power, not as theretofore by his own independent action, but thereafter only by the concurrence of the Senate. It is a regulation by the legislature of the manner in which an executive power is to be formed.

So, to, as to *ad interim* appointments, it does not purport to take away that power from the President; it only attempts to regulate the execution of the power in a special instance.

Mr. Burke, on the impeachment of Warren Hastings, speaking of the crimes for which he stood impeached, uses this significant language:—"They were crimes, *not* against *forms*, but against those eternal laws of justice which are our rule and our birth-right. His offenses are *not* in *formal, technical* language, but in *reality*, in *substance* and effect, high crimes and high misdemeanors."

Now, Senators, if the Legislative Department had a constitutional right thus to regulate the performance of executive duties, and to change the mode and form of exercising an executive power which had been followed from the beginning of the government down to the present day, is a refusal of the executive to follow a new rule, and, notwithstanding that, to adhere to the ancient ways, that sort of high crime and misdemeanor which the Constitution contemplates, is it just ground for impeachment? Does the fact that such an act is called by the legislature a high crime and misdemeanor necessarily make it such a high crime and misdemeanor as is contemplated by the Constitution? If, for instance, the President should send a military order to the Secretary of War, is that an offense worthy of impeachment? If he should remove an officer on the 21st of February, and nominate one on the 22d, would that be an impeachable misdemeanor? Now, it **must be admitted, that if the President had sent the name** of Mr. Ewing to the Senate on the 21st, in the usual way, in place of Mr. Stanton removed, and had not absolutely ejected Mr. Stanton from office, but had left him to await the action of the Senate upon the nomination, certainly in mere matter of form there would have been no violation of this Tenure of Office act.

Now, what did he do? He made an order for the removal of Mr. Stanton on the 21st, but did not eject him from office, and sent a nomination of Mr. Ewing to the Senate on the 22d. Is it possible that thereby he had committed an act that amounted to a high crime and misdemeanor, and deserved removal from office. And yet that is just what the President has done. He has more closely followed the mere matter of form prescribed by the Tenure of Office act than, according to the learned manager who opened this prosecution, was necessary. For, if he had made an order of removal, and at once had sent to the Senate his reasons for making such removal, and had stated to them that his purpose was to make this removal in order to test the constitutionality of the Tenure of Office act, then, says the honorable manager, "Had the Senate received such a message, the Representatives of the people might never have deemed it necessary to impeach the President for such an act, to insure the safety of the country, even if they had denied the accuracy of his legal positions." How, then, can it be deemed necessary to impeach the President for making an order of removal on one day, advising the Senate of it the same day, and sending the nomination of a successor the next day? Was ever a matter more purely formal than this? And yet this is the only act. Is this, in the words of Mr. Burke not in merely *technical* language, "but in reality, in substance, and effort" a high crime and misdemeanor within the meaning of the Constitution?

The first clause of the first section declares that every person then or thereafter holding any civil office under an appointment with the advice and consent of the Senate and due qualification, shall hold his office until a successor shall have been in like manner appointed and qualified.

If the act contained no other provisions qualifying this general clause, then it would be clear—

1. That it would apply to all civil officers who held by appointment made by the President with the advice of the Senate, including judicial officers as well as executive officers. It gives all of them the same right to hold, and subjects all of them to the same liability to be removed. From the excercise of the power of *suspension* by the independent act of the President made applicable to any officer so holding, by the second section, judges of the United States are expressly excepted. We find no such exception, express or implied, as to the exercise of the power of *removal* declared in the first section. Judicial officers, as well as executive officers, are made to hold by the same tenure. They hold during the pleasure of the President and the Senate, and cease to hold when the President and the Senate appoint a successor.

2. It applies equally to officers whose tenure of office, as fixed prior to the act, was to hold during the pleasure of the President, as to those who were to hold for a fixed term of years, or during good behavior.

3. It purports to take from the President the power to remove any officer, at any time, for any cause, by the exercise of his own power alone. But it leaves him a power of removal with the concurrence of the Senate. In this process of removal, the separate action of the President and the Senate is required. The initiatory act must come from the President, and from him alone. It is upon his action *as taken* that the Senate proceeds, and they give or withhold their consent to what he *has* done. The manner in which the President may exercise his part of the process is merely formal. It may be simply by the nomination of a successor to the incumbent, or the officer intended to be removed. Then, upon the confirmation by the Senate of such nomination, and the issuance of a commission to him, the removal becomes complete. Or the President may exercise his part of the process by issuing an order of removal, followed by a nomination. Neither the order for removal or the nomination works a change in itself. Both are necessarily conditional upon the subsequent action of the Senate. So, too, the order of removal, the nomination, and the confirmation of the Senate, are not final. A further act remains to be done before the appointment of the successor is complete, and that is an executive act exclusively the signing of the commission by the President. Up to this point, the President has a *locus penitentiæ*; for, although the Senate have advised him to appoint his nominee, the President is not bound by their advice, but may defeat all the prior action by allowing the incumbent to remain in office.

Thus far we have considered the first clause of the first section of the act, without reference to the context. Standing alone, it seems to have a universal application to all civil officers, and to secure *all* of them who hold by the concurrent action of the President and the Senate, against removal, otherwise than by the same concurrent action, and to make all of them liable to removal by that concurrent action.

Are there exceptions to the universality of the tenure of office so declared? We say there are—

1. Exceptions by *necessary implication.* Judicial officers of the United States come within this exception; for their tenure of office is fixed by the Constitution itself. They cannot be removed either by the President alone, or by the President and Senate conjointly. They alone hold for life or during good behavior, subject to only one mode of removal, and that is by impeachment.

2. Exceptions *made expressly* by the provisions of the act; which make it manifest that it was not intended for all civil officers of the United States. First of all, this purpose is indicated by the *title* of the act. It is entitled "An act regulating the Tenure of *certain* Civil offices"—not of *all* civil offices. Next we find, that immediately succeeding the first clause, which, as has been shown, is in terms of universal application, comprehending "every person holding any civil office," the purpose of restraining or limiting its generality, is expressed in these words, "except as herein otherwise provided for." This puts us at once upon inquiry. It advises us that all persons and all officers are not intended to be embraced in the comprehensive terms used in the first clause—that some persons and some officers are intended to be excepted and to be "otherwise provided for"—that some who do hold by the concurrent action of the President and the Senate, are not to be secured against removal by any other process than the same concurrent action.

What class of officers embraced by the general provisions of the first clause are made to come within the clause of exception? The *proviso* which immediately follows answers the question. It is in these words:—"*Provided* That the Secretaries of State, of the Treasury, of War, of the Navy, and of the Interior, the Postmaster-General, and the Attorney-General, shall hold their offices respectively for and during the term of the President by whom they may have been appointed, and for one month thereafter, subject to removal by and with the advice and consent of the Senate."

We see that these seven heads of departments are the only civil officers of the United States which are especially designated. We see a clear purpose to make some special provision as to them. Being civil officers holding by the concurrent appointment of the President and the Senate, they would have been embraced by the first general clause of the section, if there had been no exception and no *proviso*. The argument on the other side is, that notwithstanding the declared purpose to make exceptions, these officers are not made exceptions; that notwithstanding there is a *proviso* as to them, in which express provision is specially for *their* tenure of office, we must still look to the general clause to find their tenure of office. It is a settled rule of construction that every word of a statute' is to be taken into account, and that a *proviso* must have effect as much as any other clause of the statute.

Upon looking into this *proviso*, we find its purpose to be the fixing a tenure of office for these seven officers. And how is that tenure fixed? We find it thus declared, some of them are given a tenure of office, others are not. But as to the favored class, as to that class intended to be made safe and most secure, even *their* tenure is not so ample and permanent as the tenure given to all civil officers who, prior to the act, held by the same tenure as themselves. By the general clause, all civil officers are embraced and protected from executive removal, including as well those who hold by no other tenure than "the pleasure of the President." This tenure, "during the pleasure of the President," was the tenure by which all these Cabinet officers held prior to the passage of this law. Now, for the first time, this *proviso* fixed another and safer tenure for certain Cabinet officers, not for all. It gave to some of them the right to hold during the term of one President and for one month of the term of the succeeding President, but it did not give that right to all of them. It was given only to a favored class, and the new tenure so given to the favored class was not so favorable as that given to other civil officers who had theretofore held by precisely the same uncertain tenure, that is to say, "the pleasure of the President," for these other civil officers were not limited to the term of one President and one month afterwards, but their tenure was just as secure from "the pleasure of the President" after the expiration of one Presidential term and after the expiration of the first month of the succeeding Presidential term, as it was before.

We see, then, that in fixing a new tenure of of office for Cabinet officers, the tenure given to one class of them, and that the most favored, was not as favorable as that given to other civil officers theretofore holding by the same tenure with themselves. This favored class were not to hold one moment after the expiration of the month of the second Presidential term. At that punctual time, the right of the President to select his Cabinet would, even as to them, return to him. If they were to remain after that, it would be that it would be his pleasure to keep them and to give them a new tenure by his choice, in the regular mode of appointment.

But, as we have seen, the *proviso* makes a distinction between Cabinet officers, and divides them into two classes, those holding by appointment of the President for the time being, and those not appointed by him, but by his predecessor, and holding only by his sufferance or pleasure. If ever an intent was manifest in a statute, it is clear in this instance. There is a division into two classes, a tenure of office given to one class, and withheld from the other. Before the passage of this act, all Cabinet officers holding under any President, whether appointed by him or his predecessor, held by the same tenure, "the pleasure of the President." This *proviso* makes a distinction between them never made before. It gives one class a new and more secure tenure, and it leaves the other class without such new tenure. One class was intended to be protected, the other not.

Now comes the question, Upon what ground was this distinction made? Why was it that a better title, a stronger tenure was given to one class than to the other? The answer is given by the *proviso* itself. The officers in the Cabinet of a President, who were nominated by him who were appointed by him with the concurrence of the

Senate, are those to whom this new and better tenure is given. They are officers of his own selection; they are his chosen agents. He has once recommended them to the Senate as fit persons for the public trust, and they have obtained their office through his selection and choice. The theory here is, that having had one free opportunity of choice, having once exercised his right of selection, he shall be bound by it. He shall not dismiss his own selected agent upon his own pleasure or caprice. He is, in legal language, "estopped" by the selection he has made, and is made incapable by his own act of dissolving the official relation which he has imposed on himself. Having selected his Cabinet officer, he must take him as a man takes his chosen wife, for better or worse.

But as to such Cabinet officers as are not of a President's selection—as to those who have been selected by a former President—as to those whose title was given by another—as to those he never appointed, and, perhaps, never would have appointed—as to those who came to him by succession and not by his own act—as to those who hold merely by his acquiescence as sufferance—*they* are entitled to no favor, and receive none. They stand as step-children in his political family, and are not placed on the same level with the rightful heirs entitled to the inheritance.

The construction claimed by the managers leads to this inevitable absurdity: that the class entitled to favor are cut off at the end of the month, while those having a less meritorious title, remain indefinitely. What was intended for a benefit, becomes a mischief, and the favored class are worse off than if no favor had been shown them. Their condition was intended to be made better than that of their fellows, and has been made worse. From those entitled to protection, it is taken away to be given to those not entitled.

Now, when President Johnson was invested with his office, he found Mr. Stanton holding the office of Secretary of War. He had been appointed by Mr. Lincoln during his first term, and was holding in the second month of Mr. Lincoln's second term under the old appointment. Mr. Stanton was neither appointed by Mr. Lincoln or Mr. Johnson for that second term; so that we are relieved from all question whether the fractional term, counting from the accession of Mr. Johnson, is to be called the unexpired term of Mr. Lincoln, or the proper term of Mr. Johnson, and whether, if he had been appointed or re-appointed by Mr. Lincoln during his second term, he might not have claimed that he was entitled, as against Mr. Johnson, to hold on to its end. Mr. Stanton never had any tenure of office under the Tenure of Office act for the current Presidential term, never having been appppointed for that term by either Mr. Lincoln or Mr. Johnson. He, therefore, does not come within the category of those members of Mr. Johnson's Cabinet who have been appointed by Mr. Johnson.

At the date of the passage of the Tenure of Office act, the Cabinet of Mr. Johnson was composed as follows:—The Secretaries of State, of the Treasury, of War, and of the Navy, held by appointment of Mr. Lincoln made in his first term; the Secretary of the Interior, the Postmaster-General, and the Attorney-General, held by the appointment of Mr. Johnson made during his current term. There was, then, as to the entire seven, a difference as to the manner and time of their appointment. Four had been appointed by Mr. Lincoln, and the other three by Mr. Johnson. All of them held by the same tenure, "the pleasure of the President." All of them, without reference to constitutional provisions, were, by existing laws, removable by the independent action of the President. The acts of Congress creating the offices of Secretaries of State, of War, and of the Navy, expressly recognize the Executive authority to remove them at pleasure. The acts of Congress creating the four other heads of departments place them on the same footing as to tenure of office. All these acts remained, in this particular, in full force. This Tenure of Office act introduces a distinction made applicable to Cabinet officers alone, never made before. For the first time, it gives to those appointed by the President for the time being, a new tenure. It secures them from removal at his pleasure alone. It repeals, as to them, the existing laws, and declares that they shall thereafter be entitled to hold during the remainder of the term of the President by whom they were appointed, and for one month of the succeeding Presidential term, exempt from removal by the sole act of the President, and only subject to removal by the concurrent act of the President and Senate. But it gives them no right to hold against the pleasure of the succeeding President, one moment after the expiration of that punctual time of one month. When that time has arrived, their right to hold ceases, and their offices become vacant. The policy here declared is unmistakable, that notwithstanding anything to the contrary in the act, every President shall have the privilege of his own choice, of his own selection of the members of his Cabinet. The right of selection for himself is, however, qualified. He may not, as theretofore, enjoy this right throughout his term. For the first month he must take the Cabinet of his predecessor, however opposed to him in opinion or obnoxious to him personally. Then, too, while the right is given to him, it can be exercised but once. It is a power that does not survive, but expires with a single execution.

Now, as to the three members of Mr. Johnson's Cabinet, appointed by his own exercise of this independent power, he having, as to them, once exercised the power, it is, as to them, exhausted. The consequence is, that these three officers no longer remain subject to *his pleasure* alone. They are entitled to hold in defiance of his wishes, throughout the remainder of his term, because they are his own selected officers; but they are not entitled to hold

during the whole term of his successor, but only for a modicum of that term, just because they were not selected by that successor. So much for these three.

Now, as to the other four, as to whom Mr. Johnson has not exercised his right of choice even by one appointment. May they hold during the residue of his term in defiance of his wishes? Do they come within that clear policy of giving to every President one opportunity at least to exercise his independent right of choice? Surely not. Then, if, as to them, he has the right, how can he exercise it, if, as in the case of Mr. Stanton, the Cabinet officer holds on after he has been requested to resign? What mode is left to the President to avail himself of his own independent right, when such an officer refuses to resign? None other than the process of removal; for he cannot put the man of his choice *in* until he has put the other *out*. So that the independent right of choice cannot, under such conditions, be exercised at all without the corresponding right of removal; and the one necessarily implies the other.

We have seen that the tenure of office fixed by the *proviso* for Cabinet officers applies only to those members of Mr. Johnson's Cabinet appointed by himself. It, therefore, does not apply to Mr. Stanton. If there is any other clause of the act which applies to Mr. Stanton, it must be the first general clause, and if that does not apply to him, then his case does not come within the purview of the act at all, but must be ruled by the pre-existing laws, which made him subject at all times to the pleasure of the President and to the exercise of his independent power of removal. And this is precisely what is claimed by the managers. They maintain, that, although the *proviso* does not give Mr. Stanton a new tenure, yet the first general clause does, and that he is put by that clause on the same footing of all other civil officers who, at the date of the act, held by the concurrent appointment of the President and Senate by no other tenure than "during the pleasure of the President." But all the officers intended to be embraced by that first clause, who held by that tenure before, are declared to hold by a new tenure. Not one of them can be removed by the President alone. Whether appointed by the President for the time being or by his predecessor, they must remain in defiance of the President until removed by the concurrent action of the President and the Senate. In effect, so far as the power of the President is concerned, *they* may hold for life. If Mr. Stanton comes within the protection of that clause, if his tenure of office is fixed by that clause, it follows inevitably that Mr. Johnson cannot remove him. It follows as inevitably that no succeeding President can remove him. He may defy Mr. Johnson's successor as he has said to Mr. Johnson, "I am compelled to deny your right under the Constitution and laws of the United States, without the advice and consent of the Senate." If the successor of Mr. Johnson should point him to the *proviso*, and at the end of the month require him to leave, his answer, according to the managers, would run thus:—"That *proviso* did not fix my tenure of office. It did not apply to me, but only to those appointed by Mr. Johnson. They must go out with the month; I do no not. My tenure is fixed by the first clause, and you cannot get clear of me without the advice and consent of the Senate."

Without concluding, Mr. Stanbery gave way to a motion to adjourn. He had read only nineteen pages out of fifty-five.

PROCEEDINGS OF SATURDAY, MAY 2.

The Senate met at noon, and the court was immediately opened in due form.

Mr. STANBERY resumed the floor, introducing the continuance of his remarks by thanking the Senate for the courtesy shown him in an early adjournment last evening, and saying he had been greatly benefited by the consequent rest, and then expressing in advance his confidence in a speedy acquittal, proceeded with his argument.

At 1·15 P. M., Mr. Stanbery showing evident signs of fatigue, Senator Johnson approached him and apparently made a suggestion, in reply to which Mr. Stanbery said it would relieve him very much if his young friend would be permitted to read his remarks.

Senator ANTHONY said, in order to relieve the counsel, he would move that the Senate adjourn until Monday.

Several Senators—No, no!

In reply to an inquiry from the Chief Justice, Mr. STANBERY said he did not ask it, and Mr. W. F. Pedrick, formerly of the Attorney-General's Office,

and who has assisted the counsel during the trial, then proceeded to read from the printed speech in a clear voice.

Mr. Stanbery's Address.

It is only in the first article that any charge is made in reference to Mr. Stanton's removal. That article nowhere alleges that Mr. Stanton has been removed either in law or in fact. It does allege that on the 21st of February Stanton was "lawfully entitled to hold said office of Secretary for the Department of War," and that on that day the President "did unlawfully and in violation of the Constitution and laws of the United States, issue an order in writing for the removal of Edwin M. Stanton from the office of Secretary for the Department of War." It is the issuance of this order for a removal that is made the gravamen of the charge. It is not followed by any allegation that it had the effect to work a removal either in law or in fact. On the contrary, in the very next article which is founded on the order to Thomas, which purports to be made after the order for the removal of Stanton, it is alleged that Stanton still held the office lawfully, and that notwithstanding the order of removal to Stanton, and the order to Thomas to act as Secretary, Stanton still held the office, and no vacancy was created or existed. This is the tenor of every article, that Stanton never has been removed, in law or in fact; that there never has been an ouster, either in law or in fact, and that there has been at no time a vacancy. The proof shows that Stanton remains in possession, and that his official acts continue to be recognized. Now if the order *per se* operated a removal in law, it must follow that the order was valid and in conformity with the Constitution and laws of the United States, for no order made contrary thereto could take effect in law. If there was a removal in law the executive order which accomplished it was a valid, not an invalid act. But if the order did not operate a removal *per se*, and if a removal in fact, though not in law, might be held sufficient to constitute an offense, and if it were alleged and were proved that under the illegal order an ouster or removal was effected by force or threats, the answer to be given in this case is conclusive. No ouster—in fact, no actual or physical removal—is proved or so much as charged. Mr. Stanton has never to this day been put out of actual possession. He remains in possession as fully since the order was as before, and still holds on. Now, we look in vain through this Tenure of Office act for any provision forbidding an attempt to cause a removal, or making it penal to issue an order for such purpose. The sixth section is the only one on the subject of removal, and that provides "that every removal * * * made * * * contrary to the provisions of this act * * * shall be deemed, and is hereby declared, to be a high misdemeanor, and is made punishable by fine not exceeding ten thousand dollars, or imprisonment not exceeding five years, or both, at the discretion of the court. No latitude of construction can torture an attempt to make a removal into an actual removal, or can turn an abortive effort to do a given thing into an accomplished fact. Such a latitude of construction could not be allowed when the rule of construction is least restricted, and least of all in a penal statute where the rule of construction is the most restrictive. It seems a waste of words to argue this point further. There is a total failure of the case upon the first article on this point, if we had none other. And yet this article is the head and front of the entire case. Strike it out and all that remains is "leather and prunella." But, Senators, if you should be of opinion that the Tenure of Office act protected Mr. Stanton, and that the attempt to remove him was equivalent to a removal, we next maintain—First, that the President had a right to construe the law for himself, and if, in the exercise of that right, he committed an error of construction, and acted under that error, he is not to be held responsible. Second, if he had so construed the law as to be of opinion that Mr. Stanton was intended to be protected by it against his power of removal, and was also of opinion that the law in that respect was contrary to the Constitution, he is not to be held responsible if he therein committed an error. I proceed to argue these points in the order in which they have been stated. First, then, is the President responsible for an official act done by him under an erroneous construction of an act of Congress? I agree that ignorance or misconception of the law does not, in general, excuse a party from civil or criminal liability for an act contrary to law. But this well-established rule has exceptions equally well established, and the case here falls within one of the exceptions, and not within the rule where a law is passed which concerns the President and touches his official duties, it is not only his right, but his duty to determine for himself what is the true construction of the law, and to act, or refuse to act, according to that determination, whatever it may be. He is an executive officer, not a mere ministerial officer. He is invested with a discretion, with the right to form a judgment and to act under his judgment so formed, however erroneous. No such distinction is allowed to a ministerial officer. His business is not to construe the law, but merely to perform it, and he acts at his peril if he does not do that which is commanded by reason of an erroneous construction, however honestly entertained. Mr. Stanbery then claimed that the Constitution clearly gives the President the power to construe laws, and argued at length that Mr. Johnson had no right to go to the Supreme Court to ascertain whether the law was constitutional, nor was he obliged to take advice from his Cabinet as to what course he should pursue. Proceeding, he said:—Besides this late authoritative exposition, as to the discretionary power of the President, there is abundance of other authority entitled to the gravest consideration, which might be adduced to the same effect, and which I propose to introduce upon the next point, which I now proceed to consider, and that point is that if the President had so construed this Tenure of Office act as to be satisfied that Mr. Stanton came within its provisions, but was also of opinion that the law in that respect was contrary to the Constitution, he is not to be held responsible if therein he committed an error. The case, in that aspect, stood thus:—Here was an act of Congress, which, in the construction given to it by the President, was for the removal of Mr. Stanton from the War Department. The President, in the exercise of his executive functions and of his duty to see that the laws were faithfully executed, came to the conclusion that in the execution of so much of this executive duty as had relation to the administration of the War Department it was expedient to place it in the hands of another person. His relations with Mr. Stanton were such that he felt unwilling any longer to be responsible for his acts in the administration of that department, or to trust him as one of his confidential advisers. The question at once arose whether this right of removal, denied to him by this law, was given to him by the Constitution; or, to state it in other words, whether this law was in this respect in pursuance of the Constitution. Now, it appears that his opinion upon this question has been made up deliberately. When this same law was on its passage and had been presented to him for his approval, his opinion was formed that it was in violation of the Constitution. He refused to approve it, and returned it to Congress with a message in which this opinion was distinctly announced. It passed, notwithstanding, by a constitutional majority in both Houses. No one doubts that then, at least, he had a perfect right to exercise a discretion, and no one has ever yet asserted that an error in an opinion so formed involved him in any liability. The exercise of that veto power exhausted all his means of resistance to what he deemed an unconstitutional act in his legislative capacity, and so far as the law provided a rule of action for others than himself no other means of resistance were left to him. But this law was directly aimed at him and the exercise of the executive power vested in him by the Constitution. When, therefore, he came a second time to consider it, it was in the discharge of an executive duty. Had he then no discretion of any sort? Was he bound to act in a merely ministerial capacity? Having once finally exercised a discretion in his legislative capacity to prevent the passage of the law, was he thereby deprived of his discretion in his executive capacity, when he was called upon to act under it? It has been said that a law passed over a President's veto by a majority of two-thirds, has a greater sanction than a law passed in the ordinary way by a mere majority. I know that there are those who, whilst they admit that as to a law passed in the ordinary mode by the concurrent acts of the two Houses and the President, it may be questioned on the score of unconstitutionality, yet maintain that a law not passed by such a concurrence but by the separate action of the two Houses without the concurrence of the Executive or against his will, is something superior to ordinary legislation, and takes the character of a fundamental or organic enactment. But this is a modern heresy unsustained by the slightest reason or authority. It is at least but a legislative act. It stands upon an equal footing with other legislative acts. It cannot be put upon higher ground or lower ground. No distinction is allowable between the one and the other. But if it were, it certainly would seem more reasonable that such a law passed by one co-ordinate department would stand on lower ground than a law passed with full concurrence of both departments. The question then recurs, is the President invested with a discretion in his executive capacity? In the exercise of that discretion may he compare the law with the Constitution, and if in his opinion the law vests him with a power not granted by the Constitution, or deprives him of a power which the Constitution does not grant, may he refuse to execute the power so given or proceed to exercise the power so taken away? We have already cited a late decision of the Supreme Court directly in point, that presented the direct question, whether as to the reconstruction acts passed like this Tenure of Civil Office act, by a vote of two-thirds in each House, the President had, notwithstanding, in reference to those laws an executive discretion? The decision maintains that he had. I proceed to show that this is no modern doctrine. The authorities which I shall cite go beyond the necessities of this case. Some of them go to the length of asserting that this executive discretion survives even after the passage of the law by the legislative department.

It has been construed by the judicial department, and in that extreme case leaves the President at last to act for himself in opposition to the express will of both the other departments. I will first cite some opinions upon this extreme position. Mr. Stanbery then quoted from Presidents Jefferson, Jackson, Van Buren, from the Federalists, and from a large number of loyal authorities and decisions of the Supreme Court of the United States to sustain his position. Continuing, he said:—Quotations from opinions of the Supreme Court maintaining that the executive power is in no sense ministerial, but strictly discretionary, might be multiplied indefinitely. And indeed, it is easy to show, from repeated decisions of the same Court, that the heads of departments, except where the performance of a specific act or duty is required of them by law, are in no sense ministerial officers, but that they too are clothed with a discretion, and protected from responsibility for error in the exercise of the discretion. Thus:—Decatur vs Paulding, 14 Peters; Kendall vs. Stokes, 3 Howard; Brashear vs. Mason, 6 Howard; in which latter case the Cour say;—"The duty required of the Secretary by the resolu tion, was to be performed by him as the head of one of the executive departments of the Government, in the ordinary discharge of his official duties; that in general, such duties, whether imposed by act of Congress or by resolution, are not merely ministerial duties; that the head of an executive department of the Government, in the administration of the various and important concerns of his office, is continually required to exercise judgment and discretion; and that the Court could not, by mandamus, act directly upon the officer, to guide and control his judgment and discretion in matters committed to his care in the ordinary discharge of his official duties."

I will now ask your attention, Senators, to the remaining articles, and first, the four conspiracy articles. These allege that the President unlawfully conspired with Lorenzo Thomas, and others to the House of Representatives unknown, on the 21st of February, 1868, first, to hinder and prevent Edwin M. Stanton, Secretary of War, from holding the office of Secretary for the Department of War, contrary to the Conspiracy act of July 31, 1861, and in violation of the Constitution of the United States; second, to prevent and hinder the execution of the "act regulating the tenure of certain civil offices," and in pursuance of this conspiracy did unlawfully attempt to prevent Edwin M. Stanton from holding the said office; third, by force to seize, take and possess the property of the United States in the Department of War in the custody and charge of Edwin M. Stanton, Secretary thereof, contrary to the Conspiracy act of July 31, 1861, and of the Tenure of Office act: fourth, with intent unlawfully to seize, take and possess the property of the United States in the Department of War in the custody of Edwin M. Stanton, the Secretary thereof, with intent to violate the "act regulating the tenure of certain civil offices." It will be seen that these four conspiracy counts all relate to the same subject matter—the War Office, the Secretary of the War Office and the public property therein situated—and this is all that is necessary to be said about these articles, for not a scintilla of proof has been adduced in their support. The case attempted to be made out under these conspiracy articles by the managers was, in the first place, by the production of orders issued on the 21st of February. But as these of themselves did not amount to evidence of a conspiracy, as they carried the idea of no unlawful agreement, but simply stood upon the footing of an order given by the President to a subordinate, the managers, in order to make some show of a case, offered to introduce the declarations of General Thomas, made on the night of the 21st and on the 22d of February and other days, intending to show a purpose on his part to obtain possession of the department and the property of the department by intimidation and force. Objection was made at the time to the introduction of these declarations without laying a foundation upon which the President could be made liable by such declaration. Impressed with this objection, the manager who opened the prosecution, after some consideration, at length answered an inquiry of a Senator that he expected to follow up the proof of the declarations by proof connecting the President with them. Upon that assurance he was allowed to give the declarations of General Thomas in evidence. But that is the last we have heard of any supporting proof so promised. Not a scintilla of proof has been obtained from General Thomas or from any other quarter, under the conspiracy charge, of any authority given or intended to be given by the President to General Thomas to resort to force, intimidation or threats, in the execution of the order which the President had given. This is quite enough to say with regard to these articles. Next, as to the ninth article, usually known as the Emory article. It had no substance in itself from the beginning, and since the testimony of Mr. Welles remains without the slightest foundation. Next, as to the tenth article, relative to the speeches made at the Executive Mansion, at Cleveland and at St. Louis, in the months of August and September, 1866. It is in the name of the people of the United States that you, Senators, are in this article called upon to hold the President of the United States criminally responsible, even to the loss of his office, for speaking, as the article has it, with a loud voice to an assemblage of American citizens what is called scandalous matter touching the Thirty-ninth Congress of the United States. Mr. Stanbery held that the Thirty-ninth Congress having taken no notice of the alleged scandal, this Congress could not, and quoted from an English case to sustain his position.

The tenth article, he said, carried us back five hundred years to the days when men were punished for expressing their religious opinions. He then continued as follows:—Upon the formation of the Constitution of the United States, our fathers were not unmindful of what had happened in the past. They had brought with them the traditions of suffering and persecution for opinion's sake, and they determined to lay here for themselves the foundations of civil liberty, so strong that they never could be changed. When our Constitution was formed and was presented to the various States for adoption, the universal objection made to it was not so much for what it contained as for what it omitted. It was said we find here no bill of rights; we find here no guarantee of conscience, of speech, of the press. The answer was that the Constitution itself was, from beginning to end, a bill of rights; that it conferred upon the government only certain specified and delegatad powers, and among these was not to be found any grant of any power over the conscience or over free speech or a free press. The answer was plausible, but not satisfactory. The consequence was that at the first Congress held under the Constitution, according to instructions sent from the various State Conventions, ten amendments were introduced and adopted, and first in order among them is this amendment:—

Article 1. Congress shall make no law respecting an establishment of religion or prohibiting the free exercise thereof, or abridging the freedom of speech or of the press; or the right of the people peaceably to assemble and to petition the government for a redress of grievances.

There, in that article, associated with religious freedom, with the fredom of the press, with the great right of popular assemblage and petition—there we find safely anchored forever this inestimable right of free speech. Mark, now, Senators, the prescient wisdom of the people! Within ten years after the adoption of the Constitution the government was entirely in the hands of one party. All of its departments, executive, legislative and judiciary, were concentrated in what was then called the Federal party. But a formidable party had begun to show itself, headed by a formidable leader, a party then called the Republican, since known as the Democratic party. Nothing was left to them but free speech and a free press. All the patronage was upon the other side. But they made the most of these great engines. So much, however, had the dominant party lost discretion, confident in its party strength, that, irritated to folly and madness by the fierce attacks made upon its executive, its judiciary and its Houses of Congress, in an evil hour it passed an act, July 14, 1798, entitled "An act for the punishment of certain crimes against the United States." The second section of this act provides:—"That if any person shall write, print, utter, publish * * * any false, scandalous and malicious writing or writings against the Government of the United States, or the President of the United States, with intent to defame the said government, or either House of the said Congress, or the said President, or to bring them or either of them into contempt or disrepute, or to excite against them or either or any of them the hatred of the good people of the United States * * * such persons * * * shall be punished by a fine not exceeding two thousand dollars, and by imprisonment not exceeding two years." No act has ever been passed by the Congress of the United States so odious to the people as this. Mr. Hamilton, and other great Federalists of the day, attempted in vain to defend it before the people. But the authors of the law and the law itself went down together before the popular indignation, and this act, which was gotten up by a great and powerful party in order to preserve itself in power, became the fatal means of driving that party out of power, followed by the maledictions of the people. History continues to teach us now as heretofore, that "eternal vigilance is the price of liberty." There is now, as there has been in the past, a constant tendency to transfer power from the many to the few. There the danger lies to the permanence of our political institutions, and its source is in the Legislative Department alone. Guard that well and we are safe. And to guard it well, you must guard the other departments from its encroachments. Without the help of the people they cannot defend themselves. This last attempt manifested in this tenth article to again bring into play the fearful privilege of the legislative department, is only a repetition of what has happened from the dawn of history. Wherever that has been the governing element, it has always been jealous of free speech and a free press. It has not been so with the absolute monarch. He feels secure surrounded by physical power, sustained by armies and navies. Accordingly, we find that such a monster as Tiberius pardoned a poor wretch who had lampooned his authority and ridiculed his conduct; while the Decemvirs remorselessly put to death a Roman satirist who was bold enough to attack and bring into contempt their authority. The eleventh article is the only one that remains to be considered. I confess my inability to make anything out of that article. And now, Senators, after this review of the articles of impeachment, we are prepared to form some idea of the nature of this impeachment itself. Where now is the mischief? Where now is the injury to any individual or to any officer of the government brought about by the action of the President? Whether actuated by good motives or bad, no injury has followed; no public interest has suffered; no officer has been changed, either rightfully or wrongfully; not an item of public property or public money has passed out of the custody of law or has been appropriated to improper uses. To all this it is said that it is enough that the law has been violated, that powers have been assumed by the President not conferred upon him by the Constitution of the United States. It is in the order of the 21st of February, 1868, that it is claimed on the part of the managers that the President usurped a power not granted by the Constitution. If that proposition could be established the managers would still be a great way off from a conviction for an impeachable offense. Much more must be made out besides the actual violation by the President of the constitutional provisions; first of all, the criminal intent to violote; and secondly, the existence of an act of Congress providing that such violations with criminal intent should amount to a high crime and misdemeanor.

But I hasten to meet the managers upon the main proposition, and I maintain with confidence that the order issued on the 21st of February, 1868, for the removal of Mr. Stanton was issued by the President in the exercise of an undoubted power vested in him by the Constitution of the United States. No executive order issued by any President, from the time of Washington down to the present, comes to us with a greater sanction, or higher authority, or stronger indorsements than this order. If this order is indeed, as it is claimed, a usurpation of power not granted by the Constitution, then Washington was a usurper in every month of his administration, and after him every President that ever occupied that high office from his day to that of the present incumbent, for every one of them has exercised, without doubt and without question, this executive power of removal from office. So far as this question stands upon authority, it may be said to have been more thoroughly and satisfactorily settled than any one that has at any time agitated the country; settled first in 1789 by the very men who framed the Constitution itself; then after the lapse and acquiescence of some forty years brought again and again into question in 1826, in 1850 and in 1835. But in the worst party times it was never changed by the Legislature, but left as it was until the 2d of March, 1867, when, after the lapse of almost eighty years, a new rule was attempted to be established which proposes to reverse the whole past. Mr. Stanbery argued that although the Constitution was silent about the power of removals, it plainly implied that power. The purpose of making appointments subject to the advice and consent of the Senate was to prevent corruption and favoritsm, but not to give the Senate power to control the Executive. Continuing, he said:—I stand, then, Senators, on the constitutional power of the President to remove Mr. Stanton from office. If he did in fact possess that power, what becomes of the Tenure of Office act or anything else in the way of legislation? If it is a constitutional power which he possesses, how can it be taken away by any mode short of a constitutional amendment? Then, too, if he deems it his constitutional power, how can you punish him for following in good faith that oath which he has been compelled to take, that he "will preserve, protect and defend the Constitution of the United States." Look, Senators, at what has happened since the beginning of this trial. During the progress of the case, on March 31, 1868, a question arose in which the Senate as an Impeachment Court were equally divided. Thereupon the Chief Justice decided the question in the affirmative by his casting vote. I make now the following extract from the minutes of the next day, April 1. Mr. Stanbery then quoted from the proceedings relative to Mr. Sumner's resolution declaring that the Chief Justice had no authority to vote, and continued:—How near, Mr. Chief Justice, did you come to the commission of an impeachable offense, according to this modern doctrine announced here by the managers? But it is said on behalf of the managers, that although each department may have a right to construe the Constitution for itself in the matter of its own action, that being so the legislative department may carry out its own opinions of the Constitution to their final results, even if thereby they totally absorb every power of the Executive department. They are the sole judges of their own powers when called upon to act, and must decide for themselves. But if they have this ultimate power of decision, so also has the Executive; and if they have a right to enforce their construction against the Executive, so also has the Executive a right to enforce its construction against theirs. It was to meet that very contingency, it was to save us from such fatal consequences, that the wisdom of our forefathers introduced the Judicial Department as the final arbiter of all such questions. That failing, there is but one alternative —an actual collision or a resort to the people themselves. This last is the great conservative element in our government. When this fails us all is gone. When the voice of the people ceases to be appealed to, or, being appealed to, ceases to be listened to, then faction and party will have accomplished their perfect work, and this frame of government will, like a worthless thing, be cast away. Mr. Stanbery declared that nothing was plainer than that it was the duty of the President to resist all encroachments on the Constitution. Continuing, he said:—And now, Senators, I ask your close attention to what seems to me a most singular characteristic of this case. How does it happen that for the first time in the history of our country the President of the United States has been suddenly subjected to such punitive legislation as that which was passed on the 2d of March, 1867? Laws were passed on that day purporting to change the order of Executive action, Such laws have not been uncommon, either in our national or State Legislatures. It has often happened that the legislative department has made changes in the manner of administration of the executive department, oftentimes imposing duties never imposed before; oftentimes prescribing action in the most direct and explicit terms; but where before has legislation of this sort been found attended with such pains and penalties as we find here? Now observe, Senators, that neither in the primitive clauses of the second section of that Military Appropriation act, nor in the sixth section of that Tenure of Office act, is the President of the United States so much as mentioned. Whoever drew these acts shrunk from referring to the office by name. It is under the general description of "person" or "civil officer" that he is made liable to fine and imprisonment for failing to carry out the new provisions of the law. But there is no question that it is the President, and the President alone, that is meant. The law was made for him. He is left no choice, no chance of appeal to the courts, no mode of testing the validity of the new law. In these pregnant words the whole matter is settled. There is, first of all, an enumeration of what crimes are in the contemplation of the Constitution—treason and bribery; and they are the highest of official crimes that can be committed. If the Constitution had stopped there, no doubt could exist. Would anything short of treason have sufficed for an article of impeachment—anything even amounting to misprison of treason or even that modern crime in English law, treason felony? Could any case have been made against the President under an article alleging treason, short of actual levying of war or giving aid and comfort to the enemies of the United States? Then as to bribery, would anything short of actual bribery have sufficed? Would an attempt to bribe—an act almost equal to bribery, yet just short of it? Certainly not. They are crimes and misdemeanors, says Mr. Burke, not of form, but of essence. You cannot call that a high crime and misdemeaner which, in the nature of things, is not. There is no room for cunning manufacture here. If a legislative act should undertake to declare that the commonest assault and battery should be a high crime and misdemeanor under the Constitution, that would not change its essence or make it the high offense which the Constitution requires. Look through all the correlative provisions of the Constitution on the subject, as to trial, conviction, judgment and punishment, as to pardons, and last of all, to that provision that, "the trial of all crimes, except in cases of impeachment, shall be by jury," and that other provision, that after conviction on impeachment, "the party convicted shall nevertheless be liable and subject to indictment, trial, judgment and punishment according to law." If you are not yet satisfied, examine the proceedings of the convention that framed this article, and see how studiously they rejected all impeachment for misbehavior in office, and how steadily they adhered to the requisition that nothing but a high crime and misdemeanor should suffice. Mr. Stanbery then referred to the promise of the managers that they would show that the President had made no attempt to carry the Tenure of Office law before the courts, and said:—Senators, where has this been shown on the part of the managers? Where is there even a feeble attempt to show it? But look now to the proof on the part of the President. Cabined, cribbed and confined as we have been by the rulings of the Senate upon this question, yet what appears? From first to last the great fact forces itself upon our attention that this was no subterfuge of the President, no afterthought to escape the consequences of an act, but, on the contrary, that this wholesome and lawful purpose of a resort to the proper tribunal to settle the difficulty between Congress and himself was in the mind of the President from the very beginning. They proved it by his own declarations, introduced by themselves in his letter to General Grant, dated February 10, 1868, which may be found on page 234 of the printed record. One extract from that letter will suffice. The President says:—"You knew the President was unwilling to trust the office with any one who would not, by holding it, compel Mr. Stanton to resort to the courts. You perfectly understood that in this interview, some time after you accepted the office, the President, not content with your silence, desired an expression of your views, and you answered him that Mr. Stanton would have to appeal to the courts."

If this is not enough, Senators, remember the testimony of General Thomas, of General Sherman, of Mr. Cox, of Mr. Merrick, and see throughout the purpose of the President, declared at all times, from first to last, to bring this question to judicial arbitrament. After all this, what a shocking perversion of testimony it is to pronounce it an afterthought or a subterfuge. And after the proof of what took place on the trial of Thomas, how can the managers be bold enough to say that they will "show you that he has taken no step to submit the matter to any court, although more than a year has elapsed since the passage of the act." Senators, it was not at all necessary for the defense of the President that, in the exercise of that discretion which the law allows to him, he should be put to prove that his intentions were all right. He has gone far beyond the necessities of his case. Never were good intentions and honest motives more thoroughly proved than they have been proved in this case. I repeat it, that if everything else were made out against him, this great exculpatory fact must absolve him from all criminal liability. And now, Senators, I have done with the law and the facts of the case. There remains for me, however, a duty yet to be performed—one of solemn and important obligation—a duty to my client, to my former chief, to my friend. There may be those among you, Senators, who cannot find a case of guilt against the President. There may be those among you who, not satisfied that a case for impeachment has yet arisen, are fearful of the consequences of an acquittal. You may entertain vague apprehensions that, flushed with the success of acquittal, the President will proceed to acts of violence and revolution. Senators, you do not know or understand the man. I cannot say that you wilfully misunderstand him; for I, too, though never an extreme party man, have felt more than once, in the heat of party conflicts, the same bitter and uncompromising spirit that may now animate you. The time has been when I looked upon General Jackson as the most dangerous of tyrants. The time has been when, day after day, I expected to see him inaugurate a revolution; and yet, after his administration was crowned with success and sustained by the people, I have lived to see him gracefully surrender his great powers to the hands that conferred them, and under the softening influences of time, came to regard him, not as a tyrant, but as one of the most honest and patriotic of men.

Now listen for a moment to one who, perhaps, understands Andrew Johnson better than most of you, for his opportunities have been greater. When nearly two years ago he called me from the pursuits of a professional life to take a seat in his Cabinet, I answered the call under a sense of public duty. I came here almost a stranger to him and to every member of his Cabinet, except Mr. Stanton. We had been friends for many years. Senators, need I tell you that all my tendencies are conservative? You, Mr. Chief Justice, who have known me for the third of a century, can bear me witness. Law, not arms, is my profession. From the moment that I was honored with a seat in the Cabinet of Mr. Johnson not a step was taken that did not come under my observation, not a word was said that escaped my attention. I regarded him closely in Cabinet and in still more private and confidential conversation; I saw him often tempted with bad advice; I knew that evil counsellors were more than once around him; I observed him with the most intense anxiety, but never in word, in deed, in thought, in action, did I discover in that man anything but loyalty to the Constitution and the laws. He stood firm as a rock against all temptation to abuse his own powers or to exercise those which were not conferred upon him. Steadfast and self-reliant in the midst of difficulties, when dangers threatened, when temptations were strong, he looked only to the Constitution of his country and to the people. Yes, Senators. I have seen that man tried as few have been tried. I have seen his confidence abused. I have seen him endure day after day provocation such as few men have ever been called upon to meet. No man could have met them with more sublime patience. Sooner or later, however, I knew the explosion must come. And when it did come my only wonder was that it had been so long delayed. Yes, Senators, with all his faults, the President has been more sinned against than sinning. Fear not, then, to acquit him. The Constitution of the country is safe in his hands from violence, as it was in the hands of Washington. But if, Senators, you condemn him, if you strip him of the robes of office, if you degrade him to the utmost stretch of your power, mark the prophesy! The strong arm of the people will be about him. They will find a way to raise him from any depths to which you may consign him, and we shall live to see him redeemed and to hear the majestic voice of the people:—"Well done, faithful servant, you shall have your reward!" But if, Senators, as I cannot believe, but as has been boldly said with almost official sanction, your votes have been canvassed and the doom of the President is sealed, then let that judgment not be pronounced in this Senate chamber; not here, where our Camillus in the hour of greatest peril, single-handed, met and baffled the enemies of the Republic; not here, where he stood faithful among the faithless; not here, where he fought the good fight for the Union and the Constitution; not in this Chamber, whose walls echo with that clarion voice that in the days of our greatest danger carried hope and comfort to many a desponding heart, strong as an army with banners. No, not here. Seek out rather the darkest and gloomiest chamber in the subterranean recesses of this Capitol, where the cheerful light of day never enters. There erect the altar and immolate the victim.

At quarter to three P. M. Mr. Stanbery resumed the floor himself, and concluded his address at ten minutes past three o'clock.

The court then, on motion of Senator HOWARD, adjourned until Monday next.

PROCEEDINGS OF MONDAY, MAY 4.

A large audience was early assembled this morning to hear the closing arguments of Mr. Manager Bingham. No business was attempted to be done, and by direction of the Chief Justice the argument immediately began.

Judge Bingham's Argument.

Mr. BINGHAM said:—Mr. President and Senators:—I protest, gentleman, that in no mere partisan spirit, in no spirit of resentment, or prejudice, do I come to the argument of this great issue. A Representative of the people, upon the obligation of my oath by order of the people's Representatives, in the name of the people, and for the defense of their Constitution and laws, this day speaking, I pray you, Senators, to hear me for my cause. But yesterday, the supremacy of the Constitution and laws was challenged by armed Rebellion; to-day the supremacy of the Constitution and laws is challenged by Executive usurpation, and this attempted to be defended in the Senate of the United States.

For four years millions of men disputed by arms the supremacy of American law and American soil. Happily for our common country, on the 9th day of April, in the year of our Lord 1865, the broken battalions of treason, the armed resistance to law, surrendered to the victorious legions of this country. On that day, Senators, not without sacrifice, not without suffering, not without martyrdom, the laws were vindicated. On that day went all over our sorrow-stricken land and to every nationality, that the republic, the last refuge of constitutional liberty, the last sanctuary of inviolable justice, was saved, forever saved by the sacrifice, the virtue and the valor of its children.

On the 14th day of April, 1865, here in the Capital amidst the joy and gladness of the people fell Abraham Lincoln, by an assassin's hand. A President of the United States slain, not for his crimes but for his virtues, and especially for his fidelity to duty, that highest word revealed by God to man. By the death of Abraham Lincoln Andrew Johnson, then Vice President of the United States, became President. Upon taking the prescribed oath, faithfully to execute the office of President, and preserve, protect, and defend the Constitution of the United States, the great people, bowing with uncovered heads in the presence of that strange grief and sorrow which came upon them, forgot for the moment the disgraceful part which Andrew Johnson had played upon this tribune of the Senate, on the 4th day of March, 1865, and accepted his oath as successor of Abraham Lincoln, his affirmation and assurance that he would take care that the laws be faithfully executed.

It is, Senators, with the people, an intuitive judgment, the highest conviction of the human intellect, that the oath, faithfully, to execute the office of President, and preserve, protect and defend the Constitution of the United States, means, and must forever mean, while the Constitution remains as it is, that the President will himself obey and compel others, by the whole power of the people, to obey the laws which shall be enacted by the people, through their Representatives in Congress, until the same shall have been duly repealed by the law-making power—shall have been actually reversed by the Supreme Court of the United States within the limitations and restrictions of the Constitution itself. For these purposes and of this argument, Senators, we must accept this as the general judgment of the people of this country. Assumedly, it is the pride of every American, that no man is above the laws and no man beneath them. That the President himself is as much the subject of law as the humblest citizen in the remotest frontier of your ever advancing civilization,

I need not say in this presence, surrounded by the representatives of the people, that among the American people there is no sovereign save God, except the laws enacted by themselves, obligatory alike upon each and all, official and unofficial, the obligation of which ceases only with their repeal, or their actual reversal in the mode prescribed by the people themselves. This, Senators, and I am almost fearful that I may offend in saying it, but this is one of the traditions of the Republic, and is understood from the Atlantic to the Pacific shore by the five and thirty millions of people who dwell between those shores, and hold in their hands to-day the greatest trust ever committed, in the providence of God, to any political society. I feel myself justified, entirely justified, in saying that it rests not simply upon the traditions of the people, but is embodied in their written records from the day when the fiery strife began on the field of Lexington to this hour.

It is not declared in that immortal Declaration which will live as long as our language lives, as one of the causes of the move against the King of Great Britain, that he had permitted the governors of these colonies to withhold the execution of the laws of the land until they should have received his assent, and that they should be suspended. Furthermore, I use the words of the Declaration, which, like the words of Luther, were half battles; they should be suspended until they had received his assent, and that was the first voice of those immortal men with whom God walked through the night and storm and darkness of the Revolution, and whom he taught to lay here to the going down of the sun, the foundation of those institutions of civil and religious liberty which have since become the hope of the world. I quote that written record further.

Still asking pardon of the Senate, praying them to remember that I speak this day not simply in the presence of Senators, but in the presence of an expectant and waiting people, who have commissioned you to discharge this high trust and who have committed to you, Senators, the issues of life and death to this republic. I refer you to the words of Washington, first of Americans and foremost of men, who declared that the Constitution, which at all times exists, unless changed by the act of the whole people, "is sacredly obligatory upon all." I refer next to a higher authority, which is the expression of the collective powers and will of the whole people of the United States, in which it is asserted that this Constitution, and the laws made in pursuance thereof, and all treaties made, or which shall be made by the authority of the United States, shall be the supreme law of the land, and the judges in every State shall be bound thereby, anything in the Constitution or laws of any State to the contrary notwithstanding.

That is the solemn declaration of the Constitution itself, and pending this trial, without a parallel in the history of nations, it should be written upon these walls and considered not simply by the Senators, but by that portion of the people who look down from these galleries upon this grave proceeding. The Constitution and the laws passed in pursuance thereof shall be the supreme law of the land, anything in the Constitution or laws of any State to the contrary notwithstanding. How are these propositions, so plain and simple that the wayfaring man, though a fool, could not err therein, met by the retained counsel, who appear for hire to defend this treason and this betrayal of trust of an outraged people. The proposition is met by stating to the Senate with an audacity that has scarcely a parallel in judicial proceedings, that every official may challenge at his pleasure the supreme law of the land, and especially that the President of the United States charged by his oath, charged by the express letter of the Constitution, shall take care that the laws be faithfully executed, is nevertheless invested with the power to interpret the Constitution for himself, and determine judicially.

Senators, I use the words used by the learned gentleman who opened the case for the accused, and "determine judicially whether the laws declared by the Constitution to be supreme, or are not null and void because they do not happen to accord with his judgment." That is the defense which is presented here before the Senate of the United States, upon which they are asked to declare that the Executive is clothed with powers judicial. I repeat their own words, and I desire that it may be twined into the brain of the Senators when they come to deliberate upon this question, that the President may judicially construe the Constitution for himself, and judicially determine finally for himself, whether the laws which, by your Constitution are declared to be such, are not after all null and void, of no effect, and not to be executed because it is not his pleasure.

When his highness, Andrew Johnson, first king of the people of the United States, in imitation of George III, attempts to suspend their execution, he ought to remember that it was said by those who set the Revolution in motion, and who contributed to the organization of this government, that Cæsar had his Brutus; that Charles I had his Cromwell, and he would do well to profit by that example.

Nevertheless, the position is assumed in the presence of the Senate, in the presence of the people of the United States, and in the presence of the civilized world, that the President of the United States is invested with the judicial power of determining the force and effect of the Constitution, the force of his obligation under it, and the force and effect of every law passed by the Congress of the United States. Senators, if the President may declare an act unconstitutional without danger to his official position, I respectfully submit that the Constitution which we have been taught to revere as the sacred charter of our liberties is at last a Constitution of anarchy, and not a Constitution of order; a Constitution which authorizes the violation of law, and of the Constitution which enjoins obedience to law; and I further respectfully submit to you, Senators, that when you shall have established any such rule by your solemn judgment which you will pronounce at the close of these proceedings, it needs no prophet of the living God to foresee that you will have proved yourselves the architects of your country's ruin; that you will have transformed this land of law and order, of light and knowledge, into a land of darkness, the very light whereof will be darkness; into a land where "night and chaos, the ancestors of nature, will hold eternal anarchy amid the noise of endless war."

Gentlemen, they may glaze them over as they may, they may excuse with specious pretexts and arguments, as they may, the acts of this guilty President, the fact nevertheless, remains patent to the observation of all right-minded men, in this country, that the question on which the Senate must, as the issue joined between the people of the United States and the President, is whether the President may at his pleasure and without peril to his official position, set aside and annul both the Constitution and the laws of the United States, and thereby inaugurate anarchy. That is the issue. No matter what demagogues may say of it in this Chamber; no matter what retained counsel may say of it inside of this Chamber—that is the issue, and the recording angel of history has already struck it into the adamant of the past, there to abide forever.

On that issue, Senators, you, the House of Representatives, and their representatives at this bar, will stand or fail before the final tribunal of the future. That is the issue. It is all there is of it. What is embraced in these articles of impeachment is all that there is in it. In spite of the technicalities of counsel, in spite of the fatal pleas that have been interposed here in his defense, that is the issue —it is the head and front of Andrew Johnson's offending, that he has assumed to himself the exclusive prerogative of interpreting the Constitution and of deciding on the validity of the laws at his pleasure.

Stripping the defense of all specious reasoning, it is based on this startling proposition that the President cannot be held to answer, by the people or by their representatives, on impeachment for any violation of the Constitution, or of the laws, because of his asserted constitutional right to interpret for himself, and to execute and disregard, at his discretion, any provision, either of the Constitution or of the laws of the United States. I say it again, Senators, with every respect to the gentlemen who sit here as the representatives of States and as representatives as well of that great people who are one people, that the man who has heard this prolonged discussion, running through days and weeks, who does not understand this to be the plain, simple proposition at last, made in the hearing of Senators, insisted upon in defense of the President, is one of those unfortunates, to whom God, in his providence, has denied the usual measure of intelligence, and of that faculty which we call reason. The power to decide this great question between the people and the President, is vested solely and exclusively in the Senate. The responsibility, Senators, to decide aright, rests exclusively upon the Senate. That responsibility can be divided by the Senate with no human being outside of this Chamber.

It is all important to the people of the United States, as it is all important to their representatives in Congress assembled, and certainly is all important to the Senators sworn to do justice in the premises, between the people and the President, that this great issue, which touches the national life, shall be decided in accordance with the letter of the Constitution. It is all important that it should be decided in accordance with that justice, to establish which the Constitution itself was ordained—that justice, before the majesty of which we this day bow, as before the majesty of that God whose attribute it is—that justice which dwelt with Him before the worlds were, which will exist with Him when worlds are no longer, by which we shall be judged for this day's proceedings.

The Senate having the sole power to try impeachment, is necessarily vested by every intendment of the Constitution with the sole and exclusive power to decide every matter of law and of fact involved in the issue, and yet, Senators, although that would seem to be a self-evident proposition, hours have been spent here to persuade the Senate of the United States that the Senate at last has not the sole power to try every issue of law and of fact arising on the question between the people and the President. The ex-Attorney-General well said, the other day, and quoted a familiar canon in interpretation when he said it, that effect must be given to every word in a written statute. Let effect be given to every word of the written statute of the people's fundamental law—the Constitution of the United States—and there is an end of all controversy about the exact power of the Senate to decide here questions of law and of fact arising on this issue.

Why, then, this long-continued discussion on the part of the counsel for the President, resting on a remark of a colleague, in his opening in behalf of the people, that this was not a court. Was it an attempt to divert the Senate from the express provision of the Constitution that they shall be the sole and final—I add another word to the argument— the final arbiters between the people and the President? What meant this empty criticism about the words of my colleague that this was not a court, but the Senate of the United States? My colleague, Mr. Chief Justice, simply followed the plain words of the Constitution, that the Senate shall have the sole power to try impeachment.

I propose neither to exhaust my strength nor the patience of the Senate by dwelling upon this miserable distinction to be made between the Senate and the court. That is what it results in at last, although it came after a deal of deliberation, after a great many days of incubation, and after many utterances on many subjects concerning things both in the heavens above and in the earth beneath, and in the waters under the earth. (Laughter.) I do not propose to imitate the example of the learned and accomplished counsel for the President on the trial of this grave issue, which carries with it so grave results to all the people of the United States, not only of this day, but all generations hereafter. I hope to be saved, in the providence of God and by His grace, from becoming, as was the counsel for the President in this august presence, a mere cater up of syllables, a mere snapper up of unconsidered trifles. (Laughter.)

I propose to deal in this discussion with principles, not trifles light as air. I care not if the gentlemen choose to call the Senate, sitting in a trial of impeachment, a court. The Constitution calls it a Senate. I know, as every other intelligent man knows, that the Senate of the United States, sitting on the trial of impeachment, is the highest judicial tribunal in the land. That is conceding enough to put an end to all that was said on that subject; some of it most solemnly, like the stately argument of the learned gentleman from Massachusetts (Mr. Curtis); some of it most tenderly by the affecting and adroit argument of my learned and accomplished friend from Ohio (Mr. Groesbeck) and some of it most wittily, so witty that he held his own sides lest he would explode with laughter at his own wit, by the learned gentleman from New York (Mr. Evarts) who displayed more of Latin than of law in his argument, more of rhetoric than of logic, and more of intellectual pyrotechnics than of either. (Laughter.) Senators, I am not to be diverted by these fireworks, by these Roman candles, by these fiery serpents that are let off at pleasure and to order by the accomplished gentleman from New York. Upon the point made here between the people and the President by his advocates, I stand upon the plain, clear letter of the Constitution. When it declares that the Senate shall have the sole power to try impeachments, it necessarily invests the Senate with the sole and exclusive power to determine finally and forever, every issue of law and of fact arising in the case. This is one of those self-evident propositions arising under the Constitution of the United States which Hamilton states, in words clear and strong, and which must carry conviction to the mind of every man. This is one of those truths which, to a correct and unprejudiced mind, carries its own evidence along with it, and may be obscured, but cannot be made plainer by argument or reason. It rests on maxims as simple as they are universal.

The persons from whose agency the attainment of an end is expective, ought to possess the means by which it is to be attained. The end is expected, by the letter of your Constitution, from the Senate of the United States, to decide finally and for themselves every issue of law and of fact arising between the people and their accused President. What comes then, I want to know, Senators, of that argument of the learned gentleman from New York (Mr. Evarts)? The most significant thought of which was this, that the right way, and the effectual way by which a man may make his speech immortal, is to make it eternal. (Laughter).

What becomes of his long-drawn out sentences here about the right of the accused and guilty man who stands this day clothed with perjury as with a garment in the presence of the people, to be tried first in the Supreme Court of the United States, before the Senate shall proceed to trial and judgment?

Senators, the people of the United States, through their representatives in Congress assembled, have made provisions for such unfortunates as are not able to take care of themselves across the Eastern Branch, on the crown of yonder green hill, where they can be cared for—alluding to the Insane Asylum. The Senate is vested with the sole and exclusive power to try this question, and the Supreme

Court of the United States has no more power to intervene or to have judgment of the premises than has the Court of of St. Petersburg to the people of the United States.

I hesitate not to say, will hold, nevertheless, clear and manifest as this proposition is, that has been insisted upon here from the opening of this defense to its close, by all the counsel who have participated in this discussion, that the Supreme Court is the final arbiter for the decision of all questions arising under the Constitution. I do not state the propositions too broadly. Senators, my occupations have been of such a nature, since the commencement of the trial to this hour, that I have relied more upon my memory of what counsel said, than upon any reading which I have given to their voluminous and endless arguments in defense of the accused; but I venture to say that the proposition is not more broadly stated by me than it has been stated by them. I submit to the Senate that there are many questions arising under the Constitution which by no possibility can be considered as original questions, either in the Supreme Court, or in any other court of the United States. For example, my learned and accomplished friend, who honors me with his attention, and who represents the great and growing Commonwealth of Illinois on this floor, Senator Trumbull, is here, and is to remain here, not by force of any decision that the Supreme Court has made or may hereafter make. It is not a question within their jurisdiction. Illinois, one of those great commonwealths, which, since the organization of the Constitution, and within the memory of living man, has sprung from the shores of the beautiful Ohio and the golden sands of the Pacific, is here, under the direct obligation of the Constitution of the United States. The people by their Constitution did provide that the Congress shall have power to admit new States into this Union, and when the Congress passed upon the question of whether the people of Illinois had organized a government republican in form and well entitled to assume their place in the sisterhood of commonwealths, the decision was final, and the judge of the Supreme Court who dares to challenge the great seal of the State which the Senator represents would be instantly ejected from his place—which he would thereby dishonor and disgrace—by the supreme power of the people speaking and acting through the process of impeachment. It does not belong in any sense of the word to the judicial power of the United States to decide all questions arising under the Constitution and laws. According to the logic of the counsel for the President, the Supreme Court would come to sit in judgment at last on the power given exclusively to each House to judge of the election and qualifications of its own members. Senators, the judicial power of the United States is entitled to all respect and to all consideration, here and everywhere else, but that judicial power, as is well known to Senators, is defined and limited by the terms of the Constitution, and beyond that limitation or outside of it, that tribunal cannot go. I read from the Constitution the provisions in answer to the argument of the gentleman touching the judicial power of the United States:—

Section 1. The judicial power of the United States shall be vested in one supreme court and in such inferior courts as the Congress may from time to time ordain and establish. The judges both of the Supreme and inferior courts shall hold their offices during good behavior, and shall at stated terms receive for their services a compensation, which shall not be diminished during their continuance in office.

Section 2. The judicial power shall extend to all cases in law and equity arising under this Constitution, the laws of the United States, and treaties made, or which shall be made, under their authority; to all cases affecting ambassadors and other public ministers and consuls; to all cases of admiralty and maritime jurisdiction; to controversies to which the United States shall be a party; to controversies between two or more States; between a State and citizens of another State; between citizens of different States; between citizens of the same State, claiming lands under grants of different States, and between a State or the citizens thereof, and foreign States, citizens or subjects; in all cases affecting ambassadors and other public ministers and consuls, and those in which a State shall be a party, the Supreme Court shall have original jurisdiction; in all the other cases before mentioned the Supreme Court shall have appellate jurisdiction, both as to law and fact, with such exceptions and under such regulations as the Congress shall make. The trial of all crimes, except in cases of impeachment, shall be by jury, and such trial shall be held in the State where the said crimes shall have been committed; but when not committed within any State, the trial shall be at such place or places as the Congress may by law have directed.

Section 3. Treason against the United States shall consist only in levying war against them, or in adhering to their enemies, giving them aid and comfort. No person shall be convicted of treason unless on the testimony of two witnesses to the same overt act, or on confession in open court. The Congress shall have power to declare the punishment of treason; but no attainder of treason shall work corruption of blood, or forfeiture, except during the life of the person attainted.

As I said before, inasmuch as 'the Senate of the United States has the sole power to try impeachment, and therefore the exclusive power finally to determine all questions thereon, it results that its decision can neither be restricted by judgments in advance, made either by the Supreme Court, or by any other court of the United States, nor can the final judgment of the Senate on impeachment be subjected to review by the several courts of the United States, or to reversal by the executive pardon, for it is written in the Constitution that the pardoning power shall not extend to impeachment, and impeachment is not a case in law and equity, within the meaning of the term; as employed in the third article of the Constitution, which I have just read.

It is in no sense a case within the general judicial power of the United States. Senators, no one is either bold enough or weak enough to stand in the presence of the United States, and clearly and openly proclaim and avow that the Supreme Court has the power to try impeachments. Nevertheless, the position assumed in this defense for the accused—that he may suspend the laws without peril to his official position, and may interpret and construe the Constitution for himself, without peril to his official position, if he states, either after the crime or after the fact, that his only object in violating the Constitution or in suspending the law was to obtain at some future day a judicial construction of the one or a judicial decision on the validity of the other, and that, therefore, the Senate is not to hold him to answer an impeachment for a high crime and misdemeanor — does involve the proposition, and no man can get away from it, that the court at last has a supervising power over this unlimited and unrestricted power of impeachment, vested by the people in the House of Representatives, and over this unrestricted power of trial of impeachment, vested by the people in the Senate of the United States. On that proposition I am willing to stand, defying any man here, and my learned friend, to challenge it successfully. The position assumed by the accused means that or it means nothing. If it does not mean that it is a tale told by an idiot, full of sound and fury, and means nothing.

Now I ask you, Senators, what colorable excuse there is for presenting any such monstrous proposition as that to the consideration of the Senate of the United States. I think myself justified in reiterating the words of John Marshall, that it is respectful to conclude that the Senate knows something. The original jurisdiction of the Supreme Court cannot by any possibility extend to a case of impeachment. Senators will recollect the text of the Constitution which I have already read, that the original jurisdiction of the Supreme Court is, by the express letter of the Constitution restricted to "foreign ambassadors, other public ministers and consuls," and to cases to which a State may be a party. The accused is not a foreign ambassador; the accused is not a foreign minister; the accused is not a consul, and the accused is not as yet, thank God, the State. Therefore, the accused is not within the original jurisdiction of the Supreme Court of the United States. The counsel for the President, who dwelt so learnedly and so long on this question, quoting from the great case of Marbury vs. Madison, ought to have recollected that the Chief Justice, who pronounces that decision, and whose intellect shed a steady and luminous light on the Judiciary of the country for a third of a century, declared what no man has since questioned, that the original jurisdiction of the Supreme Court, as laid down in the text of the Constitution, can neither be enlarged nor restricted by Congressional enactment.

Those gentlemen should have recollected, further, when they invoked the intervention of the Supreme Court, or of any other court, between the people and the accused President, that the appellate jurisdiction of the Supreme Court, by innumerable decisions, depends exclusively, under the Constitution, upon the will of Congress; so that they must go to some other tribunal for a settlement of this great question between the people and the President, unless Congress choose to let them go to the Supreme Court by a special enactment for their own benefit. The appellate jurisdiction of the Supreme Court, as defined in the Constitution by words clear and plain, and incapable of any misunderstanding or misconstruction, excludes the conclusion that a case of impeachment can, by any possibility, be within the jurisdiction of any of the courts of the United States—either its District, or Circuit, or Supreme Court.

The Senate will notice that by the terms of the Constitution the appellate jurisdiction of the District and Circuit Courts is limited and restricted to the cases in law and in equity, and the other cases specifically named in the Constitution, none of which embrace the case of impeachment. There is, therefore, Senators, no room for invoking the decision of the Supreme Court of the United States on any question touching the liability of the President to answer impeachment by the people's representatives at the bar of the Senate. What excuse, therefore, I ask, for the pretense that the President may set aside and dispense with the execution of the laws, all or any of them enacted by the Congress, under the pretext of defending the Constitution by invoking a judicial inquiry in the court of the United States. But I know, Senators, that the only two questions which by possibility could become a subject of judicial decision and which have been raised by the learned and astute counsel who have attempted to make this defense, have already been decided by the Supreme Court.

The first is that the heads of departments are the mere registering secretaries of the President, and are bound to recognize his will as their sworn duty. I deny it. I deny that proposition, and I think the learned gentleman from New York (Mr. Evarts) did well, did remarkably well, as he does everything well, to quote in advance for our instruction when we would come to reply to him on this point, those divine words of the great Apostle of the Gentiles, where he speaks of charity as patient and long suffering. It requires, Senators, charity broader than the charity of the gospel, to sit patiently by and hear those gentleman invoke the decision of the Supreme Court upon either of the questions involved in that issue, when we know that those gentlemen, overflowing as thy manifestly are, with all learning, ancient and modern, the learning of the dead as well as the learning of the living, knew right well that the Supreme Court had solemnly decided both questions against them.

Now for the proof. As to the obligation of the heads of departments to learn their duty under the law from the will of the Executive, the Senate will recollect that the learned gentleman from New York quoted the great case of Marbury and Madison with wondrous skill and dexterity. He took good care, however, not to quote that part of the decision which absolutely settled this question as to the liability of the Secretaries to respond to the will of the Executive. He took care to keep that in the background. Perhaps he assumed that he knew all that the managers of the House knew about this case, and then, that he knew all that he knew himself besides. (Laughter.) He gathered from the past, from Cicero against Cataline, and from Cicero against Verres, and from that speech of Cicero in defense of Milo, which happened never to have been made until after poor Milo was convicted, for he was made to cry out that if Cicero had made that speech for him on his trial, he would not, on that day be undergoing punishment.

I will read now the decision of Chief Justice Marshall, in the case of Marbury and Madison, touching this alleged obligation of the heads of departments, to take the will of the Executive as their law. Chief Justice Marshall says (page 158, 1st Cranch):—"It is the duty of the Secretary of State to conform to the law, and not to obey the instructions of the President." This only illustrates the proposition that neither the President nor his Secretaries are above the Constitution, or above the laws which the people enacted. As to the other proposition, Senators, set up in the defense of this accused and guilty President, that he may with impunity, under the Constitution and laws of the United States interpret the Constitution and sit in judicial judgment, as the gentleman from Massachusetts (Mr. Curtis) words it, on the validity of your laws. That question has also been ruled upon by the Supreme Court of the United States, and from that hour to this the decision has never been challenged. Although an attempt was made to drag the illustrious name of the Chief Justice who presides at this moment over this deliberative and judicial assembly to their help, it was made in vain, as I shall show before I have done with this part of the matter. I say that the point assumed for the President, by his counsel, that he is the judiciary to interpret the Constitution for himself; that he is the judge to determine the validity of laws, and to execute them or suspend them, or to dispense with their execution at his pleasure; and to defy the power of the people to bring him to trial and judgment, has been settled against him thirty years ago by the Supreme Court of the United States, and that decision has never been questioned since by any authoritative writer on the Constitution, or by any subsequent decision of the courts.

Mr. Bingham, in this connection, referred to the case of Kendall vs. the United States, reported in 12th Peters, where Justice Thompson, pronouncing the judgment of the court, declared that the claim of the President to suspend the execution of a law, growing out of the constitutional provision that he shall take care that the laws be faithfully executed, was a doctrine which could not receive the sanction of that court, as it would be vesting the President with dispensing power which had no countenance for its support in any part, and the effect of which would be to clothe the President with power to control the legislation of Congress, and to paralyze the administration.

Mr. Bingham continued:—I ask you, Senators, whether I was not justified in saying that it was a tax upon one's patience to sit here and listen, from day to day and from week to week, to those learned arguments made in defense of the President, all resting upon his asserted executive prerogative to dispense with the execution of the laws and to protect himself from trial and impeachment because he said he only violated the law in order to test its validity in the Supreme Court, when that court had already decided, thirty years ago, that any such assumed prerogative would enable him to sweep away all the legislation of Congress, and to prevent the administration of justice itself, and that it found no countenance in the Constitution. I suppose, Senators, that the learned ex-Attorney-General thought that there was something here which might disturb the harmony and order of their arguments, and so, in his concluding arguments for the accused, he attempted to fortify against such conclusion by calling to his aid the decision of the present Chief Justice of the United States, in what is known as the Mississippi case.

Now with all due respect to the learned ex-Attorney-General, and to all his associates engaged in this trial, I take it upon me to say that the decision pronounced by His Honor the Chief Justice of the United States in the Mississippi case has no more to do with the question involved in this controversy than has the Koran of Mahomet, and the gentleman was utterly inexcusable for attempting to force that decision into this case in aid of any such proposition as that involved in this controversy. What did His Honor the Chief Justice decide in the Mississippi case? Nothing in the world but this, which is well known to every lawyer in America, even to every student of the law versed or not, beyond the horn books of his profession, that when the law vested the President with discretionary power, his judgment in the exercise of his discretion, until that judgment be overruled by the legislative power, necessarily concludes all parties. In that we agree. The learned Senator

from New York, Mr. Conkling, who honors me with his attention, knows that before he was born that question was decided precisely in the same way in the great State which he so honorably represents here to-day, and is reported in 12 Wheaton. But it does not touch the question at all, and the proposition is so foreign to the question that it is like one of those propositions referred to by Mr. Webster on one occasion, when he said that to make it to a right-minded man was to insult his intelligence.

Mr. BINGHAM read some extracts from the opinion of the Chief Justice, in the Mississippi case, bearing upon the point for which he was contending, and continued:—What on earth has that to do with the question? I maintain that the law which is called in question here to-day—the Civil Tenure act—leaves no discretion whatever in the Executive, and, in the language of his Honor, the Chief Justice, imposes on the Executive a plain, unequivocal duty. I account myself justified, therefore, at this stage of the argument, in reiterating my assertion, that the decision in the Mississippi case has nothing to do with the principle involved in this controversy, and that the President finds in that decision no excuse whatever for an attempt to interfere with, or to set aside, the plain mandates or requirements of the law. There is no discretion left in him whatever, and none of his counsel even had the audacity to argue here that the act of 1867, which is called in question, gives to the Executive any discretion whatever.

The point they make is that it is unconstitutional, and no law, and that is the very point which is settled in Kendall vs. the United States, which I have just quoted, that the power vested in the President, to take care that the laws be faithfully executed, vests in him no power to set aside a law of the United States, or to direct the head of a department to disobey it. It is written in the Constitution that he shall take care that the laws be faithfully executed. Are we to mutilate the Constitution, and, for the benefit of the accused, to interpolate into it a word which is not there, and the introduction of which would annihilate the whole system? That is to say, that the President shall take care that the laws, and only the laws which he approves, shall be faithfully executed. This is at last the position assumed for the President by himself in his answer, and assumed for him by his counsel in his defense, and the assumption conflicts with all that I have already read from the Constitution, with all that I have already read of judicial interpretation and construction, conflicts as well with the expressed text of instrument itself. It is useless to multiply words to make plain a self-evident proposition. It is useless to attempt to imply this power of the President to set aside or dispense with the execution of a law in the face of the express words of the Constitution that all legislative power granted by this Constitution shall be vested in a Congress which consist of a Senate and a House of Representatives, and in the face of the world, that he shall be sworn to execute faithfully the office of President, and, therefore, faithfully to discharge every obligation which the Constitution enjoins, first and foremost of which obligations is this, written on the very front of the instrument, that he shall take care that the laws enacted by the people's Representatives, assembled in Congress, shall be executed, not some of the laws, not the laws which he approves, but that the laws shall be faithfully executed, until the same shall have been reviewed by the power which made them, or shall have been constitutionally reversed by the Supreme Court of the United States, acting within the limits and under the restrictions of the Constitution itself.

We have heard much, Senators, in the progress of this discussion about the established customs of the people of this country. We have heard much about the long-continued practice of eighty years under the Constitution and laws of the United States. You have listened in vain, Senators, for a single citation of a single instance in the history of the republic, where there was an open and defiant violation of the written law of this land, either by the Executive, by States, or by combinations of men, which the people did not crush and put down at the very outset. That is a fact in our history, creditable to the American people. It is a fact which ought to be considered by the Senate when it comes to sit in judgment upon this case.

I need not remind Senators of that fact in our early history when General Washington was called from the quiet and seclusion of his home to put down the Whisky Insurrection in Pennsylvania, which was the first uprising of insurrection against the majesty of the law. Counsel for the President have attempted to summon to their aid the great name of the hero of New Orleans. It is fresh within the recollection of Senators as it is fresh within the recollection of millions of the people of this country, that when the State of South Carolina, in the exercise of what she called her sovereign power as a State, attempted by ordinance to set aside the laws of the United States, Andrew Jackson, not unmindful of his oath, although the law was distasteful to him, and it is a fact which has passed into history that he even doubted its constitutionality, issued his proclamation and swore by the Eternal that the "Union must and shall be preserved."

There was no recognition here of the right either in himself or in the State of South Carolina to set aside a law. Senators, there is a case still fresh within your recollections, and within the recollections of all the people of this country, which attests more significant than any other, the determination of the people to abide by their laws, however odious they may be. The gentleman from New York (Mr. Evarts) took occasion to refer to the Fugitive Slave bill of 1850, a bill that was disgraceful to the Congress which enacted it; a bill that was in direct violation of the letter and spirit of the Constitution; a bill of which I can say at least, although I doubt much whether the gentleman from New York can, that it never found an advocate in me; a bill of which Mr. Webster said that, in his judgment, it was unwarranted by the Constitution; —a bill which offered a bribe out of the common Treasury of the nation to every magistrate who sat in judgment on the right of a fleeing bondman to that liberty which belonged to man when God breathed into his notrils the breath of life and he became a living soul—a bill which offered a reward to the ministers of justice to sharpen the judgment of the poor—a bill which, suiting the conscience of the American people and the conscience of the civilized world, made it a crime to give shelter to the houseless or a cup of water to him who was ready to perish—a bill enacted for the purpose of sustaining that crime of crimes, that sum of all villanies, which made merchandise of immortality, which transformed a man into a chattel, a thing of trade, into what, for want of a better name, we call a slave, with no acknowledged right in the present, with no hope of inheritage in the great hereafter, and to whose darkened soul the universe was voiceless, and God himself seemed silent—a bill under the direct violation of which that horrible tragedy was enacted within our own noble commonwealth, within the sight, Mr. Chief Justice, of your own beautiful city, when Margaret Gardner, with her babe lashed upon her breast, pursued by the officers of the law, in her wild frenzy forgot her mother's affection in the joy she felt at sending, before the appointed time, by her own hand, the spotless soul of her child back to the God who gave it, rather than allow it to be tossed back into the hell of human bondage under the American law—a bill sustained, nevertheless, by the American people. Even on that day when Anthony Burns walked in chains, under the shadow of Bunker Hill, where every turf beneath your feet is a soldier's sepulchre, and where sleep the first greatest martyrs in the cause of American independence, to be tried before a magistrate, in a temple surrounded itself with chains and guarded with bayonets, and yet the people stood by and said:—"Let the law be executed until it be repealed."

Talk to me about the American people recognizing the right of any President to set aside the law. Who does not know that two years after this enactment of 1852 the terrible blasphemy was uttered in the platform of the party whose representatives to-day insist on the Executive prerogative to set aside your laws and annihilate your government, that all discussion in Congress and out of Congress, touching this very Fugitive Slave bill, should be suppressed.

The body that adopted that resolution should have remembered that there is something stronger, after all, than the resolution by mere partisans, in convention assembled. They ought to have remembered that God is not in the earthquake nor in the fire, but in the still small voice, speaking to the enlightened conscience of men, and that voice is omniponent. God allows, that for the honor of our common country, I would take the step backward and cover the nakedness and the shame of the American people in that day of American disgrace. They nominated their candidate for President, and he accepted their terms and was carried into the Presidential chair by the votes of all the States in this Union.

With such a record as that, with such a law, offensive to the judgment and conscience of the people of the United States, and of the civilized world, executed, how dare gentlemen come before the American Senate and tell us that it is the traditional policy of the American people to allow their laws to be defied by an Executive? I deny it. There is not a line in our history that does not give that denial to the assumption. It has never been done, never.

In this connection, Senators, I feel constrained to depart from the direct line of argument to notice another point that was made, in order to bolster up this assumption of executive prerogative, to suspend or dispense with the execution of a law. That is the reference made to your lamented and honored President, Abraham Lincoln. In God's name, Senators, was it not enough to be reminded in that darkest hour of your trials, when the pillars of your temple trembled in the storm of battle, of that oath which in its own simple words was registered in Heaven, and which he must have taken on the peril of his soul? Was it not enough that he kept his faith to the end, and finally laid down his life a beautiful sacrifice in the defense of the Republic and of the laws, without his name being slandered and calumniated, now that he is dead, that his tongue is mute, and that he is no longer able to speak for himself, by the bold, naked and false assertion that he violated the laws of his country.

I speak earnestly, I speak warmly, Senators, on this subject, because the man thus slandered and outraged in the presence of the Senate, and of the civilized world, was not only my own personal friend but was the friend of our common country and of our common humanity. I deny that, for a single moment, he was regardless of the obligation of his oath or of the requirements of the Constitution. I deny that he ever violated your laws. I deny that he ever assumed to himself the power claimed by this apostate President, this day, to suspend the laws and dispense with their execution. Though dead, he yet speaks from the grave, and I ask Senators, when they come to consider this accusation against their murdered President, to ponder on the words of his first inaugural, when manifestly alluding to the Fugitive Slave law, he said to the American people that however much we may dislike laws upon our statute books, we are not at liberty to defy them,

or to disregard them, or set them aside, but must await the action of the people and their repeal by the law-making power. Oh! but, say the gentlemen, he suspended the habeas corpus—the gentlemen were too learned not to know that it has been settled law from the earliest times to this hour that in the medst of arms the law is silent. You cannot suppress war by a magistrate's warrant or a constable's staff. Abraham Lincoln simply followed the accepted law of the civilized world in doing what he did.

I answer further, for I want to leave no particle unanswered, I would consider myself dishonored, being able to speak here for him when he cannot speak for himself, if I left any colorable authority for that assault on his character unanswered and unchallenged. But, say the gentlemen, you have passed your indemnity. Who is there so weak as not to know that it is in vain that you pass indemnity acts to protect the President?

If, after all, his acts were unconstitutional, you must go a step further than that. You must deny jurisdiction to the courts; you must shut the doors of your temples of justice; you must silence your ministers of the law before you pass an indemnity act that will protect them, if his act at last was unconstitutional. That was not the purpose of the act, if it was the general indemnity act that was referred to. I had the honor to draw it myself, although I claim no personal credit for it. It is not unknown in the legislation of this country or any other country.

Congress passed a similar act in 1862. The general act to which I refer was passed in 1867. That act was simply declaring that the acts of the President in the premises, and of those who were acting under the President in the premises, shall be barred prosecution against them in the courts. If it be in the power of the nation to defend itself; if it be constitutional to defend the Constitution; if it be constitutional for the President to summon the people to the defense of their own laws, of their own firesides, and of their own nationality, the law said that that should be an authority for the court to dismiss the proceeding on the ground that the act was done under order of the President.

I will not stop to argue the question. It has been argued by wager of battle, and it has been settled beyond the review of this tribunal or any tribunal, that the public safety is the highest law, and that it is part and parcel of the Constitution of the United States. I have answered, Senators, and I trust I have answered satisfactorily all that has been said by the counsel of the President, for the purpose of giving some color of justification to the monstrous plea which they have interposed for the first time in history, that it pertains to the Executive prerogative to interpret the Constitution judicially for himself, and to determine judicially the validity of every law passed by Congress, to execute or to suspend, or to dispose with its execution at his pleasure."

The court here took a recess for fifteen minutes.

After the recess Mr. BINGHAM repeated the point at which he had suspended his remarks and continued, as follows:—I beg pardon of the Senate for having forgotten to notice the very astute argument, made by the learned counsel from New York on behalf of the President, touching the broker's refusal to pay the license under the tax law by the advice of the learned counsel and who was finally protected in the courts. I may say again, that the introduction of such an argument as that was an insult to the indulgence of the American Senate.

It does not touch this question, and the man who does not understand that proposition is not fit to stand in the presence of this tribunal and argue for a moment any issue involved in this case. Nothing is more clearly settled—and I ought to ask pardon at every step for making such a reference to the Senate—nothing is more clearly settled, under the American Constitution and its interpretation, than that the citizen upon whom the law operates is authorized by the Constitution to decline compliance, without resistance, and appeal to the courts. That was the case of the New York broker to which the learned counsel referred, and desperate must be the case of his client if it stands upon any such slender defense.

Who ever heard, Senators, of that law of universal application in this country: of the right of the citizen quietly without resistance, without meditating resistance, to appeal to the courts against the oppression of the law being applied to the sworn executor of the law? The learned gentleman from New York would have given more light on this subject, if he had informed us that the collector, under your revenue law, had dared, under the letter of authority of Andrew Johnson, to set aside your Constitution, and upon his own authority, coupled with that of the chief, to defy your laws.

The questions are as wide as life and death, as light and darkness, and no further word need be said by me to the American Senate in answer to that. I may be pardoned now, Senators, for referring to other provisions of the Constitution which sustain and make clear the position which I assume as the basis of my argument, that the letter of the law passed by the people's representatives in Congress assembled includes the Executive.

I have given you already the solemn decision of the Supreme Court of the United States upon this subject, unquestioned or unchallenged from that day to this. I now turn, Senators, to a higher and more commanding authority. I refer to the supreme law of the land, ordained by the people, and for the people, in which they have settled this question between the people and the Executive beyond the reach of a colorable doubt. I refer to the provisions of the Constitution, which declared "that every bill which shall have passed the House of Representatives and the Senate, shall, before it shall become a law, be presented to the President of the United States, and if he approves he shall sign it, but if not he shall return it, with his objections, to the house in which it shall have originated, who shall enter the objections upon their journal, and proceed to reconsider it, and if after such reconsideration two-thirds of the house shall agree to pass the bill, it shall be sent, together with the objections, to the other house, by which it shall likewise be reconsidered, and if passed by two-thirds of that house it shall become a law.

If any bill shall not be returned by the President within ten days, Sundays excepted, after it shall have been presented to him, the same shall be a law in like manner as if he had signed it, unless the Congress by its adjournment prevents its return, in which case it shall not be a law. I ask the Senators to please note in this controversy between the Representatives of the people and the advocates of the President, that it is there written in the Constitution so plainly that no mortal man can gainsay it, that every bill which shall have passed the Congress of the United States, and been presented to the President, and shall receive his signature, shall be a law. And it further provides, that every bill which he shall disapprove and return to the house in which it had originated, if reconsidered and passed by the Congress of the United States, shall become a law; and that every bill which shall have passed the Congress of the United States, and shall have been presented to the President for his approval, which he shall retain for more than ten days (Sundays excepted) during the session of Congress, shall become a law.

That is the language of the Constitution. It shall be a law if he approves; it shall be a law if he disapprove it and Congress pass it over his veto it shall be a law. Says the Constitution:—If he retain a bill for more than ten days during the session of Congress, Sundays excepted, it shall be a law. It is in vain altogether—in vain against this bulwark of the Constitution that the gentlemen come in—not with their rifled ordnance, but with their small armsplaying upon it, and telling the Senate of the United States and the people of the United States, in the face of the plain words of the Constitution, that it shall not be a law.

The people meant precisely what they said, that it shall be "a law." Though the President gives ever so many reasons why, by veto, he, deemed it unconstitutional, nevertheless, if the Congress, by a two-thirds vote, pass it over his veto, it shall be a law. That is the language of the Constitution. What is their answer? Oh, it is not to be a law unless in pursuance of the Constitution. An unconstitutional law, they say, is no law. We agree to that. But the President, and that is the point in controversy here, is not the department of the government to determine that issue between the people and their representatives, and the man is inexcusable, absolutely inexcusable, who ever had the advantage of common schools and learned to read the plain text of his native vernacular, who dares to raise the issue in the plain text of the Constitution, that the President, in the face of the Constitution, is to say it shall not be a law, despite his veto, though the Constitution says expressly it shall be a law. I admit that when an enactment of Congress shall have been set aside by the constitutional authority of this country, it thenceforward ceases to be law, and the President himself may well be protected for not thereafter recognizing it as law.

I admit it. Gentlemen on that side of the chamber (Democratic) will pardon me if I make an allusion I have no disrespect to propose, in saying—I say it rather because it has been pressed into this controversy by the other side—that it was the doctrine taught by the man called the great apostle of Democracy in America, that the Supreme Court of the United States could not decide the constitutionality of a law for any department of this government; that they only decided for themselves and the suitors at their bar; and what earthly use this citation from Jefferson was intended to be put by the learned gentleman from Tennessee, who first referred to it, and by the learned Attorney-General, I cannot for the life of me, comprehend. In the light of the answer interposed here by the President, he tells you, Senators, by his answer, that he only violated the law, he only asserted this prerogative that would have cost any crowned head in Europe this day his life, that he only violated it innocently, for the purpose of taking the judgment of the Supreme Court, and here comes his learned advocate, the Attorney-General, quoting the opinion of Thomas Jefferson, to show that at least the declaration of the Supreme Court could not control at all, that it could not decide any question. I am not disposed to cast reproach upon Mr. Jefferson. I know well that he was one of the framers of the Constitution. I know well that he was one of the builders of the fabric of American liberty; one of those who worked out the emancipation of the American people from the domination of British rule, and that he deserved well of his country as one of the authors of the Declaration of Independence. Yet I know well that his opinions on that subject are not accepted at this day by the great body of the American people, and find no place in the authorities and in the writers upon the Constitution.

He was a man, doubtless, of fine philosophical mind; he was a man of noble, patriotic impulses; he rendered great service to his country, and deserved well of his country, but he is not an authoritative exponent of the principles of your country, and never was. I may be pardoned further, here, for saying in connection with this claim that is made here, right in the face of the answer of the accused that his only object in violating the law was to have the decision of the Supreme Court upon the subject, that there was another distinguished man of the Demo-

cratic party, afterwards lifted to the Presidency of the United States, who, in his place in the Senate Chamber, years ago, in the controversy about the constitutionality of the United States Bank, stated that, while he should give respectful attention to the decisions of the Supreme Court touching the constitutionality of an act of Congress, he should nevertheless, as a Senator upon his oath, not hold himself bound by it at all. That was Mr. Buchanan.

One thing is very certain, that these authorities quoted by those great men do sustain, in some sort, if it gives any support at all, the position that I have ventured to assume before this Senate, that upon all trials of impeachment presented by the House of Representatives the Senate of the United States is the highest judicial tribunal of the land, and is the exclusive judge of the law and the fact, no matter what any court may have said touching any question involved in the issue.

Allow me now, Senators, to take one step further in this argument, touching this position of the President, for I intend in every step I take to stand with the Constitution of my country, the obligations of which are upon me as a representative of the people. I refer to another provision of the Constitution, that which defines and limits the executive powers of the President.

The President shall be Commander-in-Chief of the Army and Navy of the United States, and the militia of the several States when called into the actual service of the United States. He may require the opinion in writing of the principal officers of each of the Executive departments upon any subject relating to their respective offices, and he shall have power to grant reprieves and pardons for offenses against the United States, except in cases of impeachment. He shall have power by and with the advice and consent of the Senate to make treaties, provided two-thirds of the Senators present concur, and shall nominate by and with the advice and consent of the Senate, shall appoint ambassadors, other public ministers, and Consuls, and Judges of the Supreme Court, and all other officers of the United States, whose appointments are not herein otherwise provided for, and which shall be established by law. But the Congress may, by law, vest the appointment of such inferior officers as they think proper in the President alone, in the courts of law, or in the heads of departments. The President shall have power to fill all vacancies that may happen during the recess of the Senate, by granting commissions, which shall expire at the end of their next session. He shall, from time to time, give to the Congress information of the state of the Union, and recommend to their consideration such measures as he shall judge necessary and expedient. He may, on extraordinary occasions, convene both Houses, or either of them, and in case of disagreement between them, with respect to the time of adjournment, he may adjourn them to such time as he shall think proper, &c.

These are the specific powers conferred upon the President by the Constitution. I shall have occasion hereafter in the course of this argument to take notice of that other provision which says that the executive power shall be vested in the President. This provision of the Constitution grants to the President of the United States neither legislative nor judicial power. Both of these powers—legislative and judicial—are necessarily involved in the defense which is attempted to be set up by the Executive, first, in the words of his own counsel, that he may judicially interpret the Constitution for himself and judicially determine upon the validity of every enactment of Congress; and, second, in the position assumed by himself, and for which he stands charged here at your bar as a criminal, to repeal—I use the word advisedly—to repeal by his own will and pleasure the laws enacted by the representatives of the people. This power of suspending those laws, and dispensing with their execution until such time as it may suit his pleasure to test their validity in the courts of justice, is a repeal for the time being, and, if he be sustained by the Senate, may last during his natural life, if the American people should so long tolerate him in the office of Chief Magistrate of the nation.

Why should I stop to argue the question whether such a power as this legislative and judicial may be rightfully assumed by the President of the United States under the Constitution, when that Constitution expressly declares that all legislative powers granted by it should be vested in the Congress, and that all judicial powers shall be vested in the Supreme Court, and in such inferior courts as the Congress may, by law, establish, subject, nevertheless, to the limitations and donations of power embraced in the Constitution. The assumption upon which the defense rests that he shall only execute such laws as he approves is an assumption which invests him with legislative and judicial power in direct contravention of the express words of the Constitution itself.

If the President may dispense with one act of Congress upon his own discretion, may he not in like manner dispense with every act of Congress? I ask you, Senators, whether this conclusion does not necessarily result as necessarily as effect follows efficient cause? If not, pray why not? Is the Senate of the United States, in order to shelter this great criminal, to adopt the assumption of unrestricted prerogative—the wild and guilty phantasy that "the king can do no wrong," and thereby clothe the Executive of the American people with power to suspend and dispense with the execution of their laws at his pleasure; to interpret their Constitution for himself, and thereby inherit their government.

Senators, I have endeavored to open this question before you in its magnitude. I trust that I have succeeded. Be assured of one thing—that according to the best of my ability, in the presence of the representatives of the nation, I have not been unmindful of my oath; and I beg leave to say to you, Senators, in all candor, this day, that in my judgment no question of mightier import was ever before presented to the American Senate, and to say further, that no question of greater magnitude ever can come by possibility before the American Senate, or any question upon the decision of which graver interests necessarily depend.

In considering, Senators, this great question of the power of the President, by virtue of his executive authority, to suspend the laws and dispense with their execution, I pray you consider that the Constitution of your country, essential to your national life, cannot exist without legislation, duly enacted by the representatives of the people in Congress assembled, and duly executed by their chosen Chief Magistrate. Courts, neither supreme nor inferior, can exist without legislation.

Is the Senate to be told that the department of the government essential to the peace of the republic, essential to the general administration of justice between man and man, those ministers of justice, who, in the simple oath of the purer days of the republic, were sworn to do equal justice between the poor and the rich, shall not administer justice at all, if perchance the President of the United States may choose when Congress comes to enact a law for the organization of the judiciary, and pass it despite his objection to the contrary in accordance with the Constitution, by a two-third vote, to declare that, according to his judgment and convictions, it violates the Constitution of the country, and, therefore, it shall not be put into execution?

Senators, if he has the power to sit in jugment judicially' and I use the words of his advocate, upon the Tenure of Office act of 1867, he has like power to sit in judgment judicially upon every other act of Congress. I would like to know, in the event of the President of the United States interfering with the execution of the Judiciary act, whereby, for the first time, if you please, in your history, or for the second time, if you please, by some strange intervention of Providence, by which the existing judges have perished from the earth, I would like to know what becomes of this wicked and bold pretense, unfit to be played upon children, that the President only violated the law innocently to have the question decided in the courts, and he has the power to prevent any court sitting in judgment upon it. Representatives to the Congress of the United States cannot be chosen without legislation:—First. The legislation of Congress appertaining to representation among the several States according to the whole number of representative population in each.]

Second. The enactment either by Congress or by the legislatures of the several States, fixing the time, place and manner of holding the elections. Is it possible that the President of the United States, in the event of such legislation by Congress, clearly authorized by the very terms of the Constitution, and essential to the very existence of the governmnnt, is permitted, in the exercise of his judicial executive, authority to sit down in judgment upon your Constitution and say that it shall not be executed?

Why, this power, given by the Constitution to the Congress, to prescribe the time, place and manner of holding elections for representatives in Congress, in the several States, was, in the words of the framers of the Constitution, to enable the people, through the National Legislature, to perpetuate the legislative department of this government, and we are to be told here, and we are to deliberate upon it from day to day, and from week to week, that the President is by virtue of his executive office, his executive prerogative, clothed with the authority to determine the validity of your law, to suspend it and dispense with its execution at his pleasure, Again, a President of the United States, to execute the laws of the people, enacted by their Represensatives in Congress assembled, cannot be chosen without legislation. Are we to be told the President at every step is vested with authority to dispense with the execution of the laws and to suspend with its operation until he can have a decision, if you please, in the courts of justice?

If the President may set aside the laws and suspend their action at pleasure, it results that he may annul the Constitution and annihilate the government. That is the issue before the American Senate. I do not go outside of the President's answer to establish it. The Constitution itself, according to this assumption, is at his mercy, as well as the laws, and the people of the United States are to stand by and to be mocked and derided in their own Capital, when, in accordance with the express provisions of their Constitution, they bring him to the bar of the Senate to answer for his great crime, than which none greater was ever committed since that day when the first crime was committed on this planet, as it sprung from the hand of its Creator, that crime which covered one man's brow with the ashy paleness of death, and covered the brow of another man with the damning blotch of fratricide. The people of the United States are not to be answered at this bar. It is in vain that they have put into the hands of their representatives the power to impeach such a malefactor, and by the express words of their Constitution have given to the Senate the power, the exclusive power, the sole power, to try him for his high crimes and misdemeanors.

The question touches the nation's life, but I know, Senators, that your matchless Constitution of the government, the hope of the struggling friends of liberty in all lands, and for the perpetuity and triumph of which millions of hands are lifted this day in prayer to the God of nations, can no more exist without laws duly enacted by the law-making power, than can the people of the United States themselves exist without air or without that light of Heaven which shines above us, filled with the light and breath of the Almighty. A Constitution and laws which are not and cannot be enforced, are dead.

The vital principle of your Constitution and laws is that they shall be the supreme law of the land—supreme in every State, supreme in every territory, supreme in every rood, supreme on every deck covered with your flag, in every zone of the globe; and yet we are debating here today whether a man whose breath is in his nostrils, a mere servant of the people, may not suspend the execution both of the Constitution and of the law at his pleasure, and defy the power of the people.

If I am right in the proposition that the acts of Congress are law, and are to be executed until repealed or reversed in the mode prescribed by the Constitution, in the courts of the United States, acting within their jurisdiction and under the limitations of the Constitution, it results that the violation of such acts by the President of the United States and his refusal to execute them, is a high crime and misdemeanor within the terms of the Constitution, for which he is impeachable, and for which, if he be guilty, he ought to be convicted and removed from the office which he has dishonored. It is not needful to inquire whether only crimes and misdemeanors, specially made such by the Constitution of the United States, are impeachable, because by the laws of the United States all crimes and misdemeanors at common law, committed within the District of Columbia, are made indictable.

I believe it is conceded on every hand that a crime or misdemeanor made indictable by the laws of the United States, when committed by an officer of the United States, in his office, after violation of his sworn duty, is a high crime and misdemeanor, within the meaning of the Constitution. At all events, if that be not accepted as a true and self-evident proposition by the Senate, it would be in vain that I should argue further, for I might as well expect to kindle life under the throes of death as to persuade a Senate so lost to every sense of duty, and to the voice of freedom itself, as to come to the conclusion that after all it is not a high crime and misdemeanor, under the Constitution, for the President of the United States, deliberately and purposely, in violation of his oath, in violation of the plain letter of the Constitution that he should take care that the laws should be faithfully executed, to set aside the laws, and to declare defiantly that he will not execute them.

Mr. BINGHAM in this connection referred to the act of 1801 extending the common law of Maryland to the District of Columbia, and argued from it, and from the opinion of the court in the Kendall case, that the President's acts were indictable in the District, and that being indictable they must therefore be impeachable. He then continued:—I do not propose, Senators, to waste words in noticing what but for the respect I bear to the learned counsel from Massachusetts (Mr. Curtis) I would call the mere lawyers' quibble of the defense, that even if the President be guilty of the crimes laid to his charge in the articles presented by the House of Representatives, still they are not high crimes and misdemeanors within the meaning of the Constitution, because they are not kindred to the great crimes of treason and bribery.

It is enough, Senators, for me to remind you of what I have already said, that they are crimes which touch the life of the nation, which touch the stability of our institutions; that they are crimes which, if tolerated by this the highest tribunal of the land, would vest the President, by its solemn judgment, with a power under the Constitution to suspend, at his pleasure, all laws upon your statute books, and thereby to annihilate your government. They have heretofore been held crimes in history, and crimes of such magnitude, that they have cost their perpetrators their lives; not merely their offices, but their lives.

Of that I may have more to say hereafter, but I return to my proposition, the defense of the President is not whether indictable crimes or offenses are laid to his charge, but it rests upon the broad proposition, as already stated, that impeachment does not lay against him for any violation of the Constitution or of the laws, because of his asserted constitutional right judicially to intepret every provision of the Constitution for himself, and also to interpret for himself the validity of every law, and to exclude or disregard, at his election, any provision either of the Constitution or of the law, and especially if he declares at the fact or after the fact, that his only purpose in violating the one or the other, is to have a true construction of the Constitution in the one case, and a judicial determination of the validity of the other in the courts of the United States.

I do not state this, as the position of the President, too strongly, although I pray Senators to notice, for I would account myself a dishonorable man, if purposely, here or elsewhere, I should misrepresent the position assumed by the President that the counsel for the defense, Mr. Curtis, in his opening, attempts to gainsay the statement as I have just made it, that the defense of the President rests upon the assumption as stated in his answer.

Mr. Curtis, in his opening address says:—"But when, Senators, a question arises whether a particular law has cut off a power confided to him by the people through the Constitution, and he alone can raise that question, and he alone can cause a judicial decision to come between the two branches of the government, to say which of them is right, and after due deliberation, with advice of those who are his proper advisers, he settles down firmly upon the opinion that such is the character of the law, it remains to be settled by you whether there is any violation of his duty when he takes the needful steps to raise that question and have it peacefully decided."

Now, I ask, Senators, in all candor, what there is to hinder the President, if by force of the Constitution, as the learned counsel argues, he is vested with judicial authority to interpret the Constitution and to decide on the validity of any law of Congress, what there is to hinder him to say of every law of the land that it cut off some power confided to him by the people. The learned gentleman from Massachusetts was too self-raised, and he is manifestly too profound a man to launch ont on this wild stormy sea of anarchy, careless of all success, in the manner in which some of his associates did. You may remember, and I give it only from memory, but it is burned into my brain and will only perish with my life, you will remember the utterances of the gentleman from New York (Mr. Evarts), who was not so careful of his words, when he stood before you and said, in the progress of his argument, that the Constitution of the United States had invested the President with the power to guard the people's rights against Congressional usurpation.

You recollect that as he kindled in his argument, he ventured on the further assertion, in the presence of the Senate of the United States, that if you dared to decide against the President on this issue, the question would be raised by the people under the banner of the supremacy of the Constitution in defense of the President, and of the supremacy or authority of Congress on the other side. The supremacy of the Constitution is to be the sign under which the President shall conquer against the unlimited authority of Congress to bind him, by laws enacted by themselves in the modes prescribed by the Constitution.

Senators, I may be pardoned for summoning the learned counsel from Massachusetts, Mr. Curtis, as a witness against the assumption of his client, and against the assumption of his associate counsel touching this power of the President to dispense with the execution of the law. In 1862 there was a pamphlet published, bearing the name of the learned gentleman from Massachusetts, touching limitations on the executive power, and I will read an extract or two from that pamphlet to show the difference between the current of a learned man's thoughts when he speaks for the people according to his own convictions and a similar man when he speaks under a retainer.

His pamphlet is addressed "to all persons who have sworn to support the Constitution, and to all citizens who guard the principles of civil liberty, which that Constitution embodies, and for the preservation of which it is our only security, these speeches are respectfully dedicated. Benjamin W. Curtis." The President, he says, is "the Commander-in-Chief of the Army and Navy, not only by force of the Constitution, by under and subject to the Constitution, and to certain restrictions therein contained, and to every law enacted by its authority as completely and clearly as the private in the ranks.

"He is General-in-Chief, but can a General-in-Chief disobey any law of his own authority? When he can, he superadds to his right as commander the power of being a judge, and that is military despotism. The mere authority to command an army is not an authority to disobey the laws of the country. Besides, all the powers of the President are executive merely, He cannot make a law, he cannot repeal one; he can only execute a law; he can neither make, nor suspend, nor alter it; he cannot even make an inquiry."

That is good law; not good law exactly in the midst of the Rebellion, but it is good law enough under the Constitution—in the light of the interpretation given to it by that great man, Mr. John Quincy Adams, whom I have before cited—when the limitations of the Constitution are in operation, and when the land is covered with the serene light of peace; whenever a human being, citizen or stranger, within our gates is under the shadow of the Constitution. It is the law and nothing but the law, that the claim on the part of the Executive to suspend, at his discretion, all the laws on your statute book, and to dispense with their execution, is the defense, and the whole defense of the President seems to me clear, clear as that light in which we live, and so clear, that whatever may be the decision of this tribunal, that will be the judgment of the American people.

It cannot be otherwise. It is written in this answer; it is written in the arguments of his counsel, and no mortal man can evade it. It is all that there is of it, and to establish this assertion that it is all there is of it, I ask Senators, to consider what articles the President has denied. Not one. I ask the Senate to consider what offense charged against him in the articles presented by the House of Representatives, he has not openly by his answer confessed, or what charge is not clearly re-established by the proof. Not one.

Who can doubt that when the Senate was in session, the President in direct violation of the express requirement of the law, which, in the language of the honorable Chief Justice, in the Mississippi case, left no discretion in him, but enjoined a special duty upon him, did purposely, deliberately violate the law and defied its authority, in that he issued an order for the removal of the Secretary of War, and issued a letter of authority for the appointment of a successor, the Senate being in session and not consulted in the premises.

The order and the letter of authority are written witnesses of all the guilt of the accused. They are confessions of reference, and there is no escape from them. This order is a clear violation of the Tenure of Office act. The President is manifestly guilty in manner and form, as he stands charged in the first, second, third, eighth and eleventh articles of impeachment, and no man can deny it except a man who accepts as the law's assumption in his answer, that it is an executive prerogative, judicially, to interpret the Constitution, and to set aside, to violate and to defy the law when it vests no discretion in him whatever, and to challenge the people to bring him to trial and punishment.

Senators, on this question, at the magnitude and character of the offenses charged against the President, I may be permitted, inasmuch as the gentleman from New York referred to it, to ask your attention to what was ruled and settled, and I think well settled, on the trial of Judge Peck. The counsel took occasion to quote a certain statement from the record of that trial, and took especial pains to evade in their statement of what was actually settled by it. I choose to have the whole of the precedent. If the gentleman insists on the law in that case, I insist on all its forms and on all its provisions. In the trial of the Peck case Mr. Buchanan, speaking for the managers on the part of the House of Representatives, made the statement that an impeachable violation of law could consist in the abuse as well as in the usurpation of authority; and if you look carefully through that record, you will find none of the learned counsel who appeared in behalf of Judge Peck questioning for a moment the correctness of the proposition.

I think it capable of the clearest demonstration that that is the rule which ought to govern the decision in this case, inasmuch as all the offenses charged were committed within this district, and as I have already shown, are indictable. It is conceded that there is a partial exception to this rule. A judge cannot be held accountable for an error of judgment, however erroneous his judgment may be, unless fraud be asserted and proved.

No such rule ever was held to apply to an executive officer. That is an exception running through all the law in favor of judicial officers. A mere executive officer, clothed with no judicial authority, would be guilty of usurpation without fraud. An error of judgment would not excuse an executive officer. I refer to the general rule of law, as stated by Sedgwick in his work upon statutory and constitutional law, in which he says:—"Good faith is no excuse for the violation of a statute. Ignorance of the law cannot be set up in defense, and this rule holds good in civil as well as in criminal cases."

The gentleman from New York, Mr. Evarts, entered upon a wonderful adventure here when he undertook to tell the Senate that that rule which holds the violator of law answerable, and necessarily implies a guilty purpose, applies to offenses which are *mala in se*. The gentleman should have known when he made that utterance that the highest writer on law in America, a man second to no writer on law in the English tongue in any country, has truly recorded in his great commentaries on the law that the distinction between *mala prohibita* and *mala in se*, has been long ago exploded, and that the same rule applies to the one as to the other. I refer to 1 Kent's Commentaries, p. 529, and really I cannot see why it should not be so, and I doubt very much whether it is within the compass of the mind of any Senator to see why it should not be so.

Mr. Bingham went on to argue that the limitation of six months within which an office must be filled would be evaded if the President were allowed to make an *ad interim* nomination, and at the end of six months make another *ad interim* nomination, and so on to the end of his term of office.

He then continued—But it has been further stated here by the counsel for the defense, by way of illustration and answer, suppose the Congress of the United States should enact a law, in clear violation of the express power conferred in the Constitution, as for example, a law declaring that the President shall not be Commander-in-Chief of the Army, or a law declaring that he shall not exercise the pardoning power in any case whatever, is not the President of the United States to intervene to protect the Constitution? I say, no! The President is not to intervene and protect the Constitution.

The people of the United States are the guardians of their own Constitution; and if there be one thing in that Constitution more clearly written and more firmly established than another, it is the express and clear provision that the Legislative Department of the government is responsible to no power on earth for the exercise of its legislative authority and for the discharge of its duty save the people.

It is a new doctrine altogether, that the Constitution is exclusively in the keeping of the President. When that day comes, Senators, that the Constitution of this country, so essential to your national existence, and so essential to the peace, happiness and prosperity of the people, rests exclusively on the fidelity and patriotism, and integrity of Andrew Johnson, may God save the Constitution, and save the Republic. (Laughter.) No, sir, there is no such power vested in the President of the United States. It is only coming back to the old proposition. But, say the gentleman, certainly it would be unconstitutional for Congress so to legislate. Agreed; I admit that it would be not only unconstitutional, but that it would be criminal.

But the question is, before what tribunal is the Congress to answer? Only before the tribunal of the people. Admit that Congress passed such a law corruptly, and yet every one at all conversant with the Constitution of the country, knows well that it is written in that instrument that the members of Congress shall not be held to answer in any place, or before any body whatever, for their official acts in Congress assembled, save before their constituents. That is the end of it. They answer to the people, and the people alone can apply the remedy.

You cannot answer in the courts, and, of course, when a majority votes that way in each House you cannot expect very well to expel them. Their only responsibility is to the people; the people alone have the right to challenge them. That is precisely what the people have written in the Constitution, and every man in the country so understands that proposition.

I might make another remark which shows the utter fallacy of any such proposition as that contended for by the counsel for the President, and that is that if Congress were so lost to all sense of justice and duty as to take away the pardoning power from the President, it would have it in its power to take away all right of appeal to the courts of the United States on that question, so that there would be an end of it, and there would be no remedy but with the people, except indeed the President is to take up arms and set aside the laws of Congress.

Having disposed of this proposition, the next inquiry to be considered by the Senate, and to which I desire to direct your attention is, that of the power of the President under the Constitution to remove the heads of the departments, and to fill the vacancies so created during the session of the Senate of the United States, without its consent and against the express authority of law.

At this stage of his argument, Mr. Bingham yielded to a motion to adjourn, and the court, at ten minutes before four o'clock adjourned.

PROCEEDINGS OF TUESDAY, MAY 5.

When the Senate was called to order, Mr. CAMERON moved that the members of the National Medical Association be admitted to places in the gallery. In reply to a question of Mr. Morrill, of Vermont, he said there were about two hundred of them.

Senator DRAKE opposed the motion, saying that Senators and Representatives could furnish them tickets, and thus avoid thronging the galleries.

After some further talk the motion was lost, and the chair was vacated for the Chief Justice.

Mr. Bingham Resumes.

The court having been opened in due form Mr. Bingham proceeded with his argument.

In his opening remarks, indistinctly heard, he was understood to repeat the view taken by him yesterday, that no man, in office or out of office, is above the law, but that all persons are bound to obey it; that the President, above all others, is bound to take care that the laws be faithfully executed, and that the suspending and dispensing power asserted by the President is a violation of the rights of the people, and cannot for a moment be allowed.

Mr. BINGHAM continued as follows:—

When I had the honor to close my remarks yesterday, I called the attention of the Senators to this proposition:— That their inquiries were to be directed, first, to the question whether the President has power, under the Constitution, to remove the heads of departments and to fill the vacancies so created by himself, during the session of the Senate, in the absence of express authority, or law authorizing him so to do? If the President has not the power, he is confessedly guilty, as charged in the first, second, third, eighth and eleventh articles, unless, indeed, the Senate is to come to the conclusion that it is no crime in the President of the United States, deliberately and purposely, and defiantly, to violate the express letter of the Constitution of the United States, and the express prohibition of the law of Congress.

I have said that the act was criminal, for it was done deliberately, purposely and defiantly. What answer has been made to this, Senators? The allegation that the violation of law charged in these articles was not with criminal intent, and the learned counsel stood here, from hour to hour, and from day to day, to show that the criminal intent is to be proved. I deny it. I deny that there is any authority which justified any such assumption. The law declares, and has declared for centuries, that any act done deliberately in violation of law, that is to say, any unlawful act done by any person of sound mind and understanding, responsible for acts, necessarily implies that the party doing it intended the necessary consequences of his own act. I make no apology, Senators, for the insertion of the word "intent" in the articles.

It is a surplusage, and is not needful, but I make no apology for it. It is found in every indictment. Who ever heard of a court where the rules are applied with more strictness than they can be expected to be applied in the Senate of the United States? Who ever heard of a court demanding of the prosecution in any instance whatever that he should offer testimony of the criminal

intent specially averred in the indictment, when he had proved that the act was done, and that the act was unlawful? It is a rule not to be challenged here or elsewhere among intelligent men, that every person, whether in office or out of office, who does an unlawful act, made criminal by the very terms of the statutes of the country in which he lives, and to the jurisdiction of which he is subject, intends all that is involved in the doing of the act, and the intent, therefore, is already established.

No proof is required. Why to require it would simply defeat the ends of justice. Who is able to penetrate the human intellect, to spy into its secret and hidden recesses in the brain or heart of man, and there witness that which it meditates and which it purposes? Men, intelligent men, and especially the ministers of justice, judge of men's purposes by their acts, and necessarily hold that they intend exactly that which they do, and then it is for them—not for their accusers—to show that they do it without intention; to show that they did it under a temporary delirium of the intellect, by which in the providence of God they were for the time being deprived of the power of knowing their duty, and of doing their duty under the law.

Senators, on a remarkable occasion, not unlike that which to-day attracts the attention of the people of the United States, and attracts the attention of the people of the civilized world, the same question was raised before the tribunal of the people, whether intent was to be established, and one of those men on that occasion when Strafford knelt before the assembled majesty of England, arose in his place, and answered that question in words so clear and strong that they ought to satisfy the judgment and satisfy the conscience of every Senator. I read the works of Pym on the trial of Strafford as to the intent.

"Another excuse," says Pym, "is this—that whatsoever he hath spoken was out of good intention. Sometimes, my lords, good and evil, truth and falsehood, lie so near together, that they are hardly to be distinguished. Matters fraught with danger may be accompanied with such circumstances as may make them appear useful and convenient, and in all such cases good intentions will justify evil consequences. But where matters are evil in their own nature, such as the matters are wherewith the Earl of Strafford is charged, breaking the public faith and subverting laws and government, they can never be justified by any intention of good, of whichsoever they may be pretended."

Is there no endeavor here to break public faith? Is there no endeavor here to subvert laws and government? I leave Senators to answer that question upon their own consciences and upon their oaths. On this subject of intent, I might illustrate the utter futility of the position assumed here by the learned counsel, but I will refer to a notable instance in history where certain fanatics in the reign of Frederic II put little children to death with the intent of sending them to heaven, because the Master had written "of such is the Kingdom of Heaven." It does not appear that there was any intention of staying the innocents, with their sunny voices and sunny hearts, but that they could send them at once to heaven was of no avail in the courts of justice.

I read also of a Swedish Minister who found within the kingdom certain subjects who were the beneficiaries of charity, upon whose heads Time's frosty fingers had scattered the snows of five and seventy winters, whom he put brutally and cruelly to death with the good intent of thereby increasing the charity in the interest of the living with a longer measure of years before them. I never read, Senators, that any such plea as that availed in the courts of justice against the charge of murder with malice aforethought. It is a puerile conceit, unfit to be uttered in the hearing of Senators, and condemned by every letter and line and word of the common law, "the growth of centuries, the gathered wisdom of a thousand years."

It is suggested by one of my colleagues, and it is not unfit that I should notice it in passing, that, doubtless, Booth on the 14th day of February, 1865, when he sent the pure spirit of your martyred President back to the God who gave it, declared—declared is the proper word, because the case here rests upon declarations—declared that he did that act in the service of his country—in the service of liberty—in the service of law—in the service of a common humanity. If the avenging hand of justice had not cut him off upon the spot where he stood, instantly, as though overtaken by the direct judgment of offended humanity, I suppose that he would have had this sort of argument interposed in his behalf, that his intentions were good, and therefore the violated law itself ought to justify the act, and allow him to depart, not a condemned criminal, but a crowned and honored man.

I really feel, Senators, that I ought to ask your pardon for having dwelt at all upon this proposition, but you know with what pertinacity it has been pressed upon the consideration of the Senate, and with all respect to the learned and accomplished gentleman who made it, I feel it due to myself to say here that I think it was unworthy of them, and unworthy of the place. Again I ask you, Senators, has the President this power under the Constitution and the laws during the session of the Senate to create vacancies in the heads of departments, under your Constitution, and fill them without the authority of an express law, without the advice and consent of the Senate? If he has not, he has violated the Constitution, he has violated, as I shall show you hereafter, the express law of the land, and is, therefore, criminal. Criminal in his conduct and in his intention before this tribunal, where he stands by the order of the people.

First, then, is this violation by the act of removal and appointment, and, here, Senators, although I shall have occasion to notice it more specially hereafter, I ask to be excused for referring at this time to the fact that it cannot have escaped your notice that the learned and astute counsel of the President took care all the time, just from the beginning to the end of this controversy, not to connect together the power of removal and the appointment during the session of the Senate. Every word in the voluminous argument of the learned and ingenuous counsel for the President bears witness to the truth of what I now assert, that the appointing power is, by the express terms of the Constitution, during the session of the Senate put beyond the power of the President, save and except when it is expressly authorized by law.

I thank the gentlemen for making this concession, at least, to the Senate, for it is a confession of guilt on the part of their client. When no answer can be made they act on the ancient time-honored and accepted maxims, that "silence is golden," and so on that point they were silent on, and all without exception. There was an appointment made here, in direct violation of the express law; in direct violation of the express letter of the Constitution; in direct violation of every interpretation ever put upon it by any commanding intellect in this country, and the gentlemen know it.

It is in vain, Senators, that they undertake to meet that point in this case by any reference to the speech of my learned and accomplished friend who represents the State of Ohio in this Senate (Mr. Sherman). Not a word escaped his lips in the speech which they have quoted, touching the power of appointment, during that session of the Senate, and in direct violation of the express letter of the Tenure of Office act; nor did any such words es- escape from the lips of any Senator. I am not surprised; it is a credit to the intellectual ability of the learned and accomplished counsel who appear for the President, that they kept that question out of sight in their elaborate and exhaustive arguments.

I read now, Senators, from the provision of the Constitution on this subject. "He shall have power by and with the advice and consent of the Senate to make treaties, provided two-thirds of the Senators present concur; and he shall nominate, and with the advice and consent of the Senate shall appoint ambassadors and other public ministers and consuls, Judges of the Supreme Court and all officers of the United States whose appointments are not herein expressly provided for, and which shall be established by law: but the Congress may by law vest the appointment of such inferior officers, as they think proper, in the President alone, in the courts of law, or in the heads of departments."

Can any one doubt that this provision clearly restricts the power of the President in the appointment of heads of departments—in this, that it expressly requires that all appointments not otherwise provided for in the Constitution, enumerating ambassadors and others, shall be by and with the advice and consent of the Senate. It is useless to waste words with the proposition, it is so plain and clear. It must be so unless the appointments of heads of departments are otherwise provided for in the Constitution, and I respectfully ask Senators wherein are they otherwise provided for? The heads of departments are named by that title, and it is provided by the very terms of the Constitution, that Congress may, by law, vest in the heads of departments the power to appoint, without the consent of anybody but the authority of the laws of Congress, all the inferior officers. Can anybody, in light of that provision, stand before this Senate and argue that the heads of departments are inferior officers.

If, then, their appointment is not otherwise provided for by law, whether it was ever otherwise provided by law, I am not unmindful of the fact that some of the learned counsel for the President have said that there was no appointment, that this was only an authority to fill a vacancy. The counsel are not strong enough for their client. They cannot get rid of his answer. He declares that he did make an appointment, that he made a removal and filled a vacancy—an appointment *ad interim* more than once escaped the lips of counsel. I do not, however, propose to rest this case upon any quibble, or any technicality, or any controversy about words.

I rest it on the broad spirit of the Constitution, and I stand here this day to deny that there was ever an hour since the Constitution went into operation, that the President of the United States had authority to authorize anybody, even temporarily, to exercise the functions of the head of a department save by the authority of express law. It certainly is a self-evident proposition which must be understood by Senators, that that power which created the law may repeal it.

I make this here and now, because the President's defense is stated more clearly in his answer, and more distinctly than in any of the arguments of the learned counsel, which is that he asserts and exercises this power by virtue of the implied executive prerogative judicially to interpret the Constitution for himself, and judicially to determine the validity of all the laws of the land for himself, and, therefore, to appoint just such ministers as he pleases and for such period as he pleases, in defiance alike of Constitution and of the law. The language of his answer is that he indefinitely vacated the office.

I read a paragraph from the President's answer on this point:—And this respondent further answering, says that it is provided in and by the second section of an act to regulate the tenure of certain civil offices, that the President may suspend the officer from the performance of the duties of the office held by him, for certain causes therein designated, until the next meeting of the Senate, and until the case shall be acted upon by the Senate; that this respondent, as President of the United States, was advised, and he verily believed and he still believes, that the executive power of removal from office confided to him by the Constitution, as aforesaid, includes the power of suspension from office, at the pleasure of the President; and this respondent, by the order aforesaid, did suspend the Secretary of War, Edwin M. Stanton, from office, not until the next meeting of the Senate, or until the Senate should have acted upon the case, but by force of the power and authority vested in him by the Constitution and laws of the United States indefinetely and at the pleasure of the President, and the order in form aforesaid was made known to the Senate of the United States on the 12th day of December, A. D. 1867, as will be more fully hereinafter stated, that in his answer he claims this power under the Constitution. On that subject, Senators, I beg leave to say in addition to what I have already uttered, that it was perfectly well understood when the Constitution was on trial for its deliverance before the American people, that no such power as this was lodged in the President of the United States. On the contrary, that for every abuse, that for every usurpation of authority, that for every violation of the laws, he was liable at all times to the unrestricted power of the people to impeach him through their Representatives, and to try him before their Senate without let or hindrance from any tribunal in the land. I refer to the clear utterances of Mr. Hamilton, as recorded in his seventy seventh letter to the *Federalist*.

Mr. BINGHAM having read the extract referred to, continued:—I agree with Mr. Hamilton that it is an absurdity, indeed, after what has been written in the Constitution, for any man, whatever may be his attainments and whatever may he his pretensions, to say that the President has the power, in the language of his answer, of indefinitely vacating the executive offices of the country, and, therefore, of indefinitely filliing them without the advice and consent of the Senate, in the absence of an express law so to do. Here I leave that point for the consideration of the Senate, and for the consideration of that great people whom the Senate represent on this trial.

I also ask the judgment of the Senate on the weighty words of Webster, who the counsel for the President conceded is entitled to some consideration in this body which he illustrated for long years, American institutions, by his wisdom, his genius and his learning—a man who while having stood alone among living men by reason of his intellectual stature, a man who when dead sleeps alone in his tomb by the surrounded sea, meet emblem of the majesty and sweep of his matchless intellect. I ask the attention of Senators to the words of Mr. Webster on this appointing power conferred upon the President under the Constitution by and with the advice and consent of the Senate. "The appointing power," said Mr. Webster, "is vested in the President and Senate."

This is the general rule of the Constitution. The removing power is part of the appointing power. It cannot be separated from the rest but by supposing that an exception was intended, but all exceptions to general rules are to be taken strictly, even when expressed; and, for a much stronger reason, they are not to be employed when not expressed, unless the inevitable necessity of construction requires it. What answer, I pray you, Senators, has been given; what answer can be given to this interpretation by Hamilton and Webster? None, except a reference to the acts of 1789 and 1795 and to the opinions expressed in the debates of the first Congress.

Neither of these acts, nor the debates, justify the conclusion that the President, during the session of the Senate, may vacate and fill the executive departments of the government at pleasure. The acts, themselves, will bear no such interpretation. I dismiss, with a single word, all reference to the debate on the occasion, for the Senate is not unadvised that there were differences of opinion expressed in that debate. Nor is the Senate unadvised that it has been ruled by the Supreme Court of the United States that opinions expressed by Representatives or Senators in debate in Congress, pending the discussion of any bill, are not to be received as any apology of instruction or interpretation whatever to be given to the act.

It would be a sad day for the American people if the time should ever come when utterances in an excited debate are to be received as the true construction and interpretation of law. Look to the act, Senators, and say whether gentlemen are justified in attempting to quote either from the Legislature of 1789, or from the Legislature of 1795, or from any other Legislature, that at any time there existed upon the statute books of the country, this executive prerogative in direct violation of the express letter of the Constitution, to vacate all the executive offices of the government at his pleasure, and to fill them during the session of the Senate, and thereby to control all the patronage of the government, amounting to millions of dollars, at his pleasure, and to put it into the hands of irresponsible agents to become only the subtle tools of his mad ambition.

I admit that, during the session of the Senate, such a statute should be always on the statute books. So long as you have a President who cannot be trusted, the man who betrays his trust ought to be suspended from his office by a temporary removal, for reasons appearing to the President to justify it. That is precisely the law to-day. What one of the President's counsel ventured to say here, that the President of the United States at any time had power during the session of the Senate to vacate the offices of the head of a department, even under the act of 1789, and to fill the office indefinitely at his pleasure. What practice of government was cited here to support any such pretension of power in the Executive? None whatever. To be sure, reference was made to the case of Pickering, but the gentleman ought to remember that that was expressly authorized by the act of 1789.

It does not follow by any means that because this power of removal was exercised by the elder Adams, that he thereby furnished a precedent in justification of the violation of another and a different statute, which, by every intendment, repealed the act of 1789, and stripped the President of any colorable excuse for exercising any such authority. That is my first answer to the points made by the counsel, and my still further answer to it, is that the elder Adams himself, as his letter to the Secretary of State clearly discloses, did not consider it proper even under the law of 1789 for him to make a removal during a session of the Senate, and, therefore, those significant words are incorporated in his letter requesting Secretary Pickering that he should resign before the session of the Senate, so that on the incoming of the Senate he might name his successor, showing exactly how he understood his obligations under the Constitution.

Although the reference, so far as anybody has been able to see to trace it, is somewhat imperfect, I deem it but just to the memory of that distinguished statesman to say that the whole transaction justifies me in asserting here that Mr. Adams did dot issue the order for the removal of Mr. Pickering after the Senate had commenced its session. It is true that he issued it on the same day, but he did not ssue it after the Senate had commenced its session; and on the next day John Marshall was confirmed as Secretary of State, and succeeded Timothy Pickering, removed by the advice and consent of the Senate. Nor does it appear that John Marshall exercised the functions of his office, or attempted to exercise the functions of the office until the Senate had passed upon the question of his appointment, and had therefore necessarily passed upon the question of Mr Pickering's removal.

All the facts that arose in the case of the removal of Pickering, go to disprove everything that has been said here by way of apology, or justification, or even excuse for the action of the President of the United States, in violating the Constitution and the existing laws of the country. But the other provision of the Constitution, which I recited yesterday, pour a flood of light on this question, of the power of the President to vacate executive offices, and to fill them at his pleasure, and dispels the mist with which the subtleness of counsel have attempted to envelop it. That is the provision, that the President shall have power to fill up all vancancies that may happen during the the recess of the Senate, and to issue commissions to his appointees, which commissions shall expire at the end of the next session.

Now, I ask, Senators, what possible sense is there in this express provision of the Constitution if, after all, as is claimed by the President in his answer, he is invested by the Constitution with power to make vacancies at his pleasure, even during the session of the Senate. I ask, Senators, further, to answer what sense is there in the provisions that the commissions which he shall issue to fill vacancies happening during the recess shall expire at at the end of the next session, if, after all, notwithstanding this limitation in the Constitution, the President may, during the session, create vacancies and fill them indenitely.

If he has any such power as that, I must be allowed to say in the words of John Marshall, "Your Constitution at last is but a splendid bauble. It is not worth the paper on which it is written." It is a matter of mathematical demonstration from the text of that instrument, that is, the President's power to fill vacancies is limited to vacancies which may arise during a recess of the Senate, save where it is otherwise provided for by the express law. That is my answer to all that has been said here by gentlemen on that subject. They have brought here a long list of appointments and of removals from the foundation of the government to t is hour, which is answered by a single word, that there was an existing law authorizing it all, and that that law no longer exists.

This provision of the Constitution necessarily means what it declares—that the President's power of appointment, in the absence of every express law, is limited to such vacancies as may happen during the recess of the Senate; and it necessarily results that the appointment of the head of a department, made during the session of the Senate without the advice and consent of the Senate, had to be made temporarily, or otherwise it must be a commission, according to the President's own claim of authority, arising under this unlimited executive prerogative, which can never expire but by and with his consent. If anybody can answer that proposition, I should like to have an answer now.

If, notwithstanding all that is on your statute books; if, notwithstanding this limitation of the Constitution, that his commission to fill vacancies arising during the recess shall expire at the end of the next session, he may, nevertheless, make vacancies, and fill them, then, I say, that such commission cannot expire without the consent of the Executive. If that proposition can be answered by any one I desire it to be answered now. I want to know by what provision of the Constitution the commission would expire on the plane of this? I want to know by what provision of law they would expire on the plane of this? Answer. And if they do not expire, without the consent of the Executive, I want to know what becomes of the appointing power, lodged jointly in the Senate, with the Executive, for the protection of the peoples' rights and the protection of the peoples' interests?

It cannot be answered here or anywhere by a retained advocate of the President, or by a volunteer advocate of the President, in the Senate or out of the Senate; nor shall I demand to know again what provision of the Constitution under the claim set up in the President's answer, terminates the commission. I took occasion to read from the answer that I might not be misunderstood. The President puts his claim of power directly on the Constitution. Nobody is to be held responsible for that assumption, but this guilty and accused President. It was an authority the like of which has no parallel in centuries, for him to come before the custodians of the peoples' power and defy even their written Constitution, in its plainest sense and its plainest letter. I have endeavored, Senators, and I have thought over the subject carefully, considerately and conscientiously, to find out any where in the text of the Constitution, any tolerable excuse for that claim of power by the President, so dangerous to the liberties of the people, and I can find, from the beginning to the end of that great instrument, no letter on which the claim can, for a moment, be based, save the words that all Executive power, under this Constitution, shall be vested in the President.

But that gives no colorable excuse for the assumption. What writers on your Constitution, what decision of your courts, what argument of all the great statesmen, who have in the past illustrated our history, has ever intimated that that provision was a grant of power? No human ingenuity can torture into anything more than a mere designation of the officer or person to whom shall be committed under the Constitution, and subject to its limitation and subject to the limitations of the laws enacted in pursuance of the Constitution, the executive powers of the government. Is it not as plainly written that all legislative power herein granted shall be vested in a Congress, which shall consist of a Senate and the House of Representatives?

But is anybody to reason from that designation of the body to which the legislative power is assigned that that is a special and indefinite authority to Congress to legislate on such subjects as it pleases, and without regard to the Constitution? Is it not also just as plainly written in the Constitution that the judicial power of the United States shall be vested in one Supreme Court and in such inferior court as the Congress may from time to time assign by law, and is anybody thence to infer that that is an indefinite grant of power, authorizing the Supreme Court or the inferior courts of the United States to sit in judgment on any and all conceivable questions, and even to reverse by their decision the power of impeachment, lodged exclusively in the House of Representatives, and the judgment of impeachment, authorized to be pronounced exclusively and only by the Senate of the United States?

It will never do for any man to say that that provision of the Constitution is a grant of power. It is simply the designation of the officer to whom the executive power of the government is committed, under the limits of the Constitution and laws, as Congress is the designation of the department of the government to which shall be committed the legislative power, and as the court is the designated department to which shall be committed judicial power. Says Mr. Webster on this subject:—"It is perfectly plain and manifest, that although the framers of the Constitution meant to confer executive power on the President, yet they meant to define and to limit that power, and to confer no more than they did thus define and limit."

Does not the Constitution, Senators, define and limit the Executive power; in this, that it declares that the President shall have power to grant reprieves and pardons; in this, that it declares that the President shall have power to appoint, by and with the advice and consent of the Senate, foreign embassadors and other public officers; in this, that it provides he shall have power to make treaties, by and with the advice and consent of the Senate, and does it not limit his power; in this, that it declares that all legislative power shall be vested in a Congress, which shall consist of a Senate and House of Representatives; in this, that it declares that the President shall take care that the laws which the Congress enact, shall be faithfully executed; in this, that it declares that every bill which shall have passed the Congress of the United States with or without his consent, shall always remain a law, to be executed as a law until the same shall have been repealed by the power which made it, or shall have been actually reversed by the Supreme Court of the United States in a case clearly within its jurisdiction and within the limitations of the Constitution itself. It has been a settled law in this country from a very early period, that the constitutionality of a law shall not be tampered with, much less adjudged against the validity of the law, by a court charged by the Constitution with jurisdiction in the premises, except for a case so clear as to clearly admit of a doubt.

But what is the result, Senators? It is that there is not—I feel myself justified in saying it, without having recently very carefully examined the question—one clear, unequivocal decision of the Supreme Court of the United States against the constitutionality of any law whatever enacted by the Congress of the United States—not one. There was no such decision as that in the Dred Scott case; lawyers will understand me when I use the word decision what I mean; I mean a judgment pronounced by the court upon issue joined on the record. There was no such decision in that case, nor in any other case, so far as I recollect.

On that subject, however, I may be excused for reading one or two decisions from the courts. Chief Justice Marshall, in the case of Fletcher vs. Peck, 6 Cranch, p. 87, says, "The question whether a law be void for its repugnance to the Constitution, is at all times a question of much delicacy, which ought seldom, if ever, to be decided in the affirmative in a doubtful case. All opposition between the Constitution and the law, should be such that the judge feels a clear and strong conviction of their incompatibility with each other." Mr. Bingham also read the opinion of the court, reported in 3 Denio, p. 389, to the effect that the presumption is always in favor of the validity of the law, if the contrary is not clearly demonstrated.

He then continued:—I have read this, Senators, not that it was really necessary to my argument, but to answer the pretensions of the President, who comes here to set aside a law and to assume the prerogative of duty, in order to test its validity in the courts of justice, when the courts have never ventured on that dangerous experiment themselves; and, on the contrary, have, thirty years ago, as I showed the Senate yesterday, solemnly ruled that the assumption of power claimed by the President would defeat justice itself and anticipate the laws of the people.

I have done it, also, to verify the text of your Constitution, and to make plain its significancy, when it declares that every bill which shall have passed Congress with or without the President's approval, and then over his veto, shall be a law. The language is plain and simple. It is a law until it is annulled; a law to the President; a law to every department of the government—legislative, executive, and judicial; a law to all the people. It is in vain for gentlemen to say that it is only constitutional laws which bind; that simply begs the question. The presumption, as I have shown you, is that every law is constitutional until by authority it is declared otherwise.

The question here is, whether that authority is in Andrew Johnson. That is the whole question. Your Constitution says it shall be a law. It does not mean that it shall remain a law after being reconsidered by the law-making power and repealed, or after it shall have been adjudged unconstitutional in the Supreme Court of the United States, under limitations of the Constitution and within its express jurisdiction. But it does mean that, until that judgment be pronounced authoritatively in your tribunals of justice, or until that power be exercised authoritatively by the people's Representatives in Congress assembled, it shall be a law to the people, to every head of e department—as the court ruled in the case of Kendall, to which I referred yesterday—to every Representative in Congress, to every Senator, and every human being within the jurisdiction of the laws.

Why do the gentlemen make this distinction, that it is only laws passed in pursuance of the Constitution that are to bind? Why make it at all? Why not follow their premises to their logical conclusion—that the President of the United States is, by virtue of the prerogative of his office, vested with power judicially to interpret the Constitution for himself, and judicially to decide for himself on the validity of every law, and may, therefore, with impunity set aside every law on your statute books, for the reason—in the words of his advocate, Mr. Curtis—that he has come deliberately to the conclusion that it conflicts with some power vested in him by the people.

Well, Senators, consider it from the operations of the President's mind, as manifested in his past official conduct, God only knows to what absurd conclusions he may arrive. Hereafter, if by your judgment, you recognize this omnipotent prerogative in him, when he comes to sit in judicial judgment on all the laws on your statute book, he may come to the conclusion that all those statutes cut off some power given to him by the Constitution. Such an idea conflicts with every principle of law and with every principle of common sense. If this discretionary power is in the President no man can lay his hand upon him.

That was exactly the ruling of his honor, the Chief Justice, in the Mississippi case, touching the exercise of certain discretionary powers vested in the President by the Reconstruction acts. His judgment includes everybody. The courts cannot reverse his decision, and unless you charge him with corruption there is an end of the matter. It was settled more than thirty years ago, in the case to which I referred yesterday, and has never been challenged from that day to this.

I deny any such discretion in the Executive, because such discretion is incompatible with public liberty; because it is in direct conflict with the express letter of the Constitution; because it is a discretion which vests him with kingly prerogatives; because it is a discretion which puts the servant above his master; because it is a discretion which clothes the creature with power superior to that of the creator. The American people will tolerate no such discretion in an Executive, by whomsoever sanctioned or by whomsoever advocated.

When that day comes that the American people will tamely submit to that assumption of authority, that their President is above their Constitution and above their law, and may defy each or both at his pleasure with impunity, they will have proved themselves unfit custodians of that great trust which has been committed to their care in the interests of their children and in the interests of the millions that are to come after them, I have no fear of the result with the people. Their instincts are all right. They understand perfectly well that the President is but their servant, to obey their laws in common with themselves, to execute their laws in the mode and manner prescribed in the laws themselves, and not to sit in judgment day by day on their authority; to legislate for themselves, and to govern themselves by laws duly enacted through their representatives in Congress assembled; and this brings me, Senators, to the point made by the learned and accomplished gentleman from New York (Mr. Evarts), when he talks of that common struggle in which the President and his friends, headed, doubtless, by the learned gentleman himself, would march under the banner of the supremacy of the Constitution against the omnipotence of Congress. I have uttered no words, nor have my associates uttered any words which justify any suggestion about the omnipotence of Congress.

I can understand very well something of the omnipo-

tence of a Parliament under the protection of a corrupt hereditary monarch, of whom it may be said, and is said by the retainers, that he rules by the grace of God and by Divine right; but I cannot understand, nor can plain people anywhere understand what significance is to be attached to this expression:—"The Omnipotence of Congress," the popular branch of which is chosen every second year by the suffrages of freemen. I intend to utter no word, as I have uttered no word from the beginning of the contest to this hour, which will justify any man in intimating that I claim for the Congress of the United States any omnipotence—I claim for it simply the power to do the people's will, as required by the people in their written Constitution, and as enjoined by their oaths.

It does not result that because we deny the power of the Executive to sit in judgment on the legislation of Congress, an unconstitutional enactment, passed in plain usurpation of authority by Congress, is without remedy. The first remedy under your Constitution is in the courts of the United States, in the mode and manner prescribed by the Constitution; and the last great remedy under your Constitution is with the people who ordained Constitutions, who appoint Senates, who elect Houses of Representatives, who establish courts of justice, and abolish them at their pleasure. Gentlemen will astonish nobody by talking about an omnipotent Congress. If the Congress is corrupt, let it be held to answer for it; but in God's name, let Congress answer somewhere else than to the President of the United States.

The Constitution of the United States has declared that members of Congress shall answer to no man for their legislation, or for their words uttered in debate, save to their respective houses, and to that great people which elected them. That is my answer to the gentleman's claim about an omnipotent Congress. Among the American people there is nothing omnipotent and nothing eternal but God, and no law save His and the laws of their own creation, subject to the requirements of those that were written on tablets of stone, and to which the gentleman from New York so eloquently referred, and a part of which, I deeply regret to say, the gentleman forgot and broke. We are the keepers of our own consciences.

It was well enough for the gentleman to remind the Senators of the obligation of their oaths. It was well enough for the gentleman to suggest to them, as earnestly as he did, the significance of these great words, justice, law, oath, duty. It was well enough for him to read, in the hearing of the Senate, and in the hearing of this listening audience, those grand words of the common Father of us all:—"Thou shalt not take the name of the Lord thy God in vain; for the Lord will not hold him guiltless that taketh his name in vain."

But it was not well for the gentleman in the heat and fire of his argument to pronounce judgment upon the Senate, to pronounce judgment upon the House of Representatives, and to say, if he did say, that, unmindful of the obligation of our oaths, regardless of the requirements of the Constitution, forgetful of God, and forgetful of the rights of our fellow man, in the spirit of hate we had preferred these articles of impeachment. It was not well for the gentleman to intimate that the Senate of the United States had exercised a power which did not belong to them, when, in response to the message of the President of the 21st of February, 1868, it was resolved that the act done by the President, and communicated to the Senate, to wit:—the removal of the head of the Department of War, and the appointment of a successor thereunto without the advice and consent of the Senate, was not authorized by the Constitution and laws. It was the duty of the Senate, if it had any opinions on the subject, to express them, and it is not for the President of the United States, either in his own person or in the person of his counsel, to challenge the Senate as disqualified to sit in judgment under the Constitution as his tryers on articles of impeachment because the Senate discharged another duty and pronounced against him.

The Senate pronounced a right. The people of the United States will sanction its judgment, whatever the Senate itself may think about it. Senators, all that I have said in this general way, as to the power claimed by the President and attempted to be justified here over this whole question between the people and this guilty President, no man can gainsay.

First. He stands charged with a misdemeanor in office, in that he issued an order in writing for the removal of the Secretary of War during the session of the Senate, without its advice or consent, in direct violation of express law, and with intent to violate the law.

Second. He stands charged with having, during the session of the Senate, without its advice or consent, in direct violation of the express letter of the Constitution and of the act of March 2, 1867, issued a letter of authority to one Lorenzo Thomas, authorizing him and commanding him to assume and exercise the functions of Secretary of the Department of War.

Third. He stands charged with an unlawful conspiracy to hinder the Secretary of War from holding his office, in violation of the law, in violation of the Constitution, and in violation of his own oath; and with a further conspiracy to prevent the execution of the Tenure of Office act, in direct violation of his oath, as well as in direct violation of the express provisions of the statutes, and to prevent also the Secretary of War from holding the office, and with a further conspiracy, by force, threat, or intimidation, to possess the property of the United States, and unlawfully control the same, contrary to the act of July 20, 1861.

He stands charged, further, with an unlawful attempt to influence Major-General Emory to disregard the requirements of the Army Appropriation act of March 2, 1867, and which expressly provides that a violation of its provisions shall be a high misdemeanor of office. He stands further charged with a high misdemeanor, in this, that on the 18th of August, 1866, by a public speech, he attempted to incite resistance to the Thirty-ninth Congress, and to the laws which it enacted. He stands further charged with a high misdemeanor, that he did affirm that the Thirty-ninth Congress was not a Congress of the United States, thereby denying and intending to deny the validity of the legislation, except in so far as he saw fit to approve it, denying its power to propose an amendment to the Constitution of the United States, devising and contriving means by which to prevent the Secretary of War, as required by the act of 2d of March, 1867, from resuming, forthwith, the functions of his office, and suspending him after the refusal of the Senate to concur in his suspension. He is charged further with devising to prevent the execution of the act making appropriations for the support of the act of March 2, 1867, and also to prevent the execution of the act providing for the more efficient government of the Rebel States.

That these several acts so charged, Senators, are impeachable has been shown. To deny that they are impeachable is to place the President above the Constitution and above the laws—to change the servant of the people into their master—the Executive of their laws into the violator of their laws. The Constitution has otherwise provided, and so it has been otherwise interpreted by one of the first writers on the law—Chancellor Kent—who says:—" In addition to all the precautions that have been mentioned to prevent abuses of the Executive trust, the Constitution has also rendered him amenable directly by law for mal-administration."

That is a text from Kent which the gentlemen were careful not to read. The inviolability of any officer of government is incompatible with these remarks of Chancellor Kent, as well as with the principles of justice. The Constitution provides that " The President and Vice President and all civil officers of the United States may be impeached by the House of Representatives for treason, bribery and other crimes and misdemeanors, and on conviction thereof by the Senate, removed from office."

" If, then," continues Chancellor Kent, " neither the guise of duty or force of public opinion, nor the transitory nature of the office are sufficient to secure a faithful discharge of the executive trusts; but if the President will use his authority to violate the Constitution and the law of the land, the House of Representatives can arrest him in his career by resorting to the power of impeachment." What answer is made when we bring the President here? When we show him guilty of maladministration as no man ever was before in the country; when we show that he violated the laws; when we show that he has defied the power of the Senate, even after it had admonished him of the danger impending over him, the answer is, that he is vested with the unlimited prerogative to decide all these questions for himself, and to suspend even your power of impeachment, in the courts of justice until some future day, when it may suit his convenience to test the validity of your law, and to show the uprightness of his own conduct.

There never was a bolder proposition since man was on the face of the earth. It is simply an insult to the human understanding to press any such defense in the presence of his triers. I have said enough, and more than enough, to show that the matter charged against the President is impeachable. I waste no words upon the frivolous question whether the articles have the technical requisites of an indictment. There is no law anywhere that requires it. There is enough in the past precedents of the Senate of the United States, sitting as a high court of impeachment, that condemns any such suggestion.

I read, however, for the perfection of the argument rather than for the instruction of the Senate, from the text of Rawle on the Constitution, who declares that articles of impeachment need not be drawn with the strictness of indictments; but that it is sufficient for the charges to be distinct and intelligible. They are distinct and intelligible. They are well enough understood, even by the smallest children of the land who are able to read their mother tongue, and who knows that the President stands charged with usurpation of power, with violation of the Constitution, with violation of his oath, with violation of the laws, that he stands charged with the attempt to subvert the Constitution and the laws, and to usurp to himself all the power of the government which is vested in the legislative and judiciary as well as in the executive departments.

Touching the proofs, Senators, little need be said. The charges are admitted substantially by the answer, although the guilty intent is formally denied by the answer, and attempted to be denied in argument. The accused submits to the judgment of the Senate that, admitting all the charges to be true—admitting them to be established—nevertheless he cannot be held to answer, before the Senate, for high crimes and misdemeanors, because it is his prerogative to construe the Constitution for himself, and to determine the validity of your laws for himself, and to suspend the power of impeachment until it suits his convenience to lay the question in the courts of justice.

That is the whole case. It is all that there is to it, or of it, or about it. After all that has been said here by his counsel, that was the significance of the opening argument—that he could be only convicted of such high crimes and misdemeanors as are kindred with treason and bribery. I referred to that suggestion yesterday, and I asked the Senate that the crimes whereof he stands charged—which are proved against him and which he confesses—are offenses which touch the nation's life, endanger the public liberty, and cannot be tolerated for a day or an hour by the American people. I proceed, then, gentlemen, as rapidly as possible, for I myself am growing weary of this discussion.

Senator SHERMAN interposed and suggested a recess.

Mr. BINGHAM said he hoped to be able to close his argument to-day, and unless it was the pleasure of the Senate to take the recess now, he would proceed with his argument for another hour. Mr. Bingham proceeded. The first question, Senators, that arises under the first article is, whether Mr. Stanton was the Secretary of War? That he was duly appointed by and with the advice and consent of the Senate is conceded. About that there is no question. As the law then stood he was entitled to hold the office until removed by the authority of the act of 1796, or by authority of some other existing act in full force at the time of his removal, but otherwise he was not removable at all without the advice and consent of the Senate; that is the proposition I take in reference to the matter, and I venture to say before the Senate that there is not one single word in the record of the past history of the country to contradict it.

The act of 1789, as I said before, authorizes the removal. We will see whether that act authorized the removal in 1867. Gentlemen seem to think that the tenure of office depends upon the words of the commission. If that were so I would surrender the question, but I deny it. The tenure of office depends upon the provisions of the Constitution and upon existing laws. There is no vested power in the President of the United States over that subject. He never had any power whatever over the question, except that joint power with the Senate, to which I have referred, in the Constitution, and the power expressly conferred by legislation of Congress. It is clearly the power which conferred it—made it a law. The Tenure of Office act changed the law of 1789.

Gentlemen have made elaborate arguments to show that the act of 1863 did not necessarily repeal the act of 1789, and that part of the argument was very significant as confessing that it was competent for the Congress of the United States to put an end to all this talk about the tenure of office depending in any sense on the language of the commission. It depends exclusively upon the provisions of existing law. The act of 1867 repealed both the acts of 1789 and 1795. It provided for the suspension of all officers theretofore appointed or commissioned by and with the advice and consent of the Senate, and no kind of sophistry can evade the plain clear words of the law. The gentleman undertook to get out of this pinch by suggesting a distinction between the office and the officer.

But no such distinction will avail them; this act of 1867 puts an end to all such quibbling. The office and the person who fills it are alike under the protection of the law, and beyond the reach of the Executive, except as limited and directed by the law. No man can gainsay that.

Mr. Bingham referred to the Tenure of Office act, and continued:—There is a law so plain that no man can misunderstand it. There is a plain, clear, distinct provision in the law, that in such case, and no other, to wit, during the recess, and for reasons, the President may suspend from office any person heretofore, or who may thereafter be appointed by and with the advice and consent of the Senate. It is admitted that the Secretary of War, and every other officer appointed with the advice and consent of the Senate, holds his appointment within the provisions of the body of the act; and being within the provisions of the body of the act, the President himself is prohibited by the act from removing them, as he is authorized by the act of 1789 to make removal. There is no escape from the provisions of the law.

What next? It is attempted to be said here that from the body of this act the Secretaries appointed by Mr. Lincoln were excepted. Who, pray, says that? I have just read to you the words of Mr. Webster—"That exceptions, unless clearly expressed in the law, are never to be implied unless a positive necessity exists for that application." That is a sound rule of construction. Who says that the heads of departments appointed by Mr. Lincoln are by the proviso excepted from the body of this act? Why the gentleman, in the absence of any farther reason, undertook to quote a speech of my learned and accomplished friend, the Senator from Ohio (Mr. Sherman), forgetting that one line of that speech declares expressively, or by necessary intendment, that the existing Secretaries and heads of departments were within the operations of the law.

He says:—If a secretary would not withdraw and resign on the politest suggestion from the new President, he would consent to his removal. What significance can be attached to these words, if they do not mean this. To be sure, by this law, the President, after all, may not be permitted to remove a Secretary of War; but if he politely requests him to resign, and if the Secretary refuses to resign, I would, myself, consent to his removal. As the matter then stood, the Senator was doubtless entirely justified before the country in coming to that conclusion, for facts had not sufficiently disclosed themselves then to show the necessity of the Secretary of War maintaining the office.

Times have changed. The President has more fully developed his character. It is understood now of all the country, and of the whole civilized world, that he has undertaken to usurp all the powers of the government, and to betray the trust committed to him by the people through their Constitution. This idea of his being excepted by the proviso from the body of the law is an afterthought. The President himself in his message notified the Senate that if he had supposed any member of his Cabinet would have availed himself of the law, and retained the office against his will, he would have removed him without hesitation before it became a law. He supposed then that Mr. Stanton was within the law again.

The President is concluded on this question, because, on the 12th of August, 1867, he issued an order suspending Edwin M. Stanton, Secretary of War, under this act. What provision in the Constitution was there authorizing the President to suspend anybody for a day or an hour? Has anybody ever claimed it? Has anybody ever exercised it? It is a thing unheard of altogether in the past history of the country. It never was authorized in any way before except by the act of 2d of March, 1867, the Tenure of Office act. I do not intend that this confessedly guilty man shall change front in the presence of the Senate in order to cover up his villainy.

In his message to the Senate he not only quotes the words of the statute, that he had suspended Mr. Stanton, but he quotes the other words of the statute when he says the "suspension was not yet revoked."

I ask you again, Senators, whether that word ever occurs before in the Executive papers of the United States? It is the word of the Tenure of Office act. It is too late for any man to come before the Senate and say that the President of the United States did not himself believe that the Secretary of War was within the operations of the statute. He was not excepted from its provisions by the proviso more than that his letter to the Secretary of the Treasury, Mr. McCulloch, reciting the eighth section of the Tenure of Office act and notifying him that he had suspended Edwin M. Stanton, was a further recognition of the fact, on his part, that Mr. Stanton was within the provisions of this act.

But that is not all. His own counsel who opened the case (Mr. Curtis) declared that there are no express words within the proviso that bring the Secretary of War, Edwin M. Stanton, within that proviso. That is his own proposition, and that being so, he must be within the body of the statute. There is no escape from it. There has been a further argument, however, on this subject, namely, that the President did not intend to violate the law; and if he believed that Mr. Stanton was in the statute, and suspended him under the statute, and reported him in obedience to the statute, the reasons of his suspension to the Senate within twenty days, and the evidence on which he made the suspension, it will not do to come and say now that the President did not intend to violate the law, that he did not think it obligatory on him. If not, why did he obey it in the first instance? Why did he exercise power under it at all? There is but one answer which can be given to it, and that answer itself covers the President with ignominy and crime and reproach. It is this:— I will break my oath; I will avoid the law; I will suspend the head of a department under its express authority, for the first time in the history of the Republic; I will report his suspension to the Senate, together with the reasons and the evidence on which the suspension was made, and if the Senate concur in the suspension, I will abide by the law; if the Senate non-concur in the suspension, I will defy the law, and fling my old record in their faces, and tell them that it is my prerogative to sit in judgment, judicially on the validity of the statute. That is the answer, and it is all the answer that can be made to it by anybody.

Now, Senators, I admit on this construction of the law, that the President in the first instance is himself the judge of the sufficiency of the reasons and evidence on which he makes the suspension, and that he is not to be held impeachable for any honest errors of judgment in coming to that conclusion. It would be gross injustice to hold him impeachable for any honest error of judgment in coming to the conclusion that the Secretary of War was guilty of a misdemeanor or crime in office, or that he became incapable or otherwise disqualified to hold office.

But the President is responsible if, without any of the reasons assigned by the law, he, nevertheless, availed himself of the power conferred under the law to suspend the Secretary of War, although he knew that there was no colorable excuse for charging that the Secretary was guilty of any misdemeanors or crime, or that he had become in any way legally disqualified.

This is the very crime charged against him in the eleventh article of impeachment—that he did attempt to violate the provisions of the Tenure of Office act, in that he attempted to prevent Edwin M. Stanton, Secretary of War, from his resuming the functions of his office, and from exercising the duties of the office to which he had been appointed by and with the consent and advice of the Senate, in direct violation of the provisions of the act itself.

Now, what are the reasons? The President is concluded by his record, and in the presence of the American people is condemned upon his record. What were his reasons? Let the Senate answer, when they come to delivery, what evidence did he furnish to this Senate in the communication made to it that Edwin M. Stanton had become in any manner disqualified to discharge the duties of his office? What evidence did he furnish to the Senate that Mr. Stanton had been guilty of any misdemeanor or crime in office? What evidence was there that he was legally disqualified in the way stated? None whatever.

The result, therefore, Senators, is that the President of the United States, on his own showing, judged by his own record, suspended Edwin M. Stanton from the office of Secretary of War, and appointed a successor without the presence of the reasons named in the statute, and is confessedly guilty before the Senate and the world, and no man can acquit him.

The court here, at quarter past two, took a recess for a quarter of an hour.

After the recess Mr. BINGHAM continued:—I have said about all that I desire to say, to show that the President of the United States, upon his own messages sent to the Senate of the United States, has been guilty in manner and form as he stands charged in the first, second, third, eighth and eleventh articles of impeachment. It does seem hard, Senators, and yet the issue involved in this question is so great that I do not feel myself at liberty to fail to utter a word in furtherance of it, but it seems hard to be compelled to perform so sad a duty as to insist that the man, who stands convicted on the evidence, should be pronounced guilty.

It touches the concern of every man in this country whether the laws are to be vindicated, whether they are to be enforced; or whether, at least, after all that has passed before our eyes, after all the sacrifices that have been made, after the wonderful salvation that has been wrought by the sacrifices of the people in vindication of the people's cause, their own Chief Magistrate is to renew the Rebellion, and violate the laws and set them at defiance. When the Senate took its recess I had shown, I think, to the satisfaction of every fair-minded man within the hearing of my voice, that the President, without colorable excuse, assumed to himself authority not conferred by the laws of the republic to suspend the head of an office, and has disregarded at the same time the express limitations of the law, which declares that he shall not suspend it save during the recess of the Senate, and that only for the reason that from some cause he has become incapacitated to fill the office as by the visitation of Providence, or has become legally disqualified to hold the office, or is guilty of a misdemeanor, or of a crime. Without the least shadow of evidence that your Secretary of War was incapacitated, without the shadow of evidence that he was guilty of a misdemeanor or a crime, the President dared to suspend him, and to defy the people in the presence of the people's tribunes who have held him to answer for the violation of his oath, for the violation of the Constitution, and for the violation of the laws. Senators, whatever may be the result of this day's proceedings, impartial history, which records and perpetuates what men do and suffer in this life, will do justice to your slandered and calumniated Secretary of War. The gentleman spoke of him but yesterday as being a thorn in the heart of the President. The people know that for four years of sleepless vigilance he was a thorn in the heart of every traitor in the land who lifted his hands against your flag and against the sanctuary of your liberties.

He can afford to wait. His time has not come. His name will survive the trial of this day, and will be remembered with the names of the demi-gods and the heroes who, through an unprecedented conflict, saved the Republic alive. And yet I charge your recusant President with calumny, with slander, when he suspended the Secretary of War, under the pretense, in the words of your statute, that he was guilty of a misdemeanor, or a crime in office, or had become legally disqualified. He was legally disqualified, undoubtedly, judging him by the President's standard, if the qualification for an office is an utter disregard for the obligations of an oath.

He was guilty of misdemeanor and crime undoubtedly, according to the President's standard, if he was guilty of claiming that neither the Executive of the United States nor any other man might at pleasure suspend the people's laws, which were enacted by themselves, and for themselves, and are for their protection both while they wake and while they sleep, at home and abroad, on the land and on the seas. Your Secretary of War, Senators, whatever may be the result of this day's proceeding, will stand, as I said before, in the great hereafter upon the page of history as one who has deserved well of his country— a man equal in the discharge of his office, in every quality that can adorn or ennoble, or elevate human nature to any man of our own time, or of any time, a man who was clear in his great office, a man who organized victory for your battalions in the field as man never organized victory before in the Cabinet councils of the people since nations were upon the face of the earth. And this man is to be suspended by a guilty, and corrupt, and oath-breaking President, under a law which he defied under the hollow and hypocritical pretense that he was guilty of misdemeanor, or crime, or, in the language of the law, had become otherwise disqualified for holding office. I dismiss the subject. The Secretary needs no defense from me, and yet I will state in passing that I shall take this notice of what the President has done, not simply to his hurt, but to the hurt of the republic.

I have said enough, Senators, to satisfy you and to satisfy all reasonable men in this country that the President when he made this suspension of the Secretary of War had no doubt of the validity of this law and its obligation upon him, and that the Secretary was within its provisions; for, availing himself of its express provisions, he did suspend him, and made report, as I have said, to the Senate. Now, what apology, what excuse can be made for this abuse of the powers conferred upon the President, for which he stands charged this day, in that he has abused, in the language of the authority, which I read yesterday before the Senate, and which was used on the trial of Justice Peck, without a dissenting voice—"Who has abused the power conferred upon him by the statute?"

The counsel may have doubted the validity of the Tenure of Office act; the President never doubted it until he was put on trial, after he had vetoed it. Of course, when it was presented to him for approval it was a question whether it was in accord with the Constitution; but after Congress had passed it by a two-thirds vote over his veto, in the mode prescribed by the Constitution, the President of the United States thenceforward until he was impeached by the people's representatives, recognized the obligation of the law, in the plain, simple words of the Constitution, that if a bill be passed by a two-thirds vote over his veto it shall become law to himself and to everybody else in the Republic.

The counsel, however, doubt the validity of the law. They raise the question in the answer; they raise it in the argument; they intimate to the Senate that it is unconstitutional, and they take a very plain and simple proposition, and it is really, to me, a very grateful thing to be able to agree with the counsel for the President in any single proposition whatever. They did state one proposition to which I entirely assent, and that is that an unconstitutional law is no law; but it is only no law to the President; it is only no law to the Congress; it is only no law to the courts; it is only no law to the people after its unconstitutionality shall have been decided in the mode and manner prescribed by the Constitution, and the gentleman who so adroitly handled that text as obtained from the mighty name of Marshall, knew that that rule governed the case just as well as anybody else knows. It is a law until it shall have been reversed. It has not been reversed, and to assume any other position would be to subject the country at once to anarchy, because, as I have had occasion to say in the progress of this argument, the humblest citizen in the land is as much entitled to the immunity which that propositions brings as the President of the United States. It does not result, however, that the humblest citizen of the land, in his cabin on your Western frontier, through whose torn thatch the rains beat down and the winds play at pleasure, is at liberty to defy the laws, on the ground that they are unconstitutional. The same rules applies to the President. The Constitution is no respecter of persons. Is this law constitutional? Is it valid, and did the President really intend to violate its provisions? Senators, I said before that the rule of the common law and the common sense of mankind is, that whenever a man does an unlawful act, he being a man of sound mind and understanding, he intends precisely what he does, and there is an end to all further controversy. It sometimes happens, however, because, in the providence of God, truth is stronger than falsehood, that a guilty conscience sometimes makes revelations, and thereby contributes to the vindication of violated law and the administration of justice between man and man in support of the right. So it has happened, Senators, that the accused at your bar—the President of the United States—was no exception to that rule that "murder will out." He could not keep his secret. It possessed him and it compelled him, in spite of himself, to stammer out his guilty purpose and his guilty intent, and thereby silence the tongue of every advocate in this Chamber, and of every advocate outside of this Chamber.

Who undertakes to excuse the poor man that he did not know the necessary consequences of his own act? He did intend it. Why he confessed it? Now, I ask the Senate to note what is recorded on page 234 of the record, in his letter to General Grant, to see what becomes of this pretense that the intent is not proved; that he did not intend to violate the law; that he did not intend, in defiance of the express words of the law, which are, "That the Secretary shall forthwith resume the functions of the office in the event that the Senate shall non-concur in the suspension, and inform the Secretary of the fact of non-concurrence," all of which appears on the record.

Mr. BINGHAM here read the letter of the President to General Grant, dated February 10, in which he claims that General Grant was aware of his intention to force Mr. Stanton to resort to the courts, or to prevent his resuming the office of Secretary of War. He continued:—How could he know it, if that was not his purpose? It would be, it seems to me—and I say it with all reverence—beyond the favor of Omnipotence to know a thing that was not and could not possibly be. You know it was the President's purpose to prevent Mr. Stanton from resuming the office.

What says the law? That it shall be the duty of the suspended Secretary, if the Senate shall non-concur in the suspension, forthwith to resume the functions of the office. And yet the Senate is to be told that we must prove the intent. Well, we have, and in God's name what more are we to prove before this man is convicted and the people justified in the judgment of their own Senators. "It was my purpose, and you knew it, to prevent Mr. Stanton from resuming the duties of the office." I have given him the benefit of his whole confession.

There is nothing in this stammering confession of this violator of oaths, and violator of constitutions, and violator of laws, that can help him, either before this tribunal or any other tribunal constituted as this is, of just and upright men. He says:—"You know the President was unwilling to trust the office with any one who would not, by holding it, compel Mr. Stanton to resort to the courts;" and he knew as well as he knew anything—if he does, indeed, know anything at all—(laughter)—and if he does not, then order an inquest on lunacy, and dispose of him in that manner. He knew, if he knew anything at all, if he prevented Mr. Stanton from resuming the office, Mr. Stanton could not any more test that question in your courts of justice than can the unborn child, and the man that does not know it ought to be turned out of the office which he disgraces and dishonors for natural stupidity. (Laughter.) He has abused the powers that have been given him. A man that had sense enough to find his way to the Capitol ought to have sense enough to know that. (Laughter.) Yet the gentleman's office goes on here, and the people are mocked and

insulted day by day by this pretense, that we are prosecuting an innocent man, a defender of the Constitution, a lover of justice, a respecter of oaths.

I have had occasion to say before, Senators, in the progress of this discussion, that this pretence of the President is an after-thought. The letter which I have just read, dated February 10, 1868, says that his object was to prevent Mr. Stanton from resuming the office, and then the after-thought is to drive him to the courts to test the validity of the law. Had he prevented the resumption of the office there would have been an end of it. Stanton never could have got in, and that question has been discussed long enough, and is no longer an open question, and the President knew it when he babbled this stuff in order to deceive the grandlings. Let him babble it to the winds. He need not babble it to the Senate. The question has been settled long ago.

Mr. BINGHAM quoted from the opinion of Chief Justice Marshall, 5 Wheaton, 291, to the effect that the writ of *quo warranto* can be maintained only at the instance of the government. This High Court of Impeachment, Senators, is the only tribunal to which this question could by any possibility be referred. Mr. Stanton could not bring that question here. The people could and the people have. And the people await your judgment.

Now Senators, I ask you another question, and that is this: How does the President's statement, that it was to compel Mr. Stanton to resort to the courts that he suspended him, compare with the pretence of his answer that his only purpose was to have the Supreme Court pass upon the constitutionality of the law? Tender regard this for the Constitution. That his only purpose in breaking the laws, the validity and the obligation of which in the most formal and solemn manner he had recognized; availing himself of its express grant to suspend the head of a department from the functions of his office, and to appoint temporarily a successor, and reporting the fact to the Senate, he now comes with his answer, and says that his only purpose was that he might test the validity of the law in the Supreme Court.

Surely, the President felt a very tender regard for the Constitution. If that was the sole purpose, how comes it that the President did not institute the proceedings? The Senate will answer that question when they come to pass upon the defense which the President has incorporated in his plea. I think if the honorable Senator from Maryland (Mr. Johnson) were to respond here now to that inquiry, full of learning as he is full of years, he would answer that it was because it was impossible that the President instituted proceedings. Mr. Chief Justice, it is well known to every jurist of the country, as the question stands, and as the President left it, that there is no colorable excuse under the Constitution and laws of this country to say that he would institute proceedings.

If he had not instituted proceedings, then I ask again' why insult the people by mocking them with this cold hypocritical assertion that his only purpose in doing the act was to institute a proceeding in his own mode, in the Supreme Court of the United States, to test the validity of the people's laws? Senators, it is only another illustration, surrounded as the President is by those learned in the law, and I cast no reproach on them in saying it. It was their duty to defend him; it was their duty to bring to his defense all their experience, and all their learning, and all those great powers of intellect with which it has pleased Providence to endow them; but it is only another evidence of what I said before, that notwithstanding the learning and ingenuity of his accomplished defenders, truth is at last stronger than falsehood.

When he comes before this Senate and says that his purpose in violating your laws was that he might test the validity of the statute in the Supreme Court of the United States when he knew he had no power under the Constitution or laws to raise the question at all, the written order for the removal of the Secretary of War, and the written letter of authority for the appointment of Lorenzo Thomas to the office of Secretary for the Department of War, are simply written conclusions of his guilt, in the light of that which I have already read from the record, and no man can gainsay it.

Mr. Bingham here quoted from Russell's Criminal Law, on the question of intent:—"To the extent that were an act, and in itself unlawful, the proof of justification or excuse lies on the defendant, and that the law in such cases implies a criminal intent." Was the act unlawful? If your statute was valid, it certainly was. Mr. Bingham read the sixth section of the statute, declaring its violation to be a high misdemeanor, &c. Then, is it an unlawful act within the text of Greenleaf? That surely is an unlawful act, the doing of which is, by the express law of the people, declared to be a penal offense, punishable by fine or imprisonment in the penitentiary. What answer do gentlemen make, and how do they attempt to escape from this provision of the law? Why, they say the President attempted to remove the Secretary of War, but he did not succeed. Are we to be told, Senators, that if a man makes an attempt upon your life here in the District of Columbia, although if you were to search never so closely the Constitution of the United States, you would not find the offense definitely defined and its punishment prescribed by statute.

Are we to be told, because he did not succeed in murdering you outright, that he must be acquitted, to try what success he may have on another day and in another place, in accomplishing his purpose. Senators, I have reminded you already of that which you knew, that your act of 1801, as well as of 1831, declares that all offenses, indictable at the common law, committed within the District of Columbia, shall be crimes or misdemeanors, according to their grades, and shall be indictable and punishable in the District of Columbia in your own courts.

I listened to the learned gentleman from New York the other day, upon this point, and for the life of me—and I beg his pardon for saying so—I could not understand what induced the gentleman to venture upon the intimation that there was any such thing possible as a defense of the President for the unlawful attempt to violate this law.

By admitting the order to be an unlawful attempt, I say with all respect to the gentleman, that it has been settled through the current century and longer, by the highest courts of this country and of England, that the attempt to commit a misdemeanor, whether the misdemeanor be one at common law or a misdemeanor by statute law, the attempt is itself a misdemeanor.

Mr. BINGHAM quoted Russell, 84, to the above effect. I would like to see a book brought into this Chamber to contradict that rule. It is common law as well as common sense. But, further, what use is there for raising a question when the further provision of the statute is "That the making, signing, sealing, countersigning or issuing any commission, letter of authority, or ownership of any such appointment or employment shall be assumed, and are hereby declared to be a high misdemeanor." Who is to challenge this, here or elsewhere?

What answer has been made? What answer can be made to this? None, Senators, none. When the words of a statute are plain there is an end to all controversy, and in this, as in every other part of this discussion touching the laws of the land, I stand upon that accepted canon of construction stated by the learned Attorney-General in his defense of the President last week, when he said effect must be given to every part of the written law.

I have discharged my duty—my whole duty. The question which now remains is whether the Tenure of Office act is valid? If it is, whatever gentlemen may say about the first article, there is no man in America but knows that under the second and third and eighth articles, by issuing a letter of authority, the President was guilty of a high misdemeanor in the words of the statute. He did issue the letter of authority, and he has written it down on the 10th of February that his object and purpose was to violate that very law and to prevent the Secretary of War from resuming the functions of his office, although the law says he shall forthwith resume the functions of his office, in case the Senate non-concurred in the suspension. And yet gentlemen wriggle here about this question as if it was an open question. It is not an open question. It is a settled, closed question this day, this hour, in the judgment of every enlightened, intelligent man who has access to your record, and it is useless, and worse than useless, to waste time on it. The question now is, is the act valid? Is it constitutional? Senators, I ought to consider that question closely. I ought to assume that the Congress of the United States which passed the act will abide by it. Congress acted on the responsibility of its oath. It acted under the limitations of the Constitution. The Thirty-ninth Congress, not unmindful, I trust, of its obligation, and not incapable of judging and considering the grants and limitations of the Constitution, passed this law because, first, it deemed itself authorized to do so by the Constitution, and because, secondly, it deemed that its enactment was necessary, and that is the language of the Constitution itself.

To the public welfare, and the public interest Congress sent it, in obedience to the requirements of the Constitution, to the President for his approval. The President, in the exercise of his power, and of his right under the Constitution, considered it, and returned it to the House in which it originated, with his objections. When he had done this we claim that all his power over the question of the validity of that law terminated. He returned it to the House, and with it his objections. He suggested that it was unconstitutional. Congress reconsidered it in obedience to the Constitution, and it was again passed by a two-thirds vote of both Houses, and, in the words of the Constitution, it thereby became a law—a law to the President of the United States—and it will forever remain a law until it is repealed by the law-making power or reversed by the courts. And now what took place?

These gentlemen come before the Senate with their answer, and tell the Senate the law was unconstitutional. They ask the Senate, in other words, to change their record. They ask to have this journal read hereafter at the opening of the court:—"The People of the United States against the Senate and House of Representatives, charged with high crimes and misdemeanors, in this, that, in disregard of the Constitution, in disregard of their oath of office, they did enact a certain law, entitled, 'An act to regulate the tenure of certain civil offices,' to the hurt and injury of the American people, and that they are thereby guilty of high crimes and misdemeanors in office."

Well, gentlemen, we have had our lessons here on charity in the progress of this trial, and really it does seem to me that this would be a stretch of that charity which requires you to give your coat, &c. I never knew before that it went beyond your outer garments, your bread, and the money in your purse; but it seems that you are to make a voluntary surrender of your good name, of your character, and of your conscience, in order to accommodate this accursed culprit, and to say, after all that, it is not the President of the United States who is impeached, but that it is the Senate, which is sitting in judgment upon him that is impeached, and that you will accommodate this unfortunate man by making a confession before the gods and before men, that we violated our own oath; that we violated the Constitution of our country, in that we did enact into a law, despite the President's veto to the contrary, a certain act passed March 2, 1867. Well, when it comes to that it is not for me to say what becomes of the Senate. This is an attempt to gibbet us all in eternal infamy for making up the record of this case deliberately and of malice aforethought, to the injury of the rights of a whole people, and to the disconcern and shame and disgrace of human nature itself.

And yet the question is made here that the law is unconstitutional. If the law be valid the President is guilty, and there is no escape for him. It is needless to make the issue, but having it, it is enough that the Senate decided. If the Senate decide that the law is constitutional there is an end of it. It has decided it three times. It decided it when it first passed the law. It decided it when it re-enacted the law over the President's veto, and it decided it again, as it was its duty to do, when he sent his message to the Senate on the 21st of February, 1868, telling the Senate that he had violated it and defied the provisions of the law. It was the duty of the Senate te decide it.

The Senate needs no apology, and I am sure will never offer an apology to any man in this life, or to any set of men, for what it did on that occasion. What! is the President of the United States deliberately to violate the law, to disregard the solemn action of the Senate, to treat with contempt the notice served upon him by the Senate in accordance with that law, and is he then to come into their own chamber and insult them, and defiantly challenge them in regard to this law? To this challenge the Senate made answer, as was its duty, Sir, the thing that you have done is not warranted by the Constitution and the laws of the country. This, Senators, is my answer to that challenge in the prosecution of this impeachment.

The representatives of the people, and others who have thought it worth while to notice my own official conduct touching this matter of impeachment, knew well that I kept myself back, and endeavored to keep others back from rushing madly into this conflict between the people and their President. The Senate, also, acting in the same spirit, gave him this notice that he might retrace his steps and thereby save the institutions of the country from this great shock. But no, it was needful that he should illustrate that Pagan rule:—"Whom the gods mean to destroy they first make mad," and so he went on, and here we are to-day to try this issue.

I return to the question of the validity of this law with the simple statement that by the act of the Constitution, as I have already read it, it is provided that all appointments not otherwise provided for in the Constitution, shall be made by and with the advice and consent of the Senate. It necessarily results, as Mr. Webster said, that the removing power is incident to the appointing power until otherwise provided by law. I have shown to the Senate that the removing power has never been otherwise exercised from the first Congress to this hour, except in obedience to the express provisions of law. I have shown the Senate that the act of 1789 authorized removals, and the act of 1795 authorized temporary appointments.

I add further that I have cited the fact of this provision of the Constitution that the President shall have power to fill up all vacancies that happen during the recess of the Senate, by issuing commissions which shall expire with the end of the next session, which very necessarily implication means, and means nothing else, that he shall create vacancies without authority of law during the session of the Senate, and shall not fill them at his pleasure without the consent of the Senate.

I have but one word further to add in support of the constitutionality of this law, and that is the express grant in the Constitution itself that the Congress shall have power to pass all laws necessary and proper. Interpreting that word "proper," in the words of Judge Marshall himself, in the great case of McCulloch vs. Maryland, as meaning "adapted to the execution of all the powers granted by this Constitution to the United States, or to any department thereof," I think that grant of power is plain enough and clear enough to sanction the Tenure of Office act.

Even admitting that the power of removal and appointment, "subject to law of course," was conferred upon the President, I do not stop, Senators, to argue the proposition further, but I refer to the authority of Mr. Webster, in volume 4, page 199, in which he recognizes the same principles most distinctly and clearly—that it is proper for the Congress of the United States to regulate this very question by law. I add, that the Congress of the United States, from the First Congress to this hour, has approved the same thing by its legislation. That is all there is of this question. The law, I take it, is valid, and will remain valid forever, if its validity is to depend upon the judgment of the Senate, which twice passed it under the solemn obligations of its oath.

Something has been said here, Senators, about the continued practice of eighty years. I have said enough on that subject to fully answer all that has been said, and so well said, by the learned counsel for the President. I have shown that the act of 1789, by the interpretation and construction of one of the first men in America, Mr. Webster, did really, by direct operation, separate the removing from the appointing power, and was itself a grant of power. I have shown that the Constitution confers that power on the Senate. Then there is no practice of eighty years adverse to this Tenure of Office act, so that I need say no word further on that subject, but leave it there.

all the acts from 1780 to 1867 bear witness to one thing, and that is that Congress has full power under the Constitution, by law, to confer upon the President the power of temporary or permanent removal, or to withhold that power. That is precisely what Congress has done, and I stand upon it here, as a representative of the people, prosecuting for the people these articles of impeachment, and declare here, this day, upon my conscience and on what little reputation I may have in this world, that the whole legislation of the country, from 1789 to 1867, altogether bears one common testimony to the power of Congress to regulate, by law, the removal and appointment of all officers within the general limitation of the Constitution and the supervisory power of the Senate that the act of 1789, as Mr. Webster stated, conferred upon the President of the United States the power of removal, and thereby separated that power from the power of appointment, of which it was a necessary incident. The act of 1795, on the other hand, gave him power to make certain temporary appointments limited here to over six months for any vacancies, thereby showing that it was no power under the Constitution and beyond the limitation and restrictions of law. The act of 1863 limited and restricted him as did also the act of 1789.

If, therefore, the President of the United States has this power by force of the Constitution, independent of law, I say, tell me, Senators, how it comes that the act of 1789 limited and restricted him to the chief clerk of the department? How comes it that the act of 1795 limited and restricted him to the period of six months only for one vacancy, if, as if claimed in his answer, he has power ot indefinite removal, and therefore the power of indefinite appointment? How comes it that the act of 1863 limited him to certain officials of the government, and did not leave him at liberty to choose from the body of the people?

I waste no further words on the subject. I consider the question fully closed and settled; and all the legislation shows the power of the President to be subject to the limitations of such enactments as the Congress may make, which enactments must bind him as they bind everybody else, whether he approves them or not, and until they be duly reserved by the courts of the United States or they shall be repealed by the peoples' representatives, in Congress assembled.

I may be pardoned, Senators, in having gone very heavily in this way over the general facts of the case, for saying that the President's declarations are here interposed to shield him from the conseqence of his guilt under the first three, the eighth, and eleventh articles of impeachment. These declarations of the President are declarations of the fact. Most of them were excluded by the Senate, and were properly, in my judgment, excluded. Some of them were admitted. I do not regret that; it showed that the Senate was willing, even if it were a doubtful question, or if it were not a doubtful question to modify the rules of evidence in the exercise of a discretion to see what explanation the Chief Executive could possibly give of his conduct.

The Senate allowed him, contrary to the rules of evidence, to be a witness in his own case, and that not under the obligation of an oath. The counsel produced his declarations. They amounted to no more than I have referred to already—that his purpose in violating the law was merely to test its validity in the courts. That is all there is of it. There was nothing more in the declarations of the President, as witnessed by himself on this trial. They cannot by any means excuse him in the light of the facts to which they have referred before, namely, that it was simply imposible for him to test questions in the courts in the manner proposed. There is an end of it. There is no use of pressing the question, and the farther

The President has no right to challenge the laws, and to suspend their execution until it is his pleasure to test their validity in a court of justice. But, Senators, what more is there? He is charged with conspiracy here. A conspriracy is proved upon him by his letter of authoritv to General Thomas, and by Thomas' acceptance under his own hands. Both of these papers are before the Senate, and in evidence. What is a conspiracy? A simple agreement between two or more persons to do an unlawful act, either with or without force, and the offense is completed the moment the agreement is entered into.

It is a misdemeanor at common law, and it is a misdemeanor under the act of 1801. It is a misdemeanor under the act of 1831. It is a misdemeanor for which Andrew Johnson and Lorenzo Thomas are both indictable after these proceedings shall have closed. And it is a misdemeanor, an indictment for which would be worth no more than the paper on which it would be written, until after this impeachment trial shall have closed, and the Senate shall have pronounced the righteous judgment of guilty on this offender against your laws, and for this simple reason, Senators, that it is written in your Constitution that the President shall have power to grant reprieves and pardons for all offenses against the United States save in cases of impeachment. Indeed, if Lorenzo Thomas were to-morrow indicted for a conspiracy with Andrew Johnson to prevent Edwin M. Stanton from resuming the functions of his office, all that would be wanted would be for Andrew Johnson with a mere wave of his hand to issue a general pardon and to dismiss the proceedings.

I say again, this is the tribunal of the people, in which to try this great offender, this violator of oaths, of the Constitution and the laws. Well, say gentlemen, it is a very little offense, and you may forgive him that. It is a very little offense when the pardoning power does not happen to be conferred upon him, and these tender and tearful appeals to the Senate on the ground of its being a little thing, do not amount to very much; but, say the gentlemen, you have also charged him, under the act of 1861, with having conspired with Lorenzo Thomas in the one article with force, and in the other with threats and intimidations, to work out the same result in preventing the execution of the law.

So we have, and we say that he is clearly proved

gnilty. How? By the confession made by his co-conspirator. I have said that the conspiracy is established by the written letter of authority and by the written acceptance of that letter of authority by Thomas, and the conspiracy being established, I say that the declaration of the co-conspirator made in the prosecution of the common design is evidence against both.

Mr. Bingham, in this connection, read some extracts from the testimony of General Thomas in reference to the mode in which he proposed to gain possession of the papers of the War Department, and particularly in reference to the draft of a letter which he submitted for the President's consideration on the 10th of March. Mr. Bingham, referring to the date of this draft letter, remarked that this was after the President was impeached, and that it showed that the President was still defying the power of the people to check him.

The Senate will notice, he said, that these two confederates and co-conspirators have not only been deliberately conferring together about violating the Tenure of Office act, and the act making appropriations for the army, but that one of the conspirators has written out an order for the very purpose of violating the law, and that the other conspirator, seeing the handwriting on the wall, and apprehensive after all that the Senate of the United States, in the name of all the people, may pronounce him guilty, concludes to whisper in the ear of his co-conspirator, "Let it rest until after the impeachment."

Give him, Senators, a letter of authority, and he is ready to renew this contest, and again to sit in judicial judgment on all your statutes, and to say in the language of his accomplished and learned advocate (Mr. Curtis), that he has deliberately settled down in the Constitution that your law regulating the army, fixing the headquarters of its general in the Capitol, not removable without the consent of the Senate, does impair certain rights conferred upon him by the Constitution, and that bv his profound judicial judgment he had come to the conclusion to set aside that law and to order General Grant to California, or to the Oregon, or Maine, and defy you again to try him. Senators, I trust you will spare the people any such exhibition.

Now, Senators, it has been my endeavor to finish to-day all that I desire to say on this matter. I know that if I were in possession of my strength I could finish all I have to say in the course of an hour or an hour and a half. It is now, however, past four o'clock, and if the Senate will be good enough to indulge me, I promise that I shall conclude my arguuent before recess to-morrow.

The court then adjourned.

PROCEEDINGS OF WEDNESDAY, MAY 6.

The court was opened in due form, and Mr. Bingham resumed his argument as follows:—

Senators:—On yesterday I had said nearly all that I had to say touching the question of the power of the President to assume legislative power for the executive office of this government. For the better understanding of my argument, however, Senators, I will read the provisions of the acts of 1789 and 1795 in the presence of the Senate, and will show by the law, as read by the counsel for the President on this trial, that the act of 1789, and the act of 1795 have ceased to be laws, and that the President can no more exercise authority under them to-day than can the humblest private citizen.

I desire also, Senators, in reading these statutes to reaffirm the position which I assumed on yesterday, with perfect confidence, that it would command the judgment and conscience of the Senate, to wit, that the whole legislation of this country, from the first Congress, in 1789, to this hour bears uniform witness to the fact that the President of the United States has no control over the executive offices of this government, except such control as is given by the text of the Constitution which I read yesterday, to fill up such vacancies as may occur during the recess of the Senate with limited commission to expire with the next session, or such power as is given him by express authority of law. I care nothing for the conflicting speeches of the representatives in the first Congress upon this question; the statute of the country conclude them, and conclnde us, and conclude as well every officer of this government from the Executive down.

What, then, Senators, is the provision of this act of 1789? I may be allowed, in passing, to remark that the act establishing the Department of Foreign Affairs contains precisely the same provision, word tor word, as the act to establish the Department of War.

Mr. Bingham read the act of 1789, and continued:—

Standing upon that statute, Senators, and upon the continued and unbroken practice of eighty years, I want to know, as I inquired yesterday, where it appears that this vacancy thus created by authority of the act of 1789, could be filled during the session of the Senate by the appointment of a new head to that department, without the consent of the Senate as prescribed in the Constitution?

I remarked yesterday, what I repeat now, in passing, that the vacancy was filled without the consent of the

Senate, and that was the end of this unbroken current of decisions, upon which the gentleman relied to sustain this assumption of power on the part of the accused President, I repeat, Senators, the act of 1789 excludes the conclusions which they attempted to impress upon the minds of the Senate in defense of the President. Why, the law restricted the appointment to the Chief Clerk. Could he over-ride that law? Could he give the papers of that department to any human being but the chief clerk, not appointed by him—by the head of the department? There stands the law, and in the light of that law the defense made by the President turns to dust and ashes in the presence of the Senate. I say no more upon that point, reminding the Senate that the act of 1789, establishing the War Department, contains the same provision, giving him no power to fill the vacancy by appointment during the session of the Senate.

I pass now to the act of 1795. The act of 1792 is obsolete; has been superseded, and was substantially the same as the act of 1795, and what I have to say, therefore, on the act of 1795 applies as well to the act of 1792.

Mr. Bingham read the law from the Statutes at Large, and continued:—There stood the law of 1798 unrepealed up to this time, I admit, expressly authorizing the President to fill the vacancy, but restricting him, under the control of the department after it was created, to the Chief Clerk of the department. This act expressly repeals the act of 1789, in so far as it expressly provided that "It shall be lawful for the President of the United States, in case he shall deem it necessary, to authorize any person or persons, at his discretion, to perform the duty of the said respective office until a successor be appointed."

It was a grant of power—and no grant of power could be more plainly given. What is the necessity of this grant if the reason, made by the President, as charged in his answer, and read by me yesterday, that the power is his by virtue of the Constitution, is correct? and if it be, I ask to-day, as I asked yesterday, how comes it that this constitutional power was restricted to appointments not to exceed six months for any one vacancy? That is the language of the statute. Am I to argue, Senators, that this term—"any one vacancy"—excludes the conclusion that the President could, upon his own motion, multiply vacancies *infinitum*, creating another at the end of six months, and making a new appointment? Senators, there is no unbroken current of decision to support any such assumption, and here I leave it.

I ask the attention of Senators now to the act of 1863, which affirms "the absolute control of the Legislative department over the whole question of removal and appointments, except the express provisions of the Constitution, which Congress cannot take away, that the President shall fill vacancies which may happen during the recess of the Senate by limited commission, to expire at the end of such commission.

Mr. BINGHAM read the act of 1863, and said:—Senators, what man can read the statute without being forced to the conclusion that the Legislature thereby reaffirmed the power that they had affirmed in 1867—the power that they had affirmed in 1795, to control and regulate by the law this asserted unlimited power of the Executive over appointments or removals either. Why look at the statute if it be permitted to choose at large from the body of the community to fill temporarily these vacancies? Not at all. It is restricted by the very terms of the statute to the heads of departments, or to such inferior officers of the several departments as are by law subject to his own appointment, and by that act he can appoint no other human being; and yet gentlemen stand here and say, the acts of 1789 and 1795 are not repealed, when they read authority themselves to show that when two statutes are altogether irreconcilable, the last must control. For the purpose of my argument it is not needful that I should rest upon the repeal of the act of 1795 any further, more than it relates to the vacancies which arise from the causes enumerated in the act of 1783.

It is a reassertion of the power of the Legislature to control this whole question, and that is the unbroken current of decision from the first Congress to this day, that the President can exercise no control over this question, except by authority of law, and subject to the express requirement of law. This brings me then, Senators, to the act of 1867, for the purpose of completing this argument upon this question, as to the limitation imposed by law upon the President of the United States, touching this matter of the appointment and removal of heads of departments, and of all other officers whose appointment is under the Constitution and laws, by and with the advice and consent of the Senate.

My chief object in referring again this morning to show to the Senate what I am sure must have occurred to them already, and rather to perfect my own argument than to suggest any new points to them at this very rule of interpretation by every letter and word read in the progress of these arguments on behalf of the President by his counsel. The act of 1867, by necessary implication, beyond the shadow of a doubt, repeals the acts of 1789 and 1795, and leaves the President of the United States subject to the requirement of the law as to all that class of officials.

Mr. Bingham read the act of 1789, and the Tenure of Office bill, and said, what becomes of this grant of power in the act of 1789 to the President to remove? What becomes of this grant of power, in the act of 1795, to make temporary appointments for six months?

Mr. BINGHAM went on to argue at great length, supporting his argument on the Constitution and on the statute of 1867, that the meaning of the clause in the Tenure of Office act, by which the Secretaries were to hold their offices during the term of the President by whom they were appointed, was, that they should hold their offices during the term for which Mr. Lincoln was elected, and that if a President should happen to be elected for two, or three, or four successive terms, the law would operate in giving the offices to the Secretaries until the expiration of the term of the President.

On this latter point, he said, I read the law literally as it is. The Secretaries are to hold their offices during the entire term, if it should be eight years, or twelve years or sixteen years, of the President by whom they were appointed. That is my position in regard to the appointment. There is no person who has a term but the President, elected by the people, and there is no person, therefore, whose appointment can by any possibility be within the provision of the proviso in the Tenure of Office act but such a President. If Mr. Lincoln had lived he could not have availed himself of the act of 1789 or of 1795, to remove a single head of a department appointed by himself at any time during the term.

I do not care how often his term was renewed, it was still the term, and answered to the statute, and he was still the President by whom those officers were appointed. When his term expired, whether it was his first, second, third or fourth term, the proviso then took effect according to its express language, and the offices became vacant one month after the expiration of that term; but that term never does expire until the end of the time for which the President was elected.

What else is there about this matter? Counsel for the defense argued here, and have put in the answer of the President, that the Tenure of Office act is unconstitutional and void. They talked for hours, in order to convince the Senate that no man can be guilty of crime—for the violation of an unconstitutional act—because it was no law which was violated. But why all this effort to prove the Tenure of Office act to be unconstitutional, if, after all, it did not embrace Mr. Stanton; if, after all, there was no violation of this provision; if, after all, it was no crime for the President to make an *ad interim* appointment; if, after all, the acts of 1789 and of 1795 remained in full force? Senators, I have no patience to pursue an argument of this sort.

The position assumed is utterly inexcusable, and utterly indefensible. I ask you Senators, to consider also, whether the counsel for the President were not too fast in saying, that even admitting that the Secretary of War had ceased to be entitled to the office, and was not to be protected in it, under the operation of the Tenure of Office act, the President, nevertheless, must go acquit of the conspiracy into which he had entered, and must go acquit of issuing the letter of authority to Thomas, in direct violation of the sixth section of the act.

The Senate will recollect the language of the counsel of the President (Mr. Stanbery) to the effect that this act was odious, offensive and unconstitutional, and that it attempted to impose penalties on the Executive for discharging Executive functions, and made it a crime and misdemeanor for him to exercise his undoubted discretionary power under the Constitution as claimed in his answer. He affirmed here, with emphasis, that the fifth section of the act makes it a crime to every man who participates with the President voluntarily in the breach of the law, and makes it a high misdemeanor for any person to accept any appointment under such circumstances.

I do not understand, Senators, why this line of argument was entered upon, if my friend from Ohio was right in coming to the conclusion that there was nothing in the conspiracy, and that there was nothing in issuing the letter of authority in violation of the express provisions of the law.

Mr. Bingham alluded to a remark made by Mr. Nelson, to the effect that it was his opinion, and was also the opinion of the President, that the House of Representatives, as now organized, had no power under the Constitution to impeach him, and that the Senate of the United States, as now organized, had no power under the Constitution to to try him on impeachment.

We are very thankful, continued Mr. Bingham, that the President of his grace permits the Senate to sit quietly to deliberate on this question presented by the articles of impeachment by the people's representatives.

But I ask Senators to consider whether the President, at least, is not notifying us through his counsel—for I observed that counsel did not intimate that the President was willing to abide the judgment of the Senate, but only that he was willing to wait the trial—of what we may expect, and whether he is not playing the same role which he did play, when he availed himself of the provisions of the Tenure of Office act to suspend E. M. Stanton from office, and to appoint a Secretary *ad interim*, and afterwards, when the Senate did not concur in the suspension of Mr. Stanton, refused to recognize the binding force of the Tenure of Office act.

I think it would have been well for the President of the United States when he was informing us of his opinion, through his learned counsel, to have gone a step further and informed us whether he will abide the judgment of the Senate.

Mr. Bingham also referred to a remark made by Mr. Curtis in sustaining his argument, to the effect that the letter of authority to General Thomas could not be strictly called a military order; but that the habitual custom of the officers of the army to obey all the orders of their superior officers gave it, in some sense, the force of a military order. In that connection, Mr. Bingham said:—It would not surprise me, Senators, at all, if the President were to issue an order to-morrow, to his Adjutant-General to disperse the Senate, after his sending here such an utterance, by the lips of his counsel, that the Senate has no constitutional right to try him, by reason of the absence of twenty Senators, excluded by the action of this body, elected by ten States and entitled to representation on this floor. That is a question which the President of the United States has no more right to decide or to meddle with than has the Czar of Russia, and it is a piece of arrogance and impudence for the President of the United States to send to the Senate a message that it is not constitutional according to the Constitution, and that it has no right to decide for itself the qualifications and elections of its own members, when it is the express language of the Constitution that the Houses of Congress shall have that power, and no man on earth should challenge it.

I trust, Senators, that to that utterance of the President, which is, substantially, that you shall suspend judgment in the matter, and defer to his will until it shall suit his convenience to inquire in the courts as to the rights of the people to have their laws executed, the Senate will return, by its judgment in this matter, an answer of the grand heroic spirit of that which the Deputies of the French nation returned in 1789 to King Lous XVI, when he sent his order that they should disperse, and when, on that occasion, the illustrious President, rising in his place, was hailed by the king's usher with the question:—"Did you not hear the king's order?" "Yes, sir," replied the President, and he immediately turned to the Deputies and said I adjourn the Assembly until it has deliberated upon the matter. "Is that your answer?" said the usher. "Yes sir," and he immediately followed it with the further words, "It appears to me that the assembled nation cannot receive an order," and this was followed by the words of the great tribune of the people, Mirabeau, addressing the king's usher and saying, "Go back to those who sent you, and tell them that bayonets have no power over the will of the nation." That sir, continued Mr. Bingham addressing himself to the President's counsel, is our answer to the arrogant words of your client. I have said, Senators, all that I have occasion to say touching the first eight articles preferred against the President, as to his having issued this order of removal unlawfully, and having issued this letter of authority unlawfully.

It was necessary that the President should take another step in his guilty march, and he proceeded very cautiously, as conspirators always do, in the experiment of corrupting the conscience and staining the honor of a gallant soldier, who was in command of the military forces in the district. He had an interview with him the day after he issued this letter of authority. In that interview he says to him:—"Sir, this act of 1867 making appropriations for the army, which requires all military orders to pass through the General of the Army, and which requires also that any violation of its provisions shall be a high misdemeanor in office, is an unconstitutional law, and is not within the purview of your commission."

It was simply a suggestion to the General that his commander-in chief would stand by him in violating the law of the land. It was a suggestion to him that it would be a very great accommodation to the President if the commandant of the forces of the District would receive his orders directly from the President, and not from the General of the army. It was a confession, Senators, indirectly to be sure, "that confession, however, which always syllables itself in the confession of the guilty, when guilty speaks at all"—that General Grant, the hero of the century, who led your battalions to victory on a hundred stricken fields, having vindicated the supremacy of the law by wager of battle, would surely here in the capital be faithful to the obligations and requirements of law, and refuse to strike hands with him.

More than that, he has put it in writing to this effect:—"You knew, General Grant, that my object and purpose was to violate and defy the law, and you accepted the office of Secretary of War *ad interim* in order to circumvent me." That is his language in his letter to General Grant of the 10th of February; and yet gentlemen say that this is a miserable accusation. Is it? It is so miserable an accusation, sirs, that in any other country than this, where the laws are enforced rigidly, it would have cost an executive or a military officer his head to suggest to any subordinate that he should violate a law, and a penal law at that, touching the movements of troops and military orders, and so plain that no mortal man could mistake its meaning. I say no more on that point, but I leave it with the Senate.

I approach article ten, about which a good deal has been said, both by the opening counsel and the concluding counsel. The President is, in that firticle charged with an indictable offense, in this, that in the District of Columbia, he uttered seditious words—I am stating the substance and legal effect of the charge—intending to excite the people to revolt against the Thirty-ninth Congress, and to a disregard of its legislation, asserting in terms that it was not a Congress, that it was a body assuming to be a Congress, hanging on the verge of the government.

He is charged also with committing acts of public indecency, which, as I showed to the Senate yesterday, is, at common law, an indictable misdemeanor, showing a purpose on his part to violate the law himself, and to encourage and incite others to violate it also. In other words, his language was the language of sedition. What did the counsel for the President say about it? They referred to the sedition act of 1798, which had expired by its own limitation, and talked about its being a very odious law. I do not know but what they intimated that it was a very unconstitutional law Pray what court of the United States ever so decided? There were prosecutions under it, and what Court, I ask, ever so decided, or what commanding authority on the Constitution ever ruled that the law was unconstitutional?

I admit that no such law as that should be on your statute-books of general application and operation, except in the day of national peril, and that was a day of national peril. There was sedition in the land. The French Minister was abroad all through the republic, everywhere attempting to stir up the people to enter into combinations abroad, hurtful and dangerous to the security of the republic. But I pass from that. The gentleman (Mr. Evarts) referred to Mr. Jefferson coming into power and exhibiting his hostility to the Sedition act of 1798. But he had no sooner got into power than he re-enacted that law as to every officer in your army, and it stands the law of the republic, unchallenged, from that day to this.

I read from the act of 1806, "any officer or soldier who shall use contemptuous or disrespectful words against the President of the United States, against the Vice President thereof, against the Congress of the United States, or against the Chief Magistrate or Legislature of any of the United States in which he may be quartered, if a commissioned officer, shall be cashiered or otherwise punished as a court martial may direct; and if a non-commissioned officer or soldier, shall suffer such punishment as may be inflicted upon him by the sentence of a court-martial, even unto death." The gentleman read from the Constitution, in the hope, I suppose to show that it was utterly impossible for the Congress of the United States to inflict pains and penalties by law for seditious utterances, either by the President or anybody else.

If it was competent for Congress, in 1806, to enact that law, it was equally competent for the Congress of 1798 to enact the Sedition law, and by the act of 1801 those seditious utterances made in the District of Columbia are indictable as misdemeanors, whether made by the President or anybody else, and especially when made by any officer charged with the execution of the laws, for, as I read yesterday, the refusal by an officer to do an act required by the law, is, at common law, indictable. An attempt on the part of such officer to procure others to violate a law, is also indictable; and, in general, seditious utterances by an executive officer are always, at the common law, indictable—such as inciting the people to resistance, inciting an officer of the army to mutiny, in disregard of the law; and that was the attempt, and that is the language of the President.

But, say counsel, this was his guaranteed right under the Constitution. The freedom of speech is not to be restricted by a law of Congress. How is that answered by the act of 1806, which subjects every soldier and every officer in your army to court-martial for using disrespectful language of the President, of Congress, or his superior officer? The freedom of speech guaranteed by the Constitution to all the people of the United States, and to be protected from any unjust restraint, is that freedom of speech which respects first the rights of the nation itself, which respects next the supremacy of the nation's laws, and which finally respects the rights of every citizen of the Republic.

I believe, too, in that freedom of speech; that is, the freedom of speech to which the learned gentleman from New York referred when he quoted the words of Milton, saying 'Give me the liberty to know, to argue and to utter freel'A according to conscience—above all liberties." That is the liberty which respects the rights of the nation and the rights of individuals. It is called that virtuous liberty, "a day, an hour of which is worth a whole eternity of bondage." That is your American constitutional liberty, the liberty in defense of which the noblest and the best of our race—men of whom the world was not worthy—suffered hunger and thirst, cold and nakedness, the jeer of hate, the frown of power, the gloom of the dungeon, the torture of the wheel, the agony of the faggott, the ignominy of the scaffold and the cross, and by their living and their dying glorified human nature, and attested its claim to immortality; and I stand, Senators, for that liberty. But I stand against that sedition which would disturb the peace of nations, and disturb the repose of men even in their graves.

There is, Senators, but one other point in this accusation which I deem it my duty to discuss further; that is the eleventh article, which alleges specifically the attempt, not the accomplishment of the acts, and which rests on all the evidence which applies to all the other articles preferred against this accused and guilty man. It charges the attempt, by advice, to incite the people to resistance against their own Congress and its laws, by declaring that it was a Congress of only a part of the States; the attempt to prevent the ratification by the Legislatures of several States of the fourteenth article of amendment proposed by the Thirty-ninth Congress, on the same ground that it was not the Congress of the nation, and had no power to propose an article of amendment to the Constitution; the position asserted by the President in his message to Congress, and reasserted in his speech; the attempt to prevent the execution of the Tenure of Office act; the attempt to prevent the execution of the act making appropriations for the army, and the attempt to defeat the operation and execution of the act for the better and more efficient government of the Rebel States.

The gentleman from Ohio (Mr. Groesbeck) asserted that the evidence which was introduced to support this last averment in the eleventh article, was evidence of an act done by the President six months or more before the law was passed. The gentleman was entirely right in his dates, but he was altogether wrong in his conclusions. We introduced the telegram to Governor Parsons for no such purpose. We introduced it in order to sustain that averment of the eleventh article, which charges an attempt to defeat the ratification of the fourteenth article or amendment—an amendment essential to the future safety of the Republic by the judgment of twenty-five millions of men, who have so solemnly declared by its ratification in twenty-three organized States of the Union. This fourteenth article or amendment was passed in June, 1866, by the Thirty-ninth Congress.

After it had been passed, and after it was ratified, even by some of the States, the President sent this telegram to Governor Parsons:—

"UNITED STATES MILITARY TELEGRAPH, EXECUTIVE OFFICE, WASHINGTON, January 17, 1867.—What possible good can be obtained by reconsidering the Constitutional amendment; I know of none in the present posture of affairs, and I do not believe the people of the whole country will sustain any set of individuals in an attempt to change by enabling acts or otherwise?"

Any set of individuals; not the Congress, but simply a mob, a set of individuals. Is that the language of an honest man, or the language of a conspirator?

"I believe, on the contrary, that they will eventually uphold all who have patriotism and courage to stand by the Constitution, and who place their confidence in the people. There should be no faltering on the part of those who are honest in their determination to sustain the several co-ordinate departments of the government, in accordance with its original design.   "ANDREW JOHNSON."

Now what is all that, coupled with his message to Congress and coupled with his utterances? What is all that but a confirmation on the part of the President that these Rebel States, lately in insurrection, hold, after all, a power over the people of the organized States of the Union, to the extent that the people can neither legislate for the government of those disordered communities nor amend their own Constitution even for the government and protection of themselves?

If it does not mean that it means nothing. It is an attempt, in the language of the learned gentleman from New York (Mr. Evarts), who appears to-day as the able advocate of the President at this bar—it is an attempt on the part of the President to revive an expiring rebellion, the Lost Cause. It is an utterance of his to the effect that, unless the ten States lately in insurrection, or the eleven States, if you please, choose to assent to it, the people of the organized States cannot amend their constitution, and the President calls upon them to rally to the standard and to support the co-ordinate departments of the government against those encroachments of "a set of individuals on the rights of the people."

Mr. Bingham read to the Senate the text of the fourteenth article of the amendment, and then proceeded:—That is the article which the people desired to adopt, and which the President by co-operation and combination with those lately in rebellion seeks to defeat, What right had he to meddle with it? The gentleman undertook to draw a distinction between Andrew Johnson the citizen, and Andrew Johnson the President. I thought at the time that I could see some significance in it. It was a little hard for them to stand here to advocate the right of the President under his sworn obligations to take care the laws be faithfully executed, to make these utterances, and to excuse him, as President, for them.

It was a much more easy matter apparently to excuse him as a private citizen, than Andrew Johnson, for saying that the people were without a Congress, and that being without a Congress all legislation was void, and, of course, not to be enforced except so far as he saw fit to approve or enforce it; that even Congress had no right to propose this article of amendment as essential to the future life of the republic. What was this at last but saying that rebellion worked no loss of political rights? What was it but saying that by acts of secession and rebellion, if one-fourth of all the States persistently refuse to elect members of Congress, they may deprive the people at large of the power to propose amendments to their Constitution?

No utterances more offensive than these were ever made by the Executive officer of this country or of any other country. They are understood by the common plain people as the utterances in aid of a suppressed rebellion, of a lost cause, of hostility to the amendment—and why? Because, among other things, it made slavery forever impossible in the land. Because, among other things, it made repudiation of the plighted faith of this nation, either to its living or to its dead defenders, forever impossible in the land. Because, by its very provisions, it makes the payment of any debt or liability in aid of the Rebellion, either by States or by Congressional legislation, forever impossible in the land. Because it makes compensation for slaves forever impossible in the land, either by Congressional enactment or by State legislation.

Is that the secret of the hostility? If not, what is it? What is it but simply a declaration that you have no Congress and have no right to amend your Constitution; that your nation is broken up and destroyed? The President's immediate adviser and counsellor, Mr. Nelson, took she same ground in this presence, only he attempted to qualify it by saying that you may have power of ordinary legislation and yet have no power of impeachment, and he gave us notice in advance that what was the President's opinion, that you have no right to pronounce judgment unless you pronounce judgment and acquit. As I said before, Senators, all the facts in the case support the averment of the eleventh article of impeachment.

I do not propose to review the facts. I have already referred to them at sufficient length. I only ask the Senate to recollect, when it comes to deliberate, that there are several averments in the eleventh article of these attempts to violate the law, which are, by the act of 1801, indictable in the District that those offenses were committed

within, and that the averments are divisible. You may find him guilty of one of the averments in the eleventh article, and not guilty of another. If you hold it to be a crime for the President to attempt to prevent the execution of a law of Congress by combination or conspiracy, with or without force—with or without intimidation—you must, under the eleventh article, find this man guilty of having entered into such combination to prevent the execution of the Tenure of Office act, and especially to prevent the Secretary of War from resuming the functions of his office.

It is no matter whether Secretary Stanton was within the act or without the act. It was decided by the legislative department of the government, the Congress of the United States and its decision, under the law, should have controlled the President. The law was mandatory. It commanded the Secretary in the decision of the Senate, and a notice given to him forthwith to resume the functions of his office, and for disobedience to its command, after such judgment of the Senate, and after such notice, the Secretary would himself have been liable to impeachment.

This fact being established and confessed, how is the Senate to get away from it, when the President himself puts in writing and confesses, on the 10th of April, 1868, that as early as the 12th July, 1867, it was his purpose to prevent Edwin M. Stanton from resuming the functions of that office. It was his purpose, therefore, as alleged in the eleventh article, to pervert, if he could, the execution of the law.

Senators, I can have no further words on the subject. It is useless for me to exhaust my strength by further argumentation. I assume, from all that I have said on the subject, that I have made it clear to the comprehension of every Senator, and to the entire satisfaction of every Senator, that the substantial averments in the various articles presented by the House of Representatives against the President are established by the proof, and are substantially confessed by the answer of the President himself, in this, that the President did issue his order for the removal of the Secretary of War during the session of the Senate, in violation of the provision of the act of March 2, 1867, regulating the tenure of civil offices, and with the intent to violate it, which intent the law implies, and which intent the President expressly confesses: that his guilt is further established in this, that he did issue his letter of authority to General Thomas in violation of the Tenure of Office act, with the intent, as declared by himself, to prevent the Secretary of War to resume the functions of his office; that he is guilty further in this, that he did unlawfully conspire with Lorenzo Thomas, as charged in the fourth, fifth, sixth and seventh articles, with or without force, with or without intimidations, to prevent and hinder the Secretary of War from holding his office, in direct violation of the terms of the Tenure of Office act. That he is guilty, further, in this, that he did attempt to induce General Emory to violate the act making appropriations for the support of the army, a violation of which, is by the second section, declared a high misdemeanor in office; that he is guilty further in this that by his indecorous and scandalous harrangues he was guilty of great public indecency and of an attempt to bring the Congress of the United States into contempt, and to incite the people to sedition and anarchy; that he is guilty in this, that by denying the constitutionality of the Thirty-ninth Congress, and by the acts before referred to, he did assume to himself the prerogative of dispensing with the laws and of suspending their execution at his pleasure until such time as might suit his own convenience to test the question of their validity, or to ascertain the true construction of the Constitution in the courts of the United States; and that by conspiring with those lately in insurrection he did further attempt to prevent the ratification of the fourteenth article of the amendment to the Constitution, and that by all these several acts he did attempt to prevent the execution of the Tenure of Office act, the execution of the Army Appropriation bill, and the execution of the act for the efficient government of the Rebel States.

These facts being thus established, will not only enforce conviction on the mind of the Senate, but will, in my judgment, enforce conviction on the mind of the greater part of the people of this country. Nothing remains, Senators, for me to consider further in this transaction but the confession and attempted avoidance of the President, as made in his answer. It is only needful for me to remind the Senate that the President claims, in his answer, the power indefinitely to suspend the heads of departments during the session of the Senate, without its advice and consent, and to fill the offices by appointments ad interim; that he claims the right to interpret the Constitution for himself, and in the exercise of that right to pronounce for himself on the validity of every act of Congress that may be placed upon the statute books, and that, therefore, in the exercise of his prerogative as the Executive of the United States, in defiance of your law, and in defiance of that transcendent power of impeachment vested by the people in the House of Representatives and the Senate, may suspend the laws and dispense with their execution at his pleasure. That is the position of the President; these are the offenses with which he stands charged. The effect of the charge against the President is usurpation in office, suspension of the people's laws, dispensation of their execution here, and corruptly and purposely, with intent to violate them, and, in the language of the articles, to "hinder and prevent their execution." The defense set up is that of implied judicial power, as it is called by the learned counsel for the President, judicially to determine for himself the true construction of the Constitution, and judicially to determine for himself the validity of all your laws.

I have endeavored to show, Senators, that this assumption of the President is incompatible with every provision of the Constitution; that it is at war with all the traditions of the republic; that it is in direct conflict with the cotemporaneous and continued construction of the Constitution, legislative, executive and judicial. I have endeavored also, to impress you, Senators, with my own conviction, that this assumption of the President to interpret the Constitution and laws for himself, and to suspend the execution of the laws at his pleasure, is an assumption of power simply to set aside the Constitution, to set aside your laws and to annihilate the government of the people.

This is the President's crime, that he has assumed this prerogative, dangerous to the people's liberties, violative of his oath, of the Constitution and of the laws. I have also endeavored to show that these offenses, as presented in the articles, are impeachable. They are declared by the law of the land to be high crimes and misdemeanors, indictable and punishable as such; yet the President has the audacity, in his answer—I go not beyond that to convict him—to come before this Senate and declare, admitting all the charges against me to be true, admitting that "I did suspend the execution of the laws; that I did enter into conspiracy with intent to prevent the execution of the laws; that I did issue a letter of authority, in direct violation of the law; nevertheless, I say it was my right to do so, because, by force of the Constitution I may interpret the Constitution for myself, and decide upon the validity of the law, as to whether it conflicts with the power conferred upon me by the Constitution, and, if it does, take the necessary steps to test its validity in the courts of justice."

I have endeavored further to show, Senators, that the civil tribunals of the country can by no possibility have any power, under the Constitution, to determine any such cause between the President and the people. I do not propose to repeat my argument, but I ask Senators to consider that if the courts are to be allowed to intervene and to decide, in the first instance, any question of the sort between the people and an accused President, it would necessarily result that the courts at last, acting on the suggestion of the President, may decide every question of impeachment that can possibly arise by reason of malfeasance of the President in office, and that the President may defy the power of the people to impeach and to try him in the Senate.

The Supreme Court cannot decide questions of that sort for the Senate, because the Constitution declares that the Senate shall have the sole power to try all impeachments, and that necessarily includes the sole power to decide every question of law and of fact, finally and forever, between the President and the people.

That is our argument; that is the position which we assume here, in behalf of the people, before the Senate. If we are wrong, and if after all you can cast on the courts the burden which the Constitution imposes on you, and on you alone, and can thereby deprive the people of the power of removal of an accused and guilty President, it is for you to say. We do not entertain for a moment the belief that the Senate will give any sort of countenance to that position assumed by the President in his answer, and and which at last constitutes his sole defense.

The acts charged, Senators, are acts of usurpation in office, criminal by reason of the Constitution and laws of the land, and, inasmuch as they are committed by the Chief Magistrate of the nation, they are the more dangerous to the public liberties. The people, Senators, have declared in words too plain to be mistaken, too strong to be evaded by the subtleties of false logic, that the Constitution, ordained for themselves, and the laws enacted by their representatives in Congress assembled, shall be obeyed, shall be executed or enforced by their servant, the President of the United States, until the same shall be amended or repealed in the mode prescribed by themselves.

They have written this decree of theirs all over this land, in the tempest and the fire of battle. When twelve millions of men, standing within the limits of eleven States of the Union, entered into a confederation and an agreement against the supremacy of the Constitution and the laws, conspired to suspend their execution and annul them within the territorial limits of their respective States, from ocean to ocean, by a sublime uprising, the people stamped out in blood the atrocious assumption that even millions of men can be permitted, even through State organizations, to suspend for a moment the supremacy of the Constitution and the laws, or the execution of the people's laws.

Is it to be supposed for a moment that this great and triumphant people, who but yesterday wrote this decree of theirs all over this land, amid the flames of battle, are now, at this time of day, tamely to submit to the same assumption of power in the hands of a single man, and that their own sworn Executive? Let the people answer that question, as they surely will answer it, in the coming elections. Is it not in vain, I ask you, Senators, that the people have thus vindicated by battle the supremacy of their Constitution and law, if, after all, their own President is permitted to suspend their laws, to dispense with their execution at his pleasure, and to defy the power of the people to bring him to trial and judgment before the only tribunal authorized by the Constitution to try him?

That is the issue which is presented before the Senate for decision by these articles of impeachment. By such acts of usurpation on the part of the rulers of the people the peace of nations is broken, as it is only by obedience to law that the peace of nations is maintained and their existence perpetuated. The seat of law is the bosom of God, and her voice the harmony of the world. All history is but philosophy teaching by example; God is in it, and through it teaches to men and nations the profoundest lessons that they learn."

It does not surprise me, Senators, that the learned counsel for the accused ask the Senate, in the consideration of this question, to close that volume of instruction—not to look into the past—not to listen to its voice. Senators, from that day, when the inscription was written on the graves of the heroes of Thermopylæ:—"Stranger, go tell the Lacedemonians that we lie here in obedience to their laws," to this hour no profounder lesson has come down to us than this, that through obedience to laws comes the strength of nations and the safety of men.

No more fatal provision, Senators, ever found its way into the constitutions of States than that contended for in this defense, which recognizes the right of a single desperate man, or of the many, to discriminate in the administration of justice between the ruler and the citizen—between the strong and the weak.

It was by that unjust discrimination that Aristides was banished, because he was just. It was by that unjust discrimination that Socrates, the wonder of the Pagan world, was doomed to drink the hemlock, because of his transcendant virtues. It was an honorable protest against that unjust discrimination that the great Roman Senator, the father of his country, declared that the force of law consisted in its being made for the whole community.

Senators, it is the pride and boast of that great people, from whom we are descended, as it is the pride and boast of every American, that the law is the supreme power of the State, and is for the protection of each by the combined power of all. By the Constitution of England the hereditary monarch is no more above the law than the humblest subject; and by the Constitution of the United States the President is no more above the law than the poorest and most friendless beggar in your streets. The usurpations of Charles I, to which reference has been made by my associate, inflicted untold injuries on the people of England, and finally cost the usurper his life.

The subsequent usurpation of James II—and I only refer to that, Senators, because there is between his official conduct and that of the President the most remarkable parallel that I have ever read in human history—filled the brain and heart of England with the conviction that new securities must be taken to restrain the prerogative asserted by the Crown if the people would maintain their ancient Constitution and perpetuate their liberties.

It has been well said that the usurpation of James swept away the solemn ordinances of the legislature. Out of that usurpation came the great revolution of 1688, which resulted in the dethronement and banishment of James. In the elevation of William and Mary, in the immortal declaration of rights, of which it is well said, "it is the germ of the law which gave religious freedom to the dissenters; which secured the independence of the churches; which limited the duration of Parliament; which is based on liberal principles, under the protection of juries; which prohibited the slave trade; which abolished the sacramental test; which removed the Roman Catholic disabilities; which reformed the representative system, and of every good law which has been passed during one hundred and sixty years, in England, and of every good law which may hereafter, in the course of ages, be found necessary to promote the public weal and to satisfy the demand of public opinion."

Senators, that great declaration of rights records these words against this accused King of England:—

"He has endeavored to subvert the liberties of the country in this, that he has suspended and dispensed with the execution of the laws; in this, that he has issued commissions under the great seal, contrary to the laws; in this, that he has levied money for the use of the Crown, contrary to law; in this, that he has caused cases to be tried in the King's Bench, which are cognizable only in the Parliament."

I ask the Senate to notice that these charges against James are substantially the charges presented against this accused President, and confessed here by record. That he has suspended the laws and dispensed with the execution of the laws, and in order to do it, has usurped authority as Executive of the nation, declaring himself entitled, under the Constitution, to suspend the laws and dispense with their execution.

He has further, like James, issued commissions contrary to law; he has further, like James, attempted to control the appropriated money of the people contrary to law, and he has further, like James, though that is not alleged against him in the articles of impeachment—it is confessed in his answer—attempted to cause the question of his responsibility to the people to be tried, not in the king's bench, but in the Supreme Court, while it is alone triable and alone cognizable in the Senate of the United States.

Surely, Senators, if these usurpations and these endeavors on the part of James thus to subvert the liberties of the people of England were sufficient to dethrone him, the like offenses committed by Andrew Johnson ought to cost him his office and to subject him to that perpetual disability pronounced by the people, through the Constitution, upon him for his high crimes and misdemeanors.

Senators, you will pardon me—but I will detain you only a few minutes longer—for asking your attention to another view of the question between the people and the Executive.

I use the words of England's brilliant historian when I say:—"Had not the legislative power of England triumphed over the usurpations of James, with what a crash, felt and heard to the farthest ends of the world, would the whole vast fabric of society have fallen." May God forbid that a future historian shall record of these days proceedings, that by reason of the failure of the legislative power of the people to triumph over the usurpations of an apostate President, through defection in the Senate of the United States, the great fabric of American empire fell and perished from the earth.

That great revolution of 1688 in England was but a forerunner of your Constitution. The declaration of rights to which I have referred but reasserted the ancient Constitution of England, not found in any written instrument, but scattered through statutes of four centuries. The great principle thus reasserted by the declaration of rights in 1688, was, that no law shall be passed without the consent of the representatives of the nation; no tax shall be kept up; no citizen shall be deprived for a single day of his liberty by the arbitrary will of the Sovereign; no officer shall plead the royal mandate in justification of a violation of any legal right of the humblest citizen. It forever swept away the assumption that the executive prerogative was the fundamental law. Those were the principles, Senators, involved that day in the controversy between the people and their recusant sovereign. They are precisely the principles this day involved in this controversy between the people and their recusant President, and, without revolution, "like the great Parliament of 1688," you are asked to reassert the principles of the Constitution of the country, not to be searched for through statutes of centuries, but to be found in that great sacred written instrument, given to us by the fathers of the republic.

The Constitution of the United States, as I have said, embodies that act. In the English declaration of rights and in the English Constitution and laws, it was ordained by the people, amid the convulsions and agonies of nations, by its express provisions, all men within its jurisdiction are equal before the law, and are equally entitled to those rights of persons which are as universal as the material structure of man, and are equally liable to answer to its tribunals for every injury done either to the citizen or to the State. It is that spirit of justice, of liberty, of equality, Senators, that makes your Constitution dear to freemen in this and in all lands, in that it secures to every man his rights, and to the people at large the inestimable right of self-government.

That is the right which is this day challenged by the usurping President; for, if he be a law unto himself, the people are no longer their own law-makers, through their Representatives in Congress assembled. He simply becomes their dictator. If so, he becomes so by the judgment of the Senate, not by the Constitution; not by any interpretation heretofore put upon it; not by any act of the people, nor by any act of the people's Representatives. They have discharged their duty; they have presented him at the bar of the Senate for trial, in that he has usurped and attempted to combine in himself the legislative and executive powers of this great people, thereby claiming for himself a power by which he might annihilate their government. We have seen that when the supremacy of the Constitution was challenged by battle the people made such sacrifices to maintain it as has no parallel in human history.

Senators, can it be that, after this triumph of law over anarchy, of right over wrong, of patriotism over treason, the Constitution and laws are again to be assailed in the Capitol of the nation by the Chief Magistrate, and that he is to be by the judgment of the Senate protected in that usurpation? I say, Senators, that you are deliberately asked by the President in his answer, and by the lips of his counsel, to set the accused through your judgment above the Constitution which he has violated, and to set him above the people, whom he has betrayed, and that, too, on the pretext that the President has the right judicially to construe the Constitution for himself, and judicially to decide for himself the validity of your laws, and to plead justification at your bar, that his only purpose in violating the Constitution and the law was to test the validity of the law, and to ascertain the construction of the Constitution on his own motion, in the courts of justice, and thereby to suspend these proceedings.

I ask you, Senators, how long men would deliberate on the question, whether a private citizen, arraigned at the bar of one of your tribunals of justice for a criminal violation of the law, should be permitted to interpose as a plea in justification of his criminal act, that his only purpose was to interpret the Constitution and law for himself; that he violated the law in the exercise of his prerogative, to test its validity hereafter at such time as might suit his own convenience, in the courts of justice?

Surely, Senators, it is as competent for the private citizen to interpose such justification in answer to a criminal charge, in any of your tribunals of justice, as it is for the President of the United States to interpose it, and for the simple reason that the Constitution is no respecter of persons, and vests neither in the President nor in the private citizen judicial powers. Pardon me, Senators, for saying it. I spoke in no offensive spirit. I speak it from a sense of duty; I utter it in my own conviction, and desire to place it on record, that for the Senate to sustain any such plea would, in my judgment, be a gross violation of the already violated Constitution and laws of a free people.

Can it be, Senators, that by your decree you are at last to make this discrimination between the ruler of the people and the private citizen, and allow the President to interpose his private right of interpretation, judicially, of your Constitution and laws. I put away, Senators, the possibility that the Senate of the United States, equal in dignity to any tribunal in the world, is capable of recording any such decision, even upon the petition and the prayer of this accused and guilty President. Can it be that by reason of his great office, the President is to be protected in those high crimes and misdemeanors, violative alike of his oath, of the Constitution, and of the express letter of your written law.

Senators. I have said perhaps more than I ought to say; I have said perhaps more than there was occasion to say; I know that I stand in the presence of men illustrious in our country's history; I know that I stand in the presence of men who for long years have been in the nation's counsels; I know that I stand in the presence of men who, in some sense, may be called to-day the living fathers of the republic; and I ask you, Senators, to consider that I speak before you this day in behalf of that violated law of a free people who commissioned me.

I ask you to remember that I speak this day under the obligation of my oath; I ask you to consider, Senators, that I am not insensible to the significance of those words of which mention was made by the learned gentleman from New York (Mr. Evarts)—"Justice, duty, law, oath." I ask you, Senators, to consider that we stand this day pleading for the violated majesty of law by the graves of half a million of murdered hero patriots, who met death in battle by the sacrifice of themselves for their country, the Constitution and the laws, and proved by their sublime example that all must obey the law; that none are above the law; that no man lives for himself alone, but each for all; that some may die in order that the State may live; that the citizen is at best for to-day, while the Commonwealth is for all time, and that no position, however high, no patronage however great, can be permitted to shelter crime to the peril of the Republic.

It only remains for me, Senators, to thank you, as I do, for the honor you have done me by your kind attention, and to demand, in the name of the House of Representatives and of the people, judgment against the accused for the high crimes and misdemeanors in office whereof he stands impeached, and of which, before God and men, he is clearly guilty.

Mr. Bingham concluded his remarks at half-past two o'clock.

As he ceased speaking, a large number of the spectators in the galleries applauded him by clapping of hands, and persisted in these manifestations, in spite of the efforts of the Chief Justice to restore order. Finally, the Chief Justice directed that the galleries should be cleared. Even after the order was given, and in apparent defiance of it, many of the spectators continued to clap their hands, while some few indulged in hisses.

Senator GRIMES arose and moved that the order of the Chief Justice to clear the galleries be immediately enforced.

The Chief Justice renewed the order to the Sergeant-at-Arms to clear the galleries, but even after that second order the spectators continued to manifest their sentiments, the most part by applause, and a very few by hissing.

Senator TRUMBULL, amid the excitement caused by the disregard of the rules of the court, and of the orders of the Chief Justice, rose and moved that the Sergeant-at-Arms be directed to arrest all who were thus offending.

The impossibility of doing anything of the kind caused the proposition to be received by the spectators with laughter and derision.

Senator CAMERON then arose in spite of repeated calls to order by Senator Fessenden and Senator Johnson and the Chief Justice, and persisted in expressing the hope that the galleries would not be cleared; he added that a large proportion of the spectators had a very different feeling from that expressed by the clapping of hands, and that as it was one of the most extraordinary cases in our history, some allowance should be made for the excitement natural to the occasion. Finally Senator Cameron, on the Chief Justice ruling that he was out of order, took his seat.

During all this time there was no indication on the part of the spectators of any intention on their part to obey the order directing the galleries to be cleared.

Senator CONNESS, as the simplest mode of getting over the difficulty, moved that the Senate take a recess, but that motion was met with the expression, by several Senators, "No; not till the galleries are cleared."

The motion, however, was put and rejected.

Senator DAVIS then rose, and insisted that the order to have the galleries cleared should be enforced.

The Chief Justice stated that orders to that effect had been given to the Sergeant-at-Arms.

Still no motion was made by any person in the crowded galleries to leave his or her seat.

Senator SHERMAN, apparently influenced by the same motive as Senator Conness, asked the Chief Justice whether it was in order to move that the Senate retire for deliberation; if so, he would make that motion.

The Chief Justice remarked, in reply to Senator Sherman, that until the order to clear the galleries was enforced, the Senate could not, with self-respect, make any other order.

Senator SHERMAN expressed the opinion that many persons in the galleries did not understand that they were ordered to leave the galleries. The spectators showed themselves not at all disposed to take the hint, and not one made a movement towards leaving.

Finally the Chief Justice informed the persons in the gallery that the Senate had made an order for the galleries to be cleared, and that it was expected that they would respect the order and leave the galleries.

This direct appeal, backed as it was by the ushers and police officers, had the effect at last of inducing the elegantly dressed ladies and their attendants to rise from their seats and move towards the doors, but they did so with evident reluctance and discontent.

The spectators in the diplomatic gallery were not interfered with while the other galleries were being cleared, but finally their turn came too; and last of all the representatives of the newspaper press were required to leave the reporters' gallery.

While this clearing out process was going on, and when all but those in the diplomatic galleries and the reporters had left—

Senator ANTHONY moved that the order be suspended.

Senator HOWARD protested against its suspension.

Senator CONKLING inquired whether the suspension of the order would open all the galleries to those who had been turned out?

Several Senators remarked that it would have that effect.

Senator HOWARD continued to protest against the suspension of the order, and the the motion was voted down.

Senator MORRILL (Me.), then submitted the following order:—

Ordered, That when the Senate, sitting for the trial of impeachment, adjourn this day, it will adjourn till Saturday next at twelve o'clock.

Senator CONNESS, seeing the reporter of the Associated Press coolly taking notes of the proceedings, objected to any business being done until the order for clearing the galleries was fully carried out.

The reporters, yielding to the force of circumstances, departed, leaving the Senate Chamber in the sole occupation of the Chief Justice, the Senators, the managers, the members of the House, the President's counsel, and the officers of the Senate.

While the doors were closed, the motion offered by Mr Morrill (Me.) to adjourn the court until Saturday next was lost by a vote of 22 to 29.

In answer to a question by Senator Conkling (N. Y.), the Chief Justice said it had not been his intention to exclude the reporters and that he was about to submit the question to the Senate when the inquiry was made.

Pending the consideration of the various orders in regard to the mode of voting and the admission of the reporters during the final deliberations, a motion to take a recess prevailed, and at three o'clock the doors were opened to the public. It was some twenty minutes before the Senate was again called to order.

The Chief Justice said that he understood the case to be closed on both sides, that nothing further was to submitted. The next business in order was the several pending propositions.

Senator HENDRICKS said he believed the pending questions would be considered in secret session, but he would desire that the Senate proceed by unanimous consent to consider them as if it had retired.

The Chief Justice—The only motion in order is that the Senate retire for deliberation, and that the doors be closed.

Senator FESSENDEN (Me.)—I would suggest that the motion be modified; that the audience retire and that we consider them in secret session.

Mr. HENDRICKS—I move that the Senate retire, without disturbing the audience, by unanimous consent.

Chief Justice—If there is no objection.

Mr. HENDRICKS moved that we consider this in public as if we had retired, so that what is said in regard to these rules shall be said in public.

Mr. CONNESS—That is, that debate shall be allowed.

Mr. HENDRICKS—Debate to the extent of ten minutes.

The Chief Justice—The Chief Justice thinks it proper to state to the Senate that that reverses the whole order of proceeding, but if there is no objection it can be done.

Several Senators objected.

The Chief Justice stated the question to be on the motion of Mr. Hendricks.

Mr. EDMUNDS moved as an amendment that the doors be closed.

Mr. HENDRICKS said his sole object was to remove the limit of debate.

The Chief Justice interrupted, to say that debate was not in order, and put the question on the motion of Mr. Edmunds, which was carried, and at half-past three o'clock the doors were closed for deliberation.

The Secret Session.

When the Senate went into Secret Session this afternoon, crowds besieged the doors, evidently in expectation of a result being reached on the Impeachment question to-day. There was considerable speculation among the outside parties as to the matter at issue, and much excitement in all. Particular was the earnest inquiries made when the doors were opened, in relation to the result of the Senatorial deliberation.

It was ascertained that the following took place in secret session.

Chief Justice Chase announced that the first question would be on the following proposition of Senator Edmunds:—

Ordered, That after the arguments shall be considered, and when the doors shall be closed for deliberation upon the final question, the official reporters of the Senate shall take down the debates upon the final question, to be reported in the proceedings.

Senator WILLIAMS offered an amendment that no member shall speak longer than fifteen minutes.

Senator FRELINGHUYSEN moved to lay the whole subject on the table, which was agreed to as follows:—

YEAS.—Messrs. Cameron, Cattell, Chandler, Conkling, Conness, Corbett, Cragin, Drake, Ferry, Frelinghuysen, Harlan, Henderson, Howe, Morgan, Morrill, (Me.,) Morton, Norton, Patterson, (N. H.,) Pomeroy, Ramsey, Ross, Stewart, Sumner, Thayer, Tipton, Trumbull, Williams, and Yates.—28.

NAYS.—Messrs. Anthony, Bayard, Buckalew, Davis, Dixon, Doolittle, Edmunds, Fessenden, Fowler, Grimes, Hendricks, Johnson, McCreery, Morrill (Vt.), Patterson (Tenn.), Saulsbury, Sprague, Van Winkle, Vickers and Willey—20.

The following is the vote on the motion to adjourn the court of impeachment till next Saturday, the question being decided in the negative:—

YEAS.—Messrs. Anthony, Cattell, Cragin, Doolittle, Fessenden, Foster, Frelinghuysen, Grimes, Henderson, Howard, Johnson, Morrill (Me.), Norton, Patterson (N. H.), Patterson (Tenn.), Ross, Saulsbury, Sprague, Trumbull, Van Winkle and Willey.—22.

NAYS.—Messrs. Buckalew, Cameron, Chandler, Conkling, Conness, Corbett, Davis, Drake, Edmunds, Ferry, Harlan, Hendricks, Howe, McCreery, Morgan, Morrill (Vt.), Morton, Nye, Pomeroy, Ramsey, Sherman, Stewart, Sumner, Thayer, Tipton, Vickers, Williams, Wilson and Yates.—29.

PROCEEDINGS OF THURSDAY, MAY 7.

The court was opened at noon with the usual formalities. A very small attendance was visible in the galleries.

Mr. Nelson, of the counsel for the President, occupied a seat at their table.

Closing the Doors.

After the reading of the journal, the Chief Justice said the doors would now be closed unless some order to the contrary was made.

Mr. HOWE did not see any necessity for closing the doors, and hoped the order would not be executed,

Mr. SUMNER raised the question of order whether the Senate can deliberate with closed doors now, except by another vote, the court having now commenced in open session.

The Chief Justice said he would put the question to the Senate.

Mr. SHERMAN asked whether the Senator from Massachusetts (Mr. Sumner), proposed to vote upon the pending question without debate.

Mr. SUMNER replied that he had no intention of making any proposition in that respect, but simply wished that what was done should be done under the rules.

The Chief Justice, checking the discussion with the gavel, said there could be no debate until the doors were closed.

The Sergeant-at-Arms, from the floor, directed the doorkeepers to clear the galleries, and all but the reporters' gallery were speedily cleared. Finally, however, the officers turned out the reporters also. As they were leaving,

Mr. TRUMBULL was raising a point of order that under the rules the deliberations must be had with closed doors.

The Senate in Secret Session.

The following is the record of proceedings in the secret session of the Senate to-day, which occupied about six hours.

The Chief Justice stated that the unfinished business from yesterday was on the order of Mr. Sumner submitted by him on the 25th of April as follows:—

"That the Senate, sitting on the trial of Andrew Johnson, President of the United States, will proceed to vote on the several articles of impeachment, at 12 o'clock, on the day after the close of the argument."

Mr. MORRILL (Me.) moved to amend the order of Mr. Sumner so as to provide in addition, that when the Senate, sitting to try the impeachment of Andrew Johnson, President of the United States, adjourns to-day, it be to Monday next, at noon, when the Senate shall proceed to take the vote by yeas and nays, on the articles of impeachment, without debate, and any Senator who may choose shall have permission to file a written opinion to go on the record of the proceedings.

Mr. DRAKE moved to amend by adding, after the

word "permission," the words "at the time of giving his vote."

After debate, Mr. CONKLING moved that the further consideration of the subject be postponed.

Pending which, Mr. TRUMBULL moved to lay the subject on the table, and the question was decided in the affirmative.

Mr. MORRILL (Vt.) submitted the following:—

Ordered, When the Senate adjourns to-day, it adjourns until Monday, at eleven o'clock A. M., for the purpose of deliberating on the rules of the impeachment; and that, on Tuesday, at twelve o'clock meridian, the Senate shall proceed to vote, without debate, on the several articles of impeachment, and each Senator shall be permitted to file, within ten days after the vote is taken, his written opinion to go in the record.

Mr. ANTHONY added an amendment that the vote be taken on or before Wednesday.

This was decided in the negative; yeas, 13; nays, 37, as follows:—

YEAS.—Messrs. Anthony, Buckalew, Davis, Dixon, Doolittle, Fowler, Hendricks, McCreery, Patterson (Tenn.), Ross, Saulsbury, Sprague and Vickers—13.

NAYS.—Messrs. Cole, Conkling, Conness, Corbett, Cragin, Drake, Edmunds, Ferry, Frelinghuysen, Harlan, Henderson, Howard, Howe, Johnson, Morgan, Morrill (Me.), Morrill (Vt.), Morton, Norton, Nye, Patterson (N. H.), Pomeroy, Ramsey, Sherman, Stewart, Sumner, Thayer, Tipton, Trumbull, Van Winkle Willey, Williams, Wilson and Yates—37.

Mr. SUMNER moved that the further consideration of the subject be postponed, and that the Senate proceed to consider the articles of impeachment.

The question was decided in the negative, by the following vote:—

YEAS.—Messrs. Cameron, Conkling, Conness, Drake, Harlan, Morgan, Nye, Pomeroy, Stewart, Sumner, Thayer, Tipton, Williams, Wilson and Yates—15.

NAYS.—Messrs. Anthony, Bayard, Buckalew, Cattell, Cragin, Davis, Dixon, Doolittle, Edmunds, Ferry, Fessenden, Fowler, Frelinghuysen, Grimes, Henderson, Hendricks, Howard, Howe, Johnson, McCreery, Morrill. (Me.), Morrill (Vt.), Morton, Norton, Patterson (N. H.), Patterson (Tenn.), Ramsey, Ross, Saulsbury, Sherman. Sprague, Trumbull, Van Winkle, Vickers and Willey—38.

Mr. SUMNER moved to amend Mr. Morrill's order by striking out the word "Monday," and inserting "Saturday," as to the time to which the Senate will adjourn.

This was determined in the negative, as follows:—

YEAS.—Messrs. Cameron, Chandler, Cole, Conkling, Conness, Drake, Harlan, Howard, Morgan, Pomeroy, Stewart, Sumner, Thayer, Williams, Wilson, and Yates—16.

NAYS.—Messrs. Anthony, Bayard, Buckalew, Cattell, Corbett, Cragin, Davis, Dixon, Doolittle, Edmunds, Ferry, Fessenden, Fowler, Frelinghuysen, Grimes, Henderson, Hendricks, Howe, Johnson, McCreery, Morrill (Me.), Morrill (Vt.), Morton, Norton, Patterson (N. H.), Patterson (Tenn.), Ramsey, Ross, Saulsbury, Sherman, Sprague, Tipton, Trumbull, Van Winkle, Vickers, and Willey—36.

Mr. SUMNER moved to amend by striking out the following words from Mr. Morrill's order, namely:— "And each Senator shall be permitted to file within two days after the vote is taken, his written opinion to go on the record."

Mr. DRAKE moved to further amend by striking out the above words, and inserting, "at the time of giving his vote." This was determined in the negative, as follows:—

YEAS.—Messrs. Cameron, Chandler, Conkling, Conness, Drake. Harlan, Howard, Morgan, Ramsey, Stewart, Sumner and Thayer—12.

NAYS.—Messrs. Anthony, Bayard, Buckalew, Cattell, Cole, Corbett, Cragin, Davis, Dixon, Doolittle, Edmunds, Ferry, Fessenden, Fowler, Frelinghuysen, Grimes, Henderson, Hendricks, Johnson, McCreery, Morrill (Me.), Morrill (Vt.), Morton, Norton, Patterson (N. H.), Patterson (Tenn.), Ross, Saulsbury, Sherman, Sprague, Tipton, Trumbull, Van Winkle, Vickers, Willey, Williams, Wilson and Yates—38.

The question was then taken on Mr. Sumner's motion to strike out the words "and each Senator shall be permitted to file, within two days after the vote is take, his written opinion to go on the record," and the question was determined in the negative, as follows:—

YEAS—Messrs. Drake, Harlan, Ramsey, Stewart, Sumner and Thayer—6.

NAYS—Messrs. Bayard, Buckalew, Cameron, Cattell, Chandler, Cole, Corbett, Davis, Dixon, Doolittle, Edmunds, Ferry, Fessenden, Fowler, Frelinghuysen, Grimes, Henderson, Hendricks, Howard, Howe, Johnson, McCreery, Morgan, Morrill (Me.), Morrill (Vt.), Morton, Norton, Patterson (N. H.), Patterson (Tenn.), Pomeroy, Ross, Saulsbury, Sherman, Sprague, Tipton, Trumbull, Van Winkle, Vickers, Willey, Williams, Wilson and Yates—42.

Mr. MORRILL (Vt.) then modified his order, as follows, which was agreed to, namely:—

Ordered, That when the Senate adjourns, it adjourns until Monday at twelve o'clock, meridian, for the purpose of deliberating on the rules of the Senate, setting on the trial of the impeachment, and that on Tuesday next following, at twelve o'clock, meridian, the Senate shall proceed to vote, without debate, on the several articles of impeachment, and each Senator shall be permitted to file, within two days after the vote is taken, his written opinion, to be printed with the proceedings.

The Senate then proceeded to the consideration of Mr. Drake's proposition to amend the twenty-third rule, so that the fifteen minutes therein allowed for debate shall be for the whole deliberation on the final question, and not on each article of impeachment; and this was agreed to.

The Senate then proceeded to the consideration of the following additional rules proposed by Mr. Sumner on April 25:—

Rule 23. In taking the vote of the Senate on the articles of impeachment, the presiding officer shall call each Senator by his name, and upon each article proposed the following question in the manner following:—Mr. ——, how say you, is the respondent guilty or not guilty, as charged in the —— article of impeachment? Whereupon each Senator shall rise in his place and answer, "guilty" or "not guilty."

Mr. CONKLING moved to insert "of a high crime or misdemeanor," as the case may be.

After some debate, Mr. SUMNER modified his rule accordingly, by inserting after the words "guilty or not guilty," the words "of a high crime or misdemeanor," as the case may be.

Mr. BUCKALEW suggested an amendment, which Mr. Sumner accepted, as follows:—

Mr. ——, how say you, is the respondent, Andrew Johnson, guilty or not guilty of a high crime or misdemeanor, as charged in the articles of impeachment, etc.

Mr. CONNESS moved further to amend the rule by striking out certain words and adding others, so as to read:—

In taking the votes of the Senate on the first, second, third, fifth, seventh, eighth, ninth, tenth and eleventh articles of impeachment, the presiding officer shall call each Senator by his name, and propose the following question:— "Mr. ——, how say you, is the respondent, Andrew Johnson, President of the United States, guilty or not guilty of high crimes and misdemeanors, as charged in these articles?" and on the fourth and sixth articles:—"Mr. ——, How say you, is the respondent. Andrew Johnson, President of the United States, guilty or not guilty, as charged in these articles?" And each Senator will rise in his place, and answer, "guilty," or "not guilty."

Mr. HENDRICKS moved an amendment by inserting the following at the end:—

"But on taking the vote on the eleventh article, the question shall be put as to each clause of said article, charging a distinct offense."

After debate, the question on Mr. Hendricks' amendment was agreed to as follows:—

YEAS.—Messrs. Anthony, Davis, Doolittle, Drake, Edmunds, Ferry, Fowler, Frelinghuysen, Harlan, Henderson, Hendricks, Johnson, McCreery, Morton, Patterson (Tenn.), Ross, Sprague, Tipton, Trumbull, Van Winkle, Vickers and Willey—23.

NAYS.—Messrs. Buckalew, Cole, Conness, Corbett, Cragin, Morton, Patterson (N. H.) Pomeroy, Ramsey, Stewart, Sumner, Thayer, Williams, Wilson and Yates—15.

After further debate, the question being on agreeing to the amendment of Mr. Conness as thus amended, on motion of Mr. JOHNSON the whole subject was laid on the table by the following vote:—

YEAS.—Messrs. Bayard, Buckalew, Cameron, Cattell, Conness, Davis, Doolittle, Drake, Harlan, Henderson, Hendricks, Johnson, McCreery, Norton, Patterson (Tenn.), Saulsbury, Sprague, Thayer, Tipton, Trumbull, Van Winkle, Vickers, Willey and Yates—24.

NAYS.—Messrs. Cole, Corbett, Cragin, Edmunds, Ferry, Pomeroy, Ramsey, Ross, Sumner, Williams and Wilson—11.

The Chief Justice said it would place him in an embarrassing position to frame the questions, and that he should like to have the advice of the Senate on the subject, and would be obliged to them if they would adjourn until 10 o'clock on Monday, whereupon, on motion of Mr. YATES, the time for meeting was fixed at 10 o'clock on Monday.

On motion of Mr. COLE, the court then adjourned.

PROCEEDINGS OF MONDAY, MAY 11.

The Senate met at ten o'clock, pursuant to order, with about twenty Senators in their seats at the opening.

After the reading of the journal the Chief Justice said:—The Senate meets this morning under the order for deliberation, and the doors will be closed, unless some Senator makes a motion now,

Mr. SHERMAN—Before the doors are closed I will submit a motion that I believe will receive the unanimous consent of the Senate. To-morrow will be a day of considerable excitement, and I move that the Sergeant-at-Arms be directed to place his assistants through the galleries with directions, without further order from the Senate, to arrest any person that violates the rules of order.

Mr. EDMUNDS—It is a standing order.

Mr. SUMNER—An intimation and the Sergeant-at-Arms would be sufficient.

The Chief Justice—The Chief Justice will state that the Sergeant-at-Arms has already taken that precaution.

Mr. SHERMAN suggested that notice be given in the morning papers.

Mr. WILLIAMS suggested that, as there will probably be many strangers in the galleries to-morrow, the Chief Justice, before the call of the roll, admonish all persons that no manifestation of applause or disapproval will be allowed in the Senate under penalty of arrest.

This proposition met with general approbation, and Mr. SHERMAN withdrew his motion.

The doors were closed at 10·20 o'clock.

The doors having been closed the Chief Justice stated that in compliance with the decree of the Senate he had prepared the questions to be addressed to Senators upon the articles of impeachment, and that he had reduced his views to writing, which he read.

Mr. BUCKALEW submitted the following motion, which was considered by unanimous consent and agreed to:—

Ordered, that the views of the Chief Justice be entered upon the journal of proceedings of the Senate for the trial of impeachment.

Address of the Chief Justice.

The Chief Justice then arose and addressed the Senate as follows:—

Senators:—In conformity with what seemed the general wish of the Senate, when it adjourned on last Thursday, the Chief Justice, in taking the vote on the articles of impeachment, will adopt the mode sanctioned by the practice in the case of Chase, Peck and Humphreys. He will direct the Secretary to read the several articles successively, and after the reading of each article will put the question of guilty or not guilty to each Senator, rising in his place—the form used in the trial of Judge Chase:—Mr. Senator ——, how say you, is the respondent, Andrew Johnson, President of the United States, guilty or not guilty of a high misdemeanor, as charged in this article?

In putting the questions on articles fourth and sixth, each of which charges a crime, the word "crime" will be substituted for the word "misdemeanor." The Chief Justice has carefully considered the suggestion of the Senator from Indiana (Mr. Hendricks), which appeared to meet the approval of the Senate, that in taking the vote on the eleventh article, the question should be put on each clause, and has found himself unable to divide the article as suggested. The articles charge several facts, but they are so connected that they make but one allegation, and this charges as constituting one misdemeanor; the first act charged in substance, that the President publicly declared in August, 1866, that the Thirty-ninth Congress was a Congress of only part of the States, and not a constitutional Congress, intending thereby to deny its constitutionality to enact laws or propose amendments to the Constitution, and this charge seems to have been made as introductory, and as qualifying that which follows, namely:—That the President, in pursuance of this declaration, attempted to prevent the execution of the Tenure of Office act by contriving and attempting to contrive means to prevent Mr. Stanton from re-

suming the functions of Secretary of War, after the refusal of the Senate to concur in his suspension, and also by contriving and attempting to contrive means to prevent the execution of the Appropriation act of March 2, 1867; and also to prevent the execution of the Rebel States Government's act of the same date.

The gravamen of the article seems to be that the President attempted to defeat the execution of the Tenure of Office act, and that he did this in pursuance of a declaration which was intended to deny the constitutional competency of Congress to enact laws or propose constitutional amendments, and by contriving means to prevent Mr. Stanton from resuming his office of Secretary; and also to prevent the execution of the Reconstruction acts in the Rebel States. The single substantive matter charged is the attempt to prevent the execution of the Tenure of Office act and the other facts alleged, either as introductory, and exhibiting his general purpose, or as showing the means contrived in furtherance of that attempt. This single matter, connected with the other matters previously and subsequently alleged, is charged as the high misdemeanor of which the President is alleged to have been guilty.

The general question of guilty or not guilty of high misdemeanor, as charged, seems fully concurred in as charged, and will be put to this article, as well as to the others, until the Senate direct some mode of division. In the tenth article the division suggested by the Senator from New York (Mr. Conkling) may be more easily made. It contains a general allegation to the effect that on the sixteenth of August, and on other days, the President, with intent to set aside the rightful authority of Congress and bring it into contempt, uttered certain scandalous harangues and threats and bitter menaces against Congress, and the laws of the United States enacted by Congress, thereby bringing the office of President into disgrace to the great scandal of all good citizens, and sets forth in three distinct specifications the harangues, threats and menaces complained of in this respect to the several specifications; and then the question of guilty or not guilty of high misdemeanor, as charged in the article, can also be taken. The Chief Justice, however, sees no objection in putting general questions on this article, in the same manner as the others; for whether particular questions be put on the specifications or not, the answer to the final question must be determined by the judgment of the Senate, whether or not the acts alleged in the specifications have been sufficiently proved, and whether, if sufficiently proved, they amount to a high misdemeanor within the meaning of the Constitution.

On the whole, therefore, the Chief Justice thinks that the better practice will be to put the general question on each article, without attempting to make any subdivision, and will pursue this course, if no objection is made. He will, however, be pleased to conform to such directions as the Senate may see fit in the matter.

Whereupon, Mr. SUMNER submitted the following order, which was considered by unanimous consent:—

That the questions be put as proposed by the presiding officer of the Senate, and each Senator shall rise in his place and answer, "Guilty" or "Not Guilty" only.

On motion of Mr. SUMNER, the Senate proceeded to consider the following resolution, submitted on the 25th of April last:—

Resolved, That the following be added to the rules of procedure and practice in the Senate, when sitting at the trial of impeachment:—"On a conviction by the Senate, it shall be the duty of the presiding officer, forthwith, to pronounce the removal from office of the convicted person, according to the requirements of the Constitution. Any further judgment shall be on the order of the Senate."

After debate, the Chief Justice announced that the hour, eleven o'clock A. M., fixed by the order of the Senate for deliberation and debate had arrived, and that Senators could now submit their views upon the several articles of impeachment, subject to the limits of debate fixed by the twenty-third rule.

And, after deliberation, on motion of Mr. CONNESS, at ten minutes before two o'clock, the Senate took a recess of twenty minutes, at the expiration of which time, after further deliberation, on motion of Mr. CONNESS, at half-past five o'clock the Senate took a recess until half-past seven o'clock P. M.

While the Senate was in secret session excited crowds were in the lobby, anxious to know the course of the debates inside. Frequent inquiries were made of all who were supposed to know anything of the matter, and from time to time additional information was received by them, and soon traveled to the House of Representatives, where groups were occasionally formed discussing the subject. The inquiry was made of everybody coming from the direction of the Senate, "What's the latest news?" or "Who has last spoken, and what course had he taken?" Answers were given according to the ability of the person interrogated. It was ascertained that numerous Senators had spoken, but the views of the Republicans excited the most interest.

It was ascertained that Messrs. Grimes, Trumbull and Fessenden had clearly expressed themselves against the conviction of the President, while Mr. Henderson was against all the articles of impeachment except the eleventh. Messrs. Sherman and Howe, according to the general account, supported only the second, third, fourth, eighth and eleventh articles. Messrs. Edmunds, Stewart, Williams and Morrill (Me.) sustained all the articles, while Messrs. Hendricks, Davis, Johnson and Dixon opposed them.

Midnight.—A large number of persons were in the Rotunda of the Capitol to-night, waiting to hear from the Senate, which resumed its secret session at half-past seven o'clock. Only those privileged to enter the Senate side of the building, including members of the House and reporters for the press were permitted to approach the immediate vicinity of the Senate. Some occupied the adjacent rooms, while others stood in the passage ways, all anxious inquirers after important intelligence.

It was ascertained that Senator Conness, Harlan, Wilson and Morton spoke in favor of, and Mr. Buckalew in opposition to the conviction of the President.

The expectation by the outside parties was that those who are regarded as *doubtful* on the Republican side would express their views.

Mr. Edmunds submitted the following order:—

That the order of the Senate that it will proceed at twelve o'clock, noon, to-morrow, to vote on the articles of impeachment, be rescinded.

This was not acted on.

Mr. WILLIAMS offered the following:—

Ordered, That the Chief Justice, in directing the Secretary to read the several articles of impeachment, shall direct him to read the eleventh article first, and the question shall be then taken upon that article, and thereafter the other ten successively as they stand.

This lies over.

A motion that the Senate meet at half-past eleven o'clock to-morrow morning to sit with open doors, was agreed to.

The Senate adjourned at eleven o'clock.

PROCEEDINGS OF TUESDAY, MAY 12.

The chair was taken at half-past eleven precisely by the President pro tem., and the Chaplain, Rev. Dr. Gray, then opened the proceedings with prayer. After an invocation on behalf of the nation, he concluded as follows:—

"Prepare the mind, O, Lord, of the President for the removal or the suspense connected with this day's proceedings; prepare the minds of the people for the momentous issues which hang upon the decisions of the hour; prepare the minds of Thy servants, the Senators, for the great responsibility of this hour; may they be wise in counsel; may they be clear and just, and correct in judgment, and may they be faithful to the high trusts committed to them by the nation, and may the blessing of God be upon the people everywhere; may the people bow to the supremacy of the law; may order, and piety, and peace prevail throughout all our deliberations, and may the blessing of God rest upon the nation. God preserve the people. God preserve the government and save it. God maintain the right, to-day and forevermore. Amen."

Messrs. Stanbery and Evarts entered the Chamber. In the meantime the Chief Justice assumed the chair, and the court was opened by proclamation.

Senator CHANDLER immediately arose and addressed the Chair, but the Chief Justice directed the Secretary to proceed with the reading of the journal. After the reading had progressed for some minutes,

Mr. EDMUNDS moved that the further reading be dispensed with, but

Mr. DAVIS objected, and the journal was read through.

Mr. EDMUNDS moved to take up the pending order, which was as follows:—

Ordered, That the standing order of the Senate, that it will proceed at twelve o'clock, noon, to-morrow, to vote upon the articles of impeachment, be reconsidered.

Mr. CHANDLER asked unanimous consent to make a statement. No objection being made he said:—My colleague, Mr. Howard, is taken suddenly ill, and was delirious yesterday. He was very ill this morning, but he told me that he would be here to vote, even at the peril of his life. Both of his physicians, however, objected, and said it would be at the peril of his life. With this statement, I desire to move that the Senate, sitting as a court, adjourn until Saturday next, at twelve o'clock.

Mr. HENDRICKS moved to amend by making it to-morrow at twelve o'clock.

Mr. CHANDLER—There is no probability that he will be able to be up; he had a very high fever and was delirious; he said he would be here to-day if the Senate insisted on having him come.

Mr. FESSENDEN inquired whether the postponement would leave the order with reference to filing opinions after the final vote applicable to-day?

The Chief Justice—The Chief Justice understands that it applies to the final vote.

Mr. CONNESS—And two days thereafter?

The Chief Justice—And two days thereafter.

Mr. HENDRICKS then suggested that Mr. Chandler modify his motion so as to provide for an adjournment till Thursday, when, if the Senator should not be well enough, a further adjournment could be had.

Mr. CHANDLER asked would Friday suit the Senator?

Several Senators—"No;" "no."

The motion of Mr. Hendricks was lost.

Mr. TIPTON moved to amend by making it Friday, but the motion was not agreed to, Senator Sumner and mover apparently being the only Senators voting affirmatively.

Mr. BUCKALEW suggested that Mr. Chandler modify his motion to read, "that when the Senate adjourn it be to Saturday."

Mr. CHANDLER so modified it, and it was agreed to, with only one or two nays on the Democratic side.

Mr. EDMUNDS moved that the Secretary be directed to inform the House the Senate will proceed further in the trial on Saturday next, at twelve o'clock. He withdrew the motion, however, after a few minutes.

On motion of Mr. DRAKE, the court was adjourned at ten minutes before twelve o'clock.

PROCEEDINGS OF SATURDAY, MAY 16.

WASHINGTON, May 16.—The Senate met at 11·30 A. M. The galleries were full, and policemen were stationed in all the aisles.

At 12 M., the Chief Justice assumed the Chair, and called the court to order. In the meantime, Managers Stevens, Bingham and Logan, and Mr. Evarts, of the counsel for the President, had entered and taken their places. Mr. Conkling, Mr. Grimes and Mr. Howard were present, making a full Senate.

The following is the vote on the adoption of an order, offered by Mr. Williams, to take the vote on the eleventh article, first:—

YEAS—Messrs. Anthony, Cameron, Cattell, Chandler Cole, Conkling, Conness, Corbett, Cragin, Drake, Edmunds, Ferry, Frelinghuysen, Harlan, Howard, Howe, Morgan, Morill (Me.), Morrill (Vt.), Morton, Nye, Patterson (N. H.), Pomeroy, Ramsey, Sherman, Sprague, Stewart, Sumner, Thayer, Tipton, Wade, Williams, Wilson and Yates—34.

NAYS—Messrs. Bayard, Buckalew, Davis, Dixon, Doolittle, Fessenden, Fowler, Henderson, Hendricks, Johnson, McCreery, Norton, Patterson (Tenn.), Ross, Saulsbury, Trumbull, Van Winkle, Vickers and Willey—19.

Senator JOHNSON inquired whether the order of Senator Williams was debateable.

The Chief Justice replied that it was not.

Senator JOHNSON said he would like to make a remark on it.

Senator CONNESS objected.

The question was then put on taking up Senator Williams' order for action, and it was decided. Yeas, 34; nays, 19.

Senator Wade voted for the first time, and voted in the affirmative. Senator Grimes was not then present.

The vote was then taken on the Eleventh Article of impeachment, and resulted as follows:—

GUILTY.

Anthony,
Cameron,
Cattell,
Chandler,
Cole,
Conkling,
Conness,
Corbett,
Cragin,
Drake,
Edmunds,
Ferry,

Frelinghuysen,
Harlan,
Howard,
Howe,
Morgan,
Morton,
Morrill (Me.),
Morrill (Vt.)
Nye,
Patterson (N.H.),
Pomeroy,
Ramsey,

Sherman,
Sprague,
Stewart,
Sumner,
Thayer,
Tipton,
Wade,
Williams,
Willey,
Yates.

NOT GUILTY.

Bayard,
Buckalew,
Davis,
Dixon,
Doolittle,
Fessenden,
Fowler,

Grimes,
Henderson,
Hendricks,
Johnson,
McCreery,
Norton,

Patterson (Tenn.)
Ross,
Saulsbury,
Trumbull,
Van Winkle,
Vickers.

The vote stood 35 for conviction, and 19 for acquittal. So Andrew Johnson was acquitted on that article.

Immediately on the declaration of not guilty on the eleventh article, Mr. Williams moved an adjournment to Tuesday, 26th inst.

Mr. HENDRICKS claimed it to be out of order.

The Chair so decided.

Mr. DRAKE appealed from the decision of the Chair, and it was overruled. Yeas, 34; nays, 20.

The votes of the Senators were waited for with the utmost anxiety, though nothing more than a general motion as of suspense relieved, was made manifest when the vote of a doubtful Senator was given. It was noticed that Senator Cameron voted ahead of time. The Chief Justice had not concluded the formal question before the Senator's vote of guilty was pronounced. Senators Fessenden, Fowler, Grimes, Ross, Trumbull, and Van Winkle, among the Republican Senators, voted not guilty. Senator Wade, when his name was called, stood up unhesitatingly, and voted guilty.

Before the result of the vote was announced, but when it was known, Mr. WILLIAMS rose and moved that the Senate, sitting as a Court of Impeachment, adjourn till Tuesday, May 26, at twelve o'clock.

Senator JOHNSON addressed the Chief Justice.

The Chief Justice said that debate was not in order.

Senator JOHNSON—Is it in order to adjourn the Senate when it has already decided on one of the articles.

The Chief Justice—The precedents are, except in one case, "the case of Humphreys," that the announcement was not made until the end of the cause. The Chair will, however, take the direction of the Senate. If the Senate desire the announcement to be made now, it will be made.

Senator SHERMAN — The announcement of the vote had better be made.

Senator DRAKE—I submit, as a question of order, that a motion to adjourn is pending, and that that motion takes precedence of all other things.

The Chief Justice—The Senator from Missouri is perfectly right. A motion to adjourn has been made, and that motion takes precedence.

Mr. HENDRICKS—The motion to adjourn cannot be made pending a vote, and the vote is not complete until it is announced.

Senator CONKLING—A motion cannot be made pending the roll call.

Several Senators—Certainly not; let the vote be announced.

Senator JOHNSON—I ask that the vote be announced.

The Chief Justice—The vote will be announced. The Clerk will read the roll.

The roll having been read by the Clerk, the Chief Justice rose and announced the result in these words:—"On this article there are 35 Senators who have voted guilty and 19 Senators who have voted not guilty. The President is, therefore, acquitted on this article.

No manifestation of sentiment was made on either side of the question. Whatever were the feelings of Senators, members and spectators, they were thoroughly suppressed.

Senator Williams' motion to adjourn till Tuesday, the 26th inst., was then taken up.

Senator HENDRICKS submitted as a question of order, that the Senate was not executing an order already made, which was in the nature and had the effect of the previous question; and, therefore, the motion to adjourn otherwise than simply to adjourn, was not in order.

Calls of "Question!" "Question!"

The Chief Justice—The motion that when the Senate adjourn it adjourn to meet at a certain date, cannot now be entertained, because it is in process of executing an order. A motion to adjourn to a certain day, seems to the Chair to come under the same rule, and the Chair will, therefore, decide the motion not in order.

Senator CONNESS—From that decision of the Chair I appeal.

The Chief Justice put the question, and directed the Clerk to read the order adopted to-day on motion of Senator Edmunds, as follows:—

Ordered, That the Senate do now proceed to vote on the articles, according to the rules of the Senate.

Senator Howard called for the yeas and nays on the question whether the decision of the chair should be sustained. The vote was taken and resulted, yeas, 24; nays, 30, as follows:—

YEAS.—Messrs. Anthony, Bayard, Buckalew, Conkling, Davis, Dixon, Doolittle, Ferry, Fessenden, Fowler, Grimes, Henderson, Hendricks, Johnson, McCreery, Morgan, Norton, Patterson (Tenn.), Saulsbury, Sherman, Trumbull, Van Winkle, Vickers and Willey—24.

NAYS.—Messrs. Cameron, Cattell, Chandler, Cole, Conness, Corbett, Cragin, Drake, Edmunds, Frelinghuysen, Harlan, Howard, Howe, Morrill (Me.), Morrill (Vt.), Morton, Nye, Patterson (N. H.), Pomeroy, Ramsey, Ross, Sprague, Stewart, Sumner, Thayer, Tipton, Wade, Williams, Wilson and Yates—30.

So the decision of the Chief Justice was reversed and the order to adjourn over was ruled to be in order.

Mr. HENDERSON moved to amend the order by striking out the words "Tuesday, the 26th inst.," and inserting in lieu thereof the words "Wednesday, the first day of July next."

The amendment was rejected by the following vote:—

YEAS.—Messrs. Bayard, Buckalew, Davis, Dixon, Doolittle, Fessenden, Fowler, Grimes, Henderson, Hendricks, Johnson, McCreery, Norton, Patterson (Tenn.), Ross, Saulsbury, Trumbull, Van Winkle, Vickers and Willey—20.

NAYS.—Messrs. Anthony, Cameron, Cattell, Chandler, Cole, Conkling, Conness, Corbett, Cragin, Drake, Edmunds, Ferry, Frelinghuysen, Harlan, Howard, Howe, Morgan, Morrill (Me.), Morrill (Vt.), Morton, Nye, Patterson (N. H.), Pomeroy, Ramsey, Sherman, Sprague, Stewart, Sumner, Thayer, Tipton, Wade, Williams, Wilson and Yates—30.

Mr. McCREERY moved to amend the order by making it read "adjourn without day."

The question was taken, and the amendment was rejected. Yeas, 6; nays, 47, as follows:—

YEAS.—Messrs. Bayard, Davis, Dixon, Doolittle, McCreery, and Vickers—6.

NAYS.—Messrs. Anthony, Buckalew, Cameron, Cattell, Chandler, Cole, Conkling, Conness, Corbett, Cragin, Drake, Edmunds, Ferry, Fessenden, Fowler, Frelinghuysen, Harlan, Henderson, Hendricks, Howard, Howe, Johnson, Morgan, Morrill (Me.), Morrill (Vt.), Morton, Norton, Nye, Patterson (N. H.), Patterson (Tenn.), Pomeroy, Ramsey, Ross, Saulsbury, Sherman, Sprague, Stewart, Sumner, Thayer, Tipton, Trumbull, Van Winkle, Wade, Williams, Wilson, and Yates—47.

Senator BUCKALEW moving to amend the order by providing for an adjournment till Monday, 25th inst. Rejected without a division, and the question recurred on the order as originally offered by Senator Williams, to adjourn the court till Tuesday, the 26th inst.

The vote was taken, and resulted—yeas, 32; nays, 21, as follows:—

YEAS.—Messrs. Anthony, Cameron, Cattell, Chandler, Cole, Conness, Corbett, Cragin, Drake, Edmunds, Frelinghuysen, Harlan, Howard, Howe, Morrill (Me.), Morrill (Vt.) Morton, Nye, Patterson (N. H.), Pomeroy, Ramsey, Ross, Sprague, Stewart, Sumner, Thayer, Tipton, Van Winkle, Wade, Williams, Wilson and Yates—32.

NAYS—Messrs. Bayard, Buckalew, Conkling, Davis, Dixon, Doolittle, Ferry, Fessenden, Fowler, Johnson, Henderson, Hendricks, McCreery, Morgan, Norton, Patterson (Tenn.), Saulsbury, Sherman, Trumbull, Vickers and Willey—21.

The Chief Justice announced the result, and said:—"So the Senate, sitting as a Court of Impeachment, stands adjourned till the 26th inst., at twelve o'clock."

The Chief Justice then left the chair, and the members of the House retired to their own chamber.

The spectators who had filled every seat and standing place in the galleries immediately began to pour out into halls and corridors, and the curtain fell on the national drama of impeachment.

The closing scene was not marked by the slightest breach of decorum or of good order.